THE CAMBRIDGE HISTORY OF

IRISH LITERATURE

*

VOLUME I

TO 1890

This is the first comprehensive history of Irish literature in both its major languages, Irish and English. The twenty-nine chapters in this two-volume history provide an authoritative chronological survey of the Irish literary tradition. Spanning fifteen centuries of literary achievement, the two volumes range from the earliest Hiberno-Latin texts to the literature of the late twentieth century. The contributors, drawn from a range of Irish, British and North American universities, are internationally renowned experts in their fields. The *Cambridge History of Irish Literature* comprises an unprecedented synthesis of research and information, a detailed narrative of one of the world's richest literary traditions, and innovative and challenging new readings. No critical work of this scale and authority has been attempted for Irish literature before. Featuring a detailed chronology and guides to further reading for each chapter, this magisterial project will remain the key reference book for literature in Ireland for generations to come.

This first volume covers early to late medieval texts in Latin and Norman French as well as Irish, the literature of English settlement in the early modern period, and the developments of the eighteenth and nineteenth centuries.

MARGARET KELLEHER is Senior Lecturer in the Department of English at the National University of Ireland, Maynooth. She has previously held the John J. Burns Visiting Chair in Irish Studies at Boston College. She is the author of *The Feminization of Famine* (1997), editor of *Making It New* (2000) and co-editor of *Nineteenth-Century Ireland: A Guide to Recent Research* (2005).

PHILIP O'LEARY is Associate Professor of Irish Studies at Boston College. He is the author of *Prose Literature of the Gaelic Revival 1881–1921: Ideology and Innovation* (1994), which won the ACIS First Book Prize, *Déirc an Dóchais: Léamh ar Shaothar Phádhraic Óig Uí Chonaire* (1995) and *Gaelic Prose in the Irish Free State, 1922–1939* (2004), which won the Michael J. Durkan Prize.

THE CAMBRIDGE
HISTORY OF
IRISH LITERATURE

★

VOLUME 1
TO 1890

★

Edited by
MARGARET KELLEHER
and
PHILIP O'LEARY

CAMBRIDGE
UNIVERSITY PRESS

CAMBRIDGE UNIVERSITY PRESS
Cambridge, New York, Melbourne, Madrid, Cape Town, Singapore, São Paulo

Cambridge University Press
The Edinburgh Building, Cambridge CB2 2RU, UK

Published in the United States of America by Cambridge University Press, New York

www.cambridge.org
Information on this title: www.cambridge.org/9780521822244

First published 2006

Printed in the United Kingdom at the University Press, Cambridge

A catalogue record for this book is available from the British Library

Library of Congress Cataloguing in Publication data
The Cambridge history of Irish literature / edited by Margaret Kelleher and Philip O'Leary.
p. cm.
ISBN 0-521-82224-6 (2-vol. hardback set)
1. Irish literature – History and criticism. 2. English literature – Irish authors – History and criticism.
3. Northern Ireland – Intellectual life. 4. Northern Ireland – In literature. 5. Ireland – Intellectual
life. 6. Ireland – In literature. I. Kelleher, Margaret, 1964–. II. O'Leary, Philip, 1948– III. Title.
PB1306.C36 2006
820.9'9417 – dc22 2005006448

Volume I 0-521-82222-X
Only available as a two-volume set
ISBN-13 978-0-521-82224-4
ISBN-10 0-521-82224-6

Contents

Contributors

Neil Buttimer University College Cork
Marc Caball Irish Research Council for the Humanities and Social Sciences
Matthew Campbell University of Sheffield
Andrew Carpenter University College Dublin
Claire Connolly Cardiff University
Gearóid Denvir National University of Ireland, Galway
Anne Fogarty University College Dublin
Kaarina Hollo University of Sheffield
Margaret Kelleher National University of Ireland, Maynooth
Mícheál Mac Craith National University of Ireland, Galway
Christopher Morash National University of Ireland, Maynooth
Máire Ní Mhaonaigh St John's College, Cambridge
Tomás Ó Cathasaigh Harvard University
Clare O'Halloran University College Cork
Philip O'Leary Boston College
Ian Campbell Ross Trinity College, Dublin
Donna Wong University of California, Berkeley

Acknowledgements

Firstly, our thanks to all of our contributors: the excellence of their scholarship was the mainstay of our work throughout. We acknowledge with gratitude our editor, Dr Ray Ryan, Cambridge University Press, who first conceived of this project and who encouraged us to the finish. Our thanks also to the anonymous readers of our initial prospectus who offered very useful suggestions, and to the Syndicate of Cambridge University Press for their support. We gratefully acknowledge the expert assistance of Alison Powell, Carol Fellingham Webb, David Watson and Maartje Scheltens of Cambridge University Press in the preparation of these volumes for publication.

To those who offered comments on specific chapters and assistance to individual contributors, sincere thanks; these include David Berman, Michael Clarke, Peter Denman, Aileen Douglas, Peter Garside, Raymond Gillespie, Nicholas Grene, the members of the Harvard Postgraduate Colloquium 2002–3, Siobhán Kilfeather, Carla King, David Latané Jr., Joep Leerssen, James H. Murphy, Jane Moody, Jane Moore, Máirín Ní Dhonnchadha, Nollaig Ó Muraíle, Pádraig Ó Riain, Erich Poppe, John Valdimir Price, Paige Reynolds, Maria Luisa Ross, Diego Saglia and John Strachan. Our special thanks to Máire Ní Mhaonaigh who offered wise counsel throughout. We acknowledge with gratitude the work of Matthew Stout who provided the maps for this history. Amanda Bent, Denis Condon, Mike Cronin, Feargus Denman, Michael Kelleher, Niamh Lynch, Brian Ó Catháin and Andy Storey provided invaluable assistance in the production of these volumes. The views expressed, and any errors, are, of course, our responsibility.

We are very grateful for the support provided by our colleagues in the Irish Studies Program, Boston College, and the English Department, National University of Ireland, Maynooth. We gratefully acknowledge the assistance provided through the granting of the John J. Burns Visiting Chair in Irish Studies, Boston College to Margaret Kelleher in the academic year 2002–3. Once again, we are indebted to the staff of the Burns Library and O'Neill

Library, Boston College; the staff of Maynooth University Library; and the staff of the National Library, Dublin. Financial assistance towards this volume was received from the Publications Fund of the National University of Ireland and we gratefully acknowledge this assistance.

To Joyce Flynn, the Kelleher family (Mallow, County Cork) and the O'Leary family (Worcester, MA) we owe personal thanks. We acknowledge with gratitude the warm and longstanding hospitality provided by friends in Ireland and the USA: Angela Bourke, Eleanor Byrne, Patrick Ford, Marie Kearney, Gemma Kelleher, Maeve Lewis, Tomás Mac Anna, Nollaig Mac Congáil, Deirdre McMahon, Mohsen Marefat, the Ní Mhaonaigh / Meißner family, Brian Ó Conchubhair, the O'Shea / Curtin family, the O'Sullivan / Fleming family, Kathleen Rush, Mary Ann and Bud Smith, Leslie Swanson, Alan Titley, Terri Trafas, Maura Twomey and Unn Villius. Our work on this project is dedicated to the memory of two distinguished friends and mentors, Professor Adele M. Dalsimer, Boston College and Professor John V. Kelleher, Harvard University.

Ár mbeannachtaí leat, a scríbhinn . . .

Margaret Kelleher and Philip O'Leary
Dublin and South Yarmouth

Chronology

837–76	Intense Viking activity in Ireland; semi-permanent bases established, including encampment in Dublin (*c.* 841)
900–1200	Middle Irish linguistic period
916–37	Renewed Viking activity in Ireland
1002–14	Reign of Brian Bóruma mac Cennétig
1014	Battle of Clontarf (Good Friday, 23 April)
c. 1100?	Compilation of *Lebor na hUidre* (The Book of the Dun Cow)
1101	Council of Cashel
1127–34	Building of Cormac's chapel at Cashel
c. 1130	Compilation of Leinster codex, Rawlinson B502
1142	First Irish Cistercian house founded at Mellifont
c. 1160–1200	Compilation of the Book of Leinster
August 1170	Richard de Clare (Strongbow) arrives in Ireland
c. May 1171	Death of Diarmait Mac Murchada; Strongbow (his son-in-law) succeeds as king of Leinster
November 1171	Henry II in Dublin; receives submission of kings of north Leinster, Bréifne, Airgialla and Ulster
February 1183	First visit to Ireland of Giraldus Cambrensis (Gerald of Wales)
c. 1200–*c.* 1650	Early Modern Irish linguistic period
November 1216	Magna Carta issued for Ireland
1224	First Irish Dominican foundations (at Dublin and Drogheda)
c. 1224–30	First Irish Franciscan foundations (at Cork and Youghal)
c. May 1316	Edward Bruce crowned king of Ireland (defeated and killed October 1318)
c. 1330	Compilation of British Library Manuscript Harley 913
February 1366	Statute of Kilkenny promulgated
1446	First known use of 'Pale' to denote area under Dublin control
1494	'Poyning's Law' enacted by parliament at Drogheda
1534–5	Silken Thomas's rebellion
February 1537	Silken Thomas executed in London

October–December 1537	Acts for the suppression of Irish monasteries
June 1541	Henry VIII declared 'king of Ireland' by statute of Irish parliament
June 1549	Order for use of English Book of Common Prayer in Ireland
1550–7	Plantations in Laois (Leix) and Offaly (established as Queen's County and King's County in 1556)
1555	Papal Bull of Pope Paul IV declares Ireland a kingdom
1561–7	Rebellion of Shane O'Neill; English campaigns led by Sussex and Sir Henry Sidney
1568–73	First Desmond rebellion
June 1571	First printing in the Irish language, in Dublin
1579–83	Second Desmond rebellion
December 1585	Scheme for plantation in Munster drawn up (amended scheme passed by Elizabeth I, June 1586)
September 1588	Ships of Spanish Armada wrecked off Irish coast
March 1592	Charter incorporates Trinity College, Dublin
1595–1603	Rebellion of Hugh O'Neill, earl of Tyrone
September 1601	Spanish army lands at Kinsale
December 1601	Tyrone and 'Red Hugh' O'Donnell defeated at Kinsale; O'Donnell leaves Ireland for Spain
March 1603	Surrender of Tyrone at Mellifont
September 1607	Flight of the Earls (including Tyrone and Tyrconnell) from Lough Swilly
1608–10	Preparations for plantations in Ulster counties
January 1621	Patents granted for plantations in Leitrim, King's County (Offaly), Queen's County (Laois) and Westmeath
August 1632	Compilation of the Annals of the Four Masters completed
October 1641	Outbreak of rebellion in Ulster
1642–9	'Confederation of Kilkenny': government of Catholic Confederates
August 1649	Oliver Cromwell arrives in Dublin as civil and military governor of Ireland

September 1649	Massacre at Drogheda
October 1649	Massacre at Wexford
November 1649	Death of Eoghan Ruadh Ó Néill (Owen Roe O'Neill)
May 1650	Cromwell returns to England
August 1652	Act for the settlement of Ireland
1652–3	Cromwellian land confiscations
1660–5	Restoration land settlement
July 1663	First of series of acts restricting Irish trade and exports
March 1689	James II arrives in Ireland
April 1689	Siege of Derry begins; ends in July
July 1690	Forces of James II defeated by those of William III at River Boyne
July 1691	Battle of Aughrim: Williamite victory
October 1691	Treaty of Limerick, allowing evacuation of Irish army to France and promising toleration to Irish Catholics
1691–1703	Williamite land confiscations
September 1695	Beginning of 'Penal Laws': Acts restricting rights of Catholics to education, to bear arms or to possess a horse worth more than five pounds.
March 1704	Further 'Penal Law' introduced, including 'tests' on Catholics and Protestant dissenters for holding of public office; amended and strengthened August 1708.
June–July 1718	Beginning of large-scale migration of Ulster Scots to American colonies
November 1719	Toleration Act for Protestant Dissenters
April 1720	Declaratory Act defines right of English parliament to legislate for Ireland
Winter 1740–spring 1741	'Bliadhain an Áir' ('The Year of the Slaughter'): large-scale famine, with mortality estimated at over 200,000, from a population of approximately two million
June 1758–April 1759	Acts removing restrictions on some Irish exports
March 1760	Catholic Committee established in Dublin to advance Catholic interests
c. October 1761	Beginning of Whiteboy movement in Munster

March 1778	Beginning of Volunteer movement (local independent military forces); first company enrolled in Belfast
August 1778	Catholic Relief Act grants rights of leasing and inheritance
June and July 1782	Repeal of 1720 Declaratory Act and Poyning's Law amended
April 1783	British Renunciation Act acknowledges exclusive right of Irish parliament to legislate for Ireland (inaugurates 'Grattan's parliament', to 1800)
May 1785	First meeting of Irish Academy ('Royal Irish' after January 1786)
October 1791	Foundation of Society of United Irishmen in Belfast
April 1792 and April 1793	Catholic Relief Acts allow Catholics to practise law and give parliamentary franchise
June 1795	Act passed for establishment of Catholic seminary at Maynooth
September 1795	Foundation of Orange Order
December 1796	French fleet, with Wolfe Tone, at Bantry Bay
1798	United Irishmen rising: rebellion begins in Leinster (May); outbreaks in Ulster in June; French force lands in Killala (August); French force surrenders (September)
August 1800	Act of Union dissolves Irish parliament and declares legislative union
January 1801	Act of Union takes effect
July 1801	Copyright Act renders illegal the publication of pirate Irish editions of British publications
July 1803	Robert Emmet's rebellion in Dublin; Emmet executed in September
Autumn 1816	Failure of potato crop leads to first major famine since 1742; widespread typhus epidemic continues until late 1819
Autumn 1821	Failure of potato crop; fever follows in west of Ireland in summer 1822
May 1823	Foundation of Catholic Association by Daniel O'Connell
1825–41	Ordnance Survey of Ireland carried out

July 1828	Daniel O'Connell elected MP for Clare
April 1829	Catholic Emancipation Act enables Catholics to enter parliament and to hold civil and military offices
September 1831	State system of National Education introduced
June 1837	Accession of Victoria
July 1838	English system of Poor Law is extended to Ireland
April 1840	Repeal Association founded
June 1841	Census of Ireland: population of island 8,175,124
1844	Queen's University founded, with colleges in Belfast, Cork and Galway.
1845–51	*An Gorta Mór* ('The Great Irish Famine'): mortality estimated at in excess of 1 million
September 1845	Arrival of potato blight in Ireland first noted
June 1846	Repeal of the Corn Laws
August 1846	Recurrence of potato blight, leading to large mortality in winter of 1846–7
May 1847	Death of O'Connell
July 1848	Abortive rising by William Smith O'Brien at Ballingarry, Co. Tipperary: beginning of short-lived Young Ireland rebellion
March 1851	Census of Ireland: population of island 6,552,385
March 1858	James Stephens founds Irish Republican Brotherhood (IRB) in Dublin
April 1859	Fenian Brotherhood established in USA
1867	Fenian rebellion: disturbances in England and Ireland in February; execution of Fenian 'Manchester Martyrs' in November
July 1869	Irish Church Act disestablishes Church of Ireland
May 1870	Isaac Butt founds Home Government Association: beginning of Home Rule movement
August 1870	Gladstone's first Land Act
1876	Society for the Preservation of the Irish Language founded
August 1877	Charles Stuart Parnell elected president of Home Rule Confederation of Great Britain
August 1879	Foundation of National Land League of Mayo by Michael Davitt
October 1879	Foundation of Irish National Land League by Davitt and Parnell

May 1880	Parnell elected chairman of Irish Parliamentary Party (IPP)
October 1880	Foundation of Ladies' Land League in New York
January 1881	Ladies' Land League established in Ireland
August 1881	Gladstone's second Land Act
May 1882	'Phoenix Park murders' of Lord Frederick Cavendish and Thomas Burke
November 1884	Foundation of Gaelic Athletic Association (GAA)
August 1885	Ashbourne Land Purchase Act
June 1886	Gladstone's Home Rule Bill defeated
October 1886	Announcement of 'Plan of Campaign' to withhold rents on certain estates
1877	National Library of Ireland established
1890	National Museum of Ireland opened
December 1890	Split in IPP, with majority opposing Parnell
October 1891	Death of Parnell
August 1892	National Literary Society established
July 1893	Foundation of Gaelic League (Conradh na Gaeilge)
September 1893	Second Home Rule Bill passed by House of Commons but defeated in House of Lords
August 1898	Irish Local Government Act
May 1899	First production by Irish Literary Theatre
September 1900	Foundation of Cumann na nGaedheal led by Arthur Griffith
March 1901	Census of Ireland: population 4,458,775
August 1903	Wyndham Land Act
December 1904	Opening of Abbey Theatre
April 1907	Cumann na nGaedheal and Dungannon clubs become Sinn Féin League
December 1908	Foundation of Irish Transport Workers' Union (later ITGWU)
April 1911	Census of Ireland: population 4,381,951
May 1908	Irish Women's Franchise League formed
April 1912	Third Home Rule Bill passed by House of Commons; twice defeated in House of Lords (January and July 1913)
September 1912	Solemn League and Covenant signed in Ulster
January 1913	Foundation of Ulster Volunteer Force
August 1913	Beginning of ITGWU strike in Dublin, becomes general lockout

November 1913	Formation of Irish Citizen Army and Irish Volunteers
March 1914	'Curragh Mutiny': resignation by sixty cavalry officers in the British army at Kildare
April 1914	Ulster Volunteer Force gunrunning
April 1914	Foundation of Cumann na mBan (women's auxiliary league)
May 1914	Home Rule Bill passes again in Commons
July 1914	Howth gunrunning by Irish Volunteers
August 1914	United Kingdom and Germany go to war
September 1914	Home Rule Bill suspended; John Redmond calls on Irish Volunteers to support British war; movement splits into National (pro-Redmond) and Irish (anti-Redmond) Volunteers
April 1916	Easter Uprising
May 1916	Execution of rebel leaders
December 1918	Sinn Féin victory in general election
January 1919	First meeting of Dáil Éireann at Mansion House, with Eamon De Valera elected president
1919	Irish Volunteer organisation increasingly known as Irish Republican Army (IRA)
1919–21	Irish War of Independence / Anglo-Irish War
January 1920	First recruits of British ex-soldiers and sailors ('Black and Tans') join Royal Irish Constabulary
December 1920	Government of Ireland Act provides for creation of separate parliaments in Dublin and Belfast
June 1921	George V opens Northern Irish Parliament
July 1921	Truce between IRA and British Army
December 1921	Anglo-Irish Treaty signed
January 1922	Treaty approved by Dáil Éireann (sixty-four to fifty-seven): establishment of Irish Free State
June 1922	Beginning of Irish Civil War between pro-Treaty (Free State) and anti-Treaty (Republican) forces
April 1923	Cumann na nGaedheal (political party) founded as first new post-independence party
April 1923	Suspension of Republican campaign
July 1923	Censorship of Films Act
September 1923	Irish Free State enters League of Nations
1923	W. B. Yeats is awarded the Nobel Prize for Literature

1925	George Bernard Shaw is awarded the Nobel Prize for Literature
November 1925	Findings of Boundary Commission leaked
April 1926	Census of Ireland: population of Irish Free State 2,971,992; population of Northern Ireland 1,256,561
May 1926	Foundation of Fianna Fáil
1928	Irish Manuscripts Commission founded
July 1929	Censorship of Publications Act
1930	Ireland elected to the Council of the League of Nations
February 1932	Fianna Fáil win general election
June 1932	Thirty-First International Eucharistic Congress held in Dublin
September 1933	Foundation of Fine Gael (replaces Cumann na nGaedheal)
June 1936	IRA declared illegal
June 1937	De Valera's new constitution (Bunreacht na hÉireann) approved; Éire declared official name of state
June 1938	Douglas Hyde becomes first president of Ireland
September 1939	Éire's policy of neutrality announced
1939–1945	'Emergency' years
April and May 1941	Air-raids on Belfast
February 1948	Fianna Fáil loses overall majority; replaced by Coalition government under John A. Costello
December 1948	Republic of Ireland Act under which Éire becomes Republic of Ireland and leaves Commonwealth
April 1951	Catholic hierarchy condemns 'Mother and Child' Scheme; resignation of Dr Noël Browne as Minister of Health
December 1955	Republic of Ireland joins United Nations
December 1956	IRA begins campaign on Northern border
1958	Programme for Economic Expansion introduced, encouraging exports along with private and foreign investment in manufacturing
June 1959	De Valera elected president
December 1961	RTÉ (Radio Telefís Éireann) begins television service
March 1963	Terence O'Neill becomes prime minister of Northern Ireland

1966	Ulster Volunteer Force (UVF), loyalist paramilitary group (taking its name from the 1913 movement), founded
January 1967	Foundation of Northern Ireland Civil Rights Association
August–October 1968	Civil rights marches in Northern Ireland; clashes between marchers and police in Derry mark beginning of 'the Troubles'
1969	Samuel Beckett is awarded the Nobel Prize for Literature
January 1970	IRA splits into Official IRA and Provisional IRA
August 1970	Foundation of Social Democratic Labour Party (SDLP) in Northern Ireland
August 1971	Internment introduced in Northern Ireland
October 1971	Ian Paisley founds Democratic Unionist Party (DUP)
March 1972	Stormont parliament in Belfast suspended; direct rule from London introduced
30 January 1972	'Bloody Sunday': fourteen civilians killed and twelve wounded in Derry by British army
21 July 1972	'Bloody Friday': twenty-two bombs set off in Belfast by IRA; nine people killed and some hundred and thirty wounded
January 1973	Republic of Ireland joins European Economic Community (EEC)
May 1974	Ulster Workers' Council declares general strike
December 1975	Suspension of internment without trial in Northern Ireland
29 September–1 October 1979	Pope John Paul II visits Ireland
October–December 1980	Hunger strikes in Maze and Armagh prisons
May–August 1981	Ten IRA and Irish National Liberation Army (INLA) hunger-strikers die, including Bobby Sands (elected MP, April 1981)

September 1983	Amendment to constitution passed by referendum, seeking to prevent any possible legalisation of abortion
May 1984	Report of the New Ireland Forum is published
November 1985	Anglo-Irish Agreement signed by Garret FitzGerald and Margaret Thatcher
June 1986	Referendum upholds constitutional ban on divorce
May 1987	Referendum approves Single European Act
November 1990	Mary Robinson elected president of Ireland
November 1992	Referendum held on three abortion-related issues: the right to travel and the right to information supported
December 1993	Downing Street Declaration signed by Albert Reynolds and John Major
August and October 1994	IRA and Loyalist paramilitaries declare ceasefires (later suspended and restored)
October 1995	Seamus Heaney is awarded the Nobel Prize for Literature
November 1995	Referendum allowing divorce is carried
October 1997	Mary McAleese elected president of Ireland
April 1998	Good Friday Agreement is negotiated and endorsed in referendums in Republic of Ireland and Northern Ireland (May)
December 1999	Northern Irish Assembly meets
2001	Census of population of Northern Ireland: 1,685,267
April 2002	Census of population of Republic of Ireland: 3,917,203

For a fuller chronology, to which this chronology is indebted, see T. W. Moody, F. X. Martin and F. J. Byrne, eds., *A New History of Ireland, vol. VIII: A Chronology of Irish History to 1976* (Oxford University Press, 1992). For a detailed comparative chronology of Irish and international literary history, 1800–2000, see Joseph Cleary and Claire Connolly, eds. *The Cambridge Companion to Modern Irish Culture* (Cambridge University Press, 2005).

Map 1. Map of Ireland.

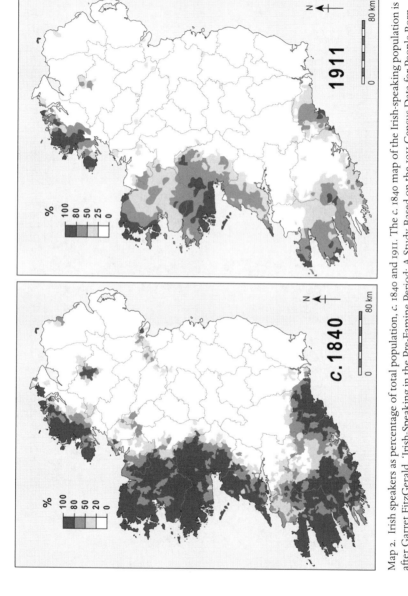

Map 2. Irish speakers as percentage of total population, c. 1840 and 1911. The c. 1840 map of the Irish-speaking population is after Garret FitzGerald, 'Irish-Speaking in the Pre-Famine Period: A Study Based on the 1911 Census Data for People Born before 1851 and Still Alive in 1911', in *Proceedings of the Royal Irish Academy*, 103 C, 5 (2003), pp 191–283, map 2. The 1911 map is after Brian Ó Cuív, 'Irish Language and Literature, 1845–1921', in W. E. Vaughan, ed. *A New History of Ireland, vol. VI: Ireland under the Union, II, 1870–1921* (Oxford: Clarendon Press, 1996), pp 385–435. p. 399, map 3. Maps by Matthew Stout.

Introduction

MARGARET KELLEHER AND PHILIP O'LEARY

In 1875, one year short of the centennial of the American republic, the publisher George H. Putnam asked Moses Coit Tyler to produce a 'manual' of American literature. Tyler was to do much more than that. Convinced that it was now time to write an account of what he called 'the most confidential and explicit record' of the American mind, the record preserved in the nation's literature, he undertook a full-scale history of American literature from 1607 to 1765, a pioneering effort that was to mark the beginning of the serious study of that literature. Tyler himself was in 1881 to join the faculty of Cornell University as the holder of the first professorship in the United States devoted to American history.

We believe that now is the time for a similar pioneering effort to create a coherent and authoritative history of Irish literature in the two major languages of the island. The publication in 1991 of the three-volume *Field Day Anthology of Irish Writing*, the first attempt to formulate a standard if not definitive anthology of Irish literature, has in effect established a canon of Irish literature, a canon since expanded with the appearance in 2002 of the fourth and fifth volumes of the anthology, volumes dedicated to writing by and about women. The existence of such a canon, however contested, only makes more compelling – even urgent – the need for an accessible and reliable historical framework within which the newly canonical texts can be read, and marginalised texts, together with the reasons for their marginalisation, can be explored. Indeed the *Field Day Anthology* has created the anomalous situation in which Ireland now has a chronologically organised literary canon but no comprehensive literary history in light of which to think about it.

Of course that does not mean that there are not sound works of Irish literary history available. Unlike Tyler, we face a situation in which there is an almost baffling profusion of histories, biographies, critical monographs, and so on, dealing with various aspects of the literatures of Ireland. Yet for all this wealth of scholarly material, we have as yet no definitive literary history. To be sure, there are important and useful surveys like those by Jeffares and Deane for Irish writing in English, and for Irish writing in Irish by Hyde, de Blacam and J. E. Caerwyn Williams (the last translated into Irish and English from the original Welsh). In addition, there are, of course, histories of individual periods, movements, genres, themes, etc. But for the scholar or general reader trying to make sense of the bigger picture, looking for a reliable overview of the Irish literary tradition as it has developed in both Irish and English, there has been next to nothing.

Given the enormous scholarly and popular interest in Irish literature at present, now is the time to remedy this deficiency. Ireland's literary tradition spans more than fifteen hundred years. As we begin the new millennium, we have both a need and an opportunity to make sense of that long tradition by providing an authoritative chronological history that will enable readers to check facts on specific authors and literary works, to trace in meaningful detail stylistic and thematic developments and influences through time, or to explore the often neglected interrelationships between the two literary traditions that have shared the island over the past five hundred years. For as Homi Bhabha has pointed out in *The Location of Culture*, 'what is theoretically innovative, and politically crucial, is the need to think beyond narratives of originary and initial subjectivity and to focus on those moments or processes that are produced in the articulation of cultural differences'.[1]

At the moment, Irish culture is experiencing unprecedented visibility and acclaim on the world stage. Simultaneously, Irish Studies has developed as a respectable academic discipline in many universities, most notably in North America and Great Britain, but also in Australia, continental Europe and, curiously belatedly, in Ireland itself. Yet despite this visibility, not all those engaged with Irish culture share the confidence, even occasional complacency, that is the predictable by-product of such striking accomplishments. In fact, some have experienced a nagging ambivalence, a concern that superficial successes, however impressive, are actually obscuring rather than illuminating an authentic understanding of crucial questions called forth by those very successes. Are Irish writers in English the Anglophone flavour-of-the-moment for jaded cosmopolitan readers? Is translation a vital transfusion of cross-cultural energy that will make writing in Irish more visible and ultimately more viable, or is it a lethal injection leading to linguistic redundancy? Do the plays of Martin McDonagh give new voice to the ever-evolving vitality of Irish theatre, or do they cynically parasitise that tradition to propagate a (not all that) new species of stage Irishism? What does the controversy over the

Field Day Anthology say about the possibility of thinking about Irish writing as a distinct and coherent literary entity?

It is, however, difficult, if not impossible, to think clearly and creatively, much less authoritatively, about these and other questions, large and small, without a specifically Irish context in which to read the literary works all too often seen as curious offshoots from a normative English tradition. At present, scholars and general readers alike lack such a context, with even those professionally involved in the study of Irish culture often experiencing an insecurity about finding a proper approach to thinking about Irish literature, about whether and how current developments relate to an ongoing tradition, and indeed about the existence and nature of that tradition itself. Given that those previous histories that do exist have concentrated exclusively on one or the other of Ireland's two major literary traditions, we see *The Cambridge History of Irish Literature* as a pioneering as well as a timely project. Far more than simply supplementing existing and forthcoming histories of English literature, it provides the first systematic and comprehensive overview of the Irish literary tradition as it has achieved expression over the centuries in both Irish and English.

The adherence to a chronological structure of organisation for the history means that the earlier chapters focus almost exclusively on Irish-language texts and writings in insular Latin and Norman French. Later chapters alternate between the Irish and English language traditions, with literature in English playing a considerably – and appropriately – more prominent, though never exclusive, role from the seventeenth century on. Our approach should, by its very novelty, generate new comparative insights, particularly in areas such as oral tradition, antiquarianism, translation or bilingualism, where the two languages have been, and still are, in direct and fruitful contact.

For general readers and even teachers and students, many of whom know only of an Irish literature in English, the relevant chapters provide a thorough and authoritative discussion of both familiar and less well-known texts along with an analysis of historical trends and current developments in the different periods. At the same time, readers of the *History* will also be introduced, many for the first time, to the diversity of the Irish-language tradition, a tradition many may have only encountered previously at second-hand through the uses and misuses to which it has been subjected by Irish writers of English. The older Irish-language material will thus not only be of interest to those with a special interest in the Gaelic past or to medievalists and scholars of comparative literature seeking access to seminal texts previously denied them. It should also enable those primarily interested in Irish literature in English to see how that literature has been influenced right up to the present by the older native tradition. We do not, then, see this as two discrete histories sharing the same covers, but rather as an integrated narrative addressing the needs of a wide readership from many different backgrounds. On the other hand, we have not tried to construct a unitary or teleological 'metanarrative' from the rich and often refractory reality of Irish literature. Rather, our intention is to offer a comprehensive and accessible survey of two thousand years of Irish literature in two principal and several incidental languages.

One controversy that the editors have had to face from the title page itself concerns the complex and often contested definitions of what an 'Irish' writer is. Our primary criterion for inclusion has been that authors were born on the island of Ireland or lived a significant and formative period of their lives there. Thus we include writings by Spenser, Moryson, Davies, Swift, Sterne, Goldsmith, Trollope and many others as important contributions to the history of Irish literature. In the case of representations of Ireland by English and other commentators (Carlyle, Engels, Gaskell, Asenath Nicholson, etc.), we are interested in the shaping role acquired by such representations, in particular their influence in Ireland and the response they generated from Irish authors. Obviously this definition by its very flexibility generates its own ambiguities. In cases of genuine uncertainty as to whether writers should be considered 'Irish' in any meaningful sense, we would prefer to err on the side of generous inclusion rather than to impose any kind of ethnic or ideological litmus test. Indeed, in some ways the very fact that an author's 'Irishness' is an issue worthy of debate is itself proof that he or she belongs in the *History*!

By defining Irishness on an inclusive island-wide basis, we are also asking our contributors to be sensitive to the existence of differing cultural, political and literary traditions on the island. By no means should this be seen as a genuflection to a transient political correctness. Given the rapid changes affecting Ireland today, in particular the still-embryonic growth of a newly multi-cultural society as a result of increasing immigration, this question of creating and living with a more fluid and embracing sense of Irish identity may well be the most important new theme in Irish literature confronting the editors of the successor to these volumes in the future. For now, however, we are attempting to subvert more familiar dichotomies. Thus, for example, we do not intend to marginalise writing from the unionist tradition in Northern Ireland by relegating it to a separate chapter as a regional or provincial offshoot of a putative dominant national tradition.

In keeping with the practice adopted in other *Cambridge History* volumes, we use the term 'literature' in an expansive sense, not limited to *belles lettres*, but also encompassing where appropriate a wide range of other forms of literary expression. We are not seeking to denigrate or subvert the term 'literature', finding it instead both a useful and a necessary term. The traditional genres of poetry, prose and drama are, as is proper, at the heart of this project. Yet by adopting a more comprehensive working definition of what constitutes literature, we make room for several forms of literary expression that have been more prominent in Irish literature than in that of other predominantly Anglophone countries. Could any comprehensive history of Irish literature fail to engage with autobiographical writings such as those by Wolfe Tone, Yeats, George Moore or Sean O'Casey in English, or the so-called 'Blasket auto-biographies' in Irish, a genre memorably parodied by 'Myles na gCopaleen' in *An Béal Bocht* (The Poor Mouth)? In like manner, any discussion of Irish literature in either of the island's languages would be poorer for the absence of the many adaptations and reworkings of early Irish heroic tales by authors such as Standish James O'Grady, Lady Gregory, Thomas Kinsella and Seamus Heaney. And of course such adaptations provide a particularly rich illustration of an ongoing cross-fertilisation between the two traditions. Another example of an ongoing Irish cultivation of less traditional genres is the popularity of political writing from Swift and Burke, to the Young Ireland writers of the *Nation* newspaper in the mid-nineteenth century, to the contemporary social and cultural critics associated with Field Day and the Raven Arts Press.

We have asked contributors to address the question of generic ambiguity as a persistent and positive quality of Irish literature in both Irish and English. We hope to show that the Irish tendency to challenge, subvert, redefine and/or merge traditional genres is one of the major forces that gives Irish literature its distinctiveness and vitality, and by no means an indication that Irish writers have either failed to master the canonical genres or devoted an inordinate effort to the cultivation of miniaturist adaptations of major genres from the dominant English tradition. In fact, Irish experimentation with genre goes back to the very origins of Irish literature, to the often anti-climactic heroic tales that represent the oldest vernacular literature north of the Alps and that, despite the example of classical models of the epic, are almost entirely in prose. In this light, one could see Swift's satires, Wilde's subversions of the well-made play, Synge's violent comedies, Yeats's experiments with the *Noh* drama, O'Casey's blendings of high tragedy and farce, and the stylistic experiments of Joyce, Beckett and Flann O'Brien as only a few of the most conspicuous examples in a mainstream Irish tradition of revisioning and revising conventional genres.

The part played by literary works in the broader cultural sphere in Ireland, and their relation to the history and politics of their time, is of necessity an essential theme throughout. Chapter titles are used to help place the literary texts under discussion into a recognisable historical context. A fundamental theme of this *History* is the role of literature in the formation of Irish identities. (And again it should be noted here that we are not positing any unitary or essentialist definition of what it means to be Irish.) Of particular interest throughout the *History* is how literature has been shaped by and in turn has helped shape the political and social developments of its time. Literature in Ireland has often provided a forum in which issues suppressed or neglected in the political arena can continue to circulate. On the other hand, literature has also been the subject of state control and censorship under both colonial and native governments. One of the more fruitful contributions of the *History* is its exploration of these themes through history, showing, for example, how intricately contemporary political issues were woven through the early literature in Irish, how the works of writers as diverse as Swift, Goldsmith, Wilde and Shaw take on different resonances when read in a specifically Irish context, and how Free State censorship blended moral and political objections to suppress dissident voices in the first decades of native rule in the South. By no means do we read the interplay between literature and politics as straightforward and unambiguous. Rather, we hope to explore how this interplay has generated its own traditions in Irish writing – past and present, in Irish and in English, North and South – traditions shaped by diverse, complex and shifting impulses which somehow manage to co-exist, however uneasily and at times all but invisibly.

The contents of this history span work from the sixth century to the year 2000, interweaving literature in Irish and English. Using this scheme readers should be empowered, in a way that was never possible while the two linguistic traditions were treated in isolation, to note and trace the existence of parallel or contradictory trends in the literary development of two languages sharing a single small landmass. Needless to say, the complexities and discontinuities of Irish life as expressed in two very different languages under the stress of a colonial hegemony seen very differently by different segments of the population often render any simplistic linear narrative inadequate, if not downright misleading. But these gaps and disjunctions are at the very heart of the Irish experience, and can therefore be far more interesting, challenging and suggestive, not only for specialists in Irish literary studies, but also for an international audience. Among the practical consequences of the acknowledgement of such gaps is that chapters do not always flow together seamlessly, a development we see as inevitable and beneficial.

The break between volumes occurs just before the commencement of the Literary Revival (*c.*1890). Volume I ends with a transitional chapter on the reciprocal relationships between oral and literary traditions in Irish and English. This chapter looks back to the nineteenth century (and earlier) and forward to the twentieth century from this dual-language perspective. The opening chapter in volume II is also organised around a crucial theme, in this case the interplay between literature and politics in Ireland. In like manner, the final two chapters of the entire *History* are intended to continue this thematic focus and indeed extend it into the future. These chapters, one dealing with literature in Irish, the other with literature in English, provide an assessment of the current state of Irish writing as well as a projection of possible future trends, all in light of current critical and theoretical methodologies that have radically changed the way we think about Irish literature at the turn of the new millennium.

The allocation of an entire volume to the period 1890–2000 obviously represents a bias. We are aware of this bias, and see it as almost inescapable. Many readers will doubtless consult the *History* for an understanding of the place and significance of modern and contemporary authors in an evolving tradition. Deprived of the luxury of a critical consensus formed over time, we may well have attributed an importance to writers of the recent past and the present that future historians will find inappropriate. But thus has it always been. We believe our decision to devote so much space to twentieth-century literature is justified both by the extent and quality of that literature and by what we believe will be significant reader interest in it. Moreover, readers drawn to the *History* primarily by an interest in the recent past may find especially illuminating and empowering the opportunity to explore the traditions and circumstances that shaped twentieth-century Irish literature in both languages.

One of the potentially more enlightening and provocative aspects of the *History* is its commitment to acknowledging the centrality of canonical figures, while also noting and discussing the contributions of less well-known writers, including those in the process of being retrieved from what now seems inexplicable obscurity and those previously marginalised for reasons having nothing to do with literary merit, but instead based on religion, gender or sexual preference. Indeed a recuperative impulse has been a fundamental motive throughout these two volumes.

Moses Coit Tyler's 1875 history was a pioneering effort, although one whose path can no longer be blindly followed, in large part because he was so sure of where that path would lead – to an ever-clearer, uncontested definition of what it meant to be American. The American tradition in literature will be more accurately explored in the pluralist and multivalent *New Cambridge History of American Literature* (edited by Sacvan Bercovitch) than it ever could be, even in its own time, by the monochromatic and teleologic approach of Tyler. Of course an emphasis on living tradition always looks to the future as well as the past, though the parameters of that future can only be suggested, never defined, much less guaranteed. Nevertheless, as Linda Hutcheon points out in her essay 'Rethinking the National Model', the traditional national model of literary history, one that lays down 'a familiar bedrock of development' and 'historically guarantees a sense of cultural legitimacy', may have to be created 'before competing, correcting, or even counterdiscursive narratives can be articulated'.[2] In this *History* we have tried both to lay down that 'familiar bedrock' and to suggest where 'competing, correcting, or even counterdiscursive narratives' might begin to reshape our understanding of the past. A future *Cambridge History of Irish Literature* will look very different from this one. We hope, however, that its editors will not find their intellectual forebears an embarrassment.

Notes

1. Homi Bhabha, *The Location of Culture* (New York: Routledge, 1994), p. 1.
2. Linda Hutcheon, 'Rethinking the National Model', in Linda Hutcheon and Mario J. Valdés, *Rethinking Literary History* (Oxford and New York: Oxford University Press, 2002), p. 13.

I

The literature of medieval Ireland to *c.*800: St Patrick to the Vikings

TOMÁS Ó CATHASAIGH

Historical introduction

Literature and scholarship, in Irish and in Latin, were prized and cultivated in early Christian Ireland: what has come down to us from the years AD 600 to 800 is most impressive, in both range and quality. These early texts are the products of an intellectual elite that comprised clerical and secular scholars and authors. There were already some Christians in Ireland early in the fifth century, for in 431 Pope Celestine sent Palladius as first bishop to the Irish who believed in Christ. Since Christianity is a religion of the Book, these Irish Christians must have had individuals among them who were literate in Latin. Some degree of literacy in the Irish language was present even earlier than the fifth century. The oldest surviving records of the Irish language are inscriptions incised in stone in the ogam script. Something under four hundred of these inscriptions survive, and they generally consist of a personal name in the genitive case, accompanied, more often than not, by the name of that person's father or other ancestor. The earliest inscriptions probably date to the fifth and sixth centuries, and some may belong to the fourth.[1] The invention of the ogam alphabet cannot have occurred later than the fourth century,[2] and it has been suggested that it may date to the end of the second century or the beginning of the third.[3] We know nothing of the identity of the inventor of this alphabet, but we can be sure that he knew Latin and that his invention entailed an analysis of the Irish language.

The relatively early date of the invention of the ogam alphabet indicates that literacy in Irish may have predated the introduction of Christianity. Ogam was probably invented to be used on wood, and it is possible that it may have been used to inscribe on wooden tablets what D. A. Binchy called 'an elementary type of written literature'.[4] There is evidence in Irish hagiography that the normal notebook in Irish schools of this period was the waxed wooden tablet inscribed with a metal stylus. As F. J. Byrne has observed, these tablets were cheap and expendable;[5] they were of course also perishable. Happily, however, six waxed yew tablets bearing portions of the Psalms have survived. Known as the Springmount Bog tablets after the bog (near Ballymena in County Antrim) in which they were found in 1913, they have been dated to the later years of the sixth century.[6] But while these tablets provide material evidence of early inscription on wood, their content is ecclesiastical and their language and script are Latin: they do not support the notion that vernacular literary texts actually were inscribed in ogam on wood. What we can say is that literacy in the vernacular has a very long history in Ireland, and that it was established long before the end of the sixth century, which is when our oldest extant vernacular texts are believed to have been composed.

Ireland was never a part of the Roman empire, so the establishment of Latin literacy in Ireland represents the expansion of the Latin script for the first time beyond the imperial limits.[7] The oldest vellum manuscripts come from about the same time as the Springmount Bog tablets, and contain liturgical and other ecclesiastical texts in Latin.[8] A manuscript written towards the end of the seventh century contains some Irish words and phrases: this is the liturgical book now known as the *Antiphonary of Bangor*, which is preserved in Milan and is believed to have been written c.680–90. In some of the manuscripts of the period between the seventh century and the eleventh, we find glosses written in Irish, which explain or comment upon the Latin texts; as well as the interlinear glosses there are some short continuous passages, and scribal marginalia and notes. This material constitutes the contemporary basis of our knowledge of Old Irish (the language of the period roughly from AD 600 to 900). Comparison with the language of the glosses provides us with approximate dates for early texts that do not survive in contemporary manuscripts. We can be reasonably sure that vernacular texts were being written in Latin script by AD 600, but none of these texts has survived in early manuscripts. The gap in time between the date of composition of a given text and that of the recording of it in the earliest extant manuscript has profound consequences for our attempts to reconstruct the history of the literature. We shall see presently that this is especially true of the early vernacular narrative texts.

The works of St Patrick

The earliest Latin texts known to have been composed in Ireland are the works of St Patrick, the *Confession* and *Letter to the Soldiers of Coroticus*.[9] The earliest manuscript of these works is the ninth-century Book of Armagh. It is virtually certain, however, that Patrick lived in the fifth century, and that his mission to Ireland followed that of Palladius. Patrick, according to his own account, was born into a privileged family in Roman Britain. He was captured as a teenager by Irish raiders and taken to Ireland as a slave. In the six years of his captivity in Ireland, Patrick came to love God with growing intensity. Guided by a vision, he escaped and contrived to return to his homeland, where he became a cleric. His return as a missionary to the land of his former captivity was also prompted by a vision, in which he was summoned to Ireland by the voice of its people. He spent the rest of his life spreading the gospel in Ireland. Patrick's works do not tell us everything we would wish to know: they do not, for example, give us any dates for the events that they relate. He evidently had certain detractors in Britain, and in his works he defends himself and his apostolate with passionate conviction. What we have here are the authentic meditations of an early and influential evangelist, who was later to be revered as the national apostle of Ireland. The figure of Patrick soon became encrusted in legend, but none of that can diminish the strength of personality and the devotion to Christ that make his own words so compelling.

Monastic literature

In the generations immediately following Patrick's mission, the crucial institutional development in the Irish church was the foundation, mainly in the sixth century, of monasteries in Clonard, Clonmacnoise, Bangor, Glendalough, Lismore and elsewhere throughout the country – and also in Scotland with the foundation by Colum Cille of the monastery of Iona. Monasteries such as these, together with those at Armagh and Kildare, became the spiritual and intellectual centres of the Irish church. The Bible, Latin grammar and computistics were intensively studied in the Irish monastic schools, and numerous exegetical tracts were taken from Ireland to Europe where they were often ascribed to authorities such as Augustine or Jerome. The Irish monastic schools exerted an influence beyond the shores of Ireland. They did this in the first place by attracting students from Britain, and secondly, and most spectacularly, through the work of alumni who for love of Christ went into exile in Britain and Europe. Of those who went to Europe in the early period the best known is St Columbanus, a Leinsterman who spent many years as a disciple of St Comgall at Bangor before he set out for Europe around the year 591. Columbanus set up a number of monasteries on the continent, culminating in the establishment of the monastery of Bobbio in Italy not long before his death in 615. A learned and effective writer of Latin, Columbanus composed poems, two sets of rules for the monastic life, a penitential (a text that gives the penalties appropriate for various sins), sermons and letters.[10]

Saints' Lives

The classes of texts that were produced and preserved in the monastic schools included the Lives of the founders of monasteries, disciplinary regulations, devotional compositions, homiletic literature, imaginative religious literature, and many more besides.[11] There are early Lives in Latin of Brigit, Patrick and Colum Cille. Muirchú moccu Machthéni wrote a Life of Patrick in the second half of the seventh century.[12] The early hagiographers were generally interested in glorifying the churches of which the saints were patrons, and Muirchú was promoting the interests of Armagh. One of his sources was the saint's *Confession*, but the meagre biographical details that Patrick supplied are subsumed in a hagiographical narrative that formed the basis of what has become known as the legend of St Patrick. Muirchú includes such episodes as those in which Patrick lights the paschal fire for the first time in Ireland, proves himself better than the druids at miracle-working, and converts the king of Tara, Loígaire mac Néill. Muirchú tells us that when Patrick first entered the king's banqueting hall, the only man who rose to welcome him was Dubthach moccu Lugair, 'an excellent poet'. The saint blessed him, and he was the first on that day to believe in God. Dubthach was accompanied by a young poet named Fiacc, who afterwards became a bishop.[13] What Muirchú has to say casts light on his own time rather than that of Patrick, and it is highly significant that a seventh-century propagandist for Armagh should claim that the poets, unlike the druids, and for a time even the king, should immediately convert to Christianity and that a young poet went on to become one of the first bishops.

Hymns and religious poems in Latin and Irish

Among the hymns and versified prayers composed in Latin, pride of place may perhaps be given to the *Altus Prosator*,[14] which is attributed to Colum Cille, and has been described as 'a kind of early "Paradise Lost"'.[15] All the great topics of the teaching of the early medieval church on the nature of the world are dealt with in this poem – the nature of God, the creation of the universe, the fall of Lucifer, the seduction of Adam and Eve, the terrors of the Day of Judgement, and so on. The validity of the attribution of the *Altus Prosator* to Colum Cille is disputed by Jane Stevenson, who argues that this 'outstandingly ambitious' poem was probably composed in Ireland in the second half of the seventh century.[16] The form of the poem is 'abecedarian', with each of its twenty-three stanzas beginning with successive letters of the alphabet. This form was particularly attractive to Hiberno-Latin authors. The influential hymn in praise of St Patrick, 'Audite Omnes Amantes', is also abecedarian and is attributed to St Secundinus (Sechnall in Irish), who is said to have been a fifth-century missionary to Ireland. It is not impossible that it was indeed composed in the fifth century; it is in any case early, and may well be the first hymn composed in Ireland.[17]

The earliest hymn in Irish may be *Brigit Bé Bithmaith* (Brigit Ever Excellent Woman), sometimes known as Ultán's Hymn.[18] The poet invokes St Brigit's protection against the flesh and the devil. He praises her as a golden sparkling flame, as a true virgin, as saint of the Leinstermen and (with St Patrick) as one of the two 'pillars of sovereignty'. She is said to be *in máthair Ísu* (the mother of Jesus), a conceit that is found also in an early genealogical poem where she is described as *alaMairi . . . morChoimded mathair* (second Mary, mother of the great Lord).[19] In the manuscripts various suggestions are offered regarding the authorship of *Brigit Bé Bithmaith*. Of these, the most plausible is perhaps Ultán of Ardbraccan (in County Meath), who died in 657 or 663. Stokes and Strachan said of *Brigit Bé Bithmaith* that it is 'the only one of the Irish hymns which shews high poetic art', and that there is nothing in its language to show that it cannot go back to the seventh century AD.[20]

One of the other authors to whom *Brigit Bé Bithmaith* is attributed is Brocán, who is said to have been a pupil of Ultán. Brocán is credited with the authorship of a much longer poem of fifty-three quatrains *Ní car Brigit búadach bith* (Victorious Brigit Loved not the World).[21] This latter poem mainly comprises allusions to miracles performed by Brigit and its content has much in common with that of the seventh-century Latin Life by Cogitosus. Stokes and Strachan suggested that Cogitosus based his narrative on the hymn.[22] There are some linguistic forms in the hymn that are incompatible with anything like so early a date, but Stokes and Strachan considered that these may be put down to interpolation, which in an essentially disconnected string of miracles could easily be accomplished.[23] James Carney included this poem among those that can be dated between the years AD 630 and 700.[24] Perhaps the most that can be said, pending further work on the poem, is that *Ní car Brigit búadach bith* contains a very early stratum, which may be one of the earliest extant specimens of hagiography in the vernacular.

Three early Irish poets composed poems on Christ; each of them is highly accomplished in its way, and also quite different from the others. One is a metrical version of the Apocryphal Gospel of St Thomas.[25] David Greene and

Frank O'Connor have justly described this as 'one of the most delightful things in early Irish', and said that 'the language is used with a sort of morning freshness that reminds us of some of the early English carols'.[26] The poem narrates episodes from Christ's childhood. He is presented as an impish prankster, who is concerned above all with protecting his own interests. He miraculously slays another boy who annoys him, and when upbraided he replies that only the wicked are put to death. When he is sent to school he cockily shows up his teacher, who finds to his dismay that he has taken on a master rather than a pupil. The young Christ soon puts a stop to anyone who chastises him: he ensures that deafness seizes their ears, blindness their eyes. The only healing miracle with which he is credited here occurs when Christ is wrongly blamed for the death of a boy who has fallen over a cliff. He revives the boy so that he can testify to Christ's innocence, and when this has been done the boy dies again. An understanding gradually develops, however, of Christ's role as saviour. At first it seems to Joseph that his son is such a misfit that he deserves to die on a cross or in some other way. His teacher Zacharias comes to learn that this little boy is the being destined for the cross, and Christ himself reveals that he will suffer the cross in order to redeem every creature.

In the eighth century, probably in the years 750–70, Blathmac son of Cú Brettan son of Congus of the Fir Roiss in what is now County Monaghan wrote at length about Christ in verse that he addressed to Christ's mother, Mary. His work survives only in a seventeenth-century manuscript in the National Library of Ireland, and it comprises two poems (one of them incomplete).[27] The first poem comprises 149 quatrains; James Carney suggested that a quatrain may have been lost, and that the original work may have consisted of three poems, each of 150 stanzas. In the first of them, *Tair cucum a Maire boíd* (Come to Me, Loving Mary), Blathmac invites Mary to come to him so that he may keen her son. The second poem, *A Maire, a grian ar clainde* (Mary, Sun of our Race), is expressly presented as a sequel to the keen, and its theme is expressed in the fourth line: *sech is bithbéo, is bithflaith* (he [Christ] lives eternally, is eternal prince). Both poems refer to successive events in the life of Christ, but in the first of them the emphasis is on his suffering and death, and on the need to lament what has been done to him, whereas the second stresses Christ's lordship, his resurrection, his ascension and the promise of his second coming.

Blathmac depicts Christ as an omnicompetent hero: he is a bishop and sage; an abbot (to his apostles and disciples); better than a prophet, wiser than a druid; more vigorous than any carpenter, more just than any judge. He has the qualities of a warrior and the generosity of a king. His life (and death) is presented episodically as a heroic biography, using the terms and categories of

Irish storytelling.[28] The poet applies the norms of Irish society to the aftermath of the crucifixion: in an Irish household cries of lamentation are raised and hands are beaten over the body of a deceased lord, and that is therefore what the apostles, had they been permitted, would have done over the body of Christ.

The relationship between the Israelites and Christ is depicted in terms of Irish concepts of lordship and kinship. An essential feature of Irish society was the contractual relationship between lord and client: the lord gave a gift to the client, the acceptance of which bound the client to return a counter-gift to the lord, in the form of food-rent and certain services. As Blathmac sees it, the contractual relationship between Jesus and the Israelites had its origin in the covenant (*cotach*) that God made with Abraham, and in fulfilment of which he granted them the Promised Land (*Tír Tairngiri*). Their slaying of Christ is a repudiation of their legal obligation to him as lord. The fact that Christ was himself an Israelite allows the poet to class his death as *fingal*, which is the crime of slaying a member of one's own kindred. This was a heinous crime in early Ireland, as it was the duty of the kindred to avenge the death of one of their members. This was not practicable if the perpetrator of the crime was also a kinsman.

Blathmac expresses some surprise that the death of Christ was not avenged by the elements. The notion that Christ's death should have been avenged is explored in the poem *Ba haprainn nan dáil cu Artrig n-arnac* (Alas that I Did Not Get to Meet the High-King),[29] which is embedded in the prose narrative of *Aided Chonchobuir* (The Violent Death of Conchobor). This tale survives in a number of versions.[30] According to one of them,[31] an emissary from imperial Rome, who was a Christian, tells the Ulster king, Conchobor, about Christ's divine nature, his mission on earth and his crucifixion. Conchobor becomes a believer. The poem is prompted by his anger upon hearing of the crucifixion. He regrets that he did not have the opportunity to protect Christ and that he must die without avenging him. He boasts of the warlike deeds that he would have performed had he been given the opportunity. The odds against him would have been insuperable, but he would happily have died. Martyrdom would have been easier for him than living on after Christ had been put to death in redemption of humankind. Conchobor's willingness to die for Christ earns him salvation. Johan Corthals has shown that this is an expression of 'baptism by blood' as it was accepted in early Christianity: Conchobor was a martyr by intention, and the blood which he would have shed as a martyr is a substitute for the baptism by water which of course was not available to him.

The poem in *Aided Chonchobuir* is in early Old Irish, and is tentatively dated by Corthals to the early eighth century. It is in rhymeless alliterative metre, and it is a very difficult work, the vocabulary and syntax being very far removed from the prosaic. In these respects it is very different from the other poems on Christ that we have been looking at. Another point of difference is that the *Aided Chonchobuir* poem has been transmitted and was presumably composed as part of the Ulster Cycle of tales. As Kim McCone has observed, the hallowing of the Ulster king in the service of Christ provides a charter for the monastic cultivation of the Ulster Cycle as a whole.[32]

Christ is intimately invoked in the metrical prayer known as 'Patrick's Breastplate',[33] which is a specimen of the *lorica* (Irish *lúirech*), a term deriving from the reference to spiritual armour in the writings of St Paul. The poem is probably to be dated to the eighth century. As John Carey has observed, the efficacy of the *loricae* depends on exhaustive enumeration: God and all the powers of heaven are invoked to protect every part of the suppliant against a multitude of spiritual and physical dangers.[34] The perils of which the poet speaks show us a world in which paganism, idolatry and 'the spells of women and smiths and druids' must be guarded against; the suppliant will be protected by the eye, ear, tongue and hand of God, Christ will be within him and all around him, in every eye that sees him and in every ear that hears him.

Féilire Óengusso (The Martyrology of Oengus),[35] a calendar of the feast-days and festivals of the church, with an entry for each day of the year, may belong to the end of the eighth, or the early part of the ninth century. In the epilogue, the *Féilire* is said to be a *lúirech*, and the author makes extravagant claims for the beneficial power of his verse. It is in the prologue to the *Féilire*, however, that Oengus shows real poetic power. The most celebrated lines are those in which Oengus draws a contrast between the pagan sites, which have fallen into disuse, and the Christian ones, which are now triumphant.[36]

Other religious texts in Irish

The use of vernacular prose for religious literature can be dated to the beginning of the seventh century on the evidence of the *Apgitir Chrábaid* (The Alphabet of Piety).[37] This is the work of Colmán moccu Béognae, who died in 611.[38] It has recently been shown that two consecutive sections of the *Apgitir Chrábaid* are in non-rhyming alliterative verse.[39] Prosimetrum, which combines prose and verse, is found also in the vernacular law texts and in the sagas.

The earliest sermon in Irish, dated on linguistic grounds to the second half of the seventh century, is the Cambrai Homily,[40] so called because it is preserved in Cambrai in a manuscript of the Collection of Irish Canons. The continental scribe was copying from an Irish manuscript into which there must have been inserted a stray leaf or two containing part of the homily, and he wrote on as though it formed part of the Collection. The end of the text is lacking, but enough survives to show that the homily was skilfully constructed. Pádraig Ó Néill has shown that its author drew on two 'long and digressive' homilies by Gregory the Great, from which he culled a short and effective piece of exegesis on a passage in Matthew's gospel.[41] This he combined with a discussion of three forms of martyrdom, which are described as white, green and red. The early Irish church was acutely aware of its lack of martyrs, but some compensation was to be found in the notion of white martyrdom, which entails separating for the sake of God from everything one loves, or green martyrdom, when by means of fasting and labour one separates from one's desires, or suffers toil in penance and repentance.

The scriptural quotations and the passages from Gregory are in Latin; the rest is in Old Irish. The Latin parts are paraphrased in Old Irish, and this suggests an audience that was not altogether familiar with Latin. This is all the more striking when it is considered that the content of the homily suggests that it was directed at a monastic community. In any case, this homily, which survives by the merest accident, is of such quality as to show that the seventh-century Irish church had mastered the art of homiletics in the Irish language.

Secular literature in Irish: poetry

What is most noteworthy about the Irish church in the context of literary history is its extraordinary openness to secular literature. An anecdote which Adomnán relates in his Life of Colum Cille (*Vita Columbae*) is emblematic of the rapport that was possible in the sixth century between a venerable cleric and a secular poet. Adomnán tells us that a poet named Crónán visited the saint as he sat with some of his monks beside Lough Key.[42] The monks were surprised that Colum Cille did not 'according to the custom ask [the poet] for a song of his own composition sung to a tune'. The saint explained that he did not do so because he knew that the poet was about to be slain by his enemies, and it would have been inappropriate to ask him for a happy song in those circumstances. Colum Cille, of royal blood and founder of the monastery at Iona, is one of the great figures of the early Irish church. He is commonly believed to have died in 597. His biographer Adomnán, a kinsman and a successor as abbot of Iona, wrote the *Vita Columbae* about a hundred years after Colum Cille's death. Adomnán, writing in Latin, describes Colum

Cille's visitor Crónán as a *scoticus poeta*, an Irish-language poet, the equivalent of Old Irish *fili* (plural *filid*). For Adomnán's purposes, the anecdote exemplifies the saint's prophetic power: the poet died as Colum Cille said he would. It has an added significance for us in that it shows that Adomnán considered it customary for Colum Cille to entertain Irish-language poets, and to ask them to sing songs of their own composition. We may assume that the songs in question would have been poems of praise, since the purveying of praise (and, where appropriate, blame) was a primary function of the *fili*. In his summary of Colum Cille's 'miracles of power', Adomnán says that certain guilty and blood-stained men were miraculously delivered from their enemies through the chanting of certain songs of his praise in the Irish tongue, the only ones who perished being the few who declined to sing; this miracle happened at various places and times, in Ireland and Britain.[43]

Adomnán thus establishes a clear association between Colum Cille and vernacular praise poetry. In later centuries, the saint is depicted as friend and patron of poets, and a large number of poems in the vernacular are credited to him. Most if not all of these attributions are false, but James Carney was prepared to entertain the possibility that Colum Cille was indeed the author of a short poem in Irish, *Sét no tíag* (The Path I Walk).[44] If poems in his praise really were composed in his own lifetime, they have not survived, but we do have poems of praise that were composed after his death. The earliest of these is the *Amra Choluim Chille* (Eulogy of Colum Cille), which is generally believed to have been composed shortly after the saint's death. Two very fine eulogies of the saint have come down to us from the seventh century; they are attributed to Bécan mac Luigdech, who (like Colum Cille himself) was a direct descendant of Níall Noígíallach, ancestor of the powerful Uí Néill.[45]

Amra Choluim Chille is attributed to Dallán Forgaill. Nothing is known with certainty about him, but according to legend he was 'the chief-poet of Ireland', and was defended by Colum Cille when the poets were threatened with banishment from Ireland. The *Amra* repeatedly honours Columba's royal ancestry, but he is praised as a spiritual rather than a secular leader, a faithful follower of the cross of Christ, ascetic and virtuous in his daily life, and protector of the naked and the poor. Special emphasis is placed on his learning and scholarship, and on his role as a teacher. No mention is made of the saint's miracles, which are such an important component in the hagiographical record. Nevertheless, the content of the *Amra* might suggest that it is the work of a cleric. If the author was a *fili*, whether called Dallán or by some other name, then it is clear that at least some of the traditional poets and the clerics were on very good terms by the end of the sixth century.

Another poet whose work points to the same conclusion is Colmán mac Léneni (died c.606). Some fragments of Colmán's verse survive,[46] and James Carney has suggested that his writings could date from about 550 onwards.[47] One of the fragments is a quatrain in praise of a king named Domnall, whose kingship excels that of others 'as swans excel blackbirds, or the shapeliness of aristocratic ladies the form of peasant women'.[48] Colmán is said to have been an *athláech* (an ex-layman), which indicates that he became a cleric late in life. In one of the surviving quatrains that clearly dates from his time as a cleric, Colmán uses legal language to say that his poem has been composed not for earthly reward, but rather for the grace of God.[49] The word used for 'grace' in this connection is not (as one might expect) a borrowing from Latin, but rather a native Irish word, *rath*, that is used of the fief given by a lord to his vassal or 'client'. Colmán's talent and skill as a *fili*, which he had used in the service of secular kings, will henceforth be devoted to praise of God.

The *fili* was a central figure in the political and cultural establishment of early Ireland. We know this from a wide variety of sources: for the early period the law tracts give us a great deal of information, and this is true in particular of the texts that, according to D. A. Binchy, emanate from a poetico-legal school that may have been located in Munster.[50] These include two tracts that bear the title *Bretha Nemed* (Judgements Concerning Privileged Persons), and two tracts concerning status: one of these, the *Uraicecht Becc* (Small Primer), is especially concerned with the status of certain kinds of privileged person, including the *filid*; the other, *Uraicecht na Ríar* (The Primer of Stipulations), deals with the various grades of *fili*, their qualifications and their privileges.[51] Seven grades of *fili*, and three sub-grades, are recognised in *Uraicecht na Ríar*. The highest grade is the *ollam*, who 'has three hundred and fifty compositions . . . he is knowledgeable in all historical sciences, and he is knowledgeable in the jurisprudence of Irish law'.[52] The other grades are classified according to the number of compositions that they have mastered. The precise meaning in this context of *drécht* (composition) is not entirely clear, but there is some evidence to suggest that it means 'tale'.[53] The traditional tales – *togla* (destructions), *tána* (cattle raids), *tochmarca* (wooings) and so on – evidently formed a central part of the poets' curriculum, and the later lists of tales give us some indication of their storytelling repertory.[54]

In the conferring of a grade upon a poet, as it is described in *Uraicecht na Ríar*, the king and his *ollam* both play a part. While it is the king who actually confers the grade, he does so upon the recommendation of his *ollam*, who is proficient in the knowledge proper to each of the seven grades. The recommendation is based in part on the poet's compositions, which he displays to the *ollam* – it is not clear from the wording whether this is done orally or in writing – but the *ollam* also takes account of certain aspects of the poet's professional and personal conduct. The poet must be learned, and he must be innocent of unjust defamation and of theft, plunder and illegality; he must have only one wife, with whom he may have intercourse on the nights when it is lawful to do so.[55] The latter provision shows that the poet's conduct was in some measure dictated by the church. Formally, the profession of *filidecht* seems to have been self-regulating, subject always to the final authority of the king, but the pervasiveness of clerical influence is also clear.[56]

The role of the *fili* as purveyor of praise and blame was inherited from pre-Christian times. We can be sure too that the traditional poets and learned men conserved the narrative and genealogical lore of the ruling classes. What is not clear is the precise nature of the relationship in early Christian Ireland between the *filid* and the clerics, but there is no doubt that there was a considerable degree of overlap between the two. The patrons of the *filid* were either the kings and nobles, or the church.[57] There is a good deal of evidence that the clerics, the *filid* and the jurists exercised their respective roles within a single literary and scholarly establishment. For one thing, our sources for Early Irish, abundant as they are, show very few features that could be described as dialectal. As David Greene has said, it is 'in the highest degree improbable' that the ordinary speech of the people showed no dialect variations whatsoever, for that is not the normal situation in any linguistic community.[58] We do not know how this standard written language was brought into existence. One suggestion is that Old Irish began as a single dialect which was then given a special status;[59] another is that a literary ecclesiastical standard was forged around the later sixth century.[60] Whichever of these explanations is preferred, the existence of a standard presupposes the intervention of a learned elite with the requisite prestige and authority to impose it. That elite must have had its institutional base in the monasteries.

The study of Latin grammar, as we have seen, was one of the major disciplines in the Irish schools, but Irish was also studied in a scholarly way. The work of bilingual Irish scholars, which had its first fruits in the invention of the ogam alphabet, continued with the adaptation of the Latin alphabet for the purpose of writing Irish. The Old Irish linguistic tract *Auraicept na n-Éces* (The Primer of the Poets)[61] deals with the alphabets of Irish and Latin, and with a limited number of grammatical categories in the two languages. It is an extraordinary work for its time, for it treats the vernacular as a serious subject of study, worthy of comparison with Latin. Even more remarkable is the author's proud proclamation that the Irish language was composed of what was best in other languages: *a mba ferr íarum do cach bérlu 7 a mba leithiu 7 a mba caímiu, is ed do-reped isin nGoídilc* (what was best then of every language and what was widest and finest was cut out into Irish).[62] These are the words of a man who knows the strength and value of his own culture. Moreover, the author of the *Auraicept* goes on to say that after Fénius Farsaid had carried out this task at the Tower of Babel, the subsequent dispersal from the Tower was on the basis of a common language: 'it was everyone who spoke the same language that went from there and not everyone of the same descent'.[63] Irish identity, and the unity of the Irish people, derives from the Irish language.[64]

The metres used by the *filid* are those found in the works of churchmen and lawyers. Two different kinds of metre are used in the *Amra Choluim Chille*. The bulk of the poem is written in unrhymed alliterative verse, which in Irish is known as *retoiric* or *roscad*. The *Amra* has an introduction that combines stanzaic structure and rhyme with sporadic alliteration. Here then we have the two broad categories of Irish verse, which are defined by the presence or absence of rhyme. Of the rhyming verse, the predominant types have regular syllable count in the lines, and also in the rhyming words. Syllabic metres of this type are known as *nua-chrotha* (new-forms), and they were to continue in use until the end of the classical Modern Irish period.

Poetry and ecclesiastical learning are treated together in a text now known as 'The Caldron of Poesy',[65] dated to the early eighth century.[66] A more appropriate title, as Liam Breatnach has suggested, would be 'The Three Cauldrons of Poetry and Learning'.[67] The author of this text is primarily concerned with the source of poetic art and of learning. He addresses the question of whether the source of poetic art is in the body or in the soul. He notes that two different answers are current: some say that the source is in the soul, since the body cannot act independently of the soul, and others say it is in the body, since the poetic craft is inherited from one's father and grandfather. He steers clear of both these positions, and asserts instead that the source of poetic art is present in all corporeal persons, but manifests itself only in every second person. Poetic art and all knowledge have their source in three cauldrons that are generated in each person. The first of them is the source of knowledge of grammar, metrics and writing, and the second is the source of knowledge of every other art besides poetic art. It is the third cauldron that receives most attention. The only individuals to benefit from this will be those who experience sorrow or joy. Sorrow, as our author conceives it, seems to have to do with purely personal experience, longing, grief, the sorrow of jealousy and that of exile for the sake of God. As Liam Breatnach has pointed out, what appears to be involved here is 'personal poetry' as opposed to 'professional poetry', and it is noteworthy that such poetry should have been held in such esteem.[68] Joy, we are told, is of two kinds, human and divine. Human joy, in this context, comprises the successive stages of training in poetry, culminating in the arrival of the quintessential poetic quality known as *imbas*, which has its origin in the well of Segais, here as elsewhere said to be an Otherworld habitation (*síd*).

The development of a 'synthetic history' for all the Irish was a major enterprise of the Irish schools. This entailed a sequence of invasions, culminating in that of Míl Espáine, whose two sons, Éber and Éremón, divided Ireland between them. This enterprise was already under way in the seventh century.[69] Three of the Milesian invaders of Ireland are mentioned in the first poem of 'The Caldron of Poesy': its speaker identifies himself as Amairgen, and he uses the knowledge derived from his caldron to compose poetry for Éber and Donn.

Secular literature in Irish: legal texts and wisdom literature

One of the greatest achievements of early Christian Ireland lay in the field of law. The Irish church developed its own law and this culminated in the text known as *Collectio canonum Hibernensis* (The Collection of Irish Canons), dated to the first quarter of the eighth century. The churchmen used the vernacular for ecclesiastical legislation, as in the case of *Cáin Adamnáin* (The Law of Adamnán),[70] which was promulgated in Ireland in 697 by Adamnán of Iona. The secular law texts cover a wide range of topics, and illuminate many aspects of early Irish society. They are of interest in their own right: to mention but one of them, Thomas Charles-Edwards has said of *Críth Gablach* (Branched Purchase) that 'it is one of the few outstanding pieces of social analysis in early medieval Europe'.[71] They also provide invaluable insight into the mindset of the authors of our poetic and narrative texts. Moreover, the authors of the law tracts sometimes drew on Irish tales (as well as the Bible) for 'precedents' or 'leading cases', and it is to this propensity on their part that we owe the preservation of some of the tales, most notably the remarkable early version of *Echtra Fergusa maic Leti* (The Adventure of Fergus mac Leti).[72]

Early Irish wisdom literature, in Latin and in Irish, is closely akin to the law. *Audacht Moraind* (The Testament of Morann) is a seventh-century example of the genre known as *Speculum Principum* (Mirror of Princes).[73] It consists of advice supposedly sent by the legendary judge Morann mac Móin to Feradach

Find Fechtnach, who is about to be made king. A central concept in the text is that of *fír flathemon* (the ruler's truth/justice): it keeps plagues and lightning from the people, it ensures peace and prosperity in the realm, as well as abundance of milk and corn and fish, and fertility among the people. This emphasis on the king's truth and justice is echoed in the laws and in the tales. The ruler is also required to be merciful: he must not allow riches or treasures to blind him to the weak or their sufferings. As a matter of honour he must feed his people; it is also his duty to defend them against others. The king and his people are interdependent, and this too is a theme in the literature and the laws.

Secular literature in Irish: history

The Irish schools were deeply committed to the study of *senchas* 'knowledge of the past'. Genealogy was an abiding concern, and early records survive in the form of pedigrees, synchronisms and origin legends. Many of the more significant ancestral figures have several tales devoted to them, and the historical tales are sometimes classed as 'cycles of the kings'. One of the richest cycles has to do with the eponymous ancestors of the Éoganachta and the Dál Cuinn. An early text is *Immathchor nAilella 7 Airt* (Mutual Restitution between Ailill and Art).[74] A short prose introduction explains that a dispute has arisen between Ailill Aulomm and his wife, Sadb, daughter of Conn Cétchathach, regarding the children of the marriage. Ailill has put aside his wife, and she has reared the children. Ailill and Sadb's brother Art submit the matter of the subsequent responsibility for the children's upbringing to Ollam, 'the judge of Ireland'. What follows is an account of the successive stages of a court case, all of the speeches being in *roscad*. (In the event, the judge assigns sole responsibility for the children to their father.) Johan Corthals argues that this text can be regarded as a reflex of a literary genre that in the rhetorical schools of antiquity was called *controversia*.[75] The body of the work consists of judicial dialogue. In the context of early Irish law, the judgment given by Ollam can be seen to follow the second of 'five paths of judgment' that are attributed to a poet called Cermna who flourished in the first half of the eighth century.[76] The judgment includes a maxim on the honourable basis of dynastic descent that is reminiscent of prescriptions found in the *Collectio canonum Hibernensis* and in the influential Irish wisdom text, *De XII abusivis saeculi*.[77]

The concern with family relationships that is reflected in this early text is a continuing one in the cycle of tales relating to the Éoganachta and the Dál

Cuinn.[78] The language of some of the tales in this cycle has been dated to the first half of the ninth century, but it has been suggested that there are elements within them that point to early sources, perhaps as early as 700.[79]

Secular literature in Irish: prose tales

The historical tales are among the great number of anecdotes and tales that have come down to us in Irish manuscripts. We can justly speak of a great tradition of storytelling in the Irish language: while tales vary greatly in their quality and in their appeal to the modern reader, many of them are literary compositions of a high order. The titles of some of the surviving tales occur also in the lists of the tales that the *filid* are said to have known. Some of these have to do with major events in the life of an individual, such as *comperta* (conceptions), *aitheda* (elopements), *tochmarca* (wooings), *echtrai* (expeditions [to the Otherworld]), *immrama* (sea voyages), and *aitte/aideda* (violent deaths). Others relate momentous or cataclysmic events in the social and political history of population groups, such as *catha* (battles), *tomadmann* (eruptions [of lakes or rivers]), *tochomlada* (migrations), *oircne* (slaughters, destructions), *togla* (destructions) and *tána bó* (cattle raids). We cannot now know what relationship there may have been between the tales that have come down to us in the manuscripts and those which would have been known by the *filid*.

The history of early Irish narrative is not recoverable. One of the difficulties has already been mentioned, which is that the manuscripts in which we find the texts are quite late. In fact none of the narrative texts survives in a manuscript written before the end of the eleventh century. The difficulties thus posed are compounded by the nature of the manuscript transmission of the texts. The authors of the tales are not named, and the manuscript transmission was a creative process comprising the expansion and contraction, reshaping and redaction of matter, much of which must have been received into the literature from indigenous oral tradition, but some of which is of learned ecclesiastical provenance. We can assume that a good deal of the material has perished; as for the rest of what was composed in our period, some of it has doubtless been modernised beyond recognition, while more of it survives as early strata in composite texts.

Some of the tales that have come down to us may nevertheless be assigned with some degree of confidence to the eighth, or perhaps even to the seventh century. There is a group of texts which appear to be early, and which are known as the *Cín Dromma Snechtai* (The Book of Drumsnat) texts. This is because they were believed to have belonged to a manuscript of that name that is now lost; the date of that manuscript and the list of surviving texts that may have been contained in it are matters of controversy, but it is likely that the designation will survive as a convenient way to refer to these early texts.[80]

Three of the texts in this group are *comperta*, including two that belong to the Ulster Cycle, *Compert Conchobuir* (The Conception of Conchobor) and *Compert Con Culainn* (The Conception of Cú Chulainn). The *Compert Conchobuir* in its early form is recounted in about one hundred words; there are no attributive adjectives, no descriptive adverbs, and the name of the hero is given only in the title. That an early eighth-century monastic author should concern himself with the story of the conception of Conchobor is interesting, but what is really revealing is the manner in which he tells the story. The tale as we have it would have a point only if it has an unspoken relationship to a narrative world, some knowledge of which is shared by the writer and the reader. The writer assumes that his reader will know who Conchobor is, and this requires an acquaintance with other stories about (or at least involving) Conchobor, in other words with other items from what we now call the Ulster Cycle. This tells us something about the nature of literary activity in the early eighth century, for it shows that at that time the Ulster tales subsisted as a cycle, demanding and enabling the proliferation of tales such as *Compert Conchobuir*, which are formally self-contained but which have as their *raison d'être* an intertextual relationship with other items in the cycle.[81]

The greatest tale of the Ulster Cycle, *Táin Bó Cúailnge*, has a complex textual history. *Compert Conchobuir* and *Compert Con Culainn* are classed among the tales that in Irish are said to be 'prefatory tales to *Táin Bó Cúailnge*' (*remscéla Tána Bó Cúailngi*).[82] There are two other texts that may be described as precursors to the *Táin*. One of these is *Conailla Medb Míchuru* (Medb Enjoined Evil Contracts), a *roscad* by the poet Luccreth moccu Chíara.[83] The other one is the *Verba Scáthaige* (The Words of Scáthach), a *Cín Dromma Snechtai* text.[84] It is a prophecy uttered in *roscad* by Scáthach, the Amazonian warrior who instructed Cú Chulainn. She foretells Cú Chulainn's adventures when he is called upon to defend Ulster against the invading army of Ailill and Medb. She alludes laconically to many of the events that are narrated in detail in *Táin Bó Cúailnge*, culminating with the fight of the two bulls. This poem shows that the story of Cú Chulainn's epic defence of Ulster must have been in existence in the eighth century in a form bearing some resemblance to that in the extant versions of *Táin Bó Cúailnge*. Much the same can be said of *Togail Bruidne da Derga* (The Destruction of Da Derga's Hostel), another one of the great Irish tales, which is represented in the *Cín Dromma Snechtai* by a laconic summary of its main events.[85]

That the short Irish saga was already a subtle and sophisticated literary form in the eighth century is shown by *Echtrae Chonnlai* (The Expedition of Connlae).[86] This is mainly in the form of stylised dialogue, with some brief linking sentences of prose narrative. Some of the dialogue is in a fairly free type of *roscad*, and it culminates in three quatrains in syllabic metre. A woman from the Otherworld comes to Connlae son of Conn and invites him to go away with her to the 'Plain of Delights'. Conn's druid uses his spells to make the woman disappear, but Connlae has now been smitten by 'longing' (*éolchaire*) for the woman, and he will take no drink nor food except for an apple which has been thrown to him by the woman, and which sustains him for a month. The woman then reappears, and once again invites Connlae to join her. He says that it is not easy for him, because he loves his people, but he declares that longing for the woman has seized him and he leaps away from them. The two of them leave, never to be seen again.

This story is the earliest example of the *echtrae*, a genre describing an Otherworld journey or experience, which is well represented in Irish literature. For Conn and his people this is a bleak story: 'the people of the sea' choose Connlae as their champion or hero, and have the woman take him away from his land and kin. Unlike the protagonists of some of the other *echtrai*, Connlae does not return from the Otherworld with treasures for his people. For the hero, however, there is a promise not only of love but also of paradise – a land that is without grief, without woe, and where there is neither death nor sin. And for Conn and his people the woman does hold out the promise of better things to come. She prophesies the coming in a short while of 'the Great High King's righteous and decent one', and of his law, and promises that 'he will destroy the spells of the druids of base teaching / In front of the black bewitching devil'.[87]

A distinguishing feature of Irish culture in the seventh and eighth centuries was the confidence and apparent ease with which external elements were combined with inherited ones. This is true of scholarship, literature and art. We encounter some towering figures in these centuries, but much of what survives is anonymous. Many of the individual works are of a high order, and only a small number of them could be noticed here. It was during this period that patterns were set that were to endure in Irish literature for many centuries to come: in language, in metre, in narrative and in much else. We owe the vitality and exuberance of the earliest Irish literature to the churchmen, scholars and *filid* who brought it into being. In doing so, they laid the foundations for much of what will be described in the other chapters of this book.

Notes

1. Damian McManus, *A Guide to Ogam*, Maynooth Monographs IV (Maynooth: An Sagart, 1991), p. 40.
2. McManus, *A Guide*, p. 41.
3. Anders Ahlqvist, *The Early Irish Linguist: An Edition of the Canonical Part of the Auraicept na nÉces*, Societas Scientiarum Fennica: Commentationes Humanarum Litterarum LXXIII 1982 (Helsinki: Societas Scientarum Fennica, 1983), p. 10.
4. D. A. Binchy, 'The Background of Early Irish Literature', *Studia Hibernica* 1 (1961), pp. 7–18, p. 9.
5. F. J. Byrne, 'Introduction', in Timothy O'Neill, *The Irish Hand: Scribes and their Manuscripts from the Earliest Times to the Seventeenth Century with an Exemplar of Irish Scripts* (Portlaoise: Dolmen Press, 1984), pp. xi–xxvii, p. xiii.
6. Brian Ó Cuív, 'Ireland's Manuscript Heritage', *Éire-Ireland* 19, 1 (1984), pp. 87–110, p. 87.
7. B. Bischoff, *Latin Palaeography: Antiquity and the Middle Ages* (Cambridge: Cambridge University Press, 1990), p. 83.
8. Ibid., pp. 83–4.
9. D. R. Howlett, ed. *The Book of Letters of Saint Patrick the Bishop* (Dublin: Four Courts Press, 1994).
10. G. S. M. Walker, ed. *Sanctae Columbanae Opera*, Scriptores Latini Hiberniae II (Dublin: Dublin Institute for Advanced Studies, 1970).
11. For a fuller list see James F. Kenney, *The Sources for the Early History of Ireland: Ecclesiastical* (1929; reprinted with addenda and corrigenda, New York: Octagon Books, 1966), pp. 1–2.
12. Ludwig Bieler, ed. *The Patrician Texts in the Book of Armagh*, Scriptores Latini Hiberniae X (Dublin: Dublin Institute for Advanced Studies, 1979), pp. 61–123.
13. Ibid., p. 93.
14. Thomas Owen Clancy and Gilbert Markus, *Iona: The Earliest Poetry of a Celtic Monastery* (Edinburgh: Edinburgh University Press, 1995), pp. 39–68.
15. Kenney, *Sources*, p. 264.
16. Jane Stevenson, 'Altus Prosatur', *Celtica* 23 (1999), pp. 326–68. Clancy and Markus, *Iona*, make the case for Colum Cille's authorship.
17. Andy Orchard, '"Audite Omnes Amantes": A Hymn in Patrick's Praise', in David N. Dumville with Lesley Abrams, T. M. Charles-Edwards, Alicia Corrêa, K. R. Dark, K. L. Maund and A. P. McD. Orchard, *Saint Patrick, AD 493–1993* (Woodbridge: The Boydell Press, 1993), pp. 153–73.
18. Whitley Stokes and John Strachan, eds. *Thesaurus Palaeohibernicus: A Collection of Old-Irish Glosses Scholia Prose and Verse*, 2 vols. (Cambridge: Cambridge University Press, 1901–3), II, pp. 325–6.
19. M. A. O'Brien, *Corpus Genealogiarum Hiberniae, vol. I* (Dublin: Dublin Institute for Advanced Studies, 1962), p. 81.
20. Stokes and Strachan, *Thesaurus*, II, p. xxxviii.
21. Ibid., II, pp. 325–49.
22. Ibid., II, p. xxxix.
23. Ibid.

24. James Carney, 'The Dating of Early Verse Texts, 500–1100', *Éigse* 19 (1992–3), pp. 177–216.
25. James Carney, ed. 'Two Old Irish Poems', *Ériu* 18 (1958), pp. 1–43. There is a new edition and translation by Máire Herbert in M. McNamara, C. Breatnach, J. Carey, M. Herbert, J.-D. Kaestli, B. Ó Cuív, P. Ó Fiannachta and D. Ó Laoghaire, eds. *Apocrypha Hiberniae I. Evangelia Infantiae*, 2 vols. Corpus Christianorum Series Apocryphorum XIII and XIV (Turnhout: Brepols Publishers, 2001), XIII, pp. 455–83.
26. David Greene and Frank O' Connor, eds. and trans. *A Golden Treasury of Irish Poetry: AD 600 to 1200* (London: Macmillan, 1967), p. 23.
27. James Carney, ed. *The Poems of Blathmac Son of Cú Brettan: Together with The Irish Gospel of Thomas and A Poem on the Virgin Mary*, Irish Texts Society XLVII (Dublin: The Educational Company of Ireland, 1964); Nessa Ní Shéaghdha, ed. 'The Poems of Blathmac: The "Fragmentary Quatrains"', *Celtica* 23 (1999), pp. 227–30.
28. See Brian Lambkin, 'The Structure of the Blathmac Poems', *Studia Celtica* 20 / 21 (1985–6), pp. 67–77, p. 76.
29. Johan Corthals, ed. 'The *retoiric* in *Aided Chonchobuir*', *Ériu* 40 (1989), pp. 41–59.
30. Kuno Meyer, ed. *The Death-Tales of the Ulster Heroes*, Todd Lecture Series XIV (Dublin: Royal Irish Academy, 1906), pp. 2–21.
31. Meyer, *Death-Tales*, pp. 12–13.
32. Kim McCone, *Pagan Past and Christian Present in Early Irish Literature*, Maynooth Monographs III (Maynooth: An Sagart, 1990), p. 75.
33. Stokes and Strachan, *Thesaurus*, II, pp. 354–8; John Carey, *King of Mysteries: Early Irish Religious Writings* (Dublin: Four Courts Press, 1998), pp. 130–5.
34. Carey, *King of Mysteries*, p. 127.
35. Whitely Stokes, ed. *Félire Óengusso Céli Dé: The Martyrology of Oengus the Culdee* (London: Henry Bradshaw Society, 1905).
36. See Greene and O'Connor, *Golden Treasury*, pp. 61–6.
37. Vernam Hull, ed. 'Apgitir Chrábaid: The Alphabet of Piety', *Celtica* 8 (1968), pp. 44–89.
38. Pádraig P. Ó Néill, 'The Date and Authorship of Apgitir Chrábaid: Some Internal Evidence', in Próinséas Ní Chatháin and Michael Richter, eds. *Irland und die Christenheit. Ireland and Christendom* (Stuttgart: Klett-Cotta, 1987), pp. 203–15.
39. Ó Néill, 'Date and Authorship', pp. 212–13.
40. Stokes and Strachan, *Thesaurus*, II, pp. xxvi, 244–7; see F. W. H. Wasserschleben, ed. *Die Irische Kanonensammlung*, 2nd edn (Leipzig: Bernard Tauchnitz, 1885).
41. Pádraig P. Ó Néill, 'The Background to the *Cambrai Homily*', *Ériu* 32 (1981), pp. 137–47.
42. Alan Orr Anderson and Marjorie Ogilvie Anderson, eds. *Adomnán's Life of Columba*, revised by Marjorie Anderson (Oxford: Oxford University Press, 1991), pp. 76–7.
43. Anderson and Anderson, *Adomnán's Life*, pp. 16–17.
44. James Carney, 'Three Old Irish Accentual Poems', *Ériu* 22 (1971), pp. 23–80, p. 26.
45. Fergus Kelly, ed. 'A Poem in Praise of Columb Cille', *Ériu* 24 (1973), pp. 1–34; Fergus Kelly, ed. 'Tiughraind Bhécáin', *Ériu* 26 (1975), pp. 66–98.
46. R. Thurneysen, 'Colmán mac Lénéni und Senchán Torpéist', *Zeitschrift für celtische Philologie* 19 (1933), pp. 193–209.
47. Carney, 'Accentual Poems', pp. 63–4.
48. The paraphrase is Carney's, 'Accentual Poems', p. 64.
49. See Calvert Watkins, 'The Etymology of Irish *Dúan*', *Celtica* 11 (1976), pp. 270–7, p. 276.

50. D. A. Binchy, 'Bretha Nemed', *Ériu* 17 (1955), pp. 4–6, and 'The Date and Provenance of *Uraicecht Becc*', *Ériu* 18 (1958), pp. 44–54.

51. Liam Breatnach, ed. and trans. *Uraicecht na Ríar: The Poetic Grades in Early Irish Law*, Early Irish Law Series II (Dublin: Dublin Institute for Advanced Studies, 1987).

52. Breatnach, *Uraicecht na Ríar*, pp. 102–3.

53. See Proinsias Mac Cana, *The Learned Tales of Medieval Ireland* (Dublin: Dublin Institute for Advanced Studies, 1980), p. 113, note 122.

54. See Mac Cana, *Learned Tales*, and Gregory Toner, 'Reconstructing the Earliest Irish Tales Lists', *Éigse* 32 (2000), pp. 88–120.

55. Breatnach, *Uraicecht na Ríar*, pp. 104–5.

56. See Donnchadh Ó Corráin, Liam Breatnach and Aidan Breen, 'The Laws of the Irish', *Peritia* 3 (1984), pp. 382–438, pp. 400–4.

57. Breatnach, *Uraicecht na Ríar*, p. 89.

58. David Greene, 'Irish as a Vernacular before the Norman Invasion', in Brian Ó Cuív, ed. *A View of the Irish Language* (Dublin: Stationery Office, 1969), pp. 11–21, p. 16.

59. Thomas Charles-Edwards, 'Language and Society among the Insular Celts 400–1000', in Miranda Green, ed. *The Celtic World* (London: Routledge, 1995), pp. 703–36, p. 728.

60. Kim McCone, 'The Würzburg and Milan Glosses: Our Earliest Sources of "Middle Irish"', *Ériu* 36 (1985), pp. 85–106, p. 103.

61. Ahlqvist, *Early Irish Linguist*. The 'canonical' text, composed in the seventh or eighth century, was greatly expanded in later centuries by the addition of glosses and commentary. These accretions are included in the edition by George Calder, *Auraicept na n-Éces: The Scholars' Primer* (Edinburgh: John Grant, 1917; reprinted Dublin: Four Courts, 1995).

62. Ahlqvist, *Early Irish Linguist*, p. 48 (text and translation).

63. Ibid., p. 47.

64. T. M. Charles-Edwards, 'The Context and Uses of Literacy in Early Christian Ireland', in Huw Pryce, ed. *Literacy in Medieval Celtic Societies* (Cambridge: Cambridge University Press, 1998), pp. 62–82, pp. 76–77.

65. Liam Breatnach, ed. 'The Caldron of Poesy', *Ériu* 32 (1981), pp. 45–93; addenda and corrigenda, *Ériu* 35 (1984), pp. 189–91. The text is also edited by P. L. Henry, 'The Caldron of Poesy', *Studia Celtica* 14/15 (1979/80), pp. 114–28.

66. Breatnach, 'Caldron', p. 55.

67. Ibid., p. 52.

68. Ibid., p. 51, note 10.

69. John Carey, *The Irish National Origin-Legend: Synthetic Pseudohistory*, Quiggin Pamphlets on the Sources of Medieval Gaelic History I (Cambridge: Department of Anglo-Saxon, Norse and Celtic, University of Cambridge, 1994), pp. 9–10.

70. Kuno Meyer, ed. *Cáin Adamnáin: An Old-Irish Treatise on the Law of Adamnán*, Andecdota Oxoniensia, Mediaeval and Modern Series 12 (Oxford: Clarendon Press, 1905); Máirín Ní Dhonnchadha, 'The Law of Adomnán: A Translation', in Thomas O'Loughlin, ed. *Adomnán at Birr, AD 697: Essays in Commemoration of the Law of the Innocents* (Dublin: Four Courts Press, 2001), pp. 53–68.

71. Thomas Charles-Edwards, '*Críth Gablach* and the Law of Status', *Peritia* 5 (1986), pp. 53–73, p. 73.

72. D. A. Binchy, ed. 'The Saga of Fergus mac Léti', *Ériu* 16 (1952), pp. 33–48.

73. Fergus Kelly, ed. *Audacht Morainn* (Dublin: Dublin Institute for Advanced Studies, 1976).
74. Johan Corthals, ed. 'Affiliation of Children: *Immathchor nAilella 7 Airt*', *Peritia* 9 (1995), pp. 92–124.
75. Ibid., p. 93.
76. Ibid., pp. 101–2.
77. Ibid., pp. 103, 122.
78. Four of these tales are in M. O Daly, ed. *Cath Maige Mucrama*, Irish Texts Society L (Dublin: Irish Texts Society, 1975). See also Tomás Ó Cathasaigh, *The Heroic Biography of Cormac mac Airt* (Dublin: Dublin Institute for Advanced Studies, 1977).
79. O Daly, *Cath Maige Mucrama*, p. 18.
80. See John Carey, 'On the Interrelationships of Some *Cín Dromma Snechtai* Texts', *Ériu* 46 (1995), pp. 71–92, especially pp. 71–2.
81. See Tomás Ó Cathasaigh, 'Reflections on Compert Conchobuir and Serglige Con Culainn', in J. P. Mallory and G. Stockman, eds. *Ulidia*, Proceedings of the First International Conference on the Ulster Cycle of Tales (Belfast: December Publications, 1994), pp. 85–9, pp. 86–7.
82. Kevin Murray, ed. 'The Finding of the *Táin*', *Cambrian Medieval Celtic Studies* 41 (2001), pp. 17–23, p. 22.
83. P. L. Henry, ed. 'Conailla Medb Míchuru and the Tradition of Fiacc Son of Fergus', in Séamus Mac Mathúna and Ailbhe Ó Corráin, eds. *Miscellanea Celtica in Memoriam Heinrich Wagner*, Acta Universitatis Upsaliensis, Studia Celtica Upsaliensia II (Uppsala: Uppsala University, 1997), pp. 53–70.
84. P. L. Henry, ed. 'Verba Scáthaige', *Celtica* 21 (1990), pp. 191–207.
85. Tomás Ó Cathasaigh, 'On the *Cín Dromma Snechta* Version of *Togail Bruidne Uí Dergae*', *Ériu* 41 (1990), pp. 103–14.
86. Kim McCone, *Echtrae Chonnlai and the Beginnings of Vernacular Narrative Writing in Ireland: A Critical Edition with Introduction, Notes, Bibliography and Vocabulary*, Maynooth Medieval Irish Texts I (Maynooth: Department of Old and Middle Irish, National University of Ireland Maynooth, 2000).
87. McCone, *Echtrae Chonnlai*, p. 122.

Select bibliography

Ahlqvist, Anders, *The Early Irish Linguist: An Edition of the Canonical Part of the Auraicept na nÉces*, Societas Scientiarum Fennica: Commentationes Humanarum Litterarum LXXIII 1982, Helsinki: Societas Scientarum Fennica, 1983.

Doherty, Charles, 'Latin Writing in Ireland (*c.*400–*c.*1200)', in Seamus Deane, general ed. *The Field Day Anthology of Irish Writing*, 3 vols. Derry: Field Day, 1991, I, pp. 61–140.

Kelly, Fergus, *A Guide to Early Irish Law*, Dublin: Dublin Institute for Advanced Studies, 1988.

Kenney, James F., *The Sources for the Early History of Ireland: Ecclesiastical*, first printed 1929; reprinted with addenda and corrigenda, New York: Octagon Books, 1966.

Mac Cana, Proinsias, 'Early and Middle Irish Literature (*c.*600–1600)', in Seamus Deane, general ed. *The Field Day Anthology of Irish Writing*, 3 vols. Derry: Field Day, 1991, I, pp. 1–60.

The Learned Tales of Medieval Ireland, Dublin: Dublin Institute for Advanced Studies, 1980.

McCone, Kim, *Pagan Past and Christian Present in Early Irish Literature*, Maynooth Monographs III, Maynooth: An Sagart, 1990.

McManus, Damian, *A Guide to Ogam*, Maynooth Monographs IV, Maynooth: An Sagart, 1991.

Mallory, J. P. and G. Stockman, eds. *Ulidia*, Proceedings of the First International Conference on the Ulster Cycle of Tales, Belfast: December Publications, 1994.

Ní Dhonnchadha, Máirín, 'Mary, Eve and the Church, *c*.600–1800' and 'Eve and her Sisters, *c*.550–1800', in A. Bourke, S. Kilfeather, M. Luddy, M. MacCurtain, G. Meaney, M. Ní Dhonnchadha, M. O'Dowd and C. Wills, eds. *The Field Day Anthology of Irish Writing, vol. IV and V: Irish Women's Writing and Traditions*, Cork: Cork University Press in association with Field Day, 2002, IV, pp. 45–165.

Ó Corráin, Donnchadh, 'Early Medieval Law, *c*.700–1200', in A. Bourke et al. eds. *The Field Day Anthology of Irish Writing, vol. IV and V: Irish Women's Writing and Traditions*, Cork: Cork University Press in association with Field Day, 2002, IV, pp. 6–44.

Ó Corráin, Donnchadh, Liam Breatnach and Aidan Breen, 'The Laws of the Irish', *Peritia* 3 (1984), pp. 382–438.

Ó Cuív, Brian, 'Ireland's Manuscript Heritage', *Éire-Ireland* 19, 1 (1984), pp. 87–110.

2

The literature of medieval Ireland, 800–1200: from the Vikings to the Normans

MÁIRE NÍ MHAONAIGH

Introduction

The literary landscape of the period defined in linguistic terms as Classical Old Irish (*c*.800–900) and Middle Irish (*c*.900–1200) is remarkable both for its size and for the sheer variety of its terrain.[1] Conventionally anchored historically by means of reference to the arrival of two groups of outsiders, Vikings and Normans, marking its beginning and its end, external influences form but one of its many fertile layers. The imaginative authors who continued to embrace European intellectual activity as their predecessors had done in the pre-Viking era were firmly grounded also in an insular inheritance which they continually made new. Earlier traditions may have been revered but their value lay primarily in their continued relevance in an ever-changing environment. Thus was the heritage of which such creators were keenly aware of being a part perennially translated into a current cultural context in which it continued to serve a role, being enlivened in the process by the host of other influences to which the tradition moulders were open. Analysis of their diverse literary output, therefore, must take into account, in John Carey's formulation, their outward, as well as their backward look.[2]

Similarly worthy of consideration is what might be termed their inward look, manifested most clearly in the vivid allusions to other works which permeate the literature.[3] Working within a highly developed creative tradition, each weaver had access to the same well-worn fabric of his forebears and cut his cloth with pre-existing garments in mind. The result is a patchwork of repeating patterns in new imaginative guises which can only be properly assessed in an intertextual context. This is no easy task in view of the extent of the literary output of which no estimate in its entirety has yet been undertaken. Its best-known feature, a significant body of narrative literature, has been calculated as comprising roughly one hundred and fifty tales.[4] It is this corpus which has been traditionally identified as medieval Irish literature since it accords best with modern literary tastes. Also included in the canon, on similar aesthetic grounds, was a group of much anthologised lyric poems.[5] Medieval anthologies, however, in the form of our surviving manuscripts, generally display a far greater heterogeneity. Moreover, since access to the literature is provided solely by such manuscripts they must surely constitute our ultimate guide. It is with an overview of the all-important manuscript tradition, therefore, that our account of the literature of this period will begin.

Manuscripts and their creators

Despite displaying considerable diversity in matters such as language and subject matter, the collection of extant manuscripts is united by the ecclesiastical nature of the environment in which they were given form. This is evident in the titles given to many of them: *Liber Ardmachanus* (The Book of Armagh), a Latin manuscript from the very beginning of our period concerned primarily with documents pertaining to St Patrick, was commissioned by an abbot of Armagh, Torbach, and written there by the scribe Ferdomnach in 807.[6] Armagh continued to be a scriptorium of significance; it was there too that Harleian 1802, a twelfth-century copy of the Latin gospels, containing poems and glosses in Irish, also came into being.[7] The monastic affiliations of the predominantly vernacular manuscripts are equally evident. *Lebor na hUidre* (The Book of the Dun Cow), the original provenance of which may have been south-east Ulster and north-east Leinster, has an association with Clonmacnoise.[8] One of its three scribes, Máel Muire mac Célechair (d.1106), may well have been the son of a bishop of Clonmacnoise.[9] Moreover, the manuscript later acquired its name from the hide of a dun cow belonging to the patron saint of that monastery, Cíarán.[10] The more prosaically named Rawlinson B502 is linked with a Leinster ecclesiastical establishment, either Killeshin or Glendalough, where it was put together by a single anonymous scribe *c.*1120.[11] The precise provenance of the Book of Leinster is more difficult to determine. Its clerical connections, however, are not in doubt: Áed mac Crimthainn was *comarba* (coarb) of the monastery of Terryglass, County Tipperary. Another of its scribes, Finn, with whom Áed corresponded, has been traditionally identified as the bishop of Kildare, Finn mac Gormáin, who died in 1160.[12]

Yet this ecclesiastical dominance was not to last. The second half of the twelfth century, during which time the Book of Leinster as we know it was compiled, constitutes a period of remarkable change in the Irish church, encompassing intellectual activity, including manuscript production, as well as organisational matters and theological developments. While the beginnings of this externally inspired reform movement can be traced to the eleventh century, its influence increased as the twelfth century progressed. Chief among its effects was the arrival in Ireland of new continental orders whose commitment to learning, particularly in the vernacular, was nothing like that of the old established ecclesiastical institutions they sought to supplant. While the Augustinians and Cistercians thrived in their new environment, native monasteries went into decline. By a complex process not yet fully understood, but in which the reform movement certainly played a part, the learning they had so carefully nurtured became the preserve of secular learned families who may themselves have had their origins in hereditary ecclesiastical families of previous generations.[13] In hindsight, it is clear that the Book of Leinster was 'the last fling of the learned ecclesiastics of the unreformed Irish church', in William O'Sullivan's memorable words.[14] Henceforth, secular learning was in the hands of highly educated laymen who sought to match the accomplishments of their clerical predecessors. Indeed, in many cases they drew directly on their work. There is a manifestly close relationship between the versions of some texts in the collection of sixteen manuscripts which has come to be known as the Yellow Book of Lecan and those in the Book of Leinster.[15] Moreover, later codices often preserve texts which bear the linguistic and historical hallmarks of having been composed in an earlier period. Any account of the literature of the pre-twelfth-century period, therefore, will also be reliant on manuscripts of a later date.[16]

While the language of these later codices is Irish, in the case of manuscripts of the twelfth century and earlier, a distinction is frequently drawn between those in Latin, on the one hand, and those in the vernacular, on the other. Although one or other language may dominate, bilingualism is a common and important trait. Irish glosses and additions in the 'Latin' Book of Armagh, for example, furnish important evidence for the state of the vernacular in perhaps the early eighth century. Furthermore, scribe 'T' in the 'Irish' Book of Leinster concludes his copy of *Táin Bó Cúailnge* (The Cattle Raid of Cúailnge (Cooley)) with a flourishing colophon in Latin in which he appears to distance himself from the entire narrative.[17] In both cases, the change of language was deliberate and effective. In the same way, the manuscript collection known as the *Liber Hymnorum* (Book of Hymns), eleventh- and twelfth-century copies of which survive, contains compositions in both Latin and Irish; as noted by

Máire Herbert, language choice in this instance may have been determined by theme.[18]

In their discriminating use of language, the mediators of our literature thus prove themselves to be skilful interpreters of texts. Similarly, their literary sensibilities are also seen in other ways. While they seldom engage in value judgements on the material in hand – the Latin colophon to *Táin Bó Cúailnge* just referred to being a rare exception – the part played by aesthetic concerns in the choice of document to be transmitted to an expensive vellum folio should not be underestimated. Ultimately, however, the range of material included depended on the purpose to which the valuable, prestige-endowing manuscript would be put (though this too may have been influenced by literary fashions of the day). Moreover, this also affected the particular lay-out of a manuscript. To this end, attempting to discern the organising principles at work in a given codex can shed light on how a particular work was read by the manuscript's creator. The early fifteenth-century manuscript, the *Leabhar Breac* (Speckled Book) is primarily concerned with religious works, though it also preserves a number of saga narratives.[19] At least some of these, however, have a strong religious dimension: *Caithréim Chellaig* (The Battle Triumph of Cellach) provides a coded commentary on the progress of reform, particularly in Connacht.[20] *Aislinge Meic Con Glinne* (The Dream of Mac Con Glinne), on the other hand, is a pious tale with a twist: among the many groups mocked in this twelfth-century satire are the unreformed monks of the author's own time.[21] For Muiris Ó Cuindlis, compiler of the codex, it may well have been their 'religious' theme that determined their inclusion in the manuscript.

Few extant medieval manuscripts display the thematic unity of the *Leabhar Breac*. Great compendia of diverse and apparently disparate material for the most part, they were likened by Gerard Murphy to modern-day museums.[22] Implicit in this comparison is an assumption that the extant codices are primarily antiquarian in character, the scribes' main motivating force being a desire to preserve as much as possible for posterity in the face of an increasingly uncertain future. However, evidence for this degree of historical foresight on the part of the learned classes is lacking. Moreover, their engagement with the past as exemplified in their recording of earlier texts takes the form of an active ongoing dialogue with the work of previous generations. Their placing of particular narratives adjacent to one another on the manuscript page was an act of textual interpretation, designed to ensure that certain groups of narratives were read and assessed collectively. In addition, they copiously annotated and glossed the material in hand, having recourse to well-known expository techniques of the day. Paramount among these was the formulaic location of the composition in question by means of *locus* (place), *tempus* (time), *persona* (characters) and *causa scribendi* (reason for writing). Of classical antiquity in origin, this method of analysis was to become popular in biblical exegesis in particular in the early Middle Ages. From there its use was extended by Irish scribes to texts of other types: as Herbert has demonstrated, the Latin and Irish hymns in *Liber Hymnorum*, for example, were furnished with prefatory material of this kind.[23] In this way too the scribe provided an interpretative context for the literature, guiding his reader or hearer to view a certain text or group of texts in a very specific light.

Furthermore, the scribe's direct involvement with his material was not confined to the level of critical commentary. Manuscript creators-turned-authors also revised and reinvented that which had come down to them: new tastes had to be catered for, contemporary political and social concerns had to be accommodated. An extant genealogy might be expanded, therefore, to include a dynasty recently arrived on the political stage; lists of kings and heroes were brought down to the scribe's own time. Thus, on copying a tenth-century poem by Cináed úa hArtacáin into the Book of Leinster, Finn, bishop of Kildare, for example, 'updated' his exemplar. The stanzas he added to the poetic composition, *Fianna bátar i nEmain* (Heroes who were in Emain (Navan Fort)), include a reference to the Battle of Móin Mór fought in 1151. Whereas Finn helpfully signalled his authorial intervention in the margin, however,[24] scribal creativity is elsewhere manifested in a variety of more subtle ways. Only by a close, detailed comparison of the various manuscript versions of the tenth-century Leinster tale, *Esnada Tige Buchet* (The Melodies of Buchet's House), for example, could Tomás Ó Concheanainn show that the two rhetorical passages in the narrative are actually the work of our Book of Leinster redactor, Áed mac Crimthainn.[25] There is no reason why the admittedly industrious Áed should have been exceptional in this regard.

In short, Áed and his colleagues were proactive men of letters, concerned not merely with preserving a literary tradition but with making a significant contribution to that tradition in the process. In this they were aided by other participants in the vibrant intellectual world of medieval Ireland, many of whom may have also been scribes. That they were members of a cultural elite is evident from the obit notices of *filid* (scholars, literally 'poets') and *fir léiginn* (learned men, frequently translated 'lectors') in contemporary chronicles: Máel Mura Othna, who died in 887, was accorded the title *righfiled Erenn* (chief poet of Ireland); a later colleague, Flann Mainistrech mac Echthigirn, was described as *airdfer leighinn ocus sui senchusa Erenn* (eminent learned man and master of the historical lore of Ireland) on his death in 1056.[26] That both these men, like most of their learned colleagues, were clerics underlines what the provenance of our early manuscripts has indicated: this vigorous scholarly environment was firmly ensconced in an ecclesiastical embrace. All-encompassing in nature, the church's grip sustained intellectual endeavours in a multitude of scholarly spheres. That it should have concerned itself with sacred matters is unsurprising, but for most of the period in question it was an equally staunch supporter of secular learning. Máel Mura Othna, for example, is best known for his pseudo-historical poem, *Can a mbunadas na nGáedel* (What are the Origins of the Irish?), in which the biblical wanderings of the Irish and their eventual conquest of Ireland are described at length.[27] Flann Mainistrech's work can be fitted into a similar semi-historical framework.[28] Nor was the world of learning unusual in this regard. Close cerebral ties between secular and religious are mirrored by the intimate co-operation of the two domains at a political and social level. Intellectual interdependency, therefore, formed one aspect of a complex, mutually beneficial relationship.

How the cultural dimension of that relationship worked, however, is not always clear. In the case of an *ollam*, the highest grade of poet, his was a royal appointment whose status was determined by that of his official patron.[29] In return, he furnished his chieftain with a variety of texts frequently designed to bolster the latter's claim to power. Did he retire to the ecclesiastical establishment where he received his education to engage in composition? Alternatively, or additionally, might a work have been dictated to a professional recorder in the scriptorium of a nearby dependent monastery to be read aloud to the royal assembly on a suitable occasion? If so, who might do the reading or reciting? In a poem ascribed to a ninth-century king of Brega, Flannacán mac Cellaig, *Innid scél scaílter n-airrich* (Tell the Tale to a Leader), it is a cleric who is asked to tell the tale.[30] The literature also resounds with eloquent *filid* delivering their wares.[31] Basic though they are, such questions have yet to be fully addressed. Nor have the complex changes which affected the intricate web of learning in the course of our four-hundred-year period been clearly delineated. Answers to these queries and others like them can only emerge from a close reading of the texts themselves in their own intellectual setting and against the backdrop of historical developments of the time. Detailed elucidation of the sources is necessary to provide the literary landscape, now visible in outline, with much needed contours.

This ongoing process is undoubtedly hampered by a lack of modern scholarly editions of very many of the sources, an analysis of the transmission history of a text and of its language being necessary prerequisites to an evaluation of its content. Moreover, in an Irish context added difficulties are presented by the late date of much of the manuscript evidence, as we have seen, as well as by the accommodating nature of Middle Irish (900–1200), the language in which the majority of the texts of our period were written.[32] Incorporating both earlier (Old Irish) and later forms, the language as we have it exhibits a wide variety of registers, all of which find expression in our literary texts, making precise dating by linguistic means almost an impossible task. Evaluation of a narrative's historical content can sometimes provide a chronological anchor; nonetheless key narratives float freely in a three- or four-hundred-year time-span awaiting the philological analysis which may secure them at a particular point therein. Given these scholarly circumstances, it is not surprising that certain 'accessible' texts have received a significant degree of attention, while other equally worthy works lie languishing in undeserved obscurity. Fortunately, this need not be a permanent state of affairs; a new edition or scholarly article can reconfigure the canon and bring a neglected narrative centre stage. In this changing critical climate, any attempt at literary history may seem premature. Taking stock of the road we have travelled, however, may serve at the very least to strengthen us for the long but ultimately rewarding journey ahead.

Irish writing abroad

We may begin with the journeying of the medieval Irish themselves since much key writing was undertaken by them in Britain and on the continent, where they frequently functioned as pivotal players in contemporary European scholarship. One such traveller was the monk Dícuil, who, following a long-established tradition, travelled abroad sometime about the year 800 and appears to have spent the remaining years of his life working as a scholar in Carolingian circles. To judge from his extant writings, his academic interests ranged from grammar to astronomy, subjects with which his contemporaries were similarly engaged.[33] In addition, he concerned himself with geography and, drawing for the most part on earlier writers, compiled the earliest medieval treatise on the topic in 825.[34] In general, however, Dícuil has been overshadowed by two slightly later compatriots, both of whom were connected to the court of Charles the Bald. The more literary of these was Sedulius Scottus (*fl.*850), to whom is attributed a considerable body of effective Latin poetry.[35] His colleague, Johannes Scottus Eriugena (810–77), also composed verse, as well as biblical commentary and other writings. Linguistically remarkably gifted, he was renowned as a scholar of Greek and compiled a bilingual Latin and Greek biblical glossary as a pedagogical tool. It is as a philosopher-theologian, however, that this erudite thinker is best known, as a result primarily of his dialogic work *De divisione naturae* (On the Divisions of Nature) or *Periphyseon* in which he brought Neoplatonic and Christian ideas together in a truly distinctive fashion.[36] Perhaps because of his striking originality, Eriugena has been studied very much as a scholar apart; yet, he and his fellow exiles continued to influence thinking in their homeland, at the very least through contact with travellers who may have returned to Ireland bearing books from abroad.[37] That these were treasured is indicated by passing references in literary texts: Brían Bórama deliberately sent messengers to acquire such foreign reading matter according to his twelfth-century heroic biography, *Cocad Gáedel re Gallaib* (The War of the Irish against the Foreigners).[38] Moreover, the author of *De Fhaillsiugud Tána Bó Cúailnge* (Concerning the Revelation of *Táin Bó Cúailnge*) depicted the last remaining copy of the *Táin* being exchanged for an exemplar of Isidore of Seville's seventh-century best-seller *Etymologiae* (Etymologies).[39]

As a result of the achievements of Eriugena in particular, the ninth century is often seen as marking the summit of Ireland's considerable contribution to intellectual activities overseas; nevertheless, the following centuries saw scholars and pilgrims continue to tread the continental path. Admittedly, few were as successful as their Eriugenian predecessor. A presumptuous poet, Moriuht (a rendering perhaps of Murchad), aroused the considerable ire of his Gallic hosts if a deliciously invective satire against him can be believed.[40] And if, as seems likely, this is creative composition of the most skilful kind, it nonetheless bears witness to the probable participation of Irishmen in Norman learned circles around the year 1000 when the poem was composed. Moriuht is depicted as having spent time in England as well as in France and, for many of his colleagues, it was the neighbouring island that provided them with institutional support. Bishop Patrick, for example, who ruled the Hiberno-Norse diocese of Dublin for a decade from 1074, received his education under Wulfstan in Worcester and appears to have maintained ties with that monastery. His literary output reflects these various influences: a poem on the wonders of Ireland may well be a translation of a vernacular work; another can be categorised as dream literature, a popular allegorical genre with which he may first have come into contact abroad.[41] Other scholars similarly drew on the full range of their international experience in their writings: Marcus of Regensburg had recourse to medieval vision literature, as well as vernacular voyage tales when producing his literary masterpiece, *Visio Tnudgali* (The Vision of Tnudgal), around the year 1149.[42] Moreover, contemporary local affairs also colour his composition. That Tnudgal on his Otherworld voyage should meet Cormac Mac Carthaig and his brother, Donnchad, may reflect the interests of their kinsman, Christianus, who was abbot of St James's in Regensburg at the time.[43] In addition, it may reveal Marcus's own political bias: having left Ireland only a short time previously he may well have favoured the Meic Carthaig siblings over the third king mentioned in the text, their Ua Briain rival, Conchobar.[44]

The languages of medieval Irish literature

Marcus's primary audience, however, was non-Irish, his patron and dedicatee a certain abbess 'G';[45] hence, not surprisingly, Latin was his medium of literary expression, as it was that of other Irishmen working in a similar intellectual environment. By contrast, works produced in Ireland in the same period display greater linguistic diversity. Old Norse may well have been cultivated as a literary language in the Hiberno-Norse colonies, just as Norman French certainly was among later settlers.[46] Nevertheless, it was Latin and Irish that formed the dominant duo of languages, and in fact the vernacular which had been employed as a written scholarly language from the early seventh century gradually became pre-eminent. Thus, hagiographical texts in Irish are attested from the ninth century, as is vernacular biblical commentary.[47] Furthermore, the linguistic balance in annalistic writing shifts in favour of Irish at about the same time.[48] Complex cultural changes undoubtedly underlie this mental metamorphosis at the heart of which may lie a redefinition of what the learning of a clerical scholar actually entailed.[49] Yet, while Latin may have lost its pivotal position in the curriculum, training therein continued to be an important part of an ecclesiastical education. Moreover, its use remained a literary prerogative down through our period. Saints' Lives, homilies and apocryphal works, for example, continued to be produced in both languages, as did hymns. Indeed Máel Ísu Úa Brolcháin, a scholar at Armagh, is proclaimed on his death in 1086 as *sui in ecna ocus in crabaid ocus i filidhecht i mberlai cechtardhai* (eminent in wisdom and piety and in poetry in both languages).[50] In addition to Latin and Irish compositions surviving from his hand, a macaronic hymn attributed to him is also extant, indicating an audience well able to appreciate his verbal dexterity.[51] Bilingual readers and hearers were also clearly envisaged for such texts as the ninth-century Life of Brigit, *Bethu Brigte*, one quarter of which is in Latin, and the eleventh-century vision text, *Fís Adamnáin* (The Vision of Adamnán), whose author deliberately employed various sentences in Latin in a predominantly Irish text.[52] An ability to read and assimilate Latin texts is further attested by the intimate knowledge of a wide range of sources displayed by the authors of vernacular material. Furthermore, some of them at least were in sufficient command of the language to enable them skilfully to adapt a number of complex classical texts.

Literary style

Attracted perhaps by the historical dimension of these classical compositions, the main events of which were also accorded a place in their chronological scheme of world history,[53] the Irish were among the first to create vernacular versions of these influential texts. The Alexander saga may have been adapted in the tenth century;[54] one recension of the Irish rendering of Dares Phrygius's *De Excidio Troiae* could well be eleventh-century in date, and may be based on an earlier adaptation.[55] A taste for such material developed: Lucan's *Pharsalia* and Statius's *Thebaid* assumed their Irish forms in the twelfth century, as *In Cath Catharda* (The Civil War) and *Togail na Tebe* (The Destruction of Thebes).[56] *Merugud Uilix meic Leirtis* (The Wanderings of Ulysses son of Leirtes), loosely based on the Odyssey, came into being at about the same time.[57] Notwithstanding the diversity of this material, certain common stylistic features have been observed to a greater or lesser extent in the various texts belonging to this corpus of adapted or 'translated' narratives. Characterised by extensive use of ornamental repetition, rhythmical runs of alliterating adjectives and nouns, as well as by a wide and varied lexis, this style, at its most developed, is a bombastic celebration of the written word. Such flamboyance is not confined to so-called translation texts: pleonastic pairings, elaborate ornamentation and a general diffuseness are symptomatic of a number of eleventh- and twelfth-century longer narratives of native inspiration, including the version of *Táin Bó Cúailnge* preserved in the Book of Leinster. Moreover, they are not confined to any one genre. Thus, saga-narratives share certain aspects of their stylistic appearance with the bilingual vision tale, *Fís Adamnáin*, as well as with the duo of religious texts it precedes in the Book of the Dun Cow, *Scéla Laí Brátha* (Tidings of Doomsday) and *Scéla na hEsérgi* (Tidings of the Resurrection).[58]

While the exact development of this distinctive style is difficult to determine, its increase in popularity in the twelfth century in particular is certainly linked with a growing trend towards composition of longer, more discursive texts, as Uáitéar Mac Gearailt has observed.[59] This may well be a natural step in a literary evolutionary process; outside influences too, however, may have had a part to play. Classical texts of epic proportion could have provided Irish authors with models for the production of extended narratives, as Mac Gearailt and Hildegard Tristram have suggested;[60] yet the fact that it was precisely such lengthy compositions that were chosen for transposition into an Irish literary setting surely indicates a predilection for such texts in the first place. In any event, the act of translating, however loosely, would have served to increase the linguistic sensibilities of those engaged with the material, alerting them to patterns of speech in both host and target languages. One result of this may have been their exploitation of rhythmical phrases from contemporary storytelling, as Mac Gearailt has claimed.[61] Moreover, the forging of a new type of translation text would have provided an ideal, convention-free environment for engaging in such stylistic experimentation. But other factors too must be considered: familiarity with convoluted Hiberno-Latin prose may have played a secondary role.[62] More significantly, elaborate descriptive passages had long since been a feature of vernacular narrative prose; these too may have contributed to the evolution of a more expansive style.

Whatever its precise genesis, this bold new prose style is common to a wide range of narratives, as we have seen. Uniting this heterogeneous conglomeration of works is the fact that all stand in stylistic contrast to an equally varied collection of generally shorter texts displaying a terse, relatively unadorned narrative technique.[63] While many of the latter are ninth- and tenth-century in date, brisk, basic prose was also composed in the two centuries that followed.[64] Furthermore, certain compositions do not readily find a place at either end of the stylistic divide. *Togail Bruidne Da Derga* (The Destruction of Da Derga's Hostel), for example, which is of eleventh-century date in its present form, creatively combines fast-flowing, uncluttered sentences with detailed description of the most elaborate form.[65] The author of *Cocad Gáedel re Gallaib* adopted a straightforward approach in the first part of his literary biography, prompted perhaps by the annalistic sources on which he so heavily drew, before displaying considerable ornamental virtuosity in the remainder of his tale.[66] Scribal schools may have favoured one stylistic strategy above another; ultimately, however, choice of a particular discursive technique was a matter of aesthetic purpose.

In this regard, we may compare the deliberate employment of a specific metre to achieve a desired literary effect. Non-rhyming verse termed *rosc(ad)*, once thought to be oral and archaic, has been shown to be well within the creative powers of Old and Middle Irish authors.[67] Adoption of this poetic register where the emphasis is on alliteration and a fixed number of stressed words, rather than the less marked one of rhyming syllabic verse, therefore, was a conscious creative act. In *Togail Bruidne Da Derga* its use punctuates a long poignant passage in which the sons of Donn Désa, foster-brothers of the tale's main character, the king, Conaire Mór, are gradually made to realise the calamitous consequences of their earlier actions.[68] In *Esnada Tige Buchet*, on the other hand, the stylised intricate exchange between Buchet and his despoiler, the more highly ranked King Catháir, is couched in similar stressed phrases and serves to give both men a way out of their legal and social difficulty.[69] A passage of summarising *rosc* forms a fitting conclusion to a companion tale of the latter, *Orgain Denna Ríg* (The Destruction of Dinn Ríg).[70] Tomás Ó Cathasaigh has drawn attention to the significance of its being attributed to Ferchertne *file*, an eyewitness to the tale's events and a survivor of the final destruction.[71] It serves a very different function, therefore, to the two stanzas of syllabic verse preceding it which form part of the ninth-century poem, *A chóicid choín Chairpri crúaid* (Fair Province of Stern Cairpre), by Orthanach úa Cóelláma.[72] Described as evidential by Proinsias Mac Cana, these serve to corroborate what has been told in the preceding prose.[73]

Literary form

The prosimetrum form in which these tales are cast is typical of much writing composed in our period. In fact, as far as narrative literature is concerned, there is scarcely a tale extant which does not intersperse some element of verse with the usually predominant prose. Apart from altering the tempo of a narrative, we may generalise that recourse to poetic language set the passage in question apart. Its artistic effect can only be properly evaluated, however, as part of an overall analysis of the creative whole. Thus, in the carefully crafted historical romance *Scéla Cano meic Gartnáin* (The Story of Cano son of Gartnán), the author turned to verse to depict critical moments in Cano's life.[74] In the same way poetry functions as a powerful emotive force in the tenth-century king tale, *Fingal Rónáin* (Rónán's Kinslaying), as evidenced by the polished, evocative, long lament which precedes the final example of kinslaying at the end of the tale.[75] Additionally, it forms a crucial plot device: an innocent game of verse-capping becomes the means by which Rónán is wrongly persuaded to accept his son's guilt.[76] Poetry similarly permeates the fabric of *Buile Shuibne* (Suibne's Frenzy), a twelfth-century prosimetrum in which verse is more voluminous than prose.[77] In this dramatic account of Suibne's inner journey from sacrilegious king to sacred poet, verse passages are used to explore his inner torment to great effect. Moreover, his tortuous voyage is seen to have a happy end: mishandling of a cleric may have caused him to lose his royal status in the first place, but in his new guise as a poet he achieves complete reconciliation through the agency of another powerful ecclesiastic, Moling.

The theme of conversion also lies at the core of *Immram Curaig Maíle Dúin* (The Voyage of Máel Dúin's Boat), a literary gem in which a revenge-seeking expedition is transformed into a rewarding quest for forgiveness.[78] Its broad agenda of peace promotion would have resonance in many an age, not least in the turbulent times of ninth-century Ireland when the prose version of the tale was probably composed.[79] A century or so later it was reworked in verse by Áed, whom Thomas Owen Clancy has speculatively identified with Áed úa Raithnén (d.923), a scholar at the monastery of Saigir.[80] We must assume, therefore, that there was an audience for narrative literature in poetic form. Áed's metrical composition may in fact have been inspired by another versified voyage-tale of similar date, *Immram Snédgusa ocus Meic Ríagla* (The Voyage of Snédgus and Mac Ríagla), a religious tract designed to draw attention to the nature of God's mercy.[81] Snédgus and Mac Ríagla's wanderings were also recounted in prose; in this case, however, the poetic text appears to have primacy. Furthermore, in recasting its form, later craftsmen also altered the original emphasis of the tale and the resulting eleventh-century prose recension acquired a new shift in setting and sympathy in turn in the following century.[82] Poetry was an equally suitable medium for updating a tale: towards the end of the twelfth century, a scholar associated with the Ua Conchobair king of Connacht, Cathal Crobderg (d.1224), audaciously appropriated an earlier origin-legend of the Uí Néill, *Echtra mac nEchdach Mugmedóin* (The Adventure of the Sons of Eochaid Mugmedón). In his rhymed retelling, provocatively entitled *Tairnic in sel-sa ac Síl Néill* (The Time of the Uí Néill is at an End), the Uí Néill are declared to be finished, the kingship having reverted to Níall's brother, Bríon, ancestor of the Uí Chonchobair.[83] Moreover, the story which served as the source has been preserved in both prose and poetic versions.[84] Indeed the earlier metrical work is attributed to one of the foremost poets of his day, the Uí Néill propagandist, Cúán úa Lothcháin, who was murdered by neighbouring Tethba men in 1024.[85]

Cúán is perhaps best known for his topographical texts (*dinnshenchas*, 'lore of notable places'), many of which form part of the extensive collection of material known as *Dinnshenchas Érenn* (The Lore of Ireland's Notable Places), in which Ireland's prominent geographical features are given literary life.[86] Significantly, this textual translation of the landscape was also accomplished in prose and verse, both of which occur side by side in manuscript sources.[87] Thus, Carman, the site of an *óenach* (assembly) in Leinster, for example, commemorates a female marauder of that name who plundered Ireland with her three sons before dying in captivity, and for whom an annual fair was held in the place. Of the fair itself, however, the poetic version of the legend provides greater detail. Moreover, the prose includes an alternative explanation of the place-name, claiming that it marked the spot where Sengarman (Old Garman) fell while on a cattle raid.[88] Any attempt at understanding this evolving tradition, therefore, must involve a consideration of these dual-medium stories as an integrated whole.

In the same way, reading both prose and metrical versions of the twelfth-century compilation known as the *Banshenchas* (Women-lore) in tandem can only enhance our knowledge of this important catalogue of prominent women.[89] Containing the names of husbands and offspring, alongside those of both mythological and historical women alike, this detailed list is an important source of information on royal marriages, which formed the backbone of many a political alliance. It is with one particular couple that the author of the poetic version of the tract, Gilla Modutu Úa Casaide, was concerned to judge from the tribute to Tigernán Úa Rúairc, king of Bréifne, and his wife, Derbforgaill, with which he ends his work. Indeed, he may have intended his artistic offering for Queen Derbforgaill, best known for her abduction by Tigernán's sworn enemy, Díarmait Mac Murchada.[90]

Other compositions by Úa Casaide have also survived: a long poem of his entitled *Ériu óg inis na ríg* (Perfect Ireland, Island of the Kings), written in 1143, forms part of one version of *Lebor Gabála Érenn* (The Book of the Taking of Ireland, commonly known as The Book of Invasions), an imaginative, influential account of the origins of the Irish in prose and verse.[91] Some centuries in the making, this elaborate construct achieved final form towards the end of the eleventh century at the hands of an enterprising scholar who interspersed pre-existing historical poems with prose passages to mould a masterful account of the history of the world, and Ireland's place within it, from creation down to his own day.[92] So popular was it that it was copied and revised extensively: a twelfth-century reworking saw its king lists extended down to Rúaidrí Úa Conchobair (d.1184), as well as the incorporation of material by contemporary poets, including Úa Casaide.

Historical and pseudo-historical writing

As a complex compendium of myth and history intricately integrated in a chronological structure of biblical inspiration, *Lebor Gabála* exemplifies many of the themes that characterise medieval Irish literature in the period upon which we are focused. In particular, its preoccupation with genealogical synthesis, combined with its emphasis on kingship, echoes the dynastic concerns that underlie much of the writing of the age. Additionally, its desire to locate Ireland's history within a worldwide setting by linking indigenous ruling families with foreign counterparts and by dating local events with reference to international affairs is fully in accord with the all-encompassing perspective found in other compositions. Moreover, since the poetic texts making up a substantial part of the treatise predate its late eleventh-century genesis, we may assume that the ideas reflected therein had been developing for some time. Indeed Máel Mura Othna's poem *Can a mbunadas na nGáedel* is a ninth-century attempt at the creation of a national history, albeit on a much smaller scale.[93] His literary descendants, Eochaid úa Flainn (d.1004), Gilla Cóemáin mac Gilla Shamthainne (*fl.*1072), as well as the Monasterboice historian Flann Mainistrech, whom we have encountered already, refined the genre of synchronistic scholarship. Their work and that of other synthetic historians supplied the skilful synthesiser of *Lebor Gabála* with his staple fare. The tastes provided were varied: over the centuries of its cultivation, the historical verse tradition expanded and evolved. As Peter Smith has shown, chronology became an increasingly important criterion from the tenth century onwards; he views an anonymous poem on the Christian kings of Leinster, *Cóic ríg trichat tríallsat róe* (Thirty-five Kings who tried the Field of Battle), as a turning point in this regard.[94] Previous work provided an impetus for further elaboration: Gilla Cóemáin's two poems *Ériu ard inis na ríg* (Noble Ireland, Island of the Kings) and *Atá sund forba fessa* (Here Follows the Greater Part of Knowledge) supplement earlier versified king lists by Flann Mainistrech, as Smith has noted.[95] A third poem, *Annálad anall uile* (All Computation Hitherto), composed by him in 1072, incorporates Irish regnal history within a broader framework to a hitherto unknown degree.[96] It need hardly surprise us that *Lebor Gabála*, which marks the summit of this literary development, came into being at about the same time.

While integrated history of this kind was being developed as a discipline, its core areas continued to be cultivated individually as well. These include genealogical writing which is preserved in the Book of Leinster, Rawlinson B502, and in later manuscripts. These voluminous, varied records, which remain to a large extent unedited, preserve information concerning some 20,000 individuals, alongside 2,000 dynasties.[97] It has been suggested that much of this material was already in existence by the ninth century, composed in response to changes in the political order requiring retrospective justification by a centrally implicated learned elite.[98] In addition, it provided the impetus for a collection of saints' genealogies, the earliest recension of which Pádraig Ó Riain has dated to the second half of the tenth century.[99] This too was prompted by current developments: as Herbert has noted, 'the shared origin ascribed to saints and rulers serves to legitimize the manner in which ecclesiastical and secular office-holding and succession had become closely interlinked'.[100] These documents proved remarkably durable: an ever-changing social landscape necessitated constant refinement of what were pliable pedigrees and later scholars proved more than equal to the task. Embedded, therefore, in the extant versions are various chronological strata, the disentangling of which has barely begun. Moreover, such extensive editorial activity is indicative of a wide, receptive audience, as is the incorporation of genealogical information into a range of other texts. Saints' ancestral lineages frequently form part of eleventh- and twelfth-century vernacular hagiographies,[101] while the story of a dynasty's origin is often embedded in a secular tale. Indeed in certain cases, the imparting of such knowledge becomes an end in itself.[102] Thus, *Aided Crimthainn meic Fhidaig* (The Death Tale of Crimthann son of Fidach), a twelfth-century companion-piece to the Uí Néill propaganda tract, *Echtra mac nEchdach Mugmedóin*, aims to set out clearly the perceived pecking order of various Connacht royal lines at the time of its composition.[103]

That genealogical concerns are central to such narratives as *Aided Crimthainn* is not in doubt; whether they may be taken as 'the starting point of much medieval Irish literature'[104] is another matter. Given the heterogeneous nature of our literary remains, and the intellectual openness of its creators, allowing for diverse, multiple origins is surely the safest course of action. Notwithstanding this, the eleventh and twelfth centuries saw the creation of extended propaganda tracts whose imaginative rewriting of history was designed to cast a particular ruling family in a favourable light.[105] To this end, eponymous ancestors were exalted and previous heroic deeds were extolled, the implication being that descendants of such giants were of the same mould. That their historically conscious, manipulative authors were steeped in a tradition of chronicle writing is indicated by the annalistic packaging in which such texts are placed. Furthermore, a literary model of sorts could have been provided by existing king tales recounting the imaginary exploits of a host of historic and prehistoric kings, and to a lesser extent by praise poetry composed for royal patrons. Despite being conceived in a recognisable literary context, however, the genesis of such texts represents something of a new departure. While Uí Néill political hegemony had long since been threatened, it was not until the tenth century that their premier position was effectively usurped, and as other dynasties came to the fore to enjoy new-found prominence, so too did their men of learning who responded to uncustomary challenges with characteristic creativity. Familiarity with foreign texts may have provided inspiration;[106] in any event a markedly different kind of Irish royal biography was born.

Inventiveness, however, was not the sole prerogative of those serving recently arrived masters. The tenth and eleventh centuries in particular saw the active promotion of Tara as an immemorial centre of sovereignty long since linked to the Uí Néill, driven in part by a desire to silence Munster upstarts, as Ó Riain has suggested.[107] Moreover, a variety of traditions, old and merely made to appear so, became effective weapons in this literary strike. A sovereignty goddess figure is made to bestow legitimacy on all Uí Néill kings since the eponymous Níall in *Echtra mac nEchdach Mugmedóin*; her made-over relative, wedded to the more powerful deity Lug, assumes a similar role in an eleventh-century reworking of an originally tenth-century prophecy, *Baile in Scáil* (The Phantom's Frenzy).[108] Neither the acclaimed man of learning Cenn Fáelad, nor the authoritative five elders of Ireland are deemed to have knowledge of the privileges of Tara in the roughly contemporary narrative, *De Shuidiugud Tellaig Temro* (Concerning the Settling of the Manor of Tara); it therefore befalls the most ancient authority of all, the primeval Fintan mac Bóchra, to accord Uí Néill aspirations the necessary authentication.[109] That this should be considered unimpeachable is further highlighted by the ascription of Fintan's knowledge to the mysterious Trefuilngid Tre-eochair, an angel of God or indeed God himself, according to the tale.[110]

Kingship

This literary preoccupation with royal power, which Kim McCone has termed 'the almost obsessive concern of medieval Irish writers with kingship',[111] reflects both the pivotal position of that institution in society and the dominant role played by monarchical patrons in shaping the tradition. Despite its abundance, and in particular its variety, key elements recur throughout the texts articulating a conceptual framework within which this multi-faceted material must be read. Thus, the sacral nature of the office of king is underlined by the controlling influence accorded to the Otherworld, whose representative on earth the rightful ruler was. In *Togail Bruidne Da Derga*, for example, Conaire Mór's accession to the kingship of Tara is carefully orchestrated by his bird-deity father, Nemglan. Furthermore, a series of all-important *gessi* (taboos) imposed upon Conaire constitutes in effect a supernatural contract which the young, inexperienced king is destined to break. Ultimately, however, responsibility lies with the reigning monarch himself: Conaire's fatal flaw is an inability to balance familial concerns with the welfare of his subjects, as a result of which his judgments become increasingly unjust. Obviously lacking *fír flathemon* (the truth/justice of a ruler), a crucial ideological concept directly linking the prosperity of a territory to the fitness of its sovereign, King Conaire is doomed and the detailed account of his downfall serves as a textbook lesson in how not to rule.[112] Paradigmatic examples of good kingship also abound: the nexus of texts dealing with the prehistoric king of Tara, Cormac mac Airt, portray a wise and wily ruler, in every regard a model monarch.[113] Moreover, such was his fame in this regard that a series of ninth-century gnomes on the proper conduct of a king was put into his mouth.[114]

In reality, however, the art of kingship constituted a delicate balancing act, as many of the narratives attest. A blemished and thus less than ideal king may be prohibited from ruling as Núadu was, according to the ninth-century tale, *Cath Maige Tuired* (The Battle of Mag Tuired). Yet through the example of the oppressive Bres (literally 'Beauty'), the same story also warns of the dangers of being enticed by a superficially beautiful sovereign without paying due regard to other aspects of his pedigree. Of mixed parentage, Bres was afforded access to the kingship through the maternal line alone, unlike his *alter ego* in the tale, the equally hybrid Lug, upon whom his paternal inheritance bestowed the right to rule.[115] Furthermore, Bres's mother, significantly named Ériu (Ireland), was raped by his foreign father, the contemporary resonance of which can scarcely have been lost on the tale's first audience. Indeed, as Carey has argued, the tale can be read as a literary reverberation of ongoing conflict between Vikings and the Uí Néill at the time of its composition.[116]

That particular echo may well have become too distant for later consumers to hear; nonetheless they invested the tale with meaning relevant to their own time. Thus, an eleventh-century reworking of *Cath Maige Tuired* adds introductory material which anchors it firmly to the scheme of invasions set out most fully in *Lebor Gabála*.[117] As texts proved recyclable so too did their adaptable narrative components. One of the most enduring symbols of kingship in the literature is that of a female goddess bestowing sovereignty upon the rightful king. Embodying the land, she entered into a divine marriage with her chosen sovereign as a result of which both king and kingdom flourished. That such a myth should hold attractions for rulers attempting to hold sway over increasingly greater tracts of territory is not surprising. Indeed we may suspect that its elaboration and popularity owe much to a growing perception that kings were controllers of land rather than peoples. Moreover, as the nature of kingship continued to evolve so too did the literary imagery with which it was connected. The sovereignty goddess survived but, as Herbert has demonstrated, she is made subservient to the male in a number of eleventh- and twelfth-century narratives underlining the king's personal role rather than that of the divine in the attainment of sovereignty.[118] Furthermore, the church is accorded an increasingly dominant role. In the twelfth-century tale, *Aided Muirchertaig meic Erca* (The Death-tale of Muirchertach son of Erca), the association of the goddess with the sixth-century king in effect brings about his demise since it involves Muirchertach's rejection of the church in whose hands the ordination of kingship now properly lies. Natural order is restored when the devilish deity, Sín, confesses, enabling St Cairnech to rescue the sovereign's soul from the torments of hell.[119]

The Otherworld

A supernatural sorceress Sín may be, but she is also accorded earthly ancestors of the *senthúatha Temrach* (the old/vassal peoples of Tara) whose defeat at the hands of Muirchertach she sought to avenge.[120] Her embodiment of both mortal and immortal reflects the ubiquitous nature of the Otherworld whose palpable presence imaginative authors sought actively to convey. According to one learned view, universal, all-seeing gods were rendered invisible through *teimel imorbuis Adaim* (the darkness of Adam's sin).[121] For the medieval Irish, therefore, the all-important boundary between the two realms was, in Carey's words, 'not of time and space but of perception'.[122] Be that as it may, the transformational experience was frequently delineated in terms of a journey to one of the many areas supernatural beings were deemed to inhabit. An expedition to a series of wondrous islands overseas is commonly depicted in *immrama* (voyage tales).[123] It is as dwellers of nearby hills and lakes that the *áes síde* (people of the *síd* (Otherworld)) appear in other tales.[124]

Both island and overland locations are envisaged in *Serglige Con Culainn* (The Wasting Sickness of Cú Chulainn), a composite text, the perhaps eleventh-century part of which contains a remarkably lyrical description of the mysterious, marvellous realm to which Cú Chulainn's charioteer, Láeg, and the great hero himself are openly enticed.[125] Yet for all its beauty, eternity has an evil edge: its female representatives combine seductive smiles with merciless beatings.[126] Furthermore, its delights are but mere diabolical delusion, for such was the power of demons *co taisfēntais aíbniusa ocus díamairi dóib, amal no betis co marthanach* (that they could show them (people) beautiful and secret things, as if they were permanent).[127] In fact, Cú Chulainn himself intimates as much in a tenth- or eleventh-century text, *Síabarcharpat Con Culainn* (The Magical Chariot of Cú Chulainn), similarly preserved in *Lebor na hUidre*, in which he urges the recalcitrant Láegaire, king of Tara, to abandon paganism and to believe in God.[128] Significantly, the power of the church is such that the encounter between the two men is made possible by the authority of St Patrick who not only releases the hero from Hell but enables the dumbstruck monarch to relate what he has seen.

Heroic literature

As the church's muted mouthpiece in *Síabarcharpat Con Culainn* bewailing the hardships of eternal damnation, Cú Chulainn cuts a very different figure to the invincible warrior he represents in the longest and best-known of medieval Irish narratives, *Táin Bó Cúailnge*. Furthermore, the indications are that the *Táin*'s popularity is of long standing. In the first place, it engendered a body of *remscéla* (foretales) with which it has a narrative association of sorts and which are related consecutively in the Book of Leinster.[129] In addition, allusions to it are found in a variety of early sources.[130] While elements of the tale appear to be reflected in seventh-century poetry,[131] the core of the *Táin* may well be ninth century in date.[132] The text as we know it, however, constitutes an eleventh-century version incorporating additional material preserved in *Lebor na hUidre* and later manuscripts[133] and an elaborately reworked twelfth-century recension, for which the Book of Leinster is our primary witness.[134] As well as creating an aesthetic unified whole, the author of the later version highlighted certain themes. Thus, Queen Medb's shortcomings, painfully obvious in the earlier text, are further underlined. He also attached considerable importance to a fair and functioning warrior code, as Éamonn Greenwood has shown.[135] Heroic prowess is, of course, a central concern of the text in all its manifestations, yet it is far from being a simple exultation of military might. Cú Chulainn's magnificent exploits may be celebrated and his unswerving loyalty lauded, but emphasis is also placed on the scale of the destruction wrought. Indeed the calamitous final scene in which the sought-after Donn Cúailnge kills not only his fellow bull, In Finnbennach, but also women and children on its own side raises questions about the futility of the entire expedition in the first place.[136]

In all this Cú Chulainn's kinsmen, the Ulaid, are almost innocent bystanders. This was a conflict foisted on them by a foolhardy female monarch in which a curious affliction, the *cess noínden*, prevented them initially from taking part. Thus, their territory was defended by an under-age hero exempt from the debility, in whose glorious victories his countrymen undoubtedly basked. Such uncritical adulation is not a feature of the entire corpus of tales in which the Ulaid play a role, many of which were composed in our period.[137] Indeed the imposition of the *cess noínden* in the first place is depicted in a ninth-century narrative as Macha's revenge for having been forced by them at her husband's instigation to race against horses while heavily pregnant.[138] Other contemporary compositions also cast them in a less than favourable light. The author of *Fled Bricrenn* (Bricriu's Feast) takes delight in depicting a mock-heroic competition between the three premier Ulaid wives: Emer, wife of Cú Chulainn, Fedlem Noíchride, wife of Láegaire Buadach and Finnabair, wife of Conall Cernach. Ultimately, it is their husbands who are ridiculed, however, since their desire to ensure their own partner's victory results in the destruction of the fort of Bricriu.[139] The latter, whose mischief-making activities earn him the soubriquet *nemthenga* (poison-tongued), is portrayed as similarly salacious in *Mesca Ulad* (The Intoxication of the Ulaid), ninth- and twelfth-century versions of which survive. In the later text, the would-be warriors are comically presented as engaging in a drunken night-march which brings them not to Cú Chulainn's citadel, their intended destination, but to far-away Temair Lúachra in the south-west, where many of them are burned to death in an iron house.[140]

The portrayal of women

Not surprisingly, such humour highlights issues of more serious import: *Mesca Ulad* probes the heroic hierarchy and gently questions the position of Conchobar mac Nessa as king. His character is more aggressively assailed in another ninth-century narrative, *Loinges mac nUislenn* (The Exile of the Sons of Uisliu), in which his treachery and venom drive the demented Deirdre to her death. In fact this story is as much a damning indictment of his catastrophic rule as a taut, well-woven account of the doomed relationship between the tragic heroine and her shadowy 'suitee'. Moreover, it is Deirdre, not the Ulaid king, who grows in stature throughout the tale, from an instinct-driven innocent for whom direct action is the primary means of expression to an eloquent, worldly-wise woman as exemplified most clearly in her powerful, poignant lament for the slain Naíse.[141] Her verbal artistry is matched by that of another tragic figure, Derbforgaill, as portrayed in the latter's tenth-century death-tale.[142] However, the real force of this complex composition lies in its stark presentation of women turning on each other on adoption of the manners of men. The mutilation that ensues is reminiscent of the havoc wrought by Medb when she too usurps a male guise, as pointed out to her in no uncertain terms by Fergus towards the end of the *Táin: Is bésad . . . do cach graig remitéit láir, rotgata, rotbrata, rotfeither a moín hi tóin mná misrairleastair* (This is what usually happens . . . to a herd of horses led by a mare. Their substance is taken and carried off and guarded as they follow a woman who has misled them.)[143]

That misogyny should be detected in a literary corpus controlled by male clerics for the most part is predictable; rather it is the many sympathetic studies of women that cause surprise. One of the most powerful is a dramatic poem of perhaps tenth-century date put into the mouth of the *Caillech Béirre* (Hag/Nun/Spouse/Widow[144] of Béirre (the Beare peninsula, County Cork)), in which the decrepit speaker contrasts times past and present as she calmly awaits death, reassured by her belief in an eternal life.[145] While it has been argued that this work may in fact have been written by a woman, Digde of the Corcu Duibne,[146] the common literary convention of donning a poetic mask, frequently female, means that this may not necessarily be the case.[147] Nonetheless, the provision for women scholars in the law tracts, coupled with occasional death notices of these *banfhili* in the chronicles, points strongly to their existence on the fringes at least of what was predominantly a male domain.[148] One such recorded poet was Líadan, whose fraught union with Cuirither is lyrically recounted in a tenth-century series of poems bound by brief prose passages. Their futile attempts to reconcile their physical love of one another with their spiritual love of God is exquisitely and excruciatingly captured in this finely wrought piece.[149] Furthermore, their dilemma was far from unique: a ninth-century poem attributed to an abbot of Lismore and Cork, Daniél úa Líathaiti (d.863), has the cleric defiantly declare to a woman whose mind was evidently set on pleasurable pursuits, *ríched ní renaim ar chol* (I sell not Heaven for sin).[150]

Religious writing

While úa Líathaiti is presented as attempting to convince himself as much as the unnamed woman of the folly of being *for seilg neich nád maith* (in pursuit of that which is not good),[151] an anonymous colleague can smugly state his preference for keeping a tryst with a melodious bell rather than a wanton woman.[152] This vibrant, vital literature accommodates, not surprisingly, a wide spectrum of views. One particularly distinctive one is illustrated by the body of ascetic literature attributed to the *céli Dé* (servants/clients of God) much of which was written in the years immediately preceding the Vikings' arrival.[153] The influence of these prodigious proponents of a more austere way of life, however, was pervasive, not least because of their wholesale use of the vernacular for devotional works. Indeed, Óengus mac Óengobann, the ninth-century author of the metrical martyrology that bears his name, can still claim to belong to their number, having been taught by the pre-eminent ecclesiastic among them, Máel Rúain, founder of the monastery of Tallaght.[154] In this case, the student may well be said to have surpassed the master for *Féilire Óengusso* is an imaginative, innovative, highly intricate saints' calendar whose popularity is indicated not only by the relatively large number of surviving manuscript copies, but by the series of notes and additional preface with which it was later augmented.[155]

An Óengus *céli Dé* is also said to be the author of another remarkable religious poem, the biblical narrative *Saltair na Rann* (The Psalter of the Quatrains), preserved in its entirety in a sole manuscript copy, Rawlinson B502.[156] However, the hundred and fifty poems which make up the body of this work appear linguistically to be tenth rather than ninth century in date, though whether they were written by Airbertach mac Coisse Dobráin (d.988), as Gearóid Mac Eoin has alternatively suggested, is far from clear.[157] Whoever the author was he had access to a wide range of sources, many of them apocryphal, in his versification of what Carey has described as 'the full sweep of Christian sacred history'.[158] In his use of apocrypha he was followed by other creative authors. One of the most inventive of the period, the tenth-century composer of a cosmological homily, *In Tenga Bithnua* (The Evernew Tongue), is indebted to a lost Apocalypse of Philip, as Carey has shown.[159] In vividness and sheer dramatic power his text resembles a later masterly work in a very different genre: the eleventh-century vision put into the mouth of the seventh-century abbot of Iona, Adamnán.[160] Moreover, like the earlier narrative, *Fís Adamnáin* too is structured as a sermon and its author, 'an Irish precursor of Dante',[161] was similarly skilful in his extensive employment of apocryphal and other sources.[162] The portrayal of Eve in *Mé Éba* (I am Eve), a dramatic lyric penned about the same time, is also enhanced by non-canonical biblical works.[163] Furthermore, her guilt-induced apologia in which she takes responsibility for a significant number of the world's ills (*eigred in cach dú . . . geimred gáethmar glé . . . iffern . . . brón . . . oman*, 'ice in every place . . . glistening, windy winter . . . hell . . . sorrow . . . fear') is perfectly in keeping with the misogynistic mindset we have observed in other compositions.[164]

Almost an anti-hymn, *Mé Éba* deliberately invokes a body of devotional poetry addressed to God, Mary and the saints which continued to be composed throughout our period.[165] One of the most delightful is a ninth- or tenth-century lyric put into the mouth of St Íte in which she rejoices in her role as foster-mother to the child Jesus. Significantly, it is preserved as part of the later commentary added to *Féilire Óengusso*, in this case to the entry for Íte's own feast-day.[166] It is as foster-mother to the Irish that St Brigit is presented in another short hymn which may be somewhat earlier in date.[167] Brigit's poetic popularity endured, however: a lively composition of perhaps tenth- or eleventh-century date presents her fervently wishing for an ale-feast with a difference, comprising *dabcha ainmnet . . . lestra déirce . . . escra trócaire* (casks of forbearance . . . cups of charity . . . jorums of mercy).[168] Desire of a different sort permeates a corpus of eleventh- and twelfth-century poetry allegedly spoken by St Colum Cille. As Ireland's premier exile, this sixth-century founder of the monastery of Iona was cast as the mouthpiece of all travellers longing *ascnam tar tuinn topur ndílenn / dochum nÉrenn* (to travel over the deluge-fountained wave to Ireland).[169]

Hagiography

This aspect of Colum Cille's persona is less marked in his vernacular Life composed about the same time. In fact, the hagiographer places emphasis on the saint's work in Ireland before his departure for Iona, and in particular on his establishment of monastic foundations, beginning with Derry.[170] The position of the latter church which assumed the leadership of Colum Cille's federation in 1150 is significant for, as Herbert has shown, a primary aim of the text was to legitimate Derry's claims over a network of Columban dependencies.[171] Political and ecclesiastical concerns similarly inform the composition of other Lives, a large number of which survive in both Latin and Irish. This genre of writing was established early and it maintained its popularity to the end of the twelfth century and beyond, being considerably developed in the process. One notable change concerns the language of the Lives, vernacular examples becoming commonplace from the ninth century, as we have seen. Yet Latin *vitae* continued to be composed, aimed in part presumably at an ecclesiastical audience rather than the lay public of some of the Irish *bethada*. Both strands, however, are far from distinct. In the case of the multiple Lives of Máedóc, for example, as elucidated by Charles Doherty, the earliest, an eleventh-century Latin text, appears to be a translation of a lost Irish original designed to subsume the cult of a rival, identically named saint. As the fortunes of those promoting the holy man's cause continued to rise, local issues gave way to metropolitan matters. Thus, a twelfth-century *vita*, based in part on the earlier Latin Life, is concerned with promoting Máedóc's Leinster seat, Ferns, among the faithful as a future episcopal see. This in turn was translated into the vernacular and augmented in the process to underline the saint's northern associations under the auspices of the Uí Ruairc. Moreover, the hagiographer in this instance was none other than the loyal poet of that dynasty we have encountered already, Gilla Modutu Úa Casaide.[172]

As a proponent of both *senchas* (lore) and its more specific offshoot *náemshenchas* (lore of saints), Úa Casaide was not unique, as indicated not least by the similar strokes with which the secular hero and his saintly counterpart are drawn in a variety of compositions.[173] What Máirín Ní Dhonnchadha has termed their common 'function of exemplarity' is certainly important in this regard;[174] we may also note the broadly comparable ideologies of what are first and foremost literary texts. Recourse to the same inspirational font may explain much of the parallel patterning and recurrence of motifs, but literary borrowing was also widespread, though the precise direction of influence is not always easy to ascertain. The dramatic account of the cursing of Tara by Rúadán, for example, forms part of the eleventh-century death tale of King Díarmait mac Cerbaill whose actions raised the ire of the saint, as well as being contained in Rúadán's own *vita* composed about the same time and in the twelfth-century *betha* of his companion-curser, St Brendan of Birr.[175] Furthermore, an identical tale involving a different pair of protagonists, Saint Adamnán and his royal opponent, Conaing of Brega, is recounted both in the former's tenth-century *betha* and in the Fragmentary Annals.[176]

Notwithstanding such striking affinities, hagiographical models served as a first port of call in the construction of new representatives of sainthood, generic convention acting as a tried and tested guide. That Adamnán, biographer of Colum Cille, should be partially created in the image of his spiritual forefather is not surprising and to this end, echoes of the seventh-century *Vita Columbae* (The Life of Colum Cille) permeate *Betha Adamnáin* (The Life of Adamnán).[177] In truth, however, as one of Ireland's holy trinity, the first Iona abbot features prominently in the hagiographical record, as do his fellow luminaries, Brigit and Patrick. Thus, Íte is specifically described as a second Brigit in her Latin Life[178] and encounters with the Kildare saint are frequent. An even greater number of saints are brought into contact with Ireland's leading patron and the Patrician legacy may well be greater still. As 'the first Irish saint's Life to have been framed as a homily', as Herbert has noted,[179] the Tripartite Life of Patrick, or more specifically the Armagh school that produced it and much other homiletic material,[180] was surely instrumental in popularising what was to become the vernacular hagiographer's preferred structural form. The influence of the *Vita Tripartita* in this regard on one particular Life, *Betha Coluim Chille*, has been demonstrated by Herbert in her discussion of a range of similarities between both texts. Among the most striking is their adoption of a geographical format first attested in seventh-century Patrician material by Tírechán, to structure the list of foundations attributed to the two saints.[181]

Fíanaigecht

The self-same itinerary motif also underlies the elaborate journey around Ireland undertaken by Patrick and his recently acquired warrior-companions in *Acallam na Senórach* (The Colloquy of the Ancients), an ambitious compendium in which Caílte and Oisín, miraculous survivors of a pagan past, provide the saint with an engaging map of their far-distant domain.[182] The atmosphere evoked in the outdoor universe of Finn mac Cumaill, to whose *fian* (warrior band) the raconteurs belong, is decidedly different from that depicted at the royal court of Conchobar mac Nessa which houses the Ulaid heroes. Dynastic ties are looser, for example; natural and supernatural worlds prevail. Yet in their aristocratic tenor and literary execution both settings resemble each other in many ways. Thus, Finn, too, is ultimately presented as the greatest of warriors and, like many another hero, he is furnished with a birth- and death-tale, both independent of the *Acallam*.[183] Furthermore, the twelfth-century account of his youthful exploits is termed *macgnímrada* in its sole fifteenth-century manuscript copy, perhaps in deliberate imitation of Cú Chulainn's similarly titled boyhood deeds.[184] In essence, therefore, the two corpora occupy adjoining creative space, as exemplified by their contiguous focal points outside and within the kin-centred court, as well as by their elucidation of two consecutive phases of human existence, the experimental adolescence of the *fénnid* (warrior) and the responsible adulthood of the committed *láech* (hero). That the spheres undoubtedly overlap is graphically illustrated not only by the adoption by the youth Cú Chulainn of a fully mature role in the *Táin*, as we have seen, but by Finn's permanent transitional state, albeit one in which he is allowed some of the trappings of adulthood, most notably marriage.

The composition of both types of narrative follows a similarly concentric chronological pattern. The Ulaid were celebrated in story as early as the eighth century and continued to form the subject of creative writing down through our period. Finn and his *fiana*, on the other hand, appear to have entered the literary record later. That they were known by the ninth century at the latest is indicated by references to Finn among others in a variety of sources.[185] It was in the tenth century and later, however, that they were accorded a more prominent place in the canon, although at the point of entry *fianaigecht* literature seems relatively mature. Thus, two of its main characters, Finn himself and his royal lord, King Cormac mac Airt, appear in familiar roles in the tenth-century wooing tale *Tochmarc Ailbe* (The Wooing of Ailbe).[186] In addition, Finn also takes his place alongside other well-known literary heroes in Cináed úa hArtacáin's tenth-century poem, *Fíanna bátar i nEmain*.[187] That his literary pre-eminence was not yet quite established, however, is indicated by an early *fianaigecht* poem, *Reicne Fothad Canainne* (The Poem of Fothad Canainne), in which Fothad rather than Finn is depicted as *fían* leader supreme.[188] Moreover, as Ann Dooley and Harry Roe have noted, his gradual movement centre stage may well have been facilitated by his convergence with another Leinster literary figure, Finn *file* (poet), as a result of which Finn mac Cumaill was accorded his notable visionary persona.[189]

It is in the increasingly numerous *fianaigecht* (later fianaigheacht) narratives that the literary evolution of Finn can be traced, although this branch of literature did not become dominant until the later medieval period. Notwithstanding this, the existence of the *fían* as a social institution containing aristocratic young males yet to claim their inheritance is alluded to in early texts, as has been demonstrated by Richard Sharpe and Kim McCone.[190] Many of these highlight its negative characteristics and this has been cited to explain its sidelining in a literary culture dictated by a clerical intelligentsia.[191] If so, the opposition weakened as time progressed. Significantly, it is the positive aspects of character development afforded by life in the *fían* that are emphasised in *fianaigecht* narratives, with a host of would-be brigands acquiring wisdom, generosity and humility in the process.[192] This new sanitised version held widespread appeal, as indicated by the increased popularity of such tales. Their innovative style, however, suggests that shifting aesthetic sensibilities also had a role to play in their development. In addition, the casting of Finn and his *fiana* as aetiological artisans of the natural world ensured a crucial link with the favoured genres of place-name lore and nature poetry, a factor which added considerably to their attraction.

Both *dinnshenchas* material and metrical compositions celebrating life outdoors form key aspects of *Acallam na Senórach*, a masterly creation from the very end of our period, which marks *fianaigecht* literature's coming of age. Skilfully shifting between three chronological levels, that of the *fiana*, St Patrick and his own present, our time-travelling author had recourse to some earlier texts in composing his elaborate construct of interlocking tales. Recurring core themes demonstrate the essential unity of the work, however, as do numerous narratorial devices, including the inventive frame-tale which sees Patrick, in the company of the extraordinarily long-lived Caílte and Oisín, embark on an imaginative circuit of Ireland, as mentioned above. What their fictional journey throws into relief, of course, are issues of concern in the Ireland of the author's own day, the narrative's Connacht focus and its espousing of reformist ideals being particularly noteworthy in this regard.[193] In this connection, it need not surprise us that the cultural changes instigated by ecclesiastical reform are also reflected in the text. Specifically, the assurance received by Patrick from none other than his guardian angel that engagement with Caílte was a worthwhile pursuit and that the *fiana*'s tales should in fact be recorded for posterity[194] highlights the increasingly self-conscious air of the church's association with secular learning. With the benefit of hindsight, it is clear that the *Acallam*'s eloquent justification constitutes a defiant last gasp.

Conclusion

In the event, lay learned families proved worthy successors to their predominantly ecclesiastical predecessors and secular literature continued to thrive, the blossoming of *fianaigecht* material in the post-twelfth-century period being a notable case in point. In the creative works of the preceding period, later medieval authors had inspiring literary models, as this summary description of a mere selection of the products composed between the ninth and thirteenth centuries has hopefully revealed. Writing predominantly in two languages, with Irish gaining the upper hand over Latin as the period progressed, in an ever-evolving variety of styles and genres, the vibrant verbal artistry and subtle skill of these highly trained literary craftsmen is manifestly clear. Obvious too is the fact that their qualities were both valued and influential in a strictly stratified society which accorded intellectual activity a central place, embracing learning in a multitude of forms. That it did so underlines the contemporary relevance of these narratives whose authors were informed by, but also seeking to inform, the diverse currents of their own time. In their quest, they drew freely on all aspects of their rich and varied inheritance, native as well as foreign, old alongside new, producing complex literary constructs in the process directed at a significant body of the community. Indeed many of the most accomplished of these texts were designed to function on a variety of levels. Detailed cross-referencing across a broad literary spectrum suggests at least in part an appreciative literate audience at whom such conscious text-play was directed. Inevitably those whose literary frame of reference was less expansive engaged differently with the self-same work. Similarly, the political nuances and social commentary encoded in certain compositions were directed at specific audiences; that did not necessarily preclude their enjoyment by others less well informed.[195] As modern readers of the literature, our engagement with it is understandably of a very different order, since of the world of its creators we are accorded no more than a restricted view. All is far from lost, however, and reinserting the texts as far as possible in their proper space and context will certainly bring us closer to them, as well as increasing our appreciation of the sophisticated society they so eloquently represent. Furthermore, such is the richness and vitality of this extraordinary material, that a bespectacled view of it is far, far better than none.

Notes

1. Linguistically, Archaic Irish and Early Old Irish precede Classical Old Irish; while Early Modern Irish follows Middle Irish.
2. John Carey, *King of Mysteries: Early Irish Religious Writings* (Dublin: Four Courts Press, 1998), p. 10.
3. Examples include material from the eleventh-century narrative, *Bórama Laigen* (The Tribute of the Leinstermen), being incorporated into the Life of St Máedóc, as well as references to Vergil and medieval bestiary literature in *Immram Curaig Maíle Dúin* (The Voyage of Máel Dúin's Boat), and to the furies in *Táin Bó Cúailnge* (The Catttle Raid of Cúailnge) and *Fled Dúin na nGéd* (The Feast of Dún na nGéd (the Fort of the Geese)).
4. Johan Corthals, *Altirische Erzählkunst*, Forum Celticum I (Münster: Lit, 1996), p. 7.
5. Gerard Murphy, ed. and trans. *Early Irish Lyrics* (Oxford: Clarendon Press, 1956); James Carney, ed. and trans. *Medieval Irish Lyrics* (Dublin: Dolmen Press, 1967); David Greene and Frank O'Connor, eds. and trans. *A Golden Treasury of Irish Poetry AD 600–1200* (London: Macmillan, 1967; reprinted Dingle: Brandon Press, 1990).
6. John Gwynn, *Liber Ardmachanus* (Dublin: Royal Irish Academy, 1913).
7. The Irish material has been edited by Whitley Stokes, ed. and trans. *The Tripartite Life of Patrick with Other Documents Relating to that Saint*, Rolls Series, 2 vols. (London: Stationery Office, 1887).
8. Tomás Ó Concheanainn, 'Textual and Historical Associations of Leabhar na hUidhre', *Éigse* 29 (1996), pp. 65–120, p. 67.
9. R. I. Best and Osborn Bergin, eds. *Lebor na hUidre: Book of the Dun Cow* (Dublin: Royal Irish Academy, 1929), p. xii.
10. Ó Concheanainn, 'Textual and Historical Associations', pp. 67–71.
11. Francis J. Byrne argues for Killeshin in *A Thousand Years of Irish Script: An Exhibition of Irish Manuscripts in Oxford Libraries* (Oxford: Bodleian Library, 1979), p. 13, whereas Edel Bhreathnach has suggested that sources for the codex originated in that monastery: 'Killeshin: An Irish Monastery Surveyed', *Cambrian Medieval Celtic Studies* 27 (1994), pp. 33–47, p. 43. Pádraig Ó Riain has associated the manuscript with Glendalough and has argued that it is none other than the 'lost' codex, 'The Book of Glendalough': 'The Book of Glendalough or Rawlinson B502', *Éigse* 18 (1981), pp. 161–76. For an alternative view, see Caoimhín Breatnach, 'Rawlinson B502, Lebar Glinne Dá Locha and Saltair na Rann', *Éigse* 30 (1997), pp. 109–32 and 'Manuscript Sources and Methodology: Rawlinson B502 and *Lebar Glinne Dá Locha*', *Celtica* 24 (2003), pp. 40–54, as well as the response by Ó Riain to Breatnach's first article, 'Rawlinson B502 alias Lebar Glinne

Dá Locha: A Restatement of the Case', *Zeitschrift für celtische Philologie* 51 (1998), pp. 130–47.

12. Edel Bhreathnach has argued, however, that Finn úa Cíanáin is intended: 'Two Contributors to the Book of Leinster', in Michael Richter and Jean-Michel Picard, eds. *Ogma: Essays in Celtic Studies in Honour of Próinséas Ní Chatháin* (Dublin: Four Courts Press, 2002), pp. 105–11, pp. 105–7.

13. Proinsias Mac Cana, 'The Rise of the Later Schools of *Filidheacht*', *Ériu* 25 (1974), pp. 126–46. The role of the church in secular learning did not become entirely insignificant, however; see Katharine Simms, 'An Eaglais agus Filí na Scol', *Léachtaí Cholm Cille* 24 (1994), pp. 21–36.

14. William O'Sullivan, 'Notes on the Scripts and Make-up of the Book of Leinster', *Celtica* 7 (1966), pp. 1–31, p. 26.

15. Tomás Ó Concheanainn, 'The Manuscript Tradition of Two Middle Irish Leinster Tales', *Celtica* 18 (1986), pp. 13–33.

16. In addition to the Yellow Book of Lecan (Robert Atkinson, *The Yellow Book of Lecan, A Collection of Pieces (Prose and Verse) in the Irish Language, In Part Compiled at the End of the Fourteenth Century* (Dublin: Royal Irish Academy, 1896)), these include the fourteenth-century Book of Lecan and Book of Ballymote: Kathleen Mulchrone, *The Book of Lecan: Leabhar Mór Mhic Fhir Bhisigh Lecáin* (Dublin: Irish Manuscripts Commission, 1937); Robert Atkinson, *The Book of Ballymote, A Collection of Pieces (Prose and Verse) in the Irish Language, Compiled about the Beginning of the Fifteenth Century* (Dublin: Royal Irish Academy, 1887).

17. Cecile O'Rahilly, ed. and trans. *Táin Bó Cúalnge from the Book of Leinster* (Dublin: Dublin Institute for Advanced Studies, 1967), p. 136, lines 4921–5, p. 272; Pádraig Ó Néill, 'The Latin Colophon to the "Táin Bó Cúailnge" in the Book of Leinster: A Critical View of Old Irish Literature', *Celtica* 23 (1999), pp. 269–75.

18. J. H. Bernard and Robert Atkinson, *The Irish Liber Hymnorum* (London: Henry Bradshaw Society, 1898); Máire Herbert, 'The Middle Irish Preface to *Amra Choluim Chille*', in Donnchadh Ó Corráin, Liam Breatnach and Kim McCone, eds. *Sages, Saints and Storytellers: Celtic Studies in Honour of Professor James Carney* (Maynooth: An Sagart, 1989), pp. 67–75, p. 67.

19. Joseph O'Longan, *Leabhar Breac, the Speckled Book, Otherwise Styled Leabhar Mór Dúna Daighre, the Great Book of Dun Doighre; A Collection of Pieces in Irish and Latin, Compiled from Ancient Sources about the Close of the Fourteenth Century* (Dublin: Royal Irish Academy, 1872–6).

20. Máire Herbert, 'Caithréim Cellaig: Some Literary and Historical Considerations', *Zeitschrift für celtische Philologie* 49–50 (1997), pp. 320–32.

21. Kenneth Jackson, ed. *Aislinge Meic Con Glinne* (Dublin: Dublin Institute for Advanced Studies, 1990).

22. Eleanor Knott and Gerard Murphy, *Early Irish Literature* (London: Routledge and Kegan Paul, 1966), p. 101.

23. Herbert, 'Middle Irish Preface'.

24. *Find episcopus Cilli Dara hoc addidit* (Find, bishop of Kildare, added this): R. I. Best, Osborn Bergin, M. A. O'Brien and A. O'Sullivan, eds. *The Book of Leinster formerly Lebar na Núachongbála*, 6 vols. (Dublin: Dublin Institute for Advanced Studies, 1954–83), I, p. 132.

25. Ó Concheanainn, 'Manuscript Tradition', pp. 21–33.
26. Seán Mac Airt and Gearóid Mac Niocaill, eds. and trans. *The Annals of Ulster (to AD 1131), Part I Text and Translation* (Dublin: Dublin Institute for Advanced Studies, 1983), pp. 342–3, 492–3.
27. Best and O'Brien, *Book of Leinster*, III, pp. 516–23.
28. Ibid., pp. 504–15; ibid., IV, pp. 791–6.
29. Liam Breatnach, ed. and trans. *Uraicecht na Ríar: The Poetic Grades in Early Irish Law*, Early Irish Law Series II (Dublin: Dublin Institute for Advanced Studies, 1987), p. 92.
30. Kathleen Mulchrone, 'Flannacán mac Cellaich Rí Breg Hoc Carmen', *Journal of Celtic Studies* I (1949), pp. 80–93, pp. 86, 88 (stanza 28).
31. Mary E. Byrne, ed. 'Airec Menman Uraird maic Coisse', in Osborn J. Bergin, R. I. Best, Kuno Meyer and J. G. O'Keeffe, eds. *Anecdota from Irish Manuscripts, vol. II* (Halle: Max Niemeyer, 1908), pp. 42–76.
32. See Liam Breatnach, 'An Mheán-Ghaeilge', in Kim McCone, Damian McManus, Cathal Ó Háinle, Nicholas Williams and Liam Breatnach, eds. *Stair na Gaeilge: in Ómós do Pádraig Ó Fiannachta* (Maynooth: Department of Old Irish, St Patrick's College, 1994), pp. 221–333.
33. See Charles Doherty, 'Latin Writing in Ireland (c.400–c.1200)', in Seamus Deane, general ed. *The Field Day Anthology of Irish Writing*, 3 vols. (Derry: Field Day, 1991), I, pp. 61–140, pp. 104–7, 138–9.
34. J. J. Tierney, ed. and trans. *Dicuili, Liber de Mensura Orbis Terrae*, Scriptores Latini Hiberniae VI (Dublin: Dublin Institute for Advanced Studies, 1967).
35. Doherty, 'Latin Writing', pp. 117–23, 139–40.
36. I. P. Sheldon Willliams, ed. and trans. *Iohannis Scotti Eriugenae, Periphyseon, Liber primus, Liber secundus* and *Liber tertius*, Scriptores Latini Hiberniae VII, IX and XI (Dublin: Dublin Institute for Advanced Studies, 1968, 1972, 1981); Édouard Jeauneau and J. J. O'Meara, ed. and trans. *Iohannis Scotti Eriugenae, Periphyseon, Liber IV*, Scriptores Latini Hiberniae XIII (Dublin: Dublin Institute for Advanced Studies, 1995).
37. John Carey has compared Eriugena's *Periphyseon* to the tenth-century vernacular work *In Tenga Bithnua* (The Evernew Tongue), though he thinks it highly unlikely that the latter was influenced directly by the former: Carey, *A Single Ray of the Sun: Religious Speculation in Early Ireland* (Aberystwyth and Andover: Celtic Studies Publications, 1999), pp. 75–106.
38. James Henthorn Todd, ed. and trans. *Cogadh Gaedhel re Gallaibh: The War of the Gaedhil with the Gaill or The Invasions of Ireland by the Danes and Other Norsemen*, Rolls Series (London: Longmans, Green, Reader and Dyer, 1867).
39. Best and O'Brien, *Book of Leinster*, V, p. 1119.
40. C. J. McDonough, ed. and trans. *Warner of Rouen, Moriuht: A Norman Latin Poem from the Early Eleventh Century*, Studies and Texts CXXI (Toronto: Pontifical Institute of Medieval Studies, 1995).
41. Aubrey Gwynn, ed. *The Writings of Bishop Patrick 1074–1084*, Scriptores Latini Hiberniae I (Dublin: Dublin Institute for Advanced Studies, 1955).
42. Albrecht Wagner, ed. *Visio Tnudgali, Lateinisch und Altdeutsch* (Erlangen: Deichert, 1882); Jean-Michel Picard and Yolande de Pontfarcy, trans. *The Vision of Tnudgal* (Dublin: Four Courts Press, 1989).

43. Picard and de Pontfarcy, *Vision*, p. 15.
44. On what is known of Marcus's life, see ibid., pp. 27–9.
45. 'G' has been tentatively identified with Gisila, abbess of the convent of St Paul in Regensburg between 1140 and 1160: ibid., p. 13.
46. George H. Orpen, ed. and trans. *The Song of Dermot and the Earl: An Old French Poem about the Coming of the Normans to Ireland* (Oxford: Clarendon Press, 1892).
47. Donncha Ó hAodha, ed. and trans. *Bethu Brigte* (Dublin: Dublin Institute for Advanced Studies, 1978); Kuno Meyer, *Hibernica Minora being a Fragment of an Old-Irish Treatise on the Psalter*, Anecdota Oxoniensia Medieval and Modern Series VIII (Oxford: Clarendon Press, 1894).
48. David N. Dumville, 'Latin and Irish in the Annals of Ulster', in Dorothy Whitelock, Rosamund McKitterick and David N. Dumville, eds. *Ireland in Early Medieval Europe: Studies in Memory of Kathleen Hughes* (Cambridge: Cambridge University Press, 1982), pp. 320–39.
49. See Thomas Charles-Edwards, *Early Christian Ireland* (Cambridge: Cambridge University Press, 2000), pp. 592–9 where he sets out political developments that may also have had a role to play.
50. Mac Airt and Mac Niocaill, *Annals of Ulster*, pp. 520–1.
51. Murphy, *Early Irish Lyrics*, pp. 52–4.
52. Ó hAodha, *Bethu Brigte*; Ernst Windisch, ed. and trans. 'Fís Adamnáin: Die Vision des Adamnán', in Ernst Windisch, ed. *Irische Texte mit Wörterbuch*, vol. I (Leipzig: Hirzel, 1880), pp. 165–96.
53. See Leslie Diane Myrick, *From the* De Excidio Troiae Historia *to the* Togail Troí: *Literary-cultural Synthesis in a Medieval Irish Adaptation of Dares' Troy Tale* (Heidelberg: Winter, 1989), pp. 70–1.
54. Erik Peters, ed. and trans. 'Die irische Alexandersage', *Zeitschrift für celtische Philologie* 30 (1967), pp. 71–264.
55. Gearóid Mac Eoin, 'Das Verbalsystem von *Togail Troí* (H.2.17)', *Zeitschrift für celtische Philologie* 28 (1960–1), pp. 73–136, 149–223, p. 202.
56. Whitley Stokes, ed. and trans. 'In Cath Catharda: The Civil War of the Romans. An Irish Version of Lucan's Pharsalia', in Whitley Stokes and Ernst Windisch, eds. *Irische Texte mit Übersetzungen und Wörterbuch*, IV.2 (Leipzig: Hirzel, 1909); George Calder, ed. and trans. *Togail na Tebe: The Thebaid of Statius* (Cambridge: Cambridge University Press, 1922).
57. Robert T. Meyer, ed. *Merugud Uilix maic Leirtis*, Mediaeval and Modern Irish Series XVII (Dublin: Dublin Institute for Advanced Studies, 1958).
58. Whitley Stokes, ed. and trans. 'Tidings of Doomsday: An Early Middle Irish Homily', *Revue celtique* 4 (1880), pp. 245–57; Whitley Stokes, ed. and trans. 'Tidings of the Resurrection', *Revue celtique* 25 (1904), pp. 232–59.
59. Uáitéar Mac Gearailt, 'Change and Innovation in Eleventh-century Prose Narrative in Irish', in Hildegard L. C. Tristram, ed. *(Re)oralisierung*, ScriptOralia 84 (Tübingen: Gunter Narr, 1996) pp. 443–96, p. 492.
60. Uáitéar Mac Gearailt, 'On Textual Correspondences in Early Irish Heroic Tales', in Gordon W. MacLennan, ed. *Proceedings of the First North American Congress of Celtic Studies held at Ottawa from 26th–30th March 1986* (Ottawa: Chair of Celtic Studies, University

of Ottawa, 1988) pp. 343–55, p. 351; Hildegard L. C. Tristram, 'Latin and Latin Learning in the *Táin Bó Cuailnge*', *Zeitschrift für celtische Philologie* 49–50 (1997), pp. 847–77, p. 872.

61. Mac Gearailt, 'Change and Innovation', p. 492.

62. Tristram, 'Latin', p. 872.

63. Examples include *Scéla Muicce Meic Dathó* (The Tale of Mac Dathó's Pig), ed. Rudolf Thurneysen, Mediaeval and Modern Irish Series VI (Dublin: Dublin Institute for Advanced Studies, 1935); *Loinges mac nUislenn* (The Exile of the Sons of Uisliu), ed. and trans. Vernam Hull (New York: Modern Language Association of America, 1949); *Bethu Brigte*, ed. and trans. Ó hAodha.

64. Examples include the twelfth-century versions of *Cath Almaine* and *Tochmarc Becfhola*.

65. Eleanor Knott, ed. *Togail Bruidne Da Derga*, Mediaeval and Modern Irish Series VIII (Dublin: Dublin Institute for Advanced Studies, 1936).

66. Todd, *Cogadh Gaedhel*.

67. Liam Breatnach, 'Canon Law and Secular Law in Early Ireland: The Significance of *Bretha Nemed*', *Peritia* 3 (1984), pp. 439–59 and 'An Edition of *Amra Senáin*', in Ó Corráin et al., *Sages*, pp. 7–31.

68. Knott, *Togail*, pp. 20–42; see Kim McCone, *Pagan Past and Christian Present in Early Irish Literature*, Maynooth Monographs III (Maynooth: An Sagart, 1989), pp. 39–40.

69. David Greene, ed. *Fingal Rónáin and Other Stories*, Mediaeval and Modern Irish Series XVI (Dublin: Dublin Institute for Advanced Studies, 1955), pp. 27–44, pp. 28–9.

70. Greene, *Fingal Rónáin*, pp. 16–26.

71. Tomás Ó Cathasaigh, 'The Oldest Story of the Laigin: Observations on *Orgain Denna Ríg*', *Éigse* 33 (2002), pp. 1–18, pp. 10–12.

72. Best et al., *Book of Leinster*, i, pp. 202–5.

73. Proinsias Mac Cana, 'Prosimetrum in Insular Celtic Literature', in Joseph Harris and Karl Reichl, eds. *Prosimetrum: Crosscultural Perspectives on Narrative in Prose and Verse* (Cambridge: D. S. Brewer, 1997), pp. 99–130, p. 111.

74. Tomás Ó Cathasaigh, 'The Theme of *Ainmne* in *Scéla Cano Meic Gartnáin*', in Ó Corráin et al. *Sages*, pp. 233–50, p. 240.

75. Greene, *Fingal Rónáin*, pp. 1–15, pp. 8–10.

76. For discussion of the tale, see Thomas Charles-Edwards, 'Honour and Status in Some Irish and Welsh Prose Tales', *Ériu* 29 (1978), pp. 123–41; Tomás Ó Cathasaigh, 'The Trial of Mael Fhothartaig', *Ériu* 36 (1985), pp. 177–80 and 'The Rhetoric of *Fingal Rónáin*', *Celtica* 17 (1985), pp. 123–44; Erich Poppe, 'Deception and Self-deception in *Fingal Rónáin*', *Ériu* 47 (1996), pp. 137–51.

77. J. G. O'Keeffe, ed. and trans. *Buile Suibhne, The Frenzy of Suibhne being The Adventures of Suibhne Geilt, A Middle-Irish Romance*, Irish Texts Society XII (London: Irish Texts Society, 1913), pp. 142–3; Seamus Heaney, trans. *Sweeney Astray* (Derry: Field Day Publications, 1983; reprinted London: Faber and Faber, 2001).

78. H. P. A. Oskamp, ed. and trans. *The Voyage of Máel Dúin: A Study in Early Irish Voyage Literature* (Groningen: Wolters-Noordhoff Publishing, 1970).

79. Ibid., pp. 47–8.

80. Thomas Owen Clancy, 'Subversion at Sea: Structure, Style and Intent in the *Immrama*', in Jonathan Wooding, ed. *The Otherworld Voyage in Early Irish Literature: An Anthology of Criticism* (Dublin: Four Courts Press, 2000), pp. 194–225, p. 208.

81. Ibid., p. 198, pp. 213–22.

82. Ibid.

83. Brian Ó Cuív, ed. and trans. 'A Poem Composed for Cathal Croibhdhearg Ó Conchubhair', *Ériu* 34 (1983), pp. 157–74; see also Donnchadh Ó Corráin, 'Legend as Critic', in Tom Dunne, ed. *The Writer as Witness: Literature as Historical Evidence*, Historical Studies XVI (Cork: Cork University Press, 1987), pp. 23–38.

84. Whitley Stokes, ed. and trans. 'The Death of Crimthann Son of Fidach, and the Adventures of the Sons of Eochaid Mugmedóin', *Revue celtique* 24 (1903), pp. 172–207, pp. 190–203; Maud Joynt, ed. and trans. 'Echtra mac Echdach Mugmedóin', *Ériu* 4 (1908–10), pp. 91–111.

85. Mac Airt and Mac Niocaill, *Annals of Ulster*, pp. 462–3.

86. See, for example, Edward J. Gwynn, ed. and trans. *The Metrical Dinnshenchas*, 5 vols. Todd Lecture Series VIII–XII (Dublin: Royal Irish Academy, 1903–35), VIII, pp. 14–27. Indeed Tomás Ó Concheanainn has suggested that he may in fact have compiled one version of the *Dinnshenchas* which was later elaborated by other poets: 'A Pious Redactor of Dinnshenchas Érenn', *Ériu* 33 (1982), pp. 85–98.

87. See, for example, Best and O'Brien, *Book of Leinster*, III, pp. 639–760. Metrical and prose versions have been edited separately: Gwynn, *Metrical Dinnshenchas*; Whitley Stokes, ed. and trans. 'The Prose Tales in the Rennes Dindshenchas', *Revue celtique* 15 (1894), pp. 271–336, 418–84; 16 (1895), pp. 31–83, 135–67; 'The Bodleian Dindshenchas', *Folk-Lore* 3 (1892), pp. 467–516; 'The Edinburgh Dindshenchas', *Folk-Lore* 4 (1893), pp. 471–97.

88. Gwynn, *Metrical Dinnshenchas*, x, pp. 2–25; Stokes, 'Rennes Dindshenchas', *Revue celtique* 15, pp. 311–15.

89. Margaret E. Dobbs, ed. and trans. 'The Ban-shenchus', *Revue celtique* 47 (1930), pp. 282–339; 48 (1931), pp. 163–234; 49 (1932), pp. 437–89.

90. Muireann Ní Bhrolcháin, 'The *Banshenchas* Revisited', in Mary O'Dowd and Sabine Wichert, eds. *Chattel, Servant or Citizen: Women's Status in Church, State and Society* (Belfast: Institute of Irish Studies, Queen's University of Belfast, 1995), pp. 70–81.

91. R. A. S. Macalister, ed. and trans. *Lebor Gabála Érenn: The Book of the Taking of Ireland*, 5 vols. (London and Dublin: Irish Texts Society, 1938–56).

92. John Carey, *The Irish National Origin-legend: Synthetic Pseudohistory*, Quiggin Pamphlets on the Sources of Mediaeval Gaelic History I (Cambridge: Department of Anglo-Saxon, Norse and Celtic, 1994).

93. Best and O'Brien, *Book of Leinster*, III, pp. 516–23.

94. Peter Smith, 'Early Irish Historical Verse, the Evolution of a Genre', in Próinséas Ní Chatháin and Michael Richter, eds. *Ireland and Europe in the Early Middle Ages, Texts and Transmission: Irland und Europa im früheren Mittelalter, Texte und Überlieferung* (Dublin: Four Courts Press, 2002), pp. 326–41, p. 335.

95. Ibid., p. 340.

96. Ibid., pp. 339–40.

97. M. A. O'Brien, ed. *Corpus Genealogiarum Hiberniae* (Dublin: Dublin Institute for Advanced Studies, 1962); Robert Welch, ed. *The Oxford Companion to Irish Literature* (Oxford: Clarendon Press, 1996), p. 213.

98. Francis J. Byrne, 'Tribes and Tribalism in Early Ireland', *Ériu* 22 (1971), pp. 128–66, p. 153.

99. Pádraig Ó Riain, ed. *Corpus Genealogiarum Sanctorum Hiberniae* (Dublin: Dublin Institute for Advanced Studies, 1985), p. xvii.

100. Máire Herbert, 'Hagiography', in K. McCone and K. Simms, eds. *Progress in Medieval Celtic Studies* (Maynooth: St Patrick's College, 1996), pp. 79–90, p. 88.

101. Ó Riain, *Corpus*, pp. xlvii–l.

102. See Donnchadh Ó Corráin, 'Historical Need and Literary Narrative', in D. Ellis Evans, J. G. Griffith and E. M. Jope, eds. *Proceedings of the Seventh International Congress of Celtic Studies held at Oxford, from 10th to 15th July, 1983* (Oxford: Clarendon Press, 1986), pp. 141–58.

103. Ó Corráin, 'Legend as Critic', pp. 33–5.

104. Welch, *Oxford Companion*, p. 214.

105. These texts are Todd, *Cogadh Gaedhel*; Alexander Bugge, ed. and trans. *Caithreim Cellachain Chaisil: The Victorious Career of Cellachan of Cashel or the Wars between the Irishmen and the Norsemen in the Middle of the 10th Century* (Christiania [Oslo], 1905); Joan Newlon Radner, ed. and trans. *Fragmentary Annals of Ireland* (Dublin: Dublin Institute for Advanced Studies, 1978).

106. Donnchadh Ó Corráin has drawn attention to the possible role of Asser's Life of King Alfred and Einhard's *Vita Karoli* in this regard: '*Caithréim Chellacháin Chaisil*: History or Propaganda?', *Ériu* 25 (1974), pp. 1–69, p. 69.

107. Pádraig Ó Riain, 'The Psalter of Cashel: A Provisional List of Contents', *Éigse* 23 (1989), pp. 107–30.

108. See Máire Herbert, 'Goddess and King: The Sacred Marriage in Early Ireland', in Louise O. Fradenburg, ed. *Women and Sovereignty* (Edinburgh: Edinburgh University Press, 1992), pp. 85–98.

109. R. I. Best, ed. and trans. 'The Settling of the Manor of Tara', *Ériu* 4 (1910), pp. 121–72.

110. Ibid., pp. 152–3.

111. McCone, *Pagan Past*, p. 107.

112. Knott, *Togail*.

113. See Tomás Ó Cathasaigh, *The Heroic Biography of Cormac mac Airt* (Dublin: Dublin Institute for Advanced Studies, 1978).

114. Kuno Meyer, ed. and trans. *The Instructions of King Cormac Mac Airt*, Todd Lecture Series XV (Dublin: Royal Irish Academy, 1909).

115. Elizabeth A. Gray, ed. and trans. *Cath Maige Tuired: The Second Battle of Mag Tuired*, Irish Texts Society L (Dublin: Irish Texts Society, 1982).

116. John Carey, 'Myth and Mythography in *Cath Maige Tuired*', *Studia Celtica* 24–5 (1989–90), pp. 53–69.

117. Ibid., pp. 53–5.

118. Herbert, 'Goddess and King'.

119. Lil Nic Dhonnchadha, ed. *Aided Muirchertaig meic Erca*, Mediaeval and Modern Irish Series XIX (Dublin: Dublin Institute for Advanced Studies, 1964). See also Joan Newlon

Radner, 'The Significance of the Threefold Death in Celtic Tradition', in Patrick Ford, ed. *Celtic Folklore and Christianity: Studies in Memory of William W. Heist* (Santa Barbara: McNally and Loftin, 1983), pp. 180–200, pp. 195–8, and Máire Herbert, 'The Death of Muirchertach mac Erca: A Twelfth-Century Tale', in Folke Josephson, ed. *Celts and Vikings: Proceedings of the Fourth Symposium of Societas Celtologica Nordica*, Meijerbergs Arkiv för Svensk Ordforskning XX (Göteborg, 1997), pp. 27–39.

120. Edel Bhreathnach has suggested that this 'may carry a contemporary political message regarding the relationship in the eleventh century between the tributary tribes of Brega and the Uí Néill': *Tara: A Select Bibliography*, Discovery Programme Reports III (Dublin: Royal Irish Academy, 1995), p. 6.

121. Osborn Bergin and R. I. Best, eds and trans. 'Tochmarc Étaíne', *Ériu* 12 (1934–8), pp. 137–96, pp. 180–1; Carey, *Single Ray*, pp. 27–38.

122. John Carey, 'The Waters of Vision and the Gods of Skill', *Alexandria* 1 (1999), pp. 163–85, p. 169.

123. Oskamp, *Voyage*, and the earlier *Immram Brain* (The Voyage of Bran) on which *Immram Maíle Dúin* is partly based: Séamas Mac Mathúna, ed. and trans. *Immram Brain: Bran's Journey to the Land of Women*, Buchreihe der Zeitschrift für celtische Philologie II (Tübingen: Niemeyer, 1985).

124. John Carey, 'The Location of the Otherworld in Irish Tradition', *Éigse* 19 (1982), pp. 36–43, and Patrick Sims-Williams, 'Some Celtic Otherworld Terms', in A. T. E. Matonis and Daniel F. Melia, eds. *Celtic Language, Celtic Culture: A Festschrift for Eric P. Hamp* (Van Nuys: Ford and Bailie, 1990), pp. 57–81.

125. John Carey, 'The Uses of Tradition in Serglige Con Culainn', in J. P. Mallory and G. Stockman, eds. *Ulidia: Proceedings of the First International Conference on the Ulster Cycle of Tales, Belfast and Emain Macha 8–12 April 1994* (Belfast: December Publications, 1994), pp. 77–84.

126. Myles Dillon, ed. *Serglige Con Culainn*, Mediaeval and Modern Irish Series XIV (Dublin: Dublin Institute for Advanced Studies, 1953), pp. 3–4.

127. Ibid., p. 29; translation by Carey, 'Uses of Tradition', p. 78 whose interpretation of the passage is followed here. See also Tomás Ó Cathasaigh, 'Reflections on Compert Conchobuir and Serglige Con Culainn', in Mallory and Stockman, *Ulidia*, pp. 85–9, pp. 88–9.

128. Best and Bergin, *Lebor na hUidre*, pp. 278–87.

129. Best and O'Brien, *Book of Leinster*, v, pp. 1119–70.

130. Kuno Meyer, ed. and trans. *The Triads of Ireland*, Todd Lecture Series XIV (Dublin: Royal Irish Academy, 1906), pp. 8–9, §62; Proinsias Mac Cana, *The Learned Tales of Medieval Ireland* (Dublin: Dublin Institute for Advanced Studies, 1980), pp. 42, 52, 65.

131. Kuno Meyer, ed. 'The Laud Genealogies and Tribal Histories', *Zeitschrift für celtische Philologie* 8 (1912), pp. 291–338, pp. 305–7. See also Ruairí Ó hUiginn, 'The Background and Development of Táin Bó Cúailnge', in J. P. Mallory, ed. *Aspects of the Táin* (Belfast: December Publications, 1992), pp. 29–67, pp. 58–61.

132. John V. Kelleher has argued that it reflected political events in Louth at the beginning of the ninth century: 'The Táin and the Annals', *Ériu* 22 (1971), pp. 107–27. For an elaboration and refinement of this view, see Pádraig Ó Riain, 'The Táin: A Clue to its

Origins', in Mallory and Stockman, *Ulidia*, pp. 31–8. On date, see also Patricia Kelly, 'The Táin as Literature' in Mallory, *Aspects*, pp. 69–102, pp. 88–9.

133. Cecile O'Rahilly, *Táin Bó Cúailnge Recension I* (Dublin: Dublin Institute for Advanced Studies, 1976).

134. O'Rahilly, *Táin Bó Cúalnge*.

135. Éamonn Greenwood, 'Some Aspects of the Evolution of Táin Bó Cúailnge from TBC I to LL TBC', in Mallory and Stockman, *Ulidia*, pp. 47–54.

136. Joan Newlon Radner, 'Fury destroys the World: Historical Strategy in Ireland's Ulster Epic', *Mankind Quarterly* 23 (1982), pp. 41–60.

137. This corpus commonly known as the 'Ulster Cycle' comprises about eighty narratives, poems and shorter works: Ó hUiginn, 'The Background', p. 29.

138. Vernam Hull, ed. and trans. '*Noínden Ulad*: The Debility of the Ulidians', *Celtica* 8 (1968), pp. 1–42.

139. George Henderson, ed. and trans. *Fled Bricrenn: The Feast of Bricriu* (London: Irish Texts Society, 1899).

140. J. Carmichael Watson, ed. *Mesca Ulad*, Mediaeval and Modern Irish Series XIII (Dublin: Dublin Institute for Advanced Studies, 1941), pp. 1–40.

141. Hull, *Loinges*, pp. 48–50, 66–68.

142. Carl Marstrander, ed. and trans. 'The Deaths of Lugaid and Derbforgaill', *Ériu* 5 (1911), pp. 211–18.

143. O'Rahilly, *Recension I*, p. 124, lines 4123–4, p. 237.

144. On the many meanings of the term *caillech*, see Máirín Ní Dhonnchadha, '*Caillech* and Other Terms for Veiled Women in Medieval Irish Texts', *Éigse* 28 (1994–5), pp. 71–96.

145. Donncha Ó hAodha, ed. and trans. 'The Lament of the Old Woman of Beare', in Ó Corráin et al., *Sages*, pp. 308–31.

146. Máirín Ní Dhonnchadha, ed. 'Medieval to Modern, 600–1900', in Angela Bourke et al., eds. *The Field Day Anthology of Irish Writing, vols. IV and V: Irish Women's Writing and Traditions* (Cork: Cork University Press in association with Field Day, 2002), IV, pp. 1–457, p. 111.

147. Maria Tymoczko, 'A Poetry of Masks: The Poet's Persona in Early Celtic Poetry', in Kathryn A. Klar, Eve E. Sweetser and Claire Thomas, eds. *A Celtic Florilegium: Studies in Memory of Brendan O Hehir* (Lawrence and Andover: Celtic Studies Publications, 1996), pp. 187–209.

148. Thomas Owen Clancy, 'Women Poets in Medieval Ireland: Stating the Case', in C. E. Meek and M. K. Simms, eds. '*The Fragility of her Sex*'?: Medieval Irish Women in their European Context* (Dublin: Four Courts Press, 1996), pp. 43–72.

149. Kuno Meyer, ed. and trans. *Liadain and Curithir: An Irish Love-story of the Ninth Century* (London: Nutt, 1902). For a modern reworking see Gerardine Meaney, ed. 'Identity and Opposition: Women's Writing, 1890–1960', in Bourke et al., *The Field Day Anthology of Irish Writing'*, v, pp. 976–1045, pp. 1026–8.

150. Murphy, *Early Irish Lyrics*, pp. 6–9.

151. Ibid., pp. 8–9.

152. Ibid., p. 4.

153. For one of the key works written in the ninth century see E. J. Gwynn and W. J. Purton, eds. and trans. 'The Monastery of Tallaght', *Proceedings of the Royal Irish Academy* 29C (1911), pp. 115–80.

154. Whitley Stokes, ed. and trans. *Félire Óengusso Céli Dé: The Martyrology of Oengus the Culdee* (London: Henry Bradshaw Society, 1905). For discussion of the precise date of the work, see Pádraig Ó Riain, 'The Tallaght Martyrologies Redated', *Cambridge Medieval Celtic Studies* 20 (1990), pp. 21–38, and David N. Dumville, '*Félire Óengusso*: Problems of Dating a Monument of Old Irish', *Éigse* 33 (2002), pp. 19–48.

155. Carey translates a version of the preface added a century or so after the text was written: *King of Mysteries*, pp. 182–4.

156. Whitley Stokes, ed. *Saltair na Rann: A Collection of Middle Irish Poems*, Anecdota Oxoniensia Medieval and Modern Series III (Oxford: Clarendon, Press, 1883). Sections of the text have been translated in David Greene and Fergus Kelly, eds. and trans. *The Irish Adam and Eve Story from Saltair na Rann* (Dublin: Dublin Institute for Advanced Studies, 1976) and in Carey, *King of Mysteries*, pp. 98–124.

157. Gearóid Mac Eoin, 'The Date and Authorship of *Saltair na Rann*', *Zeitschrift für celtische Philologie* 28 (1960–1), pp. 51–67. See also James Carney, 'The Dating of Early Irish Verse Texts, 500–1100', *Éigse* 19 (1983), pp. 177–216, pp. 207–16.

158. Carey, *King of Mysteries*, p. 97.

159. Carey, *King of Mysteries*, p. 75; see also Carey, *Single Ray*, pp. 75–106 where he highlights the homiletic nature of the work. For the text, see Whitley Stokes, ed. and trans. 'The Evernew Tongue', *Ériu* 2 (1990), pp. 96–162.

160. Windisch, 'Fís Adamnáin'; Carey, *King of Mysteries*, pp. 261–74.

161. C. S. Boswell, *An Irish Precursor of Dante: A Study on the Vision of Heaven and Hell ascribed to the Eighth-century Irish Saint Adamnán* (London: Nutt, 1908).

162. David N. Dumville, 'Towards an Interpretation of Fís Adamnáin', *Studia Celtica* 12–13 (1977–8), pp. 62–77.

163. Martin McNamara, *The Apocrypha in the Irish Church* (Dublin: Dublin Institute for Advanced Studies, 1975), p. 24.

164. Murphy, *Early Irish Lyrics*, pp. 50–2.

165. For examples, see ibid., pp. 46–65.

166. Ibid., pp. 26–9.

167. Kuno Meyer, ed. and trans. *Miscellanea Hibernica* (Urbana: University of Illinois, 1917), p. 45.

168. David Greene, ed. and trans. 'St Brigid's Alefeast', *Celtica* 2 (1952), pp. 150–3.

169. Murphy, *Early Irish Lyrics*, pp. 66–8; see also pp. 64–5, 68–71.

170. Máire Herbert, *Iona, Kells and Derry: The History and Hagiography of the Monastic Familia of Columba* (Oxford: Clarendon Press, 1988), pp. 218–43 (text), 248–65 (translation), pp. 229–36, 255–65.

171. Ibid., pp. 184–202 where she dates the text to the middle of the twelfth century.

172. Charles Doherty, 'The Transmission of the Cult of St Máedhóg', in Ní Chatháin and Richter, *Ireland and Europe*, pp. 268–83.

173. For examples, see McCone, *Pagan Past*, pp. 179–202.

174. Ní Dhonnchadha, 'Medieval to Modern', p. 2.

175. Standish Hayes O'Grady, ed. and trans. *Silva Gadelica*, 2 vols (London and Edinburgh: Williams and Norgate, 1892), I, pp. 72–82, II, pp. 76–88; Charles Plummer, ed. *Vitae Sanctorum Hiberniae*, 2 vols. (Oxford: Clarendon Press, 1910; reprinted Dublin: Four Courts Press, 1997), II, pp. 240–52, 245–9; Charles Plummer, ed. and trans. *Bethada*

Náem nÉrenn: Lives of Irish Saints, 2 vols. (Oxford: Clarendon Press, 1922), I, pp. 80–90, II, pp. 85–7.

176. Máire Herbert and Pádraig Ó Riain, eds. and trans. *Betha Adamnáin: The Irish Life of Adamnán*, Irish Texts Society LIV (Dublin: Irish Texts Society, 1988), pp. 50–1; Radner, *Fragmentary Annals*, pp. 46–9.

177. John Carey, 'Varieties of Supernatural Contact in the Life of Adamnán', in John Carey, Máire Herbert and Pádraig Ó Riain, eds. *Saints and Scholars: Studies in Irish Hagiography* (Dublin: Four Courts Press, 2001), pp. 49–62, pp. 53–5.

178. Plummer, *Vitae*, II, pp. 116–30, p. 130; Ní Dhonnchadha, 'Medieval to Modern', pp. 76–80.

179. Herbert, *Iona*, p. 195.

180. Frederic Mac Donncha, 'Medieval Irish Homilies', in Martin McNamara, ed. *Biblical Studies: The Medieval Irish Contribution* (Dublin: Irish Biblical Association/Dominican Publications, 1976), pp. 59–71.

181. Herbert, *Iona*, pp. 193–9.

182. Whitley Stokes, ed. 'Acallamh na Senórach', in Whitley Stokes and Ernst Windisch, eds. *Irische Texte mit Übersetzungen und Wörterbuch*, IV.1 (Leipzig: Hirzel, 1900); Ann Dooley and Harry Roe, trans. *Tales of the Elders of Ireland*, Oxford World Classics (Oxford: Oxford University Press, 1999).

183. *Fotha Cath Cnucha* (The Cause of the Battle of Cnucha) includes the story of his birth: Best and Bergin, *Lebor na hUidre*, pp. 101–3, and Joseph Falaky Nagy, *The Wisdom of the Outlaw: The Boyhood Deeds of Finn in Gaelic Narrative Tradition* (Berkeley, Los Angeles and London: University of California Press, 1985), pp. 218–21; Kuno Meyer, ed. and trans. 'The Death of Finn mac Cumaill', *Zeitschrift für celtische Philologie* 1 (1897), pp. 462–5.

184. Kuno Meyer, ed. 'Macgnimartha Find', *Revue celtique* 5 (1882), pp. 195–204, and Nagy, *Wisdom*, pp. 209–18.

185. Kuno Meyer, ed. and trans. *Fiannaigecht, being a Collection of hitherto inedited Irish Poems and Tales relating to Finn and His fian, with an English Translation*, Todd Lecture Series XVI (Dublin: Royal Irish Academy, 1910; reprinted, Dublin: DIAS, 1993), pp. xvi–xxii.

186. Rudolf Thurneysen, ed. and trans. 'Tochmarc Ailbe: "Das Werben um Ailbe"', *Zeitschrift für celtische Philologie* 13 (1920–1), pp. 251–82.

187. Whitley Stokes, ed. and trans. 'On the Deaths of Some Irish Heroes', *Revue celtique* 23 (1902), pp. 303–48.

188. Meyer, *Fiannaigecht*, pp. 1–21.

189. Dooley and Roe, *Tales*, p. xiv.

190. Richard Sharpe, 'Hiberno-Latin *laicus*, Irish *láech* and the Devil's Men', *Ériu* 30 (1979), pp. 75–92, and Kim McCone, 'Werewolves, Cyclopes, *Díberga* and *Fíanna*: Juvenile Delinquency in Early Ireland', *Cambridge Medieval Celtic Studies* 12 (1986), pp. 1–22.

191. McCone, *Pagan Past*, p. 223.

192. Nagy, *Wisdom*, p. 78.

193. See, for example, Dooley and Roe, *Tales*, pp. xxviii–xxx.

194. Stokes, 'Acallamh', p. 9; Dooley and Roe, *Tales*, p. 12.

195. For the many readings of the twelfth-century narrative, *Fled Dúin na nGéd* (The Feast of Dún na nGéd (the Fort of the Geese)), for example, see Máire Herbert, '*Fled Dúin na nGéd*: A Reappraisal', *Cambridge Medieval Celtic Studies* 18 (1989), pp. 75–87, pp. 80–1.

Select bibliography

Bhreathnach, Edel, *Tara: A Select Bibliography*, Discovery Programme Reports III, Dublin: Royal Irish Academy, 1995.

Breatnach, Caoimhín, 'Rawlinson B502, Lebar Glinne Dá Locha and Saltair na Rann', *Éigse* 30 (1997), pp. 109–32.

Breatnach, Liam, 'An Mheán-Ghaeilge', in Kim McCone, Damian McManus, Cathal Ó Háinle, Nicholas Williams and Liam Breatnach, eds. *Stair na Gaeilge: in Ómós do Pádraig Ó Fiannachta*, Maynooth: Department of Old Irish, St Patrick's College, 1994, pp. 221–333.

Byrne, Francis J., *A Thousand Years of Irish Script: An Exhibition of Irish Manuscripts in Oxford Libraries*, Oxford: Bodleian Library, 1979.

Carey, John, *The Irish National Origin-legend: Synthetic Pseudohistory*, Quiggin Pamphlets on the Sources of Mediaeval Gaelic History I, Cambridge: Department of Anglo-Saxon, Norse and Celtic, 1994.

'The Location of the Otherworld in Irish Tradition', *Éigse* 19 (1982), pp. 36–43.

A Single Ray of the Sun: Religious Speculation in Early Ireland, Aberystwyth and Andover: Celtic Studies Publications, 1999.

Carney, James, 'The Dating of Early Irish Verse Texts, 500–1100', *Éigse* 19 (1983), pp. 177–216.

Charles-Edwards, Thomas, *Early Christian Ireland*, Cambridge: Cambridge University Press, 2000.

'Honour and Status in Some Irish and Welsh Prose Tales', *Ériu* 29 (1978), pp. 123–41.

Clancy, Thomas Owen, 'Women Poets in Medieval Ireland: Stating the Case', in C. E. Meek and M. K. Simms, eds. *'The Fragility of her Sex'?: Medieval Irish Women in their European Context*, Dublin: Four Courts Press, 1996, pp. 43–72.

Corthals, Johan, *Altirische Erzählkunst*, Forum Celticum I, Münster: Lit, 1996.

Dumville, David N., 'Latin and Irish in the Annals of Ulster', in Dorothy Whitelock, Rosamund McKitterick and David N. Dumville, eds. *Ireland in Early Medieval Europe: Studies in Memory of Kathleen Hughes*, Cambridge: Cambridge University Press, 1982, pp. 320–39.

Herbert, Máire, 'Goddess and King: The Sacred Marriage in Early Ireland', in Louise O. Fradenburg, ed. *Women and Sovereignty*, Edinburgh: Edinburgh University Press, 1992, pp. 85–98.

Iona, Kells and Derry: The History and Hagiography of the Monastic Familia of Columba, Oxford: Clarendon Press, 1988.

'The World, the Text, and the Critic of Early Irish Heroic Narrative', *Text and Context* 3 (1988), pp. 1–9.

Mac Cana, Proinsias, *The Learned Tales of Medieval Ireland*, Dublin: Dublin Institute for Advanced Studies, 1980.

'Prosimetrum in Insular Celtic Literature', in Joseph Harris and Karl Reichl, eds. *Prosimetrum: Crosscultural Perspectives on Narrative in Prose and Verse*, Cambridge: D. S. Brewer, 1997, pp. 99–130.

'The Rise of the Later Schools of *Filidheacht*', *Ériu* 25 (1974), pp. 126–46.

McCone, Kim, *Pagan Past and Christian Present in Early Irish Literature*, Maynooth Monographs III, Maynooth: An Sagart, 1989.

'Werewolves, Cyclopes, *Díberga* and *Fíanna*: Juvenile Delinquency in Early Ireland', *Cambridge Medieval Celtic Studies* 12 (1986), pp. 1–22.

McCone, Kim and Simms, Katharine, eds. *Progress in Medieval Irish Studies*, Maynooth: Department of Old Irish, St Patrick's College, 1996.

Mac Gearailt, Uáitéar, 'Change and Innovation in Eleventh-century Prose Narrative in Irish', in Hildegard L. C. Tristram, ed. *(Re)oralisierung, ScriptOralia 84*, Tübingen: Gunter Narr, 1996, pp. 443–96.

'On Textual Correspondences in Early Irish Heroic Tales', in Gordon W. MacLennan, ed. *Proceedings of the First North American Congress of Celtic Studies held at Ottawa from 26th–30th March 1986*, Ottawa: Chair of Celtic Studies, University of Ottawa, 1988, pp. 343–55.

Mallory, J. P., ed. *Aspects of the Táin*, Belfast: December Publications, 1992.

Mallory, J. P. and Stockman, G., eds. *Ulidia: Proceedings of the First International Conference on the Ulster Cycle of Tales, Belfast and Emain Macha 8–12 April 1994*, Belfast: December Publications, 1994.

Nagy, Joseph Falaky, *The Wisdom of the Outlaw: The Boyhood Deeds of Finn in Gaelic Narrative Tradition*, Berkeley, Los Angeles and London: University of California Press, 1985.

Ní Chatháin, Próinséas and Richter, Michael, eds. *Ireland and Europe in the Early Middle Ages, Texts and Transmission: Irland und Europa im früheren Mittelalter, Texte und Überlieferung*, Dublin: Four Courts Press, 2002.

Ó Cathasaigh, Tomás, *The Heroic Biography of Cormac mac Airt*, Dublin: Dublin Institute for Advanced Studies, 1978.

'Pagan Survivals: The Evidence of Early Irish Narrative', in Próinséas Ní Chatháin and Michael Richter, eds. *Irland und Europa, Die Kirche im Frühmittelalter: Ireland and Europe, The Early Church*, Stuttgart: Klett-Cotta, 1984, pp. 291–307.

Ó Concheanainn, Tomás, 'A Pious Redactor of *Dinnshenchas Érenn*', *Ériu* 33 (1982), pp. 85–98.

'Textual and Historical Associations of Leabhar na hUidhre', *Éigse* 29 (1996), pp. 65–120.

Ó Corráin, Donnchadh, 'Historical Need and Literary Narrative', in D. Ellis Evans, J. G. Griffith and E. M. Jope, eds. *Proceedings of the Seventh International Congress of Celtic Studies held at Oxford, from 10th to 15th July, 1983*, Oxford: Clarendon Press, 1986, pp. 141–58.

'Legend as Critic', in Tom Dunne, ed. *The Writer as Witness: Literature as Historical Evidence*, Historical Studies XVI, Cork: Cork University Press, 1987, pp. 23–38.

Ó Corráin, Donnchadh, Liam Breatnach and Kim McCone, eds. *Sages, Saints and Storytellers: Celtic Studies in Honour of Professor James Carney*, Maynooth: An Sagart, 1989.

Ó Riain, Pádraig, 'The Book of Glendalough or Rawlinson B502', *Éigse* 18 (1981), pp. 161–76.

'Early Irish Literature', in Glanville Price, ed. *The Celtic Connection*, Princess Grace Irish Library VI, Gerrards Cross: Colin Smythe, 1992, pp. 65–80.

'Rawlinson B502 alias Lebar Glinne Dá Locha: A Restatement of the Case', *Zeitschrift für celtische Philologie* 51 (1998), pp. 130–47.

Poppe, Erich, 'Reconstructing Medieval Irish Literary Theory: The Lesson of *Airec Menman Uraird maic Coise*', *Cambrian Medieval Celtic Studies* 37 (1999), pp. 33–54.

Radner, Joan Newlon, 'Fury Destroys the World: Historical Strategy in Ireland's Ulster Epic', *Mankind Quarterly* 23 (1982), pp. 41–60.

Sharpe, Richard, 'Hiberno-Latin *laicus*, Irish *láech* and the Devil's Men', *Ériu* 30 (1979), pp. 75–92.

Medieval Irish Saints' Lives: An Introduction to Vitae Sanctorum Hiberniae, Oxford: Clarendon Press, 1991.

Sims-Williams, Patrick, 'Some Celtic Otherworld Terms', in A. T. E. Matonis and Daniel F. Melia, eds. *Celtic Language, Celtic Culture: A Festschrift for Eric P. Hamp*, Van Nuys: Ford and Bailie, 1990, pp. 57–81.

Thurneysen, Rudolf, *Die irische Helden- und Königsage bis zum siebzehnten Jahrhundert*, Halle: Max Niemeyer, 1921.

Welch, Robert, ed. *The Oxford Companion to Irish Literature*, Oxford: Clarendon Press, 1996.

3

The literature of later medieval Ireland, 1200–1600: from the Normans to the Tudors

Part I: Poetry

MARC CABALL

The literature of Ireland in the period covered by this chapter is characterised by a remarkable intellectual and artistic diversity shaped by a dynamic and not infrequently tense interaction between Gaelic, English and French cultures. Indeed such is the varied composition of the ethnic cultures of later medieval Ireland that discussion of the contemporary literature within a specific insular framework risks disregarding the diffuse and permeable boundaries of cultural expression. While literatures in French and English produced in Ireland constitute a local expression of vibrant metropolitan cultures, the ideological and aesthetic focus of the majority culture of the Irish-speaking population was centred on the island itself. Even in the case of Irish Gaelic culture, however, its reach and influence extended to the Gaelic-speaking regions of western and northern Scotland.[1] Conscious of the strikingly modern cultural resonances of this obscured and little-known phase in Ireland's literary history, the present chapter seeks to explore the development of writing in both prose and poetry in Irish and other languages within an inclusive framework of analysis. The literature of later medieval Ireland provides vivid testimony for contemporary ideological, social and religious beliefs; but perhaps more strikingly and affectingly, it provides a rare and valuable insight into the world-view and varied human emotions of the late medieval Irish literati and the men and women for whom they composed.

The pre-eminence of professional praise poetry

The composition of poetry in Irish in the period 1200–1600 was dominated by the formal and highly stylised genre known loosely as bardic or praise poetry. Such is the preponderance of poetry of the social elite in the surviving corpus

of late medieval and early modern verse, that only an occasional extant popular composition and some stray references to women poets offer a tantalising
glimpse of Gaelic popular culture.[2] Accordingly, it is the highly technical and
conventional work of a professional learned class which commands primary
attention in a survey of the period 1200–1600 on account of its volume in the
surviving archival record, technical accomplishment, aesthetic verve and pivotal ideological relevance to Gaelic culture and polity in the later medieval
and early modern periods.[3] The essentially occasional and dynastic nature of
professional composition is vividly reflected in a strikingly nuanced prose insertion in a poem addressed to Féilim O'Byrne (d. 1630), lord of the O'Byrnes
of Gabhal Raghnuill in Wicklow.[4] Possibly composing in the last decade of
the sixteenth century, the poet Domhnall Carrach Mac Eochaidh relates to
O'Byrne the tale of a Dublin merchant who, on a visit to O'Connor Sligo,
had been greatly impressed by how generously the latter had paid for a poem
which had been recited formally in his presence.[5] Later, when the merchant had
returned to Dublin, he was approached by a band of poets on a provisioning
trip. Mindful of O'Connor Sligo's earlier lavish reimbursement of his learned
guests, the merchant offered to purchase a poem from his poet clients. Having
procured from them for the sum of £10 a poem which had been composed
over a hundred years previously, the entrepreneurial, if culturally naïve, Palesman departed westwards for O'Connor Sligo.[6] Unwilling to contravene the
conventional Gaelic etiquette of bardic patronage, O'Connor purchased the
poem for twice the amount the merchant had expended on it. Mac Eochaidh
stresses that O'Connor bought the poem notwithstanding the fact that it had
not been composed for him or any member of his family. Consequently, he
literally had no 'use' for it.[7]

Mac Eochaidh's purpose in recounting this possibly apocryphal story is simply to note that the merchant would have found a ready and more geographically accessible buyer for the poem in O'Byrne, such was his commitment
to the professional art. However, he does also, perhaps unintentionally, highlight something of the philosophy underpinning professional composition in
medieval and early modern Ireland. Firstly, a bardic poem was perceived as
a commodity which could be bought and sold. Secondly, a bardic poem was
deemed to have a function or purpose in so far as it related to its purchaser or his
family. Thirdly, it was assumed that a Gaelic nobleman would unquestioningly
support the bardic art. An incident described by Lughaidh Ó Cléirigh in his life
of the northern Gaelic dynast Hugh Roe O'Donnell (d.1602) corroborates Mac
Eochaidh's portrayal of the respect accorded the classical poetic institution.
It appears that sometime in 1599 a detachment of O'Donnell's followers had

seized cattle from the Thomond poet Maoilín Óg Mac Bruaideadha. The latter lost no time in presenting himself to O'Donnell and reciting a poem in his honour, thus securing immediate and generous compensation for his earlier losses at the hands of O'Donnell's retainers. The inherently political quality of praise poetry is emphasised by the fact that Mac Bruaideadha centred his poem on a venerable prophecy attributed to Colum Cille which foretold how depredations against the O'Donnells by the O'Briens of Thomond would be avenged in due course by a warrior of the O'Donnells called Hugh.[8] The testimony of both Mac Eochaidh and Ó Cléirigh illustrates that the professional *oeuvre* was conceived within and predicated on a broader cultural and political framework appropriate to what was, in many respects, a corporate literature.

A vignette drawn by the Elizabethan adventurer and writer Thomas Churchyard (d.1604) offers a dramatic, if decidedly hostile, view of bardic poets and their work. In his *A generall rehearsall of warres* published in London in 1579, Churchyard describes the poets as a 'kinde of supersticious prophesiers of Irelande'.[9] He relates how a group of English gentlemen, namely Masters Malbie, Anthony Poore, Robert Hartpole and Thomas Masterson, being in Kilkenny, heard of a group of poets who had recently been richly rewarded by their patrons 'for telling them fables and lyes'. On their way home, the poets, transporting their newly acquired silver plate, jewels and horses, were intercepted by the English party and forcibly diverted to Kilkenny. Within the relative safety of the city's precincts, the English gentlemen divested the poets of their goods, whipped them and then drove them from Kilkenny. The poets, infuriated by the treatment meted out to them by their tormentors, 'swore to rime these gentlemen to death, but as yet God be thanked, they have taken no hurt, for punishing such disordered people'.[10] Churchyard's account of the poets, at once fearful and contemptuous, underlines both their status and power within Gaelic society and their alien liminality in the context of English articulation of civility in Ireland at this period.[11] In contrast, the Palesman, historian and priest Richard Stanihurst (d.1618) offers a more considered view of the poets in his account of Ireland published in Antwerp in 1584. He observes that among the Gaelic Irish the praise of a poet secures a certain sense of immortal glory, while in a curious echo of Churchyard, Stanihurst says a poet's denigration was somewhat akin to death for his victim. Consequently, the status of poets among the Gaelic Irish was assured.[12] Corroboration of the standing of professional poets in Gaelic society comes also from Edmund Spenser, a jaundiced if not unperceptive critic of Gaelic culture. In his *A View of the Present State of Ireland*, written between 1596 and 1598 though not published until 1633, he stresses the public role of the poets in setting forth the virtues of those addressed in their compositions and like previous commentators, he alludes to the high degree of ignominy attached to those reviled by them.[13] Spenser the poet, as opposed to colonial theorist, comes to the fore when he admits that, having had examples of poetry in Irish translated to English, he was surprised to find that they 'savoured of sweet wit and good invention'.[14] Importantly, both Gaelic and English sources are in agreement in emphasising the social and cultural importance of the poets among the insular elite. Before proceeding to review the work of the poets themselves, it is necessary to establish the origins and historical context of a literary canon which is crucial to understanding the ideological framework of late medieval Gaelic society.[15]

Twelfth-century origins of professional praise poets

The emergence in the twelfth century of a cohort of professional praise poets was not a chance phenomenon. Their characteristic poetic style and form was given definition at a time of profound political, religious and cultural flux in Ireland. In particular, it is possible to attribute the immediate intellectual and institutional rationale of such professional composition to two seminal developments: the reorganisation of the Irish church during the course of the twelfth century and the Anglo-Norman conquest of 1169 and onwards. Both of these processes, entailing a crucial reorientation of older Gaelic habits of ecclesiastical and political expression, influenced and facilitated the development of the poetic discourse characteristic of the period 1200–1600. Evidently the pre-Norman order of poets known as *filid* were linked intimately to the monasteries and were participants in the diverse scholarship which these institutions patronised. Some indication of the interrelated nature of the various manifestations of scholarship in Ireland in the pre-Norman period is evidenced by the four categories of learned expert of primary interest to the monastic compilers of obituaries: the *ecnae* or scholar of scriptural Latin-mediated scholarship, the *brithem* or jurist, the *senchaid* or chronicler, and the *fili* or poet.[16] It is also apparent that *filid* were often actually attached to monasteries, as were members of the other learned professions.[17] The relationship between the poets and the monasteries represented a form of intellectual symbiosis in so far as boundaries between monastic learning and secular scholarship were porous.[18]

The rapid spread of continental monastic orders, particularly the Cistercians, in Ireland in the twelfth century, while primarily constituting a process of ecclesiastical reform, also powered a critical cultural reordering in so far as the vernacular scholarship of the traditional monasteries was gradually obliged to function within a relatively secular environment.[19] The reorganisation of the church transformed a venerable nexus linking the monasteries with lay scholarship. The council of Cashel in 1101 was the first of a number of reforming councils which underpinned critical changes in the canon law and ecclesiastical structure of the Irish church. Unlike its continental counterpart, the church in Ireland was not organised along territorial diocesan lines. Instead, monasteries, presided over by abbots, who were sometimes also bishops and not infrequently laymen, constituted the structural framework of the pre-reform church.[20] These monasteries were repositories of Gaelic learning.[21] It was partly in the context of such an ecclesiastical metamorphosis that a distinct cohort of professional poets developed from the merged ranks of the learned *filid* and the secular non-literate poets known as *baird*.[22] As the physical fabric of the Irish church was in the process of transformation with the introduction of a new architectural style for the building of Cormac's chapel at Cashel between 1127 and 1134, and the consequent spread of the Hiberno-Romanesque style in the midlands in the 1160s and 1170s, a contemporaneous and no less fundamental reordering of Gaelic scholarship was under way.[23]

The precise intellectual and cultural provenance of the professional poets in the twelfth century can be delineated only tentatively. Robin Flower suggested that the professional praise poets were the successors of the monastic scribes and scholars of the midlands monasteries, notably Terryglass and Clonmacnoise. According to him, these scholars, members of hereditary learned families such as the Uí Chléirigh, Uí Dhálaigh and Uí Mhaolchonaire, subsequently spread outwards from central Ireland bringing with them their learned traditions.[24] If Flower's theory is attractive in terms of its simplicity, the actual evolution of the bardic apparatus was undoubtedly more complex in terms of its composition and chronology.[25] There is no doubt that a self-conscious and audacious merger of traditions took place in the twelfth century, resulting in the emergence of learned hereditary families with expertise in poetry, law and history.[26] The promulgation of a standard poetic language in the second half of the twelfth century, based on the spoken Irish of the day, and the composition of strict versification in syllabic metres (*dán díreach*) in this language exemplifies a daring and extraordinary act of cultural inventiveness. The bardic literary medium, characterised by standardised linguistic and metrical features, remained in use by poets down to the first half of the seventeenth century. In effect, from about 1200 onwards there is a clear distinction between poetry composed in syllabic metres with emphasised rime, consonance and alliteration, and other looser metres such as *óglachas* and *brúilingeacht*.[27] Details of the logistics of this remarkable process of cultural and linguistic management have been lost from the historical record. However, the fact that poets in following centuries adhered to the discipline of a standardised language suggests a high degree of foresight and organisational ability on the part of its architects.[28] The achievement of these literary architects is all the more impressive when it is considered how enduring the classical literary medium proved as the spoken language diverged from it in terms of pronunciation, grammar and vocabulary over the succeeding centuries.[29]

Recent research on the provenance of Gaelic professional families of later medieval Ireland indicates that they emerged from the ranks of the minor nobility, church tenants and pre-Norman professionals.[30] Not surprisingly, in view of the historic links between the monasteries and secular learning, a significant number of the classical learned families were descended from the hereditary monastic officials known as *airchinnigh* ('erenaghs') who remained in possession of church lands.[31] The documented role of many medieval poets as keepers of guest houses is mirrored by the obligation of the monastic church officials to dispense hospitality.[32] A further link between the monastic schools and the secular learned elite centred on the transmission of the study of synthetic history, most notably in the case of the historical compilation known as *Lebor Gabála Érenn*, from the monastic scholars to their lay successors.[33] The impressive diversity of secular learning cultivated in the older monastic system is evident in the late twelfth-century manuscript compilation known to modern scholars as the Book of Leinster. Containing a monumental range of prose (including versions of *Táin Bó Cúailnge* and *Lebor Gabála Érenn*), poetry, pseudo-history, place-name lore and genealogical material, this twelfth-century treasury of Gaelic learning may be said to constitute the high watermark of clerical vernacular scholarship.[34] Whether the emergent poets of the twelfth century simply incorporated the vernacular scholarship of the monastic schools within their repertoire or whether the pre-classical *filid* and the monastic scholars effectively combined their scholarly expertise in a creative act of cultural self-determination remains unclear.[35]

The coming of the Anglo-Normans: a new political dispensation

The Cistercian and Augustinian expansion in Ireland displaced an integral support of Gaelic scholarship as the older monasteries declined. The banishment of the historian and poet Ó Maolchonaire from Clonmacnoise around the year 1200 to seek alternative patronage from the king of Connacht, Cathal

Crobderg O'Conor, is emblematic of a cultural watershed in Gaelic Ireland.[36] Henceforth, a new learned elite (ironically many of whom continued as tenants on church lands), trained within lay professional schools, operated in a secular environment of patronage.[37] In the case of professional poets, in particular, their work and its ideological and aesthetic rationale were intimately linked to the political and dynastic imperatives of post-invasion Gaelic Ireland. The landing of the Anglo-Normans in 1169 near Wexford at the invitation of the sometime exiled king of Leinster, Diarmait MacMurrough, heralded a transformation of political power and its organisational expression in Ireland. The fall of Dublin in 1170 to the Anglo-Welsh nobleman Strongbow, his marriage to MacMurrough's daughter Aífe and his assumption of the kingdom of Leinster on the death of his father-in-law in 1171, underlines the rapidly established success of the militarily superior newcomers. The arrival of Henry II in the same year culminated in the submission of the Irish kings of the south-east and his recognition as their highest lord by the clergy assembled in Cashel. On his return to England, Henry had effectively established his writ in Ireland apart from the provinces of Connacht and Ulster. In 1175, Ruaidrí O'Conor of Connacht submitted to Henry under the terms of the Treaty of Windsor in return for overlordship of those areas remaining unconquered. In 1177, Henry appointed his son, John, Lord of Ireland (*Dominus Hiberniae*).[38]

The intrusion of the Anglo-Normans required a reassessment of the configuration of political authority on the part of the Gaelic Irish.[39] The high kingship was effectively subsumed by the Plantagenets and their justiciars, and the provincial kingships were supplanted by Anglo-Norman overlords such as Fitzgerald in Desmond and de Burgh in Connacht and Ulster. The power and status of Gaelic provincial magnates like O'Neill, O'Brien and O'Conor were diminished as their former vassals now held land on an equal basis with them as tenants of Anglo-Norman overlords who actively encouraged rival claimants to Gaelic titles.[40] The post-invasion Gaelic polity developed as a fragmented mosaic of autonomous lordships ('lordship' known as *oireacht* or *pobal* in Irish) underpinned by an economy which was largely pastoral, dependent as it was on cattle and horses.[41] Such was the fissured nature of seigneurial imperium that in 1515 it was estimated that the country contained some sixty Gaelic and thirty gaelicised Anglo-Norman lordships of varying degrees of magnitude and strength.[42] In the course of the thirteenth century, Gaelic rulers were obliged by force of circumstance to recast gradually the traditional articulation of authority by substituting the terminology of kingship for that of lordship.[43] With control of the church resting to a large extent with the monarchy and the continental monastic orders, Gaelic dynasts drew on the services of the secular learned elites, in particular professional praise poets, to provide them with an overarching ideological validation of their political status or aspirations.[44]

There is some evidence to suggest a certain degree of cultural refashioning in an effort to evoke continuity with an untainted pre-Norman Gaelic past by reference to selected antique customs and scholarship. Ideological manipulation and revival of arcane inauguration rites for Gaelic lords, and the collation of supposedly authoritative dynastic pedigrees for Gaelic noble families in the fourteenth century, attest to a deliberate reworking of tradition to reaffirm the integrity and vitality of the indigenous polity.[45] The revival of Gaelic political fortunes in the fourteenth and fifteenth centuries was complemented by a concurrent flowering of Gaelic literary culture. Already, given the contemporary ideological concerns of the Gaelic elite, it can have been no coincidence that professional poetry flourished in the thirteenth century under the influence of master poets such as Donnchadh Mór Ó Dálaigh, Muireadhach Albanach Ó Dálaigh and Giolla Brighde Mac Con Midhe. The consolidation of the prestige of the bardic institution in the second half of the fourteenth century is contemporaneous with a cognate political revival on the part of the Gaelic lords.[46] A new political confidence informed a historic expansion of patronage. This period witnessed the compilation of great manuscript codices such as the Yellow Book of Lecan, the Book of Uí Mhaine, and the Book of Ballymote.[47] The antiquarian content of these manuscripts reflects the importance accorded the learning of pre-Norman Ireland and illustrates the significance and no doubt the social prestige attached to patronage of literature. Professional poets were key agents of change in the reformulation of Gaelic ideology which occurred during the course of the thirteenth and fourteenth centuries. The following section will touch on the role of praise poets in the validation of lordship down to the effective dismantlement of the Gaelic system in the aftermath of the Battle of Kinsale in 1601, while also highlighting the contribution of the poets to the development of an ethnic consciousness which culminated ultimately in the predication of a politicised sense of Irish nationality in the face of early modern Tudor aggrandisement.

Gaelic society and political poetry

The historical and cultural significance of professional poetry derives from its communal compositional context and politicised function. Such poetry is characterised by an explicit commitment to the social and political legitimation of its patron and his kindred. Praise poetry genres such as eulogy and elegy offer an unrivalled glimpse of the mores and political assumptions which informed the late medieval Gaelic aristocratic world-view.[48] In the absence of an indigenous centralised framework of governance and, initially at least, in the face of ecclesiastical indifference, political poetry articulated a model of lordship which enabled the seigneurial elite to articulate their aspirations on the basis of a common discourse. The lucrative role of professional poets in the articulation of a communal Gaelic ideology secured for them an exclusive and formalised relationship with the elite.[49] The key overarching role of the poets as political counsellors in the transmission of the dynastic rationale of Gaelic lordship marked them out for particular denigration by the crown administration in Dublin from the mid-sixteenth century onwards as it sought, through a mixture of persuasive and coercive means, to incorporate Gaelic lordships within the jurisdiction of a central administration.[50] There is also some evidence to suggest that poets occasionally combined the role of ideologue with that of administrative functionary.[51]

The thirteenth-century poet Giolla Brighde Mac Con Midhe highlighted the political rationale of professional eulogy when he observed that were poetry to be suppressed it would result in anarchic historical amnesia and the consequent collapse of social hierarchies sustained by traditional lore and genealogy. In such a scenario, the standing of the progeny of the nobleman and the kennel-keeper would be conflated at the lowest common level without the essential social markers provided by poetry (*an dán*) and history (*seanchas*).[52] In the absence of the dynastic validation provided by the poets, every Irishman would be of insignificant status, every nobleman reduced to the level of churl:

> Fir Éireann más é a rathol
> ionnarbadh na healathon
> gach Gaoidheal budh gann a bhreath,
> gach saoirfhear ann budh aitheach.

(If it be the great desire of the men of Ireland to expel the poets, every Irishman would have an insignificant birth, every nobleman would be a churl.)[53]

This underlying premise of ideological endorsement remained central to the professional repertoire down to the beginning of the seventeenth century, when the defeat of the Gaelic Irish at Kinsale in 1601, and the subsequent departure of the earls of Tyrone and Tyrconnell to the continent in 1607, signalled the ultimate triumph of the English crown in Ireland. In a piece preserved in the poem book of Cú Chonnacht Mag Uidhir (Maguire) (d.1589), lord of Fermanagh, an unidentified poet predicates the status and distinction of Mág Uidhir on his reputation as a patron. In the case of the latter, his fame is attested to by the numbers of poets who attend on him to celebrate his martial qualities.[54] The distinguished master poet Tadhg Dall Ó hUiginn (d.1591) elaborated on the enduring fame accruing from patronage of poetry in a piece beginning 'Maith an ceanduighe Cormac' (Cormac is a skilled merchant) which he addressed to Cormac Ó hEadhra (O'Hara) (d.1612), sometime lord of Leyny in present-day County Sligo. Casting Cormac in the role of a shrewd merchant, the poet stresses that his subject has reaped a handsome reward on his investment in bardic eulogy. In return for his disbursement to them of transitory material wealth, Cormac has secured lasting praise from the poets.[55] In a wonderfully evocative quatrain, Tadhg Dall speaks of Cormac in terms of a merchant who has exchanged an ephemeral flower for lasting encomium. Moreover, Ó hEadhra's patronage of poetry has also ensured the reputation of his kindred until doomsday:

> Go lá an bhráich biaidh ar marthain
> 'n-a bharr shéin is shobharthoin
> don tslógh ó bheannuibh Bladhma
> ar cheandoigh d'ór ealadhna.

(Till the day of doom all that he has purchased of the gold of poetry will remain as an augmentation of fortune and prosperity for the host from *Bladhma's* peaks.)[56]

The case of Uilliam Ó Ceallaigh's (O'Kelly) famous Christmas feast for the poets of Ireland in 1351, commemorated vividly in Gofraidh Fionn Ó Dálaigh's 'Filidh Éireann go haointeach' (The Poets of Ireland to One House), was possibly an exceptional act of patronal largesse, yet Aonghus Ó Dálaigh's advice to Féilim Ó Tuathail (O'Toole) (*fl.*1590s) that no man was of account unless the subject of bardic encomium ('Ní háirmheach duine ar domhan / gan leannán fir ealadhan') will have informed countless acts of patronage over the centuries.[57]

A poem in praise of Raghnall, the Norse king of the Isle of Man, possibly composed in the period 1187–1208, is a very early example of bardic eulogy and its layered political texture.[58] The seigneurial credentials of the subject to reign in his territory, and in this case to assume the overlordship of Ireland, are emphasised by reference to what were to remain conventions of the genre. The martial attributes, physical agility, bravery and beauty of the subject are delineated in detail: Raghnall is lauded for his prowess and his steadfastness ('Maith th'engnam, cruaid do chraide'). A virile warrior, Raghnall subdues all who dare confront him ('Do shlegh derg ar do dernainn / gach fer a serc ré slimrinn').[59] Raghnall's stereotypical beauty attracts the love and admiration of women ('Ní terc, a chraebh úr étrom / serc dot chúl tsaer mar shédbharr'). Naturally, in keeping with a venerable Gaelic emphasis on the protocols of hospitality, Raghnall is portrayed as a selfless and generous host, particularly to the poem's author ('Ar ndol damsa ót deaghthoigh / m'almsa nír almsa dochraid').[60] Such is the legitimacy of Raghnall's rule that the natural world flourishes bountifully on the Isle of Man by way of validation.[61] The poet's depiction of Raghnall as the lover of his territory reflects a conceit common in praise poetry whereby a lord's dominion was endorsed by his marriage to the female personification of his territories. This conceit is intimately linked to the Gaelic perception of *Ériu* as a goddess who symbolised the sovereignty of the island.

The notion of Ireland as a woman wedded to her true king is complemented by the idea of the local lord's espousal to his own territories.[62] Maoilín Ó'n Cháinte's poem for Cú Chonnacht Mág Uidhir (d.1589) beginning 'Leis féin moltar Mág Uidhir' (Maguire is praised by himself) is a richly textured political poem of endorsement. In this skilfully wrought encomium, the author argues that it is not so much the poets' promotion of him nor his subject's own self-promotion which accounts for his distinction: rather his innate noble traits speak for themselves ('a shaoirthréighe ac labhra lais / caoimhchéile badh-bhdha Bernais'). The lord of Fermanagh, grandly styled spouse of Ireland ('céile Achaidh Iúghoine'), is capable of both warrior-like bravery ('cruas láimhe re lind catha') and gentleness when appropriate ('is réidhe athaigh oile').[63] Moreover, Mág Uidhir is a man of justice ('céile connmhála an chomhthruim') and a stout defender of Ulster ('maith choimhédus craobh Uladh').[64] Deploying a device common in professional verse, the poet adduces an exemplum by way of broader historical context in which to locate his subject and to highlight the essence of his argument. In this case, he argues that the lord of Fermanagh is most appropriately compared to Alexander the Great, for in both cases their innate character has justified their praise:

> Inand d'airrghenaibh iad sin
> Mág Uidhir, Alax-anndair;
> fiú a dtréighe méd a molta
> dá ghéig réidhe riaghalta.

(They are equal in signs, Maguire and Alexander; their character has justified the amount of their praise, two smooth obedient branches.)[65]

Clearly, Mág Uidhir is presented in the guise of an eminent Gaelic grandee shaped by a specific paradigm of lordship.

In a polity composed of fragmented lordships and lacking indigenous centralised institutions of governance and administration which might have underpinned later state formation, the broader role of the poets in articulating a collective sense of identity and cultural consciousness grew in importance over the later medieval and early modern periods. Indeed, it is possible to argue that a sense of Irish national consciousness is evident in the poetry and, to a remarkable degree, the poets articulated an overarching socio-cultural identity which linked the mosaic-like network of Gaelic lordships within a transcendent cultural continuum. Adrian Hastings's argument for a medieval origin to nationalism, which has typically been dated to the eighteenth century in Europe, inspired and moulded in its evolution by biblical religion and vernacular literatures, is particularly compelling in the Irish context.[66] The 1317 remonstrance of the Irish lords to Pope John XXII in which Domnall O'Neill outlined the grievances of the Gaelic Irish in the face of Anglo-Irish oppression and prejudice attests to a self-confident Gaelic awareness of ethnicity and its political and administrative implications.[67] A late sixteenth-century poem such as Aonghus Fionn Ó Dálaigh's 'Iomdha éagnach ag Éirinn' (Ireland Has Many Reasons for Lamentation) exemplifies the culmination of the development of the concept of Irish territorial and cultural integrity in the face of the early modern colonial intrusion. In a startlingly contemporaneous presentation of the antique conceptualisation of the female embodiment of sovereignty, Ireland has been prostituted by the newcomers ('meas méirdrighe ar mhnaoi Chobhthaigh / a-tá ag gach aon d'allmhurchaibh') and abandoned by her own Gaelic Irish children.[68] Crucially, the construct of Irish nationality which had emerged by the late sixteenth century was inclusive of both the Gaelic Irish and the gaelicised descendants of the twelfth-century colonists. This reordering of the theoretical underpinning of Gaelic ethnic and cultural supremacy in Ireland as enshrined in the magisterial *Lebor Gabála Érenn* was undertaken by innovative sixteenth-century poets of the calibre of Tadhg Dall Ó hUiginn (d.1591) in poems such as 'Fearann cloidhimh críoch Bhanbha' (Ireland is Swordland) in which he elaborated on the traditional predication of Gaelic dominance to incorporate the Anglo-Irish.[69] If the political structures which adduced the rationale for professional eulogy had been fatally undermined by crown expansion, the intellectual engagement of the Gaelic literati with the Renaissance complemented internal refashioning to produce a new literature in the seventeenth century which was at once profoundly indebted to its antecedents and enriched by Renaissance and Counter Reformation influences.[70]

Diverse literary cultures in medieval Ireland

The arrival of the Anglo-Normans introduced new and distinct cultural influences to Ireland. The dialect of French brought to the island by Strongbow, Henry II and their followers is known as Anglo-Norman. The surviving examples of literary activity in Anglo-Norman are neither as extensive nor as imaginative as contemporary work in Irish.[71] Indeed, such material as survives in Anglo-Norman is largely factual. Appropriately, the earliest and fullest composition which is extant is a verse chronicle which recounts the deeds of those Normans who first arrived in Ireland. 'The Song of Dermot and the Earl' begins with Diarmait MacMurrough's abduction of Derbforgaill, wife of Tigernán Ua Ruairc of Bréifne and continues down to the siege of Limerick in 1175. Possibly composed sometime between 1200 and 1225, this somewhat unsophisticated work was evidently intended to be recited or read aloud to an unlearned audience.[72] The poem's anonymous chronicler speaks of having sought first-hand information from MacMurrough's personal interpreter, Muiris Ua Riacáin. This unique instance of a French speaker engaging directly with an Irish speaker provides a tantalising glimpse of the historically opaque encounter between Gaelic and Hiberno-Norman cultures.[73] It is not until the end of the thirteenth century that there is evidence of an author of Irish provenance writing in French for Frenchmen. Jofroi (Geoffrey), a Dominican from Waterford, is the co-translator of three classical texts on government and the histories of Greece and Rome respectively. His translations, now extant in a single manuscript, were apparently undertaken in Paris and his style is heavily influenced by a north-eastern dialect of French. It seems that Jofroi's work also circulated in England and Ireland. In the fourteenth century, the English poet Gower was influenced by his translation of the *Secretum Secretorum* (a letter on governance supposedly written by Aristotle to Alexander) while in 1422 James Yonge translated the same work into Hiberno-English at the request of James Butler, earl of Ormond.[74]

Although politically unsettled, particularly as a result of Edward Bruce's invasion of Ireland which ended in his defeat and death in 1318, the early fourteenth century was an especially creative phase in the history of Hiberno-Norman literature in French and English. Such was the contemporary intellectual vibrancy that Pope John XXII confirmed the foundation of a university in Dublin in 1320.[75] The most remarkable surviving manuscript from the period, British Library Manuscript Harley 913, was compiled around the year 1330 and contains mainly religious and satirical material in French, English and Latin.[76] On the basis of its contents and history, it has been suggested that Harley 913 was a Franciscan portable preaching book, parts of which were collated in or collected from Franciscan priories in Kildare, New Ross and Waterford in the early fourteenth century.[77] The French material in Harley 913, namely *Proverbie Comitis Desmonie* and the poem titled 'The Walling of New Ross', is of interest more for its historical significance than any literary merit it may possess. The *Proverbie* comprise two short poems which have been attributed to Maurice fitz Thomas, created first earl of Desmond in 1329. These moralising maxims are reflective of the wide popularity of proverbs in the medieval period.[78] On the basis of internal evidence, 'The Walling of New Ross' has been dated to 1265 and it was possibly composed by a Franciscan. The poem celebrates a collective municipal achievement and was clearly intended to flatter the south-eastern town's citizens.[79] The French material in Harley 913 may well be indicative of a high point in literary composition in French in Ireland. In the second half of the fourteenth century, the use of French as a literary medium in Ireland more or less ceases.[80]

The Hiberno-English poems in Harley 913 are early fourteenth-century in provenance and while essentially reflective of the western European Christian tradition, especially as mediated by Franciscan friars of the period, they also manifest the local influence of Irish culture.[81] The moralising thrust of many of these poems is exemplified in a composition which uniquely for the manuscript contains the author's name and status. Friar Michael of Kildare warns of the corrupting impact of material wealth and its adverse effect on men's spiritual well-being. Even the most powerful and exalted individuals will not live for ever and all are destined to face divine judgement. Michael urges immediate repentance on the part of his audience if they are to avoid eternal damnation.[82] The anonymous poem known as 'The Land of Cokaygne' is quite different in tone and content. Possibly drawing on similar material in French and English, the author playfully satirises the sexual adventures of monks and nuns in a land of pleasure and material abundance.[83] The depiction of this quasi-paradise may well have been influenced by the Gaelic notion of the Otherworld. The poem has been compared to the late eleventh-century Gaelic text *Aislinge Meic Con Glinne* which also mocks clerical foibles in a somewhat fantastic manner.[84] It seems possible that 'The Land of Cokaygne' was composed by a Franciscan intent on satirising the lax mores of a Gaelic Irish Cistercian establishment.[85] The survival of a Dublin Latin liturgical drama known as *Visitatio Sepulcri* in two mid- to late fourteenth-century manuscripts underlines the extent to which the extant medieval literature of Ireland composed in languages other than Irish is largely religious, moralistic or factual in content.[86] This play with a functional liturgical purpose enacting the visit to Christ's tomb by the three

Marys on Easter Sunday morning also underlines the communal emphasis of such texts.[87] While the range of contemporary poetry in Irish is considerably richer in thematic and imaginative terms, it shares with material in English and French a similar communal framework of composition and reception.

The composition, delivery and reception of literary material in Norman-French and perhaps more influentially in Hiberno-English in late medieval Ireland did not unfold within a hermetically sealed cultural space. In the same sense that Irish Gaelic influences may be discerned in the Hiberno-English poems of Harley 913, it may be safely assumed that material and themes derived from other traditions were incorporated within literature in Irish on the basis of either self-conscious imitation or unconscious osmosis. In this process of cultural interchange, a central role of transmission and dissemination may be ascribed to Franciscan preachers. Highly mobile, the friars constituted an important preaching elite which transcended dynastic, political and ethnic boundaries. Mendicant preachers such as the mid-thirteenth-century Franciscan Tomás Ó Cuinn reflect the extent to which cultures intersected as a result of the friars' evangelical commitment to preaching the gospel. Sometime guardian of the Franciscan house in the English-speaking town of Drogheda, this Gaelic Irishman is also known to have ministered to Irish speakers. It is recorded that Ó Cuinn preached against superstition to a congregation in the diocese of Clonfert in Connacht. In preaching in both Irish and English and no doubt by drawing on the Latin learned tradition, friars such as Ó Cuinn acted as agents of cultural interchange whose efficacy was much enhanced by mobility and linguistic aptitude.[88] Likewise, the manuscript now known as Trinity College, Dublin, MS 667, probably copied around 1455 in a Franciscan conventual house in Clare, contains material in English, Irish and Latin which attests to creative interchange between cultures.[89] This veritable compendium of ecclesiastical scholarship contains a number of Irish translations of continental works in Latin, the originals of which are also included in the manuscript.[90] Yet, however innovative the role of the Franciscans as cultural interlocutors in late medieval Ireland, it is ironic that Gaelic culture profited from the Hiberno-Norman patrimony while establishing an unchallenged supremacy by the fourteenth century.[91] The passing of the Statutes of Kilkenny in 1366 underlines the progressive hibernicisation of the Anglo-Norman settlers. Ironically, while the Statutes were written in Norman French, they make no mention of this language. English had by now displaced French, which survived merely in the form of a historicised legal jargon.[92] In turn, English was threatened by Irish and the intention of the Statutes was to reverse this situation. The late fourteenth century witnesses a concomitant resurgence of Gaelic political power: indeed, the traditional historical perception of Gaelic reconquest possibly involved as much a hibernicisation of the Anglo-Norman elites as a revival of Gaelic political fortunes.[93]

Gaelicised Anglo-Norman literati such as Gerald fitz Maurice (d.1398), third earl of Desmond, and Richard Butler in the fifteenth century, attest to high-level inculturation of the settler elite.[94] Of course, Anglo-Norman patrons were also consumers of Gaelic literature as the library catalogue most likely compiled in the late fifteenth century for Gerald Mór Fitzgerald (d.1513), eighth earl of Kildare, indicates in its impressive listing of books and manuscripts in Latin, English, French and Irish.[95] Earlier still, the Psalter of MacRichard Butler, a nephew of the White Earl of Ormond, was compiled in counties Tipperary and Kilkenny around the period 1453–4. It contains diverse historical, hagiographic and saga material. Marginalia in this manuscript record that Edmund MacRichard Butler had been fostered by the Irish archbishop of Cashel, Risdeárd Ó hÉidigheáin, and they also testify to his close friendship with its Mac Aodhagáin and Ó Cléirigh scribes.[96] Other Gaelic manuscript miscellanies compiled at the behest of Anglo-Norman patrons include the Book of Fermoy commissioned around 1457–61 by David Mór Roche, lord of Fermoy and the fifteenth-century manuscript now known as British Library Additional 30512 which was variously owned by the earls of Desmond and the Butlers of Cahir in the sixteenth century. The contents of both compendia – whether it be diverse prose tales and tracts and bardic poetry, including poems addressed to David Mór Roche and his wife Ellen Butler, in the case of the Book of Fermoy, or the largely devotional material in Irish in Additional 30512 – attest to an unself-conscious inculturation of the descendants of the twelfth-century colonists.[97] Moreover, in purely linguistic terms, by the sixteenth century Irish was completely dominant, with the English language effectively restricted to the Pale, a narrow coastal strip extending northwards from Dublin to Dundalk.[98]

Religious poetry

A considerable body of devotional poetry in syllabic metres is extant – complemented by devotional prose material as discussed later by Kaarina Hollo. If the immediate political and ideological function of praise poetry is evident, the compositional rationale for poetry of a religious nature is less amenable to definitive categorisation. On the one hand, it is obvious that some of this work is the product of the personal beliefs of the authors, while on the other hand, it may be likely also that such verse was commissioned by patrons in much the same way as secular eulogies and elegies. It is possible that ecclesiastical patrons may have engaged poets to compose works to celebrate specific religious events or personages in much the same way as Gaelic lords employed the poets to legitimate their status. Moreover, the distinction between the sacred and the profane in medieval and early modern cultures was not clearly etched and accordingly both spheres overlapped unself-consciously. The vibrance of lay devotional poetry in Irish may well have derived from the extrusion of traditional Irish learning from the monasteries in the twelfth century and the consequent development of a vernacular devotional culture within a lay environment. Given that in the immediate post-Norman period, control of the church was for the most part within the preserve of the English monarchy and the continental monastic orders, Gaelic lords may well have turned to the praise poets to articulate a demotic religious expression in much the same way as they required them to articulate the ideology of lordship.[99] Such a disjunction between the new religious dispensation and praise poets is reflected in the anti-clerical sentiment of some poems composed in the thirteenth and fourteenth centuries.[100] However, the expansion of the Franciscan friars throughout Gaelic Ireland in the fifteenth century inaugurated a major devotional and cultural realignment of the sacred and the profane. The influential preaching mission of the friars and the growth of the Franciscan Third Order underpinned a new lay piety characterised by a Gaelic articulation of a European religious culture.[101] Key themes emblematic of a common European devotional culture, such as the doctrine of the Holy Trinity, divine omnipotence, devotion to the Virgin Mary, figure prominently in these poems.[102] The appearance in poetry and prose of apocryphal material and various motifs characteristic of popular devotional sentiment like the origin of the holy cross, the wonders of the flight into Egypt, the fifteen signs before doomsday, the harrowing of Hell, and the three tears of the Virgin serve further to emphasise the place of Gaelic popular religion within a broader European culture.[103]

The case of Donnchadh Mór Ó Dálaigh suggests that the custom of composing religious poetry in the classical idiom was an early development which is contemporaneous with the first flourishing of professional poetry in the thirteenth century. It is recorded in the annals that Ó Dálaigh died in 1244 and was buried in the monastery of Boyle.[104] The poetic *tour de force* attributed to him beginning 'Gabham deachmhaidh ar ndána' (Let me compose the tithe of my poetry) explicitly links the composition of poetry with divine worship.[105] Acknowledging God as the sole source of his poetic gift, the poet reflects on the constant proximity of death, like an unanticipated snare awaiting a bird ('a-tá an bás re béal gach fhir / mar shás re n-éan gan fhaicsin'), and such is the transience of this world that Ó Dálaigh vows to dedicate a tenth of his poetic work to God to secure his salvation.[106] A similarly personal tone, perhaps all the more moving for the intensely vulnerable note struck by the poet, dominates Giolla Brighde Mac Con Midhe's poem 'Déan oram trócaire, a Thríonnóid' (Holy Trinity, Have Mercy on Me).[107] A member of a bardic family settled at Ardstraw in modern County Tyrone, Mac Con Midhe (c.1210–c.1272) is known to have composed poetry for the noble houses of O'Donnell and O'Neill. Like Donnchadh Mór, he was evidently remembered as a master practitioner in the subsequent professional tradition.[108] In this poem, he laments the passing of his infant children and prays that the Almighty may grant him offspring in this life and eternal reward in heaven. Through a series of images illustrating divine omnipotence in the natural world, Giolla Brighde brilliantly evokes his predicament and his complete acquiescence in God's will. The startling emotional immediacy of this poem transcends its historic compositional context in contrast to so many examples of bardic eulogy artistically constrained by circumstance and ideology. More lyrical, perhaps, but also permeated by a deep sense of religious conviction, is the thirteenth-century pilgrim's poem which has been tentatively ascribed to Muireadhach Albanach Ó Dálaigh (fl.c.1213):

> Do chros féin duit, a Dhúilimh,
> a ghealbhráighdigh ghormshúiligh,
> mo lochta dhuid 'na deaghaidh,
> a chorcra bhuig bhairrleabhair.
>
> A-tá mise, a mhala sheang,
> 'gá hiomchar dhuit go ndícheall,
> dá bhliadhain ar mo dhruim dhi
> gan bhuing re fiadhain Féine.

(I offer to you your own cross, my creator, blue-eyed one of the bright throat, and I offer you my faults with it, generous slender-topped red one.

I carry it assiduously for you, you of the slender brow, it has been two years on my back without meeting anyone from Ireland.)[109]

This short work brilliantly evokes the loneliness and weariness of an Irish pilgrim who over a period of two years has travelled to the Mediterranean area, possibly to the Holy Land, and yet remains steadfast in his faith.

The rapid spread of the Franciscan movement in Ireland in the fifteenth and sixteenth centuries is of key significance in Irish cultural history of the period. Unlike the earlier and equally rapid and comprehensive Franciscan expansion in the Anglo-Irish colony in the thirteenth century, the second wave of diffusion was primarily Gaelic in character. The later phase of expansion was also different in so far as it embraced both the reforming Observant and more traditional Conventual forms of Franciscan organisation. The later flowering also encompassed the Franciscan Third Order which resulted in the emergence of groups of lay tertiaries who chose to live together in religious communities.[110] The Franciscans in Ireland, especially the tertiaries and the Observant friars, forming part of a highly influential European religious and cultural network, acted as local agents in the transmission of continental devotional texts and ideas.[111] The core commitment of the mendicant friars to evangelisation through preaching ensured that such ideas reached a wide audience, both literate and non-literate. The primary preaching concerns of the friars centred on the fundamental elements of late medieval religion: the eucharist, the life, death and resurrection of Christ, repentance, salvation, fear of damnation, and so on.[112] The survival of the Youghal friary library catalogue which was compiled in the period between 1491 and 1523 provides a fascinating glimpse of some of the intellectual interests of the friars and hints at some of the influences which surely had a broader impact on the learned culture of late medieval Gaelic Ireland. This library of 150 volumes included collections of sermons and exempla as well as seminal texts such as the *Gesta Romanorum*, a compilation of anecdotes and stories assembled in the late 1330s, and James of Voragine's (*c.*1230–98) popular work on the lives of saints known as the *Legenda aurea*.[113] A manuscript collection of sermons and sermon notes in Irish compiled at the Observant friary at Kilcrea in 1475 provides evidence of the direct linkage of Franciscan preaching with vernacular culture.[114] In a reversal of previous mutual antipathy between the church and the bardic elite in the aftermath of the twelfth-century ecclesiastical reform, the Franciscans in Gaelic Ireland were untrammelled by ethnic or linguistic divisions. The links of the Ó Maolchonaire learned family with the friars of Elphin in the fifteenth century suggest a unified cultural and social sphere where intellectual boundaries overlapped.[115]

The poet and Observant friar Pilib Bocht Ó hUiginn (d.1487) is an outstanding example of the embodiment of the bardic and Franciscan traditions. Described in his obituary in the Annals of Ulster as the best and most prolific religious poet of his time, Ó hUiginn displayed a mastery of syllabic metres, indicating that he trained as a poet before joining the Franciscan order.[116] His poems, generally characterised by concluding dedicatory quatrains to his patrons St Francis and St Michael, draw on scripture and various spiritual subjects for their themes. Not surprisingly in view of his bardic training, Pilib Bocht remained firmly embedded within tradition. In the poem beginning 'Dlighthear deachmhadh as an dán' (I Owe a Tithe of My Art), he echoes Donnchadh Mór Ó Dálaigh's commitment to the dedication of a proportion of his poetry to God to secure his salvation.[117] The conceptual framework of this poem, underpinned as it is by the ideological function of poetry within society, and his treatment of quintessentially Irish subjects such as the mission of St Patrick to pagan Ireland, illustrate the self-confident vitality of the bardic craft.[118] In his monumental poem 'Tuar feirge foighide Dhé' (God's Patience is an Omen of Wrath), Pilib Bocht articulates an impassioned plea for repentance in the face of impending divine retribution. Given its distinctly apocalyptic tone, it is not altogether surprising that it should have been selected as a printer's trial piece in advance of the Dublin publication of an Irish primer of religion by the Anglican reformer Seaán Ó Cearnaigh in 1571.[119] Notwithstanding his Franciscan allegiances, Pilib Bocht is just as readily classed in terms of style and intellectual outlook with professional poets such as Tadhg Óg Ó hUiginn (d.1448) and the late sixteenth-century Aonghus Fionn Ó Dálaigh, who composed religious verse as a secondary activity to their primary poetic role of dynastic validation.[120] By the late sixteenth century, the impact of the Reformation in Ireland, effectively an ecclesiastical ancillary to the crown's programme of centralisation, dramatically reconfigured Franciscan attitudes to literary composition in Irish. Franciscan poets such as Eoghan Ó Dubhthaigh and Giolla Brighde Ó hEodhusa, animated by a polemical sense of Counter Reformation Catholicism, worked assiduously to promote a distinctive interlinking of Gaelic culture and Roman Catholicism which was in explicit contrast to the apparently anglocentric cultural focus of the established church.[121] Ironically, while in the twelfth century the church had sought to sever its links with Gaelic culture, by the early seventeenth century its survival was to a large extent predicated on a self-conscious and strategic presentation of Catholicism and Gaelic culture as an organic continuum.

Heroic poetry

If praise poetry may be said to articulate the ideological priorities of the Gaelic elite, the rich and fascinating corpus of heroic ballads and prose collectively known as *fianaigheacht* reflects an alternative, to some extent dissident, worldview. Fionn, the central character of this cycle, is largely depicted as a mortal, although long-lived, being who in his diverse capacity as leader, warrior, huntsman, poet and sage, champions mortals against the wiles and onslaughts of nefarious agents, the latter often emanating from the Otherworld.[122] Fionn, in whom it seems merges an archaic blend of liminal poet and outlaw, leads a band of warriors known as *fiana* through various adventures which straddle the supernatural and secular.[123] The origins of this retinue of martial heroes have been traced to bands of transitional warrior-youths who apparently occupied a liminal space in early Irish society. The ambivalent social status of the *fiana* as marginal warrior-hunters, which contrasts with the clearly etched social gradations reflected in praise poetry, may well explain why the lore of Fionn and his companions constituted a vibrant and valued inheritance among ordinary people in Gaelic Ireland and Scotland down to modern times.[124] Although the compilation of *Acallam na Senórach* (Tales of the Elders) in the early thirteenth century marks the rise to prominence of *fianaigheacht* literature in both oral and written format, the survival of some pre-Norman Fionn material attests to the ancient lineage of this tradition.[125] The topos of the Viking threat to Ireland, which is an important theme in the ballads, possibly derives from the contemporary impact on the Fionn tradition of early and mid-ninth-century Viking raids, and may well have acquired a new resonance in the context of twelfth-century Norman aggrandisement.[126] The inclusion of two *fianaigheacht* narrative poems or *laoithe* in the twelfth-century Book of Leinster preserves early examples of a genre which was to figure in subsequent manuscripts and in the oral tradition.[127] Two major manuscript sources for such material are extant: the Book of the Dean of Lismore compiled between 1512 and 1542 by Perthshire scribes, in particular James MacGregor, dean of Lismore, and his brother Duncan; and the early seventeenth-century *Duanaire Finn* (The Poem-Book of Fionn). The latter compendium was compiled in Ostend around 1627 by the scribe Aodh Ó Dochartaigh for his patron, Captain Sorley MacDonnell of Antrim.[128]

Although *fianaigheacht* enjoyed considerable popularity among Gaelic speakers of all classes in eighteenth- and nineteenth-century Ireland and Scotland, it would seem that in the later medieval period such material was composed and circulated within a cultivated milieu. Equally, given the opaque synergy between the oral tradition and written literature so characteristic of Gaelic culture through the ages, the impact of such a cultivated tradition on popular oral culture in the medieval and early modern periods should not be underestimated.[129] While references to *fianaigheacht* themes in praise poetry are admittedly scant, the very fact that the ballads were composed in loose forms of bardic syllabic verse suggests that neither tradition was mutually exclusive of the other.[130] Alan Bruford's suggestion that the ballads were composed by professional storytellers, historians and poets, and transmitted generally though not exclusively in oral form, further supports the impression that the ballads straddled two cultures: popular and learned.[131] Unlike praise poetry, however, the ballads were complemented by a body of prose literature. Indeed, sometimes both a prose and verse version of the same story can be found and some ballads may originally have had a prose introduction by way of location of the plot.[132] Emblematically, in *Acallam na Senórach*, a seminal text of the tradition discussed more fully later in this chapter, in which the surviving heroes Caílte and Oisín relate various adventures of the *fiana* to St Patrick, prose is interspersed with verse.[133]

The best examples of such ballads combine an intricate sense of narrative tension with compelling thematic development and their engaging artistry stands in contrast to the occasionally stilted formality of the professional genres. In the sixteenth-century 'Chase above Lough Derg' (*In ccúala tú Fiana Finn*) Caílte delivers to St Patrick an eye-witness account of how the lake acquired its name. One day while hunting in the hills above Lough Derg, Fionn's warrior band encounters a fearsome and grotesque monster. Among Fionn's men was Albhaidh an Óir, son of the king of Greece, who understood the language of monsters. However, a delay in acting on Albhaidh's advice to Fionn that the monster would be sated with fifty horses or fifty cows every day proves disastrous when a ravenous beast awakes the following morning.[134] A ferocious battle rages until midday between Fionn's men and the voracious beast. Grievous losses are inflicted on the warrior band:

> Eidir sin 7 meadhón don ló
> Do budh lía ar mairbh ná ar mbeó
> Budh samhail ré slúagh oile
> Uireasbadh ar láochraidhe

(Between that and midday those of us who had fallen were more numerous than those who still lived. Our missing warriors were like a second army.)[135]

Fionn, infuriated, rushes the monster and in an instant flips her around on her back. Seizing an opportune moment, Dáire, son of Fionn, leaps into the monster's gullet and hacks his way out through her armpit. This feat of daring enables the escape of two hundred of Fionn's battered warriors, including Oisín and the son of the king of Greece. Caílte reminds his listeners that the lake had been called 'Fionnloch' (White Lake); however, it is now known as 'Loch Dearg' (Red Lake) because of that day's slaughter of the *fiana*. In the final quatrain, as at the outset of the poem, Caílte addresses St Patrick directly and on this occasion concludes by stating simply that the tale he has told has been heard by many ('na sgéla do innsim dhuit, iomdha duine do-chúalaidh').[136] Importantly, these remarks also remind the modern reader that such poems were in their time a vibrant and earthy manifestation of popular Gaelic culture which surely delighted, provoked and entertained countless nobles and commoners in late medieval and early modern Ireland.

Love poetry: a merger of traditions

The putative influence of the love poetry which emerged from the *amour courtois* tradition practised in its purest form by *troubadours* in northern France and Provence in the period 1100–1250 on the Irish poems collected together by T. F. O'Rahilly in *Dánta Grádha* (1926) remains a subject of debate among scholars.[137] In a highly influential introduction to O'Rahilly's collection, Robin Flower's characterisation of these poems composed in syllabic quatrains as the product of 'the learned and fantastic love of European tradition, the *amour courtois*, which was first shaped into art for modern Europe in Provence', introduced to Ireland by the Anglo-Normans, unwittingly served to homogenise a somewhat miscellaneous corpus of poems which take as their broad theme the interaction of the sexes.[138] Curiously, this influential anthology contains just as many examples of poems denigrating love as it does works which are celebratory in this regard.[139] Indeed, one critic has argued that these poems are heavily influenced by misogyny, such is their presentation of women as anonymous and disenfranchised objects subject to male control.[140] The late date of composition of most of the poems, largely of sixteenth- and seventeenth-century provenance, further complicates their unquestionable attribution to a Gaelic flowering of *amour courtois*.[141]

Seán Ó Tuama has argued that the influence of *amour courtois* is manifest among some of the poems in O'Rahilly's collection. Such a manifestation is a development of the courtly love tradition in Irish which he suggests occurred in the period 1400–1550 thanks to the influence of imported contemporary literary works.[142] Furthermore he claims that an earlier phase of composition of love poetry in Irish between 1200 and 1400, directly influenced by the popular genre of *carole* introduced by Anglo-Norman settlers, prefigured such a later flowering.[143] While the earliest phase of *amour courtois* in Ireland was popular and oral in character, the later phase attracted the participation of classical bardic poets and as a consequence was learned in inspiration and expression. If the earlier wave of transmission reached Ireland through the medium of

French, the second wave was disseminated through literary material in French and English, with the latter dominating from approximately 1550 onwards.[144] The research of Mícheál Mac Craith has certainly supported such an emphasis on the influence of English literature on Gaelic lyrics dating to the sixteenth and seventeenth centuries. However, given the late date of the majority of the poems in O'Rahilly's canon, Mac Craith has discounted the direct impact of French exemplars on these works, arguing that decontextualised comparisons of motifs deployed both in the *dánta grá* and in the French courtly tradition are unsatisfactory and inconclusive in so far as they collectively pertain to a common European literary patrimony.[145] In making a case for the direct impact of contemporary literature in English on these poems between 1550 and 1650, Mac Craith identifies the descendants of the Anglo-Norman settlers as a key node of cultural transmission in this regard.[146]

In fact, the earliest poems in *Dánta Grádha* which it is possible to date approximately are of fourteenth-century provenance. In the case of both of these compositions, attributed to the somewhat elusive Anglo-Norman magnate Gerald fitz Maurice, third earl of Desmond (1357–98), and the obscure Fearchar Ó Maoilchiaráin (*fl.*1395?), the influence of *amour courtois* seems negligible.[147] An extensive landowner in south-west Munster and remembered in the subsequent Gaelic oral tradition as Gearóid Iarla, it is recorded that Desmond was lord chief justice of Ireland between 1367 and 1369. The evidence of a bardic poem addressed via the young Gerald to his father, Maurice fitz Thomas, first earl of Desmond (1329–56) and possible author of the eponymous proverbs in Harley 913, by Gofraidh Fionn Ó Dálaigh, indicates the extent to which the Anglo-Norman elite had been incultured within Gaelic society, and in the case of Gerald suggests that he would have been conversant with professional poetry from an early age.[148] Gerald's significance in Irish literary history is further confirmed by the fact that poems attributed to him in the mid fifteenth-century Book of Fermoy and the early sixteenth-century Book of the Dean of Lismore manuscript collections highlight the existence of a non-professional stream of Gaelic literary culture coterminous with the professional poetic apparatus.[149] However, the evident familiarity of Gerald with the heroic saga lore of Cú Chulainn and the warriors of the Red Branch and with Fionn and the *fiana* demonstrates that both the professional literati and amateur littérateurs drew from a common cultural inheritance.[150] While the historical record has no doubt been sundered over the centuries and as such provides a distorted retrospective overview, the survival of work by an aristocratic Gaelic gentleman poet such as Diarmaid Ó Briain (d.1364) suggests that Gerald of Desmond's cultural interests may not have been as atypical contemporaneously as his historical exceptionalism implies.[151]

The earl of Desmond's poem beginning 'Mairg adeir olc ris na mnáibh' (Woe to him who speaks ill of women) initially eulogises the non-violent and eirenic disposition of the female gender while unexpectedly sketching a reverse scenario in the final two quatrains when women are reviled for preferring the company of virile young men to that of older and less active men ('annsa leó an buinneán óg bocht').[152] The poem ascribed to Fearchar Ó Maoilchiaráin is a very charming piece in which the author holds that his beloved Mór is deserving of a precious brooch in place of her simple wooden pin.[153] The emblematic reference to the mythological smith Gaibhniu suggests that this composition, like Gerald of Desmond's work, is more accurately viewed as a product of a native environment than an early Gaelic interpretation of courtly love.[154] In the sixteenth century, Desmond's role as cultivated patrician poet is replicated in the case of Manus O'Donnell (d.1563). Five poems ascribed to this Ulster dynast are included in *Dánta Grádha*. Succeeding his father as lord of Tyrconnell in 1537, O'Donnell's shrewd diplomatic skills, ecclesiastical patronage of the reforming Franciscan Observants and sophisticated cultural interests underpin the argument for his reputation as a 'Renaissance prince' in the context of a historiography which has until recently largely depicted late medieval and early modern Gaelic Ireland as archaic and isolated from contemporary Europe.[155] While Seán Ó Tuama has suggested that two of the five poems ascribed to O'Donnell in the O'Rahilly collection are not actually love poems, the remaining three compositions are certainly conventional products of the courtly love tradition.[156] These works describe the depredations wrought on his mind and body as a result of unrequited love. Love is conventionally portrayed as a disease ('Dar liom, is galar é an grádh') which leaves its victim broken-hearted ('an croidhe-se uaim do bhris') and such is his misery that he bitterly laments that he had not offered hate in place of love and received the same in exchange from the object of his affections ('Is truagh nách fuath thugas uaim').[157] Nevertheless, while supposedly composed at a point of personal despair, these poems seem too contrived and verbally dextrous to have emerged from unreflective crisis. Self-focused in the extreme, O'Donnell speaks self-pityingly of his own emotions while his ostensible subject remains a distinctly elusive presence.[158] His work may be contrasted with a composition attributed to the enigmatic countess of Argyll, Isibeul Ní Mhic Cailín. While she also depicts love as a disease in 'Mairg darab galar an grádh' (Woe to the Person Whose Sickness is Love), she adroitly, and in an altogether more rebarbative frame of mind than O'Donnell, demands that the man who has caused her pain should suffer a hundred times more so ('dá gcuire sé mise i bpéin, go madh dó féin bhus céad mairg!').[159]

The amalgam of traditions influencing the poems rather loosely titled *dánta grádha* is perhaps most apparent in such material composed in the sixteenth century by bardic poets. Verse in the *dánta grádha* idiom by bardic poets such as Laoiseach Mac an Bhaird, Eochaidh Ó hEódhusa, Tadhg Ó Cobhthaigh and Cearbhall Ó Dálaigh among others indicates that it is more appropriate to speak of a cosmopolitan combination of Gaelic, English and broader European literary cultures rather than seeking to categorise their work as originating exclusively from the courtly love movement. Mícheál Mac Craith's erudite sifting through layers of literary accretions within some of the early modern poems has demonstrated the extent to which these poems bear the impress of contemporary literature in English. For example, Mac Craith has made a convincing case that Cearbhall Ó Dálaigh's (*fl.*1597) poem 'A mhacalla dheas' (Pleasant Echo) is most appropriately located within a broader European genre of echo poems composed in Italian and French in the early modern period. In such poems, an echo generally occurs at the beginning and end of each quatrain. More specifically, Mac Craith has argued on the basis of similarities in style and vocabulary that Ó Dálaigh drew on an echo poem in English titled 'What is the Fair' composed by William Percy in 1594.[160] Other contemporary early modern influences may also be discerned. The broader issue of sectarian division is evident in a poem composed by Mac Con Ó Cléirigh in which he bitterly laments his unhappy marriage and separation. An intriguing reference to his wife's procurement of a marital separation from the reformed primate of Armagh highlights the extent to which poets composed within specific historical and cultural circumstances.[161] While the varied and fascinating intellectual pedigree of the *dánta grádha* will no doubt continue to be debated by scholars, the brilliant artistry and stark emotional immediacy of many of these poems will ensure them a central position in Irish literary history. When Tadhg Ó Cobhthaigh spoke of love as an unquenchable flame, he could have been but partially conscious of how his sentiments would still resonate some four centuries later.[162]

Notes

1. Wilson McLeod, *Divided Gaels: Gaelic Cultural Identities in Scotland and Ireland c.1200–c.1650* (Oxford: Oxford University Press, 2004).
2. For examples of popular poetry see David Greene, ed. 'Un Joc Grossier' in Irish and Provençal', *Ériu* 17 (1955), pp. 7–15; E. G. Quin, ed. 'Truagh truagh an Mhuc', *Hermathena* 101 (1965), pp. 27–37; Pádhraic Ó Ciardha, ed. 'The Lament for Eoghan Mac Criostail',

The Irish Sword 13, 53 (1979), pp. 378–81; Máirín Ní Dhonnchadha, ed. 'The Poem Beginning *"A Shláine Inghean Fhlannagáin"'*, *Ériu* 46 (1995), pp. 65–70. For evidence of Gaelic women poets see Herbert F. Hore, 'Irish Bardism in 1561', *Ulster Journal of Archaeology* 6 (1858), pp. 165–7, pp. 202–12, p. 167; Réamonn Ó Muireadhaigh, ed. 'Aos dána na Mumhan 1584', *Irisleabhar Muighe Nuadhat* (1960), pp. 81–4; Pádraig Ó Fiannachta, *Lámhscríbhinní Gaeilge Choláiste Phádraig Má Nuad* iv (Maynooth: An Sagart, 1967), p. 26.

3. Douglas Hyde, *A Literary History of Ireland from Earliest Times to the Present Day* (London: T. Fisher Unwin, 1903), pp. 479–97; E. C. Quiggin, 'Prolegomena to the Study of the Later Irish Bards, 1200–1500', *Proceedings of the British Academy* 5 (1911–12), pp. 89–142; Aodh de Blacam, *Gaelic Literature Surveyed* (Dublin: Talbot Press, 1933), pp. 99–162; Gerard Murphy, *Glimpses of Gaelic Ireland* (Dublin: C. J. Fallon, 1948); Eleanor Knott, *Irish Syllabic Poetry* (Dublin: Dublin Institute for Advanced Studies, 1957); Eleanor Knott, *Irish Classical Poetry* (Cork: Mercier Press, 1957); David Greene, 'The Professional Poets', in Brian Ó Cuív, ed. *Seven Centuries of Irish Learning 1000–1700* (Cork: Mercier Press, 1961), pp. 38–49; James Carney, *The Irish Bardic Poet* (Dublin: Dublin Institute for Advanced Studies, 1967); Osborn Bergin, *Irish Bardic Poetry*, compiled and ed. David Greene and Fergus Kelly (Dublin: Dublin Institute for Advanced Studies, 1970); J. E. Caerwyn Williams, 'The Court Poet in Medieval Ireland', *Proceedings of the British Academy* 57 (1971), pp. 85–135; James Carney, 'Society and the Bardic Poet', *Studies* 62 (1973), pp. 233–50; Brian Ó Cuív, 'The Irish Language in the Early Modern Period', in T. W. Moody, F. X. Martin and F. J. Byrne, eds. *A New History of Ireland, vol. III: Early Modern Ireland 1534–1691* (Oxford: Clarendon Press, 1976), pp. 509–45; J. E. Caerwyn Williams and Máirín Ní Mhuiríosa, *Traidisiún Liteartha na nGael* (Dublin: An Clóchomhar, 1979), pp. 147–200; Brian Ó Cuív, *The Linguistic Training of the Mediaeval Irish Poet* (Dublin: Dublin Institute for Advanced Studies, 1983); James Carney, 'Literature in Irish, 1169–1534', in Art Cosgrove, ed. *A New History of Ireland, vol. II: Medieval Ireland 1169–1534* (Oxford: Clarendon Press, 1987), pp. 688–707.

4. The genre characterised by an amalgam of prose and verse is called *crosántacht* in Irish: see Alan Harrison, *An Chrosántacht* (Dublin: An Clóchomhar, 1979). (Names of historical figures in this period have been standardised in accordance with the usage in *New History of Ireland*.)

5. Seán Mac Airt, ed. *Leabhar Branach* (Dublin: Dublin Institute for Advanced Studies, 1944), no. 58, pp. 211–19; Liam P. Ó Caithnia, *Apalóga na bhFilí 1200–1650* (Dublin: An Clóchomhar, 1984), pp. 119–20.

6. Colm Lennon, *The Life of Richard Stanihurst the Dubliner 1547–1618* (Dublin: Irish Academic Press, 1981), p. 145.

7. 'Bíodh nách raibhe feidhm aige ris': Mac Airt, *Leabhar Branach*, p. 216.

8. Paul Walsh, ed. *Beatha Aodha Ruaidh Uí Dhomhnaill*, 2 vols. (London: Irish Texts Society, 1948, 1957), i, pp. 208–11.

9. Thomas Churchyard, *A generall rehearsall of warres, wherein is five hundred several services of land and sea* (London: Edward White, 1579), Dii (verso); Churchyard, art. *DNB*.

10. Churchyard, *A generall rehearsall of warres*, Dii (verso).

11. An entry in the Annals of Connacht for the year 1414 relates how the English monarch's lieutenant in Ireland, John Stanley, had unwisely plundered the Ó hUiginn bardic family of Uisneach in Meath and how Stanley subsequently supposedly died from the venom

of the satire directed against him by the Ó hUiginn family. See Dáithí Ó hÓgáin, *An File: Staidéar ar Osnádúrthacht na Filíochta sa Traidisiún Gaelach* (Dublin: Oifig an tSoláthair, 1982), pp. 335–63.

12. Lennon, *Richard Stanihurst*, p. 158.

13. Edmund Spenser, *A View of the State of Ireland*, ed. Andrew Hadfield and Willy Maley (Oxford: Blackwell, 1997), pp. 75–7; Richard A. McCabe, 'Edmund Spenser, Poet of Exile', *Proceedings of the British Academy* 80 (1991), pp. 73–103.

14. Spenser, *A View of the State of Ireland*, p. 77.

15. Katharine Simms, 'Bardic Poetry as a Historical Source', in Tom Dunne, ed. *The Writer as Witness: Literature as Historical Evidence* (Cork: Cork University Press, 1987), pp. 58–75; Katharine Simms, 'Literary Sources for the History of Gaelic Ireland in the Post-Norman Period', in Kim McCone and Katharine Simms, eds. *Progress in Medieval Irish Studies* (Maynooth: Department of Old Irish, St Patrick's College, 1996), pp. 207–15.

16. Kim McCone, *Pagan Past and Christian Present in Early Irish Literature* (Maynooth: An Sagart, 1990), p. 22.

17. Ibid., p. 23.

18. Ibid., p. 24.

19. For continued interaction between the church and secular learning see Katharine Simms, 'An Eaglais agus Filí na Scol', *Léachtaí Cholm Cille* 24 (1994), pp. 21–36; Simms 'The Brehons of Later Medieval Ireland', in Daire Hogan and W. N. Osborough, eds. *Brehons, Sergeants and Attorneys: Studies in the History of the Irish Legal Profession* (Dublin: Irish Academic Press, 1990), pp. 51–76, p. 70.

20. John Watt, *The Church in Medieval Ireland*, 2nd edn (Dublin: University College Dublin Press, 1998), pp. 1, 8–10; Michael Richter, *Medieval Ireland: the Enduring Tradition* (Basingstoke: Macmillan, 1988), pp. 126–9; Katharine Simms, 'Frontiers in the Irish Church – Regional and Cultural', in T. B. Barry, Robin Frame and Katharine Simms, eds. *Colony and Frontier in Medieval Ireland: Essays Presented to J. F. Lydon* (London: Hambledon Press, 1995), pp. 177–200, pp. 191–2.

21. Robin Flower, *The Irish Tradition* (Oxford: Oxford University Press, 1947), p. 85.

22. McCone, *Pagan Past*, p. 27.

23. Watt, *The Church in Medieval Ireland*, pp. 26–7.

24. Flower, *Irish Tradition*, pp. 85–6.

25. Moreover, there is no evidence of a midlands lineage for many of the leading hereditary bardic families. Proinsias Mac Cana, 'The Rise of the Later Schools of *Filidheacht*', *Ériu* 25 (1974), pp. 126–46, pp. 137–8.

26. Ibid., pp. 126–7; Liam Mac Mathúna, 'The Designation, Functions and Knowledge of the Irish Poet: A Preliminary Semantic Study' in *Anzeiger der phil.-hist. Klasse der Österreichischen Akademie der Wissenschaften, 119. Jahrgang* (Vienna: Verlag der Österreichischen Akademie der Wissenschaften, 1982), pp. 225–38. See also Liam Breatnach, 'Poets and Poetry', in McCone and Simms, eds. *Progress in Medieval Irish Studies*, pp. 65–77.

27. Ó Cuív, *Linguistic Training*, pp. 3, 17–18. *Brúilingeacht* is syllabic verse on the pattern of *dán díreach* but allowing simpler forms of rime. *Óglachas* is a loose imitation of *dán díreach* with simpler forms of rime and no rules of alliteration or consonance: Knott,

Syllabic Poetry, p. 2; Cáit Ní Dhomhnaill, *Duanaireacht* (Dublin: Oifig an tSoláthair, 1975), pp. 41–4. For an overview of normative bardic grammar and versification see Lambert McKenna, ed. *Bardic Syntactical Tracts* (Dublin: Dublin Institute for Advanced Studies, 1944).

28. Ó Cuív, *Linguistic Training*, p. 4.

29. Ibid. Brian Ó Cuív, 'A Mediaeval Exercise in Language Planning: Classical Early Modern Irish', in Konrad Koerner, ed. *Progress in Linguistic Historiography*, Studies in the History of Linguistics XX (Amsterdam: John Benjamins B. V., 1980), pp. 23–34.

30. Simms, 'The Brehons of Later Medieval Ireland', pp. 60–1.

31. Mac Cana, 'The Rise of the Later Schools', pp. 131–3.

32. Ibid., p. 131.

33. Gearóid Mac Niocaill, *The Medieval Irish Annals* (Dublin: Dublin Historical Association, 1975), pp. 21–5; John Carey, *A New Introduction to Lebor Gabála Érenn* (London: Irish Texts Society, 1993), Subsidiary Publication Series, 1.

34. One of the four main scribes of the Book of Leinster (TCD MS 1339), Áed mac Crimthainn, was *comarba* of the monastery of Terryglass. Another of its scribes, Finn, has been identified with Finn mac Gormáin (d.1160), bishop of Kildare. William O'Sullivan, 'Notes on the Scripts and Make-up of the Book of Leinster', *Celtica* 7 (1966), pp. 1–31; Gearóid Mac Niocaill, 'The Irish Language-Manuscripts', in Peter Fox, ed. *Treasures of the Library: Trinity College Dublin* (Dublin: Royal Irish Academy, 1986), pp. 57–66, pp. 59–60; Edel Bhreathnach, 'Two Contributors to the Book of Leinster: Bishop Finn of Kildare and Gilla na Náem Ua Duinn', in Michael Richter and Jean-Michel Picard, eds. *Ogma: Essays in Celtic Studies in Honour of Próinséas Ní Chatháin* (Dublin: Four Courts Press, 2002), pp. 105–111.

35. Mac Cana, 'The Rise of the Later Schools', p. 139.

36. Simms, 'Frontiers in the Irish Church', p. 192; R. I. Best, 'The Graves of the Kings at Clonmacnois', *Ériu* 2 (1905), pp. 163–71; Alan Harrison, *The Irish Trickster* (Sheffield: Sheffield Academic Press, 1989), pp. 49–50.

37. Katharine Simms has noted that it is not possible to document flourishing secular schools of vernacular law, history, poetry and medicine until the fourteenth century: 'Literacy and the Irish Bards', in Huw Pryce, ed. *Literacy in Medieval Celtic Societies* (Cambridge: Cambridge University Press, 1998), pp. 238–58, p. 242.

38. Richter, *Medieval Ireland*, pp. 132–4.

39. Francis John Byrne, *Irish Kings and High-Kings* (London: Batsford, 1987), pp. 270–2.

40. Katharine Simms, *From Kings to Warlords: the Changing Political Structure of Gaelic Ireland in the Later Middle Ages* (Woodbridge: The Boydell Press, 2000), pp. 14–15.

41. Kenneth Nicholls, *Gaelic and Gaelicised Ireland in the Middle Ages* (Dublin: Gill and Macmillan, 1972), pp. 22–3.

42. Patrick J. Duffy, David Edwards and Elizabeth FitzPatrick, 'Introduction: Recovering Gaelic Ireland, *c*.1250–*c*.1650', in Duffy et al., *Gaelic Ireland: Land, Lordship and Settlement c.1250–c.1650* (Dublin: Four Courts Press, 2001), pp. 21–73, p. 39.

43. Ibid., p. 40.

44. Simms, *From Kings to Warlords*, pp. 15–16; Robin Frame, '"Les Engleys nées en Irlande": The English Political Identity in Medieval Ireland', *Transactions of the Royal Historical Society* 3, sixth series (1993), pp. 83–103, p. 89.

45. Simms, *From Kings to Warlords*, pp. 16–17; K. W. Nicholls, 'Anglo-French Ireland and After', *Peritia* 1 (1982), pp. 370–403, p. 392.
46. Simms, 'Literacy and the Irish Bards', p. 250.
47. R. A. Breatnach, 'The Book of Uí Mhaine', in *Great Books of Ireland* (Dublin: Clonmore and Reynolds, 1967), pp. 77–89; Brian Ó Cuív, *The Irish Bardic Duanaire or 'Poem-Book'* (Dublin: National Library of Ireland Society, 1973); H. P. A. Oskamp, 'The Yellow Book of Lecan Proper', *Ériu* 26 (1975), pp. 102–19; William O'Sullivan, 'Ciothruadh's Yellow Book of Lecan', *Éigse* 18 (1980–1), pp. 177–81; Tomás Ó Concheanainn, 'The Book of Ballymote', *Celtica* 14 (1981), pp. 15–25; Carney, 'Literature in Irish', pp. 690–2.
48. Katharine Simms, 'The Poet as Chieftain's Widow: Bardic Elegies', in Donnchadh Ó Corráin, Liam Breatnach and Kim McCone, eds. *Sages, Saints and Storytellers: Celtic Studies in Honour of Professor James Carney* (Maynooth: An Sagart, 1989), pp. 400–11.
49. Pádraig A. Breatnach, 'The Chief's Poet', *Proceedings of the Royal Irish Academy* 83C, 3 (1983), pp. 37–79.
50. Marc Caball, 'Innovation and Tradition: Irish Gaelic Responses to Early Modern Conquest and Colonization', in Hiram Morgan, ed. *Political Ideology in Ireland 1541–1641* (Dublin: Four Courts Press, 1999), pp. 62–82, pp. 64–6.
51. Daniel MacCarthy, ed. *The Life and Letters of Florence MacCarthy Reagh* (London: Longmans, 1867), p. 362; Maura Carney, ed. 'Select Documents III. Agreement between Ó Domhnaill and Tadhg Ó Conchobhair concerning Sligo Castle (23 June 1539)', *Irish Historical Studies* 3 (1942–3), pp. 282–96; K. W. Nicholls, ed. 'The Lisgoole Agreement of 1580', *Clogher Record* 7 (1969), pp. 27–33.
52. N. J. A. Williams, ed. *The Poems of Giolla Brighde Mac Con Midhe*, Irish Texts Society LI (London: Irish Texts Society, 1980), no. xviii, pp. 204–13, p. 208, quatrain 21.
53. Ibid., pp. 212–3, quatrain 33.
54. David Greene, ed. *Duanaire Mhéig Uidhir* (Dublin: Dublin Institute for Advanced Studies, 1972), no. viii, pp. 68–77.
55. Lambert McKenna, ed. *The Book of O'Hara* (Dublin: Dublin Institute for Advanced Studies, 1951), no. iv, pp. 58–75, p. 58, quatrain 5.
56. Ibid., p. 60, quatrain 9; p. 70–1, quatrain 42.
57. Eleanor Knott, ed. 'Filidh Éireann go hAointeach', *Ériu* 5 (1911), pp. 50–69; Éamonn Ó Tuathail, ed. 'A Poem for Felim O'Toole', *Éigse* 3 (1941–2), pp. 261–71; Ann Dooley, 'The Poetic Self-fashioning of Gofraidh Fionn Ó Dálaigh', in Richter and Picard, *Ogma*, pp. 211–23.
58. Brian Ó Cuív, ed. 'A Poem in Praise of Raghnall, King of Man', *Éigse* 8 (1956–7), pp. 283–301.
59. Ibid., p. 292, quatrains 21–2.
60. Ibid., pp. 295–7, quatrains 37, 48.
61. Ibid., pp. 288–9, quatrains 1–8.
62. T. F. O'Rahilly, 'On the Origin of the Names Érainn and Ériu', *Ériu* 14 (1946), pp. 7–28, p. 18.
63. Greene, *Duanaire Mhéig Uidhir*, no. xxii, pp. 204–15, pp. 204–6, quatrains 6, 8.
64. Ibid., no. xxii, pp. 206–8, quatrains 11, 16.
65. Ibid., no. xxii, pp. 212–13, quatrain 30.

66. Adrian Hastings, *The Construction of Nationhood: Ethnicity, Religion and Nationalism* (Cambridge: Cambridge University Press, 1997), p. 18.

67. Edmund Curtis and R. B. McDowell, eds. *Irish Historical Documents 1172–1922* (London: Methuen, 1943), pp. 38–46; J. R. S. Phillips, 'The Remonstrance Revisited: England and Ireland in the Early Fourteenth Century', in T. G. Fraser and Keith Jeffery, eds. *Men, Women and War* (Dublin: Lilliput Press, 1993), pp. 13–27.

68. Lambert McKenna, ed. *Dánta do chum Aonghus Fionn Ó Dálaigh* (Dublin: Maunsel and Co., 1919), no. liii, pp. 73–5, p. 73, quatrain 6.

69. Eleanor Knott, ed. *The Bardic Poems of Tadhg Dall Ó hUiginn (1550–1591)*, 2 vols, Irish Texts Society XXII and XXIII (London: Irish Texts Society, 1922, 1926), no. 17.

70. Mícheál Mac Craith, 'Gaelic Ireland and the Renaissance', in Glanmor Williams and Robert Owen Jones, eds. *The Celts and the Renaissance: Tradition and Innovation* (Cardiff: University of Wales Press, 1990), pp. 57–89; Marc Caball, *Poets and Politics: Reaction and Continuity in Irish Poetry, 1558–1625* (Cork: Cork University Press, 1998); Clare Carroll, *Circe's Cup: Cultural Transformations in Early Modern Ireland* (Cork: Cork University Press, 2001); Patricia Palmer, *Language and Conquest in Early Modern Ireland* (Cambridge: Cambridge University Press, 2001).

71. Evelyn Mullally, 'Hiberno-Norman Literature and its Public', in John Bradley, ed. *Settlement and Society in Medieval Ireland* (Kilkenny: Boethius Press, 1988), pp. 327–43, p. 328. See also Edmund Curtis, 'The Spoken Languages of Medieval Ireland', *Studies* 8 (1919), pp. 234–54; Alan Bliss, 'Language and Literature', in James Lydon, ed. *The English in Medieval Ireland* (Dublin: Royal Irish Academy, 1984), pp. 27–45; Alan Bliss and Joseph Long, 'Literature in Norman French and English to 1534', in Art Cosgrove, ed. *A New History of Ireland, vol. II: Medieval Ireland 1169–1534* (Oxford: Clarendon Press, 1976), pp. 708–36; Terence Dolan, 'Writing in Ireland', in David Wallace, ed. *The Cambridge History of Medieval English Literature* (Cambridge: Cambridge University Press, 1999), pp. 208–228; Jean-Michel Picard, 'The French Language in Medieval Ireland', in Michael Cronin and Cormac Ó Cuilleanáin, eds. *The Languages of Ireland* (Dublin: Four Courts Press, 2003), pp. 57–77.

72. Bliss and Long, 'Literature', p. 715.

73. Mullally, 'Hiberno-Norman Literature', pp. 328–9; Goddard H. Orpen, ed. *The Song of Dermot and the Earl: An Old French Poem about the Coming of the Normans to Ireland* (Oxford: Clarendon Press, 1892); Evelyn Mullally, ed. *The Deeds of the Normans in Ireland* (Dublin: Four Courts Press, 2002).

74. Mullally, 'Hiberno-Norman Literature', pp. 330–2; Bliss and Long, 'Literature', p. 735.

75. Mullally, 'Hiberno-Norman Literature', p. 332; Art Cosgrove, *Late Medieval Ireland, 1370–1541* (Dublin: Helicon, 1981), p. 1.

76. Angela M. Lucas, ed. *Anglo-Irish Poems of the Middle Ages* (Dublin: Columba Press, 1995), p. 14; Alan J. Fletcher, 'Preaching in Late-Medieval Ireland: The English and the Latin Tradition', in Alan J. Fletcher and Raymond Gillespie, eds. *Irish Preaching 700–1700* (Dublin: Four Courts Press, 2001), pp. 56–80, p. 71.

77. Lucas, *Anglo-Irish Poems*, p. 21.

78. Mullally, 'Hiberno-Norman Literature', pp. 332–3.

79. Ibid., p. 333; Bliss and Long, 'Literature', pp. 718–19. For an edition of the poem see Hugh Shields, ed. 'The Walling of New Ross – a Thirteenth-Century Poem in French', *Long Room* 12–13 (1975–6), pp. 24–33.

80. The prevalence of spoken French in Ireland at this period is difficult to gauge. Richard Ledred, an English Franciscan who was bishop of Ossory from 1317 to c.1361, composed hymns in Latin recorded in the Red Book of Ossory. Innovatively and possibly indicative of at least a passive knowledge of French in Kilkenny in the 1320s, he appended the opening lines of popular vernacular songs in French to indicate the airs to which his hymns were to be sung. Mullally, 'Hiberno-Norman Literature', pp. 334, 339; Bliss and Long, 'Literature', pp. 709–10; Richard Leighton Greene, ed. *The Lyrics of the Red Book of Ossory* (Oxford: Basil Blackwell, 1974); Edmund Colledge, ed. *The Latin Poems of Richard Ledrede, O. F. M., Bishop of Ossory, 1317–1360* (Toronto: Pontifical Institute of Mediaeval Studies, 1974).

81. Lucas, *Anglo-Irish Poems*, p. 9.

82. Ibid., pp. 66–73.

83. Ibid., pp. 46–55; Bliss and Long, 'Literature', pp. 727–8.

84. Lucas, *Anglo-Irish Poems*, p. 175; Kenneth Hurlstone Jackson, ed. *Aislinge Meic Con Glinne* (Dublin: Dublin Institute for Advanced Studies, 1990), pp. xxvi–xxvii; Vivian Mercier, *The Irish Comic Tradition* (London: Souvenir Press, 1991), pp. 17–18.

85. Lucas, *Anglo-Irish Poems*, pp. 176–9.

86. *Visitatio Sepulcri* is extant in Dublin, Marsh's Library, MS Z.4.2.20 and in Oxford, Bodleian Library, MS Rawlinson liturg. D. 4. Both the *Visitatio* and the Dublin Hiberno-English play *The Pride of Life*, possibly early fifteenth century in date, were probably composed under the auspices of Dublin's Augustinian canons. See Alan J. Fletcher, *Drama, Performance, and Polity in Pre-Cromwellian Ireland* (Cork: Cork University Press, 2000), pp. 62, 84.

87. Fletcher surmises that the *Visitatio* was constructed in Dublin in the late thirteenth or early fourteenth century from various imported elements which are paralleled in church drama in England and on the continent. Fletcher, *Drama*, p. 62.

88. Fletcher, 'Preaching in Late-Medieval Ireland', p. 56.

89. Flower, *Irish Tradition*, pp. 122–3; Fletcher, 'Preaching in Late-Medieval Ireland', p. 58. It has recently been suggested that Trinity College, Dublin, MS 667 may have originated from a Franciscan house in Limerick or Nenagh patronised by the O'Briens of Thomond. Colmán N. Ó Clabaigh, 'Preaching in Late-Medieval Ireland: The Franciscan Contribution', in Fletcher and Gillespie, *Irish Preaching*, pp. 81–93, p. 90.

90. Ó Clabaigh, 'The Franciscan Contribution', p. 90.

91. Bliss and Long, 'Literature', p. 735; Andrew Carpenter, *Verse in English from Tudor and Stuart Ireland* (Cork: Cork University Press, 2003), pp. 1–32.

92. Bliss and Long, 'Literature', p. 713.

93. Nicholls, 'Anglo-French Ireland and After', p. 392; J. A. Watt, 'Gaelic Polity and Cultural Identity', in Cosgrove, *A New History of Ireland, vol. II: Medieval Ireland 1169–1534*, pp. 314–51; Katharine Simms, 'The Norman Invasion and the Gaelic Recovery', in R. F. Foster, ed. *The Oxford Illustrated History of Ireland* (Oxford: Oxford University Press, 1989), pp. 53–103. The historiographical 'two-nation theory' which held that after c.1200 the island was demarcated by self-contained territories defined by Anglo-Norman and English settlement and Gaelic settlement is now considered overly simplistic. In fact, social interchange between the Gaelic Irish and gaelicised Anglo-Irish was a marked feature of later medieval Ireland outside the Pale. Duffy et al., 'Recovering Gaelic Ireland', pp. 38–9, p. 44. See also Art Cosgrove,

'Hiberniores ipsis Hibernis', in Art Cosgrove and Donal McCartney, eds. *Studies in Irish History* (Dublin: University College Dublin, 1979), pp. 1–14; Frame, 'Les Engleys nées en Irlande'; James F. Lydon, 'Nation and Race in Medieval Ireland', in Simon Forde, Lesley Johnson and Alan V. Murray, eds. *Concepts of National Identity in the Middle Ages* (Leeds: Leeds Texts and Monographs, 1995), pp. 103–24.

94. Flower, *Irish Tradition*, pp. 133–5; Gearóid Mac Niocaill, 'Dhá Dhán le Risteard Buitléir', *Éigse* 9 (1958–61), pp. 83–8.

95. Mícheál Mac Craith, *Lorg na hIasachta ar na Dánta Grá* (Dublin: An Clóchomhar, 1989), pp. 228–32; Gearóid Mac Niocaill, ed. *Crown Surveys of Lands 1540–41 with the Kildare Rental begun in 1518* (Dublin: Irish Manuscripts Commission, 1992), pp. 355–6.

96. Myles Dillon, 'Laud Misc. 610', *Celtica* 5 (1960), pp. 64–76; Myles Dillon, 'Laud Misc. 610 (cont.)', *Celtica* 6 (1963), pp. 135–55; Katharine Simms, 'Bards and Barons: The Anglo-Irish Aristocracy and the Native Culture', in Robert Bartlett and Angus MacKay, eds. *Medieval Frontier Societies* (Oxford: Clarendon Press, 1989), pp. 177–97, pp. 190–1.

97. Simms, 'Bards and Barons', p. 190; Standish Hayes O'Grady and Robin Flower, *Catalogue of Irish Manuscripts in the British Library [formerly British Museum]* 2 vols. (reprinted Dublin: Dublin Institute for Advanced Studies, 1992), ii, pp. 470–505.

98. It appears that English continued to be used in only two rural districts: in the area north of Dublin known as Fingall and in the two adjacent baronies of Forth and Bargy in south-east Wexford. Bliss, 'Language and Literature', pp. 28–30.

99. Simms, *From Kings to Warlords*, p. 16.

100. Simms, 'The Brehons of Later Medieval Ireland', p. 54; Simms, 'Literacy and the Irish Bards', in Huw Price, ed. *Literacy in Medieval Celtic Societies* (Cambridge: Cambridge University Press, 1998), pp. 238–58, p. 250; Brian Ó Cuív, ed. 'An Appeal on Behalf of the Profession of Poetry', *Éigse* 14 (1971–2), pp. 87–106.

101. Colmán Ó Clabaigh, *The Franciscans in Ireland, 1400–1534* (Dublin: Four Courts Press, 2002), pp. 56–7, 105. Cf. Michael J. Haren, ed. 'Select Documents XXXIX: The Religious Outlook of a Gaelic Lord: A New Light on Thomas Óg Maguire', *Irish Historical Studies* 25, 98 (1986), pp. 195–7.

102. Lambert McKenna, ed. *Dán Dé* (Dublin: Educational Company of Ireland, 1922), pp. xiii–xv.

103. McKenna, *Dán Dé*, p. xi; J. E. Caerwyn Williams, ed. 'An Irish Harrowing of Hell', *Études celtiques* 9 (1960), pp. 44–78; William Gillies, ed. 'An Early Modern Irish "Harrowing of Hell"', *Celtica* 13 (1980), pp. 32–55; Andrew Breeze, 'The Virgin's Tears of Blood', *Celtica* 20 (1988), pp. 110–22; Máire Herbert and Martin McNamara, eds. *Irish Biblical Apocrypha* (Edinburgh: T. & T. Clark, 1989), pp. xxiii–xxvii.

104. A. Martin Freeman, ed. *Annála Connacht: The Annals of Connacht (AD 1224–1544)* (Dublin: Dublin Institute for Advanced Studies, 1944), sub anno 1244, p. 83.

105. McKenna, *Dán Dé*, no. xxv, pp. 46–51, 113–17.

106. Ibid., p. 47, quatrain 10.

107. Williams, *Mac Con Midhe*, no. xix, pp. 214–23.

108. Ibid., pp. 2–5.

109. Brian Ó Cuív, ed. 'A Pilgrim's Poem', *Éigse* 13 (1969–70), pp. 105–9, pp. 105–6, quatrains 1–2. Regarding Ó Dálaigh see Brian Ó Cuív, 'Eachtra Mhuireadhaigh Í Dhálaigh', *Studia Hibernica* 1 (1961), pp. 56–69.

110. Ó Clabaigh, *Franciscans in Ireland*, p. 15.

111. Ibid., p. 102.

112. Ó Clabaigh, 'The Franciscan Contribution', p. 91.

113. Ibid., pp. 85–8.

114. For this manuscript, now in Rennes, see Pádraig de Brún, *Lámhscríbhinní Gaeilge: Treoirliosta* (Dublin: Dublin Institute for Advanced Studies, 1988), p. 32.

115. Ó Clabaigh, *Franciscans in Ireland*, p. 45. A scholar such as Iorard Ó Maolchonaire (d.1482), a poet and chronicler, credited with an interest in astronomy and with having translated part of the scriptures from Latin into Irish, is clearly an example of such cultural interchange: Freeman, *Annála Connacht*, sub anno 1482, p. 585.

116. Lambert McKenna, ed. *Philip Bocht Ó hUiginn* (Dublin: The Talbot Press, 1931), pp. ix–xiv.

117. Ibid., no. 7, pp. 28–31, pp. 146–9.

118. Ibid., no. 10, pp. 41–6, pp. 154–8.

119. Brian Ó Cuív, ed. *Aibidil Gaoidheilge & Caiticiosma* (Dublin: Dublin Institute for Advanced Studies, 1994), pp. 191–208.

120. McKenna, *Dán Dé*, p. vii; McKenna, *Aonghus Fionn Ó Dálaigh*; Cuthbert McGrath, 'Ó Dálaigh Fionn cct.', *Éigse* 5 (1945–47), pp. 185–95.

121. Cuthbert Mhág Craith, ed. *Dán na mBráthar Mionúr*, 2 vols. (Dublin: Dublin Institute for Advanced Studies, 1967–80); Cainneach Ó Maonaigh, 'Scríbhneoirí Gaeilge Oird San Froinsias', *Catholic Survey* 1 (1951), pp. 54–75.

122. Joseph Falaky Nagy, *The Wisdom of the Outlaw: The Boyhood Deeds of Finn in Gaelic Narrative Tradition* (Berkeley: University of California Press, 1985), p. 17; William Gillies, 'Heroes and Ancestors', in Bo Almqvist, Séamas Ó Catháin and Pádraig Ó hÉalaí, eds. *The Heroic Process: Form, Function and Fantasy in Folk Epic* (Dún Laoghaire: The Glendale Press, 1987), pp. 57–73, p. 61; Gerard Murphy, *The Ossianic Lore and Romantic Tales of Medieval Ireland*, rev. edn (Cork: Mercier Press, 1971).

123. Nagy, *Wisdom of the Outlaw*, p. 17; Alan Bruford, 'Oral and Literary Fenian Tales', in Almqvist et al., *The Heroic Process*, pp. 25–56, p. 32.

124. Donald E. Meek, 'Development and Degeneration in Gaelic Ballad Texts', in Almqvist et al., *The Heroic Process*, pp. 131–60, pp. 135–6; Nagy, *Wisdom of the Outlaw*, p. 13; Ann Dooley and Harry Roe, trans. *Tales of the Elders of Ireland (Acallam na Senórach)* (Oxford: Oxford University Press, 1999), p. xi–xiii; Katharine Simms, 'Gaelic Warfare in the Middle Ages', in Thomas Bartlett and Keith Jeffery, eds. *A Military History of Ireland* (Cambridge: Cambridge University Press, 1996), pp. 99–115, pp. 102–5.

125. Proinsias Mac Cana, 'Fianaigecht in the Pre-Norman Period', in Almqvist et al., *The Heroic Process*, pp. 75–99; Bruford, 'Oral and Literary Fenian Tales', p. 29; Dooley and Roe, *Tales of the Elders*, p. viii.

126. Mac Cana, 'Fianaigecht', pp. 90–1; Bruford, 'Oral and Literary Fenian Tales', p. 34.

127. Nagy, *Wisdom of the Outlaw*, pp. 6–7.

128. Meek, 'Development and Degeneration', p. 138; Eoin MacNeill and Gerard Murphy, eds. *Duanaire Finn*, 3 vols., Irish Texts Society VII, XXVIII and XLIII (London and Dublin: Irish Texts Society, 1908, 1933, 1953), iii, pp. x–xi.

129. Nagy, *Wisdom of the Outlaw*, p. 2.

130. Meek, 'Development and Degeneration', p. 135; Ó Caithnia, *Apalóga na bhfilí*, pp. 20–3.

131. Bruford, 'Oral and Literary Fenian Tales', pp. 26–7.
132. Meek, 'Development and Degeneration', pp. 134–5.
133. Bruford, 'Oral and Literary Fenian Tales', pp. 34–5.
134. Murphy, *Duanaire Finn*, ii, no. lx, pp. 234–9, p. 234.
135. Ibid., pp. 236–7.
136. Ibid., pp. 238–9.
137. T. F. O'Rahilly, ed. *Dánta Grádha: An Anthology of Irish Love Poetry* (AD 1350–1750) (Cork: Cork University Press, 1926); Mac Craith, *Lorg na hIasachta*, pp. 11–41; Grace Neville, 'Les *Dánta Grádha* et la poésie des troubadours: un genre littéraire paradoxal', in Jean-Michel Picard, ed. *Aquitaine and Ireland in the Middle Ages* (Dublin: Four Courts Press, 1995), pp. 161–72.
138. Flower, in O'Rahilly, *Dánta Grádha*, pp. xi, xvi–xvii.
139. Seán Ó Tuama, *An Grá i bhFilíocht na nUaisle* (Dublin: An Clóchomhar, 1988), p. 41; James Carney, *Studies in Irish Literature and History* (Dublin: Dublin Institute for Advanced Studies, 1955), pp. 243–75.
140. Grace Neville, 'Medieval Irish Courtly Love Poetry: An Exercise in Power-Struggle?', *Etudes Irlandaises* 7 (1982), pp. 19–30, p. 28.
141. Flower, in O'Rahilly, *Dánta Grádha*, p. xii; Ó Tuama, *An Grá i bhFilíocht na nUaisle*, p. 23.
142. Ó Tuama, *An Grá i bhFilíocht na nUaisle*, pp. 23, 60.
143. Seán Ó Tuama, *An Grá in Amhráin na nDaoine* (Dublin: An Clóchomhar, 1960), pp. 205–14.
144. Ó Tuama, *An Grá i bhFilíocht na nUaisle*, pp. 55–6, p. 61.
145. Mac Craith, *Lorg na hIasachta*, pp. 7–8.
146. Ibid., p. 9.
147. Gearóid Mac Niocaill, ed. 'Duanaire Ghearóid Iarla', *Studia Hibernica* 3 (1963), pp. 7–59, pp. 8–11; Mac Craith, *Lorg na hIasachta*, pp. 59–60.
148. Láimhbheartach Mac Cionnaith, ed. *Dioghluim Dána* (Dublin: Oifig an tSoláthair, 1938), pp. 201–6.
149. The Book of Fermoy is now Dublin, Royal Irish Academy, MS 23 E 29. For the Book of the Dean of Lismore see E. C. Quiggin and J. Fraser, eds. *Poems from the Book of the Dean of Lismore* (Cambridge: Cambridge University Press, 1937); William J. Watson, ed. *Scottish Verse from The Book of the Dean of Lismore* (Edinburgh: Scottish Gaelic Texts Society, 1937); William Gillies, 'Courtly and Satiric Poems in the Book of the Dean of Lismore', *Scottish Studies* 21 (1977), pp. 35–53; Mícheál B. Ó Mainnín, 'Gnéithe de Chúlra Leabhar Dhéan Leasa Mhóir', in Máirtín Ó Briain and Pádraig Ó Héalaí, eds. *Téada Dúchais: Aistí in Omós don Ollamh Breandán Ó Madagáin* (Inverin: Cló Iar-Chonnachta, 2002), pp. 395–422.
150. Simms, 'Bards and Barons', p. 182. The thirty poems attributed to Gerald in the Book of Fermoy are composed in the less technically complex *ae freislighe* and *óglachas* metres: Mac Niocaill, 'Duanaire', p. 8.
151. Bergin, *Irish Bardic Poetry*, no. 12, pp. 60–1; Simms, 'Literacy and the Irish Bards', pp. 249–50. Cf. Brian Ó Cuív, 'The Poetic Contention about the River Shannon', *Ériu* 19 (1962), pp. 89–110.

152. O'Rahilly, *Dánta Grádha*, no. 4, p. 4. The earliest copy of the poem is extant in the Book of the Dean of Lismore. Gillies, 'Courtly and Satiric Poems', p. 50, note 18; Mac Craith, *Lorg na hIasachta*, pp. 43–7.

153. O'Rahilly, *Dánta Grádha*, no. 14, p. 18; Mac Craith, *Lorg na hIasachta*, pp. 59–60.

154. Mac Craith, *Lorg na hIasachta*, p. 60. Seán Ó Tuama has argued that specific poems attributed to Gerald in the Book of Fermoy correspond to the *chanson d'amour* and *le salut d'amour* genres associated with courtly love. Seán Ó Tuama, 'Gearóid Iarla –"the First Recorded Practitioner"?', in Seosamh Watson, ed. *Féilscríbhinn Thomáis de Bhaldraithe* (Dublin: An Coláiste Ollscoile, 1986), pp. 78–85.

155. Brendan Bradshaw, 'Manus "the Magnificent": O'Donnell as Renaissance Prince', in Art Cosgrove and Donal McCartney, eds. *Studies in Irish History* (Dublin: University College Dublin, 1979), pp. 15–36, pp. 15–17; Duffy et al., 'Recovering Gaelic Ireland', p. 38.

156. Ó Tuama, *An Grá i bhFilíocht na nUaisle*, pp. 37–8.

157. O'Rahilly, *Dánta Grádha*, no. 50, pp. 71–2.

158. Ó Tuama argues that O'Donnell may have composed these poems subsequent to the death of his first wife, Siobhán (d.1535), and prior to his marriage to Eleanor Fitzgerald in 1537: *An Grá i bhFilíocht na nUaisle*, pp. 38–9.

159. O'Rahilly, *Dánta Grádha*, no. 54, pp. 74–5; Gillies, 'Courtly and Satiric Poems'.

160. O'Rahilly, *Dánta Grádha*, no. 19, pp. 26–8; Mac Craith, *Lorg na hIasachta*, pp. 62–77. For Ó Dálaigh see James E. Doan, 'The Poetic Tradition of Cearbhall Ó Dálaigh', *Éigse* 18 (1980–1), pp. 1–24.

161. O'Rahilly, *Dánta Grádha*, no. 97, pp. 129–31. Given that Ó Cléirigh claims to have composed this poem while in the throes of death, it may be assumed it dates to approximately 1595, the year his passing was recorded in the Annals of the Four Masters. The Anglican primate referred to in the poem is most probably John Garvey (d.1595), who was translated from Kilmore to Armagh in 1589. Marc Caball, 'The Gaelic Mind and the Collapse of the Gaelic World: An Appraisal', *Cambridge Medieval Celtic Studies* 25 (Summer 1993), pp. 87–96, p. 90, note 10.

162. O'Rahilly, *Dánta Grádha*, no. 69, pp. 93–4, p. 93. For the Uí Chobhthaigh bardic family see Basil Iske, *The Green Cockatrice* (Dublin: Meath Archaeological and Historical Society, 1978), pp. 179–82.

Part II: Prose literature

KAARINA HOLLO

Introduction

The movement of manuscript production, and the learned culture attendant upon it, from the purview of the monasteries to that of the secular learned families is central to the development of prose literature during the later medieval period in Ireland. The motivations behind the preservation, adaptation and creation of prose literature may have remained to some extent the same in this new milieu. It is unimaginable, however, that they did not change to at least some degree. The extent and nature of that change is open to debate, and will be discussed below. The Norman conquest of 1169 is also, of course, of great significance in this context. As is shown below, the introduction of Norman French and English and their associated literatures into the Irish cultural milieu, and the hybridisation of culture that followed, had a significant impact upon Irish prose literature.

The major generic innovation of this period has commonly been seen as that of *Rómánsaíocht* or the Romantic tale. The usefulness of this term has been called into question by scholars over the past twenty years, but it continues in use.[1] In addition, various tales relating to Cú Chulainn and the other characters of the early medieval Ulster Cycle continue to be written and reworked during this period, and the literature relating to the hero Fionn Mac Cumhaill (*Fíanaigheacht*) enters a phase of great creativity. Translations and adaptations of various types abound, and historical, religious and medical writing flourishes as well. All these types of writing are considered below, although particular attention is given to *Rómánsaíocht* and the problems of definition attendant upon the use of this term.

The dyadic themes of continuity and innovation will inform this discussion of the prose literature of the four centuries under consideration here. These terms, of course, are in themselves problematic. What is meant when we speak of the 'continuity' of a literary tradition? The fact that a tale may be extant in eleventh-century and sixteenth-century versions does not tell us anything about its currency in the intervening period.[2] Also, we must not confuse apparent continuity in subject matter, character or plot with continuity in style or function. A later reworking of an Old or Middle Irish tale could be more innovative in these latter respects than a highly assimilated translation of a continental romance.

Authorship and context

To say that at the beginning of our period the secular learned families have become the locus for manuscript production and its associated culture generates its own set of questions. Who in particular was responsible for the production of prose narrative? For whom or to what purpose were prose tales written, modified and preserved? By the fourteenth century there is clear evidence for 'the existence of flourishing secular schools of vernacular law, history, poetry and medicine run by hereditary practitioners under the patronage of lay chieftains'.[3] But what of the substantial body of prose literature that seems to fall outside these categories? There is no separate and distinct specialisation in literary prose narrative, nor indeed a term that designates specifically the author of such work.

We have various references to the *telling* of tales. In the thirteenth century Giolla Pádraig Mac Cnáimhín mentions in a poem that his patron listened to *tiompánaigh* (instrumentalists upon the *tiompán*, a stringed instrument) recite tales of the *fiana*.[4] There are other references to the role of the storyteller in the households of the nobility and to poets reciting bedtime tales to noble individuals or assemblies.[5] The telling of tales is, of course, not the same as involvement with written narrative. As discussed in chapter 2, we do find an association between the poet or *fili* and both the knowledge of and the telling of tales during the earlier medieval period. The continuation of this association into the later medieval period is evidenced by the relatively frequent references to prose tales and their characters in the work of the professional poets.[6] It would not be unreasonable to assume that the writing of prose tales during this period was fostered in the secular schools of poetry. The fact that there seems to be no specific term for one with a mastery of this particular type of written material (unlike the other areas of law, history and poetry) could indicate that it was understood to be an integral yet subsidiary aspect of the poet's repertoire.

To what end were tales preserved, reworked or newly composed during our period? The traditional view has been one that conflates the oral and written traditions and assigns to the narratives of this period a primary function of entertainment.[7] More recently it has been suggested that, just as certain Old and Middle Irish tales can be seen as responsive to contemporary political circumstance, so too can the tales written during our period.[8] If the bardic poetry of this period was written for individual patrons, the argument continues, could not perhaps the prose tales be as well? As Caoimhín Breatnach puts it, '[w]hy should members of the literary profession write poetic compositions for individual patrons but choose to do otherwise in the case of prose tales?'[9] This is perhaps somewhat overstated. Not all literary production during this period was necessarily at the behest of individual patrons. Yet it is reasonable to allow that at least some of the prose tales composed or reworked during our period were written in response to needs other than that for entertainment of groups or individuals and a convincing case can be made in the case of certain texts.

The manuscripts

The period gets off to a slow start, as there are no extant manuscripts in Irish (apart from occasional annotations) or in a traditional Irish script that can be assigned with any certainty to the thirteenth century.[10] When we do find firm evidence for manuscript activity in Irish again, in the fourteenth century, the continuity with the pre-Norman tradition is, as Françoise Henry and Geneviève Marsh-Micheli have noted, 'near perfect, but we know that the whole background has changed.' Manuscript production moved from the monastic scriptoria into the hands of secular learned families, working under noble patronage.[11]

Among the manuscripts which appear on the other side of the thirteenth-century gap is the Book of Uí Mhaine, which James Carney has observed 'may well be the earliest great book of the Irish revival'.[12] It is part of an impressive group of manuscripts produced in the late fourteenth to mid-fifteenth century that echo in their form the great compilatory manuscripts of the twelfth century such as *Lebor na hUidre* (the Book of the Dun Cow) and the Book of Leinster; among them are the Yellow Book of Lecan (TCD MS 1318), the Book of Lecan (RIA MS 23 P 2), the Book of Ballymote (RIA MS 23 P 12), the Leabhar Breac (RIA MS 23 P 16) and the Liber Flavus Fergusorium (RIA MS 23 O 48). The manuscript tradition remains strong throughout the later part of our period as well, with important collections such as BL MS Egerton 1782 and the Book of Lismore being produced in the late fifteenth and early sixteenth centuries. Not all collections were heterogeneous in nature, with many manuscripts focused on specific areas of knowledge (medical or theological, for example). The established Munster Anglo-Norman families were notable sponsors of manuscripts in Irish, with the fifteenth-century Book of Fermoy written for the Roches of that locality. The beautifully produced Book of the White Earl was written between 1410 and 1452 for James Butler, the fourth earl of Ormond (obit 1452). It passed to his nephew, Edmund, with whose Book of Pottlerath, written for him between 1453 and 1454, it now makes up Bodleian MS Laud Misc. 610. The contemporary value of this combined manuscript is reflected in its use as a ransom payment for Edmund in 1462, when he had been taken prisoner by the eighth earl of Desmond. The colophons and marginal notes in the Book of Pottlerath show that the scribes, in the words of Brian Ó Cuív, 'shared very closely the life of their patron, travelling with him to his various houses in Kilkenny, Waterford and Tipperary'.[13]

It should be noted that many tales and other texts composed during the period 1200–1600 are preserved only in manuscripts of seventeenth-century date or later. The discussion below focuses primarily on material preserved in manuscripts from the period itself.

Style and critical issues

There has been relatively little serious study of the prose style of this period. The sort of analysis done by Uáitéar Mac Gearailt of the prose of the eleventh and twelfth centuries has not been carried out widely on the later material.[14] A general consensus exists that many narrative texts written from the thirteenth through to sixteenth century partake of the 'highly ornamental and florid style' (discussed in chapter 2) which developed during the Middle Irish period, which numbers the use of synonyms and alliterating pairs and triplets of modifiers among its characteristics.[15] Also typical of this style is the inclusion of often bravura set pieces in a heightened rhythmical prose style in which these characteristics are taken to extremes; such a passage is known as a run in English or by various terms in Irish (e.g. *cóiriú catha, culaith ghaisge, ruith*). These are introduced at certain set points in a text and can be classified under various headings: there are opening, battle, dialogue and travelling runs and those descriptive of people, nature and celebrations.[16] Similarities between this prose style and the style of oral storytellers of the nineteenth and twentieth century have been used by some to support arguments for the essentially oral character of much of Old and Middle Irish narrative literature.[17] Conversely, others have pointed to these similarities and argued for the literary origin of these features of the oral storytelling style. The reality is probably more complex. It is likely that the prose style referred to here has its origins in oral storytelling. But I would agree with Erich Poppe that this style had become 'a conscious literary and literate device' by the beginning of our period,[18] and further that it developed as such in interaction with the oral tradition over the course of the four centuries in question. Models in which the influence is all one way or limited to a certain time period are inadequate.

Much of the prose literature produced from the thirteenth to sixteenth century refers back in various ways to that of the pre-Norman period. Some tales are new versions or reworkings of older texts (for example, the third recension of *Táin Bó Cúailnge* (The Cattle Raid of Cooley)). Others, although the plot may be new, employ a milieu or characters found in the earlier literature (for example, the thirteenth / fourteenth century *Tochmarc Treblainne* (The Wooing of Treblann)). This referencing has often been seen as a weakness in the later literature, as a lack of originality. However, it can be shown that the earlier literature itself is heavily intertextual and that this was seen by its creators as a positive attribute. To be able to supply one's readership or audience with 'new wine in old skins' might have been seen as a considerable achievement and have put the weight of tradition behind any message that the author was sending. Also, as mentioned in Marc Caball's preceding discussion of the poetry of this period, the harking back to earlier materials may have been in part a conscious attempt to assert a cultural continuity with a pre-Norman Gaelic past at a time of rapid social, cultural and political change.

The critical tendency to view later versions of Old and Middle Irish tales as inferior to their precursors has greatly hindered the understanding of the prose literature of the period under consideration here. Very often these later reworkings were not considered worthy of serious discussion by modern editors and were simply mentioned in passing or printed without comment in the introductions to the canonical versions (see, for example, Rudolf Thurneysen's treatment of the later version of *Scéla Muicce Meic Dá Thó* (The Tidings of Mac Dá Thó's Pig)).[19] This tendency has often been paired with a prejudice against tales newly composed or translated during this period, on account of what is perceived as their foreignness or decadence (often represented as one and the same thing).[20] In order to write a comprehensive literary history of this period, a great deal of basic textual and critical work remains to be accomplished; meanwhile, the emphasis is put here upon texts that have already received some critical attention.

In reading what follows, it should also be kept in mind that one should be wary of claiming continuous circulation or popularity during our period for any given text on the basis of relatively scanty manuscript evidence. Tales could conceivably lie in manuscript form unread and unnoticed for centuries and then be reintroduced into circulation for a variety of reasons. Conversely, there is good reason to believe that many manuscripts have been lost over the past eight hundred years and that this has led to the evidence for many tales looking far thinner than it would have appeared otherwise. A full understanding of the reception of these tales is really beyond the reach of modern scholarship, given the fragmentary nature of our evidence for the manuscript tradition.

Ulster Cycle

The two major recensions of the chief text of the Ulster Cycle – *Táin Bó Cúailnge* (The Cattle Raid of Cooley) – belong to the period prior to that under discussion here. There is general agreement that the incomplete third recension, extant in fifteenth- and sixteenth-century manuscripts, is to be dated to the late twelfth or the thirteenth century.[21] Uáitéar Mac Gearailt notes in it, in comparison to Recension II on which he plausibly argues it is based, 'a much simpler style typical of the late twelfth and early thirteenth century'.[22] Recension IIb, more commonly known as the Stowe Recension,[23] is dated to the fifteenth century, although the earliest extant manuscript is of the seventeenth century.[24] Critics have noted its clarity and readability.[25] The circumstances of the writing of these versions are unknown to us; as Feargal Ó Béarra notes of Recension III, 'is cinnte gur ag freastal ar ghá agus ar phobal nua a bhí an té a chum' (whoever wrote it must have been serving a new need and a new audience).[26]

It has been argued that the story of Cú Chulainn's killing of his son (*Aided Óenfir Aífe*, The Death of Aífe's Only Son, in its earliest version[27]) enjoyed widespread popularity from the ninth or tenth century onwards.[28] This claim is based on scanty evidence. During our period, there is a fifteenth- or sixteenth-century retelling of the tale in a commentary on a law tract,[29] and the tale is used as an exemplum in an elegy for Aongus Óg, king of the Hebrides, in 1490.[30] The earliest manuscript of the later version of the tale, *Oidheadh Chonnlaoich* (The Death of Connlaoch), is of the early seventeenth century.[31]

Oidheadh Chloinne Uisnigh (The Death of the Children of Uisneach),[32] a recasting of the Old Irish Ulster Cycle tale *Loinges mac nUislenn* (The Exile of the Sons of Uisliu), is one of three tales which come to be referred to collectively in the later manuscript tradition as 'trí truagha na sgéalaigheachta' (the three sorrows of storytelling). There is a copy preserved in the Glenmasan Manuscript (NLS Adv. 72.2.3), which has been dated to c.1500. It has long been suggested that the interest in this tale during our period was a result of a general predilection for romantic themes characteristic of the age.[33] However, much material in the earlier tale concerning Deirdre, a pivotal character and the love interest, is omitted in the Glenmasan version and it has been persuasively argued that this version of the tale should be seen as part of a longer narrative (including the late version of *Táin Bó Flidais* (The Driving of the Cows of Flidais) which follows it in the manuscript) focused instead on the figure of Fergus mac Róich, the Ulster hero whose betrayal causes the death of the eponymous sons of Uisneach.[34] The renewed focus on Deirdre in numerous seventeenth- and eighteenth-century versions can be explained as derived from Geoffrey Keating's version in his *Foras Feasa ar Éirinn* (A Basis for Knowledge about Ireland) which in turn is based on the earlier *Loinges mac nUislenn*.[35]

A later version of *Scéla Muicce Meic Dá Thó* (The Tidings of Mac Dá Thó's Pig) may have been created in the context of the mid-sixteenth-century conflict between Shane O'Neill and the MacDonnells and written for the latter.[36] New tales relating to the Ulster Cycle include the thirteenth- or fourteenth-century *Tochmarc Treblainne* (The Wooing of Treblann), which draws freely on earlier material concerning the hero Fráech mac Fidaig, as well as on other tales.[37]

Fíanaigheacht

During this period there is considerable growth in the corpus of both prose and verse relating to Fionn Mac Cumhaill and the *fiana*. As Kim McCone has noted, *Acallam na Senórach* (The Conversation of the Elders), which sits on the linguistic divide between the Middle and Early Modern Irish periods and the historical divide between pre-Norman and Norman Ireland, marks a watershed in the history of this body of material.[38] Whatever the reasons for the relative scarcity of this body of literature prior to the end of the twelfth century (including possible clerical aversion to the institution of the *fían*), *Acallam na Senórach*, with its internal imprimatur from God and St Patrick, marks the full integration of this material into the body of literature considered suitable for manuscript preservation and transmission.

Around 1400 a new version of the *Acallam* was created, by an author who essentially stitched together the two Late Middle Irish versions, adding a few extra poems and stories and slightly modernising the language in the process.[39] Like the shorter of the two Late Middle Irish versions on which it is based, this new *Agallamh Déanach* (Late Agallamh) is structured primarily around the dialogue between St Patrick and Oisín, a theme which becomes quite dominant in the later manuscript and folk Fenian lays (our text is primarily prose). As is quite common for tales of this period, the earliest extant copy of the *Agallamh Déanach* is in a seventeenth-century manuscript.

Cath Fionntrágha (The Battle of Ventry)[40] is one of the many tales referred to in the *Acallam*. The stress in the *Acallam* is placed entirely upon the tragic death of the warrior Cáel in the eponymous battle and the resultant lament of his lover. In *Cath Fionntrágha* itself Ireland is attacked by the King of the World, Dáire Donn, and a large force of foreigners all seeking revenge upon Fionn, who had eloped with the wife and daughter of the king of the Franks. The greater part of the tale is taken up with accounts of massed battles and individual combats. Fionn is shown as at odds with Cormac mac Airt, the king of Ireland, who accuses him of levying unfair charges upon his people and refuses to come to the aid of the forces defending Ireland against the foreign onslaught. At the tale's end, Fionn is on his deathbed. Cáel swims out to the departing boat carrying the King of the World away and manages, in a heroic but suicidal act, to drag Dáire Donn to the bottom of the sea. Finally, Gelges sings her lament for Cáel and herself dies of grief.

Cath Fionntrágha is commonly accepted as of fifteenth-century date.[41] The earliest version of the tale is found in the late fifteenth-century Bodleian MS Rawlinson B 487; all other manuscript copies are of the eighteenth century and later. Rawlinson B 487 is of Connacht provenance and was written for a female patron, Sadhbh Ní Mháille of Mayo, who also has a praise poem addressed to her which immediately follows *Cath Fionntrágha* in the manuscript.[42] The O'Malleys were associated with the Anglo-Norman Bourkes of Mayo and there is a possibility that Sadhbh was married to a member of the family.

The text takes on an interesting aspect when read against the provenance detailed above. Caoimhín Breatnach notes that the term used throughout the tale to describe the defenders of Ireland is *Éireannaigh* (Irishmen) rather than *Gaedhil* (Gaels) and points to the use as early as 1419 of the former term to describe a mixed force of Gaelic and Anglo-Norman soldiers fighting under Butler leadership in France.[43] The term is also used frequently in fifteenth- and sixteenth-century poems addressed to Anglo-Norman patrons. Breatnach also notes a distinct ambiguity in the attitude taken to Ireland's defenders and attackers. The attack is precipitated by Fionn's misconduct and the defenders are in disarray, with the high king refusing to participate. Breatnach sees the international nature of the attacking force, with *Lochlannaigh* (Vikings), French and English among them, as significant and cites Katherine Simms' analysis of the frequent references to the successive invasions which texts such as *Lebor Gabála Érenn* held had populated Ireland as 'a device that set the Normans' land-rights on the same legal footing as those of the Milesian Celts'.[44] He also notes as significant in its emphasis on intermarriage between natives and incomers a passage in which Bodhbh Dearg, a member of the Tuatha Dé Danann, declines to help in the fight against the invaders (on the basis that he owes no loyalty to the *Éireannaigh*[45]) and is reminded by his interlocutor of the intermarriage between the women of the Tuatha Dé Danann and the men of the *fiana* (and is thus persuaded to join in Ireland's defence).

The overall thrust of Breatnach's argument is that these tensions and issues around identity and loyalty within the tale would make it of particular interest and relevance to a fifteenth-century patron such as Sadhbh Ní Mháille, an aristocratic woman of Gaelic stock with close connections with the Anglo-Norman nobility. More generally, it can be argued that the usage of the term *Éireannaigh* in *Cath Fionntrágha* provides further evidence that a notion of Irishness which encompassed those of both Gaelic and Anglo-Norman backgrounds was already current in the fifteenth century.

The structure and style of *Cath Fionntrágha* would be considered typical of tales of this period. In form, the tale is episodic, with one combat or consultation listed after the other. Such episodes could be added or subtracted from the text without essentially altering the plot. Alliterating synonyms or near-synonyms are freely used throughout (e.g. *rí ro gabasdar flaitheas 7 forlamhas* 'a king assumed sovereignty and possession'[46], *ro thionoileadar imoro 7 ro thimsaigeadar sluaig in domain* 'the hosts of the world gathered and assembled'[47]). Lists of warriors and place-names are found throughout, as are battle and travel runs. In these latter passages in *Cath Fionntrágha* the use of alliterating modifiers is more frequent than in the rest of the text, in which a somewhat simpler, less adjectival style is employed.

Unlike *Cath Fionntrágha*, *Tóruigheacht Dhiarmada agus Ghráinne* (The Pursuit of Diarmaid and Gráinne)[48] is not directly referred to in the *Acallam*, although the boar that is fated to kill Diarmaid is mentioned.[49] The tale has been dated to the fourteenth century, although the earliest extant manuscript is of the mid-seventeenth century. The tale is clearly the work of an accomplished literary author. It tells of the wooing of King Cormac's daughter Gráinne by Fionn, her revulsion at being betrothed to an older man, her placing of Diarmaid under *geassa*, or magical injunctions, to elope with her and their flight through the wilderness and pursuit by Fionn. With the help of Aonghus of Brú na Bóinne, one of the chief members of the Tuatha Dé Danann and Diarmaid's foster-father, a truce is effected between Fionn and Diarmaid and Gráinne and Diarmaid settle down and raise a family.

This seeming resolution, however, is only a temporary resting point for the narrative. In the next, penultimate, episode the author's skill is displayed particularly clearly, so some space is devoted to examining it here.[50] At this point Diarmaid, awakened several times during one night by the sound of a dog hunting, can't resist arising early in the morning to join the chase, despite

Gráinne's attempts to prevent him. He finds Fionn in pursuit of a boar. Fionn reminds Diarmaid that it is taboo for him to hunt boar, but Diarmaid persists nevertheless. Fionn departs, leaving Diarmaid alone and it is at this point that Diarmaid realises that he is doomed. He is mortally wounded by the animal, against which his weapons are useless. Fionn and his men then reappear and Fionn bitterly says that he is happy to see Diarmaid in such a plight:

> 'Is maith leam t'fheicsin mar sin, a Dhiarmaid,' ar sé, '7 is truagh leam nach ffuilid mná Éreann uile dot fhéachain anois, ór tucais maisi ar mhí-mhaisi 7 dealbh mhaith ar droch-dheilbh.'[51]

> ('I like to see you like that, Diarmaid,' said he, 'and I regret that all the women of Ireland are not looking at you now, for your beauty is turned to ugliness and your good form to deformity.')[52]

Diarmaid beseeches Fionn for some water from his hands, known to have healing properties. Fionn only agrees after his grandson, Osgar, pleads with him. Twice he lets the water trickle out between his fingers halfway between the spring and the dying Diarmaid. Finally Osgar threatens Fionn with death if he does not bring Diarmaid the water.

> Do thill Fionn an treas feacht ar ceann in uisge leis in ccomhrádh sin go Diarmaid, 7 tuc lán a dhá bhos don uisge leis. Agus ag teacht do láthair dó do sgar a anam rena chorp ag Diarmaid.[53]

> (Fionn returned for the water the third time for Diarmaid because of that speech and he brought with him the full of his two palms of water. And as he was coming to the place the life parted from the body of Diarmaid.)[54]

The emotional intensity of this scene continues unabated, with Osgar kept from killing his grandfather only by his father's intervention. Fionn and the *fiana* leave the hill. Osgar, Oisín, Caoilte and Mac Lughach, the four most prominent of the warriors, slip away from the group to place their cloaks over Diarmaid's body and then follow the rest. A wrenching scene follows, in which the heavily pregnant Gráinne sees Fionn and his men approaching. Fionn is holding Diarmaid's dog, Mac an Chuill, and Gráinne surmises from this that Diarmaid is dead. She falls in a faint over the rampart of the enclosure and gives birth to three still-born boys.

> Mar do-chonnairc Oisín an bhean go n-iodhnuibh do chuir sé Fionn 7 an Fhian ón láthair. Ag fághbháil na láithreach d'Fhionn 7 don Fhéin do thóguibh Gráinne a ceann 7 do iarr ar Fionn Mac an Chuill d'fhágbháil aice féin. Adubh-airt Fionn nac ttiubhradh, 7 nachar mór leis an oiread sin d'oighreacht

Diarmada uí Dhuibhne do bheith aige féin. Do-rinne Oisín air 7 do bhean an cú a lláimh Fhinn 7 tuc leis go Gráinne hí, 7 do lean sé fén a mhuintir.[55]

(When Oisín saw the woman in travail he sent Fionn and the *fiana* away from the place. As Fionn and the *fiana* were leaving the place Gráinne lifted up her head and she asked Fionn to leave Mac an Chuill with herself. Fionn said he would not and that he did not think it too much that he himself should have that much of Diarmaid Ó Duibhne's inheritance. Oisín made for him and he took the hound from Fionn's hand and he brought it with him to Gráinne and he himself followed his people.)[56]

The story continues with an account of Aonghus's removal of Diarmaid's body to Brú na Bóinne and ends with Gráinne rallying her children to avenge themselves on Fionn.

The skill with which the author of the *Tóruigheacht* represents the intensity and conflicted nature of Fionn's feeling towards Diarmaid is remarkable. The rest of the *fiana* act as a counterbalance throughout, throwing Fionn's emotional excess into sharp relief through their reasonable and compassionate behaviour and words. There is an ambiguity in the water scene that makes it all the more effective. The first time Fionn attempts to bring back the water, he says he isn't able to do it and Osgar accuses him of letting the water run through his fingers on purpose. When he brings the water for the third time, is he actually intending to give it to Diarmaid? If so, is it only because of Osgar's threat? The reader will never know. The scene with Gráinne and the hunting hound, Mac an Chuill, is equally accomplished. Although a modern reader may well find the depiction of Gráinne's reaction to her husband's death excessive, the emotional truth of the scene strikes home. Fionn's callousness in claiming the dog for himself is intermingled with a sense that he too is mourning the death of one who was once among his dearest friends. We arguably have here one of the great depictions of jealousy, hate, rage and disappointment in world literature, well able to stand alongside that of Shakespeare's *Othello*.

The structure of the tale is simple. A good proportion of it is taken up by the relation of 'in-tales', or stories told by characters. Even as Diarmaid lies dying, he narrates in some detail some of the good turns that he had done for Fionn in the past.[57] Thus the *Tóruigheacht* is similar to the *Acallam* in its use of a relatively simple narrative as a frame on which to hang numerous others.

The style of the tale displays a moderate version of that described as 'ornamental' above. Dialogue generally is simpler, unless the speaker is narrating an in-tale, in which case the style is identical with that of the frame narrative. At various key points in the narrative, such as those quoted above, the language becomes more economical and modifiers and synonyms are largely dispensed with.

References to the elopement of Diarmaid and Gráinne exist from the tenth and eleventh centuries, so the tale clearly has its origins in the earlier medieval period. The earliest references to Diarmaid's death are those in *Acallam na Senórach* and hence of the twelfth/early thirteenth century.[58] Scholars vary in their identification of the main focus of the tale, with some seeing it as a tragedy of 'a young girl betrothed to an old man and of the conflict between passion and duty on the part of her lover',[59] and others seeing the focus of the tale on Diarmaid and his life-story.[60] Based on the earlier evidence, one can suggest that there were originally two distinct sources or traditions, one telling of Gráinne's betrothal to Fionn and her elopement with Diarmaid, the other concerned with the life-story and *oidheadh* or violent death of Diarmaid.[61] These two sources were then brought together, possibly for the first time by the fourteenth-century author of the *Tóruigheacht*.

As Diarmaid lies dying, he reminds Fionn of how he helped him out of trouble in the Bruidhean Chaorthainn, or Rowan-Tree Hostel.[62] There is a tale extant with this name (*An Bhruidhean Chaorthainn*), the earliest manuscript copy of which can be dated to 1603 and has a Scottish provenance.[63] This is representative of a sub-type of Fenian tale in which the *fiana* are lured into a hostel or *bruidhean* by an enemy with magical powers and then make their escape. In *Feis Tige Chonáin* (The Feast of Conán's House) the initial hostility comes from human hosts who are mollified by storytelling, providing the author with an ideal opportunity for the introduction of a number of in-tales.[64]

Romantic tales

The Romantic tale has been defined memorably by Gerard Murphy as follows:

> When scholars speak of the Romantic tales of Early Modern Irish they are thinking mainly of a group of tales whose main traits are the prevalence of magic and the piling of unbelievable incident upon incident. They are akin in this respect to the wonder-tales of native folklore . . . They resemble French *romans d'aventure* in so far as knightly adventures in distant lands and the winning of wives, are normal features in them . . . [T]he sixteenth and seventeenth centuries may be looked upon as the period in which they enjoyed their greatest popularity . . . Their closest parallels in European literature are the Icelandic 'lying sagas' of the thirteenth and following centuries.[65]

This description, although a *locus classicus*, is none the less problematic. In terms of subject matter, Murphy includes tales in which the hero is drawn from Irish history or pseudo-history or earlier so-called king tales, on the one hand, and tales with 'some fictitious non-Irish character' in the leading role on the other.[66] As his argument proceeds, however, the limits of the category begin to become unclear. Although seeing the popularity of this type of tale as dependent upon 'continental influence' from the late fifteenth century onwards, Murphy notes correctly that there are Old and Middle Irish tales, such as *Tochmarc Emire* (The Wooing of Emer) and *Loinges mac nDuíl Dermait* (The Exile of the Sons of Dóel Dermait), that exhibit the characteristics of the Romantic tale as he has described it.[67]

The model of literary history in which a heroic or epic phase, corresponding to a heroic phase of society, is followed by one of romance is a well-established and powerful, if somewhat discredited, one and clearly underlies the historical usage of the term Romantic tale in the Irish context.[68] The heterogeneity of the material described under this heading, however, in terms of subject matter and milieu makes the term of questionable use, especially as not all scholars subscribe to Murphy's parameters. Alan Bruford, for example, includes under the rubric 'all the late medieval and later romances found in Irish manuscripts from the fifteenth to the nineteenth centuries and the related folk tales',[69] (romances are 'rambling episodic stories of battle and magic, sometimes loosely unified by a quest theme'[70]), or alternatively 'all original prose hero-tales written in Gaelic from the late twelfth to the early nineteenth centuries which were not intended to be read principally as history or allegory'.[71] Dáithí Ó hÓgáin seems to include only those stories to which an Aarne-Thompson folk-tale type-number can be assigned.[72]

As the references to 'continental influence' and the French *romans d'aventure* above indicate, the Romantic tale is seen as related to medieval romance as commonly understood in the greater European context, a genre described by one scholar as 'the shape-shifter par excellence among medieval genres, a protean form that refuses to settle into neat boundaries prescribed by modern critics'.[73] Perhaps it is no surprise, then, that we have difficulty in defining the parameters of the Irish genre most closely related to romance.[74]

There can be no doubt that tales from continental and English sources were known and disseminated by various means in Ireland during this period. The houses of the Anglo-Norman patrons of Gaelic poetry and learning would have been foci of such cultural exchange, providing opportunities for both oral and written transmission and performance of such material. Tendencies already present within the Irish literary tradition – particularly the interest in foreign material already exemplified by the translations and adaptations from Latin narrative sources in the Middle Irish period and the expansion of the stylistic and compositional repertoire of Irish literati attendant upon the creation of these works – coincided with the opportunities represented by the influx of foreign material during our period to produce the literature which we are considering here under the rubric of the Romantic tale. If we accept the term as describing more of an attitude towards material rather than the material itself, a mode rather than a genre, we may find it of greater use.[75] Tales that some might not wish to classify as Romantic (*Tóruigheacht Dhiarmada agus Ghráinne*, for example) have clearly been influenced by the same conditions and influences that created the Romantic tales and share many characteristics with them. For the purposes of this chapter, we will discuss as Romantic tales texts which conform to Murphy's definition, while keeping in mind its limited usefulness.

Some Romantic tales are to be found in fifteenth- and sixteenth-century manuscripts. All have as their protagonists characters associated with royal dynasties that figure already in the prose literature of Old and Middle Irish. *Eachtra Airt Meic Chuind*[76] (The Adventure of Art son of Conn) appears in the Middle Irish tale lists,[77] but the language of the sole copy of the tale in the Book of Fermoy is clearly Early Modern Irish. The hero is the son of Conn Cétchathach, who had a place in the Irish historical schema as high king of Ireland during the second century. *Eachtra Airt* is typical of the Irish Romantic tale in its overseas quest to win a wife, but echoes the earlier literature in many ways, including its preoccupation with the theme of just kingship. Stylistically it is quite restrained, with the ornamental style primarily reserved for descriptive passages and travelling and battle runs. The hero of another transmarine adventure tale, *Eachtra Thaidhg mhic Chéin* (The Adventure of Tadhg son of Cian; Book of Lismore, *c.*1500), figures in the earlier literature as a contemporary of Cormac, Art's son.[78] In the *Eachtra* he travels overseas, encountering various marvels on the way, to rescue his wife and brothers from marauders who have kidnapped them. *Leigheas Coise Céin* (The Healing of Cian's Leg) is found in Egerton 1781 (*c.*1484–7).[79] The hero, Cian, is a historical figure associated with the tenth-century Irish king Brian Boru. Although Brian figures as high king in *Leigheas Coise Céin*, the plot of the tale has nothing to do with the known historical facts and it is a loosely constructed and entertaining episodic tale, full of fantastic incident and detours through various in-tales. *Stair Nuadat Find Femin* (The History of Fair Nuadu of Femin) also is placed in a context drawn from Irish pseudo-history.[80] It is in the hand of Uilleam Mac an Leagha (see the discussion of translations and adaptations below) and in the same manuscript as his versions of the lives of Hercules, Guy of Warwick and Beves of Hamtoun; it may well have been conceived by him as the native counterweight to the classical story.[81]

The earliest manuscript copy of *Eachtra Chonaill Ghulban* (The Adventure of Conall Gulban) is of the late seventeenth century, but the tale is thought to have a sixteenth-century Donegal provenance.[82] Its hero, Conall Gulban, figured prominently in the genealogy of the O'Donnells and Alan Bruford has suggested, on the basis of references in the tale to events in Spain and Germany, that the romance may have been written 'with some thought of encouraging the young Manus O'Donnell, who succeeded in 1537, to join an anti-English league'.[83]

Translations and adaptations

The Norman invasion of 1169 and the subsequent settlements brought Norman-French and English speakers into Ireland in considerable numbers. As discussed earlier in this chapter, the relative importance and prevalence of the two languages is hard to ascertain, but it is safe to say that by the early fourteenth century the dominant spoken idiom among these settlers was English.[84] During the fourteenth century we see a resurgence of Gaelic culture and the increasing Gaelicisation of Anglo-Norman families, against which the Statutes of Kilkenny was promulgated (in Norman French, now a language reserved primarily for legal and business use)[85] with little effect in 1366. In such a hybridised milieu, it is not surprising to see flourishing a lively culture of literary translation from English (and to a lesser extent from Latin) into Irish. There is no evidence for translation from French into Irish; all known translations of originally French texts can be shown to be based on English intermediaries.[86]

The output of one fifteenth-century scribe, author and translator in particular, Uilleam Mac an Leagha, is worth looking at in some detail. There are seven manuscripts in his hand extant, and the majority of texts in these are religious. Non-religious texts figure too and he has been identified as the creator of the Irish versions (based on English sources) of the lives of Hercules, Beves of Hamtoun and Guy of Warwick, all found in one of his manuscripts, TCD MS H.2.7.[87]

Study of Mac an Leagha's version of Beves can provide us with some understanding of the *modus operandi* of the medieval Irish translator, who, in Erich Poppe's words was more of a redactor who kept the basic structure and the events of his source text, but who felt free to cast it into a form which would be based to a considerable extent on native literary conventions and expectations and which would therefore appeal directly to the intended audience.[88]

The Irish version of Beves, *Bibus*, is based on a Middle English verse source.[89] The translator chose to write his version in prose. This is consistent with the aesthetic of the target culture (that is, the culture into which the tale is being introduced through translation, in this case that of fifteenth-century Ireland), in which prose is the primary vehicle for narrative.[90] The tale is written in the ornamental style discussed above. References to towns in the source text are generally altered to references that seem more applicable to fortified Irish tower-houses.[91] Added references and changes relating to royal counsellors, the institution of fosterage, a woman's ability to voice an opinion on a match made for her by her parents, royal tribute as opposed to feudal vassalage and the obligation to provide hospitality all reflect an acculturation of the text into the Irish context, as does a passage which reflects the notion, central to the Irish ideology of kingship, that the prosperity of the realm is linked to the just behaviour of a rightful king.[92]

Some of Mac an Leagha's manuscripts can be associated with the Anglo-Norman Butler family and with the notably Gaelicised Edmund Mac Richard Butler, nephew of the fourth earl of Ormond, in particular. Bibus's stay with the prior of Rhodes, not found in Beves, could have been of special interest to anyone associated with the Knights Hospitallers of St John of Jerusalem (who were based in Rhodes). In Ireland the Knights Hospitallers were drawn from among the Anglo-Norman aristocracy and the Butler family had various connections with the order during the fifteenth century.[93] Overall, Erich Poppe has noted, the Butlers' tastes 'would appear to be well-reflected in the combination of the English interest of the plot of Beves of Hamtoun and its gaelicized presentation'.[94]

Mac an Leagha is also credited with the Irish version of the Life of St Mary of Egypt and possibly some other religious texts, found in BL Add. MS 30512, of which he is the scribe.[95] Again, Mac an Leagha's approach to translation is typical of his period, in which the translator attempts to integrate the text into the culture of the target language. Mac an Leagha does this in his version of the Life of St Mary by writing it in the ornamental style discussed above. Erich Poppe notes that 'the cultural transfer is very much a transfer into a specific mode of narrative expression'.[96] As in *Bibus*, this transfer is effected not only through stylistic means but also through substantive changes and additions to the material of the tale; for example, Mary is introduced in Uilleam's text as the daughter of a king,[97] which brings her more clearly into the aristocratic realm of the popular romances of the period. The description of Mary's transformation into bestial form while in the desert resonates with Irish literary representations of the figure of the wild man or woman,[98] and particularly with texts in which women, such as Gormlaith and Mis, repair to the wilderness (usually in a state of grief), wander in rags, are torn by thorns and, in more extreme cases, grow animal fur and claws.[99]

The Arthurian literature of this period in Ireland comprises one clear translation and a handful of tales of Irish origin in which an Arthurian milieu and characters are employed. The original tales (or, at least, those without a known foreign source) include *Eachtra an Mhadra Mhaoil*[100] (The Adventure of the Crop-eared Dog / Wolf), which employs an Arthurian werewolf theme, and relates how '[t]he son of the King of India, transformed into a werwolf by a wicked stepmother, seeks the aid of a knight of Arthur's court [Gawain] to hunt down the Knight of the Lantern, the son of the enchantress, who alone can effect his retransformation'.[101] It is found in Egerton 1782, a substantial manuscript written for the greater part in 1517 in Roscommon by members of the learned family of Ó Maoil Chonaire. The *Eachtra* keeps company with a wide range of material here, including religious poetry and prose, Ulster Cycle texts including *Táin Bó Cuailnge* and Fenian material. Another possible Arthurian tale of Irish origin from our period is *Céilidhe Iosgaide Léithe* (The Visit of the Grey-hammed Lady),[102] which is listed in the sixteenth-century table of contents drawn up for the mid-fifteenth-century manuscript Egerton 1781; unfortunately, the portion of the manuscript containing it is missing. There is an Arthurian tale of the same name preserved in a seventeenth-century manuscript, but its relationship to the earlier text is unknown.[103]

The sole proven Arthurian translation, by an unknown author, is based on an early English version (now lost) of the Quest for the Holy Grail and has been dated to the mid-fifteenth century.[104] Its simple style and deliberate use of archaic linguistic forms set it aside from other Irish translations of romances from this period, although there is occasional use made of the ornamental style (for example, when describing a sea journey).[105] This difference is no doubt partly a response to the critique of romance inherent in the source text.[106] However, it may also be a result of the circumstances of its translation into Irish and its intended audience. Could it have been created within an ecclesiastical, perhaps Franciscan, environment? The 'heightened spiritual atmosphere' of the Irish version in comparison to others has been noted.[107] This emphasis on the spiritual aspect of the text and the downplaying of its romance nature (including a deliberate avoidance of the prose style most commonly associated with secular prose narrative in this period) would be consistent with an Irish adaptor writing within a religious context.

Genres other than romance were widely translated into Irish during our period, including travel literature (versions of the Travels of Marco Polo[108] and the armchair wanderings of Sir John Mandeville[109]) and a good quantity of medical, scientific and philosophical material.[110] Religious translations are discussed separately below.

Two fifteenth-century English-language versions of earlier Latin works give us an insight into the mentality of the Anglo-Irish community of that period. The first is a loose translation of Giraldus Cambrensis' late twelfth-century *Expugnatio Hibernica*.[111] Its representation of the barbarity of the Irish and the superiority of the Normans no doubt served to reinforce the Anglo-Irish sense of entitlement to the land of Ireland.[112] The second is James Yonge's (*fl.*1420s) *The Gouernance of Prynces*,[113] a very free version of the pseudo-Aristotelian *Secreta Secretorum*, based to a great extent upon the thirteenth-century French version of the latter by the Dominican Geoffrey (Jofroi) of Waterford. Yonge's translation was made for James Butler, the fourth earl of Ormond, and is notable for additions which emphasise the right of the English crown to the land of Ireland.[114]

Religious literature

A wide range of religious material was produced during this period, with the fifteenth century seemingly the most active for Irish-language material.[115] Activity peaks sooner in Latin, with, among others, a tract on the Seven Deadly Sins by the Franciscan Malachy of Armagh (*fl.c.*1310) and an *Itinerarium* of a journey from Ireland to the Holy Land in 1322 by another friar, Symon Simeonis.[116] The Franciscan and bishop of Ossory Richard Ledrede (*obit c.*1361), who presided over the trial for witchcraft in 1324 of Alice Kyteler and figures in the Latin account of the proceedings, is the author of sixty devotional poems in Latin.[117] Of particular interest from the substantial Latin *oeuvre* of Richard Fitzralph, archbishop of Armagh from 1346 to 1360, is a series of sermons against the friars that he preached (in both English and Latin, of which only the Latin versions survive) from 1350 onwards. These culminate in the *Defensio Curatorum* delivered before the Pope at Avignon in 1357, which has been described as 'one of the most important anti-mendicant documents of the Middle Ages'.[118]

Hagiography in both Latin and Irish is well represented. There are about twenty saints' Lives in Irish of various periods extant in fourteenth- to sixteenth-century manuscripts and others from our period preserved only in copies made later.[119] The early fifteenth-century *Leabhar Breac* contains, among much other religious material, the Lives of Patrick, Brigit and Columba in homiletic form. The Book of Fermoy (*c*.1450–60) and Laud Misc. 610 (1453–5) count saints' Lives among their contents, as does the later fifteenth-century Book of Lismore. As Pádraig Ó Riain has noted, the interest in this material is shared by secular patrons of Gaelic and Anglo-Norman descent alike.[120]

Any discussion of hagiography of this period is usually capped by a consideration of Maghnus Ó Domhnaill's (?–1563) *Betha Coluim Chille* (Life of Columba) with which, in Richard Sharpe's memorable words, '[m]edieval Irish hagiography may reasonably be thought to end'.[121] It has been convincingly argued by Brendan Bradshaw that Ó Domhnaill's Life of Columba, written in 1532, five years before his accession to the lordship of Donegal, is a Renaissance document in the attitude reflected in it towards sources, its authorship by a noble amateur, its use of simple straightforward language and its reflection of a humanist ethos.[122] Bodleian Library MS Rawlinson B 502, which comprises a copy of the Life and an Ó Domhnaill *duanaire*, is thought by some scholars to have been written for Ó Domhnaill himself.[123] The lay-out of the beautifully written and illustrated text may owe something to contemporary printed works.[124] Bradshaw also shows that Ó Domhnaill, to whom a handful of accomplished lyric poems are also attributed, had extensive contacts with the continent, Scotland and the south of England. The presence of Observant Franciscans in Donegal from the 1480s has also been highlighted as a significant locus for the transmission of Renaissance Christian humanism in the area.[125]

Devotional tracts translated into Irish from English and Latin are plentiful, with *Smaointe Beatha Chríost*[126] (Thoughts upon the Life of Christ), a mid-fifteenth-century translation of the *Meditationes Vitae Christi* (Meditations upon the Life of Christ), among the most popular, to judge from the number of manuscript copies.[127] The Irish versions of *De Contemptu Mundi* (Concerning Contempt for the World) and *Instructio pie Vivendi et Superna Meditandi* (Instruction in Holy Life and Heavenly Thought) were made at around the same time.[128] The style of these translations is generally simple and direct, with ease of comprehension clearly the primary goal. Colophons to the *Smaointe* and *Instructio* may indicate, in one reading, that the translation process in each case involved two men, one translating out loud and the other transcribing, but this is not certain. The importance of these translations and those of medical, philosophical and scientific works, in the development of Irish prose style should not be underestimated.[129]

Medical and historical writing

Over one hundred fifteenth- to seventeenth-century manuscripts containing Irish-language medical texts (mostly translations of Latin works) are extant.[130] These tracts were produced in the context of a flourishing network of schools of medicine associated with hereditary medical families.[131] Tadhg Ó Cuinn (probably of the Munster family of that name), who wrote in the early fifteenth century, was responsible for the translation of three Latin medical works into Irish.[132] Cormac Mac Duinnshléibhe (*fl.c.*1459), like Ó Cuinn a holder of a baccalaureate in medicine and whose family were physicians to the O'Donnells, was notable in this field, translating nine Latin works, among them Bernard of Gordon's *Lilium Medicum* (The Medical Lily) (1305) and the first book of Guy de Chauliac's *Chirurgia Magna* (Great Surgery).[133]

Annals continued to be kept during this period. In addition to the Irish-language annals, we find the Latin *Annales Hiberniæ*, by the Kilkenny Franciscan John Clyn, which is occupied primarily by an eye-witness account of the plague in that city during the years 1348–9.[134] Just as the Middle Irish period has, in addition to works written in annal format, a great narrative prose historical work (*Cogadh Gaedhel re Gallaibh* (The War of the Gaels with the Foreigners)) so too does our period, in *Caithréim Thoirdhealbhaigh* (The Triumphs of Turlough).[135] This tells of two intertwined conflicts in Thomond in the late thirteenth and early fourteenth century: the internecine struggle within the Uí Bhriain dynasty between the Toirdhealbhach of the title and his uncle Brian Ruadh; and that between the established Anglo-Norman Irish family of the de Burgh and Toirdhealbhach's faction, the Clann Taidhg, on the one side, and newcomer Thomas de Clare, granted Thomond by Edward I in 1276, and Clann Bhriain Ruaidh, on the other.[136] The *Caithréim*, composed in the mid-fourteenth century, ends with the victory of Muirchertach, Toirdhealbach's son, at Disert O Dea in 1318. The conflict between the two branches of the Uí Bhriain continued until at least 1350, however, and Aoife Nic Ghiollamhaith argues convincingly that the *Caithréim* was probably 'commissioned by a king from among Clann Taidc to discredit Clann Briain Ruaid for good and to prove his own impeccable pedigree'.[137] De Clare and his men are represented as the real villains of the piece, with Clann Bhriain Ruaidh represented as their dupes.[138] On the other hand, the *Caithréim*'s 'fusion of the old idea of the Gaelic king with the new concept of the feudal vassal', in Nic Ghiollamhaith's words, and the emphasis put upon the 'kingly' and 'Irish-natured' qualities of Clann Taidhg's allies the de Burghs reflect the political reality of the time, in which 'collaboration with the Anglo-Irish was obviously a policy of the utmost respectability'.[139]

The period 1200–1600 was one of great political and demographic change in Ireland. The production of manuscripts containing Irish-language literature had, by the beginning of the period, passed from the monasteries into the hands of secular learned families and it stayed with them throughout this time. These centuries also saw continued writing in Latin in Ireland and the introduction of writing in Anglo-Norman French and Hiberno-English. The dominant language, however, by the sixteenth century was still Irish, with English concentrated within the Pale. The professional poets wrote in Irish for lords of Gaelic, Anglo-Norman and mixed ancestry, sure of their place within a traditional system of patronage. Prose literature in Irish continued to be produced, with several new genres coming to the fore and English and continental works were assimilated into the Irish corpus through translation. Great manuscript compilations were created to rival those of the earlier period. As will be seen in the next chapters, the political and military events of the first few years of the seventeenth century had a profound effect upon this literary culture.

Notes

1. See Joseph Nagy, 'In Defense of *Rómánsaíocht*', *Ériu* 38 (1987), pp. 9–27, p. 12, and Bianca Ross, 'Uilleam mac an Leagha's Versions of the Story of Mary of Egypt', in Erich Poppe and Bianca Ross eds. *The Legend of Mary of Egypt in Medieval Insular Hagiography* (Dublin: Four Courts Press, 1996), pp. 259–78, p. 278.
2. Caoimhín Breatnach, *Patronage, Politics and Prose: Ceasacht Inghine Guile, Sgéala Muice Meic Dá Thó, Oidheadh Chuinn Chéadchathaigh*, Maynooth Monographs V (Maynooth: An Sagart, 1996), p. 12.
3. Katharine Simms, 'Literacy and the Irish Bards', in Huw Pryce, ed. *Literacy in Medieval Celtic Societies* (Cambridge: Cambridge University Press, 1998), pp. 238–58, p. 242.
4. Lambert McKenna, ed. and trans., *The Book of Magauran* (Dublin: Dublin Institute for Advanced Studies, 1947), ll. 827–8.
5. See Proinsias Mac Cana, *The Learned Tales of Medieval Ireland* (Dublin: Dublin Institute for Advanced Studies, 1980), pp. 13–14.
6. See Osborn Bergin, ed. and trans. *Irish Bardic Poetry: Texts and Translations together with an Introductory Lecture* (1970; Dublin: Dublin Institute for Advanced Studies, 1984), pp. 64, 76–80, 110–11, 163–4.
7. Mac Cana, *The Learned Tales*, p. 80.
8. Breatnach, *Patronage*, p. 2
9. Ibid., p. 5.

10. Harley MS 193, which contains material in Norman French and English, is discussed elsewhere in this chapter.

11. Françoise Henry and Geneviève Marsh-Micheli, 'Manuscripts and Illuminations, 1169–1603', in Art Cosgrove ed. *A New History of Ireland*, vol. II: *Medieval Ireland 1169–1534* (Oxford: Clarendon Press, 1987), pp. 780–815, p. 789.

12. James Carney, 'Literature in Irish, 1169–1534', in Cosgrove ed., *Medieval Ireland*, pp. 688–707, p. 691.

13. Brian Ó Cuív, *Catalogue of Irish-Language Manuscripts in the Bodleian Library at Oxford and Oxford College Libraries*, 2 vols. (Dublin: Dublin Institute for Advanced Studies, 2001), I, p. 63.

14. See Uáitéar Mac Gearailt, 'Change and Innovation in Eleventh-Century Prose Narrative in Irish', in Hildegard Tristram, ed. *(Re)Oralisierung*, ScriptOralia 84 (Tübingen: Gunter Narr, 1996), pp. 443–96.

15. E.g. Erich Poppe, 'Favourite Expressions, Repetition and Variation: Observations on *Beatha Mhuire Eigptacdha* in Add. 30512', in Poppe and Ross, *The Legend of Mary of Egypt*, pp. 279–99, p. 281.

16. Alan Bruford, *Gaelic Folk-tales and Medieval Romances: A Study of the Early Modern Irish 'Romantic Tales' and their Oral Derivatives* (Dublin: The Folklore of Ireland Society, 1969), pp. 37–9.

17. Nagy, 'In Defense', pp. 12–13.

18. Poppe, 'Favourite Expressions', p. 298.

19. Rudolf Thurneysen, ed. *Scéla Mucce Meic Dathó*, Mediaeval and Modern Irish Series VI (Dublin: The Stationery Office, 1935; reprinted Dublin Institute for Advanced Studies, 1975).

20. For parallels in the study of continental medieval literature see John M. Ganim, 'The Myth of Medieval Romance,' in Howard P. Bloch and Stephen G. Nichols, eds. *Medievalism and the Modernist Temper* (Baltimore: The Johns Hopkins University Press, 1996), pp. 148–66, pp. 156–8.

21. Feargal Ó Béarra, 'Táin Bó Cúailnge III: Abach Aimrid?', in James Mallory and Gerard Stockman, eds. *Ulidia: Proceedings of the First International Conference on the Ulster Cycle of Tales, Belfast and Emain Macha* (Belfast: December Publications, 1994), p. 74; Uáitéar Mac Gearailt, 'The Relationship of Recensions II and III of the Táin', in Mallory and Stockman, *Ulidia*, pp. 55–70, p. 70.

22. Mac Gearailt, 'The Relationship of Recensions II and III', p. 70.

23. Cecile O'Rahilly, ed. *The Stowe Version of Táin Bó Cuailgne* (Dublin: Dublin Institute of Advanced Studies, 1961).

24. Rudolf Thurneysen, *Die irische Helden- und Königsage bis zum siebzehnten Jahrhundert* (Halle: Max Niemeyer, 1921), p. 117.

25. Ibid., pp. 116–17; Hildegard Tristram, 'What is the Purpose of Táin Bó Cúailnge?', in Mallory and Stockman, *Ulidia*, pp. 12–13.

26. Ó Béarra, 'Abach Aimrid', p. 76.

27. Kuno Meyer, ed. and trans. 'The Death of Conla', *Ériu* I (1904), pp. 113–21.

28. Ruairí Ó hUiginn, 'Rúraíocht agus Rómánsaíocht', *Éigse* 32 (2000), pp. 77–87, pp. 77–9.

29. James G. O'Keeffe, 'Cuchulinn and Conlaech', *Ériu* I (1904), pp. 123–7.

30. Cited in Ó hUiginn, 'Rúraíocht agus Rómánsaíocht', p. 83.

31. For an edition and translation of this version see Paul Walsh, 'Oidheadh Chonlaoich mic Con gCulainn', *Éigse Suadh is Seanchaidh* (Dublin: M. H. Gill [1909]), p. 13.

32. Caoimhín Mac Giolla Léith, ed. and trans. *Oidheadh Chloinne hUisneach*, Irish Texts Society LVI (London: Irish Texts Society, 1993).

33. Gerard Murphy, *The Ossianic Lore and Romantic Tales of Medieval Ireland*, rev edn, Irish Life and Culture XI (Cork: Mercier Press, 1971), pp. 30–1.

34. Caoimhín Breatnach, 'Oideadh Chloinne Uisnigh', *Ériu* 45 (1994), pp. 99–112.

35. Ibid., pp. 111–12.

36. Breatnach, *Patronage*, pp. 27–9.

37. Thurneysen, *Die irische Helden- und Königsage*, p. 296.

38. Kim McCone, 'Werewolves, Cyclopes, *Díberga* and *Fíanna*: Juvenile Delinquency in Early Ireland,' *Cambridge Medieval Celtic Studies* 12 (Winter 1986), pp. 1–22, p. 1.

39. Nessa Ní Shéaghdha, ed. *Agallamh na Seanórach*, 3 vols., Leabhair ó Láimhsgríbhnibh VII, X and XV ed. Gerald Murphy (Dublin: The Stationery Office, 1942–5), I, p. xxxi.

40. Kuno Meyer, ed. and trans. *Cath Finntrága or Battle of Ventry, edited from MS. Rawl. B 487 in the Bodleian Library*, Anecdota Oxoniensia, Mediaeval and Modern Series, I. IV. (Oxford: Clarendon Press, 1885); Cecile O'Rahilly, ed. *Cath Finntrágha*, Mediaeval and Modern Irish Series XX (Dublin: Dublin Institute for Advanced Studies, 1962).

41. Caoimhín Breatnach, 'Cath Fionntrágha', in *Léachtaí Cholm Cille* XXV (Maynooth: An Sagart, 1995), pp. 128–43, p. 132.

42. O'Rahilly, *Cath Finntrágha*, pp. viii–x, 63–4.

43. Breatnach, 'Cath Fionntrágha' p. 141.

44. Katharine Simms, 'Bards and Barons: The Anglo-Irish Aristocracy and the Native Culture', in Robert Bartlett and Angus MacKay, eds. *Medieval Frontier Societies* (Oxford: Oxford University Press, 1989), pp. 177–97, p. 182, cited in Breatnach, 'Cath Fionntrágha', p. 138.

45. Breatnach, 'Cath Fionntrágha', pp. 140–1.

46. Meyer, *Cath Finntrága*, p. 1.

47. Ibid.

48. Nessa Ní Shéaghdha, ed. and trans. *Tóruigheacht Dhiarmada agus Ghráinne*, Irish Texts Society XLVIII (Dublin: Educational Company of Ireland for the Irish Texts Society, 1967).

49. Ní Shéaghdha, *Tóruigheacht*, p. xii.

50. Ibid., pp. 81–97.

51. Ibid., p. 90.

52. Ibid., p. 91.

53. Ibid., p. 94.

54. Ibid., p. 95.

55. Ibid., p. 96.

56. Ibid., p. 97.

57. Ibid., pp. 90–5.

58. Cited in ibid., p. xii.

59. Myles Dillon, *Early Irish Literature* (Chicago: University of Chicago Press, 1948; reprinted Dublin: Four Courts Press, 1994), pp. 42–3.

60. Donald Meek, 'The Death of Diarmaid in Scottish and Irish Tradition,' *Celtica* 21 (1990), pp. 335–61, p. 338; also Tomás Ó Cathasaigh, 'Tóraíocht Dhiarmada agus Ghráinne', in *Léachtaí Cholm Cille* XXV (Maynooth: An Sagart, 1995), pp. 30–46, p. 39.

61. Ibid., p. 39.

62. Ní Shéaghdha, *Tóruigheacht*, pp. 92–5.

63. See S. H. O'Grady and R. Flower, *Catalogue of Irish Manuscripts in the British Library [formerly British Museum]*, 2 vols. (London: British Museum, 1926; reprinted Dublin: Dublin Institute for Advanced Studies, 1992), II, pp. 343–4 for discussion of MSS containing the tale. There is no full published edition based on the oldest manuscript.

64. Maud Joynt, ed. *Feis Tighe Chonáin*, Mediaeval and Modern Irish Series VII (Dublin: The Stationery Office, 1936).

65. Murphy, *Ossianic Lore*, pp. 39–40.

66. Ibid., p. 42.

67. Ibid., pp. 45–8.

68. For a classic statement of this model in a continental European context, see W. P. Ker, *Epic and Romance: Essays on Medieval Literature*, 2nd rev. edn (London: Macmillan, 1908), pp. 3–15; for the linking of a heroic phase of society with the production of epic literature, see H. Munro Chadwick and N. Kershaw Chadwick, *The Growth of Literature*, 3 vols. (Cambridge: Cambridge University Press, 1932–40), I, and Kenneth Jackson, *The Oldest Irish Tradition: A Window on the Iron Age* (Cambridge: Cambridge University Press, 1964).

69. Bruford, *Gaelic Folk-tales*, p. 1.

70. Ibid.

71. Alan Bruford, 'Eachtra Chonaill Gulban', *Béaloideas* 31 (1963), pp. 1–50, p. 1.

72. Dáithí Ó hÓgáin, *Myth, Legend and Romance: An Encyclopædia of the Irish Folk Tradition* (New York: Prentice Hall, 1991), pp. 374–7.

73. Matilda Tomaryn Bruckner, 'The Shape of Romance in Medieval France,' in Roberta Krueger, ed. *The Cambridge Companion to Medieval Romance* (Cambridge: Cambridge University Press, 2000), pp. 13–28, p. 13.

74. See Erich Poppe, '*Stair Nuadat Find Femin*: Eine Irische Romanze', *Zeitschrift für celtische Philologie* 49–50 (1997), pp. 749–59, for the problem of the relationship of Irish literature to European romance.

75. See Pamela Gradon, *Form and Style in Early English Literature* (London: Methuen, 1971), pp. 269–7; also Bianca Ross, *Bildungsidol-Ritter-Held: Herkules bei William Caxton und Uilleam mac an Lega*, Brittanica et Americana, dritte Folge, Bd. 10, eds. Rudolf Haas and Claus Uhlig (Heidelberg: Carl Winter Universitätsverlag, 1989), pp. 207–12.

76. Richard. I. Best, ed. and trans. 'The Adventures of Art Son of Conn and the Courtship of Delbchæm', *Ériu* 3 (1907) pp. 149–73.

77. Mac Cana, *Learned Tales*, p. 53.

78. Standish Hayes O'Grady, ed. and trans. *Silva Gadelica, A Collection of Tales in Irish with Extracts illustrating Persons and Places*, [I–XXXI], 2 vols. (London: Williams and Norgate, 1892), I, pp. 342–59 (text); II, pp. 385–401 (trans.).

79. O'Grady, *Silva Gadelica*, II, pp. 296–305 (text); II, pp. 332–42 (trans.)

80. Käte Mueller-Lisowski, ed. and trans. 'Stair Nuadat Find Femin', *Zeitschrift für celtische Philologie* 13 (1920), pp. 195–250.

81. Poppe, '*Stair Nuadat Find Femin*', pp. 758–9.

82. G. Lehmacher, ed. and trans. 'Eine Brüsseler Handschrift der *Eachtra Conaill Gulban*', *Zeitschrift für celtische Philologie* 14 (1923), pp. 212–69.

83. Bruford, *Gaelic Folk-tales*, p. 88, note 2.

84. Alan Bliss and Joseph Long, 'Literature in Norman French and English to 1534', in Cosgrove, *Medieval Ireland*, pp. 708–36, pp. 711–13.

85. Terence Dolan, 'Writing in Ireland', in David Wallace, ed., *The Cambridge History of Medieval English Literature* (Cambridge: Cambridge University Press, 1999), pp. 208–28, p. 214.

86. Sheila Falconer, ed. and trans. *Lorgaireacht an tSoidhigh Naomhtha, an Early Modern Irish Translation of the Quest of the Holy Grail* (Dublin: Dublin Institute for Advanced Studies, 1953; reprinted 1997), p. xxxi.

87. Poppe, '*Stair Nuadat Find Femin*', p. 750.

88. Erich Poppe, 'The Early Modern Irish Version of Beves of Hamtoun', *Cambridge Medieval Celtic Studies* 23 (Summer 1992), pp. 77–98, pp. 78–9.

89. Ibid., p. 80.

90. Ibid., p. 81.

91. Ibid., p. 88.

92. Ibid., pp. 90–6.

93. Ibid., pp. 97–8.

94. Ibid., p. 98.

95. Poppe, 'Favourite Expressions', pp. 279–80.

96. Ibid., p. 298.

97. Ross, 'Uilleam mac an Leagha's Versions', p. 263–4.

98. Ibid., p. 269.

99. For Gormlaith, see Bergin, ed. and trans. *Irish Bardic Poetry* (1984), pp. 207–8, 310; for Mis, see Brian Ó Cuív, ed. 'The Romance of Mis and Dub Ruis', *Celtica* 2 (1954), pp. 325–33; trans. in Angela Bourke et al., eds. and trans. *The Field Day Anthology of Irish Writing, vols. IV and V: Irish Women's Writing and Traditions* (Cork: Cork University Press in association with Field Day, 2002), IV, pp. 238–41.

100. R. A. S. Macalister, ed. and trans. *Two Arthurian Romances: Eachtra Mhacaoimh-an-Iolair and Eachtra an Mhadra Mhaoil*, Irish Texts Society X (London: David Nutt, 1908).

101. Robin Flower, *Catalogue of Irish Manuscripts in the British Library, vol. II* (1926; reprinted Dublin: Dublin Institute for Advanced Studies, 1992), p. 271.

102. Máire Mhac an tSaoi, ed. *Dhá Sgéal Artúraíochta, mar atá Eachtra Mhelóra agus Orlando, agus Céilidhe Iosgaide Léithe* (Dublin: Dublin Institute for Advanced Studies, 1946; reprinted 1984), pp. 42–70.

103. Martje Draak, 'Sgél Isgaide Léithe', *Celtica* 3 (1956), pp. 232–40.

104. Falconer, *Lorgaireacht*, pp. xxxii, xiv.

105. Ibid., p. 151.

106. See Simon Gaunt, 'Romance and Other Genres', in Krueger, ed. *The Cambridge Companion to Medieval Romance*, pp. 45–59, pp. 55–7.

107. Falconer, *Lorgaireacht*, p. xvi.

108. Whitley Stokes, ed. and trans. 'The Gaelic Abridgement of the Book of Ser Marco Polo', *Zeitschrift für celtische Philologie* 1 (1896–7), pp. 245–73, 362–438, 603; *Zeitschrift für celtische Philologie* 2 (1898), pp. 222–3 (corrigenda).

109. Whitley Stokes, ed. and trans. 'The Gaelic Maundeville', *Zeitschrift für celtische Philologie* 2 (1898), pp. 1–63, 226–312, 603–4.

110. See Michael Cronin, *Translating Ireland: Translation, Languages, Cultures* (Cork: Cork University Press, 1996), pp. 25–30.

111. Frederick Furnivall, ed. *The English Conquest of Ireland. AD 1166–1185: Mainly from the 'Expugnatio Hibernica' of Giraldus Cambrensis*, Early English Texts Society [original series] CVII (London: K. Paul, Trench, Trübner & Co., for the Early English Texts Society, 1896).

112. Dolan, 'Writing in Ireland', p. 225.

113. Robert Steele, ed. *Three Prose Versions of the Secreta Secretorum*, Early English Texts Society Extra Series LXXIV (London: Kegan Paul, 1898).

114. Dolan, 'Writing in Ireland', p. 225.

115. Canice Mooney, *The Church in Gaelic Ireland: Thirteenth to Fifteenth Centuries*, A History of Irish Catholicism II, general ed. Patrick Corish (Dublin: Gill & Macmillan, 1969), p. 62.

116. Dolan, 'Writing in Ireland', p. 226; Mario Esposito, ed. *Itinerarium Symonis Semeonis ab Hybernia ad Terram Sanctam*, Scriptores Latini Hiberniae IV (Dublin: Dublin Institute for Advanced Studies, 1960).

117. Dolan, 'Writing in Ireland', p. 226; Edmund Colledge, ed. *The Latin Poems of Richard Ledrede, Bishop of Ossory, 1317–1360, edited from the Red Book of Ossory* (Toronto: Pontifical Institute of Mediaeval Studies, 1974).

118. Terence Dolan, 'The Literature of Norman Ireland', in Seamus Deane, general ed. *The Field Day Anthology of Irish Writing* (3 vols., Derry: Field Day Publications, 1991), I, pp. 140–70, p. 148; Aaron Perry, ed. *Dialogus inter Militem et Clericum [here taken to be by William of Ockham], Richard FitzRalph's Sermon: Defensio Curatorum, 'and Methodius: 'þe Bygynnyng of þe World and þe Ende of Worldes' by John Trevisa*, Early English Texts Society [original series] CLXVII (London: Oxford University Press for Early English Texts Society, 1925).

119. Richard Sharpe, *Medieval Irish Saints' Lives: An Introduction to Vitae Sanctorum Hiberniae* (Oxford: Clarendon Press, 1991), p. 6.

120. Pádraig Ó Riain, ed. and trans. *Beatha Bharra, Saint Finbarr of Cork: The Complete Life*, Irish Texts Society LVII (London: Irish Texts Society, 1994), p. 41.

121. Sharpe, *Medieval Irish Saints' Lives*, p. 37; A. O'Kelleher and Gertrude Schoepperle, *Betha Colaim Chille*, University of Illinois Bulletin 15, 48 (Urbana: University of Illinois, 1918).

122. Brendan Bradshaw, 'Manus "the Magnificent": O'Donnell as Renaissance Prince', in Art Cosgrove and Donald McCartney, eds. *Studies in Irish History* (Dublin: UCD Press, 1979), pp. 15–36, pp. 25–7.

123. Ó Cuív, *Catalogue*, I, p. 270.

124. Henry and Marsh-Micheli, 'Manuscripts and Illuminations', p. 808.

125. Bradshaw, 'Manus O'Donnell', pp. 18–19.

126. Cainneach Ó Maonaigh, ed., *Smaointe Beatha Chríost, .i. Innsint Ghaelge a Chuir Tomás Gruamdha Ó Bruacháin (fl.c.1450) ar an Meditationes vitae Christi* (Dublin: Dublin Institute for Advanced Studies, 1944).

127. Mooney, *The Church*, p. 33.

128. James Geary, ed. and trans. *An Irish Version of Innocent III's De Contemptu Mundi: A Dissertation* (Washington, DC: Catholic University of America, 1931); John MacKechnie, ed. and trans. *Instructio Pie Vivendi et Superna Meditandi*, 2 vols., Irish Texts Society XXIX (London: Irish Texts Society, 1946).

129. Cainneach Ó Maonaigh, *Smaointe Beatha Chríost*, p. x; Cronin, *Translating Ireland*, p. 30.

130. Aoibheann Nic Dhonnchadha, 'Irish Medical Writing, 1400–1600', in Bourke et al., *The Field Day Anthology of Irish Writing*, IV, pp. 341–57, p. 341.

131. Ibid.

132. Ibid., p. 357.

133. Ibid., p. 356.

134. Dolan, 'The Literature of Norman Ireland', p. 147.

135. S. H. O'Grady, ed. and trans. *Caithréim Thoirdhealbhaigh*, 2 vols., Irish Texts Society XXVI and XXVII (London: Irish Texts Society, 1929).

136. Aoife Nic Ghiollamhaith, 'Dynastic Warfare and Historical Writing in North Munster, 1276–1350'. *Cambridge Medieval Celtic Studies* 2 (1981), pp. 73–89, p. 75.

137. Ibid., p. 77.

138. Ibid., p. 79.

139. Ibid., pp. 87–8.

Select bibliography for Parts I and II

Bergin, Osborn, *Irish Bardic Poetry*, compiled and edited by David Greene and Fergus Kelly, Dublin: Dublin Institute for Advanced Studies, 1970.

Bliss, Alan and Joseph Long, 'Literature in Norman French and English to 1534', in Art Cosgrove, ed. *A New History of Ireland, vol. II: Medieval Ireland 1169–1534*, Oxford: Clarendon Press, 1976, pp. 708–36.

Bradshaw, Brendan, 'Manus "the Magnificent": O'Donnell as Renaissance Prince', in Art Cosgrove and Donal McCartney, eds. *Studies in Irish History*, Dublin: University College Dublin, 1979, pp. 15–36.

Breatnach, Caoimhín 'Cath Fionntrágha', in *Léachtaí Cholm Cille* XXV, Maynooth: An Sagart, 1995, pp. 128–43.

   'Oideadh Chloinne Uisnigh', *Ériu* 45 (1994), pp. 99–112.

   Patronage, Politics and Prose, Maynooth Mongraphs V, Maynooth: An Sagart, 1996.

Bruford, Alan, *Gaelic Folk-tales and Medieval Romances: A Study of the Early Modern Irish 'Romantic Tales' and their Oral Derivatives*, Dublin: The Folklore of Ireland Society, 1969.

Caball, Marc, 'Innovation and Tradition: Irish Gaelic Responses to Early Modern Conquest and Colonization', in Hiram Morgan, ed. *Political Ideology in Ireland 1541–1641*, Dublin: Four Courts Press, 1999, pp. 62–82.

Poets and Politics: Reaction and Continuity in Irish Poetry, 1558–1625, Cork: Cork University Press, 1998.

Carney, James, *The Irish Bardic Poet*, Dublin: Dublin Institute for Advanced Studies, 1967.

'Literature in Irish, 1169–1534', in Art Cosgrove ed., *A New History of Ireland, vol. II: Medieval Ireland 1169–1534*, Oxford: Clarendon Press, 1987, pp. 688–707.

'Society and the Bardic Poet', *Studies* 62 (1973), pp. 233–50.

Studies in Irish Literature and History, Dublin: Dublin Institute for Advanced Studies, 1955.

Dolan, Terence, 'The Literature of Norman Ireland', in Seamus Deane, general ed., *The Field Day Anthology of Irish Writing*, 3 vols. Derry: Field Day, 1991, I, pp. 140–70.

'Writing in Ireland', in David Wallace, ed., *The Cambridge History of Medieval English Literature*, Cambridge: Cambridge University Press, 1999, pp. 208–28.

Dooley, Ann, 'The Poetic Self-fashioning of Gofraidh Fionn Ó Dálaigh', in Michael Richter and Jean-Michel Picard, eds. *Ogma: Essays in Celtic Studies in Honour of Próinséas Ní Chatháin*, Dublin: Four Courts Press, 2002, pp. 211–23.

Fletcher, Alan J., *Drama, Performance and Polity in Pre-Cromwellian Ireland*, Cork: Cork University Press, 2000.

Gradon, Pamela, *Form and Style in Early English Literature*, London: Methuen, 1971.

Greene, David, 'The Professional Poets', in Brian Ó Cuív, ed. *Seven Centuries of Irish Learning 1000–1700*, Cork: Mercier Press, 1961, pp. 38–49.

Harrison, Alan, *An Chrosántacht*, Dublin: An Clóchomhar, 1979.

Henry, Françoise and Geneviève Marsh-Micheli, 'Manuscripts and Illuminations, 1169–1603', in Art Cosgrove ed., *A New History of Ireland, vol. II: Medieval Ireland 1169–1534*, Oxford: Clarendon Press, 1987, pp. 780–815.

Knott, Eleanor, ed. *The Bardic Poems of Tadhg Dall Ó hUiginn (1550–1591)*, 2 vols., Irish Texts Society XXII and XXIII, London: Irish Texts Society, 1922 and 1926.

Irish Classical Poetry, Cork: Mercier Press, 1957.

Irish Syllabic Poetry, Dublin: Dublin Institute for Advanced Studies, 1957.

Lucas, Angela, M., ed. *Anglo-Irish Poems of the Middle Ages*, Dublin: Columba Press, 1995.

Mac Cana, Proinsias, *The Learned Tales of Medieval Ireland*, Dublin: Dublin Institute for Advanced Studies, 1980.

'The Rise of the Later Schools of *Filidheacht*', *Ériu* 25 (1974), pp. 126–46.

Mac Craith, Mícheál, 'Gaelic Ireland and the Renaissance', in Glanmor Williams and Robert Owen Jones, eds. *The Celts and the Renaissance: Tradition and Innovation*, Cardiff: University of Wales Press, 1990, pp. 57–89.

Lorg na hIasachta ar na Dánta Grá, Dublin: An Clóchomhar, 1989.

Mac Gearailt, Uáitéar, 'Change and Innovation in Eleventh-Century Prose Narrative in Irish', in Hildegard Tristram, ed. *(Re)oralisierung*, ScriptOralia LXXXIV, Tübingen: Gunter Narr, 1996, pp. 443–96.

'The Relationship of Recensions II and III of the Táin', in J. P. Mallory and Gerard Stockman, eds. *Ulidia: Proceedings of the First International Conference on the Ulster Cycle of Tales, Belfast and Emain Macha, 8–12 April 1994*, Belfast: December Publications, 1994, pp. 55–70.

MacNeill, Eoin and Gerard Murphy, eds. *Duanaire Finn*, 3 vols., Irish Texts Society VII, XXVIII and XLIII, London and Dublin: Irish Texts Society, 1908, 1933 and 1953.

Mercier, Vivian, *The Irish Comic Tradition*, London: Souvenir Press, 1991.

Mhág Craith, Cuthbert, ed. *Dán na mBráthar Mionúr*, 2 vols., Dublin: Dublin Institute for Advanced Studies, 1967–80.

Mullally, Evelyn, 'Hiberno-Norman Literature and its Public', in John Bradley, ed. *Settlement and Society in Medieval Ireland*, Kilkenny: Boethius Press, 1988, pp. 327–43.

Murphy, Gerard, *The Ossianic Lore and Romantic Tales of Medieval Ireland*, Irish Life and Culture XI, 1955; rev. edn, Cork: Mercier Press, 1971.

Nagy, Joseph, 'In Defense of *Rómánsaíocht*', *Ériu* 38 (1987), pp. 9–27.

Nic Dhonnchadha, Aoibheann, 'Irish Medical Writing, 1400–1600', in A. Bourke, S. Kilfeather, M. Luddy, M. MacCurtain, G. Meaney, M. Ní Dhonnchadha, M. O'Dowd and C. Wills, eds. and trans., *The Field Day Anthology of Irish Writing, vols. IV and V: Irish Women's Writing and Traditions*, Cork: Cork University Press in association with Field Day, 2002, IV, pp. 341–57.

Nic Ghiollamhaith, Aoife, 'Dynastic Warfare and Historical Writing in North Munster, 1276–1350', *Cambridge Medieval Celtic Studies* 2 (Winter 1981), pp. 73–89.

Nicholls, Kenneth, *Gaelic and Gaelicised Ireland in the Middle Ages*, Dublin: Gill and Macmillan, 1972.

Ó Béarra, Feargal, 'Táin Bó Cuailnge III: Abach Aimrid?', in James Mallory and Gerard Stockman, eds. *Ulidia: Proceedings of the First International Conference on the Ulster Cycle, Belfast and Emain Macha*, Belfast: December Publications, 1994, pp. 71–6.

Ó Caithnia, Liam P., *Apalóga na bhFilí 1200–1650*, Dublin: An Clóchomhar, 1984.

Ó Clabaigh, Colmán, *The Franciscans in Ireland, 1400–1534*, Dublin: Four Courts Press, 2002.

Ó Cuív, Brian, 'Eachtra Mhuireadhaigh Í Dhálaigh', *Studia Hibernica* 1 (1961), pp. 56–69.

The Irish Bardic Duanaire or 'Poem-Book', Dublin: National Library of Ireland Society, 1973.

'The Irish Language in the Early Modern Period', in T. W. Moody, F. X. Martin and F. J. Byrne, eds. *A New History of Ireland, vol. III: Early Modern Ireland 1534–1691*, Oxford: Clarendon Press, 1976, pp. 509–45.

The Linguistic Training of the Mediaeval Irish Poet, Dublin: Dublin Institute for Advanced Studies, 1983.

O'Rahilly, T. F., ed. *Dánta Grádha: An Anthology of Irish Love Poetry (AD 1350–1750)*, Cork: Cork University Press, 1926.

Ó Tuama, Seán, *An Grá i bhFilíocht na nUaisle*, Dublin: An Clóchomhar, 1988.

Poppe, Erich, 'The Early Modern Irish Version of Beves of Hamtoun', *Cambridge Medieval Celtic Studies* 23 (Summer 1992), pp. 77–98.

'Favourite Expressions, Repetition and Variation: Observations on *Beatha Mhuire Eigptacdha* in Add. 30512', in Erich Poppe and Bianca Ross, eds. *The Legend of Mary of Egypt in Medieval Insular Hagiography*, Dublin: Four Courts Press, 1996, pp. 279–99.

'*Stair Nuadat Find Femin*: Eine Irische Romanze', *Zeitschrift für celtische Philologie* 49–50 (1997), pp. 749–59.

Ross, Bianca, *Bildungsidol-Ritter-Held: Herkules bei William Caxton und Uilleam mac an Lega*, Brittanica et Americana, dritte Folge, Bd. X, eds. Rudolf Haas and Claus Uhlig, Heidelberg: Carl Winter Universitätsverlag, 1989.

Sharpe, Richard, *Medieval Irish Saints' Lives: An Introduction to Vitae Sanctorum Hiberniae*, Oxford: Clarendon Press, 1991.

Simms, Katharine, 'Bardic Poetry as a Historical Source', in Tom Dunne, ed. *The Writer as Witness: Literature as Historical Evidence*, Cork: Cork University Press, 1987, pp. 58–75.

'Bards and Barons: The Anglo-Irish Aristocracy and the Native Culture', in Robert Bartlett and Angus MacKay, eds. *Medieval Frontier Societies*, Oxford: Oxford University Press, 1989, pp. 177–97.

From Kings to Warlords: The Changing Political Structure of Gaelic Ireland in the Later Middle Ages, Woodbridge: The Boydell Press, 2000.

'Literacy and the Irish Bards', in Huw Pryce, ed. *Literacy in Medieval Celtic Societies*, Cambridge: Cambridge University Press, 1998, pp. 238–58.

Thurneysen, Rudolf, *Die irische Helden- und Königsage bis zum siebzehnten Jahrhundert*, Halle: Max Niemeyer, 1921.

Watt, J. A., 'Gaelic Polity and Cultural Identity', in Art Cosgrove, ed. *A New History of Ireland*, vol. *II: Medieval Ireland 1169–1534*, Oxford: Clarendon Press, 1987, pp. 314–51.

Williams, J. E. Caerwyn, 'The Court Poet in Medieval Ireland', *Proceedings of the British Academy* 57 (1971), pp. 85–135.

4

Literature in English, 1550–1690: from the Elizabethan settlement to the Battle of the Boyne

ANNE FOGARTY

Faced with the massed heaps of state papers about Irish affairs awaiting his attention on his accession in 1603, James I reportedly declared that there is 'more ado about Ireland than all the world beside'.[1] The overriding impression fostered by current historical accounts of sixteenth- and seventeenth-century Ireland is that political, diplomatic and propagandist writing predominates and that literary production is fitful and even at times non-existent. The assumption persists too that Ireland was in the main untouched by the cultural transformations and creative energies of the continental and English Renaissances. This chapter sets out to redress such views by charting the diversity of Anglophone writing in the early modern period and by tracing the complex generic interconnections between texts by Irish authors from various ethnic backgrounds, by English writers who incorporate Irish scenes and characters despite lack of first-hand experience of Irish society, and by English travellers, soldiers, settlers and colonists who spent periods of time in the country. It will further be contended that Irish writing in this era, despite its intimate links with English literary practices, constitutes a discrete tradition whose peculiar characteristics are instigated by local political and social concerns. In short, this overview of Irish literature in English will chart the first emergence of a circumscribed, indigenous Anglophone culture during the sixteenth century and its subsequent growth and further development by the end of the seventeenth century. By 1690 a distinctive but multi-faceted corpus in English had evolved that was shaped by the modalities of local experience and the turbulent cultural and political interactions of the Renaissance age.

The degree to which writing in the early modern period may easily be aligned with national allegiances and lines of demarcation has been much debated. For some it is anachronistic to import nineteenth-century notions of the nation-state and the related phenomenon of a unitary and self-contained national culture into analysis of the sixteenth and seventeenth centuries. Moreover, simply using place of birth as a means of fixing the provenance of an author or of staking out the boundaries of Irish writing proves insufficient in this era. Many of the writers examined in this chapter led peripatetic existences and produced work that evinced a complex awareness of the precarious and conflicted nature of identity and of the divided readerships that they target, situated severally in Ireland and in England. Even though lines of affiliation could be signalled by dedications to patrons and friends and by subtle permutations and inflections of literary genres, early modern writings nonetheless tend to straddle boundaries, whether geographical, artistic, ideological or political. Hence, *The Faerie Queene* (1596) by Edmund Spenser may be seen at once as a veiled rendering of the anxieties of the New English planter in late sixteenth-century Ireland and as a product of the charged, self-fashioning aesthetics of the Elizabethan court. In a similar manner, the heroic tragedies of Roger Boyle, first earl of Orrery (1621–79), *The Generall* (1661) and *Henry V* (1664), and his sprawling romance, *Parthenissa* (1651–69), while catering for English tastes and perspectives also unfold plots that capture the shifting and unstable political allegiances that typify Restoration Ireland.

Even though such doubleness may be mooted as one of the primary hallmarks of Irish writing in the one hundred and forty years of literary production surveyed here, this chapter will be concerned less with pinpointing an unchanging set of features linking the multiple texts under review than with tracing their involvement in a varying array of conflicts over 'symbolic power'. According to Pierre Bourdieu, symbolic power operates in two ways: it allows groups to achieve coherence by inculcating in their members a unifying set of mental structures and tastes, and it also aids them in the quest for political and ideological dominance when they impose this world-view and use it as a gauge for devaluing alternative value systems and cultures.[2] Questions of fealty and allegiance are, as a consequence, of foremost concern in the works treated here. Sixteenth- and seventeenth-century Irish writing establishes its pedigree through prominent and elaborate dedications to patrons and powerful associates, through aligning itself with a precisely configured network of political interests and by foregrounding and playing with its literary affiliations and antecedents. Further, it will be contended that these texts are distinguished by a pronounced readiness to remould literary conventions and genres to encode the entangled historical and political contexts which inflect them.

The Anglophone literature of early modern Ireland thus constitutes what Arthur Marotti terms a 'social textuality' in which the exchange of manuscripts or printed works enacts a struggle over perception, symbolic capital and political power.[3] Moreover, while the circulation of texts permits the consolidation of group identities, it also opens up fissures within them. Irish writings and the discourse about Ireland in this period have often been seen as neatly according with the *mentalités* of four main cohorts, the English, the Old English, that is descendants of the original twelfth-century Anglo-Norman invaders, the native Irish and the New English, those colonists who settled in the country in the late sixteenth century and were fired with a new urgency to control and dominate it.[4] Although the existence of these clashing cultural and ideological fields of interest will certainly be borne out by the historical survey that follows, their friability and points of convergence will also become evident.

Tudor Ireland, 1550–1603

A statute passed by a meeting of the Irish parliament on 18 June 1541 declared that Henry VIII 'shall in future be reputed and acknowledged to be the King of Ireland, as in truth he always was'.[5] This milestone declaratory act was aimed at reinforcing English sovereignty, curbing papal jurisdiction and ensuring greater obedience on the part of both Old English and native Irish subjects. It marked a significant shift in the relations between the two countries and ushered in an active policy of cultural and political assimilation that was to be pursued by successive Tudor monarchs and their Irish viceroys throughout the sixteenth century. However, the legislative transformation of Ireland from a refractory lordship into a unified kingdom governed by the English crown could not by fiat create consensus or resolve the problem of enforcing the religious and political conformity that this new prerogative demanded. Moreover, a striking feature of the Dublin parliamentary proceedings of 1541 was that they were translated into Irish, thereby paradoxically endorsing the biculturalism of many of the Old English representatives in the house.

The experimental narratives written during the late Edwardian reign variously shadow this altered political vision which views Ireland both as an indivisible aspect of the realm of England and as a place apart. The poet, printer and Protestant apologist William Baldwin (*c*.1518–63?) is primarily remembered as the chief author of *A Mirror for Magistrates* (1559), but he is also credited with creating the first English prose fiction, *A Marvelous Hystory Intitulede, Beware the Cat*.[6] Although completed by 1553, this latter work was probably suppressed under the Marian regime and not finally published until 1570. It is telling that Baldwin's protean text, which melds beast fable, satire, oral narrative, a medieval tale of wonders, anti-Catholic invective and earnest Protestant apologetic, jumpcuts from its setting, a printing house situated beside a public gallows in Aldersgate in London, to Ireland. The text hence shifts from scenes of division in Edwardian England – suggestively encapsulated in the reference to the thriving printing trade and the spectacle of the bodies of those recently hung for their role in the 1551 Prayerbook rebellions – to its neighbouring colony. The initial instalment of Baldwin's intricate series of embedded narratives concerns the fateful strangling of a hapless Irish kern by his own cat. This violent fate is a retaliation for his killing of the legendary Grimalkin, the king of the cats, during a raid on his master's enemy. Through this inaugural narrative, cats are associated, not only with barbarity and Catholic superstition, but also with the internal dissension in Irish society. The kern 'Patrick Apore' is identified as a servant of John Butler who is engaged in a feud with Cahir Mac Art Kavanagh. The subversive anti-world of necromancy and lethally anthropomorphic cats is hence intertwined with local power struggles between Anglo-Norman and native Irish chieftains. Ironically too, these were the very factions courted by successive viceregal regimes in Ireland. Cahir Mac Art Kavanagh, for example, was amongst the Irish lords present in the Commons when the 1541 act asserting Henry VIII's jurisdiction over the country was approved.

After an excursus on Irish werewolves and witches, the topsy-turvy world of malevolent, shape-changing animals and humans is tracked back to London. Master Streamer, the naïve prelate who is the main protagonist, becomes privy to the cacophonous language of local cats by dint of taking a magic potion and eavesdrops on the trial of Mouse-Slayer who recounts her meddlesome exploits in self-defence and is subsequently acquitted. Even though the violent unruliness of the feline world in part exemplifies the potential threat represented by Catholics, the Irish and domestic recusancy, the political allegory of Beware the Cat remains curiously indeterminate, especially as in some cases the cats act not out of malice but in order to redress wrongdoing or to seek justice. In like manner, Ireland has an ambivalent valency in this text: it functions as a displaced version of English religious disputes and is itself depicted as a site of intractable conflict. However, it also provides a necessary frame for Baldwin's own subversive imaginings and doctrinal views and anchors the new mode of fictionality that he invents.

The degree to which the Reformation reinforced negative stereotypes about the Irish becomes increasingly evident in other Protestant mid-century writings. In the work of John Bale (1495–1563) religious prejudices compound political and cultural divides. Bale, who was born in Suffolk, was originally a Carmelite priest but converted to the reformed faith in the 1530s and thereafter became an assiduous champion of this new religion. He was appointed bishop of Ossory on 2 February 1553 but his ill-fated proselytising mission was cut short when, by his account, he was forced to flee for his life in August of the same year. *The Vocacyon of Johan Bale to the Bishoprick of Ossorie His Persecucions in the Same and Finall Delyveraunce* was completed shortly afterwards and published in December 1553.[7] Its frontispiece, which depicts a peaceable 'English Christian' confronted by a sword-wielding 'Irish Papist', sums up the dichotomies that define his pungent autobiographical account of his stay in the country with its attacks on priests who are 'unshamfast whorekeepers' and 'playe the buggery knaves'. His narrative is a fusion of saint's life, historical chronicle and spiritual diary. It prefigures the Puritan spiritual autobiographies of the seventeenth century and like them blends a vigorous realism with religious reflection. Bale styles himself as a beleaguered divine who valiantly combats Irish resistance to the new religious dispensation. He tries to offset the slackness of local clergy, whom he roundly denounces for their gluttony, lechery and idolatry, with his zealous preaching. As in Baldwin's text, the narrative resorts readily to fantastical anecdote. Thus, a story about how the drunken bishop of Galway was tricked into baptising a dog who had been disguised in a sheet serves to ridicule Catholic ritual.

The crisis which precipitated Bale's departure from Kilkenny was the murder of five of his servants whom he had dispatched to harvest hay on the feast of the Virgin's nativity. The narrative quickly converts the affecting description of this violent loss into an exemplum of Irish apostasy and of miraculous escape by the author. Likewise, the conclusion attempts to cast his Irish experiences and subsequent exile as a providential story of deliverance from an Irish Babylon and as a token that the 'sorrowful church of England' will prevail. However, a digression about the 'crueltie and fearcenesse' of native kerns and gallowglasses, who are key tropes of Irish otherness in the colonial texts of this period, indicates the difficulty of seamlessly subsuming violent conflict into a consolatory homily.[8]

As Alan Fletcher has shown, there was a long-standing tradition of religious pageantry in Dublin and elsewhere, particularly in association with prominent church feast-days such as Corpus Christi.[9] A collateral effect of Bale's short sojourn in Kilkenny was the impetus that he gave to a renewed tradition of public theatrical performance there. On 20 August 1553, three of his plays, *God's Promises, Johan Baptystes Preachynge* and *The Temptacyon of Our Lorde*, which had been published in 1547, were enacted for the first time at the market cross in the town.[10] Notwithstanding his contempt for the false theatricality of the Catholic mass, Bale in these works appropriated the stagecraft and affective structures of medieval mystery plays but injected them with the doctrinal fervour of the new reformed religion. The author himself acted the part of the Prolocutor who declaimed the hortatory and pointedly anti-Catholic prologues and epilogues. The injunction in *God's Promises* to abandon superficial belief in favour of a truth that can guide the 'inwarde stomake' captures the ideological intent of these texts and the altered values that Bale wished to disseminate, while their frequent scenes of conversion, virtuous resistance and repentance symbolically re-enact the means by which he hoped to implant this new faith. However, equally, unyielding figures such as Pharisaeus and Sadducaeus in *Johan Baptystes Preachynge*, who refuse the benefits of reform and are consequently denounced as 'Hypocrytes' and 'Sodomytes', gesture at the hostilities in which the author found himself embroiled and the opposition that he encountered during his brief career in Ireland.

The Image of Ireland with a Discoverie of Woodkarne (1581) by John Derricke (*fl.* 1578) is a multi-form text that celebrates Sir Henry Sidney's second term as lord deputy in Ireland (1575–8) by casting him as a crusading hero who defeated intractable Irish rebels, including Shane O'Neill and Rory Óg O'More, and forced Turlough Luineach O'Neill into submission, thereby achieving peace in Ulster. In thus aligning his work with a militant Protestantism, Derricke obscures the troubled nature of Sidney's Irish political career, which had been beset by disputes especially about his taxation regime and came to an abrupt end when he was recalled from his post. The successive layers of the text span several self-exculpatory epistles dedicatory, variously directed at Sir Philip Sidney (son of Henry Sidney), an Irish audience and a general English readership, a sequence of poetic segments devoted to a history of the Irish woodkern and the defeat of Rory Óg O'More, and a concluding array of woodcuts with accompanying emblematic verses. The irregularity and episodic nature of this text thus mirror the prevarications and divisions of New English writing as it attempts to curry favour in court, reconcile events in Ireland with colonial ideology and appease Old English sensitivities. Ultimately, the composite structure of *The Image of Ireland*, its playful mythographies and genealogies of Irish savagery and the detailed precision of its engravings are at odds with its apocalypticism and promulgation of a virulent Protestant rhetoric of reproof and retribution.[11]

Likewise, Derricke's amplification of the familiar image of the Irish woodkern or footsoldier threatens to turn it into an all-encompassing cipher of evil. The poem, however, counters the vision of unremitting barbarism which it courts, by conjuring up a lurid prosopopoeia in which Rory Óg O'More in the manner of a convicted traitor denounces himself; his self-confession, as Patricia Palmer has argued, acts as a carefully contrived fantasy of submission and endorses the zealous militancy attributed to Sidney.[12] This strategy of containment, whereby the demonised rebel passes sentence on himself, suppresses many aspects of the historical record. In particular, it silently masks Sidney's infamous use of brutality in March 1578 when a gathering of the O'Mores was lured to a mass assembly at Mullaghmast and then killed by English forces.[13] The engravings further conceal these contradictions by underscoring the ability of the Irish viceroy to unite the countervailing facets of the worthy Renaissance governor in his several functions as diplomat, politician and man of action. The scenes in Plate XII in which he parleys with Turlough Luineach O'Neill symmetrically offset the martial vigour imbuing the depiction of Sidney's exit from Dublin Castle in Plate VI.

Derricke's pointed mythologisation of an Elizabethan deputy as a compound of loyal servant and reforming zealot provides a key to understanding the allegiances evidenced in the numerous dedications of sixteenth-century Irish texts to the Sidney family and their circle. These inscriptions track not just the pathways of literary clientage but also the peculiarly vexed interaction of cultural exchange and political influence in early modern Ireland. Symbolically such invocations reference the ideals of humanism, fealty and ardent Protestantism linked with prominent figures such as the Sidneys, but they also necessarily imbricate themselves in the struggles for power, clashing loyalties and ideological battles of Elizabethan courtiers and colonial administrators. The extensive but unfinished memoir by Sir Henry Sidney (1529–86) describing his Irish service, *Sir Henry Sidney's Book 1582*, composed as a missive to Sir Francis Walsingham, captures the nature of such intrigues and provides a telling counter-perspective to Derricke's account of him as the all-conquering scourge of Irish rebels.[14] Contrary to *The Image of Irelande*, he characterises his terms as lord deputy not as an apocalyptic clash between the godly and the ungodly but as a spiralling cycle of losses rather than gains. Images of the voluntary submission of loyal Irish subjects to Sidney alternate with descriptions of his campaigns against traitors such as Shane O'Neill and Rory Óg O'More and his conflicts with both Irish and English political enemies, including Thomas Butler, tenth earl of Ormond and Sir William Gerrard. The providentialism of Derricke's poem is replaced by a view of history as a 'tragical discourse' and an inevitable sequence of failure and disappointment. Sidney's self-construction as a loyal statesman, undermined by Irish treachery and English factionalism, allows him in his retrospective summation to style himself as a tragic victim of fortune and of the contingencies of political rivalry. Despite his exercise of a Machiavellian *virtù* or civic spirit, his aggrieved reckoning shows him merely to have garnered royal disfavour and material loss; in the discourse of Ireland loyalty and disaffection dangerously shadow each other.

Similar patterns emerge in the writings of Sir Philip Sidney (1554–86) who visited Ireland in July 1576 in the company of Walter Devereux, first earl of Essex, the journey occasioned by the latter's acquisition of Irish estates despite the bloody debacle of the massacre of Rathlin island that had ended his attempts to create a plantation in Antrim. During his sojourn, Sidney came into contact in addition with the warring aspects of Irish society as he was involved in the campaigns against Richard Burke, second earl of Clanrickard, and also had occasion to meet Granuaile (Grace O'Malley), 'a most famous feminine sea captain' as his father's memoirs style her. In Sonnet 30 of *Astrophel and Stella* (1591) Sidney lists the question as to 'How Ulster likes of that same golden bit / Wherewith my father once made it half tame' in a catalogue of the perplexing political issues that distract him from the contemplation of his love for Stella. Notwithstanding his vigorous and pragmatic defence of his father's plan to impose 'cess' or land tax in an earlier tract, 'Discourse of Irish Affairs' (1577), his later poetic assessment portrays Ireland as an emblem of futility, significant only as a counterpoint to the constancy of his secret love. Metonymically, the problem of Irish disorder is commuted in Sidney's sonnet but its residual legacy is still evident in the painful wrangles of Petrarchan love that are equally incurable.

Chronicles of England, Scotlande and Irelande (1577 / 87) by Raphael Holinshed (d.1580?) had the revolutionary aim of producing a compendium containing the histories of the three kingdoms of the British realm in answer to the Renaissance vogue for universal cosmographies. However, the uneasy juxtaposition of Old English and New English narratives in the revised 1587 edition foregrounds the dichotomies as much as the commonalities within the *Irish Chronicles*. While the sections on Ireland in the 1577 volume are compiled by Sir Richard Stanihurst (d.1618), a member of a powerful Old English, Dublin Catholic family, the expanded 1587 text ends with a 'Supplie of the Irish Chronicles extended to this present yeare of Our Lord 1586' by the English Protestant John Hooker (1526–1601) who represents many of the values espoused by New English settlers. Both Holinshed and Stanihurst pay homage to Henry Sidney in their epistles dedicatory, thus linking their undertaking with the regime of conquest and plantation with which Sidney was coupled. Stanihurst, however, complicates this association by prominently acknowledging his indebtedness to *Two Bookes of the Histories of Ireland* (1633) by Edmund Campion (1540–81). This text was composed in Dublin in 1570–1 while the author, still an Anglican divine, was a guest of the Stanihurst family and was first published posthumously in Ireland in 1633 by Sir James Ware. In creating this cross-alliance, Stanihurst advertises the dependence of his 'iagged hystorie of a ragged Wealepublicke' on the thinking of his former teacher at Oxford, whose activities as recusant and agent of the Catholic Counter Reformation would lead to his execution in 1581.

Consonant with this insistence on dissent, Stanihurst's narrative centrally concerns itself with outlining the development of the Old English as a distinctive ethnic group and with asserting their hegemony over Irish history and culture. To this end, his chorography depicts the country as divided into 'an English pale and Irishry', and hence as split between civilisation and savagery. For Stanihurst the roots of this divide are as much cultural as political: above all, he opposes the purity and ancient pedigree of the Chaucerian English of the Pale and elsewhere to the 'gybbrishing' of the Irish. Unlike later New English commentators, his dismissive treatment of the habits and customs of the 'meere Irish commonly called the wyld Irish' is perfunctory; he concentrates instead on the ethnography and history of the Pale in general and of Dublin in particular, 'the beautie and eye of Irelande'. A foreshortened survey of the history of Ireland prior to 1169 is followed by a lengthy description of the twelfth-century Norman invasion, while his detailing of the reign of Henry VIII focuses on several notable Old English families including the Ormonds and the Barnewalls but gives particular prominence to the Geraldines, the Kildare Fitzgeralds, for whom he had acted as schoolmaster. Amongst the numerous catalogues of towns and families that he compiles is a key listing of the 'names or surnames of the learned men and authors of Ireland'. In Stanihurst's portrayal, the Old English, while remaining loyal to the crown, possess a separate and distinctive cultural history; their Englishness runs in parallel to, and athwart, an Irish identity whose lineaments he also insistently traces.

By the time the supplement to the *Irish Chronicles* appeared in 1587 Campion had been beheaded in Tyburn and Stanihurst, under suspicion of intrigue and necromancy, had been driven into exile on the continent. Irish historiography had become a similarly devalued mode in the eyes of John Hooker. In an epistle dedicatory addressed to Sir Walter Ralegh, he describes Irish historical records as a 'tragedy of cruelties to be abhorred' in contradistinction to the inherently moral structures of British history. The Irish past is of value only for its admonitory function in yielding examples of God's 'severe judgement' against traitors and rebels. Hooker first travelled to Ireland in 1567 as the legal agent of Sir Peter Carew to press his claims to estates in Munster and Leinster on the basis of titles traced back to the twelfth century. If the Norman conquest of Ireland is of moment for Stanihurst as a legitimation of the Old English families in Ireland, it is of importance to Hooker as a ratification for the colonising aims of the New English. Consequently, he supplements the *Irish Chronicle* with his translation of Giraldus Cambrensis's *The Conquest of Ireland* (*Expugnatio Hibernica*), an apologia for the Anglo-Norman invasion written around 1169, that assesses the reasons for the partial nature of Henry II's annexation of the country. If, as Richard McCabe claims, Giraldus's text has an almost typological status for Hooker, then his retracing and updating of the trajectories posited by Stanihurst allows him further to extend his biblical remodelling of events with its reliance on a vehement Protestantism.[15] Recent Irish history is thus reconfigured as a spiritual drama revolving around conflicts between good and evil. Through this Reformation optics, the heroic activities of the spiritual elect, a succession of lord deputies and military commanders, including Sir Edward Bellingham, Sir Henry Sidney, Sir Humphrey Gilbert and Sir John Perrot, are opposed to the innate depravity and rebelliousness of the fallen, both the native Irish and the Old English. Panegyric for English leaders alternates with denunciations of the treacherous inhabitants who atavistically relapse into evil 'as dogs . . . returne to their vomit and as swine to their durt and puddles'. Where Stanihurst concludes his chronicle with the reconciliation of the Ormonds and Fitzgeralds, Hooker terminates his 'short discours and rhapsodie' with a climactic account of the defeat of the house of Desmond. He construes the devastating famine in Munster ensuing from the rebellion of the Fitzgeralds 'as a iust iudgement of God upon such a Pharoicall and stifnecked people'. Irish history is thus co-opted to a drama of salvation in which only the virtuous, primarily the New English, prevail.

Many of those involved in the sixteenth-century colonisation of Ireland had recourse to the resources of humanist scholarship and learning in order imaginatively to reframe their experiences and to provide them with ideological underpinnings. Lodowyck Bryskett (*c.*1546–1612) served as clerk of the council of Ireland under Sir Henry Sidney in 1571 and was appointed secretary of the Munster council by Sir Arthur Grey in 1582. His *A Discourse of Civill Life: Containing the Ethike Part of Morall Philosophie. Fit for the Instructing of a Gentleman in the Course of a Virtuous Life* (1606), written in Ireland in the 1580s and dedicated to Sir William Cecil and Sir Arthur Grey, is a translation of Giovanni Battista Giraldi's *Tre Dialoghi della Vita Civile*, a text about the moral training of young gentlemen in the service of the commonwealth. Bryskett interleaved the Italian original with the philosophical exchanges of the visitors, including Edmund Spenser, Captain Warham St Leger and Sir Thomas Norris, to his cottage possibly on the outskirts of Dublin. Through such juxtaposition, Bryskett's Irish garden is transformed into a vista of Renaissance order, while conversely the discussion of the moral qualities of a civil society becomes implicitly a commentary on their absence in Ireland. Bryskett's 'The Mourning Muse of Thestylis', a pastoral elegy on the death of Philip Sidney, similarly transposes a classical form to an Irish context and includes Irish nymphs and the 'gurgling sound / Of Liffies tumbling streames' in a universal cosmography of grief on the loss of a friend who is also a model of heroic virtue.

The Irish career of Sir Geoffrey Fenton (c.1539–1608) began in 1580 during the Munster rebellion. From then until his death in Dublin in 1608 he was active in several military campaigns and held various posts including that of surveyor-general. Fenton's translation of Francesco Guicciardini's *Storia D'Italia* (1561), *The Historie of Guicciardin Containing the Warres of Italie*, was first published in 1579 but subsequently revised during the course of his Irish residence. A third, corrected edition was published posthumously in London in 1618. In dedicating his work to Elizabeth I as 'soveraign Emperesse over several nations and languages', Fenton links his translation with colonialist and humanist expansiveness and deems it especially apposite for an English readership because the density of Guicciardini's treatment of Italy in the decades following the French invasion in 1494 and his probing of human motivation allow a widened understanding of international politics and of the forces of history. The author of *Eclogues, Epitaphs, and Sonnets* (1563), Barnabe Googe (1540–94), who first visited Ireland in 1574 and held the post of provost-marshal of Connacht from 1582 to 1584, sees the function of translation in another light. His 'increased' version of Konrad Heresbach's *Res Rusticae Libri Quatuor, Four Books of Husbandries* (1577), which is dedicated to Lord Deputy Sir William Fitzwilliam, styles itself as an eclectic compendium about the *otium* of country life that is a necessary counterweight to the rigours of public office and of military engagements in Ireland. The most remarkable translation emanating from sixteenth-century Ireland is Richard Stanihurst's *The First Four Bookes of Virgil His Aeneis*, a rendering into hexameters of the Latin epic, which was published in Leiden in 1586. The linguistic exuberance of his text is its overriding feature; its use of archaisms, neologisms, the intermingling of the vernacular and the lofty and the frequent resort to protracted onomatopoeia all add to its deliberately overdetermined and disorienting quality. Ultimately, his idiosyncratic version of the *Aeneid* may be seen as a literary experiment that interfuses the energies of Tudor English and Hiberno-English in order to create a hybrid work that manifests its Irish as well as its classical and European origins.

By contrast, Edmund Spenser (1552–99) seems at pains to efface the historical contexts of *The Faerie Queene* (1590/96), an allegorical epic which was written against the backdrop of the Munster rebellion and plantation. The panoply of dedicatory sonnets to members of inner court circles in Britain, such as Sir Christopher Hatton and Lord Burleigh, and to prominent Old English and New English lords, such as Thomas Butler, tenth earl of Ormond, and Sir John Norris, as well as the dual dedications of the 1590 edition to Elizabeth I and Sir Walter Ralegh also seem designed to obscure the poem's allegiances. However, notwithstanding this overt reticence, Ireland may be claimed to be bound into the ideological anxieties, symbolic patterns and narrative dynamics of *The Faerie Queene*. It is at once a referential field haunting the text and a generative core for the intricate plots and allegories that Spenser sets in motion. In particular, the obdurate indeterminacies of *The Faerie Queene* and its obsessive revisiting of ambiguous clashes between the forces of good and evil and of civility and savagery replicate New English assessments of the intractability of Ireland and of its endemic and contagious wildness. The moral and theological questions that the poem debates and the mythographic narratives that it unfurls hence restage the political and ideological problems of colonial Ireland.

Many scenes may be cited to exemplify the complex operations of Spenserian allegory and the slippage which constantly threatens to undermine its coherence. In I.vi, Una, the embodiment of truth and of the Protestant church, is rescued from the Saracen knight Sansloy by a race of satyrs and fauns who have many of the traits attributed to the Irish. This 'salvage nation' is depicted as uncouth, devoid of language or culture and prone to obdurate errancy. Instead of recognising the revealed truth, they turn Una into an idol and start to worship her. Their credulousness hence, on one level, denotes ignorance and superstition; yet, on another level, their primitive innocence has the power to subvert and misrecognise the unity that she symbolises. The text castigates their difference of view but it cannot wholly erase its effects. Similar ambiguities emerge in II.xii when Guyon, the knight of temperance, destroys 'with rigour pittilesse' the Bower of Blisse, the island dwelling of Acrasia, who epitomises the evils of lust, enervation and female depravity against which he is pitted. His act of regenerative violence akin to the military campaigns pursued by successive Elizabethan viceroys is designed to restore order and to obliterate the evil of this savage other world. However, in a discomfiting aftermath, the 'donghill kind', the people turned into beasts by Acrasia, refuse to be redeemed and have to be abandoned to their abjection and apostasy. While their degeneracy merely reinforces the probity of Spenser's crusading knight of temperance, it also marks the limits of his political efficacy and of the moral economy of the poem.

Spenser came to Ireland as secretary to Lord Arthur Grey in 1580. He held several administrative offices including clerk of the Faculties in the Court of Chancery and clerk of the council of Munster. In 1589, as an undertaker in the Munster plantation, he took up residence in Kilcolman, County Cork on an estate of 3,028 acres deriving from the escheated lands of the earl of Desmond. The first three books of *The Faerie Queene* were published in 1590 and the following three in 1596. The latter section of the poem is hence composed in part against the backdrop of the crisis in Ulster precipitated by the increasing resistance of Hugh O'Neill, earl of Tyrone, to English rule. A growing pessimism about the course of Irish affairs is evident as a consequence in the second instalment of the poem. In Book V, Artegall, the representative of justice, and his confederate, the Iron Man, Talus, consistently use physical force and resort to beheadings and dismemberings to establish equitable governance. Although Artegall's release of the suppliant Irena from the tyrannical Grantorto is in part a vindication of Arthur Grey's aggressive Irish campaigns, his emasculation by the Amazonian queen, Radigund, who forces him to wear women's weeds and perform the demeaning task of sewing, raises the spectre of engulfment by the forces of otherness. Moreover, the joyous reception of the liberated Irena by her people who claim 'her as their true Leige and Princesse naturall', while it mobilises an ideal image of a united body politic and of native Irish submission to English rule, also opens up questions about the problem of dominion in the country. Close scrutiny reveals Irena to be a complex allegorical aggregate: she is at once a symbol of English sovereignty, a figure of Elizabeth I in her role as queen of Ireland, a projection of the New English political vision, a blank abstraction for the people and land of Ireland and a myth of colonial dominance. The failure of Artegall to retain his heroic status at the end of Book V is an indication that the friction between all of these competing aspects of Irish affairs cannot readily be dissipated. *Two Cantos of Mutabilitie* also projects the Irish landscape as a mythic space which is disrupted by the rival territorial claims of Mutabilitie and of Jove. The judgement of Dame Nature against the goddess sanctions the necessity for dispossession, but the correspondent tale of the trespass of Faunus suggests that Ireland remains a fallen world rather than a site of cosmic order. Spenser's shorter poems similarly construct competing views of Ireland. *Amoretti and Epithalamion* (1595), marking his courtship of and marriage to Elizabeth Boyle in June 1594, depicts his Munster home as a place of pleasure and erotic dalliance, while the political complaint 'Colin Clouts Come Home Againe' (1595) sees Ireland not only as a place of exile but also, as Louis Montrose has contended, as a kind of homeland or 'domestic domain'.[16]

Although allusions to Ireland in the plays of Shakespeare (1564–1616) seem simply to mirror negative stereotypes – such as Dromio of Syracuse's cartographic blazon charting the body of Nell, Adriana's kitchen maid, in *The Comedy of Errors* (1594) which locates the country 'in her buttocks . . . out by the bogs' (act 3, scene 2, 115–16) – the two historical tetralogies evince a preoccupation with colonial politics that goes beyond such conventionalism.[17] In these plays Ireland functions as an ambiguous off-stage site which exerts an impalpable but fateful influence. Its very invisibility paradoxically signals its determining role in British dynastic conflicts. Thus, in *Henry VI Part II* (c.1590), Jack Cade's rebellion and York's usurpation of the throne are both represented as an outcome of their engagement in Irish military action. In *Richard II* (1595), the king's pursuit of his 'Irish wars' (act 2, scene 1, 155) is portrayed as a misplaced absorption crystallising inherent flaws within his authority. The disruptive potential of encounters with 'rough rug-headed kernes' (act 2, scene 1, 156) is borne out by the coincidence of Bolingbroke's deposition of Richard with the latter's return from his Irish sortie. In *Henry V* (1599), Irishness similarly both delimits and threatens to undermine English identity. The ambiguous reply of Macmorris, the Irish soldier of Anglo-Norman descent, to Fluellen's question about the basis of his nationality positions him at once as a loyal British subject and as a disaffected Other, while the prospect of Essex's heroic return from Ireland 'bringing rebellion broachèd on a sword' (act 5, Chorus, 32) overlays desire for colonial dominance with the fear of anarchy transmitting itself to the realm of England.[18] Traces of the political anxieties inspired by the Elizabethan wars in Ireland are also evident in the peripheral figures and sub-plots of other plays of the period, such as the revengeful Irish kern who is the ally of Mordred in Thomas Hughes's *The Misfortunes of Arthur* (1587) and the involvement of the English adventurer Thomas Stukeley in a papal conspiracy to invade Ireland in *The Battle of Alcazar* (1589) by George Peele (1556–96).

A proliferation of texts anatomising Ireland and debating how it might most effectively be conquered was produced by English travellers, New English colonial administrators and soldiers in the Irish wars throughout the Tudor period. These include Andrew Boorde (1490–1549), *The Fyrst Boke of the Introduction of Knowledge* (c.1548), Edward Walshe (fl.1522), 'Conjectures Concerning the State of Ireland' (1552), Roland White, 'Discors Touching Ireland' (1569) and 'The Dyssorders of the Irishry' (1571), Robert Payne, 'A Briefe Description of Ireland'

(1590), Captain Thomas Lee, 'A Brief Declaration of the Government of Ireland' (c.1594), Nicholas Dawtrey, 'A Book of Questions and Answars Concerning the Warrs or Rebellions of the Kingdome of Irelande' (1597), the anonymous 'A Discourse of Ireland' (c.1599), and John Dymmok, 'A Treatice of Ireland' (c.1600). The copious works of the soldier-adventurer Thomas Churchyard (d.1604), who served in several Irish campaigns from the 1550s onwards, include *A Generall Rehearsall of Warres Called Churchyards Choise* (1579), *The Most True Report of James Fitz Morrice Death, and Other Like Offenders with a Brief Discourse of Rebellion* (1579), *The Miserie of Flaunders, Calamitie of Fraunce, Misfortune of Portugall, Unquietnes of Ireland, Troubles of Scotlande: and the Blessed State of England* (1579), *A Scourge For Rebels* (1584) and *The Fortunate Farewell to the Most Forward and Noble Earl of Essex* (1599). They combine vivid accounts of combat with panegryrical lyrics on the military prowess of figures such as Thomas Butler, earl of Ormond, and the earl of Essex.

Undoubtedly, the paramount Tudor discourse about Ireland is Edmund Spenser's *A View of the Present State of Ireland*, completed by 1598 but not published until 1633 by Sir James Ware. In their dialogue about the 'fatall destiny of that land', Spenser's interlocutors personify two seemingly divergent positions: the intemperate Irenius – the man of ire – is the mouthpiece for the New English experience of Ireland and radical Protestant thinking, while Eudoxus – the person of sound judgement – is the Englishman who upholds the precepts of enlightened humanism. Irenius's extremism, however, wins the day. His account of the lawlessness, 'licentious barbarism' and debased customs of the Irish is offered as unassailable proof that they can be saved only by violent means. *A View* ultimately presses home ancient rights of conquest sanctioned by Arthurian myth and Henry II's renewed subjugation of the Irish. The brutal logic of the insistence that reform can be brought about only 'by the sword' is exposed in the unflinching representation of famine in Munster in the aftermath of the Desmond rebellions which insinuates that the destitution of the Irish natives is not a side-effect of war but rather an expression of their moral condition. Sympathy shades seamlessly into revulsion in the haunting image of skeletal figures creeping forth from 'every corner of the woods and glynnes' to cannibalise their dead companions. The reality of suffering is thus converted into a gruesome admonitory parable. Yet, despite this advocacy of a seemingly absolutist political solution, *A View* is an inherently fractured text that veers between a vision of irremediable Irish barbarism and a prospect of a 'people so humbled and prepared . . . that they will and must yeeld to any ordinance that shall be given to them'. Further, its implicit critique of Elizabethan policy and contention that the Irish lord deputy should have 'uncontrouled power' suggest that the loyalism of the queen's New English subjects is conditional and that the ruthless expediency of its reformist proposals might mask an underlying disaffection. Similar faultlines are evident in *Solon His Follie, Or A Politique Discourse Touching the Reformation of Common-Weales Conquered, Declined or Corrupted* (1594), a dialogue by Richard Beacon (fl.1590–1611) who was likewise an undertaker in the Munster plantation and owned an estate in Waterford and Cork. Comparing Ireland to the Greek colony of Salamina, Beacon's allegory draws on Plutarch's apologia for Solon as a just lawgiver and leader and Machiavellian republicanism in order to validate the bellicose methods deemed requisite to effect a full reformation of the country. As in Spenser, the multiple contradictions of this discourse preclude closure. Beacon's narrator is jolted out of his colonising dream vision by 'the great noise and clattering of the weapons, and armour of the souldiers'. This culminating image both gestures at the urgency of the problems in Ireland and betrays the insidious reliance of the reformed Irish commonweal that he envisages upon military force.[19]

The literature of the late 1590s is coloured by the crisis of the Nine Years War and bears the strain of a period of conflict that threatened to topple English rule in Ireland. As a consequence, figurations of ambiguous rebels and treatments of atrocity predominate in this era. The anonymous play *Captain Thomas Stukeley* (1596) includes a portrait of a menacing Shane O'Neill as he lays siege to Drogheda. In 'Report of a Journey into the North of Ireland Written to Justice Carey' (1599) Sir John Harington (1560–1612) sketches his role in Sir William Warren's mission in October 1599 to broker peace with Hugh O'Neill. His fissured intelligence report on the Irish rebel alternates between suspicion, fascination with his exotic pastoral environment and admiration for his *sprezzatura*. Harington's gift of his 'English translation of Ariosto' to O'Neill's sons symbolically denotes his cultural ascendancy over them, but Tyrone's active interest in the text subtly subverts this authority and hints at his expert manipulation of his anglicised persona.[20] *The Dialogue of Silvynne and Peregrynne* (1597–8) by 'H.C.', Henry Chettle (fl.1560–1607), and the anonymous *The Supplication of the Blood of the English Most Lamentably Murdered in Ireland, Cryeng Out of the Yearth for Revenge* (1598), however, reject even such tentative attempts at reformation. In keeping with the pessimism and apocalyptic outrage induced by the struggles of the late 1590s, they stress the unremitting bloodthirstiness of the Irish and luridly rehearse the atrocities perpetrated by opponents cast now not just as uncouth but as indisputably evil and diabolic.[21]

The accession of James I to the Civil War period, 1603–1640

Ric: Nugent's Cynthia Containing Direfull Sonnets, Madrigalls, and Passionate Intercourses, describing his repudiate affections expressed in Love's Owne Language (1604) was composed by Richard Nugent (*c*.1564/5–1615), a member of a long-established Old English dynasty with estates in County Westmeath. Although little is known about his personal biography, his familial history typifies the hybrid and warring loyalties of the descendants of the Anglo-Normans. His father, Nicholas Nugent (*d*.1582), was charged with involvement in the rebellion led by his nephew William Nugent and hanged for treason in Dublin in 1582. Similarly, his cousin Christopher Nugent (1544–1602) aroused constant suspicion on account of his recusancy and intimate knowledge of Gaelic society and culture and died in Dublin Castle while awaiting trial for treason. Likely to have been written in the closing years of the sixteenth century, Nugent's sonnet sequence which records his hopeless love for an unyielding mistress subtly transposes and recontours many of the reigning conceits of Tudor poetry. His Cynthia unites the dual roles of Elizabeth I and a local Irishwoman, the abstract Petrarchan topography is infiltrated by shadowy images of the landscapes of the Pale, and the exile that he laments is not the displacement of the New English colonist but the deracination brought about by removal to England or Europe. In superimposing a painful Irish love affair on English courtly entanglements, it is implied that Cynthia simultaneously allegorises the poet's love of Ireland and his loyalty to the English crown. His account of the psychic damage wrought by his beloved's cruelty points to the strain involved in maintaining these dual and often incompatible allegiances. Nugent's sonnets thus indirectly limn the disgruntlement of the Old English who are frequently forced into loyal rebellion throughout this period and constantly have to absolve themselves of charges of treachery and recusancy. The exchange of sonnets amongst an imagined coterie of friends that concludes the volume adds further dimensions to its suggestive politics while playfully unravelling many of its metaphors. Despite the cyncial dismissal of his love affair by his correspondents, Nugent reasserts his devotion but leaves moot whether the Cynthia he serves is the English monarch or the locally rooted ethnic and tribal attachments of the Old English. The Petrarchan themes of loss, supplantation and anguished devotion are thus deftly remodelled in *Cynthia*. They provide an expressive but oblique rhetoric that allows the identity and patriotic fervour of the Old English to be etched, while also charting the embattled political fortunes of this community.

The career of the soldier and writer Barnaby Rich (1542–1617) similarly straddles the Elizabethan and Jacobean eras. His prodigious output, encompassing accounts of warfare in Ireland, Protestant polemic and stirring satirical and ethnographical descriptions of the country and its inhabitants, includes *Allarme to England foreshewing what perilles are procured, where the people live without regarde of martiall lawe* (1578), *Greenes Newes both from Heaven and hell Prohibited the first for writing of bookes, and banished out of the last for displaying of conny-catchers* (1593), *A Short Survey of Ireland truly discovering who it is that hath so armed the hearts of that people with disobedience to their Prince* (1609), *A New Description of Ireland wherein is described the disposition of the Irish wherunto they are inclined* (1610), *A Catholicke Conference Betweene Syr Tady Mac Mareall, A Popish priest of Waterforde and Patricke Plaine, a young student in Trinity Colledge by Dublin in Ireland* (1612), *The Irish Hubbub, or, the English Hue and Crie breifely pursuing the base conditions, and most notorious offences of this vile, vaine and wicked age* (1617), *A True and a Kind Excuse written in defence of that booke, intituled A New Description of Ireland* (1612), *The honestie of this age prooving by good circumstance, that the world was never honest till now* (1614), and *My ladies looking glass wherein may be discerned a wise man from a bad: and the true resemblance of vice masked under the vizard of vertue* (1616). As Eugene Flanagan has argued, this is a singular body of work, not just because it spans a period of forty years, but because it evidences a consistent and self-conscious appropriation of radical Protestant rhetoric and a playful engagement with the hidden politics and symbolic dimensions of form.[22] Conjoining the roles of soldier and self-appointed lay evangelist, Rich is insistent on his adherence to revealed truth and, contrary to the secularism of other New English commentators, his account of the altering circumstances in Ireland is shaped by an unswervingly religious stance. His trenchant denunciations of the depravity of native culture are fuelled by his detestation of the corruption and falsehood of Catholicism. Even though in *A New Description of Ireland* Rich protests his affection for his Dublin Catholic friends, he nonetheless insists on the need for a complete religious reformation of the country. Likewise, his rueful reflections on his vituperative anti-papistry in *A True and a Kind Excuse* point to the self-reflexive nature of his writing and his awareness of the sensitivities of his Irish readership, but do not allow him to relinquish his sectarian righteousness. Rich's impassioned advocacy of Protestantism is complemented by his adroit manipulations and inventive reworkings of literary structures. *Greenes Newes* uses the device of a cony-catching pamphlet to launch an attack on the laxity of the Church of Ireland, *A Catholic Conference* subtly transposes a humanist dialogue into a treatise about religious reform and *A Short Survey of Ireland* produces a vigorous tract about the Pope as Antichrist in lieu of the topographical overview flagged in the title. Eschewing religious denunciations, *A Discourse of Ireland* (1620) by Luke Gernon (*fl.*1620) also fuses literary modes, albeit in a more haphazard manner. It uneasily blends chorographical description with ethnographic commentary and uses a triumphalist colonialist rhetoric to convey personal animus and an adversarial politics that does not harbour any prospect of reconciliation or reform.

By contrast, the discussion by Sir Francis Bacon (1561–1626) and Sir John Davies (1569–1626) of the unfolding schemes for the plantation of Ulster in the wake of the defeat of Hugh O'Neill and Hugh O'Donnell at the Battle of Kinsale in 1601 and the subsequent flight of the Northern leaders in September 1607 affects a more measured assessment of things.[23] Bacon's 'Certain Considerations Touching the Plantation in Ireland Presented to His Majesty, 1606' (1609) rationalises the conquest of Ireland in the light of the new polity of Britain represented by the Stuart state. The symbolic union of the three kingdoms of England, Ireland and Scotland brought about by the succession of James I is seen also as indemnifying the further prospect of harmony heralded by the plantation of Ulster. Bacon pointedly rejects militarism and the possibility of an 'effusion of blood'. Instead the Northern plantation is to be effected through the smooth replacement of the harp of Ireland by the civilising force of the British 'harp of Orpheus', thereby cancelling native opposition and barbarism.[24] The poet and lawyer John Davies occupied the posts of solicitor general and attorney general in Ireland between 1603 and 1619 and was one of the chief legal strategists behind the plantation of Ulster. In a manner akin to Bacon he uses the resources of forensic rhetoric in *A Discovery of the True Causes Why Ireland Was Never Entirely Subdued and Brought Under Obedience of the Crown of England Until the Beginning of His Majesty's Happy Reign* (1612) to elucidate the conflicts of Irish history and to corroborate the 'perfection of the conquest' realised by the Jacobean regime. To his eyes, the extension of the common law to Ireland is a crucial factor in its subjugation as it transforms the Irish from rebels and outlaws into British subjects. Like many other texts of this period, *A Discovery* deploys tropes of concord in order to erase the inveterate divisions fostered by the country such as the split between the Old and New English, 'the English in bloud and the English in birth'. Even geography is put to account in Davies's rational mythography that aims to glorify a triumphantly united polity. The ultimate goal of colonialism is thus declared to be such a thoroughgoing political and cultural assimilation of the Irish that 'there will bee no difference or distinction, but the Irish sea betwixt us'.

Representations of Irishness in early Jacobean theatre, however, continue to stress the inassimilable alterity of the country. The London-born playwright and pirate Lording Barry (1580–1629) is reputedly of Irish descent and his city comedy *Ram-Alley, or, Merrie Tricks* (1611) has traditionally been seen as the first Irish play on the English stage. It was performed by the boys' theatre company, the Children of the King's Revels, at the Whitefriars venue that he co-owned. The gulling plot unfolds the stratagems of William Small-Shanks as he tricks Throat, the lawyer who has ruined him, into marrying his 'punk', and inveigles Taffata, a wealthy, lascivious widow, into accepting him as consort in lieu of his elderly father. In keeping with the defiantly anti-puritanical stance of the prologue and epilogue, the action depicts a giddily amoral urban under-world of schemers and prostitutes in which pleasure and deceit are rewarded rather than held up for castigation. The thief and murderer Macshane in *The First Part of The True And Honorable History Of The Life of Sir John Oldcastle, The Good Lord Cobham* (1599) by Michael Drayton, Richard Hathway, Antony Munday and Robert Wilson also belongs to a criminal counter-sphere, while the minor Irish characters in the plays of Thomas Dekker (*c.*1572–1632) derive from the marginal domain of servants and vagrant tradesmen such as Bryan the footman in *Honest Whore, Part 2* (*c.*1605) and the costermongers Andelocia and Shadowe in *Old Fortunatus* (1599). However, the drama from the later Jacobean period indicates a possible shift in attitudes. *The Welsh Embassador* (1623) by Dekker stresses the loyalty of Ireland and its leaders such as Leinster.[25] Although often disreputable and grotesque, the Irish figures portrayed by Ben Jonson (*c.*1573–1637), such as Captain Whit in *Bartholomew Fair* (1614) or Lady Frampul's adopted persona of an Irish beggarwoman in *New Inn* (1629), are imbued with a similar integrity. His *The Irish Masque at Court* (1613), which was performed for royal festivities on 29 December 1613 and 3 January 1614 to cele-brate the ill-fated marriage of Frances Howard to Robert Carr, earl of Somerset, presents a quartet of Irish characters, Dennice, Donnell, Dermock and Patrick, who possess a disturbing, carnivalesque energy. Their comic inability to make out their surroundings and especially to identify the king is transformed into unquestioning obeisance when they cast off their Irish cloaks and reveal them-selves to be English courtiers in disguise. While the startling metamorphosis appears to endorse the myth of a harmonious body politic, their prolonged misrecognition of their monarch and the exact rendering of Hiberno-English dialect in their exchanges suggest that the dissonance of Ireland cannot readily be expunged by the persuasive political rhetoric of the period. The comment by John Chamberlain in a letter of 30 December 1613 to Alice Carleton that it was 'no time (as the case stands) to exasperat that nation by making yt ridiculous' gestures at the political divisions hidden by the carefully contrived sycophancy of these self-effacing Irish courtiers.[26] The bitter struggles in the Irish parliament in 1612–13 about the appointment of John Davies as speaker and the undermining of the Old English majority through the creation of new Protestant boroughs contrast sharply with the illusion of collective harmony that Jonson fosters but also implicitly lays bare in his courtly entertainment.[27]

Richard Bellings (c.1603–77), a member of an Old English family with extensive estates in Dublin, Wicklow and Kildare, was educated as a Catholic despite his father's conformity. In June 1642, he was indicted of rebellion and was expelled from the House of Commons along with forty other Catholic members. Thereafter, he became secretary to the supreme council of the Catholic Confederation and acted as its principal ambassador and peace negotiator. The diversity of his writing is indicative not just of a versatile talent but of a quest for apposite and malleable modes with which to express the upheavals of seventeenth-century Ireland and the volatile fortunes and slowly eroding power of the Old English. His works include commendatory verse, occasional poetry, romance and history. His two most important creations, *A Sixth Booke to the Countesse of Pembrokes Arcadia* printed in Dublin in 1624 and a multi-volume history of the Irish Confederation which was unpublished in his lifetime, evidence his skill in exploiting and remoulding literary genres to suit his artistic and political purposes. His continuation of Philip Sidney's *Arcadia* is dedicated to Elizabeth Cary (1585/6–1639), Viscountess Falkland, wife of Henry Cary, who was Irish lord deputy 1622–9. In her posthumously published autobiography, *The Lady Faulkland Her Life*, Cary, who notoriously converted to Catholicism in 1626, interprets the failure of her altruistic ventures during her brief Dublin residence in 1624–5 as divine disapproval of her attempts at Protestant proselytism.[28] In thus associating his work with Cary's defiant recusancy and championing of Catholic Ireland, Bellings signals his intent not only to supplement but also to recast Sidney's text. Just as the reception of *Arcadia* becomes a site for warring ideological viewpoints in seventeenth-century England – the quotation by Charles I of Pamela's prayer in *Eikon Basilike* (1648) is the most famous instance of such appropriation – so too it is subtly reinscribed to reflect the specific dilemmas of Old English Catholics in the 1620s as they find themselves constantly torn between loyalism and rebellion.[29]

Although the Old English community constantly battled exclusion from public office as a result of royal insistence on religious conformity and the enforcement of the oath of supremacy, the prospect of war with Spain in the 1620s and of a Catholic marriage for Charles I raised hopes of a shift in the balance of power. Old English loyalty and financial support were important bargaining tools in the religious resettlement and international and internal alignments of the Caroline regime. Deana Rankin has noted that a key impetus of Bellings's revision of *Arcadia* is to achieve closure through tying up its loose ends and enacting constant scenes of reconciliation.[30] Hence *A Sixth Booke to the Countesse of Pembrokes Arcadia* completes all of the unfinished business of Sidney's work: Basilius and Gynecia return from pastoral exile to take control of their kingdom and the long-delayed nuptials of Pamela and Pyrocles and of Musidorus and Philoclea take place. Marriage is used as a sign not just of social concord but also of political rehabilitation. Amphialus, an erstwhile traitor, is forgiven and his marriage to Helen of Corinth, the woman he once spurned, is sanctioned. When he initially appears on the scene, the armour that he wears simulates a naked, wounded body, thus externalising the bloody civil conflicts that had been the mainstay of Arcadian society. Similarly, his union with Helen permits the interplay of the harmony of romance with the discord of tragedy, as before their marriage both partners recount at length their recent experiences of wars of usurpation, blighted love and murderous conflict. In *The Defence of Poesy*, Philip Sidney declares that tragedy 'openeth the greatest wounds and showeth forth the ulcers that are covered with tissue'.[31] In a parallel manner, the dual perspectives of Bellings's revisionary fiction shift between utopian moments of reconciliation, in which traitors and usurpers such as Amphialus and Tanarus may be forgiven, and the terrible spirals of revenge and hatred conjured up by retrospection. The tissue of romance provides a thin covering for the ulcers of history. The epilogue containing the doleful eclogues of the Aracadian shepherds continues this sense of political existence as a teetering construct. The mood of optimism generated by the magical reconciliations with former enemies is neatly counterpointed by the bleak poetic disquisition of Agelastus on honour as a 'spongie idol'. If Bellings's narrative toys with the possibility of a common cause between the Old English and the crown it does so with the awareness that such moments of integration depend on political ideals that are as fragile and ambiguous as the fictional metaphors which give expression to them.

The poetry, fiction and autobiographical writings of English settlers in Ireland throughout the early decades of the seventeenth century document a diverse spectrum of political opinion and experience and attest to the heterogeneous nature of literary production in the country. A native of Northamptonshire, Parr Lane (*fl.*1621) came to Ireland to fight in the campaign against Tyrone and thereafter settled in Munster. His *News from the Holy Isle* (*c.*1621) picks up on the irony noted in many New English texts, including those of Spenser, that the Latin adjective 'sacer' variously means blessed and cursed.

Because of the English failure to impose religious uniformity, far from being a holy isle, Ireland is in Lane's imagining a dystopian realm ruled by kerns, Jesuits and priests. His fervent poetic apostrophe unites satire, millenarian urgency and vivid polemic and ends with a compelling image of a spiritual revolution which would transform the country from an infernal domain into 'Jehovas temple'. Gervase Markham (c.1568–1637) likewise spent a term of service as a soldier in Ireland during the 1590s. His *The Newe Metamorphosis* is a lengthy unpublished poem composed between 1600 and 1615 which tells of travels in Ireland, Flanders and Spain. It combines pungent Chaucerian fabliaux with unrelenting anti-Catholic invective. The metamorphoses described are not Ovidian tales of dalliance and escape but punishments meted out for deleterious sins. Unlike Lane, Markham sees Ireland as a place of ineradicable evil and sexual depravity. Numerous counter-myths are interspersed throughout his narrative to pinpoint its wickedness. In one such invention, Jove is forced to destroy 'Bernia Lande' because of the bestiality of its king. As a punishment the royal city is plunged into an abyss and the immoral inhabitants are turned into wolves who can assume human shape. In Markham's hands the pervasive Jacobean trope of social transformation is used to denote the Irish descent into evil rather than any process of positive change.

Francis Quarles (1592–1644) was born in Essex and his literary career began in England where he published moral poetry on biblical themes. It continued after his appointment in 1626 as secretary to James Ussher, archbishop of Armagh. His residence possibly in Dublin extended until 1630. Despite his association with Ussher he utilised his stay in the country to turn from religious to secular material by composing *Argalus and Parthenia*, a poetic romance based on an episode in Sidney's *Arcadia*. In his dedication to his reader, written from Dublin on 4 March 1628, Quarles suggests that his sojourn in Ireland is responsible for a change in the underlying principles of his aesthetic which is not simply a casual shift in focus. The Parthenia he has invented, he tells his female readers, 'hath crost the Seas for your acquaintance'. Indeed, as David Freedman notes, his romance is distinctive because of the dual fascination that it evinces with the moral themes of love and honour on the one hand and with scenes of burlesque anti-heroism on the other.[32] Although these opposing emphases have forerunners in the classical epic, where the comic and the heroic are frequently juxtaposed, they are also adopted as the primary vectors of Irish Renaissance versifying.[33] In Quarles's Sidneian romance, the interweaving of a scabrous mock-heroic vision with a high-flown moralising rhetoric becomes the means by which he adapts English heroic epic to Irish circumstance and the concerns of an early seventeenth-century imaginary. His concluding account of his noble lovers united in death through the posthumous honour they have garnered turns the original tale of romantic love into a transcendent myth of 'public service' as well as 'private rites'. Lady Anne Southwell (née Harris) (1573–1636) was born in Cornworthy in Devon where her family was politically allied with Sir Walter Ralegh. Through his auspices, her first husband, Thomas Southwell, acquired property in Youghal. In 1603 the couple settled at Castle Poulnelong or Shippool in County Cork. Following the death of her first spouse in 1626, she married Captain Henry Sibthorpe and they resided in Ireland for two further years. Her commonplace book is a patchwork of original and transcribed verse which affords a remarkable insight into female practices of private composition in the period.[34] It unites anti-Catholic polemic, spiritual meditation and domestic description and is marked by its vehemence of tone. To capture her sense of horror at the prospect of dying in 'Hibernia', she conjures up a vision of a tumultuous native presence at her funeral who will 'crye / and teare theyr hayres like furyes sent from hell'. Countering the stridency of her moral reflections are intimate poems and epistles directed to Irish acquaintances and friends. In a letter to Cicely MacWilliams, Lady Ridgeway, she vehemently defends the art of poetry because 'Imagination goes before Realitye', while a mock-elegy to this friend who later became Countess of Londonderry uses the animating fear of loss to conjoin metaphysical speculation, robust *contemptu mundi* and sapphic playfulness.

Early modern history writing is characterised by a shift from annalistic modes of recording towards more searching accounts of the past that privilege individual style, the status of the author and selective emphasis.[35] Many early seventeenth-century Irish histories take the form of personal memoirs or testamentary narratives that return to the crisis of the Nine Years War and endeavour to explicate the role of its key players, above all, Hugh O'Neill. The vitriolic poem 'A Discourse occasioned upon the late defeat, given to the Archrebels, Tyrone and Odonnell, by the right Honourable, the Lord Mountjoy, Lord Deputie of Ireland', by Ralph Birchensa (*fl.*1602), however, puts forward a crudely providentialist account of the recent battle which is perceived in triumphalist terms 'as a just revenge for bloud'.[36] Fynes Moryson (1566–1630), who was chief secretary to Charles Blount, Lord Mountjoy (1563–1606) from 1600 to 1606, constructs a more objective but equally jaundiced overview of this crucial period. The second volume of his *Itinerary* (1617) is devoted to a history of Ireland from 1599 to 1603 with specific focus on the Battle of Kinsale. As in his negative ethnographical assessment of native culture in the first part of this work, Moryson portrays the Irish as weak and barbarous and as 'perfidious friends' even to their Spanish allies. Through opposing the strategic finesse of Mountjoy to the duplicity of Tyrone, the 'arch-traitor', his exact chronicle of events, which is supported throughout by quotations from official correspondence and documents, serves further to mould reportage to the ideological aim of celebrating the 'absolute subjection' of the country in the wake of the defeat at Kinsale. Thomas Gainsford (*fl.*1624) in *The True, Exemplary, and Remarkable History of the Earle of Tirone* (1619), by contrast, constructs an ambivalent and emotionally charged account of O'Neill as a duplicitous over-reacher and as a tragically heroic figure 'groveling to the earth' at Mellifont. Thomas Stafford (*fl.*1633) also tracks the course of the Nine Years War in *Pacata Hibernia* (1633), but is insistent on the role of accurate observation in unlocking the meaning of events. His declared goal is to balance expectations by advancing the honour of both nations. While the suppression of the rebellion will appeal to his English audience, his Irish readership, he contends, will take solace from his emphasis on the fundamental loyalty of the country. With a similar view to clarity, William Farmer resorts to an annalistic listing of events in *Chronicles of Ireland from 1594 to 1613* (1587). *Britain, or, A Chorographicall Description of the Most Flourishing Kingdomes, England, Scotland, and Ireland* (1637), a translation by Philemon Holland (1552–1637) of *Britannia* (1586) by William Camden (1551–1623), signals the continuities as well as the differences between Tudor and Jacobean and Caroline historiography. However, *The Historie of Ireland* (1633) by Sir James Ware (1594–1666) is self-consciously innovative. By marrying in one volume *The Chronicle of Ireland* by Meredith Hanmer (1543–1604), Edmund Campion's *History of Ireland* and Edmund Spenser's *A View of the Present State of Ireland*, he harnesses the modish antiquarianism of his day to effect a revolutionary confluence of opinions. In a rare instance of scholarly ecumenism, views of Irish history by an English divine who settled in Ireland, an English recusant and a New English poet and planter are interlinked and nudged into uneasy dialogue with each other.

Ironically, Ware's history was dedicated to the controversial Irish lord deputy, Sir Thomas Wentworth (1593–1641), earl of Strafford. The policies that he pursued while in office from 1632 to 1639 alienated all elements of Irish society and the dissension that he inspired was eventually to lead to his execution as a traitor in 1641. Wentworth's quest for religious and political reform through the policy of 'Thorough' and the furthering of schemes for plantation was matched by his ambition to be acknowledged as patron of the arts and to achieve authoritative expression in the cultural sphere.[37] He appointed John

Ogilby, the English dancing master, as Master of the Revels in Ireland and instructed him to found a theatre in Dublin. Although the proximity of the Werburgh Street theatre to the viceregal court in Dublin Castle suggests that it was akin to the intimate private playhouses in London frequented by an exclusively upper-class audience, the political faultlines in the city precluded such cohesion. The English Catholic playwright James Shirley (1596–1666) was imported for the initial season and three of his plays, *The Royall Master* (1638), *Rosania or Love's Victory* (1652) and *St Patrick for Ireland* (1640), were staged during its brief opening season as well as works by Ben Jonson and John Fletcher. *The Royall Master*, which centres on a Neapolitan king who extricates himself by wise counsel from the deceptions and intrigues of his retainer Montalto, is at once an endorsement of royal power and a portrayal of its inherent flaws. Like much of Shirley's theatrical work it is poised uneasily between compliment and critique.[38] However, his distrust of Irish society and growing hostility towards his audience seem to have increasingly exerted pressure on these polarities in his writing.

The placatory tone assumed in London is swapped for the open disgruntlement of his Irish presentations. In the prefatory verse for a lost play, *The Irish Gentleman*, he complains that 'wit and soul-enriching poesy' are fated to die in Ireland, while in the prologue to *No Wit To A Woman's* he declares that, though an inhabitant of the Irish capital, he 'knows not where / To find the city'. His final Dublin composition, *St Patrick for Ireland*, was designed to mollify his audience by using Irish material but its conflicting allegories exacerbate rather than diminish the political divides within which it operates. On one level, St Patrick's conversion of the native Irish, who are depicted as pagan and readily given to necromancy, murder and rape, seems a vindication of Catholicism but, on another level, the reformation effected by this British saint symbolically enacts the transformation from barbarism to civility desired by English colonialism.[39] The counterpointing of country and city that, as Martin Butler observes, provides the basis for subtle moments of dissent in Shirley's London productions does not have the same purchase in Dublin.[40] Instead his play appears merely to be at odds with itself. While it endorses the ascetic pastoralism of Patrick, it shamelessly exploits the lurid possibilities for extravagant stage effects of the courtly Irish pagan world which it nonetheless condemns.

Landgartha (1640) by the Catholic royalist Henry Burnell was composed as a direct rejoinder to Shirley's failed drama. The complex equation of female chastity with honour in Caroline theatre is pressed into service in this text. The Amazonian warrior and Norwegian queen, Landgartha, forms an alliance with Reyner, king of Denmark, who rescues her country by killing Frollo, the Swedish king, who has overrun it. She reluctantly consents to marriage only later to be deserted and betrayed by Reyner. Despite this, she goes to his aid when Denmark comes under attack. Although the couple are nominally reconciled at the end of the play, she refuses either to sleep or to live with him, thereby winning back a partial autonomy. In his epilogue, Burnell pointedly draws attention to the suspended nature of the conclusion which is consonant with the equivocal nature of tragi-comedies that, as he states, 'neither end Comically or Tragically but betwixt both'. Landgartha's conditional loyalty and her belated and unrealisable attempt to reclaim her chastity thus project the complicated position of the Old English who are caught between fealty to England, political compromise and the desire for self-government.[41] The wedding celebration for Reyner and Landgartha similarly orchestrates a number of competing undercurrents. It is graced by the bluff, good-hearted, but vaguely threatening Marfisa, dressed in an Irish gown, 'broags on her feet her hayre dishevell'd' and wearing a sword and spurs, who dances 'the whip of Donboyne', thus providing a fleeting reminder of the native Irish who are also part of Landgartha's dominion. Marfisa's energetic performance is counterbalanced by the 'grand Dance' of the courtly couples present. The masque performed on this occasion is split between two classical subjects, the Trojan wars and the peaceable foundation of a British empire by Aeneas. A prophecy foretells the union of Reyner and Landgartha but warns that 'their own sad dissentions' may undo this alliance. Burnell's play thus canvasses the uncertainties of a multi-ethnic politic and delicately points to the impasses that might occur if traditional Old English loyalty to the crown is disregarded or eroded.

The Irish civil wars and their aftermath, 1641–1660

The ruptures caused by the 1641 rebellion and the ensuing civil wars in Ireland created a sense of irreparable crisis with which all of the writers of the mid-century of whatever persuasion struggled to come to terms. The military contestations of this period were restaged and refracted by a textuality that derived a new combativeness and vigour from the urge for explication and clarity. Wounds and words became contiguous in a war-torn world where the need to transform recent trauma into coherent memory was imperative. On 23 October 1641, the Catholics of Ulster led by Sir Phelim O'Neill captured a number of key towns and garrisons. The insurgents, driven by privation and an accumulation of political grievances, killed Protestant neighbours, drove many more from their homes and seized their properties. This insurrection quickly spread to the rest of the country and led to prolonged unrest between the Catholic alliance of Gaelic and Old English landowners and the Protestant forces of the New English and English which was not allayed until 1653. The rebellion immediately became the fuel for divisive propaganda, conflicting reckonings of the death toll and the brutality of the violence used and strained historical reconstructions. Because of its polemical vehemence and graphic portrayal of the atrocities, *The Irish Rebellion* (1646) by Sir John Temple (1600–1677) quickly established itself as an authoritative assessment of events. Drawing on his legal training, Temple in his preface announces his intention to construct a 'true impartiall relation' of recent happenings. The text he constructs, however, does not follow a single trajectory but shifts between narrative modes, intermingling history, forensic disquisition and the eye-witness reports recounted in the depositions. The numerous rebellions of the Irish through the ages are cited as examples of their inherent treachery, while the barbarity and the premeditated nature of the uprising are corroborated by the vivid testimonials cited in full. The additional animus inspired by papistry serves to heighten inherited images of native savagery. This enhanced perfidy of the Irish is borne out by a compendious catalogue of the violent attacks and the relentless listing of heinous acts such as rapes, the butchering of unborn children, the stripping of innocent victims and the callous prevention of proper burial rites. Such undeviating interrogation of motives and actions is at variance with another mode of commentary deployed by Temple that insists on the unspeakable nature of the 'most notorious Cruelties and bloody Massacres'. Irish papist depravity is thus depicted in this text as an unfathomable excess. The cataclysmic nature of the violent onslaught turns the dead into spectral witnesses whose vengeful, sword-wielding ghosts, as in the case of those killed at the river Bann, noisily demand retribution. Taking his cue from these restless spirits, Temple depicts the perpetrators of the rebellion as a final enemy or Antichrist beyond the reach either of mercy or redemption. As Raymond Gillespie has demonstrated, the fractured nature of this work made it amenable to selective interpretation.[42] It could be read variously for the frisson of massacre literature, the clarifying logic of scholarly history, didactic edification or the coded reassurances of a providential narrative. Protestant memorialising polemic, for all its desire to achieve ideological fixity, cannot foreclose on hermeneutic ambiguity or limit the variable political appropriations that its persuasive rhetoric readily courts.

Temple's tract, moreover, belonged to a general outpouring of anti-papist pamphlets decrying the monstrosity of the 1641 rebellion and castigating the satanic nature of the Irish, including *A Perfect Relation of the Beginning and Continuation of the Irish Rebellion* (1642) by Henry Jones (1605–82), *An Exact Relation of all such occurences as have happened in the severall counties of Donegall, London-Derry, Tyrone and Fermanagh in the North of Ireland since the beginning of this horrid, bloody and unparaleld rebellion there* (1642) by Sir Audley Mervyn (*fl.*1675), *The Mysterie of Iniquity yet Working in the Kingdomes of England, Scotland, and Ireland for the destruction of religion truly Protestant* (1643) by Edward Bowles (1613–62), *Israels Tears or Distressed Zion* (1645) by John Whincop (*fl.*1647), *The Irish Massacre or A True narrative of the unparallel'd Cruelties exercised in Ireland upon the British Protestants* (1646) by Henry Parker (1604–52), *King Charls his Case* (1649) by John Cook (d.1660), and *A Brief Narration of the Plotting, Beginning & Carrying on of the execrable rebellion and butcherie in Ireland* (1651) by Thomas Waring (*fl.*1651).

Partisanship left its firm imprint on all of the writing of this period. Additionally, writers struggled to accommodate the traumatic effects of the bloody military struggles of confederate Ireland and the regime of torture and revenge instituted by English government in reprisal for 1641. The anonymous manuscript *An Aphorismical Discovery of Treasonable Faction* (1652–60) depicts the events of the rebellion from the Catholic perspective and also covers much of the history of the Confederacy, 1641–50. The scrawled initials of the author, 'R.S.', do not permit reliable identification, although his allegiances with Counter Reformation Catholicism and Ulster politics are patent. The unfinished manuscript may have been composed in exile after the Cromwellian conquest 1649–50. Its provenance within the defeated Catholic community may explain why a contemporary publication was not realised, a first edition of the text by Sir John T. Gilbert appearing only in the late nineteenth century.[43] The frontispiece dedicates the work to Sir Owen Roe O'Neill (*c.*1582–1649) who is also styled Don Eugenius ONEALE, thus casting him in the dual role of Counter Reformation Prince and Ulster leader. The text sets out to heroicise him 'as another Jason of Thesaly', who has returned from Spain to recover the Golden Fleece of the 'libertie of a free borne nation', and to prove the integrity of his cause by establishing him as an epic hero. Simultaneously, however, it exposes with impassioned intensity the treacherous factionalism that thwarted O'Neill, particularly that of James Butler, earl of Ormond (1610–88) who led the royalist forces during the war, and the prevarications of Old English leaders within the Confederacy such as Richard Bellings. As a consequence, the text seems divided between two opposing impulses: the vituperation of the Irish enemies of the Ulster leader and the glorification of his methods. Further the chapters purposively combine moral philosophy and history. Each opens with a brief aphorism, culled from a compilation of quotations by Sir Robert Dallington (1561–1637) from Francesco Guicciardini's history of the Italian wars, which is then followed by a detailed analysis of political events. Contrary to the predominant New English view of Irish history as malign and disordered – evident in the political tracts of Edmund Spenser and John Davies – this alternating pattern highlights the universal dimensions of Irish affairs and produces successive moral frames within which to view the unfurling narrative. The gnomic nature of many of these pronouncements, however, also signals the difficulty of steering a course through the morass of contemporary conflicts. Even though the text constantly stresses the probity of O'Neill's mission it also foregrounds the chaos of war, 'for be the title never soe cleere, and the cause just yett the meanes are not without fire and sworde nor the end without horrour and bloudshed'. As Deana Rankin has noted, this deliberate interplay of clashing perspectives is most evident in the account of the Battle of Benburb (5 June 1646), which moves from the epic crescendo of O'Neill's address to his troops to the bathos of a street ballad sung 'to the tune of blewe bonnett and bobtaile' that describes the macabre scene of the female camp-followers searching 'the stript dead bodies' in order to identify their one-time paramours.[44] Instead of glorying in this key victory by the Ulster general, the text lingers on the sobering bathos of the battlefield and the pain of loss. The anonymous discoverer's vigorous defence of this Irish military leader who fights selflessly in the Catholic cause is further truncated by O'Neill's sudden death in 1649. Epic heroism is at once vitiated by the inveterate divisions of Irish domestic politics and by the adversity of fortune. The narrative tracks the declining fortunes of the O'Neill clan after the demise of its leader and the further undermining of the key purpose of the Catholic alliance and war by fruitless diplomatic negotiations. Symbolically, the manuscript is incomplete and its final half page is illegible. Its lack of closure is a telling commentary on the deep-seated animosities and internal strains of confederate Ireland that foil any effort to impose narrative coherence.

Observations on Articles of the Peace with the Irish Rebels (1649) by John Milton (1608–74) was his first official piece of writing for the Rump parliament. He was commissioned to decide on the urgency of sending troops to Ireland, especially in the light of the threat posed by the 'Articles of Peace' that had been negotiated after protracted discussion by the earl of Ormond with Charles I and proclaimed in Kilkenny in July 1646. Milton's tract enunciates the tenets of a newly emerging republicanism through its painstaking refutation of its Irish enemies. His righteous anger is directed severally at Ormond, the recently executed English monarch, the 'inhumane Rebels and Papists of Ireland' and the 'pretended Brethren', the Scottish Presbyterians of Belfast. Even though all these groups and figures are differentiated, they also ironically melt into one another and are condemned with equal ferocity. The Protestant Ormond inspires as much ire as the recalcitrant Catholics and Presbyterians. The 'unexampl'd virulence' of the 1641 massacre has lastingly stamped the Irish in Milton's eyes. Treachery, barbarity and a propensity to rebelliousness and devious sedition are seen as inherent aspects of all of the opponents that he attacks. Irishness in this essay is opposed to a new vision of Englishness that is founded on rectitude, militant godliness and a dedication to truth and freedom. Republicanism, as a result, construes itself not just by articulating a credo of liberty but by pitting itself against the demonic forces that it opposes, including monarchists, 'Irish barbarians' and the heretical demands of 'High-land theevs and Red-shanks'.[45]

The campaign of the New Model Army in Ireland from late summer 1649 drew on the apocalypticism evoked by Milton's *Observations*. Oliver Cromwell in his letters and speeches viewed himself as engaged in a divinely appointed mission to destroy the forces of darkness on Irish soil. In a letter of 17 September 1649 to Honourable William Lenthall, he defended the mass killing of soldiers, priests and civilians at Drogheda as 'a righteous judgement of God', while in a speech delivered at Clonmacnoise in 1650 he roundly denounced Irish Catholic prelates, declaring that they 'are a part of Antichrist, whose Kingdom the Scripture so expressly speaks should be laid in blood; yea in the blood of the Saints'. A similar providentialism is evident in 'An Horation Ode upon Cromwell's Return from Ireland' (1650) by Andrew Marvell (1621–78) which depicts the taming of the Irish by Cromwell as an irrefutable aspect of his revolutionary heroism. By contrast, *The Memoirs of Ann Lady Fanshawe* (1676) provide a vividly secular counter-perspective on the Cromwellian era and its trenchant religious polemics. Forced into exile because of their royalism and close connections with the king, Ann Fanshawe (1625–80) and her husband fled to Ireland and found a new home in Red Abbey in Cork City. Her diary details the anguish caused by their second dispossession during the sacking of Cork in 1649. Her purported sighting of a banshee-like apparition, 'a woman . . . in white, with red hair and pale, gastly complexion', while staying subsequently in the house of Lady Honor O'Brien curiously appropriates Irish folklore, which is insistently dismissed as superstition, to render concrete her own sense of fear and displacement during the turmoil caused by the Cromwellian campaigns.

James Ussher (1581–1656), the leading theologian, antiquarian and scholar of his age, was likewise forced into exile. He lost his lands and income as a result of the 1641 rebellion and spent the latter half of his life in England. An Old English Protestant, educated in Trinity College, his work exhibits the divided views of a Church of Ireland prelate who professes loyalty to the crown but is simultaneously at pains to account for the alternative standpoint of the Irish ministry to which he belongs. Ussher's early works, *A Discourse of the Religion Anciently Professed by the Irish and British* (1622/31) and *An Answer to A Challenge Made by a Jesuite in Ireland* (1624), mine his deep-seated knowledge of church history and Irish antiquity to delineate the fundamental characteristics of Irish Protestantism. Royalism, ancient precedence and anti-papistry are the cornerstones of the world-view that he propounds. In the preface to *A Discourse* he laments 'the strange kinde of credulities' of Irish Catholics and presents his revisionary history as a corrective to their misguided beliefs. His readjusted narrative claims that the Protestant and not the Catholic faith is the direct descendant of the ancient religion founded by St Patrick. Protestantism thus has the weight of historical authority and ancient pedigree; its purity is opposed to the adulteration of papistry which is dismissed as a 'forraine doctrine' imposed by Rome. Even though Ussher ends his tract with the pious wish that 'wee may all bee gathered into one fold', the unity that he envisions involves the obliteration of the historical and spiritual aberration of Catholicism. *An Answer to A Challenge Made by a Jesuite in Ireland* similarly uses sectarianism in order to define the specificities of Irish Protestantism. The dedicatory preface to James I praises the monarch's dexterity in exposing the 'frauds of the Romish Church' and positions Ussher's refutation on the frontier of Reformation battles between two inimical confessional views. In this tract, too, Irish Catholicism is condemned on the grounds of its historical illegitimacy and baseless self-deceptions. It is Protestantism, as Ussher argues, that has retained the essence of the ancient church and that therefore has the only pretensions to truth. Although he fell out with Strafford in 1634 about the imposition of the thirty-nine ecclesiastical articles on the Church of Ireland because he resolutely favoured local autonomy and feared the subsumption of Irish ordinances into English structures, Ussher's devotion to English monarchism remained unwavering and in the 1640s he served the household of Charles I. The posthumous publication from the 1660s onwards of sermons delivered to the king and of texts such as *The Power Communicated by God to the Prince and the Obedience Required of the Subject* (1661) and *The Great Necessity of Unity and Peace Among all Protestants and the bloody Principles of the Papists* (1688) effect a further shift in Ussher's legacy as they capitalise on his loyalism to promote the restoration of the monarchy. Such appropriations, moreover, reveal how textual instability is conducive to variant ideological readings. James Tyrill, the editor of *The Power Communicated*, dedicates the text on Ussher's behalf to Charles II and notes that it was originally composed for the monarch's father. He thus neatly aligns textual transmission with royal succession. In so doing, he commutes the monarchism of the 1640s to the altered circumstances of the Restoration period and erases in the process the difference of Irish Protestantism for which Ussher had acted as a central mediator and promulgator.[46]

Little is known about Henry Burkhead (*fl.*1645–6), the author of *A Tragedy of Cola's Furie or Lirenda's Miserie* (1646). One of the commendatory verses describes him as a merchant, while the dominant themes and sympathies of this unique work associate him with the Catholic Confederacy which had its headquarters at Kilkenny. The text unites features of the history play, masque and revenge tragedy. It also deploys thinly veiled allegory to render the events and leading figures of the Irish wars prior to the Ormond cessation of 1643 and presupposes an audience capable of deciphering these coded references. The action centres on the skirmishes between the Lirendeans, or Confederate Irish, who are defending their state against the cruel oppression of the Puritan Angoleans, the English and New English. The title character, Sir Carola Cola, is a representation of Sir Charles Coote Senior who was infamous for his exploitativeness and the brutality of the reprisals that he authorised in County Wicklow in the wake of the 1641 rebellion. Like the hero-villains of Senecan tragedy, he is portrayed as demonically possessed by the rage 'like Ioves violent thunder' which propels him. His anguished self-torment is an index of his evil and a means of externalising the hidden dynamics of a corrupt authority. The play depicts the Angoleans as savagely inhuman and fired by a relentless mission to exterminate their opponents. Cola on first entrance with 'his weapon drawne' declares his intention 'to hang, to racke, to kill, to burne, to spoile / until I make this land a barren soile'. This rapacious cruelty is captured in reports of his merciless killing of civilians, his refusal to honour agreements granting quarter to soldiers who have surrendered and his racking of the Lirendean commanders, Cephalon and Rufus. The graphic torture of Barbazella by Tygranes, an Angolean leader, in which 'shee is drawne aloft, with burning matches between each finger' affords a further searing manifestation of an irreparably embattled world. Although Burkhead underlines the worthiness and patriotic devotion of the Lirendeans who struggle both to defend 'the drooping state, of this our native / Clime' and to maintain their loyalty to the Angolean king, they are also depicted as motivated by an unyielding resolve. Only divine intervention is capable of calling this apocalyptic theatre of war to a halt. Following a heavenly parley which is decided in favour of the Lirendeans, Cola in a surreal encounter is confronted by the figure of Revenge 'with a sword in one hand' and three ghostly embodiments of those he has killed. Mirroring the conventional logic that dictates that revenger figures must themselves be avenged, Cola's all-consuming vindictiveness rounds on him and demands requital for his actions. This neatly fashioned allegorical reversal turns the punitive immorality of Angolean revenge into the retaliatory justice desired by the Lirendeans.[47] The subsequent providential killings of Cola and Tygranes satisfy the urgings of this climactic scene. Burkhead's ending, however, does not achieve even the unsatisfactory resolution effected by the rough justice of revenge tragedies. Instead, competing moments are held in suspension to underline the sense of indeterminacy caused by the ongoing strife of a fatally torn polity. An angel in the culminating epilogue grants the laurels of victory to the courageous Lirendeans. The contrivance of this cosmic vindication runs counter to the parting recognition of Abner, a Lirendean commander, that tragedy must necessarily renew itself if Angolean injustice and oppression continue. A further Catholic drama, *Titus or the Palme of Christian Courage* (1644), the text of which is not extant, is known to have been staged at the Jesuit school in Kilkenny in 1644.[48] Set in Japan, its plot centres on the heroic constancy of Titus and his family who refuse to cede to the demands of the king of Bungo that they abandon their faith. Their steadfastness and 'couragious Christian resolution' are ultimately rewarded. Akin to *Cola's Furie*, this play also implicitly legitimises the Catholic alliance and reinforces the oppositional stance that it feels constrained to adopt.

A key body of English scientific and philosophical writings in the 1650s is concerned with the expropriation of the lands of Irish insurgents ousted during the Cromwellian wars. The scientist and economist Sir William Petty (1623–87) was appointed surveyor general in 1654 to carry out the 'down survey' of forfeited properties. Petty himself acquired substantial estates in County Kerry as the result of his own scientific mapping of the country. His later writings, including *History of the Down Survey* (c.1659) and *The Political Anatomy of Ireland* (1691), draw upon his knowledge of Ireland to develop an empirical method. Dedicated to the duke of Ormond, the latter text sets out to describe Ireland in objective, scientific terms and in accordance with a philosophy of social improvement. While the country is a palimpsest of discarded pasts for earlier commentators, for Petty it is 'a political animal scarce twenty years old' and hence akin to a modern laboratory in which he can test his ideas. Mathematics and econometrics have replaced history and religious fulmination. His anatomy quantifies and measures every aspect of Irish life from the number of chimneys on Dublin Castle and the quantity of people fit for trade to the number of working days achieved by Catholics and Protestants. The proper management of the economy of the country and the controlled exploitation of its resources are for Petty the key to 'transmuting' and anglicising the Irish. However, his rationalist belief in material progress is belied by his insistence on the need to retain social hierarchies. Although he recommends the improvement of living conditions for the native Irish, he ultimately argues against parity as this would 'beget anarchy and confusion'.

Ireland's Naturall History (1652) by the Dutch doctor Gerald Boate (1604–50) was in part co-authored by his brother, Arnold Boate (*c.*1600–53), who had lived in Ireland during the civil wars and served as physician-general to the army in Leinster. Their work sets out programmatically to fulfil the ideals of Samuel Hartlib with whom they were associated by adopting the precepts of empirical observation and utilitarianism. In concentrating rigorously on the physical geography of the country, it deliberately erases the effects of human presence or the role of culture and religion. Instead, their natural history is a compendious catalogue of Irish harbours, rivers, roads, bogs, promontories, hills, mines and varieties of manure, all of which, it is implied, can be more effectively exploited than heretofore once fully surveyed. Baconian pragmatism, however, becomes a new means of justifying racial animus. The Boates, in frequent asides, denounce the Irish as 'one of the most barbarous nations on the whole earth' and accuse them of mismanaging the natural resources at their disposal. Even the wetness of the climate and the large number of bogs are deemed to be the result of native indolence and lack of enterprise. *The Great Case of Transplantation in Ireland Discussed* (January 1655) by the New English Munster landowner Vincent Gookin (*c.*1616–59) similarly draws on rationalist principles but does so in order to dismantle received prejudices rather than to reinforce them. Disputing the viability and moral necessity of the transplantation to Connacht, Gookin develops a sympathetic portrait of the Irish while castigating the failure of British governance. Above all, he questions the notion of Irish national blood-guilt and the continuing pursuit of punitive rather than reformist policies. Although Gookin, like Petty and the Boates, is motivated by self-interested utilitarianism and a belief in cultural assimilation, his enlightened and even-handed treatise refuses to see the native Irish as monstrous and Other. Counter to the bloodthirstiness of the civil wars, he declares that 'the conversion of that nation will be a more pious work than their eradication'. He was immediately taken to task by Richard Lawrence (d.1684) in *The Interest of England in the Irish Transplantation* (1655) and accused of sedition. Gookin vehemently defended and restated his views in *The Author* *and Case of Transplanting the Irish into Connaught Vindicated* (May 1655) while exposing the spurious logic of Lawrence's plans which he held would turn Ireland into a wilderness.[49]

The eldest son of a Protestant clergyman, Faithful Teate (*c.*1626–61) was born in Ballyhaise, County Cavan. His family lost its holdings during the 1641 rebellion and took refuge in Dublin only subsequently to be displaced once again, possibly because of his father's combative Puritanism. The anti-Catholicism and gift for emphatic polemic of the elder Teate are evident in his sermon *Nathanael, or an Israelite Indeed* (1657). Faithful Teate was educated in Cambridge and held various livings in England and possibly in Ireland from 1650 to 1666. In 1655, a collection of his sermons was published as *A Scripture-map of the wildernesse of sin*, which, as Angelina Lynch has discovered, also contains his first printed poem, 'Epithalamium; or a Love Song of the Leaning Soul'.[50] Two further sermons, dedicated to Cromwell, *The Character of Cruelty in the Workers of Iniquity* and *The Cure of Contention among the People of God*, appeared in 1656. A first edition of Teate's most significant composition, *Ter Tria*, an extended metaphysical poem, was published in 1658. The full title of this singular text, *Ter Tria or The Doctrine of the Three Sacred Persons, Father, Son, and Spirit; Principal Graces, Faith, Hope and Love; Main Duties, Prayer, Hearing and Meditation*, itemises its multiple sub-divisions and suggests that it is designed as a series of practical spiritual meditations on an array of key theological topics. The prefatory verse addressed to the reader announces Teate's intention of moulding 'leud Poetrie' to spiritual ends. This moral stringency, however, belies the inventive liveliness of the ensuing poems, which are characterised by their conversational intimacy, plangent imagism, frequent yoking of the homely and the exalted and startling metaphorical analogies. Thus, the section on faith depicts faltering belief as a disorder of the blood which can only be cured when the guilt-laden veins of the sinner are washed and phlebotomised, while the meditation on prayer variously describes it as a bellows, lute, limbeck, bucket and pump that enable the believer to address heaven. The engaging devotionalism of this dramatic spiritual autobiography contrasts sharply with the stridency of Teate's final two Dublin sermons, *The Uncharitable Informer charitably informed that Sycophancy is a Sin* (1664) and *The Thoughts of the Righteous are Right* (1666), which attack the 'angry humors' and 'tongue-dysenteries' infecting the country. Embitterment seems to have clouded the end of his life. The family name was regularised to Tate by his descendants. Although one of the most expressive and original poets of seventeenth-century Ireland, Teate's literary achievements have ironically been eclipsed by those of his son, the playwright Nahum Tate.

The Restoration to the Battle of the Boyne,
1660–1690

Pompey. A tragoedy, by the English royalist poet and playwright Katherine Philips (1631–64), was staged in Smock Alley Theatre in Dublin in 1663 in the presence of the duke of Ormond, then lord lieutenant of Ireland, and his retinue and followers. Philips had come to Dublin to pursue land claims on behalf of her father who had invested in the Company of Adventurers set up by Cromwell. She produced this translation of Corneille at the instigation of a coterie of her New English friends, including Wentworth Dillon, earl of Roscommon, and Roger Boyle, earl of Orrery. It at once panders to the *préciosité* and francophilia of this circle and enunciates the many tensions and strains of a society adapting to the restoration of the Stuart monarchy and coming to terms with the disruptions of decades of political upheaval and division. The prologue delivered by Roscommon casts the Dublin audience not just as spectators but as adjudicators on the bloody rivalry of Caesar and Pompey. Although the play promises a clear moral reckoning with the past, its ambiguities preclude any one-sided readings. Indeed, its predominant feature is the opacity of its allegories. The plot depicts the aftermath of Caesar's victory at Pharsalia as he pursues his defeated opponent, Pompey, to Egypt. The latter realm is ruled conjointly in an uneasy alliance by Cleopatra and her brother, Ptolomy. Ptolomy's rivalry with Cleopatra convinces him of the expediency of killing the vanquished Roman general in the hopes of improving his own political standing. Inevitably recalling the execution of Charles I, the image of the violent assassination of Pompey by beheading haunts the text. The Roman leader remains a political force after his death even though the disturbing undercurrents with which he is linked are intractably double, given that he is at once a symbol of deposed monarchy and an embodiment of republicanism. The traumatic core of Philips's political drama thus refuses to adopt a reliable shape. Rather it is the confused merging and ambivalent overlay of loyalties that concerns her. Even though the text reflects on the irony of Caesar turning his rival into a hallowed martyr after his death, the chief tensions accrue around the female figures, Cleopatra and Pompey's widow, Cornelia, each of whom is forced into undesirable political compromises. Above all, the problematic sovereignty which Cleopatra achieves at the end when she assumes the throne of Egypt raises uncomfortable questions about an attenuated Irish polity and the nature of colonial dependency.[51] Two plays by the army officer and translator John Dancer (*fl.*1660–75), *Nicomède, A Tragi-comedy Translated out of the French of Monsieur Corneille* (1671) and *Agrippa King of Alba* or *The False Tibernius . . . from the French of Monsieur Quinault* (1675), staged in the Theatre Royal in Dublin in the late 1660s, continued this engagement with the unresolved themes of insurrection, treachery and political marginality.

Several vital strands of Irish Restoration poetry are associated either with the patronage of the Ormond circle or with the cultural and political aspirations of an interconnected but multifarious group of New English writers. 'To the Excellent Orinda', the only surviving poem by the unknown author 'Philo-Philippa', is an Irish eulogy to Katherine Philips that provides an insight into the suppressed feminist pretensions of the female artists of this period. Philo-Philippa, while granting that Corneille and Philips are equals, also wonders what the latter would achieve if her muse were not 'fetter'd'.

Encomiastic exchange in other poetic texts of the period similarly allows for a subtle yoking of politics and aesthetics through debating questions of priority and value. In many instances, it is suggested that the transposition of literary forms to an Irish context permits a return to their pristine essence and the concomitant rescue of erstwhile patrician virtues. John Dryden in a commendatory poem prefaced to *An Essay on Translated Verse* (1684) by Wentworth Dillon, earl of Roscommon (1637–85), praises him for restoring the 'Muses Empire' and deems the Irish art of translation to be a distinctive aesthetic bolstering the authority of Britain from without. Roscommon – who also composed occasional and devotional verse – propounds in *An Essay* and *Horace's Art of Poetry* (1679) a theory of translation that calls for a reinstatement of its core concerns with decorum, cultural pluralism and the development of a 'sympathetick' bond between the translator and his text. The English painter and aesthete Thomas Flatman (1635–88) in *Poems and Songs* (1686) likewise makes a case for recuperating pre-existent forms and adapting them to modern needs. In particular, he favours the reintroduction of the 'Pindarique strain' because its loftiness and openness liberate the writer. His volume contains elegaic pindaric odes on the premature demise of Thomas, earl of Ossory (1634–80) and the deaths of Katherine Philips, Charles II and the duke of Ormond which stress the heroic dimensions of these figures. In similar vein, John Dryden (1631–1700) in *Absalom and Achitophel* (1681) enlists references to Barzillai and his deceased son, the duke of Ormond and Thomas, earl of Ossory. Rather than belonging to a perverted anti-world, they provide an index of the aristocratic values of honour, nobility, bravery and immutable loyalty.[52] The Dublin-born John Denham (1614/15–69) espoused two contrasting kinds of poetic style, royalist panegyric and burlesque. His pastoral *Coopers Hill* (1642) defines the London landscape in terms of a fundamental monarchism, while *The Famous Battel of the Catts in the Province of Ulster* (1668), by contrast, is a grotesque fable about the spread of anarchy from Ireland to England.

The Irish Hudibras or Fingallian Prince (1689) is of uncertain provenance and has been variously attributed to James Farewell and Francis Taubman.[53] Written in burlesque mode, it parodies the journey of Aeneas to the underworld in the sixth book of the *Aeneid* by recounting the hapless descent of Nees, an Irishman, into St Patrick's purgatory at Lough Derg. Lively satiricism is eclectically mingled with bawdy humour, historical diagnosis and racist clichés. The poem derives its energy, in large part, from its attempt to capture the nuances of Hiberno-English which contradictorily are registered as devalued pastiche and as a discrete and ebullient idiom.

If topicality exerted an unremitting pressure on the aesthetic in the late seventeenth century, by the same token writing could be used to reflect on the volatility and ever-modulating loyalties of the individual subject. Roger Boyle (1621–79), first earl of Orrery, was paradigmatic in this respect; his multi-faceted public career was complemented by his prolific literary output. His *oeuvre* – which encompasses poetry, drama, romance, political pamphlets and a military tract, *A Treatise of the Art of War* (1677) – interrogated the mutable nature of honour and notions of service and probed the gaps between private affect and public duty.[54] Boyle was a member of one of the most powerful Protestant, New English dynasties in seventeenth-century Ireland. An expert and slippery politician and active soldier, he survived the political ruptures of the mid-century by constantly shifting allegiance, serving Charles I, Cromwell and Charles II with equal ability. His transfer to the parliamentary side in the 1640s is symbolic of his adaptive ability and skill for refashioning his identity. However, as Patrick Little has argued, Orrery was motivated throughout these fluctuations in his political position by an enduring belief in monarchical structure and in the necessity for achieving union within the British state.[55] As a consequence, his literary writings thematise the struggle for an ideal of transcendent order as well as the chaos caused by compromised loyalties and civic conflict. Orrery is credited with spearheading the vogue for heroic tragedy on the London stage and two of his early plays performed in Smock Alley Theatre are written in this vein. *The Generall: a Tragi-Comedy* (1664; originally titled *Altemera*) was staged in 1663 shortly after Philips's *Pompey*. Depicting a civil war between the citizens of Leptis and Mora, it explores the complex interassociations of love and honour troubling the central figures, especially the hero, Clorimum. Divided loyalty is a key theme of the play. Clorimum is forced initially to serve the usurper king of Leptis and to save his rival in love, Lucidor, in order to maintain his reputation and prove himself in the eyes of his beloved, Altemera. His culminating feat is a further deed of self-abnegation as he agrees to renounce his love and sanction the marriage of Lucidor and Altemera. Thus, revenge and rivalry are abandoned in the interests of social concord. Clorimum's embattled progress has, however, enabled the restoration of the true king, Melizer, who duly kills the usurper who has displaced him. A strained admixture of military aggression and Platonic idealism is hence seen as the crucial fundament of the state. In *Henry V* (1664), Orrery similarly introduces a sub-plot tracing the conflict of love and duty; Owen Tudor is forced to suppress his feelings for Princess Katherine in the interests of political stability.[56] The complex narratives of his convoluted fiction *Parthenissa, A Romance in Four Parts* (1651–69), which was expanded to six volumes in its final edition, centre on the intertwined amatory and military adventures of four Platonic heroes. Orrery's experiences of Cromwellian campaigns in Ireland are refracted in the tales of combat and of military engagement punctuating the multiplying plots of this romance; the political exchanges of his protagonists – such as the dispute between Ventidius and Artavasdes in Book III as to the relative merits of commonwealths and monarchies – restage and obsessively revisit the key conflicts that had dominated Irish and English affairs from the 1640s onwards.[57]

The tumult of the civil war period haunts the writings of the Restoration period and is evident in their perennial negotiation of the rules of permissible conduct and anxious formulations of identity as torn between contingency and order. Drawing on the conventions of rogue literature and of picaresque fiction, Richard Head (c.1637–86) created a host of vagrant figures who migrate between worlds and veer between a debased amorality and a desire to accord social sympathies with ethical impulses. Born in Ireland, Head was the son of a Church of Ireland clergyman who was murdered in the 1641 rebellion. He graduated from Oxford but seems to have moved back and forth between Ireland and England during his later career. His fortunes were equally variable as he alternated between periods of prosperity because of his expertise as a book-seller and of penury resulting from an addiction to gambling. The travel tales and fantastical voyages of discovery *The English Rogue Described in the Life of Meriton Latroon* (1665), *The Floating Island, or A new discovery relating the strange adventure on a late voyage from Lambethana to Villa Franca alias Ramallia* (1673) and *The Western Wonder, or, O Brazeel, an Inchanted Island Discovered* (1674), capture his sense of the radically dislocated nature of Irish identity. His play *Hic et Ubique; or, the Humours of Dublin* (1663) remoulds Jonsonian city comedy to reflect the economic realities and social dynamics of colonial Dublin. It depicts a seamy urban world peopled by wastrels, prostitutes, con-men and travellers who are motivated by greed and an irrepressible instinct for survival. A motley group of London outcasts who arrive in Dublin at the start of the play to try their fortunes render concrete the exploitative relations between the two countries as well as mirroring the processes of social and cultural exchange that mutually define Irish and English identities. Head represents the colonial capital as populated by rootless individuals who thrive on various forms of corruption, several of whom like Hic et Ubique and Phantastick are on the verge of monetary and moral bankruptcy. The abusive relationship between Captain Kil-tory and his voluble but disaffected Irish servant Patrick provides another perspective on the imbalances of this shady community. The criminalised licence and carnivalesque anarchy of the characters are, however, ultimately reined in by the moral imperatives of comedy. Kil-tory is defeated by the superior wiliness of the Hopewells, while the deracinated Peregrine and Hic et Ubique find suitable spouses. In contrast, English libertinism becomes the grounds of its own exploitation in *The Miss Betrayed With all Her Wheedling Arts and Circumventions* (1675) which details the fluctuating fortunes of the Irish prostitute Cornelia.[58] The titillating adventures of the heroine earn her, not opprobium or destitution, but a flourishing business in London.

The prose of the later seventeenth century continues to worry about questions of religious and historical legitimacy and to capture the altering divisions between ethnic and religious identities. The Church of Ireland theologian and divine William King (1650–1729) debates aspects of Protestant identity through his contestations of Catholic precept. His early tracts *An answer to the considerations which obliged Peter Manby . . . to embrace, what he calls the Catholick religion* (1687), *A Vindication of the Answer* (1688) and *A Vindication of the Christian Religion and Reformation* (1688) are a refutation of Catholicism and a defence of the necessity and truth of the Protestant faith. Several histories provide a retrospective on the mid-century debacles and use them to mediate and articulate the experiences and values of particular social groupings. Writing in exile, the Catholic bishop and former Confederate Nicholas French (1604–78), in *A Narrative of the Settlement and Sale of Ireland whereby the just English Adventurer is much prejudiced, the antient proprietor destroyed, and publick faith violated* and *The Bleeding Iphigneia or an Excellent preface of a Work Unfinished*, casts the events of the civil war period as a tragic sequence of loss and dispossession, while Edmund Borlase (fl.1682) in *The History of the Execrable Rebellion Trac'd from many preceding Acts to the Grand Eruption the 23 of October, 1641 And thence pursued to the Act of Settlement* (1680) sets out to disclose a consequential history that vindicates a Protestant triumphalism.

Partisan discourse is thus deployed not just to corroborate preconceived political and religious oppositions but to crystallise notions of identity that are constantly subject to slippage. The *History of the Irish Confederation and The War in Ireland, 1641–1643* by Richard Bellings, which was composed in the latter half of his life but remained unpublished until the nineteenth century, retells in painstaking detail the story of the Catholic alliance.[59] It immerses the reader in an unforeclosed but carefully weighted narrative that moves from the fragmentation of the opening, with its highlighting of a 'warr of many parts . . . perplexed with such diversity of rents and divisions, among those who seemed to be of a side', to the grim foreboding of the suspended ending in which Cromwell remains poised with his New Model Army to march on Drogheda. In his reconstruction of the Confederation, Bellings is at pains to distinguish the Old English at once from the Gaelic Irish, the royalism of Ormond, and the Catholic nationalism of Rinuccini and his party. Yet despite this quest for coherence, the ordering of the historian seems at a loss finally to contain and explicate the fractures of the past.[60] A similar counterpointing of futility and coherence is evident in the autobiographical writings of Mary Boyle Rich, countess of Warwick (1625–78), whose private diaries and religious contemplations, *Occasional Meditations Upon Sundry Subjects: With Pious Reflections Upon Several Scriptures* (1678), awkwardly shift from the pain of subjective experience to the transcendence of spiritual consolation. Thus, her comparison of the spider and the bee opposes the worthlessness of webs to the enduring value of honey, but registers the difficulty in the ensuing moral of relinquishing the self in favour of the liberating truths of the soul.[61] The letters of Boyle's sister, Lady Katherine Jones, viscountess of Ranelagh (1615–91), similarly bear testament to the necessity for a disciplined introspection but also give an insight into her rationalist non-conformism and lively engagement with the intellectual debates of her day.[62] The *Commonplace Book* and *Memoir* of Elizabeth Freke (*c.*1640–1714) are composed from a resolutely secular vantage point by contrast. They record her sense of wounded betrayal caused by her unhappy marriage and afford a vivid insight into the alienation of colonial experience in County Cork from the viewpoint of the wife of a New English settler.

The political conflicts of the Stuart regime and of the Williamite wars inflect the texts written in the latter decades of the seventeenth century. *The Loyal Brother or The Persian Prince. A Tragedy* (1682) by the playwright Thomas Southerne (1660–1746) uses an orientalist tale to shadow the divisions between Charles II and his brother, the future James II. His second play, *The Disappointment Or The Mother in Fashion* (1684), was performed in the Smock Alley Theatre in January 1685 shortly before the death of Charles II in February of that year. Its thematisation of intrigue, revenge and virtue under trial symbolically presages the battle between opposing creeds and political world-views enacted in the clash between James II and William of Orange. The entrenched sectarianism unleashed by the Williamite wars (1689–91) and the symbolic defeat of Jacobite forces at the Boyne in July 1690 is evident in contemporaneous writings. Thus, the self-aggrandising *A True Account of the Siege of Londonderry* (1689) by the Church of Ireland minister George Walker (1618–90) is immediately disputed by the Presbyterian John Mackenzie in *A Narrative of the Siege of London-Derry, or, The late memorable transactions of that city faithfully represented to rectifie and supply the omissions of Mr Walker's account* (1690), while the anonymous pamphlet plays from 1690, *The Royal Flight or the Conquest of Ireland a new farce*, *The Royal Voyage or the Irish expedition a tragicomedy*, *The Late Revolution or the Happy Change a tragi-comedy*, *The Abdicated Prince or The adventures of 4 Years a tragi-comedy*, and *The Bloody Duke or The adventures for a Crown a tragi-comedy*, welcome the advent of a new Protestant dispensation and reinvoke anti-papist stereotypes. The confessionalisation and ideological battles of Irish literature in English continue apace in this period, but equally the instability of symbolic representation and the fissile nature of local identities are evident in the internal strains of the pointed political rhetoric of these late seventeenth-century texts.

Although the Anglophone literature of Ireland from 1550 to 1690 is marked by its diversity and protean qualities, the history of cultural production tracked in this chapter also reveals continuities and consistent lines of influence. It is notable that particular forms are regularly adopted by the Irish writers of this era – whatever their background or persuasion – and refashioned to bear the weight of local interests and preoccupations. Thus, the anti-pastoral of Edmund Spenser's *Two Cantos of Mutabilitie* connects with that of Richard Bellings's *A Sixth Booke to the Countesse of Pembrokes* and of Francis Quarles's *Argalus and Parthenia*. Similarly, the rhetoric of satire and of sectarian polemic unites writers as disparate as Barnaby Rich, John Temple, Nicholas French, Richard Bellings and the unknown author of *The Irish Hudibras*. As the English tradition of the playhouse becomes an established feature of seventeenth-century Irish society, it is striking that dramatists commonly resort to the hybrid and unstable form of tragi-comedy as the most congenial and expressive mode because of its capacity to resonate with the political conditions of the country. James Shirley, Henry Burnell, Roger Boyle, earl of Orrery and the anonymous playwrights of the 1690s all write plays in this manner. The writings of early modern and Restoration Ireland are interconnected, moreover, not just by convergences in political and religious allegiance but by the symbolic ties of fealty signalled through the invocation of literary patrons. Just as sixteenth-century bardic poetry, as Marc Caball has shown, is imbricated in the dynastic systems of Gaelic Ireland, so too literature in English is variously aligned with strategic political circles in Ireland and in England and with the variable policies of successive Irish viceroys.[63] Moreover, the vital role of women as cultural facilitators becomes visible in these symbolic dedications as in the instance of the multiple female benefactors invoked by Bellings in the prefaces to his successive works or the female readers implicated in the reception of Katherine Philips's *Pompey*.[64]

Above all, writing in Ireland in the sixteenth and seventeenth centuries is characterised by the interpenetration of politics and aesthetics. Partisanship is an inseparable aspect of textuality in this era and the borderlines of literature and polemic are abidingly blurred.[65] Even though ideology as a consequence is an inescapable dimension of much of the literature produced between 1550 and 1690, it is also the case that these compositions refract and reimagine political struggles, thereby opening them up – at least partially – to scrutiny. Thus, visible and hidden relations to history enhance rather than curtail the symbolic density and suggestive ambiguities of writing in this era.[66] Ultimately, too, the shadow of military conflagrations, including the Nine Years War, the 1641 rebellion and the Confederate and the Williamite wars, leaves its mark on the texts composed in or about sixteenth- and seventeenth-century Ireland. The recent memory of trauma inscribes itself indelibly in this literature which can never disengage itself from the dissensions endemic within colonial communities.

Notes

1. 'March 10, 1619, Sir Thos. Wilson to the King', *Calendar of State Papers, Domestic Series, of the Reign of James I, 1623–1625, with Addenda* (London: Longman, Brown, Green, 1859), p. 555.

2. Pierre Bourdieu, 'Social Space and Symbolic Power', in *In Other Words: Essays Towards a Reflexive Sociology*, trans. Matthew Adamson (Stanford: Stanford University Press, 1996), pp. 123–39.

3. Arthur F. Marotti, *Manuscript, Print, and the English Renaissance Lyric* (Ithaca: Cornell University Press, 1995), pp. 135–208.

4. See Vincent P. Carey and Ute Lotz-Heumann, eds. *Taking Sides?: Colonial and Confessional Mentalités in Early Ireland: Essays in Honour of Karl S. Bottigheimer* (Dublin: Four Courts Press, 2003).

5. *Calendar of Carew Manuscripts Preserved in the Archiepiscopal Library of Lambeth 1515–1624*, ed. J. S. Brewer and W. Bullen, 6 vols. (London: Longman, Green, Reader and Dyer, 1867–73), I, p. 180.

6. William A. Ringler, Jr. and Michael Flachmann, eds. *Beware the Cat: the First English Novel* (San Marino, CA: Huntington Library, 1988).

7. Peter Happé and John N. King, *The Vocacyon of John Bale* (Binghampton, NY: Renaissance English Text Society, 1990).

8. For a discussion of Bale in terms of the rhetorical traditions of Protestantism see Andrew Hadfield, *Literature, Politics and National Identity: Reformation to Renaissance* (Cambridge: Cambridge University Press, 1994), pp. 51–80.

9. Alan Fletcher, *Drama, Performance, and Polity in Pre-Cromwellian Ireland* (Cork: Cork University Press, 2000), pp. 161–74. This ground-breaking study uncovers a richly varied and continuous tradition of dramatic performance in Ireland which has hitherto been largely ignored.

10. Peter Happé, ed. *The Complete Plays of John Bale, Vol. II* (London: D. S. Brewer, 1986), pp. 1–63.

11. For analysis of the rhetoric and politics of Derricke's text, see Maryclaire Moroney, 'Apocalypse, Ethnography, and Empire in John Derricke's *Image of Irelande* (1581) and Spenser's *View of the Present State of Ireland* (1596)', *English Literary Renaissance* 29 (1999), pp. 355–74.

12. Patricia Palmer, *Language and Conquest in Early Modern Ireland: English Renaissance Literature and Elizabethan Imperial Expansion* (Cambridge: Cambridge University Press, 2001), pp. 57–9.

13. For a discussion of the violence of Sidney's regime see Vincent Carey, 'John Derricke's *Image of Irelande*, Sir Henry Sidney, and the Massacre at Mullaghmast, 1578', *Irish Historical Studies* 31 (1999), pp. 305–27.

14. See Ciaran Brady, ed. *A Viceroy's Vindication?: Sir Henry Sidney's Memoir of Service in Ireland, 1556–78* (Cork: Cork University Press, 2002).

15. Richard A. McCabe, 'Making History: Holinshed's Irish *Chronicles*, 1577 and 1587', in David J. Baker and Willy Maley, eds. *British Identities and English Renaissance Literature* (Cambridge: Cambridge University Press, 2002), pp. 51–67.

16. Louis A. Montrose, 'Spenser's Domestic Domain: Poetry, Property, and the Early Modern Subject', in Margreta De Grazia, Maureen Quilligan and Peter Stallybrass eds. *Subject and Object in Renaissance Culture* (Cambridge: Cambridge University Press, 1996), pp. 83–130.

17. Stanley Wells, Gary Taylor, John Jowett and William Montgomery, eds. *William Shakespeare: The Complete Works* (Oxford: Clarendon Press, 1988). All references are to this edition and will be noted in parentheses. For discussion of the varying dimensions of the depiction of Ireland in Shakespeare's plays see Mark Thornton Burnett and Ramona Wray, *Shakespeare and Ireland: History, Politics, Culture* (Houndmills: Macmillan, 1997) and Christopher Highley, *Shakespeare, Spenser and the Crisis in Ireland* (Cambridge: Cambridge University Press, 1997).

18. For an analysis of the censorship of the potentially seditious allusions to Ireland in *Henry V* and other history plays of the period see Janet Clare, 'Art Made Tongue-Tied by Authority': Elizabethan and Jacobean Dramatic Censorship* (Manchester: Manchester University Press, 1999), pp. 24–75.

19. For an account of the rhetorical strategies of this dialogue see Richard Beacon, *Solon His Follie, Or A Politique Discourse Touching The Reformation of Common-Weales Conquered,*

Declined or Corrupted, ed. Clare Carroll and Vincent Carey (Binghampton, NY: Medieval and Renaissance Texts and Studies, 1996), pp. xiii–xliii.

20. For an analysis of this text, see David Gardiner, '"These Are not the Thinges Men Live By Now a Days": Sir John Harington's Visit to the O'Neill, 1599', *Cahiers Élisabéthains* 55 (1999), pp. 1–17.

21. See Henry Chettle, *Dialogue of Silvynne and Peregrynne*, ed. Hiram Morgan (http:///www.ucc.ie/celt/published/texts/E590001-001/nav.html) and *The Supplication of the Blood of the English Most Lamentably Murdered in Ireland, Cryeng Out of the Yearth For Revenge*, ed. Willy Maley, *Analecta Hibernica* 36 (1995), pp. 1–77. Morgan speculates that Chettle's text is an intelligence exercise, while Maley proposes that Spenser may have been the author of *The Supplication*.

22. Eugene Flanagan, 'Captain Barnaby Rich (1542–1617): Protestant Witness in Reformation Ireland', unpublished Ph.D thesis, University of Dublin, (1995) and 'The Anatomy of Jacobean Ireland: Captain Barnaby Rich, Sir John Davies and the Failure of Reform, 1609–22', in Hiram Morgan, ed. *Political Ideology in Ireland 1541–1641* (Dublin: Four Courts Press, 1999), pp. 158–80. For further discussion of Rich see Willy Maley, 'Gender and Genre: Masculinity and Militarism in the Writings of Barnaby Rich', *Irish Studies Review* 13 (1995–6), pp. 2–6.

23. Hiram Morgan notes the symbolic difference of the periodisation adopted by the English and Irish camps. The Battle of Kinsale is dated 24 December 1601 in the old calender deployed by Protestant England but 3 January 1602 in the reformed Gregorian system used by both the Irish and the Spanish. See 'Introduction', in Hiram Morgan, ed. *The Battle of Kinsale* (Bray, County Wicklow: Wordwell, 2004), p. 1.

24. Willy Maley analyses the rhetoric and political sub-texts of this tract. See '"Another Britain"?: Bacon's *Certain Considerations Touching the Plantation in Ireland* (1609)', *Prose Studies: History, Theory, Criticism* 18 (1995), pp. 1–18.

25. On the Jacobean attempt to forge a British consciousness and unify the realms under the dominion of James I, see Tristan Marshall, *Theatre and Empire: Great Britain on the London Stages under James VI and I* (Manchester: Manchester University Press, 2000). For a contrasting view of the underlying politics of depictions of Britishness on the English stage, see J. O. Bartley, *Teague, Shenkin and Sawney: Being an Historical Study of the Earliest Irish, Welsh and Scottish Characters in English Plays* (Cork: Cork University Press, 1954).

26. See C. H. Herford and Percy and Evelyn Simpson, eds. *Ben Jonson, Volume X* (Oxford: Clarendon Press, 1950), pp. 541–2.

27. On the strained politics of this masque, see David Lindley, 'Embarrassing Ben: The Masques for Frances Howard', *English Literary Renaissance* 16 (1986), pp. 343–59; Margaret Rose Jaster, 'Staging a Stereotype in Gaelic Garb: Ben Jonson's *Irish Masque*, 1613', *New Hibernia Review* (1998), pp. 87–98; Elizabeth Fowler, 'The Rhetoric of Political Forms: Social Persons and the Criterion of Fit in Colonial Law, *Macbeth* and *The Irish Masque at Court*', in Amy Boesky and Mary Thomas Crane, eds. *Form and Reform in Renaissance England: Essays in Honor of Barbara Kiefer Lewalski* (Newark, N.J.: University of Delaware Press, 2000), pp. 70–103; James M. Smith, 'Effaced History: Facing the Colonial Contexts of Ben Jonson's Irish Masque at Court', *English Literary History* 65 (1998), pp. 297–321.

28. Elizabeth Cary, Lady Falkland, *Life and Letters*, ed. Heather Wolfe (Tempe, AZ: Renaissance Texts from Manuscripts, 2001), pp. 119–25.

29. Annabel Patterson surveys the varying seventeenth-century interpretations of *Arcadia* in *Censorship and Interpretation: The Conditions of Writing and Reading in Early Modern England* (Madison: University of Wisconsin Press), pp. 24–43.

30. Deana Rankin, 'The Art of War: Military Writing in Ireland in Mid-Seventeeth-Century Ireland', unpublished D.Phil. thesis, Oxford (1999), pp. 116–21.

31. Philip Sidney, *The Defence of Poesy*, in Katherine Duncan-Jones, ed. *Sir Philip Sidney: The Major Works* (Oxford: Oxford University Press, 1989), p. 230.

32. Francis Quarles, *Argalus and Parthenia*, ed. David Freedman (Washington, DC: The Renaissance English Text Society, Associated University Presses, 1986), pp. 23–8.

33. For reflections on the cohesive traditions as well as the generic diversity of early modern Irish poetry see Andrew Carpenter, ed. *Verse in English from Tudor and Stuart Ireland* (Cork: Cork University Press, 2003), pp. 1–32. This pioneering anthology documents the vitality of poetic creation in Renaissance Ireland.

34. For accounts of Southwell's biography and poetics, see Jean Klene, ed. *The Southwell-Sibthorpe Commonplace Book, Folger MS. V.b.198* (Tempe, AZ: Medieval and Renaissance Texts and Studies, 1997); Danielle Clarke, *The Politics of Early Modern Women's Writing* (Essex: Longman, 2001), pp. 10–11; Sidney L. Sondergard, ' "Tears Woundes and Blood": Lady Anne Southwell's Caustic Meditation on Domestic Survival', *Sharpening Her Pen: Strategies of Rhetorical Violence by Early Modern English Writers* (Selinsgrove: Susquehanna University Press, 2002); Erica Longfellow, 'Lady Anne Southwell's Indictment of Adam', in Victoria E. Burke and Jonathan Gibson, eds. *Early Modern Women's Manuscript Writing: Selected Papers from the Trinity/Trent Colloquium* (London: Ashgate, 2004), pp. 111–33.

35. D. R. Woolf charts the changes in historiography in this period. See *Reading History in Early Modern England* (Cambridge: Cambridge University Press, 2000).

36. For an assessment of the insidious rhetoric of this text, see Hiram Morgan, 'Birchensa's Discourse', in Morgan, *The Battle of Kinsale*, pp. 391–407.

37. On the interconnections between politics and culture in Strafford's regime, see Hugh Kearney, *Strafford in Ireland 1633–41: A Study in Absolutism* (Manchester: Manchester University Press, 1959); J. F. Merritt, ed. *The Political World of Thomas Wentworth, Earl of Strafford 1621–41* (Cambridge: Cambridge University Press, 1996).

38. For discussion of the politics of Shirley's writing see Sandra A. Burner, *James Shirley: A Study of Literary Coteries and Patronage in Seventeenth-Century England* (Lanham, NY: University Press of America, 1988).

39. St Patrick was declared a Catholic saint in the seventeenth century but was also celebrated in the Protestant tradition. See Mike Cronin and Daryl Adair, *The Wearing of the Green: A History of St Patrick's Day* (London: Routledge, 2002), pp. 1–3.

40. Martin Butler, *Theatre and Crisis 1632–1642* (Cambridge: Cambridge University Press, 1984), pp. 166–80.

41. On the political tensions in the Werburgh Street theatre see William Smith Clark, *The Early Irish Stage: The Beginnings to 1720* (Oxford: Clarendon Press, 1955), pp. 26–40; Christopher Morash, *A History of Irish Theatre 1601–2000* (Cambridge: Cambridge University Press, 2002), pp. 3–10.

42. Raymond Gillespie, 'Temple's Fate: Reading *The Irish Rebellion* in Late Seventeenth-Century Ireland', in Jane H. Ohlmeyer and Ciaran Brady, eds. *British Interventions in Early Modern Ireland* (Cambridge: Cambridge University Press, 2005), pp. 315–33.

43. For this edition of *An Aphorismical Discovery of Treasonable Faction* see John T. Gilbert, ed. *A Contemporary History of Affairs in Ireland, from 1641 to 1652* (Dublin: Irish Archaeological and Celtic Society, 1879–80).

44. Rankin, 'The Art of War', pp. 177–81.

45. For discussion of the politics of Milton's tract see Thomas N. Corns, 'Milton's *Observations upon the Articles of Peace*: Ireland under English Eyes', in David Loewenstein and James Grantham Turner, eds. *Politics, Poetics and Hermeneutics in Milton's Prose* (Cambridge: Cambridge University Press, 1990), pp. 123–34; Willy Maley, 'Rebels and Redshanks: Milton and the British Problem', *Irish Studies Review* 6 (1994), pp. 7–11; David Loewenstein, *Representing Revolution in Milton and His Contemporaries: Religion, Politics and Polemic in Radical Puritanism* (Cambridge: Cambridge University Press, 2001), pp. 191–201.

46. For varying accounts of Ussher's politics and career see Alan Ford, 'James Ussher and the Creation of an Irish Protestant Identity', in Brendan Bradshaw and Peter Roberts, eds. *British Consciousness and Identity: The Making of Britain, 1533–1707* (Cambridge: Cambridge University Press, 1998), pp. 185–212; John McCafferty, 'St Patrick for the Church of Ireland: James Ussher's *Discourse*', *Bullán* 3 (1998), pp. 87–102.

47. Patricia Coughlan analyses the historical and political intricacies of this play. See '"Enter Revenge": Henry Burkhead and *Cola's Furie*', *Theatre Research International* 15, 1 (1990), pp. 1–17 and '"The Modell of its Sad Afflictions": Henry Burkhead's Tragedy of *Cola's Furie*', in Micheál Ó Siochrú, ed. *Kingdoms in Crisis: Ireland in the 1640s* (Dublin: Four Courts Press, 2001), pp. 192–211.

48. Notes on the staging of this play survive. See Timothy Corcoran, *State Policy in Irish Education, 1536 to 1816* (Dublin: Fallon Brothers, 1916), pp. 208–11.

49. For discussion of the intellectual contexts of these works by William Petty, Arnold and Gerard Boate and Vincent Gookin see T. C. Barnard, *Cromwellian Ireland: English Government and Reform in Ireland 1649–1660* (Oxford: Oxford University Press, 1975), pp. 213–48; Patricia Coughlan, '"Cheap and Common Animals": The English Anatomy of Ireland in the Seventeenth Century', in Thomas Healy and Jonathan Sawday, eds. *Literature and the English Civil War* (Cambridge: Cambridge University Press, 1990), pp. 205–23; Coughlan, 'Counter-Currents in Colonial Discourse: The Political Thought of Vincent and Daniel Gookin', in Jane H. Ohlmeyer, ed. *Political Thought in Seventeenth-Century Ireland: Kingdom or Colony* (Cambridge: Cambridge University Press, 2004), pp. 36–82; Coughlan, 'Natural History and Historical Nature: The Project for a Natural History of Ireland', in Mark Greengrass, Michael Leslie and Timothy Raylor, eds. *Samuel Hartlib and Universal Reformation: Studies in Intellectual Communication* (Cambridge: Cambridge University Press, 1994), pp. 298–317.

50. I am grateful to Angelina Lynch for sharing the findings of her University College Dublin doctoral dissertation on *Ter Tria* with me.

51. On the rich sub-texts of *Pompey*, see Morash, *A History of Irish Theatre*, pp. 21–9; Deana Rankin, '"If Egypt Now Enslav'd Or free A Kingdom or a Province Be": Translating Corneille in Restoration Dublin', in Sarah Alyn Stacey and Véronique Desnain, eds.

Culture and Conflict in Seventeenth-Century France and Ireland (Dublin: Four Courts Press, 2004), pp. 194–209.

52. On the history and cultural attainments of the Ormonds see Toby Barnard and Jane Fenelon, ed. *The Dukes of Ormonde 1610–1745* (Woodbridge: Boydell Press, 2000).

53. For a discussion of the history and manuscript variants of this elusive text see Andrew Carpenter, 'Sectarianism in Marsh's Ireland: Some Literary Evidence', in Muriel McCarthy and Ann Simmons, eds. *The Making of Marsh's Library: Learning, Politics and Religion in Ireland, 1650–1750* (Dublin: Four Courts Press, 2004), pp. 187–208.

54. Kathleen M. Lynch provides an overview of Orrery's life and career. See *Roger Boyle, First Earl of Orrery* (Knoxville: The University of Tennessee Press, 1965).

55. Patrick Little, *Lord Broghill and the Cromwellian Union with Ireland and Scotland* (Woodbridge: Boydell Press, 2004).

56. For an examination of Orrery's revival of the history play see Tracey E. Tomlinson, 'The Restoration English History Plays of Roger Boyle, Earl of Orrery', *Studies in English Literature 1500–1900* 43 (2003), pp. 559–77.

57. John Kerrigan discusses the Irish dimension of this romance. See 'Orrery's Ireland and the British Problem, 1641–1679', in David J. Baker and Willy Maley, eds. *British Identities and English Renaissance Literature* (Cambridge: Cambridge University Press, 2002), pp. 197–225.

58. For an extended analysis of this text, see Raymond Gillespie, 'Richard Head's *The Miss Display'd* and Irish Restoration Society', *Irish University Review* 34 (2004), pp. 213–28.

59. Richard Bellings, *History of the Irish Confederation and the War in Ireland*, ed. John T. Gilbert, 7 vols. (Dublin: M. H. Gill and Son, 1882–91).

60. On the political values underlying Bellings' history, see Raymond Gillespie, 'The Social Thought of Richard Bellings', in Ó Siochrú, *Kingdoms in Crisis*, pp. 212–28.

61. For an account of the representation of subjectivity in the countess of Warwick's journals see Ruth Connolly, '"The Amaseing Surprise of my Pation": Mastering the Self in the Diaries of Mary Boyle Rich, Countess of Warwick', unpublished M.A. dissertation, National University of Ireland, Cork (2001).

62. For an analysis of Ranelagh's correspondence see Elizabeth Anne Taylor, 'Writing Women, Honour, and Ireland: 1640–1715', unpublished Ph.D thesis, University College Dublin (1999), pp. 273–369.

63. See Marc Caball's discussion in chapter 3.

64. For a commentary on the role of women as readers, auditors and recipients of literature in medieval and early modern Ireland, see Máirín Ní Dhonnchadha, 'Medieval to Modern, 600–1900', in A. Bourke, S. Kilfeather, M. Luddy, M. Mac Curtain, G. Meaney, M. Ní Dhonnchadha, M. O'Dowd and C. Wills, eds. *The Field Day Anthology of Irish Writing, vols. IV and V: Irish Women's Writing and Traditions* (Cork: Cork University Press, 2002), IV, pp. 4–5.

65. For a related argument about the polemicisation of English literary culture between the civil wars and the Glorious Revolution see Steven N. Zwicker, *Lines of Authority: Politics and English Culture 1649–89* (Ithaca: Cornell University Press, 1993).

66. On the multiple ways in which political thinking is encoded in the writings of this era see Raymond Gillespie, 'Political Ideas and their Social Contexts in Seventeenth-Century Ireland', in Ohlmeyer, *Political Thought in Seventeenth-Century Ireland*, pp. 107–27.

Select bibliography

Barnard, Toby, *A New Anatomy of Ireland: The Irish Protestants, 1649–1770*, New Haven and London: Yale University Press, 2003.

'"Parlour Entertainment in an Evening"?: Histories of the 1640s', in Micheál Ó Siochrú, ed. *Kingdoms in Crisis: Ireland in the 1640s*, Dublin: Four Courts Press, 2001, pp. 20–43.

Bradshaw, Brendan, Andrew Hadfield and Willy Maley, eds. *Representing Ireland: Literature and the Origins of Conflict, 1534–1660*, Cambridge: Cambridge University Press, 1993.

Brady, Ciaran, ed. *A Viceroy's Vindication?: Sir Henry Sidney's Memoir of Service in Ireland, 1556–78*, Cork: Cork University Press, 2002.

Canny, Nicholas, *Making Ireland British: 1580–1650*, Oxford: Oxford University Press, 2001.

Carroll, Clare, *Circe's Cup: Cultural Transformations in Early Modern Ireland*, Cork: Cork University Press in association with Field Day, 2001.

Carpenter, Andrew, 'Sectarianism in Marsh's Ireland: Some Literary Evidence', in Muriel McCarthy and Ann Simmons, eds. *The Making of Marsh's Library: Learning, Politics and Religion in Ireland, 1650–1750*, Dublin: Four Courts Press, 2004, pp. 187–208.

ed. *Verse in English from Tudor and Stuart Ireland*, Cork: Cork University Press, 2003.

Coughlan, Patricia, '"Cheap and Common Animals": The English Anatomy of Ireland in the Seventeenth Century', in Thomas Healy and Jonathan Sawday, eds. *Literature and the English Civil War*, Cambridge: Cambridge University Press, 1990, pp. 205–23.

'Counter-Currents in Colonial Discourse: The Political Thought of Vincent and Daniel Gookin', in Jane Ohlmeyer, ed. *Political Thought in Seventeenth Century Ireland*, Cambridge: Cambridge University Press, 2000, pp. 56–82.

'"The Modell of its Sad Afflictions": Henry Burkhead's Tragedy of *Cola's Furie*', in Micheál Ó Siochrú, ed. *Kingdoms in Crisis: Ireland in the 1640s*, Dublin: Four Courts Press, 2001, pp. 192–211.

Gillespie, Raymond, 'Political Ideas and their Social Contexts in Seventeenth-Century Ireland', in Jane Ohlmeyer, ed. *Political Thought in Seventeenth Century Ireland*, Cambridge: Cambridge University Press, 2000, pp. 107–27.

Reading Ireland: Print, Reading and Social Change in Early-Modern Ireland, Manchester: Manchester University Press, 2005.

'The Social Thought of Richard Bellings', in Micheál Ó Siochrú, ed. *Kingdoms in Crisis: Ireland in the 1640s*, Dublin: Four Courts Press, 2001, pp. 212–28.

Gillespie, Raymond, and Andrew Hadfield, eds. *History of the Irish Book, vol. III: 1500–1800*, Oxford: Oxford University Press, 2005.

Hadfield, Andrew, *Spenser's Irish Experience: Wilde Fruit and Salvage Soyl*, Oxford: Clarendon Press, 1997.

Kerrigan, John, 'Orrery's Ireland and the British Problem, 1641–1679', in David J. Baker and Willy Maley, eds. *British Identities and English Renaissance Literature*, Cambridge: Cambridge University Press, 2002, pp. 197–225.

McCabe, Richard, 'Making History: Holinshed's Irish *Chronicles*', in David J. Baker and Willy Maley, eds. *British Identities and English Renaissance Literature*, Cambridge: Cambridge University Press, 2002, pp. 51–67.

Maley, Willy, *Nation, State and Empire in English Renaissance Literature: Shakespeare to Milton*, London: Palgrave Macmillan, 2003.

Morgan, Hiram, ed. *Political Ideology in Ireland 1541–1641*, Dublin: Four Courts Press, 1999.

Ohlmeyer, Jane, *Civil War and Restoration in the Three Stuart Kingdoms*, Cambridge: Cambridge University Press, 1993.

O'Neill, Stephen B. 'Staging Ireland: Representations of Ireland in English Renaissance Drama, c.1587–1603', unpublished Ph.D thesis, National University of Ireland, 2003.

Palmer, Patricia, *Language and Conquest in Early Modern Ireland: English Renaissance Literature and Elizabethan Imperial Expansion*, Cambridge: Cambridge University Press, 2001.

Rankin, Deana, *Between Spenser and Swift: English Writing in Seventeenth-Century Ireland*, Cambridge: Cambridge University Press, 2005.

"'If Egypt Now Enslav'd or free A Kingdom or a Province Be": Translating Corneille in Restoration Dublin', in Sarah Alyn Stacey and Véronique Desnain, eds. *Culture and Conflict in Seventeenth-Century France and Ireland*, Dublin: Four Courts Press, 2004, pp. 194–209.

5

Literature in Irish, c.1550–1690: from the Elizabethan settlement to the Battle of the Boyne

MÍCHEÁL MAC CRAITH

Introduction

As crown officials began to exercise more and more control over Ireland in the second half of the sixteenth century, the Tudor state considered the spread of Protestantism to be an essential element of its political and civilising role. Given the Protestant Reformation's insistence on the vernacular for scripture and public worship, and its alacrity in exploiting the recently discovered resources of print technology to disseminate bibles and other religious material in the vernacular, it is not surprising that it was the Reformation that introduced printing to the Gaelic world. The first Irish book in print, however, did not appear until 1567, printed in Edinburgh and not in Dublin, and it was not until 1602 that an Irish translation of the New Testament was printed in Dublin.

The first section of this chapter examines the attempts of the state authorities to publish Protestant religious works in Irish and provides a context for their less than enthusiastic efforts. Catholic reaction to Protestant religious propaganda was not really organised on a systematic basis until the second decade of the seventeenth century. Spearheaded in particular by the Observant Franciscans who were fortunate to have a number of exceptionally talented members of the Gaelic literati join the order at this time, the campaign to counteract Protestant religious work in Irish was centred on the Irish Franciscan College which was founded in Louvain in 1607. The second section of this chapter deals with the religious works written and printed in Louvain, works which also led to the production of grammars and dictionaries as the use of print led the friars to engage in serious reflection on vernacular languages in general and on Irish in particular. These reflections of an émigré community, forced to dwell abroad for religious and political reasons, also led to deeper speculation on the nature of Irish identity. Living in the centre of the northern European Renaissance and Counter Reformation, the Irish friars were not immune to the renewal of interest in hagiography and history that had been inspired by both evangelical humanism and the Renaissance. Stimulated by this intellectual current, the Louvain Franciscans carried out serious research on the lives of Irish saints and on Irish history and the fruits of their labours in these fields are the subject of the next section of this chapter.

The foundation of an Irish regiment in the Spanish service in 1605 and the location of its headquarters in Brussels led to the establishment of an Irish community there. Acting as chaplains to the Irish regiment, the Franciscans in Louvain maintained close links with their compatriots. Some of these exiles brought literary manuscripts with them from Ireland; some poems and prose texts were actually composed in exile. While neither specifically Franciscan nor religious, this literature emanated from the same general Louvain ambience, and is dealt with as such in the fourth section of this chapter.

Perhaps the great achievement of the Gaelic literati of the seventeenth century was the forging of an Irish communal identity that fused Roman Catholicism with Gaelic consciousness, uniting those of Gaelic descent and those of Anglo-Norman descent under a common religion, a common culture and a common monarch. While Irish clerics on the continent played a major role in creating this identity, it can already be traced in embryonic form in the verse of professional and amateur poets composing in Ireland from the last years of the previous century. The final section of this chapter traces the elaboration of this sense of Irishness up to the accession of James II in 1685, placing particular emphasis on the work of Dáibhí Ó Bruadair, the greatest poet of the second half of the century and one who experienced at first hand the major socio-political disturbances of the period.

Print, prose and Protestantism

When the Irish parliament passed the Act of Uniformity in 1560, restoring Protestantism as the state religion with the accession of Elizabeth I to the throne, it added a rider permitting church functionaries who did not know English to continue conducting services in Latin and specifically forbidding the use of Irish. Seeing that the use of the vernacular for scripture and public worship was one of the most significant features of the Protestant Reformation, the attitude of the Dublin parliament seems bizarre. Had evangelisation really been a priority, the advantages of targeting the Gaelic literati should have been obvious, and the arguments offered by the Dublin officials on the difficulties of getting Gaelic into print and the low level of literacy are but flimsy excuses. In Gaelic Ireland, however, evangelisation went hand in hand with military conquest and anglicisation. Cultivating the Gaelic language, even for evangelical reasons, could only be construed as disloyalty to the crown, with the result that the principles of evangelisation had to yield to the exigencies of conquest.

Given the hostility of the authorities it is little wonder that the first book in Gaelic was printed not in Ireland but in Scotland. The work in question was John Carswell's *Foirm na n-Urrnuidheadh* (Edinburgh, 1567), a translation of the *Book of Common Order* (Edinburgh, 1562 and 1564), which was in turn a revision of the *Geneva Book*, sometimes called John Knox's Liturgy, printed in Geneva in 1556.[1] In his epistle to the reader and introductory poem Carswell refers six times to the Gaels of Ireland and the Gaels of Scotland, stating that his work was intended for dissemination in both countries. Choosing classical common Gaelic as his medium, with relatively few concessions to Scotticisms, he would have been equally intelligible in both countries. Carswell, highly literate in Gaelic, Scots and Latin, has been aptly described by John Bannerman as perhaps 'the most notable practitioner of the three cultures in the sixteenth century'.[2] Like his patron, Archibald Campbell, the fifth earl of Argyll (1538–73), he interacted with the Lowland south, an area in which the principles of the Renaissance and the Reformation were highly valued. Carswell was able to present the Reformation in terms that were acceptable to a Gaelic world-view, showing a flexibility that may not have pleased many of his fellow Reformers. In his dedicatory epistle to Argyll, Carswell utilises the traditional Gaelic mode of panegyric in address to a chief, but is innovative in changing the medium from poetry to prose. Further innovation is demonstrated by choosing exemplary figures from the Old Testament instead of legendary Gaelic warriors as suitable role models for a chief. The ideal Gaelic chief is thus transformed by Carswell into a godly prince supporting the Reformation.[3] In his epistle to the reader Carswell laments that the Gaelic language has not benefited from the advantage of the printing press. Especially regrettable is the absence of a Gaelic Bible in print. Even the traditional Gaelic scribes would save time and labour in transferring to the new technology.[4]

While acknowledging the value of historical lore, Carswell goes on to attack the scribes' preoccupation with secular tales, making particular reference to stories about Fionn mac Cumhaill and the *fiana*. Instead of pursuing worldly gain they would be much better employed in writing down 'the faithful words of God and the righteous path of truth'. These strictures on the Gaelic literati, however, can be seen less as an out and out attack, than as a call to reorder their priorities and put their talents at the disposal of the Reformation, particularly for the production of a Gaelic Bible. In stressing the need for a Gaelic Bible Carswell is a promoter of the Reformation; in emphasising the advantages of print culture, he is a promoter of the Renaissance.[5]

Carswell's approach was completely at variance with that displayed by the Dublin authorities, but his work was greatly facilitated by his patron. Not only was Argyll a committed supporter of the Reformation, but he was also one of the most powerful nobles in these islands, with 5,000 trained soldiers at his disposal. Argyll had close relations with the MacDonalds of Antrim, the O'Donnells of Tyrconnell and the O'Neills of Tyrone. His aunt Lady Agnes Campbell was married to James MacDonald of Dunivaig and the Glynnes. Following the latter's death in 1565, Argyll arranged two very strategic marriages, one between Lady Agnes and Toirdhealbhach Luineach O'Neill of Tyrone, the other between her daughter Fionnuala Campbell and Hugh O'Donnell, the earl of Tyrconnell. These marriages, taking place together in August 1569, had the important consequence of reconciling the traditional enmity between the O'Neills and the O'Donnells. Both brides were very dominant characters and were responsible for most of the traffic of Scottish mercenaries to Ulster at this time.[6]

Given Argyll's strong Ulster links, it is little wonder that Carswell addressed his work to the Gaels of Ireland as well as those of Scotland. Under his influence it was quite reasonable to expect that Gaelic Ulster, if not Gaelic Ireland altogether, could be persuaded to adopt the Genevan Order, thus posing a threat to Elizabeth's Anglican settlement. It was this potential challenge that finally galvanised the authorities in Dublin into providing spiritual material for the native Irish.

Some time before 1567 Elizabeth had sent the not inconsiderable sum of £66 13s. 4d. to Adam Loftus, archbishop of Armagh, and Hugh Brady, bishop of Meath, 'for the making of character to print the New Testament in Irish'.[7] When nothing had happened by the end of 1567 she threatened to demand that the money be returned 'unless they presently put the same in print'.[8] In 1571 Seán Ó Cearnaigh, treasurer of St Patrick's cathedral in Dublin, published the first Gaelic book to be printed in Ireland, *Aibidil Gaoidheilge 7 Caiticiosma*.[9] In addition to an epistle to the reader, this work contained a brief account of the Gaelic alphabet, a translation of the catechism of the *Book of Common Prayer* (1559), various prayers for private recitation, and a Gaelic version of Archbishop Matthew Parker's twelve articles of religion (1561). Whereas Carswell's work was printed in roman script by Robert Lekprevik, printer to the General Assembly of the Reformed Church, Ó Cearnaigh used a Gaelic typeface that was specifically cut for the purpose. Archbishop Matthew Parker, a member of the privy council that bore the cost of this Gaelic typeface, and the first to use a specially cut typeface for printing Anglo-Saxon characters, would have known that Anglo-Saxon letters were similar to Gaelic ones. It was cost-effectiveness that prompted the use of Gaelic script, even though some of the material had already appeared in Scotland in roman characters.[10] It seems that two hundred copies of this work were printed, but only two have survived. The reference to Queen Elizabeth as 'our pious all-powerful supreme prince' must be one of the earliest acknowledgements in the Gaelic language of the English monarch's legitimacy in Ireland.

Seán Ó Cearnaigh was also involved in the translation of the New Testament into Gaelic and, although conceived as far back as the 1560s, progress on the project was slow. Two members of the team died before it was brought to completion: Nioclás Bhailís in 1585 and Ó Cearnaigh himself in 1587. In 1587 the privy council in England wrote to the lord deputy, Sir John Perrot, to encourage the work, 'consydering how godlie and necessary a mater yt was for the instruccion of that Realme to have the Scriptures in their vulgar tongue'. Fearganainm Ó Domhnalláin's involvement was curtailed as a result of his appointment as archbishop of Tuam in 1595. By 1597 only the gospels as far as the sixth chapter of St Luke had been printed. While the rest of Luke's gospel and the gospel of John were available in manuscript, the remainder of the New Testament had still to be translated. It was left to Uilliam Ó Domhnaill, one of the first three students to enter Trinity College, Dublin, on its establishment in 1592, to bring the work to completion and to see it through the press. Ó Domhnaill acknowledged the collaboration of Domhnall Óg Ó hUiginn in this final stage. The printing was done by Uilliam Ó Cearnaigh, a kinsman of Seán, who had a printing-shop in Trinity College, and it was completed in 1602. In his dedicatory epistle to James I, Ó Domhnaill explained that his translation was based on the Greek version of the New Testament: 'Vnder which burden how carefully and conscionably I have groned, they onely can judge that can confer this translation with the original Greeke, vnto which I tyed my selfe, as of dutie I ought.'[11]

The 'original Greeke' was in fact the *Textus Receptus* published by Erasmus in 1516. This was a major breakthrough in biblical scholarship, even though some of the 'original Greeke' was composed by Erasmus himself. In addition to the *Textus Receptus*, Ó Domhnaill also made use of the Latin Vulgate and the English *Geneva Bible* (1557). The team of translators were all university men trained in the classics and Ó Domhnaill's willingness to work from the best Greek text available at the time marks this Gaelic New Testament as a work of evangelical humanism. It seems that only five hundred copies were printed and even then demand does not appear to have been great as copies were still available in 1628 when Sir William Usher bestowed twelve on Trinity College for the use of Gaelic-speaking students there.[12]

Under the inspiration of Sir Arthur Chichester, lord deputy since 1605, Ó Domhnaill undertook a translation of the Book of Common Prayer. This work appeared in 1608 and is remarkable for its faithful transmission of Cranmer's dignified prose into a natural, fluent Gaelic style. *Leabhar na nVrnaightheadh gComhchoidchiond* contains some noteable omissions, however. The ceremonies for the ordination of priests and deacons and for the consecration of bishops are lacking. The psalter is also wanting. Given that only the New Testament was available in Gaelic by this time, Ó Domhnaill omitted the lessons from the Old Testament.

In 1627 William Bedell (1571–1642) was called from his parish in East Anglia to be provost of Trinity College, Dublin. As a conformist Puritan who was fluent in Hebrew, Bedell was well qualified for the post. A further advantage was his three years' experience in Venice, as chaplain to Sir Henry Wotton, James I's ambassador to the Venetian Republic. After spending two years in Trinity, Bedell was appointed bishop of Kilmore and Ardagh and until his death in 1642 proved himself an assiduous promoter of the Reformation in his diocese, conscious of the need to provide Gaelic-speaking ministers and Gaelic religious material for his flock. His most ambitious project, the translation of the Old Testament into Gaelic, was completed by 1638. As provost of Trinity he learned Gaelic from Muircheartach Ó Cionga, a member of a hereditary learned family from County Westmeath, and it was on this scholar and his assistant Séamus de Nógla that he laid the task of rendering the Old Testament into 'plain Irish'. It bears emphasising that Ó Cionga's translation was not just a slavish adherence to the King James version of 1611. Bedell compared the English text with the Hebrew Torah and with Giovanni Diodati's annotated translation of the Bible into Italian (Geneva, 1603). Correcting the Irish wherever the English was found wanting, the bishop's method of translation meant that he was using the best biblical scholarship available at the time. It seems that Bedell had purchased a printing press at his own expense and had it installed in his own residence by 1641. As a result of the Confederate wars and Bedell's death in 1642, the Old Testament was not published until 1685, the original manuscript undergoing many changes in the course of its preparation for the press.[13]

Catholic reaction in exile

The initial Gaelic Catholic reaction to the Protestant initiatives was rather disparate. In 1560 Richard Creagh, archbishop of Armagh, produced the first Irish catechism, a trilingual work in Gaelic, Latin and English. Written on the continent, this work, entitled *Epitome officii hominis christiani*, was never published and is only known to us through the writings of O'Sullivan Beare. In focusing on printed material, however, one should not overlook the influence of preaching friars. Eoghan Ó Dubhthaigh (d.1590), provincial of the Irish Franciscans from 1581 to 1583, was a well-known preacher who used to sum up the substance of his teaching in Irish verse.[14] Stanihurst referred to him in 1577 as 'a preacher and a maker in Irishe', this surely being one of the earliest references to an amateur Irish poet by name.[15] Only two of Ó Dubhthaigh's poems have survived, unfortunately. One of them, *A Bhanbha, is truagh do chor* (Ireland, Pitiful is your Plight), while only a short undated poem of seven quatrains, both laments the English presence in Ireland and depicts the Reformation as alien and English. The poet implores Ireland not to become a little England (*Saxa óg*). He depicts the religious struggle as one between *Cáiptín Lúitér* and *Cáiptín Cailbhín* on one hand and *Pádruig do ghénerál féin* on the other, thus linking the faith brought by Patrick to Ireland with that of Counter Reformation Catholicism.[16]

Ó Dubhthaigh's other poem, composed late in 1578, is a long piece of more than eighty quatrains that combines a paean of praise to the Virgin Mary with a scathing attack on three Irishmen who have turned their backs on Roman Catholicism to become bishops in the Church of Ireland. In this work devotion to Mary becomes a yardstick of allegiance to Tridentine Catholicism, while abandoning her entails the abandonment of other essential features of Roman Catholic doctrine. Ó Dubhthaigh expressly links Anglicanism with conquest when he states in one quatrain that the Virgin Mary would only receive a slap in the face were she to visit Dublin Castle, the centre of alien rule as well as of alien religion. His use of English words on four occasions is not only significant as one of the earliest occurrences of English words in poetry in Irish, but the negative connotations of their use suggest that the Reformation has political and cultural implications over and above its religious consequences.[17] A popular preacher who would as provincial have met with the elite of Irish society, both of Gaelic and Anglo-Norman stock, Ó Dubhthaigh's poems spell out in no uncertain terms for his flock the religious, cultural and political implications of the Tudor conquest. If Anglicanism and anglicisation go hand in hand, Roman Catholicism and Gaelic culture are equally inextricably linked.

There is in fact very little difference ideologically between the views expressed orally by Ó Dubhthaigh in the 1570s and those expressed in print by his more famous colleagues in Louvain forty years later, and Ó Dubhthaigh's evidence suggests that Franciscan opposition to Tudor proselytism and conquest had crystallised by a very early stage.

In 1593 Flaithrí Ó Maolchonaire (Conry) (1560–1629) translated the Jesuit Jerónima de Ripalda's catechism, *El texto de la doctrina Cristiana*, into Irish, perhaps while attending the University of Salamanca. A member of a professional Gaelic learned family that served the O'Connors and McDermots of Connaught, Ó Maolchonaire practised the craft of poetry for some time before departing for the continent to study for the priesthood. Finding the Old English bias of Thomas White, rector of the Irish College at Salamanca, little to his liking, Ó Maolchonaire left to join the Franciscans who had a prestigious college in the same city.[18] He sent his text to an unnamed recipient in Ireland in 1598 but it seems to have survived in only one seventeenth-century manuscript.[19] This is a very simple work intended for children, as indicated by the forms of address, *child* and *master*. It is difficult to know if Ó Maolchonaire really envisaged publication when he sent his catechism to Ireland, but in 1606 he successfully petitioned Phillip III of Spain for permission to open a college for Irish Franciscans in the university town of Louvain, then the leading intellectual centre of the Catholic Counter Reformation in northern Europe.[20] The first community took up residence the following year and was joined on 1 November 1607 by the former professional poet Giolla Brighde Ó hEodhasa (d.1614) who took the name Bonabhentura in religion.

Within four years Bonabhentura had put his literary talents at the service of the Catholic Counter Reformation and published *An Teagasg Críosdaidhe* or Catechism in Antwerp in 1611.[21] In seeking permission to publish this work Ó hEodhasa said it was intended primarily *'pour la jeunesse et aultres braves gens dicelluys pays contre la faulse doctrine des aultres religions contraires à nostre saincte foy et nostre mère la Saincte Eglise de Rome . . .'* (for the young and other fine people of this country against the false doctrine of other religions contrary to our holy faith and mother, the Holy Catholic Church of Rome),[22] while the approbation given by the archbishop of Malines, clearly stated the aim of the work: *'ut conatibus haereticorum ad pervertendam gentem Hibernicam iam libros hoc idiomate conscriptos evulgantium contraeatur'* (to oppose the attempts of the heretics who have already published books in this language to pervert the Irish people).[23] Whereas Carswell was trying to enlist the support of the Gaelic *literati* in favour of the Reformation, Ó hEodhasa's Counter Reformation strategy was directed at a much younger and popular audience. Influenced by the works of Peter Canisius and Robert Bellarmine, Ó hEodhasa's book does not follow the question-and-answer format, but is divided into five sections comprising a commentary on the Creed; the Our Father and the Hail Mary; the Ten Commandments; the sacraments; and virtues and vices, good works and sins. The catechism's most novel feature is the summary in verse of the doctrine contained in the following prose sections. This ensured that Ó hEodhasa's teaching would reach a much wider audience than those literate in Irish. While catechetical works in verse were not unknown on the continent, Ó hEodhasa may have been thinking of the didactic techniques of Eoghan Ó Dubhthaigh already mentioned.

Despite Ó hEodhasa's express intention of writing 'pour la jeunesse', his catechism seems to have been in sufficiently wide circulation among Irish soldiers stationed in the Spanish Netherlands to warrant the following remarks from the English spy Richard Morres in a letter to Lord Salisbury in 1611:

> After his coming from Prague, he saw one of the books among the Irish soldiers, printed in Irish at Antwerp, and set forth by the friars of Louvaine confirming their own religion, and to the contrary infirming and refuting that of the Protestants, in such sort that infinite readers and hearers of the Irish will presently believe the contents thereof to be true.[24]

The Franciscans eventually procured their own printing press, despite the efforts of the English authorities to persuade Archduke Albert to refuse permission, and a second posthumous edition of Ó hEodhasa's catechism appeared in 1614/15. A letter from Sir Ralph Winwood to William Trumbull, dated 9 July 1614, refers to the failure of the archduke to prevent 'the unworthy proceedings of the Irish friars at Louvain in printing and publishing these seditious libels, and that in their own language'.[25] The only hope, as far as Winwood was concerned, was 'that all copies of such books be called in and publicly burned'.[26]

The next work to come off the press was Flaithrí Ó Maolchonaire's *Desiderius* in 1616.[27] Ostensibly a translation of a popular Spanish religious text, Conry took considerable liberties with his original, making both omissions and additions. One particularly lengthy passage, nearly one-quarter the length of the original, was composed for the express purpose of encouraging Irish Catholics to persevere in their faith. Of particular interest is an extract where Conry declares that civil government derives its authority from the governed:

For it is not to the princes, but to Peter that Christ gave the spiritual powers . . . and Paul had them as he says himself, one who had not civil powers. And it is certain that the spiritual powers and the temporal powers originated in a different and dissimilar way for the reason that it is the people or their ancestors who gave the kings whatever power they now possess; and it is Christ himself and not the people who gave the spiritual powers to Peter and to the other apostles; through whom the same powers were given to the bishops, without any permission being sought from the people, as can be proved from Paul's epistle to Titus and from his other epistle to Timothy.[28]

Ó Maolchonaire's theological training on the continent put him in touch with the latest thinking of Counter Reformation Europe. Robert Bellarmine in the University of Louvain claimed that a pope under certain circumstances could depose a heretical ruler and absolve his subjects from their allegiance, while Suarez, a theologian from the University of Salamanca, had advanced the revolutionary theory that power derived from the people. This theory cut right across the doctrine of the divine right of kings, a doctrine very clearly enunciated by James VI of Scotland and future king of England in his *Trew Law of Free Monarchies* (1598). The insertion of a clause into the oath of allegiance in 1607, deliberately framed to counteract Bellarmine's claim, led to a protracted controversy between James and Bellarmine, and Ó Maolchonaire's work is best situated within this debate. While the latter's reference to 'oaths that they are wont to ask of poor people .i. that the princes are head of the church'[29] refers more to the Elizabethan Oath of Supremacy (1563) than the Oath of Allegiance, his denial of the divine right of kings was not destined to win him any favours from James.

Desiderius was followed by Aodh Mac Cathmhaoil's work on the sacrament of penance, *Scáthán Shacramuinte na hAithridhe* in 1618.[30] Better known as Aodh Mac Aingil (1571–1626) he studied law in the Isle of Man. He was engaged as tutor to the sons of Hugh O'Neill, and Sir John Harrington refers to him in his description of his encounter with O'Neill in 1598.[31] Mac Aingil accompanied Henry O'Neill to Spain when he was sent there as a hostage by his father in 1600 to ensure that Spanish aid would reach Ireland. Studying at the University of Salamanca he joined the Franciscans around 1603, becoming a teacher of theology in the university soon after his ordination. Appointed to Louvain in June 1607, he was heavily involved in diplomatic activities from 1609 to 1614 on behalf of O'Neill and other Irish interests.[32]

Scáthán Shacramuinte na hAithridhe is based on the teaching of the four-teenth session of the Council of Trent (15 October 1550 to 25 November 1551), with the incorporation of recent material from the *Rituale Romanum* of 1614.

In the words of the censors, the aim of the work was *ad instructionem cleri & populi afflictae patriae* (for the instruction of the clergy and people of the afflicted homeland) and it contained *omnia tam confessoribus quam poenitentibus necessaria ad forum poenitentiae* (all that was necessary regarding the forum of penance for the clergy as well as the laity).[33] This prioritising of the laity is borne out in the body of the text itself when the author states that the penitent should be aware of the nature of absolution, even though this properly pertains to the role of the priest. The doctrinal nature of the work notwithstanding, closer perusal yields some very interesting evidence of shifts in Gaelic political ideology. In his introduction Mac Aingil states that while every other Catholic nation, *gach náision Chatoilic eili*,[34] has printed religious books, they are more necessary in Ireland than elsewhere because of the dearth of priests and preachers. His description of Ireland as a Catholic nation is most interesting, as is the frequency of the word *nation* in the text, the term occurring sixteen times in all.

While Mac Aingil adopts a most polemical stance in his introduction, the body of the text is remarkably free from controversy until the final section which treats of indulgences.[35] The author alerts the reader to the fact that he is writing in 1617, exactly one hundred years after the outbreak of the Reformation, which is depicted as originating from Luther's pique at being passed over in favour of Tetzel to preach the indulgence granted by Pope Leo X to those who would support the war against the Turks. Turning polemical once more, Mac Aingil accuses both Luther and Calvin of gross indecencies, based for the greater part on Johannes Cochlaeus's *Commentaria de actis et scripits Martini Lutheri* (1549). The real aim of this invective, however, is less to discredit Luther and Calvin, than to highlight the contrast between them and James I. Though brought up in the faith of Luther and Calvin, he cannot be held culpable for his education. More importantly, he did not follow the paths of these two malicious masters in pride and arrogance. James, in fact, is our noble illustrious king, (*ar rí uasal óirdheirc*).[36] Through a highly selective use of James's own work, the *Praefatio monitoria* (1609), and through studiously avoiding passages that would prove offensive to Catholics, Mac Aingil demonstrates to his own satisfaction that the content of James's faith is either explicitly or implicitly the same as that held by Roman Catholics. In thus manipulating the king's own words, Mac Aingil concludes that James is a Catholic in fact if not in name, and that Irish Catholics are therefore justified in granting him their allegiance as their lawful sovereign. If Irish Catholics are being forced to obey laws that go against their conscience, it is the king's officials who are guilty, not the king himself.[37]

For Mac Aingil Ireland is a Catholic nation, but this spiritual allegiance to Rome is in no way incompatible with temporal allegiance to the English crown, nor is this allegiance incompatible with Gaelic culture. This description of Ireland as a Catholic nation seems also to apply to Gaelic Scotland, since the author specifically refers to Ireland and her dear daughter Scotland (*Éri . . . agus a hinghean ionmhuin Alba*)[38] as the only countries to have received the privilege of being free from all taint of heresy.

The Louvain friars obtained a new printing press in 1641 and an Irish translation of the Rule of the Third Order of St Francis was the first work to be printed on it. In 1645 Antoin Gearnon published *Parrthas an Anama*, a work that is both a catechism and a prayer book, the catechetical section being very much indebted to Ó hEodhasa's catechism.[39] Subsequent devotional works such as Séan Ó Dubhlaoich's *Suim Bhunudhasach an Teagaisc Chriosdaidhe* (Louvain, 1663) and Francis Molloy's *Lucerna Fidelium* (Rome, 1676) also borrowed from Gearnon.[40] The prayers in *Parrthas an Anama* proved very popular in the later manuscript tradition of Munster. Gearnon's work is quite free of the polemical bitterness that characterises Ó Maolchonaire and Mac Aingil and seems to be more a manual of devotion for Irish Catholic gentlemen living in tranquillity than a work encouraging Irish Catholics to persevere in the face of persecution. Perhaps the hope engendered in the early years of the Confederation of Kilkenny (1642–50) had led Gearnon to believe that the days of persecution were over. An interesting feature of the work is the presence of eighty-six woodcuts illustrating the text. Though the illustrations were used in other religious works published in Louvain, and do not refer to specifically Irish settings, their presence adds to the general aura of tranquillity that the work presumes.

While the actual output from Louvain is rather meagre, it seems that other publications were envisaged. In 1650 Fr Philip O'Reilly, guardian of the Irish Franciscan community in Prague, a daughter house of Louvain, translated St Francis de Sales's religious classic *Introduction à la vie dévote* into Irish as *De Theacht isteach air an mBeathaidh Chrábhaidh*. The original manuscript has not survived, but the fact that it was copied by another Franciscan in Flanders in 1710 suggests that O'Reilly was hoping to have his work published in Louvain.

Apart from their theology and the political implications of their militant Catholicism, the most striking feature of the first three Louvain productions is the deliberate rejection of the studied artificial language of the *fileadha* (professional poets) in favour of a direct, simple style. Ó hEodhasa, Ó Maolchonaire and Mac Aingil were very aware of this innovatory aspect and, as if anticipating censure, use their prefaces to defend themselves. Ó hEodhasa spells out in verse his fears that the splendour of fine words would only obscure the splendour of divine teaching:

> I have not – it would not be right – dulled, with the shine of words, the glistening array sparkling with gems, from heaven – the radiant words of the Creator.
>
> Were I engaged in gilding words, I should obscure many of them: rings of precious stones conceal a scabbard completely.[41]

Ó Maolchonaire, in support of his contention that his main aim was to be understood by simple people not skilled in the subtleties of the literary tongue, has recourse to a quotation from his favourite author, St Augustine:

> Of what profit is the golden key unless it opens that which we need to open, when that is the only use we have for it; and why should we reject a wooden key if it opens that thing for us?[42]

Mac Aingil defends his choice of language in the following terms:

> If it is said that it is impertinent for us to write anything in Irish because we have not cultivated that language in the traditional way: our answer is this, that it is not to teach Irish that we write but to inculcate repentance and we deem it sufficient to be understood even though our Irish is not quite correct.[43]

While arguing, however self-consciously, in favour of a simpler form of language, all three authors refrain from open criticism of the cultivators of the literary language. Much less muted in his criticism was the secular priest Theobald Stapleton, who published a catechism in Irish and Latin in Brussels in 1639.[44] Of Old English extraction, the author's knowledge of Irish would have been confined to the vernacular, and he castigates the literati for cultivating obscurity. Ignoring the merits of the literary language, he was acutely conscious of its disadvantages for the spread of the faith in a new world dominated by printing. Interestingly enough, he is equally stringent on the use of Latin for religious instruction and he vividly describes the ordinary people trying to recite the Our Father and the Creed in Latin chattering like a parrot or a jackdaw trying to talk (*acht a gogalluig amhail Pioraide, no caoga do chuirfeadh chum cainte*).[45] As for *an Tuata bocht simplidh Erenach* (the poor simple Irish peasant),[46] both Latin and literary Gaelic were equally unintelligible to him, and therefore useless in furthering the Counter Reformation.

We have little information as to the number of copies printed of each of the Louvain books.[47] We also lack precise information on the levels of literacy in Irish in the early seventeenth century. The use of verse in Ó hEodhasa's catechism suggests that the dissemination of the contents would occur much more by rote than by reading. In recusant England, the master of the house would instruct both family and servants, so it was possible that one literate person, either cleric or lay person, could reach quite a large audience. Robert Darnton's comment is quite instructive regarding the oral reception of printed material: 'For the common people in early modern Europe, reading was a social activity. It took place in workshops, barns and taverns . . . for most people throughout most of history, books had audiences rather than readers. They were better heard than seen.'[48]

In most European countries the growth of humanism and the invention of printing encouraged the cultivation of the vernacular for literary purposes. The advent of the Reformation and the demand for translating the scriptures into the vernacular accelerated this trend. But whereas in other countries it was a matter of the vernacular vying with Latin, in Gaelic Ireland the vernacular had to contend with two languages, Latin and *bérla na bhfileadh*, the artificial literary language of the poets. The printing revolution, however, meant that knowledge had become democratised and was no longer the preserve of an intellectual elite. As the Gaelic literati struggled to come to terms with the consequences of the printed word, their whole concept of learning and literacy had to change, this change being accelerated by the exigencies of the Counter Reformation. The prefaces to the Louvain works are thus dominated by a mixture of humanistic values and Counter Reformation strategy. The self-conscious apologia of the authors is all the more acute, given that Ó Maolchonaire and Ó hEodhasa both belonged to the traditional learned caste, and even Aodh Mac Aingil may have received some training in a bardic school. They all felt the same need to justify themselves to their peers as did many a continental author when abandoning Latin for the vernacular. Though Ó Maolchonaire had practised as an *ollamh* (master poet) before departing for Spain, his long absence from Ireland may have caused him to feel overawed at Ó hEodhasa's literary skills. Ironically enough, there is a major divergence between the self-styled simplicity of *Desiderius* (1616) and the real simplicity of the former's unpublished catechism of 1593, which he felt no need to explain. This raises the possibility that Ó Maolchonaire's admission of lack of skill and fluency is not genuine, but a mere trope in accordance with the stylised professions of humility common in literary introductions of the time. Even Ó hEodhasa's apologia rings somewhat hollow given his avowed intention of writing 'pour le jeunesse'.

Mac Aingil, the least 'professional' of the three authors, is also the least self-conscious in his apology: my first priority is to teach repentance, not language. Yet it is obvious that he held Ó hEodhasa's linguistic skills in great esteem if not awe, and he deeply regretted the poet's premature death in November 1614:

> He had intended to write much for the salvation of souls and for the secular honour of our nation had he lived, but, alas, through God's anger with his sinful people, he was called at the time of his fruitfulness when he was beginning to put his work into print and before he managed to instruct us in our mother tongue, so that we could succeed in writing something that would benefit souls, since the severity of the persecution prevents from teaching by word of mouth. He left no one behind for the nation who was able to achieve what he had intended to do. For, though our nation, glory to God, has many learned people, and though many of our youth are being educated in universities of learning and piety, nevertheless, not one of them is as skilled and as illustrious as Bonabhentura in learning, in Gaelic and in piety, and there has not been such for a long time.[49]

The invention of printing and the consequent cultivation of vernacular tongues resulted in the standardising of these languages, thus introducing the necessity for grammars and dictionaries. Ó hEodhasa played a central role here too and he produced the first formal grammar in Irish, *Rudimenta grammaticae hiberniae* in Louvain, sometime between 1607 and 1614. Despite its great influence on subsequent grammarians of the Irish language, this was all achieved through the manuscript tradition, and it was only in 1968 that this grammar was finally published.[50] Given Mac Aingil's reference to Ó hEodhasa's intention of instructing 'us in our mother tongue', it is possible that his grammar was composed solely for the Louvain community, but neither can it be ruled out that publication and consequent dissemination to a wider public were also envisaged. In the light of the new-found cultivation of the vernacular, it is little wonder that the first Gaelic dictionary was also printed in Louvain, Micheál Ó Cléirigh's *Foclóir nó Sanasán Nua* (1643). The full title of the work, *Foclóir nó Sanasán Nua ina mínighthear cáil dfoclaibh cruaidhe na gaoidheilge, arna scriobhadh ar urd aibghitre* . . . . (A Dictionary or New Wordbook in which the Meaning of Difficult Words in Irish is Explained, Written in Alphabetical Order) suggests that the author was mainly preoccupied with archaic and difficult words, but Robert Cawdrey, publisher of the first English dictionary in 1604, expressed similar aims: '*A Table Alphabetcall, conteyning and teaching the true writing, and understanding of hard usuall English wordes . . . Whereby they may the more easilie and better understand many hard English wordes . . .*' Most of the English dictionaries published in the seventeenth century had like objectives, and maybe Ó Cléirigh's intention needs to be re-evaluated in the light of this knowledge.[51]

Other Franciscan lexicographers of the period were Muiris Ó Maolchonaire, Baolach Mac Aogáin, Seán Ó Cuirnín and Risteard Pluincéad. The last made good use of Ó Cléirigh's work in compiling his Latin–Irish dictionary at the Franciscan convent of Trim in 1662. All these dictionaries still remain in manuscript form, though contemporary writers expressed the hope of seeing at least some of them in print.

While the friars' main preoccupation was the production of religious material, it seems that they also intended to cultivate secular literature. A manuscript now held in the university library of Giessen in Germany indicates that the contents were intended for publication in Louvain with a title page containing the words *iar na chur a ccló a mainisdir na mbrathair neirionach a Lobhain maille hughdardhás MDLXXXV* (printed in the monastery of the Irish friars at Louvain 1585), the date 1585 being an obvious error for 1685.[52] The manuscript contains four courtly love poems and an amount of Ossianic material in both verse and prose, including the earliest known Irish version of the famous ballad *Cnoc an Áir*. Despite the emphasis on secular literature, however, the first item in the manuscript is a long poem by Bonabhentura Ó hEodhasa, *Truagh liomsa, a chompáin, do chor*, one of three poems inserted into the Louvain edition of his catechism. Allegedly a lament for a friend who has fallen into heresy, the poem is really an elucidation of Roman Catholic doctrine and a strenuous refutation of the reformers.[53]

While the intention to publish Irish secular literature would have marked a new and welcome development, it seems that the compiler of the manuscript felt that he could not do so at the expense of the original aim behind the Louvain publishing venture, promotion of the Counter Reformation in Ireland through the publication of religious works. Ó hEodhasa's use of the Gaelic language and his claim that Catholicism was the religion of the tradition encapsulated in that language were vital ingredients in the creation of a faith and fatherland ideology. If Gaelic and Catholic were now synonymous, English and Protestant were equally synonymous and equally alien.[54] The addition of this poem to the second edition of the catechism only served to accelerate the formation of an Irish national identity that was to become even more explicit in the works of Ó Maolchonaire and Mac Aingil. While its appearance in the Giessen manuscript is further confirmation of the constructed symbiosis of language, culture and religion that became the essence of Irish identity during the seventeenth century, it bears recalling that this construct of Irish identity had already been elaborated in Eoghan Ó Dubhthaigh's oral verse in the final quarter of the previous century. Additional important iconographical evidence for this construct is found in St Isidore's

Irish Franciscan College, Rome, a sister college of Louvain founded by Luke Wadding in 1625. The grave-slabs of Mac Aingil (d.1626), Wadding (d.1657) and Molloy (d.1677) refer to each of them as *de religione e patria benemerito* (distinguished for love of religion and country), while the grave-slab of Rory O'Donnell, earl of Tyrconnell (d.1608) and his brother Cathbharr (d.1609) in the church of San Pietro in Montorio in Rome carries an even more explicit reference to this ideology in specifically referring to Red Hugh O'Donnell (d.1602) as thinking of faith and fatherland (*pro fide et patria cogitante*).

The would-be title page for the publication of the Giessen manuscript refers to the Irish Franciscan house in Louvain as *mainisdir na mbrathair neirionach* (the monastery of the Irish brothers). The title page of Mac Aingil's work on the sacrament of penance (1618) refers to the author as *leaghthóir diadhachta a ccoláisdi na mbráthar néirionnach a Lobháin* (a lecturer in theology in the college of the Irish Franciscans at Louvain). When the Ulster chieftains Hugh O'Neill, Rory O'Donnell and Cúchonnacht Maguire left Ireland for good in September 1607, thus paving the way for the plantation of Ulster and the final subjugation of the province, Maguire's chronicler Tadhg Ó Cianáin kept a record of their travels.[55] In his entry for November 1607, Ó Cianáin describes the first encounter in seven years between Henry O'Neill and his father at Notre Dame de la Halle beside Waterloo. Henry had been appointed colonel of the Irish regiment in the Spanish forces in 1605 and the text describes going to meet the refugees *go mbuidhin ndermhair ndeighinnill do chaiptínibh, do dhaoinibh uaisle do Spáinneachaibh agus d'Eirinnchaibh 7 do gach nasión archena dia mbátor* (with a large well-equipped company of captains and of noblemen, Spanish and Irish and of every other nation).[56] It bears noting that Ó Cianáin uses the word *Éireannach* (Irish person) here rather than the ethnic signifier *Gael* (or *Gaoidheal*) and that the words *Éireannach* and *nasión* (nation) occur together. The text has a further reference to Henry O'Neill as *coronél na nEirinnach a fFlonndrus*,[57] and the Irish college at Douai is referred to as a *coláiste Eireannach*.[58]

Another important document associated with Louvain is the will made by Robert Chamberlain on 7 February 1611 prior to his entry into the Franciscans. In his will he leaves his money *le h-aghaidh an Clódh-Ghaoidheilge agus neithe do chur a ccló do rachas an onóir do Dhia, a cclú dár násion agus d'órd San Froinsias* (for the Gaelic press and for the printing of things that will redound to the honour of God, the fame of our nation and of the order of St Francis).[59] We have already referred to Mac Aingil's description of Ireland as a Catholic nation in his work on the sacrament of penance and his use of the word 'nation' sixteen times in all in the course of the text. The use of the marker *Éireannach* to describe the members of the Irish Catholic nation seems to have developed in Irish émigré circles in the Spanish Netherlands in the early years of the seventeenth century, circles associated with the Franciscans in Louvain and O'Neill's Irish regiment. Both in the Franciscan community and among the Irish aristocratic exiles tensions arose between those of Gaelic stock and those of Old English origin. The use of the geographical marker *Éireannach* appears to have been a deliberate choice of terminology to overcome ethnic tensions in the cause of a common homeland, common culture and common religion. William Trumbull, an agent of the English crown in Brussels, had deftly assessed the situation in referring to the 'perfidious Machiavellian friars of Louvain', who 'seek by all means to reconcile their countrymen in their affections and to combine those that are descended of the English race and those that are mere Irish in a league of friendship and concurrence against your majesty and the true religion now professed in your kingdom'.[60]

Ó Cianáin's association of *nasión* and *Éireannach* is highly significant as this is the earliest example known to me of the concept *nation* itself in Irish, of the word *Éireannach* in its new meaning, and of the two words together in combination. In his study on the construction of nationhood Adrian Hastings notes that English people felt themselves to be a nation from the fourteenth century onwards, and suggests that the English Bible and the Book of Common Prayer reinforced both the use of the word and the understanding of the concept in the English mind. Furthermore the depiction of Israel itself in the Old Testament presented a very clear model of what it meant to be a nation, understood as a unity of people, language, religion, territory and government.[61] This formative influence of the Bible on political concepts was, of course, much stronger in Protestant countries than in Catholic ones. The word *natio* occurs but seven times in the Vulgate version of the New Testament, but on quite significant occasions, such as the first Pentecost: *erant autem in Jerusalem habitantes Judaei, viri religiosi ex omni natione, quae sub coeli est* (Acts 2:5). The Gaelic New Testament of 1602, however, translating from the Greek *ethnos* rather than the Latin *natio*, uses *cineadh* (race) five times, *ceineúl* (stock) once and a circumlocution on the final occasion. The Gaelic use of the word seems to have derived from continental sources – indeed Tadhg Ó Cianáin's spelling could well be suggestive of a Spanish origin – but we cannot rule out the fact that the Franciscan intellectuals would have been familiar with both the Latin Vulgate and Spanish political thought.

Marc Caball has traced the growing sense of Irish national consciousness from the middle years of Elizabeth I's reign, the key elements of this consciousness being a common homeland and a common Gaelic culture shared between those of Gaelic stock and gaelicised descendants of Anglo-Norman origins, coupled with a growing realisation that Roman Catholicism was an essential component of this shared culture.[62] This consciousness becomes more acute, it seems to me, in Irish émigré circles in the Spanish Netherlands in the early years of the seventeenth century, with a deliberate attempt being made to forge this national consciousness through the adoption of specific semantic markers such as *nasión* and the adoption of the inclusive term *Éireannach* at the expense of ethnic markers such as *Gaoidheal* and *Gall*. In fact this apparently inclusive term contained its own exclusivity as it did not extend to all the inhabitants of the island of Éire but deliberately excluded the Nua-Ghaill, or the new planters who were hostile to both Catholicism and Gaelic culture. And as *Éireannaigh* gradually accepted the Stuart dynasty as their legitimate sovereign the term eventually came to exclude those who were supporters of parliament and opposed to Charles I.

Breandán Ó Buachalla has noted the first use of this new meaning of *Éireannach* in formal verse in a poem composed by Eoghan Ruadh Mac an Bhaird around 1626. Mac an Bhaird had translated the famous military handbook of Justus Lipsius, *De militia Romana libri cinque*, for Aodh Ó Domhnaill, a son of one of the exiled earls. The poet's hope was that Lipsius's advice would benefit Ó Domhnaill in an invasion of Ireland. In a dedicatory poem accompanying the handbook, *A leabhráin ainmnighthear d'Aodh*, the poet expresses his hope that those of Irish and Old English stock would unite together as *Éireannaigh*. What is perhaps most significant about this poem is that the author was residing in Louvain at the time, the very same crucible that forged this new terminology in the first place.[63] In the preface to his catechism already discussed, Stapleton uses *Éireannach* for *Hibernus* throughout his introduction and *Gaoilaig* for *Hibernus lingua*. This new usage grew popular in the homeland as well as is evidenced from the following account by a French traveller in Ireland in 1644:

> les naturels sont connus des Anglois sous le nom d'Iriche, des Francois sous celuy d'Hibernois que l'on tire du latin, ou d'Irois que l'on tire du nom de l'Isle, parce que Land signifie terre, ils se nomment Ayrenacke, ce qui'il faut apprendre par la practique, parce qu'ils n'escrivent point leur langue & n'apprennent le Latin que sur le pied de l'Anglois.
>
> (The indigenous population is known by the English under the name Irish, by the French under the name Hibernois which is derived from Latin, or Irois which is derived from the name of the island, because land means 'terre'. They call themselves 'Éireannach' which must be learned from practice as they do not at all write their language and only learn Latin on the back of English.)[64]

Though primarily composing works of religious instruction to advance the Catholic Counter Reformation, the Louvain authors could not remain untouched by the world around them, and their writings have political, cultural and ideological implications apart altogether from their religious content.

The creative impulse in Louvain was highly admired in the homeland as is indicated by a letter written in 1642 by Rory O'Moore, one of the leaders of the 1641 rising: 'If we may before Flan Mac Egan dies, we will see an Irish school oppened, and therefore could wish heartily that those learned and religious fathers in Louvayn did come over in hast with their monuments and with an Irish and Latin print.'[65] O'Moore's hopes were unfortunately not realised. Lack of funds and the diversion of promised funds to the war effort slowly strangled the literary projects in Louvain itself and the resulting Cromwellian conquest ensured that there would be no creation of a similar foundation in Ireland.

The Louvain contribution to hagiography and history

Promoting Counter Reformation teaching in the vernacular was only one aspect of the work of the Louvain Franciscans. Their other great contribution lay in the fields of hagiography and history. The study of hagiography was given a fresh boost by the growth of evangelical humanism and the Reformation, and a scientific critical approach to the discipline had begun in Brussels in the early seventeenth century under the direction of a group of Jesuit scholars known as the Bollandists, some of whom were known to the Franciscans at Louvain. Closer to the bone were the activities of some learned but erratic Scottish writers who, through a misinterpretation of the Latin words *Scotia* and *Scot(t)us* were claiming Irish saints for their own country. The most active of these propagandists was Thomas Dempster with his publications *Menologium Scotticum* (Bologna, 1619) and *Historia ecclesiastica gentis Scotorum* (Bologna, 1627). His extravagant claims prompted a number of Irish scholars to undertake the kind of research necessary to repudiate the Scotsman's assertions.[66] Henry Fitzsimon had already published a catalogue of the principal saints of Ireland in 1611 but the first work to tackle Dempster's claims was David Rothe's *Hibernia resurgens* (Rouen, 1621). In the spring of 1623, Thomas Messingham, rector of the Irish College in Paris, met with two Irish Franciscans, Aodh Mac an Bhaird (Ward) (1593–1635), a member of a literary family that were hereditary poets to the O'Donnells, and Patrick Fleming (1599–1631). Messingham had already been collecting materials relating to the lives of the Irish saints, and was interested in enlisting the co-operation of the Franciscans for his project. An agreement was reached but subsequently fell through. Messingham later reproached Mac an Bhaird for his slowness of work, while the Franciscans felt that Messingham published material without acknowledging their contribution. (Messingham published his *Florilegium insulae sanctorum* in Paris in 1624.) As well as refuting Dempster, Messingham believed that a properly researched corpus of national hagiography would both strengthen Irish Catholicism in the battle against heresy and also facilitate the presentation of a united Catholic *natio* for European readers.[67]

When the arrangement with Messingham fell through, the Franciscans decided to initiate their own project. Mac an Bhaird had already collected much hagiographical material in France and went to Louvain in the autumn of 1623. Accompanying Aodh Mac Aingil to Rome for the General Chapter of the Order that same year, Patrick Fleming noted items of Irish hagiographical interest in all the monasteries in which they stayed en route and corresponded regularly with Mac an Bhaird. A great boost to the project came when Micheál Ó Cléirigh (*c.*1592–1643), a trained historian, joined the Franciscan order in Louvain.[68] In 1626 he was sent back to Ireland to collect as much material as he could. For the next eleven years he traversed the country, visiting friaries and lay schools, and collecting, transcribing and checking material, before sending it back to Louvain. Ó Cléirigh's travels took place during the summer, but in winter he returned to Drowes, the refuge of the former friary of Donegal, where he made fair copies of the material he had collected. The task of editing the manuscripts fell to John Colgan (1592–1658) and in 1645 he published a large folio volume, *Acta Sanctorum Hiberniae*, the Lives of those Irish saints whose feast-days fell between the first of January and the end of March. The Lives of Patrick (17 March) and Brigid (1 February) were excluded from this volume, but together with the Life of Columba (9 June), they were published as a separate work dealing with Ireland's three major patron saints in 1647, *Triadis thaumaturgae*. It was intended to publish the Lives of the Irish saints for the whole twelve months of the year as well as many other works, but lack of funds in particular hindered the undertaking.

Given that an awareness of evidence was one of the essential components of the new sense of history that emerged during the Renaissance, Colgan's work shows him to be very much a scholar of this period. Faithful to the Renaissance rallying cry, *ad fontes*, he was most diligent in searching out manuscripts not only in Ireland, but all over Europe. On the minus side, his critical faculty was somewhat disarmed by the fact that he was dealing with the lives of saintly people. Religious credulity tended to blunt the healthy scepticism needed to analyse documents objectively. Yet his intention of editing the best text, instead of producing a critical edition, shows him to be at one with the humanist tradition.

Like Colgan, Mícheál Ó Cléirigh was equally aware of the importance of primary sources. During the eleven years he spent in Ireland collecting and transcribing manuscripts, he was always careful to cite his source, the place and date of transcription, and the actual owner of the document. Given the fact that his work was undertaken under the vow of obedience, it is not always easy to assess the sharpness of his critical faculty. While sometimes admitting that he finds certain aspects of the saints' lives absurd, nevertheless, he faithfully transcribes what was written before him in accordance with his orders: *óir do haithnitheadh dhíom lorg na seinleabhar do leanmhain* (since I was commanded to follow the pattern of the old books).[69] Ó Cléirigh's emphasis on obedience notwithstanding, his tendency to omit material that reflected badly on the O'Donnells indicates that he was not always a mere transcriber.

If Ó Cléirigh's initial brief was to gather material for an ecclesiastical history of Ireland, it soon became obvious that a civil history of Ireland would complement the latter. In addition to hagiographical material, he transcribed martyrologies and genealogies. He completed *Réim Ríoghraidh* (Succession of the Kings) in November 1630 and *Lebor Gabála* (Book of Invasions) in December 1631. In 1632 he initiated his major work, *Annála Ríoghachta Éireann* (Annals of the Kingdom of Ireland), a history of Ireland in annalistic form from the earliest times until 1616. The whole work took four years to complete and since Ó Cléirigh had the assistance of three other important scholars, Cúchoigríche Ó Cléirigh, Fearfeasa Ó Maolchonaire and Cúchoigríche Ó Duibhgeannáin, Colgan gave the history its more popular title, the Annals of the Four Masters.

Though a contemporary letter expressed surprise that Ó Cléirigh was not hanged during his travels in Ireland, this does not mean that he was working under extremely difficult conditions. His accomplishments indicate that his research was undertaken with the support of distinguished patrons in an atmosphere conducive to study, research and writing. Toirdhealbhach Mag Cochláin, who gave his patronage to *Seanchas Ríogh Éireann* and *Geinealuighi na Naomh* in 1630, was both a member of parliament and a wealthy landowner.[70] Brian Mag Uidhir, lord of Fermanagh, who gave his patronage to Ó Cléirigh for the re-edition of *Lebor Gabála Éireann* in 1631, was chosen as king's commissioner in County Fermanagh, an office that entailed collecting the royal taxes. Mag Uidhir and his cousin were the only persons of Gaelic origin to be given this appointment.[71] Sir Fergal O'Gara, a member of parliament for County Sligo, was the patron for the Annals and could well have instigated the work. An alumnus of Trinity College, O'Gara may have provided the link between Ó Cléirigh and Archbishop Ussher.[72] Fr. Thomas Strange, guardian of the Franciscan convent in Dublin from 1626 to 1629, was on particularly friendly terms with Ussher, who indicated his willingness, despite the religious tensions of the time, to make his library available to Irish Franciscan scholars.[73] Despite Ussher's generosity, Strange felt he could not mention him by name in a letter to Luke Wadding, giving him instead the ironic sobriquet Jacobus de Turrecremata (Torquemada), adding that this man 'could harm us more than any in the kingdom'.[74]

Ó Cléirigh was working under the patronage of men of substantial means, men of considerable standing in the land, men who had come to terms with the new political settlement. Far from making a last stand for Gaelic culture, *Annála Ríoghachta Éireann* is best seen as an authoritative history for the new Irish Catholic nation that had come into being under the *síoth coitcheann* (common peace) established by James I and continued by Charles I. A copy of the Annals was presented to Sir Fergal O'Gara, another sent to Louvain for printing. Once again the lack of proper funding and the diversion of promised funds to the military campaign of 1642–9 resulted in failure to carry the grandiose scheme through to completion. It was only in the middle of the nineteenth century that the Annals were eventually published.

The Annals cannot be properly discussed in isolation from Seathrún Céitinn's (Geoffrey Keating) *Foras Feasa ar Éirinn* composed between 1629 and 1634. Eschewing the traditional annalistic format in favour of a continuous narrative, Céitinn (c.1580–c.1644) adopts the invasion framework of *Lebor Gabála* to accommodate and include the Old English community in the national myth. Like Ó Cléirigh, Céitinn was writing for the new Catholic Irish nation that had come into being, *ríocht Éireann* (the kingdom of Ireland). That nation was a community of *Éireannaigh*: persons born in Ireland. It included all those of Gaelic or Anglo-Norman descent who were Irish-born and Catholic. It excluded those who were not Irish-born, in particular the recently arrived, usually Protestant, settlers, and disregarded the minority who were Old English and Protestant. In this sense the history was designed to define a select 'nation' in opposition to others who were deemed to be outside of, and hostile to, that nation.[75] In completing his history with an account of the twelfth-century reform of the Irish church, the author's aim in focusing on this reform is really to vindicate the efforts of the Catholic Counter Reformation diocesan clergy of his own day. A diocesan priest himself and of Old English stock, Céitinn was trained in France and is associated with Rheims and Bordeaux. Returning to Ireland in 1613 he was the author of a number of unpublished devotional works in Irish that entered and influenced the manuscript tradition.

Céitinn's *Foras Feasa* immediately entered this tradition and is contained in approximately thirty manuscripts of the seventeenth century alone, one-third of these from before 1650. Apart from the interest this text generated among Gaelic secular scholars, Irish Franciscan scholars were also avid readers of Céitinn's history. One of the very early copies seems to have been in the hand of Mícheál Ó Cléirigh himself, transcribed in the Franciscan convent in Kildare not later than September 1636. This copy was taken to Louvain, used, annotated and actually cited by Colgan in *Acta Sanctorum Hiberniae* (1645). Another copy with Franciscan associations is dated between 1638 and 1641. A Franciscan working in County Leitrim made a copy in 1644 which also made its way to the continent, while a copy was transcribed in the Irish Franciscan house in Prague in 1663. The surviving evidence indicates that Franciscan scholars were among the first and keenest readers of Céitinn's *Foras Feasa*.[76]

Overshadowed by Ó Cléirigh and Céitinn, Dubhaltach Mac Fhirbhisigh (c.1600–71) has not yet received the prominence he merits. The last of his family to practise learning, Mac Fhirbhisigh, though trained as a poet, was more interested in history and law. He made his learning available to some of the most prominent people of his time, such as Mother Bonaventure Brown, abbess of the Poor Clares in Galway for whom he translated a copy of the Rule of St Clare into Irish; the historian John Lynch (c.1599–c.1677), for whom he made a copy of *Chronicon Scotorum*; the antiquarian Sir James Ware (1594–1666), for whom he translated from Irish, making lists of bishops available to him; and the famous Galway lawyer and politician Patrick Darcy. Mac Fhirbhisigh apparently did not highly regard *Foras Feasa*: '(a work which) the judicious Mac-Firbis (in a letter to Dr Lynch) observes ought never to be published'.[77] Despite this disparagement, however, Mac Fhirbhisigh would have been of one mind with Céitinn's political ideology. His most important work, *Leabhar na nGenealach*,[78] the book of genealogies, gives prominence to families of Anglo-Norman descent as well as to those of Gaelic origin, but studiously omits the New English and the Ulster planters. *Leabhar na nGenealach* also provides five different Gaelic genealogies for Charles II, thereby aligning Mac Fhirbhisigh with the same allegiance to the Stuart dynasty evinced by Mícheál Ó Cléirigh in his *Annála Ríoghachta Éireann*.

Secular literature in the Louvain ambience

The literature compiled and composed by the Franciscans themselves was not the only literature compiled in the Louvain ambience. Somhairle Mac Domhnaill of the Glens of Antrim (c.1586–1632), having been implicated in the abortive rising of 1615, fled to the continent and after numerous adventures became a captain in the Irish regiment in Flanders commanded by his cousin John O'Neill, earl of Tyrone. Commended by the emperor for bravery at the battle of the White Mountain outside Prague in 1620, Mac Domhnaill demonstrated that he was not just a swashbuckling adventurer. In the years 1626–7 he commissioned the compilation of a collection of Ossianic ballads known as *Duanaire Finn*, the poem book of Fionn.[79]

Comprising sixty-nine ballads in all, *Duanaire Finn* is the largest and most important source of Ossianic ballads that survives. Transcribed in Ostend by Aodh Ó Dochartaigh, a member of the Irish regiment in Flanders, it is preceded in the manuscript by an incomplete copy of another Ossianic text, *Agallamh na Seanórach*, a collection of a hundred episodes in prose and verse allegedly recounted by Oisín or Caoilte to St Patrick. The *Agallamh* was mainly transcribed by a different scribe, one Niall Gruama Ó Catháin, before alternating with Aodh Ó Dochartaigh and another scribe between 7 August 1626 and the end of the year. Two references, one to St Francis, the other to Louvain, indicate that this section of the manuscript had close links with the Irish Franciscan college, though it is unlikely that Ó Catháin himself was a Franciscan. Between the *Agallamh* and the *Duanaire*, the manuscript contains in a different hand a fragment of a prose tale concerning Fionn, Oscar and Maghnus, son of the king of Lochlainn. In compiling *Duanaire Finn* Ó Dochartaigh drew material from manuscripts carried by Irish exiles to the continent. Joseph Falaky Nagy, however, has suggested that Ó Dochartaigh may have taken down some of the ballads from oral recitations in Flanders and further speculates that he might have actually composed a few ballads for the *Duanaire*.[80] When Captain Somhairle died he was buried in the cloister of St Anthony's Franciscan College at Louvain and the manuscript came into the possession of the community. A reference in the college financial accounts dated 16 April 1632 noted that Somhairle owed 150 florins to the college and it is possible that he gave his manuscripts to the friars as a contribution to clearing his debts. Somhairle's manuscript is a good indication of the popularity of *fianaigheacht* among seventeenth-century Gaelic aristocracy, a popularity no doubt enhanced by the similarity between Somhairle's own military career and that of a *féinnidh* (outlaw).[81]

In 1631 Aodh Ó Dochartaigh received another commission from Captain Somhairle and produced another manuscript in Ostend that is known to us as the *Book of the O'Conor Don*. Douglas Hyde, the first person to examine the manuscript with care, noted the scholarly, beautiful and painstaking nature of Ó Dochartaigh's handwriting.[82] This anthology is a collection of 342 poems, with a further 28 that have since been lost. When one considers that approximately 2,000 poems in all have survived from the classical bardic period, about 1,000 of them dating from 1566 onwards, the importance of the *Book of O'Conor Don* becomes obvious.[83] Containing just under 20 per cent of the extant total, and bearing in mind that many of the poems occurring in this manuscript are found nowhere else, its importance becomes greater still.

Despite the fact that the poems date back to the twelfth century, one of the most striking features of the manuscript's contents is its contemporaneity. Two of the poets were members of the Louvain community, discussed earlier: Bonabhentura Ó hEodhasa and Aodh Mac Aingil, the former's poems composed before he entered religious life. Fearghal Óg Mac an Bhaird (*c.*1550–1620) has thirty poems ascribed to him; Eochaidh Ó hEodhasa (*c.*1568–1612), twenty-five; Tadhg Dall Ó hUiginn (1550–91), twenty-four; Eoghan Ruadh Mac an Bhaird (b.*c.*1570), eleven; Brian Ó Corcráin (*fl.* 1609–24), seven. Though poets from all over Ireland are included, the anthology, unsurprisingly, has a strong northern bias. In all eighty-five poets are mentioned.

Many of the poems deal with contemporary political events, such as a poem by Eoghan Ruadh Mac an Bhaird for the success of Red Hugh O'Donnell's mission to the king of Spain, seeking further aid after the defeat at Kinsale. One can treat this simply as a political poem, but when we realise that Red Hugh O'Donnell and Somhairle Mac Domhnaill were cousins, the poem takes on a new sense of urgency and poignancy, where it becomes almost impossible to separate the personal from the political. This would equally apply to a number of poems dealing with the Flight of the Earls and its impact on Gaelic Ireland, Mac Domhnaill's own exile being a direct consequence of the exile of his illustrious relations. Matters like this raise very interesting questions as to the working relationship between patron and scribe. Did Captain Somhairle influence the choice of poems, or was it left to Aodh Ó Dochartaigh's good judgement? One striking feature of the compilation is the absence of any poems relating to the Mac Domhnaills themselves, though there were many such poems available. One plausible explanation for this lacuna is that Somhairle envisaged another *duanaire* (poem book) specifically devoted to such poems. If the captain's other manuscripts were given to the Franciscans to help redeem his debts, this family *duanaire* would have been the one book that he would not have surrendered. Unfortunately without the Franciscans to safeguard it, this manuscript, if it existed, suffered the fate of countless other Gaelic manuscripts and was lost to posterity.[84]

Further tantalising questions come to mind. Is it sheer coincidence that the two poems, one by Tadhg Óg Ó hUiginn and the other by Fearghal Mac Domhnuill Ruaidh Mac an Bhaird, from which Carswell quoted at the conclusion of *Foirm na n-Urrnuidheadh* are found *in toto* in the *Book of the O'Conor Don?*[85] Even more remarkable is the fact that the manuscript contains two poems by the Scottish poet Athairn Mac Ceóghuin, *Maircc dar compánach an colann* and *Maircc doní uaill as óige*. These two poems were included in the translation of Calvin's Geneva Catechism, *Adtimchiol an Chreidimh*, published by the Synod of Argyll around 1631, the printed copies thus being contemporaneous with the earliest known manuscript copies.[86] The translator was Athairn's son, Niall. Did Aodh Ó Dochartaigh transcribe these poems directly from the printed text? If so, what was a Gaelic copy of Calvin's catechism doing in the Spanish Netherlands? Given that the first aim of the Louvain friars was to counteract Protestant publications in Gaelic, it would have made very good sense to study this literature, a strategy made all the more imperative with the instigation of a Franciscan mission to the Scottish Highlands and Islands in 1619.[87] Confessional differences aside, the friars may well have been envious of the economic advantages accruing from the roman font used in Scottish publications compared with the Gaelic type of the Louvain press. A possible link explaining the presence of *Adtimchiol an Chreidimh* in Flanders would have been the arrival of Archibald Campbell, seventh earl of Argyll, in Brussels in 1618. Converted to Catholicism in secret by his English wife in 1610, the patron of the Mac Ceóghuin poets fled to the continent heavy in debts, having giving his lands to his sons to prevent their forfeiture.

If the modernising Carswell lauded the advantages of print technology over the slow cumbersome method of transcription by hand, it is surely ironic to see Ó Dochartaigh now transcribing from print to manuscript, from roman to Gaelic script. Could Ó Dochartaigh and his patron have been trying to reclaim Mac Ceóghuin's Calvinist poems for the Catholic side or was it simply a realisation that good poetry transcended all confessional rivalries?

Another interesting feature of the *Book of the O'Conor Don* is that it contained twenty-seven poems that deal with courtly love. Unfortunately the majority of these poems belonged to the missing section of the manuscript, but it is a significant number, in all 25 per cent of the *amour courtois* type poems published in T. F. O'Rahilly's famous anthology *Dánta Grádha*.[88] Here too is a Scottish connection, as one of the poems still extant in the manuscript is Niall Mór

Mac Muireadhaigh's *Soraidh slán don oidhche a-réir* (Farewell Forever to Last Night).[89]

Somhairle Mac Domhnaill is associated with another manuscript compiled in Flanders: *Leabhar na hInghine Uí Dhomhnaill* (the Book of O'Donnell's Daughter).[90] An anthology of thirty-seven poems on the O'Donnells, this work belonged to Nuala Ní Dhomhnaill, sister of Maghnus, Aodh Ruadh, Rudhraighe and Cathbharr Ó Domhnaill. Nuala was in Rome when her brothers Rudhraighe and Cathbharr died in 1608 but had returned to Louvain by 1613. An interesting example of female patronage, it seems that this collection was made in Flanders between 1622 and 1650, the famous poet Eoghan Ruadh Mac an Bhaird being one of the scribes who copied poems into the manuscript. Of interest is a note on folio 152 from John O'Neill, colonel of the Irish regiment in Flanders, referring to his second cousin 'Sorle mc donnell Captin of Musskedtre the best of the Irish wither the will or nott'.[91] All but five of the poems are also found in the *Book of the O'Conor Don* and the exact relationship between the two manuscripts merits further study.

The O'Donnell book also contains a copy of a prose tale on the adventures of Conall Gulban. Paul Walsh noted a marked similarity in style and substance between this text and Lughaidh Ó Cléirigh's *Beatha Aodha Ruaidh Uí Dhomhnaill* (the Life of Red Hugh O'Donnell).[92] Though exhibiting many of the features of traditional Gaelic narrative, the text is highly innovative in its emphasis on motivation and character, thus making it an early example of Renaissance biography. The author's emphasis on the pivotal role of Red Hugh's memory of his captivity in the formation of his character conveys a very modern flavour to this work.[93] Recently described as 'a eulogy of Red Hugh which at many points is a gross misrepresentation of the historical record',[94] this misrepresentation can be more easily understood if the Life is seen as a deliberate work of propaganda to promote the claims of Red Hugh's nephew as head of the projected Spanish invasion force of 1627.[95] If this interpretation is correct, the *Beatha*, though composed in Ireland, seems to be very closely associated with the Irish Franciscan milieu of Louvain and particularly with Flaithrí Ó Maolchonaire, who lived there between 1623 and 1626.

Forging an Irish identity at home

Acknowledging the achievements of the Louvain literary milieu, however, is not to deprecate developments in the homeland. Some of the poems of Tadhg Dall Ó hUiginn (d.1591) advocate a fusion of Gaelic and gaelicised Anglo-Norman interests in resisting Tudor encroachment.[96] While bardic poetry does not suggest intense engagement with the theological implications of the Reformation, such reflection is to be found among a new group of non-professional poets. We have already discussed the warning of the Franciscan preacher-poet Eoghan Ó Dubhthaigh (d.1590) that the Reformation was alien and intrusive to Gaelic Ireland, and if successful would result in Ireland becoming a *Saxa óg*. This symbiosis of Gaelic and Catholic with its counterpoint of English and Protestant was to become a vital factor in defining Irish identity throughout the seventeenth century. The two poems of Maolmhuire Ó hUiginn, archbishop of Tuam (1586–90), brother of the famous Tadhg Dall, evince the spirit of the Counter Reformation while presenting Roman Catholicism and Gaelic consciousness as 'indivisible components of communal identity'.[97] Uilliam Nuinseann (d.1625), son of Baron Delvin of Westmeath and of Old English stock, was one of the first to compose poems of exile at this time, a theme that was bolstered by the Renaissance's recovery of the concept of *patria* as well as by personal experience. Nuinseann's description of an idealised Ireland is equally remarkable in its fusion of Gaelic culture with Catholicism and in its assumption that this Gaelic Catholic patrimony belongs to both those of Gaelic origin and those of Old English stock.[98]

Neither the Battle of Kinsale nor the Treaty of Mellifont was seen as a pivotal event by the Gaelic literati. Poets like Eochaidh Ó hEoghusa and Fearghal Óg Mac an Bhaird actually celebrated the accession of James VI and I to the crown on the demise of Elizabeth, feeling that a monarch with a Gaelic pedigree might even exercise some restraint on the activities of crown officials in Ireland. The Flight of the Earls in 1607, however, and the subsequent plantation of Ulster soon put an end to this optimism. With the departure of O'Neill, O'Donnell and Maguire from Ulster, the amount of patronage available to the poets was severely curtailed. As more and more of the elite class became anglicised, the exercise of patronage would henceforth belong to minor families. With the diffusion throughout the country of the norms of English common law and of primogeniture in particular, the traditional legitimising role of the poets was no longer essential. This mortal blow to the institution of the *fileadha* paradoxically resulted in a prolific and impassioned creative outburst as the poets strove to come to terms with the ferment of socio-political and socio-economic changes that were affecting their country. If the institution was reduced to a state of corporate paralysis, the poetry is characterised by a more individual note and by ideological innovation. Elements of ideological change that were discernible only in embryonic form in the final quarter of the previous century are deliberately and consciously firmed up in the first quarter of the seventeenth century. The gaelicised Anglo-Normans and Old English are formally incorporated into the framework of the *Lebor Gabála* and come to participate in the origin myth of the Gaels. Under the common marker of *Éireannaigh* both *Gael* and *Sean-Ghall* achieve a common politicised identity whose essential components are Counter Reformation Catholicism, adhesion to Gaelic social mores and a consciousness of territorial insular sovereignty. While these ideological innovations may have attained semantic exactitude in the intellectual crucible of Louvain, the ideas were originally moulded by the *literati* at home. Poets like Eoghan Ruadh Mac an Bhaird, Fearflatha Ó Gnímh and Lochlann Ó Dálaigh adopted the concept of providentialism to explain the communal upheavals of the early seventeenth century. In this view, *Fearg Dé* (God's anger) was punishing the Irish for their sins, especially that of pride. Far from being a fatalistic reaction, however, God's anger could be assuaged by repentance, with communal punishment yielding to communal liberation, a theme that was enhanced by a comparison between the Irish and the Israelites.[99]

Originally developed among the professional *fileadha*, these fundamental changes of mindset were taken up by the new amateur poets, both laymen and clerics, who came to the fore in the second quarter of the seventeenth century. And while the initial reaction of the professionals to the gradual replacement of syllabic metres by stressed metres was one of dismay at the perceived demoticisation of their craft, their ideological innovations were enthusiastically taken up by the amateurs. Not content with merely copper fastening the innovations of their professional colleagues, these amateurs introduced innovations of their own, especially in the areas of love poetry and poetry of friendship. Piaras Feiritéar (*c*.1600–53)[100] and his Dominican contemporary Pádraigín Haicéad (*c*.1604–54)[101] belong to the same world as Thomas Carew and Robert Herrick. Feiritéar's poems to his male friends exhibit an atmosphere of relaxation and warmth that are more striking than his formal courtly love productions to female personae. His prioritisation of the individual at the expense of the communal almost single-handedly subverts the ethos which the professional bardic system validated, and his celebration of the dignity of the human person makes Feiritéar a worthy representative of the Renaissance. Haicéad, a fierce supporter of the Rinuccini faction during the Confederate wars, could also compose tender heterosexual love poems and celebrate male friendship.

An unusual feature of the early seventeenth century is a poetical dispute known as *Iomarbhágh na bhFileadh* (the Contention of the Bards)[102] Initiated in 1616 by Tadhg mac Dáire Mac Bruaideadha (*c*.1570–*c*.1652) in a poem asserting the superiority of the southern part of the country, the honour of the northern half was immediately taken up by Lughaidh Ó Cléirigh (c.1580–c.1630), *ollamh* to the O'Donnells since 1595, with various poets on both sides subsequently joining the debate. Twentieth-century commentators have wondered at the amount of energy wasted on such a trivial concern at a time of unprecedented upheaval for Gaelic society. Recent commentators, however, have taken a more nuanced view of the contention. Mac Bruaideadha's patron, in fact, was none other than Donnchadh Ó Briain, fourth earl of Thomond, and president of Munster. A Protestant and loyal servant of the crown who supported the authorities in the struggle against the northern leaders, Thomond was the only earl of native stock to have carved out a successful niche for himself under the new dispensation. The northern literati were deeply shocked at Mac Bruaideadha's use of the panoply of Gaelic learning to eulogise the very person who posed the greatest threat to that same tradition. It was this deep sense of shock that led to the contention. Mac Bruaideadha, however, gave priority to survival over all other considerations.[103]

While the last word has still to be said on the Contention, investigation into the role of Mathew de Renzy (1577–1634) in the proceedings might prove fruitful. A German planter who came to Ireland in 1605, de Renzy learned Irish from a number of sources, including Tadhg mac Dáire Mac Bruaideadha. Deeply ambiguous in his approach to native culture, de Renzy was sufficiently interested in it to learn the language to a high degree of proficiency, while at the same time quite anxious regarding the political and cultural influence of the Gaelic learned classes. De Renzy's example shows that the attitude of other New English settlers to Gaelic culture merits close scrutiny.[104]

While dispossession of their patrons and encroachments by new planters were matters of grave concern to the Gaelic literati, they were equally distressed at the rise of the Irish lower classes whose conditions actually improved through the political and social upheavals. It was this dismay that gave rise to the anonymous prose satire *Pairlement Chloinne Tomáis* (the Parliament of Clann Thomas).[105] Written in two parts, *Pairlement Chloinne Tomáis* I was composed around 1610–15 by a member of a professional learned family from southern Munster, possibly one of the O'Dinneens, hereditary historians to the McCarthys, an author who was equally familiar with the Gaelic literary tradition and with contemporary English literature. Rejecting the traditional understanding of the *Pairlement* as an attack on agricultural labourers, however, Marc Caball considers the satirist's skilful manipulation of the burlesque elements of the indigenous prose tradition to be aimed at a Gaelic *arriviste* class ready to espouse English values and benefit from the social flux, in particular at one Patrick Crosbie (d.1611) who earned the gratitude of the authorities for helping to transfer seven Gaelic families *en masse* from Leix to lands in north Kerry in 1608–9.[106] *Pairlement Chloinne Tomáis* II was composed in the early 1660s, possibly by a member of the Nugent family of County Westmeath. Though lacking the rumbustious and slapstick elements of its predecessor, it is the first of a number of anti-peasant satires in post-Cromwellian Ireland and beyond to draw inspiration from *Pairlement Chloinne Tomáis* I.

Cromwell's military campaign in Ireland from August 1649 until May 1650 was particularly severe because of both the use of artillery to the greatest extent ever seen in Ireland and the practice of laying waste the land as a military tactic. The outbreak of bubonic plague exacerbated the suffering, with people dying at the rate of thirteen hundred per week in Dublin alone during the height of the plague. With typhus and dysentery already endemic in the armies, it is little wonder that the poet Seán Ó Conaill described it as *an coga do chríochnaigh Éire* (the war that finished off Ireland).[107] Ó Conaill's poem *Tuireamh na hÉireann* (The Lament of Ireland), written between 1655 and 1659, proved extremely popular in the manuscript tradition over the following century. Virtually a summary in verse of Céitinn's *Foras Feasa*, the course of Irish history is presented from the perspective of post-Cromwellian Ireland.[108] While the *Tuireamh* is written from an Old English perspective, an anonymous contemporary clerical poet wrote *An Síoguidhe Rómhánach* (The Roman Fairy)[109] giving the reaction of the Gaelic Ulster Confederates. Michelle O Riordan has pointed out striking similarities between this poem (in some sense a lament for the death of Eoghan Ruadh Ó Néill in 1649) and Abraham Cowley's *A discourse by way of Vision concerning the government of Oliver Cromwell* (1661), and emphasises the need for enlarging the interpretative framework against which these Irish poems belonging to the aftermath of the Cromwellian settlement should be evaluated.[110]

Were it just for the extent of his corpus alone, Dáibhí Ó Bruadair (1625–98) merits recognition as the major poet of the second half of the seventeenth century.[111] Eighty poems are ascribed to him, though only fifty-two lines out of six thousand are in his autograph.[112] Experiencing at first hand the major disturbances of the period, from the Confederate wars to the Cromwellian settlement, from the Restoration to the popish plot, from the accession of James II to the Revolution of 1688, from the Battle of the Boyne to the Penal Laws, Ó Bruadair not only gives very important witness to the effect of these disjunctures on the Gaelic Catholic landed classes, but in addition his tendency to address these matters almost exclusively in terms of their effect on his own personal plight adds a tone of intense bitterness and invective to his

verse. As Joep Leerssen succinctly puts it in a comparison between Ó Bruadair and his eighteenth-century successor Aodhgán Ó Rathaille: 'Ó Bruadair
registered social upheaval *in*, Ó Rathaille registered it *through* his personal
plight.'[113]

Ó Bruadair's work falls into four main periods. Along with his contemporaries, the poet of the 1650s registers the misfortunes of the Irish as God's
punishment for their sins. Unlike his contemporaries, however, who used
Céitinn's *Foras Feasa* with its version of Ireland's past to explain the present,
Ó Bruadair notes a complete discontinuity between what he perceived to be
an idyllic past and the grimness of the present.[114] The 1670s and particularly
the famine of 1674–6 mark a change of emphasis in the poet's verse. While
the new misfortune is still represented as divine punishment, the response is
much more personal. Ó Bruadair evinces no interest in a glorious past and his
only hope of salvation is to be found in prayer and trust in God.[115]

A new optimism pervades Ó Bruadair's verse in the 1680s that is markedly
present in the poem *Searc na suadh*, a piece composed in May 1682 to celebrate
the accquittal of a number of Munster gentlemen accused of complicity in the
popish plot.[116] Writing in praise of one of the judges, John Keating, Ó Bruadair
is able to draw analogies between the judge's role and that of his more famous
namesake, the author of *Foras Feasa*:

> D'fhoillsigh onóir ardfhlath Éireann
> Iul a bpréamh sa ngéaga gaoil
> Tug anall dá mbladh ar bhradadh
> Ar nach gann re cabghall claoin
>
> (The honour he revealed of Erin's princes
> The knowledge of their stems and families
> Restoring to their fame what has been pilfered
> No trifling task, 'gainst mouthers' vaunts.)[117]

With the accession of James II to the throne and the emergence of Irish
heroes like Patrick Sarsfield, Ó Bruadair's optimism becomes even more palpable. In some poems of this period he seems to envisage the restoration of
Ireland's idyllic past, though in others he is less interested in resorting to the
past than in focusing on the present now that God's judgement is lifted from
the Irish.[118]

The 'Purgatory'[119] of the 1680s with its promise of Paradise regained gave
way, however, to the 'Shipwreck' of the 1690s.[120] As Pádraigín Riggs deftly
remarks: 'The poet of the 1690s is a victim of despair and despondency, finally

succumbing to historical amnesia.'[121] Such is the overwhelming nature of defeat and the corresponding social disjuncture that it marks the end of history. Ó Bruadair himself is so traumatised by the debacle that he resolves to write no more:

> ós críoch di mo stríocadh go seanabhrógaibh
> Fínis dom scríbhinn ar fhearaibh Fódla
>
> (But since I am reduced to old shoes as the result of it all
> Finis be unto my writing for the men of Fódla's land.)[122]

National catastrophe and personal catastrophe coincide. Even more, the very craft of poetry is unable to function any longer. Whereas Ó Bruadair complained of lack of patronage in his earlier compositions, this concern for the very future of the art itself is a new element in his work. Historical amnesia gives way to cultural amnesia and Ó Bruadair's loss of faith in the capacity of art to deal with unprecedented tragedy is strangely reminiscent of that of Adorno and Steiner in the second half of the twentieth century.[123]

While the last two periods of Ó Bruadair's *oeuvre* belong chronologically to the seventeenth century, his poetry from the accession of James II can be more properly seen as initiating the Jacobite era of Gaelic literature. That Ó Bruadair should be the harbinger of a new era at the very moment when he plunged the depths of personal and professional despair is most paradoxical. Such phoenix-like renewal, however, is an essential component of Jacobitism, the full story of which properly pertains to a following chapter.

In summarising the achievements of the Gaelic literati from the time of the Elizabethan conquest, it is hardly an exaggeration to claim that perhaps their most enduring legacy was the forging of an Irish identity that equated Irishness with Catholicism. In *Hibernia Anglicana*, written in England between 1685 and 1689, Sir Richard Cox, a strong supporter of the Protestant interest in Ireland, described the country's religio-political situation as follows:

> At this day we know no difference of nation but what is expressed by papist and Protestant, if the most ancient natural Irishman be a Protestant, no man takes him for other than an Englishman, and if a cockney be a papist, he is reckoned in Ireland, as much an Irishman as if he were born on Slevelogher; the earls of Inchiquin and Castlehaven are examples thereof.[124]

That even their enemies accepted their invention of Irishness is no mean testimony to the forcefulness and tenacity of the Gaelic literati. They themselves would wish for no better tribute.

Notes

1. R. L. Thomson, ed. *Foirm na n-Urrnuidheadh: John Carswell's Gaelic Translation of the Book of Common Order* (Edinburgh: Scottish Gaelic Texts Society, 1970).
2. John Bannerman, 'Literacy in the Highlands', in Ian B. Cowan and Duncan Shaw, eds. *The Renaissance and Reformation in Scotland: Essays in Honour of Gordon Donaldson* (Edinburgh: Scottish Academic Press, 1983), p. 234.
3. Donald E. Meek, 'The Reformation and Gaelic Culture: Perspectives on Patronage, Language and Literature in John Carswell's Translation of "The Book of Common Order"', in James Kirk, ed. *The Church in the Highlands* (Edinburgh: Scottish Church History Society, 1998), pp. 42–7.
4. Meek, 'The Reformation and Gaelic Culture', pp. 47–8.
5. Ibid., pp. 48–51.
6. For Argyll's career see Jane Dawson, *The Politics of Religion in the Age of Mary, Queen of Scots: The Earl of Argyll and the Struggle for Britain and Ireland* (Cambridge: Cambridge University Press, 2002), especially chapter 5, 'The Reconfiguration of British Politics, 1566–1568', pp. 144–69.
7. Breandán Ó Madagáin, 'Bíobla: An Bíobla i nGaeilge', *Diagacht don Phobal* 1 (1986), p. 43.
8. Ibid.
9. Brian Ó Cuív, ed. *Aibidil Gaoidheilge & Caiticiosma: Seán Ó Cearnaigh's Irish Primer of Religion Published in 1571* (Dublin: Dublin Institute for Advanced Studies, 1994).
10. N. J. A. Williams, 'Review of Brian Ó Cuív, ed. *Aibidil Gaoidheilge & Caiticisioma: Seán Ó Cearnaigh's Irish Primer of Religion Published in 1571'*, *Studia Hibernica* 28 (1994), pp. 165–6.
11. N. J. A. Williams, *I bPrionta i Leabhar: na Protastúin agus Prós na Gaeilge 1567–1724* (Dublin: An Clóchomhar, 1986), p. 32.
12. Ibid., p. 34.
13. Terence McCaughey, *Dr Bedell and Mr King: The Making of the Irish Bible* (Dublin: Dublin Institute for Advanced Studies, 2001).
14. Colmán N. Ó Clabaigh OSB, *The Franciscans in Ireland 1400–1534: From Reform to Reformation* (Dublin: Four Courts Press, 2002), p. 144.
15. Stanihurst's comment occurs in chapter 7 of *The Description of Ireland* (1577): 'The Names or Surnames of the Learned Men and Authors of Ireland'; see Liam Miller and Eileen Power, eds. *Holinshed's Irish Chronicle* (Dublin: Dolmen Press, 1979) p. 106. The only other Irish-language poet mentioned is 'David fitz Geralde, vsually called David Duffe . . . a maker in the Irish' (p. 100). Stanihurst alludes to William Nugent's 'diuers Sonets' (p. 105) in English (p. 106), poems which have not survived, while he makes no acknowledgement at all of his poems in Irish, at least some of which have survived. See Éamonn Ó Tuathail, 'Nugentiana', *Éigse* 2 (1940), pp. 4–14; Gerard Murphy, 'Poems of Exile by William Nuinseann Mac Barún Dealbhna', *Éigse* 6 (1959), pp. 8–15.
16. For the text of this poem see Cuthbert Mhág Craith, ed. *Dán na mBráthar Mionúr, vol. I* (Dublin: Dublin Institute for Advanced Studies, 1967), pp. 151–3. For commentary see the following by Marc Caball: *Poetry and Politics: Reaction and Continuity in Irish Poetry, 1558–1625*, Critical Conditions: Field Day Monographs (Cork: Cork University Press, 1998), p. 79; 'Faith, Culture and Sovereignty: Irish Nationality and its Development, 1558–1625', in Brendan Bradshaw and Peter Roberts, eds. *British Consciousness and Identity*

(Cambridge: Cambridge University Press, 1998), pp. 134–5; 'Innovation and Tradition: Irish Gaelic Responses to Early Modern Conquest and Colonization', in Hiram Morgan, ed. *Political Ideology in Ireland* (Dublin: Four Courts Press, 1999), p. 77.

17. For the text of this poem see Mhág Craith, *Dán na mBráthar Mionúr*, pp. 127–51. For commentary see Caball, *Poetry and Politics*, pp. 78–9; 'Irish Nationality', pp. 134–5; 'Innovation and Tradition', p. 77.

18. Thomas O'Connor, '"Perfidious Machiavellian Friar": Florence Conry's Campaign for a Catholic Restoration in Ireland, 1592–1616', *Seanchas Ard Mhacha* 19, 1 (2002), pp. 91–195, pp. 92–3.

19. Brian Ó Cuív, 'Flaithre Ó Maolchonaire's Catechism of Christian Doctrine', *Celtica* 1 (1950), pp. 169–74.

20. Tomás Ó Cléirigh, *Aodh Mac Aingil agus an Scoil Nua-Ghaedhilge i Lobháin* (1935; new edn Dublin: An Gúm, 1985); Canice Mooney OFM, 'St Anthony's College, Louvain', *Donegal Annual* 8 (1969), pp. 18–48; Bernadette Cunningham, 'The Culture and Ideology of Irish Franciscan Historians at Louvain 1607–1650', in Ciaran Brady, ed. *Ideology and the Historians* (Dublin: Lilliput Press, 1991), pp. 11–30.

21. Fearghal Mac Raghnaill, ed. *Bonabhentura Ó hEodhasa, An Teagasg Críosdaidhe* (Dublin: Institute for Advanced Studies, 1976).

22. Brendan Jennings and Cathaldus Giblin, eds. *Louvain Papers, 1606–1827* (Dublin: Stationery Office, for the Irish Manuscripts Commission, 1968), pp. 32–3.

23. Mac Raghnaill, *An Teagasg Críosdaidhe*, p. 95.

24. *Calender of State Papers relating to Ireland in the Reign of James I, 1611–1614* (London, 1877).

25. Mac Raghnaill, *An Teagasg Críosdaidhe*, p. xiv.

26. Ibid., p. xv.

27. T. F. O'Rahilly, ed. *Desiderius* (Dublin: Dublin Institute for Advanced Studies, 1941).

28. Ibid., p. 128, lines 3895–3908.

29. Ibid., p. 128, lines 3910–12.

30. Cainneach Ó Maonaigh, ed. *Scáthán Shacramuinte na hAithridhe* (Dublin: Dublin Institute for Advanced Studies, 1952).

31. Norman Egbert McClure, ed. *The Letters and Epigrams of Sir John Harrington* (Philadelphia: University of Pennsylvania Press, 1930; reprint, 1972), Letter 10: To Justice Carey, October 1599, p. 77.

32. Cathaldus Giblin, OFM, 'Hugh McCaghwell, OFM, Archbishop of Armagh (+1626): Aspects of his Life', *Seanchas Ard Mhacha*, 11, 2 (1983–5), pp. 259–90.

33. Ó Maonaigh, *Scáthán Shacramuinte na hAithridhe*, p. 219.

34. Ibid., p. 4, line 68.

35. Mícheál Mac Craith, 'Scáthán Shacramuinte na hAithridhe: Scáthán na Sacraiminte Céanna', *Léachtaí Cholm Cille* XXX (Maynooth: An Sagart, 2000), pp. 28–64.

36. Ó Maonaigh, *Scáthán Shacramuinte na hAithridhe*, p. 166, line 5456.

37. Mícheál Mac Craith, 'Scáthán Shacramuinte na hAithridhe: Saothar Reiligiúnda nó Saothar Polaitíochta,' *Irisleabhar Mhá Nuad* (1993), pp. 144–54.

38. Ó Maonaigh, *Scáthán Shacramuinte na hAithridhe*, p. 190, lines 6287–8.

39. Anselm Ó Fachtna, OFM, ed. *Parthas an Anma* (Dublin: Dublin Institute for Advanced Studies, 1953).

40. Pádraig Ó Súilleabháin, ed. *Lucerna Fidelium* (Dublin: Dublin Institute for Advanced Studies, 1962).

41. Mac Raghnaill, *An Teagasg Críosdaidhe*, p. 2, lines 21–8. The following translations are by the present author.

42. O'Rahilly, *Desiderius*, p. 2, lines 44–8.

43. Ó Maonaigh, *Scáthán Shacramuinte na hAithridhe*, p. 5, lines 74–8.

44. Theobald Stapleton, *Catechismus, seu Doctrina Latino-Hibernica* (Brussels, 1639; reflex facsimile Dublin: Irish Manuscripts Commission, 1945).

45. Ibid., Introduction, paragraph 28.

46. Ibid., Introduction, paragraph 27.

47. A reference to the auction of a clergyman's library in Erris, County Mayo in 1845 states that it contained 66 copies of Ó hEodhasa's catechism and 278 copies of Molloy's *Lucerna Fidelium*. See Máire Ní Mhurchú and Diarmuid Breathnach, eds. *1560–1781 Beathaisnéis* (Dublin: An Clóchomhar, 2001), p. 158. These figures, unfortunately, are not open to verification.

48. Robert Darnton, 'History of Reading', in Peter Burke, ed. *New Perspectives in Historical Writing*, 2nd edn (Cambridge: Polity Press, 2001), p. 150.

49. Ó Maonaigh, *Scáthán Shacramuinte na hAithridhe*, pp. 94–5, lines 3080–94.

50. Parthalán Mac Aogáin, OFM, ed. *Graiméir Ghaeilge na mBráthar Mionúr* (Dublin: Dublin Institute for Advanced Studies, 1968), pp. 3–106.

51. Alan Harrison, 'Graiméir agus Foclóirí Scuitbhéarla', in Seosamh Watson, ed. *Féilscríbhinn Thomáis de Bhaldraithe* (Dublin: Coiste Fhéilscríbhinn Thomáis de Bhaldraithe, 1986), pp. 51–2.

52. Ludwig-Christian Stern, 'Le manuscrit irlandais de la Bibliothèque universitaire de Giessen', *Revue celtique* 16 (1895), p. 9.

53. Mhág Craith, *Dán na mBráthar Mionúr*, pp. 38–51.

54. Caball, *Poetry and Politics*, pp. 104–6.

55. Paul Walsh, ed. *The Flight of the Earls by Tadhg Ó Cianáin* (Dublin: Gill, 1916). While this event has gone down in history as the Flight of the Earls, it bears noting that Ó Cianáin himself does not use this charged term. Recent analysis by Micheline Kerney Walsh of Hugh O'Neill's correspondence in exile led her to consider his departure as 'a planned, tactical retreat' rather than a precipitous flight, 'an attempt by O'Neill to secure military aid by pressing his case in person to King Philip'. See Micheline Kerney Walsh, *An Exile of Ireland: Hugh O'Neill Prince of Ulster* (Dublin: Four Courts Press, 1996), pp. 133. Cf. also her earlier work *'Destruction by Peace': Hugh O'Neill after Kinsale* (Armagh: Cumann Seanchais Ard Mhacha, 1986).

56. Walsh, *The Flight of the Earls*, pp. 42–3.

57. Ibid., pp. 24–5.

58. Ibid., pp. 36–7.

59. Colm Ó Lochlainn, *Tobar Fíorghlan Gaedhilge* (Dublin: At the Sign of the Three Candles, 1939), p. 97.

60. C. P. Meehan, *The Fate and Fortunes of the Earls of Tyrone and Tyrconnell* (Dublin: J. Duffy, 1868), p. 328.

61. Adrian Hastings, *Construction of Nationhood, Ethnicity, Religion and Nationalism* (Cambridge: Cambridge University Press, 1997), pp. 14–19.

62. Caball, *Poetry and Politics*, pp. 40–82.

63. Breandán Ó Buachalla, 'Cúlra is Tábhacht an Dáin *A Leabhráin Ainmnighthear d'Aodh*', *Celtica* 21 (1990), pp. 402–16.

64. De la Bovlaye le Gouz, *Les Voyages et Observations dv Sievr de la Bovlaye le Gouz, Gentle Homme Angevin* (Paris, 1653), p. 456.

65. Ó Cléirigh, *Aodh Mac Aingil*, p. 27.

66. Fr. Canice Mooney, OFM, 'Father John Colgan, OFM, his Work and Times and Literary Milieu', in Terence O' Donnell, ed. *Father John Colgan OFM* (Dublin: Assisi Press, 1959), pp. 13–20; Mooney, 'St Anthony's College, Louvain', pp. 29–32.

67. Thomas O'Connor, 'Towards the Invention of the Irish Catholic *Natio*: Thomas Messingham's *Florilegium* (1624)', *Irish Theological Quarterly* 64, 2 (1999), pp. 169–75.

68. Brendan Jennings, *Michael O Cleirigh, Chief of the Four Masters, and his Associates* (Dublin: Talbot Press, 1936).

69. MS Bibliothèque Royale, Bruxelles, 2324–40, f. 273.

70. Breandán Ó Buachalla, '*Annála Ríoghachta Éireann* is *Foras Feasa ar Éirinn*: An Comhthéacs Comhaimseartha', *Studia Hibernica* 22–3 (1982–3), p. 94.

71. Ibid.

72. Ibid. Alexander Boyle, 'Fearghal Ó Gadhra and the Four Masters', *Irish Ecclesiastical Record* 50, 2, 5th series (1963), pp. 109–10, 112–13.

73. Fr Aubrey Gwynn, SJ, 'Archbishop Ussher and Father Brendan O'Connor', in Franciscan Fathers, eds. *Father Luke Wadding Commemorative Volume* (Dublin: Clonmore and Reynolds, 1957), pp. 270–2. Further information on Ussher's attitude to Gaelic culture can be found in J. Th. Leerssen, 'Archbishop Ussher and Gaelic Culture', *Studia Hibernica*, 22–3 (1982–3), pp. 50–8.

74. Gwynn, 'Archbishop Ussher', p. 272.

75. Bernadette Cunningham, *The World of Geoffrey Keating: History, Myth and Religion in Seventeenth-Century Ireland* (Dublin: Four Courts Press, 2000), pp. 109–10.

76. Ibid., pp. 177–8.

77. Nollaig Ó Muraíle, '"Aimsir an Chogaidh Chreidmhigh" – An Dubhaltach Mac Fhirbhisigh, a Lucht Aitheantais agus Polaitíocht an Seachtu hAois Déag', in Máirín Ní Dhonnchadha, ed. *Nua-Léamha Gnéithe de Chultúr, Stair agus Polaitíocht na hÉireann c.1600–c.1900* (Dublin: An Clóchomhar, 1996), p. 100. The eighteenth-century scholar Charles O'Conor of Belanagare is the sole source for Mac Fhirbhisigh's view of Céitinn. Ó Muraíle provides a comprehensive account of Mac Fhirbhisigh's career in *The Celebrated Antiquary, Dubhaltach Mac Fhirbhisigh (c.1600–1671): His Lineage, Life and Learning*, Maynooth Monographs VI (Maynooth: An Sagart, 1996).

78. Nollaig Ó Muraíle, *The Great Book of Irish Genealogies*, 5 vols. (Dublin: de Búrca Books, 2004).

79. Eoin MacNeill and Gerard Murphy, eds. *Duanaire Finn: The Book of the Lays of Fionn*, 3 vols., Irish Texts Society VII, XXVIII and XLIII (London, 1908–53).

80. Joseph Falaky Nagy, 'The Significance of the *Duanaire Finn*', in John Carey, ed. *Duanaire Finn: Reassessments*, Irish Texts Society, Subsidiary Series XIII (Dublin: Elo Press, 2003), pp. 42, 47.

81. Ibid., 40; Ruairí Ó hUiginn, 'Patron and Text', in Carey, *Duanaire Finn: Reassessments*, pp. 98–9, 104.

82. Douglas Hyde, 'The Book of the O'Conor Don', *Ériu* 13, 1 (1915), p. 79.

83. Caball, *Poets and Politics*, p. 2.

84. Hector McDonnell, *The Wild Geese of the Antrim MacDonnells* (Dublin: Irish Academic Press, 1996), p. 31; Ó hUiginn, 'Patron and Text', pp. 104–6.

85. The opening quatrain of Tadhg Óg Ó hUiginn's poem *Mairg darab soirbh an saoghal* is found in Thomson's edition of Carswell's *Foirm na n-Urrnuidheadh* on p. 113, lines 3967–70. Two couplets from Mac an Bhaird's poem *Olc íocthar ar luach leighis* are found on p. 113. lines 3971–2 and 3979–80. Cf. also the notes on pp. 171–2.

86. R. L. Thomson, ed. *Adtimchiol an Chreidimh: The Gaelic Version of John Calvin's Catechismus Ecclesiae Genevensis* (Edinburgh: Scottish Gaelic Texts Society, 1962). *Mairee doní uaill as óige* is found on pp. xiv–xv.; *Mairee dar compánach an colann* on p. xvii.

87. Cathaldus Giblin, *Irish Franciscan Mission to Scotland 1619–1646: Documents from Roman Archives* (Dublin: Assisi Press, 1964).

88. T. F. O'Rahilly, *Dánta Grádha: An Anthology of Irish Love Poetry (AD 1350–1750)*, (Cork: Cork University Press, 1926).

89. Ibid., no. 38, pp. 51–2. Derick Thomson argues that Niall Mór lived between *c.*1550 and *c.*1630 and that he composed *Soraidh slán don oidhche a-réir* before 1600; see his 'Niall Mór MacMhuirich', *Transactions of the Gaelic Society of Inverness* 49 (1974–6), pp. 9–25.

90. Kuno Meyer, 'A Collection of Poems on the O'Donnells', *Ériu* 4 (1910), pp. 183–90; Paul Walsh, *Irish Men of Learning* (Dublin: At the Sign of the Three Candles, 1947), pp. 179–205.

91. Ibid., p. 195.

92. Ibid., p. 204; Paul Walsh, ed. *Beatha Aodha Ruaidh Uí Dhomhnaill*, 2 vols., Irish Texts Society XLIII and XLV (London, 1948 and 1957).

93. Mícheál Mac Craith, 'The *Beatha* in the Context of the Literature of the Renaissance', in Pádraig Ó Riain, ed. *Beatha Aodha Ruaidh: The Life of Red Hugh O'Donnell: Historical and Literary Contexts*, Irish Texts Society, Subsidiary Series XII (Dublin: Elo Press, 2002), pp. 36–45.

94. Hiram Morgan, 'The Real Red Hugh', in Ó Riain, *Beatha Aodha Ruaidh*, p. 2.

95. Mac Craith, 'The *Beatha* in the Context of the Literature of the Renaissance', pp. 43–53.

96. Caball, *Poetry and Politics*, pp. 45–50; 'Innovation and Tradition', pp. 72–3; 'Faith, Culture and Sovereignty', pp. 125–8.

97. Caball, *Poetry and Politics*, p. 80; 'Innovation and Tradition', p. 77; 'Faith, Culture and Sovereignty', pp. 117–18.

98. Caball, *Poetry and Politics*, pp. 66–8; 'Innovation and Tradition', pp. 74–5; 'Faith, Culture and Sovereignty', pp. 118–19.

99. Caball, *Poetry and Politics*, pp. 107–11; Marc Caball, 'Providence and Exile in Early Seventeenth-Century Ireland', *Irish Historical Studies* 29, 114 (1994), pp. 174–88; Caball, 'Innovation and Tradition', p. 80.

100. Pádraig Ua Duinnín, ed. *Dánta Phiarais Feiritéir* (1903; 2nd edn Dublin: Government Publications, 1934).

101. Máire Ní Cheallacháin, ed. *Filíocht Phádraigín Haicéad* (Dublin: An Clóchomhar, 1962).

102. Lambert McKenna, ed. *Iomarbhágh na bhFileadh: The Contention of the Bards*, 2 vols., Irish Texts Society XX and XXI (London: Irish Texts Society, 1918).

103. J. Th. Leerssen, *The Contention of the Bards (Iomarbhágh na bhFileadh) and its Place in Irish Political and Literary History*, Irish Texts Society, Subsidiary Series II (London: Irish Texts Society, 1994), pp. 14–15, 68. Cf also Anne Dooley, 'Literature and Society in Early Seventeenth-Century Ireland: The Evolution of Change', in C. Byrne, M. Harry and P. Ó Siadhail, eds. *Celtic Languages and Celtic Peoples. Proceedings of the Second North American Congress of Celtic Studies* (Halifax, Nova Scotia: St Mary's University, 1992), pp. 513–34; Bernadette Cunningham, 'Native Culture and Political Change in Ireland, 1580–1640', in C. Brady and R. Gillespie, eds. *Natives and Newcomers: The Making of Irish Colonial Society* (Dublin: Irish Academic Press, 1986), pp. 163–4.

104. Brian Mac Cuarta, 'Mathew de Renzy's Letters on Irish Affairs, 1613–1620', *Analecta Hibernica* 34 (1987), pp. 107–82; Mac Cuarta, 'A Planter's Interaction with Gaelic Culture: Sir Mathew de Renzy (1577–1634)', *Irish Economic and Social History* 20 (1993), pp. 1–17; Mac Cuarta, 'Conchubhar Mac Bruaideadha and Sir Mathew de Renzy (1577–1634)', *Éigse* 27 (1993), pp. 122–6. Caball, *Poets and Politics*, pp. 128–9.

105. N. J. A. Williams, *Pairlement Chloinne Tomáis* (Dublin: Dublin Institute for Advanced Studies, 1981).

106. Marc Caball, 'Pairlement Chloinne Tomáis I: A Reassessment', *Éigse* 27 (1993), pp. 47–57.

107. Cecile O' Rahilly, ed. *Five Seventeenth-Century Political Poems* (Dublin: Dublin Institute for Advanced Studies, 1952; reprinted 1977), p. 75, line 353.

108. Ibid., pp. 50–82.

109. Ibid., pp. 12–32.

110. Michelle O Riordan, 'A Seventeenth-Century Political Poem', in Myrtle Hill and Sarah Barber, eds. *Aspects of Irish Studies* (Belfast: Institute of Irish Studies, 1990), pp. 117–26; O Riordan, '"Political" Poems in the Mid-Seventeenth-Century Crisis', in Jane H. Ohlmeyer, ed. *Ireland from Independence to Occupation 1641–1660* (Cambridge: Cambridge University Press, 1995), pp. 126–7.

111. John Mac Erlean, ed. and trans. *Duanaire Dháibhidh Uí Bhruadair: The Poems of David Ó Bruadair*, Part I, Irish Texts Society XI (London, 1910); Part II, Irish Texts Society XIII (London, 1913); Part III, Irish Texts Society XVII (London, 1917).

112. Breandán Ó Conchúir, 'The Manuscript Transmission of Ó Bruadair's Poetry', in Pádraigín Riggs, ed. *Dáibhí Ó Bruadair: His Historical and Literary Context*, Irish Texts Society, Subsidiary Series XI (London: Irish Texts Society, 2001), pp. 49–50.

113. Joep Leerssen, *Mere Irish and Fíor-Ghael: Studies in the Idea of Irish Nationality, its Development and Literary Expression prior to the Nineteenth Century*, Field Day Monographs, (Cork: Cork University Press, 1996), pp. 151–294, p. 234.

114. Bernadette Cunningham and Raymond Gillespie, 'Lost Worlds: History and Religion in the Poetry of Dáibhí Ó Bruadair', in Riggs, ed. *Dáibhí Ó Bruadair*, pp. 27–32.

115. Ibid., pp. 33–7.

116. Mac Erlean, *Duanaire Dháibhidh Uí Bhruadair*, Part II, pp. 264–88.

117. Ibid., Part II, pp. 264–5.

118. Cunningham and Gillespie, 'Lost Worlds', pp. 37–41.

119. Mac Erlean, *Duanaire Dháibhidh Uí Bhruadair*, Part III, pp. 12–23.

120. Ibid., Part III, pp. 164–81.

121. Riggs, *Dáibhí Ó Bruadair*, p. vi.

122. Mac Erlean, *Duanaire Dháibhidh Uí Bhruadair*, Part III, p. 181.

123. Cunningham and Gillespie, 'Lost Worlds', pp. 41–4.
124. Richard Cox, *Hibernia Anglicana or the History of Ireland from the conquest thereof by the English to this Present Time*, 2 parts (London, 1689–90), sig. c2.

Select bibliography

Binéid, Dara, *Searc na Suadh: Gnéithe de Fhilíocht Dháibhí Uí Bhruadair*, Dublin: An Clóchomhar, 2004.

Caball, Marc, *Poets and Politics: Reaction and Continuity in Irish Poetry, 1585–1625*, Critical Conditions, Field Day Monographs, Cork: Cork University Press, 1998.

Cunningham, Bernadette, *The World of Geoffrey Keating: History, Myth and Religion in Seventeenth-Century Ireland*, Dublin: Four Courts Press, 2000.

Jennings, Brendan, *Michael O Cleirigh, Chief of the Four Masters, and his Associates*, Dublin: Talbot Press, 1936.

Leerssen, J. Th. (Joep), *The Contention of the Bards (Iomarbhágh na bhFileadh) and its Place in Irish Political and Literary History*, Irish Texts Society, Subsidiary Series II, London: Irish Texts Society, 1994.

Mere Irish and Fíor-Ghael: Studies in the Idea of Irish Nationality, its Development and Literary Expression prior to the Nineteenth Century, 1986; reprinted Field Day Monographs, Cork: Cork University Press, 1996, pp. 151–294.

Mac Craith, Mícheál, *Lorg na hIasachta ar na Dánta Grá*, Dublin: An Clóchomhar, 1989.

Mooney, Canice, 'St Anthony's College, Louvain', *Donegal Annual* 8 (1969), pp. 18–48.

Ní Mhurchú, Máire and Diarmuid Breathnach, eds., *1560–1781 Beathaisnéis*, Dublin: An Clóchomhar, 2001.

Ó Buachalla, Breandán, *Aisling Ghéar: Na Stíobhartaigh agus an tAos Léinn, 1603–1788*, Dublin: An Clóchomhar, 1997.

'James our True King: The Ideology of Irish Royalism in the Seventeenth Century', in D. G. Boyce, ed., *Political Thought in Ireland since the Seventeenth Century*, London: Routledge, 1993, pp. 1–30.

Ó Cléirigh, Tomás, *Aodh Mac Aingil agus an Scoil Nua-Ghaedhilge i Lobháin*, 1935; newly edited by Tomás de Bhaldraithe, Dublin: An Gúm, 1985.

Ó Cuív, Brian, 'The Irish Language in the Early Modern Period', in T. W. Moody, F. X. Martin and F. J. Byrne, eds., *A New History of Ireland, vol. III; 1534–1691*, Oxford: Clarendon Press, 1976, pp. 509–45.

Ó Dushláine, Tadhg, *An Eoraip agus Litríocht na Gaeilge, 1600–1650: Gnéithe den Bharócachas Cultúrtha i Litríocht na Gaeilge*, Dublin: An Clóchomhar, 1987.

Ó Muraíle, Nollaig, *The Celebrated Antiquary, Dubhaltach Mac Fhirbhisigh (c.1600–1671): His Lineage, Life and Learning*, Maynooth Monographs VI, Maynooth: An Sagart, 1996.

Ó Riain, Pádraig, ed., *Beatha Aodha Ruaidh: The Life of Red Hugh O'Donnell: Historical and Literary Contexts*, Irish Texts Society, Subsidiary Series XII, London: Irish Texts Society, 2002.

Riggs, Pádraigín, ed. *Dáibhí Ó Bruadair: His Historical and Literary Context*, Irish Texts Society, Subsidiary Series XI, London: Irish Texts Society, 2001.

Williams, N. J. A., *I bPrionta i Leabhar: na Protastúin agus Prós na Gaeilge 1567–1724*, Dublin: An Clóchomhar, 1986.

6

Prose in English, 1690–1800: from the Williamite wars to the Act of Union

IAN CAMPBELL ROSS

The defeat of the Jacobite forces in 1691, confirmed by the Treaty of Limerick, was soon followed by varied attempts by the Protestant (and particularly Anglican) minority in Ireland to justify their position of dominance over the country's Roman Catholic majority, at times in defiance of the terms of the treaty. This they did by appeal to Providence, by the assertion of the Irish parliament's legislative independence of the parliament in London, and by means of penal legislation directed against the economic interests as well as the political, religious, and educational freedoms of Catholics. Though working in a cultural context marked by an uneasy admixture of self-confidence and defensiveness, Protestant writers of varying beliefs produced literary work – political, philosophical, theological, economic and scientific – of remarkable assurance for an audience that extended, at times, far beyond those like themselves, to include pre-eminent figures in Great Britain, continental Europe and North America.

Enlightenment and Counter Enlightenment,
1690–1750

Attempts to legitimise Protestant ascendancy in Ireland began early. In his *State of the Protestants of Ireland under the late King James's Government* (1691), the Trinity College, Dublin-educated William King (1650–1729), archbishop of Dublin from 1703, gave a damning account of the oppression suffered by Protestants during the earl of Tyrconnel's Roman Catholic administration in the late 1680s. Attributing the triumph of Protestantism to divine providence, King offered a justification of the change of allegiance from James II to William and Mary, but he was not himself notably hostile to Roman Catholicism, later voting against a great part of the penal legislation. Though he retained an active interest in politics throughout his life – sharing common cause in the 1720s with Jonathan Swift – King's later contribution to Irish writing was predominantly in philosophical theology. *De origine mali* (1702) was among the most celebrated theodicies of the age: an attempted justification of God in the face of perceived evils that attracted responses by many writers, including Leibniz, Bayle, Berkeley, Hume and Alexander Pope. King returned to central questions of Christian belief in *Divine Predestination and Foreknowledge* (1709), attempting a reconciliation of divine omniscience with human free will.

In articulating Irish claims to legislative independence, the most significant work was *The Case of Ireland's being bound by Acts of Parliament in England, Stated* (1698) by William Molyneux (1656–98). A Whig lawyer and MP for Trinity College, Dublin, Molyneux drew variously and inconsistently on arguments including historical and legal precedent, the particularities of the historical moment, and an appeal to the natural right of men not to be ruled without their consent. It was this last argument, drawn from Locke's *Two Treatises of Government* (1690), that resulted in the *Case* being frequently republished at crucial political moments throughout the following century: in the 1720s, following the Declaratory Act (1720) by means of which the British parliament restated its claim to a right to legislate for Ireland, and during the 'Wood's Half-pence' controversy of 1722–5 when Swift gave eloquent voice in the *Drapier's Letters* (1724–5) to the arguments advanced by Molyneux; in 1749 by the Dublin city politician and later member of parliament Charles Lucas; at the time of Grattan's parliament in the 1780s; and as a central point of reference in the debate that preceded the Act of Union. On first publication Molyneux's work provoked sharp reaction in England, including condemnation by the House of Commons and a number of pamphlet attacks. In Ireland, by contrast, some believed it conceded too much to England and Molyneux, who appears to have had second thoughts about his work, could scarcely have envisaged the appeal his more radical arguments would hold for colonists in North America in the following century.

The *Case* was Molyneux's last work. Almost two decades earlier, however, he had published a translation of Descartes's *Meditations* (1682) and had made significant contributions to physics through his optical studies *Sciothericum Telescopicum* (1686) and *Dioptrica Nova* (1692). Molyneux was also active in the Dublin Philosophical Society, forerunner of the Dublin Society (1731), along with the English-born political economist Sir William Petty (1623–87), a founder of the Royal Society in London. Petty's works included the *Political Arithmetic* (1690), a seminal work of modern political thought that suggested land and population rather than precious metals to be the basis of a nation's wealth, and the *Political Anatomy of Ireland* (1672; pub. 1691), a survey of Ireland's inhabitants and natural resources.

In the 1690s, Molyneux was a correspondent of, among others, John Locke, through whom he made a more curious contribution to Irish (and western) philosophy. In the second edition of his *Essay on Human Understanding* (1690; 2nd edition 1694), Locke introduced a problem sent him by 'that very ingenious and studious promoter of real knowledge, the learned and worthy Mr *Molyneux*' (II, ix). The 'Molyneux problem' supposes a man who, born blind, has been taught to distinguish by touch between a cube and a sphere of the same metal; gaining his sight as an adult, would he be able to distinguish by sight alone the two objects, placed together on a table? Molyneux thought not, and Locke agreed, but the problem exercised numerous eighteenth-century philosophers, including Berkeley – who extended Locke's answer to conclude that the objects of the senses of touch and sight are quite different – Edward Synge the elder and Hutcheson in Ireland, Joseph Priestley in England, Leibniz in Germany, and Voltaire and Diderot in France.

While a defence of the new Protestant order was important to Irish writing in English during the 1690s, Protestants did not always speak with a single voice. So, Robert, later Viscount, Molesworth (1656–1725), a supporter of William III, who restored his confiscated estate and made him a privy councillor, wrote in his *Account of Denmark, as it was in the year 1692* (1694) a robust attack on the connection between church and state that had evident implications for Ireland. Declaring that the 'Want of *Liberty* is a Disease in any Society or Body Politick',[1] Molesworth argued that it was a mistake to believe Catholicism unique among 'Christian sects' in permitting the establishment of 'Slavery in a Nation'.[2] In Denmark, where he had served as envoy in 1692, Lutheranism did likewise – and Molesworth's argument that there was no essential difference between it and the established church in Ireland, equally entrenched in opposition to Catholicism and Protestant dissent, earned him public mistrust and royal disfavour. A fuller statement of Molesworth's Old Whig views is to be found in his preface to the second edition of his translation of Francis Hotoman's *Franco-Gallia*.[3] Despite his sympathy for dissent, Molesworth retained the personal approbation of many political opponents and Jonathan Swift addressed one of his *Drapier's Letters* to him in 1725.

Roman Catholic opinion, political or religious, was much less frequently to be found in print in Ireland in the late seventeenth and early eighteenth century.[4] An exception was the work of the Dublin-based priest Cornelius Nary (1658–1738). His *Modest and True Account of the Chief Points of Controversie between Roman Catholics and Protestants* (1699) originally appeared in London and Antwerp, though the powerful, if ineffectual, attack on the Penal Laws, *The*

Case of the Roman Catholics of Ireland (1724), was published in Dublin. Personally respected, he corresponded with Edward Synge the elder, whom he addressed publicly in *Letter to . . . Edward Lord Archbishop of Tuam in answer to his Charitable Address* (1728). Nary also published a *New History of the World* (1720).

The most radical voice of the 1690s was that of John Toland (1670–1722). Born an Irish-speaking Roman Catholic on the Inishowen peninsula in Donegal, Toland abandoned his earliest faith at the age of fifteen; subsequently, he professed a variety of religious beliefs, including Presbyterianism, Latitudinarianism, deism, and a personal form of pantheism that he took care, in his writing, to distinguish from the covert atheism that has been attributed to him. Schooled in the north of Ireland, Toland attended Glasgow and Leiden universities. Author of some one hundred published works, he wrote on a vast range of religious, philosophical, historical, literary, linguistic and political topics – though his precocious reputation for learning was quickly overshadowed by the publication of his most famous work, *Christianity not Mysterious* (1696). Arguing the merits of a wholly rational religion, this provoked instant controversy, becoming a central point of reference in the deist controversy that spread throughout Europe in the following century.

As with many contemporaries, Toland was profoundly influenced by the writings of John Locke, who knew and initially esteemed the young man. *Christianity not Mysterious*, however, yokes together elements of Locke's thought – particularly his privileging of reason over human or divine authority as guides to true knowledge, and the distinction between real and nominal essence – putting them to far more radical ends than had Locke himself. For Toland, Christian mysteries were to be understood neither as contrary to reason, to be received by faith alone, nor even as consonant with, but above, human reason. Revelation, which marks out Christianity's unique claims, Toland argued to be a 'means of Information' making clear, rather than enjoining deferral to, Christian mysteries. Nothing, Toland insisted, on Lockean grounds, 'ought to be call'd a Mystery, because we have not an adequate Idea of all its Properties, nor any at all of its Essences',[5] summing up his argument in the words that *there is nothing in the Gospel contrary to Reason, nor above it; and that no Christian Doctrine can be properly called a Mystery*'.[6] Had such views been expressed obscurely, at length or in Latin, the controversy that *Christianity not Mysterious* engendered might have been less immediate or less furious. Toland, however, wrote clearly, succinctly and in English, allowing readers easy access to views that struck at the heart of the confessional states of Ireland and England. Locke broke with him, as did Molyneux, and the Irish parliament directed that *Christianity not Mysterious* be burned by the common hangman. Toland himself was forced to leave Ireland, dividing the remainder of his life between England and continental Europe.

Although they attacked him, contemporaries could not easily dismiss Toland; the religious and political implications of *Christianity not Mysterious* and subsequent associated writings – *A Defence of Mr Toland in a Letter to Himself* (1697), *An Apology for Mr Toland* (1702) and *Vindicius Liberius* (1702) – were too subversive simply to be ignored. So, in Ireland William King, Peter Browne, Edward Synge the elder, Jonathan Swift, George Berkeley and Philip Skelton all replied to Toland, in the interests both of the Church of Ireland and of a political establishment still in the process of confirming its ascendancy through penal laws. The result was to stimulate a flourishing of Irish philosophy without parallel in modern times. Nor was the debate entirely one-sided for Toland's anti-sectarian and rationalist arguments appealed to Irish philosophical liberals such as the Presbyterian Francis Hutcheson and, later, even the Anglican bishop Robert Clayton – as well as commanding the attention and admiration of continental Enlightenment figures from Leibniz to Voltaire, Diderot, d'Holbach, Herder and Lessing.

Some features of Toland's early writings remained largely constant in his later work. A ferocious anti-clericalism, for instance, is apparent in *Letters to Serena* (1704) and *Adeisidaemon* (1709), which attacks superstition. It is evident too in *Nazarenus* (1718), a work of biblical scholarship that affronted many by appearing to question the authenticity even of the gospels, *Tetradymus* (1720), a defence of the former work (and one in which Toland introduces his distinction between esoteric and exoteric knowledge), and the posthumously published *Account of the Druids* (1726). Toland's religious allegiances, by contrast, underwent transformations that occasional prudential protestations of orthodoxy make hard to follow with certainty. So, the pantheism that he openly avowed in *Pantheisticon* (1720) was anticipated almost two decades earlier in *Letters to Serena* and *Socianism Truly Stated* (1705), which Toland signed with one of his many pseudonyms, here 'A Pantheist'.

Toland's political views are similarly difficult to pin down clearly: there is considerable irony in the fact that so prominent a republican as Toland, who described himself as a '*great Commons-wealths-man* . . . wholly devoted to the self-evident Principle of *Liberty*, and a profest Enemy to *Slavery* and *arbitrary Power*',[7] should have been received with such favour by the Electress Sophia of Hanover and the Queen of Prussia, of whose courts he published a laudatory account in 1704. Yet Toland's radical politics were at once a consequence of, and spur to, his attack on the mysteries of religion and clerical privilege. If there were no religious mysteries then sectarian differences had no basis in reason, a position which cut across Anglicanism's attempts to maintain its own privileged position against both Protestant dissent and Roman Catholicism. All priesthoods he considered 'calculated to beget Ignorance and an Implicite Disposition in the people, no less than to procure power and profit to the Priests'.[8] His own politico-religious ideal he described in *Nazarenus*, which drew creatively on his knowledge of early Irish language and culture to proffer a view of ancient Irish Christianity – epitomised by the beliefs of the 'Keldees' (i.e. Culdees), an order of 'Lay Religious' – as deistical and anti-Roman.[9]

Forced out of Ireland in his twenties, Toland continued to show both a personal and public interest in the country throughout his life. Though he affected to have no particular regard for his own people – he gave the place of publication of one of his works as Cosmopoli – he procured a testimonial from Franciscan friars in Prague in 1708 asserting him to have been born on the Inishowen peninsula to an old and noble family, and dedicated part of his antiquarian studies to showing that the ancient Irish 'were neither more ignorant nor barbarous . . . than the politest of nations, the Greecs and the Romans'.[10]

Two years before his death, Toland declared that 'Civil Liberty and Religious Toleration, as the most desirable things in this World, the most conducing to peace, plenty, knowledge, and every kind of happiness, have been the two main objects of all my writings'.[11] It was an ironic literary epitaph since the immediate importance of Toland's work for Irish literature was to be found less in the writings themselves than in the reaction they provoked.

John Toland stands as the most powerful Irish proponent of Enlightenment thought in the late seventeenth and early eighteenth century. In time, and in significantly different ways, he would be joined by others, including Francis Hutcheson and Robert Clayton. Against these, and often in specific opposition to Toland, were ranged important proponents of Counter Enlightenment values. Many of these, including William King, were Church of Ireland clergymen whose successful careers were launched by their defence of the established church and its doctrines. So, Edward Synge the elder (1659–1741), future bishop of Raphoe (1714) and archbishop of Tuam (1716), argued in the *Appendix* (1698) to his *A Gentleman's Religion* (1693–7), that while 'nothing contrary to our Reason can possibly be the Object of our Belief', it is 'no just Exception against some of the Doctrines of Christianity, that they are above our Reason'.[12] A similarly direct response to Toland came from Peter Browne (d.1735), provost of Trinity College, Dublin, later bishop of Cork (1709), in his *A Letter in Answer to a Book entitled Christianity not Mysterious* (1697), whose arguments he extended in

The Procedure, Extent and Limits of Human Understanding (1728) and *Things Divine and Supernatural conceived by Analogy with things Natural and Human* (1728).

The greatest of all Irish philosophers, George Berkeley (1685–1753), transcends any overly schematic account of an Enlightenment versus Counter Enlightenment split in early eighteenth-century Irish thought. Politically conservative and a life-long (though notably charitable) opponent of Roman Catholicism, Berkeley was a fierce anti-free thinker in religion whose rationalism nevertheless led him to oppose what he regarded as the facile responses to Toland's deism by some of his senior ecclesiastical contemporaries.

A student at, and later Fellow of, Trinity College, Dublin, Berkeley published two minor mathematical works in 1707. Already, though, he was formulating the core ideas of his mature philosophy: his rejection of abstraction and of Locke's distinction between the 'intellectual and material world' is anticipated in embryonic form in the *Philosophical Commentaries*, written 1705–8. As a young man, Berkeley was caught up in what he perceived to be the deistical or atheistical tendencies of Descartes's separation of mind and matter, as developed by Malebranche and Locke. As a philosophical theologian, Berkeley believed that there were solid arguments for God – even for the Christian God.

Alert to the likelihood that his arguments would not find immediate or easy acceptance, Berkeley introduced them in stages in his earliest major works: *A New Theory of Vision* (1709), the *Treatise Concerning the Principles of Human Knowledge* (1710) and *Three Dialogues between Hylas and Philonous* (1713). So, he began by arguing that the visible world exists only as it is known by the percipient mind, though allowing that the tangible world exists outside the mind (*New Theory*, sect. 45). In the *Treatise*, Berkeley went much further, asserting the ideas of touch – distance, tangible figure and solidity – to be themselves mind-dependent. Thus, Berkeley came to state clearly his doctrine of Immaterialism, famously writing of physical things: 'Their *esse* is *percipi*, nor is it possible they should have any existence out of the minds or thinking things which perceive them.'[13] In thus denying the existence of matter, independent of perception, Berkeley hoped to cut out the scepticism increasingly engendered by contemporary materialistic philosophy. In taking so radically simple an approach to the problems of materialism, Berkeley was alert to the kinds of objections he might face, endeavouring to pre-empt them.[14] To those who would object that his principles meant that things were, in a manner repugnant to common sense, 'every moment annihilated and created anew', Berkeley posited the necessary existence of 'that eternal invisible Mind which produces and sustains all things' (1, sect. 94), i.e. God.[15]

Though anxious to obtain widespread assent to his philosophy, Berkeley was aware of the difficulties of framing his theories for 'common use', especially among those whose vision was blinkered by prejudice. His response was *Three Dialogues between Hylas and Philonous*, in which he both rehearsed and developed his Immaterialism. Set in an idealised version of the Fellows' garden in Trinity College, Dublin, the work is in the Socratic dialogue form to which he would return two decades later in *Alciphron* (1732; 3rd edn 1752). In the *Dialogues*, Philonous – who represents Berkeley – propounds his philosophy to Hylas, causing the latter's belief in independent matter gradually to crumble before his amiably articulated but finally irresistible arguments. If his principles are admitted as true, Berkeley averred, 'the consequences which . . . evidently flow from thence, are, that *atheism* and *scepticism* will be utterly destroyed, many intricate points made plain, great difficulties solved, several useless parts of science retrenched, speculation referred to practice, and men reduced from paradoxes to common sense'.[16] Whether Berkeley's hopes were as sanguine as he implied, they were scarcely fulfilled. The *New Theory*, *Principles*, and *Three Dialogues* commanded only modest attention in the short term and were later read in a manner that ran quite counter to his intention. Perhaps prophetically aware of the difficulties to which his thought might lead him Berkeley had recorded in the *Philosophical Commentaries*: 'I am the farthest from Scepticism of any. man.'[17] Yet David Hume did little more than echo the sentiments of Hylas in the Second Dialogue when he declared that Berkeley's arguments tended rather to foster scepticism in that they 'admit of no answer and produce no conviction'.[18]

The elegant and lucid style of the *Dialogues* was to stand Berkeley in good stead in his continuing attempts to rebut contemporary free-thinking, most notably in a series of essays in Addison and Steele's periodical *The Guardian* (1713). With the Dublin-born Steele, Berkeley also collaborated on *The Ladies Library* (1713), a popular work of educational and religious instruction.

For some years, Berkeley published little, a second part of the *Treatise* having been apparently lost during his extended travels in Italy. However, the short Latin treatise *De Motu* (1721), originally written as a submission for a French scientific prize, embodied ideas to which he would return in his philosophical writing, while the *Essay towards Preventing the Ruine of Great Britain* (1721) – prompted by the South Sea Bubble scandal – anticipated the social concerns of later years, articulated in works as varied as *Alciphron*, *Siris* and *The Querist*.

Just as Berkeley's philosophy served always to support Christianity, then Christian faith served in turn to encourage good works. Chief among these in the 1720s was the idea of founding a university in Bermuda for the better evangelising of North America. In the year Berkeley was appointed dean of Derry, he expounded the idea at length in *A Proposal for the better supplying of churches in our foreign plantations* (1724), four years prior to settling in Rhode Island on the first stage of what would ultimately prove an abortive venture.

Shortly after his return to Ireland, Berkeley published a work which was the fruit of his years of comparative isolation in North America: *Alciphron; or the Minute Philosopher . . . Containing an Apology for the Christian Religion against those who are called Free-Thinkers* (1732). A series of seven Socratic dialogues, *Alciphron* picked up on ideas Berkeley had tackled in his early philosophy, while foregrounding the social concerns that had previously remained largely implicit. Whereas, in the *New Theory*, *Principles* and *Three Dialogues*, he had engaged principally with Descartes, Malebranche and Locke, Berkeley now set his sights on Hobbes, Spinoza, Shaftesbury, Mandeville and Anthony Collins, as well as on Irish contemporaries including William King and Peter Browne. In *Three Dialogues*, Berkeley had advanced his own position under the guise of Philonous. *Alciphron*, by contrast, consists of debates between two 'minute philosophers', or free-thinkers – Alciphron (= strong-mind) who, in Dialogue Three, articulates Shaftesbury's argument concerning the beauty of virtue, and decadent Lysicles who, in Dialogue Two, attempts to defend Mandeville's alleged philosophy, as epitomised by the tag 'Private Vices, Public Benefits' – and the arguments of Euphranor, who advances the reasonableness of Christianity, in the presence of Crito and the largely silent Dion (whom Mandeville took to be the author's representation of himself[19]). Throughout *Alciphron*, Berkeley seemed to acknowledge that readers – such is the strength of received prejudice – might prove more refractory than his youthful self had hoped, yet he was correspondingly more forthright in arguing that Christianity, properly understood, is to be considered the true 'free-thinking'. If Shaftesbury and Mandeville are the most celebrated of those whom Berkeley sought to refute in *Alciphron*, then in Dialogue Four, he engaged most explicitly with the argument, repeatedly articulated by King and Browne, that human beings can only have *analogical* knowledge of God, by attempting to clarify what is to be understood by *analogy* (Fourth Dialogue, sect. 21). Browne rejoined the debate in 1733 with *Things Divine and Supernatural conceived by Analogy with Things Natural and Human* (1733), while a younger man, Philip Skelton, endeavoured to engage both Browne and Berkeley in his *Letter to the Author of the Divine Analogy and the Minute Philosopher* (1734).

Though *Alciphron* opens with a primary emphasis on moral philosophy, the concluding dialogues find Berkeley once more concerned to assert the reasonableness of theistic belief and to maintain – though not without manifest difficulty – the particular reasonableness of Christianity, mysteries and all. Berkeley's mastery of the Socratic dialogue form is evident throughout, not least in those flashes of humour that – his reiterated attack on the prevalence of wit in modern writing notwithstanding – are a notable feature of many of his works.

The first of Berkeley's works to be translated (into French in 1734), *Alciphron* also brought Berkeley's earlier philosophy back into public awareness – for instance, in the *Gentleman's Magazine* in the mid-1730s. His next important work, *The Analyst* (1734), represented a return to his earliest interests, revealing the essential unity of Berkeley's extensive writings. Ostensibly a contribution to advanced mathematics, the critique of Newton's theory of fluxions saw Berkeley again attacking free-thinkers, here in the person of the 'infidel mathematician' who, Berkeley alleges, happily accepts what (he alleges) is incomprehensible in mathematics while denying what he cannot immediately understand in religion, though the benefits to be gained from the latter infinitely outstrip those conferred by the former. The next decade saw a pamphlet controversy of considerable proportions, mostly critical of Berkeley – who was drawn into replying to some attacks, at times with a testiness uncharacteristic of the man and the writer – while the controversy lingered on even longer in the periodicals and even finds unexpected and querulous expression in Thomas Amory's novel *Memoirs of Several Ladies of Great Britain* (1755).

Appointed bishop of Cloyne, Berkeley published the first part of his socioeconomic work, *The Querist* (1735–7; final edn 1752), in which he manifested an interest in the common good founded on religious conviction and a civic humanism of the kind represented by other contemporary clergymen, William King, Jonathan Swift and Thomas Sheridan the elder among them. A series of discrete questions – a total of more than nine hundred in all – concerning the present economic state of Ireland, *The Querist* is only apparently at odds with Berkeley's usual fluidity of expression. While his youthful *Philosophical Commentaries* open with a query, Berkeley's philosophy – founded in empirical enquiry – more generally insists that the truth can only be found by those willing to ask questions for themselves. A significant contribution to contemporary economic thought, *The Querist* also revealed Berkeley's imaginative engagement in Irish affairs.

His final major work, however, suggests the extent to which the unity of Berkeley's thought is never achieved at the expense of a willingness to rethink his position. *Philosophical Reflexions and Inquiries concerning the Virtues of Tar-Water and Divers other Subjects connected together and arising one from another*

(1744) is the evocative and accurate title of the work now generally known as *Siris* (an addition to the second edition). *Siris* – a chain – offers an impassioned plea for the medical virtues of tar-water as a panacea. That the metaphysical subjects the work deals with are connected may be allowed if we accept that the connections are to be found principally in Berkeley's own well-stocked mind. It is indeed a remarkable feature of Berkeley's work that its author begins with reference to relatively few and mainly modern authors, only to expand its range of reference until, in *Siris*, the philosophers of Greek and Roman antiquity, the eastern philosophers, hermetic philosophy, and a panoply of Renaissance and modern thinkers – the fruits of reading going back many decades – mingle as Berkeley's work moves its reader engagingly if not effortlessly from tar-water to God.

Berkeley's miscellaneous writings include some few sermons, a travel journal and youthful enquiries into natural history. His apparently inconsistent contributions to political philosophy, beginning with *Passive Obedience* (1712) – which led, almost certainly wrongly, to accusations of Jacobitism – ended with notably tolerant addresses to the clergy and people, and to the Roman Catholic clergy, of his diocese of Cloyne during the 1745 Jacobite rebellion.[20]

In his early twenties, anxious to make a reputation for himself yet aware of the task he was about to undertake in opposing himself to Locke and the most esteemed thinkers of his age, Berkeley wrote that his disagreements with those he admired must be understood as arising from the same source as his admiration: the love of truth. In the 'Conclusion' to *Siris*, he offered a later reflection on the same theme: 'Truth is the cry of all, but the game of a few . . . He that would make a real progress in knowledge might dedicate his age as well as youth, the later growth as well as first fruits, at the altar of Truth.'[21] For Berkeley, the great truth was that of Christianity and, as he asserted the great mark of that truth to be its tendency to do good, so too do his writings aim to promote 'the general well-being of mankind' (*Alciphron*, 1.16).

While no subsequent philosopher or philosophical theologian had the stature of Berkeley, there were younger men of undeniable talent who made their own contributions to contemporary debate. Philip Skelton (1707–87) engaged with both Browne and Berkeley in his *Letter to the Author of the Divine Analogy and the Minute Philosopher* (1734), hoping to persuade his distinguished fellow-clergymen to end their disagreement in the interest of presenting a unified front against deism. In his major work, *Ophiomaches; or Deism Revealed* (1749; rev. 1751), Skelton swung behind Browne, however, arguing in a series of eight dialogues for a radical confrontation between 'real Deism, and real Christianity',[22] the former understood as natural religion based on a belief in the sufficiency of human reason, and the latter revealed religion, wholly dependent on faith. *Some Proposals for the Revival of Christianity* (1736) was initially taken as being a work by Swift and in his forthright repudiation of the idea of man as a rational and self-sufficient being, Skelton provides a link in a chain of conservative thought that runs throughout the eighteenth century from Swift to Burke.

A quite different theological trajectory is to be observed in the writings of Robert Clayton (1695–1758). Like Skelton, Clayton was a student at, and later Fellow of, Trinity College, Dublin. Though his ecclesiastical career was as conventional as it was distinguished – he was, in turn, bishop of Killala (1730), Cork and Ross (1735), and Clogher (1745) – only his death prevented Clayton's arraignment on charges of heresy. His principal work, the *Essay on Spirit* (1750), developed an imaginative metaphysical theory of spirits which, widely attacked, prompted the *Defence of an Essay on Spirit* (1752). Subsequently, Clayton became increasingly heterodox, publishing *Some Thoughts on Self-Love, Innate Ideas, Free Will, Occasion'd by Reading Mr Hume's Works* (1753) and *Vindication of the Old and New Testaments* (1752–7), the third and final part of which invokes Toland in its discussion of religious mysteries. The Arianism that increasingly marked these works – and would end with Clayton proposing the removal of the Athanasian and Nicene creeds from the Book of Common Prayer – also resulted in an increased call for toleration of those who remained outside of the established church, including not only Roman Catholics and Quakers but also Jews.

The toleration Clayton advocated in the 1750s was a far cry from the position adopted by most of his peers in the Church of Ireland in the first half of the eighteenth century. Even Berkeley, who engaged in published debate with many of his Irish contemporaries, ignored the greatest of them completely. Francis Hutcheson (1694–1746), however, came from a quite different religious and political tradition. Moreover, though he was highly regarded personally in his lifetime, his influence was principally felt in the half-century or so after his death, and in Scotland and North America as much or more so than in Ireland. Hutcheson was born in County Down, son and grandson of Presbyterian ministers of Scottish descent. After schooling in the north of Ireland, he studied at the University of Glasgow from 1710 to 1716. Licensed as a minister, Hutcheson was sent to Dublin, following the passing of the Toleration Act of 1719, to open the Dissenting Academy in the Irish capital that he ran until 1729, when he was appointed professor of moral philosophy at his old university. That he was, in other words, marginal to the ascendancy culture of the Anglican establishment is a key to an initial understanding of why

Hutcheson's work made so little impact on the outstanding writers among his Irish contemporaries. This is not to say that Hutcheson was altogether unknown in Dublin. Indeed, the liberal political and theological circle centred on Robert Molesworth constituted the original audience for Hutcheson's early writings, especially his *Inquiry into the Original of our Ideas of Beauty and Virtue* (Dublin, 1725) and *An Essay on the Nature and Conduct of the Passions* (Dublin, 1728), and Hutcheson's place in Irish literature is now as well established as the older claim fostered on him as Father of the Scottish Enlightenment – teacher of Adam Smith and model for David Hume, Thomas Reid, Dugald Stewart and others.

Given the very different philosophical and religious traditions in which he was educated, it was most likely through Molesworth that Hutcheson developed his interest in the philosophy of Anthony Ashley Cooper, third earl of Shaftesbury, best known for his *Characteristicks of Men, Manners, Opinions and Times* (1711; 1714). For a Glasgow-educated Presbyterian, Shaftesbury was an unlikely source of influence, for his writing was more influenced by deism than by Calvinist theology, promoting a view of human beings as inherently benevolent, possessed of an innate moral sense and naturally attracted to the beauty of virtue. In following Shaftesbury's lead, Hutcheson was setting himself both against the older philosopher's principal targets – Hobbes and Mandeville – and against the Calvinist doctrine of man's natural corruption. Far from conceiving of human beings as depraved – and hence utterly dependent on divine grace – or governed only by self-interest (i.e. egotism), Hutcheson argued that human beings were possessed of an innate moral sense that made them naturally inclined to benevolence (i.e. altruism). In articulating such a position, Hutcheson placed himself so much in the vanguard of the liberal wing of Presbyterianism – the 'New Light' movement – that in 1737 the Glasgow Presbytery charged him with (though it eventually cleared him of) teaching false doctrine.

The stimulus to Hutcheson of Mandeville's challenge to Shaftesbury in the revised version of his *Fable of the Bees* (1709; 1714; 1723) may be gauged both by the title page of the first edition of the *Inquiry* and by three letters published in the *Dublin Journal* in February 1726. In the latter, Hutcheson attacked the *Fable* in a manner quite scathing for so mild-mannered a writer, his criticism prompting Mandeville subsequently to defend his own position. In contrast to the fashionable neo-Epicurean view that self-love was the mainspring of human action, Hutcheson argued for an innate moral sense that led human beings to take disinterested pleasure in the good of others: a view he supported by both frequent appeals to the authority of classical writers – poets as well as philosophers – and common human experience. This, in turn, led Hutcheson to challenge the long-standing belief – classical as well as Christian – in the necessity of a system of rewards and punishments, secular and divine, as encouragement to virtue. Virtue rewarded (or virtue that *demands* reward) is not virtue at all, Hutcheson suggests. A still more optimistic counterpart to such ideas in Hutcheson's thought is to be found in his assertion that humans have a 'moral sense of beauty in actions and affections', drawing them naturally away from vice and towards virtue. This entwining of the moral and aesthetic – again developed from Shaftesbury – was to influence Burke, among others.

His position as a Dublin schoolmaster in the 1720s seems certain to have militated against a wider engagement with Hutcheson's ideas in print. So, Berkeley made no mention of Hutcheson in his rejection of Shaftesbury's advocacy of the beauty of virtue in Book III of *Alciphron*. Paradoxically, the move to Glasgow marked both a break in Hutcheson's published work and a simultaneous increase in his influence, especially through his teaching. Although he insisted on the primary importance of the human individual, Hutcheson signalled his interest in man in society in his inaugural lecture, *De naturali hominum Socialitate* (On the Social Nature of Man) (1730) which, like most of his late work, was published in Latin – though Hutcheson was a pioneer in lecturing in English at Glasgow. Challenging the neo-Hobbesians, Hutcheson argued against the misuse of the idea of the 'state of nature' and Hobbes's definition of the life of man as 'solitary, poor, nasty, brutish and short'.[23] Human beings are naturally sociable, Hutcheson declared, God having 'implanted the seeds of almost all virtues or . . . motives to virtue of every kind'.[24] In considering humans as sociable by nature, Hutcheson does not mean that they are in search of pleasure or self-interest; rather, human nature is 'benevolent, kind and sociable, even in the absence of any calculation of advantage or pleasure to oneself' (p. 137). From his initial consideration of man in the state of nature, Hutcheson would go on to discuss both the causes and origin of civil society.

Hutcheson's last works, the Latin *Compend* (1742) – translated by James Moor as *A Short Introduction to Moral Philosophy* (1747) – and the posthumously published *A System of Moral Philosophy* (1755), enlarged on his consideration of man in society to include civil and political society. Though, in his insistence on innate ideas, Hutcheson turned his back on Lockean epistemology, he followed and developed Locke's political philosophy – especially his contractual theory of government – to a considerable degree. The speculative origins of his interest in the sociable nature of man give way to more practical concerns as he argued, for example, that whereas humans may come together in civil society for their own benefit, they are not bound to continue in any existing political union if this proves to be counter to their own interests: 'no endowments, natural or acquired, can give a perfect right to assume power over others, without their consent',[25] and if the people grant power in error they may 'justly abolish it again, when they find it necessary to their safety to do so'.[26]

After his death, Hutcheson's belief in natural rights made wide impact. In North America, part of a chapter (III, vii) of the *Short Introduction to Moral Philosophy* was reprinted in *The Massachusetts Spy* in 1772 and his ideas helped underpin the movement for American independence. At home, William Drennan, son of Hutcheson's friend Thomas, was instrumental in creating the United Irishmen with his proposal for a society based on 'the Rights of Man, and the Greatest Happiness of the Greatest Number' – a phrase (usually accredited to Jeremy Bentham) coined by Hutcheson in connection with his own proto-utilitarianism. That Hutcheson himself could scarcely have foreseen such use of his ideas does little to diminish the importance either of his thought or of the impact of his years in Ireland, 'my dearly beloved native soil', for his own liberalism owed much to his experience of marginalisation as a Presbyterian in the Ireland, and especially the Dublin, of the early years of the eighteenth century. It was this experience that led both to Hutcheson's advocacy of religious and political toleration and to his belief that it is in the realm of civil society rather than the state that virtue – unforced and unrewarded – may alone be practised.

Swift and his contemporaries

Jonathan Swift (1667–1745) was educated at Kilkenny School and Trinity College, Dublin, graduating in 1686. The landing of the deposed James II at Kinsale led the twenty-two-year-old to join thousands of other Protestants of English descent who left hurriedly for England, fearful of a repetition of the massacres of 1641 (the exaggerated extent of which was already entrenched in Protestant mythology). Though he returned to Ireland the following year, Swift spent much of the next decade attempting to find some suitable post in England. An early stay at the home of his relative Sir William Temple, at Moor Park in Surrey, producing nothing, Swift reluctantly entered the Church of Ireland, taking priestly orders in 1695. His experience in his first living at Kilroot, in a Presbyterian stronghold near Belfast, proved so discouraging that he soon returned to Moor Park, where he acted as secretary to Temple until the latter's death in 1699.

It was at Moor Park that Swift's first significant prose works were conceived and written. *The Battle of the Books* (begun *c.*1696; published 1704) was an attempt to support his patron's conservative position in the debate between the Ancients and the Moderns. This cultural clash had its origins in France, in the *Querelle des Anciens et Modernes*, but Temple had become known as the foremost English defender of the cause of the Ancients – i.e. the writers of classical antiquity – against the Moderns. Though Swift's contribution was influenced by evident self-interest as well as his reading in Temple's library, the position he adopted was one from which he scarcely deviated in later life – though his engagement with Modernity would become both more subtle and more troubled in his later writings. Though derivative, the *Battle of the Books* is a well-managed comic allegory – the battle takes place in the library of St James's palace – and contains some of Swift's most memorable passages, such as that describing the Ancients and the Moderns as the wide-ranging bee and the self-sufficient spider respectively, where the bee alone brings home honey and wax: i.e. 'Sweetness *and* Light'.[27]

Following his patron's death, Swift remained in England long enough to edit Temple's correspondence (1700) and to publish his own earliest political work, *The Contests and Dissensions between the Nobles and the Commons in Athens and Rome* (1701), before returning to Ireland.

In 1704, the *Battle of the Books* was first published, along with the *Mechanical Operation of the Spirit*, in the first edition of one of Swift's two greatest works, *A Tale of a Tub* (London, 1704; 5th edn 1710). Like its companion piece, the *Tale* is, above all, an attack on Modernity, taking in religion, politics, philosophy and literature. In religion, the *Tale* challenges contemporary free-thinking, epitomised by Toland's *Christianity not Mysterious*. Constructed around an allegory of religious division, represented by the figures of Peter, Martin and Jack (for St Peter / Roman Catholicism, Martin Luther / Episcopalianism and John Calvin / Presbyterianism), who variously interpret and misinterpret the will of their Father according to their own lights, Swift's work may be read as a defence of his own belief in revealed religion, as found in the Anglican teachings of, in Swift's case, the Church of Ireland. Devout contemporaries, though, as much as more sceptical modern readers, found the defence of the established church to be, at best, lukewarm – though the vehemence of Swift's attack on Catholicism and Protestant dissent was never in doubt. Accordingly, Anglicans hit back at the (then) anonymous author of the *Tale*, causing Swift to take up the pen again in defence of his own orthodoxy.

Religion aside, Swift's conservative mistrust of the modern world centred on the contemporary commercialisation of literature. Thus the supposed author of the *Tale* is a hack, writing in a garret, for bread. Especially in the final shape it reached, in its fifth edition – replete with dedication, an Epistle Dedicatory to

Prince Posterity, a preface, the 'Bookseller to the Reader', and advertisements for other works by the same writer – Swift's digressive satire takes on the loose, baggy form of the debased modern literature it sets out to parody. A version of the *Battle*'s spider, the Hack is an exemplary Modern who ends up 'trying an Experiment very frequent among Modern Authors; which is, to *write upon Nothing*; When the Subject is utterly exhausted, to let the Pen still move on . . .'[28]

In the *Battle of the Books*, Swift had written that 'Satyr is a sort of *Glass*, wherein Beholders do generally discover every body's Face but their Own.'[29] Since the *Tale*'s criticism of Modernity takes in both contemporary philosophy (Locke's empiricism, for example) and the new experimental science (associated with the Royal Society), many who praised the book were, in fact, the targets of its satire. Lauded and criticised by turn, the *Tale* nevertheless made Swift's name.

In 1707, the Church of Ireland sent him on a political mission to London, where Swift consolidated his reputation as a writer of works that simultaneously exploited and criticised the novel world of mass print culture. Writing as Isaac Bickerstaff, in the *Bickerstaff Papers* (1708), Swift impersonated the fashionable astrologers of his time so successfully that his prediction of the imminent death of one of their number – Swift's political enemy, John Partridge – was widely credited, much to Partridge's discomfiture. *An Argument against Abolishing Christianity* (1708) offered a critique of contemporary (ir)religion so audacious as still to dazzle readers, who find it hard to know where, exactly, its author stands on the real value of Christianity to the modern world.

Such works brought Swift further renown; when Richard Steele started *The Tatler* in 1709, he did so under the name of Isaac Bickerstaff. Swift's credit increased still further when the new Tory ministry led by Robert Harley granted the Church of Ireland the tax concessions Swift had sought in vain for the previous three years. Harley's motive was to acquire an able writer for his own ministry. Swift remained in England and, in a series of intimate letters, known as the *Journal to Stella* (written 1710–13; published 1779), he offered Hester Johnson, 'Stella', a captivating, if sometimes self-deceiving, account of his success in the English capital.

Soon, Swift was editing the Tory newspaper *The Examiner* (1710–11). More influential still was the pamphlet *The Conduct of the Allies* (1711), which did much to swing national opinion behind the Tory ministry's desire to end involvement in the War of the Spanish Succession – though it caused Swift to break with friends like Steele and Addison, while incurring the enduring enmity of other Whigs. Swift's account of the period, the principal historical work of a man who once aspired to the post of Historiographer Royal (a position then held by the Dublin-born and Trinity College, Dublin-educated poet, dramatist and translator Nahum Tate), was posthumously published as the *History of the Four Last Years of the Queen* (1713; published 1758).

Between Swift and real preferment, however, stood *A Tale of a Tub*, which Queen Anne thought too subversive to countenance Swift's elevation to the bench of bishops. Instead, he was given the deanery of St Patrick's cathedral, Dublin. The queen's death in 1714, following so closely on the collapse of the Tory ministry, sealed Swift's fate. In 1714, he left England and, with the exception of two short visits there in 1726 and 1727, spent the remainder of his life in Ireland.

To see Swift's celebrated involvement in Irish affairs as no more than the effect of rage or personal disappointment does less than justice to the writer's complex and troubled relationship to Ireland. His first surviving work, the *Ode to the King: On his Irish Expedition and the Success of his Arms in General* (1691), related directly to his experience of Ireland in 1689–90. In 1707, he wrote his first extended prose work on Irish affairs, *The Story of the Injured Lady*, depicting Ireland as an unhappy woman jilted by her unfaithful lover, England, for the ill-favoured Scotland – a transparent, though deftly handled, account of the negotiations leading up to the 1707 Act of Union between England and Scotland. At the time of writing, Swift was himself sympathetic to the suggested parliamentary union between England and Ireland. Conscious, however, of his own modest prospects in the church, he chose not to publish his account of an Ireland undone 'half by Force, and half by Consent'.[30]

Swift's championing of Irish political rights – always to be understood in terms of a colonial nationalism based on arguments most famously expressed in Molyneux's *Case of Ireland* – did not follow immediately on his return to Ireland in 1714. It was the passing of the Declaratory Act of 1720, restating England's alleged right to legislate on behalf of Ireland, that stung him to reply in print. The widely circulated *Proposal for the Universal Use of Irish Manufacture* (1720) was designed to encourage the purchase of home-produced goods as a means of promoting economic self-interest in the face of repressive English commercial legislation. The pamphlet having been published anonymously, the response of the English administration in Ireland was to have the printer tried for seditious libel. So fierce a response resulted not simply from the *Proposal*'s implied repudiation of the Declaratory Act but from the provocative way Swift chose to express his opinion (characteristically he did so by means of a joke). 'I heard', declares the author of the *Proposal*, 'the late Archbishop of *Tuam* mention a pleasant Observation of some Body's; that Ireland *would never be happy 'till a Law were made for* burning *every Thing that came from* England, *except their* People *and their* Coals: Nor am I *even* yet for lessening the Number of those Exceptions.'[31] These are in every sense the most inflammatory words Swift wrote on Irish affairs. It is not necessary to believe he ever seriously envisaged endorsing an armed rising against England to acknowledge that his pamphlet plays on English fears of rebellion that were real enough (the *Proposal* was written only five years after the 1715 Jacobite rebellion when troops were rushed to Ireland for fear that the country would rise in support of the Pretender). Certainly, the seditious import of the passage was sufficiently clear for it to be changed and softened when the pamphlet was reprinted, even in less tense political circumstances, as part of George Faulkner's 1735 edition of Swift's *Works*.[32]

The Drapier's Letters (1724–5) represent the fullest expression of Swift's attempt to rally Irish resistance to what he increasingly came to perceive as English political and economic oppression of the country. The affair of 'Wood's Halfpence' – in which an English ironmaster, William Wood, purchased a patent to manufacture copper coinage for Ireland from a mistress of George I – had begun as early as 1722. For two years it smouldered, a source of resentment in Ireland that engaged the interest of influential figures including Archbishop King. Swift's intervention was, if anything, tardy. Yet from the moment the first Drapier's letter appeared anonymously in March 1724, his became the best-known and most widely circulated of all publications on the issue. Once more assuming a *persona* – a device he had adopted in such diverse works as *A Tale of a Tub* and the *Bickerstaff Papers* – Swift posed as a Protestant linen-draper, living in the Dublin liberties, around St Patrick's cathedral. In this guise, the draper addresses tradesmen like himself – drawing arguments from constitutional history and natural law – for the right of the Irish to refuse the debased copper currency. Two further letters – to the nobility and gentry of Ireland, and to the printer John Harding, respectively – kept the issue a live one throughout the summer of 1724. It was the fourth letter, however, ambiguously addressed to 'The Whole People of Ireland', that particularly roused the English government's wrath. No longer was copper coinage even nominally the issue at stake; rather Swift questioned the entire constitutional relationship between Great Britain and Ireland, as understood in terms of Poynings's Law and the Declaratory Act. Addressing the 'Whole People' he declared provocatively:

The Remedy is wholly in your own Hands; and therefore I have digressed a little, in order to refresh and continue that *Spirit* so seasonably raised amongst you; and to let you see, that by the Laws of GOD, of NATURE, of NATIONS, and of your COUNTRY, you ARE and OUGHT to be as FREE a people as your brethren in *England*.[33]

Swift's authorship being known but not proved, the printer was charged with seditious libel (and would die in prison). Eventually, the new lord lieutenant of Ireland, the earl of Carteret, known to Swift from his days in London, announced the suspension of the patent at the opening of the Irish parliament in September 1725.

Swift became the 'Hibernian Patriot' but there is no hint of self-congratulation in his later writing. In narrow economic terms Swift had been successful, for Wood's coinage was withdrawn, yet Swift saw further, aware that nothing in the constitutional relationship between Ireland and Great Britain had changed (nor would it for another sixty years). With the later 1720s marked by repeated crop failure and extensive famine, Swift's writing evidenced a deepening pessimism about the state of Ireland. In 1729, he published *A Modest Proposal*, perhaps the most celebrated ironic essay in the language. Swift had written several contributions to emerging economic theory in a non-ironic vein but now, masquerading as an economic projector, he famously offered an extreme solution appropriate to the famine years of the late 1720s: the raising of Irish infants for human consumption. The Proposer develops his ideas at length, rejecting in the process such remedies as Swift, *in propria persona*, had put forward in published works for many years. If there is a despairing quality in such writing, then it was not unjustified. Stung by complacent contemporary reports of Ireland as a flourishing kingdom, Swift offered, in *A Short View of the Present State of Ireland* (1728), an account of a desolate nation that begins ironically, only to abandon forced humour with the poignant words 'my Heart is too heavy to continue'.[34]

That Swift continued to engage with Irish social and economic problems until the late 1730s is the more remarkable, given the extent to which he felt such works to be at odds with his own conception of the writer's real task. In his 'Letter to the Lord Chancellor Middleton' (written 1724; published 1735), Swift declared the three common motives of writers to be 'profit, favour, and reputation'. Opposition writing, however, brought no ecclesiastical preferment and Swift disdained monetary reward as incompatible with his gentlemanly notion of the disinterested author – the principled counterpart of the *Tale of a Tub*'s mercenary Hack. And, Swift added, 'as to Reputation, certainly no Man of Worth and Learning, would employ his Pen upon so transitory a

Subject, and in so obscure a Corner of the World, to distinguish himself as an Author'.[35]

So, while engaged in the Wood's Halfpence affair, Swift had also been composing what he intended would be the most universal of all his writings: *Travels through Several Remote Nations of the World* (1726). Now commonly known as *Gulliver's Travels* (the title was never Swift's), this book also has a claim to be not only the most famous work of the author but the most widely read book written in Ireland or by an Irish writer. Its fame was immediate but Swift had taken care to ensure that fame, making his first trip to England in a dozen years in order personally to take the manuscript to London. That *Gulliver's Travels*, unlike so much of his recent work in verse and prose, first appeared in London is very much in line with Swift's belief that issues of real substance must be addressed from the metropolitan centre rather than the margins (his frequent disparagement of those of his works in which he engaged directly with the problems of contemporary Ireland is unsettling to read).

It is clear, though, that Swift did not understand *Gulliver's Travels* as an 'English' work: the satirical account of English politics during the reign of Queen Anne in Book I (the 'Voyage to Lilliput') is granted no more significance than the account of 'Wood's Halfpence' in Book III. Rather, Swift moved from the essentially local and practical concerns of the first three books to engage, in Book IV, with the universal question of human nature itself, the 'Voyage to the Land of the Houyhnhnms' offering a challenge to the optimistic benevolist assumptions gaining ground in contemporary philosophy. Indeed, he went further, striking at one of the central beliefs of the classical-humanist tradition: the idea that humankind, as a species, is to be defined by reason. To Alexander Pope, Swift declared that, in writing the *Travels*, he had 'Materials Towards a Treatis proving the falsity of that Definition *animal rationale*; and to show it should be only *rationis capax*'.[36] In defiance of the school logics, with their assertion that '*homo est animal rationale*', Swift insisted that man be defined *not* as a 'rational being' but merely as a being 'capable of reason'. (Paradoxically, this universal truth is articulated in terms directly traceable to Swift's own education in Trinity College, Dublin during the 1680s and to the logic book he studied there, authored by the-then provost of the college, and later archbishop of Dublin, Narcissus Marsh.) To a twenty-first-century reader, the change might seem slight. Even the most cursory acquaintance with the response of readers and critics from the eighteenth to the twentieth century will show otherwise, for the account of the brutish Yahoos in the land of the rational, horse-like Houyhnhnms has been frequently and savagely attacked as a libel on human nature.

If Swift has retained the power to shock it is because he articulates throughout his work a profoundly anti-Modern sensibility, couched in language that,
more than other writers of his age and class, he strove to make accessible to the
new reading public of his day. Language was a life-long concern of Swift – not
least in his preoccupation that, like all else, it was subject to decay, and hence
liable soon to render his works, like those of his friends and contemporaries, as
obscure and inaccessible as those of the English Middle Ages. Such concerns
remained with Swift throughout his life, articulated in works including the
Proposal for Correcting the English Tongue (1712) and *Polite Conversation* (1738).
'Proper Words in proper Places', he declared in *A Letter to a Young Gentleman,
Lately Entered into Holy Orders* (1720), 'makes the true Definition of a St[y]le'[37] –
and Swift tried out his own prose on his servants, to ascertain its ready intelli-
gibility.

For a writer whose capacity for intolerance so often led to a fierce, alienating
authoritarianism, it was a paradoxical yet not uncharacteristic stance. Swift's
writing is suffused with the 'fierce indignation' he attributed to himself in his
Latin epitaph. Yet such an attitude co-exists throughout Swift's writing – from *A
Tale of a Tub* to his *Directions to Servants* (1745) – alongside an extraordinary ability
to imagine himself in the position of those whom he desired to subordinate.
Of all eighteenth-century Irish writers – of all writers in the English language –
Swift remains the most insistently subversive of moral, religious or political
complacency, and of unexamined belief in the human capacity for progress.

Even more than Berkeley, Swift dominated Irish writing in English in the
first half of the eighteenth century. He was not, however, without talented
contemporaries, though none had his range or imagination. Like Swift a pupil
at Kilkenny School and student at Trinity College, Dublin, Thomas Prior (1682–
1751) seconded the efforts of Swift and the work of older men, such as Robert
Molesworth's *Considerations for Promoting Agriculture and Employing the Poor*
(1723), to find practical solutions to the country's economic ills. Prior published
his frequently revised and reprinted *List of Absentees* (1729) and helped found
the Dublin (later Royal Dublin) Society in 1731. His public-spirited contribution
stimulated others in turn, so that, for example, Sir Richard Cox's thoughts on
linen manufacture were published as *A Letter . . . to Thomas Prior, Esq.* (1749).
Prior was also a friend and admirer of Berkeley, whose views he seconded in the
Authentic Narrative of the Success of Tar-water (1746). A co-founder of the Dublin
Society was Samuel Madden (1686–1765), a Trinity College, Dublin-educated
landowner who dramatised his patriotic principles in *Themistocles, the lover of
his country* (1729) and backed the campaign against absenteeism in *Reflections
and Resolutions Proper for the Gentlemen of Ireland* (1738). Madden was also author

of the fantastic *Memoir of the Twentieth Century* (1732), influenced by *Gulliver's Travels*. Along with Swift, Thomas Sheridan the elder (1687–1738) co-edited the Dublin periodical *The Intelligencer* (1728–9), which offered coruscating accounts of contemporary social and economic conditions, including a reprinted version of Swift's 'particular Description of our present misery', *A Short View of the State of Ireland*, with an introduction by Sheridan. The interests of Dr Patrick Delany (1685/6–1768), one-time professor of oratory at Trinity College, Dublin and later dean of Down, meanwhile, were predominantly scholarly. Author of several eccentric works including *Revelation Examined with Candour* (1732–63), *Defence of Polygamy* (1738) and *An Historical Account of the Life and Writings of King David* (1740–2), Delany also wrote one of the first biographical accounts of Swift. Among those female writers whose work Swift encouraged in defiance of contemporary convention – the poet Mary Barber and Laetitia Pilkington were others – the classical scholar Constantia Grierson (*c*.1705–1732) wrote Latin prefaces to her editions of Virgil (1724), Terence (1727) and Tacitus (1730).

In the different circumstances of the 1740s, the Dublin apothecary, local politician and later member of parliament Charles Lucas (1713–71) made Swift's political concerns of the 1720s his own while also fighting aldermanic privilege in the Irish capital. His published works included *Divelina Libera: An Apology for the Civil Rights and Liberties of the Commons and Citizens of Dublin* (1744), *The Political Constitutions of Great Britain and Ireland asserted* (1751) and *Seasonable advice to the electors of members of parliament at the ensuing general election* (1760), this last prompted by the death of George II, which heralded the first general election to be called in Ireland since the death of George I in 1727. Lucas was also responsible for reprinting Molyneux's *Case of Ireland* in 1749. In 1763, he founded the influential and long-lived *Freeman's Journal*, which in the following decade would publish essays by Henry Grattan and other 'patriots'.

Biography and memoir

After the deaths of Swift and Berkeley there was no established writer of remotely comparable stature. If the bishop of Cloyne's reputation as a major philosopher and truly virtuous man was secure, however, Swift's posthumous reputation was more uncertain than ever. As a result, he was the occasion of a number of biographical essays that endeavoured to reconcile his perceived genius with writing often thought morally perverse, and his notable charity with behaviour allegedly unbefitting a clergyman. The first biography proper was *Remarks on the Life and Writings of Dr Jonathan Swift*, written by John Boyle, fifth earl of Cork and Orrery (1707–62) in the unpromising (and possibly unique) form of a series of letters to his son. Though much criticised for presenting a view of Swift as mad and bad, Orrery's awkward but honest account remains a source of much unique material as well as offering vivid insights into the contemporary reception of Swift's extensive output. Biography – of modern writers, at least – was still in its infancy in the mid-eighteenth century, yet two further biographical accounts quickly appeared in response to Orrery's: Patrick Delany's *Observations upon Lord Orrery's Remarks on the Life and Writings of Dr Jonathan Swift* (1754), and Deane Swift's *An Essay upon the Life, Writings and Character, of Dr Jonathan Swift, Interspersed with some occasional Animadversions upon the* Remarks *of a late critical Author, and upon the* Observations *of an anonymous Writer on those Remarks* (1755). Among later lives of Swift by Irish writers, those by Thomas Sheridan the younger, the first volume of a complete volume of an edition of the *Works* (1784) and George Monk-Berkeley's *Literary Relics . . . To which is prefix'd, An Inquiry into the Life of Dean Swift* (1789) deserve mention. No other Irish writer attracted the same degree of biographical attention, though Oliver Goldsmith, who wrote numerous short biographical accounts for magazine publication, was author of lives of Robert Boyle, the poet and prelate Thomas Parnell, and 'Some original MEMOIRS of the late famous Bishop of CLOYNE [i.e. Berkeley]'.[38]

Swift was a special case but the growing interest in individual lives bore fruit also in letters, diaries and autobiographies. Early examples include accounts of his experience in Ireland by the English bookseller John Dunton (1659–1732), especially *The Dublin Scuffle* (1699); his 'Teague-Land, or a Merry Ramble to the Wild Irish' recalls earlier attitudes to the native Irish of Gaelic stock, and remained unpublished in his lifetime. That 'Teague-Land' remained in manuscript was uncharacteristic. Female writers, though, were of necessity more reticent in publishing their work. Exceptionally, Laetitia Pilkington (c.1709–50) did publish her informative and entertaining *Memoirs* (1748–54),[39] which include valuable information on Swift's last years; she did so, though, at some cost to herself, for the memoirs were considered the scandalous work of a scandalous author, Pilkington's offence being that she was a woman writing for money (and an unfaithful wife to Swift's one-time friend, Matthew Pilkington). The most extended, valuable and interesting account of an 'ordinary' Irish existence (if that of a genteel, English-born Protestant may be so termed) is contained in the autobiography and letters of the English-born Mary Delany (1700–88), who came to Ireland in 1743 when she married, as her second husband, Patrick Delany. Her work is a source of much valuable and entertaining material concerning the life of mid-century Ireland, which also reveals Delany's extensive knowledge of flowers and gardening, yet contemporary notions of propriety ensured that the correspondence and account of her life remained unpublished until the mid-nineteenth century.[40]

Notable among (mostly) posthumously published memoirs or autobiographical fragments are such varied works as Swift's 'Account of the Swift Family'; Laurence Sterne's *Memoirs* (1775), which give glimpses of the novelist's childhood in counties Dublin, Wicklow and Westmeath; the *Recollections of the Life of John O'Keeffe, Written by himself* (1826) by the actor and playwright John O'Keeffe (1747–1833); and the *Reminiscences* (1826) of the tenor Michael Kelly (1762–1826), who premiered the roles of Basilio and Curzio in Mozart's *Le nozze di Figaro*. In quite different vein, the autobiographical *Life* (1826), first edited by his son, is the most lasting literary testament to Theobald Wolfe Tone.[41] Among other memoirists and letter-writers, whose correspondence ranges from high politics in Ireland and England, through church affairs, to the social life of Protestants and Roman Catholics, the following names are particularly worthy of note: George Berkeley,[42] Jonathan Swift,[43] Charles O'Conor of Belanagare,[44] Dorothea Herbert,[45] Mary Leadbeater,[46] Betsy Sheridan,[47] James Caulfeild, earl of Charlemont,[48] Edmund Burke[49] and Richard Lovell Edgeworth.[50]

Goldsmith, cosmopolitanism and national pride

After Swift, the first truly distinguished imaginative writer in English was Oliver Goldsmith (1728–74), poet, dramatist, essayist, reviewer, historian and novelist. His career, however, offers a very different model to those discussed above. Goldsmith seems, from his youth, to have felt himself doubly provincial: an Irishman from County Longford who aspired to a literary career at a time when cultural life was increasingly centred on the British metropolis of London. After graduating from Trinity College, Dublin, in 1749, Goldsmith studied medicine in Edinburgh and later toured the continent, visiting France, Germany, Switzerland and Italy, as well as the Low Countries. Failing in his aim of becoming an East India Company surgeon, Goldsmith took a post as usher at a school in Peckham. Though he subsequently settled in the English capital, this unfixed early period of his life prefigures Goldsmith's literary career, in which he not only made a significant reputation as a poet and dramatist but wrote on an exceptionally wide range of topics in his extensive prose. In part, he had little choice. His earliest forays into literature were as a jobbing writer, contributing to the *Monthly Review*, where one of his earliest notices was of Edmund Burke's

On the Sublime and Beautiful (1757).[51] Subsequently, he contributed to Tobias Smollett's *Critical Review* and the *British Magazine*. *The Bee* (1759), a weekly journal he founded himself, was short-lived, yet a prodigious undertaking for he penned most of the content personally. At times, Goldsmith wrote with Johnsonian gravitas on such subjects as 'The Characteristics of Greatness' or 'On the Instability of Worldly Grandeur'. Elsewhere, his essays followed more closely the models established by Steele and Addison. Thus, Goldsmith wrote notably on aspects of everyday life – the theatre, education, pulpit eloquence, opera and luxury – while offering biographical sketches of subjects as diverse as Charles XII of Sweden and Maupertuis. There are also many fictional set-pieces, at times tinged with autobiography. His essay asserting the reign of Queen Anne to be the 'Augustan Age' of English literature offered a highly influential piece of critical shorthand that retains currency today.[52]

As a periodical essayist in London, Goldsmith was by no means alone. Irish contemporaries engaged in magazine publishing included Arthur Murphy (1727–1805), with the *Gray's Inn Journal* (1756) and, later, the *Test* and the *Auditor*, Edmund Burke, who edited the *Annual Register* from 1758, and Hugh Kelly (1739–77), with the *Ladies' Museum*, the *Court Magazine* and the *Babler* in the 1760s and 1770s. In a crowded market, *The Bee* enjoyed only modest success and folded after eight numbers (though the essays were quickly republished in collected form). A more commercially successful venture in periodical essay-writing is represented by the letters – modelled on Montesquieu's *Lettres Persanes* (1721) – purportedly written by a Chinese philosopher to his friends at home, published initially in the *Public Ledger* (1760–1). The characteristically gentle humour, often at the philosopher's expense, that pleased a wide public is ultimately deceptive, however. Goldsmith's sharp observation of contemporary England offered a complex critique of the increasing insularity and tendency to self-congratulation that Goldsmith believed to characterise the new polity of Great Britain. Here, as elsewhere, the writer exhibited too a reserve about the growth of empire: 'When a trading nation begins to act the conqueror, it is then perfectly undone.'[53]

Goldsmith's own stance is best indicated by the title, *The Citizen of the World*, under which the letters were reprinted in 1762. Influenced by his own youthful experience of travel, the writer argued against the gathering tendency to proffer accounts of other peoples in terms of supposed *national* characteristics, in favour of a more precisely detailed, and hence juster, notion of nations, based on 'experimental enquiry'. In a series of four essays offering a comparative view of races and nations that appeared in the *Royal Magazine* in 1760, Goldsmith declared that he would feel well rewarded if his travels could 'enlarge one mind, and make the man who now boasts his patriotism, a citizen of the world'.[54] Though partly attributable to his own notoriously defensive sensibility, such ideas are integral to Goldsmith's conception of the writer's proper role – one prefigured by Fougeret de Monbron, from whose *Le cosmopolite; ou le Citoyen du Monde* (1750) Goldsmith most likely borrowed his title. 'It is the duty of the learned', Goldsmith averred, 'to unite society more closely and to persuade men to become citizens of the world.'[55]

One result of Goldsmith's elective cosmopolitanism was to turn the writer away from any particular concern with Ireland – though shafts of nostalgia for his childhood haunts light up many passages of his published and private writings, in prose and verse. Writings on Irish subjects include 'A Description of the Manners and Customs of the Native Irish' to the *Weekly Magazine* in 1759,[56] and a much-cited essay on Carolan. The latter is perhaps no more representative of Goldsmith than Swift's rendering of Hugh Mac Gauran's 'Pléaráca na Ruar-cach' as 'Description of an *Irish-Feast*' is of Swift – though the latter, at least, was far from uninformed about the Gaelic world, having, through his friend Anthony Raymond, contacts with the important Irish-language manuscript culture of the Dublin of his day, centred on Seán Ó Neachtain and his son Tadhg.[57] In the essay, Goldsmith, who elsewhere attacked contemporary luxury as corruption, compared 'Celtic simplicity with modern refinement', and characterised the Gaelic-speaking Celts of his native land as 'still untinctured with foreign refinement, language, or breeding'.[58]

Like many contemporaries in a commercial age, marked by social and cultural flux, Goldsmith was deeply conflicted. In his *Enquiry into the Present State of Polite Learning in Europe* (1759; 2nd edn 1774), he self-consciously offered readers a familiar narrative of cultural decline – thereby recalling, though in different terms, the farewell to Poetry that concludes Goldsmith's best-known poem, *The Deserted Village* (1770). Yet, marked as it is by an insistence on the powerful influence of imaginative and historical writing on society, the *Enquiry* may also be understood as one of many works that defer to Enlightenment ideas of progress and popular enlightenment. The assertion that '[t]he poet and the historian, are they who diffuse a lustre upon the age, and the philosopher scarce acquires any applause, unless his character be introduced to the vulgar by their mediation'[59] embodies what would become a familiar notion in Goldsmith's writing and an important impulse to his own later work of popularisation. Arguing that 'The generality of readers fly from the scholar to the compiler',[60] he himself compiled, abridged, projected or wrote prefatory materials to works as varied as a *New and Accurate System of Natural History* (1763), a *History of England in a Series of Letters from a Nobleman to his*

Son (1764), a *General History of the World* (1764), the *Roman History* (1769; abridged 1772); the *History of England, from the Earliest Times to the Death of George II* (1771; abridged 1774) and a *History of the Earth, and Animated Nature* (1774). Though lamenting perceived cultural decline, Goldsmith nowhere suggested that readers should be denied the materials for self-improvement. In his preface to the *History of the Earth, and Animated Nature* (1774), he acknowledged his personal desire for the approbation of scholarly naturalists, but insisted – with a glance at the Addison of the *Spectator* – that his principal ambition was 'to drag up the obscure and gloomy learning of the cell to open inspection; to strip it from its garb of austerity, and to shew the beauties of that form, which only the industrious and inquisitive have been hitherto permitted to approach'.[61]

Personal insecurities aside, Goldsmith's literary cosmopolitanism might be understood as a reaction to the growing interest in *national* literatures within these islands, which encompassed work in English, Irish, Welsh and Scots Gaelic – this last exemplified most obviously by the Ossianic cult started by James Macpherson. In Ireland, James Arbuckle (1700–34) was among the first to engage with the idea of a specifically national literature. A Dublin-born and Glasgow-educated Presbyterian schoolmaster and journalist, he was associated with the 'New Light' movement that included also Francis Hutcheson, a contributor to the *Dublin Weekly Journal* (1725–33), edited by Arbuckle, whose own essays were collected in *Hibernicus's Letters* (1729). Many of the issues Arbuckle addressed were familiar enough in the 1720s, including the alleged spread of luxury or the extent to which, in addition to the obstacles put in their way by England, the Irish were responsible for their own problems. While Swift lamented the fact that Ireland welcomed English writers no matter how bad, Arbuckle inveighed against the fact that many distinguished 'English' writers were in fact natives of Ireland. 'England boasts among her illustrious names that have excelled in arts as well as arms, multitudes that had the misfortune to be born in Ireland,'[62] he declared, and encouraged the publication of work by Irish authors in the *Journal*. Thirty years later, Thomas Campbell would advance a similar argument, in relation to painting, in *An Essay on Perfecting the Fine Arts in Great Britain and Ireland* (1767).[63]

A more positive attempt to construct an Irish literary tradition was made in the mid-century by Paul Hiffernan (1719–77) in his miscellany, *The Hiberniad* (1754). Hiffernan had studied for the Roman Catholic priesthood before turning first to political journalism, as editor of *The Tickler* (1747–8). In the *Hiberniad*, Hiffernan argued that the two principal motives for '*national Pride*' were the beauties of Ireland's landscape and the 'extraordinary talents' of its natives.

(Given that his standard of beauty was derived from the Wicklow countryside, his position took him close to that of the painter George Barret, then working in the wilder parts of that county, and looked forward, via Burke's *On the Sublime and Beautiful* (1757), to James Barry, whose *Works* were eventually published in 1809.[64]) Though crude, the literary tradition Hiffernan attempted to construct was remarkable for its breadth of sympathies, so that Ireland's 'illustrious' writers include not only Ussher, Denham, Roscommon, Boyle, Congreve, Southerne, Steele, Farquhar, Berkeley, Parnell and Swift, but also Constantia Grierson, Mary Barber, Laetitia Pilkington and Carolan.

Hiffernan hoped to foster 'National Pride', a term soon to be familiar in European discourse, following the publication of *Von dem Nationalstolze* (1758) by the Swiss Johann Georg Zimmermann, later translated as *On National Pride* (1771). Like Hiffernan, Zimmermann was aware of the extent to which (though not exclusively) the Irish suffered from tenacious negative characterisations. English prejudice was a particular problem: Zimmermann noted the English view of the Irish as '*blood-thirsty . . . bog-trotter*[*s*]'.[65] Attempts to redress such pejorative understandings of Ireland or to construct an Irish literary tradition were not confined to miscellaneous writers like Hiffernan. So, in his *Discorso sopra le vicende della letteratura* (1760; 2nd edn 1763), the Italian comparativist Carlo Denina affirmed that natives of the British metropolis erred in priding themselves on exclusive possession of propriety of expression in polite letters and learning alike. If luxury can be resisted, then 'IRELAND might become the seat of science and literature . . . the example of USHER [*sic*], SWIFT, BERKELEY, HUTCHESON, and several others, is a proof that the Irish are capable of equalling any of the northern nations in erudition and elegance, in criticism and philosophy'.[66]

Denina's argument, however, was increasingly undermined by a general drift towards London by Irish writers, including Hiffernan himself. Others who, sooner or later, took the boat to Holyhead included many of the best-known authors of historical, critical, biographical and scholarly prose in the second half of the eighteenth century: Thomas Sheridan the younger, Edmond Malone, Richard Brinsley Sheridan and, above all, Edmund Burke.

A rare exception was the Trinity College, Dublin-educated Henry Brooke (?1703–83) who made a name for himself in London as a poet, translator and dramatist – for *Universal Beauty* (1735), Tasso's *Gerusalemme Liberata*, 1–3 (1738), and the controversial *Gustavus Vasa* (1739) – before returning to Ireland in the 1740s. There he aspired to make an ambitious collection of Irish tales – *Ogygian Tales: or a curious collection of Irish Fables, Allegories and Histories from the Relation of Fintane the Aged* (1743) – and a history of Ireland (1744), though neither work got further than the published proposal. The Jacobite rebellion of 1745 prompted *The Farmer's Six Letters to the Protestants of Ireland* (1745), to be followed by *The Spirit of Party* (1753), both of which articulate Brooke's early anti-Catholicism. Among Brooke's critics was Charles O'Conor (1710–91) of Belanagare, who, in the *Cottager's Remarks on the Spirit of Party* (1754), emphasised Catholic loyalty to the Hanoverians in 1745. Brooke subsequently changed his position, later publishing *The Tryal of the Cause of the Roman Catholics* (1761), which examines the arguments for and against the Penal Laws and concludes by arguing for their relaxation.

A younger contemporary of Brooke, the historian Thomas Leland (1722–85) would also find himself in conflict with Charles O'Conor. Professor of oratory at Trinity College, Dublin, from 1763, Leland notably translated the *Orations of Demosthenes* (1754–70), which – together with the *Principles of Human Eloquence* (1765) – would provide a pattern for the admired parliamentary oratory of Trinity-educated students such as Edmund Burke and Henry Grattan, among others. A classical historian, author of the *Life of Philip of Macedon* (1758), Leland also wrote an ambitious *History of Ireland from the Invasion of Henry II* (1773). In this undertaking he was encouraged by Charles O'Conor, though the latter subsequently criticised the traditional Protestant bias of Leland's treatment of such key events as the 1641 rebellion. With the Jacobite *Histoire de l'Irlande* (Paris, 1758–62) by the Abbé James MacGeoghegan (1702–64) still untranslated, a Roman Catholic critique of Leland's *History* was offered by both John Curry in *An Historical and Critical View of the Civil Wars in Ireland* (1775) and Sylvester O'Halloran.

Making his career in Ireland, Leland was increasingly in a minority. Thomas Sheridan the younger (1719–88), son of Swift's friend, travelled back and forth between Ireland and England for many years, in his capacities as actor and theatre-manager, before leaving Ireland in the late 1750s. Sheridan's work as educationalist, elocutionist and apologist for the new polity of Great Britain is best represented in his *British Education* (1756), *Plan of Education for the Young Nobility and Gentry of Great Britain* (1769), and *Lectures on the Art of Reading* (1775). As well as short works on Dublin theatrical politics, he also published *A View of the State of School-Education in Ireland* (1777). His 'Life' of Swift forms the first volume of Sheridan's important seventeen-volume edition of Swift's *Works* (1784).

An edition of Goldsmith's *Works* (1777), just three years after the author's death, was the first literary production of the Shakespearean scholar and textual editor Edmond Malone (1741–1812). It appeared in Dublin shortly before the Trinity College-educated Malone left his Irish law practice for London; editions of Reynolds (1797) and Dryden (1800) followed. A year later, he published *An Attempt to Ascertain in which Order the Plays of Shakespeare were Written* (1778), the first example of the scholarship that was to establish Malone's reputation. The *Historical Account of the Rise of the English Stage* (1780) followed and in 1790 Malone published his edition of Shakespeare in eleven volumes. Malone also aided Boswell with the latter's *Life of Johnson* (1791), adding substantial footnoted material to later editions; Boswell's son, James Boswell the younger, repaid the compliment, seeing the massive twenty-one-volume revision of Malone's edition of Shakespeare through the press in 1821.

Burke, politics and revolution

Of all prose writers, it was Edmund Burke (1729–97) who dominated the second half of the eighteenth century. The son of a Protestant, but possibly convert, lawyer who had married a Roman Catholic, Burke had a mixed Catholic and Protestant schooling and attended Trinity College, Dublin before heading to London to study law. While a student in Dublin, Burke had founded, edited and largely written a journal, *The Reformer*, and soon found himself immersed in literary life in the English capital. His earliest work, the ironically entitled *A Vindication of Natural Society* (1756), looked backwards to conservative attacks on natural religion in the early part of the century – though Burke's principal target was Henry St John, Viscount Bolingbroke. In the second, revised edition of 1759, Burke made his intentions plain: 'The Design was, to shew that, without the Exertion of any considerable Forces, the same Engines that were employed for the Destruction of Religion, might be employed with equal success for the Subversion of Government.'[67]

In the *Philosophical Enquiry into the Origin of our Ideas of the Sublime and Beautiful* (1757), Burke drew on varied sources of eighteenth-century aesthetic theory, encompassing both Addison's *Spectator* series, the 'Pleasures of the Imagination' (1712), and Hutcheson's *Inquiry into the Original of our Ideas of Beauty and Virtue*. In the introductory section, 'On Taste', added to the second, revised edition of his book in 1759, Burke defined 'taste' as the human faculty that forms a judgement of works of imagination and the 'elegant' arts. The scope of his enquiry is to determine whether there are any principles on which the imagination is affected that are common to all individuals, so that we may usefully reason about them. Answering in the affirmative, Burke declared that where the passions – love, grief, fear, anger or joy – are represented, 'natural human sympathy' ensures that all men respond in the same manner, 'upon certain, natural and uniform principles'. They are also driven by the competing ideas of pleasure and pain, which Burke associates with the Beautiful and the Sublime. For Burke, the (feminine) Beautiful is associated with order and harmony – what is comparatively small, smooth, clear, light and delicate, and founded on pleasure; the (masculine) Sublime is disorder and menace – what is vast, rugged, dark, massive, and founded on pain.[68] Of the Sublime, Burke writes: 'Whatever is fitted in any sort to excite the ideas of pain, and danger, that is to say, whatever is any sort terrible . . . is a source of the *sublime*; that is, it is productive of the strongest emotion which the mind is capable of feeling.'[69] To experience the Sublime, however, pain and danger must not be too immediately present, else human instinct for self-preservation will take over. Rather, the cultivation of a 'sort of tranquillity tinged with terror' requires the employment of the finer senses, resulting in 'delightful horror' (the implications of Burke's sexualised aesthetics for later eighteenth-century literature – the Gothic or emerging Romanticism – are clear). The centrality of the non-rational to Burke is made explicit in the *Enquiry*'s conclusion, which maintains that language may affect the mind of the hearer not by raising distinct images or by standing for ideas but by engaging the passions. Such a position is closely related to, and perhaps derives from, Berkeley's use of an emotive theory of language in support of religious mysteries (*Alciphron*, vii). For Burke, who declared that he knew of nothing Sublime that was not 'some modification of power', there were also strong political implications, since the Sublime also comes, inexorably, to involve not only the omnipotence of God but the might of kings.[70]

The immediate influence of Burke's early works was modest. Among Irish thinkers, the *Enquiry* perhaps had most impact on James Usher (1720–72), a Protestant-born and Trinity College, Dublin-educated convert to Catholicism. An obscurantist writer, Usher published *A New System of Philosophy* (1764), the ironical *Free Examination of the Common Methods employed to Prevent the Growth of Popery* (1766) and *An Introduction to the Theory of the Human Mind* (1771), in which he celebrated music for its peculiar power to move its hearers through its very failure to communicate any clear idea (an extension of Berkeley's emotive theory of language as taken up by Burke). *Clio; or a Discourse on Taste* (1767), in which Usher returns to the subject of music, now described as 'a language directed to the passions',[71] retained its popularity into the first decades of the nineteenth century.

In 1759, Burke entered politics when he became private secretary to William Gerard Hamilton, chief secretary to the Irish viceroy. Six years later, he became private secretary to the prime minister, the earl of Rockingham, and entered the British House of Commons. Burke's career was henceforth pursued in

England – though his varied political concerns, articulated both in pamphlets and in printed versions of celebrated parliamentary speeches, famously comprehended British, American, Indian and Irish affairs. On the first, *Thoughts on the Cause of the Present Discontents* (1770) is an impassioned assertion of parliamentary rights against the perceived absolutist tendencies of George III; in the speech on economical reform (1780), Burke argued for a curb on monarchical influence on parliament exercised through the distribution of sinecures. Such matters were, however, linked in Burke's mind with America, his views on which he had begun to formulate in the mid-1760s. In 1770, his hope was to avert a taxation crisis and the move toward revolution he believed it would portend; a decade later, his aim was to persuade the king to accept the fact of American independence. In the intervening years, Burke had argued strongly and repeatedly in favour of conciliation with the colonists, notably in his impromptu contribution against the proposed imposition of a tea tax, subsequently published as *On American Taxation* (1774).

Concerning Indian affairs, on which he first spoke in 1767, Burke's most famous role was in the impeachment of Warren Hastings, governor general of Bengal, whom Burke held chiefly responsible for what he termed 'the present most corrupt and oppressive system' of government in the subcontinent, still largely under the control of the East India Company, itself heavily influenced by vested interests. Burke made his first move towards impeachment in 1785, managed the Commons' case before the House of Lords two years later, and in 1794 made the *Speech in Reply*, which closed the case (Hastings was acquitted the following year). Among many notable contributions, Burke's *Speech on the Nabob of Arcot's Debts* (1785) was one of his finest orations.

Burke's family background gives his involvement in Irish affairs a particular interest, not least since members of his mother's family – the Nagles of County Cork – were implicated in the Whiteboy agrarian agitation of the early 1760s. Having acquired the seat for Bristol in 1774, Burke lost it after supporting Irish free trade against the perceived interests of his constituents, arguing that, without relaxation of trade restrictions, Ireland might one day follow America's example (*Speech at the Guildhall in Bristol* (1780)). Yet, among his many speeches and writings on Irish affairs, *To a Peer of Ireland on the Penal Laws* (1782) reveals the ambivalence towards Protestant ascendancy that led Burke to be lukewarm in his support for Irish legislative independence in that year. Such concerns were of long standing: his posthumously published 'Fragment of a Tract on the Popery Laws' was composed in or before

1764 and he returned to the subject throughout his life. In the 'Fragment', he problematically recalled Swift's famous apothegm that 'government without the consent of the governed is the true definition of slavery' in arguing that:

> As a Law directed against the mass of the Nation has not the nature of a reasonable institution, so neither has it the authority: for in all forms of Government the people is the true Legislator; and whether the immediate and instrumental cause of the Law be a single person or many, the remote and efficient cause is the consent of the people, either actual or implied; and such consent is absolutely essential to its validity.[72]

The support Burke offered the Catholic Committee in the 1780s was strengthened in the wake of the French Revolution, resulting in *A Letter to Sir Hercules Langrishe* (1792), in which he argued for a gradual easing of the franchise to admit Roman Catholics as a necessary bulwark against revolution in Ireland. By 1795, his mistrust of Protestant ascendancy would lead him to equate its pernicious effects in Ireland with those of Jacobinism in France,[73] while by the following year he was prepared to see Catholic defenderism as the sole check on ascendancy.[74]

Despite his reputation, in fact, Burke was much more than a philosopher of conservatism. His final position, however, was greatly influenced by his sharp and immediate sense that the French Revolution represented too abrupt and too complete a break with the past. Certainly, this helps explain those features of *Reflections on the Revolution in France* (1790) – the vehemence of its heightened rhetoric, its deviation from strict truthfulness in detail, its ultimate appeal to sentiment – that provoked immediate and widespread reaction, caused Burke to break with friends of long-standing, such as Charles James Fox, and led some to believe its author to be simply mad. This was a man who had defended the rights of American colonists against the imperial power, of Indians suffering under the tyranny of the East India Company, and the political and economic interests of the Irish, both Protestant and Roman Catholic. The peculiar force of Burke's passionate engagement with injustice had always, however, resided not in any abstract theory of rights – a concept Burke scorned – but in a concern with the political implications of failing to deal with instances of injustice in their specific circumstances, in a timely and appropriate fashion. Now, Burke was anxious to insist that English applause for, or complacency about, the events then taking place across the Channel was misplaced; the conditions that allowed for revolution in France were present too, he believed, in contemporary England. He was not, he insisted, against change per se, for 'a state without the means of some change is without the means of its conservation' – a sentiment he would express in still broader terms in the *Letter to Sir Hercules Langrishe*: 'We must all obey the great law of change, it is the most powerful law of nature, and the means perhaps of its conservation.'[75] Change, however, must be gradual and entrusted to men alert to custom and tradition, possessed of practical experience of statecraft, with proven models of utility before them, and human nature always in mind. Here, Burke recalled Swift explicitly, citing Laputa and Balnibarbi (*Gulliver's Travels*, III) as examples of states unhappily fallen into the hands of foolish philosophers whom Burke compares to the 'literary cabal' of the *Encyclopédistes*.[76]

In line with the young writer's belief in the power of language to work on readers' emotions, much of the *Reflections* – cast in the form of a personal letter to a youthful French correspondent – subordinates rational argument to an impassioned appeal to the reader's sensibility, a contrast to the 'unfeeling heart' of the contemporary French legislator. In what is perhaps the single most celebrated passage in the *Reflections*, Burke drew on recollections of his visit to France in the 1770s and employed all his rhetorical power to call on the sensibility of readers whose responses had been shaped by the fashion for the literature of sentiment:

> It is now sixteen or seventeen years since I saw the queen of France, then the dauphiness, at Versailles; and surely never lighted on this orb, which she hardly seemed to touch, a more delightful vision. I saw her just above the horizon, decorating and cheering the elevated sphere she just began to move in, – glittering like the morning-star, full of life and splendor, and joy. Oh! what a revolution! and what an heart must I have, to contemplate without emotion that elevation and that fall![77]

Increasingly without influence in his party and alienated from friends, Burke wrote on regardless. Both the *Letter to a Member of the National Assembly* (1791) and *Letters on a Regicide Peace* (1796) find Burke arguing that a stop could be put to the excesses of the Revolution only by foreign intervention and he urged Britain to defend the existing order in Europe. In the *Letter to a Noble Lord* (1796), he defended his own integrity against attacks of inconsistency and venality (in 1794, the proposer of economical reform had accepted a civil-list pension), recalling that he had rejected the authority of instructions from constituents, while seeking re-election in Bristol, thereby asserting the independence of members of parliament who were to be understood not as delegates but as representatives. Reflecting on his career as a whole, Burke makes his most impassioned defence of his personal independence: 'I was not made for a minion or a tool.'[78]

Independent he may have been but at the end of his life Burke was under attack from many sides. Just as a century before, John Toland's directness and clarity in *Christianity not Mysterious* provoked innumerable writers to attempt a defence of Christian mysteries, so, conversely, the obscure power of Burke's emotive attack on the French Revolution in the *Reflections* – which went through eleven editions within a year of publication – spawned dozens of rejoinders by radicals, most notably Mary Wollstonecraft's *Vindication of the Rights of Man* (1790) and Thomas Paine's *The Rights of Man* (1791).

Among political friends who broke with Burke, as a result of the *Reflections*, two were Irishmen who had likewise made their careers primarily in England. The elder was the Dublin-born and Trinity College-educated Sir Philip Francis (1740–1818), who was also active in the impeachment of Warren Hastings, with whom he had earlier fought a duel. Francis is now best known as the long-unidentified author of the *Letters of Junius* (1769–72), attacking the administration of the duke of Grafton. The fame of Richard Brinsley Sheridan (1751–1816), son of Thomas Sheridan the younger and Frances Sheridan, rests on the dramatic works written while he was still in his twenties. However, Sheridan entered the British parliament in 1780, where he served for almost thirty years, holding ministerial office and establishing a reputation as one of the best speakers in the House of Commons. Some of his finest speeches were made on Irish affairs or in support of the impeachment of Warren Hastings – his oratorical skills occasionally supplemented by his histrionic ones as when, on completing one major speech, he sank back into the arms of Burke.[79] Sheridan's speeches were collected in 1816.[80]

Burke's death in 1797 meant that he did not live to see the alliance of Roman Catholic and Protestant dissenters result in the Irish rebellion he had predicted. While Burke, Sheridan and Francis pursued their political careers in England, however, a very different kind of politics was occupying many of their Irish contemporaries. In the Irish House of Commons, Henry Grattan (1746–1820) consolidated his early 'patriot' credentials by involvement in the Volunteer movement of 1779–81 and by the extent to which the legislative independence the Irish parliament gained in 1782 was identified with him personally. He sat largely in opposition for the next eighteen years and opposed the United Irishmen, though initial reserve on Catholic emancipation eventually turned to unconditional support. Grattan, who opposed the Act of Union, later served in the British parliament. As with other Irish politicians, his speeches were edited on a number of occasions subsequently and gathered by his son in

The Life and Times of the Rt. Hon. Henry Grattan (1839–46); the extent to which they were rewritten for posterity remains a live topic of debate, leaving in doubt the authenticity even of such celebrated phrases as 'Spirit of Swift! spirit of Molyneux! your genius has prevailed. Ireland is now a nation.'[81] Other celebrated 'patriot' orators included John Philpot Curran (1750–1817), who spoke on behalf of Catholic emancipation in the Irish House of Commons and defended several United Irishmen, including Hamilton Rowan, William Drennan, Napper Tandy and Wolfe Tone, before moving to England following the Union; his 1794 speech in Rowan's defence is among the greatest of those posthumously collected as *The Speeches of the Right Hon. John Philpot Curran* (1846).

Of those who devoted themselves to radical politics in the 1780s and 1790s, the Presbyterian William Drennan (1754–1820), son of Francis Hutcheson's associate, Thomas Drennan, made his name with *Orellana; or Letters of an Irish Helot* (1784–5), in which he addressed his readers as 'Fellow Slaves!' and argued for an increased politicisation of Ireland in the wake of legislative independence; he was also a poet and later editor of the *Belfast Monthly Magazine* (1808–15). Following the French Revolution, the United Irishman Arthur O'Connor (1763–1852) more optimistically addressed his most considerable work, *The State of Ireland* (1798), to his 'Fellow Citizens'. Closely associated with French intellectual circles, O'Connor also published translations of French republican works in *The Press*, which he edited.[82] Most significant in literary as well as political terms was Theobald Wolfe Tone (1763–98). His *Argument on behalf of the Catholics of Ireland* (1791) sought to effect a rapprochement between radical Protestants and radical Catholics, with Tone arguing that 'no reform can ever be obtained, which shall not comprehensively embrace Irishmen of all denominations'.[83] In 1792, he became secretary of the Catholic Committee, taking over from Edmund Burke's son, Richard (1758–94), and thereby having contact with both the United Irishmen, whose ranks he had joined the previous year, and the Catholic Defenders. Tone had wide literary interests, revealed in his letters and in his most important work, his *Autobiography*, the earliest version of which was published by his son in 1827.

One of Tone's least-known and most surprising literary efforts was the sentimental novel *Belmont Castle; or, Suffering Sensibility* (1789). In turning his hand to fiction, albeit sceptically, Tone was contributing to one of the few literary genres to flourish rather than decline in late eighteenth-century Ireland. Throughout the second half of the eighteenth century, writers increasingly, and often with great success, devoted attention to the 'new species of writing' that developed in the wake of the success of the work of Richardson, Fielding, Smollett and others in Britain and Ireland in the 1740s.

Prose fiction

The early history of Irish prose fiction reveals multiple influences: ancient and modern, classical and Christian. In the 1680s, Nahum Tate (1652–1715) collaborated in a translation of Heliodorus' *Aethiopian History*, published as *The Triumphs of Love and Constancy* (1687), and Robert Boyle (1627–91) wrote the *Martyrdom of Theodora, and of Didymus* (1687). William Congreve's *Incognita; or, Love and Duty Reconciled* (1692), which effects a partial shift from romance into novel form, was supposedly written while he was an undergraduate at Trinity College, Dublin. One of the earliest works to deal with specifically Irish themes is the anonymous *Vertue Rewarded; or, the Irish Princess* (1693), which has also been credited with influencing Samuel Richardson's *Pamela* (1740).[84] Historically and geographically, the setting of *The Irish Princess* – Clonmel in the 1690s, following the Williamite victory – suggests a foregrounding of Irish subject matter in fiction that the following decades would not entirely bear out. Author of several novels written after 1700, Mary Davys (1674–1732) scathingly asserted that readers' knowledge that she was Irish would occasion 'a general Dislike to all I write'[85] and departed for England. Strikingly, then, *Irish Tales* (1716) by Sarah Butler (d. before 1716) offers a Jacobite critique of Protestant rule, by means of an ingenious retelling of episodes of much earlier Irish history, culminating in Brian Boru's death at the Battle of Clontarf in 1014. Intriguingly, Butler's primary source was the *Foras Feasa ar Éirinn* by Geoffrey Keating (Seathrún Céitinn), then still available only in manuscript, whether in the original Irish or in English translation (the first printed text, the translation by Dermod O'Connor, in which Toland may have had a hand, would not appear until 1723). A rather different fictional engagement with Irish politics is to be found in Swift's *Story of the Injured Lady* (c.1707; published 1746).

Only following the growing popular success of the novel in the 1740s, however, did Irish fiction gather strength. *The History of Jack Connor* (1752) by William Chaigneau (1709–81) draws on Alain-René Le Sage's *Gil Blas* (1715–47) as well as works by Fielding and Smollett, as it grapples with the problematic issue of Irish identity, using the sentimentalised picaresque form to recount the adventures of the eponymous hero, son of a Protestant English father and Irish Catholic mother, in the Ireland, England and continental Europe of the 1740s. English prejudice against Ireland is one of Chaigneau's themes, as it is also in the fiction of Charles Johnstone (c.1719–c.1800) whose *Chrysal; or*

the Adventures of a Guinea (1760–5) draws intriguingly for its central concept –
the spirit that informs the novel's it-narrator – on Bishop Robert Clayton's
Essay on Spirit (1752). A *roman-à-clef*, *Chrysal* was a considerable popular (and
scandalous) success. Johnstone's other fiction includes his oriental tale *Arsaces,
Prince of Betlis* (1774), which, despite its American setting and anti-colonialist
tone, is strangely reticent in hinting at possible parallels with contemporary
Ireland. Yet Johnstone's subsequent career in England and India did not lead
him to neglect Irish subject matter and his fiction includes further examples of
updated picaresque in *The Adventures of Anthony Varnish* (1781) and *John Juniper*
(1786). The Ireland depicted in these novels is not, as befits the Limerick-born
author, restricted to Dublin but includes counties Limerick, Tipperary and
Meath.

Nothing in Charles Johnstone's works, however, would prepare the reader
for the fictional portrayal of the west and of the old Gaelic order offered by
Thomas Amory (1690/1–1788) in his fantastical compendium novel *The Life of
John Buncle, Esq.* (1756–66). The geographical location and much of the Gaelic
subject matter, evidenced too by the earlier *Memoirs of Several Ladies of Great
Britain* (1755), has no contemporary parallel in English-language fiction and
no obvious successors before Sydney Owenson's early works, *St Clair* (1803)
and *The Wild Irish Girl* (1806), or Edgeworth's attempt to depict both Gaelic
and Anglo-Irish culture in *Ormond* (1817). Nor has the work's narrative organisation, which owes much to Irish-language oral tradition. Blending fictional
autobiography with flights of extreme fancy, *John Buncle* contains many tantalising hints of Amory's own experiences in Ireland, to which he claimed to have
been brought as an infant and where he learned the Irish language. Whether
Amory really read Keating's history in manuscript, or feasted with the Knight
of Glin and the White Knight in County Kerry, to the accompaniment of a
blind harper – as John Buncle informs the reader was his own case – may
be doubted. It seems certain, however, that Amory knew the Dublin of the
1720s and 1730s, and his anecdotal fiction is full of vivid glimpses of contemporary life in the capital. It is full too of (often querulous) allusion to some of
Ireland's most famous writers of the time, with many of whom the Unitarian
Amory claimed acquaintance: Swift, Constantia Grierson, Hugh MacCurtin
(Aodh Buí Mac Cruitín) and 'my friend, worthy John Toland'.[86] Though John
Buncle eventually leaves Ireland he does so for a landscape which, a year before
Burke published his *On the Sublime and Beautiful*, privileges the sublimity of
the English Peak and Lake districts, as well as the west of Ireland, while the
'England' through which Buncle wanders is populated to a remarkable degree
by the Irish friends of his youth.

Amory's sprawling, digressive fantasy is hard to accommodate even within the flexible conceptions of English fiction in the 1750s. Other early Irish novels likewise suggest alternative sources of influence to those of their contemporary English counterparts. So, Sarah Butler and Thomas Amory invoke Geoffrey Keating, while the Huguenot Chaigneau's *Jack Connor* draws on Le Sage's *Gil Blas*. *Memoirs of Miss Sidney Bidulph* (1761–7) by Frances Sheridan (1724–66), meanwhile, is marked both by the European sentimentalism of Marie-Jeanne Riccoboni and the abbé Prévost (who in turn translated *Bidulph* into French) and by that of Samuel Richardson's *Clarissa* (1748–9). Though influenced by Richardson's epistolary technique and moral concerns, Sheridan is no mere imitator and in *Sidney Bidulph* she subjects the English novelist's conception of female virtue to a critique of unequalled power and cogency. Set primarily in England, *Sidney Bidulph* also offers an oblique comparison of national character. While England is represented by the heroine's dull, faithless husband, Mr Arnold, Sheridan's homeland is associated with Sidney Bidulph's ardent Irish lover, the romantic Orlando Faulkland. Like Charles Johnstone, Sheridan also essayed the oriental tale; and *Nourjahad* (1767) is arguably the finest example of its kind in English after Johnson's *Rasselas*.

The Fool of Quality; or, the History of Henry, Earl of Moreland (1765–70) by Henry Brooke is a *roman-à-thèse* of a kind that would soon become familiar among Irish Enlightenment writers, Maria Edgeworth chief among them. *The Fool of Quality* offers a fictionalised account of education that owes much to the example of Rousseau's *Emile* (1762), while presenting the first extended fictional portrayal of childhood in English-language fiction. (The eighteenth-century's continuing concern with education, stimulated by the work of Locke and Rousseau in particular, later manifests itself in *Practical Education* (1798), co-authored by Richard Lovell Edgeworth (1744–1817) and his daughter Maria Edgeworth (1767–1849), whose pedagogic interests are evident too in *Letters for Literary Ladies* (1795), *Early Lessons* (1801) and *Moral Tales* (1801).) Brooke's other principal source of influence was Laurence Sterne's *Tristram Shandy*. *The Fool of Quality* opens with a droll dialogue between author and reader which is little more than a superior imitation of Sterne's facetious style, common enough in the wake of the extraordinary critical and commercial success of the early volumes of *Tristram Shandy*. Increasingly, though, Brooke developed his own concerns – taking the theme of education more didactically than would Sterne with the young Tristram – and subordinating wit to sensibility (a pattern which conforms only in part to the development of Sterne's novel through its later volumes or in *A Sentimental Journey*). Best known among Brooke's later fiction, *Juliet Grenville* (1774) is a work of full-blown sentiment.

Whether *The Life and Opinions of Tristram Shandy, Gentleman* (1759–67) and *A Sentimental Journey through France and Italy* (1768) by Laurence Sterne (1713–68) are usefully considered part of Irish literary history is debatable. Sterne was born in Ireland by chance when his father, a junior army officer, was posted there and left the country aged nine or ten, never to return. Yet it cannot be overlooked that the most notable contemporary imitators of Sterne's fiction – with its fluid, conversational construction, and its teasing combination of facetiousness and sentiment – were themselves Irish. Sterne's friend Richard Griffith (d.1788) wrote both the Shandaic *The Triumvirate* (1764) and *The Koran*, which was published with Sterne's *Works* in 1775 and was taken for his. Leonard MacNally (1752–1820) penned a short play, *Tristram Shandy: A Sentimental, Shandean Bagatelle* (1783), and later Irish writers who responded directly to Sterne include James Joyce and Flann O'Brien. Griffith had first come to attention as co-author with Elizabeth Griffith (1727–93) of the hugely popular *Series of Genuine Letters between Henry and Frances* (1757), a semi-autobiographical fiction based on the authors' courtship letters, which spawned sequels and was a possible influence, in turn, on Sterne's letters to the much-younger (and married) Elizabeth Draper, belatedly published as *Journal to Eliza* (1904), after the example of Swift's *Journal to Stella*. Elizabeth Griffith produced many other successful novels, of which *The Delicate Distress* (1769) is perhaps best known, as well as translations, criticism, and editions of the work of earlier women writers.

The 1760s saw Irish fiction shifting – at times uneasily – between comic realism and a sentiment that risked enervating its readers. Oliver Goldsmith intended his distinction between 'laughing' and 'sentimental' comedy to apply to drama, yet it has resonance too in a more general shift in sensibility in the 1760s and 1770s. *The Vicar of Wakefield* (1766) relates the story of the fortunes and misfortunes of the benevolent clergyman Dr Primrose and his accident-prone family, while articulating the moral qualities Goldsmith thought appropriate to the 'new species of writing'. Yet for all that *The Vicar of Wakefield* is written with an eye to reforming the age (and Goldsmith's fellow novelists), the irony that suffuses the work cannot disguise a serious, if now unfashionable, faith in divine providence. Goldsmith had touched on the theme often before, as in 'The Story of Alcander and Septimius', in the first number of *The Bee*, which likewise insists that *'no circumstances are so desperate, which Providence may not relieve'*.[87]

Less amiably, Hugh Kelly's *Memoirs of a Magdalen* (1767) offers readers the kind of moral dilemma that the mid-century loved: should the hero still marry his intended bride after consummating their marriage shortly *before* the wedding? A twenty-first-century sensibility might easily imagine the protracted agonising that takes place on the part of both parties to be facetious but there is little in the book itself to bear out such a reading. *Memoirs of a Magdalen* is a novel that warns against the dangers of novel-reading – or at least of the dangers of reading the wrong novels in the wrong circumstances – so that on the fateful evening in question, the bridegroom and bride are to be found reading *Clarissa* and *Tristram Shandy*, respectively (with what results we know).

Historical fiction was attempted too. The historian Thomas Leland (1722–85) wrote *Longsword, Earl of Salisbury* (1765) and later Anne Fuller (d.1790) published *Alan Fitz-Osborne: An Historical Tale* (1786) and *The Son of Ethelwolf: An Historical Tale* (1789). Frequently, however, historical, sentimental and Gothic fiction overlap, as in the case of *The Children of the Abbey* (1796), by Regina Maria Roche (1764–1845), a novel whose influence Jane Austen acknowledged, and which was one of over a dozen Roche published between 1789 and 1836. Exoticism of a different kind is to be found in *Letters of a Hindoo Rajah* (1796) by Elizabeth Hamilton (1758–1816).

Since the British Copyright Act of 1709 had never applied to Ireland, Irish booksellers had been quick to reprint popular English fiction for domestic consumption in pirated editions. So, as with other kinds of prose writing, some novels by Irish authors were published in England and reprinted in Ireland, but others first appeared in Dublin (less frequently, in Cork or even Drogheda) to be taken up later by London publishers, or were published in Ireland alone. The first two volumes of Henry Brooke's *Fool of Quality*, which achieved great popularity on both sides of the Irish Sea, were first published privately for the author in Dublin in 1765, before appearing in London the following year. Moreover, as the century progressed, there is considerable evidence that Irish readers were developing a taste for national fiction related to but distinct from that of British novel readers. Chaigneau's *Jack Connor* went through just two English editions while reaching a fourth Irish edition by 1766. John O'Keeffe reported Sheridan's *Sidney Bidulph* to have been 'more read and admired in Ireland' than any other novel.[88] At times, publishers might silently adjust texts first published in England to accommodate Irish interests, so that a comment on Garrick's acting in Smollett's *Sir Lancelot Greaves* was silently changed, in Dublin editions, to a comparable comment on the Irish favourite, Spranger Barry.[89] Less covertly, even mildly critical accounts of Ireland or its inhabitants were editorially glossed to salve wounded domestic sensibilities.[90] More pointedly, the last three decades of the century saw a clutch of novels boasting avowedly 'patriotic' titles: *The Irish Guardian* (1776), *The Fair Hibernian*

(1789) or *The Irish Heiress* (1797); the 'national tale' was born. At times, national pride went further, with writers variously articulating in fiction overt patriotic nationalism and ardent feminism, as in *The Triumph of Prudence over Passion* (?1781), set amid the Volunteer movement in the year preceding Grattan's parliament, or conservative reaction, as in *The Rebel* (1799), a prompt fictional response to the 1798 rebellion.

With some outstanding exceptions – especially the writings of Goldsmith and Burke – Irish prose of the second half of the eighteenth century reveals a dimming of the intellectual and imaginative brilliance of the period 1690–1750. In these changing circumstances, eighteenth-century Irish fiction is doubly notable. Firstly, it anticipated and made possible the work of novelists of the early nineteenth century: Maria Edgeworth, Sydney Owenson, Charles Robert Maturin and the Banims, for example. Secondly, in a cultural climate that, especially after the Act of Union, tended to privilege imaginative writing over the historical, political, philosophic or scientific, Irish fiction pointed out, however hesitantly, the principal direction Irish prose would take in the decades and even centuries to come.

Notes

1. Robert Molesworth, 'Preface' to *An Account of Denmark, as it was in the year 1692* (London, 1694), p. [vii].
2. Ibid., 'Conclusion', p. 258.
3. 'Preface' (pp. i–xxxvi) to Francis Hotoman, *Franco-Gallia: or, An Account of the Ancient Free State of France* [1574], trans. Robert Molesworth (1711; 2nd edn, London, 1721).
4. Fuller accounts of Roman Catholic writing in the eighteenth century appear in chapters 8 and 14 of the present *History*.
5. John Toland, *Christianity not Mysterious*, in Philip McGuinness, Alan Harrison and Richard Kearney, eds. *John Toland's* Christianity not Mysterious (Dublin: Lilliput, 1997), p. 58.
6. Ibid., title page (and p. 17).
7. John Toland, *Vindicius Liberius*, in McGuinness et al. *John Toland's* Christianity not Mysterious, pp. 186, 187.
8. John Toland, *A Specimen of the Critical History of the Celtic Religion and Learning: containing An Account of the Druids*, in *A Collection of Several Pieces of Mr John Toland*, 2 vols. (1726; reprinted New York and London: Garland, 1977), i, p. 8.
9. John Toland, *Nazarenus*, ed. Justin Champion (Oxford: Voltaire Foundation, 1999), pp. 217, 229–32.
10. Toland, *An Account of the Druids*, i, p. 101.
11. 'Advertisement' in *The Post-Man*, 30 January – 2 February 1720, in Toland, *Collection*, i, p. xxxiii.
12. Edward Synge, *Appendix* to *A Gentleman's Religion*, 4th edition (London, 1710), p. 275.

13. *Treatise Concerning the Principles of Human Knowledge*, vol. 1, sect. 3, in *The Works of George Berkeley, Bishop of Cloyne*, eds. A. A. Luce and T. E. Jessop, 9 vols. (1948–55; reprinted Nendeln: Kraus Reprints, 1979), II, p. 42.

14. Ibid., I, pp. 34–84.

15. Ibid., II, p. 82.

16. 'Preface' to *Dialogues*, in *Works*, II, p. 168.

17. *Works*, I, p. 70.

18. David Hume, *Enquiries concerning Human Understanding*, ed. L. A. Selby-Bigge, 3rd edn, revised P. H. Nidditch (Oxford: Clarendon Press, 1975), section 12, part 1, p. 155 note.

19. See Bernard Mandeville, *Letter to Dion* (London, 1732).

20. See *Two Letters on the Occasion of the Jacobite Rebellion 1745*: 'A Letter to his Clergy' and 'A Letter to the Roman Catholics of his Diocese', in *Works*, VI, pp. 227–8, 228–9; the letters were originally published in the *Dublin Journal*, 15–19 October 1745 (no. 1942), and 19–22 October 1745 (no. 1943) respectively.

21. *Works*, V, p. 164.

22. Philip Skelton, *Ophiomaches; or Deism Revealed*, ed. David Berman (1749; rev. 1751; reprinted Bristol and Tokyo: Thoemmes and Kinokuniya, 1990), 'Preface', p. xvii.

23. Thomas Hobbes, *Leviathan*, ed. J. C. A. Gaskin (Oxford: Oxford University Press, 1996), p. 84.

24. Francis Hutcheson, *On the Social Nature of Man* (1730), p. 126.

25. Francis Hutcheson, *A System of Moral Philosophy*, repr. with an introduction by Daniel Carey (Bristol: Thoemmes, 2000), pp. 300–1.

26. Francis Hutcheson, *A Short Introduction to Moral Philosophy*, trans. James Moor (Glasgow, 1747), p. 302.

27. *The Prose Writings of Jonathan Swift*, ed. Herbert Davis et al., 16 vols. (Oxford: Basil Blackwell, 1948–74), I, p. 151.

28. Ibid., I, p. [140].

29. Ibid., I, p. 133.

30. Ibid., IX, p. 5.

31. The text given follows that of the first edition of 1720; in *Prose Writings*, IX, p. 17, the editor Louis Landa prints the revised text of 1735, giving the original in 'Textual Notes' (IX, p. 369).

32. See note 31 above.

33. *Prose Writings*, X, p. 63.

34. Jonathan Swift, '*Intelligencer* 15', in Jonathan Swift and Thomas Sheridan, *The Intelligencer*, ed. James Woolley (Oxford: Clarendon Press, 1992), p. 179.

35. *Prose Writings*, X, p. 114.

36. *The Correspondence of Jonathan Swift*, ed. Harold Williams, 5 vols. (Oxford: Clarendon Press, 1963–5), III, p. 103.

37. *Prose Writings*, IX, p. 65.

38. *Weekly Magazine*, 1 (29 December 1759) and 2 (5 January 1760); see *Oliver Goldsmith: Collected Works*, ed. Arthur Friedman, 5 vols. (Oxford: Clarendon Press, 1966), III, pp. 34–40.

39. Laetitia Pilkington, *Memoirs of Laetitia Pilkington*, ed. A. C. Elias Jr. (Athens, GA and London: University of Georgia Press, 1997).

40. *The Autobiography and Correspondence of Mary Granville, Mrs Delany*, ed. Lady Llanover, 6 vols. (London, 1861–2); see also *The Correspondence of Emily, Duchess of Leinster (1731–1814)*, ed. Brian Fitzgerald (Dublin: Irish Manuscripts Commission, 1949–57).

41. Thomas Bartlett, ed. *Life of Theobald Wolfe Tone: Memories, Journals and Political Writings, compiled and arranged by William T. W. Tone* (1826) (Dublin: Lilliput, 1998); see also Theobald Wolfe Tone, *The Writings of Theobald Wolfe Tone, 1763–98, vol. I: Tone's Career in Ireland to June 1795*, ed. T. W. Moody, R. B. McDowell and C. J. Woods (Oxford: Clarendon Press, 1998), and *The Writings of Theobald Wolfe Tone, 1763–98, vol. II: America, France, and Bantry Bay, August 1795 to December 1796*, ed. T. W. Moody, R. B. McDowell and C. J. Woods (Oxford: Clarendon Press, 2001).

42. *Works*, vols. VIII and IX.

43. See note 36 above; a new edition of Swift's correspondence is in progress: *The Correspondence of Jonathan Swift, DD*, ed. David Woolley, 4 vols. (Frankfurt am Main: P. Lang, 1999–).

44. *The O'Conor Papers*, ed. G. and J. Dunleavy (Madison, WI: University of Wisconsin Press, 1977); *Letters of Charles O'Conor of Belanagare*, ed. Robert E. Ward, John F. Wynn, SJ, and Catherine Coogan Ward (Washington, DC: The Catholic University of America Press, 1988).

45. Dorothea Herbert, *Retrospections of Dorothea Herbert 1770–1806*, ed. L. M. Cullen (Dublin: Town House, 1988).

46. *The Leadbeater Papers*, ed. Elizabeth Leadbeater, 2 vols. (London, 1862; reprinted in facsimile London: Routledge, 1998).

47. *Betsy Sheridan's Journal: Letters from Sheridan's sister 1748–1786 and 1788–1790*, ed. W. R. Le Fanu (Oxford: Oxford University Press, 1986).

48. *Manuscripts and Correspondence of James, First Earl of Charlemont. [Containing 'Lord Charlemont's Memoirs of his political life, 1755–1783', and a catalogue of, and extracts from his correspondence, 1747–1799]*, ed. Sir John T. Gilbert, 2 vols. (London, 1891–4).

49. *The Correspondence of Edmund Burke*, general ed. T. W. Copeland, 10 vols. (Cambridge and Chicago: Cambridge University Press and Chicago University Press, 1958–78).

50. *Memoirs of R. L. E. . . . begun by himself, and concluded by his daughter, M. Edgeworth*, 2 vols. (London, 1820).

51. *Monthly Review* 16 (May 1757), pp. 473–80.

52. *The Bee* 8 (24 November 1759); *Collected Works*, III, pp. 498–505.

53. *The Citizen of the World*, no. xxv; *Collected Works*, II, p. 106.

54. *Royal Magazine* 2 (June 1760), pp. 285–8; *Collected Works*, III, p. 68.

55. *The Citizen of the World*, no. xx; *Collected Works*, II, p. 86.

56. *Weekly Magazine* 1 (29 December 1759); *Collected Works*, III, pp. 24–30.

57. See Alan Harrison, *The Dean's Friend: Anthony Raymond 1675–1726, Jonathan Swift and the Irish Language* (Blackrock, County Dublin: Caisleán an Bhúrcaigh, 1999).

58. 'The HISTORY of CAROLAN, the last Irish Bard', *British Magazine* (July 1760); *Collected Works*, III, p. 118.

59. *Collected Works*, I, p. 269.

60. Ibid., p. 306.

61. *Collected Works*, V, p. 355; cf. Joseph Addison, *The Spectator* 4 (12 March 1711).

62. *Hibernicus's Letters*, 2 vols. (Dublin, 1729), I, p. 3.

63. [Thomas Campbell], *An Essay on Perfecting the Fine Arts in Great Britain and Ireland* (1767), esp. pp. 38–9.

64. James Barry, *The Works of James Barry . . . containing his correspondence*, 2 vols. (London, 1809).

65. Johann Georg Zimmermann, *An Essay on National Pride* (1758; trans. London, 1771), p. 46; this passage was particularly noted in the review of Zimmermann's work published by the *Hibernian Magazine* 2 (June 1772), p. 328.

66. Carlo Denina, *An Essay on the Revolutions in Literature*, trans. John Murdoch (London [1771]), pp. 284–5.

67. Paul Langford, general ed. and William B. Todd, textual ed. *The Writings and Speeches of Edmund Burke*, 10 vols. (Oxford: Clarendon Press, 1981–2000), vol. I: *The Early Writings*, eds. T. O. McLoughlin and James T. Boulton, p. 134.

68. Ibid., p. 281.

69. Ibid., p. 216.

70. Ibid., pp. 236–41.

71. James Usher, *Clio; or a Discourse on Taste*, ed. J. Mathew (1767; reprinted [London] 1803), p. 156.

72. *Writings and Speeches*, vol. IX, Part 2: *Ireland*, ed. R. B. McDowell, p. 454.

73. 'Letter to Sir Hercules Langrishe', 26 May 1795, in *Correspondence of Edmund Burke*, VIII, p. 254.

74. 'Letter to Hussey', 18 January 1796, in *Correspondence of Edmund Burke*, VIII, p. 378.

75. *Writings and Speeches*, vol. IX, Part 2, p. 634.

76. *Writings and Speeches*, vol. VIII, ed. L. G. Mitchell, p. 182 note.

77. Ibid., p. 126.

78. *Writings and Speeches*, vol. IX, Part 1: *The Revolutionary War 1794–1797*, ed. R. B. McDowell, p. 160.

79. See Fintan O'Toole, *A Traitor's Kiss: The Life of Richard Brinsley Sheridan* (London: Granta, 1997), p. 229.

80. *The Speeches of the late Right Honourable Richard Brinsley Sheridan*, 5 vols. (London, 1816).

81. Henry Grattan [the younger] ed., *The Speeches of the Right. Honourable Henry Grattan in the Irish and the Imperial Parliament*, ed. by his son, 4 vols (London, 1822), I, p. 123.

82. See Arthur O'Connor, *The State of Ireland*, ed. James Livesey (1798; reprinted Dublin: Lilliput, 1998).

83. Theobald Wolfe Tone, *An Argument on behalf of the Catholics of Ireland* (Belfast, 1791), p. 16.

84. See *Virtue Rewarded; or The Irish Princess*, ed. Hubert McDermott. Princess Grace Irish Library Series VII (Gerrards Cross: Colin Smythe, 1992).

85. *The Merry Wanderer*, in *The Works of Mrs Davys*, 2 vols. (London, 1725), I, p. 161.

86. Thomas Amory, *Memoirs of Several Ladies of Great Britain* (London, 1755), p. 75.

87. *The Bee* 1 (6 October 1759); Goldsmith: *Collected Works*, I, p. 367.

88. *Recollections of the life of John O'Keeffe, Written by Himself*, 2 vols. (London, 1826), I, p. 86.

89. See Ian Campbell Ross and Barbara Laning Fitzpatrick, 'David Garrick or Spranger Barry? A Dramatic Substitution in Irish Editions of Smollett's *Sir Launcelot Greaves*', *Long Room* 30 (1985), pp. 6–10.

90. See [Anon], *The History of Ned Evans: Interspersed with Moral and Critical Remarks . . . and Incidental Strictures on the Present State of Ireland*, 2 vols. (Dublin, 1797), I, p. 224.

Select bibliography

Ayling, Stanley, *Edmund Burke: His Life and Opinions*, London: John Murray, 1988.

Barry, Kevin, 'James Usher and the Irish Enlightenment', *Eighteenth-Century Ireland* 3 (1988), pp. 115–22.

Bartlett, Thomas, ed. *Life of Theobald Wolfe Tone: Memoirs, Journals and Political Writings, compiled and arranged by William T. W. Tone (1826)*, Dublin: Lilliput, 1998.

Bataille, Robert R., *The Writing Life of Hugh Kelly: Politics, Journalism, and Theater in Late-Eighteenth-Century London*, Carbondale, IL: Southern Illinois University Press, 2000.

Berman, David, 'Berkeley, Clayton, and *An Essay on Spirit*', *Journal of the History of Ideas* 32, 3 (1971), pp. 367–78.

'The Culmination and Causation of Irish Philosophy', *Archiv für Geschichte der Philosophie* 64 (1982), pp. 257–79.

'Enlightenment and Counter-Enlightenment in Irish Philosophy', *Archiv für Geschichte der Philosophie* 64 (1982), pp. 148–65.

George Berkeley: Idealism and the Man, Oxford: Clarendon Press, 1994.

'Introduction', in Philip Skelton, *Ophiomaches; or Deism Revealed*, Bristol and Tokyo: Thoemmes and Kinokuniya, 1990, pp. v–xiv.

'The Irish Counter-Enlightenment', in Richard Kearney, ed. *The Irish Mind*, Dublin: Wolfhound Press, 1985, pp. 119–40, 335–7 notes.

Berman, David and Andrew Carpenter, 'Eighteenth-Century Irish Philosophy', in Seamus Deane, general ed. *The Field Day Anthology of Irish Writing*, 3 vols. Derry: Field Day, 1991, I, pp. 760–806.

Boyce, D. G., R. Eccleshall and V. Geoghegan, eds. *Political Thought in Ireland since the Seventeenth Century*, London: Routledge, 1993.

Boyle, Frank T., *Swift as Nemesis: Modernity and its Satirist*, Stanford, CA and Cambridge: Stanford University Press and Cambridge University Press, 2000.

Bredvold, Louis I. and Ralph G. Ross, eds. *The Philosophy of Edmund Burke*, Ann Arbor: University of Michigan Press, 1967.

Brown, Michael, *Francis Hutcheson in Dublin, 1719–1730*, Dublin: Four Courts Press, 2002.

Carey, Daniel, 'Method, Moral Sense, and the Problem of Diversity: Francis Hutcheson and the Scottish Enlightenment', *British Journal for the History of Philosophy* 5, 2 (1997), pp. 275–96.

'Swift among the Freethinkers', *Eighteenth-Century Ireland* 12 (1997), pp. 88–99.

Carpenter, Andrew, *The Irish Perspective of Jonathan Swift*, Wuppertal: Hammer, 1978.

'Jonathan Swift (1667–1745)', in Seamus Deane, general ed. *The Field Day Anthology of Irish Writing*, 3 vols. Derry: Field Day, 1991, I, pp. 327–94.

Carpenter, Andrew and Seamus Deane, 'The Shifting Perspective (1690–1830)', in Deane, *The Field Day Anthology of Irish Writing*, I, pp. 961–1010.

Carpenter, Andrew, Seamus Deane and W. J. McCormack, 'Political Prose: Cromwell to O'Connell', in Deane, *The Field Day Anthology of Irish Writing*, I, pp. 855–960.

Connolly, S. J., ed. *Political Ideas in Eighteenth-Century Ireland*, Dublin: Four Courts Press, 2000.

Crane, R. S., 'The Houyhnhnms, the Yahoos, and the History of Ideas', in Crane, *The Idea of the Humanities and other Essays*, Chicago: University of Chicago Press, 1967.

Craven, Kenneth, *Jonathan Swift and the Millennium of Madness: The Information Age in Swift's A Tale of a Tub*, Leiden and New York: E. J. Brill, 1992.

Crowe, Ian, ed. *Edmund Burke: His Life and Legacy*, Dublin: Four Courts Press, 1997.

Cullen, Louis, 'Burke, Ireland and Revolution', *Eighteenth-Century Life*, 16, 1, new series (1992), pp. 21–42.

Daniel, Stephen H., *John Toland: His Method, Manners and Mind*, Kingston: McGill-Queen's University Press, 1984.

Deane, Seamus, 'Edmund Burke', in Deane, *The Field Day Anthology of Irish Writing*, 1, pp. 658–81.

   'Oliver Goldsmith: Miscellaneous Writings 1759–74', in Deane, *The Field Day Anthology of Irish Writing*, 1, pp. 658–81.

   A Short History of Irish Literature, London: Hutchinson, 1986.

   Strange Country: Ireland, Modernity and Nationhood 1790–1970, Oxford: Clarendon Press, 1999.

   'Swift and the Anglo-Irish Intellect', *Eighteenth-Century Ireland* 1 (1986), pp. 9–22.

Dickson, David, Dáire Keogh and Kevin Whelan, eds. *The United Irishmen*, Dublin: Lilliput, 1993.

Doody, Margaret Anne, 'Frances Sheridan: Morality and Annihilated Time', in Mary Anne Schofield and Cecilia Macheski, eds. *Fetter'd or Free*, Athens, OH: Ohio University Press, 1986, pp. 324–58.

Douglas, Aileen, 'Britannia's Rule and the It-Narrator', *Eighteenth-Century Fiction* 6, 1 (1993), pp. 65–82.

   'Fiction before 1800', in John Wilson Foster, ed. *Cambridge Companion to the Irish Novel*, Cambridge: Cambridge University Press, 2006.

Douglas, Aileen, Patrick Kelly and Ian Campbell Ross, eds. *Locating Swift: Essays from Dublin on the 250th Anniversary of the Death of Jonathan Swift*, Dublin: Four Courts Press, 1998.

Duddy, Thomas, *A History of Irish Thought*, London and New York: Routledge, 2002.

Ehrenpreis, Irvin, *Jonathan Swift: The Man, his Works, and the Age*, 3 vols. London: Methuen, 1962–83.

Elliott, Marianne, *Wolfe Tone: Prophet of Independence*, New Haven: Yale University Press, 1989.

Eshelman, Dorothy Hughes, *Elizabeth Griffith: A Biographical and Literary Study*, Philadelphia: University of Pennsylvania Press, 1949.

Fabricant, Carol, *Swift's Landscape*, 1982, reprinted Notre Dame: University of Notre Dame Press, 1995.

Fagan, Patrick, *Dublin's Turbulent Priest, Cornelius Nary (1678–1738)*, Dublin: Royal Irish Academy, 1991.

Fox, Christopher and Brenda Tooley, eds. *Walking Naboth's Vineyard: New Studies of Swift*, Notre Dame: University of Notre Dame Press, 1995.

Fuchs, Michel, *Edmund Burke, Ireland, and the Fashioning of Self*, Oxford: Voltaire Foundation, 1996.

Furniss, Tom, *Edmund Burke's Aesthetic Ideology: Language, Gender, and Political Economy in Revolution*, Cambridge: Cambridge University Press, 1993.

Geoghegan, Vincent, 'A Jacobite History: The Abbé MacGeoghegan's *History of Ireland*' *Eighteenth-Century Ireland* 6 (1991), pp. 37–56.

Gibbons, Luke, *Edmund Burke and Ireland: Aesthetics, Politics and the Colonial Sublime*, Cambridge: Cambridge University Press, 2003.

Harrison, Alan, *Béal Eiriciúil an Inis Eoghain: John Toland (1670–1722)*, Dublin: Coiscéim, 1994.

   The Dean's Friend: Anthony Raymond 1675–1726, Jonathan Swift and the Irish Language, Blackrock, County Dublin: Caisleán an Bhúrcaigh, 1999.

Hill, Jacqueline, 'Ireland without Union: Molyneux and his Legacy', in John Robertson, ed. *A Union for Empire: The Union of 1707 in British Political Thought*, Cambridge: Cambridge University Press, 1995, pp. 271–96.

Hoppen, Theodore K., *The Common Scientist in the Seventeenth Century: A Study of the Dublin Philosophical Society 1683–1708*, Charlottesville: University of Virginia Press, 1970.

Kearney, Richard, ed. *The Irish Mind*, Dublin: Wolfhound Press, 1985.

Kelly, Ann Cline, *Swift and the English Language*, Philadelphia: University of Pennsylvania Press, 1988.

Kelly, James, 'Jonathan Swift and the Irish Economy in the 1720s', *Eighteenth-Century Ireland* 6 (1991), pp. 7–36.

Kelly, Patrick H., 'Ireland and the Critique of Mercantilism in Berkeley's *Querist*', *Hermathena* 139 (1985), pp. 101–16.

   'Recasting a Tradition: William Molyneux and the Sources of *The Case of Ireland . . . Stated*', in Jane H. Ohlmeyer, ed. *Political Thought in Seventeenth-Century Ireland*, Cambridge: Cambridge University Press, 2000, pp. 83–106.

   'William Molyneux and the Spirit of Liberty in Eighteenth-Century Ireland', *Eighteenth-Century Ireland* 3 (1988), pp. 38–53.

Kilfeather, Siobhán, 'Beyond the Pale: Sexual Identity and National Identity in Early Irish Fiction', *Critical Matrix* 2, 4 (1986), pp. 1–31.

   'The Profession of Letters 1700–1810', in A. Bourke, S. Kilfeather, M. Luddy, M. Mac Curtain, G. Meaney, M. Ní Dhonnchadha, M. O'Dowd and C. Wills, eds. *The Field Day Anthology of Irish Writing, vols. IV and V: Irish Women's Writing and Traditions*, Cork: Cork University Press, 2002, v, pp. 772–832.

Kilroy, Phil, 'Memoirs and Testimonies: Non-conformist Women in Seventeenth-Century Ireland', in Bourke et al., *The Field Day Anthology of Irish Writing*, IV, pp. 480–9.

   Protestant Dissent and Religious Controversy in Ireland 1660–1714, Cork: Cork University Press, 1992.

Leerssen, Joep, *Mere Irish & Fíor-Ghael*, Amsterdam and Philadelphia: John Benjamins, 1986.

Lock, F. P., *Edmund Burke, vol. I*, Oxford: Clarendon Press, 1998.

Lytton Sells, A., *Oliver Goldsmith: His Life and Works*, London: George Allen & Unwin, 1974.

McDowell, R. B., *Grattan: A Life*, Dublin: Lilliput, 2001.

McGuiness, Philip, Alan Harrison and Richard Kearney, eds. *John Toland's* Christianity not Mysterious: *Text, Associated Essays and Critical Essays*, Dublin: Lilliput, 1997.

McKee, Francis, 'Francis Hutcheson and Bernard Mandeville', *Eighteenth-Century Ireland* 3 (1988), pp. 123–33.

McMinn, Joseph, *Jonathan Swift: A Literary Life*, London: Macmillan, 1991.

Martin, Peter, *Edmond Malone, Shakespearean Scholar*, Cambridge: Cambridge University Press, 1995.

O'Brien, Conor Cruise, *The Great Melody: A Thematic Biography and Commented Anthology of Edmund Burke*, London: Sinclair-Stevenson, 1992.

O'Dowd, Mary, 'The Political Writings and Public Voices of Women, *c.*1500–1850', in Bourke et al., *The Field Day Anthology of Irish Writing*, v, pp. 6–68.

O'Halloran, Clare, *Golden Ages and Barbarous Nations: Antiquarian Debate and Cultural Politics in Ireland, c. 1750–1800*, Cork: Cork University Press, in association with Field Day, 2004.

O'Regan, Philip, *Archbishop William King of Dublin (1650–1729) and the Constitution in Church and State*, Dublin: Four Courts Press, 2000.

Pollard, Mary, *Dublin's Trade in Books 1550–1800*, Oxford: Clarendon Press, 1989.

Raughter, Rosemary, 'Eighteenth-Century Catholic and Protestant Women', in Bourke et al., *The Field Day Anthology of Irish Writing*, iv, pp. 490–516.

Ross, Angus, 'The Hibernian Patriot's Apprenticeship', in Clive T. Probyn, ed. *The Art of Jonathan Swift*, London: Vision, 1978, pp. 83–107.

Ross, Ian Campbell, 'Fiction to 1800', in Deane, *The Field Day Anthology of Irish Writing*, i, pp. 682–759.

'Irish Fiction before the Union', in Jacqueline Belanger, ed. *The Irish Novel in the Nineteenth Century: Facts and Fictions*, Dublin: Four Courts Press, 2005, pp. 34–51.

'An Irish Picaresque Novel: William Chaigneau's *The History of Jack Connor*', *Studies* 71, 283 (1982), pp. 270–9.

Laurence Sterne: A Life, Oxford and New York: Oxford University Press, 2001.

'"One of the Principal Nations in Europe": The Representation of Ireland in Sarah Butler's *Irish Tales*', *Eighteenth-Century Fiction* 7, 1 (1994), pp. 1–16.

'Rewriting Irish Literary History: The Case of the Irish Novel', *Etudes Anglaises* 39, 4 (1986), pp. 385–99.

'Thomas Amory, *John Buncle*, and the Origins of Irish Fiction', *Éire-Ireland* 18, 3 (1983), pp. 71–85.

'*The Triumph of Prudence over Passion*: Nationalism and Feminism in an Eighteenth-Century Irish Novel', *Irish University Review* 10, 2 (1980), pp. 232–40.

Simms, J. G., *William Molyneux of Dublin (1656–1698)*, ed. P. H. Kelly, Dublin: Irish Academic Press, 1982.

Spector, Robert D., *Arthur Murphy*, Boston: Twayne, 1979.

Spencer, Christopher, *Nahum Tate*, Boston: Twayne, 1972.

Sullivan, Robert E., *John Toland and the Deist Controversy*, Cambridge, MA: Harvard University Press, 1982.

Trumpener, Katie, *Bardic Nationalism: The Romantic Novel and the British Empire*, Princeton, NJ: Princeton University Press, 1997.

Zimmermann, Everett, *Swift's Narrative Satires: Author and Authority*, Ithaca, NY: Cornell University Press, 1983.

7

Poetry in English, 1690–1800: from the Williamite wars to the Act of Union

ANDREW CARPENTER

In December 1690, five months after the Battle of the Boyne, a little-known Dublin printer called John Brett printed the first poem of what was to be a golden age for Irish verse in English. The grandiloquent and florid 'Ode to the King on his Irish Expedition' was intended to flatter the unattractive but victorious Dutchman whom the Protestants of Ireland were hailing as their 'Providential deliverer' from the horrors of popery and tyranny under Jacobite rule.

> What can the Poet's humble Praise?
> What can the Poet's humble Bays?
> (We Poets oft our Bays allow,
> Transplanted to the Hero's Brow)
> Add to the Victor's Happiness?

asked the poet, in a flourish of rhetorical exuberance. Whatever William of Orange might have answered to these – and many other similarly euphuistic – questions, the poet (a 23-year-old graduate of Trinity College, Dublin named Jonathan Swift) hoped that this – his first printed work – would be sufficiently well regarded by those around the king to bring him some reward for the trouble of writing it, and presumably for the expense of having it printed.[1] Even though, it seems, nothing came of Swift's efforts to attract patronage by the poem, the verse itself marks an important moment in the history of Irish poetry. Not only is it the first appearance in print of the poet who was to dominate Irish poetry in English for the first half of the eighteenth century, but it is also the first poem of the new Williamite era, one in which peace and prosperity in Ireland would provide a nurturing environment not only for the writing and reading of verse but for its printing. Between the Battle of the Boyne and the Act of Union, the muse of poetry was very busy in Ireland.

Irish printers and publishers were well placed to take advantage of the peace that followed the Williamite wars. Restrictions on the book trade, which had prevented its development for much of the seventeenth century, had been removed at the end of the reign of Charles II, and the copyright laws which operated in England did not apply in Ireland. Dublin, an increasingly prosperous city with a substantial middle class, was particularly fertile ground for this burgeoning industry. Here were two houses of parliament, a substantial civil service, various military headquarters, coffee houses and schools, an expanding university, law courts, a port and scores of small industries and shops. The city provided a ready-made market for books of all kinds. Dublin printers soon began to take advantage of the freedom they had to reprint material which had appeared in England, and the Irish printing and publishing industries grew rapidly.

During the 1690s and the first years of the new century, little indigenous verse was available for publication, but an anthology of verse written in Ireland entitled *A New Miscellany of Poems and Translations* appeared in Dublin in 1716 and, by the 1720s, much of the poetry printed by Dublin booksellers was the work of poets living in the city. Overall, the market in Dublin for poetry, imported or domestically produced, was remarkably buoyant throughout the eighteenth century; in fact, during the first forty years of the century, over 130 separate printers of verse were active in Dublin, and the city ranked second only to London for the production of verse in English. Poetry was printed outside Dublin too, in Armagh, Belfast, Cork, Drogheda, Limerick, Rathfarnham and Templeogue – the last two because the writing and printing of poetry appealed to those taking the waters at the spas there.[2] In the latter half of the century, the quantity of Irish-printed verse of all kinds, including collected editions of the major English poets, continued to increase until, by the 1790s, a bewildering variety of material was available for those seeking to buy verse in Ireland. With the Act of Union, of course, the cultural and economic climate changed, and many of those who had been steady purchasers of poetry moved from Dublin to London; Dublin bookshops would not again be so impressively stocked with poetry until the last decade of the twentieth century.

The early period

For the first twenty-five years of the period under consideration, most poetry by Irish writers was printed in London – where, indeed, many of them lived.[3] The oldest of these poets was Nahum Tate (1652–1715) who had been at Trinity College, Dublin in the 1660s but had moved in the 1670s to London, where he was making his living as a poet and dramatist. Though Tate was more successful at this than most of his compatriots and was appointed poet laureate in 1692, he maintained his connection with Ireland and published, in 1694, an interesting ode on the centenary of the foundation of Trinity College which was set to music by Henry Purcell. Other Irish poets published in London at this time include Ellis Walker (fl.1677–99), a schoolmaster whose fine – and for many years very popular – verse translation of the *Enchiridion* of the Greek poet Epictetus was published in 1695, and the two sons of the bishop of Derry, Ezekiel Hopkins (1634–90). The elder of these, Charles (*c*.1664–*c*.1700), had distressed his father by joining 'the rebels' in Ireland in 1689, but he had gone on to become a popular poet in London – Dryden being among his admirers. Charles Hopkins specialised in witty verse paraphrases from Ovid, but his fondness for women and for strong drink brought him to an early grave – 'a martyr to the cause', according to an early biographer.[4] His younger brother, John (*c*.1675–*c*.1700), was also a prolific and popular poet, but is remembered now for his ill-advised attempt to rewrite Milton's *Paradise Lost* in rhyming couplets.[5] These poets were just some of those treading the path from Dublin to London, a path later well worn by dozens of Irish-born poets – George Farquhar, Jonathan Swift, William Congreve, Thomas Parnell, Mathew Concanen and Oliver Goldsmith, among them.

In Ireland, even before the publication of the first anthology of Irish verse in 1716, locally written verse began to appear on the streets in the form of broadsides – poems about hangings in Dublin Castle (Dublin, 1701), about the Dublin visit of the famous Italian castrato Nicolo Grimaldi (Dublin, 1711), and about the 'Old Wash-Women of Dunlary' (Dublin, *c*.1720), for instance.[6] There are also interesting descriptions of life in Ireland, including a colourful account of the triennial procession of the mayor and the members of the trades guilds 'Riding the Franchises' and marking the limits of the city jurisdiction (Dublin, *c*.1717). The most entertaining of these poems, which are usually cast in mock-heroic or burlesque modes, is by the English writer and wit William King (1663–1712), who spent some months at the country house of a certain Judge Upton at Mountown, seven miles south-east of Dublin in 1701. The rural tranquillity of the place enchanted him and he wrote a memorable eulogy on Mully, the magnificent cow that provided milk for the household. Though King's description of life near Dublin is conventional enough, there is no reason to suppose that it was not based on fact:

> MOUNTOWN! Thou sweet Retreat from *Dublin* Cares,
> Be famous for thy *Apples* and thy *Pears*;
> For *Turnips, Carrots, Lettice, Beans* and *Pease*;

> For *Peggy*'s Butter, and for *Peggy*'s Cheese.
> May Clouds of *Pigeons* round about thee fly;
> But condescend sometimes to make a *Pye*.

As for Mully herself, despite the fact that she was the generous provider of 'Milk that equal'd Cream', and despite the entreaties of her minder, Peggy, and Peggy's fellow-servants Daniel and Terence, she was destined for the butcher:

> What Ribs, what Rumps, what Bak'd, Boil'd, Stew'd and Roast!
> There shan't one single Tripe of her be lost!

Other poets whose work gives an insight into life in early eighteenth-century Ireland include James Ward (1691–1736), who wrote an elegant descriptive poem entitled '*Phoenix* Park' (1718) as well as a lively account of 'The Smock Race at Finglas'; the latter poem, which describes three girls, Oonah, Nora and Shevan, competing in a running race for the prize of a smock or chemise, contains the memorable couplet 'The Butcher's soggy Spouse amidst the throng, / Rubbed clean, and tawdry dressed, puffs slow along.' Another entertaining mock-heroic poem, this time on a game of football between teams from Swords and Lusk – two towns in Fingall, north of Dublin – was the work of the playwright, poet and anthologist Matthew Concanen (1701–49);[7] the poem is full of detail and shows clearly that the rules of the game were somewhat more permissive in the 1720s than they are today.

> Le'nard observing, stood upon his Guard,
> And now to Kick the rolling Ball prepared,
> When careful Terence, fleeter than the Wind,
> Ran to the Swain, and caught his Arm behind;
> A Dextrous Crook about his leg he wound,
> And laid the Champion Grov'ling on the Ground,
> Then tossed the Foot-Ball in the Ambient Air,
> Which soon was stopp'd by nimble Paddy's care . . .

Life in the north of Ireland, slowly returning to normal after the wars of the seventeenth century, is vividly portrayed in 'The North Country Wedding' (1722) by Nicholas Browne (*c*.1699–1734), a poem which describes, among other things, the peculiar behaviour of the bride's father on the wedding night. Browne was celebrating the multiple cultures of Irish life – which he knew from first hand, having been brought up in County Fermanagh where his father was an Irish-speaking Church of Ireland minister.

Several poets of this period – Matthew Concanen, James Ward, Jonathan Smedley, Patrick Delany, William Dunkin and Thomas Sheridan, for instance, all of whom were born, brought up and educated in Ireland – were equally shaped by their experience of the dual realities of the country in the late seventeenth and early eighteenth century. These men were Protestant and English speaking, but they were loyal to the Church of Ireland rather than to the Church of England, to Trinity College, Dublin rather than to Oxford or Cambridge and, particularly when the English administration was enacting anti-Irish legislation, to Ireland rather than to England. Once they had left Trinity College, most of them made their livelihoods in Ireland, as clergy or as schoolmasters, and they saw themselves as part of its fabric. As poets, they remained under the spell of their time at university: they were inspired by classical precedent and, in favouring the mock-heroic and the satiric, were reflecting the mood of Trinity College from which, during the first quarter of the eighteenth century, poured a stream of verse lampoons, squibs and burlesques. The best of this material is clever, witty and original, and any study of the cultural life of early eighteenth-century Ireland must take account of it and of the environment in which it was created.

Swift and his circle

The most influential of these Trinity College graduates, and indeed, the most important poet of eighteenth-century Ireland, was Jonathan Swift whose Irish verse is central to his poetic achievement. Though he was sometimes disparaging about the verses he wrote in Ireland – once describing them as 'trifles' which fell from him, 'amusements in hours of sickness or leisure, . . . never intended for publick view'[8] – Swift took considerable pains over his Irish poems and translations and corrected material for the printer with great care. He was not only the foremost poet of his time but also the leading figure in the intellectual and poetic life of Dublin between about 1718 and the end of the 1730s; around him gathered many active poets, men like Thomas Sheridan (1687–1738), William Dunkin (c.1709–65) and Patrick Delany (c.1685–1768), and women like Mary Barber (c.1685–1755), Constantia Grierson (c.1705–32) and Laetitia Pilkington (c.1709–50). Swift acted as a kind of mentor to this group, an avuncular chairman of a *Senatus Consultum*, prepared to give advice on the shaping of verses and on much else.[9] He obviously enjoyed being the senior poet of his age.

Behind the verse of Swift, and that of the poets with whom he was in contact, was the assumption that the writing of verse was a civilised and a civilising activity. The male poet, in particular, felt himself linked to the world of the classics, ancient and modern: Horace and Martial, Dryden and Pope breathed over his shoulder. Wittily chosen classical epigraphs headed each poem, the muses were invoked, classical gods and goddesses were constantly referred to, and the whole exercise of communicating with one's friends in verse was carried on with an air of relaxed urbanity. Thomas Sheridan, the most energetic and scholarly punster of the circle, summed up the tone of these many verses when he wrote to Swift in 1726:

> You will excuse me, I suppose,
> For sending rhyme instead of prose,
> Because hot weather makes me lazy,
> To write in metre is more easy.
> While you are trudging London town,
> I'm strolling Dublin, up and down;
> While you converse with lords and dukes,
> I have their betters here, my books.

The poets and the readers of this informal verse all recognised when the fine line between the heroic and the mock-heroic was being crossed, and relished that moment when the writer's savage (or merely venomous) indignation turned an innocent-looking description into a devastating personal attack. The affair of Wood's Halfpence – in which the English government sought to impose a debased copper coinage on Ireland – gave Swift a perfect opportunity to extend his influence over Irish affairs in verse as well as in prose. Following his powerful prose pamphlets now known as the *Drapier's Letters*, Swift wrote and circulated, as broadsheets, a series of scurrilous poems on William Wood, the English iron-merchant authorised to mint the copper coinage for Ireland – a man described in the title of Swift's 1724 'Serious Poem upon William Wood' as a 'Brasier, Tinker, Hard-Ware-Man, Coiner, Counterfeiter, Founder and Esquire':

> When Foes are o'ercome, we preserve them from Slaughter,
> To be Hewers of Wood and Drawers of Water;
> Now, although to Draw Water is not very good,
> Yet we all should Rejoyce to be Hewers of Wood . . .
> I hear among Scholars there is a great Doubt
> From what kind of Tree this Wood was Hewn out.
> Teague made a good Pun by a Brogue in his Speech,
> And said: *By my Shoul, he's the Son of a Beech.*

As Swift returned to harass Wood and his pay-masters with an extended barrage of songs and epigrams, mock translations and insulting jibes, the power of this kind of poetry to influence politics in Ireland became clear not only to the politicians who were the target of Swift's verse but to all those who enjoyed reading it. These readers not only were familiar with the biblical texts which are so often echoed in Swift's own verse but had also (if they were men) received a classical education. It was this loosely knit group of educated men which provided the main audience for the mock-heroic and the mock-pastoral verse produced during the first thirty years of the Irish eighteenth century; they enjoyed not only the material which came from Swift and his circle but also such poems as James Ward's 'The Smock Race at Finglas', Matthew Concanen's 'A Match at Football', and Nicholas Browne's 'The North Country Wedding'; they would also have been tickled by Swift's translation of the Irish poem on O'Rourke's feast ('O'Rourk's noble Fare / Will ne'er be forgot, / By those who were there, / Or those who were not') for some of them, particularly the clergymen, would have had a working knowledge of Irish.[10] These middle-class readers would have agreed with Swift when he wrote to his friend Patrick Delany that 'Three Gifts for Conversation fit / Are Humor, Raillery and Witt'; there must have been many gatherings in Dublin and around the country at which entertaining squibs and witty adaptations of the classics were passed from hand to hand.

The female poets who were part of Swift's coterie came with different skills and a different agenda. Most of them had received a haphazard, practical education involving little or no study of the classics, and it is notable that they did not, in their poetry, seek to emulate the men in their classicism. Even Constantia Grierson – classical scholar as well as midwife – did not try to write with the Horatian urbanity of the male poets of the group. Grierson, Mary Barber and Laetitia Pilkington sometimes used classical allusions to give point to their poems, but they were not showing off their learning or their ingenuity: instead, they sought to articulate their experiences as women, writing about their children, about motherhood, about getting old, about being lonely, or about the need to champion the feminine. They wrote with an enviable lightness of touch, however, and with wit. Mary Barber – a draper's wife who often wrote poems for the entertainment of her children – reflected on her changing appearance in a poem addressed to Miss Frances-Arabella Kelly, a noted Dublin beauty of the day:

> Today as at my Glass I stood,
> To set my Head-cloths, and my Hood,
> I saw my grizzled Locks with Dread,

> And call'd to mind the Gorgon's Head.
> Thought I, whate'er the Poets say,
> Medusa's Hair was only gray:
> Tho' Ovid, who the Story told,
> Was too well-bred to call her old;
> But, what amounted to the same,
> He made her an immortal Dame.

But Constantia Grierson used a similar poem to express markedly more feminist feelings:

> To you, Illustrious Fair, I tune my song;
> To you alone, of right, my lays belong;
> Attend and Patronise a work design'd
> To free you from the Oppression of mankind.
> And ye harmonious Nine, whose heavenly Fire
> Does Mortal breasts with Godlike thoughts inspire,
> To whom are Learning, Wit and Arts assign'd
> To show th'extensive pow'rs of woman's Mind,
> By your enliv'ning force assist my Lays;
> Who praises Women does the Muses praise.[11]

Attractive and interesting though the work of these female Irish poets from Swift's circle is, the Dean himself stands head and shoulders above his contemporaries – both male and female – not only because he wrote so well but also because he was not afraid to rail against the rottenness of the institutions of eighteenth-century Ireland, and to name and shame those who propped them up. Swift's courage in standing up against corruption in Irish political life gained him enemies in high places but admiration among those who thought as he did, and undying hero-worship from the poor. An instance of Swift's willingness to name the sins of the powerful occurred in 1729; his friend Patrick Delany had sent a foolish verse epistle to the lord lieutenant requesting ecclesiastical preferment. Swift first sent Delany a verse letter in which he gently chided him for his lack of tact, but he followed this with a much more significant, second poem entitled 'A Libel on D[r] D[elany] and a Certain Great Lord'. In this work (which a contemporary reported he heard being 'cry'd about the streets'), Swift turned on the whole tribe of politicians, the English ones sent to drain Ireland dry and their obsequious, sycophantic Irish counterparts. He reserved particular scorn for the lord lieutenant – though he made an exception for his friend Lord Carteret who happened to occupy the office at the time of the poem.

> He comes to *drain* a *Beggar's Purse*:
> He comes to tye our Chains on faster,
> And shew us, *England* is our Master:
> Caressing Knaves and Dunces wooing,
> To make them work their own undoing.

And later, again, in the same poem:

> So, to effect his *Monarch's* ends,
> From *Hell* a *Viceroy* DEV'L ascends,
> His *Budget*[12] with *Corruptions* cramm'd,
> The Contributions of the *damn'd*;
> Which with unsparing Hand, he strows[13]
> Through *Courts* and *Senates* as he goes;
> And then at *Beelzebub's Black-Hall*,[14]
> Complains his *Budget* was too small.

This sense of outrage at the venality and corruption of politicians finds its most memorable expression in Swift's famous attack on members of the Irish House of Commons, 'A Character, Panegyric, and Description of the Legion Club'.[15] This withering depiction of the parliamentarians as madmen remains the most powerful poem of eighteenth-century Ireland for its unremitting stripping bare of the hypocrisies of the age. The poet starts by observing the magnificent new parliament house, designed by Sir Edward Lovet Pearce, now the headquarters of the Bank of Ireland and still, as it was in the 1730s, one of the most impressive public buildings in Dublin.

> As I strole the City, oft I
> Spy a Building large and lofty,
> Not a Bow-shot from the College,
> Half the Globe from Sense and Knowledge . . .
> Tell us what this Pile contains?
> Many a Head that holds no Brains.
> These Demoniacs[16] let me dub
> With the Name of *Legion Club*.

The main body of the poem catalogues the vices of individual members of parliament and, not surprisingly, the poet affirms that the best outcome for Ireland would be if the roof of the building crashed down upon this 'Den of Thieves' and killed the lot of them. Here, addressing itself to the situation in Ireland, we can see the pen that created the Yahoos and feel the power of the savage indignation that Swift claimed, in the epitaph he is said to have written for himself, used to lacerate his breast.

Swift's verse also includes interesting poems written to or for his friends, among them poems for the two women in his life, Esther Johnson ('Stella') and Esther Van Homrigh ('Vanessa'). For Stella, Swift wrote a series of birthday poems which give a fascinating insight into the Dublin lives of Swift, Stella and their friends, who included Swift's close confidant, Charles Ford. For Vanessa, Swift wrote a long, indiscreet poem about their relationship, 'Cadenus and Vanessa'. Though this poem was written at Windsor before Swift's return to Ireland in 1713, its first printed appearance was in Dublin in 1726 and it is clear from Swift's correspondence that copies had been circulating in Ireland for some time before that date. Dubliners would have found the poem particularly interesting as Vanessa had followed Swift from England to Ireland shortly after his return in 1713, and had settled near Dublin. There were persistent rumours of a romantic relationship between Swift and Vanessa from the time of her arrival in Ireland until, baffled and embittered by her treatment at Swift's hands, she died in 1723; nothing could have fuelled those rumours more effectively than the clandestine circulation, in Dublin, of a poem which told of how the beautiful Vanessa 'not in Years a Score' had fallen in love with Cadenus, a 'decay'd' old doctor of 'forty-four'.

The best of the younger poets encouraged by Swift was William Dunkin. As a young man, Dunkin was a member of a group of lively young undergraduates in Trinity College who entertained each other, and those who frequented the Dublin coffee houses, by publishing scurrilous verse satires. He joined the circle around Swift, and was described by the Dean as 'a Gentleman of much Wit, and the best English as well as Latin poet in this Kingdom'.[17] Dunkin's English verse is certainly ebullient, original and witty and he exploited his classical learning by translating his own English poems into Latin, then from Latin to Greek and finally from Greek back into English.

Dunkin is best known for clever long poems including 'The Parson's Revels' and 'The Murphaeid'. In the first of these, he uses stanzas made up of jaunty tetrameters and suggestive double rhymes (mating 'Papish' with 'apish' and 'Planxsty' with 'Small thanks t'ye', for example) to rush the reader through a vivid account of an extended, riotous party given by an Irish country squire and attended by the local parish priest. The nature of each character is brilliantly captured in his speech – the parish priest speaking a wonderfully incompetent Latin and some of the other characters addressing each other in a barely intelligible Hiberno-English; in general, the poem shows how much Dunkin and his readers relished the absurd juxtaposition of musty book learning and bawdy, demotic speech. The Irish mock-heroic has one of its finest hours in this poem; yet Dunkin's other works, particularly 'The Murphaeid' – a burlesque account of epic struggles involving the porter of Trinity College – can also offer entertainment to the modern reader. A good example of his ironic wit can be seen in the following short poem, 'On the Omission of the Words *Dei Gratia* in the late Coinage of Half-Pence' – written to mark the issue, in 1736, of an Irish halfpenny coin which, though it did carry the head of George II, did not carry the customary words 'Dei Gratia', 'by the grace of God'.

> No Christian king, that I can find,
>   However queer and odd,
> Excepting our's, has ever coin'd
>   Without the grace of God.
>
> By this acknowledgement they shew
>   The mighty King of Kings,
> As him, from whom their riches flow,
>   From whom their grandeur springs.
>
> Come then, Urania,[18] aid my pen,
>   The latent cause assign;
> All other kings are mortal men,
>   But GEORGE, 'tis plain's, divine.

Dunkin's mischievous rhyming of 'God' with 'odd', his parody of an Anglican hymn in the second stanza as well as his neat redefinition of 'divine' in the last line – together with his fine sense of timing and confidence in the whole piece – show him to be one of the finest Irish poets of his age, second only to – and occasionally surpassing – Swift.

The Hibernian muse hard at work

Many interesting poetic descriptions of life in Ireland have survived from the middle years of the eighteenth century. These were all printed and published in Dublin, by this time a thriving centre of literary activity with dozens of printers specialising in the publication of verse. The 'king' of these printers was George Faulkner (*c.*1703–75), famous not only as the proprietor of the widely read *Dublin Journal* but as the most successful Dublin publisher and bookseller of the eighteenth century. Faulkner not only managed to obtain important texts through his willingness to deal with members of the London book-trade but also gained Swift's trust sufficiently to be allowed to bring out a four-volume collection of Swift's works in 1735. Faulkner established himself as Swift's Irish publisher and continued to bring out his works in multiple editions for the next forty years – and to make a large amount of money in the process. Swift read the proofs of Faulkner's 1735 edition and authorised many changes to the text, particularly in the volume that contained his poems. On the basis of his acquaintance with Swift, Faulkner moved up the social ladder and was jocularly referred to, regularly, as 'Sir' George. Faulkner printed a very large quantity of verse during his long career and took to 'editing' the texts of writers such as Pope – mainly by adding explanatory notes to them – for the Irish market.

In this flourishing market-place, many Irish poets were eager to put forward their work for publication. Among the most interesting material to survive from the middle of the century are a poem describing the Dublin debtors' prison ('The Humours of the Black Dog' by Wetenhall Wilkes (fl.1737)) and a lively poem advocating the establishment of a whale fishery off the west coast of Ireland ('A Friend in Need is a Friend in Deed . . .' by James Stirling (1701–63)). There are also several volumes by individual poets including Laurence Whyte (c.1683–c.1753) and John Winstanley (1677–1750).

The first of these, Laurence Whyte, who was born in County Westmeath, became a teacher of mathematics in Dublin. He wrote a prodigious quantity of verse and described himself on the title pages of his two volumes as 'A Lover of the Muses and of Mathematics'. He was the author of two fascinating long poems, 'The Parting Cup', which gives a detailed description of the life of a substantial farming community in early eighteenth-century Ireland, and 'A Dissertation on Italian and Irish Musick, with some Panegyrick on *Carralan* our late Irish Orpheus'. In the second of these poems, Whyte links Irish and Italian culture in a way unique in Irish eighteenth-century verse, asserting that 'There's scarce a *Forthman* or *Fingallian*, / But sings or whistles in *Italian*', – which would be fascinating, if we knew it were true.

'The Parting Cup or the Humours of Deoch an Doruis' (Ir. *deoch an dorais*, a stirrup-cup or parting drink) is a poem of enduring interest. The first two cantos depict life in County Westmeath in the early years of the eighteenth century and describe, in considerable detail, the world of a substantial Catholic farmer. By the fourth canto of the poem, the farmer and his neighbours have been reduced to abject poverty by rack-renting landlords and unfavourable economic conditions. The contrasts in Whyte's poem between a life of plenty in the past and a life of want in the present, and the analysis of the economic and social causes of these devastating changes, were to be echoed eloquently in Goldsmith's *The Deserted Village* a generation later. As Whyte puts it, farmers who used to live like gentlemen are:

> Now beggar'd and of all bereft,
> Are doom'd to starve, or live by Theft,
> Take to the Mountains or the Roads,
> When banish'd from their old Abodes;
> Their native Soil were forc'd to quit,
> So Irish Landlords thought it fit,
> Who without Cer'mony or Rout,
> For their Improvements turn'd them out.

This bleak picture of the situation for Catholics trying to make a living off the land is in stark contrast to the carefree picture the unconventional James Winstanley painted of life for Catholic schoolgirls in Dublin in the 1740s. Winstanley was a gentle poet whose eccentricities are well illustrated by the fact that he habitually placed the letters A.M.L.D. (standing for 'Apollo's and the Muse's Licensed Doctor') after his name and used the title 'Doctor' when it suited him. He was a Catholic himself and one of the girls in his poem is given a 'Cross with jewels at the end on't'. In the mornings, the 'obstrep'rous' and loquacious schoolgirls

> Saunter an Hour or two to School;
> And when they come there, play the Fool . . .
> Call Masters 'Bastard' or such Name,
> And ev'ry little Miss defame . . .

Winstanley's works contain fascinating glimpses of life in mid-century Dublin, including a fine portrait of the poet and his cat, and a lively verse account of a Captain Molineux who was 'most barbarously strangled by an inhuman Strumpet with his own Wig'. Winstanley also penned a moving elegy on the 'much lamented Death of Jenny the Fish who departed this Life at Ring's-End the 19th of January 1718' where she had been kept in an underwater cage so that mothers-to-be could stoke her sides; such an action was meant to ensure that this 'best of Midwives' – 'So soft! so sleek! so beautifully plump! / Nine foot, at least, in length from Nose to Rump' – would help them when they went into labour. Winstanley may not have been a great poet, but he was an entertaining recorder of the world around him. 'A Brother Bard' sent him the following facetious verse: 'I've read your Book of Poems o're, / And thank you for the Pleasure; / I wish of them there had been more, / For ev'ry Line's a Treasure.'

Though Winstanley was one of those who went out of his way to put his name before the book-buying public, many Irish poets – including Swift – preferred their verse to appear anonymously or under false names. Among the anonymous Dublin-printed poems of the early and middle years of the eighteenth century are scores of entertaining and revealing verses – ballads, drinking-songs, accounts of sporting events, descriptions of patterns, satires on individuals and institutions, burlesque accounts of trials and drunken orgies and of enormous feasts, and poems seeking to influence the politicians of the day. Throughout the eighteenth century, the towns and cities of Ireland were full of the sounds of poems being sung or recited by hawkers, while anyone who wanted to buy poetry in a pamphlet or bound volume had an impressive array to choose from in the 'bulks' or shop-front stalls set up outside the printing shops. Poetry in English was embedded in the cultural life of eighteenth-century Ireland.

Irish-born poets continued to make a name for themselves in London as well. A long philosophical poem entitled *Universal Beauty* was praised by Alexander Pope on its appearance in London in 1736 and its young Irish author, Henry Brooke (*c.*1703–83), found himself fêted in literary and political circles in England, as Oliver Goldsmith would be a generation later. Henry Brooke was born in County Cavan, the son of a clergyman. He was educated at Trinity College, Dublin and soon became a prolific writer. In addition to *Universal Beauty*, Brooke wrote plays (including the famous *Gustavus Vasa*, which was banned in London by Walpole because of its apparent criticism of him), novels (including *The Fool of Quality*) and many political pamphlets; as a pamphleteer, Brooke wrote in support of differing points of view at various times. His daughter Charlotte, famous for her *Reliques of Irish Poetry*, edited his works for publication and they appeared in four volumes shortly before he died in Dublin in 1783. *Universal Beauty* is a remarkable poem in which, in heroic couplets of great flexibility, Brooke surveys God's creation in the universe, and gives an account of the forms of knowledge and of the nature of man. In the last of the six books of the poem, he contemplates the beauty of the design of the universe and expresses a typically Augustan wonder at the social order which exists in the world of bees; there are, the reader soon learns, lessons here for humankind.

> High on her throne, the bright Imperial Queen[19]
> Gives the prime movement to the state machine;
> Around, the drones who form her courtly train,
> Bask in the rays of her auspicious reign;
> Beneath, the sage consulting peers repair,
> And breathe the virtues of their prince's care;
> Debating, cultivate the publick cause,
> And wide dispense the benefit of laws . . .

At about the same time as Brooke was making a name for himself in London, the most famous Irish expatriate poet of the century, Oliver Goldsmith, was growing up near Lissoy in County Westmeath where, like other poets considered in this chapter, he experienced the bilingual and bicultural life of eighteenth-century rural Ireland. After some time at Trinity College, Dublin, Goldsmith travelled widely on the continent and eventually settled in London in the 1760s where he made a precarious living as a writer and became a member of Samuel Johnson's famous literary 'Club'. Goldsmith's 'Irishness' was a characteristic often remarked on by his London companions and his exploitation of his early background is clearly seen in his plays, particularly *She Stoops to Conquer*. Goldsmith's awareness of the multiple cultures of Ireland is also seen in two of his essays, 'The History of Carolan, the Last Irish Bard' (1760) and 'A Description of the Manners and Customs of the Native *Irish*' (1759). Most of all, however, Goldsmith's Irishness is reflected in his famous poem, *The Deserted Village*. Here he drew on his memories of childhood in the Irish midlands in lamenting the lost innocence of life in an untainted countryside; although, as Katharine Balderston has pointed out, there was probably a considerable difference between 'the coarse reality of the 1730s' and the 'refined and idealised memories' of the poem,[20] generations of readers have seen a reflection of eighteenth-century Irish rural life in sweet Auburn.

> Sweet AUBURN, loveliest village of the plain,
> Where health and plenty cheared the labouring swain,
> Where smiling spring its earliest visit paid,
> And parting summer's lingering blooms delayed;
> Dear lovely bowers of innocence and ease,
> Seats of my youth, when every sport could please,
> How often have I loitered o'er thy green,
> Where humble happiness endeared each scene!
> How often have I paused on every charm,
> The sheltered cot, the cultivated farm,
> The never failing brook, the busy mill,
> The decent church that topt the neighbouring hill,
> The hawthorn bush, with seats beneath the shade,
> For talking age and whispering lovers made!

The fact that the rural idyll of Goldsmith's poem turns into a nightmare helps strengthen the sense of identification that readers felt between the world of *The Deserted Village* and the changing face of eighteenth-century Ireland. But other poetic texts circulating at the same time as Goldsmith's poem describe a rather different reality. A long anonymous poem entitled 'Hesperi-neso-graphia: or

A Description of the Western Isle',[21] for instance, which was printed several times during the eighteenth century, contains an extended, burlesque – but nonetheless convincing and factually rich – account of a substantial Catholic farmer and of the daily life of his prosperous household somewhere in the Irish countryside. Although this poem first appeared long before Goldsmith's *Deserted Village*, it was, in its later printings, competing for its audience with Goldsmith's poem and, with its vivid details and rough energy, provided a very different experience for its readers. In the one poem, gentle pentameters describe the sheltered cot and the cultivated farm; in the other, rough tetrameters describe spirited events of various kinds in Gillo's house, at one end of which 'he kept his Cows, / At th'other End he and his Spouse / On Bed of Straw, without least Grumble, / Nay, with delight, did often tumble.' Equally vividly, Laurence Whyte's description of the plight of farmers in County Westmeath gives the reader a more specific and convincing picture of eighteenth-century rural life than does Goldsmith's famous poem. If texts other than Goldsmith's were made more readily available than they are, critics might be able to reassess and compare the verse descriptions of eighteenth-century Irish life available to the readers of the day. *The Deserted Village* is certainly a greater poem than the others we are considering and, in its general treatment of the theme of rural depopulation, enduringly appealing to a general audience – particularly an English one. But the 'Hesperi-neso-graphia' was regularly reprinted in the eighteenth century; like Laurence Whyte's poem, it was popular with contemporary readers who must have enjoyed its unpretentious account of the lost world of Irish rural prosperity and hospitality. Clearly more work needs to be done on the genre of the eighteenth-century Irish landscape poem, on its authors and on its readership; though it is not surprising that Goldsmith's romantic and inoffensive treatment of the theme of rural decline should have remained popular from the day of its publication until now, it seems unfortunate that distinctively Irish works such as Laurence Whyte's 'Parting Cup' and the 'Hesperi-neso-graphia', with which it makes an interesting comparison, remain largely unread and wholly unassessed today.

As the century progressed, the work of many middle-class poets living throughout Ireland was printed, often at their own expense. The Corkman James Eyre Weekes (*c.*1720–*c.*1754) wrote volumes of suggestive love songs, and Thomas Newburgh (*c.*1695–1779) published an interesting description of St Stephen's Green in Dublin in his volume *Essays Poetical, Moral and Critical* (Dublin, 1769); Samuel Whyte (1733–1811), Gerald Fitzgerald (1740–1819), William Preston (1753–1807), the eccentric James Delacourt (1709–81) and George Sackville Cotter (1755–81) all published volumes of enjoyable verse –

the last of these including in his *Poems, consisting of Odes, Songs, Pastorals, Satyrs &c* . . . (Cork, 1788), a highly entertaining account of high-jinks at the fashionable spa at Swanlinbar, County Cavan. In other poems in the same collection, Cotter gave a long, satirical description of an Irish country house of the 1780s and depictions of night-life in Cork, with accounts of its alcoholics, its coffee houses and its gambling.

Among those who published their poems by subscription was John Anketell (*c*.1750–1824). Anketell, who was originally from County Monaghan, was a self-important clergyman in the Church of Ireland, obsessed with his low income and the fact that he was constantly passed over for promotion. At the beginning of his *Poems on Several Subjects* is a long and entertainingly tetchy essay 'To my Subscribers' in which he gives accounts of being repulsed from various noblemen's doors when he attempted to solicit subscriptions for his book in person. Lord Clonmel, for instance, assured him, 'without blushing', that he 'had taken an oath never to read a line of poetry'. Many of Anketell's potential, middle-class subscribers refused him – he quotes their various excuses – and a grocer in Armagh declared that 'hurry of business absolutely prevented him from reading any thing except his daybook and ledger'. Nevertheless, this obstinate and persistent man succeeded in assembling over 1,200 subscribers who did pay their five shillings for his rather dull book. The list is headed by the archbishop of Cashel, the duke of Leinster and several bishops, and includes subscribers from fourteen counties, among them clergymen, landed gentry, surgeons, army officers, lawyers, academics, tradesmen and a considerable number of women – who presumably found it harder to get rid of the Revd Anketell than did their menfolk. Though it is safe to say that not all the people listed actually read Anketell's poems, it is also clear that there was a considerable market for poetry in English – 'of Irish manufacture' as Anketell described his effusions – among the middle classes in eighteenth-century Ireland.[22]

The female muse

It was at this time too that volumes of verse by Irish women began to appear on the Dublin bookstalls with greater regularity. Earlier in the century, poetry by Irish women, including *Marinda* by Mary Monck, daughter of Robert, Lord Molesworth, and the initial volumes by Mary Barber and Laetitia Pilkington, had been published in London, and little poetry known to be by women had been printed in Dublin.[23] However, in 1764, Dublin readers were startled by a powerful volume entitled *Poems on Several Occasions by a Lady of Quality* – who turned out to be Dorothea Dubois (1728–74), the seriously wronged daughter of an Irish nobleman. Like most volumes of verse by women, this was published by subscription but unlike most such volumes, this one asserted forcefully that men were the cause of the wrongs of the world – as they certainly were the cause of Dorothea's own sufferings. One of her best short poems is entitled 'The Amazonian Gift'.

> Is Courage in a Woman's Breast,
>   Less pleasing than in Man?
> And is a smiling Maid allow'd
>   No Weapon but a Fan?
>
> 'Tis true, her Tongue, I've heard 'em say,
>   Is Woman's chief Defence;
> And if you'll b'lieve me, gentle Youths,
>   I have no Aid from thence.
>
> And some will say that sparkling Eyes,
>   More dang'rous are than Swords;
> But I ne'er point my Eyes to kill,
>   Nor put I trust in Words.
>
> Then, since the Arms that Women use,
>   Successless are in me,
> I'll take the Pistol, Sword or Gun,
>   And thus equip'd, live free.
>
> The Pattern of the *Spartan* Dame
>   I'll copy as I can;
> To Man, degen'rate Man, I'll give
>   That simple Thing, a *Fan*.

Other distinctive female poets to emerge in Ireland in this period include the Quaker Mary Shackleton Leadbeater (1758–1826) and two satirists – the Meath-born Henrietta Battier (1751–1813) (who once described herself, unfairly, as 'a better housewife than a poet') and Mary O'Brien, an Englishwoman who lived in Ireland for several years around 1790. In addition, Henrietta O'Neill née Boyle (1758–93) wrote a number of delicate poems including a fine ode to the opium poppy, to which she was addicted: 'I hail the goddess of the scarlet flower,' she wrote: 'Thou brilliant weed! . . . should'st spread / Thy spell around my aching head.' Another woman who made a major contribution to Irish poetry in the latter part of the eighteenth century was Charlotte Brooke (*c*.1740–93), whose pioneering anthology of translations of Irish verse, *Reliques of Irish Poetry*, was printed in Dublin in 1789. A remarkable feature of the volume is Brooke's far-seeing preface in which she makes what were at the time unprecedented claims for the beauty of poetry written in the Irish language. 'It is really astonishing,' she wrote, 'of what various and comprehensive powers this neglected language is possessed . . . The British muse is not yet informed that she has an elder sister in this isle; let us introduce them to each other!' Brooke was in the vanguard of those prepared to acknowledge what she called the 'genius' of Irish poetry.

One of the more unexpected female voices of the age belongs to Ellen Taylor whose *Poems by Ellen Taylor, the Irish Cottager* appeared in 1792. Though she later seems to have kept a school, Taylor was employed as a house-maid when she wrote the verse in her book. She explains, in the introduction to the volume, that it was a guest in the house who encouraged her to write poetry. The same unknown benefactor may have been behind the attempt to raise money for her through the publication of her work. Only forty copies of her *Poems* were printed and it is remarkable that such a slight, cheaply printed pamphlet has survived. The best poem in this fragile little book was written by the side of the river Barrow in County Kilkenny where the poet had been 'sent to wash Linen'.

> Thy banks, O Barrow, sure must be
>   The Muses' choicest haunt,
> Else why so pleasing thus to me,
>   Else why my soul enchant?
>
> To view thy dimpled surface here,
>   Fond fancy bids me stay;
> But Servitude, with brow austere,
>   Commands me straight away.

The language and feeling of this poem may be conventional, but the context of its composition makes it of particular interest.

Another woman who would be completely forgotten were it not for the poetry she wrote is Olivia Elder, who lived on a farm in County Derry. Elder, whose work remains in manuscript, seems to have been at ease in both the Ulster Scots dialect and English since she wrote in both. In a lively verse letter to a friend (in standard English), she explained how she sought to balance writing poems with her other daily tasks; these included cleaning the house, making hay, sewing, knitting, and visiting the squire and the 'stupid Rector'.

> Oft from my hand the Pen I whisk out
> And in its place take up the Dishclout;[24]
> For spite of all sublimer wishes,
> I needs must sometimes wash the dishes . . .

Unfinished I must leave a fable,
To go and scour the kitchen table,
Or from the writing of a Poem,
Descend my neighbour's Turf to throw in . . .

Though Olivia Elder was 'never at a school or college', she had gained some knowledge of classical mythology and remarked, disarmingly, that she must sometimes

. . . like the Shepherd God Apollo,
Leave wit and verse a Cow to follow.

Like Mary Barber and Constantia Grierson a generation before her, Olivia Elder used her daily work as the material for her verse with remarkable ingenuity and imagination. The astonishing thing is that this self-educated woman, living on a farm in a remote part of Ireland, should not only have written verse but have preserved it. Yet Olivia Elder penned verse letters to her friends as if this were the most natural way of communicating; it is highly likely that other manuscripts of verse by eighteenth-century Irish female poets await discovery and publication. Until such material is revealed, it will not be possible to undertake any full assessment of the culture of eighteenth-century Ireland.

Poetry in Ulster Scots

Eighteenth-century Ulster produced many fine male poets too, quite a number of them weavers; their verse often celebrated daily life through the medium of the energetic and robust dialect of Ulster Scots. In an early example from a poem entitled 'Tit for Tat, or the Rater Rated' – which might be explained as 'Tit for Tat or the berating of those who demand tithes' – the wife of a County Donegal farmer of the 1750s who has been berating the wife of the rector – to whom all farmers, much against their will, had to pay tithes – tells her husband precisely what she said to the rector's wife:

'While dressing ye're and pinning,
I'll spin, and bleach my linnen,
And wear my ain hands winning,
    Ye rector's lazy daw.

Shame fa' them wad change marrows,
    For rector's gown and chaise.'

A rough paraphrase of this passage might be: 'While you are dressing and beautifying yourself, I spin and bleach my linen, and wear my own hands [to the bone] gathering crops – you're the rector's lazy slut. Shame fall on those who would exchange their equals for the comforts of life with a rector.' The implication in this passage is that the rector's wife was herself from a farming family.

Direct speech and dialogue are particularly effective in Ulster Scots and some of the most entertaining poems in the dialect – 'To a Hedge-hog' by Samuel Thomson (1766–1816), for instance – exploit this to the full. In the passage which follows, the poet is addressing the hedgehog.

> Thou grimest far o' grusome tykes,
> Grubbing thy food by thorny dykes,
> Gudefaith *thou* disna want for *pikes*,
>> Baith sharp an' rauckle;
> Thou looks (L—d save's) array'd in spikes,
>> A creepin' heckle!
>
> Some say thou'rt sib kin to the sow,
> But sibber to the de'il, I trow;
> An' what thy use can be, there's few
>> That can explain;
> But naithing, as the learn'd allow,
>> Was made in vain.
>
> Sure Nick begat thee, at the first,
> On some auld *whin* or thorn accurst;
> An' some horn-finger'd harpie nurst
>> The ugly urchin;
> The Belzie, laughin, like to burst,
>> First ca'd thee *Hurchin*!

A rough paraphrase of these wonderfully rich and earthy stanzas might be: 'You, by far the grimmest of the rough-looking creatures, grubbing your food by stone walls covered with thorn bushes, Good heavens!, you are not short of spines, both sharp and strong. Arrayed in your spikes, you look (Lord save us!) like a creeping flax-comb. Some say you are a blood relation of the sow, but I think you are more closely related to the devil, and what use you serve, few can explain; but the learned maintain that nothing was made in vain. Sure, in the beginning, if the devil was your father then your mother was some cursed old thorn or gorse bush, and some monstrous old hag with horny fingers nursed the ugly brat; it was Beelzebub himself who, laughing, first called you "hurchin" or hedgehog.'

Though he was a radical in politics, like most of his brother Ulster Scots poets, Thompson was not a weaver but a hedge-schoolmaster. He lived at

Carngranny near Templepatrick, County Antrim in a small thatched cottage called 'Crambo Cave'; this house became a meeting place for many of the weaver poets who, together, brought about the remarkable renaissance in Ulster Scots poetry which took place towards the end of the century. The best known of these weaver poets was James Orr (1770–1816) – patriot, United Irishman, 'New Light' Presbyterian and a man with a deep social conscience. The short visit he paid to America in 1799 provided him with the subject matter for two interesting descriptions of life on an emigrant ship sailing from Ulster to Delaware. One of these, in standard English, is a comparatively tame piece of work, but the account of the voyage which Orr wrote in Ulster Scots exploits to the full the energy of the vernacular. Here he describes the behaviour of the passengers:

> Meanwhile, below, some count their beads,
>   While prudes, auld-light sit cantin';
> Some mak' their beds; some haud their heads,
>   An' cry wi' spite, a' pantin'!
> 'Ye brought us here, ye luckless cauf!
>   ('Aye did he; whisht my darlin'!)
> L—d sen' me hame! wi' poke an' staff,
>   I'd beg my bread thro' Airlan',
>   My lane, that day'.

A rough paraphrase of this stanza might be: 'Meanwhile, below decks, some say the rosary while the prudish ones [members of the strict 'Old Light' Non-conformist sects] sit chanting; some make their beds, some hold their heads and cry with disappointment, blurting out "You brought us here, you stupid idiot (Yes he did so – hush, my darling!); Lord, send me home! I'd prefer to beg for bread throughout Ireland, on my own, with a beggar's bag and a staff."'

Orr wrote a large quantity of verse, including memorable descriptions of ordinary life in Ulster; a recent admirer of his work, the Ulster poet John Hewitt, described two of Orr's poems, 'The Penitent' and 'The Irish Cottier's Death and Burial', as 'the major successes in scale in our vernacular literature'.[25] Like the demotic verse from the rest of eighteenth-century Ireland, the verse of the Ulster weaver poets reflects a life far more vigorous and full of fun than official cultural histories suggest. The idea that rural Ireland under the Penal Laws was a place of unrelieved gloom is belied by this spirited, life-enhancing writing and it is time that cultural historians looked seriously at the environment that produced it.

The rural muse

Some of the poetry written in English outside the major cities and towns of Ireland in the second half of the eighteenth century provides clear evidence that, in the countryside at least, communities with differing backgrounds were interacting with each other. It also shows that the widespread idea that there were only two cultures in eighteenth-century Ireland – the culture of English speakers and the culture of Irish speakers – is quite inadequate to explain the actual situation in rural Ireland. In fact, eighteenth-century Ireland – including Ulster – was made up of many distinct but interdependent and interwoven social and cultural communities in which two main languages, English and Irish, or versions of them, were living side by side with each other, and influencing each other at a local level. There were many forms of English and many forms of Irish, many places (hedge-schools, for instance) where, in their local forms, these languages and dialects rubbed against and influenced each other. As the century progressed, economic conditions changed and travel became easier, which meant that rural communities gradually became less isolated from each other and cultural interaction occurred on an ever-widening stage; but still, as the new language of commerce and progress came up against the older ways of Irish life, strange, culturally hybrid forms of writing came into existence in many parts of Ireland. Some of the most memorable English-language verse of the age is the product of this cross-pollination of form, syntax and vocabulary between the cultures and languages of eighteenth-century Ireland.

While demotic poems from Ulster tend to be in Ulster Scots, texts from other provinces tend to be in Hiberno-English – as English influenced by the Irish language is usually called. There are, however, two kinds of Hiberno-English: a contrived or 'Stage-Irish' form, designed to make fun of the speaker by exaggerating the mistakes in syntax and vocabulary which an Irish speaker might make when trying to speak English, and the 'natural' Hiberno-English used by such a speaker when attempting to express him- or herself in the unfamiliar medium. This more natural and spontaneous Hiberno-English is found in anonymous ballad sheets and chapbooks printed mostly in Irish provincial towns during a comparatively short period of time – between about 1770 and 1800. It is clear that those who composed these songs composed also in Irish – indeed some interesting material can be found in bilingual poems in which Irish and Hiberno-English are interwoven. Though the knowledge these poets had of English was considerable, it was incomplete, and the use they made of the language was unconventional. They were also using the

Irish *amhrán* or song metres, which meant that they would sometimes choose a word more for its sound or metrical value than for its meaning. Some of the songs they wrote are comic or bawdy, but others tell of the horrors of dipsomania, of hopeless love, of forced emigration or of unhappy marriages. The poems reflect real and powerful emotions, and the Hiberno-English in which they are written is entirely unselfconscious and natural. Like many writers in postcolonial environments who start working in the language of the cultural coloniser, these poets knew nothing of lexical definitions or of rules about writing 'correct' English. The poet who wrote 'The Maiden's Resolution', for example, was expressing her unrequited love in an unfamiliar medium, borrowing vocabulary and modes of expression from her native Irish as she did so. The effect is poignant, powerful and fresh:

> Draw near each constant female, while I my ruin revealing,
> My grief's beyond concealing, for ever I'm undone;
> As on my bed I leaned, of my darling's pain I dreamed,
> My mind was then enflamed to love my Farmer's Son . . .
>
> Blessed was the hour, I entered his sweet bower,
> Bedeckt with fragrant flowers where silver streams do run;
> And Sol's beams were shining with beauty most surprising,
> All things were still delighting my country Farmer's Son.
>
> Tho' my ambitious parents doth like for to make varience,[26]
> Who said he was inferior to their great dignity;
> Cupid has inspir'd me and Hyme [27] has desir'd me,
> To hail[28] the wound I gave him with sweet chestity.

Though this particular poem comes from a chapbook printed in Dublin in 1784, most of the chapbooks and ballad sheets in which songs like these occur were printed in provincial towns such as Monaghan, Limerick, Newry, Tralee and Wexford. The chapbooks would be bought from the printer by chapmen who hawked them around the towns and in the countryside, selling them on to ballad-singers. The songs would then be sung on street corners, at fairs and patterns,[29] in cottages, kitchens and shebeens or wherever an audience could be found. Whereas the Irish-language tradition had been one of manuscript and oral transmission, these songs in English (or Irish and English) were transmitted in printed form.[30] The verse is often of immediate interest – commemorating local or national events – and seems to have been written close to the place where it was printed. The texts are sometimes incomplete or garbled, and often contain compositors' mistakes which were not corrected before printing. Some of them also address issues that are not

addressed anywhere else in Irish poetry in English until the twentieth century
– domestic misery or the horrors of a reliance on alcohol. 'The Coughing
Old Man', for instance, tells of a young farmer's daughter forced to marry an
elderly man:

> The very first night that he came to bed to me,
> I longed for a trial at Venus's game,
> But to my sad vexation and consternation,
> His hautboy was feeble & weak in the main.
> For instead of pleasing he only kept teazing;
> To him then I turned my back in a huff,
> But still he did cry, 'twill do by-and-by,
> *A chusla se sthere!*[31] I am killed with the cough . . .
>
> His breath it does stink like asafœtadu,[32]
> His blobbring and slobbring I can't bear,
> For each night when I lie beside him,
> He must have a spitting cup placed on his chair;
> His nose and his chin are joined together,
> His tawny old skin is yellow and tough,
> Both trembling and shaking like one in the ague,
> Still smothering and spitting and killed with the cough.

The chapbooks also contain early, unedited texts of songs which respectable,
nineteenth-century editors later forced into metrical and lexical straitjackets.
Take, for instance, the following wonderfully fresh and unsophisticated version
of a famous Irish song, 'The Colleen Rue'. The poet, who has 'roved out on a
summer's morning, / A specalating most curiously', comes across 'a charming
fair one'. He accosts her thus:

> 'Are you Aurora or goddess Flora,[33]
>   Eutarnatia or fair Venus bright
> Or Helen fair beyond compare,
>   That Paris stole from the Grecians sight?'
> 'Kind sir, be easy and do not tease me,
>   With your false praises most jestingly;
> Your dissimulation or invocation,
>   Are vaunting praises seducing me.
> I'm not Aurora or beautious Flora,
>   But a rural female to all men's view,
> That's here condoling my situation,
>   My appelation is the Colleen Rue.'

This text, strongly influenced by the *amhrán*, includes many elements borrowed from Irish; in particular, it demonstrates an imperfect understanding of English vocabulary, pronunciation and syntax – suggesting that English was not the first language of the person who composed it. It is not just the English and Irish languages that are intertwined with each other in these texts but the two cultural traditions.

In fact, though English was not the normal language for communication in the Irish countryside in the last thirty years of the eighteenth century, it was taught, after a fashion, by hedge-schoolmasters who had often learned the language from books and not from native speakers.[34] The value of English as the language of commerce was widely acknowledged and many people strove to acquire some competence in it.[35] The evidence of the chapbooks and ballad sheets is that the singing of songs in English was a popular occupation, even if not all the audience could understand all the words all the time. Evidence of practical bilingualism can be found in surviving macaronic songs, for the appreciation of which knowledge of both English and Irish was needed.[36] If language acquisition in Ireland followed the patterns usual elsewhere – and there is no reason to suppose that it would not have done so – the parents of these songwriters and their audience would have been monoglot Irish speakers. Though the poets themselves and the compositors who set the texts in type would, by the 1780s, have been able to speak English fairly fluently, they would have had little formal schooling in it, which would explain why their texts exhibit considerable orthographical uncertainties.

A typical example is 'The Rake's Frolick or *Stauka an Varaga*', a poem which appears in a chapbook printed in Limerick in about 1785.[37] The metrical elements of the poem are borrowed from Irish *amhrán* or song metres and the poet's grasp of standard English syntax and vocabulary is less than perfect. Though poems like this were intended for a bilingual audience and were the work of bilingual poets, those who printed the texts did not expect those who sang them to be able to read Irish. They printed the Irish passages as an English speaker would spell them out if he heard them; thus when they are read aloud by someone who can read English, an Irish speaker should be able to understand them as Irish.

> . . . When first I set sail to range the barony,
> From sweet Farihy to Kildoray,[38]
>> Oro,[39] and from that to red chair.
> It's there the fair maids do treat me heartily,
> With full glasses free and impartiality,
>> Oro, the truth I'll declare.

On the high road to Castle Oliver[40]
I met a coaxing, roving froliker,
Her mode denoted she was a Palentine,[41]
She wore deep ribbons her clothes in fashion sir,–
    Oro, her love she received.

Boadha ma raee, three claar na Banaba,
Oan ra Chariges dhan thraid shin Chasnal,
    Oro, es ga dreliceh ra slardh.
Na danea yhan rith shin no knaulioh challiogs er,
Da har vaccasa an erraen's an arrigadh,
    Oro, es da nearing neas moe,
Been affran leh foule gagh law o haggirth aun
An Maraga's faar you laulau sathaugh thin aun,
Straidh van calkes es ee er liabha,
Mydhen d eass es mea a veh na hanea shea,
    Oro da baith ea mr [*sic*] skiole.[42]

This fascinating song gives some idea of the energy of Irish poetic culture in rural communities at the time it was printed and, more significantly, shows that, at the interface between the Irish and English languages, the energy, vitality and lack of prudery characteristic of Irish material could move without difficulty into English – dragging Irish vocabulary and syntax with it.

There is also an interesting, unedited example of an Irish praise poem in English, dating from about 1790, the work of an itinerant ballad-maker named L. O'Reilly. In form, style and subject matter, this poem is an English-language version of an Irish elegy. The poet would probably have learned what English he knew from books, rather than from native speakers, which would explain his misunderstanding of the meanings of certain English words and of the syntax of standard English; the rules he is applying throughout the poem are those of Irish rather than English prosody.

A head-note in the first printing of this poem explains how it came to be preserved. A company of ladies, who were taking an evening's walk in the Irish countryside, happened to meet 'a poor mad itinerant Ballad-maker' and purchased all his compositions from him. An elegy on the death of 'the late good and truly pious Miss Bridget Burne' happened to be the first poem read aloud, and the company amused themselves by laughing at it. A poet called William Ball, who was present, defended the poem and 'extolled its excellences'. As a penance for his remarks, Ball was required by the company to 'translate' the elegy into the conventional poetic language and metre of the day. Joshua Edkins, when he included Ball's poem in the second volume of his *A Collection of Poems, mostly original, by several hands* (two vols., Dublin, 1789–90, I, pp. 141–9), printed the original poem and the 'translation' on facing pages, and so preserved what may well be a unique example of an eighteenth-century Irish elegy in English. The natural naivety of the text is heightened by L. O'Reilly's lack of understanding of the registers of English – as well as by his unfamiliarity with the normal meaning and pronunciation of some English words. The poem begins as follows:

> Unhappy Hibernia mourn, O mourn and do not cease!
> Thus and only thus can you equitably appease
> The throbs and griefs of all that lov'd the good,
> The seraphick spirit that from you alas! is fled.
> Mourn ye widows, your comfortress is gone;
> Ye orphans mourn, thrice orphantized again;
> Lament ye poor; ye lost her tender-looking charity,
> Who pity'd your wants, distress and misery . . .

The effect of this earnest use of a half-understood language is poignant and sad, yet it reminds us that there must have been many thousands of such works in circulation in manuscript in the latter part of the eighteenth century in Ireland, and that they represent an important moment in cultural history. Though work has been undertaken on the interaction between the English and Irish languages in some popular writings of the late eighteenth and early nineteenth centuries, virtually no work has been done on the verse chapbooks or on texts such as the elegy on Miss Brigit Burne. Yet these texts present significant evidence of an important aspect of the popular culture of rural Ireland in the 1780s and 1790s; a detailed investigation of the texts themselves and a study of their reception might suggest answers to some of the uncertainties which hover over key questions about the nature of rural culture in late eighteenth-century Ireland.

The urban muse

Urban material from the latter part of the century, including 'De Nite afore Larry was Stretch'd' – one of the most anthologised of eighteenth-century Irish poems in English – is of equal interest. Conjectures about the authorship of this poem and of the several connected with it have been widespread, but it is probable that they were genuine street poems, 'collected' in Dublin by someone whose identity is unknown, and written down in a way which reflects the pronunciation and vocabulary of the speech of the late eighteenth-century

Dublin underworld. Despite – or perhaps because of – their demotic register and vulgarity, these underworld poems were 'all the *ton*' (i.e. all the rage) in Dublin in 1788. An interesting characteristic of the poems was the fact that the last line (or prose passage) in each stanza was to be said 'Newgate style' – that is, spoken rather than sung, and inserted as comic relief as happens in 'patter' songs in music halls.

Although these texts seem to exhibit a shockingly casual attitude to public executions and to street violence, life for the poor in Dublin in the late eighteenth century was nasty, brutish and short. Many accepted that they were likely to meet a violent end and retained, even in the presence of death, a sense of humour and a delight in the ridiculous. This is exemplified in a poem entitled 'A New Song call'd Luke Caffrey's Gost'; Luke's friends are waking his body after his execution when . . .

> On a sudden de wind shook de house,
> De devil was taught in a hurry,
> Dat struck us as mute as a mouse,
> I'd blew in a damnable flurry:
> But making a pitiful moan,
> We soon saw de poor Operation:
> De dust case he view'd wid a groan,
> To see himself in that condishain.

His eyes were swell'd in his brain-box, like two scalded goose-berries in a mutton tart; his face look'd for all de world like de rotten rump of a Thomas-street blue-arse, and his grinder rattled in his jaw wags, like a pair of white headed fortune tellers in an elbow-shaker's bone box.[43]

Another, equally energetic, song from the time gives an insight into bull-baiting, a common pastime in eighteenth-century Ireland. Bulls were often stolen from herds being driven into the city for slaughter, and were baited either in special bull-rings or in the streets. This particular poem, 'Lord Altham's Bull', dates from shortly after 1771 when the Brownes became earls of Altamont (i.e. Altham).

> 'Twas on the fust of sweet Magay,
> It being a high holiday,
> Six and twenty boys of de straw
> Went to take Lord Altham's bull away.

I being de fust in de field, who should I see bud de mosey wid his horns sticking in de ground. Well becomes me, I pinked up to him, ketched him by de tail, and rode him dree times round de field, as well as ever de master of de tailor's corporation rode de fringes; but de mosey being game to de back bone, de first rise he gev me in de elements, he made a smash of me collar-bone. So dere being no blunt in de cly, Madame Stevens was de word, where I lay for seven weeks in lavendar, on de broad of me back, like Paddy Ward's pig, be de hokey.[44]

It is interesting to have, in the 'patter' sequences in these poems, not only clear indications of spoken Hiberno-English of the late eighteenth century, but also an insight into the energetic and vigorous life of the city at the time. These urban poems are poems of anarchy – of language as well as of subject matter – which communicate not only infectious enthusiasm for life but also a love of vivid and colourful speech. In fact, the demotic verse of the cities and towns of eighteenth-century Ireland is as full of originality and of vital energy as that of the countryside.

Towards the next century

As the eighteenth century drew to a close, respectable verse became increasingly important in Irish middle-class life. Several anthologies of Irish verse were published in Dublin, the most comprehensive of which was Joshua Edkins's two-volume *Collection of Poems, mostly original, by several hands* (Dublin, 1789–90). The poets whose work was included – some of them making their only appearance here but others, such as Henry Grattan, Edmund Burke, Richard Brinsley Sheridan and Oliver Goldsmith, with established reputations as writers – were proud to be Irish or to be connected with Ireland; Edkins's anthology as a whole exudes a remarkable sense of cultural confidence, a reflection of the same confidence in things Irish which enabled Grattan to hail Ireland as an independent nation in his famous speech to the Irish House of Commons in 1782. For the subscribers to this important Irish publication – and they included nearly five hundred of Ireland's nobility and gentry, the sort of people who were, at about this time, having their portraits painted by Nathaniel Hone and Hugh Douglas Hamilton – Ireland was now a nation worthy to hold her head up among the nations of the earth, and one of the clear demonstrations of this was the proficiency of her poets. As Edkins wrote in his dedicatory letter to Lord Powerscourt: 'The Spirit of Poesy has, in all Countries, marked the progress of Civilization, and the Manners of the Age have taken their polish from the Genius of Song.' Ireland's genius lay, at least in part, in her poets.

More of the verse written by the Irish middle classes towards the end of the century is to be found in *The Shamrock or Hibernian Cresses, a collection of Poems, Songs, Epigrams &c., Latin as well as English, the Original Production of Ireland* . . . edited by the famous Dublin schoolmaster Samuel Whyte (Dublin, 1772). In this handsome quarto volume – the subscription list of which includes almost anyone of note in the middle or upper echelons of Irish society in the 1770s – Whyte included poems by many of the young gentlemen and ladies who had attended his school as well as some pieces from elsewhere. *The Shamrock* is an endearingly eccentric book in which odes and elegies rub shoulders with recipes for the improvement of kisses and epigrams with titles such as 'To a young Lady blowing a Turf-fire with her Petticoat'. Clearly Mr Whyte's pupils were encouraged to burst into verse at every opportunity.

In fact, the writing of poetry was remarkably widespread in late eighteenth-century Ireland. Many public figures, in addition to Grattan and Burke, published verse, among them Henry Flood (1732–91), Walter Hussey Burgh (1742–83), Theobald Wolfe Tone (1763–98) and Robert Emmet (1778–1803). Female poets whose work is still read include Mary Tighe (1772–1810), whose verse was much admired by John Keats, and Elizabeth Ryves (*c.*1750–97) whose 'Ode to Sensibility' was widely popular. An important patron of the arts in Dublin was Lady Elizabeth Hastings, dowager countess of Moira, best remembered today for her literary salons and for her patronage of the erratic but highly gifted poet, Thomas Dermody (1775–1802).[45] Dermody was a child prodigy who, by the age of ten, had learned not only Latin and Greek but also the pleasures of the bottle. As he put it in his 'Ode on Myself', his life was spent "twixt poetry and alehouse, / 'Twixt quill and can.' During his brief, passionate, self-destructive life, Dermody produced some wonderfully vivid poetry but alienated all his patrons, including the long-suffering Lady Moira, and died, in poverty, at the age of twenty-seven. Though Dermody wrote many kinds of verse and was particularly proficient at the sonnet, he was perhaps most effective as a satirist. His 'Farewell to Ireland', for instance, begins with these memorable lines:

> Rank nurse of nonsense; on whose thankless coast
> The base weed thrives, the nobler bloom is lost;
> Parent of pride and poverty, where dwell
> Dullness and brogue and calumny: – farewell!

The Ireland from which Dermody was escaping when he wrote these lines was by no means as dull as his jaundiced eye chose to see it. By any objective assessment, Dublin was a thriving centre of literary activity, well stocked with poets, printers, publishers and readers; had it not been for the political crises which rocked Ireland in the 1790s and their disastrous culmination in the Act of Union, Dublin would have remained secure in its place as the second most important centre of cultural life in the British Isles.

As the century drew to a close, however, political matters became increasingly important to poets and to their readers. The Volunteer movement of the late 1770s and 1780s spawned large amounts of anonymous, patriotic verse and the climate was also suitable for the forceful expression of divergent political opinions in verse. There are scores of partisan poems of various kinds from this period, as well as political satires from the pens of Henrietta Battier (fl.1790), Jane Elizabeth Moore (fl.1796) and Edward Lysaght (1763–1810). Even the young Thomas Moore (1779–1852) was caught up in the excitement of the United Irishmen movement through his friendship with Robert Emmet at Trinity College. Moore's youthful poetry was not political, though; he was more interested in writing polished songs and clever translations which appeared in Dublin early in the next century under his pseudonym, Thomas Little.

The most lasting poetic legacy of the final years of the eighteenth century is undoubtedly the large body of partisan songs which arose throughout Ireland as the complex and contradictory political tensions of the time gradually crystallised the people of Ireland into two main camps, those who supported the United Irishmen and the nationalists on the one side, and those who favoured the loyalists and the newly founded Orange Order on the other. In the early 1790s, many of the songs produced on either side were idealistic – reflecting on the glorious success of the revolutions against tyranny in America and in France on the one side, and on the need to safeguard freedom by maintaining passionate loyalty to king and country on the other. Freedom was the watchword of both sides but, as the political situation in Ireland as a whole became gradually more unstable, the songs – particularly on the nationalist side – made it clear that the only way to gain freedom was by force. As Georges-Denis Zimmermann put it: 'These songs call on the Irish to awake, unite, take arms and banish tyranny; the ever-recurring keywords are Liberty, Freedom, Unity.'[46] On the loyalist side, songs such as 'The Tree of Liberty' asserted that 'the Great Cause' which needed to be defended was 'Our blest Constitution, our King and our Laws'.

These songs, particularly the nationalist ones, were distributed not just by word of mouth and in broadsheets but also, for the first time, through the newspapers; the most famous collection of Irish political songs of the decade, *Paddy's Resource* – a collection which was published in New York and Philadelphia as well as in Dublin and Belfast – contained many songs which had first appeared in the pages of the radical Belfast paper *The Northern Star*. Though the songs in *Paddy's Resource* were inspired by general grievances and political aspirations, later nationalist songs were more specific and reported, in bloody detail, local skirmishes and treacheries that arose before and during the rising of 1798. Quite a number of these songs, 'The Croppy Boy', 'Dunlavin Green' and 'The Patriot Mother' for example, are still sung today: their stark narrative style, their use of vivid detail and, frequently, of direct speech not only make them highly effective at an emotional level but also make them easy to remember. The Orange songs are, on the whole, less dramatic, though some of them, too, recount tales of local skirmishes. Others repeat the view that loyalty to Ireland means loyalty to the crown:

> Sons of Hibernia, attend to my song,
> Of a tree call'd th'Orange, it's beauteous and strong;
> 'Twas planted by William, immortal is he!
> May all Orange brothers live loyal and free.
> *Derry down, down, traitors bow down.*

In the uncertain and violent years at the end of the century, most of this political verse, Orange as well as nationalist, appeared anonymously; but some famous supporters of the United Irishmen – including Revd James Porter, John Sheares and Theobald Wolfe Tone – were said to have been associated with the verse in *Paddy's Resource*. Other well-known political and legal figures put their name to their verse: Robert Emmet's 'Lines written on the Burying-Ground of Arbour Hill in Dublin where the Bodies of Insurgents shot in 1798 were interred' is one of the most powerful poems of the decade, and John Philpot Curran (1750–1817) published a fascinating poem in an Irish *amhrán* metre entitled 'The Deserter's Meditation'. A more obviously appealing poem is 'The Wake of William Orr', the work of the radical Belfast poet William Drennan (1754–1820). Orr had been executed in 1797 for nothing more serious than administering an illegal oath, and his death provoked a surge of outrage. Drennan's poem begins with the memorable and unambiguous line: 'Here our murdered brother lies' and contains this sadly accurate description of the political state of Ireland in the late 1790s:

> Hapless Nation, hapless Land,
> Heap of uncementing sand!
> Crumbled by a foreign weight,
> And by worse, domestic hate.

The horrific events of 1798 were to remain one of the principal sources of inspiration for Irish nationalist ballad-makers for generations to come and the evidence shows that, even as they were taking place, it was through verse and through song that these events were commemorated. On the other side of the divide, the Orange tradition may have produced fewer songs in the late eighteenth century and, indeed, the songs may pack less of a poetic punch; still, Orange songs of the 1790s, such as 'Croppies Lie Down' and 'The Tree of Liberty' seem to have circulated widely and, like nationalist songs, to have been an effective source of identification in a disintegrating world. In his *Memoirs of the Different Rebellions in Ireland* (London, 1802) Richard Musgrave tells a story of a woman in County Kildare who, in May 1798, urged the rebels to kill one of her neighbours: 'You should get rid of him, for his children sing "Croppies lie down".'[47] Late eighteenth-century Irish drawing-rooms may have echoed to the singing of genteel songs about the coming of spring, but the countryside echoed with songs which could bring with them the kiss of death.

In summary, it should be clear that the literary and cultural environment of eighteenth-century Ireland was kind to those who wrote verse and wanted to see it in print – as indeed it was to those who wrote songs and wanted to hear them sung. Dublin was second only to London in the English-speaking world as a centre for publishing and printing, and it also had an appreciative and active book-buying public throughout the century. But the Act of Union of 1801 changed this situation dramatically. Following the passing of that Act, Dublin sank almost overnight from being a capital city to being no more than a provincial backwater within the British empire. All its civil servants and politicians left for London as did many of its writers and, perhaps more significantly, many of its book-buying citizens. New copyright laws were enacted, the economic structure of the book-trade was entirely changed, and the vibrant literary scene which had existed throughout most of the eighteenth century disappeared. Education in English became increasingly available throughout the whole island of Ireland and the permissive rural culture which had enjoyed the lively verse of the chapbooks and broadsheets came under the puritanical influence of Catholic curates from the newly founded seminary at Maynooth. The oral culture which had produced songs of such vibrancy and vigour was changing too as the prudery of the nineteenth century began to affect even what was sung in the streets. The world which had produced and supported the poetry, the verse and the song surveyed in this chapter disappeared for ever.

Notes

1. For an account of the recent discovery of the unique surviving copy of this printing of Swift's first poem see James Woolley, 'Swift's First Published Poem: *Ode. To the King*' in Hermann J. Real and Helgard Stöver-Leidig, eds. *Reading Swift: Papers from The Fourth Münster Symposium on Jonathan Swift* (Munich: Wilhelm Fink, 2003), pp. 265–84. The text of the poem is reproduced in the article.

2. D. F. Foxon, *English Verse 1701–1750: A Catalogue of Separately Printed Poems with Notes on Contemporary Collected Editions*, 2 vols. (Cambridge: Cambridge University Press, 1975), II, pp. 194–200.

3. The texts considered in this paragraph may be found in Andrew Carpenter, ed. *Verse in English from Tudor and Stuart Ireland* (Cork: Cork University Press, 2003).

4. Giles Jacob, *The Poetical Register* (London, 1719–20).

5. John Hopkins, *The Fall of Man* (London, 1699).

6. The texts considered in the rest of this chapter may be found in Andrew Carpenter, ed. *Verse in English from Eighteenth-Century Ireland* (Cork: Cork University Press, 1998).

7. Concanen's anthology *Miscellaneous Poems* (London, 1724) is the second known anthology of Irish verse in English and includes poems by (among others) Patrick Delany, Swift, Jonathan Smedley, Thomas Sheridan, James Sterling, Thomas Parnell and James Ward.

8. Swift to Revd Henry Jenner, 8 June 1732, in *The Correspondence of Jonathan Swift*, ed. Harold Williams, 5 vols. (Oxford: Clarendon Press, 1963–5), IV, p. 27.

9. See A. C. Elias Jr., '*Senatus Consultum*: Revising Verse in Swift's Dublin Circle, 1729–35', in Hermann J. Real and Helgard Stöver-Leidig, eds. *Reading Swift: Papers from The Third Münster Symposium on Jonathan Swift* (Munich: Wilhelm Fink, 1998), pp. 249–68.

10. See Andrew Carpenter and Alan Harrison, 'Swift's "O'Rourke's Feast" and Sheridan's "Letter": Early Transcripts by Anthony Raymond', in Hermann J. Real and Heinz J. Vienken, eds. *Proceedings of the First Münster Symposium on Jonathan Swift* (Munich: Wilhelm Fink, 1985), pp. 27–46.

11. These lines are untitled in Constantia Grierson's commonplace book, but it is possible they were also addressed to Miss Kelly.

12. Satchel or bag – but also, a few lines later, with the modern meaning of money available for spending.

13. Throws or casts (as if sowing corn).

14. The Devil's Black Hall, contrasted with Whitehall, the centre of English government.

15. Luke 18:30 refers to a madman called Legion 'because many devils were entered into him'.

16. Madmen.

17. *The Correspondence of Jonathan Swift*, v, p. 86.

18. The muse of astronomy.

19. I.e. the queen bee.

20. *The Collected Letters of Oliver Goldsmith*, ed. Katharine Balderston (Cambridge: Cambridge University Press, 1928), p. x.

21. The title comes from the Greek 'graphein' (to write), 'hesperos' (western) and 'nesos' (an island).

22. See M. Pollard, *Dublin's Trade in Books 1550–1800* (Oxford: Clarendon Press, 1989), pp. 165–226, and Richard Cargill Cole, *Irish Booksellers and English Writers 1740–1800* (Atlantic Highlands, NJ: Humanities Press, 1986), pp. 23–39.

23. Only a selection of the female poets active in eighteenth-century Ireland is mentioned in this section; others of interest are included in Carpenter, *Verse in English from Eighteenth-Century Ireland* and in Siobhán Kilfeather ed., 'The Profession of Letters 1700–1810', in A. Bourke et al., eds. *The Field Day Anthology of Irish Writing, vols. IV and V: Irish Women's Writing and Traditions* (Cork: Cork University Press, 2002), v, pp. 772–832.

24. Dishcloth.

25. John Hewitt, *Rhyming Weavers* (Belfast: Blackstaff, 1974), p. 62.

26. Trouble.

27. I.e. Hymen, the classical god of marriage.

28. I.e. 'heal', a Hiberno-English pronunciation.

29. 'Pattern' or 'patron' days were the festivals of the patron saints of particular churches, noted for revelry after the religious observances.

30. Cf. L. M. Cullen, 'Patrons, Teachers and Literacy in Irish: 1700–1850', in Mary Daly and David Dickson, eds. *The Origins of Popular Literacy in Ireland: Language Change and Educational Development 1700–1920* (Dublin: Trinity College and University College, 1990), pp. 15–44, p. 38.

31. Ir. *A chuisle is a stór*, oh my pulse and my treasure. A common endearment in Irish.

32. A strongly garlic-flavoured gum used in medicine and in cooking.

33. Flora, queen of flowers, and Aurora, the dawn, often appear together in popular verse in the late eighteenth century, linked by their assonance and rhyme. In the next line, 'Eutarnatia' is probably a mistake for Euterpe, the muse who presided over music; Venus was the goddess of love.

34. For an account of the hedge-schools, see P. W. Joyce, *English as We Speak it in Ireland*, ed. T. P. Dolan (Dublin: Wolfhound Press, 1979), pp. 149–63.

35. Dáithí Ó hÓgáin, 'Folklore and Literature: 1700–1850', in Daly and Dickson, *Popular Literacy in Ireland*, pp. 1–13, p. 7.

36. See Diarmaid Ó Muirithe, *An tAmhrán Macarónach* (Dublin: An Clóchomhar, 1980). But see also the story told about Donncha Rua Mac Conmara's Gaelic and English distychs in Joep Leerssen, *Mere Irish and Fíor-Ghael: Studies in the Idea of Irish Nationality, its Development and Literary Expression prior to the Nineteenth Century*, 2nd edn (Cork: Cork University Press, 1996), p. 242.

37. 'Stauka an Varaga' means the market post or stake. This poem, and others like it, were common throughout the midlands at the time: for instance, 'The Answer to Stauka an Varaga' was printed in Monaghan about two years later. See Carpenter, *Verse in English from Eighteenth-Century Ireland*, pp. 420–4, 610.

38. Farahy and Kildorrery are communities in north County Cork, near the Limerick border.

39. An exclamation like 'Oho!'

40. Near Kilfinane, County Limerick.

41. A Palatine. Several hundred German Protestant families from the Palatine settled in County Limerick in the early eighteenth century.

42. Though it is impossible to reconstruct the full Irish text of this second stanza, a rough paraphrase might be: 'My road shall be through the plain of Ireland from the foot of Carrig [possibly a local name for a peak in the Galtee or Knockmealdown Mountains] to that street of Cashel. Yoho! . . . The people of that journey . . . She was better than I saw all over Ireland and across the sea; Yoho! and if I were to say more! There's a mass to be got there every day from a priest; it's the best market ever . . . A stately woman [or 'a street woman'], her skin chalk-white, and she on the bed having good desire, and me to be beside her; Yoho! that was the story!'

43. A rough paraphrase of this stanza might be: 'Suddenly, the wind shook the house – we thought the devil must have been in a hurry! That struck us mute as a mouse, and I was pretty frightened immediately. But we soon saw the poor apparition, moaning pitifully; he looked into the coffin with a groan to see himself in that condition. His eyes were all swollen in his head, like two scalded gooseberries in a mutton tart; his face looked, for all the world, like the rotten backside of a blue-bottle fly from Thomas Street [famous for butchers' stalls], and his teeth rattled in his jaws like a pair of little white dice when shaken by a gambler in a dice-box.'

44. A rough paraphrase of this stanza might be: 'It was on the first day of the sweet month of May, a high holiday, that twenty-six straw-boys went to take Lord Altham's bull away. I was first into the field, and who should I see but the bull with its horns sticking in the ground. As befits me, I crept up to him, caught him by the tail and rode him three times round the field, as well as ever the master of the tailor's corporation rode the franchises. But the bull was full of life, and the first time he tossed me up in the air, I smashed my collar-bone. Since I had no money in my pockets, I had to go to Mrs Stevens's hospital where I lay for seven weeks in luxury, flat on my back like Paddy Ward's pig, by heaven!' [Some explanatory notes: 'boys of de straw' = boys employed in the Dublin straw-market at Smithfield; 'Lord Altham' = Lord Altamont; 'mosey' = a common name for a bull; 'de master of de tailor's corporation rode de fringes' refers to the triennial beating of the bounds of the liberties of the city by members of the Dublin guilds; 'Madame Stevens was de word' refers to Dr Steevens' Hospital, endowed by Dr Richard Steevens (1653–1710) and built by his sister, Grizell (the 'Madam Stevens' of the text).]

45. James Grant Redmond, *The Life of Thomas Dermody*, 2 vols. (London, 1806), I, pp. 112–30.

46. Georges-Denis Zimmermann, *Songs of Irish Rebellion: Political Street Ballads and Rebel Songs 1780–1900* (Dublin: Allen Figgis, 1967), p. 38.

47. Richard Musgrave, *Memoirs of the Different Rebellions in Ireland*, 2 vols. (London, 1802), I, p. 314. Quoted in Zimmermann, *Songs of Irish Rebellion*, p. 310.

Select bibliography

Brooke, Charlotte, ed. *Reliques of Irish Poetry*, Dublin, 1789.

Carpenter, Andrew, ed. *Verse in English from Eighteenth-Century Ireland*, Cork: Cork University Press, 1998.

ed. *Verse in English from Tudor and Stuart Ireland*, Cork: Cork University Press, 2003.

Cole, Richard Cargill, *Irish Booksellers and English Writers 1740–1800*, Atlantic Highlands, NJ: Humanities Press, 1986.

Concanen, Matthew, ed. *Miscellaneous Poems*, London, 1724.

Edkins, Joshua, ed. *A Collection of Poems, mostly original, by several hands*, 2 vols. Dublin, 1789–90.

Elias, A. C. Jr., ed. *Memoirs of Laetitia Pilkington*, 2 vols. Athens, GA: University of Georgia Press, 1997.

Hogan, Robert, ed. *The Poems of Thomas Sheridan*, London and Newark, NJ: Associated University Presses and University of Delaware Press, 1994.

Lonsdale, Roger, ed. *Eighteenth-Century Women Poets*, Oxford: Oxford University Press, 1989.

ed. *The New Oxford Book of Eighteenth-Century Verse*, Oxford: Oxford University Press, 1984.

A New Miscellany of Poems and Translations, Dublin, 1716.

Paddy's Resource, Belfast, 1795.

Pollard, M., *Dublin's Trade in Books 1550–1800*, Oxford: Clarendon Press, 1989.

Rawson, Claude and F. P. Lock, eds. *Collected Poems of Thomas Parnell*, London and Newark, NJ: Associated University Presses and University of Delaware Press, 1989.

Whyte, Samuel, ed. *Poems on Various Subjects*, Dublin, 1795.

ed. *The Shamrock or Hibernian Cresses, a collection of Poems, Songs, Epigrams &c., Latin as well as English, the Original Production of Ireland*, Dublin, 1772.

Williams, Harold, ed. *The Poems of Jonathan Swift*, 3 vols. 2nd edn, Oxford: Clarendon Press, 1958.

Zimmermann, Georges-Denis, *Songs of Irish Rebellion: Political Street Ballads and Rebel Songs 1780–1900*, Dublin: Allen Figgis, 1967.

8

Literature in Irish, 1690–1800: from the Williamite wars to the Act of Union

NEIL BUTTIMER

Practical as well as conceptual difficulties lie in the way of describing this phase of writing in the Irish language.[1] More manuscript sources survive for the eighteenth and nineteenth centuries together than for any other stage in the Gaelic past. While influenced by print and showing traces of interaction with the oral world, barriers to publishing, accompanied, paradoxically, by the spread of literacy, ensured that the handwritten documentary tradition inherited from medieval times remained the main means of transmission for all forms of creative composition. Most of these original codices have yet to be described (properly or even at all), with their full complement of texts professionally extracted from them. Work in this regard has been under way, particularly from the beginning of the 1900s, approximately, but it too poses its own problems. Early twentieth-century scholarship is characterised by the shortcomings of a newly developing domain: incompleteness of coverage, the tentative nature of either text or translation, and the restricted context in which the material is discussed. Because these editions are often still the only immediate point of contact with the evidence, the present chapter will have to rely on them frequently (and does not underestimate their consider-able strengths), without the opportunity to comment in full on any identifi-able deficiencies. A brocade of previously unpublished original material must therefore be introduced from time to time to augment the account where necessary.[2]

The practice also arose at the start of the twentieth century of employing the Irish language itself in major scholarly writing on post-classical topics. This may have been a result of the involvement in the Gaelic revival movement of many researchers active in the field. They would have intended almost certainly to place their findings at the disposal of this most recent renaissance.[3] The custom of employing Irish in such a fashion endures to the present. While its use for the purpose in question is no more blameworthy than discoursing in modern Greek on the literary inheritance of that country, the inescapable consequence is that those who are unacquainted with the contemporary language are faced with the challenge of accessing an unknown subject via an unfamiliar medium. Deploying the panoply of scholarship in Irish such as is carried out here is not done to cause further hindrance but to reflect the state of play as one finds it.

A third obstacle is arguably of greatest import. This is how later stages of Gaelic are viewed within the totality of Irish studies itself. The medieval period has attracted most enquiry in Irish, a pattern discernible from the nineteenth century onwards and consistently involving substantial cohorts of international scholars as well as those based in Ireland. They may have been drawn towards it on account of its earliness, its richness or what could be seen, *a priori* at any rate, as its relatively integral or unimpaired nature. The time horizon under review here could seem less appealing as a result of the onset of contraction and decline. It might also have been felt that, in light of its lateness, fewer research skills (linguistic, comparative or codicological) are required in describing it. Historians or others concerned with the age may have stayed away in the belief that, because power would no longer reside with Irish speakers in society, limitations consequent on their social standing almost axiomatically assign their world-view itself a secondary status.[4] This chapter does not question the incontrovertible reality that the re-establishment of English authority in Ireland in and from the 1690s had negative implications for the Gaelic-speaking community. There would be no apparent reversal of those downward tendencies following upheavals in overseas and domestic affairs from the 1780s onwards, despite whatever hopes to the contrary might have been entertained at the time. It is such circumstances precisely which shape the writings we shall be considering and give them their distinctive quality. One finds in them the testimony of people coming to terms with major adversity while also getting on with existence as they found it. Doing so involved no less complicated a reaction than coping with such instances of success or self-governance as may have been at issue on other occasions.

Verse

Various aspects of Irish literary composition, in earlier times or during the period discussed here, would have been intended for presentation or have had a performance element, as we shall see again later. Some Gaelic speakers were themselves actors, while certain scribes record their attendance at the theatre or similar spectacles. However, the writing of plays, together with an accompanying stagecraft, familiar in England or on the European mainland, is to all intents and purposes unattested in Irish-language records until revival interests supported the creation and realisation of dramatic works from the late 1800s onwards. Therefore, poetry and prose remain the two dominant media in which the literature of the age is found. The quantity, complexity and diversity (in social, geographic and other terms) of the former of these require that our discussion treat verse initially and also at greatest length.

The contents of the poetic material will be examined to begin with, so that the impression gained of what the items are about may facilitate investigation of how they were put together. Three broad categories of subject matter may be identified. Works which record incidents in this transitional phase of Irish life, as well as their impact at a human level on those who witnessed them, are looked at first and most extensively, because of their distinctive character and their prominence within the tradition. A second and closely related assemblage, namely texts giving their composers' thoughts on the political setting in which such events took place, or their reflections about what an alternative polity could look like, are then briefly examined. The third sub-set comprises items focusing on the everyday activities of those who completed them, again touched on in summary form mainly. Public affairs could shape these, but such considerations are more likely to be in the background, if present at all. The compartmentalisation is offered as a guide only and ought not to be viewed as watertight. A particular author or a single piece may be entered in one or more of the different groupings as circumstances dictate.

Thematics I: Events

A range of Gaelic texts dating from just before the beginning of the 1700s and extending throughout the eighteenth century shows ongoing clashes between various forms of state interest (strategic, ecclesiastical, commercial and legal) and undertakings in which Irish speakers were involved. While each episode is unique in its own right, all seem to have taken place against a backdrop of international occurrences which, to a greater or lesser extent, may be shown to have influenced how they evolved. Even in the Gaelic world itself, there would appear to be no absolute uniformity in attitude towards the merits of its representatives' participation in the incidents in question, nor agreed opinion about them as individuals. Nevertheless, a cluster of generically divergent poems shares the same dominant notes of dismay and disarray at the happenings with which they are concerned.

Works by the poet Dáibhidh Ó Bruadair (1625–98)[5] reveal a keen awareness of current affairs in the 1680s and later. Possibly a native of east Cork, this writer had the benefit of a good early education and enjoyed contact with local notables. He relocated to Limerick in the 1660s where he composed poetry for members of traditional learned families and the offspring of the aristocracy, comprising laments, marriage celebrations and the like. He experienced a significant reversal in his own personal fortunes in the mid-1670s, possibly arising from fractious relations with patrons. The following decade saw Ireland become the venue for strife centring on control of Britain and Ireland and involving continental European protagonists as well as contestants from both islands. Ó Bruadair's verse chronicles these developments after the largely pro-Catholic James II (1633–1701) was deposed as king of England in 1688: the attempted suppression of Irish Protestant settlers loyal to the new, Dutch-born ruler, William III (1650–1702); efforts to raise military forces in Ireland in favour of the dethroned leader; the success of Patrick Sarsfield (c.1655–93) in early August 1690 against a Williamite army which had sought to prevent Ireland becoming an anti-English and pro-French dependency, together with other moments in the affray.

The war effectively came to an end with the surrender of the Irish in October 1691, when their army was allowed safe passage to France under the terms of the Treaty of Limerick. Ó Bruadair appears subsequently to have composed *Le ciontaibh na healta ag ar dalladh a gcluastuigse* (For the Sins of that People whose Earsense was Rendered Dull)[6] which takes a retrospective look at the course and outcome of the conflict. The struggle did not have a positive ending from the composer's point of view, but left the country desolate and directionless, with certain sections of the population having experienced particular suffering during the fighting:

> D'imircibh leanbh is mbanaltran mbuaidheartha
> ó Shionainn go Leamhain fá ainimh ag ualfartaigh
> gan siolla ar bith eatartha is rabharta an ruadhchoilg
> acht inneamh an fheartaigh is faire na n-uasal sin.
> (stanza 8)

> (Children and women migrating in fear and dread
> From Shannon to Leamhain, bemoaning their misery,
> Having nought betwixt them and the rush of the mighty sword
> But the Mighty One's strength and those noblemen's vigilance.)

Much of the difficulty arose from the failure of certain Irish to assist their fellow countrymen:

Innmhe ag Gallaibh ní machtnamh dom thuairimsi
is cunnail a gcaingean sa gcaradas buan gan scur
ní hionann is clanna na n-ainnear ór ghluaiseasa
do rithfeadh a gceangal go rantaibh le ruainne fuilt.

(st. 2)

(The success of the Galls is no wonder at all to me;
Discreet is their compact, unbroken their friendship lasts,
Not like the sons of the women from whom I spring,
Whose bonds would, if pulled by a hair, be dissolved in bits.)

The work deplores the renegades' activities: taking advantage of troubled conditions to plunder goods, remove stock from farmyards, rob the defenceless elderly, behave as badly as 'British roughs' ('gairbh na Breatan', st. 18), and abscond with herds and crops. Failure to support the efforts of a monarch who had expended energy and income on their behalf when seeking to establish justice in the land revealed their myopic selfishness.

The text's evocation of a pastoral way of life, however disturbed, coupled with the emphasis in the writer's earlier works on landscape, settlement and gentry households, is so prominent that the poem's core image comes as a surprise. The piece came to be known as 'An Longbhriseadh' (The Shipwreck). The maritime references implicit or incorporated in it nonetheless show it as a product of its time. Unprecedented numbers of the soldiery of many nationalities had just been ferried into Ireland, with James II himself, here spoken of as a 'skipper' ('luamaire', st. 25), docking at Kinsale. When his ventures and those of his adherents were unsuccessful, the bulk of the Irish military departed from ports and estuaries in Ó Bruadair's immediate hinterland. Apparently alluding to their transportation in 'cheerless ships' ('i bhfuarlongaibh', st. 34), this composer does not condemn any, particularly youths who had fought the good fight, wishing to embark. Even if matters may have been felt more acutely at home, the exiles shared a common experience with those left behind. For all, their universe had come apart and was foundering, with Ó Bruadair's own spirits shaken 'mightily' ('chrithnigh mo mheanma', st. 39). His poem and its heading therefore express in an archetypal manner a major overturning of indigenous Irish culture. The turbulence to which they allude was the ultimate consequence of actions set in train from the early sixteenth century onwards, as Ireland was enmeshed in inter-state competition for control of the Atlantic seaboard and of territories on both sides. The country's destiny, such as this writer envisioned it, indicates that civilisations in the Old World could fall victim to Europe's expansionism and internecine strife as readily as their counterparts in the New.

Aogán Ó Rathaille (*c.*1670–1729),[7] a younger contemporary of Ó Bruadair's, presented events at the turn of the 1700s in a shorter but similarly emblematic utterance. From the Sliabh Luachra district east of Killarney, County Kerry, he would seem to have been raised in good circumstances and may have enjoyed the support of prominent settler and local landholders like the Brownes and the McCarthys.[8] The decline in their status resulting from the Williamite wars foreshadowed his own. Denied leaseholds in his home area, he was obliged to migrate to poorer parts of the Dingle peninsula or seek sustenance from more prosperous supporters in travels throughout west and south Munster. A hospitable welcome might be found even in the most unexpected quarters, but the poet's personal distress and upset at the reduction of families who had previously shown him favour are his verses' dominant notes.

Ó Rathaille would have considered his, or possibly his patrons', fortunes to be closely intermingled with that of Ireland itself, whom he represents allegorically in one concise, nine-stanza poem as a forlorn female figure.[9] This and others of his pieces established the *aisling* or 'vision' poem as one of the most popular forms in eighteenth-century Irish composition. After a brief conversation with her, the composer speaks of this character being snatched away and incarcerated in a desolate dungeon-like structure, one created through 'wizard sorcery' ('draoidheacht dhruadha', line 20). Ó Rathaille was also borne off to the same venue. The work then outlines the hostility which awaited them both:

> Brisid fá scige go scigeamhail buidhean ghruagach
> Is fuireann do bhruinnealaibh sioscaithe dlaoi-chuachach;
> I ngeimhealaibh geimheal me cuirid gan puinn suaimhnis;
> 'S mo bhruinneal ar bruinnibh ag bruinnire bruinn-stuacach.
> (ll. 21–4)

> (They burst into laughter, mockingly – a troop of wizards
> And a band of maidens, trim, with plaited locks;
> In the bondage of fetters they put me without much respite,
> While to my maiden clung a clumsy, lubberly clown.)

Aogán urged the young girl not to become united to this 'awkward, sorry churl' ('slibire slím-bhuaidheartha', l. 26), but to no avail. While he was released, the maiden remained 'Held by a horned, malicious, croaking, yellow clown, with a black troop!' ('Ag adharcach fuireann-dubh mioscaiseach cóirneach buidhe', l. 35). The concluding colour coding thus confirms the key contrast at issue. The maiden is introduced in the work's first line and subsequent title as 'Brightness of Brightness' ('Gile na Gile') personified, with the text going on to place her at the heart of darkness. The poem reads accordingly like a statement of detention, powerlessness and defilement. The fact that it became the most frequently copied of its author's compositions[10] could indicate the extent of the response to its symbolism as much as to its inherent expressiveness.

The aforementioned text may have a fantasy or dreamlike aspect, but it also appears to reflect one commonly occurring underlying phenomenon. Incarceration of the Irish throughout Britain or Ireland had become particularly prevalent from Tudor times onwards, a fact confirmed by the abundance of associated Gaelic records, from poetry to graffiti.[11] A set of compositions linked with the writer Seán Ó Neachtain (c.1640–1729) exhibits the ongoing reality of imprisonment during the lifetime of this approximate coeval of Ó Rathaille's. Confiscation in Cromwellian times deprived the Ó Neachtain family of hereditary historians of their landholdings in County Roscommon. Seán worked as an itinerant labourer in County Meath and subsequently took up residence near central Dublin. His son, Tadhg (c.1671–c. 1749), and certain of his grandchildren continued to cultivate Irish letters as part of a circle of scribes and scholars active in the metropolis and elsewhere down to and beyond mid-century.[12]

Three compositions directed to members of this *cénacle* or their associates detained in Dublin's well-known Black Dog Prison have come down to us.[13] This facility, formerly an inn bearing this name and located in the south-west quarter of the city, functioned until the late 1790s as the marshalsea of the sheriff of Dublin, holding both debtors and dissenters. Two items are attributed to Seán Ó Neachtain. He wrote the first (*A shearc is 'annsacht gach saoi*) to one Pól Mac Aodhagáin as well as five other companions, and it elicited a reply from Pól (*An moladh uait do fhuaras*). The second (*Tabhair mo bheannacht, a pháipéir*) may also have been directed to the same group of individuals. While both are in Irish, in the latter Seán speaks of sending a 'blessing' to one acquaintance who did not know the mother tongue ('teanga dhílis mo mháthar', quatrain 3), while also conveying his greetings to the others. In his first address to Mac Aodhagáin, Seán professes himself to be 'moist-eyed' ('súil-fhliuch', *A shearc is 'annsacht*, q. 1), shedding tears like salt water (*Tabhair mo bheannacht*, 'deora mar sáile', q. 4) at the plight of his friend, whose capture is manifestly unfair ('i mbruid le éageart shoiléir', q. 4). He is stated to be kept in a narrow space, without any attention being paid to him ('[i] gcarcar chael, gan aird, gan chaoi', st. 11), in an institution which the second item, gaelicising its sobriquet, claims to be distressful and large (*Tabhair mo bheannacht*, 'san Mhada mhéalach mhór', st. 13).

Apart from this, the poems contain no direct evidence of the conditions under which the individuals were held. However, concluding wishes in Ó

Neachtain's second composition that their captors might in turn experience beating, striking, weakening and bloodshed ('Bualadh, basgadh, lagar léir, is cró', st. 13), or the appeal in Mac Aodhagáin's response that they should come to know want, confinement, crying and weeping (*An moladh uait*, 'Easbuidh . . . amhgar, gáradh is guil', st. 4), could hint at what they themselves had encountered. All the detainees in question were ecclesiastics, Franciscans mainly, members of the religious order which enjoyed the greatest popularity of all in Ireland from the later Middle Ages onwards. They would have been incarcerated under various forms of anti-popery legislation dating from the late 1690s, affecting the promotion of Catholicism and the standing of its personnel, the code to which the term 'Penal Laws' is now applied.[14] Seán's son, Tadhg, himself also a Dublin city resident and schoolteacher, continued for many years afterwards to monitor (mainly from newspapers)[15] accusations against the Catholic clergy and community, as a record of mid-1726 indicates.[16] This note speaks of rumours that a sermon preached in the capital by a Gaelic churchman ('aon da neagluisibh') encouraged Irish speakers to engage in murder and mayhem, leading to Protestants in turn cleaning and readying their firearms, with Ó Neachtain arguing that the Gaelic Irish had in fact long since been deprived of any significant offensive weaponry. Material like this illuminates how the image of closeness between a people and its besieged priesthood could have come to form part of popular consciousness and official church remembrance alike in later generations.

Mid-century experiences

It might have been felt that the consolidation of ascendancy control as the 1700s progressed would have resulted in a diminution in a sense of beleaguerment in contemporary Irish-language versification. Occurrences during the latter part of the century meant that the topic remained live throughout the period, however. This may be seen in the case of Muircheartach Óg Ó Súilleabháin (c.1710–54).[17] A native of the Beara peninsula (a district shared between the counties of Cork and Kerry) who may have been educated in Spain, he served in the Austrian military and was on the victorious side against the English in the Battle of Fontenoy in 1745. Following his return to his home area, he was later engaged in coastal trading, smuggling and the press-ganging of local youths for service in the Wild Geese regiments of continental European armies. In March 1754, he and some companions assassinated John Puxley, a tax official who had sought to curtail dealing in contraband throughout the region, even though his family had been involved in it previously. Government forces pursued and shot Muircheartach Óg dead in May, and arrested two of his collaborators.

Ó Súilleabháin's body was attached to the back of a boat and drawn into Cork harbour from Berehaven, a detail still related in oral tradition upwards of two hundred years later. His colleagues were hanged in late August, all three being decapitated and their heads placed on spikes in Cork Gaol near the city's South Gate Bridge.

His extortionary conduct towards certain persons in his own hinterland (also recalled in subsequent centuries)[18] meant that the Beara man's demise was not unequivocally mourned. However, three extant texts give an alternative impression of the event's impact on close associates.[19] One poem (*Is doilg liom saoithe de phrímhshliocht Gaeil Ghlais*) is by an unnamed author who, it is felt, may have wished to remain anonymous lest the vehemence of his support for Muircheartach Óg's anti-establishment outlook also incriminate him. His work speaks of the composer's dismay at Ó Súilleabháin's departure (ll. 1–29), points to the natural environment being fruitless following his death (ll. 45–52), outlines the deceased's aristocratic lineage (ll. 77–100) and the resultant negative impact of his removal on the poor, the church and men of art like himself (ll. 117–24). The poet's learned background may be seen in the listing of classical mythological figures who had bestowed their gifts of strength, intelligence and resourcefulness on his honorand (ll. 29–44), as well as in allusion to the privileges he previously enjoyed in the patron's entourage but would probably no longer do so now that the latter was gone.

The second poem (*Osna go cruaidh le guais na scéal so ag rith*) is ascribed to one Muirn Ní Shúilleabháin, who apparently acted as Muircheartach Óg's foster-mother in his youth. It is less amenable to analysis in thematic blocks than the first item, but shares the same concerns. The work contains an equivalent mention of its composer's personal upset, talks about the elegance of her charge's appearance, snowy skin and bright eyes, together with the sadness of the learned at his demise, stating his region had lost a decisive protector. It points to the close association of women with the tradition of lament, further instances of which will be reviewed in due course in this section. The third piece (*Mo chreach agus mo chás bhocht mar thána' ar an saol so*) differs substantially from the previous pair. It is not principally a eulogy of Ó Súilleabháin as such, but focuses on his attendant, Domhnall Ó Conaill, one of the two aforementioned followers killed in Cork. This poem (also by an unknown author) recreates, *post mortem*, Ó Conaill's sentiments such as they may have been envisioned in the days leading up to his execution. The latter reminisces affectionately on his slain leader, stating where he travelled and worked with Muircheartach Óg and how, had he lived, Ó Súilleabháin would have sympathised with him in his current plight. What the thoughts of Ó Conaill's own people might be like as his destiny was about to unfold are also broached.

Information in all of the poems supplements evidence available elsewhere for the same affair. *Is doilg liom* indicates that Ó Súilleabháin did not take flight after killing Puxley to seek assistance in his own difficulty, and curses the named individual who arranged for Muircheartach Óg's shooting. *Osna go cruaidh* speaks of the latter being wounded and burned, when those who besieged his house set fire to the building to cause its defenders to flee. The presence of these otherwise corroborated details may lend a greater degree of credibility to additional elements, such as their representation of the punishment and detention in question. The third text especially attempts to reconstruct what befell Domhnall Ó Conaill during his last days, as when he addressed his former employer, Ó Súilleabháin, thus:

> A mháistir na n-áran ba thruagh leatsa mise,
> Le slabhraí ar mo lámha 'gam is glas trom ar mo cuislinn;
> Madraí na sráide, im cháibleadh air fuaid ghutaigh,
> A' ciorrbhadh air gach spearra dhíom, 'gus a' búirtheach le mustar.
>
> (st. 7)

(Beloved master, you would have pitied me, with chains on my hands and a heavy lock on my wrist; the dogs of the street drawing me by a cable throughout the mire, mutilating me on each spike and baying with arrogance.)

He imagines the rope being placed around his neck and the crowd's deafening noise at the scaffold ('Beid na sealáin 'nár bhfásgadh, agus na táinte 'nár mbodhradh', st. 2). Of particular concern is the fact that, for him, no consoling lament ('caoineadh', st. 10) would be heard or wake ('tórramh', st. 12) conducted in the traditional style by his relatives or clergy. He was to have been prayed for by a minister representing another religion, dressed in unfamiliar attire, a person he would wish to challenge rather than greet. Ó Conaill talks of his own head and those of his colleagues being put on show and exposed to snow and other inclement elements ('Tré shneachta na hoíche agus gach síne eile (d)á ngeobhaidh leis', st. 9). Ó Súilleabháin's foster-mother was also distressed at the lack of customary obsequies in remembrance of him (*Osna go cruaidh*, st. 4), as well as at the ostentatious display of his headless remains for the delectation of Cork city's bursars ('lucht sparán i gCorcaigh', st. 7). Those characteristics in turn both complement and augment similar features in other poems considered here.

The following decade again witnessed confrontation with the authorities which elicited corresponding reactions in the Gaelic world. A County Tipperary priest, Fr Nicholas Sheehy (1728/9–66), had been active in campaigns against the payment of tithes and other grievances organised by secretive, mainly rural-based protest groups like the Whiteboys.[20] These entities were suppressed for seditious conduct, and persons thought to be linked with them or sympathetic to their aims brought before the courts. Sheehy was indicted for high treason, with his first arraignment taking place in Dublin, where he was acquitted. A second trial, held in Clonmel, in the county at the epicentre of Whiteboy unrest and where feelings ran high, resulted in conviction and his subsequent hanging, drawing and quartering. The cleric's decapitated head remained by the town's prison gate for a number of decades afterwards.

Reaction to his career is expressed in a set of compositions of which three in particular may again be summarily reviewed. Parallels between them as a grouping and those connected with Muircheartach Óg Ó Súilleabháin show the breadth of the elegiac base underpinning the act of mourning in the tradition. The first text (commencing *Ag taisteal liom fá smúit im aonar*)[21] is once more somewhat learned in nature, even though completed by a composer, Seán Cúndún, from nearby Kildorrery in north Cork, who was, as his concluding colophon admits, a youthful, apprentice artist ('duine óg san ealaíon'). Its literary character may be seen in the topos of the poet walking out one day and meeting a beautiful, Venus-like figure who subsequently identifies herself as Ireland (stt. 1–16). The death of Nicholas Sheehy, scion of the nobility, is the source of her grief (stt. 19–24). She indicates this paragon of priestly virtue, piety, learning and preaching (stt. 25–35) was lamented by his church, his people and even such deities (male and female) of the local landscape as Donn Fírinne or Aoibheall (stt. 35–41). Cúndún's interlocutor claims it would have been better to foresake the country than witness the clergyman's demise or to be reduced to the despair and desolation which continue to weigh her down. The piece ends with prayers for the acceptance into paradise of Sheehy's soul (stt. 65–8), together with a précis of his qualities of a kind which might constitute a suitable verse epitaph for his gravestone ('Feartlaoi', stt. [69]–[70]).

The second item (*A Athair Nioclás, mo chás id luí thú*) is also a lament attributed to a female associate, in this instance the priest's sister, Cáit de Búrca, recorded from oral narration in the twentieth century.[22] Among other issues, she dwells on her sibling's widespread repute, his melodious voice and bravery in facing the charges levelled against him when he might have chosen to abscond. De Búrca speaks of the calibre of Sheehy's forebears and the welcome awaiting him among his own in the resting-place of his paternal and maternal antecedents. The third poem (*Is gearr do bhí mé ar leabaidh im luí nuair ghlaoigh amuigh*)[23] recalls the Muircheartach Óg Ó Súilleabháin assemblage, even if only indirectly. Its manuscript rubric speaks of the priest's 'Awakening' ('Múscladh'), when an unidentified ally who arrived at the cleric's house at night asked him to arise and inspect his amassed followers. The composition shows Sheehy mounting his black steed and reviewing a troop of two thousand orderly, armed agents. Having been emboldened by the turn of international events, these were ready to reaffirm their ancestral entitlements under the direction of their foremost huntsman ('máistir géim', st. [5]), presumably the priest himself. Unlike in the aforementioned Domhnall Ó Conaill poem, the clergyman is not stated to be deceased, nor is his demise imminent. However, the title's evocation of a rising may suggest a Sheehy, after death, being imaginatively resurrected to function figuratively again in an inspirational if not an obviously real leadership role.

The tenor of *Is gearr do bhí mé* is largely optimistic, in contrast to that of the Ó Conaill elegy. However, the other Sheehy poems are *ad idem* with the Ó Súilleabháin material overall and with earlier verse compositions considered here as far as the negativity of their reportage of the incidents under discussion is concerned. Cúndún's text repeatedly suggests the priest's conviction was secured by treachery, perversity and lies ('le fórsa is feall le cam is éitheach', st. 14), or by trickery, bribery and falsehood ('le gangaid is ceilg is claonchlis / foireann do bhreabadh léar spalpadh an t-éitheach', st. 44). The poem uses joint Irish and English terms (the latter italicised here) to depict the deed as '*murder* dubh' (st. 42). His female interlocutor had hoped that her spirits would improve over time, but reveals that, for her, and by extension Ireland, each advancing year is worse than its predecessor (''s gur dona gach bliain ná an bhliain thréigeas', st. 54). Aspects of the clergyman's demise feature in his sister's lament. This contains scathing criticism of those it views as having contributed to it, including clerical colleagues who refused to give character references on his behalf, or the named witness who testified against him, whom she would wish to grind like a mill. She hopes those responsible for placing the rope ('córda', st. [1]) around his neck will themselves choke, and speaks of her brother's fair head turning black in colour on the spikes outside the town gaol ('cé go mbeidh do cheann bán anocht go dubh / Ar spair an phríosúin thoir', st. [4]).

The final decade of the period under discussion witnessed a further misadventure. This is the story of the contention, in the early 1770s, between Art Ó Laoghaire (1747–73), a resident of Raleigh, near Macroom, County Cork, and a neighbour, Abraham Morris, of nearby Hanover Hall, formerly a magistrate, which resulted in Ó Laoghaire being shot dead. The grounds for the stand-off remain unclear. The antagonism could possibly have been based on a clash of personalities, or perhaps mirrors deeper contrasting interests among the differing communities from which each was drawn.[24] These tensions may have been sharpened in turn by the prospect of fresh conflict arising from colonial unrest in the New World and the clash of loyalties which this was likely to engender; Art would die within two years of what was termed in Ireland the 'New England War'. It looks as though he himself had become known for assertiveness after returning from service in the Austro-Hungarian armies in the 1760s, to judge by his securing of or bearing firearms, contrary to prescriptions then in force against Catholics under 'penal' legislation. Notices of complaint against him were placed in the public press. Demands Morris subsequently made of him included one that Ó Laoghaire give up a valuable horse, according to legal provisions which sanctioned the sequestration of assets of those felt to be potentially subversive. Matters came to a head when Art's plan to ambush his adversary as the latter was on a journey away from his own home was discovered. He was instead killed by a military detachment which Morris had mustered, with the one-time magistrate later acquitted of homicide in the matter.

The incident is the subject of one Gaelic composition only, as opposed to the cluster of works on the Ó Súilleabháin and Sheehy affairs. No verse items about it of a literary character primarily are extant and, given the still reasonably inclusive and retentive nature of contemporary manuscript transmission, some doubt must be entertained as to whether such were ever created, despite suggestions that works of this kind have been incorporated into the piece which has come down to us. Neither are there any autonomous poetic reimaginings or invocations of Art Ó Laoghaire, after his death, as a living person such as one sees in the Ó Conaill, and perhaps the Sheehy, situations. Questions thus arise as to whether the apparent lack of more formal eulogy indicates an absence of hereditary patronage on Ó Laoghaire's part, or whether, simply, it suggests the attenuation of this compositional practice had already begun to set in by that stage.

The sole famous extant item centring on the incident, *Caoineadh Airt Uí Laoghaire* (The Lament for Art O'Leary),[25] is itself a correspondingly contested text. Uncertainty surrounds the time of its composition or recording, the fidelity to any putative original of the versions which have been discovered, even the validity of its ascription to the lady who is held mainly responsible for it, Art's wife, Eibhlín Dubh Ní Chonaill (*c.* 1743–*c.* 1800), or whether its evident artistry is genuinely hers. The position is rendered more complicated by the fact that other voices, like those of Ó Laoghaire's father and sister, speak in the poem from time to time. It might be Art's wife's family connections as aunt of Daniel O'Connell (1775–1847), the most celebrated public figure in early nineteenth-century Ireland, which principally ensured an enduring near-contemporary interest in the piece. Should the poem have been supplemented or enlarged over time, such contributions may reflect in this case as well the intervention of a community otherwise prone to extensive myth-making as far as O'Connell himself was concerned.[26] The latter's Kerry origins might equally have influenced the extent of its attestation in that county. Growing historiography about Daniel O'Connell and his background may finally have caused the work to continue to receive disproportionate notice in the late 1800s when compared with other examples of its kind.

The 'Lament's' situation appears thus to foreshadow the deconstructionist dilemma of attempting to establish any ultimate or secure sense in a text, or even, in this instance, the text itself, particularly a piece on the borderland between the spoken and the written.[27] Its most recent redactor does not, in fact, collate the surviving versions to produce a composite, agreed recension, unlike the practice of an editorial predecessor, but concentrates instead on one manuscript witness only from among several.[28] While comments on the item presented here are therefore and of necessity tentative, nevertheless, a number of topics of relevance to the present discussion seem to stand out in the composition. They are highlighted here for illustrative purposes only and not in the order of their occurrence within the poem.[29] What is noteworthy is the extent of the elaboration in each. Eibhlín's unshakable affection for Art and the quality of their life together come across in the first. The terms for love and friendship and variations thereof echo repeatedly in the piece, together with the almost untranslatable concept of 'steadfastness' ('Mo ghrá go daingean tú', 'Mo chara go daingean tú', 'Mo chara thú go daingean', 'Mo chara thú 's mo shearc', 'Mo chara thú is mo shearc-mhaoin', 'Mo ghrá thú is mo chumann', ll. 1, 18, 44, 129, 151, 194 respectively), as she describes their initial meeting and in recollections of her slain husband thereafter. The ease and comfort of their household is conveyed via an inventory of domestic arrangements as concise and inclusive as one finds in Gaelic literature, when Eibhlín speaks of their rooms, parlours, sleeping quarters, sense of relaxation and diet (ll. 8–17), or how she would wish to return to or resume these, their dinner parties and musical entertainments, if her partner still lived (ll. 85–95).

The killing of Art changed all, and the particulars of his demise are a further dominant note throughout. Intimations of hostility to him accompany his wife's portrayal of his elegant appearance and attire (ll. 18–29), as people, especially in leadership positions ('Sasanaigh', l. 30), deferred to him, not out of admiration but from fear (ll. 30–35). She learned of his mishap when his horse returned home bloody and riderless (ll. 62–72), following which she herself hastened to the place where he died, stretched out like a slain animal,[30] with only the corner of an old woman's cloak as covering, and nobody to lament him (ll. 72–84). She would have wished to be by his side as the bullets pierced him (ll. 136–40), and later curses the named individual bribed into betraying him (ll. 341–57).

A third strand of the poem is particularly strong on a specific type of fragmentation after Ó Laoghaire's shooting. Eibhlín's imaginings of its impact on their children are especially prominent. The two eldest will have no father to answer them when they call (ll. 44–54). The man of the house has been taken at a time when their home is still the only environment with which this pair are immediately acquainted. Their mother is unlikely to give birth to the third infant she is carrying, from upset at the unfolding circumstances (ll. 160–6). When he embraced his two sons and wife at the gate of their residence on the occasion of his departure, Eibhlín scarcely believed he would never return alive (ll. 166–78). She seems prepared to leave the homestead desolate and unfurnished, and herself to remain destitute, in pursuit of justice (ll. 315–27).

Recurrence of such problematic happenings throughout much of the eighteenth century appears therefore to be endemic, with their underlying causes probably structural in nature. It looks as though their impact was correspondingly traumatic. *Caoineadh Airt Uí Laoghaire* comprehensively encapsulates this dimension through the extent of its emphasis on the disintegration of family, with its distinguishing exposé of the consequences for a household's youthful and most vulnerable members. A domestic context of this kind, by contrast, is not at issue in the Sheehy texts and, while scarcely absent from it, seems less evident throughout the Muircheartach Óg Ó Súilleabháin material. Crediting the 1700s on their own with full responsibility for the ontological anxiety typifying these and other forms of Gaelic writing would be inaccurate. Irish civilisation, as a review of the early literature will show, had long been innately agonistic, a competitive tendency probably augmented by the country's insular character, apart altogether from its historical experiences. However, the period from the late seventeenth century onwards did witness more definitive transfer, and, by extension, loss of control affecting substantial sections of society. The works under review suggest these systemic transformations do not seem, of necessity, to have led to any diminution in many contemporaries' feelings of uncertainty. They may rather have resulted in their questioning their actual identity. The principals involved in the episodes under consideration, clergy and the minor aristocracy, were among the more privileged in the Irish-speaking segment of the population. Fewer of their likes would, as time progressed, assign this vernacular any significant priority.

The new order

An indication of how encounters with authority could have borne on the public at large in addition to its elites may be seen in the events of 1798. It is not possible to review at length the complex background to, or the actual course of, these incidents, apart from an explanation, to follow, of certain early and revealing perspectives on them from within Gaelic tradition.[31] The revolutionary fervour of the closing decades of the eighteenth century witnessed a rise in demands in Ireland as elsewhere for more comprehensive citizenship rights and greater inclusivity in administration. The British administration became more concerned with radical groupings in the country, like the United Irishmen, when war broke out between England and France in 1793, fearing these might combine with overseas agents to overthrow the state. The arrival of a French force at Bantry Bay in 1796 heightened the concern. Concerted moves against the organisation began in late 1797, leading to rebellion in various parts of eastern Ireland throughout the next year, followed by a second French incursion in the north-west. The outbreak of hostilities occurred despite calls by members of the Catholic hierarchy for their co-religionists to desist from insurrection, as illustrated by a sermon of the Roscommon-based Dr Edmond French, bishop of Elphin, delivered in April, of which homily an Irish-language version survives.[32]

Some of the fiercest fighting took place in Wexford from Easter onwards, in the county town itself, in Enniscorthy and elsewhere. Insurgents had also assumed control of New Ross. The authorities retook this centre after an assault in early June. An account by the loyalist James Alexander, charged with clearing up in the aftermath of the siege, claims:

> The rebel carcases lay in the street unburied for three or four days; some perforated over and over with musket balls, or the bayonet; some hacked with swords; some mangled and torn with grapeshot, and worse still with *pigs*, some of which I have seen eating the brains out of the cloven skulls and gnawing the flesh about the raw wounds! Many rebels were reduced to ashes . . . and many partly burned and partly roasted.[33]

Estimates of mortality from conflict throughout Ireland at large often speak of the losses being, *pro rata*, as substantial as were experienced in France during its revolutionary era.

Alexander's statement might be read as an explanatory gloss on entries in a famous Irish-language poem, 'Sliabh na mBan', commencing *Is dubhach liom féinig bualadh an lae úd*,[34] which records moments in the campaign from the insurgent standpoint and its impact on the ordinary citizenry:

> 'Sé Ros do bhreoigh 's do chloígh go deo sinn,
> Mar a bhfúigeadh mórchuid dínn sínte lag;
> Is leanaí óga 'na smól ann dóite
> 'S an mhéid d'fhan beo dhíobh cois claí nó scairt.
>
> (st. [3])

(It is New Ross which sickened and subdued us eternally, where many of us were left stretched out, weakened; with young children there burnt to a cinder, and those of them who survived lying by ditches or thickets.)

The text goes on to speak of the fate of the captured:

> Is iomdha fear aosta 's crobhaire gléigeal
> Ó'n am go chéile do gabhadh le seal,
> A bhfuil córdaí caola 'buain lúth a ngéag díobh
> I ndoinsiúin dhaora go doimhin faoi ghlas.
>
> (st. [4])

(Many an elderly man and hearty young fellow were seized recently from time to time, the strength of whose limbs is being sapped by tight cords, locked up in deep dungeons.)

The composition subsequently seems to indicate their guards would not intervene on their behalf, either to ease the prisoners' plight or prevent their banishment from Ireland. Complementary testimony relating to this issue is extant in other Gaelic sources. The poet and scribe Mícheál Óg Ó Longáin (1766–1837) lamented the arrest of his first cousin and United Irish activist, Tomás Ó Longáin, in 1799, and the latter's transportation the following year to the new 'fatal shore' at Botany Bay. One of his poems (*Is atuirseach léanmhar mé le sealad*)[35] speaks of the episode's impact on Tomás's flock of children ('do scaoth bocht leanbh', l. [12]), who were debilitated, scattered and tearful ('faon iar scaipeadh go déarach dealamh', l. [13]) as a result, and notes the cheerless condition of his other relatives since his cousin's departure ('gan seol spóirt ó scarais-se leo', l. [17]). Thus ended the least disturbed century in the island's history since the commencement of the 1500s, with, among other matters, fresh variations on the theme of dislocation implicit in Ó Bruadair's verse responses from slightly over one hundred years earlier.

Thematics II: Politics

Thoughts on the broader context in which events such as the foregoing took place form a second component within eighteenth-century Irish poetry. The verse material can capture subtle variations in this situation over time. Reflections on how the status quo might be modified or ameliorated often appear in it as well, whether through collective action or in a person's own conduct. None of the latter deliberations is as extensive as those found in contemporary treatises on societal structures in other languages. However, a diversity of approach greater than may have been anticipated from the nature of the aforementioned incidents is detectible within the surviving poetic record.

From Jacobitism to scepticism

Support for the restoration of Stuart kings to public office is to the fore in the extant data. The enterprise became known, from the dynasty's first ruler, James VI of Scotland and I of England (1566–1625), as Jacobitism.[36] Irish-language authors throughout the seventeenth century wrote on theoretical and practical aspects of the movement, on monarchical legitimacy and on its Gaelic identity. Real financial and military assistance continued to be made available during the opening decades of the 1700s, after the defeat of James II in the Williamite wars, to later Jacobite figures like James III (1688–1766), the so-called Old Pretender, and his son, Charles Edward Stuart (1720–88), the Young Pretender, both of whom enjoyed residual support in Britain as well as Ireland.

A classic representation of the last-mentioned, in the poem *Bímse buan ar buairt gach ló*, occurs among the compositions of Seán Clárach Mac Domhnaill (1691–1754), a farmer, mill-owner and teacher associated with the Charleville area in north Cork.[37] The author of the eleven-stanza text declares himself unsettled at the lack of information about this claimant to the throne. The work was possibly composed on the occasion of Bonnie Prince Charlie's departure for Scotland prior to his participation in the ill-fated rising of 1745. The item suggests that both nature and people are aggrieved at not knowing his circumstances. Such distress is exemplified by the silencing of bird-song ('Ní haoibhinn cuach ba shuairc ar neoin', l. 9), or the darkening of the sun ('Níor éirghidh Phoebus féin ar cóir', l. 13) and moon ('Ar chaoin-chneas rae tá daol-bhrat bróin', l. 14). Poets ('éigse', l. 18) and young women ('béithe', l. 19) are also gloomy.

The chorus, repeated after each stanza, mentions the author's sleeplessness at the tidings ('ní fhuaras féin aon suan ar séan', l. 7). The refrain's wording, when found for the last time following the final stanza, is altered, but the change continues to emphasise Mac Domhnaill's ongoing unease ('cruadhtan', l. 51).

Despite this, the text's second part strikes out in a different direction as a core of five central quatrains goes on to describe the prince's characteristics. The piece's own verbal adornment underpins its positive portrayal of Charles. The work speaks, for example, of the clarity of his gaze ('Is glas a shúil . . . Mar lagán drúchta ar chiumais an róis', ll. 25–6), or his Irish-like leadership qualities ('Taoiseach Éireannach tréan ar tóir', l. 36). His majesty is noted almost mystically when Charles is compared to mythological figures like Aonghus Óg (l. 33) or the golden 'Cúraoi árd mac Dáire' (l. 35). A toast to the Young Pretender's life and health ('saoghal is sláinte', l. 48) is probably meant to induce in its readers or audience the same degree of optimism generated by the stirring musical air which its text was intended to accompany. All of these features point to royalism of the ancestral Gaelic variety as being Seán Clárach's preferred polity. The ideology may have had no intellectual novelty, but it would certainly have undermined the newly established order in reality.

Bímse buan remains well-known and sung down to the present, but the same cannot be said concerning another early eighteenth-century song ('Abhrán'), *Léimimid suas a chairde*.[38] This anonymous item lacks a refrain, but is otherwise of approximately equivalent length, at twelve stanzas. It also asks its listeners to be upstanding and to drink the health of a ruler whom they ought to endorse ('an rí dár chóir dúinn stríocadh dó', st. [1]). The poem hopes that anyone who would wish to see him defeated will himself be overturned ('bíodh leagan síos go tráth air', st. [2]). The individual so extolled is a Hanoverian ('triath Hanóbhar', st. [3]), entitled to rule in Ireland through hereditary right ('ó shinsear', st. [4]). He is to dispute the demands of, and pursue, any aberrant aspirant to authority ('ar thóir an bhréagPhretender', st. [6]). Those who do not acknowledge George's right ('a cheart', st. [7]) are to suffer pain, particularly insurgents ('rebels theann', st. [8]). Which of the eighteenth-century monarchs of the same name is at issue here is not specified, but it is most probably the first in the sequence, George Ludwig (1660–1727). The incoming king was scheduled to defend the Lord's faith ('creideamh an Tiarna', st. [9]) and merits approval accordingly for these and related measures.

The cataloguer of the manuscript where this unedited text occurs classifies it as anti-Jacobite. The poem is more likely to be the opposite, with its tone of exaggerated submission to the new dispensation, as well as its challenge to identify the one true religion, being deliberately ironic. Even if it does not imply a shift in loyalty as such, neither is its humour excessively sardonic, however. It may have been adopting a temporising attitude, awaiting the outcome of the Hanoverian prince's impact in England as much as on Ireland. It is not unlikely that certain officials dispatched to this country during George I's reign achieved a degree of acceptability among speakers of Irish. John Carteret (1690–1763), viceroy in the years 1724–30, an opponent of attempts to flood Ireland with worthless coin during the 'Wood's Halfpence' controversy, was admired for this reason by Dean Swift (1667–1745), and would in turn have been known and probably well regarded in the likes of the Ó Neachtain scribal entourage.[39]

Further distancing from what might have been assumed, a priori, to be the sole form of allegiance in Gaelic Ireland may perhaps be seen in the output of the composer Peadar Ó Doirnín (c.1700–69).[40] This writer could have had Munster connections, but he spent most of his life in the County Louth area, apparently devoting himself to poetry as much as to any other activity. His free-spirited attitude comes across in 'The Independent Man',[41] where he advocates enjoyment of life rather than a fixation with other causes:

> Here's a health to all those that at liberty goe
> That travel the road without a command,
> That drink and that sport, that sit in their clothes
> Whilst taking repose with a glass in their hand.
>
> (ll. 1–4)

It looks as though no partisanship of any kind finds absolute favour in his writings, so long as his own basic needs remain satisfied:

> A Whig or a Tory, High Church or Low Church,
> Protestant, Roman, Quaker or Clan
> Shall ne'er controul me to any other notion
> But the same motive I have in hand;
> I'll travel the road, I'll meddle with none,
> I'll let them alone by sea and by land,
> For Providence store me want of their board,
> I'm covered with clothes and that's my demand.
>
> (ll. 25–32)

The poet's editor suggests that a text published in the nineteenth century contains extra verses which ought to be linked with this work. The second such stanza clarifies the author's sentiments about those jockeying for position in society:

> In Heaven's great name, how can they blame
> The poor man, or shame him, in the long run?
> Ambition's their game, what else do they mean,
> But purchase high fame, great power and fun?
>
> (ll. 57–60)

He takes an equally jaundiced view of rivalry among European states when arguing:

> What do I care for Holland or Hague
> Or trouble my brains with packets or news
> From Germany's states to Lobquid's retreat
> Their taking of Prague, or Spaniards confuse . . .
> For kings or their guards I care not a straw
> No colour at all shall make me stand . . .
>
> (ll. 9–12, 17–18)

although he would not be particularly upset if other nations combined to assault the English. The text was apparently written as Britain was involved in the complex War of the Austrian Succession (1741–8), when it supported Maria Theresa's (1717–80) attempts to succeed her father, Charles VI (1685–1740), in controlling extensive Habsburgian possessions in central Europe against a coalition comprising France and a range of other associates. Not the least interesting aspect of the item is the extent to which access to printed journals mentioned in it could have encouraged others like this northern bard to resort to English rather than Irish in musing on the events of the day.

Subsequent testimony from alternative locations indicates that Ó Doirnín's move towards disengagement is not an isolated phenomenon. An Augustinian, Liam Inglis (1708 / 15–78), a native of either Limerick or Tipperary but who spent most of his working days in Cork city, wrote on the outbreak of the Seven Years' War in the mid-1750s in his *Cré agus cill go bhfaighe gach bráthair*.[42] In this conflict, countries which had previously been united formed different competing partnerships in response to the latest developments. France and Austria, among others, were now aligned, contending against Prussia and England as this erstwhile insignificant German statelet came to prominence. Inglis compared the stand-off about how to divide up Europe to a squabble over sharing out the multi-coloured components of a mendicant friar's keg of butter ('leastar an bhráthar', l. 12) coming into Cork city's butter market. The poem's phrasing suggests he may have put into words the visual imagery of contemporary cartoons. Various countries claimed a section of the vessel's contents to match the hues of their national emblems, according to the piece, with Ireland seeking the green stripes ('na síoga uaithne', l. 13), Britain the red ('na síoga dearga', l. 15) and France the white ('na síoga bána', l. 16). Prussia alone took umbrage ('do ghlac rí Prúise cumha', l. 21) at not having received any of the spoils, and attacked its neighbour, Austria, to claim its due portion ('roinnt', l. 22).

Inglis's parodic neutrality only altered when, during the course of the conflict, it became clear that England and its affiliates were gaining the upper hand. However, another anonymous Gaelic author, writer of *Tá scanradh ar an bhFrancach a dhóthain*,[43] seemed satisfied, albeit reluctantly, at French reversals and British advances in this campaign. He was particularly glad that the Austrians, under Maria Theresa, should have experienced difficulty:

> Mo chrá uaim go mb'fhearr liom mar shóchas
> An t-áthas seo ar Sheoirse 's a chuideachta
> 'Ná Máire dá ndáilfeadh mála óir dom
> Cé tá's ag an gcomharsain mé i n-uireasa.
>
> (st. [4])

(It troubles me that I would prefer, as a solace, that George and his company would be happy rather than Maria, even if she bestowed a bag of gold on me, although my neighbours know how sorely I am in want.)

George II (1683–1760) was in a strong position because of the reduction of his former adversaries:

> Ní heagal dó bagairt na Stíobhart
> Tá Carolus cloíte gan duine aige
> Greadfar le Sasana Laoiseach
> Má thagann sa gcoimheascar ina choinne chugainn.
>
> (st. [2])

(He is not afraid of the Stuart threat; Charles is defeated and is without anyone. Louis will be routed by England if he comes to us into the conflict against him.)

Protestantism appears triumphant and on the move:

> Tá Cailvín 's a chathbhuíon go láidir
> Gan binn ar an bPápa 'ná ar thuilleadh acu,
> Cailís i bPáiris ní fhágfam,
> ná aibíd ag bráthair gan tiomargan. (st. [3])

(Calvin and his divisions are strong, paying no heed to the pope or others. We shall not leave a chalice in Paris or a habit on a friar untaken.)

Use of various plural forms in these citations ('chugainn', 'ní fhágfam') seems intriguingly to place the composer on the British side. Should a change of loyalties on his part have been responsible for it, he may have been moved to castigate Maria Teresa for joining with England in the first instance, or, conversely, the French for their earlier abandonment of the Young Pretender when, after his Scottish debacle during the previous decade, Charles Edward Stuart was expelled in accordance with the Treaty of Aix-la-Chapelle in 1748. Whatever its origins, this striking Francophobia goes against the grain of a long-standing *entente* between France and Gaelic Ireland in the period.

Absorbing innovation

The decline of Jacobitism did not signal a curtailment of political options. Military experience gained in what they called the 'French and Indian wars', together with a reluctance disproportionately to bear the costs of this campaign, among other reasons, led Americans to revolt in the 1770s. The Irish Volunteers, formed to defend their island should the French take advantage of England's transatlantic discomfort, soon sought more favourable terms for their membership in the British federation. Less restrictive commercial conditions were conceded to Ireland in 1780. The implications of these various moves are treated in a set of English- and Irish-language poems now extant in a County Wexford document.[44] The items deal with the challenging issue of establishing harmony between Irishmen of different persuasions for the material benefit of all. It would appear as though the English text of the first work (entitled 'On the FREE TRADE of Ireland. Tune, Moggy Lauther. Paddy's Triumph') is the original, of which these are the first two verses:

> Come all you kind and loving Souls,
> and join your own dear Paddy;
> with Irish Liquour fill your Bowls,
> And drink our Friends that's steady:
> Our Parliament are Paddy's all
> Of Irish manufacture
> Who've laid the Corner-stone of all,
> Our Irish Architecture.
>
> And please the Lord, we'll raise it high,
> In spite of Opposition,
> Tho' England storm, and Sawny cry,
> We'll hold our Disposition:

> Tho' Paddy has been mock'd to Scorn,
> For being poor and needy,
> He has a Soul can stand a storm
> From Britans [*sic*] rich and greedy.

The piece subsequently speaks about the folly of the inhabitants of the country being unnecessarily divided along denominational lines, and advocates ending quarrels brought about by such sterile segmentation.

A gaelicisation of the opening stanza reads as follows:

> Tagaíg, a Ghaeil, ag comhchuidiú i bpáirt go dlúth le Pádraig
> is ólfam féin go leor dár gcrúsca, sláinte shúgach ár gcairde:
> Ár bPárlaimint atá dár gcumhdach fuair siad dúinn ar dtrád cheart,
> ag cur bunúis ar chloch an chúinne ina gcúirt go láidir.

However, the translation breaks off at a juncture corresponding to mid-way in the fourth line of its English counterpart's second verse:

> Is le cúnamh an Tiarna tógfaidh í, ainneoin a naimhde gnásmhar',
> Is i Londain, cé toirmeascach bhíd, 'fonóid 'nár n-aghaidh le Sání,
> coinneom ár . . .

There is no attempt at an Irish version of the three remaining English stanzas. The unnamed adapter seems unlikely to have been put off by the somewhat condescending tone of the source text, a type of superciliousness absent from the Gaelic copy. He goes on to furnish full parallel versions of a second composition, 'On the Free Trade granted to Ireland in 1780 by K. George IIId. Tune, the white [Y?]oke.' ('Dán ar chomhphribhléid ceannaíochta d'Éirinn, le hÚdarás Rí Sacsan, an Treas Sheoirse. 1780').

Difficulties in creating an acceptable Irish idiom for the concepts in question may be at the root of the problem in the first text. Its redactor could have come by the English material through hearing it. Like many pieces in this section, the work appears to have been intended to be sung. If this is how he encountered it, the compiler might also have learnt parts of the second composition imperfectly, as the somewhat irregular rhyming patterns of its fourth stanza, and the stanza's unusual indentation on the manuscript page (repeated below), could reveal:

> Merchant, Farmer, Mechanic may now
> Begin Bus'ness with Pleasure,
> Having a Prospect of Prosperity:
> Stings of Religion are done away,

> Friendship and union bear the sway, very
> Fairly, daily connecting them in a –
> > Bond of Amity, now
> May the Irish thrive and ever agree.

The possibility that the foregoing is in fact an anglicisation of the corresponding Irish item should be entertained as well, but such a hypothesis seems less likely.

Understanding the exchange of information between the two written or spoken linguistic media involved requires further investigation of these textual challenges. However, exploring the interface should not obscure appreciation of the significance of what is at issue. The evidence highlights the Gaelic adapter's awareness of novel forms of political rhetoric inherent in the English verses just cited, and underscores openness to an all-embracing view of society contained in them. Analysis should also bear the piece's provenance in mind. The codex containing this dual-language material is associated with south-east Ireland. It is attested here almost twenty years before the region witnessed discord of a kind alluded to in the foregoing review of the events of 1798. The English and Irish poems under discussion bespeak a growth in expectations in that area from the 1780s onwards among those who composed or recorded them. Failure to realise such aspirations, probably leading to an aggravated sense of disappointment, may be among the factors which lent the ensuing rebellion there its notorious sharpness.

The final intriguing development in the history of Gaelic writing considered in this section may also have captured the mood of the times, even if indirectly. One of the eighteenth century's most celebrated compositions would seem to have been completed by 1780. *Cúirt an Mheán Oíche* (The Midnight Court) is the work of a County Clare native, Brian Merriman (1750–1805).[45] Possibly from Ennistymon, he relocated to the neighbourhood of Feakle, near which he taught and farmed, and subsequently moved to Limerick, where he kept a mathematics school as well. The Clareman is one of the few Irish-language authors of the day whose death was the subject of a notice in the contemporary press, although it failed to mention this aspect of his interests. Very few of his original works survive (he may not in fact have been all that prolific), but this lengthy piece of more than one thousand lines more than makes up in density for the apparent scarcity of Merriman's *opera* overall.

In it, the poet takes a rest by the idyllic shores of Lough Graney close to Feakle (ll. 1–40). During his sleep, a grotesque female bailiff summons him to a court (ll. 41–134), gathered to discuss current misfortunes, among which are warfare resulting in population decline, reflecting people's unwillingness to reproduce. Obstacles to marriage become the principal debating point at the assembly, presided over by the goddess Aoibheall. A young female speaker complains about eligible younger men marrying not their nubile coevals but substantially older women (ll. 167–356). An older man then makes a submission on his experience of female wantonness (ll. 363–644), particularly his discovery, during his wedding night, of the already advanced state of his wife's pregnancy. The child was born almost immediately thereafter. The young woman counters by pointing out her male interlocutor's shortcomings, while making a further plea to the court on behalf of the welfare of womankind in general (ll. 645–854). The work appears to conclude by ordaining that the poet himself, like other youthful unwed males, be punished for not having married (ll. 855–1020), at which point he wakes up from his challenging reverie (ll. 1021–6). The text's depiction of various forms of relations between the sexes was so energetic as to cause English-language versions of the poem to be censored in Ireland in the mid-1900s, while the Gaelic original continued to circulate simultaneously, both in published, scholarly editions as well as the oral tradition.

'The Midnight Court' has proved to be uniquely resistant to interpretation of a kind which would suggest that one has extracted a definitive interpretation from it. Explicit internal testimony concerning the circumstances of its composition is scant. Determining the balance between the actual and the imaginative aspects of its contents, couched in a dream-like setting, is equally problematic. Not the least of these problems is establishing whether the poem's deliberations mirror certain of Merriman's personal concerns, such as his own possible illegitimacy. In this connection, recent studies have suggested that the high-spirited worldliness in the 'Court' represents the antithesis of certain categories of late seventeenth-century devotional poetry, preoccupied with more sombre issues like mortality and the transience of human existence. Merriman actually transcribed such material, and may be shown to have drawn upon it for certain of his poem's diction and literary references.[46]

This confirmation of the 'Court's' textual interdependence, and, arising from it, the identification of a wider remit, may also encourage speculation on its indebtedness to other broadly based formative influences, particularly those of a more recent kind.[47] The decade preceding its completion saw almost unprecedented levels of publishing on societal organisation, internationally and with respect to Ireland, by philosophers, economists and the like. Descriptions of Clare itself, reminiscent of such writings, were made by authors also active in Gaelic composition, suggesting that others from the county, such as Merriman, might not have been immune from these trends. A short five years earlier, the outbreak of the American Revolution in 1775, ongoing until 1782, would have involved widely publicised discussion of government, focusing on the need to end exclusiveness, for instance. North America, furthermore, would not have been unknown in the Irish-language community for its imagined climate of moral toleration.[48] Gaelic speakers' unenfranchised status meant they were prevented from debating these matters within fora like parliaments where they had effectively no presence. Nevertheless, in the 'Court', Brian Merriman could have set out to impart the view that his characters were not absolved of responsibility for the conduct of human affairs in matters over which they exercised some control, particularly in more personalised social contracts such as matrimony. The text seems to have been concerned with other aspects of the welfare of the individual within the community as well, like challenging prejudice towards those born out of wedlock, an attitude made to look ludicrous. Both the 'Court' and Aogán Ó Rathaille's 'Gile na Gile', examined here at the outset, are to some degree vision texts. However, the different emphasis in each is one additional measure of the extent to which debate had evolved in the intervening years. Merriman's recourse to the tried, vision-based formula to make his concrete case also appears more successful than the aforementioned Wexford texts' struggle with the comparatively abstract terminology of political balladry.

Thematics III: Quotidian life

The presentation thus far has brought together texts which throw light on pivotal events or others offering thoughts on the broader context which moulded them. Even within these categories, aspects of their authors' or communities' day-to-day affairs, surpassing specific incidents or political considerations, have already become apparent. To judge by the volume of extant verse devoted to them, those quotidian matters are likely to have been as important in the minds of most contemporaries as any reviewed hitherto. The quantity and diversity of relevant evidence is such that everyday issues cannot be treated comprehensively in the present confines, apart from one subject, religion, which like others, is frequently attested, seems distinctive to the period and exhibits acknowledged imaginative inputs.

Links between various manifestations of belief (in the form of explanatory and organising world-views) and eighteenth-century existence are in fact almost inextricable. As the case of Merriman would have indicated, the topic is ever present, if only in reaction against it. No such opposition is likely to be involved as regards an anonymous verse biography of Jesus, the central figure in the Christian tradition. *Ag so beatha agus páis agus bás ar Slánaightheóra Íosa*

Críosd (Here is the life and passion and death of Our Saviour, Jesus Christ) extends to some four thousand lines.[49] Its origins may also lie in County Clare towards the close of the 1600s, as its mixture of Munster and Connacht dialect features points to a Thomond background, in its editor's opinion. The piece circulated abundantly in manuscript during the opening quarter of the eighteenth century. The composition is divided into seven chapters, the first comprising a summary of the Old Testament Genesis and Exodus narratives (ll. 1–252), followed by an account of Christ's background and birth (ll. 253–468). Sections two to four focus on his public ministry (ll. 469–1739), with concluding segments devoted to accounts of its subject's last days (ll. 1740–2352), burial (ll. 2353–819), resurrection and ascension into heaven (ll. 2820–3999).

The piece is a poetic summary of a fifteenth-century prose compilation, *Smaointe Beatha Chríost* (comprising over six thousand lines of text), which a secular priest, Tomás Gruamdha Ó Bruacháin, of Killala, County Mayo, translated into Irish from a Franciscan-inspired Latin original, *Meditationes Vitae Christi*.[50] Codices containing Ó Bruacháin's adaptation, either in whole or in part, are attested throughout much of Ireland from the time of the work's completion onwards into the nineteenth century. Thoughts about Christ's career are furnished for each of the seven days of the week. The gaelicised recension speaks to a 'beloved disciple' ('a deisgibail ghradaigh', l. 14), who is encouraged to reflect on the themes in question within this week-based framework. Because a learner or acolyte is envisaged, the language is particularly accessible, a factor matching the popularity of the work itself when first completed.

The poem takes the latter elements further still, even if it does not follow the prose work's diurnal lay-out as such (and includes additional scriptural entries not present in its exemplar). It also adds scenes from everyday life in its depiction of an accessible Christ figure and the humanity of those associated with him. Thus after the Archangel Gabriel is sent to Mary and when the incarnation has taken place, Joseph and his spouse set out to visit her kinswoman, Elisabeth, to inform her of the news of Mary's pregnancy. They are obliged to walk the lengthy journey from Nazareth to Jerusalem despite her condition, an indication of their forbearance and humility. In conceptualising the modes of conveyance of which they could not avail, the redactor seems to reflect his own time rather than biblical antecedents:

> is ní raibh cóistí ag róduigheacht sligh' aca
> ina mbeidis iarlaidhe, ná tighearnaidh tíre,
> ruidairidhe, is sguéir, go tréan gach taobh dhi,
> marcshluagh, ná maighdeana meidhir dá coimhideacht.
>
> (ll. 325–8)

(There were no coaches travelling the road with them, in which one might find earls or landlords, knights, or squires strongly by her side, cavalry or merry courtesans accompanying her.)[51]

Recent experiences may also feature in the episode of Jesus' incarceration, such as in the description of the facility to which he is imagined to have been taken and the treatment he received there. He was brought to a tightly sealed jail ('príosún fíor-dhúnta', l. 1963) in an underground cellar ('faoi shoiléar talmhun', l. 1964) and left standing until morning, where his captors are stated to have treated him as follows:

> 'fhéasóg dá statha is dá chathamh chum gaíthe,
> doirne is basa feadh a leacan dá síne air,
> 's ag gabháil go teann 'na cheann do raoín-slait,
> do sheilidhibh an' éadan, 's ag sléachtuin síos do
> ag iarraig gach stróice a thomhas cia níodh sin.
> (ll. 1969–73)

(His beard was torn and thrown to the wind, fists and hands flailing at his cheek, and beating his head vigorously with a rigid stick, spitting at his forehead, and bowing down before him, asking with each stroke who it was that did that.)[52]

In addition to descriptive passages such as the above, some fourteen hundred lines from the total are devoted either to soliloquies or to conversations. Certain of these passages extend to over one hundred lines. This proportion of direct speech must have greatly facilitated the poem's recitation, if not actual acting out, by contemporaries.

The possibility of this having been the case may be reinforced by a consideration of a sequence of over twenty devotional poems associated with Tadhg Ó Neachtain. Many of the verses are linked with specific feast-days, such as those of John the Baptist ('For theadaibh canam go caoin'), of Peter and Paul ('Bhreaghghloir brathacht d'ordha lá'), All Saints ('Fóir do shirbhisidh Chriost chaidh') and the like. Others are part of the wider story of Christ, for instance reflections on the Virgin ('Failte Ríaghain fhlaithis Dé'). All are adaptations of Latin originals from the roman Breviary, the compendium of hymns, lessons and prayers forming part of the divine office of the Catholic church, Ó Neachtain's version of its 'Stabat mater' ('Sheas an mhathair bruite bronach') furnishing some important additional textual evidence for mariology in Gaelic tradition generally.[53] While the series could have been translated for Ó Neachtain's personal use, other reasons are also possible. Irish remained a spoken language for church purposes in the Dublin diocese even late into the eighteenth century. This scribe was also a teacher, and the material could have been provided for the benefit of his pupils, as would appear to have happened again in the early 1800s when County Kilkenny-based copyist Amhlaoibh Ó Súilleabháin (*obit* 1838) made other Gaelic versions of Latin hymnology.[54] A distinguishing characteristic of the Roman Breviary is its function as a liturgical compendium, hence one by definition intended for public performance, as aspects of the verse biography of Christ may have been equally, even if not in a strictly ecclesiastical setting.

Religious material also became more demonstrably internalised, as the writings of the poet Tadhg Gaelach Ó Súilleabháin (*c*.1715–95)[55] indicate. Data concerning him are few, but he seems to have been associated particularly with counties Limerick, Cork and especially Waterford. Patrons extolled in his works, like the Barrys and surviving branches of the Gaelic aristocracy such as the McCarthys, resided in various of these regions. His extant corpus of over fifty pieces also reveals a sensuousness for which he became renowned in both written and oral tradition. His support for the Stuart cause apparently led to his temporary imprisonment in Cork City. His poetry is best known, however, not for these secular trends but for its devotional character. It is unclear whether Tadhg Gaelach turned towards religion as the result of a damascene conversion or in a more gradual fashion. Whatever its origins and timing, the reorientation led to the production of upwards of thirty texts dealing with religious personages like Mary, the Holy Spirit and the Trinity, and Irish saints. Such material was published after his death as *The Pious Miscellany*, which came out in more than twenty editions, making it the most frequently printed book in the Irish language before the twentieth century.

Ó Súilleabháin's popularity in this area may have resided in his ability concisely to capture and re-present aspects of religious practice which were otherwise probably familiar to his readership or audience. Thus one short piece isolates a moment in the baptismal rite, during which a celebrant asks sponsors and others to renounce the Devil and his deeds for the good of the person in receipt of the sacrament and on behalf of all.[56] The procedure recurs during other transformative phases, such as at Easter. The call is made in a set of queries, balanced by matching replies. Ó Súilleabháin compresses the interchange into a short statement of denunciation and affirmation, where rejection is underpinned by immediate repetition, with the deprecated elements combining in their awfulness:

Diúltaímid, is diúltaímid, is diúltaímid do Shátan!
Diúltaímid do dhú-shaígheada, 's do chrúb chlaíonmhar an chneámhaire!
Diúltaímid do shúistí oilc, 's do sciúirsí ní' ár námhaid,
le dlúthdhíograis do ghnúis naíofa, chumhra Íosa, ár máistir.   (ll. [1]–[4])

(We renounce, we renounce, we renounce Satan! We renounce the black darts
and the perverted hoof of this crook! We renounce the evil flails and scourges
of our enemy, with firm affection for the sacred and fragrant countenance of
Jesus, our master.)

Similar compositional strategies are then evident in the assertion of what is
accepted:

Umhlaímid, is umhlaímid is umhlaímid don Ardmhac!
Is umhlaímid go humhal aoibhinn, le humhlaíocht dá Mháthair!
Dúblaímid cúig mhíle tiúin bhinn le grá di.
Is iompaímid go húrchroíoch ar Ghiúistís na nGrás ngeal.

(ll. [5]–[8])

(We submit, we submit, we submit to the Great Son! And we submit humbly
and pleasantly with obedience to His Mother! We double five thousand sweet
tunes for love of her. And we beseech wholeheartedly the Justice of bright
Graces.)

The last stanza summarises the automatic benefits flowing from this choice, as
supplicants become lustrous ('lonraímid', l. [9]) in Jesus' presence. In speaking
of being self-directed ('stiúraímid', l. [11]) into Christ's court ('cúirt Chríost',
l. [12]), the work recalls similar expressions in other texts relating to his
hope of attaining this destination, for its comforts ('Id' chúirt cheolmhar
chúmpordach'; 'cúmpord m'anama is m'aigne taobh leat'). In this connection, the author's identification of himself elsewhere as an exile ('deoraí') may
reflect genuine experience of vagrancy rather than being simply a cliché characteristic of such material.[57] Ó Súilleabháin introduces one final alteration
into the sequence of first-person plural verb forms recurring throughout his
baptismal piece by making intransitive the term *cumhraigh* ('to sweeten', 'to
purify'), when it is suggested the devout grow fragrant ('cumhraímid', l. [9])
in the company of Jesus. This brief three-quatrain work therefore seems to
encompass a range of contextual and personal references while innovating
in its style. It exemplifies the time-honoured paradox of prayer, rooted in
dogmatic system, not necessarily conducive to agapaeic openness, potentially
becoming poetry.

Its personal internalisation did not prevent Ó Súilleabháin's verse from having other public resonances. It has been argued that authors well disposed to

Jacobitism appropriated the language of love in their description of various Stuart rulers. Hints of this appeared in Seán Clárach's sentimental account of the youthful Bonnie Prince Charlie considered earlier. Ó Súilleabháin, however, would appear to have transferred such an emotional representation to the figure of Christ. This may be seen in his *Mo ghrá-sa mo Dhia, mo gharda mo lia; mo ghrá geal mo Thiarna trócaireach!*[58] in which he speaks of his affection for the Saviour's blood ('fuil a chroí', l. [2]), his eyes ('do shúil', l. [3]), his walk ('do shiúl', l. [3]), his waist ('do chúm', l. [13]), the brightness of his appearance ('do chló geal', l. [13]), his demeanour ('do mhéin', l. [14]) and nobility ('do mhórgacht', l. [14]), among other features, making him an object of desire ('Mo ghrá thú le fonn', l. [4]), an exclamatory statement not unlike some counterparts in 'Caoineadh Airt Uí Laoghaire'. Additional stanzas, also using a favoured term in the Jacobite lexicon, argue that allegiance to Jesus is more worthwhile than adherence to secular princes ('Na Saesair', l. [23]).

That the transfer does indeed manifest these levels of complexity may be sensed in a poem whose extended first line reads *Éisteadh gach eolach san Eoraip go héachtach lem' sceolta go scéithfead don tsaogal gan spás.*[59] Eighteenth-century verse asking people to listen ('Éisteadh'), while simultaneously making mention of Europe ('Eoraip') and news ('sceolta'), would have gone on to speak of continental conflicts of a kind explored earlier here, and tease out the consequence of events at issue in them for affairs in Ireland. This text, in contrast, is an invitation to follow the crucified Christ as the ultimate chieftain ('Ár gceann', l. [7]), prince ('ár bprionnsa', l. [7]) and redeemer, whose spiritual assistance is duly invoked. The poet's position could indeed mirror his own redirection in these matters. However, it might also reflect explorations of the consequence of the decline in Stuart fortunes from the 1750s. As a further token of this, the dynasty finally lost its right of consultation into the appointment of Catholic bishops during the 1770s. Ó Súilleabháin's underscoring of religion as the source of authority should perhaps be viewed as but one of a range of conclusions reached by this deliberative process.

The professionals required for the transmission of religion and the implementation of its rites feature prominently also in contemporary writings.[60] By and large, they had a positive relationship with those in their care. This may be seen in works by the Armagh-born Art Mac Cumhaigh (c. 1738–73), who, in his *A mhic Éamoinn Ruaidh, a shadharclann an tsluaigh*, praised the Franciscan Fr Seán Ó hAnluain (1720–93).[61] He apparently operated in the composer's parish in the 1760s. He is like a Moses who released his people from sorrowful diseases ('ó ghalraibh léin', l. 4). The cleric's easy, philosophic disposition ('an feallsúnach suaimhneach', l. 12) has helped remove the darkness and cloud ('teimheal is dlúimh', l. 25) overhanging those for whom he was spiritually responsible. Interestingly, Mac Cumhaigh states Ó hAnluain is unlike certain others who are unsuited to holy orders as, when they returned from seminaries to their flocks, they reverted to a type of harshness or coarseness ('cruas', l. 60) in which they may have originated in the first instance. Perhaps in this connection, Peadar Ó Doirnín would have been as scathing as Mac Cumhaigh concerning one clergyman whose exactions from the poor in his community proved the predictions of an older prophecy (*Tairngire dheárscnaí a rinneadh le Créafann mac Fhéilim an Fhíona*).[62] This had foretold the arrival in their midst of a personality as troublesome as Henry VIII or Oliver Cromwell, or as tragically ineffective, ultimately, as James II. Ó Doirnín may have also been upset at church figures because a former partner of his, Róis Nic an Bhaird, had left him to reside in the household of a local priest, as he intimates in *Cé go raibh sí, Róis, is mise 'ár gcónaí mar lánúin thart thall*.[63] His writings in this regard thus played their part in ensuring that the traditions of south Ulster continued to be as lively in the eighteenth century as they had appeared over a millennium earlier and were set to remain in subsequent generations.

Particular odium was reserved for Catholic religious (or other members of this community) who renounced their faith. This may be observed in the case of a Munster text, *Ní tarcuisne dár n-eaglais ná céim do chách* (variously attributed), on a pervert friar.[64] The transparent meaning of his surname, Ó hÉadromáin ('Light-Weight', l. 4) probably led to satire involving ironic variations of his forename, when this latter is given as 'Achrann' ('Trouble', l. 4) or 'Mearbhall' ('Delusion', l. 12). The poem goes on to describe the changes in him:

> Srathaire do mhalartuigh Mac Dé na ngrás
> An bearradh fuilt, an tAifreann 's an léine bhán,
> Ar hata dhuilleach, scairfeanna is ar dhaol-bhrat ghnáith,
> Is ar ghreammanaibh de gharbh-rolla ar dtéacht ón tsráid.
>
> (ll. 5–8)

(A layabout who exchanged the Son of God of the graces, tonsure, mass and white shirt, for a pointed hat, scarves and a common, beetle-black cloak, and for the stitchings of a rough roll in from the street.)

From the foregoing references to apparel and the hint of his taking up what looks like a disapproved version of the Bible, the suggestion would seem to be that he had become a Protestant minister. The latter appears as a form of *bête noire* in many aspects of both written and oral tradition. Stereotyping Protestant clergy, of course, masks the productive relations which existed between many established church clergy, like County Meath-based Anthony Raymond (1675–1726), and Gaelic scribes in the Dublin-centred Ó Neachtain circle, mentioned earlier, when this collaboration involved their mutual interest in Irish language and literature.[65]

Poetics

The present section now turns to the genesis of texts rather than their contents. In this regard, it has been suggested that the position of the poet in early Ireland is based on a set of reciprocal relations whereby a composer received recompense (*duais*) from his patron in return for the piece he creates, conceived of as a gift (*dúan*).[66] Such expectations are quite likely to have survived in Dáibhidh Ó Bruadair's world-view. Echoes of the first of the two terms may be present in *An ghéag dá dtug mé grá di* by Peadar Ó Doirnín, where the author states he would not part with an unnamed maiden he had fallen for and was extolling, even if he received regal riches and Greek gifts as a reward ('mar dhuais', l. 16).[67] However, a poem also had to be 'made' in the root meaning of this term rather than constituting a 'donation' as it might once have done in its Gaelic understanding. This section will thus focus on the production of materials in the period instead of dwelling on the alternative concept from previous ages, with data culled from contemporary verse as the principal testimony for these procedures.

Image and art

Ó Bruadair's writings may again serve as a point of departure for the investigation. He states that he chronicled the events underlying his 'An Longbhriseadh' poem[68] in the same way he had related Irish affairs during a forty-year period by 'weaving' them ('Níl tuisle . . . nár *fuaigheasa*', st. 37, emphasis added). References to texture occur almost everywhere throughout the work itself. In describing the destruction wrought by warfare at the turn of the 1690s, the author claimed all he saw around him were 'looms left without a thread' ('na garmain seacham gan ruaimneacha', st. 35). He blamed those he castigated for taking advantage of troubled times for robbing the poor of their rags ('giobal', st. 32), ladies of their headgear ('calla', st. 31) or elderly women of the linen garb overlaying their frail frames ('anairt a truaghchruite', st. 18). Any man who had struggled in Ireland's interest but opted to leave could do so without a stain on his character or, as the item puts it, a crease in his cloak ('tulg ina fhallainn', st. 10), in his view.

This focus on clothing and its shaping could at first glance seem remote from the marine symbolism inherent in the work's title, but closer inspection may reveal implicit linkages. As a person who probably lived inland for most of his life, Ó Bruadair might not have seen many seafaring vessels being constructed. However, he could have appreciated that manufacturing them required a kind of joining, with results not dissimilar to the binding at issue in work on cloth, as layers of ship's timbers came to resemble lining in a woollen or flaxen bundle. A shipwreck in this sense therefore becomes a kind of unravelling, a bursting of the seams. This sundering of a protective covering left Ireland 'distraught in the webs of sin' ('Banbha meascuighthe an uama chuil', st. 3), a situation in which, according to a quatrain already quoted, the bonds tying her people together were weakened to the point they might be loosed even if pulled by a hair (st. 2). While the impression may be one of disintegration, in the drawing together of the poem itself, creation and content are therefore intertwined. The end-product and how it was developed have been distinguished in this chapter only for the purposes of analysis and elucidation.

We may consequently explore the formation of others of the age's poetic texts with this Ó Bruadair concept of verse as craft in mind, even if not all composers mentioned in what follows might necessarily have concurred with his specific representation of it. Some pieces give an impression of poems developing organically from the topics represented in them. An item attributed to Seán Ó Tuama (1707/8–75), an innkeeper and small trader from the village of Croom, County Limerick, illustrates the proposition. His *Gach sáir-fhear saordha séimh-ghlic soilbh súghach*[69] issued an invitation to his acquaintances to assist him in describing Croom's high-spirited fair ('Aonach aerach', l. 4). Markets and fairs were Ireland's principal centres of exchange down to the late nineteenth century and beyond, comprising social as well as commercial components. The fair's core aspects would have been fairly similar all over the country.[70] The elements claimed by this work to be found at Croom, including many an attractive woman ('spéir-bhean mhaordha', l. 13), vigorous racing steeds ('stéid-each craosach', l. 17), animals ('stoc na dtriúcha', l. 25) such as fatted bullocks ('lán-mhairt mhéithe', l. 26) and sizeable flocks of sheep ('tréadaibh sochair-iomdhach', l. 26), or grain crops ('fás na ndéas', l. 27) and hay ('féar glas gorm-ghnúiseach', l. 27), might not be considered out of place elsewhere. Certain of the poem's remaining textual features indicate that it is more than a commonplace inventory, however. Its opening call for colleagues to help Ó Tuama depict the occasion ('Bhur ndán go léir le dréachta is cothrom conganta', l. 3) is restated in the author's final appeal not to be left unaided in realising his ambition ('Ná fágaidh mési i gcéin gan chothrom conganta', l. 35). The rewording suggests the author's concluding contribution is a conscious drawing together of his text rather than this remaining a haphazard itemisation. Well-established themes, however hackneyed, were accordingly always candidates for enhancement.

A poem might be bound tight by means other than echoing the beginning in the end. Ó Doirnín's *Ólfaidh mé sláinte an pháiste is daoire folt* concisely praises an unnamed girl.[71] It extols her hair ('folt', l. 1), forehead ('clár a héadain', l. 5), gentle eyes ('a dá rosc shéimhí', l. 13), soft hands ('a dá chrobh maothghil', l. 33) and other standard characteristics, going from head to foot. Each of its ten stanzas commences with the same three words ('Ólfaidh mé sláinte'), toasting the physical features listed. The County Clare composer Seon Ó hUaithnín (1688–?) had recourse to another iterative device to integrate his *Éistigh uaim, a chairde chroí*.[72] In this work, he appeals to his friends to give ear to his upset at Jacobite misfortunes, while wishing that those who undermined him would be routed in turn. Its core metaphor, a stock Stuart image, is one of a card player ('Fear úid', l. 6) bested in the game by unscrupulous gamblers ('idir chearrbhaigh', l. 7), among whom deceit and dissimulation reign ('Ag dearbhú éithigh is ag ceilt cirt', l. 11). The Clareman's hope that these knaves might be routed apparently led to his arraignment for treason. The charge was successfully defended when another meaning was taken from the text before a grand jury whose members knew no Irish. In *Éistigh uaim*, the last word of each stanza is repeated as either the first or second entry in the initial line of the quatrain immediately after. Thus, the poet's own sense of bitterness ('searbhas', l. 4) at the Jacobite predicament, conveyed at the end of the opening verse, is mirrored in equivalent pangs ('Searbhas', l. 5) felt throughout Ireland mentioned at the start of the second stanza. Such pairing is practised throughout the composition's six core quatrains, and is known by the term *conchlann*. It is a ubiquitous linking mechanism in poetry from all regions during this period.

Parallelism of a different kind emerges in the work of Cathal Buí Mac Giolla Ghunna (c.1680–c.1756), possibly a native of Breffney (comprising parts of counties Cavan, Fermanagh and Leitrim), who apparently spent most of his life wandering in north Connacht, north Leinster and south Ulster. He is best known for *A bhonnáin bhuí*, in which he laments a yellow bittern, lying by the roadside, which apparently died from lack of water.[73] The poet had heard it suggested that he himself would, in due course, be found stretched out like this bird, but because of an intake of alcohol rather than from thirst. He facetiously agreed that want of drink would probably not bring about his downfall. The trouble his dissipation caused Mac Giolla Ghunna and others is the subject of the less renowned *An gcluin tú mé, a Chathail Bhuí, tá an bás fá fhad téide dhuit*.[74] This argues that his death from excessive consumption was more imminent than he might have imagined, and outlines the composer's reaction to the latter proposition. Stanzas discussing the claim, attributed to his partner, Nóra, alternate with ones associated with the author himself, as the woman's prudence contrasts with the poet's profligacy. When she speaks of his preference for drunkenness ('meisce', l. 26) and disregard for her innocent children ('mo pháistí maoth', l. 26), for example, he counters that he is not going to dispute with his offspring whatever of life's riches may come his way ('ní bheirimse ábhar troda . . . do mo pháistíbh . . . fá nglacfad mo lámha de rachmas an tsaoil', ll. 29–30), the implication being that his drinking will result in his heirs having no legacy in any case. Although its editor was obliged to restore the text from the poem's often incomplete extant sources, the reconstituted version still conveys the pointed nature of the debate. The work's format, dialogue, is also omnipresent in contemporary verse tradition.

Actualisation and abandonment

While such conversation gives texts a particular coherence, it points as well to the close association between verse and the spoken word, whether in its origination or its delivery. Evidence already considered shows that many poems would have been intended for performance in this way, as works calling for listeners to hear them, noted earlier, have indicated. Alternative sources involving other forms of utterance underscore the same connection. The Limerick composer Seán Ó Tuama, also mentioned above, probably recited his *Mo gháirse mo gháire is mo ghníomh* to raise a happy cry ('gáir') at the arrival into his company of a colleague composer, Seán Clárach Mac Domhnaill.[75] Another acquaintance, Fr Nioclás Ó Domhnaill, in his *Fáilte dár n-árd-fhlaith dár ndíon*, issued a welcome ('fáilte') to the same visitor, in terms equally suggestive of *viva voce* presentation.[76] Counter-examples do not necessarily undermine the linkage between versification and speech, as what is stated (or cannot be) remains at issue. Thus Seán Cúndún's elegy on Fr Nicholas Sheehy enabled the female figure allegorically representing Ireland to vent her feelings on the priest's death.[77] The piece illustrated the lady's sorrowful depression ('táim dubhach tuirseach tréithlag', st. 63) by claiming she was distracted and unable to express herself effectively ('gan mheabhair im cheann ná labhairt i n-éifeacht', st. 63). If thoughts or sentiments could be spoken in poetry, there was an expectation that they might be done so appropriately. In the exchanges just noted, Seán Ó Tuama had earlier extolled Mac Domhnaill as an author whose output was especially euphonious ('Ughdar . . . béil-mhilis blasta binn').[78]

Ó Tuama, moreover, seemed taken by Mac Domhnaill's ability as a writer in the primary sense of that word, speaking of him as one of the best he had seen to handle a pen ('A lámh is fearra dá bhfeaca-sa ar sheoladh an phinn').[79] The feeling was mutual, as in his short *Gabhaim páirt le Seán Ó Tuama an Ghrinn*, Mac Domhnaill spoke correspondingly of Seán's competence as a scribe ('Is beartach bearrtha bláith-cheart buan do scríobhas').[80] That composing verse also literally involved writing appears clear from other indicators. In *Bhí mé ag suírí le cailín a bhí fíneálta, geanúil*, Peadar Ó Doirnín tells of how he courted a girl who initially seemed attractive, but, on getting to know her better, turned out to be somewhat fatuous ('amaid shúgach', l. 8).[81] He did not think her name worth inscribing in his work ('cha scríobhaim a hainm is níorbh fhiú liom', l. 22). His *An ghéag dá dtug mé grá di is áille í ná Helen mhór* (already referred to)[82] suggests he was more smitten by another unnamed favourite, stating that no gifted seer or poet failed to put it down that she was the most beautiful of all ('Níl draoi nó file fuair tíolacaí nach scríobhann síos', l. 21).

In generating verse, therefore, Ó Doirnín appears partially to look to written antecedents or their creators as models. Thus when speaking about a third sweetheart, Róis Nic an Bhaird (who, as we have seen,[83] apparently left him), in order to win her back, he agreed he would need what seemed to him to be Homer's skill, and material success, as a penman ('is go beacht i bhfoghlaim ar aiste Homer thuill táin lena pheann', l. 26). The only unintentional paradox here is the extent to which the latter is associated with orality rather than its opposite in later scholarship. The preferences of County Clare poet Tomás Ó Míocháin may have been for authors closer in time and space, as may be inferred when he criticises a contemporary for swearing that 'Dryden, Milton, Creech & Pope / Could spin no verse, but scribble, scratch & grope'.[84] Should he have known such composers, it is likely to have been through publications mainly. As if to show that these considerations are not merely theoretical, the message which comes through about the creation of the aforementioned verse life of Christ is one of its being scripted, as the author's frequent mention of written sources ('scríbhinn', ll. 2786, 3794, etc.), together with his fatigue from the physical act of writing ('táim cortha dom sgríobhinn', l. 3358), indicates.[85]

One forum seems to have facilitated a blending of the oral and the written in eighteenth-century verse as well as encouraging other aspects of the compositional process. To promote this activity, poets would appear to have assembled in informal sessions, as the evidence of the material they produced and accounts from external observers suggest. Some Munster gatherings replicated the justice system to the point of styling themselves a 'court' ('cúirt'), presided over by a sheriff ('Ardsirriam') or other official, sending warrants ('barántais') to summon participants, passing judgement on pieces submitted for appraisal and offering patents ('paitin(t)') to successful younger applicants.[86] This type of emulation indicates that the events were primarily for enjoyment and entertainment, particularly as many are associated with taverns. However, indicators relating to leadership, aesthetic standards and work practices may be derived from the personnel and compositions linked with them. Thus Limerick poets associated with the Maigue school near Croom looked to the aforementioned Seán Clárach Mac Domhnaill as a pre-eminent exponent ('saoi', l. 8). Mac Domhnaill spoke in turn of what he regarded as Ó Tuama's excellent output ('feabhas', l. 11).[87] Four affiliates of this grouping compiled a piece each on the death of 'Preabaire', the horse of their colleague priest, Fr Nioclás Ó Domhnaill, also mentioned above, resulting in a unity of focus with intertextuality of treatment characteristic of much other verse in the period.[88]

While most information relating to this type of networking comes from the south of Ireland, instances of interaction are also attested for the north, even if on occasion the relationships appear less harmonious. The exchanges add further to the contemporary lexicon of methodology and critical self-appraisal. Two fellow poets, Peadar Mac Giolla Fhiondain and Séamus Dall Mac Cuarta, exchanged verse messages praising the other's compositions. Peadar Ó Doirnín replied in *Más libh amháin is le mic Dághda*, stating that artistic ability was not confined to them alone.[89] His measure of what might have constituted poetic competence includes reference to the intellectual capacity ('intleacht', l. 4) of Roman writers ('saoithe Rómhánda', l. 4), with Ovid as an exemplar of acuity in these matters. If the Stuarts had greater luck, Ó Doirnín claims in *Is fada ag éisteacht mé leis an scéala-sa*,[90] he would have wished to live life like this keen Latin lyricist ('file faobhrach', l. 26). Art Mac Cumhaigh, Peadar's younger contemporary, lamented Ó Doirnín's passing (*Ar Mhullach an Átha Buí 'mo luí teacht ghairm na gcuach*).[91] He was a Gaelic 'Oracle' (l. 27), in Mac Cumhaigh's opinion, not likely to suffer gladly any foolish company ('bálach gan chéill', l. 30). He seemed more at home in the society of an intelligent conversationalist ('fear céillí', l. 31), whose likes he could regale as a consummate maker of lays and poems ('fear déanta laoi agus duan', l. 44).

Employment in the foregoing phrase of two words for 'lay' and 'poem' recalls a continuing degree of indebtedness in the later period to the verse traditions of previous eras, although the latter have been momentarily overlooked in the interests of focusing on poetic creation within our time-frame proper. It is quite likely that the 'courts' of poetry played a part in the perpetuation of the medieval inheritance, not least through the circulation and copying of manuscript materials which they apparently encouraged, even late into the 1700s. Thus, eighteenth-century authors tried their hand at replicating the syllabic metres characteristic of Early Modern Irish, in contrast to the accentual measures based on ordinary speech patterns more frequently associated with their own age. This appears from a verse exchange of 1762 linked to two County Cork writers, Séamas Mac Coitir and Conchubhar Ó Dálaigh, on the subject of ability or otherwise in the ancient poetic profession, cast in the commonly attested *deibhidhe* meter.[92] Neither is it possible to engage with many northern poets without encountering their distinctive amalgam of medieval and modern prosody in the *rann agus amhrán* ('quatrain and song') generic blend.[93] The frequence of this hybrid's attestation is, perhaps, also further evidence of the operations of organised learned poetic milieux better known from the writings of their southern colleagues. It cannot be imagined that the many unlettered composers, particularly women, for instance those associated with the Irish oral lament tradition, had, in their own right, any lesser standards or levels of interaction.

Dáibhidh Ó Bruadair may be the foremost instance of a composer grappling with the task of fusing classical and contemporary idioms as the bardic order came to a close and new horizons opened up. His resultant diction and style are highly idiosyncratic, to the point of being autistic in the primary sense of that word, centred on a deeply personalised use of language. What became of his output subsequently could be illuminating in this connection also. Just two later scribes are responsible for providing three-quarters of his extant texts.[94] His dealings with patrons and fellow composers indicate he was not completely isolated. The poet himself might have been obliged, on account of indigence, to part with autograph copies, none of which survives. One nevertheless wonders whether his works' tenuous transmission history may not indicate that accessing this material involved other challenges. The inbuilt complexity of Ó Bruadair's poetry, of itself, possibly meant that any circle of readers or auditors who could comprehend it was, arguably, relatively narrow in the first instance, with the ranks of those capable of appreciating it diminishing rather than increasing in the prevailing circumstances.

Dáibhidh brought 'The Shipwreck' to a close with the phrase 'finis dom scríbhinn ar fhearaibh Fódla' (st. 41). The disenchantment expressed in the lead-up to this sentiment suggests the line means much more than that a composition which has dealt with the men of Ireland is now ending. Our author did not completely disengage from writing during his few remaining years, but the amount produced in the interval between 1691 and 1694 seems to have lessened substantially, with nothing apparently thereafter. Age or infirmity could have played a part, but alternative explanations may be equally possible, as Ó Bruadair's predicament is not without its analogues, however indirect. Arthur Rimbaud's (1854–91) relinquishing of verse-making remains an unsolved mystery. Stéphane Mallarmé (1842–98), beset by the demands of giving any expression to reality, found taking pen to paper difficult regardless of conditions. With these parallels in mind, there is no reason not to conclude that the situation described in 'An Longbhriseadh' did not exercise a deep influence on Ó Bruadair's motivation as a composer. Silence looks to have been the sole means left to him of reacting to the fate of his civilisation. Others of his colleagues may have taken this course as well over time.

Prose

This chapter has chosen to focus on poetry primarily as, in the comparatively undeveloped domain of eighteenth-century Irish scholarship, it has received the greater share of attention, and consequently offers a platform on which to build further exposition and argumentation. The second of the two media at issue here would appear to have enjoyed far less notice. Its situation is paradoxical, because extant prose writings may surpass their verse counterparts in quantity and range, if on no other grounds. These comprise copies of early medieval sagas, including material from all the major indigenous branches like the mythology, Ulster, King and *fiannaíocht* cycles, as well as hagiography. Adaptations of overseas classical and romance works, the latter dating from post-Norman times, are represented as well. The abundant output of the 1600s reappears in full during the next century. The 1700s also generated their own new creations. Transmission, reception and invention all await further investigation, in ways which may be only sketched here in outline.

Secular prose

The taking on board of pre-existing prose matter is not a passive exercise. An instance from the Ulster Cycle helps illustrate the proposition. This series, comprising over sixty tales, concerns the affairs of a community in the northeast of Ireland at an undetermined point before the advent of Christianity, even if it may owe its recording and continuation to the writing skills brought to the island with the arrival of the new religion. Various anecdotes deal with insoluble difficulties among the people in question. *Longes Mac nUislenn* (The Exile of the Sons of Uisliu) centres on the struggles surrounding the female character, the Old Irish form of whose name is Derdriu.[95] Among these are whether, as an otherwise innocent infant, she should be saved or slain following a prophecy foretelling that she would cause trouble; the authority of the Ulster ruler, Conchobar, to spare her or by so doing counter his people's counsel; the furtherance of the girl's own, arguably legitimate, desires against the possible best interests of Noísiu, the object of her affections; their departure from Ireland; the king's dilemma regarding forgiving the elopement and allowing them to return, followed by Derdriu's suicide (and its morality) after the execution of her paramour, with, finally, the civil war generated by certain Ulstermen against their own province when their gurarantee of safe passage to Noísiu was violated. This clash of values is presented with a conciseness of expression characteristic of much early Irish narration.

Given its centrality, the tale went on to be reformulated down through the centuries. A second redaction from around 1400 casts it as melodrama, with the presentation stressing the starkness of the emotions and the nomenclature of the *dramatis personae* reflecting evolution in the language proper.[96] The text dwells on Deirdre's anxiety, the darkness of Conchobhar's treachery or the heroism of Naoise and his brothers' self-defence on their return to Ireland. A copy of this reworking was available to scribes in the later 1600s. Earlier in that century, Geoffrey Keating presented the pre-Norman recension in shortened form in his compendium of Irish history, *Foras Feasa ar Éirinn*, which became one of the most abundantly replicated documents throughout what remained of the Irish manuscript heritage. Scribes interested in the Deirdre saga during the 1700s would therefore have had a spread of models at their disposal when coming to it. These could comprise either the integral earlier redactions or précis of them, or various combinations thereof, all with their own emphases. Copyists' own best guesses as to character or motivation would often have featured in their retellings,[97] with the possibility of these end-products all entering into folk narrative as manuscript renditions were in turn read out.[98] The Deirdre story is, to date, probably the only Irish tale whose trajectory throughout the tradition and into Anglo-Irish writing has been traced even in these most summary terms. Hundreds of its prose counterparts, and particularly those associated with the 1700s, await similar rudimentary treatment.

Well-established narrative constructs could be reworked internally or also given an added external dimension. This may be seen in the case of *Eachtra na gCuradh*, a work which takes the cast of Ulster characters as its point of departure but then goes off in other directions.[99] These protagonists are, in the main, the *curaidh* ('warriors') implicit in its title, while its *eachtra* term refers to three 'excursions' they make out of Ireland. The text itself describes these voyages as 'rowings' (*ráimh*). The composition is clearly ahistorical with reference to the Ulster Cycle proper, as the journeys involve, variously, trips to Africa, Persia and Greece, among the geographically secure locations, or to a range of alternative venues more patently fictitious. The compendium provides a context for the 'adventures' also implicit in its title's first word. During its various outings, heroes like Fer Día retrieve precious stones, or the principal narrator, Conall Cearnach, other valuable heirlooms, often in single combat or in battle. The text thus gives free rein to the imagination in what is ultimately an exercise in wondrous thrillseeking. Not the least interesting aspect of it is the identity of its scribe, Pádraig Úa Pronntaigh, himself a northerner who penned the piece in October 1761. What appears to be the anglicised form of this surname, Brontë, is better known in other times and in different settings.

Other contemporary texts may have taken as their starting point prose works of relatively recent vintage rather than ones with older roots. The seventeenth-century compilation *Pairlement Chloinne Tomáis* brought the Irish peasantry more fulsomely into fiction with its aristocratic satire of upstart commoners. The latter had benefited materially from upheavals during phases like the Cromwellian period when their former rulers lost privilege and position. The uncouthness of the lower orders, however, ensured that social climbing could never make up for inferiority of birth. This work ultimately paved the way for other writers, such as Tadhg Ó Neachtain, who explored the humours of misconduct in his picaresque *Stair Éamoinn Uí Chléirigh*.[100] Its eponymous hero received, in Part 1, the hand in marriage of Iomchuibheacht inghean Fhortúin ('Decency daughter of Fortune') on agreeing to her request that he stay away from the nefarious Cuirm Searbhandeire ('Bitter-End Brew'). There follows the tale of Éamonn's unending struggle with alcoholic addiction, played out in encounters between him and Cuirm throughout different parts of Ireland, including rural Roscommon and urban Dublin, before his personal purgatory at Lough Derg, after which he opens a school to instruct speakers of broken English. One of these plays his part in introducing a further character, Cormac Mac Searraigh, who, in Part II, proceeds to relate the misadventures and marriage of persons of his own acquaintance.

References to country and city life, as well as to teaching, indicate that aspects of Ó Neachtain's affairs must have formed the basis for this account. An autobiographical strand seems more overtly present in *Eachtra Thomáis Mhic Chaiside*,[101] the life story of one Tomás Ó Casaide, also a native of County Roscommon, but of whom, curiously, almost nothing else is known apart from this prosimetrical combination. His tale is the story of a person educated as an Augustinian, but who abandoned his calling for a wandering existence. After some time travelling throughout Ireland, he went overseas and became involved in various continental military forces in the 1730s. He deserted the

French army and fled into the Black Forest with a German colleague who subsequently betrayed him to the Prussians. The hero absconded and made his way to Brunswick, and thence, following further incidents, to Hamburg, where he embarked for Bristol and later Ireland. This main character would often tell tales during his subsequent period of vagrancy in Ireland, acting the part of a dazzling distractor of those he proposed to entertain. He claims he wound up as a pitiable, troubled and sorrowful wretch ('fuad bocht faoi bhuaidhreadh . . . is me a ceisnigheadh i mbrón', l. 608). The piece may be substantially shorter than *Stair Éamoinn Uí Chléirigh* and other items, but all point to the same general conclusion. While eighteenth-century Irish prose remained weighted towards its earlier narrative forebears, modernity was in prospect. The nucleus of a Gaelic novel, realist or other, is present in these more creative undertakings.[102]

Devotional prose

Religious works form the second major strand of eighteenth-century Irish prose composition. This may also consist of reworked early material together with items closer chronologically to its own point in time. We shall take a look at the second of the two elements for the distinctive perspective it offers on different aspects of contemporary Gaelic civilisation. One particularly note-worthy feature is the recent adaptation into Irish of a number of works of French spirituality.[103] This is hardly surprising, given that France acted as the foremost training ground for Irish Catholic clergy in pre-Revolutionary days. Two Gaelic compositions may serve to indicate the nature of the material taken into that language. The first is a compendium of scripture-based history enti-tled *Stair an Bhíobla*.[104] This text is made up of a lengthy introduction, followed by a summary of the Old Testament, from the Creation to the Books of the Maccabees, with their influential doctrinal teaching on immortality, the value of suffering as a means of expiation and prayers for the dead, and onwards. The second composition, entitled *Trompa na bhFlaitheas*,[105] is a clarion-call to sinners to abandon wrongdoing and turn towards God. Its first section con-centrates on what a transgressor's attitude of mind should be in attempting to achieve this aim (pp. 5–132). Twenty-six chapters detail ways of focusing a Christian's attention on the Lord, such as through penance (pp. 50–4). Section 2 is concerned with the obstacles a believer will confront in this endeavour (pp. 133–202), listing instances of the same, like his own natural infirmity or lack of resolve (pp. 165–70), in its thirteen sub-segments. Its third section concen-trates on strategies helpful in implementing the move towards proper conver-sion (pp. 202–63), from the good works of its opening component (pp. 203–9) through to its tenth and final part's statement of an absolute requirement not to overlook prayer (pp. 256–63).

Stair an Bhíobla is probably an adaptation of *L'histoire du Vieux et du Nouveau Testament* (1670), primarily by the Port Royal Jansenist theologian Nicholas Fontaine, Sieur de Royaumont (1625–1709). Another associate of this foundation, Isaac-Louis Le Maistre de Sacy (1613–84), most likely collaborated in its production as well. The source of the second work is *La trompette du ciel*, issued posthumously in 1661 and attributed to a Provençal clergyman, Antoine Yvan (1576–1653). His peripatetic career included a period as a domestic servant and pedlar of his own artwork. His contact with the Oratorian movement and establishment of the Notre Dame de Miséricorde congregation of nuns led to the production of pious manuals of self-improvement such as the item at issue here. Reforming trends in seventeenth-century French Catholicism constitute the main threads linking these and related compositions. Their adaptation may have reflected a recognition that post-Reformation experience in France would provide the best means of strengthening devotional practice in Ireland in the 1700s, at a time when Catholicism there experienced administrative weaknesses, some anti-clericalism and other difficulties.

The names of two signatories in the manuscript copy of *Stair an Bhíobla*, those of the Roscommon-based Gaelic aristocrat Cathal Ó Conchubhair (Charles O'Conor, 1710–91) and the scribe, Brian Ó Fearghail (1715–*c*.1812), suggest the codex's associations are with the west of Ireland. Accordingly, the work's Gaelic compiler, Uaitéar Ó Ceallaigh (*c*.1726–73), may have been a Galway-based Franciscan of the same name. A Calced Carmelite prior, Tadhg Ó Conaill (obit 1779), completed *Trompa na bhFlaitheas* in Kinsale, County Cork, in the 1750s. His motivation in so doing was to combat the dearth of suitable devotional works in Irish, especially for the young, and to confront the drop in standards of religious instruction consequent on persecution. His comments in this connection may have implications beyond the sphere of religion. Ó Conaill's introduction also alludes to a reduction in the numbers of secular teachers consequent on disturbed contemporary circumstances ('do bhrígh an léirsgris do-rinneadh . . . ar na hoideadha don eagluis agus don tuath'). Their absence could equally have had implications for the production of literary as well as more devout prose composition at this time.

Conclusion

An account such as this cannot be fully inclusive in its coverage. Poets like Donnchadh Ruadh Mac Con Mara or Eoghan Rua Ó Súilleábháin have been omitted. The adventures of the former as an aspirant traveller to Newfoundland, or the latter's active, if rather ironic, service in the British navy, indicate that each shared more than the same colourful personal epithet or origins in Ireland's eighteenth-century Gaelic heartland. Adapters of historical tracts like *Stair Fhírcheart ar Éirinn*, the Irish rendition of *The Impartial History of Ireland* with which Cornelius Nary is associated, are overlooked, as are the activities of lexicographers such as Aodh Mac Cruitín or Seán Ó Briain. If it cannot become fully informative, a chapter like the present should seek, nevertheless, to be in some sense interpretative. This contribution may accordingly have demonstrated that the material it covers is intellectually and artistically challenging. The situation could hardly be otherwise. Those many composers who created it were heirs to a major cultural legacy, whatever the vicissitudes by then confronting their patrimony. The richness many of them strove to perpetuate may come, in time, to be more fittingly harvested.

Notes

1. See Cornelius G. Buttimer, 'Postclassical Modern Irish', in Máirtín Ó Murchú, ed. *Scoil an Léinn Cheiltigh Tuarascáil Leathchéad Blian / School of Celtic Studies Fiftieth Anniversary Report 1940–1990* (Dublin: Dublin Institute for Advanced Studies, 1990), pp. 119–24.

2. The language of hitherto unedited texts is modified, according to current scholarly approaches, to reflect modern standards. Gaelic citations from existing printed sources are given as their editors have presented them, unless otherwise indicated. First lines of poems are also italicised in conformity with recent procedures. 'Q.' ('quatrain') is employed in this article to distinguish segments in syllabic verse from segments in accentual verse. For accentual verse, the abbreviation 'st.' for 'stanza' is used. Quatrain or stanza or line numbers not present in manuscripts or editions are given in square brackets.

3. The emergence of the practice at a localised level may be seen in Traolach Ó Ríordáin, 'Saothrú an Traidisiúin', in Ó Ríordáin, *Conradh na Gaeilge i gCorcaigh 1894–1910* (Dublin: Cois Life Teoranta, 2000), pp. 117–76.

4. For comments on historians' engagement (or lack of it) with Gaelic materials see J. J. Lee, 'Irish History', in Neil Buttimer, Colin Rynne and Helen Guerin, eds. *The Heritage of Ireland* (Cork: The Collins Press, 2000), pp. 117–36, at pp. 131–32.

5. John C. Mac Erlean, ed. *Duanaire Dháibhidh Uí Bhruadair/The Poems of David Ó Bruadair*, 3 vols., Irish Texts Society XI, XIII and XVIII (London: Irish Texts Society, 1908–17); Pádraigín Riggs, ed. *Dáibhí Ó Bruadair: His Historical and Literary Context*, Irish Texts Society Subsidiary Series 11 (Dublin: Irish Texts Society, 2001); Dara Binéid, *Searc na Suadh: Gnéithe de Fhilíocht Dháibhí Uí Bhruadair* (Dublin: An Clóchomhar, 2003).

6. Mac Erlean, *Duanaire Dháibhidh Uí Bhruadair*, III, pp. 164–81 (text, translation and notes).

7. Patrick Dinneen and Tadhg O'Donoghue, eds. *Dánta Aodhagáin Uí Rathaille/The Poems of Egan O'Rahilly*, 2nd edn (London: Irish Texts Society, 1911); Seán Ó Tuama, *Filí faoi Sceimhle: Seán Ó Ríordáin agus Aogán Ó Rathaille* (Dublin: Oifig an tSoláthair, 1978).

8. Breandán Ó Buachalla, 'Ó Rathaille, na Cárthaigh agus na Brúnaigh', *Studia Hibernica* 31 (2000–1), pp. 119–38, argues against this patronage.
9. Dinneen and O'Donoghue, *Dánta Aodhagáin Uí Rathaille*, pp. 18–21 (text, translation and notes).
10. Breandán Ó Buachalla, '"A Line in Aogán Ó Rathile"', *Celtica* 24 (2003), pp. 225–31.
11. Neil Buttimer, 'An Irish Inscription in the Tower of London', *Journal of the Cork Historical and Archaeological Society* 107 (2002), pp. 211–16.
12. Nessa Ní Shéaghdha, 'Irish Scholars and Scribes in Eighteenth-Century Dublin', *Eighteenth-Century Ireland / Iris an Dá Chultúr* 4 (1989), pp. 41–54.
13. For these see Cuthbert Mhág Craith, ed. *Dán na mBráthar Mionúr*, 2 vols. (Dublin: Dublin Institute of Advanced Studies, 1967), I, pp. 273–8 (text, with length-marks replacing editor's macrons and most editorial square brackets removed here).
14. Thomas Bartlett, *The Fall and Rise of the Irish Nation: The Catholic Question 1690–1830* (Dublin: Gill and Macmillan, 1992), pp. 1–29.
15. Nessa O'Sullivan, 'Tadhg Ó Neachtain agus na Nuachtáin', unpublished MA thesis, University College, Cork (1990).
16. From National Library of Ireland (NLI), MS G 132, p. 92, cited in Nessa Ní Shéaghdha, ed. *Catalogue of Irish Manuscripts in the National Library of Ireland*, Fasciculus IV (Dublin: Dublin Institute for Advanced Studies, 1977), pp. 60–1.
17. Pádraig A. Breatnach, 'Muircheartach Óg Ó Súilleabháin (+ 1754): Stair, Traidisiún agus Marbhnaí', in Breatnach, ed. *Téamaí Taighde Nua-Ghaeilge* (Maynooth: An Sagart, 1997), pp. 159–237.
18. Roibeárd Ó hÚrdail, 'An Pleaintéir agus an Gael Dísheabhaithe', in Pádraigín Riggs, Breandán Ó Conchúir and Seán Ó Coileáin, eds. *Saoi na hÉigse: Aistí in Ómós do Sheán Ó Tuama* (Dublin: An Clóchomhar, 2000), pp. 105–52, especially pp. 105–6, where a previously unpublished version of a Gaelic lament for John Puxley is also provided (pp. 122–3).
19. Texts here as in Breatnach, 'Muircheartach Óg', pp. 178–225, with all translations mine; Ó hÚrdail, 'An Pleaintéir', pp. 124–31, supplies additional (whole or partial) recensions of the items.
20. Tomás de Bhial, *Oidheadh an Athar Uí Shíthigh* (Dublin: Oifig an tSoláthair, 1954).
21. Citations here based on copy in Royal Irish Academy (henceforth RIA), MS 23 B 4, pp. 9–24; see Elizabeth FitzPatrick, *Catalogue of Irish Manuscripts in the Royal Irish Academy*, Fasciculus IX (Dublin: Royal Irish Academy, 1933), pp. 1151–3, at p. 1152.
22. Cited from Angela Bourke, Siobhán Kilfeather, Maria Luddy, Margaret Mac Curtain, Geraldine Meaney, Máirín Ní Dhonnchadha, Mary O'Dowd and Clair Wills, eds. *The Field Day Anthology of Irish Writing, vols. IV and V: Irish Women's Writing and Traditions* (Cork: Cork University Press in association with Field Day, 2002), IV, pp. 1369–71 (text and translation), 1398 (notes).
23. Excerpts here from version in RIA, MS 12 E 24, pp. 67–8; see Elizabeth FitzPatrick, *Catalogue of Irish Manuscripts in the Royal Irish Academy*, Fasciculus XXI (Dublin: Royal Irish Academy, 1936), pp. 2624–33, at p. 2627.
24. L. M. Cullen, 'The Contemporary and Later Politics of *Caoineadh Airt Uí Laoire*', *Eighteenth-Century Ireland / Iris an Dá Chultúr* 8 (1993), pp. 7–38.
25. Seán Ó Tuama, ed. *Caoineadh Airt Uí Laoghaire* (Dublin: An Clóchomhar, 1961).

26. Ríonach Uí Ógáin, *An Rí gan Choróin: Dónall Ó Conaill sa Bhéaloideas* (Dublin: An Clóchomhar, 1984), translated as *Immortal Dan: Daniel O'Connell in Irish Folk Tradition* (Dublin: Geography Publications, 1995).

27. Seán Ó Coileáin, 'When Oral Becomes Literary: The Case of *Caoineadh Airt Uí Laoghaire*', Statutory Public Lecture, School of Celtic Studies, Dublin Institute for Advanced Studies, 2003. See also Donna Wong's discussion in chapter 15.

28. Angela Bourke, 'Tórramh-Chaoineadh Airt Uí Laoghaire', from University College, Dublin, Ferriter MS, no. 1, pp. 298–305, in Bourke et al., *Field Day Anthology of Irish Writing*, IV, pp. 1372–84 (text and translation), 1398 (notes).

29. References here to Ó Tuama, *Caoineadh Airt Uí Laoghaire*, unless otherwise indicated.

30. Bourke, 'Tórramh-Chaoineadh', pp. 1373 (text), 1378 (translation).

31. Thomas Bartlett et al., eds. *1798: A Bicentenary Perspective* (Dublin: Four Courts Press, 2003).

32. Brian Ó Cuív, 'Tréadlitir ó 1798', *Éigse* 11 (1964), pp. 57–64.

33. Cited from Thomas Pakenham, *The Year of Liberty: The History of the Great Irish Rebellion of 1798* (London: Hodder & Stoughton, 1969; reprinted London: Fontana, 1992), p. 209. See also Tom Dunne, *Rebellions: Memoir, Memory and 1798* (Dublin: Lilliput Press, 2004).

34. Cited from RIA, MS 23 M 5, pp. 75–7 (translation mine), by the copyist Seán Ó Dálaigh; see Elizabeth FitzPatrick, *Catalogue of Irish Manuscripts in the Royal Irish Academy*, Fasciculus XV (Dublin: Royal Irish Academy, 1935), pp. 1911–15, at p. 1914.

35. Breandán Ó Conchúir, 'Tomás Ó Longáin, Captain Steele', in John Carey, Máire Herbert and Kevin Murray, eds. *Cín Chille Cúile. Texts, Saints and Places: Essays in Honour of Pádraig Ó Riain* (Aberystwyth: Celtic Studies Publications, 2004), pp. 249–57.

36. Breandán Ó Buachalla, *Aisling Ghéar: Na Stíobhartaigh agus an tAos Léinn 1603–1788* (Dublin: An Clóchomhar, 1996); Éamonn Ó Ciardha, *Ireland and the Jacobite Cause* (Dublin: Four Courts Press, 2004).

37. Pádraig Ua Duinnín, ed. *Amhráin Sheagháin Chláraigh Mhic Dhomhnaill* (Dublin: Conradh na Gaedhilge, 1908), pp. 1–3 (text).

38. Cited from RIA, MS 23 M 46, p. 9, by the copyist Richard Tipper; see Kathleen Mulchrone, *Catalogue of Irish Manuscripts in the Royal Irish Academy*, Fasciculus IV (Dublin: Royal Irish Academy, 1929), pp. 411–14, at p. 413.

39. Thus Tadhg Ó Neachtain transcribed English-language newspaper accounts of the viceroy's address to King George I seeking aid for Ireland now that sedition had ended there, and translated into Irish press reports of Carteret's laying the foundation stone for this country's new houses of parliament in 1728; see O'Sullivan, 'Tadhg Ó Neachtain agus na Nuachtáin', pp. 81–2 and 77 respectively.

40. Breandán Ó Buachalla, ed. *Peadar Ó Doirnín: Amhráin* (Dublin: An Clóchomhar, 1969); Seán de Rís, ed. *Peadar Ó Doirnín: a Bheatha agus a Shaothar* (Dublin: Oifig an tSoláthair, 1969).

41. De Rís, *Peadar Ó Doirnín*, pp. 45–7 (text), 141–2 (notes).

42. Úna Nic Éinrí, *Canfar an Dán: Uilliam English agus a Chairde*, Dán agus Tallann 10 (Dingle: An Sagart, 2003), pp. 129–30 (text), 253–7 (notes).

43. Cited here from British Library, MS Add. 31877, f. 141 b, for which see Robin Flower, *Catalogue of Irish Manuscripts in the British Museum*, 3 vols. (London: British Museum, 1926), II, pp. 214–21, at p. 220. Neil Buttimer, 'Degrés de Perception de la France dans

l'Irlande gaélique de la pré-famine', in Catherine Laurent and Helen Davis, eds. *Irlande et Bretagne: Vingt Siècles d'Histoire* (Rennes: Terre de Brume, 1994), pp. 179–89, at pp. 183–4, explores the wider context.

44. Cited from RIA, MS 23 D 8, pp. 270–3 by the copyist Philip Gibbon; see Elizabeth Fitz-Patrick, *Catalogue of Irish Manuscripts in the Royal Irish Academy*, Fasciculus XII (Dublin: Royal Irish Academy, 1934), pp. 1450–5, at p. 1454. Séamus de Vál, 'Oidhreacht Ghaelach Loch Garman', *Irisleabhar Mhá Nuad* (1992), pp. 75–107, at p. 96, discusses the scribe.

45. Liam Ó Murchú, *Cúirt an Mheón-Oíche* (Dublin: An Clóchomhar, 1982), which supplies text and notes.

46. Liam P. Ó Murchú, 'Cúlra agus Múnla Liteartha do *Chúirt* Mherriman', in Riggs et al. *Saoi na hÉigse*, pp. 169–95.

47. Cornelius G. Buttimer, '*Cogadh Sagsana Nuadh Sonn*: Reporting the American Revolution', *Studia Hibernica* 28 (1994), pp. 63–101, at pp. 79–92; Vincent Morley, *Irish Opinion and the American Revolution, 1760–1783* (Cambridge: Cambridge University Press, 2002) discusses the general background.

48. Thus in one love poem (*An ghéag dá dtug mé grá di is áille í ná Helen mhór*), the poet Peadar Ó Doirnín states that he would have wished to walk with his sweetheart through Pennsylvania among Quakers, because they would not be speaking (or gossiping) about the couple (ll. 1–10); see de Rís, *Peadar Ó Doirnín*, pp. 16–17, at p. 16.

49. Áine Ní Chróinín, ed. *Beatha Chríost*, Leabhar ó Láimhsgríbhnibh XVII (Dublin: Oifig an tSoláthair, 1952). Editor's macrons are replaced by length-marks here.

50. Cainneach Ó Maonaigh, *Smaointe Beatha Chríost* (Dublin: Dublin Institute for Advanced Studies, 1944).

51. Compare ibid., pp. xiii–xlviii for the details of the underlying fifteenth-century text.

52. Ibid. may also be consulted to gauge the alterations in the late seventeenth-century verse rendition of this scene.

53. See NLI, MS G 135, pp. 43–55, noted in Ní Shéaghdha, *Catalogue*, pp. 72–4. Angela Partridge (Bourke) discusses the wider background in *Caoineadh na dTrí Muire: Téama na Páise i bhFilíocht Bhéil na Gaeilge* (Dublin: An Clóchomhar, 1983).

54. Michael McGrath, ed. *Cinnlae Amhlaoibh Uí Shúileabháin: The Diary of Humphrey O'Sullivan*, 4 vols., Irish Texts Society XXX–XXXIII (London: Irish Texts Society, 1937), IV, pp. 152–5 (text and translation). For the scribe see Neil Buttimer, 'Amhlaoibh Ó Súilleabháin's Writings', in Liam P. Ó Murchú, ed. *Cinnlae Amhlaoibh Uí Shúileabháin: Reassessments*, Irish Texts Society Subsidiary Series XIV (Dublin: Irish Texts Society, 2004), pp. 79–110.

55. Úna Nic Éinrí, *An Cantaire Siúlach: Tadhg Gaelach*, Dán agus Tallann VIII (Dingle: An Sagart, 2001).

56. Ibid., pp. 215 for the full text (translations here mine), 303 (notes).

57. Ibid., for poems *A Mhóirmhic cathrach cailce na soils' aoihne* (pp. 140–2, at 1. [9]) and *A Ollaimh a Íosa, naíomhaigh, neartaigh* (pp. 156–62, at 1. [27] and 1. [13]).

58. Ibid., pp. 209–11 (text), 298–300 (notes).

59. Ibid., pp. 213–14 (text), 301–3 (notes).

60. See Anna Heussaff, *Filí agus Cléir san Ochtú hAois Déag* (Dublin: An Clóchomhar, 1993).

61. Tomás Ó Fiaich, ed., *Art Mac Cumhaigh: Dánta* (Dublin: An Clóchomhar, 1973), pp. 94–6 (text), 147–8 (notes).

62. De Rís, *Peadar Ó Doirnín*, pp. 39–42 (text), 134–38 (notes).

63. Ibid., pp. 25–7 (text), 121–3 (notes).

64. Risteard Ó Foghludha, ed. *Éigse na Máighe* (Dublin: Oifig an tSoláthair, 1952), pp. 84 (text), 241 (notes).

65. Alan Harrison, *Ag Cruinniú Meala: Anthony Raymond (1675–1726), Ministéir Protastúnach, agus Léann na Gaeilge i mBaile Átha Cliath* (Dublin: An Clóchomhar, 1988).

66. Calvert Watkins, 'The Etymology of Irish *Dúan*', *Celtica* 11 (1976), pp. 270–7. For the wider context, see also Dáithí Ó hÓgáin, *An File: Staidéar ar Osnádúrthacht na Filíochta sa Traidisiún Gaelach* (Dublin: Oifig an tSoláthair, 1982).

67. De Rís, *Peadar Ó Doirnín*, pp. 16–17 (text), 115–16 (notes).

68. Above, note 6.

69. Ó Foghludha, *Éigse na Máighe*, pp. 77–8 (text), 240 (notes).

70. Patrick J. O'Connor, *Fairs and Markets of Ireland: A Cultural Geography* (Newcastle West: Oireacht na Mumhan Books, [2003]), to whose references may be added Cornelius G. Buttimer, 'Tuairisc Amhailt Uí Iartáin: An Eighteenth-Century Poem on a Fair', *Eighteenth-Century Ireland / Iris an Dá Chultúr* 7 (1992), pp. 75–94.

71. De Rís, *Peadar Ó Doirnín*, pp. 18–20 (text), 118 (notes).

72. Eoghan Ó hAnluain, ed. *Seon Ó hUaithnín* (Dublin: An Clóchomhar, 1973), pp. 37 (text), 67 (notes).

73. Breandán Ó Buachalla, ed. *Cathal Buí: Amhráin* (Dublin: An Clóchomhar, 1975), pp. 75–83 (text of two versions), 133–46 (notes).

74. Ibid., pp. 64–6 (text), 125–8 (notes).

75. Ó Foghludha, *Éigse na Máighe*, p. 79 (text).

76. Ibid., pp. 78 (text), 240 (notes).

77. Above, note 21.

78. Ó Foghludha, *Éigse na Máighe*, in the poem beginning *Ó gabhais mo pháirt san dán, a shuairc-fhir ghroidhe*, pp. 75–6 (text), 240 (notes), at l. 19.

79. Ibid., at l. 26.

80. Ibid., pp. 74–5 (text), 239 (notes), at l. 13.

81. De Rís, *Peadar Ó Doirnín*, pp. 27–8 (text), 123–5 (notes).

82. Above, note 67.

83. Above, note 63.

84. From the poem *My Learned Friends What Source of Dull Despair*, in Diarmuid Ó Muirithe, ed. *Tomás Ó Míocháin: Filíocht* (Dublin: An Clóchomhar, 1988), pp. 65–6 (text), 93 (notes), at ll. 27–8.

85. Ní Chróinín, *Beatha Chríost*, pp. 145, 170.

86. Breandán Ó Conchúir, 'Na Cúirteanna Éigse i gCúige Mumhan', in Riggs et al., eds. *Saoi na hÉigse*, pp. 55–81. For the legislative resonances, see further Damien Ó Muirí, 'An Cúlra Dlíthiúil leis an Bharántas', in Máirtín Ó Briain and Pádraig Ó Héalaí, eds. *Téada Dúchais: Aistí in Ómós don Ollamh Breandán Ó Madagáin* (Inverin: Cló Iar-Chonnachta, 2002), pp. 423–44.

87. See *Fáilte dár n-árd-fhlaith dár ndíon* and *Gabhaim páirt le Seán Ó Tuama an Ghrinn* in Ó Foghludha, *Éigse na Máighe*, pp. 78 and 74–5 (text), and 240 and 239 (notes) respectively.

88. Ibid., pp. 85–92 (texts), 241–2 (notes).

89. De Rís, *Peadar Ó Doirnín*, pp. 3 (text), 101–3 (notes).

90. Ibid., pp. 8–10 (text), 106–7 (notes).

91. Ó Fiaich, *Art Mac Cumhaigh*, pp. 116–17 (text), 158–60 (notes).

92. Breandán Ó Conchúir, 'Comhfhreagras sa Deibhidhe ón mBliain 1762', in Ó Briain and Ó Héalaí, *Téada Dúchais*, pp. 275–93. For additional insights on versification and composition probably of relevance to the 'courts' of poetry see Tadhg Ó Donnchadha, *Prosóid Gaedhilge* (Cork: Cló Ollsgoile Chorcaighe, 1925) and *Bhéarsaidheacht Gaedhilge* (Dublin: Brún agus Ó Nualláin, 1936).

93. Éamonn Ó Tuathail, *Roinn agus Amhráin* (Dublin: Brún agus Ó Nualláin, 1944).

94. Breandán Ó Conchúir, 'The Manuscript Transmission of Ó Bruadair's Poetry', in Riggs, *Dáibhí Ó Bruadair*, pp. 46–55.

95. For references to editions and studies of this work see Cornelius G. Buttimer, '*Longes mac nUislenn* Reconsidered', *Éigse* 28 (1994–5), pp. 1–41.

96. See Caoimhín Mac Giolla Léith, ed. *Oidheadh Chloinne hUisneach: The Violent Death of the Children of Uisneach*, Irish Texts Society LVI (London: Irish Texts Society, 1992).

97. See ibid., pp. 9–62 *passim* for an exploration of these issues.

98. See further for this general area Alan Bruford, *Gaelic Folktales and Medieval Romances: A Study of Early Modern Irish 'Romantic Tales' and their Oral Derivatives* (Dublin: Folklore of Ireland Society, 1969).

99. Meadhbh Ní Chléirigh, ed. *Eachtra na gCuradh*, Leabhair Ó Láimhsgríbhinibh I (Dublin: Oifig an tSoláthair, 1941).

100. Eoghan Ó Neachtain, ed. *Stair Éamuinn Uí Chléire* (Dublin: Mac an Ghuill, 1918). William J. Mahon, *The History of Éamon O'Clery* (Inverin: Cló Iar-Chonnachta, 2000) has provided a valuable translation, annotation and standardised version of Ó Neachtain's edition.

101. Maighréad Nic Philibín, *Na Caisidigh agus a gCuid Filidheachta* (Dublin: Oifig an tSoláthair, 1938), pp. 23–43 (text), 149–59 (notes).

102. For a seminal initiation of debate on this topic see Cathal Ó Háinle, 'An tÚrscéal nár Tháinig', *Léachtaí Cholm Cille* 4 (1975), pp. 1–29.

103. Cornelius G. Buttimer, 'The French Sources of Religious Teaching in Pre-Famine Gaelic Ireland', in *Transactions of the Eighth International Congress on the Enlightenment, Studies on Voltaire and the Eighteenth Century* 303–5 (1992), pp. 620–4.

104. Máire Ní Mhuirgheasa, *Stair an Bhíobla*, 4 vols., Leabhair ó Láimhsgríbhinní IV, V, VIII and XIV (Dublin: Oifig Díolta Foillseacháin Rialtais, 1941–5).

105. Cecile O'Rahilly, ed. *Trompa na bhFlaitheas* (Dublin: Institute for Advanced Studies, 1955).

Select bibliography

Breatnach, R. A., 'The End of a Tradition: A Survey of Eighteenth-Century Gaelic Literature', *Studia Hibernica* 1 (1961), pp. 128–50.

Buttimer, Cornelius G., 'Gaelic Literature and Contemporary Life in Cork, 1700–1840', in Patrick O'Flanagan and Cornelius G. Buttimer, eds. *Cork, History and Society: Interdisciplinary Essays on the History of an Irish County*, Dublin: Geography Publications, 1993, pp. 585–654.

Caerwyn-Williams, J. E. and Máirín Ní Mhuiríosa, *Traidisiún Liteartha na nGael*, Dublin: An Clóchomhar, 1979.

Corkery, Daniel, *The Hidden Ireland: A Study of Gaelic Munster in the Eighteenth Century*, Dublin: Gill and Macmillan, 1924.

Cullen, L. M., *The Hidden Ireland: Reassessment of a Concept*, Mullingar: Lilliput Press, 1988.

de Blacam, Aodh, *Gaelic Literature Surveyed*, Dublin: Talbot, 1933.

de Brún, Pádraig, *Lámhscríbhinní Gaeilge: Treoirliosta*, Dublin: Dublin Institute for Advanced Studies, 1988.

Hyde, Douglas, *A Literary History of Ireland from Earliest Times to the Present Day*, London: T. Fisher Unwin, 1899.

Kiberd, Declan, *Irish Classics*, London: Granta, 2001.

Ní Mhurchú, Máire and Diarmuid Breathnach, eds. *1560–1781 Beathaisnéis*, Dublin: An Clóchomhar, 2001.

eds. *Beathaisnéis 1782–1881*, Dublin: An Clóchomhar, 1999.

Ó Buachalla, Breandán, *I mBéal Feirste Cois Cuain*, Dublin: An Clóchomhar, 1968.

Ó Conchúir, Breandán, *Scríobhaithe Chorcaí 1700–1850*, Dublin: An Clóchomhar, 1982.

Ó Cuív, Brian, 'Irish Language and Literature, 1691–1845', in T. W. Moody and W. E. Vaughan, eds. *A New History of Ireland, vol. IV: Eighteenth-Century Ireland (1691–1800)*, Oxford: Clarendon Press, 1986, pp. 375–423.

Ó Fiannachta, Pádraig, *Léas ar Ár Litríocht*, Maynooth: An Sagart, 1974.

Léas Eile ar Ár Litríocht, Maynooth: An Sagart, 1982.

Ó Madagáin, Breandán, *An Ghaeilge i Luimneach 1700–1900*, Dublin: An Clóchomhar, 1974.

Ó Tuama, Seán, *Repossessions: Selected Essays on the Irish Literary Heritage*, Cork: Cork University Press, 1995.

Ó Tuama, Seán, and Thomas Kinsella, *An Duanaire: Poems of the Dispossessed*, Portlaoise: Dolmen Press, 1981.

Welch, Robert, *The Oxford Companion to Irish Literature*, Oxford: Clarendon, 1996.

9

Theatre in Ireland, 1690–1800: from the Williamite wars to the Act of Union

CHRISTOPHER MORASH

'For the amusement of the plundered people': Irish theatre in 1691

Shortly before Christmas in the winter of 1691, announcements for a production of *Othello* at Dublin's Smock Alley Theatre appeared in the taverns, coffee houses and printers' shops clustered in the narrow streets between Dublin Castle and the river Liffey. For the people of Dublin, this was yet another sign of civil society re-emerging, for – like so much else in the city – Smock Alley had lain dark and empty during the three years of warfare and plague since William of Orange's landing in England in November 1688. Anyone reading those notices would have known that reopening the theatre in the months immediately after the Treaty of Limerick involved much more than airing the musty seats and dusting off the scenery. For the audiences who made their way through the thin winter light to that production of *Othello*, there would have been an uncanny sense of returning to something familiar, and yet anomalous in its familiarity, for all around it had changed.

The theatre in which the play was to be performed, Smock Alley was only the second public theatre building to have been constructed in Ireland. Its predecessor had been established (probably in 1635)[1] in Werburgh Street (just behind Dublin Castle) by the lord lieutenant of the time, Thomas Wentworth, earl of Strafford, and was managed by a member of Wentworth's retinue, John Ogilby. Although it lasted only until 1640, the Werburgh Street Theatre was part of a culture of theatre-going in the Stuart court; Smock Alley, also built by Ogilby, was a continuation of that tradition, and had been built as part of the process of establishing a Stuart viceregal court in Restoration Dublin. Consequently, when the Stuarts were defeated in 1690, there must have been some doubt as to whether the theatre would reopen. As it happened, the new administration chose the pragmatic course of action, and not long after his appointment in 1692 as the first lord lieutenant under William, Viscount Henry

Sidney began promoting (as one observer put it) 'Plays, Sports, and Interludes for the Amusement of the Plundered People'.[2] So, when *Othello* was staged in 1691, there would have been cautious optimism that the theatre would survive the demise of the regime that had created it. In the long term, its survival would depend upon its ability to adapt to the tectonic ideological shifts set in motion by the Williamite wars. For much of the next century this ongoing process would give the act of theatre-going in Ireland a political resonance that exceeded the content of individual plays.

When the curtain rose on *Othello* that winter's afternoon in 1691, the first actor in three years to step on to the Smock Alley stage was Joseph Ashbury, playing the role of Iago. Ashbury was a living link to the theatre's past, having taken over management of the theatre from Ogilby in 1675. Acting opposite Ashbury, in the role of Othello, was a young clerk in the King's Guard who had travelled to Ireland with William's army: Robert Wilks. Wilks's success as Othello would convince him to give up his commission to become a professional actor, initially at Smock Alley, but later in London, where by 1709 he was co-manager of the Drury Lane Theatre. These two men can stand as emblems of past and future in the changing theatre world of the 1690s: for Ashbury, the theatre was a place of sinecure and patronage; for Wilks, it was a business – and a business more profitably carried out in London than in Dublin.

Wilks's career, with its movement between Dublin and London (and a stint in the army along the way) is typical of the Irish theatrical generation who came of age in the 1690s. For instance, Thomas Southerne, who was born in 1660 in Oxmantown, on the north side of Dublin, had a hit on the London stage with *The Disappointment* in 1685. He used the success of this first play to gain a commission in the army of James II in England, returning to the theatre after the Stuart defeat with a series of popular plays, including *The Fatal Marriage* (1694) and *Oroonoko* (1695). Born in Leeds a decade later, William Congreve (1670–1729) grew up in Kilkenny and was educated at Trinity College, Dublin, while his father was stationed as a garrison commander in Ireland. Like Southerne, his short writing career – from *The Old Bachelor* (1693) to *The Double Dealer* (1700) – was exclusively based in London. Richard Steele's early life is almost a mirror image of Congreve's, in that Steele was born in Dublin in 1672, but educated in England, at Charterhouse, and later Merton College, Oxford. A committed Whig and supporter of the Williamite settlement, he too joined the army, serving in the Life Guards, before writing a series of plays, beginning with *The Funeral* in 1701, and concluding with his last (and most successful) comedy, *The Conscious Lovers* (1722). His long career (which for a time involved control of the patent for Drury Lane), was punctuated by writing and editing a series of periodicals, notably *The Tatler* (1709–11) and *The Spectator* (1711–12), on which he collaborated closely with Joseph Addison. For his part, Addison served as chief secretary for Ireland for two terms, during the latter of which he may have begun planning his influential verse tragedy, *Cato* (1713). Both Addison and Steele knew Susannah Centlivre (another Whig), who was born in 1667 in County Tyrone, where her family took up a grant of land after the Restoration. Like Steele, she reputedly spent time at university in England (disguised as a boy, since women were not permitted to attend), and went on to write eighteen plays, of which the most popular were *The Busie-Body* (1709) and *The Wonder, A Woman Keeps a Secret* (1714).

Of course, other names could be added to this list of playwrights of the period with Irish connections. However, even if we limit ourselves to these major figures, we are forced to confront a basic question: is there any meaningful sense in which any of them can be described as Irish playwrights? It would be possible to argue that accidents of birth, education or employment do nothing to alter the substantial fact that they all wrote primarily in London for a London audience, none of their plays is set in Ireland, and none contains more Irish characters, or a more original treatment of such characters, than one would expect from any other writer at the time. However, there is another way of looking at the situation. Steele's *Conscious Lovers* was performed at Smock Alley not long after its London premiere, and would go on to be staged in twenty-six separate Irish runs between 1722 and 1745. Southerne's *Fatal Marriage* was also staged in the 1722 season, and was revived annually from 1740 to 1744. Congreve's *Double Dealer* would appear on Dublin stages in twelve productions between 1720 and 1745, as would Centlivre's *The Busie-Body*, while Addison's *Cato* would appear nineteen times in the same period.[3] Even when these plays were not being performed in Irish theatres (sometimes owing to the departure of an actor with whom a particular role was associated), they were being read and published in Ireland. For instance, there were at least four Dublin editions of Steele's *Conscious Lovers* in 1722 alone, a 1725 Dublin imprint of Centlivre's *Busie-Body* claims to be the 'fourth edition', while Addison's *Cato* (although a play with only the most tenuous claim to Irishness) would appear in an Irish imprint at least thirteen times in the century. As late as 1772, the Dublin bookseller William Smith was advertising Southerne's *The Funeral*, Centlivre's *Busie-Body*, Addison's *Cato* and Congreve's *Double Dealer* – the latter as part of an edition of the author's complete works.

Looked at in this way, there is no denying that all of these writers were part of eighteenth-century Irish theatre culture, extending from the stage of Smock Alley to the booksellers in the streets surrounding the theatre, to the drawing rooms around the country where plays were read. By the same token, none of these writers is unproblematically Irish in the way that would be true of most twentieth-century playwrights. No matter what criteria we apply in the early eighteenth century, we are bound to find exceptions. If our criterion is birth in Ireland, we exclude Congreve; if it is a sustained period of residence in Ireland, we exclude Centlivre; if it is meaningful Irish subject matter in their plays, we exclude both. In short, clear-cut rules as to who is and who is not an Irish playwright in the decades immediately after the Battle of the Boyne are not very helpful here, if only because who was Irish was far from clear to contemporaries in a period in which there are the beginnings of an attempt to define an Irish identity based not on birth or heredity, but on the Lockean grounds of a commitment to an Irish community of interests, however partial.

'A mere Wolf-dog': Farquhar and the beginnings of Irish comedy

Perhaps the best way of unravelling the question as to who qualifies as Irish during the reigns of William and Anne is to look more closely at a playwright who, at least early in his short career, qualifies on most grounds: George Farquhar. Although he died in penury in 1707, Farquhar's posthumous career makes him arguably the most successful Irish-born playwright in Ireland during the first half of the eighteenth century. In their calendar of the Irish stage for the years 1720–45, John C. Greene and Gladys L. H. Clark record 116 Irish productions of plays by Farquhar – a total for the period exceeded only by Shakespeare (279) and Colley Cibber (144). During the 1737/8 season alone, the Dublin theatres staged five of his seven full-length plays. Even on those rare occasions when Farquhar's works were absent from the stage, they were being read in more than fifty editions of individual plays published in Ireland over the course of the century, as well as in two multi-volume collected editions of his work, the first of which, published by the Dublin bookseller George Risk, had run to eight printings by 1755.

We gain a sense of the extent to which Farquhar was considered Irish in a later edition of his collected works, printed in Dublin for Thomas Ewing in 1775, where the introduction emphasises Farquhar's Irish origins:'born in Derry, in the kingdom of Ireland, in the year 1678; his father was a Clergyman, who had a living in that diocese, of about one hundred and fifty pounds a year, and had a family of seven Children'.[4] Farquhar attended Trinity as a sizar, but was expelled for writing an essay about Christ walking on water, in which he concluded that 'the man can not be drowned who was born to be hanged', after which he turned to acting, taking over Robert Wilks's role as Othello at Smock Alley, and beginning what would be a life-long friendship with the actor. It was also while in Dublin (or shortly thereafter) that he started work on his first play, *Love and a Bottle*, which premiered in Drury Lane in December 1698.

Love and a Bottle opens with George Roebuck, 'an Irish gentleman, of a wild roving temper, newly come to London' (as he is described in the published script), meeting a young Englishwoman 'of considerable fortune', Lucinda. Within minutes of the curtain rising, Roebuck introduces himself as an Irishman, to which Lucinda responds with mock-horror: 'Oh horrible! an *Irishman*! a mere Wolf-dog, I protest.' The dialogue then proceeds to set up a series of reversed expectations that establish a template for almost a century of Irish stage comedy. 'I have heard the strangest Stories [of Ireland],' Lucinda taunts him. 'That the People wear Horns and Hoofs.' 'Yes, 'faith, a great many wear horns,' Roebuck responds, 'but we had that among other laudable fashions, from London . . .'[5] In the history of Irish dramatic writing, this is an important moment in that it assumes, for the first time, that an English audience will have certain assumptions about Irish society, but that those assumptions exist in a tension with an opposing view, which can be invoked with laughter.

In *The Stage Irishman*, a pioneering study published in 1937, G. C. Duggan traced the history of Irish characters on stage from George Peele's *Battle of Alcazar* in 1594, through Captain MacMorris in Shakespeare's *Henry V* (and his oft-quoted question, 'What ish my nation?'), through to early post-Restoration characters, including Teague in John Howard's *The Committee* (1662) and the title character in Thomas Shadwell's *The Lancashire Witches and Teague O'Divelly, the Irish Priest* (1681) – all almost invariably figures of derision, clearly defined as specific types, such as the bumbling servant or the scheming priest.[6] More recent work by Joep Leerssen suggests that there is a developmental taxonomy of Irish characters, in which the negative stereotypes of the seventeenth century are ultimately answered (although never entirely displaced) by the 'counter-stage Irishman', an Irish character who is able to demonstrate that the apparent peculiarity of Irish characters is the product of a misunderstanding '*between* the parties rather than *within* either of the parties concerned'.[7] Leerssen argues that the first counter-stage Irishman appears in Thomas Sheridan's afterpiece *The Brave Irishman* (1743). However, there is a case to be made that Roebuck, more than forty-five years earlier, is in fact the first counter-stage Irishman.

Admittedly, like many other Irish characters on the eighteenth-century stage, Roebuck is a fortune-hunter, on the prowl in London for a wealthy wife.

However, even from this opening exchange, he demonstrates a verbal skill – clearly signalling to a post-Restoration audience that they are to sympathise with his character – that is the antithesis of the garbled pronunciation and muddled logic of a conventional Irish character like Teague in *The Committee*. It is worth reminding ourselves here that Farquhar was capable of creating entirely generic Irish characters when it suited his dramatic purposes. There is, for instance, MacShane, a lecherous Irish priest disguised as a Frenchman, who swears by his 'shoul' in *The Beaux' Stratagem* (1707), as well as the servant Teague in *The Twin Rivals* (1702). 'Dear Maishter,' exclaims Teague, 'have a care upon yourself. Now they know you are dead, by my shoul they may kill you.'[8] Teague's name, his diction and his logical blundering (the 'bulls' that would become such a favourite subject of belletrists later in the century) all mark him out as a conventional stage Irish character. By contrast, Roebuck's name signals a different dramaturgical lineage (Roe + buck = roving buck; a 'roebuck' is also a male deer, suggesting his wildness and virility); he is, in short, a Restoration libertine adapting to the post-1688 world by becoming a Whig libertarian.[9] He speaks in standard stage English, and his verbal jousting gets the better of every character with the exception of Lucinda. At the same time, in his first appearance on the stage, Roebuck announces that he is Irish, he defends his Irishness by putting Irish foibles in the context of English ones, and the subsequent plot hinges on his acquisition of an Irish estate.

The temptation here is to reduce *Love and a Bottle* to autobiography, reading Roebuck as a cipher for Farquhar, a young, impoverished Irishman, arriving in London with a ready wit and little else – and this is an approach not without its legitimacy. At the same time, Roebuck is unique in Farquhar's dramatic writing only in his explicit Irishness; in other respects, he is the archetypal Farquhar character, variously manifested as Sir Harry Wildair in *The Constant Couple* (1699) and *Sir Harry Wildair* (1701), and Captain Plume in *The Recruiting Officer* (1706), through to Aimwell and Archer in *The Beaux' Stratagem* (1707) – all characters who are 'free from the rigidness of teachers, and the pedantry of schools',[10] as a character describes Wildair in *The Constant Couple*. For Farquhar, these characters are not so much a projection of his own personality, as a demonstration of his ideological understanding of the theatre's social function after 1691. 'You are the Rules by which he writes his Plays,' he tells the audience in the prologue to *Sir Harry Wildair*. 'From musty Books let others take their View, He hates dull Reading, but he studies You.'[11] While this is couched in the language of a conventional flattery of the audience, it is equally an application of Lockean political theory to the theatre, just as characters such as Roebuck are living demonstrations of its principles.

As he makes clear in his *Discourse Upon Comedy* (1701), Farquhar believed that comedy was a fundamentally modern genre, ideally suited to the new Whig dispensation. Unlike tragedy, its rules were not laid down by dogma or tradition; the rules of comedy were determined by an audience, gathered together as a community, who showed their approval or disapproval by applauding or cat-calling in a public arena in which liberty of expression was guaranteed by the monarch. For Farquhar, the theatre was the perfect model of the libertarian marketplace, just as the characters who thrive in his plays, untrammelled by tradition, are living embodiments of its ideology. 'All we can say for the credit of its institution', Farquhar writes of comedy, 'is the stress of its charter for liberty and toleration.'[12]

When looked at in this way, the Irishness of a character like Roebuck, who arrives on stage without 'one farthing' and leaves it married to an heiress with an estate in Ireland, can be understood within the very specific sense of the terms 'liberty and toleration' that underscored Irish life in the wake of the Treaty of Limerick. By an act of massive political misrecognition, the same changes in landownership that dispossessed the majority of the population were seen as creating 'liberty' and unprecedented opportunities for social advancement among that section of the population not bound by the traditions of Catholicism or Jacobitism. Indeed, for Farquhar or most of the audience at Smock Alley (at least in the early part of the century) to be considered Irish at all required a way of thinking about identity that explicitly denied the validity of the ties of tradition. Within this fundamentally modern world, it was possible for the son of a blacksmith (such as William Connolly, who built Castletown House) or the grandson of a brewer (such as the earl of Milltown, who built Russborough House) to rise to immense wealth – just as Farquhar's friend Robert Wilks rose from being an army clerk to manage the largest theatre in London.

Farquhar was among the first dramatists to realise that he was living in a world of rapid social transformation that had made identity malleable in a way ideally suited to stage comedy, and this awareness runs through almost all of his work. In *The Twin Rivals* (1702), the slippages of identity would take a dark turn, veering towards tragi-comedy when a brother is mistaken for his evil twin. In his least narrative-driven play, *The Recruiting Officer* (1706), Captain Brazen is married to a servant, mistaking her for a lady. Finally, Farquhar's last play, *The Beaux' Stratagem* (1707), dedicated to Wilks, pushes these confusions of social status even further, in a plot that hinges around a gentleman, Archer, who passes himself off as a servant, while his friend Aimwell passes himself off as his own older (and titled) brother, Lord Aimwell. The possibilities for this kind of personal transformation were not unique in Ireland at the period; however, the scale of land transfer after 1691 was far greater than in England, so possibilities for creating a new identity existed on a larger scale. *Love and a Bottle* may end with an antiquarian 'Irish Entertainment of three Men and three Women dress'd after the Fingallian Fashion',[13] but the Irish context of the play was nonetheless resolutely modern, mercantile and libertarian. It is thus possible to read Farquhar's plays, with their London settings, as pioneering the kind of coded engagement with Irish society that would re-emerge later in the century in plays such as Frances Sheridan's *The Discovery* (1763), Oliver Goldsmith's *She Stoops to Conquer* (1773), Arthur Murphy's *Three Weeks After Marriage* (1776), and R. B. Sheridan's *School for Scandal* (1777).

'Of Irish distraction': comedy from Farquhar to Sheridan and Goldsmith

As was so often the case in the final years of his life, Farquhar was nearly penniless late in 1704, so he had taken up an army commission and returned to Dublin to stay with his brother, who was a bookseller on Castle Street, a short distance away from Smock Alley. Although impoverished, Farquhar was still a celebrity, and his friends were able to arrange a benefit performance of *The Constant Couple* at Smock Alley in which Farquhar himself took the role of Sir Harry Wildair. The script of *The Constant Couple* may clearly indicate that Wildair is English, and yet, when Farquhar stood on the Smock Alley stage on that winter's afternoon in 1704, there was a very real sense in which Sir Harry Wildair was Irish – at least for those few hours. Seven years later, in 1711, the character would be Irish again, when Robert Wilks returned to Smock Alley to play Wildair, in a performance so popular that it ran for eighteen successive nights.

If there are no obvious criteria by which we can decide who is, and who is not, an Irish playwright in the early eighteenth century, these Dublin productions of *The Constant Couple* should remind us that the same is true of individual plays. When we read today comedies of the eighteenth century written by writers associated with Ireland, it is difficult to see how there is any meaningful sense in which many of them can be considered Irish. And yet, on any given evening, at a particular historical moment, the relevance of an otherwise conventional dramatic situation would flash before an audience's eyes. In part, this was a result of the stability of dramatic conventions. In the eighty years between *Love and a Bottle* in 1698 and *The Rivals* in 1775 change took place only within very limited parameters – notwithstanding constant complaints from actors, playwrights and managers that 'Things now-a-days are chiefly governed by Fashion, Novelty and Whim.'[14] Few comic playwrights deviated from the same basic settings (a domestic interior, either rural or urban, with occasional forays to an alehouse, park or fashionable thoroughfare), in which a shared palette of character types (including the various hues of stage Irishmen) worked their way through subtle variations on a standard set of situations, almost invariably involving marriage, inheritance or both. Within these boundaries, there were some exceptions and some fluctuations of taste, as well as the emergence of cognate genres such as ballad-opera (of which the Irish-born Isaac Bickerstaffe was a prolific writer) or pantomime, but little evolutionary change within the main comic genre itself. Hence, even minor innovations took on an exaggerated significance.

For instance, in 1722 Sir Richard Steele's *The Conscious Lovers* had helped to establish a fashion for what became known as 'sentimental' comedy, in which laughter was less important than moral instruction. Half a century later, in 1773, the debate over comedy's moral function would still be open enough to provoke Goldsmith's 'Essay on the Theatre; or A Comparison between Laughing and Sentimental Comedy'. By the same token, the success of Goldsmith's 'laughing comedy' *She Stoops to Conquer* in 1773 did not prevent Steele's 'sentimental comedy' from continuing to hold the stage, or from being reprinted in Dublin, in 1777, and again in 1793; nor did it prevent the writing of new sentimental comedies.

The persistence of this particular debate over the course of more than half a century not only indicates the relative stability of dramatic conventions; the continuous interaction between print and performance also suggests why this stability existed. While playwrights made a point of publishing their plays, both individually and in collected editions, and revised them for publication, eighteenth-century comedy was written to be performed. As long as theatrical conditions remained essentially the same, a play could be revived with the right actor, again and again, long after the appearance of plays which might be said to have superseded it in dramaturgical terms. This meant that comic drama could only begin to undergo real change in the final decades of the century, when changes in theatre architecture made auditoria so large and the forestage so small that witty dialogue became less effective than music or stage spectacle.

To a greater degree than other forms of Irish writing in the period, therefore, drama's dependence on theatrical performance meant that it was driven by the marketplace. A long prose work, or a collection of poetry, might sit on a bookseller's shelves over a period of years, eventually recovering its costs along with a coating of dust. By contrast, a play had to persuade one of the actor-managers who ruled the theatre world that it could draw an audience; in order for the playwright to profit, the play had to run for at least three nights, because playwrights were only paid from the proceeds of the third, sixth or ninth night of a run. If there was any money to be made from publication of the script (as there often was not, given the legal quagmire of Irish copyright legislation), it could only be generated by a play that had been a success in the theatre. So, when Farquhar told his audience 'You are the Rules by which he writes his Plays,' he was doing more than paying a polite compliment; he was also recognising that writing stage comedy was closer to journalism than to other forms of literary endeavour in terms of its intimacy with the market.

Audience demand meant that a play designed to appeal to London audiences was always going to be more profitable than one set in Dublin. By the time George I was crowned in 1714, there were three major theatres in London: Drury Lane, the Haymarket and the newly opened Lincoln's Inn Fields, whose first production was a revival of Farquhar's *The Recruiting Officer*. In Dublin, by contrast, there remained only Smock Alley, still under the management of John Ogilby's successor, the venerable Joseph Ashbury. A second theatre opened on Dublin's Aungier Street in 1734, but soon merged with the Smock Alley company. It was not until 1736 that the first permanent Irish theatre outside Dublin was established in Cork – by which point the 1,897-seat Covent Garden Theatre had opened in London, and there were theatres in Bath, Bristol, York and Ipswich. Only when Spranger Barry, a Dublin-born actor, returned from London to open a theatre in Crow Street in 1758 did Dublin finally have two fully functioning theatres. Even so, as late as 1790, the manager of the Crow Street Theatre, Frederick Jones, would argue: 'The experience of many years has sufficiently evinced that Dublin can afford no more than one audience; it therefore must consequently follow, that when two theatres contend for existence, one of them must fall.'[15] While Jones was far from unbiased, and Helen M. Burke has recently argued that government efforts to use the theatre as an instrument of hegemonic control worked against the proliferation of theatres,[16] the experience of several generations of eighteenth-century Irish theatre managers gave substance to Jones's argument.

These market conditions would have had less impact on Irish dramaturgy if the conventions of eighteenth-century comedy either had been more flexible or had been more like those of the early seventeenth century, with their fantasised Italian and Athenian settings – in which case there would have been no reason not to set a play intended for a London audience in Ireland. However, the persistence of comic conventions over decades had the effect of consolidating eighteenth-century comedy's defining feature: its essential modernity. While it was certainly not realistic (at least in the sense in which 'realism' has been used since Zola and Ibsen), the world of eighteenth-century comedy was an extension of the world of its audience, who sat in boxes level with the stage (and in some cases sat on the stage itself) in an auditorium that illuminated the audience as fully as the actors. Most comic characters wore versions of the same clothes as the audience, actors frequently borrowed behavioural ticks from real public figures, while the frequent use of double plots, involving servants and their masters, reflected the same divisions that existed in the theatre auditorium between the upper galleries and the boxes. Finally, the whole event was framed with prologues and epilogues that addressed sub-groups in the audience ('the ladies', 'the pit', etc.), inviting their direct identification with characters in the play.

As a consequence, the conditions that had made it more profitable for an Irish playwright to live and work in London at the beginning of the century not only continued, they became even more pronounced as the gap between the London and Dublin theatre worlds widened. So, as we move into the middle of the eighteenth century, the most successful Irish playwrights continued to leave Ireland. Among them was Arthur Murphy (1727–1805), who was born in Cloonyquin, County Roscommon, and raised in Dublin and Cork, but who – like many of his contemporaries – hoped a career in the London theatre and journalism would lead to a career in politics. Murphy managed to attract political controversy through his journalism, but little patronage. He did, however, write a number of very successful farces and comedies, among them the afterpiece *All in the Wrong* (1763) and *Three Weeks After Marriage* (1764), and his reputation would survive into the nineteenth century. The same was true of the Killarney-born Hugh Kelly (1739–77), whose political ambitions came to little, but whose *School for Wives* (1773) was a success. By the same token Frances Sheridan (1724–66), who had remained very much in the shadow of her husband, Thomas Sheridan (1719–88), while he was managing Smock Alley in the 1750s, began to write for the London stage after the couple moved to that city, and her play *The Discovery* ran for six nights during the 1775/6 season. Indeed, even an Irish writer such as Henry Jones, author of *The Earl of Essex* (1753), no sooner gained the patronage of Lord Chesterfield in Dublin, than he left for London; the same was true of Mary Davys (1674–1732), author of *The Self Rival* (1725), who moved to York as she began to achieve success as a writer. There are a few rare exceptions to this pattern, notably Robert Jephson (1736–1803). Born in Mallow, County Cork, he returned to Ireland to take up the post of Master of the Horse, perpetuating the long relationship between the colonial administration at Dublin Castle and Smock Alley by writing plays such as

The Count of Narabone (1781) and *The Hotel* (1784) for the Dublin stage. However, Jephson was something of an exception, and the case of the wife and husband Elizabeth (1727–93) and Richard Griffith (d.1788), who lived in Bennettsbridge, County Kilkenny, indicates why this was so. Although talented and prolific writers in a range of genres, their dramatic careers – Elizabeth acted and wrote plays including *The Platonic Wife* (1763) and Richard wrote a comedy, *Variety* (1782) – struggled without the hobnobbing in the green room that was so necessary for a new writer to succeed in the intimate, gossipy world of the theatre.

To make matters worse for an Irish playwright, while eighteenth-century English audiences went to the theatres to see themselves, they also went there to be confirmed in the belief that their own behaviour – however it might be in need of improvement – was the norm by which all human behaviour was to be judged. This meant that while an English comic character could be (and often was) as cantankerous, foolish or tongue-tied as a corresponding Irish character, in the English character such faults were ascribed to a general human nature (which, in sentimental comedy, it was the task of the play to reprimand or cure), whereas in the Irish character every trait was attributable to Irishness (and was hence incurable). With the exception of a small number of exceptionally jingoistic characters, Englishness was invisible; by the same token, every other form of ethnic or national identity became locked into a fixed set of behaviours.

There were a few attempts in the early decades of the eighteenth century to create a corresponding invisible Irishness by writing plays set in Ireland, notably William Philips's *St Stephen's Green* (1700) and Charles Shadwell's *Irish Hospitality* (1717–18). Philips (1675–1734) was a Jacobite, son of the governor of Derry at the time of William's landing, and he wrote in a tradition with obvious affinities to earlier Restoration comedy. Shadwell (1675–1726), by contrast, was born in England, son of the English dramatist Thomas Shadwell, but in a reversal of the usual pattern, lived in Dublin and wrote for a Dublin audience. His *Irish Hospitality* prefigures Steele's *The Conscious Lovers* as part of a wave of anti-Jacobite sentimental comedies in which characters exercised their liberty by acting morally. 'As our Politick Notions of the World teach us to hate Tyranny and Slavery, and to make noble Stands for the preserving of our Liberty,' announces the character Goodlove, 'so we should Subdue the Arbitrary Power of the Flesh . . . to depose the Corrupt Monarchy of Sin.'[17] And yet, where a play with an English setting (*The Conscious Lovers*, for instance) can treat the world of the play as unproblematically normative, by choosing to set *Irish Hospitality* in Finglas (at that point, open countryside on the outskirts of

Dublin), Shadwell finds himself opening up issues that highlight the difference between England and Ireland, and the relative deficit of liberty in the latter.

For instance, *Irish Hospitality* mentions a character named 'Sir Run-away-Spend-thrift', an improvident landowner with a long generic genealogy on the post-Restoration stage. However, because Sir Run-away is Irish, when we are told that he 'was Fool enough to go to the Bath for his Health, and he no sooner got it, but he whipt to *London*, and there lost that, and his Estate too',[18] the play opens up a real political issue of absentee landownership (which would become worse later in the century) that raises more serious questions about the relative rights and opportunities of English and Irish landowners. These are precisely the issues opened up by Philips's *St Stephen's Green*, from the other side of the political spectrum. In Philips's play, Bellmine, 'a Gentleman of Ireland', is met by the 'pert conceited [Irish] fop' Vainly, who, mistaking him for an English visitor, declares that 'Breeding and Conversation' are not to be had in Ireland. Bellmine then proceeds to question him about the quality of Irish wine, food, society and ladies – all, according to Vainly, excellent. 'Why thou worthless Contemptible Wretch!' Bellmine explodes. 'Do you entertain Strangers with your aversion for your Country, without being able to give one Reason for it?'[19]

In spite of their political differences, Philips and Shadwell faced a structural problem in attempting to use stage comedy to write about Ireland. Issues such as the relative values of Irish and English cultures were discussed, frequently and vociferously, in other forms of Irish public debate at the time, and a different kind of stage comedy could have made an active contribution to such debates. However, the tradition of stage comedy that playwrights inherited from the Restoration could not address the fundamental differences between English and Irish life on an equal footing, because to do so would be to upset the deeply rooted assumptions about universal human nature, going back to Jonsonian comedy of humours, and naturalised as thoroughly by Irish as by English audiences through decades of theatre-going.

Consequently, Irish playwrights found themselves in the paradoxical situation that Irish characters could be most fully explored against a background that appeared normative: England. In many cases, the function of Irish characters in such plays, with their brogues and their bulls, was simply to reinforce the normative nature of their English counterparts. In a few cases, however, the process was reversed, as was the case with Roebuck in *Love and a Bottle*, and with the character of Captain O'Blunder in *The Brave Irishman* (1743), by Thomas Sheridan. Although he later went on to write dictionaries, dissertations on grammar and education, and a biography of Swift, Sheridan appears to have written *The Brave Irishman* (his only play) when he was still a student at Trinity College, shortly before taking over as the manager of Smock Alley in the 1745/6 season. 'I look upon the Country where a Man is born to be the Place pointed out by Providence for his Scene of Action,' wrote Sheridan a few years later,[20] and it is in the context of a growing sense of Irish patriotism in the 1740s that we can read *The Brave Irishman*. Like *Love and a Bottle*, it places an exuberant Irish gentleman – Captain O'Blunder – in a London full of frauds and fops. Although the play ran to nine Irish editions in the century, it is really a performance piece, winning its audience to its Irish hero by setting him up in confrontations with characters such as Cheatwell and a pair of quack physicians, Gallypot and Clyster. 'Suppose we use Phlebotomy, and take from him thirty Ounces of Blood?' suggests Clyster. 'Flay my Bottom,' exclaims an affronted O'Blunder. 'Ye Sons of Whores – ye Gibberish Scoundrels (*Drives them out*).'[21] O'Blunder fumbles over language, waves his 'shillela', and is woefully rustic in his knowledge of London society; at the same time, in his honesty and generosity, he is the play's moral centre. The final effect is like a painting in which the foreground and background have been reversed: the picture remains the same, but the perspective has been radically altered.

Having said this, Captain O'Blunder in *The Brave Irishman* does not banish from the stage cruder forms of Irish character. Indeed, the opposite is true, for the dramatic effect of a character such as Captain O'Blunder relies upon the contrapuntal existence of his less flattering counterparts, and thus the play both conjures up and inverts the audience's expectations in the same gesture. The same had been true, of course, of Farquhar's Roebuck in *Love and a Bottle* in 1698; and it would be equally true of Haffigan in Shaw's *John Bull's Other Island* in 1904. There is, in short, no single moment (at least in the eighteenth, or, indeed, nineteenth, century) when the stage Irish character is forever shamed from the stage. Instead, there is an ongoing dialectic of subversion and reinforcement, in which the reversal of expectations produced by the counter-stage Irishman is a theatrical effect in its own right, depending upon the continuing parallel existence of the unreconstructed stage Irishmen.

This juggling of expectations was certainly close to the way in which eighteenth-century audiences experienced *The Brave Irishman* in the theatre, for Sheridan's play was an afterpiece, to be performed after a longer play as part of an evening's entertainment. On any given evening it could have been performed on the same stage (possibly even using the same set and actors) as a play such as Howard's *The Committee* (1662), with its blundering Teague, whose popularity continued undiminished in the 1740s and 1750s. The afterpiece's potential for creating this kind of meta-dramatic commentary would be even more apparent four years later in *The New Play Criticiz'd* (1747) by Charles Macklin (?1699–1797), the Donegal-born actor, manager and playwright, whose lengthy career stretched from the 1720s until 1789. Set 'an hour after the play', *The New Play Criticiz'd* is one of Macklin's self-reflexive plays about the theatre, in which a group of fops, critics, jealous playwrights and ladies of fashion discuss a new play.

Among them is Sir Patrick Bashfull, a polite, considerate gentleman who will not admit to being Irish (he claims to be French, but 'of Irish distraction'). 'I am no Irishman at all,' he protests, 'but my Mother was one . . . I an Irishman – no, no, no, I'faith you may know by my Tongue that I am no Irishman.'[22] As well as providing an occasion for comedy, Sir Patrick Bashfull gives Macklin a means of exploring the impossibility of an invisible Irishness on the English stage. It is clear that Sir Patrick Bashfull in *The New Play Criticiz'd* is proud of his country; in denying that he is Irish, he is rejecting not Ireland, but a way of looking at Irish characters that sees only their Irishness; a way of hearing that pays no heed to their words, but hears only their 'Tongue'. However, as it becomes apparent that Sir Patrick embodies ideals of generosity and civility to a greater extent than any other character in the play, the other characters (and, by extension, the audience) are made aware that they have failed to see the gentleman behind the Irishman. In short, *The New Play Criticiz'd* is a critique of a theatrical convention that could not countenance an Irish character who wished to be something other than simply Irish. Equally, it acted as a sly commentary on those Irish playwrights (including Robert Jephson, Arthur Murphy and Isaac Bickerstaffe) whose writing for the theatre was an effective denial that they were Irish.

Macklin's exploration of characters who deny that they are Irish continued after he moved back to Dublin, when he staged *The True-Born Irishman* at Barry's Crow Street Theatre, where it ran for a creditable six nights in 1760, and became a fixture in the repertoire. Macklin found himself the toast of Dublin society after the success of this play in which an Irishman (O'Dogherty, played by Macklin himself) must persuade his wife (who calls herself Mrs Diggerty, and denies that she is Irish) to give up her foreign affectations, which are encouraged by a conniving English fop, Count Mushroom (who was based on a real person, the earl of Halifax, who was resident in Dublin at the time). In terms of plot, *The True-Born Irishman* does not break new ground, in that characters had been mocked for making a fetish of foreign (particularly French) fashions since the Restoration. However, by setting the play in Ireland, Macklin subverts this generic situation, so that the normative behaviour is Irish, and Englishness becomes a foreign affectation.

Macklin would realise just how unsettling to English audiences this inversion would be when the play (retitled *The Fine Irish Lady*) opened at Covent Garden on 28 November 1767, and the audience objected so strongly that it was withdrawn after one performance. Between *The New Play Criticiz'd* in 1747, and *The True-Born Irishman* in 1760, it is possible to see Macklin testing the limits to which the conventions of comedy would permit him to use an Irish character to question the genre's universalising foundational assumptions. 'I believe the audience are right,' conceded Macklin after the London debacle of *The Fine Irish Lady*. 'There's a geography in humour, as in morals, which I had not previously considered.'[23]

Nonetheless, Irish playwrights working in London increasingly recognised the extent to which an Irish character like Sir Patrick Bashfull, even in a relatively minor part, could put deeply rooted cultural assumptions about the normative nature of English civility in an unexpected frame. Macklin continued to explore the possibilities of such characters in his most popular afterpiece, *Love à la Mode* (1759), where the character of Sir Callaghan O'Brallaghan, 'an Irish-Englishman', defines an Irishman as an 'outlandish Englishman'.[24] With variations, similar characters appear in Richard Cumberland's *The West Indian* (1771) and Dublin-born Isaac Jackman's *The Milesian* (1777). Jackman's play, for example, makes use of a running gag involving the sensitivity of the hero, Captain Cornelius O'Gollagher, to having his name mispronounced (as all of the English characters invariably do).

Similarly, in Hugh Kelly's *School for Wives* (1773), the playwright claims to be attempting 'to remove the imputation of a barbarous ferocity, which dramatic writers, even meaning to compliment the Irish nation, have connected with their Idea of that gallant people', and goes on to make his Irish character, Connolly, the means by which a duel is prevented. ''Tis not very customary, Sir,' comments the English Captain, 'with gentlemen of Ireland to oppose an affair of honour' – to which Connolly replies reasonably: 'They are like the gintlemen of England, Sir, they are brave to a fault; yet I hope to see the day that it will be infamous to draw the swords of either, against anybody but the enemies of their country.'[25] In such a moment, when the Captain insists on discerning a national trait in Connolly's behaviour, while Connolly speaks of their common 'country', we glimpse the fatal strategy at work in the decree that Irish characters must make a spectacle of their Irishness. By insisting on Irish difference, comic plays since the 1690s had insisted on an Irish difference that could not be denied (as Macklin had shown in characters like Sir Patrick Bashfull). For most of the century, this inveterate Irishness had confirmed English audiences in their own normativity; from the 1770s onwards, however, it increasingly carried the implication that if England and Ireland were different, they should be legislatively separate.

Richard Brinsley Sheridan's first play, *The Rivals* (1775), can thus be read as a response to Kelly's mollifying attempt to iron out Irish difference. The son of Thomas Sheridan and Frances Sheridan, R. B. Sheridan (1751–1816) is in more than one sense the heir to a tradition of Irish comic writing; in retrospect, his plays seem very much like the end of a tradition, his characters conforming to convention so closely that they become almost figures of pastiche, with a sly awareness of their own artifice. So, the Irish character in *The Rivals*, Sir Lucius O'Trigger, boasts that he could 'shew you a range of ancestry, in the O'Trigger line . . . every one of whom had killed his man!'[26] Where Kelly's ameliorative Connolly had been applauded in Drury Lane, Sheridan's unashamedly bloodthirsty Irish duellist picks up where Thomas Sheridan's Captain O'Blunder had left off, outraging the Covent Garden audience when *The Rivals* premiered on 17 January 1775. 'It is the first time I ever remember to have seen so villainous a portrait of an Irish Gentleman, permitted so openly to insult the country upon the boards of an English theatre,' fumed 'A Briton' in *The Morning Post*.[27]

Sheridan was forced to rewrite the part; however, even in his capitulation, he made clear the politics of the initial gesture of creating an irreconcilably Irish character. 'If the condemnation of this comedy (however misconceived the provocation) could have added one spark to the decaying flame of national attachment to the country supposed to be reflected on,' wrote Sheridan, 'I should have been happy in its fate.'[28] As the howls of derision rang out through Covent Garden that evening, there was a collective moment of recognition that decades of insisting that Irish characters could never be other than Irish had, almost imperceptibly, helped create a world of national differences, in which England and English values looked less and less central. From that point onwards, Irish characters on stage – no matter how ludicrous – carried an implicit threat: the threat of difference.

When audiences in 1775 watched *The Rivals*, they brought to it a social context, rich in gossip and inside knowledge, that could make plays with little or no overt Irish content appear to be interventions in Irish culture: knowing Sheridan's Irish connections made all the difference. In the same way, Fintan O'Toole has argued that Sheridan's *School for Scandal* (1777), with its contrast between the hypocritical Joseph Surface and the outwardly dissolute but virtuous Charles Teazle, can be understood as an intervention in the political debates leading up to the American Revolution, in which the English politician John Wilkes, 'a philanderer, a drinker, even a pornographer', turned out to be – in Sheridan's view – morally superior to his self-righteous opponents in his acceptance of the colonists' grievances.[29] With support for America strong among Irish patriots, the unmasking of hypocrisy in *School for Scandal* was, argues O'Toole, bound to be interpreted politically in Ireland, particularly after Sheridan began speaking out publicly on the rights of England's colonies while the play was being staged at Drury Lane. As circuitous as such an argument might appear, it is given substance by the response to *School for Scandal* in Ireland, where the scramble to have a Dublin opening was followed by an unprecedented publishing phenomenon, with at least nineteen Irish editions between 1781 and 1799. Moreover, we gain some sense of who was reading *School for Scandal* in Dublin when we turn to the final pages of a 1782 edition published in Dublin by Patrick Wogan, where we find advertisements for Wogan's editions of the American Declaration of Independence and an account of the American Revolution by Thomas Paine.

The ability of Sheridan's comedies to take on the political colouring of their time is a function of the way in which they flaunt their own theatricality, inviting their audiences to read beyond the conventions. His most memorable characters, such as Mrs Malaprop (*The Rivals*), Sir Benjamin Backbite (*School for Scandal*) and Sir Tunbelly Clumsy (*A Trip to Scarborough* (1777)) exist first and foremost in the world of the theatre, their conformity to conventional dramatic types signalled by their names and obsessive, single-note behaviour. With rare exceptions, the Englishness of these characters is as artificial and as incidental as the *faux*-Spanishness of the characters in his comic opera *The Duenna* (1777), or his last play, *Pizarro* (1799), set in Peru. It is this aspect of Sheridan's work that makes *The Critic* (1779) so much of a piece with his earlier comedies – and arguably caps his astonishing burst of creativity as a comic playwright in the late 1770s. This final comedy brandishes its theatrical artificiality by being set predominantly in Drury Lane Theatre, where characters with names such as Sneer, Dangle and Sir Fretful Plagiary (who is a caricature of the Irish-born playwright Richard Cumberland) watch a play-within-a-play, a tragedy containing characters such as Sir Walter Raleigh and the earl of Leicester. In the meta-theatrical world of *The Critic*, English tragedy is presented as a generic form enslaved by national history; the comedy which frames this tragedy, by contrast, exists in the world of its audience, taking on their concerns, adapting through performance to current events.

If we need to reconstruct something of the context in which Sheridan's plays were received in order to understand their place in an Irish dramatic canon, the same is even more so in the case of Oliver Goldsmith's two comedies *The Good Natur'd Man* (1768), and *She Stoops to Conquer* (1773). While the plots of Goldsmith's plays are no less conventional than those of Sheridan (or, indeed, those of most comic writers of the period), his characters flaunt their conventionality less openly. For the audience who watched *She Stoops to Conquer* on its opening night in Covent Garden, for instance, a character such as Hardcastle, with his bluff, commonsense dismissal of 'vanity and affectation', and his fondness for 'everything that's old: old friends, old times, old manners, old books, old wines',[30] would have suggested not so much an existing stage stereotype, as the national stereotype of the honest, plain-dealing John Bull, fond of his bottle and his home, popularised in John Arbuthnot's *History of John Bull* (1712). Lacking the kind of self-reflexive, meta-theatrical quality of the comic characters of Macklin or Sheridan, Hardcastle and Tony Lumpkin seem to sit uneasily within an Irish tradition.

Nonetheless, Christopher Murray has noted that the basic premise of *She Stoops to Conquer*, in which a gentleman's house is mistaken for an inn, was based on a real incident in Goldsmith's native Roscommon.[31] It could be argued that this kind of social confusion carried a much sharper point in Ireland than in England, where the confiscation of land after 1691 had produced a class of landowners whose gentility was planted in very thin soil. It is certainly the case that there was a string of Irish plays throughout the eighteenth century that responded to Irish slippages in class and identity, beginning with Farquhar's sustained exploration of these issues at the beginning of the century. For instance, the plot of William Philips's *St Stephen's Green* (1700) depends on its characters' inability to recognise a genuine gentleman; similarly, Charles Shadwell's comedy *The Sham Prince* (1718) centres around a character who is able to swindle large amounts of money from Dublin's freshly planted aristocracy by persuading them that he is the Prince of Passau. On the stage, Thomas Sheridan responded to the drunken provocations of a gentleman in the Smock Alley audience in 1747 by retorting: 'I am as good a Gentleman as you are.'[32] The resulting brawl sparked a riot that spread from the theatre to the streets of the capital, generating a fusillade of pamphlets that questioned whether young men whose days were spent drinking and fighting could call themselves 'Irish gentlemen'. It could be argued that Goldsmith's Tony Lumpkin – born to wealth and land, but spending his days at the tavern – touched on this nerve in Irish society. Hence, in spite of the play's foundational role in constructing one of the defining archetypes of English character, there is a sense in which it arises from an indigenous Irish dramatic tradition, and this may explain why the play was to become such a fixture on Irish stages, well into the nineteenth century.

Sheridan's *School for Scandal* and Goldsmith's *She Stoops to Conquer* are among the most popular and enduring English-language comedies of the eighteenth century. While their authors are certainly, to use Macklin's phrase, 'of Irish distraction', it is equally the case that the Irishness of these plays is not inherent in the scripts. It must be produced (either on a stage, or in the act of reading); but so too, it should be said, must their Englishness be produced. *School for Scandal* and *She Stoops to Conquer* may seem to fit readily in an English dramatic tradition (more so than in an Irish tradition), but we need to recognise that the contextualisation that makes them seem so naturally English involves an act of production that calls upon our knowledge of English class structure, rural/urban divisions and authority. Equally, today these plays can be made to work centuries after they were written on a purely theatrical level for audiences who have no idea that Sheridan or Goldsmith lived in England, or were born in Ireland.

'Those unhappy days of yore': Irish historical tragedy

If the best eighteenth-century comedies now seem to exist in a world of gleeful artificiality, the same is not true of post-Restoration tragedy. The fixed, almost cartoon-like nature of comic characters, signalled in their names – from Lady Lurewell, 'a lady of jilting temper' in *The Constant Couple*, to the trigger-happy Sir Lucius O'Trigger in *The Rivals* – is at the heart of comedy. As comic characters blindly pursue their natures, the audience's awareness of a character's blinkered view of the world produces a pleasurable ironic knowledge, in that we can see what must follow as soon as such a character enters a scene. When this kind of tunnel-vision has serious consequences, as is the case in eighteenth-century tragedy, and characters treat their situations with the utmost seriousness, explained in seemingly interminable speeches, the reader today (such plays are almost never staged) begins to wonder whether there is much difference between noble fixity of purpose and dangerously insane monomania. When translated into an Irish context, the immutable character types that become an assertion of Irish identity in comedy become predetermined destiny in tragedy – usually a destiny of defeat.

When returning to these plays today, we need to remember that when they were originally performed, in a theatre like Smock Alley, where an actor perched at the very lip of the forestage, staring into the eyes of the audience in the pit or in the boxes, while the servants in the upper gallery made their presence felt above, such plays could become very public debates on issues such as loyalty, justice and the right of possession, veering in their sheer excess into areas that could not be spoken of in the same way in any other public sphere in eighteenth-century Ireland.

It was in this very excess, however, that the problem lay in writing historical verse tragedy in eighteenth-century Ireland. The pitfalls inherent in writing a play with a historical setting were apparent from the very first play to have been written in Ireland for an Irish audience: James Shirley's *St Patrick for Ireland* (1639). Early in Shirley's play, Patrick identifies himself as 'a Briton', who has come to Ireland to 'to make this nation glorious'.[33] Although the dramatic form of *St Patrick for Ireland* (with its affinities to the Jacobean masque) had little in common with the Irish historical tragedies of the eighteenth century, it nonetheless identifies what would become their central concern: justified invasion. In the first quarter of the eighteenth century, almost all of the patrons of Smock Alley were descended from English settlers in Ireland, whose very presence on the island was the product of a series of invasions, and whose self-image as both lawful and legitimately Irish required them to justify these earlier invasions; as a consequence, any play that dealt with invasion in an Irish context was wandering into dangerous territory.

The political sensitivity of this issue in eighteenth-century Irish culture can be measured in the observation that the four major attempts to write plays dealing with Irish history in the entire eighteenth century are clustered in two critical periods: the debates leading up to the passing of the Declaratory Act, which confirmed the right of the English parliament to legislate for Ireland in 1720; and the formation of the Volunteer movement, in the mid-1770s. On either side of the Declaratory Act, we thus find two early Irish historical tragedies: Charles Shadwell's *Rotherick O'Connor* (1719) and William Philips's *Hibernia Freed* (1722). Fifty years later, as Irish patriots were beginning to see legislative independence as a possibility, two very similar plays appeared: Gorges Edmond Howard's *The Siege of Tamor* and Francis Dobbs's *The Patriot King* (both 1773/4). In terms of theatrical effectiveness, and audience popularity, all of these plays were failures by the standards of comic writers such as Farquhar or Sheridan; at the same time, these tragedies broach the key issues of Irish culture in the period with a directness simply not possible in comedy.

Like the comedies of the period, Irish tragedies were constrained by convention, and produced their meanings only in the context of wider public debate. This means that when we read Shadwell's prologue calling for indigenous Irish tragedy, we need to remind ourselves that many of his audience were also reading Swift's influential pamphlet *A Proposal for the Universal Use of Irish Manufacture*, published in 1720, and were taking part in a campaign to wear only Irish-manufactured clothing when going to the theatre.[34]

From distant Climes, each scribbling Author brings,
A Race of Heroes, and a Race of Kings . . .
Be he a *Roman, Greek,* or *Persian* Born,
Thus Foreign Stories do our Stage Adorn.

For Shadwell, these 'foreign stories' should not be acceptable to an Irish audience who were beginning to assert their Irish identity. 'Our Author tries, by Different Ways to please,' he writes, 'And shews you Kings, That never cross'd the Seas.'[35] Shadwell thus turns back to Irish history, and stages the original moment of the English presence in Ireland: the twelfth-century invasion of the Norman Strongbow at the invitation of the king of Leinster, Dermot MacMurrough, who was engaged in a civil war with a rival Irish king, the eponymous Rotherick. By putting Irish kings from the twelfth century in the context of 'Roman, Greek' and 'Persian' kings, Shadwell is attempting two contradictory things. He is suggesting that twelfth-century Ireland was every bit as noble and 'antique' (to use a favourite term of the period) as Rome or Persia, and thus a suitable subject for tragedy, while at the same time advertising his play as a piece of 'Irish manufacture'. However, as was the case with comedy (and, indeed, political theory), it was almost impossible for a play to achieve the kind of universalising timelessness to which tragedy of the time aspired within an Irish context.

To the extent that *Rotherick O'Connor* is a justification of the historical invasion of Ireland by the Normans, it must endorse the character of Strongbow. 'I come not to destroy, but give you Liberty,' Strongbow announces, 'And bring this barbarous Nation, to such Laws / As will draw Peace and plenty to your Country.' When dealing with abstractions such as 'Liberty', 'Peace' and 'plenty', Shadwell is on safe enough ground. However, when Strongbow is challenged to defend the authority by which he is to establish such laws, his response betrays the fundamental flaw at the heart of the society for which Shadwell wrote: 'The right of Conquest is the Right I own.'[36] In chapter 16 of his *Second Treatise on Government*, John Locke unequivocally refutes the arguments of anyone who may 'have mistaken the force of Arms, for the consent of the People; and reckon Conquest as one of the Originals of Government'.[37] Consequently, while the prologue to *Rotherick O'Connor* may have exhorted its audience to 'Learn then from those unhappy Days of Yore, / To scorn and hate an Arbitrary Power', by the end of the play an audience who had taken possession of their Irish property in the seventeenth century would have been uncomfortably reminded that their own much-vaunted 'Liberty' and 'Peace' rested on a series of violent conquests.

The thin ice on which a Whig playwright such as Shadwell was treading in addressing the issue of invasion becomes clear in a play from the opposite end of the political spectrum, William Philips's *Hibernia Freed*, of 1722. Philips was a Tory with Jacobite connections. Consequently, when he asks in his introduction to the published play, 'What is so noble as to free one's Country from Tyranny and Invasion?', his question would be read in a Jacobite context, in which William's landing in Ireland could be understood as an invasion. Unlike Strongbow in *Rotherick O'Connor*, Turgesius, the Viking invader in *Hibernia Freed*, is an unredeemed stage tyrant, leader of 'a savage Race, urg'd by their Wants to roam', who 'Have by insidious Arts usurp'd your Crown'. As Turgesius first invades Ireland, and then marches towards the Boyne for a decisive battle, an audience who were aware of Philips's Jacobite politics could well have found themselves wondering whether *Hibernia Freed*, with its condemnation of anyone who would depose 'lawful Kings', was a fantasised rewriting of the Battle of the Boyne, in which the invader (Turgesius / William) is defeated by the Gaelic Irish proto-Jacobites. 'Another Nation shall revenge my Death, / And with successful Arms invade this Realm,' prophesies the dying Turgesius. 'My Soul shall rejoyce to see the Land subdu'd, / And Peasants Hands with Royal Blood embru'd.'[38] Although this was bound to be well received by Philips's fellow Jacobites, still outraged at the thought of an anointed king driven from his realm by 'peasants' dripping with 'Royal Blood', Philips still had to deal with the recognition that his own family came to Ireland from England in the 1640s during a previous invasion. In the end, he is unable to employ historical allegory to denounce William's invasion without leaving open the unpleasant possibility that the same argument will be extended to all previous invaders of the island, extending back to Cromwell, Essex and Strongbow. Not surprisingly, *Hibernia Freed* fared even worse on the Irish stage than *Rotherick O'Connor*; and after a London run at Lincoln's Inn Fields in 1722, it was never given an Irish performance.

In the years following the Declaratory Act, the kinds of issues that Shadwell and Philips tried in their differing ways to address erupted in unexpected ways on the Irish stage. On 3 December 1744, for instance, *Gustavus Vasa: The Deliverer of His Country* (1739), by Irish playwright Henry Brooke, was performed in Smock Alley as *The Patriot*, after a proposed Drury Lane production was banned under the terms of the 1737 Licensing Act (which did not extend to Ireland). When Brooke's Swedish hero launches into one of his exhortations to heed 'the Call of Liberty',[39] this play – originally intended for an English audience – articulated the growing sense of patriotic identification with Ireland (even when that meant opposing the English parliament) among some Irish Protestants.

Later, Brooke's satire on Irish politicians who put self-advancement before patriotism, *Jack the Giant Queller*, was suppressed after a single Dublin performance on 27 March 1749, when a character waving a wand decorated with gold coins counselled: 'Would you silence a Patriot-committee / Touch their lips with this Magical Wand.'[40] The same Patriots that Brooke ridiculed rioted during a production of Voltaire's *Mahomet* in Smock Alley in 1754, kicking off their protest by calling for an encore of lines in which a character named Alcanor denounces 'those Vipers, / Who, singled out by a Community / To guard their Rights, shall for a Grasp of Ore, / Or paltry Office, sell'em to the Foe!'[41] All over Ireland, reading from pamphlets with titles such as *A Patrick's Pot and a Shamrogue for the Patriots of Ireland*, Irish men and women who considered themselves 'Patriots' drank toasts such as 'May Mahomet never be able to Impose on the People of Ireland', and 'May the Spirit of *Alcanor* Possess every Friend of Liberty.'[42]

Riots such as those that met the 1754 production of *Mahomet* in Smock Alley remind us that the theatre was one of the few places in eighteenth-century Ireland in which public denunciations of corruption and treachery could be made in even moderately acceptable coded terms. At the same time, in rare cases – such as the *Mahomet* riots – when the response spilled out on to the street and led to rioting, we are also reminded of the extent to which the theatre was a place of containment. This feature of the theatre becomes even more apparent when it fails, as it did with the only two dramas of the period to deal explicitly with the Williamite wars: John Michelburne's *Ireland Preserv'd; or, The Siege of London-Derry* (1705) and Robert Ashton's *The Battle of Aughrim: Or, the Fall of Monsieur St Ruth* (1728).

These two staunchly Williamite plays staged key battles using dramaturgically simple narratives, virtuous heroes, and action alternating back and forth between the two armies. Although in some ways primitive, both plays were enormously popular. There were at least ten editions of Michelburne's play between 1705 and 1774, and at least sixteen eighteenth-century editions of Ashton's, followed by several more in the early decades of the nineteenth century. Even more striking is the pattern of publication for both of these plays, for although early editions have Dublin or London imprints, in later decades they were printed in Belfast, Newry and Strabane. Moreover, there is at least anecdotal evidence, vividly conveyed in William Carleton's autobiographical memoirs, that both plays were performed by amateurs, particularly in rural Ulster, throughout the eighteenth century and into the nineteenth.[43] Where the mainstream theatre was driven by convention to strive for what were seen as universals, in barns and halls all over rural Ulster these plays rehearsed, over and over again, the specific political events that had shaped the local animosities which moulded the lives of the people who staged them.

If the historical tragedies of Shadwell and Philips can be seen as responses to debates surrounding the Declaratory Act of 1720, the swell of patriotic feeling that led to the founding of the Volunteer movement forms the context of two later historical tragedies: Gorges Edmond Howard's *The Siege of Tamor* and Francis Dobbs's *The Patriot King; Or, The Irish Chief. The Siege of Tamor* reworks the plot of William Philips's *Hibernia Freed* of 1722, in which an Irish king (named O'Brien in *Hibernia Freed*, Malsechlin in *The Seige of Tamor*) defeats a lustful invading Dane, Turgesius, by helping the king of Ulster (O'Neill in the earlier play, Niall in the latter) to infiltrate the Danish camp. Although the plots of the two plays are similar, Howard – who had lobbied for relief of the Penal Laws against Catholics, and had acted as a solicitor for the Catholic Committee – goes beyond Philips's cautious interest in the Gaelic Irish. This note is struck from the beginning, as a prologue to the play (by Peter Seguin) proclaims that 'a bard, a native bard, at last . . . / Plucks forth the tale of virtue to the light, / And gives living glory to your fight', clearly inviting his audience to identify with the Gaelic king who threw off the tyranny of the Danes. With the real possibility of a Jacobite reinvasion of Ireland effectively gone by the 1770s, it became possible to sympathise with the Gaelic noblemen who had sided with James II in 1688, and from this sympathy Irish Protestant patriots were able to define themselves in more forcefully independent language. 'We hence may learn', declares the Irish king, Malsechin, 'how they are favour'd, / Who dare for freedom and their Country bleed.'[44] Both the Irish actor-manager Henry Mossop and David Garrick promised to produce Howard's play, and when published in 1773 it was favourably reviewed in the *Hibernian Magazine*, the *Monthly Review*, the *Edinburgh Magazine* and elsewhere; however, it was never produced.

Dobbs was at least more fortunate in this regard, in that *The Patriot King* was produced in April 1773 at Smock Alley. On that evening, the actor Courtney Melmoth told his audience:

> Full oft hath honest Teague been here display'd
> And many a roar have Irish blunders made:
> The bull, the brogue, and row so common grown,
> That one would almost swear they were – your own.
> But lo! to-night, what you ne'er saw before,
> A tragic hero from HIBERNIA's shore.[45]

More than half a century after *Rotherick O'Connor*, it was still possible for an author to boast that audiences watching 'A tragic hero from HIBERNIA's shore' were seeing something novel. And yet, there are telling details in *The Patriot King* that indicate the extent to which the argument had moved on from the time of *Rotherick O'Connor*, not least in the name of Dobbs's 'patriot king': Ceallachan. Christopher Wheatley has hinted that Dobbs may have been given the idea for his play by a remark in Sylvester O'Halloran's *Introduction to the Study of the History and Antiquities of Ireland*, which had appeared in 1772. O'Halloran asks at one point: 'Where do we look for incentives to the brightest actions for national liberty?', and answers his question by pointing to the historical figure of Ceallach, recounting his selfless (and, in O'Halloran's account, patriotic) defence of Ireland against the Danes: 'How noble a subject for the Muse!'[46] Given that there are other verbal echoes of O'Halloran's work in Dobbs's piece (such as referring to Ireland as 'Iërne', the name for Ireland favoured by O'Halloran in *Iërne Defended*, 1774), the play begins to make sense as part of a wider antiquarian movement.

'The baseless fabric of a vision': forging an Irish dramatic canon

For O'Halloran or Dobbs, the recovery of the Gaelic past for Irish patriot nationalists involved a complicated process of negotiation, identification and misrecognition, in which people whose ancestors had dispossessed the Gaelic Irish in the seventeenth century made a common cause with the besieged culture of Gaelic Ireland in the late eighteenth century to attempt to forge a common Irish identity. Irish antiquarian interest in the Gaelic past coincided with a period in which theatre historians throughout Europe were formulating a wider Enlightenment narrative of the progressive development of the theatre and its role in the wider processes of civilisation. Most of these early histories take as their starting point Aristotle's claim in his *Poetics* that theatre originated when an actor – traditionally known as Thespis – stepped forward from a dithyrambic chorus reciting stories about the god Dionysus, and began impersonating characters in the narrative. For many of these early theatre historians, it was precisely this moment when hymns of praise to a pagan god became a recognisably modern art form that marked the transition from barbarism to civility. Irish antiquarianism, in tracing continuities between the pre-Norman past and contemporary Irish society, set about tracing a parallel trajectory of emergence, and with poetry, music, the decorative arts and law, this was successfully accomplished; however, when it came to the theatre, the process hit a blank wall.

We find the problem of a missing origin for the Irish already present in what is arguably the first history of the Irish theatre, published in 1749, whose full title gives an idea of its scope: *A General History of the Stage (More Particularly the Irish Theatre) From its Origin in Greece down to the present Time. With Memoirs of most of the Principal Performers, that have appeared on the Dublin Stage, for the last Fifty Years*. Its author, W. R. Chetwood, weaves together a synoptic history of the theatre for the book's first fifty pages, endorsing the standard Aristotelian origin, and trotting through the theatrical highlights of Greece, Rome and Renaissance England. 'This Kingdom of *Ireland*', he then finds himself admitting, 'is one of the last in *Europe* where establish'd *Theatres* were erected; yet I am assur'd one of the first, whose Bards, or Poets have celebrated in Verse, the illustrious Actions of their Monarchs.'[47] For Chetwood (who was variously a bookseller, dramatist and prompter at Smock Alley), this is a puzzle, but not an unduly troubling one. For Joseph Cooper Walker (a respected antiquarian who had published *Historical Memoirs of the Irish Bards* in 1786) it is a serious obstacle to the project of reclaiming a redeemed Irish past for the present. 'It is very extraordinary that we cannot discover any vestiges of the Drama amongst the remains of the Irish Bards,' admits Walker in his 'Historical Essay on the Irish Stage' (1788). 'If the Stage ever existed in Ireland previous to the middle ages, like the "baseless fabric of a vision" it has melted into air, leaving not a trace behind.'[48]

Walker tackled this problem by tracing the earliest accounts of theatrical activity in Ireland, including Corpus Christi plays documented in Dublin civic records, and the Anglican liturgical dramas of Bishop Bale, performed at the Market Cross in Kilkenny in 1553. He then looked for traces of a native drama in surviving mummers' performances and other folk dramas, but even here must concede that 'these attempts cannot be considered as vestiges of an ancient regular drama',[49] as most seem to go back no further than the late seventeenth century (a finding that has been confirmed in the more recent work by Alan Gailey and Henry Glassie).[50] Moreover, given the increasingly philological turn of antiquarian research, with works such as Charles Vallencey's *Grammar of the Hiberno-Celtic or Irish Language* (1773), the fact that the surviving folk theatre was not in the Irish language further discredited it as a indigenous source for Irish theatre. Throughout the nineteenth century, there would be scattered attempts to claim the English-language theatre of the seventeenth and eighteenth centuries as a founding tradition, notably in a series of articles by the theatre manager J. W. Calcraft in the *Dublin University Magazine*. However, it would not be until the closing years of the nineteenth century that the gaps in Irish theatre history would be fully enabling, allowing the founders of the Irish

Literary Theatre to claim that they were creating the first Irish theatre worthy of the name. In the late eighteenth century, however, the same antiquarian studies that were questioning the extent to which Irish theatre was truly Irish were also laying the groundwork for the form of theatre that would supplant the theatrical world of Farquhar, Shadwell and Sheridan.

Acting the Union: John O'Keeffe and the future of Irish drama

One of the most striking illustrations of an Irish theatre from the eighteenth century is an etching that shows the interior of the Crow Street Theatre with the forestage specially extended in the shape of a rectangular track, running out into the pit, circling around the back of the auditorium and returning to the stage. An amazed audience is shown sitting in the pit, looking up at this circuit, upon which a horse race – with half a dozen real horses – is being run as part of an unidentified play. This picture may seem like a curiosity; however, it is in fact indicative of changes taking place in the theatre that would shape the future of Irish drama over the next century.

When the Crow Street Theatre was built in 1758, the rival Smock Alley Theatre was basically the same theatre it had been when it was first built in 1662 (with a few modifications and a modest extension). With its large forestage, Smock Alley was an actor's theatre, ideally suited for placing actors and audience in the kind of close proximity to one another that gave force to the declamatory speeches of tragedy, and allowed an audience to catch every nuance of a witty comic exchange. While not significantly bigger than Smock Alley, the Crow Street Theatre was designed for the production of lavish scenic spectacles, and its first manager, Spranger Barry, quickly established a reputation for giving audiences the kinds of scenic effects that simply were not possible in the older theatre.

Among the actors performing at Smock Alley when Barry opened the Crow Street Theatre was a young man who had studied painting, John O'Keeffe (1747–1833), whose stage career was cut short when his sight began to fail. He then began to write for the stage, creating pantomimes such as *Harlequin in Waterford* (1767), *Harlequin in Derry* (1770), *The Giant's Causeway; or, A Trip to the Dargle* (1770) and *Tony Lumpkin's Ramble Thro' Cork* (1773), which brought Goldsmith's character on tour to Ireland as a means of offering Cork audiences the chance to see stage recreations of local sights such as 'the Mall, Red-House Walk, Sunday's Well, Coffee-Houses, Taverns, &c.'[51] On 15 April 1777 at Crow Street, he produced *The Shamrock*, a lost play whose attractions included (by

O'Keeffe's own account) 'Irish characters and customs, pipers, and fairies, foot-ball players, gay hurlers', all set to Irish melodies deriving from the harpist Toirdhealbhach Ó Cearbhalláin. By 1785, O'Keeffe was working in London with the most innovative scenic designer of the period, Philippe Jacques de Loutherbourg, adapting an account of Captain Cook's voyages in the South Pacific into a phenomenally popular spectacle, *Omai*; by 1800, there had been more than 1,200 performances of O'Keeffe's plays in London.

The leap from *The Shamrock* to *Omai* is not as great as it might appear. While late eighteenth-century Irish antiquarians may have run into difficul-ties when they tried to produce a coherent history of the Irish theatre, this was secondary to the wider impact of antiquarianism, which coincided with a growing appreciation of the wildness of Irish landscape and the exotic splen-dour of Irish antiquity, spurred by works such as Edmund Burke's *Philosophical Enquiry into the Origin of Our Ideas of the Sublime and the Beautiful* (1757). As with all things fashionable, the growing taste for a wild, legendary Irish past filtered its way into the drawing-rooms of comedy. We see it surface when Macklin's O'Dogherty praises 'our fine sounding Milesian names' at the end of *The True-Born Irishman*, or when Lady Greyley in Mary O'Brien's *The Fallen Patriot* (1790) enthuses that 'it's all the ton in this country' to have an 'O' in one's name: 'there are the Keelys, that never had an O in their generation, yet many of them now stile themselves O'Keelys'.

Indeed, O'Brien's play is an indication of the extent to which such patri-otism could have been made to work within existing theatrical conventions if playwrights had been content to satisfy themselves with an Irish audience. Adapting the values of sentimental comedy for overtly political ends, *The Fallen Patriot* was intended for Irish audiences, presenting them with a clear choice between Sir Richard Greyley, who has accepted a knighthood for voting against Irish interests in parliament, and his nephew, Freeport (whose name is a lightly coded reference to Irish demands for free trade with England), because Freeport refuses to compromise his principles. 'When the gilded fool shall sneer at virtue,' Freeport tells his uncle, 'I'll thunder in his ears Liberty and my Country.'[52] By equating 'Liberty and my Country' with 'virtue', *The Fallen Patriot* translates ideas which were more commonly dealt with in tragedy into the domestic sphere of comedy.

The Fallen Patriot survives as a tantalising intimation of the politicised direc-tion in which sentimental comedy might have developed after 1790; however, by the time O'Brien wrote the play, the theatre was already moving in another direction. Macklin (who had an extensive antiquarian library) was among the first to recognise the full stage potential of this new interest in the Irish (and

Scottish) past, creating a sensation in 1773 by playing Macbeth 'in the old Cale-donian habit' of cloak and kilt, as a contemporary put it. 'Previous to this period, Macbeth used to be dressed in a suit of scarlet and gold . . . in every respect like a modern military officer.'[53] When this theatrical antiquarianism combined with the fashionable idealisation of peasant life, and the develop-ment of new stage technologies, particularly in the area of colouring light, the result was a gradual transformation of the fundamental aesthetics of the theatre. So, in the same years that Sheridan and Goldsmith were writing what are in many ways the highest accomplishments of a theatrical tradition based on verbal wit (which required only an open stage, good acoustics and a skilful performer), O'Keeffe was at the forefront of those who were creating a theatre in which language was less important than exotic spectacle and music (and which required ever-larger theatres and an ever-increasing array of complex stage machinery).

The discovery that Ireland could be fashionably exotic rather than embar-rassingly provincial was to overcome at a stroke the obstacles to comic plays with Irish settings. Initially, when John O'Keeffe had written early plays like *Harlequin in Waterford*, he was simply extending to Ireland the fashion for harlequinades (a precursor of pantomime) that had been created by John Rich and John Weaver at Covent Garden in the middle decades of the cen-tury. O'Keeffe's major innovation came in 1782, when he merged the scenic attractions of one of his early Irish spectacle plays, *The Shamrock*, with the conventions of sentimental comedy. Later writers, including O'Keeffe's con-temporary, the Limerick-born Andrew Cherry, would develop this formula; however, O'Keeffe was to pioneer it.

O'Keeffe's *The Poor Soldier* (1782) is thus an important milestone in the development of Irish theatre. The plot is a variation on a familiar theme in sentimental comedy, in which a landlord, Lord Fitzroy, renounces his love for one of his tenants, Norah, when he realises that she loves Pat, the 'poor soldier' of the title. Similarly, the characters are all recycled from stock types, and the music and scenery were pulled out of the lumber room from O'Keeffe's own earlier play, *The Shamrock*. Although none of these elements was original, they combined to create a form of theatre in which an exoticised Irishness was attractive rather than an encumbrance. Where Irish characters, since at least *The Rivals*, increasingly became assertions of a distinct Irish identity, O'Keeffe neutralises the threat of difference by borrowing sentimental comedy's empha-sis on reconciliation. The result was as acceptable to Irish audiences seeking to create a common Irishness that superseded class and sectarian divisions, as it was to English (and later American audiences) who could imagine themselves welcome in this charmingly exotic pastoral world. 'We are common children of one parent,' announces Lord Fitzroy, 'and the honest man who thinks with moral rectitude, and acts according to his thoughts, is my countryman let him be born where he will.' Throughout the next century, this fantasised union of landowner and tenant (which was also at the heart of the antiquarian project) would be projected again and again, in Irish novels and plays, from Lady Morgan to Dion Boucicault. Indeed, *The Poor Soldier*'s set might stand as an emblem of much Irish writing for the next century: 'The Country . . . a large mansion at some distance – near the front, on one side . . . a Cottage.'[54] Not surprisingly, the play ran to eighteen Irish editions by 1800.

John O'Keeffe recognised – in a way not possible earlier in the century – that Ireland's lack of an indigenous theatrical tradition meant that it was possible to forge for Ireland a stage past that responded to the theatrical possibilities and tastes of his own time, and in this he is as much a precursor of the Irish Literary Theatre a century later as he is of the tradition of melodrama it sought to supplant. Unlike poetry, prose narrative, music or the visual arts, where it was possible to trace (or, at least, construct) a link to the Gaelic past, the theatre in Ireland was never going to be anything other than a creation of modernity. Irish writers of comedy, from Farquhar onwards, had embraced this condition, and it was to cost them a secure place in a narrative of Irish cultural history that increasingly demanded continuity with antiquity. Irish writers of tragedy, from Charles Shadwell to Francis Dobbs, would discover that attempting to trace lines of continuity over the fractures of Irish history was a perilous business, whose time would lie ahead. With hindsight, we can recognise that after *Rotherick O'Connor* in 1717, the next attempt to dramatise the invasion of Strongbow was Yeats's *Dreaming of the Bones* in 1919. By the same token, it was not until Douglas Hyde's *Casadh an tSúgáin* in 1901 that a play would be performed in the Irish language in a professional theatre. In the interim, the real future of Irish theatre for the century after the Act of Union would be in the dramatic descendents of John O'Keeffe's agreeable world, where elements of indigenous Irish culture that could be appropriated to stage spectacle (music, landscape and a sentimental pastoralism) combined with conventional reconciliatory plots to act out a fantasised union of those who had created Ireland's theatre culture, and those who for so many years had been excluded from it.

Notes

1. Alan J. Fletcher, *Drama, Performance and Polity in Pre-Cromwellian Ireland* (Cork: Cork University Press, 2000), pp. 262–3.

2. W. S. Clark, *The Early Irish Stage: The Beginnings to 1720* (Oxford: Clarendon Press, 1955), p. 100.

3. John C. Greene and Gladys L. H. Clark, *The Dublin Stage, 1720–1745: A Calendar of Plays, Entertainments and Afterpieces* (Bethlehem, PA: Lehigh University Press; London and Toronto: Associated University Press, 1993), pp. 426–9.

4. George Farquhar, *The Works of Geo. Farquhar*, 2 vols. (Dublin: Thomas Ewing, 1775), I, p. iii.

5. George Farquhar, *The Works of George Farquhar*, ed. Shirley Strum Kenny, 2 vols. (Oxford: Clarendon Press, 1988), I, p. 33. All subsequent references to Farquhar are to this edition.

6. G. C. Duggan, *The Stage Irishman: A History of the Irish Play and Stage Characters from the Earliest Times* (Dublin: Talbot Press, 1937), pp. 288–97.

7. Joep Leerssen, *Mere Irish and Fíor-Ghael: Studies in the Idea of Irish Nationality, its Development and Literary Expression prior to the Nineteenth Century* (Amsterdam: Benjamins, 1986; Cork: Cork University Press, 1996), p. 117.

8. Farquhar, *Works*, I, p. 539.

9. Shirley Strum Kenny, 'Farquhar, Wilks, and Wildair: or, the Metamorphosis of the "Fine Gentleman"', *Philological Quarterly* 57, 1 (1978), pp. 47–8.

10. Farquhar, *Works*, I, p. 157.

11. Ibid., I, p. 254.

12. Ibid., II, p. 377.

13. Ibid., I, p. 108.

14. Thomas Sheridan. *An Humble Appeal to the Publick, Together With Some Considerations on the Present Critical and Dangerous State of the Stage in Ireland* (Dublin: G. Faulkner, 1758), p. 40.

15. [Frederick Jones], *Reasons for a Parliamentary Regulation of the Irish Stage* (Dublin [c. 1790]), p. 1.

16. Helen M. Burke, *Riotous Performances: The Struggle for Hegemony in the Irish Theater, 1712–1784* (Notre Dame, IN: University of Notre Dame Press, 2003), pp. 282–3.

17. Charles Shadwell, *The Works of Mr Charles Shadwell*, 2 vols. (Dublin: George Risk, Joseph Leathley and Patrick Dugan, 1720), I, pp. 285–6.

18. Ibid., I, p. 267.

19. William Philips, *St Stephen's Green; or, the Generous Lovers*, ed. Christopher Murray (Dublin: Cadenus Press, 1979), pp. 102–3.

20. Sheridan, *Humble Appeal*, p. 40.

21. Thomas Sheridan, *The Brave Irishman; or, Captain O'Blunder*, in Seamus Deane, general ed. *The Field Day Anthology of Irish Writing*, 3 vols. (Derry: Field Day, 1991), I, p. 537.

22. Charles Macklin, *A Will and No Will: Or a Bone for the Lawyers and The New Play Criticiz'd* (Los Angeles: William Andrews Clark Memorial Library, 1967), p. 66.

23. William W. Appleton, *Charles Macklin: An Actor's Life* (Oxford: Oxford University Press, 1961), p. 141.

24. Ibid., p. 121.

25. Hugh Kelly, *The School for Wives*, in Deane, *Field Day Anthology*, I, p. 567.

26. Richard Brinsley Sheridan, *The Dramatic Works of Richard Brinsley Sheridan*, ed. Cecil Price, 2 vols. (Oxford: Clarendon Press, 1973), I, p. 116.

27. *Morning Post* (21 January 1775); in Sheridan, *Dramatic Works*, I, p. 47.

28. Sheridan, *Dramatic Works*, I, p. 71.

29. Fintan O'Toole, *A Traitor's Kiss: The Life of Richard Brinsley Sheridan* (London: Granta, 1997), p. 128.

30. Oliver Goldsmith, *She Stoops to Conquer*, in Deane, *Field Day Anthology*, I, p. 572.

31. Christopher Murray, 'Drama 1690–1800', in Deane, *Field Day Anthology*, I, pp. 500–657, p. 503.

32. Thomas Sheridan, *A Full Vindication of the Conduct of the Manager of the Theatre-Royal* (Dublin: S. Powell, 1747), p. 17.

33. James Shirley, *The Dramatic Works of James Shirley*, ed. W. Gifford, 4 vols. (London: John Murray, 1833), IV, pp. 373, 419.

34. Burke, *Riotous Performances*, pp. 53–84.

35. Shadwell, *Works*, II, p. 267.

36. Ibid., II, p. 328.

37. John Locke, *Two Treatises on Government*, ed. Peter Laslett (Cambridge: Cambridge University Press, 1967), pp. 402–4.

38. William Philips, *Hibernia Freed: A Tragedy* (Dublin: Pat Dugan, 1722), pp. 9, 60.

39. Henry Brooke, *Gustavus Vasa: The Deliverer of His Country: As it was to have have been Acted at the Theatre-Royal in Drury-Lane* (London: R. Dodsley, 1739), p. 12.

40. Henry Brooke, *The Songs in Jack the Gyant Queller: An Antique History* (Dublin: George Faulkner, 1749), p. 5. See Kevin J. Donovan, 'Jack the Gyant Queller: Political Theatre in Ascendancy Dublin', *Éire-Ireland* 30, 2 (1995), pp. 70–88.

41. Voltaire, *Mahomet: The Impostor*, trans. D. Miller (Dublin: W. Smith, n.d. [c. 1754]), p. 8.

42. *A Patrick's Pot and a Shamrogue for the Patriots of Ireland, &c.* (London: n.p. [1754]), p. 10. See Christopher Morash, *A History of Irish Theatre, 1601–2000* (Cambridge: Cambridge University Press, 2002), pp. 58–66.

43. William Carleton and D. J. O'Donoghue, *The Life of William Carleton*, 2 vols. (London: Downey, 1896), I, pp. 26–8. See also Niall Ó Ciosáin, *Print and Popular Culture in Ireland, 1750–1850* (New York: St Martin's Press; Houndmills: Macmillan, 1997), pp. 100–18.

44. Gorges Edmond Howard, *The Miscellaneous Works, in Verse and Prose*, 3 vols. (Dublin: R. Marchbank, 1782), I, pp. clxvii, 248.

45. Francis Dobbs, *The Patriot King: Or, Irish Chief: A Tragedy* (London: J. Bew and A. Grant, 1774), p. 9.

46. Cited in Christopher J. Wheatley, *Beneath Iërne's Banners: Irish Protestant Drama of the Restoration and Eighteenth Century* (Notre Dame, IN: University of Notre Dame Press, 1999), p. 100.

47. William Rufus Chetwood, *A General History of the Stage (More Particularly the Irish Theatre) From its Origin in Greece down to the present Time. With Memoirs of most of the Principal Performers, that have appeared on the Dublin Stage, for the last Fifty Years* (London: E. Rider, 1749), p. 49.

48. Joseph Cooper Walker, 'An Historical Essay on the Irish Stage', *Transactions of the Royal Irish Academy* 2 (Dublin: Royal Irish Academy, 1788), p. 75.

49. Ibid., p. 75 note.

50. Alan Gailey, *Irish Folk Drama* (Cork: Mercier, 1969); Henry Glassie, *All Silver and No Brass* (Dublin: Dolmen, 1976).

51. W. S. Clark, *The Irish Stage in the Country Towns: 1720 to 1800* (Oxford: Clarendon Press, 1965), p. 103.
52. Mary O'Brien, *The Fallen Patriot: A Comedy in Five Acts* (Dublin: William Gilbert [1790]), pp. 9, 5.
53. William Cooke, *Memoirs of Charles Macklin, Comedian, With the Dramatic Characters, Manners, Anecdotes, &c., of the Age in which he Lived* (London: James Asperne, 1804), pp. 283–4.
54. John O'Keeffe, *The Dramatic Works of John O'Keeffe, Esq.* 4 vols. (London: T. Woodfall, 1798), I, pp. 271, 273.

Select bibliography

Appleton, William W., *Charles Macklin: An Actor's Life*, Oxford: Oxford University Press, 1961.

Bataille, Robert R., *The Writing Life of Hugh Kelly: Politics, Journalism, and Theater in Late-Eighteenth-Century London*, Carbondale, IL: Southern Illinois University Press, 2000.

Burke, Helen M., *Riotous Performances: The Struggle for Hegemony in the Irish Theater, 1712–1784*, Notre Dame, IN: University of Notre Dame Press, 2003.

Chetwood, William Rufus, *A General History of the Stage*, London: E. Rider, 1749.

Clark, W. S., *The Early Irish Stage: The Beginnings to 1720*, Oxford: Clarendon Press, 1955.

The Irish Stage in the Country Towns: 1720 to 1800, Oxford: Clarendon Press, 1965.

Duggan, G. C., *The Stage Irishman: A History of the Irish Play and Stage Characters from the Earliest Times*, Dublin: Talbot Press, 1937.

Farquhar, George, *The Works of George Farquhar*, ed. Shirley Strum Kenny, 2 vols. Oxford: Clarendon Press, 1988.

Fitzpatrick Dean, Joan, *Riot and Great Anger: Stage Censorship in Twentieth-Century Ireland*, Madison, WI: University of Wisconsin Press, 2004.

Gailey, Alan, *Irish Folk Drama*, Cork: Mercier, 1969.

Glassie, Henry, *All Silver and No Brass: An Irish Christmas Mumming*, Dublin: Dolmen, 1976.

Greene, John C. and Gladys L. H. Clark, *The Dublin Stage, 1720–1745: A Calendar of Plays, Entertainments, and Afterpieces*, Bethlehem, PA: Lehigh University Press; London and Toronto: Associated University Presses, 1993.

Hitchcock, Robert, *Historical View of the Irish Stage*, 2 vols. Dublin, 1788–94.

Kavanagh, Peter, *The Irish Theatre*, Tralee: The Kerryman, 1946.

Leerssen, Joep, *Mere Irish and Fíor-Ghael: Studies in the Idea of Irish Nationality, Its Development and Literary Expression prior to the Nineteenth Century*, Amsterdam: Benjamins, 1986; reprinted in Critical Conditions Series, Cork: Cork University Press, 1996.

Morash, Christopher. *A History of Irish Theatre, 1601–2000*, Cambridge: Cambridge University Press, 2002.

Murray, Christopher, 'Drama 1690–1800', in Seamus Deane, general ed. *The Field Day Anthology of Irish Writing*, 3 vols. Derry: Field Day, 1991, I, pp. 500–657.

Ó Ciosáin, Niall, *Print and Popular Culture in Ireland, 1750–1850*, New York: St Martin's Press; Handmills: Macmillan, 1997.

O'Keeffe, John, *Recollections of the Life of John O'Keeffe*, 2 vols. London: Colburn, 1826.

O'Toole, Fintan, *A Traitor's Kiss: The Life of Richard Brinsley Sheridan*, London: Granta, 1997.

Sheldon, Esther K., *Thomas Sheridan of Smock Alley*, Princeton, NJ: Princeton University Press, 1967.

Sheridan, Richard Brinsley, *The Dramatic Works of Richard Brinsley Sheridan*, ed. Cecil Price, 2 vols. Oxford: Clarendon Press, 1973.

Simpson, Linzi, *Smock Alley Theatre: The Evolution of a Building*, Archaeology in Temple Bar Series, Dublin: privately published, 1996.

Stockwell, La Tourette, *Dublin Theatres and Theatre Customs (1637–1820)*, Kingsport, TN: Kingsport Press, 1938.

Victor, Benjamin, *The History of the Theatres of London and Dublin*, 3 vols. London, 1761–71.

Wheatley, Christopher, *Beneath Ïerne's Banners: Irish Protestant Drama of the Restoration and Eighteenth Century*, Notre Dame, IN: University of Notre Dame Press, 1999.

Wheatley, Christopher and Kevin Donovan, eds. *Irish Drama of the Seventeenth and Eighteenth Centuries*, London: Ganesh Publishing, 2003.

Irish Romanticism, 1800–1830

CLAIRE CONNOLLY

Ireland entered the period of Romanticism scorched by what Quaker writer Mary Leadbeater called the 'ruthless fires' of the 1798 rebellion.[1] Reacting against the threat of Ireland separating from Britain and becoming a client state of France, William Pitt's government moved quickly to draw the neighbouring island more securely to its side. Ireland was in future to send its electoral representatives (considerably reduced in number) to Westminster: the uneasy constitutional compromise that was the Dublin parliament was concluded. Other legal anomalies were cleared up also. The Copyright Act of 1709 was extended to Ireland, all but killing off an Irish publishing industry that was reliant on markets for cheap reprints in Ireland, Britain, the American colonies and the West Indies.[2] More profoundly, the Union created a professional literary culture characterised by movement between and across the two islands. A chapter such as this one therefore has to account for an 'Irish' literature that developed both outside and inside Ireland: the vast majority of the writers discussed here either lived in Britain or published there, and London and Edinburgh play as important a part in the shaping of Irish Romanticism as Dublin, Belfast or Cork. Moreover, the experience of travel and cultural bi-location was itself to become an object of interest in the literature of the period.

Romanticism and Ireland

Romanticism across Europe took its political bearings from the Enlightenment, with its radical faith in social progress and human perfectibility. At the same time, however, the cultural forms and styles favoured by Romantic writers encode a rejection of central eighteenth-century tenets; thus, the liberated imagination takes precedence over enslaved reason, natural forces threaten to overwhelm the established social order, and idealism challenges realism. Apprehending and analysing Irish Romanticism requires reading strategies alert to a series of contests: between politics and culture, progress and nostalgia, crude classificatory systems and sensuously rendered detail.

It is generally agreed that Romanticism 'occurred in national phases', as Stuart Curran puts it, its rhythms 'keyed to the distinct exigencies of national culture'.[3] Until recently, however, mainstream Anglo-American scholarship has tended to treat 'the British Isles' as forming one phase in this process. Differences between component parts of the recently United Kingdom have been largely ignored. Irish literary history, on the other hand, has preferred to seek out evidence of the late flowering of a Romantic sensibility, first glimpsed in the writings of James Clarence Mangan and Thomas Davis and coming to fruition in the early poetry of W. B. Yeats. This chapter treats Irish Romanticism both as a distinct cultural phenomenon, separate from 'British' and other literary histories in the same period, and also as a 'phase' that is temporally coincident with, and shares important connections to, the Romanticism that swept across Europe in the late eighteenth and early nineteenth century. An important effect of Romantic aesthetics was the development of Romantic nationalism. Ireland emerged from this period with a renovated reputation as a naturally distinct national culture; this in turn fostered and supported new theories of nationality and nourished the cultural nationalism of the 1830s and 1840s.

This is not, however, to sketch a smooth scene of historical change, but rather to begin to fill in the contours of the 'confused and introverted' cultural moment described by Tom Dunne in his groundbreaking essay on Irish Romanticism.[4] The intellectual origins of Irish culture in this period are to be found in the eighteenth century, especially in the antiquarian (or 'first' Celtic) revival which constitutes the enabling ground of Irish Romanticism. Books, essays and lectures by antiquarian scholars, along with cultural gatherings like the Granard and Belfast harp festivals of 1781 and 1792, allowed the writers of Irish Romanticism to negotiate a route back to the Irish past (the paths laid down by historical writings are traced in detail by Clare O'Halloran in chapter 14). Irish writers of the early nineteenth century were greatly influenced also by the cult of the bard, especially Macpherson's translations of Ossian which promised access to a hitherto unseen Celtic sensibility. Nor were these traditions entirely consigned to the past: bardic practices survived in memory and in stories for authors such as Maria Edgeworth and Sydney Owenson, while poets like Patrick O'Kelly strove to keep the legacy alive. The figure of the bard was powerfully revived for the 1790s (and for Ulster writers in particular) in the figure of Robert Burns.[5] Most influential of all were the efforts of late eighteenth-century writers such as Charlotte Brooke and

Charles Henry Wilson, who sought to give expression to a vanishing world by capturing the oral tradition in print. This sense of change and decline is significant: even as they undertook their heroic attempt to preserve and revive the fragments of Gaelic culture, the antiquarians and revivalists gave powerful expression to the idea of loss. Irish Romanticism as a whole developed new and sophisticated ways of representing defeat and enervation, while at the same time retaining the raw energy and exhibitionism characteristic of the revivalist impulse. The sense of a cultural barrier that had to be crossed was intensified by the passing of the Act of Union, memorably described by Thomas Moore as 'the phantom by which the dawn of the Nineteenth century was welcomed'.[6]

Union and identity

The Act of Union between Great Britain and Ireland passed into law on 1 January 1801 amidst a great outpouring of words. For Irish literature, the impact was swift. The Union debates, expressed in pamphlets, reprinted speeches, poems and mock-playbills, exploited the resources of print culture and quickly spilled over into literary forms. Among these the novel dominates, not only as the genre most associated with the kinds of questions ushered in with the Union, but as the pre-eminent cultural form of this period of Irish literature.

The legal formula employed in legislatively joining Ireland to Britain was, according to liberal Wicklow MP William Parnell (1780–1821), one of the Act's critics, an aggravating trick of rhetoric: 'the Union is a name, a sound, a fiction; there is no Union; the nominal Union is only an additional source of discord'.[7] Such accusations entered a literary culture sensitised to the idea of a separate national identity – a familiar theme of Irish literature since at least Swift and Molyneux – and poised to move the issue into a new and distinctly cultural register. In the place of economics, however, or abstract political concepts such as rights (found in eighteenth-century patriotic discourse), the Romantic period witnessed a turn to culture itself as the ground on which ideas of Ireland and Irishness were debated. An understanding of culture not only as vehicle for identity but as constitutive of its essence is characteristic of Romanticism across Europe; Ireland in this period begins to think of itself as Irish in ways that specifically relate to the English-language literature it produces.

Hopes that the Act might allow Catholics a greater share in public life were swiftly disappointed, and lingered as an open sore on the surface of the new body politic. The literary culture of Irish Romanticism is thus strongly marked by a sense of grievance, generated by broken political promises and failed rebellion. The note of complaint, however, was heard alongside persistent calls to mould civil society in a more progressive shape. Critics conventionally map different literary genres on to these cultural registers: the discourse of improvement finds expression in the novel, while poetry and (to the extent that it is noticed at all) drama are associated with despair and decline. Such schemata ignore the extent to which the English-language literature of early nineteenth-century Ireland – whether optimistic or elegiac in mood – comes to bear the burden of reform and change. The account offered here attempts a more wide-ranging and comprehensive treatment of the connections between cultural form and political content, and shows how the work of writing constitutes an intrinsic part of the desire to effect transformations in Irish culture.

Overall, the period sees a distinct shift in what may be termed, with equal applicability to literary history and affairs of state, the politics of representation. Catholic rights were recognised with the repeal of the Test and Corporation Acts in 1828 and the granting of emancipation in 1829; the 1820s in particular see the emergence of a distinct body of professional Catholic men of letters and a squeezing out of liberal Protestant opinion. Writing in 1823, judge and baron of the exchequer Sir William Cusack Smith (1766–1836) warned politicians and journalists no longer to 'expect that what [they] address to the public will be a sort of theatrical *aside*; which none but Protestants shall hear'.[8] Questions of representation pervade literary culture at every level. Lady Olivia Clarke's (née Owenson, ?1785–1845) play, *The Irishwoman*, performed in Dublin in 1819, compares dramatic prologues to 'those civil speeches / In which a candidate for votes beseeches'. The conceit of the play's own prologue, written by Clarke's brother-in-law, Sir Charles Morgan (*c.*1780–1843, husband of Sydney), is to introduce the performance as a candidate seeking the votes of the audience. The play's themes are presented via a series of linked references to demands for Catholic suffrage: 'On stage or hustings, when they take their station, / Both Speakers seek to gain – representation.'[9] The prologue to Clarke's play further associates calls for political change with the distinct claims, fears and feelings of women: the 1820s also saw the start of public lobbying for the rights of women, with the publication of Cork-born Anna Doyle Wheeler and William Thompson's *Appeal of One Half of the Human Race, Women Against the Pretensions of the Other Half, Men* (1825).

This sense of a broadening public stage for which new roles had to be scripted (or old truisms tested) is crucial for understanding texts as diverse as Maria Edgeworth's novels, Thomas Moore's poetry and Charles Robert Maturin's dramas. A concern with voices and their framing within narrative is a recognisable hallmark of Irish culture from the Act of Union up to Catholic emancipation, and should be understood in terms of contemporary developments: the loss of an independent legislature, and increasing agitation for proper public representation of Catholics as political subjects and, most significantly of all, as a bilingual culture on the cusp of a major shift from one language to another. Irish literary texts of this period are equipped with a strong sense of opposing audiences, and manifest an awareness of what W. J. McCormack describes as 'the dynamics of . . . rival, even irreconcilable readerships'.[10] Along with this public dimension, however, the texts discussed in this chapter are shadowed by a need for secrecy and a lingering sense of the value of illegitimate knowledges. It is thus within the genre of the novel, with its narrative mastery of social visibility and public authority, that the greatest energy is concentrated and distilled.

Prose fiction

This period of Irish literature opens with a series of ground-clearing exercises undertaken by a young but intellectually assured writer living on her family's estate in County Longford. Resident in Ireland from 1782, Maria Edgeworth (1768–1849) had an unusually liberal upbringing, largely a result of her father's radical educational theories, her reading in the French and Scottish Enlightenments, and the family immersion in Romantic print culture. The most respected novelist of her day and the benchmark by which new arrivals like Jane Austen and Walter Scott were judged, Edgeworth visited Britain, France and Switzerland and acquired a growing circle of influential correspondents. Her career was, however, largely lived out among family and friends in Longford, and she remained close to midlands gentry families like the Beauforts, who formed the first horizon of her readership. Edgeworth's literary career embraced a diverse but ultimately interrelated set of concerns, all of which can be seen in embryo in her earliest publications: *Letters for Literary Ladies* (1795), *Castle Rackrent* (1800) and *Belinda* (1801).

Letters for Literary Ladies uncovers and scrutinises assumptions about female education and authorship. Written in mock-epistolary form with a concluding essay, the text suggests that it is only women who have the leisure to be wise and to unite different professional specialisms in the domestic sphere: this is the bedrock of national unity and a strong guarantor of social progress. *Practical Education* (1798) was written with Edgeworth's father and life-long collaborator, Richard Lovell Edgeworth (1744–1817). It treats education as a public issue that ought to be debated in the full light of rational inquiry, a proposition considered radical enough to attract several negative reviews that focused especially on the Edgeworths' neglect of religion. She continued to publish works aimed at both children and educators, including *Moral Tales* (1801), *Early Lessons* (1801) and *The Parent's Assistant* (1796).

Belinda (1801), a courtship novel that endorses the contemporary ideology of companionate marriage as the only safe foundation for domestic and social happiness, carries forward Edgeworth's interest in women's social power. The novel displays Edgeworth's wide reading in 1790s feminism, and cleverly caricatures Mary Wollstonecraft and Mary Hays in the character of a hysterical advocate of the rights of woman named Harriet Freke. In *Belinda*, Edgeworth takes a measured step away from the discredited Jacobinism of her father's generation (although she continued to publish with the radical Joseph Johnson and later his nephews) and moves towards a more cautious endorsement of the virtues of domesticity, a private sphere that is always closely connected with the public world and dominated – sometimes damagingly so – by well-educated and independent women who freely transgress the threshold between private and public. In the case of *Belinda*, the invasion of the public into the private is marked via a series of extreme bodily sensations, most notably the wound and subsequent terror experienced by the character of Lady Delacour. Later fictions like *Leonora* (1803) and *Patronage* (1814) repeatedly cross the public / private boundary and her final novel, *Helen* (1834), represents a sustained examination of the limits of women's public power.

The preface to Edgeworth's experimental first-person narrative, *Castle Rackrent* (1800), surveys established literary models and coolly considers which genre might best suit the story at hand. Nothing less than Ireland's future in prose is at stake here: *Castle Rackrent* moves between established literary modes, self-consciously in search of a new style of prose fiction. Long recognised as innovative, its newness has been claimed for different traditions: the first 'regional' fiction in British literature, the first distinctively Irish novel and even, according to anecdote, the first text to help George III to understand his Irish subjects (this at the very moment he decided to refuse them religious tolerance). *Castle Rackrent* acts as a vehicle for the point of view of an Irish servant, Thady Quirke. His opinions are expressed in an English that is heavily marked by the traces of Irish syntax and vocabulary, framed by the crisp explanatory prose of the editor's preface, notes and glossary.

Despite his loquaciousness, the character of Thady Quirke retains a degree of ironic impenetrability that has generated a rich and varied critical response to the novel. *Castle Rackrent*'s framing of Thady's voice remains a subject of critical discussions that were to become increasingly heated once the embryonic Catholic energies that Edgeworth seeks to represent found their own political voice in the early years of the twentieth century. This has led to a tendency to dismiss the later Irish novels, *The Absentee, Ennui* and *Ormond*, as patrician and prescriptive fictions of progress, blind to the complex realities of Irish life. Important as part of a history of Irish cultural politics, these debates have, however, condemned readings of Edgeworth's ironic masterpiece to tread a deeply grooved but narrow-gauged circle of ideas concerning authenticity and political responsibility. Edgeworth's experiment with voice and genre is a product not only of her residence in Longford from age fifteen and her conversations with the family steward John Langan, but also of her reading in Scottish Enlightenment philosophy, French moral tales and English novels. Like Aphra Behn's *Oroonoko* or Samuel Johnson's *Rasselas, Castle Rackrent* is a sophisticated fictional experiment that seeks to convey within the medium of print culture a perspective otherwise alien to a novel-reading audience. Edgeworth's choice of an Irish peasant narrator is new, as is her Romantic interest in orality and in the politics of language. This precise sense of language and its political consequences finds further expression in *Essay on Irish Bulls* (1802), a witty and self-consciously Swiftian examination of Hiberno-English usage, co-authored with her father. The text was revised in 1803 and in 1808.

All of Edgeworth's Irish novels from *Castle Rackrent* onwards effect a transfer of land: property that had formerly belonged to the Williamite generation of Protestant landowners passes into the hands of Catholic (or strongly Catholic-associated) characters, as in her novels *Ennui* (1809), *The Absentee* (1812) and *Ormond* (1817). In each case, the mechanism of transfer is a marriage that effects an alliance between native and settler cultures. The novels end with the promise of a happier future that can be read in both domestic and national terms. This kind of doubled narrative, where sexual relations are made to relate to political ones, lends the novels an allegorical aspect that connects them most immediately to Sydney Owenson's *The Wild Irish Girl* (1806). Through Owenson, a path can be traced back to seventeenth- and eighteenth-century bardic verse and the *aisling* tradition. Another direct source may be found in radical feminist fictions of the 1790s, with their overdetermined politics of plot. More generally, allegory may be seen forming part of what Tom Dunne calls 'the colonial character of Irish Romantic literature':[11] the injunction to speak otherwise (*allos-agoreuein*) remained a powerful one throughout the nineteenth century and connects Edgeworth's and other Irish fictions of this period to twentieth-century postcolonial literatures.

The attachment to allegorical forms within Irish Romanticism marks one of its key differences from mainstream British literary trends in the same period. Critics such as Samuel Taylor Coleridge contributed to an influential and pervasive devaluation of allegory in contemporary aesthetics; meanwhile, symbol took pride of place as the most sophisticated form of metaphor. Inheritors of this Romantic distrust of the simple and simplifying effects of allegory include the many critics of Irish literature who dismiss national allegories like those of Edgeworth as having an 'analgesic' effect.[12]

Alongside this allegorical tendency, Edgeworth's novels develop a realist mode that won her wide praise. Her later Irish fictions were consistently described as offering authentic images of Irish life, and praised by liberal journals like *The Edinburgh Review* for contributing to the great project of reforming Ireland. Such praise proved short-lived, however, and did not survive even into mid-century. Negative reviews of her father's *Memoirs* (1817), combined with the masculine capturing of the novel described below, meant that Edgeworth's reputation suffered severe blows. The backlash can be witnessed from as early as *Patronage* (1814), the publication of which was greeted with accusations of impropriety and ignorance. Edgeworth was to be dogged throughout her career by similar charges of perceived breaches of propriety, whether linguistic, political or moral, and often made revisions to the text of her novels (for collected and other editions) in order to counter accusations levelled against her in public forums like the reviews.

Partly as a result of the energies unleashed by Edgeworth's experiments in prose, and partly, perhaps, as a consequence of Union itself, the Irish novel marshalled fresh energy and momentum in this period. The decade after the Union saw the emergence of the national tale, product of the precocious literary talent of Sydney Owenson (later Lady Morgan) (c.1783–1859). Her greatest success was *The Wild Irish Girl: A National Tale* (1806), the text now credited with the first use of this innovative brand or badge of generic identity. Owenson had published two earlier novels, *St Clair; or the Heiress of Desmond* (1803) and *The Novice of St Dominick* (1806). The former was first published in Dublin, and is worthy of note as one of the few novels originally published in Ireland in the years between the passing of the Act of Union and the revival of the Irish publishing industry in the 1830s. *The Wild Irish Girl* takes elements from these earlier fictions – an Irish setting, religious difference, Gothic plots and an interest in a contested past – and combines them with Owenson's extensive knowledge of antiquarian debates and contemporary politics to produce a national romance. A young English man is banished to his father's estates in Ireland. There he learns the history of those lands, which have come into his family as a result of the Cromwellian conquest. He falls in love with the daughter of the Gaelic family dispossessed by his ancestors and their marriage serves to allegorise a happier future for a divided Ireland, as well as more immediately reminding readers of the recent Union between Great Britain and Ireland. The longevity of this plot (up to and including contemporary Troubles romances and films like Neil Jordan's *The Crying Game*) suggests its resilience and flexibility; and should remind us also of the many possible meanings of Owenson's narrative manoeuvres.

The national tale's distinctive generic qualities are the result of efforts by (chiefly) Irish female writers to give fictional shape to an interrelated set of concerns, including history, property and national conduct. The national tale combines elements of feminist fictions of the 1790s with bardic verse, allegory and the contemporary novel of courtship and companionate marriage. From 1808 to 1814 may be seen as the great years of the national tale and the period evidences a set of titles that prove the instant marketability of *The Wild Irish Girl* formula. These include Charles Robert Maturin's *The Wild Irish Boy* (1808) and *The Milesian Chief* (1812), Henrietta Rouviere Mosse's *The Old Irish Baronet: or, Manners of My Country* (1808), Elizabeth Plunkett's *The Exile of Erin* (1808), Theodore Melville's *The Irish Chieftain, and His Family* (1809), John Agg's *Mac Dermot; or, The Irish Chieftain* (1810), and Ann Mary Hamilton's *The Irishwoman in London* (1810).[13]

An indicative arc can be observed in the writings of the Waterford-born Regina Maria Roche (1763/4–1845). Her Gothic bestseller *Children of the Abbey* (1798) – still in print as late as the 1890s and the basis of an early silent film – has occasional Irish references. Her home country then comes more fully into view with *Clermont: A Tale* (1798). Roche continued to write formulaic fictions for the Minerva Press, but by 1820 had moved into a recognisably Irish mode with *The Munster Cottage Boy* (1820), which draws heavily on the plot and style of *The Wild Irish Girl*. Much more than the intellectually respectable but still eccentric experiment that was *Castle Rackrent*, then, the success of *The Wild Irish Girl* is to credit (or blame) for making Ireland a recognisable location within the world of Romantic-era fiction.

Sydney Owenson was daughter to the actor-manager Robert Owenson and had travelled widely with him in Ireland. The influence of the sentimental comedies of John O'Keeffe, a staple of her father's companies, can be seen in her early Irish fictions. Owenson had an active publishing career until her death in 1859, carried on after this by her secretary Geraldine Jewsbury and her friend W. J. Fitzpatrick. Such was her success and exposure that she was a key point of contact for Irish writers moving into the London publishing scene in the 1810s to 1830s. As with Regina Maria Roche, Owenson's own first novel, *St Clair*, can help chart the process of generic and cultural change that Owenson herself instigated. In many respects, the novel is remarkably similar in form and theme to *The Wild Irish Girl*: told in letter form, *St Clair* relates how a stranger arrives in the wilds of the west of Ireland, and falls in love with the daughter of a chieftain. In *St Clair*, however, the setting, scenery and location are incidental.

A revised edition of the novel appeared in 1812, and added aspects of *The Wild Irish Girl* formula to the earlier fiction. The recipe was to be repeated in *Woman; or, Ida of Athens* (1809) and *The Missionary* (1811), each of which takes on a new national context (Greece and Goa) and has a young woman with fervent attachments to her native place come into passionate conflict with established authority and join forces with a man whose oppositional stance affirms her own. In the case of *The Missionary* in particular, the price of such affirmation is the near-annihilation of the heroine's sense of self, already rendered precarious by the experience of romantic love. The conclusion of that novel sees the heroine, a Brahmin princess, ascending the funeral pyre of the Franciscan friar with whom she had fallen in love, scenes that so affected the young Percy Bysshe Shelley that he borrowed them for his *Revolt of Islam*.

These novels fully inhabit the culture of sensibility, and Owenson fine-tunes her narratives to sound an almost unbearably high-pitched note of intense feeling. Her fluency in the language of sentiment was to lose Owenson readers once literary fashions shifted; in an attempt to recapture the market she revised *The Wild Irish Girl* (1846) and *The Missionary* (as *Luxima*, in 1858), removing what she described as 'superfluous epithets' and some of the more purple passages.

Irish literature of the Romantic period shows evidence of a sustained interest in and interrogation of the culture of sensibility, always understood in Ireland (as in the American republic) as involved in and associated with the project of nation-building. With Edgeworth and Owenson, we see the incorporation of the domestic novel, with its in-built generic focus on shaping and guiding behaviour, into the repertoire of Irish fiction, where it becomes a way of addressing issues of political as well as sexual propriety. Translating ideas of sympathy into an Irish context causes problems, however, chiefly because of its problematic link to political and religious enthusiasm. Irish writers like Elizabeth Plunkett (née Gunning, 1769–1823) and Thomas Moore (1779–1852) strive to vindicate sensibility in a climate which is already sceptical of its Jacobin and United Irishmen associations (Plunkett, *The Exile of Erin*, 1808). The figure of Lord Edward Fitzgerald is central here, especially as he is depicted in Moore's 1831 biography but also in his role as shadowy presence behind the characters of Ormsby Bethel in Maturin's *Wild Irish Boy* and Lord Walter Fitzwalter in *The O'Briens and The O'Flaherties*.

Owenson's later Irish novels (*O'Donnel* (1814), *Florence Macarthy* (1818) and *The O'Briens and The O'Flaherties* (1824)) move out of the mode of fatal sincerity and into what Ina Ferris has identified as an obliquely angled and shape-changing mode of address.[14] Owenson (by now Lady Morgan, thanks to her marriage to the physician of her Whig patrons, Lord and Lady Abercorn) creates in these novels a series of highly artificial and 'performative'[15] heroines, who translate a need for secrecy (demanded by even the most blameless of public causes) into disguise, theatricality and display. Owenson's interest in powerful women sequestered within convents or other all-female spaces allows us to connect her writings to later fictions by Kate O'Brien and Julia O'Faolain. Like them, she combines a strong interest in romance with narrative strategies that move 'on the diagonal', as Ferris puts it, and address history aslant. Her later Irish novels show evidence of a sustained engagement with recent Irish history, in particular the turbulent decades of her own youth. The 1780s and 1790s are presented almost as a series of tableaux, connected via a series of cinematic fades back into the sixteenth century.

The later fictions of both Owenson and Edgeworth were published in the context of a significant shift in the gendered hierarchies of authorship and genre. Peter Garside's authoritative bibliographical study of the Romantic-era novel identifies a 'male invasion of mainstream fiction' taking place in the early years of the nineteenth century in both Britain and Ireland, with 'female dominance' up to the 1810s reversed by the 1820s.[16] An initial female dominance of the fiction market was thus followed by what is now recognised as a masculine capturing of the novel in both Britain and Ireland.[17] This coincided with a fashion for military and naval fictions, evident by the 1820s, with Irish novelists William Hamilton Maxwell (1792–1850) and later Charles Lever (1806–72) in the forefront of this new trend.[18] Furthermore, the masculine capturing of the novel described by Garside and exemplified in the figure of Walter Scott encodes a wider cultural phenomenon, whereby the novel itself moved into the cultural mainstream.[19]

Cultural change of this sort does not occur without a degree of confusion and contradiction on the ground. A generic approach to the fictions of this period shows the Irish novel splitting across a series of fictional fashions. A great many novels in the 1810s veer between parody and pastiche. The latter include Cork-born Eaton Stannard Barrett's (1786–1820) satire of novel reading, *The Heroine; Or Adventures of a Fair Romance Reader* (1813), while Maturin's *The Wild Irish Boy* balances precariously between heartfelt emotion and camp display. Examples of pastiche include more straightforwardly imitative and far less assured novels such as Francis Higginson's *Manderville; or, The Hibernian Chiliarch* (1825).

Across this period, Gothic gives way to historical fiction,[20] but in the case of the Irish novel the latter form retains within it important elements of the former. The interpenetration of these modes can be witnessed in the novels of the Dublin-born Protestant cleric Charles Robert Maturin (1782–1824): *Fatal Revenge* (1807), *The Wild Irish Boy* (1808), *The Milesian Chief* (1812), *Women; or Pour et Contre* (1818), *Melmoth the Wanderer* (1820) and *The Albigenses* (1824). Maturin's family origins lay in the Huguenot flight from religious persecution in seventeenth-century France. The relation between religious and state power concerns him everywhere in his novels, and provides the backdrop for dynamic fictions of persecution and flight. Maturin's novels allow us to see the evolution of Irish Gothic as a fictional idiom in which excessive forms of subjective experience (passion, terror, starvation) compel the invention of new structures of feelings within which political affiliation can be reimagined.[21]

Melmoth the Wanderer uses the shadow of dissident sexualities and the bodily and mental weakness brought on by hunger to wreck any possibility of affective social bonds. Maturin thus calls into question the idealised national communities proposed in the national tales of Maria Edgeworth and Sydney Owenson. To this extent, Maturin, and nineteenth-century Protestant Gothic fiction more generally, should be understood as sharing generic ground with the O'Connellite fictions of the 1820s; like *Melmoth*, the Catholic novels 'as often blocked as enabled sympathetic attachments' and similarly seek to interrogate the processes by which closed communities are formed.[22]

Melmoth was originally conceived, Frankenstein-like, from a patchwork of different literary models. Maturin first describes it as a poem like *Lallah Rookh* (inspired no doubt by Thomas Moore's great financial success with the title), then a 'Prose Romance', and finally as a series of linked tales imitating the structure of Scott's *Chronicles of the Canongate*.[23] What was eventually published is an embedded narrative of linked stories that move backwards in time (from the roughly contemporary to the Reformation and the English Civil War) while ranging widely through Ireland, Spain and the east. Maturin's correspondence with his publisher, John Constable, helps explain the ragged nature of the text, as well as providing some insight into the working life of an author dogged by poverty and ill health.[24]

Maturin was assisted early in his career by Walter Scott, who sought to challenge the Whig dominance of the Irish question in fiction by nurturing the talents of a fellow Tory. Maturin, however, proved far from doctrinaire. Curate of St Peter's church in Dublin, he ignored Scott's advice and courted controversial religious topics with publications like *Five Sermons on the Errors of the Roman Catholic Church* (1824). Maturin's literary imagination shows evidence of a deep involvement with the forms and rituals of the Catholic faith. The anti-Catholic stereotypes characteristic of Gothic fiction are thus transmuted into something unique and troubling; connected perhaps to the interest in 'dead-alive' bodies and states of suspended animation found in later fictions by Catholic novelists Gerald Griffin and the Banim brothers.

The Milesian Chief depicts an imaginary insurgency taking place in the aftermath of the rebellions of 1798 and 1803. Borrowing details from both of these events for a rebellion taking place in a projected future, the narrative achieves a strange acceleration of temporality that contrasts strongly with the overall atmosphere of ruins and relics. Maturin, like Owenson and the Banims, also achieves some of the best writing of city life in the period; his *Women; or Pour et Contre* satirises evangelical Dublin life and contains some urban set-pieces that cast the Irish metropolis as scene of melancholy splendour.

The Church of Ireland began its steady move towards evangelical Christianity from the 1800s onwards. Proselytising novels and tales played a key part in the advance of the Protestant Crusade (also known as the Second Reformation). Short tales published and distributed by evangelical groups like the Kildare Place Society usually focus on exemplary Irish heroines, whose discovery of a copy of the Bible proves the key to their salvation. Examples include *The Irish Girl* (1814) and *The History of Mary* (1820). Evangelical novels regularly borrowed from the tropes and themes of the national tale, as in Patrick Brontë's (1777–1861: father of Charlotte, Emily and Anne) *The Maid of Killarney* (1818), which reworks *The Wild Irish Girl*, or Selina Bunbury's (1802–82) *The Abbey of Inismoyle* (1828), which imagines Ireland's north-western coast infiltrated by a Jesuit conspiracy.

The Second Reformation prompted angry ripostes from Catholic writers, including John Banim's *The Nowlans* (discussed below) and Thomas Moore's prose satire, *Memoirs of Captain Rock* (1824). *Captain Rock* opens with a description of a young man sent to Ireland, not by his parents (as in so many national tales), but by an English society of Protestant charitable ladies. He immediately encounters the eponymous hero, who presents him with a bundle of papers containing his life story and the history of his family; the Captain's memoirs form the remainder of the narrative. They are narrated by an agrarian outlaw with a long family history of rebellion, and resemble *Melmoth* in their Gothic obsession with the effects of historical trauma. Yet *Captain Rock* is quite different (from *Melmoth*, as from almost every Irish fiction that surrounds it) in seeking to make that trauma part of a coherent narrative whole, the consequences of which have been, are and always will be bruised souls, broken bodies and armed rebellion. The continuity of Irish insurgency is realised in a series of brilliant, quasi-symbolist images that illuminate a vast panorama of historical injustice, even as they disrupt the flow of the plot. Moore's fondness for iconic images that capture and condense historical processes is ascribed by Ronan Kelly to his reading in contemporary French historiography; whatever their origin, these moments in his prose connect powerfully to his *Irish Melodies* and help join up different aspects of Moore's varied literary career.[25] His next prose fiction, *Travels of an Irish Gentleman in Search of a Religion* (1833), continues in satiric mode: like *Captain Rock*, it targets evangelical Protestantism, although this time in the changed context of post-Catholic emancipation Ireland.

The 1820s is the decade in which 'an Irish *line* of fiction begins to be defined' in the British reviews, with Irishness now negatively understood as associated with an excessive political commitment.[26] This marks a move away from an earlier more positive climate, but did not stem the production of Irish titles. When Gerald Griffin (1803–40) came to publish his first fictions, the pressure of expectation and counter-expectation is clearly felt. The introduction to the first series of his *Tales of the Munster Festivals* (1826) features a conversation between an enthusiastic writer of national tales and a dour antiquarian who believes that a 'ruined people stand in need of a more potent sedative than an old wife's story'. Griffin makes the old man's 'sour' cynicism part of his narrative frame, allowing the *Tales* to voice strong and self-conscious criticism of existing modes of national fiction even as they stake out new fictional territory: 'You would, I suppose, have a typhus fever, or a scarcity of potatoes, remedied by a smart tale, while you would knock a general insurrection on the head, with a romance in three volumes.'[27]

Novelists who embark on publishing careers in the 1820s are aware of entering a crowded field, and an element of fictional meta-consciousness enters their writings. They also begin to turn in new directions for material for their 'smart tales': towards Irish folklore, being collected and made available from the 1820s, and, with a new confidence, to the recent past. The 1820s sees a spate of novels that explicitly make the rebellion of 1798 part of their plot: Lady Morgan's *The O'Briens and the O'Flaherties*, John and Michael Banim's *The Croppy* (1828), James McHenry's *The Insurgent Chief; or, O'Halloran, An Irish Historical Tale of 1798* (1828), and Eyre Evans Crowe's 'The Northerns of Ninety-Eight', part of his *Yesterday in Ireland* (1829).

The Irish novel in the Romantic period thus moves between the modes of historical fiction and national tale. Katie Trumpener has put in place a useful set of distinctions between these literary modes, contrasting their treatment of past and present. Where the national tale slides back and forth between competing modes and does not organise them hierarchically, the historical novel reorganises the opposition along chronological lines and decisively shifts the terms into a narrative of development and progress.[28] The historical novel creates a verifiable past via the presence of recognisable world-historical characters, lending to fiction a decisively evidential basis and a stiffer chronological spine.

One danger of these distinctions is that they prop up a process whereby Irish fiction by women began to be either excluded from the literary canon, or only admitted on certain terms. Maria Edgeworth's Irish novels have been a victim of this trend, as have other femino-centric fictions of Irish life. These include Sarah Isdell, *The Irish Recluse* (1809), Mrs Kelly, *The Matron of Erin* (1814), Elizabeth Plunkett, *The Exile of Erin* (1808) and Ann Hamilton, *The Modern Irishwoman in London* (1810). These novels all share an interest in the rebellion of 1798 (a decade earlier than the fictions discussed above), and offer set-piece discussions or striking images of the events of that summer. They might also be read alongside the range of non-fictional responses to the rebellion written by female loyalist witnesses like Dinah Goff and Jane Adams.[29] To these women's fictions of rebellion may be added Lady Caroline Lamb's scandalous novel *Glenarvon* (1816), which uses a Lady Morgan-inspired version of the rebellion of 1798 as a backdrop against which to replay the drama of her recent affair with Lord Byron.

Despite the considerable interest of these past-oriented fictions by female Protestant writers, however, literary historians still tend to ascribe the proper beginnings of Irish historical fiction to two middle-class Catholic men: John and Michael Banim (1798–1842 and 1796–1874), brothers from Kilkenny who collaboratively published their *Tales of the O'Hara Family* throughout the 1820s (including *The Nowlans* (1824), *The Boyne Water* (1826), *The Croppy: A Tale of 1798* (1828) and *The Anglo-Irish of the Nineteenth Century* (1828)). The Banims (like Thomas Moore and Gerald Griffin) subscribed to the cult of anonymity made fashionable by Walter Scott and published under the pseudonym 'The O'Hara Family' (as brothers Abel and Barnes O'Hara). Scholars have disputed the exact authorship of each fiction, and the precise nature of their literary collaboration remains under-researched. The novels are prefaced with letters from one (fictional) brother to the other, usually rooted in reported travels around Ireland.

The Banims' fictions broadly divide into stories of contemporary peasant life, which take the form of tales or short fictions, and large-scale historical fictions that are presented in novel form. The tales flirt with supernaturalism, but usually assign rational causes to such Otherworldly manifestations as fetches and banshees, fairy-blasts and strokes. The novels are more evidently in the tradition staked out by Edgeworth and Owenson (often specifically responding to their themes and tropes), yet also represent a new departure. Like Maturin (and the later Owenson), the Banims' novels allow us to chart 'the transformation of an allegorically flattened national character . . . into one torn apart by the contradictions of uneven development'.[30] The novels characteristically end (and sometimes begin) with a depiction of nervous and shaken individuals, their futures blighted by the invasion of politics into their lives. Most notable is their characterisation of the anguish suffered by John Nowlan, the novice priest of *The Nowlans*, who falls in love with and marries a young Protestant woman.

The Banims were not the first writers to feature the Catholic clergy in their fictions: *The Wild Irish Girl* features a genial chaplain who encourages the young lovers, and in 1819 William Parnell published *Maurice and Berghetta; or the Priest of Rahery* (1821), a controversial national romance centring around the benevolent actions of a kindly Catholic priest. Narrated by a cleric at the end of his life, the novel caused one reviewer to accuse Parnell of apostasy[31] and led another to condemn the flawed understanding of any individual who could 'speak of Popery as in itself of innocuous or of beneficial tendency'.[32] In *The Nowlans*, however, the focus falls emphatically on the psychological suffering of the priest figure, himself made the centre of the romance plot. The shadow of conversion looms large, and helps explain some of the anguish experienced by the young John Nowlan. The Revd George Brittaine's (1790–1847) virulently anti-Catholic fictions (*Reflections of Hyacinth O'Gara* (1828), *Confessions of Honor Delany* (1829), *Irishmen and Irishwomen* (1830)) belong to this world also, immersed as they are in the detail of evangelical battles and evoking the new spectre of the 'Maynooth priest': educated in Ireland, not on the continent (Maynooth College opened in 1795), and part of the machinery of O'Connellite politics.

The emergence of organised Catholic politics in the 1820s is crucial for understanding the Banims' historical fictions, published in the years just before the gaining of Catholic emancipation. *The Boyne Water* opens with news of the Catholic James II having succeeded to the throne and concludes with the end of the Williamite wars and the introduction of the Penal Code. In the place of the Glorious Revolution of popular English memory, *The Boyne Water* depicts a tripartite story of dynastic contest between Scottish, English and European interests; a struggle between Tories and Whigs for power over the islands, centred in London; and, finally, a conflict between natives and settlers in

Ireland that has a crucially religious dimension. The influence of Scott on the novel has often been noted, in particular on a narrative designed to allow opposing forces to rub up against each other until equilibrium is achieved. *The Boyne Water* does not provide any final moment of balance or harmony, however, nor can it reassure its readers that insurgency is safely consigned to the past. Published in the immediate aftermath of agrarian disturbances, the novel concludes on the open question of Ireland's political future.

With the fictions of the Banim brothers and Gerald Griffin (1803–40), the adventure story moves into prominence in Irish fiction. Griffin left his native Limerick for London in 1823, following the emigration of his parents to America. Dejected at the rejection of his tragedy *Aguire*, and his failure to make his way in the theatre, Griffin turned to journalism. He wrote prose and poetical pieces for the London papers (under 'five hundred different signatures', as he puts it),[33] and wrote and published his first tales before returning to Ireland in 1827. *Tales of the Munster Festivals* (1826–7) and *Holland-Tide; Or, Munster Popular Tales* (1827) are presented within a frame narrative that recalls *The Canterbury Tales*. An audience of Irish peasants gathered to celebrate a festival are made the narrative occasion for a set of linked tales that move Irish prose in English onto new ground: legends from myth and folklore are presented on their own terms, and, via the frame narrative, to their own audience. Griffin's tales echo the Romantic supernaturalism of James Hogg in Scotland, combining as they do uncanny tales of resurrected corpses and ghostly limbs with a detailed account of political unease and social stratification in the southern part of Ireland. Munster in the 1820s was still recovering from the economic crisis created by the ending of the Napoleonic wars and the famines of 1817 and 1822; at the time of Griffin's writing, the south of Ireland was generally considered the most lawless and troubled province. Griffin's short life involved a return to his native Limerick, where he met and (unhappily) fell in love with Lydia Fisher, the married daughter of Mary Leadbeater; he subsequently joined the Christian Brothers and died in a monastery in Dublin.

Griffin's *The Collegians* (1829) is perhaps the best representative of the new Catholic fiction: published in the year in which Catholic emancipation passed into law, it blends themes from Irish history with contemporary trial reportage and the new trend for society (or 'silver-fork') fiction. *The Collegians* depicts the densely textured social landscape of rural Ireland: landowners, strong farmers, middlemen, smugglers, lawyers, boatmen and buckeens all jostle for space in a narrative that shows how conflicting codes of conduct create moral chaos and political turmoil. The novel has a murder at its centre – innocent Eily O'Connor falls victim to the lazy morals and attractive indolence of local Protestant landowner Hardress Cregan – that puts a fatal twist on the Protestant/Catholic pairing familiar to readers of the national tale. *The Collegians* does end with a more honourable version of cross-cultural union, but the promise of the union of virtuous Catholic masculinity and chaste Protestant conscience exemplified in the alliance of Kyrle Daly and Anne Chute is far outweighed by the impact of the earlier seduction and murder. This 'coarse'[34] tendency towards melodrama and mayhem was what interested later readers of Griffin's novels such as Dion Boucicault. Like *The Davenels*, a silver-fork novel published anonymously in the same year, *The Collegians* shows how the literary consequences of emancipation may include new demands on narrative form. The frame narratives adopted by both Griffin and the Banims (and later William Carleton) all seek to produce a range of authenticity effects that might be read in terms of the consequences of Catholic authorship for what had been largely a Protestant form.

Non-fictional prose

Irish periodical literature is usually thought to have suffered with the Act of Union and the decline in the indigenous publishing industry. Around twenty new titles were launched between 1800 and 1830, however, published in Cork, Newry and Sligo as well as in Dublin and Belfast. Most were short-lived, but as a group they testify to a self-reflective interest in Irish cultural formations, and especially to the emergence of the concept of Irish literature in English as a category for debate.[35] Neither should Irish involvement in the major British periodicals be underestimated. William Maginn's contributions to *Blackwood's Magazine* (from 1819 through to the end of the 1820s) and later editorship of *Fraser's* (1830–42) make him a key figure: John Banim, Gerald Griffin and Jeremiah Joseph Callanan all turned to him for advice when looking to pursue careers in London. The most significant critical commentator of the Romantic period was the Waterford-born and Trinity College-educated John Wilson Croker (1780–1857). Croker was secretary to the Admiralty from 1809 and spokesperson for a range of Tory cultural causes through to the 1840s. These included the building of the British Museum to house the King's Library, the acquisition of the Elgin marbles and designs for Dublin's Wellington monument. He was one of the founders of *The Quarterly Review* (established in 1809 in Tory opposition to the Whiggish *Edinburgh Review*) and devoted the pages of its first number to a slashing review of Owenson's *Ida of Athens*.

If the novels of Maria Edgeworth and Sydney Owenson are marked by what Thomas Flanagan calls 'the language of explanation', the 1820s and 1830s see a range of other genres assume this responsibility.[36] Increased tourist interest in Ireland in this period can be seen in travellers' accounts by writers such as John Carr, Anne Plumptre, and the Revd James Hall as well as statistical studies like Edward Wakefield's *An Account of Ireland, Statistical and Political* (1812). The range and extent of these writings has led Glenn Hooper and Ina Ferris to make a case for a distinct post-Union travelogue, emerging as a generic response to the awkwardness of Ireland's role in the new United Kingdom.[37] In addition, Irish writers themselves began to contribute to a body of travel writing. Lady Morgan published accounts of her travels in France and Germany; Lady Blessington (1789–1849) capitalised on her success with *Sketches and Fragments* and *The Magic Lantern* to publish *Journal of a Tour through the Netherlands to Paris in 1821* (1822). Blessington moulds her observations to the established form of the 'sketch', already used by Owenson in her *Patriotic Sketches* (1807), in which femininity becomes the politicised sign of an emotional susceptibility to the effects of history and politics on landscape.[38] Blessington's accounts of London focus on civic spaces that allow for a collision of classes, manners and accents.

Although they form no part of the print culture of this period and do not constitute travel literature in any ordinary sense of the word, it is also worth noting here that the 1820s and 1830s saw the composition of Gaelic scholar John O'Donovan's (1806–61) extraordinary field reports detailing Irish place-names and local history. The letters languished in the Ordnance Survey office in Phoenix Park in Dublin until the period of the Literary Revival.[39] For readers keen to know more of the world represented in the texts of Irish Romanticism, they stand as a rich and densely textured resource with which our scholarship has yet to fully engage.

Advanced Romantic theories of education saw the development of a body of literature written especially for children. Edgeworth, who 'helped invent modern children's fiction',[40] wrote rationalist tales based on hers and her father's belief in the value of education in the home. Adelaide O'Keeffe (1776–c.1855) published poems as part of Ann and Jane Taylor's *Original Poems for Infant Minds* (1804), *National Characters Exhibited in Forty Geographical Poems* (1808), as well as biblical stories under the title *Patriarchal Times; or, The Land of Canaan* (1811). O'Keeffe was the daughter of the playwright and actor John O'Keeffe, and the amanuensis for his *Recollections* (1826). Mary Leadbeater and Harriet Beaufort (Edgeworth's step-niece) also published instructional books aimed at children, as did Edward Groves (1775–?), an ardent repealer and author of melodramatic history plays in the 1830s, who wrote adaptations of the Greek legends for children.[41] Some of the same authors – notably Edgeworth and Leadbeater – wrote tales and stories aimed at adult audiences whom they believed were in need of improvement or education. Edgeworth's *Popular Tales* (1804) target a middle-class readership, while Mary Leadbeater's *Cottage Dialogues among the Irish Peasantry* (1811) utilises a simple dialogue form to appeal to Irish peasants and warn them against adopting the mores and manners of 'the quality'. Edgeworth provided explanatory notes for *Cottage Dialogues*, which are indebted to the style (if not the politics) of Hannah More's *Cheap Repository Tracts* (1795–8).

The same moment saw the birth of Irish folklore studies, with the publication of Thomas Crofton Croker's *Researches in the South of Ireland* (1824). Croker borrowed extensively from the antiquarian researches of the Cork poet Jeremiah Joseph Callanan (discussed below). Callanan and Croker corresponded, with the young poet seeking payment for material he had collected in Cork and Kerry. Croker was also involved with the Grimm brothers: in his chapter on 'Fairies and Supernatural Agency', Croker compares 'the fairies of Ireland' to 'the elves of Northern Europe'.[42] *Daniel O'Rourke*, a pantomime in verse by Croker based on oral fairy legend, was performed at the Adelphi Theatre in London during Christmas of 1826.

Drama and the novel

The preceding discussion suggests the extent to which cultural initiative had been seized by the novel in this period. Closely linked with the powerful new English and Scottish periodicals, the Irish novel was involved in commentary on everyday life and on the still fresh facts of recent history. This is not to ignore, however, the co-existence of drama and the novel as modes of address in the imaginations of many of the writers already discussed (Edgeworth, Owenson, Maturin, John Banim and Griffin all wrote plays for performance), as well as the extent to which drama and novels developed in relation to an interrelated set of aesthetic categories and political concerns.

It is worth noting also that two of the great talents of the early period, Edgeworth and Owenson, were, as women, likely to encounter some difficulties in the exposed world of the Irish theatre. Even when a literary success, Owenson was pursued by rumours that she had herself acted in her father's touring company, and never shook off the dubious social reputation that went along with her theatrical connections. Meanwhile, Maria Edgeworth had designs on the London (although not the Dublin) stage: she wrote *The Absentee* (her most admired novel in her own time) as a play script and sent it to Richard Brinsley Sheridan for his consideration. Sheridan wrote back, warning the young author that Irish topics were not welcome in British theatres. There is, however, strong evidence of her continuing interest in drama: *Patronage* (1814) also began life as a play and Edgeworth later scripted two comic dramas, *Love and Law* and *The Rose, Thistle and Shamrock*, as well as the ambitious but unfinished *Whim for Whim*, a comedy of philosophical and political manners published for the first time in 2004 as part of a new edition of Edgeworth's works.[43] None of these plays was performed in public.

It may be that Irish novels absorb a kind of theatricality, comparable to the way in which English poetry of the same period commandeered some of the greatest dramatic impulses of its moment. Mrs Plunkett's novel *The Exile of Erin* ends with the text of a five-act play (*The Favourite*), which revisits the central themes of the novel (sympathy and the 1798 rebellion) but dresses them up as events taking place in the Swedish court, presented in blank verse. Edgeworth regularly incorporates drama inside the folds of her fiction. In *Vivian* (1812), the central characters stage Nicholas Rowe's racy drama *The Fair Penitent*. The characters' involvement in private theatricals precipitates a moral crisis in the world of the novel, a device Austen was to borrow for *Mansfield Park* (1814). Edgeworth's own interest in the theme was probably sparked by the fashion for private theatricals in post-Union Ireland (also reflected in *The O'Briens and the O'Flahertys*), and should also be read alongside Maturin and Owenson's use of theatricality as a trope for the brilliant but brittle texture of Irish political life.

The trope of theatricality may be further understood as the product of a culture in which the legitimating rules of political representation were under challenge. The rebellions of 1798 and 1803 were, as Christopher Morash remarks, to 'have long, lingering afterlives on the Irish stage';[44] more immediately, however, the rebellions, together with the Union debates and mounting calls for Catholic emancipation, contributed to a highly charged cultural climate. If England was (to paraphrase Edmund Burke) 'able to contain theatre within theatres',[45] Ireland in the late eighteenth and early nineteenth century witnessed a series of public political dramas that provoked memories of revolutionary France.

Fiction's physical medium meant that it was perhaps better equipped to handle the complex bi-cultural experience of life under the Union. A novel might be published in London or Edinburgh but still declare itself 'Irish' or 'national'; in the theatre, the physical facts of performance produce different pressures and raise issues of location and identity. Drawing drama into a narrative of Irish Romanticism thus poses challenges. What does 'Irish' mean in relation to drama of the period? Is Irishness best established at the level of content or of style? And what difference do location and institutional history make? The succeeding sections deal with theatre in Ireland and Irish dramatists and actors on the London stage, and further suggest some ways in which to combine these stories in order to create a more cohesive narrative of Irish drama in the period.

Theatre in Ireland

As Christopher Morash has shown, Irish theatre-going audiences in the late eighteenth and early nineteenth century participated in a vibrant theatrical culture in cities such as Dublin, Cork, Belfast and Waterford (although he makes no special case for Romanticism either as a period or as an aesthetic).[46] Performances were always prone to interruptions, however, the result of political unrest and economic uncertainty. Moreover, audiences who were internally divided along the lines of class and religion were, in the case of Ireland, grouped together in a small number of theatres that attempted to cater to all tastes. The volatile nature of theatre business and institutions thus had a distinctly national dimension, and the 1820s in particular were to witness repeated disturbances and riots in Dublin theatres.

A critic considering the repertoire of these theatres, however, will have some difficulties in establishing the lineaments of a national culture. Irish theatres in this period continued to stage a list of largely eighteenth-century plays, in addition to the newly fashionable Gothic melodramas. References to contemporary events, including the passing of the Act of Union, can be found in Alicia Le Fanu's *The Sons of Erin* (1812). First performed at the Lyceum Theatre in London before being taken up in Dublin, the play seeks to counter metropolitan prejudices against the Irish, especially their reputations as fortune-hunters and bad husbands. To the stock characters of stage Irish servant and charming rogue, it adds a 'Lady of science' who is an advocate for the 'rights of rational creatures'.[47] A number of Dublin-produced plays by women have not survived: these include Owenson's comic opera *The First Attempt* (1806), Sarah Isdell's *The Poor Gentlewoman* (1811) and *The Cavern* (1825), as well as Elizabeth Gunning's *The Wife with Two Husbands* (1803; never performed).

Evidence does exist of attempts to stage events or plots from Irish history, including Mary Balfour's *Kathleen O'Neil: a Grand National Melo-drame*, staged in Belfast in 1814. A now lost play by Daniel Mara entitled *Brian Boroimhe (The Victorious)* was performed in Dublin in 1810 and later adapted by Cork-born James Sheridan Knowles (1784–1862), cousin of Richard Brinsley Sheridan. Knowles moved to London with his family in 1793 and later studied medicine at Aberdeen University. Though writing from a young age, he also acted, taught and lectured and was not able to pursue a full-time career as a playwright until the 1840s. *Brian Boroimhe* (1811) and *Virginius* (1820) (first performed in Glasgow, later a success in London) successfully toured Ireland and were to become staples of American theatres. Knowles is a key figure in the development of the 'Irish play' in the nineteenth century and his significance continues to be felt right through to the century's end, especially in America.

More typical for this period though is the oblique Irishness of John Banim's *Damon and Pythias* (1821), a verse tragedy that dramatises the fall of a corrupt senate. Despite its classical credentials and debt to Joseph Addison's *Cato*, the play indexes many recognisably contemporary concerns, in particular in its depiction of a parliament that decides to 'dissolve' itself[48] alongside criticism of the heavy military presence needed to maintain the new dispensation. The senators are persuaded by threats and bribery to hand over their power to a would-be tyrant king. Chiefly consisting of lengthy speeches and containing little dramatic action, the play may further be read as a meditation on the role of rhetorical eloquence in political life. This is a topic with which both Banim and Richard Lalor Sheil (barrister and playwright, said to have assisted in the composition of this play) are stylistically as well as thematically engaged. Sheil's *Evadne or, The Statue* (1819) ends with the eponymous heroine solving all of the play's dilemmas by taking upon a Scheherazade role.

A need to establish the Irishness of the Irish theatre was keenly felt by contemporary commentators, and the period immediately after the Act of Union sees a great flurry of controversy and criticism directed at the stage. This opens with John Wilson Croker's anonymous *Familiar Epistles to Frederick Jones, Esq., on the Present State of the Irish Stage* (1804). Croker's vicious attack on the Dublin theatrical establishment supposedly brought about the death of one Irish actor (just as his later harsh review of *Endymion* in the *Quarterly* was said to have killed John Keats). Responses included Robert Owenson's *Theatrical Tears* (1804), Sydney Owenson's *A Few Reflections, Occasioned by the Perusal of a Work, entitled, 'Familiar Epistles to Frederick J – s Esq. on the Present State of the Irish Stage'* (1804) and Sydney Owenson's comic opera *The First Attempt* (1806). For Morash, this moment revolves around 'the demand for Irish material on Irish stages',[49] a pressure that finds expression in the prologues of such Dublin-produced plays as Richard Lalor Sheil's *Adelaide* (1814), Alicia Le Fanu's *The Sons of Erin* (1812) and Lady Olivia Clarke's *The Irishwoman* (1819).

The remodelling of the Theatre Royal in Hawkins Street, Dublin (opened 1821) resulted in the first major nineteenth-century Irish theatre, and signalled the arrival of the theatre of spectacle in Dublin. Another large theatre, the Adelphi, opened in 1829. Political unrest seems to have sharpened with these new larger theatres. A number of political riots and protests took place in the 1820s, most famously the bottle riot of 1822, in which Orange protestors attacked the new pro-Catholic lord lieutenant, Lord Wellesley, during a performance of Oliver Goldsmith's *She Stoops to Conquer*. Despite what Morash calls the 'unravelling' of 'the old reciprocal arrangement between the castle and the theatre', however, there remains a vital sense of the theatre as a political venue, which lasts at least until the founding of the Abbey. (In the case of the bottle riots of 1822 Chief Lord Justice Charles Kendal Bushe ruled on the difference between a 'noisy' and a 'riotous audience', a judgment that was to be invoked in the aftermath of the *Playboy* riots in 1907.)[50]

Irish drama on the London stage

The greatest Irish theatrical successes of this period were staged in London (to audiences that may of course have been partly Irish) and did not take Ireland or its history as their overt theme or plot. The stage Irish roles discussed in the preceding chapter persist into this period, for instance in Richard Butler's (earl of Glengall) popular and widely performed *The Irish Tutor, or New Lights* (1800), a one-act comedy revolving around mistaken identities that was still being performed at the Theatre Royal in Covent Garden in 1823 and 1828. Similar stage Irish characters (usually servants) appear in comedies by Eaton S. Barrett (*My Wife! What Wife?* (1815)), Joseph Sterling Coyne and the prolific James Kenney (witness the character of Mr Teddy Fitzgrallaghan Macmullinoch O'Cloghorty in his 'petit opera' of 1804, *Matrimony*).

Kenney, who wrote farces, burlettas and melodramas, was associated with the illegitimate theatre. A division between legitimate and illegitimate theatre lasted until the effective abolition of theatrical monopoly in 1833 (officially 1843), and forms a vital context for our understanding of plays by Irish writers written for London audiences. Broadly, illegitimate drama refers to plays other than tragedies and comedies that were performed in unpatented theatres (venues other than Covent Garden or Drury Lane), which proliferated across the burgeoning metropolis. Dublin also had a patented theatre, the Theatre Royal, as did Edinburgh, Bath and Liverpool. Theatrical licence in Westminster and for the provincial patents was the responsibility of the Lord Chamberlain but – in one of the anomalies of power in which post-Union Ireland abounds – the licensing of Irish-based drama remained under the control of the lord lieutenant in Dublin.

This was a period of dispute over categories and styles as much as theatrical venues. Illegitimate genres were reliant on tableaux and spectacle and went under names like melodrama, burletta, burlesque, extravaganza, pantomime, hippodrama and aquadrama (examples include *The Gheber; or the Fire-Worshippers*, based on Thomas Moore's *Lallah Rookh*).[51] Within the Romantic period, such techniques began to permeate the legitimate stage, bringing with them an emphasis on the art of the gesture and a new concern with physiology. This new emphasis on actors' bodies (rather than niceties of facial expression) was also related to the increased size of London theatres (Drury Lane and Covent Garden had both been expanded considerably in the 1790s).

A parliamentary Select Committee on Dramatic Literature met in 1832, bringing issues of dramatic style and cultural taste into the political mainstream; their findings were issued in new legislation (the Dramatic Copyright Act of 1832 and the Theatres Act of 1843). It is difficult to determine exactly the role played by Ireland in what was essentially a dispute about cultural democracy in late Georgian Britain, but it is hard to ignore the high visibility of Irish writers, plays and actors in these debates. The playwright Richard Lalor Sheil served on the parliamentary inquiry into the condition of the drama, chaired by Edward Bulwer Lytton, as did George Lamb, MP for Dungarvan, County Waterford from 1822. A Whig with O'Connellite sympathies and an amateur interest in drama, Lamb served on the Drury Lane committee and wrote the epilogue to Maturin's *Bertram*. Lamb's sister-in-law was Lady Caroline Lamb, discussed above, and his half-brother, Lord Melbourne, was chief secretary for Ireland from 1827 to 1828. The testimony gathered by the inquiry pays attention to Ireland and witnesses included professionals like Eugene McCarthy, former lessee of several Irish theatres, who cheerfully reported on the 'completely illegal' performances that took place in Fishamble Street, Dublin, and advocated 'the free trade principle' for drama; without regulation, he argued, 'everything of that kind would find its level'.[52]

The most significant Irish contribution to the legitimate drama came from Richard Lalor Sheil (1791–1851). It is possible to connect Sheil to a wider European impulse to reinvent the resources of tragic drama for a range of national cultures: writers from Germany, Italy, France, Poland and of course England all sought, as Jeffrey N. Cox puts it, 'to redefine the tragic and renew the stage'.[53] Following an early success in Dublin with *Adelaide; or The Emigrants* (1814), Sheil moved to London to pursue a career that involved politics and the law as well as the stage. His plays are built around powerful dramatic monologues that give expression to sexual jealousy, violence, black hatred, revenge, madness, intrigue and conspiracy. The surviving stage directions given (especially in the plays that followed *Adelaide*) suggest the extent to which Sheil made full use of the resources of the London stage: wing-and-backdrop scenery gives depth and colour, characters move to the front of the stage to deliver powerful speeches and there is a strong overall sense of pictorial symmetry, as when twin pillars are placed at either side of the stage to frame the closing scenes of *Bellarima*. Like Maturin, Sheil was criticised for an excessive dramaturgical vigour and an undue violence of effect.

Sheil's work returns repeatedly to the subject of religious difference, thrown into the sharpest possible relief by plays that dramatise historic conflicts between Islam and Christianity in Moorish Spain (*The Apostate* (1817)) and North Africa (*Bellamira* (1818)). No distinct confessional line emerges, however. *Bellamira* does make lavish use of orientalist and anti-Muslim stereotypes, while *The Apostate*'s depiction of the Spanish Inquisition is quite as Gothic as anything Maturin might produce. In general, the plays do not seek to defend or celebrate any one oppressed group but are rather concerned to show that the experience of oppression will inevitably generate tragic consequences and sour the futures of those who wield power as well as those enslaved by it. For the barrister and defender of Catholic rights to produce these dramas of religious oppression must have raised eyebrows. In the preface to *The Apostate*, a play that voices the anguish of a deposed Moorish king who must convert to Christianity or lose the hand of his noble Spanish love, Sheil (writing in the third person) insists that his depiction of the Inquisition should not be read as mischievous: 'He mentions this to relieve himself from the imputation of having sought the illegitimate assistance of political allusion; and he hopes that, upon reflecting on the nature of the subject, the reader will consider the introduction of the Inquisition as unavoidable.'[54] With the founding of the Catholic Association in 1829, Sheil turned his attention increasingly to political journalism and popular agitation, eventually winning a seat in the reformed post-1829 parliament.

Sheil's (and Maturin's) plays were, as Jeffrey N. Cox has noted, performed in London at the very moment when it seemed as if 'the romantics might have captured the stage'.[55] Sheil himself refers to 'the bias of the Public towards the tragic drama in this country' and, up to as late as Gerald Griffin's verse tragedy *Gisippus* (not staged until 1842), Irish playwrights made a conscious bid to create a sensation within the genre of tragic drama. But, perhaps more significantly, Sheil and Maturin were also practitioners of a Romantic dramaturgy organised around spectacle and tableaux. Both influenced and were influenced by the ways in which illegitimate genres were infiltrating the respectable stage. These are plays that emerge out of classical tragedy but have their destination in nineteenth-century melodrama, the greatest exponent of which was the Irish playwright Dion Boucicault.

First staged in Drury Lane in 1816, Maturin's *Bertram* was the controversial 'hit of the season'.[56] Seeking fresh material as part of a concerted effort to reclaim the stage, the Drury Lane committee had written to Walter Scott soliciting a new drama. He sent them *Bertram*, a play for which Maturin had sought his assistance as early as 1814. The committee, which included Byron, responded enthusiastically to the play's poetic language and sensational plot, and committee member George Lamb set about making the play stageable. This involved a series of strategic cuts and replacements, including the near-elimination of a character known in the original version as the Dark Knight. Neither Scott nor Lamb would allow Maturin to bring this satanic figure before an audience, and he survives in the play only as an ominous off-stage threat. Much else in Maturin's play was judged by Lamb to be 'too much for an Audience',[57] and even the revised version did not fail to shock.

Bertram takes from illegitimate forms such as melodrama a sense of evil as ever present and beyond reform.[58] Its hero, the leader of a robber band who has led a failed rebellion against the husband of his lover, is a characteristically Romantic tragic figure, comparable to Joanna Baillie's De Montfort and Byron's Manfred. Undoubtedly representative of a rootless spirit of Romantic agony, Bertram is also shadowed by melancholy reflections of past commitment to his country and 'the sheeted relics of mine ancestry'. His robber band are rather vaguely realised, but these 'desperate followers' help him to launch his attack from a 'wild and wooded shore'[59] that lies across a narrow gulf from Sicily, site of Aldobrand's authority. These references, along with the strongly religious terms in which his transgressions are described (false idol, perjurer, apostate and fallen archangel), help give the play some of the flavour of Irish politics, and make the passionate Bertram legible in terms of such glamorous Irish insurgents as Lord Edward Fitzgerald and Robert Emmet, as well as evoking the military prowess and charismatic public persona of the duke of Wellington.

With *Bertram*, Maturin brought melodrama and Gothic spectacle – or, in Jane Moody's words, 'the moral cacophony of illegitimate culture' – onto the stage of Drury Lane.[60] Among the play's fiercest critics was Samuel Taylor Coleridge, who launched a blistering attack on *Bertram* in a review that was later tacked onto the final section of his *Biographia Literaria*. In striving after effects that are all too literally realised on stage, Maturin endorsed a literary style that Coleridge elsewhere described as 'the material Sublime'.[61] Defined by him in opposition to the mental theatre of the great Romantic poetry where imagination can roam free, Coleridge employs this term to identify literary texts that fail to shed the cumbersome mechanics of affectivity. Irish poetry of this period similarly retains a rawly material focus that is the subject of the next section.

Poetry

Readers in search of a cohesive account of the poetry of Irish Romanticism must negotiate a route between seemingly diverse texts, contexts and reputations. The 'remarkable exfoliation of verse forms'[62] associated with British Romantic poetry extends itself in the case of Ireland into a further splitting of literary and political layers, brought about by asymmetries of languages and cultures. This section presents a constellation of Irish poets working in this period and aims to reconceptualise their relationship both to Irish literary history and to each other.

The early years of the nineteenth century saw the publication of collected editions of the work of some of the radical poets of the 1790s: these include the Ulster weaver poets James Orr and Hugh Porter, influenced by the 'tutelary' figure of Robert Burns;[63] the fugitive verse of Thomas Dermody; and the political poetry of former United Irishman William Drennan (these late eighteenth-century writers are discussed in more detail in chapter 7). Echoes of the 1798 rebellion sound throughout the English-language poetry of Irish Romanticism (although its resonance in Gaelic poetry is still in dispute); its literary legacy passes through Moore and continues through to the writings of Thomas Davis and James Clarence Mangan. United Irishmen like Belfast Dissenter and physician William Drennan, as well as the younger radical Robert Emmet, wrote directly political poems. Drennan retired from medical practice and returned from Dublin to Belfast in 1807, and in 1814 helped establish the Belfast Academical Institution; his *Fugitive Pieces in Verse and Prose* were published in Belfast in 1815.

The Glasgow-born poet Thomas Campbell (1777–1844) had met some of the exiled United Irishmen in Hamburg in 1800 (and himself incurred government suspicion because of his association with them). He subsequently wrote a poem that first frames and then voices the feelings of an 'Exile of Erin'. Sometimes criticised for easy nostalgia and moody fatalism, the poem does sound a defiant, even martial note. Three of the stanzas, including the first and last, end by invoking the United Irish motto, 'Erin go Bragh!', or, 'Ireland for ever!' (used to similar effect in Sydney Owenson's 'The Irish Harp'). The final lines of the poem move from the 'sad recollection' of a 'bruised and cold' heart through to a sound that defies silence: 'And thy harp-striking bards sing aloud with devotion / Erin mavournin – Erin go bragh!'[64] Edward Bunting, arranger of Irish tunes, used

Campbell's poem as a last-minute replacement for the potentially incendiary songs collected by Patrick Lynch, a Belfast acquaintance of Bunting's who had been arrested on suspicion of sedition.[65] Other translators employed by Bunting for the second (1809) edition of his *Ancient Music* included Mary Balfour (1780–1819) and William Drennan.[66] The post-rebellion context did not favour directly political verse, although notable exceptions include satires by Moore and John Banim,[67] as well as Balfour's *Hope: A Poetical Essay; with various other Poems* (1810), which features recognisably political emblems and events. Balfour's collection features a number of poems adapted to traditional airs collected by Bunting ('Ellen a Roon', 'I am Asleep and Don't Waken Me', 'My Lodging is on the Cold Ground'), although no musical notation is given. Eliza Ryan's 'In the Time of the Rebellion in Ireland', 'At the Time of the Irish Rebellion' and 'On Saunder's Grove at the Time of the Rebellion' appeared in her collected *Poems on Several Occasions* (1816); here, the 1798 rebellion takes its place alongside an array of occasional verse concerning marriage, fashion, morality and popular science.

Even more difficult to establish is the part played by 1798 (and radical politics in general) in the poetry of Thomas Moore. Son of a middle-class Catholic grocer and born in Dublin, Moore had been an undergraduate at Trinity College when the rising took place. He moved thereafter to distance himself from radicals like his friend Emmet. The influence of these early connections remained, however, in particular Moore's exposure to Edward Bunting's *General Collection of the Ancient Music of Ireland* (1796). Moore's orientalist poem *Lallah Rookh* (1817) presents characteristic difficulties of interpretation: details borrowed from the failed Irish rebellions of 1798 and 1803 are presented against a backdrop of sexual tyranny and eastern luxury, in language calculated to heighten the poem's exotic impact. Like Owenson's *The Missionary, Lallah Rookh* is at once deeply involved with Irish debates and fully immersed in the erotics of the British imperialist imagination. The difficulty of establishing any single reading of the poem's politics is only heightened by its popular success: written at the height of Moore's career in London, the poem garnered him an astonishing £3,000 from Longmans and went into numerous editions.

It is with Moore's *Irish Melodies* that questions of popular appeal, literary style and political meaning become most urgent. Remembered chiefly for their aestheticising of despair, the *Melodies*, published between 1808 and 1834, called up memories of Ireland's past only to banish all hope of future glory. Yet, as Matthew Campbell has argued, the *Melodies*' characteristic 'air of defeat' and 'tone of enervation' may also be read as generating symbols and sound effects that resonate through English-language poetry up to Yeats. Campbell's reading of the *Melodies* establishes that, although often associated with a kind of bland poise, movement does occur in the poems, principally experienced at the level of sound and rhythm.[68]

Moore's *Irish Melodies* recast the Romantic myth of inexpressibility to political ends. This is most powerfully the case in his poem 'Oh! Breathe not his name', which (silently, namelessly) invokes the memory of recently executed rebel leader Robert Emmet. Emmet's Dublin-centred rebellion of 1803 had been limited, short-lived and disastrous, but Moore's poem suggests a more profound meaning for Emmet's legacy even as it enjoins silence on its inheritors. The dates, names and events associated with the rebellions of 1798 and 1803 are often, for the *Melodies*, where readers can trace specific details of Irish history. 'Oh! Breathe not his name' creates a network of watery images (dew, tears, dampness) to create a kind of swell that surges through the poem: 'And the tear that we shed, though in secret it rolls, / Shall long keep his memory green in our souls.' The dynamic present in the Emmet poem, in which the vital living past washes over and begins to seep through the frozen surface of the present, is most vividly present in the first number of Moore's *Melodies* but occurs across the series, combining with repeated sonic patterns and image sequences to give the poems their distinctive atmosphere.

New on the ear as such sounds were, their wide popularity and easy recognition factor made the *Melodies* easy prey for parody. Less easily assimilable, both in their own day and now, are Moore's verse satires. Collected, arranged and edited for the first time in 2003, it is now possible to see the development of Moore's stinging wit across a range of satiric forms and styles. Composed throughout his writing life, the satires show evidence of a sustained engagement with the day-to-day politics and scandal of Regency England and Ireland. An abrasive Juvenalian satire written in heroic couplets, *Corruption and Intolerance* (1808) attacks both the Glorious Revolution itself and competing Tory and Whig claims to its legacy. The passing of the Act of Union is a specific target, and Mary Helen Thuente suggests that the poems resonate with sounds and images remembered from United Irish popular songs.[69] The greatest number of Moore's satires, however, are written in loose anapaests and correspond to gentler Horatian models: these include several squibs attacking the Prince Regent as well as his *Intercepted Letters: Or, The Two Penny Post-Bag* (1813), a witty and inventive attack on the Regent's social circle. Moore's ability to infuse verse satire with a strong narrative thread is best seen in his *Fudge Family in Paris* (1818). Organised around a linked set of characters (an Irish family), each of whom recounts her/his travels in her/his own characteristic metre, *The Fudge Family* is a *tour de force* of 'combative liberal politics'[70] and mocks Irish patriotism alongside French food and fashions, political place-seeking and fantasies of romantic love. Moore's decision to pillory the 'groups of ridiculous English people who were at that time swarming in all directions through Paris'[71] in the shape of Phil, Biddy and Bob Fudge (as well as their firebrand tutor, Phelim Connor) is, however, a curious one, and helps us to think about the persistence of Irish themes in even the most English of his writing.

Moore had a bitter political and literary enemy in the Cork-born writer William Maginn (1794–1842): hostile to Moore's luxuriant verse and to Lady Morgan's Romantic nationalism (always connected with the Whiggism of both), Maginn was a vocal spokesperson for the crusty circle that gathered around *Blackwood's Edinburgh Magazine*. The talented son of a Cork schoolmaster, Maginn began writing for *Blackwood's* from Cork (a place, remarks Mrs Oliphant, William Blackwood's daughter-in-law and memoirist, 'more associated with pigs and salted provisions than with literature'[72]), and finally moved to Edinburgh in 1823. Oliphant wonders at how he 'took up the tone, and even the local colour' of Edinburgh before even visiting there; one answer may be found in the connection (suggested by Terry Eagleton) between Maginn's beleaguered Cork Protestantism and the reactionary Toryism of the 1820s.[73] A further reason may lie in the magazine's embrace of 'the nationalist discourses of the post-Enlightenment', including antiquarianism and vernacular poetry.[74] Maginn remained deeply sceptical of the forms of literary Irishness practised by Moore and Morgan, but it is important to note that the *Blackwood's* context offered an alternative form of cultural nationalism – one better fitted for his own politics – rather than a rejection of its tenets. In a letter Maginn tries to explain to William Blackwood the particular antipathy to Catholic emancipation experienced in his native Cork: 'If you were in Ireland you would not wonder at our hostility. I never knew a traveller from the sister island, even were he bitten by the "Edinburgh Review" . . . who did not leave Ireland with the same feeling.'[75] Maginn's criticisms of Moore similarly upbraid him for a lack of local knowledge, accusing him of only paying lip-service to 'our localities' and refuting his 'absurd' and 'unIrish' *Melodies* in ringing Munster metaphors.[76] This 'crystallised Paddy' (in Mrs Oliphant's terms) quickly became the star of the *Blackwood's* scene, favourite spokesperson for its Tory politics and dislike of literary innovation.[77]

Maginn's own writings, however, roamed across a precocious range of genres and voices. 'Some Account of the Life and Writings of Ensign and Adjutant Odoherty, late of the 99th regiment' was first published in the *Blackwood's Edinburgh Magazine* of February 1818 and became a regular feature of the journal. In these admiring memoirs of a sometime poet, militiaman and soldier, Odoherty presents himself in a drunken overblown style that consistently undercuts his many claims to virtue and excellence. Maginn offers such specimens of Odoherty's verse as 'Odoherty's Garland in honour of Mrs Cook, *The Great*' and 'The Eve of St Jerry',[78] in which he stretches the resources of vocabulary and grammar to ludicrous effect. Maginn's poetry brilliantly mocks Romantic literary values (the fragment, the cult of the imagination, the elevation of subjective genius). The high disdain for literary originality, the combination of prose and poetry, the use of Arabic languages and typography, and the inebriated and eccentric range of voices deployed all prefigure the work of James Clarence Mangan. Maginn, however, left nothing as serious or politically committed as Mangan's lyrics or ringing refrains, and his cranky Cork genius soon faded from the vision of a literary establishment that became more sternly nationalist in outlook as the century progressed.

Maginn promoted the work of a fellow Cork poet, Jeremiah Joseph Callanan (1795–1829). He published Callanan's translations in the pages of *Blackwood's*, perhaps in the hope of attaching his talents to the magazine's brand of Counter Enlightenment cultural nationalism. A Catholic, Callanan had attended Maynooth Seminary in County Kildare but left after two years. He went from there to Trinity College, Dublin and then on to a short period of military service. In Cork, Callanan worked as an assistant in Maginn's father's school, only finally to die in Portugal, having travelled there as a tutor to a merchant family.

Callanan spent a period travelling around Cork and Kerry, collecting stories and songs. Remembered now chiefly for his translations of the poems he encountered, it is worth noting Callanan's quasi-anthropological relationship to his material and the extent to which, as Robert Welch reminds us, he turned his eyes to London even as he roamed the roads of west Cork.[79] Callanan's significant formal achievements are discussed by Matthew Campbell in chapter 12, but it is worth noting here how the poetry speaks from a place located somewhere between English and Gaelic cultures: the overall result is an aesthetic that moves between intimacy and distance, and calls to mind the 'migratory impulse' of the national tale.[80]

Callanan may also have written a lost manuscript novel, based on a legendary tale concerning Lough Ine (near Skibereen); he also published in the Cork-based *Bolster's Magazine* under the editorship of the antiquarian John Windele. His original poetry inhabits a characteristic rhythm: a soaring moment of hope builds up only to fall away ('But oh!') in an atmosphere of delicious agony. The influence of Moore is strong, but the poems are also reminiscent of Mary Tighe (1772–1810) (discussed below). Robert Welch has criticised Moore for producing only 'generalised moods' and being unable to delineate 'states of feeling' in his verse; in this respect, Callanan and Tighe succeed where Moore fails.[81] Their writing shares a strong desire to co-ordinate private and public meanings in the poet's search for authentic subjectivity. Like Tighe, Callanan's strongest work aestheticised solitude, as in his 'Recluse of Inchidoney', which echoes Byron's 'Childe Harold'. Like Tighe also, he is ambitious with form and metre: both court a sense of poetic purpose, only then to banish it (and with it their own selves) elaborately in verse.

Where the two poets differ is perhaps just as significant: a poet of place also, seeking to give expression to the dilemmas of a self only insecurely located in a landscape, Tighe appears to share none of Callanan's interest in the culture, peoples or languages of the Ireland she evokes. This difference has meant that she is largely omitted from surveys of nineteenth-century Irish poetry. Tighe's work is, however, coming back into view in studies of women's Romantic writing and may yet benefit from new trends in Irish feminist criticism. Like John Keats, who admired her verse passionately,[82] Tighe died young and of consumption. Born in County Wicklow to a liberal gentry family, she lived a short and unhappy life. Like the heroine of her manuscript novel *Serena*, Tighe married a cousin to cement family connections. Her miserable life was in part a consequence of the Act of Union: her husband (Henry Tighe) was one of those Irish men for whom the Act had immediate professional consequences. The indulged younger son of a proudly anti-Union family, he lost his parliamentary seat with the Union and moved with his new wife to London to study law. The move was experienced as dislocation for the poet. Charles Kendal Bushe, who owned a copy of Tighe's most famous poem, *Psyche*,[83] tried to describe the effect the Union had on his own mental health: 'Ever since', he wrote to his wife, 'my mind has been agitated in the way I have described to you. I am seven years older and my nerves twenty years older than at the period of the Union.'[84] In Mary Tighe's poetry of inner turmoil we may read an oblique commentary on the psychic as well as professional and political consequences of Union. The prevalence of poems and popular songs about maniac figures in this period should also be noted: as well as the ballad 'Mary le More' (sometimes known as 'The Maniac', or 'The Irish Maniac' and described by Siobhán Kilfeather as a 'debased *aisling*'), James Orr, James Stuart and Amelia Bristow all wrote poems that imagine fugitive (usually female) figures driven mad by the experience of political turmoil.[85]

In the few years before her final illness, Tighe moved among the burgeoning Irish social scene in post-Union London. Henry Luttrell (1768–1851) belonged to the same circles, and wrote poetry satirising social norms and fashionable life. Tighe knew Owenson and Moore (the leaders, with Lady Blessington, of the literary absentees), as well as Arthur Wellesley (later duke of Wellington), Lady Charlemont, Lady Argyll and William Parnell. Tighe's Methodist mother worried about her son-in-law's fondness for 'amusement' and 'water-drinking places',[86] but was no more approving of her daughter's literary ambitions. That Tighe's own religious convictions troubled her literary ones is borne out by a hint from her brother-in-law and literary executor, William Tighe,[87] and helps explain the distrust of her own medium that permeates the poetry:

> Vain dreams, and fictions of distress and love,
> I idly feigned, but, while I fondly strove
> To paint with every grace the tale of woe,
> Ah fool! my tears unbid began to flow.[88]

Worrying over the status of the 'real sorrow' produced by fictitious arts, Tighe prays to be allowed repose 'in the arms of truth'.[89]

Psyche was first published in 1805, in a limited edition of only fifty copies. A long narrative poem in Spenserian stanzas, it tells the story of Cupid's forbidden love for Psyche, stolen from her parents' home and confined in the Palace of Love. Tighe adopts what Marlon B. Ross calls a 'muted, arch-conventional style'[90] that nonetheless draws attention to its considerable formal achievements. These include skilled versification and a frank eroticism unusual in women's writing of the period. Keats came to think of Tighe's verse as all too agonisingly transparent or understandable. Her refusal of the mists of allegory and her decision to 'let my meaning be perfectly obvious' is better understood in relation to the thrust towards public meaning found in her male Irish contemporaries; instead Tighe privileges the 'raw nerves and emotional excess'[91] associated with the Romantic revival of the sonnet from the 1790s. The titles of her poems characteristically offer details of time and place but privatise and interiorise the moment of reflection. The majority of her sonnets join subjective experience to natural landscape but fail to achieve a restoration of completeness. 'Lines Written at Scarborough, August, 1799' closes with a characteristic note of unrelieved bleakness: 'I, like the worn sand, exposed remain / To each new storm which frets the angry main'.

Tighe died in 1810, and a year later her brother-in-law William Tighe republished *Psyche* with Longmans. The profits went to a charity residence for 'unprotected Female Servants' founded by her Methodist mother. The Welsh-born poet Felicia Hemans, living in Dublin in the 1830s, composed her 'Grave of a Poetess' on seeing Tighe's grave at Inistioge, County Kilkenny, and thus set in motion a vital chain of connection for female poets of the nineteenth century: Laetitia Elizabeth Landon and Elizabeth Barrett Browning continue the theme of graveside meditations on the life and writings of gifted women. Tighe was thus claimed in the Victorian period for an embryonic tradition of women's poetry, only to be forgotten once more when the fashion for lyrical 'poetesses' passed.

Like Tighe, Mary Shackleton Leadbeater (1758–1826) republished in a commercial edition of 1808 poems that she had written for private circulation. Leadbeater was born into the Quaker community of Ballitore in County Kildare. Her father ran the local school, founded by her grandfather who had counted Edmund Burke among his pupils. She married William Leadbeater in 1791 and throughout her life kept a daily record of the village world she inhabited. The journals were edited and published with a memoir of her family as *The Annals of Ballitore* in 1862. They vividly depict a small town shadowed by events such as the 1798 rebellion and the passing of the Act of Union; the journal records the particular difficulties of maintaining Quaker values in the face of the rebellion and its violent repression.[92] The consequences of rebellion for civil society are expressed in a range of poems written in the immediate context of rebellion, all marked by outrage at the military and especially the yeomanry: 'Yet listen to mercy; – the guilty are fled: / Oh let not the guiltless fall victims to rage!'[93] A similar anxiety about violence and its consequences informs her translation of Maffeo Vegio's continuation of Virgil's *Aeneid*, also published as part of her *Poems*.

Leadbeater's evocation of her locality is vivid and detailed, but the poems do not yield the kind of rich and intimate engagement with place that is usually associated with Romantic aesthetics. It is, however, possible to trace in Irish literature across the long eighteenth century the halting emergence of a loco-descriptive tradition that flows from the grudging 'topophobia'[94] of Jonathan Swift and gives rise to a steady trickle of imaginative writing about place in the period of Romanticism. Poems by Mary Tighe, William Tighe, Patrick O'Kelly, James Orr and Ulster writer James Stuart (1764–1840) all testify to an emergent aesthetics of place in Irish writing of this period. William Tighe's 'Lines Addressed to the River at Rosanna, in the County of Wicklow', a poem finely attuned to the way in which place forms the ground of subjectivity, represents one (slender) strand of this loco-descriptive tradition in Irish writing of this period. Echoing Mary Tighe's 'Written at Rosanna, November 18, 1799' and written in a visionary present tense, the poem pursues a line of memory along a familiar local river, transporting the poet back to his childhood and evoking thoughts of death and oblivion. Redemption eludes his 'soul depress'd' and the poem ends by evoking a precarious present existence poised at the threshold of darkness.[95]

Patrick O'Kelly's (1754–c.1835) poem about Killarney, County Kerry, represents the dominant thread in Irish topographical poetry, being chiefly concerned with place in relation to a national rather than a personal past (he describes his own travels as 'ethicographical' rather than topographical).[96] O'Kelly addresses the famous beauty spot with a conscious awareness both of its eighteenth-century reputation as tourist attraction and of the precedents set by the landscape poetry of William Cowper and James Thomson.[97] Written in rhyming couplets, his epic poem about Killarney tries to comprehend not only the place itself but the layers of history and myth that lie under its surface. The poem ends with an acknowledgement of the difficulty of such comprehensiveness, as well as a reminder of O'Kelly's claim to be considered the last of the bards: 'Sweet scenes adieu! – oh! takes your Bard's farewell, / A Bard who wishes all your scenes to tell.'[98]

A similar refusal of the 'pleasing evocative associations' of place in favour of 'an historical moral imagination' is found in Drennan's long poem 'Glendalloch'.[99] The poem creates a kind of Celtic mist of magical enchantment, borne along by incantatory rhyming couplets with few stanza breaks. The valley described in the poem serves as a metonymy for Ireland itself, surrounded by awe-inspiring dense darkness on all sides. A roll-call of history generates sublime sensations that darken and draw closer as the poem nears the present moment. Bearing the date 1802 at its head, the poem is accompanied by a stern note that explicitly attaches the significance of the ancient round tower at Glendalough, County Wicklow to the period of Union: 'Amidst a silent and melancholy waste, it still raises its head above the surrounding fragments, as if moralizing on the ruins of our country, and the wreck of legislative independence.'[100]

Conclusion

Silent, melancholy, ruin, fragments, wreck: Drennan's depiction of the ancient monument is fluent in the 'decline-speak' we now associate with Irish Romanticism. Such language derives from the early political experiences of the period (post-1798 devastation, the broken promises and forced measure of the Union, Emmet's failed rebellion, famine and agrarian disturbances), yet survives as a literary and cultural resource into more prosperous and promising times. Daniel O'Connell, who admired Owenson, Moore, Griffin and the Banims, began the exploitation of 'Romantic Ireland': his Catholic Association and later the repeal movement drew on images made familiar by the writings discussed in this chapter (round towers, harps, picturesque peasants). In the process O'Connell earned the suspicion and dislike of many of the early writers discussed here: Edgeworth, Owenson and Moore all expressed doubts as to his politics and methods, and resented his success.

This chapter thus ends on a note of contest, made intense by the broadening of the literary as well as the political franchise. By 1830, a tumult of Irish voices struggle to make themselves heard within print culture. Literary conflicts assumed a distinctly confessional dimension. 'I confess I should have see[n] the old Lady of Babylon's mouth stopd with pleasure', wrote Walter Scott in his journal in 1829, 'but now you have taken the plaister off her mouth and given her free respiration I cannot see the sense of keeping up the irritation about their right to sit in parliament.'[101] Scott's sense of a vocal if gasping Catholic body finds an echo in Owenson's view, also expressed in 1829, that '[a]mong the multitudinous effects of catholic emancipation, I do not hesitate to predict a change in the character of Irish authorship'.[102] At the same moment, however, the choice of cultural script can be seen to become narrowed and constricted. The complexities of Irish Romanticism, with its busy traffic back and forth between modes of historical feeling, were thus honed down, sharpened and split across a more specialised range of voices and genres.

Notes

1. Mary Leadbeater, 'The Summer Morning's Destruction', *Poems by Mary Leadbeater* (Dublin, 1808), p. 287.

2. See M. F. Pollard, *Dublin's Trade in Books, 1550–1800* (Oxford and New York: Clarendon Press and Oxford University Press, 1989).

3. Stuart Curran, *Poetic Form and British Romanticism* (New York: Oxford University Press, 1986), p. 209.

4. Tom Dunne, 'Haunted by History: Irish Romantic Writing 1800–1850', in Roy Porter and Miklaus Teich, eds. *Romanticism in National Context* (Cambridge: Cambridge University Press, 1988), pp. 68–90, p. 68.

5. Liam McIlvanney, *Burns the Radical: Poetry and Politics in Late Eighteenth-Century Scotland* (East Linton: Tuckwell Press, 2002), p. 221.

6. [Thomas Moore], *Memoirs of Captain Rock, the Celebrated Irish Chieftain, with Some Account of his Ancestors, written by himself* (London, 1824), p. 363.

7. William Parnell, *Inquiry into the Causes of Popular Discontents in Ireland*, 2nd edn (London and Dublin, 1805), p. 72.

8. William Cusack Smith, *Recent Scenes and Occurrences in Ireland* (London, 1823), p. 9.

9. Lady Olivia Clarke, *The Irishwoman* (Dublin, 1819).

10. W. J. McCormack, 'The Tedium of History: An Approach to Maria Edgeworth's *Patronage* (1814)', in Ciarán Brady, ed. *Ideology and the Historians* (Dublin: Lilliput Press, 1991), pp. 77–98, p. 91.

11. Dunne, 'Haunted by History', p. 70. See also Luke Gibbons, *Transformations in Irish Culture* (Cork: Cork University Press, 1996).

12. Seamus Deane, *Strange Country: Modernity and Nationhood in Irish Writing since 1790* (Oxford: Clarendon Press, 1997), p. 30.

13. Peter Garside, 'The English Novel in the Romantic Era', in Peter Garside and Rainer Schöwerling, eds. *The English Novel 1770–1829: A Bibliographical Survey of Prose Fiction Published in the British Isles, Vol. II: 1800–1829* (Oxford: Oxford University Press, 2000), p. 61.

14. Ina Ferris, *The Romantic National Tale and the Question of Ireland* (Cambridge: Cambridge University Press, 2002), p. 76.

15. Ibid., p. 75.

16. See Garside, 'The English Novel in the Romantic Era', pp. 63, 75; Ina Ferris, *The Achievement of Literary Authority: Gender, History and the Waverley Novels* (Ithaca and London: Cornell University Press, 1991).

17. Garside, 'The English Novel in the Romantic Era', p. 75.

18. Ibid., p. 63.

19. Ferris, *The Achievement of Literary Authority*, p. 1.

20. Garside, 'The English Novel in the Romantic Era', p. 62.

21. See Siobhán Kilfeather, 'Terrific Register: The Gothicization of Atrocity in Irish Romantic Writing', *boundary 2* 31, 1 (2004), pp. 49–71.

22. Ferris, *The Romantic National Tale*, p. 133.

23. Quoted in Peter Garside, Jacqueline Belanger and Sharon Ragaz, *British Fiction, 1800–1829*, http://www.british-fiction.ac.uk. Accessed 10 May 2004.

24. Full details of the correspondence can be found at Garside et al., *British Fiction, 1800–1829*.

25. Ronan Kelly, 'Thomas Moore and Irish Historiography', in Karen Vandevelde, ed. *New Voices in Irish Criticism* (Dublin: Four Courts Press, 2002), pp. 70–5.

26. Ferris, *The Romantic National Tale*, pp. 130–1.

27. Gerald Griffin, *Tales of the Munster Festivals*, 3 vols. (London, 1827), I, pp. xviii, xvii.

28. Katie Trumpener, *Bardic Nationalism: The Romantic Novel and the British Empire* (Princeton: Princeton University Press, 1997).

29. See John D. Beatty, ed. *Protestant Women's Narratives of the Irish Rebellion of 1798* (Dublin: Four Courts Press, 2001).

30. Trumpener, *Bardic Nationalism*, p. 142.

31. Review of William Parnell, *Maurice and Berghetta, Quarterly Review* (1819); quoted in R. F. Foster, *Charles Stewart Parnell: The Man and his Family* (Hassocks: Harvester Press, 1976), p. 27. William Parnell was the grandfather of Charles Stewart Parnell.

32. Review of William Parnell, *Maurice and Berghetta, Eclectic Review* 12 (1819), pp. 245–67, p. 247.

33. Gerald Griffin to his parents, London, 1 February 1826; quoted in John Cronin, *Gerald Griffin: A Critical Biography* (Cambridge: Cambridge University Press, 1978), p. 21.

34. The term is Lady Morgan's; see her *Memoirs: Autobiographies, Diaries and Correspondence*, ed. W. H. Dixon, 2 vols. (London, 1862), II, p. 288.

35. Thanks to Jacqueline Belanger for this information.

36. Thomas Flanagan, *The Irish Novelists, 1800–1859* (New York: Columbia University Press, 1956), p. 36.

37. Glenn Hooper, '"Stranger in Ireland": The Problematics of the Post-Union Travelogue', *Mosaic* 28 (1995), pp. 25–47; Ina Ferris, 'Civic Travels: The Irish Tour and the New United Kingdom', in *The Romantic National Tale*, pp. 18–45. For a representative selection of texts, see Glenn Hooper, ed. *The Tourist's Gaze: Travellers to Ireland, 1800–2000* (Cork: Cork University Press, 2001).

38. See Richard C. Sha, *The Visual and Verbal Sketch in British Romanticism* (Philadelphia: University of Pennsylvania Press, 1998).

39. See J. H. Andrews, *A Paper Landscape: The Ordnance Survey in Nineteenth-Century Ireland* (Dublin: Four Courts Press, 2002).

40. Alan Richardson, *Literature, Education and Romanticism: Reading as Social Practice, 1780–1832* (Cambridge: Cambridge University Press, 1994), p. 7.

41. *Stories from the History of Greece, From the Earliest Period to its Final Conquest by the Romans. Adapted to the Capacities of Children. By the Rev. Edward Groves, LLB*, 2 vols. (Dublin and London, 1829).

42. Thomas Crofton Croker, *Researches in the South of Ireland* (London, 1824), p. 78.

43. Marilyn Butler and Mitzi Myers, general eds. *The Works of Maria Edgeworth*, 12 vols. (London: Pickering and Chatto, 2004), XII.

44. Christopher Morash, *A History of the Irish Theatre, 1601–2000* (Cambridge: Cambridge University Press, 2002), p. 76.

45. Julie Carlson, *In the Theatre of Romanticism: Coleridge, Nationalism, Women* (Cambridge: Cambridge University Press, 1994), p. 10.

46. Morash, *A History of the Irish Theatre*; see also Peter Kavanagh, *The Irish Theatre: Being a History of the Drama in Ireland from the Earliest Period up to the Present Day* (Tralee: The Kerryman Limited, 1946).

47. For an online edition of the text and a critical introduction, see Julia M. Wright, 'Introduction to Lefanu's *The Sons of Erin*', *British Women Playwrights around 1800*, http://www.etang.umontreal.ca/bwp1800/essays/wright_sons_intro.html. Accessed: 14 July 2004.

48. John Banim, *Damon and Pythias: A Tragedy, in Five Acts. As Performed at the Theatre Royal, Covent-Garden* (London, 1821), act 2, scene 2, p. 22.

49. Morash, *A History of the Irish Theatre*, p. 76.

50. See ibid., p. 102.

51. Jane Moody, *Illegitimate Theatre in London, 1770–1840* (Cambridge: Cambridge University Press, 2000), p. 98.

52. *Report from the Select Committee Appointed to Inquire into the Laws Affecting Dramatic Literature* [1832] (Shannon: Irish University Press, 1968), pp. 174–5.

53. Jeffrey N. Cox, *In the Shadows of Romance: Romantic Tragic Drama in Germany, England and France* (Athens: Ohio University Press, 1987), p. 51.

54. Richard Sheil, *The Apostate: A Tragedy in Five Acts. As Performed at the Theatre Royal, Covent-Garden* (London, 1817), p. iii.

55. Cox, *In the Shadows of Romance*, p. 127.

56. Ibid., p. 109.

57. *The Correspondence of Sir Walter Scott and Charles Robert Maturin, with a few other allied letters* (Austin: University of Texas Press, 1937), p. 44.

58. Moody, *Illegitimate Theatre in London*, p. 98.

59. Charles Robert Maturin, *Bertram*, in *Seven Gothic Dramas, 1789–1825*, edited with an introduction by Jeffrey N. Cox (Athens, OH: Ohio University Press, 1992), p. 354.

60. Moody, *Illegitimate Theatre in London*, p. 59.

61. Coleridge on Schiller, quoted in Martin Meisel, *Realizations: Narrative, Pictorial and Theatrical Arts in Nineteenth-Century England* (Princeton: Princeton University Press, 1983) p. 167.

62. Curran, *Poetic Form and British Romanticism*, p. 214.

63. McIlvanney, *Burns the Radical*, p. 221. McIlvanney describes the 1790s as 'the decade of the Ulster-Scots literary revival' (p. 223).

64. *The Poetical Works of Thomas Campbell* (London, n.d.), pp. 153–4.

65. See Leith Davis, 'Sequels of Colonialism: Edward Bunting's *Ancient Irish Music*', *Nineteenth-Century Contexts* 23 (2001), pp. 29–57.

66. Robert Welch, A *History of Verse Translation from the Irish, 1789–1897* (Gerrards Cross and Totowa, NJ: Colin Smythe and Barnes and Noble Books, 1988), pp. 54–5.

67. On satire in the period, see Mary Helen Thuente, '"The Belfast Laugh": The Context and Significance of United Irish Satires', in Jim Smyth, ed. *Revolution, Counter-Revolution and Union: Ireland in the 1790s* (Cambridge: Cambridge University Press, 2000), pp. 67–82.

68. Matthew Campbell, 'Thomas Moore's Wild Song: The 1821 *Irish Melodies*', *Bullán* 4, 2 (2000), pp. 83–103.

69. See Mary Helen Thuente, *The Harp Re-Strung: The United Irishmen and the Rise of Irish Literary Nationalism* (Syracuse, NY: Syracuse University Press, 1994), p. 178.

70. Jane Moore, *The Satires of Thomas Moore* (London and Brookfield, VT: Pickering & Chatto, 2003), p. xxv.

71. Letter to Samuel Rogers, quoted in Moore, *The Satires of Thomas Moore*, p. xxv.

72. Mrs Oliphant, *William Blackwood and his Sons: Their Magazine and Friends, vol. I* (Edinburgh: William Blackwood, 1897), p. 362.

73. Oliphant, *William Blackwood and his Sons*, pp. 366–7; Terry Eagleton, 'Cork and the Carnivalesque', in Eagleton, *Crazy John and the Bishop: Essays in Irish Culture* (Cork: Cork University Press, 1998), pp. 165, 199–206.

74. See Ian Duncan with Leith Davis and Janet Sorensen, 'Introduction', in Leith Davis, Ian Duncan and Janet Sorensen, eds. *Scotland and the Borders of Romanticism* (Cambridge: Cambridge University Press, 2004), pp. 1–19, p. 13.

75. Quoted in Oliphant, *William Blackwood and his Sons*, I, p. 382.

76. Quoted in Patrick Rafroidi, *Irish Literature in English in the Romantic Period (1789–1850)*, 2 vols. (Gerrards Cross: Colin Smythe, 1980), I, p. 18.

77. Oliphant, *William Blackwood and his Sons*, I, p. 364.

78. *Blackwood's Edinburgh Magazine* 4 (February 1819), pp. 567–8.

79. Welch, A *History of Verse Translation from the Irish*, p. 60.

80. Ferris, *The Romantic National Tale*, p. 47.

81. Robert Welch, *Irish Poetry from Moore to Yeats* (Gerrards Cross: Colin Smythe, 1980).

82. See Earle Vonard Weller, ed. *Keats and Mary Tighe: The Poems of Mary Tighe with Parallel Passages from the Work of John Keats* (New York: The Century Co., for the Modern Language Association of America, 1928); Marlon B. Ross, *The Contours of Masculine Desire: Romanticism and the Rise of Women's Poetry* (New York and Oxford: Oxford University Press, 1989); James Chandler, *England in 1819: The Politics of Literary Culture and the Case of Romantic Historicism* (Chicago: University of Chicago Press, 1999).

83. Charles Kendal Bushe's copy of *Psyche* (1811) is held in the Houghton Library at Harvard University.

84. E. Œ. Somerville and Martin Ross, *Irish Memories* (London: Longmans, 1917), appendix. Bushe was the authors' great-grandfather.

85. See Kilfeather, 'Terrific Register', pp. 62–4. James Orr, 'The Maniac's Petition', *Poems on Various Subjects* (Belfast, 1804), pp. 86–7; James Stuart, 'The Maniac', *Poems on Various Subjects* (Belfast, 1811), pp. 42–9; Amelia Bristow, *The Maniac: A Tale, or A View of Bethlem Hospital: and the Merits of Women. A Poem from the French, with Poetical Pieces on Various Subjects, Original and Translated* (London, 1810).

86. Caroline Hamilton, 'Anecdotes of Our Family, Written for My Children', National Library of Ireland Ms 4810, quoted in Patrick Henchy, 'The Works of Mary Tighe: Published and Unpublished', *The Bibliographical Society of Ireland* 6, 6 (1957), pp. 1–14, p. 6.

87. See Mary Tighe, *Mary: A Series of Reflections during Twenty Years* (privately printed: Dublin [1811?]) and William Tighe's manuscript analysis of the dream she records there.

88. Mary Tighe, 'From Metastasio, 1791', *Mary*, p. 9.

89. Ibid.

90. Ross, *The Contours of Masculine Desire*, p. 161.

91. Curran, *Poetic Form and British Romanticism*, p. 31.

92. Kevin O'Neill, 'Mary Shackleton Leadbeater: Peaceful Rebel', in Dáire Keogh and Nicholas Furlong, eds. *The Women of 1798* (Dublin: Four Courts Press, 1998), pp. 137–62.

93. Mary Leadbeater, 'The Triumph of Terror', *Poems, by Mary Leadbeater: To which is prefixed her translation of the Thirteenth book of the Aeneid; with the Latin original by Maffaeus* (Dublin, 1808), p. 309.

94. The phrase is Carole Fabricant's. See *Swift and Landscape* (Baltimore, MD and London: The Johns Hopkins University Press, 1982), p. 11.

95. William Tighe, *The Plants: A Poem. Cantos the First and Second, with Notes; and Occasional Poems* (London, 1808).

96. Patrick O'Kelly, *The Eudoxologist; or, An Ethicographical Survey of the Western Parts of Ireland: A Poem* (Dublin, 1812).

97. 'To Mr Kelly, on his poetical dress of the celebrated Lake of Killarney', *Poems on the Giant's Causeway, and Killarney; with Other Miscellanies* (Dublin, 1808), p. 13. On Killarney in Irish culture, see Luke Gibbons, 'Topographies of Terror: Killarney and the Politics of the Sublime', *South Atlantic Quarterly* 95, Special Issue on Irish Cultural Studies, ed. John Paul Waters (1996), pp. 23–44.

98. Patrick O'Kelly, 'Killarney: An Epic Poem', *Poems on the Giant's Causeway*, p. 49.

99. Terence Brown, *Northern Voices: Poets from Ulster* (Dublin: Gill and Macmillan, 1975), p. 25.

100. William Drennan, *Fugitive Pieces in Verse and Prose* (Belfast, 1815), p. 116.

101. W. E. K. Anderson, ed. *The Journal of Sir Walter Scott* (Oxford: Clarendon Press, 1972), p. 526.

102. Lady Morgan, *The Book of the Boudoir*, 2 vols. (London: Henry Colburn, 1829), I, p. vii.

Select bibliography

Chandler, James, *England in 1819: The Politics of Literary Culture and the Case of Romantic Historicism*, Chicago: University of Chicago Press, 1999.

Deane, Seamus, 'Introduction: Poetry and Song, 1800–1890', in Seamus Deane, general ed. The *Field Day Anthology of Irish Writing*, 3 vols. Derry: Field Day, 1991, II, pp. 1–9.

  Strange Country: Modernity and Nationhood in Irish Writing since 1790, Oxford: Clarendon Press, 1997.

Dunne, Tom, 'Haunted by History: Irish Romantic Writing 1800–1850', in Roy Porter and Miklaus Teich, eds. *Romanticism in National Context*, Cambridge: Cambridge University Press, 1988, pp. 68–90.

Ferris, Ina, *The Romantic National Tale and the Question of Ireland*, Cambridge: Cambridge University Press, 2002.

Flanagan, Thomas, *The Irish Novelists, 1800–1859*, New York: Columbia University Press, 1956.

Gibbons, Luke, *Edmund Burke and Ireland: Aesthetics, Politics and the Colonial Sublime*, Cambridge: Cambridge University Press, 2003.

Kilfeather, Siobhán, 'Terrific Register: The Gothicization of Atrocity in Irish Romantic Writing', *boundary 2* 31, 1 (2004), pp. 49–71.

Leerssen, Joep, *Remembrance and Imagination: Patterns in the Historical and Literary Representation of Ireland in the Nineteenth Century*, Cork: Cork University Press, 1997.

McCormack, W. J., *From Burke to Beckett: Ascendancy, Tradition and Betrayal in Irish Literary History*, Cork: Cork University Press, 1994.

Morash, Christopher, *A History of the Irish Theatre, 1601–2000*, Cambridge: Cambridge University Press, 2002.

Rafroidi, Patrick, *Irish Literature in English in the Romantic Period (1789–1850)*, 2 vol. Gerrards Cross: Colin Smythe, 1980.

Smyth, Jim, ed. *Revolution, Counter-Revolution and Union: Ireland in the 1790s*, Cambridge: Cambridge University Press, 2000.

Thuente, Mary Helen, *The Harp Re-Strung: The United Irishmen and the Rise of Irish Literary Nationalism*, Syracuse, NY: Syracuse University Press, 1994.

Trumpener, Katie, *Bardic Nationalism: The Romantic Novel and the British Empire*, Princeton: Princeton University Press, 1997.

Welch, Robert, *A History of Verse Translation from the Irish, 1789–1897*, Gerrards Cross and Totowa, NJ: Colin Smythe and Barnes and Noble, 1988.

II

Prose writing and drama in English, 1830–1890: from Catholic emancipation to the fall of Parnell

MARGARET KELLEHER

The 1830s have been termed by some commentators as the decade in which Irish fiction faced collapse, and, in support of this view, critics commonly cite a letter written by Maria Edgeworth in 1834, the year in which *Helen*, her last novel, was published. Writing from her home in Edgeworthstown to her brother Michael Pakenham Edgeworth in India, the novelist observed: 'It is impossible to draw Ireland as she now is in a book of fiction – realities are too strong, party passions too violent to bear to see, or care to look at their faces in the looking-glass. The people would only break the glass, and curse the fool who held the mirror up to nature – distorted nature, in a fever.'[1] As chapters 8 and 10 by Ross and Connolly have shown, by 1830 Ireland was well established as a locale for fiction and Irish fiction was firmly embedded within emerging definitions of realism – trends exemplified by the success of Edgeworth's writings. While the remarks quoted above spell the end of her own novel-writing career, they greatly underestimate the tenacity of Irish fiction. Five years earlier, in an address 'to the reader' which prefaced her *Book of the Boudoir* (1829), Sydney Owenson had delivered a more accurate prediction of the future for Irish writing: 'Among the multitudinous effects of catholic emancipation, I do not hesitate to predict a change in the character of Irish authorship.'[2]

However, with the exception of the much-cited William Carleton and the undervalued George Moore, the period of 1830 to 1890 is still not readily identifiable through major prose writers or dramatists, and many of the most popular authors of the time – Charles Lever, Anna Maria Hall and Hubert O'Grady, for example – fared badly in subsequent criticism. As early as 1889, W. B. Yeats objected to what he saw as a 'loss of Irish manner' in nineteenth-century fiction after Carleton and the Banims, and this critical sidelining of writings from the second half of the nineteenth century has continued since.[3] The view expressed by Thomas Flanagan, that 'few novelists appeared in the post-famine years to "explain" Ireland to English readers', is one such example, whereby the extent and diversity of post-1850 Irish writing in English has been significantly undervalued.[4] In the decades following Catholic emancipation not only was a much larger and more influential body of writing produced than is generally acknowledged, but also an expansion in publishing venues facilitated a greater diversity of genre; hence numerous Irish-born authors ventured into the Victorian literary marketplace with their versions of the stock genres of the period, such as sensational novels, sentimental fiction, urban fiction and melodrama, in addition to the longer-established forms of the historical novel, travel narrative and peasant tale.

The socio-political conditions of post-emancipation Ireland diagnosed by Edgeworth thus had more productive literary results than she had envisaged and led in subsequent decades to a proliferation of what may be termed 'factual fictions': as novelists assumed or had forced upon them the often urgent weight of political subject matter, the line between fact and fiction proved difficult to draw. In the closing years of the century, the particular instability of nineteenth-century Irish society as a factor disabling to its literary development continued as a matter of comment among writers;[5] a hundred years later, critics still differ as to whether this explains the 'inadequacy' of the nineteenth-century Irish novel or, more positively, was the creative condition of its 'anomalous' development.[6] To date, however, such analyses have relied on a handful of examples, yet again with little detailed study of the development of the genre over the century or of its complex influences.

The years 1830 to 1890 also mark a period in which differentiations of 'English' and 'Irish' writing, whether in prose or drama, are not easily made. Many Irish-born authors moved to London or were entirely published in London; some entered the mainstream of English literature, without complication, in terms of subject matter and form; others returned to Irish themes frequently, still others intermittently, in their careers. Of the authors who remained in Ireland, few could sustain themselves solely in the domestic market and sought a wider readership, yet such an orientation towards an English, or later an American, audience has too often, in a crude simplification, been viewed as a disqualification from the history of 'Irish' literature per se. Once more the influence may be detected here of Yeats, whose stated objection to the later nineteenth-century novel lay in what he saw as the impossibility of dividing 'what is new, and therefore Irish, what is very old, and therefore Irish, from all that is foreign, from all that is an accident of imperfect culture'.[7] But, rather than being a sign of aesthetic inferiority (a conclusion not confined to Yeats), such cultural hybridity is instead where much of the richness of nineteenth-century Irish literature in English lies.

Literature and the book trade

The collapse of an Irish publishing industry in the years following the Act of Union, together with the large-scale migration of Irish authors to London markets, led other literary commentators in the 1830s to speculate as to the end of 'Irish' writing. Writing in the September 1832 issue of the pro-repeal *Irish Monthly Magazine*, the author of 'The Past and Present State of Irish Literature' observed that 'if national literature means the capability of a people to write, and the establishment of a system to publish what is written for the instruction or entertainment of the community', then Ireland's 'very existence as a nation possessing a separate literature of her own, must be denied'.[8] Such meditations on the material institutions that enabled or disabled Irish literature were a recurring concern in periodicals that themselves displayed a newly national orientation. In 1837, the *Dublin University Magazine*, in an essay which has been described as 'in effect, the first attempt at a theory of Anglo-Irish literature', offered its diagnosis of 'the past and present state of literature',[9] and lamented that 'the vast capabilities of this country for literary pursuit, are in fact concealed by the overpowering demand of the English marts'.[10] Five years later, however, a significant change could be detected, as the reflections of author William Carleton, writing in the preface to a new edition of his *Traits and Stories*, imply:

> In truth until within the last ten or twelve years an Irish author never thought of publishing in his own country, and the consequence was that our literary men followed the example of our great landlords; they became absentees, and drained the country of its intellectual wealth precisely as the others exhausted it of its rents.
>
> Thus did Ireland stand in the singular anomaly of adding some of the most distinguished names to the literature of Great Britain, whilst she herself remained incapable of presenting anything to the world beyond a school-book or a pamphlet.[11]

Carleton was the first post-Union Irish novelist to publish primarily in Ireland and his career and the re-emergence of the Irish publishing industry would prove to be closely linked. The first edition of his *Traits and Stories of the Irish Peasantry* (1830) appeared anonymously and was published by Dublin publisher William Curry in two small, duodecimo volumes; the two volumes that comprised the 'new edition' of 1843–4, in contrast, were lavishly produced in octavo by Curry together with William Orr of London, and featured illustrations by Phiz. and other 'artists of eminence'. In 1847, Carleton's *The Black Prophet* (published the previous year in serial form in the *Dublin University Magazine*) was the first work to appear in the Parlour Library series launched by Belfast publishers Simms and M'Intyre. This series, in which volumes were priced between one shilling and one shilling and sixpence, marked a key innovation in the publication of cheaply priced fiction throughout Great Britain, and was quickly imitated by English publishers such as Routledge's Railway Library, launched 1849.

While the years of the Great Famine saw the bankruptcies of many Irish publishers and printers, most famously that of William Curry in 1847, a notable survivor was the firm of James Duffy (1808–71) with a business, as Charles Benson has noted, 'firmly based on the triple pillars of Catholic piety, school-books and nationalist literature',[12] and whose marketing of fiction in decreasing prices from the 1840s onwards allowed a significant expansion in sales and readership. Meanwhile, Irish authors continued to appear in significant numbers on the lists of English publishers, including Colburn, Bentley, the Tinsley brothers, and Chapman and Hall. In the last decades of the nineteenth century, Dublin firms such as Sealy, Bryers and Walker, M. H. Gill and Son (formerly M'Glashan and Gill), and Duffy produced novels for the domestic market in ever cheaper editions: Duffy's popular 'Parlour Library of Ireland', priced at a shilling, for example, was followed by the 'Sixpenny Library of Fiction' issued by Sealy, Bryers and Walker. These affordable prices were also facilitated by their co-publication with American firms such as Sadlier, Kenedy and the Benzinger brothers, all of New York, who, along with firms such as J. Murphy of Baltimore and Flynn of Boston, served a growing Irish-American market.

The period beginning in 1830 also saw the flourishing of the literary journal in Ireland. The founding of the *Christian Examiner and Church of Ireland Magazine* by the Revd Caesar Otway and Dr J. H. Singer, in 1825, which provided the young Carleton with his first publishing outlet, was quickly followed by that of its ideological opponent, the short-lived *Irish Catholic Magazine* (1829). More recognisably literary magazines soon followed, though most were of a very short duration: the *Dublin Literary Gazette*, later *National Magazine* (1830–1); the staunchly pro-repeal *Irish Monthly Magazine of Politics and Literature* (1832–4), which was modelled on *Blackwood's Magazine*; the *Dublin University Review, and Quarterly Magazine* (1833); and *Ancient Ireland* (1835), whose stated purpose was that of 'reviving the cultivation of the Irish language' and which published

Irish-language stories and poems, with translations and glosses. Of these 1830s periodicals by far the most influential and long lasting was the *Dublin University Magazine* which appeared monthly from January 1833 to December 1877 and has been described as 'the supreme archive of Irish Victorian experience, especially that of the protestant (and oddly, protestant *southern*) middle classes'.[13]

The *DUM* was founded in January 1833 in the wake of the Reform Bill of 1832, by a group of young Trinity College Tories, including Isaac Butt, Caesar Otway, Samuel Ferguson and John Anster, with the aspiration to be 'the monthly advocate and representative of the Protestantism, the intelligence, and the respectability of Ireland'.[14] Its most famous contributors, in literary terms, were novelists William Carleton, Charles Lever (who edited the journal from 1842 to 1845) and Sheridan Le Fanu (also editor of the journal, in its later years, from 1861 to 1869), as well as poets Samuel Ferguson and James Clarence Mangan. Although most of its contributions appeared anonymously, many have since been identified; occasional contributors included Michael Banim, George Brittaine, Elizabeth Gaskell, Anna Maria Hall, Harriet Martineau, William Hamilton Maxwell and Anthony Trollope. Subtitled 'a literary and political journal', it acknowledged its politics as 'Conservatism' and its religion as 'Protestantism', but claimed, rightly as future contents would show, 'as for literature, we avow ourselves to have ever been . . . thorough latitudinarians'.[15] Thus, as Norman Vance has noted, in its early decades, at least, 'doctors, clergymen and more or less briefless barristers as well as professional journalists' could 'decorously moonlight' as 'economists, literary critics, political commentators, antiquarians, storytellers and poets'.[16] At its peak, under the editorship of Lever, the *DUM* sold 4,000 copies a month, with Irish and English purchasers.[17]

Even more long-lasting than the *DUM*, and a direct competitor, was the London-published *Dublin Review*, launched in 1836 and surviving until 1969 over three series. Backed by Daniel O'Connell, it became the leading Roman Catholic periodical in Britain, distributed by Mudie's libraries and popular among an upper-class readership in Ireland and England.[18] Many of its contributors, including Charles W. Russell, Patrick Murray and George Crolly, were drawn from the Catholic seminary at Maynooth.

The *Dublin University Magazine* was priced at half a crown; at the other end of the literary market were the many penny magazines available. The weekly *Dublin Penny Journal* (1832–6), founded by Caesar Otway and whose contributors included William Carleton, reached a peak circulation figure of some 40,000 sales. Successors included the *Irish Penny Magazine* (1833), edited by Samuel Lover and chiefly featuring his writings, and the *Irish Penny Journal*

(1840–1), in which Carleton's writings once again featured prominently. While the *Nation* (founded in 1842) was primarily a weekly newspaper, its reviews of Irish books and periodicals, and its commissioning of poetry, firmly linked emerging literature to the Irish political scene, and its circulation figures are estimated to have reached 13,000 copies a week, with a much higher number of readers. From 1847 onwards, the periodicals produced by the firm of James Duffy were an important outlet for popular fiction, all the more significant given the declining interest in Irish material among English publishers at the time; these periodicals included Duffy's *Irish Catholic Magazine, Fireside Magazine, Hibernian Magazine* and *Illustrated Dublin Journal*. Yet another penny magazine was *The Shamrock*, self-described as 'a national weekly journal of Irish history, literature, arts, &c'; founded in 1866 by Richard Pigott, later the infamous forger of the 'Parnell' letters, it provided a forum for many writers including Charles Kickham and the young Bram Stoker. Towards the end of the century, the popular *Irish Fireside* (1883–7), which promised 'fiction, amusement and instruction', published serial stories by Kickham, Rose Kavanagh and others. And most influential of all in shaping a home audience for Irish fiction was the literary periodical the *Irish Monthly* (1873–1954); founded by the Jesuit priest Matthew Russell, it provided a vital publishing outlet for many Irish authors, most especially for female writers such as Rosa Mulholland, Katharine Tynan and Attie O'Brien.

Tales of the Irish peasantry: Carleton and his contemporaries

'The Eerishers are marchin' in leeterature, *pawri pashu*': so wrote James Hogg in *Blackwood's Edinburgh Magazine* in May 1830, a comment prompted by the recent publication of Carleton's *Traits and Stories*.[19] From the mid-1820s onwards, as critic Ina Ferris has shown, contemporary periodicals in England and Scotland had begun to define 'an Irish *line* of fiction', and the 1830 publication of the first series of Carleton's stories consolidated this trend.[20] Over the course of the next decade, numerous volumes of *Sketches, Stories, Tales, True Tales* and *Legends* followed, which variously described, explained, scrutinised, critiqued and/or defended 'Irish character', 'the Irish peasantry', Ireland and 'Irish life'. Written for the most part by Irish-born authors, and generally with English or Scottish publishers, these volumes were marketed as 'real-life' representations, offering a strong social and anthropological quotient, while at a safe distance from political contention and easily digestible by their readers. Significantly, some of the earliest recognitions of this trend in

Irish prose writing came from Scottish journals – *Blackwood's Magazine*, as cited above, or its liberal rival, *Tait's Edinburgh Magazine* – in a continuation of the 'cross-pollination' between literary Ireland and Scotland of earlier decades.[21] Thus, in the February 1833 issue of *Tait's*, Christian Isobel Johnstone used the occasion of a review of the second series of *Traits* for acerbic comment on the developing genre:

> It will go hard if the Irish do not beguile or flatter their fellow-subjects into some knowledge of Ireland at last. They had pleaded, argued, expostulated, yelled, shouted, clamoured, fought, burnt and slain, wept and sung to small purpose. Little was the permanent attention they were able to gain from the people of Great Britain, till the happy device was hit upon of throwing open the castle gates, and the cabin doors, and inviting the Scotch and English to enter, hear stories tragic and mirthful, and be *amused*.[22]

A dismissal of these writings purely as light amusement, however, fails to do justice to their contemporary popularity, and to the role which they played in the years following Catholic emancipation during which the condition of the Irish poor, the continuing agrarian disturbances, and agitation for repeal of the Union moved in and out of the British public's view.

Chief among such native informants is William Carleton (1794–1869), whose reputation, from his very first publications, was built on the perceived 'authenticity' of his writings. Born in Prillisk, County Tyrone, Carleton was the son of Irish-speaking parents, his father fluent also in English and his mother less so. Writing late in life in his *Autobiography*, Carleton credited the influence of his bilingual father in enabling him as a writer 'to transfer the genius, the idiomatic peculiarity and conversational spirit of the one language into the other' and in providing him with a 'perfect storehouse' of legend, tale and historical anecdote.[23] The details of Carleton's life are difficult to disentangle from his many autobiographical constructions, the most famous being the lines he wrote as part of an application for a government pension in 1847: 'I have risen up from a humble cottage and described a whole people.'[24] The formal education received by the young Carleton was sporadic – including attendance at a local hedge-school, a 'lady's school' and various short-lived classical schools – and it was supplemented by his avid reading of whatever literature was locally available, from Fielding's *Tom Jones* and Smollett's translation of *Gil Blas* to the chapbook tales of highwayman James Freney and *Arabian Nights*. Still a teenager, and intended by his family for the priesthood, he was sent as a 'poor scholar' to be educated in Munster, but traveled only as far as Granard, County Longford, episodes fictionalised in the early stories 'The Poor Scholar' and 'Denis O'Shaughnessy Going to Maynooth'. In 1819 he arrived in Dublin where he worked as a tutor. His first sketch, 'A Pilgrimage to Patrick's Purgatory' (later to be revised as 'Lough Derg Pilgrim'), was published in Caesar Otway's *Christian Examiner* in 1828; sharply criticised for its 'anti-Catholic' subject matter, it was modified in later versions.

The publication of the first series of *Traits and Stories of the Irish Peasantry* in 1830 established Carleton's literary reputation, with positive reviews from the English and Scottish press. A second series followed in 1833, including stories such as 'The Wildgoose Lodge' and 'The Poor Scholar' that showed a considerable advance in narrative power and dramatic effect. In 1843–4 appeared the definitive two-volume edition of *Traits and Stories*, whose long autobiographical introduction ranks among Carleton's best prose writing. Viewed overall, the most successful stories in *Traits* are those that experiment with dialect and with narrative voice, for example, the use of the first-person narrator in 'Wildgoose Lodge' and the various linguistic registers recorded in stories such as 'The Hedge School' or 'Denis O'Shaughnessy'. 'Wildgoose Lodge', now Carleton's most acclaimed story, was first published in the *Dublin Literary Gazette* in January 1830 as 'Confessions of a Reformed Ribbonman', and subtitled 'An owre true tale'. The narrator recounts the horrific killing of a local farmer and his family by a group of Ribbonmen (members of an agrarian secret society), 'some of the most malignant and reckless spirits in the parish', events in which the narrator is an unwilling but implicated participant. The atmosphere of the story partakes of Gothic-like suspense and horror – frequently described by critics as reminiscent of Poe, though well preceding Poe's 'grotesque' tales of the mid- to late 1830s – and its account of the 'fearful magnificence' of the house-burning and 'conflagration' is especially memorable, shadowed by the guilt-ridden recollections of the narrating voice. What the narrator calls 'the pernicious influence of Ribbonism' would return as a theme in later writings but is never as potently portrayed.

Alongside his various collections of short fiction, including *Tales and Sketches, Illustrating the Character, Usages, Traditions, Sports and Pastimes of the Irish Peasantry* (1846), Carleton was the author of over a dozen novels, from *Fardorougha the Miser*, first published in the *Dublin University Magazine* (1837–8) and produced in volume form in 1839, to *Redmond, Count O'Hanlon, the Irish Rapparee*, published in Duffy's new *Hibernian Magazine* in 1860 and in book form in 1862. These novels, and their various political targets, record not only Carleton's shifting political allegiance during these decades, but also his acute appraisal of reader interest, during the 1830s and 1840s at least. *Fardorougha the Miser* is set in the background of a resurgence of Ribbonism in the 1830s, but characteristically for Carleton the motivation for violent deeds is presented as what he terms the 'savage principle of personal vengeance' rather than political or economic grievance. His novel *Valentine M'Clutchy, The Irish Agent; or, Chronicles of Castle Cumber* (1845) turned to a critique of Orangeism in the first decade of the nineteenth century, and its characters include as villains the agent M'Clutchy and Phineas Lucre, the local Protestant rector. In 1845 Carleton produced three shorter novels for Dublin publisher James Duffy: *Art Maguire; or, the Broken Pledge*, in support of the temperance movement of Fr Mathew; *Rody the Rover; or, the Ribbonman*, in which the evils of Ribbonism return to view; and *Parra Sastha; or, the History of Paddy Go-Easy and his Wife, Nancy*, a deeply negative portrait of a peasant family.

Following Carleton's well-known famine novel *The Black Prophet* (1847), discussed in more detail below, his *Emigrants of Ahadarra* was published in 1848. Set in the period immediately before Catholic emancipation, the novel adds to an established list of political targets – absenteeism, corrupt agents, neglect by the legislature – an extended attack on the earlier enfranchisement of forty-shilling freeholders, an event which Carleton blamed for the multiplication of a pauper population who 'like Frankenstein in the novel' now pursued their landlord creators. *The Tithe Proctor* (1849) stages yet another political revisiting, this time of the themes of *Valentine M'Clutchy*, through the story of a rebellion against tithes forty years before. In 1855 Carleton obtained his largest commercial success with the melodramatic novel *Willy Reilly and His Dear Colleen Bawn*, first serialised in the London *Independent*, but overall his writings from the last two decades of his life – such as *The Black Baronet* (1857), *The Evil Eye* (1860) or *The Double Prophecy* (1862) – show a sharp decline in narrative power.

Although his reputation became that of 'peasant novelist', Carleton's central protagonists are usually quite prosperous small farmers; of more significance to the narrative is the apprehension shared by such characters that their economic and social advancement is vulnerable, a theme deployed to comic or to serious effect. In 'The Lough Derg Pilgrim', for example, the narrator discovers both the heightened status awarded to him when his fellow pilgrims think him to be a student studying for the priesthood, and also the swift debunking that occurs as a result merely of the theft of his clothes. And while Carleton's novels frequently endorse a narrative of social progress and economic prosperity, their powerful evocation of the 'pull' of the past and of older traditions undercuts this optimism in subtle ways.[25] In *Fardorougha the Miser*, the plight of the title character ('fear dorcha' or blind man) moves between melodrama and psychological intricacy: a now well-to-do farmer, he is haunted by fear of the poorhouse, torn between 'the famine-struck god of the miser' and his love for his son. This 1839 novel is also curiously prophetic of many of the social mores attributed to post-famine Ireland in its depiction of the sexual constraint and religious conservatism of Fardorougha's society. This is by far Carleton's most successful novel, in sharp contrast to the melodrama of his later works, and unjustly overshadowed by his more famous short fiction.

In 1829, *Sketches of Irish Character*, the first published work of the author known as Mrs Hall (1800–81), appeared. Born in Dublin, Anna Maria Fielding was raised in Bannow, County Wexford by her mother's family until the age of fifteen when the family moved to London. In 1824 she married the Cork-born journalist and author Samuel Carter Hall (1800–89), who had moved to London at the age of twenty-one, and with whom she later collaborated on many Irish travel books, such as *Ireland, Its Scenery, Character, etc.* (1841–3), *A Week at Killarney* (1843) and *Handbooks for Ireland* (1853). Set in the village of Bannow, Hall's stories proved immediately popular among English readers; in 1831 a second series of *Sketches* followed, with numerous later editions. While the author was at pains to emphasise that her characters knew little 'and care less' about politics, the sketches themselves belie this assertion with frequent references to memories of the rebellion of 1798. In the fifth edition of *Sketches* published in 1854, Hall included an extensive account of the friendship between her Huguenot grandmother and a Roman Catholic priest during the rebellion.[26]

Anna Hall was an extremely prolific writer, whose work featured in diverse Irish and English periodicals such as *Chambers's Journal*, *New Monthly Magazine*, the *Westminster Review* and the *Dublin Penny Journal*. While her writings were praised at the time for their accuracy and insight, they can now appear superficial and conventional, and she may be more fairly viewed, as Riana O'Dwyer has argued, as 'the equivalent of a journalist or columnist today, rather than as a literary writer'.[27] Some of her stories contain a level of irony rarely credited to their author: in the novella *Groves of Blarney*, for example, which comprises the first volume of *Lights and Shadows of Irish Life* (3 vols., 1838), much ridicule is directed against Peter Swan, the Cockney cousin, who arrives in Ireland as a 'travelling *towerist*', in search of the picturesque. On 16 April 1838, a dramatised version of the novella began a highly successful run at London's Adelphi Theatre. Of Hall's nine novels, *The Whiteboy* (1845) is the darkest and most substantial: set in the context of agrarian agitation in 1822, it portrays the desperation of a generation with 'no hope beyond hunger, revolt and death'.[28]

Agrarian violence had continued as a popular subject for 'condition-of-Ireland' fiction in the period immediately following Catholic emancipation. It provided the subject of Charlotte Tonna's first novel, *The Rockites* (1829), and of Harriet Martineau's *Ireland: A Tale* (1832), the ninth volume in her 'Illustrations of Political Economy' series.[29] For Martineau, Whiteboy agitation demonstrated the extent of English misgovernment of Ireland; for Tonna, it was a 'poisonous excrescence formed upon the tree of her [Ireland's] national prosperity, and eaten into its heart's core'.[30] Tonna (1790–1846), born Charlotte Elizabeth Browne, lived in Kilkenny from 1819 to 1824 with her first husband, Captain Phelan, and while in Ireland began a series of religious tracts, published as the work of 'Charlotte Elizabeth', which were fiercely denunciatory of contemporary Roman Catholicism. Her most successful novel, *Derry: A Tale of the Revolution* (1833), provided a fictional retelling of the siege of Derry (1689), heavily drawn from John Graham's 1823 history; lurid but also compelling in its depiction, the novel had reached its tenth edition by 1847 and was reprinted throughout the nineteenth century. In the 1840s, Tonna's writings also became highly popular in America, with a two-volume collection of her works published in 1844, and introduced by Harriet Beecher Stowe. Along with the Irish material, the collection included reprints of Tonna's industrial novel *Helen Fleetwood* (1841) and her *Personal Recollections* (1841), together with extensive selections from her poetic writing.

Known in her day as a social reformer as well as an evangelical writer, Tonna was also the author of *The Wrongs of Woman* (1843), a denunciation, through moral tales, of contemporary working conditions for English women and children. The subject of legal discrimination against women was explored by the renowned poet and novelist Caroline Norton, model for Meredith's *Diana of the Crossways* (1885), and herself the author of such works as *The Wife and Woman's Reward* (1835), the controversial pamphlet *English Laws for Women in the Nineteenth Century* (1854), and the quasi-autobiographical novel *Stuart of Dunleath* (1851). Other significant discourses on the 'woman question' include Anna Hall's *Tales of Woman's Trials* (1835), two with Irish settings, and Sydney Owenson's historical chronicle *Woman and her Master: a History of the Female Sex from the Earliest Period* (1840). While Tonna expressed concern about her own and others' use of fictionalised examples in order to portray the conditions of the poor, the Scottish writer Christian Isobel Johnstone, now co-editor of the influential *Tait's Edinburgh Magazine*, put official evidence to powerful effect. Her pamphlet *True Tales of the Irish Peasantry, As Related by Themselves* (1836) reproduced a large number of first-person testimonies, including those of evicted tenants, unemployed labourers and widows, selected from the report of the Poor Law Commissioners and designed to prove the necessity of a Poor Law for Ireland.

The comic representations provided in the 1830s by William Hamilton Maxwell (1792–1850) and Samuel Lover (1797–1868) fared particularly well with an English public accustomed to more humorous portrayals of Ireland. The highly successful *Wild Sports of the West, with Legendary Tales and Local Sketches* (1832) by Maxwell, then a Church of Ireland rector in Balla, County Mayo, mixed lengthy accounts of fishing and shooting in Ireland with Irish legends, 'robber-tales' and various comic adventures. In contrast Maxwell's contemporary, George Brittaine (c.1790–1847), rector of Kilcommock, in the diocese of Ardagh, provided an unrelenting attack on Catholic 'priestcraft' in works such as *Irish Priests and English Landlords* (1830) and *Hyacinth O'Gara* (1830), first published in Dublin. Brittaine's writings did not become widely available to an English readership until their republication in the 1870s in editions significantly rewritten by Revd H. Seddall.

The fame of Samuel Lover rested during the nineteenth century on his reputation as *the* Irish humourist, and declined in the twentieth century as the genre fell out of fashion. His multiple careers ranged from stockbroker to painter, musician, magazine editor, book illustrator, songwriter, novelist, poet and dramatist. His *Legends and Stories of Ireland*, some of which were first published in Dublin magazines, were printed in two series (1831, 1834) with many subsequent editions. Lover's most successful and most fully realised novel, *Rory O'More* (1837), set in late 1790s Ireland, began as a song, reputedly suggested by Sydney Owenson, and was successfully dramatised later in 1837. Although the plot is largely concerned with the comic misadventures of its hero and the 1798 rebellion occurs mostly off-stage, Lover's comic targets have a more serious dimension, including various broadsides against the corrupt judicial and political system in Ireland, and his story ends with the emigration of all of its central characters. Later works included *Handy Andy: A Tale of Irish Life* (1842), previously serialised in the newly founded *Bentley's Miscellany* over a two-year period, beginning January 1837, during which time the periodical was edited by Charles Dickens.

Travel literature about Ireland also proliferated from Dublin and London publishers in the 1830s and 1840s. Selina Bunbury (1802–82), author of numerous volumes based on her travels in Europe, published two Irish narratives in the 1830s: *Tales of My Country* (1833) and *Recollections of Ireland* (1839). The many volumes by visitors to Ireland included political economist James Bicheno's *Ireland and its Economy* (1830), *Notes of Three Tours in Ireland, in 1824 and 1826* by James Glassford, a Scotsman and one of the commissioners of inquiry into Irish education of 1824–6, and *A Tour round Ireland* (1836) by John Barrow, son of the famous English explorer of the same name. *A Journey throughout Ireland during the Spring, Summer and Autumn of 1834* (1834) by the established English travel writer Henry Inglis was in its fifth edition by 1838. That same year Charlotte Tonna's *Letters from Ireland MDCCCXXXVII* appeared, prompted, according to Tonna, by the books 'perpetually coming out on Irish subjects' and 'none that meet the case'. In 1839 *Rambles in the South of Ireland during the Year 1838* by Lady Henrietta Georgiana Chatterton was published, its author the English-born wife of Sir William Chatterton of Castlemahon, County Cork. Chatterton explained to readers that her objective was to remove some of the prejudices which rendered many of her peers afraid either to travel or to reside in Ireland, and two volumes detailing the 'charming', 'pretty' and picturesque ensued; a second edition was required within two months of publication.

While Chatterton and others sought to encourage upper-class tourists to Ireland, the large-scale migration of the Irish poor to English cities generated alarm among English commentators of the period, most notably Thomas Carlyle in his 1839 essay *Chartism*: 'Crowds of miserable Irish darken all our towns . . . With an Ireland pouring daily in on us, in these circumstances; deluging us down to its own waste confusion, outward and inward.'[31] The influence of Irish migrants also became an anxious subject in a number of later English novels, for example Elizabeth Gaskell's *North and South* (1854–5) and Charles Kingsley's *Alton Locke* (1850), and received a more ambivalent treatment in Engels's *Condition of the Working Class in England* (1845) as a force that could hasten social crisis. Carlyle's comments on England's 'guilt' and injustice towards Ireland led to his being regarded by Charles Gavan Duffy and his contemporary Young Irelanders as a potential advocate of Irish national interests.[32] However, in the longer term, Carlyle's fears of the Irish as social and political contaminant are the more revealing, expressed in his now infamous depiction of the Irish national character:

> For the oppression has gone far farther than into the economics of Ireland; inwards to her very heart and soul. The Irish National Character is degraded, disordered; till this recover itself, nothing is yet recovered . . . Such a people circulates not order but disorder, through every vein of it; – and the cure, if there is to be a cure, must begin at the heart: not in his condition only but in himself must the Patient be all changed.[33]

As Amy Martin observes, Carlyle's influential representation combines tenets of cultural and biological racism to powerful effect: 'the Irish difference of which he writes is simultaneously the result of a historically contingent process of degeneration and of racial descent'.[34]

A sharper and sustained investigation of Ireland's internal political condition, specifically of the role of its 'bad aristocracy', came from the French writer Gustave de Beaumont, author of *Ireland: Social, Political and Religious* (translated 1839), based on his visits to Ireland in 1835 and 1837.[35] For the French traveller, as for many of the writers on Ireland in this period, much of Ireland's misfortune could be attributed to the delayed emergence of a middle class: according to de Beaumont, in Ireland 'where the aristocracy is at open war with the people, the middle class, from the very moment of its existence, is quite naturally the first and only national power'.[36] De Beaumont's depiction of the 'condition of unfortunate Ireland' as worse than that of 'the Indian in his forests, and the Negro in his chains' was much cited in later decades – by John Stuart Mill, Charles Gavan Duffy and many others. It was immediately echoed by German writer Johann Georg Kohl who, in his influential *Travels in Ireland* (1843), drew on his own travels in eastern Europe to deem Irish hovels worse than the 'poorest of the Lettes, Esthonians and Finlanders'.[37] Yet two years earlier, writing in 1841, Samuel and Anna Hall happily reported that Ireland was on the eve of a new era of economic prosperity, English capitalists now considering the country as 'a vast field in which judicious labour may be assured a profitable harvest'.[38] Their three-volume travel account, *Ireland: Its Scenery and Character* (1841–3), drawn from five tours of Ireland made by the authors between 1825 and 1840, sold rapidly even prior to publication.

Small wonder then that the young William Thackeray, while on a visit to Wicklow in 1842, would bitterly complain: 'A plague take them! what remains for me to discover after the gallant adventurers in the service of Paternoster Row[39] have examined every rock, lake, and ruin of the district, exhausted it of all its legends, and "invented new", most likely, as their daring genius prompted?'[40] The picaresque and mischievous narrative that Thackeray did produce, entitled *The Irish Sketchbook 1842*, proved to be an immediate success in London following its publication in May 1843. One of the liveliest accounts of pre-famine Irish society, it includes a fascinating account of the author's own 'light reading' while in Ireland and features liberal quotation from what Thackeray termed the 'Hedge school volumes' – such as *The Life and Adventures of James Freney* and *The Irish and Hibernian Tales* – once the childhood reading of William Carleton and, two generations later, still a staple of the Irish reading public.

Narratives of the Irish famine, 1845–1851

The two most famous nineteenth-century Irish famine novels are William Carleton's *The Black Prophet* (1847) and Anthony Trollope's *Castle Richmond* (1860). Yet these constitute only a small part of the many narratives of the period on the subject of famine: from the published testimonies of contemporary observers, newspaper reports and government correspondence, to the many subsequent and competing political analyses. Nor did either novel come close to rivalling the iconic status of the texts of John Mitchel, whose accounts of the Great Famine in *Jail Journal* (1854), *The Last Conquest of Ireland (Perhaps)* (1860), *An Apology for the British Government in Ireland* (1860) and *History of Ireland from the Treaty of Limerick to the Present Time* (1868) were probably the most frequently read, and most influential, interpretations in the late nineteenth century.

Published between May and December 1846, in eight instalments of the *Dublin University Magazine*, Carleton's novel is set a generation before and draws from the history of earlier famines in 1817 and 1822. Its first issues thus appeared well before the fatal recurrence of the potato blight in the autumn of 1846; by December, in a chapter entitled 'A Picture for the Present', the contemporary relevance of this 'Tale of Irish Famine' was clear. The plot of *The Black Prophet* is quite standard melodrama, featuring a murder mystery, wrongful accusation, and a consequent family feud that obstructs the love of hero and heroine. Yet the plot element of an unsolved murder from a generation past, rising to the surface in the present, eerily parallels the resurgence of famine in the late 1840s. In later chapters the narrative voice breaks out of the story's frame to address directly the responsibility of a legislature to provide 'for a more enlightened system of public health and cleanliness, and a better and more comfortable provision of food for the indigent and the poor'. Furthermore, Carleton's identification of what he calls 'an artificial famine', created by a general and culpable monopoly in food rather than simply by food shortage, differs startlingly from the views of many of his contemporaries.[41]

Carleton's novels regularly digress into political and economic commentary, usually in lengthy footnotes as in the long discourse on famine fever, drawn from the work of D. J. Corrigan, included in *The Black Prophet*. In his later famine novel, *Squanders of Castle Squander* (written 1851–2), this non-fictional material takes over in a bewildering array of texts including a lengthy regurgitation of extracts from *Valentine M'Clutchy* and *Traits and Stories*, a narrative implosion which, as Christopher Morash has argued, may render this novel 'the characteristic Famine text', illustrating the pressure of what George

Steiner has termed 'the enormity of the fact' on literary representations of atrocity.[42]

Literary representations of the famine are thus distinguished by their generic instability, and by their authors' frequent attestations to events 'too terrible to relate' – declarations that may be read as both rhetorical trope and human appeal. One of the first, and least known, accounts of the 1840s famine was Cork author Mary Anne Hoare's 'Sketch of Famine', first published in *Howitt's Journal*, the short-lived London radical weekly, on 24 April 1847.

The quasi-fictional sketch detailed the recent arrival of the potato blight and the desperate strategies for survival employed by famine victims, in comparison with which, Hoare wrote, the horrors of Dante's Ugolino 'fade into nothingness'. In 1851 her *Shamrock Leaves*, a collection of tales and sketches gathered 'from the famine-stricken fields' of Ireland, was published in Dublin and London and explicitly addressed itself to 'our English brethren', emphasising the extent of suffering in Ireland and the importance of private philanthropy.[43]

During the years of the famine, numerous eye-witness accounts – many written by visitors to Ireland – appeared in the pages of Irish and English newspapers, and some were published in volume form. A number of the most significant and detailed testimonies came from members of the Society of Friends, men like William Forster and his son William Edward Forster (later chief secretary for Ireland), James Hack Tuke and William Bennett, who were sent by Quaker colleagues in England to 'obtain trustworthy information as to the real state of the more remote districts, and through what agency to open suitable channels for relief'.[44] The large volume *Transactions of the Central Relief Committee of the Society of Friends during the Famine in Ireland, in 1846 and 1847*, first published in 1852, remains an invaluable source in this regard. A more ephemeral yet telling work was the *Narrative of a Journey from Oxford to Skibbereen during the Year of the Irish Famine*, written in February 1847 by two young Oxford students, Frederick Blackwood (future earl of Dufferin and viceroy of India) and G. F. Boyle, who fled the horrors of Skibbereen to return speedily to England. On 13 and 20 February 1847, famine engravings by the Cork-born artist James Mahony appeared in *The Times*, featuring the now famous 'matchstick figures' and accompanied by Mahony's less well-known commentary on the scenes he had witnessed.

In July 1847 the American traveller Asenath Nicholson, then on her second lengthy visit to Ireland, began a year-long journey around the famine-stricken districts in the west, north and south of Ireland; her ensuing account was first published in London in 1850 as part of her work *Lights and Shades of Ireland*

and republished in New York the following year as *Annals of the Famine*. The strength of Nicholson's reporting, evident also in her pre-famine narrative *Ireland's Welcome to the Stranger* (1847), lies in her distinctive combination of social detail and pointed political analysis. Other contemporary sources include the diaries of Scottish-born Elizabeth Grant Smith, whose husband was a County Wicklow landowner, the letters of Alexander Somerville, child of Scottish labourers and by 1847 a well-known journalist for the *Manchester Examiner* and *Morning Chronicle*, and the correspondence of the aged novelist Maria Edgeworth which featured lengthy exchanges on the topic of famine and economy with her friend, the political economist Richard Jones.

In late 1849 and 1850 the clergyman and philanthropist Sidney Godolphin Osborne visited Ireland and published accounts of his travels in the columns of *The Times*, later republished as *Gleanings in the West of Ireland* (1850). The publication of Osborne's letters prompted the young Anthony Trollope, then living in Ireland where he worked as a surveyor for the postal service, to write a series of letters to the *Examiner*, a liberal English newspaper, on the subject of 'Ireland, her undoubted grievances, her modern history, her recent sufferings, and her present actual state'. Ten years later, just prior to his final departure from Ireland where he had lived intermittently during the 1850s, Trollope completed *Castle Richmond*, his third of five novels set in Ireland.[45] As in *The Black Prophet*, for much of Trollope's novel the subject of famine is conveyed through a conventional love story: in *Castle Richmond*, the involvement of the novel's hero, Herbert Fitzgerald, in the distribution of famine relief emerges as a useful narrative strategy to differentiate him from his rakish cousin Owen Fitzgerald, rival both to the heroine's affection and to the interest of readers. On the other hand, Herbert's encounters with the starving poor, in the course of which he champions laissez-faire policies against what is termed 'promiscuous charity', prove more difficult for the narrative to assimilate, as are the detailed and disturbing examinations of victims' quasi-naked bodies included in these scenes. An authorial voice intervenes to identify the destruction of the potato firmly as the work of God, echoing providentialist views of the blight which were current in the 1840s and after. At the novel's end, a narrative of Malthusian-like progress is proclaimed in stark biblical terms:

> But if one did in truth write a tale of the famine, after that it would behove the author to write a tale of the pestilence; and then another, a tale of the exodus. These three wonderful events, following each other, were the blessings coming from Omniscience and Omnipotence by which the black clouds were driven away from the Irish firmament . . . And then the same author going on with his series would give in his last set, – Ireland in her prosperity.[46]

The 1840s famine returned intermittently as a subject for fiction in the second half of the century, and these novels offer an early insight into the controversies concerning famine's causation and significance that would come to have such significance in Irish historiography. Novelist Mary Anne (Madden) Sadlier (1820–1903) – who had emigrated from Cavan to Canada in 1844, where she married James Sadlier, the influential publisher – employed the famine as a backdrop to the evils of proselytism in her novel *New Lights; or, Life in Galway* (1853). In contrast, Limerick-born Elizabeth Hely Walshe (1835–68) focused in her famine novel *Golden Hills*, published by the London Religious Society, on the philanthropic work of a Protestant landowning family. *The Chronicles of Castle Cloyne* (1884), by Clare author Margaret Brew, is one of the most successful of such novels and presents two concurrent narratives, that of the landlord family, the Dillons of Castle Cloyne, and of their tenant Oonagh MacDermott, 'to show how universal was the action of the Famine' with effects on 'peer and peasant, landlord and tenant, the home of the great, and the cabin of the lowly'.[47] In these later narratives, scenes of individual famine deaths, which possessed such disturbing force in Carleton and Trollope's novels, largely recede from view, supplanted by meditations on famine's place in a developmental narrative of progress and modernisation. The agents of such renewal differ from novel to novel: a reinvigorated Catholic gentry in the work of Margaret Brew, or, in a plot increasingly common in Irish fiction after 1870 (Brew's *Chronicles* and Annie Keary's *Castle Daly* (1875) being among many examples), returning Irish emigrants. Yet the very recurrence of famine as a narrative subject in the years after 1850, together with the enthusiastic welcome expressed by English reviewers towards these novels as explanations of 'the abiding Irish difficulty', attest to the continuing potency of their subject in a period too often simplified as 'silent' with regard to the Great Famine.

Reading England, writing Ireland: Lever, Le Fanu and Riddell

The career of Charles Lever (1806–72), which spanned thirty-five years, offers valuable insights into the emergence of the professional Irish novelist in the mid-nineteenth century. From a Dublin middle-class family, Lever was educated at Trinity College, Dublin and studied medicine at Göttingen and Louvain; he worked as a dispensary doctor for five years in Portstewart, Derry, before moving to Brussels in 1837 where he built up a successful medical practice. The first instalment of his *Confessions of Harry Lorrequer* appeared in the *DUM* in February 1837, and single-volume publication – by Dublin firm

Curry – followed in 1839. The novel, described by Lever himself as a 'volume of anecdote and adventure', and comprising a series of loosely connected episodes, is an Irish *Tom Jones*, its picaresque series of adventures ranging from Dublin to England, France and Germany, and featuring duels, elopements, mistaken identities and a Falstaffian comic creation in the character of Arthur O'Leary. By the novel's end, Harry, a military subaltern who has been posted to Ireland in the wake of the Peninsular wars, has become heir to an English estate and private secretary to the viceroy of Ireland. The story's success was such that instalments continued in the magazine for some months following the book's publication, while the prefatory epistle to the 1839 volume drily promises a further volume, 'to be entitled "Lorrequer *Married?*"'.

The military novel, with which Lever is most frequently associated, had already become popular through the work of his friend William Maxwell, author of *Stories of Waterloo* (1834) and *Tales of the Peninsular War* (1837), and whose fore-mentioned *Wild Sports of the West* (1832) was a significant influence on Lever's early work. The popularity of Lever's second novel, *Charles O'Malley, the Irish Dragoon* (1841), written during his years in Brussels, consolidated his reputation as 'Harry Rollicker', the author of rollicking Irish novels. Their commercial popularity also earned Lever the title of 'Dr Quicksilver', and in October 1843 William Carleton authored a deeply critical, unsigned review in The *Nation* in which he accused Lever of 'selling us for pounds, shillings, and pence'.[48] *Charles O'Malley*, while retaining qualities of the picaresque, is a much grimmer novel; unlike *Harry Lorrequer*, whose military aspects are confined to garrison adventures, the novel presents a detailed account of many battle scenes from the Peninsular wars, culminating in the Battle of Waterloo, and, although drawn from conversation with Lever's military acquaintances in Brussels and from standard histories, and not from personal experience, was widely praised at the time for its accuracy of description. In 1842 Lever returned to Dublin to live by his writing, and became editor of the *Dublin University Magazine*, where he received a salary of £1,200 a year and succeeded, partly through the serial publication of his own novels such as *Jack Hinton* (1842) and *Loiterings of Arthur O'Leary* (1843), in raising circulation of the magazine to a peak of 4,000 copies a month.[49] In the novels of this period, Lever delivers a bitter critique of the contemporary Castle administration and viceregal court, often, as in *Jack Hinton*, through the familiar 'stranger-to-Ireland' plot. In *Tom Burke of 'Ours'* (1844), a fourteen-year-old orphan witnesses savage reprisals by the yeomanry in the post-1798 period, and as, in the words of one critic, 'the first young man in Lever to be serious',[50] is exiled to France where he joins the armies of Napoleon.

In 1845 Lever again left Ireland and ended his relationship with Curry, the Dublin publishing house. Early the next year, at work on his eighth novel, *Knight of Gwynne*, he negotiated with London publishers Chapman and Hall a fee of £130 a monthly number, a scale of remuneration equal to that of Dickens at the time;[51] however, the failure of that novel also marked the beginning of his career's decline. In many of his novels from the 1850s and 1860s, he employs a double setting of Ireland and the continent, the international locations unusual in Irish fiction of the period and a welcome relief to its readers. Such bi-location is skilfully handled in his 1856 novel *The Martins of Cro'Martin* which moves between the west of Ireland, in the early 1830s, and the Paris revolution of July 1830. Lever's portrait of post-emancipation Irish society in this novel is deeply pessimistic, prompted perhaps by a short visit to Ireland in 1854: the efforts by Mary Martin, niece of the local landowner, to restore feudal relationships are doomed, as the authority of the 'demagogue' has come to replace that of the landed proprietor and O'Connellite politics prevail.[52]

In 1858 Lever finally secured a long-desired government appointment, and served as British vice consul at La Spezia until 1867, and as consul at Trieste until his death in 1872. *Lord Kilgobbin* (1872), the last of his thirty-four published novels, moves from the Irish Bog of Allen, to scenes in London, Athens and Constantinople. Its Irish subject matter draws in detail from a variety of recent events back in Ireland: the Fenian rising of 1867, the Fenian Jeremiah O'Donovan Rossa's election to parliament while still a convicted felon, the disestablishment of the Church of Ireland, and the Land Act of 1870. Lever's deep cynicism regarding Liberal policy on Ireland is at its clearest in this novel: government strategy, in the words of one of its representatives, is 'to unsettle everything in Ireland, so that anybody might hope to be anything, or to own heaven knows what – to legalize gambling for existence to a people who delight in high play'.[53] As a result critics have seen *Lord Kilgobbin* as the most pessimistic of Lever's works and an elegiac tone, with regard to the loss of Tory hegemony, is certainly present. Yet ultimately the narrative viewpoint is curiously dispassionate, and concludes with a vision for the future as seen by Fenian leader Donogan (O'Donovan Rossa): Donogan, on the eve of his departure to America, prophesies that change for Ireland will be 'slow, but it is certain', made inevitable, not by an 'appeal to arms', but by 'chronic discontent'.[54]

Although criticised during his own lifetime and since for the degree of stereotype inherent within his 'rollicking' characters – what his contemporary Trollope termed 'rattling, jolly, joyous, swearing Irishmen' – Lever's early novels achieved a large commercial success, and what Tony Bareham has called 'the intelligent internationalism' of Lever's later writing earned him conspicuously less financial reward.[55] Carleton's early jibe would be long-lasting in appraisals of his work, reinforced by the negative view of Yeats who wrote of Lever that, like his contemporary Samuel Lover, he 'wrote ever with one eye on London'.[56] The counter-argument made by critic A. Norman Jeffares that Yeats and others 'got hold of the wrong Lever' has some persuasive power, and all too often comments on Lever's work are based only on a cursory knowledge of one or two of his early novels, and the significant changes and variations within his career are obscured.[57] Lever's self-assessment may come closest to capturing both his abilities and limitations: 'All I have attempted – all I have striven to accomplish', he wrote in 1857, 'is the faithful portraiture of character, the close analysis of motives, and correct observation as to some of the manners and modes of thought which mark the age we live in.'[58]

Lever's contemporary, Joseph Sheridan Le Fanu (1814–73), was raised in Phoenix Park, Dublin where his father was chaplain to the Royal Hibernian Military School. Related to the Sheridan family (his father's mother was a sister of Richard Brinsley Sheridan), his paternal line also included a Huguenot ancestor who had settled in Ireland during the Williamite wars, and the legacy of this historical period is a recurring concern throughout Le Fanu's fictional writings. Educated at Trinity College, Dublin where he became a friend of Isaac Butt, he qualified to the bar in 1839; his professional career was not as a lawyer, however, but as a journalist, writer of fiction and newspaper proprietor. Le Fanu was Tory in his politics and strongly anti-repeal, but his failure in 1852 to secure a parliamentary nomination saw his withdrawal from national politics. In his later life he was increasingly reclusive, known as the 'Invisible Prince', but his influence continued as the proprietor of newspapers, including the *Warden* and the *Dublin Evening Mail*, and most notably as editor and proprietor of the *Dublin University Magazine* from 1861 to 1869.

Between 1838 and 1840, Le Fanu published twelve stories in the *DUM*, the majority of which are set in eighteenth-century Ireland and draw from a variety of rural superstitions and sensational tales. 'Strange Event in the Life of Schalken the Painter' (May 1839) is the only story set outside of Ireland, the 'strange event' in the life of Schalken, a seventeenth-century Dutch minor painter, being a tale of satanic possession in which the spectral bridegroom carries away a young woman, Schalken's fiancée. As in much of Le Fanu's writing on the supernatural, the sensational is restrained by a distinctly matter-of-fact tone; thus the narrator refuses the conventional 'sentimental scenes . . . cruelty of guardians, or magnanimity of wards, or agonies of lovers', choosing instead a tale 'of sordidness, levity and interest'.[59] These stories – loosely connected as tales drawn from the private papers of one Father Purcell, a County Limerick Catholic priest and collector of folklore – were published after their author's death as *The Purcell Papers* (1880). Other supernatural stories, including 'The Evil Guest' and 'The Mysterious Lodger', were published in a Christmas collection, *Ghost Stories and Tales of Mystery* (1851).

Le Fanu's first novels were historical: *The Cock and Anchor, being A Chronicle of Old Dublin City* (1845) and *The Fortunes of Colonel Torlogh O'Brien: A Tale of the Wars of King James* (1847), the latter influenced by John Banim's *Boyne Water* (1826). In *The Cock and Anchor*, early eighteenth-century Dublin is vividly depicted as 'the capital of a rebellious and semi-barbarous country – haunted by hungry adventurers, who had lost every thing in the revolutionary wars'.[60] Early chapters give voice to the claims of the Catholic dispossessed, 'mercenaries and beggars abroad, and landless at home', against a 'perjured, corrupt, and robbing ascendancy, a warning and a wonder to all after times',[61] but the novel ultimately reads as a cautionary tale for the present, directed towards a mid-nineteenth-century aristocratic class then experiencing a sharp decline in its political power.

In 1863, the publication of *The House by the Churchyard* by London publisher Tinsley ended a break of sixteen years in Le Fanu's writing of novels; nine others followed in the next decade: *Wylder's Hand* (Bentley, 1864), *Uncle Silas* (Bentley, 1864), *Guy Deverell* (Bentley, 1865), *All in the Dark* (Bentley, 1866), *The Tenants of Malory* (Tinsley, 1867), *A Lost Name* (Bentley, 1868), *Haunted Lives* (Tinsley, 1868), *The Wyvern Mystery* (Tinsley, 1869), *Checkmate* (Hurst and Blackett, 1871), and *The Rose and the Key* (Chapman and Hall, 1871). Many of these appeared first as serial publications, and until 1869 usually in the *Dublin University Magazine*. Their plots and settings have some resemblances to those employed by contemporary sensation novelists, such as Charles Reade and Wilkie Collins, though W. J. McCormack, Le Fanu's biographer, has suggested 'commercialized romanticism' as a more accurate description.[62] In this later period, Le Fanu also produced two major collections of stories, *Chronicles of Golden Friars* (Bentley, 1871) and *In a Glass Darkly* (1872). *Willing to Die*, his last novel, was published posthumously in 1873.

The House by the Churchyard is unusual among Le Fanu's late novels in employing an Irish setting; here he turns once again to historical fiction, acknowledging the lure of the past – of its 'violence, follies, and hospitalities, softened by distance, and illuminated with a sort of barbaric splendour'.[63] Set in 1767 and employing the author's childhood memories of the Dublin village of Chapelizod, the novel provides a richly dramatic rendering of what its narrator terms the 'ululatus of many-voiced humanity'.[64] In this and in other aspects – for example, the characteristic Le Fanu plot of a man believed dead who returns to life – the novel would form an important shadow-text for Joyce's *Finnegans Wake*.

Since the influential commentary by Elizabeth Bowen, it has become customary to view *Uncle Silas*, Le Fanu's most famous long fiction, as an Irish novel transposed to an English setting, and with deep autobiographical origins. Writing in 1947, Bowen argued:

> The hermetic solitude and the autocracy of the great country house, the demonic power of the family myth, fatalism, feudalism and the 'ascendency' outlook are accepted facts of life for the race of hybrids from which Le Fanu sprang. For the psychological background of *Uncle Silas* it was necessary for him to invent nothing. Rather he was at once exploiting in art and exploring for its more terrible implications what would have been the norm of his own heredity.[65]

In the suspense-filled story of young orphan Maud Ruthyn, who is under threat of her life from her villainous relative, Le Fanu also revisited one of his earliest stories, 'Passage in the Secret History of an Irish Countess', first published in the *DUM* (November 1838). Through Maud's narration of her incarceration and release, the novel brings most clearly to light the sexual anxiety and terrors which afflict almost all of Le Fanu's heroines, from the pursuit of Mary Ashwoode in his first novel, *Cock and Anchor*, to the layered psychosexual implications of his vampire story 'Carmilla'. In this regard, one of the most significant, and still underrated, effects of Le Fanu's fiction is, in the words of critic Thomas Kilroy, its 'anatomy of domestic horror'.[66]

Le Fanu's last volume of short fiction, *In a Glass Darkly*, is a collection of five tales framed through the narrative persona of German physician Dr Martin Hesselius and includes the stories 'Green Tea', heavily influenced by Swedenborgianism, 'The Familiar' and 'Carmilla'. Originally published in *Dark Blue Magazine* in four instalments (1871–2), 'Carmilla' is a vampire story owing some of its detail to John Polidori's *The Vampyre* (1819), and to which Bram Stoker's *Dracula*, in its female characterisations in particular, is heavily indebted. Set in Styria, Austria, the story is told by a young woman, Laura, who, the prologue explains, has died 'in the interval'. Born to an English father and Styrian mother, Laura bears an English name although she has never seen England. At the story's end, Carmilla, whose 'home lay in the direction of the west', is revealed to be the vampire spirit of the long-dead Mircalla, Countess Karnstein (*fl.*1698); once again in Le Fanu's narrative imagination, the hauntings of the past owe their origin to the turbulences of the late seventeenth-century period.

Following the example of Bowen's reading of *Uncle Silas*, the concept of an Irish 'Protestant Gothic' – read as the literary expression of a socio-political caste that is haunted by the past and beleaguered in the present – has now become a critical commonplace, with Maturin, Le Fanu and Bram Stoker its most famous representatives.[67] The coherence and extent of such a tradition may be overstated, and its qualities as 'political unconscious' have certainly been overly generalised, yet the Gothic mode with its distinctive anxieties is a significant form in nineteenth-century Irish writing. Other Irish examples of the genre deserve some attention: the *DUM*, for example, published between 1834 and 1837 an eight-part series entitled *Chapters of College Romance* which included various sensationalist plots and Faustian themes. Published as the work of one 'Edward S. O'Brien', the stories were identified in 1840 as the work of Isaac Butt, editor of the magazine. The writings on the occult by Henry Ferris ('Irys Herfner'), a *DUM* contributor from 1839 to 1851, have been unjustly neglected, while the ghost stories of Charlotte Riddell find only occasional mention in existing histories.

During her lifetime, Antrim-born novelist Charlotte Riddell (1832–1906) was one of the most acclaimed writers in Britain of both sensation fiction and stories of the supernatural. Her longer ghost stories, such as 'Fairy Water' and 'The Haunted River', appeared in the highly popular Christmas annuals published by Routledge and by F. Enos Arnold. Riddell, heralded as 'Novelist of the City' because of her depictions of contemporary London business and trade, makes lively use of the strong materialist element underlying Gothic fiction: her heroes are usually lawyers' clerks and other humble functionaries who secure fortune as a result of their enduring Otherworldly visitations. Irish settings are employed in a handful of her works, including her 1888 novel *Nun's Curse*, its marriage plot between Irish landowner and peasant girl an especially pessimistic 'allegory of union', and also in some later stories, most notably 'The Banshee's Warning', also entitled 'Hertford O'Donnell's Warning', which has been frequently republished in anthologies of ghost fiction.

The case of Le Fanu, a successful novelist who remained living in Dublin, is unusual for the period, as the migration of novelists to London publishers continued apace in the years following the famine. William Carleton, for example, having quarrelled with his Dublin publisher, M'Glashan, in 1850, took much of his later work to London and appeared on the lists of London publishers Saunders and Oakley, Ward and Lock, and Hope. These years also saw the emergence of many professional female writers who moved from Ireland to

London to pursue literary careers. These writers included Frances Browne (1816–79), 'the blind poetess of Donegal' and author of highly successful children's stories, as well as novels such as *My Share of the World* (1861) and *The Hidden Sin* (1866). Frances Cashel Hoey (1830–1908) moved to London in 1855 and was the author of numerous sensational novels in the mode of her contemporaries Dickens and Wilkie Collins which were highly popular in the 1870s and 1880s. Many of these women moved to London because of family financial difficulties: the death of her father prompted the young Charlotte Cowan, later Riddell, to move to London in 1855; losses in income caused Annie Hector's family to leave Dublin for London when she was nineteen; and the Huguenot family of May Crommelin (*c.*1850–*c.*1930), later an acclaimed writer of fiction and of travel narratives, moved from Down to London when she was a child because of the 'land troubles'. Charlotte Riddell's autobiographical novel *A Struggle for Fame*, published by Bentley in 1883, is a valuable record of one young Irish author's struggle to become published, with vividly drawn portraits of Newby, Tinsley, Bentley and others. It was published when Riddell was at the peak of her career but her fortunes turned soon afterwards, with the decline in popularity of the three-decker novel, and by the late 1890s she was living in severely reduced circumstances, supported by a donation from the Society of Authors and from the Royal Literary Fund.[68]

Riddell and Hector, both highly prolific, ranked for a time among the most financially successful of Victorian novelists. Hector (1825–1902), who wrote as 'Mrs Alexander', was the author of over forty novels and, while of conventional plot, featuring sensational disappearances, reappearances and happy endings, they also include extended engagements with contemporary discourses on marriage and divorce, most notably in her novel *A Choice of Evils*, published in 1894. Relatively few of these women's writings were identifiably Irish in theme, and their commercial success clearly depended on their assimilation as 'English' authors. Irish fiction, as Trollope testified in the late 1850s, had to a large extent become 'drugs in the market'.[69] Of Hector's forty novels, only one has an explicitly Irish setting: *Kitty Costello* (1902), a quasi-autobiographical novel, detailing a young Irish girl's move to London, and completed just before its author's death. Frances Hoey, said to have displayed 'fierce nationalism' in her private letters, set few of her fictional writings in Ireland, causing novelist Rosa Mulholland to note regretfully that 'the clever books of Mrs Cashel Hoey show no trace of the fact that she is Irish of the Irish, not only by birth, but in faithful affection'.[70]

The careers of these authors included many notable controversies regarding copyright and authorship, linked in no small part to the subsequent eclipse and critical neglect of their work. Though Julia Kavanagh (1824–77) is now more likely to be remembered for her biographical studies in such work as *English Women of Letters* (1863), her novels achieved considerable popularity in their day, evidenced in the many international editions of her work published by Tauchnitz in whose lists she regularly appeared along with Hector, Hoey and Riddell. Kavanagh was born in Thurles, County Tipperary and spent much of her early life in France, which provides the scene for many of her novels, including *Madeline* (1848) and *Nathalie* (1850), an engaging coming-of-age novel praised by Charlotte Brontë and said to have influenced her *Villette*. In 1857, Kavanagh's reputation suffered when her father, Peter Morgan Kavanagh, falsely attributed his inferior novel *The Hobbies* to his daughter. In 1886 Frances Hodgson Burnett, author of children's stories such as *The Secret Garden*, began in the New York periodical *St Nicholas* a series entitled 'Stories from the Lost Fairy Book, Retold by the Child Who Read Them'. The 'lost' book was immediately revealed to be Irish author Frances Browne's well-known *Granny's Wonderful Chair and Its Tales of Fairy Times* (1856), editions of which, despite Burnett's claims to have searched unsuccessfully in both England and America, had appeared throughout the 1880s. In the case of Hoey, arguments regarding the ownership of copyright dogged her later career and her authorship of a number of novels more usually credited to the writer Edmund Yates remains a matter of dispute.

A striking exception to this pattern of migrant female novelists was Margaret Hungerford, known as 'The Duchess', who achieved a wide audience from her Bandon, County Cork home; of her thirty works of fiction, mainly sentimental fiction, the most famous was *Molly Bawn* (1878) which had large sales in England, America and Australia. In an 1893 interview Hungerford explained that 'first sheets of the novels in hand are bought from her for American publications, months before there is any chance of their being completed'.[71] Yet, for the most part, these careers – along with the careers of male writers such as Edmund Downey, Richard Dowling and Justin McCarthy – fit more or less the pattern described by Rosa Mulholland in her article, 'Wanted an Irish Novelist', published in the *Irish Monthly* in 1891: 'the noticeable fact that writers who produce one good Irish novel, giving promise of store to come, almost invariably cease to be Irish at that point, and afterwards cast the tributary stream of their powers into the universal river of English fiction'. And as Mulholland sardonically concluded, 'Yet how can we quarrel with any of these bright spirits if they prefer to live their lives pleasantly and in affluent circumstances in the busy, working, paying world of London, rather than content themselves with the ideally uncomfortable conditions of him who elects to chew the cud of sweet and bitter Irish fancies, with his feet in an Irish bog and his head in a rainbow?'[72]

England and 'the Irish Question': Mill and Arnold

'Once at least in every generation the question "What is to be done with Ireland?" rises again to perplex the councils and trouble the conscience of the British nation.' So begins John Stuart Mill's 1868 pamphlet 'England and Ireland' (1868), a text occasioned in part by the contemporary Irish Republican Brotherhood (IRB) bombing campaigns in England which culminated in the notorious Clerkenwell explosion of December 1867. To an English public believing Irish disaffection to be 'cured', Fenianism, in Mill's words, 'burst like a clap of thunder in a clear sky': 'The disaffection which they flattered themselves had been cured, suddenly shows itself more intense, more violent, more unscrupulous, and more universal.'[73] Mill's own prescription for Ireland's 'cure' was stark and immediately controversial; it also represented a significant advance from his earlier analyses of Ireland as published in the *Morning Chronicle* newspaper in the years 1846 and 1847, and also as featured in his *Principles of Political Economy* (1848) with its many subsequent editions. By 1868, in his view, the diagnosis was clear: 'The difficulty of governing Ireland lies entirely in our own minds; it is an incapability of understanding'; more specifically, and influenced by the writings of his friend the political economist John Elliot Cairnes, Mill now endorsed what he termed 'a permanent solution of the land difficulty', namely fixity of tenure for Irish tenant farmers.[74]

Unlike the Young Ireland movement, the literary output of Fenianism was not substantial; the reactions generated in English writers such as Mill and Matthew Arnold were therefore all the more influential. In the spring of 1867, Arnold's *On the Study of Celtic Literature* appeared in volume form, drawn from a series of lectures first delivered in his role as chair of poetry in Oxford and first published in four parts in the *Cornhill Magazine* between March and July 1866. The much-cited and controversial definitions of the 'Celtic genius' ('with its chafing against the despotism of fact, its perpetual straining after mere emotion') have tended to obscure the contemporary potency of the *Study's* conclusion: 'and let it be one of our angelic revenges on the Philistines, who among their other sins are the guilty authors of Fenianism, to found at Oxford a chair of Celtic, and to send, through the gentle ministration of science, a message of peace to Ireland'.[75] 'Provoked by Fenianism', Arnold may be judged to have 'lapsed into Celticism', as Seamus Deane has argued; but, as Deane also acknowledges, in the process the word 'Celtic' was given 'a political resonance which it has not yet entirely lost'.[76]

Less well known are Arnold's later, and more detailed, essays on Irish politics. His essay 'Irish Catholicism and British Liberalism', written in the context of the impending University Education (Ireland) Act of 1879, supported calls for an Irish Catholic university; first published in the *Fortnightly Review* in July 1878, it was reprinted in Arnold's *Mixed Essays* (1879). 'The Incompatibles', on the Irish Land Bill of 1881, was published in two parts in the *Nineteenth Century*, in April and June 1881, and was reprinted along with the essay 'An Unregarded Irish Grievance' – which argued for the introduction of a system of public education to Ireland – in his volume *Irish Essays, and Others* (1882). That same year, discontent with British policies in Ireland from a very different political perspective appears to have motivated the posthumous and, in Charles Gavan Duffy's view, the 'unhappy' publication of Thomas Carlyle's *Reminiscences of My Irish Journey*, a grimly pessimistic account of Carlyle's travels in Ireland in July 1849. As Froude, Carlyle's biographer, drily observed in his preface to the volume, 'The Irish problem has not yet been solved since Mr Carlyle's visit, nor has it been made more easy of solution by the policy of successive ministries, which has been precisely opposite to what Mr Carlyle would have himself recommended.'[77]

Arnold's Irish essays included liberal quotation from the writings of Edmund Burke, and in 1881 he edited for Macmillan publishers a collection of Burke's writings on Ireland, entitled *Letters, Speeches and Tracts on Irish Affairs by Edmund Burke*. Arnold's construction of an 'Irish Burke' was rare for its time and sharply different, for example, from the Burke excerpts chosen by Charles Read (chiefly from *Essay on the Sublime and Beautiful* and *Reflections on the French Revolution*) for inclusion in the second volume of the *Cabinet of Irish Literature* published just over a year before. For Arnold, the contemporary 'interest about Ireland which the present state of that country compels even the most unwilling Englishman to feel' offered the occasion for a 'rescuing' of the work of Burke simultaneously as an English classic and as an influence on future Irish policy: 'Our neglected classic is by birth an Irishman; he knows Ireland and its history thoroughly . . . He is the greatest of our political thinkers and writers. But his political thinking and writing has more value on some subjects than on others; the value is at its highest when the subject is Ireland.'[78]

Although Arnold himself has been 'rescued' by some recent English critics as a pioneer of multi-cultural theory, he is more likely to be dismissed by Irish scholars as a bourgeois hegemonist. Yet the detail of his writings on Ireland reveals more complex formulations still to be recovered. In 1886, writing to the

Freeman's Journal, the Fenian John O'Leary, who might seem an unlikely fan, concluded his list of 'best hundred Irish books' with the inclusion of 'the name of a most un-Dryasdustian sort of man, the celebrated apostle of sweetness and light'. O'Leary's comments are an interesting early intervention in Arnold's reception-history, expressing a useful balancing note and, at the same time, his own version of chauvinism: 'There are very good things in Matthew Arnold's essay on "Celtic Literature," as in many other papers of his on Ireland and things Irish; he is always more or less suggestive and mostly very sympathetic, if occasionally, as is almost invariably the case with his countrymen, more than a little patronizing.'[79] As Mary Jean Corbett has demonstrated, the writings of Mill and Arnold – both of whom sought to secure Ireland's place within an improved and reformed Union – proved to have an effect opposite to their writers' intentions, 'in that their work helped to articulate for broader publics the discursive grounds on which it [Union] would ultimately be broken'.[80]

Land, politics and fiction, 1870–1890

Charles Kickham's 1873 novel *Knocknagow; or The Homes of Tipperary* was the most widely read Irish novel in the late nineteenth century, and retained this popularity well into the twentieth century.[81] Kickham (1828–82), from Mullinahone, County Tipperary, was the son of a shopkeeper and farmer. His first writings included verse published in nationalist newspapers such as the *Nation* and the *Celt* and he worked for the Fenian paper the *Irish People* for two years until his arrest in 1865. Convicted in 1866 on a charge of 'treason-felony', he served three years of a fourteen-year sentence of imprisonment, released in 1869 on grounds of ill-health. Kickham was the author of four novels, including *Sally Cavanagh; or the Untenanted Graves* (1869) and *For the Old Land*, published posthumously in 1886. These novels are significantly less well known, partly because, as James Murphy has argued, they questioned some of the 'basic assumptions of lower middle-class Ireland', in the case of *For the Old Land* through an extensive critique of clericalism and in *Sally Cavanagh* where the resolution of the novel is achieved by the benevolent agency of the new Tory landlord, who allows his tenants to purchase their lands.[82] The emotional potency of *Sally Cavanagh* may have also discomfited readers in the first post-famine generation: its graveyard scene, in which Sally tends the 'untenanted graves' where she believes her children to be buried, deploys the force of some of the most horrific famine images, and was echoed many years later in Liam O'Flaherty's 1937 novel *Famine*.

Between 1870 and 1902 a series of Land Acts gradually transformed the ownership of Irish land, and the popularity of Kickham's novel may be read alongside this social change. The precise historical setting for the story of *Knocknagow* is difficult to determine: possibly the mid- to late 1840s, or perhaps the 1850s. The Great Famine is explicitly mentioned only once, and then only in the closing pages by an emigrant to America who denounces English rule. Yet curiously *Knocknagow* became fixed in the minds of many readers as the archetypal famine novel. One reason for this is the novel's nostalgic evocation of a pre-famine society, marked by conviviality, music and social harmony, and ruined by land clearances, evictions and emigration, events that are detailed in the narrative. The novel's best-loved character, Mat the Thrasher, who remains invulnerable to eviction because of an anomaly in the land laws, thus acquires the symbolic role of folk hero, or fairy-tale figure, but one through whom the peasant proprietorship of land may also be imagined. And, as R. V. Comerford, Kickham's biographer, has shown, the novel continued to appeal in the twentieth century, primarily to a rural, middle-class readership to whom it offered an attractive explanation of their origins as a landowning class.[83]

Knocknagow's historical depiction makes for a suggestive comparison with that provided by Kickham's contemporary Annie Keary (1825–79), whose *Castle Daly: The Story of an Irish Home Thirty Years Ago* (1875) was first serialised in *Macmillan's Magazine*. Keary's novel also looks back to the 1840s, with a direct account of the Great Famine and of the 1848 rebellion; in her novel, this period is presented as a crucial time of transition, between new systems of reform and an older, more feudal order fated to decline. The novel's dynamism comes from its lengthy, and well-sustained, dialogues between Irish and English characters, a structure that facilitates the close scrutiny of potentially abstract economic and social policies, as well as the acknowledgement of alternative perspectives. The future, however, is clearly in the hands of the English reforming and modernising agent, John Thornley. English reviewers of the novel welcomed the story as an illumination of current political problems, and the novel also enjoyed a large degree of popularity in Irish intellectual circles. The *Irish Monthly* recorded in April 1886 that Keary's novel 'was singled out by so un-English an Irishman as Mr John O'Leary, in a lecture at Cork, as singularly and almost solely worthy of high praise out of the hosts of so-called Irish novels written of late' and *The Cabinet of Irish Literature* (1879–80) judged it the best Irish story of the current generation.[84] Yet its Yorkshire-born author had spent a total of two weeks in Ireland, and the novel was based largely on her readings in Irish history, together with the recollections of her Irish-born clergyman father.[85]

The Fenian rebellions and political movement appear intermittently in late nineteenth-century fiction. Lever's *Lord Kilgobbin* (1870), one of the earliest fictional engagements, emerges also as one of the more sympathetic, when compared, for example, with Justin McCarthy's critical account in *A Fair Saxon* (1873) and Kickham's somewhat disillusioned recollections in *For the Old Land: A Tale of Twenty Years Ago* (1886). Charlotte Grace O'Brien's *Light and Shade* (1878) is by far the most comprehensive treatment of the disparate elements within the Fenian movement and repeatedly insists on the authenticity of its sources, its author the daughter of 1848 veteran, William Smith O'Brien, and herself a pioneering social reformer with regard to emigrants' conditions. Fenian characters and sub-plots contribute narrative frisson to later novels such as Rosa Mulholland's *Marcella Grace* (1886) and May Laffan's *Ismay's Children* (1887), but submerge the narrative in ponderous detail in William O'Brien's *When We Were Boys* (1890). The recurrence of Fenian-related bombing campaigns in 1880s London lent added weight to this subject, most notably the dynamite campaign organised by the US-based Clan na Gael from 1883 to 1885, which generated a body of 'dynamite fiction' in the closing decades of the nineteenth century.[86]

The land wars of 1879–81 and the later 'Plan of Campaign' agitation (1886–91), in contrast, received much sharper and more frequent contemporary attention from Irish novelists, the themes of agrarian conflict and social change appearing to lend themselves more readily to the established plots of domestic and sentimental fiction. Between 1880 and 1890, numerous 'land' novels appeared, in which contemporary facts and the conventions of fiction find, however, an often-uneasy combination. One of the first was *A Boycotted Household* (1881) by Letitia McClintock, published in London by the influential Smith and Elder publication house (also publishers of Matthew Arnold), and detailing the 'reign of terror' experienced by a landlord's family between late 1879 and early 1881, together with the boycotting of one of their tenants. Of the many novels that followed, the best-known remain Trollope's *The Landleaguers* (1883) – his last and unfinished novel, researched during two short visits to Ireland in 1882 – and George Moore's *A Drama in Muslin* (1886); others include William Upton's *Uncle Pat's Cabin* (1882), Edward Moran's *Edward O'Donnell* (1884) and Richard Ashe King's ('Basil') highly popular *The Wearing of the Green* (1886). Of the many land novels authored by women, Elizabeth Owens Blackburne Casey's *Hearts of Erin* (1882), Fannie Gallaher's *Thy Name is Truth* (1884), Rosa Mulholland's *Marcella Grace* (1886) and Emily Lawless's *Hurrish* (1886) are of particular interest, along with the 1888 novel *Plan of Campaign* by English novelist and historian Frances Mabel Robinson. McClintock's and Trollope's novels are the most avowedly hostile towards the newly formed Land League; many of the other novels are more sympathetic towards the League's objectives, though the violent actions of its members prove more difficult subject matter to handle.

Although these novels generally employ the standard plots of sentimental and domestic fiction, their deployment in the particular context of the Irish land war and land agitation results in narrative strains and 'discontents' that are especially revelatory. Fannie Gallaher's novel *Thy Name is Truth*, subtitled 'A Social Novel', moves from a richly textured portrait of upper middle-class Catholic Dublin society, to an increasingly sensational story of a landlord's assassination and wrongful accusation, culminating in the revelation of the heroine's identity as heir to the landed estates. Such a revelation ends many of these plots, usually accompanied by a marriage which, as in the case of Rosa Mulholland's *Marcella Grace*, may be read as an attempt to contain the more radical political implications released earlier in the narrative. In the case of McClintock's novel, the influential London journal *The Athenaeum* expressed its unease concerning this very combination of politics and sentimental fiction; as its reviewer wryly observed, 'Certain it is that, while dealing liberally in siege and arson and murder, Mrs McClintock has not refrained from mere flirtation, and that two of her girls are mated and married ere the Land Bill passes, and the curtain falls.'[87] Yet, read from another perspective, these novels attest to an important political role played in this period by domestic fiction, with implications that may belie the usual operations of the genre. If domestic fiction seeks, in Nancy Armstrong's words, to unfold 'the operations of human desire as if they were independent of political history', in these novels sexual and political relations remain hopelessly entangled, and the fate of individuals' desires inseparable from Ireland's political future.[88]

The subject matter of these 'factual fictions' was not without its dangers for the individual writer. In 1882, Elizabeth Owens Blackburne Casey (1848–94), born in Slane, County Meath, published her fifth novel, *The Heart of Erin*, having moved from the Tinsley publishing firm to the more respectable Sampson and Low house. By the early 1880s, she was an established journalist and novelist working in London, and wrote under the pen name 'E. O. Blackburne'. Subtitled 'An Irish Story of Today', her novel called for better understanding between England and Ireland, and offered a carefully negotiated analysis of the contemporary land agitation. Soon after the novel's appearance, however, the Phoenix Park murders of 6 May took place, and in a review published on 20 May 1882 the London *Athenaeum* castigated Blackburne as a 'thoroughgoing partisan of the Land League';[89] this proved to be the last novel published by Blackburne and she died in penury in Ireland twelve years later.

The inscriptions to these land novels often record their political ambition: the first edition of *Doreen* (1894) by English author 'Edna Lyall' (Ada Bayley) was dedicated to Prime Minister William Gladstone; Hester Sigerson's *A Ruined Race* (1889) was dedicated to Mrs Gladstone. In his 1892 work *Special Aspects of the Irish Question*, Gladstone expressed his gratitude to the young Emily Lawless for her novel *Hurrish*, which, in his view, conveyed 'not as an abstract proposition, but as a living reality, the estrangement of the people of Ireland from the law'.[90] Contemporary reviewers in the *Irish Times, Scotsman* and other journals also praised the novel for its realistic depiction of existing conditions in Ireland. In sharp contrast, the *Nation* accused Lawless of grossly exaggerating peasant violence; the newspaper's fierce denunciation of both novelist (condescending to the Irish peasant 'from the pinnacle of her three-generation nobility') and novel ('slanderous and lying from cover to cover') was to dog Lawless's critical reputation.[91] Yeats's more polite evaluation of Lawless as being 'in imperfect sympathy with the Celtic nature' would prove no less damning and enduring.[92]

Lawless's ascendancy ancestors had much more complex political loyalties: on her father's side, an earlier Lord Cloncurry was involved with the United Irishmen, and supported both Catholic emancipation and the anti-tithe campaign. Raised in England with childhood summers in the west of Ireland with her maternal relatives, Lawless (1845–1913), began writing with the encouragement of English novelist Margaret Oliphant, who was a friend of Elizabeth Kirwan, Lawless's mother. Her first novels, *A Chelsea Householder* (1882) and *A Millionaire's Cousin* (1885), are conventional sentimental fictions but of lively narration, both with artists as their central protagonists. *Ireland* – a historical survey in Unwin's 'Story of the Nations' series – appeared also in 1885. *Hurrish*, published by Blackwood in 1886, is set some five years earlier, towards the end of the 1879–81 land war, but written also in the context of the Ashbourne Land Act and of Gladstone's unsuccessful Home Rule Bill of 1886. Its cast of characters unfolds as a series of types: Hurrish, the Arnoldian Celt; his Caliban-like enemy, Mat Brady; the saintly heroine, Ally; the aboriginal, paternalist landlord, Pierce O'Brien; heroically loyal Phil Rooney; and the coming young man, Maurice Brady. Lawless's success in this early novel – developed to even greater effect in her later *Grania* (1892) – lies rather in her portrayal of place, the landscape of the novel emerging as more vibrant, and significantly more complex, than its inhabitants. From the contours of the land may be traced not only the layers of prehistory, which 'rejoice the soul of the antiquary in these Celtic solitudes', but also the bleak scars of the recent past: rocks as skeletons, 'starvation made visible, and embodied in a landscape'.[93]

Following *Hurrish*, Lawless turned to historical fiction: *With Essex in Ireland*, an account of the Irish campaign of Robert Devereux, second earl of Essex, in 1599, was published in 1890, and *Maelcho*, set during the Desmond rebellion of 1579–82, followed in 1894. In her now most acclaimed novel, *Grania*, geographical remoteness replaces historical distance as a narrative tool: the scene is Inis Meáin, the middle of the three Aran Islands, off the coast of Galway. Contemporary, international discourses on racial degeneracy permeate the story, as Gerardine Meaney has shown, and are evident in the doomed fate of its heroine whose passionate yearnings for self-fulfilment render her the most powerfully realised of Lawless's characters.[94] The novel clearly deploys a number of the traits of late nineteenth-century New Woman fiction, including progressive aspiration and pessimistic conclusions, but its portrait of social degradation has also distinct national implications not lost on the author's early critics.

The year 1886 saw the publication of another author's first novel on an Irish theme, in this case George Moore's *A Drama in Muslin*. The reputation of Moore (1852–1933), which entered a critical decline following his death, has grown in recent years,[95] but his bewildering variety of careers – as novelist, short-story author, dramatist, critic, essayist and memoirist– remains difficult to evaluate fully. Moore was the son of George Henry Moore, a Catholic MP and liberal landlord; earlier Moore ancestors were Protestant settlers to Ireland who had intermarried with Catholics in the middle of the eighteenth century. The young Moore spent much of the 1870s in Paris, returning briefly to Ireland in 1880 when the land war was at its height and in other sporadic trips during the early 1880s. His first novel, *A Modern Lover* (1883), fared poorly in Mudie's circulating library, whose monopoly on the purchase of fiction Moore denounced in his celebrated 1884 article 'Censorship' and in its extended version, the 1886 pamphlet *Literature at Nurse; or Circulating Morals*. His second novel, *A Mummer's Wife* (1885), even more directly challenged contemporary social mores, and also, as Adrian Frazier argues, introduced the Flaubertian art-novel to English fiction.[96] Partly as a response to the strictures of the contemporary publishing trade, Moore chose to publish *A Mummer's Wife* and *A Drama in Muslin* with the controversial Vizetelly firm, and each appeared as a single novel rather than in the conventional, and significantly more expensive, three-decker form. This first decade of Moore's writing career also saw the publication of his autobiographical *Confessions of a Young Man* (1888) and the essay collection *Parnell and his Island* (1887),[97] a series of satires on Irish society, many of which had been published previously in the French journal *Figaro*. The outrage generated by these scathing portraits of the Irish privileged classes, together with the negative reaction accorded to *Drama in Muslin*, ended Moore's literary engagement with Ireland for the following twelve years.

A Drama in Muslin, first serialised in the English periodical *Court and Society Review*, occupies a key place in various philosophical trajectories. Its author, educated by the writings of Mill, Wollstonecraft and Olive Schreiner, conceived it at least in part as a contribution to the contemporary 'Woman Question'; later he would emphasise its significance as a study of rational atheism, two aspects of his novel which may have contributed to his denunciation in 1887 by Charles Russell, attorney general and concerned Catholic parent, as a 'night-soil novelist'.[98] But it is its treatment of Irish politics – class, gender and national – that remains influential, told through the fate of Alice Barton and her school-mates who, in the first chapter of the novel, graduate from an English Catholic convent school and return to Irish upper middle-class society. Moore himself is said to have described *Drama in Muslin*, in a letter to his publisher Unwin, as 'the worst written' of his works; 'over written' may be a more accurate assessment of a novel laden with symbolism and visual detail.[99] On the other hand, many of the novel's most memorable details are conveyed through shadow and suggestion: for instance, the rent-paying scene in chapter 7 which unfolds alongside the adulterous affair of Mrs Barton; the depiction of the Bartons' journey to Dublin Castle, on streets lined by the urban poor; and the eviction scene which features in the novel's closing chapter and subtly undercuts the story's resolution. In a passage that echoes the tones of a George Eliot narrator, Moore provides his own meta-fictional commentary on the work:

> The history of a nation as often lies hidden in social wrongs and domestic griefs as in the story of revolution, and if it be for the historian to narrate the one, it is for the novelist to dissect and explain the other; and who would say which is of the most vital importance – the thunder of the people against the oppression of the Castle, or the unnatural sterility, the cruel idleness of mind and body of the muslin martyrs who cover with their white skirts the shames of Cork Hill?[100]

And yet this passage has also a mischievous quality, tempting a reader into a false hierarchy and impossible separation. Instead, Moore's skill as a novelist lies in his unerring detection of connections between social oppression and political sterility, evidenced in the 'mummery in muslin' endured by Alice Barton and the general degeneration of Irish society. Its closing chapter presents Alice as a moderately successful novelist, living a life of 'dull well-to-do-ness' in 'typical

England', a society whose foul underside Moore would in turn expose in his best-known novel *Esther Waters* (1894).

Moore's depiction of contemporary Dublin society is one of the novel's most memorable features, ranking with Le Fanu's historical depictions in the power of its urban scenes. Two female writers in this period also made a significant, and since neglected, contribution to the development of an Irish tradition of urban realism. In 1880, the *Cabinet of Irish Literature* hailed May Laffan (Hartley) as 'to some extent the precursor of a new school in Irish fiction'.[101] Her first novel, *Hogan MP* (1876), provides a sharply observed portrait of contemporary middle-class society in a manner that may have influenced Kate O'Brien's Mellick scenes. Between 1876 and 1887, Laffan published four other novels and three volumes of short fiction. Laffan and her contemporary, Fannie Gallaher (who occasionally wrote under the pseudonym 'Sydney Starr'), were also the pioneers of 'slum fiction' in Irish settings. In 1879 Laffan published 'Flitters, Tatters and the Counsellor', a day in the lives of three street children, which ran to six editions in Ireland and England and at least two in America within the first year of publication, and was approvingly cited by John Ruskin and by Yeats. Gallaher's sketch *Katty the Flash. A Mould of Dublin Mud*, which appeared the following year, is a more satirical portrait – in this case of two street vendors, mother and daughter – and approaches the grotesque at moments in the narrative. Overall, Laffan's work is the more deserving of attention, and challenges the prevalent view of fiction of this period as only rural in subject. Of her depiction of Dublin merchant life and petty politics, Robert Lee Woolf, an early champion of Laffan's work, noted that 'the nineteenth century has at last caught up with Ireland and the spectacle is not pretty'.[102]

Irish drama, 1830–1890

In 1842 the paucity of Irish drama, as evidenced by advertisements in Dublin newspapers, led to the following criticism by visitor W. M. Thackeray: 'Only one instance of Irish talent do we read of, and that, in a desponding tone, announces its intention of leaving its native country. All of the rest of the plea-sures of the evening are importations from cockney-land.'[103] That same year, the poor houses in Dublin theatres led the manager of Dublin's Theatre Royal, 'J. W. Calcraft' (stage name of John William Cole), to issue an appeal to the city's citizens 'not to suffer their national theatre to be extinguished'.[104] Yet, as Cole himself later attested, Irish-born dramatists, both past and present, were 'numerous and eminent', if not currently evident on Dublin stages. His eleven-part 'Dramatic Writers of Ireland' series, published in the *Dublin University*

Magazine in 1855–6, provides an invaluable guide to the history of Irish-born dramatists up to 1850, told through biographical sketches of numerous individuals, extending from Henry Burnell and Roger Boyle to Cole's own contemporaries Samuel Lover, J. Stirling Coyne and James Sheridan Knowles.[105]

In the years after 1830, the number of theatrical venues available in Ireland increased significantly. Dublin's Theatre Royal, Hawkins Street, running since 1821, provided audiences with the staple offerings of Shakespearean drama, grand opera (mostly Italian), visiting 'English opera' companies, and annual pantomime. The opening of the Queen's Royal Theatre on Great Brunswick Street in 1844 challenged the dominant position enjoyed by the Theatre Royal (although it would not be until the arrival of manager James W. Whitbread in 1884 that the Queen's 'golden age' would commence). Theatres Royal were founded in Wexford in 1830 and in Limerick in 1841, and in 1866 Cork's Athenaeum Theatre (later Opera House) opened.[106] Also at this time, the careers of two Irish lyric composers, Michael William Balfe (1808–70) and William Vincent Wallace (1812–65), flourished, Balfe's light opera *The Bohemian Girl* (1843) and Edward Fitzball's *Maritana* (1845) proving enduring favourites with Dublin audiences.[107] In 1871, the new Gaiety Theatre staged Goldsmith's *She Stoops to Conquer* as its first production, and over the next decades brought to Dublin both contemporary plays and touring companies from London theatres together with established classics, most notably numerous Shakespearean productions.

On the one hand, such fare differed little from that provided by London theatres at the time; on the other hand, the annals of Dublin theatre feature occasional reminders of specific Irish conditions and concerns. In 1843, the season of Italian opera was cancelled at the Theatre Royal, as a result of 'the great political agitation then existing, which so frightened the Italian Artistes they demanded so much additional terms, there would be no Italian opera that season'.[108] As late as 1870, visits to Dublin by Irish-born acting stars, including Barry Sullivan and Shiel Barry, brought the familiar complaint as to the many artists 'whom the Dublin audience left for a London audience to "find out"'.[109] And as Martin Meisel has noted, Dublin theatre in the 1870s – as experienced by the young George Bernard Shaw, for example – was an 'earlier' theatre than that of its London contemporaries, preserving for longer the 'conventions, modes, techniques and genres' of popular theatre.[110]

The interrelation of drama and novel in the early decades of the nineteenth century, as traced by Claire Connolly in chapter 10, continued until the middle of the nineteenth century but with a clear decline evident in the fortunes of classical tragedy and classical drama. In 1835 a benefit performance for the ailing John Banim was held at Dublin's Theatre Royal; two years later, his historical drama *Sylla the Dictator*, declined by London managers, was staged unsuccessfully in Dublin. *Eily O'Connor*, an early stage adaptation of Griffin's *The Collegians*, was a success for the Theatre Royal in 1834.[111] In 1842 Griffin's verse tragedy *Gisippus*, never staged during his lifetime, was performed posthumously both at Drury Lane and Dublin, with William Macready playing the title role; while well received, it failed to impress a wider audience and was revived rarely.

The dramatic career of newcomer Samuel Lover was significantly more successful. In 1831, Cole, then in his second season as manager of the Theatre Royal, commissioned *Grana Uile; or The Island Queen*, as an 'original operatic drama on an Irish subject, in which unhackneyed melodies should be freely intermixed'.[112] Lover went on to produce eight dramatic pieces in total, seven of which were musical dramas, whose commercial appeal was largely built on their popular melodies. Of these the biggest hit was *Rory O'More*, dramatised from Lover's own novel, which ran for over a hundred nights at London's Adelphi Theatre in its first season in 1837 and was staged in many of the provincial theatres throughout the country; in 1838 it was a large hit in Dublin with the main part played for some of this run by famous nineteenth-century actor Tyrone Power. A year later, the Adelphi had another popular success with Anna Hall's *Groves of Blarney*, adapted for the stage by the novella's author in collaboration with Power; following a long season at the Adelphi, it toured throughout Britain and travelled also to Ireland and America. It received a very successful revival at Dublin's Queen's Theatre in 1854. As with Lover's work, much of its appeal came from its popular songs, including 'The Blarney', 'Aileen Mavourneen' and 'Irish Invitation'.

In the midst of this successful run of fiction writers turned dramatists, one since-lost play provides a suggestive exception. In 1841 Cole urged William Carleton, then at the peak of his career, to try his hand at dramatic writing, and a three-act comedy was hastily produced called *Irish Manufacturer, or Bob MacGawley's Project*, which opened on 25 March 1841. As Cole recalled later, expectation was high because of the celebrity of its author. While billed as comedy, in the play itself pathos predominated: the scene of a family starving for want of work was 'wrought up with an appalling strength which absolutely startled the audience' and had, Cole conceded, a 'reality' that was 'too painfully explicable to existing facts to prove either agreeable or attractive'. Its author could not be induced to repeat the experience.[113]

As Christopher Morash has observed, 'If there was a problem with the Irish theatre in the middle decades of the nineteenth century, it was not the problem of finding an audience; it was the problem of finding an Irish repertoire.'[114] Thackeray's criticism was thus largely accurate: as noted above, most productions in Irish theatres were English in origin and, conversely, Irish-born dramatists moved themselves and their careers as quickly as possible to London and to the wider dramatic and economic opportunities offered by the English stage. One example is that of Joseph Stirling Coyne (1803–68), born in Birr, County Offaly, who moved to England in 1837. By 1856, Coyne had authored over fifty plays, including farces, comedies and burlesques, and specialised in topical drama on themes such as 'Our National Defences' and 'Railway Bubbles'. Only one of his plays contained an Irish character, however. This character appeared in a play called *The Tipperary Legacy*, and proved, not unlike Haffigan in G. B. Shaw's *John Bull's Other Island*, to be a 'Saxon' in disguise. During the 1830s and 1840s Cork-born and now London-based James Sheridan Knowles, his reputation secured by historical drama and tragedies, turned to newly popular domestic themes; meanwhile revivals of his most popular works, *Virginius* (1820) and *Brian Boroimhe* (1811), took place in London and in the United States.[115]

The most characteristic form of popular theatre in Victorian England and Ireland was melodrama, laden with dramatic spectacle; its elaboration, along with the other strongly visual modes of farce, pantomime, extravagance and burlesque, was facilitated by more complex stagecraft and more detailed scenic, quasi-pictorial settings. This popular drama continued to employ Irish material throughout the nineteenth century: Irish characters appeared sporadically in English drama, for example in John Baldwin Buckstone's *Green Bushes; or, A Hundred Years Ago*, produced in London's Adelphi Theatre in 1845, and frequent use was made of Irish settings in pantomime and melodrama. The recurrence of plays with an Irish subject in certain English theatres might usefully be linked to the tastes of individual managers, as Heinz Kosok has suggested,[116] one case being the frequency of 'Irish plays' in London's Adelphi Theatre in the decades preceding its 1860 triumph with *The Colleen Bawn*.

Undoubtedly the master of Victorian melodrama was actor, manager, designer and playwright Dion Boucicault (1820–90), now the most renowned nineteenth-century Irish dramatist. In 1861, following major successes in the 1840s and early 1850s in London with plays such as *London Assurance* (1841), and later in New York with such plays as *The Poor of New York* (1857) and *The Octoroon* (1859), he returned triumphantly to Ireland with the opening of his *Colleen Bawn* (loosely based on Griffin's *The Collegians*) at the Theatre Royal, Hawkins Street on 1 April.[117] Numerous parodies of the play followed almost immediately, including H. J. Byron's burlesque *Eily O'Connor* at Drury Lane in 1861, and Brough and Halliday's farce *The Colleen Bawn Settled at Last* at the Lyceum the following year. The fashion towards Irish material also benefited Boucicault's fellow actor Edmund Falconer (born Edmund O'Rourke) (1814–79) who was the author of *Peep O'Day; or Savoureen Deelish* (1861), adapted from a short story by John Banim, and set in 1798. A later play by Falconer, *Eileen Oge* (1871), became a success in Ireland at the end of the century with frequent revivals by Whitbread at the Queen's Theatre. Three years after the first Irish production of *Colleen Bawn*, Boucicault's *Arrah-na-Pogue*, set in 1798, premiered in Dublin (November 1864) and ran in London the following year, with later productions in North America, France and Australia; in 1874 *The Shaughraun*, the last in his Irish trilogy of melodramas, opened in New York. The simultaneous popularity of Boucicault's work in Ireland and England, as well as the United States, may, as Stephen Watt rightly warns, occlude the different reasons for the plays' success, as well as their 'chameleon-like' appeal to audiences of various political persuasions.[118]

By the late nineteenth century, the renewed popularity of Irish themes is evidenced by the career of Hubert O'Grady (1841–99). Born in Limerick and trained as an upholsterer, O'Grady became a famous actor and manager. In 1876–7 he came to the attention of Dublin audiences in the role of Conn in Boucicault's *The Shaughraun*. As manager of the 'Irish National Company', O'Grady and his wife toured Ireland, England and Scotland, where performances included O'Grady's own plays, most famously his melodramas with Irish subjects: *Eviction* (1879), *Emigration* (1880), *The Famine* (1886) and *The Fenian* (1888). *The Famine* and *The Fenian* attracted huge audiences at the Queen's Theatre into the early years of the twentieth century; in 1902, for example, three O'Grady plays were staged there. The fortunes of the Queen's in the last decades of the nineteenth century were built on regular revivals of Boucicault and O'Grady, along with the plays of its manager, J. W. Whitbread (1847–1916), who took over the running of the theatre in 1884. Whitbread wrote some fifteen Irish plays, including *The Nationalist* (1891) and, in the years after 1890, a number of plays dealing with the 1798 rising.[119]

O'Grady's work is an important reminder of the existence and significance of popular theatre on Irish themes prior to the formation of the Irish Literary Theatre and Abbey Theatre.[120] The popularity of his play *The Famine*, for example, casts some light on how a 'social memory' of famine was constructed and transferred in the late nineteenth century. The long prologue to the play places it in rural Ireland in 1881 at the time of the Irish Land League and No Rent Manifesto, and thus invokes the distress and famine experienced in parts of Ireland in 1879 and 1880 – very recent events for the play's first audiences.

The famine tableau that ends this scene also draws heavily on associations with the 'Great Famine' of the 1840s, and firmly establishes the play's central theme – that the suffering of a previous generation shapes the present. The closing line of the play, voiced by the soldier son recently returned from India, underscores this:

> 'And if you will only look back to the years gone by, you cannot but be convinced that all our trials and troubles can be traced to the great distress during *The Famine*' – 'picture-curtain – end'.

O'Grady's plays, performed in Dublin nearly every year from 1877 until his death in 1899, were still performed regularly to 1907, and occasionally in the following decade.

Critical constructions of nineteenth-century Irish literature

In the last two decades of the nineteenth century, the question 'what do the Irish read?' was a recurring topic among literary commentators, in both English and Irish periodicals.[121] The large volume of correspondence received by the *Freeman's Journal* in March 1886, in response to author and historian Richard Barry O'Brien's essay on the subject of 'The Best Hundred Irish Books', provides a rich array of answers. O'Brien, writing under the pen name 'Historicus', weighed his choices heavily in favour of historical writing, an emphasis which his many respondents – over forty in total, and including well-known figures such as Justin McCarthy, Matthew Russell, Charlotte Grace O'Brien, William Lecky and Samuel Ferguson – were quick to point out. Novelists qualified for inclusion on O'Brien's list only because 'the novelist who portrays national character and manners is in some degree historian too, and must not be forgotten'. His selections of Edgeworth, Banim, Griffin and Carleton are thus unsurprising; Lever he judged to be entitled to a distinguished place among Irish novelists, 'as an artist', but disqualified from the list of 'best Irish' books by his 'caricatures' – a dismissal which would become prevalent among critics of Lever over the next decade.[122]

In the letters that followed – printed in the *Freeman's Journal* over a two-week period beginning 23 March, and soon after republished in pamphlet form – contributors suggested numerous additions to O'Brien's selections, including his choice of novelists. The authors most frequently recommended are Annie Keary, May Laffan Hartley, and Charles Kickham for his novel *Knocknagow* (1879). *Hurrish*, only recently published, was nominated by Trinity

College historian William Lecky and vehemently opposed by *Irish Monthly* editor Matthew Russell because of what he saw as its 'atrocious' depiction of Irish peasant motherhood, as well as its 'caricature of Irish dialect'. Drawing from his considerable knowledge of contemporary writing, Russell himself made the longest supplement of Irish novelists, adding works by Keary, Kickham, Margaret Brew, Richard Ashe King and Richard Dowling. Meanwhile, readers of the *Irish Fireside*, in response to that journal's rival theme of 'fifty Irish works', also nominated the novels of Kickham, along with Rosa Mulholland's recently published *Wild Birds of Killeevy* (1883), and a host of Lever titles.

Other illuminating insights into the construction of a tradition of Irish writing at this period may be obtained from the four-volume *Cabinet of Irish Literature* (1879–80). The anthology, produced by Blackie publishers in an expensive and handsome 'super-royal octavo' edition, was largely the work of author and journalist Charles Read (1841–78), who did not live to see it published; the fourth volume was completed by T. P. O'Connor, newly elected Nationalist MP for Galway, with the assistance of Read's widow. The subtitle promised readers 'selections from the work of the chief poets, orators, and prose writers of Ireland' – oratorical writing, given the political climate of the time, being a special selling point. In relation to its choice of prose writers, the contents of the *Cabinet* are impressively diverse, not only in terms of the ideological stance of the authors selected but also in relation to the genres featured. Oratorical writing ranged from an 1876 speech by Isaac Butt on the subject of land tenure, and the courtroom orations of James Whiteside (defence counsel for Daniel O'Connell and Charles Gavan Duffy), to House of Commons speeches by politician Hugh Cairns on Anglo-Indian affairs. The scientific writings of Dionysius Lardner and William Rowan Hamilton (both professors of astronomy) accompanied an extract, entitled 'Scientific Limit of the Imagination', from the highly controversial, pro-Darwinian address delivered by John Tyndall (born in County Carlow) to the British Association in Belfast, August 1874. Orientalist writings – from J. L. Porter (professor of biblical criticism and opponent of Tyndall), Richard Burton (most famous as translator of *Arabian Nights*) and Meadows Taylor (author of the 1872 'Indian mutiny' novel *Seeta*) – as well as travel writing and military memoirs also featured strongly in the *Cabinet*'s contents.

In 1902, poet and fiction-writer Katharine Tynan published a revised edition of the *Cabinet of Irish Literature* in which the richness and variety of the Read/O'Connor selection of writings were reduced significantly. Tynan's omissions were in some part ideological and in large part pragmatic, given the publisher's requirement that she reduce the previous four volumes to three and add a new volume of her own. The narrowing of genre that occurs in this edition – evident in the omission of most oratorical and travel writings, and all of the scientific material, for example – is also symptomatic of wider aesthetic developments at the time, and Tynan's understanding of 'literature' to mean fiction, poetry and drama would match that employed for much of the twentieth century. In contrast, the first edition of the *Cabinet* is an important reminder of the breadth of material that the term 'Irish literature', as late as 1879–80, could signify, a breadth of inclusion that later histories of Irish literature and writing would struggle to re-establish.

Alongside the contraction in 'literature' that occurred during this period, a significant devaluation of the nineteenth-century Irish novel took place. The roll call of nineteenth-century novelists deemed worthy of consideration shrank visibly by the century's end: thus in her 1902 revised edition of the *Cabinet*, Katharine Tynan stated decisively that 'not much happened between 1848 and 1878', a view shared by successive studies of nineteenth-century Irish writing. By 1903, Horatio Krans's analysis of 'Irish life in fiction' could unapologetically deal with only the first half of the nineteenth century, and many later critics would follow his example. The influence of Yeats was again crucial here: in his famous lists of Irish books, published in the *Daily Express* and *Bookman* in February and October 1895 respectively, and more generally in his critical writings, Yeats helped to shape an evaluation of the nineteenth-century novel that continues in critical currency. For example, in his 1891 two-volume anthology, *Representative Irish Tales*, only one living writer – Rosa Mulholland – was featured, and those fictional tales that were included (Carleton, Lover, Lever, Kickham, etc.) were intended to be 'illustrative of some phase of Irish life', with the collection overall offered as 'a kind of social history'.[123]

Following Yeats, the perceived sociological character of nineteenth-century Irish fiction was quickly made by Revival critics into an argument for the aesthetic inferiority of these novels, in contrast to the ascending status of drama in the period. Writing in 1897, in an essay entitled 'Novels of Irish Life in the Nineteenth Century', Stephen Gwynn expressed his regret that 'literature in Ireland is almost inextricably connected with considerations foreign to art'. Gwynn criticised nineteenth-century writers specifically in this regard, objecting to what he called their 'morbid national sensitiveness' and the consequent 'insincerity and special pleading which has been the curse of Irish or Anglo-Irish literature'.[124] In 1904, also writing with regard to the Irish novel, Maurice Egan went further in his criticisms: the new movement 'expressing itself in Irish literature today', he argued, was sharply different – and superior – to 'that movement which influenced the Irish novelists of the eighteenth and nineteenth centuries', the differences being that the new movement 'is not a movement of reaction', it is not 'purely social', and in it 'art counts for much'.[125]

A century later, the revival of interest in nineteenth-century Irish writers that began in the mid-1990s would turn the terms of many of these complaints into literary virtues. Gwynn's declaration that 'Irishmen have always shown a strong disinclination to pure literature' became a badge of honour for Irish writing, and the Irish novel's 'anomalous' relationship to the realist tradition was celebrated at length in critical studies. Yet, even in this new critical climate, a discomfort with what Yeats had termed the 'imperfect' influence of nineteenth-century writing still lingers, whereby the nineteenth-century novel may be redeemed as 'Irish' only by its realist failures, or by its proto-modernist forms. Nor has the choice of post-1830 authors now deemed worthy of critical consideration changed notably from that made by 'Historicus', Yeats and their contemporaries – a handful of writers featuring in all cases. Only with a fuller knowledge of what was written can we accurately assess the 'difference' of nineteenth-century Irish writing, not only within an Irish–English axis but also through other comparative studies which await attention: be it comparisons with contemporary developments in Scottish writing, with nineteenth-century Canadian and American literature, or beyond European metropolitan centres to other colonial histories.[126] To conclude, the range of prose writing that was produced by Irish writers in English from 1830 to 1890, and the complexity of its origins and influences, extends far beyond the constructions that have been offered by its critics to date.

Notes

1. Maria Edgeworth to Michael Pakenham Edgeworth, 19 February 1834; reproduced in Frances Edgeworth, *A Memoir of Maria Edgeworth*, 3 vols. (privately printed, 1867), III, pp. 87–8.
2. Lady Morgan (Sydney Owenson), *The Book of the Boudoir*, 2 vols. (London: Henry Colburn, 1829), I, p. vii.
3. Yeats to Matthew Russell, [early] December 1889; reprinted in *The Collected Letters of W. B. Yeats, vol. 1: 1865–1895*, ed. John Kelly (Oxford: Clarendon Press, 1986), pp. 198–200.
4. Thomas Flanagan, 'Literature in English, 1801–91', in W. E. Vaughan, ed. *New History of Ireland, vol. V: Ireland under the Union I, 1801–1870* (Oxford: Clarendon Press, 1989), pp. 482–522, p. 509.
5. See for example Rosa Mulholland, 'Wanted an Irish Novelist', *Irish Monthly* 19 (July 1891), pp. 368–73.
6. See David Lloyd, *Anomalous States: Irish Writing and the Post-Colonial Moment* (Dublin: Lilliput, 1993), pp. 125–62; Terry Eagleton, *Heathcliff and the Great Hunger: Studies in Irish Culture* (London: Verso, 1995), pp. 145–225.

7. W. B. Yeats, 'First Principles', *Samhain* 7 (November 1908), p. 8; reprinted in *Explorations* (1962; London: Macmillan, 1989), pp. 231–44.
8. *Irish Monthly Magazine* 1, 5 (September 1832), p. 333.
9. W. J. McCormack, 'The Intellectual Revival (1830–1850)', in Seamus Deane, general ed. *The Field Day Anthology of Irish Writing*, 3 vols. (Derry: Field Day, 1991), I, pp. 1173–1300, p. 1200.
10. 'Past and Present State of Literature in Ireland', *Dublin University Magazine (DUM)* 9 (March 1837), p. 371; W. J. McCormack has attributed this essay to *DUM* editor Isaac Butt; see McCormack, 'The Intellectual Revival', p. 1200.
11. William Carleton, 'General Introduction', *Traits and Stories of the Irish Peasantry*, new edn, 2 vols. (Dublin and London: Curry and Orr, 1843–4), I, p. v.
12. Charles Benson, 'Printers and Booksellers in Dublin 1800–1850', in Robin Myers and Michael Harris, eds. *Spreading the Word: The Distribution Networks of Print, 1550–1850* (Winchester: St Paul's Bibliographies, 1990), pp. 47–59, p. 57.
13. McCormack, 'The Intellectual Revival', p. 1176.
14. *DUM* 6 (December 1835), p. 710; cited by Wayne Hall, *Dialogues in the Margin: A Study of the Dublin University Magazine* (Washington, DC: Catholic University of America Press, 1999), pp. 15–16.
15. *DUM* 41 (January 1853), p. 3; cited in Hall, *Dialogues*, p. 14.
16. Norman Vance, *Irish Literature since 1800* (London: Longman, 2002), p. 78.
17. Hall, *Dialogues*, p. 108.
18. See Barbara Hayley , 'A Reading and Thinking Nation: Periodicals as the Voice of Nineteenth-Century Ireland', in Barbara Hayley and Enda McKay, eds. *Three Hundred Years of Irish Periodicals* (Mullingar: Lilliput Press, 1987), pp. 29–48, pp. 37–8.
19. Cited in Hayley's invaluable 'British Critical Reception of Nineteenth-Century Anglo-Irish Fiction', in Wolfgang Zach and Heinz Kosok, eds. *Literary Interrelations: Ireland, England and the World*, 3 vols. (Tübingen: G. Narr, 1987), I, pp. 39–50, p. 39.
20. Ina Ferris, *The Romantic National Tale and the Question of Ireland* (Cambridge: Cambridge University Press, 2002), p. 131.
21. The phrase is Katie Trumpener's; see her *Bardic Nationalism: The Romantic Novel and the British Empire* (Princeton: Princeton University Press, 1997), p. 17.
22. *Tait's Edinburgh Magazine* 2, 11 (February 1833), p. 554; cited in Hayley, 'British Critical Reception', p. 46.
23. William Carleton, *Autobiography* (1896; new edition Belfast: White Row Press, 1996), pp. 18–19. Carleton's unfinished autobiography was first published, posthumously, in 1896, along with an account of his later life and writings by D. J. O'Donoghue. This first edition, published by Downey, included an introduction by Frances Cashel Hoey; later editions featured forewords by Patrick Kavanagh (1968) and, more recently, by the novelist Benedict Kiely (1996).
24. Cited by Christopher Morash, *Writing the Irish Famine* (Oxford: Oxford University Press, 1995), p. 157. As Morash shows, Carleton's family may be better classified as 'solid "middle-rate farmers" . . . who enjoyed what would have been a comfortable standard of living for the period' (p. 158).
25. See Norman Vance, *Irish Literature: A Social History* (1990; Dublin: Four Courts Press, 1999), pp. 148–9.

26. Maureen Keane, *Mrs S. C. Hall: A Literary Biography* (Gerrards Cross: Colin Smythe, 1997), pp. 4–5.
27. Riana O'Dwyer, 'Women's Narratives, 1800–1840', in Bourke et al., *Field Day Anthology of Irish Writing.* v, pp. 833–94, p. 847.
28. Anna Maria Hall, *The Whiteboy*, 2 vols. (1845; reprinted New York: Garland Press, 1979), II, p. 8.
29. Martineau visited Ireland for four months in 1831; in 1852 she returned on a commisson for the *Daily News* paper. The 1852 letters are republished in Glenn Hooper, ed. *Letters from Ireland: Harriet Martineau* (Dublin: Irish Academic Press, 2001).
30. Charlotte Tonna, *The Rockites* (London: Nisbet, 1829), pp. 1–2.
31. Thomas Carlyle, 'Chartism' (1839); reprinted in Thomas Carlyle, *English and Other Critical Essays* (London: Dent, 1964), pp. 182, 185.
32. Charles Gavan Duffy, *Conversations with Carlyle* (London: Sampson Low, 1892), p. 5.
33. Carlyle, 'Chartism', p. 181.
34. Amy E. Martin, 'Blood Transfusions: Constructions of Irish Racial Difference, the English Working Class, and Revolutionary Possibility in the Work of Carlyle and Engels', *Victorian Literature and Culture* 32, 1 (2004), pp. 83–102, p. 92.
35. Gustave de Beaumont, *Ireland: Social, Political and Religious*, trans. W. C. Taylor, 2 vols. (London: Bentley, 1839), I, pp. 276–87.
36. Ibid., II, p. 115.
37. De Beaumont, *Ireland*, I, p. 268. J. G. Kohl, *Travels in Ireland* (1843; trans. London: Bruce and Wyld, 1844), pp. 86–7.
38. Samuel and Anna Hall, *Ireland: Its Scenery and Character*, 3 vols. (London: How and Parsons, 1841–3), I, p. iv.
39. Headquarters of the London book trade.
40. William M. Thackeray, *The Irish Sketchbook 1842* (1843; Gloucester: Alan Sutton, 1990), p. 250.
41. William Carleton, *The Black Prophet* (1847; Shannon: Irish Academic Press, 1972), pp. 220–1.
42. Morash, *Writing the Irish Famine*, p. 186.
43. See Margaret Kelleher, *The Feminization of Famine: Expressions of the Inexpressible?* (Cork and Durham, NC: Cork University Press and Duke University Press, 1997), chapter 2.
44. *Transactions of the Central Relief Committee of the Society of Friends during the Famine in Ireland, in 1846 and 1847* (Dublin: Hodges and Smith, 1852), p. 38.
45. Trollope's first two novels set in Ireland were *The Macdermots of Ballycloran* (1847) and *The Kellys and the O'Kellys* (1848), both commercial failures; his other Irish novels were *An Eye for an Eye* (1879) and the unfinished *Landleaguers* (1883).
46. Anthony Trollope, *Castle Richmond* (1860; Oxford: World's Classics, 1989), p. 489.
47. Margaret Brew, *The Chronicles of Castle Cloyne,* 3 vols. (1884; reprinted New York: Garland Press, 1979), I, p. viii.
48. *Nation*, 7 October 1843, p. 826.
49. See Hall, *Dialogues in the Margin*, pp. 108–13.
50. Tony Bareham, 'Introduction' to Bareham, ed. *Charles Lever: New Evaluations* (Gerrards Cross: Colin Smythe, 1991), p. 9.

51. John Sutherland, *Victorian Novelists and Publishers* (Chicago: University of Chicago Press, 1976), pp. 162–3; cited in S. P. Haddelsey, *Charles Lever: The Lost Victorian* (Gerrards Cross: Colin Smythe, 2000), p. 17.

52. The novel is in turn loosely based on the biography of Mary Martin, the 'Princess of Connemara', whose family, known for its humanitarian work, was bankrupted during the famine; Mary, author of the novel *Julia Howard* (1850), died in France in 1850.

53. Charles Lever, *Lord Kilgobbin* (1872; republished Belfast: Appletree Press, 1992), p. 170.

54. Ibid., p. 415.

55. See Bareham, 'Introduction', pp. 7–9.

56. W. B. Yeats, 'Popular Ballad Poetry of Ireland' (1889), reprinted in John P. Frayne, ed. *Uncollected Prose by W. B. Yeats*, 2 vols. (London: Macmillan, 1970), I, pp. 146–62, p. 162.

57. See A. Norman Jeffares, 'Yeats and the Wrong Lever', in Jeffares, ed. *Yeats, Sligo and Ireland* (Totowa, NJ: Barnes and Noble, 1980), pp. 98–111, p. 110.

58. Lever, preface to *The Fortunes of Glencore* (1857); cited by Bareham, 'Introduction', pp. 11–12.

59. 'Strange Event in the Life of Schalken the Painter', *DUM* 13 (May 1839), p. 587.

60. Le Fanu, *The Cock and Anchor*, 3 vols. (1845; reprinted New York: Garland Press, 1979), I, pp. 133–4.

61. Ibid: I, p. 20.

62. W. J. McCormack, *Sheridan Le Fanu and Victorian Ireland* (Oxford: Clarendon Press, 1980; 2nd edn, Dublin: Lilliput Press, 1991), p. 253.

63. Le Fanu, *The House by the Churchyard* (1863; reprinted Belfast: Appletree Press, 1992), p. 3.

64. Ibid., p. 343.

65. Elizabeth Bowen, preface to *Uncle Silas* (London: Cresset Press, 1947), reproduced in *The Mulberry Tree: Writings of Elizabeth Bowen*, selected and introduced by Hermione Lee (London: Harcourt Brace Jovanovich, 1986), p. 101.

66. Thomas Kilroy, introduction to 1992 reprint of *The House by the Churchyard*, p. xiii.

67. See R. F. Foster, 'Protestant Magic: W. B. Yeats and the Spell of Irish History', in Foster, *Paddy and Mr Punch: Connections in Irish and English History* (London: Penguin, 1993), pp. 212–32; Seamus Deane, *Strange Country: Modernity and Nationhood in Irish Writing since 1790* (Oxford: Clarendon Press, 1997), p. 85; Margot Gayle Backus, *The Gothic Family Romance: Heterosexuality, Child Sacrifice, and the Anglo-Irish Colonial Order* (Durham, NC: Duke University Press, 1999), pp. 109–43.

68. See Margaret Kelleher, 'Charlotte Riddell's *A Struggle for Fame*: The Field of Women's Literary Production', *Colby Quarterly* 36, 2 (2000), pp. 116–31.

69. Trollope, *Castle Richmond*, pp. 1–2.

70. Mulholland, 'Wanted an Irish Novelist', p. 369.

71. See Helen Black, *Notable Women Authors of the Day* (Glasgow: Bryce, 1893), p. 113.

72. Mulholland, 'Wanted an Irish Novelist', pp. 369–70.

73. John Stuart Mill, 'England and Ireland' (1868), republished in John M. Robson, ed. *Collected Works of John Stuart Mill*, 33 vols. (London: Routledge and Kegan Paul, 1982), VI, pp. 507, 508.

74. Ibid., pp. 529, 532.

75. Matthew Arnold, *On the Study of Celtic Literature* (London: Smith and Elder, 1867), pp. 103, 181.

76. Seamus Deane, *A Short History of Irish Literature* (London: Hutchinson, 1986), p. 85; Deane, *Celtic Revivals* (1985; Winston-Salem, NC: Wake Forest University Press, 1987), p. 22.

77. J. A. Froude, preface to Thomas Carlyle, *Reminiscences of My Irish Journey in 1849* (London: Sampson Low, 1882), p. vii.

78. *Letters, Speeches and Tracts on Irish Affairs by Edmund Burke*, collected and arranged by Matthew Arnold (London: Macmillan, 1881), preface, pp. vi–vii. Republished as *Irish Affairs: Edmund Burke*, with an introduction by Conor Cruise O'Brien (London: Cresset, 1988).

79. See R. Barry O'Brien, ed. *Best Hundred Irish Books by 'Historicus'* (Dublin: privately printed by the *Freeman's Journal*, 1886), p. 29.

80. Mary Jean Corbett, *Allegories of Union in Irish and English Writing, 1790–1870* (Cambridge: Cambridge University Press, 2000), p. 181.

81. On the popularity of Kickham's *Knocknagow*, see R. V. Comerford, *Charles J. Kickham: A Study in Irish Nationalism and Literature* (Dublin: Wolfhound, 1979), pp. 207–11.

82. James H. Murphy, *Catholic Fiction and Social Reality in Ireland, 1873–1922* (Westport, CT: Greenwood, 1997), pp. 79–84.

83. Comerford, *Charles J. Kickham*, p. 210.

84. *Irish Monthly* 14 (1886), p. 201.

85. See Eliza Keary, *Memoir of Annie Keary* (London: Macmillan, 1882).

86. *More New Arabian Nights: The Dynamiter* (1885) by Robert Louis and Fanny Stevenson is the most famous of these works; my thanks to Deaglán Ó Donghaile, TCD, for this reference.

87. Review of *A Boycotted Household*, *Athenaeum* no. 2812 (17 September 1881), p. 365.

88. Nancy Armstrong, *Desire and Domestic Fiction: A Political History of the Novel* (Oxford: Oxford University Press, 1987), p. 9.

89. Review of *Heart of Erin*, *Athenaeum* no. 2847 (20 May 1882), pp. 632–3.

90. William E. Gladstone, *Special Aspects of the Irish Question: A Series of Reflections in and since 1886* (1892; London: The Daily Chronicle, 1912), p. 151.

91. Cited in Betty Brewer, '"She Was a Part of It": Emily Lawless, 1845–1913', *Éire-Ireland* 18, 4 (1983), pp. 119–31, p. 123.

92. W. B. Yeats, 'Irish National Literature, II: Contemporary Prose Writers', *The Bookman* (August 1895); reprinted in Frayne, *Uncollected Prose*, 1, p. 369.

93. Emily Lawless, *Hurrish* (1886; republished Belfast: Appletree Press, 1992), pp. 32, 3.

94. Gerardine Meaney, 'Decadence, Degeneration and Revolting Aesthetics: The Fiction of Emily Lawless and Katherine Cecil Thurston', *Colby Quarterly* 36, 2 (2000), pp. 157–75.

95. See Adrian Frazier's invaluable biography, *George Moore: 1852–1933* (New Haven and London: Yale University Press, 2000).

96. Ibid., pp. xiii, 106–16, 151–3.

97. See George Moore, *Parnell and His Island*, ed. Carla King (1887; new edition Dublin: Classics in Irish History series, University College Dublin Press, 2004).

98. Ibid., pp. 118, 132–6.

99. Letter to Unwin, 14 January 1902; cited in Julian Moynaghan, *Anglo-Irish: The Literary Imagination in a Hyphenated Culture* (Princeton: Princeton University Press, 1995), p. 160.

100. George Moore, *A Drama in Muslin* (1886; republished Belfast: Appletree Press, 1992), p. 159. Cork Hill is one of the entrances to Dublin Castle.

101. Charles Read and T. P. O'Connor, eds. *The Cabinet of Irish Literature*, 4 vols. (London and Glasgow: Blackie, 1879–80), IV, p. 296.

102. Robert Lee Woolf, introduction to new edition of May Laffan (Hartley), *Flitters, Tatters and the Counsellor and Other Sketches* (1881; New York: Garland Press, 1989), p. vii.

103. Thackeray, *Irish Sketchbook*, p. 7.

104. Anon., *History of the Theatre Royal Dublin* (Dublin: Ponsonby, 1870), p. 117.

105. John William Cole, 'Dramatic Writers of Ireland, I', *DUM* 45 (January 1855), p. 39. The eleven-part series was published in *DUM* 45–47, between January 1855 and March 1856.

106. See Christopher Morash, *A History of Irish Theatre 1601–2000* (Cambridge: Cambridge University Press, 2002), pp. 81–2.

107. Christopher Fitz-Simon, *The Irish Theatre* (London: Thames and Hudson, 1983), pp. 90–3.

108. R. M. Levey and J. O'Rorke, *Annals of the Theatre Royal, Dublin* (Dublin: Dollard, 1880), p. 34.

109. Ibid., p. 53.

110. Martin Meisel, *Shaw and the Nineteenth-Century Theatre* (Oxford and Princeton: Oxford University Press and Princeton University Press, 1963), pp. 3–6.

111. Anon., *History of the Theatre Royal*, p. 92.

112. Cole, 'Dramatic Writers of Ireland, XI', *DUM* 47 (March 1856), p. 364.

113. Ibid., p. 370.

114. Morash, *Irish Theatre*, p. 82.

115. Ibid., pp. 85–6.

116. Heinz Kosok, 'The Image of Ireland in Nineteenth-Century Drama', in Jacqueline Genet and Richard Allen Cave, eds. *Perspectives of Irish Drama and Theatre*, Irish Literary Studies XXXIII (Gerrards Cross: Colin Smythe, 1991), pp. 50–67, p. 66.

117. Morash, *Irish Theatre*, pp. 87–93.

118. Stephen Watt, *Joyce, O'Casey and the Irish Popular Theatre* (Syracuse NY: Syracuse, University Press, 1991), p. 53.

119. See Cheryl Herr, *For the Land They Loved: Irish Political Melodramas, 1890–1925* (Syracuse, NY: Syracuse University Press, 1991).

120. See Stephen Watt, 'The Plays of Hubert O'Grady', *Journal of Irish Literature* 14, 1 (1985), pp. 3–13; this issue also includes the republication from manuscripts of two of O'Grady's plays, *Emigration* and *Famine*, edited by Watt.

121. See Margaret Kelleher, '"Wanted an Irish Novelist": The Critical Decline of the Nineteenth-Century Novel', in Jacqueline Belanger, ed. *The Irish Novel in the Nineteenth Century: Facts and Fictions* (Dublin: Four Courts Press, 2005), pp. 187-201.

122. O'Brien, *Best Hundred Irish Books*, pp. 9–10.

123. Yeats to Russell, [early] December 1889; see note 3 above.

124. Stephen Gwynn, 'Novels of Irish Life in the Nineteenth Century' (1897), reprinted in his *Irish Books and Irish People* (Dublin: Talbot, 1919), p. 8.

125. Maurice Egan, 'On Irish Novels' (1904), reprinted in Justin McCarthy, editor in chief, *Irish Literature*, 10 vols. (Philadelphia: Morris, 1904), V, p. vii.

126. See Joe Cleary, 'The Nineteenth-Century Irish Novel: Some Notes and Speculations on Literary Historiography', in Belanger, *The Irish Novel*, pp. 202–221.

Select bibliography

Anon., *History of the Theatre Royal Dublin*, Dublin: Ponsonby, 1870.

Backus, Margot Gayle, *The Gothic Family Romance: Heterosexuality, Child Sacrifice, and the Anglo-Irish Colonial Order*, Durham, NC: Duke University Press, 1999,

Bareham, Tony, ed. *Charles Lever: New Evaluations*, Gerrards Cross: Colin Smythe, 1991.

Belanger, Jacqueline, ed. *The Irish Novel in the Nineteenth Century: Facts and Fictions*, Dublin: Four Courts Press, 2005.

Benson, Charles, 'Printers and Booksellers in Dublin 1800–1850', in Robin Myers and Michael Harris, eds. *Spreading the Word: The Distribution Networks of Print, 1550–1850*, Winchester: St Paul's Bibliographies, 1990, pp. 47–59.

Carleton, William, *Autobiography*, first published 1896, new edition Belfast: White Row Press, 1996, with a foreword by Benedict Kiely.

Comerford, R.V., *Charles J. Kickham: A Study in Irish Nationalism and Literature*, Dublin: Wolfhound, 1979.

Corbett, Mary Jean, *Allegories of Union in Irish and English Writing, 1790–1870*, Cambridge: Cambridge University Press, 2000.

Deane, Seamus, *Strange Country: Modernity and Nationhood in Irish Writing since 1790*, Oxford: Clarendon Press, 1997.

Eagleton, Terry, *Heathcliff and the Great Hunger: Studies in Irish Culture*, London: Verso, 1995.

Flanagan, Thomas, 'Literature in English, 1801–91', in W. E. Vaughan, ed. *New History of Ireland, vol. V: Ireland under the Union I, 1801–1870*, Oxford: Clarendon Press, 1989, pp. 482–522.

Frazier, Adrian, *George Moore: 1852–1933*, New Haven and London: Yale University Press, 2000.

Hall, Wayne, *Dialogues in the Margin: A Study of the Dublin University Magazine*, Washington, DC: Catholic University of America Press, 1999.

Hayley, Barbara, 'British Critical Reception of Nineteenth-Century Anglo-Irish Fiction', in Wolfgang Zach and Heinz Kosok, eds. *Literary Interrelations: Ireland, England and the World*, 3 vols. Tübingen: G. Narr, 1987, I, pp. 39–50.

Carleton's Traits and Stories and the Nineteenth-Century Anglo-Irish Tradition, Gerrards Cross: Colin Smythe, 1983.

'A Reading and Thinking Nation: Periodicals as the Voice of Nineteenth-Century Ireland', in Barbara Hayley and Enda McKay, eds. *Three Hundred Years of Irish Periodicals*, Mullingar: Lilliput Press, 1987, pp. 29–48.

Hooper, Glenn, ed. *The Tourist's Gaze: Travellers to Ireland, 1800–200*, Cork: Cork University Press, 2002.

Keane, Maureen, *Mrs S. C. Hall: A Literary Biography*, Gerrards Cross: Colin Smythe, 1997.

Kelleher, Margaret, 'The *Cabinet of Irish Literature*: A Historical Perspective on Irish Anthologies', *Éire-Ireland* 38, 3–4 (2003), pp. 68–89.

The Feminization of Famine: Expressions of the Inexpressible?, Cork and Durham, NC: Cork University Press and Duke University Press, 1997.

'Women's Fiction, 1845–1900', in A. Bourke, S. Kilfeather, M. Luddy, M. Mac Curtain, G. Meaney, M. Ní Dhonnchadha, M. O'Dowd and C. Wills, eds. *Field Day Anthology of Irish Writing, vols. IV and V: Irish Women's Writing and Traditions*, Cork: Cork University Press, 2002, v, pp. 924–75.

Kosok, Heinz, 'The Image of Ireland in Nineteenth-Century Drama', in Jacqueline Genet and Richard Allen Cave, eds. *Perspectives of Irish Drama and Theatre,* Irish Literary Studies XXXIII, Gerrards Cross: Colin Smythe, 1991, pp. 50–67.

Laird, Heather, *Subversive Law in Ireland: 1879–1920*, Dublin: Four Courts Press, 2005.

Levey, R. M. and J. O'Rorke, *Annals of the Theatre Royal, Dublin*, Dublin: Dollard, 1880.

Lloyd, David, *Anomalous States: Irish Writing and the Post-Colonial Moment*, Dublin: Lilliput, 1993.

McCormack, W. J., *Ascendancy and Tradition in Anglo-Irish History 1789–1939*, Oxford: Oxford University Press, 1985; revised and enlarged edition: *From Burke to Beckett: Ascendancy, Tradition and Betrayal in Anglo-Irish Literary History from 1789 to 1939*, Cork: Cork University Press, 1994.

'The Intellectual Revival (1830–1850)', in Seamus Deane, general ed. *The Field Day Anthology of Irish Writing*, 3 vols. Derry: Field Day, 1991, i, pp. 1173–1300.

Sheridan Le Fanu and Victorian Ireland, Oxford: Clarendon Press, 1980; second edition Dublin: Lilliput Press, 1991.

Morash, Christopher, *A History of Irish Theatre 1601–2000*, Cambridge: Cambridge University Press, 2002.

Writing the Irish Famine, Oxford: Oxford University Press, 1995.

Murphy, James H., *Catholic Fiction and Social Reality in Ireland, 1873–1922*, Westport, CT: Greenwood, 1997.

Ireland: A Social, Cultural and Literary History, Dublin: Four Courts Press, 2002.

O'Dwyer, Riana, 'Women's Narratives, 1800–1840', in Bourke et al., *Field Day Anthology of Irish Writing*, v, pp. 833–94.

Ryder, Seán, 'Literature in English', in L. Geary and M. Kelleher, eds. *Nineteenth-Century Ireland: A Guide to Recent Research,* Dublin: University College Dublin Press, 2005, pp. 118–35.

Vance, Norman, *Irish Literature: A Social History*, Dublin: Four Courts Press, 1990; new edition 1999.

Irish Literature since 1800, London: Longman, 2002.

12

Poetry in English, 1830–1890: from Catholic emancipation to the fall of Parnell

MATTHEW CAMPBELL

For the poet Thomas Kinsella, 'silence, on the whole, is the real condition of Irish Literature in the nineteenth century'. It is a common view, an Irish version of the dissociated sensibility of the modern poet: as a result of the colonial traumas of political and sectarian oppression, famine, emigration and the decline of the Irish language, the Irish poet became, in Kinsella's words, the 'inheritor of a gapped, discontinuous, polyglot tradition'.[1] Far from suffering in silence, however, the Victorian period saw much English-language Irish poetry published not only in Ireland, but also in Britain or America. From the post-Romantic ballad and the translated Gaelic song, through the sectarian or political squib, to the renovation of narrative and epic in the conditions of a growing national culture reinvigorated by antiquarian and linguistic research, a number of poets sought ways of writing original poems in English in a distinctly Irish style. The quality of this writing may be uneven, but its interest lies in the way it either marks or attempts to mask its gaps and discontinuities, and in how its polyglot tradition creates the new.

Since 1801 Ireland had ostensibly been an integral part of the United Kingdom, but it was a major source of political instability for an imperial British state undergoing the cultural and scientific golden age associated so strongly with Queen Victoria. While a number of Irish writers saw that culture could assist political integration, many others refused, and the period up to the Literary Revival saw a hardening of the dividedness that would result in both independence and the partitioning of the island. The complex linguistic, political and social concerns of the Irish poetry of this period were correspondingly gapped. So, while many writers published for the large literary market in Britain and the new, English-speaking audiences of Irish origin in the United States, the poetry was often more concerned with its responsibility in preserving the authenticity of the cultural achievements of Ireland's past. Whether unionist or nationalist, Victorian Irish poetry was consistently uncomfortable in the face of cultural integration, as it sought to establish a style to rival that which had emerged from Scotland in the late eighteenth century, poetry which could have both a distinctive linguistic identity and international renown. The concern was that Irish culture would be doomed to the margins of the UK and the empire, since Ireland had been, in the words of Thomas Davis, 'long a province'. A majority of, if not all, Irish Victorian poets preferred Davis's solution, that Ireland become 'a nation once again'.[2]

The poetry of Ulster Protestants such as Samuel Ferguson and William Allingham, who had an eye on British as well as Irish audiences, moved from lyric through social realism to the experiments in myth which laid the foundations of the Revival's interest in Celtic epic. However, the English-language poetic experiments of James Clarence Mangan, an exemplary figure for nineteenth-century cultural nationalists, self-consciously repudiated English modes and audiences. His original poems and loose translations attempted to replicate in English both the prosodic and metaphoric practices of the Jacobite traditions of eighteenth-century Irish-language poetry, and those of German Romanticism and Orientalism. In contrast with English literary innovations in realism, even given the turn of British poetry from a subjectivist Romanticism to the impersonality of monologue, the shifting identities and vocal mannerisms of poetry such as Mangan's consistently betray vices of stylistic excess. Poet and critic Seamus Deane points to the defining features of Mangan, which may apply equally to the seeming burlesque of much Irish poetry of the Victorian period: 'the fragmentariness, the inaccuracies, the extremities of the text – its deliberate careening from the sublime to the ridiculous'.[3] Nonetheless, extremities of mode and tone may be read as the aesthetic consequences of the painful arrival of modernity, given that Irish poetry in English was divided over the authentic response to the culture's polyglot linguistic inheritance. In the mid-nineteenth century, the new thinking of nationalism was itself a 'modern' intellectual development, grounded though it was in the conception of distinct cultural identities persisting from the past. In the case of Irish culture, poetry and music bore much responsibility in conceptions of an authentic Irish national culture, given the post-Ossianic conception of the 'poetic' as a near-synonym for the 'Celtic'. In 1845, Davis wrote, 'That a country is without national poetry proves its hopeless dullness or its utter provincialism. National poetry is the very flowering of the soul – the greatest evidence of its health, the greatest excellence of its beauty.'[4]

What that 'national poetry' might be was a matter for much debate throughout the nineteenth century. For literary historian Gregory Schirmer, the poetry of this period dramatises a struggle to avoid absorption into the British empire, twinning antiquarianism with 'revolutionary nationalism . . . both part of an overarching effort to establish, define, and forcefully assert a distinctive national identity'.[5] But for the poets of Victorian Ireland, the country was neither so simply a victim of imperialism nor in agreement about its 'distinctive national identity'. After the Union, for instance, Irish poets, like those novelists and critics who were aware that the reading market was British as well as Irish, published in London and Edinburgh as well as Dublin. Some concentrated solely on English audiences, and the question mark over the 'Irishness' of poets such as George Darley, Thomas Caulfield Irwin or James Henry, who wrote in a recognisably post-Byronic style or on British Victorian subject matter, has meant that they tend to be overlooked in Irish literary histories. Lady Caroline Norton, whose unhappy marriage and involvement with a British prime minister meant a certain notoriety in Victorian literary society, was born, wrote and published in England. Yet she was born Caroline Sheridan, granddaughter of Richard Brinsley Sheridan. Her sister Helen, also English-born, became Helen Blackwood, Lady Dufferin and settled in County Down. She is thus better remembered as an Irish writer than her sister for writing the synthetic dialect ballad, 'Lament of the Irish Emigrant', an Irish theme in a self-consciously 'Anglo-Irish' style. Norton's work, like that of Darley or Henry, is not so well accommodated within the national narrative.

While the identities of individual poets were broad, within Ireland publication also suggested a number of ideological contexts. Periodical publication usually preceded later collected volumes, but even here the political affiliations of the relevant journals showed complex backgrounds. Often associated with the militant aspects of Young Ireland, Mangan was an example of a poet crossing over from the Tory *Dublin University Magazine* (*DUM*) to Davis's *Nation* and then the more militant pages of John Mitchel's *United Irishman*. One of those texts which made the transition with him, his distinctly insurrectionary version of O'Hussey's ode to the sixteenth-century Gaelic chieftain Maguire, found its first home in English in the *DUM*, as Samuel Ferguson's example of the Tory virtues of feudal loyalty. Similarly, a number of 'original' texts might take on distinctly differing meanings depending on the contexts of their appearance in successive, and frequently critically competing periodicals, or as translations and re-translations. Later in the century, in the 1880s, Fr Matthew Russell's *Irish Monthly* published the Fenian verse of Ellen O'Leary, Katharine Tynan and William Butler Yeats, some of which would later be republished in the seminal anthology *Ballads and Poems of Young Ireland*. Yet it also published Shakespeare's songs translated into Latin by Russell's fellow Dublin-based

Jesuit, Gerard Manley Hopkins, rare publication anywhere in the UK for an English poet dedicated to Union and empire.

From mid-century, the waves of emigration westward also meant that Irish poetry was both published and performed across a larger English-speaking world. Late in the century, the *melos* of the hugely successful melodramas of Dion Boucicault, performed on American and British stages, was achieved through the liberal use of Irish lyric and song. This in turn was derived from the practice of sprinkling songs throughout Irish novels, as in Gerald Griffin's *The Collegians*, the source for Boucicault's biggest hit, *The Colleen Bawn*. The most internationally successful Irish poet of the century, Thomas Moore, was plagued with versions of his songs pirated for the American market. The *Irish Melodies* (published in series from 1808) told of cultural defeat just as they attempted to renovate the national music, and the series lasted right up to 1834. Moore died in 1852 in England, where he had spent most of his life, and after his death his work was edited by a serving British prime minister, Lord John Russell. Vacillating between England and Ireland, writing of Irish loss while promoting Irish interests to the Whig establishment, securing the 'wild' music of Gaelic Ireland to the symbolism of British Romanticism, the example of Moore's writing and career was to be repeated by many Irish poets who also wrote within the United Kingdom.

It was not until the emergence of William Butler Yeats in the 1880s, writing against the background of resurgent nationalism, but nevertheless working in London as much as Sligo or Dublin, that there was to be a poet with similar British or international influence. The careers of Victorian Irish poets were often carried out in disparate places across Ireland, Britain, Europe and beyond, and those who stayed in Ireland, like Mangan and Ferguson, suffered neglect throughout their careers. In parallel with the emigration which was to halve the Irish population through the century, particularly after the famine of the 1840s, a diaspora of poets existed as well. Jeremiah Joseph Callanan died penniless in Lisbon. William Maginn and Frances Sylvester Mahony worked in London, Mahony later in France and Rome. Mary Kelly, 'Eva' of the *Nation*, followed her transported husband, Kevin Izod O'Doherty, to Paris and Australia. Lady Wilde, the *Nation*'s firebrand 'Speranza', spent her last years in London society, dying in poverty while her son was in Reading gaol.

Geographically dislocated and divided by politics or sect, it is difficult to posit a single approach to poetry's role in establishing a distinctive national culture. Yeats's 1892 'Apologia addressed to Ireland in the coming days' (better known as 'To Ireland in the Coming Times') used the posterity of Irish Victorian poetry to inform his teleology of a reawakened Irish cultural nationalism.

The sweetening of Ireland's wrong was to be achieved through poetry itself: 'Ballad and story, rann and song'. Yeats sought unity in the tradition, asking that he be 'counted one / With Davis, Mangan, Ferguson'.[6] Yet even this grouping came from widely differing backgrounds and wrote in styles which were attuned to conflicting political and aesthetic purposes. According to Seamus Deane, the myriad political movements of Victorian Ireland resulted in a poetry in which 'Incoherence of purpose was disguised in the language of utopian possibility.'[7] Yeats's poem does look to a culturally coherent 'coming times', but it is a coherence founded on the gaps and discontinuities of a poetic practice inventing itself in the difficult circumstances of Victorian Ireland.

Callanan, Ferguson and the invention of 'the Irish mode'

While the variety of styles and the range of subject matter of post-Romantic Irish poetry is large, the quality is variable, and the number of poems, poets and critics who were to influence the later development of the Irish poem may be small. The initial achievement was the establishment of a new genre which followed the experiments of the British poetry of Burns, Wordsworth and Coleridge, seeking authenticity through linking lyric and narrative in the self-consciously antique forms of the regional ballad. That achievement may at first appear merely to be one of form. In the writing of 1840s ballad anthologists Charles Gavan Duffy and Denis Florence MacCarthy, the linguistic and prosodic form of Irish poetry in English came to be called 'Anglo-Irish', borrowing a term previously used to describe the landed class in Ireland. This poetry was not so much the result of the organic natural process of hybridity, or a kind of intermarriage of Irish and English. The result is more synthetic, combining the conflicting critical and political imperatives of the quest for the 'authentic' which runs through the poetics of the period, allied to the insistent and self-conscious practical inventiveness which sought the artifice of a national poetic style in the English language. Three formal changes resulted from the innovations of the synthetic form of Victorian Irish poetry in the middle of the nineteenth century: following the example of Moore, the post-Romantic writing of 'civilised' English words for the rhythm of 'wild' Irish melodies; a translating practice which strove for English prosodic effects that imitated those of Irish; and the deliberate importation of the accents of a regional and socially mixed Hiberno-English diction into the resultant new metrical forms.

In his classic *Literature in Ireland*, published after his execution in 1916, Thomas MacDonagh said that this awareness of formal difference resulted in poetry of 'the Irish Mode'. He acknowledged it as much for its limitations as for its successes: his preferred poets have merely achieved, in MacDonagh's words, 'a contribution of melody, a music that at once expresses and evokes emotion. In the whole body of their literature you find scarcely a true poem which, in the words of the book reviewers, treats adequately a serious subject.' By way of recompense, he looks to the liberated future and 'the new epics of this nation' yet to be written. To be understood, MacDonagh's Irish mode involves the recognition of the three prosodic characteristics of Irish verse in English mentioned above, based as they are in specific Irish social and linguistic conditions: that Irish subject matter and culture 'have important differences' from English 'ways of life'; that English has become the main language of those 'of Gaelic stock'; and that the Irish accent speaks English in its own way.[8] MacDonagh had liberationist reasons for claiming the formal distinctiveness of Irish poetry in English, but his is an account of a poetry we might nowadays call 'postcolonial', a synthetic form which challenges and defers from the metrical expectations, accent and lexis of the poetry of a dominant linguistic culture.

After the successes of Moore, the model for an Irish poetic career in English literary circles of the 1820s and 1830s might have been that of George Darley (1795–1846). Dublin-born, he became an active contributor to the *London Magazine* and later the fastidious drama critic of *The Athenaeum*, also showing gentlemanly interests in science and mathematics. Yet apart from 'The Flight of the Forlorn: A Romantic Ballad Founded on the History of Ireland', he wrote little 'Irish' verse. Only three roughly printed copies of his most substantial achievement *Nepenthe* (1835) survived through the nineteenth century, while his works on popular algebra and geometry were to run to numerous editions. The psychic allegory of *Nepenthe* veers between erotic fantasy and the excesses of melancholy, but it was born of a life of solitude which was the result of a debilitating stammer. It is tempting to read Darley's subsequent obscurity as a result of his provincial origins and inability to speak in a distinctive voice.[9] For other Irish poets, the self-conscious decision to write in the provincial accents of the Irish mode was to prove to have more lasting influence. Two early versions of this mode illustrate the strangeness it brings into the English poem, Jeremiah Joseph Callanan's 'The Outlaw of Loch Lene' (1828) and Samuel Ferguson's 'The Fairy Thorn' (1834). Unlike Darley, who worked in London, Callanan and Ferguson wrote regional poetry for regional journals with a conservative political agenda. Both Callanan and Ferguson first published in *Blackwood's Edinburgh Magazine*. 'The Fairy Thorn' was published in an early number of the *DUM*, a journal designed to appeal to the same Tory readership as *Blackwood's*, from a city which had competing claims to be the second city of empire.

Jeremiah Joseph Callanan (1795–1829) had a sporadic association with *Blackwood's*, mainly through several writers who moved between Cork, Edinburgh and then London: the editor and writer William Maginn (1794–1842), the antiquarian Thomas Crofton Croker (1798–1854), the artist and illustrator Daniel Maclise (1806–70) and the satirist Francis Sylvester Mahony (1804–66). Callanan was a spoilt priest and a failed lawyer, and in its Romantic mixture of idleness and ill health, his biography serves as a depressing model for other Irish poets of the Victorian period. His bilingual talent was recognised by those who strove to publish his work or to collaborate with his antiquarian researches: he wandered penniless round west Cork collecting songs and stories, much to the interest of Croker, who requested materials for his own pioneering, if not always original, research. Callanan wrote in a variety of late Romantic forms, most notably his long poem *The Recluse of Inchidoney*, written in the *Childe Harold* stanza and invoking the example of Byron, thus equating the struggle for Greek independence with that of Ireland. His Irish poems, though, show the influence of his linguistic researches, and a strong note not so much of incipient nationalism as of self-conscious provincialism. The Cork classic 'Gougane Barra' not only celebrates a famous beauty spot, but keeps the surrounding hills haunted by the ghosts of the religion and language persecuted by the Penal Laws of the previous century. The poem experiments with an English ballad form enlivened by the importation of insistent double-syllable rhyming designed to echo the very Irish-language bardic poetry whose passing it laments.

It is in his very loose 'translations', such as the 'Dirge of O'Sullivan Bear' or 'The Outlaw of Loch Lene' that Callanan chances on something new in Irish poetry in English. 'The Outlaw' was subtitled as 'From the Irish', but no single source has been found. Robert Welch says it is 'a translation of a certain *kind* of Irish poem, the love song of a youth, who has taken to living in the wild places of nature, now that his loved one is no longer with him'.[10] The first stanza runs thus:

> O many a day have I made good ale in the glen,
> That came not of stream, or malt; – like the brewing of men.
> My bed was the ground; my roof the greenwood above,
> And the wealth that I sought one far kind glance from my love.[11]

Callanan's first line is a near literal translation of the first line of the third verse of the Irish song 'Muna b'é an t-ól' (If Only for the Drink), which runs

'Is fada mé féin ag deanamh leanna sa ghleann'. The English line accentuates its own musical effects of assonance and internal off-rhyme: the slight vowel modulations in 'many a day' or the consonantal repetitions resolving towards the end of the line, 'made good ale in the glen'. The line also develops a version of what Yeats heard as the alternating 'wavering or steady rhythm' that Thomas Moore had introduced into his lengthened lyric line.[12] Thus the packed stresses and anapaestic resolution of 'made good ale in the glen' challenge English voicing and scansion. The final line of the first stanza plays these effects again, just as it mildly censors the Irish song. 'Muna b'é an t-ól' imagines itself doubly covered, by the trees overhead and the lover's body: 'rún searc mo chléibh 's a géaga tharm anall' (the secret love of my breast with her limbs spread over me).[13] For the Tory readers of Blackwood's, Callanan removes the lover to the realm of the gaze. Three anapaests and the four packed stresses of 'one far kind glance' are the compensation he provides for the bodily loss of a desire which cannot be consummated. The effect of packing stresses becomes explicitly connected with this desire by the end of the poem, and its wistful recreation of the sound of the unheard song of the loved one: 'I think as at eve she wanders its mazes along, / The birds go to sleep by the sweet wild twist of her song.'

'The Fairy Thorn', by way of geographical as much as thematic contrast, is another self-consciously provincial poem, subtitled 'An Ulster Ballad'.[14] Yet its provincialism is not just within Ireland, but within the United Kingdom as well. Its Belfast-born author, Samuel Ferguson (1810–86), was a Church of Ireland, Trinity College-educated barrister, who had a divided sense that whatever establishment influence might accrue to one of his class, that class occupied a mere province of empire. The classic statement of the case was in his 'Dialogue between the Heart and Head of an Irish Protestant', published in the *Dublin University Magazine* in 1833. In one of its most memorable speeches, 'Heart' rails against the stranded, forgotten social position of its author's class as Irish 'loyalists', 'told we are neither English nor Irish, fish nor flesh, but a peddling colony, a forlorn advanced guard that must conform to every mutinous movement of the proletarian rabble'.[15] The 'Dialogue' shows division within its *DUM* readership and division within Ireland and across the UK, while moving in the currents of the formal dividedness which is a characteristic of English and not just Irish Victorian literature.

'The Fairy Thorn' was published four months after the 'Dialogue', and it emerges from such contexts as one of Kinsella's 'polyglot' poems, mixing the diction and subject matter of Ireland, Scotland and a European Romanticism drawn to folk legend. It tells a story of the abduction of a farm girl by the fairies, a theme retold often in Irish folk-tale, and returned to throughout nineteenth-century poetry. The theme is not just an Irish one: it is the subject of Goethe's 'Erlkönig', Robert Browning's 'Pied Piper', or Christina Rossetti's 'Goblin Market'. The distinctiveness of Ferguson's contribution is the mixing of an Irish, Scots and English ballad form with the languages of the north of Ireland. The example of Robert Burns was strong in the Presbyterian radicalism of 1790s Belfast, but by the time the Church of Ireland Ferguson showed that influence, it was transmuted more into the formal elements of diction and metre. Burns's 'Tam O'Shanter', for instance, tells a supernatural story both in Scots and English, often moving between the two languages line by line. 'The Fairy Thorn' is sprinkled with a self-consciously archaic lexis, which bears witness to the mixtures of Ulster Scots, Hiberno-English and the Anglo-Saxon of English ballad.

The girls in the poem set off to 'dance a highland reel'. They are 'merry maidens fair in kirtles of the green' ('kirtles' is an old English or Old Norse word for a petticoat). There are rowan trees beside the Fairy Hawthorn, Norse rowan against Old English haw. The rowan trees gave the hawthorn 'ruddy kisses' (Old English) while the girls 'caroll'd' (Middle English from Old French) around them. We go on to encounter 'haunted braes' (Old Norse, but also a Scots poeticism) and 'the gloaming' of the light effects of the Celtic twilight (gloaming is actually a word with Old English etymology, but the *OED* is full of examples from Burns and Walter Scott). Once the girls stop dancing, and the fairies appear, though, the diction of the poem changes and becomes a much more conventional late Romantic English-language narrative. The poeticisms of 'faint enchantment . . . anguish and perilous amaze . . . quivering eyes' are followed by the beautiful archaism reserved for the waking of the remaining girls to the fact of the loss of their friend: 'When, as the mist dissolves in the yellow morning tide, / The maidens' trance dissolveth so.' Given this play with competing English and Scots etymologies in a distinctively Irish setting, it is interesting that the poem has only one English word with Gaelic etymology, in its subtitle, 'Ulster,' from the Irish, Uladh – tír.

'The Fairy Thorn' and 'The Outlaw of Loch Lene' are remarkable performances, and both share in the conditions of their publication and the expectations of their audience. For all their attempts at importing the Irish language or a mixed Ulster demotic into the English poem, the poems are self-consciously literary and were first published in journals sold to an educated English as well as Irish readership and not to the wild outlaws or farm girls which formed their subject matter. They are in the tradition of Bishop Percy's *Reliques*, the renovated songs of Burns, *Lyrical Ballads* or Walter Scott's *Minstrelsy of the*

Scottish Border. Nevertheless, they attest to an opening of this register in the English-language Irish poem, allowing the subject matter as well as the metres and forms of street and country ballad and song to mix with the more polite forms expected by their bourgeois or landed readership. A creative confrontation emerges, between the supposed barbarity or debauchery of the authentic song tradition and the drawing-room proprieties of the literate.

The exploitation of incongruity, doggerel, broad humour, obscenity or blasphemy is generic to the ballad tradition, along with the bawdy, or, more frequently, the drunk. As is the polemical: the one hundred Irish political street ballads from 1780 to 1800 collected in George Zimmermann's 1966 classic, *Songs of Irish Rebellion*,[16] mix all of the above elements with nationalist or loyalist political sentiment. It is, though, a remarkable feature of the sheer size of the popular ballad tradition that lines of demarcation on grounds of taste or class between ballad and the poetry published in the Dublin, London and Edinburgh journals may not have been that secure.

In the same year as the publication of 'The Fairy Thorn', *Fraser's Magazine* began to publish the extraordinary comic articles which were later to be collected as *The Reliques of Fr Prout*. The character of Prout, fantastically learned parish priest of Watergrasshill in County Cork, was the invention of Francis Sylvester Mahony (1804–66). Mahony was an ordained, if not practising, priest and a conservative exile from an Ireland 'liberated' by Daniel O'Connell in the emancipation of 1829. Given his attachment to the Catholic Europe of the *ancien régime*, Mahony was later to settle in Rome. The Prout articles mix bawdy and scholarly registers to high comic effect against the background of *Fraser's* characteristic editorial line of anti-liberal satire and new British conservative transcendentalism. The famous cartoon of 'The Fraserians' by Daniel Maclise has the editor William Maginn presiding over drinks in which Croker and Mahony join, among others, Coleridge, James Hogg, John Galt and the young Thomas Carlyle: *Sartor Resartus* was running in *Fraser's* at the same time as Prout.[17] The Prout papers are as much the persistence of an anti-Enlightenment British Toryism in the midst of early Victorian liberalism: Prout claims he is the illegitimate child of Swift and Stella (and Swift, of course, had himself parodied translations of Irish poetry a century earlier in his version of 'O'Rourke's Feast' (1720) as street ballad).

Mahony's articles are also early classics of Irish literary criticism, providing oblique satiric comment on antiquarianism, the demotic and liberalism. As a pillar of the Whig establishment, Thomas Moore comes in for the most savage treatment. One of the Prout articles, 'The Rogueries of Tom Moore' (1835), charges Moore with plagiarism, but not the theft that some antiquarians might have suggested, that of Irish music. Prout provides an extraordinary set of 'originals' for the lyrics to Moore's *Irish Melodies*, simply by translating the English lyrics into French and Latin. The trick was part of the *Blackwood's/Fraser's* house style, also used by fellow Corkonian Maginn, who rewrote *Chevy Chase* in Latin and large sections of *The Iliad* and *Odyssey* as *Homeric Ballads* in *Fraser's* in 1838.[18] Mahony's first rehearsal was in Prout's 'Polyglot Edition' of the ballad 'The Groves of Blarney', by Richard Milliken (1767–1815), providing French, Greek, Latin and Irish 'originals' for Milliken's song, and slipping in an extra stanza on the amatory and political eloquence imparted by kissing the Blarney stone. The 'Polyglot Edition' is described in a great piling up of parodic metaphors of interbreeding or hybridity, an affront to notions of authenticity: it is '*Siamese*', it has 'joint-stock parentage', it is 'that rare combination of the Teïan lyre and the Tipperary bagpipe – of the Ionian dialect blending harmoniously with the Cork brogue; an Irish potatoe [sic] seasoned with Attic salt, and the humours of Donnybrook wed to the glories of Marathon'.[19]

In 'The Rogueries of Tom Moore' article, Mahony accuses Moore of plagiarising one of Prout's own songs for his 'Evening Bells', set to a Russian tune in Moore's *National Melodies* (1818–22). Mahony provides the 'original', itself set to the tune of 'The Groves of Blarney'. This is 'The Shandon Bells',[20] a poem which appears to career across genuine nostalgia, extravagant simile and outrageous doggerel in four ballad stanzas which traverse the world, comparing St Anne's church at Shandon in Cork City with St Peter's, Notre Dame, St Sophia's and Turkish mosques. Each stanza resolves this global mix into the rhymes of a refrain designed to sound forced to all but those from Cork: ''Tis the bells of Shandon, / That sound so grand on / The pleasant waters / Of the River Lee.' ('Grand' is a play on the mock-sublime and the dialect sense of the conversational 'fine, splendid'.)

'The Shandon Bells' does not feature in MacDonagh's selection of 'Poems of the Irish Mode'; in fact in a footnote he admonishes those like Samuel Lover (1797–1868) who would insist on Mahony's risqué addition to 'The Groves' in any printing of the ballad.[21] Mahony's 'Shandon Bells' locates humour in the tradition, a humour which could in the hands of someone like Lover be overplayed to the extent of stage Irishry. Lover's success was in England, and as Mahony and Maginn were later to do, he wrote for the magazine set up by old *Fraser's* contributors Harrison Ainsworth and Charles Dickens, *Bentley's Miscellany*. While writing for Dublin magazines, though, he composed the popular 'Rory O'More', a dialogue song in which the rascally O'More seduces the willing Kathleen Bawn, 'Reproof on her lip but a smile in her eye'. Rory's proposal has the broad comic accent of both his and the author's knowing Hiberno-English forced rhyme: "'And I've made myself, drinking your health, quite a *baste*, / So I think, after that, I may *talk to the priest*.'"[22] He was later to return as the eponymous hero of a novel and successful play.

Lover's 1831 *Legends and Tales of Ireland* contains a lampoon on 'Ballads and Ballad Singers', which makes much play not just with the comedy of doggerel, unlikely subject matter and impropriety in the street ballads of Dublin, but also with its adventures into print. Daniel O'Connell, according to Charles Gavan Duffy, preferred the comedy of Lover to the more strident compositions of the *Nation*.[23] Lover returns the compliment as a joke: his article bemoans the loss of ballads of religious conviction after emancipation ('of the many fatal results of the relief bill, not the least deplorable'),[24] and reserves parody of the printed broadsheet ballad of political party for gentle satire of O'Connell. This extract, deliberate typographical errors included, from 'O'Connell's Farewell Meeting in the Corn Exchange' may or may not be Lover's own composition:

> Farewell Dearest Danyel Hibernias confidential frind
> Our ble*ss*in Go along wid you *u*nto the british shore,
> Nobility and Gintery to Parliamint will you attind,
> *Like*wise be accompanied wit*h* The blessings of the *P*oor.
> Our foes within the house a*s* mute as any *mouse*,
> To see the Agitator Triumphantly arranged,
> No . . . or factious cla*n* shall daunt the *p*eople's man;
> This conversation passed in the Corn Exchange.[25]

Samuel Ferguson and James Hardiman's
Irish Minstrelsy

Beginning a month after the publication of 'The Fairy Thorn', from April to November 1834 the *DUM* ran a four-part unsigned, and in the main hostile, set of review articles of a two-volume collection, edited by James Hardiman (1782–1855), *Irish Minstrelsy, or Bardic Remains of Ireland with English Poetical Translations* (1831). The final part contained an appendix of twenty English poetic versions of Irish poems, signed S.F, the 24-year-old Samuel Ferguson. It is difficult to overestimate the significance of these articles, and for Peter Denman they stand at 'the fountain-head of modern Anglo-Irish criticism and poetry'.[26] The articles are not quite the source, though, since they were predicated on a critique of Hardiman who had not just collected translations of Irish-language poems, but, as Seamus Deane has pointed out, printed the originals in a typeface that became known as the Hardiman font. *Irish Minstrelsy* was an O'Connellite project conceived during the struggle for Catholic emancipation, and one consequence of O'Connell's educational programme was to encourage the Irish to move from speaking Irish to reading English. Translations were thus required, providing the accident of the near-modernist polyglot text of *Irish Minstrelsy*, and an early example in Irish literary history of an emphasis on what Deane calls 'the materiality of the medium of language and of print'.[27]

While not fully acknowledging the debt he owed to this printing of the originals, Ferguson had two main objections: firstly, to the 'tone of petty anti-anglicism' of the prefatory comments and annotations to a volume conceived before the emancipation of 1829, though published afterwards; and secondly, to the quality of some of the English translations. The critique was grounded in what were already familiar debates over the renovation of Irish poetry and music. Ferguson reserved praise for only one contributor, the Belfast Presbyterian minister, Unitarian theologian, geologist and poet William Hamilton Drummond (1778–1865). Partial to the historical and prehistoric epic, Drummond's most singular achievement was *The Giant's Causeway* (1811), a curious contribution to the Irish genre of poems of place, mixing geology and the sublime in a text which announced its particular materiality by interspersing a hundred pages of poem in heroic couplets and a hundred pages of prefatory matter with numerous pull-out maps and elaborate engravings of the north Antrim coast. Overlooking Drummond's youthful United Irishman associations, Ferguson granted his translations praise because of 'the absence of anything like political hatred or sectarian malignity'.[28] Special scorn was reserved for the translations of Thomas Furlong (1794–1827) who died in the early stages of the project. Hardiman's 'Memoir of Thomas Furlong' prefaced *Irish Minstrelsy*, and served to establish the volume's translating practice. Hardiman deplored the convention of uniting 'vulgar ballads' to existing Irish melodies, contrasting them with the drawing-room successes of Thomas Moore.[29] For Ferguson, this imported the inauthentic, committing the artistic crime of 'elevation'. Furlong transforms poetry that Ferguson approvingly refers to throughout as showing 'savage sincerity', or as 'a maudlin jumble',[30] into 'a pitch of refined poetic art altogether removed from the whole genius and *rationale* of its composition'. The translations are 'spurious, puerile, unclassical – lamentably bad'.[31]

The Hardiman articles sought to perform a literary service for unionist readers, while not challenging their politics. Acknowledging that the materials collected by Hardiman would be foreign to the *DUM* readership, the ruling minority of a divided country, Ferguson discerned points of contact between the innate conservatism of the Irish-language material and that of his readership. In doing so, he also brought together the competing impulses of early Victorian Irish educated taste, reconstructing the feudalism of Gaelic society for his Tory readers while promoting a post-Romantic purity of diction and feeling. The articles sketch in a bardic culture while also welcoming the sentimentality of Moore and the tradition from which he gained so much: 'for sentiment is the soul of song, and sentiment is one imprescriptible property of the common blood of all Irishmen'. As a location for all these varying accommodations, Ferguson concluded his third review with the peace that culture alone might bring to the feuding parties of Irish politics, 'a green spot of neutral ground, where all parties may meet in kindness, and part in peace'. This call was followed with his version of 'The Fair Hills of Holy Ireland', positively Georgic in its vision of the generous fecundity of a supposedly impoverished land.[32]

Ferguson's appendix prints his own poetic versions of the Irish poems, some of which he had already presented throughout the articles in literal translations. The range is from the bardic dignity of the shortened English heroic couplets of 'Torna's Lament' through the flexible four-line ballad stanza adapted for narrative in 'Timoleague', to the loose refrain invented for a song of drunkenness and abject desire in 'Pastheen Finn' and the exquisite adaptation of the wavering Irish mode line in 'Cashel of Munster'. The first two lines of this last poem, a version of the song 'Caiseal Mumhan', sometimes known as the 'Clár Bog Déil' (the bare deal board or bog pine board), show the innovations which have been brought into the English poem. The first line, 'I'd wed you without herds, without money, or rich array', is nearly unscannable, so cunningly does it lengthen the line across its five stresses. The second, 'And I'd wed you on a dewy morning at day-dawn grey', plays with a sonic richness of assonance and near-anagram ('wed you . . . dewy') and packed stress ('day-dawn grey') full of the corresponding richness of its natural scene-setting. The 'bare deal board' of its alternative title is where this lover would make his marriage bed, a detail missing entirely from the more softly furnished version provided for Hardiman by Thomas Furlong.[33]

The influence of Ferguson's articles was to be felt across more than his original readership, and his subsequent career, as antiquarian as much as poet, is one which moves closer to nationalist writers and scholars. The famine was to provoke him into speaking in favour of Home Rule, a course that his fellow *DUM* founder, economist, novelist and politician Isaac Butt (1813–79) was to pursue with vigour later in the century. Ferguson's influence permeated the writers, poets and polemicists grouped around Young Ireland in the decade following his articles, but the initial achievement was to suggest a style within

English poetry for translated Irish-language originals. After the example of Hardiman too, there were a number of similar publishing projects, such as *Reliques of Irish Jacobite Poetry* (1844), published by John O'Daly (1800–78) with translations by Edward Walsh (1805–50), or O'Daly and Mangan's *The Poets and Poetry of Munster* (1849).

While seeking an even greater degree of authenticity in translation than Ferguson, *Reliques of Jacobite Poetry* also supplied 'Interlinear Translation' across the bottom of pages which presented Irish originals. *Irish Popular Songs* (1847) demonstrated Walsh's nationalist appropriation of Ferguson's strictures on the false elevation of Irish-language material into a bland poeticised English poetry. According to Walsh's principles, the translator must avoid 'the fault of not writing the translation to the exact song tune of the original'. Thus Walsh claims that he has 'embodied the meaning and spirit of each stanza' by preserving 'the caesural and demi-caesural rhymes, the use of which produces such harmonious effects in Irish verse'.[34] His version of 'Caiseal Mumhan' attempts to retain these effects of internal rhyme while establishing a lightness of rhythmical touch in the new English line. His first two lines run: 'I would wed you dear, without gold or gear, or counted kine; / My wealth you'll be, would your friends agree, and you be mine –'. The effect is repeated throughout, sounding strange in English, but not infelicitous. Walsh does not, though, follow Ferguson in the hardships of the couple's imagined lovemaking: taking advantage of an ambiguity in the Irish word 'bog', also meaning soft, the 'clár bog déil' becomes a 'soft deal board'.

It was conventional to retain Irish names of people or places to add authentic, if slightly estranging, flavour to English-language poems. The best-known ballads of the novelist Gerald Griffin (1803–40) string their titles as refrains around italicised Gaelicisms, '*Gile Machree*' or '*Eileen Aroon*'.[35] The latter shares a metre with '*Soggarth Aroon*' by John Banim (1798–1842), also better known as a novelist. Both poems sound the Irish-language phrase through their ballads as a refrain, thus repeating a phrase sonically disconnected from, because not rhyming with, the English around them. The effects differ, though: Griffin's love song returns to the name of the loved one throughout, but Banim's ballad intensifies its complaint of dispossession and slavery with echoes of 1798 composed in the campaign for emancipation. Walsh's 'Mo Craoibhin Cno' (my little nut tree branch, or nut-brown maid) goes further. Its macaronic text retains the Irish-language endearment of its source throughout as a refrain and cross-language rhyme. The penultimate stanza presents this as a sort of incomplete translation, double-rhyming after the Irish example ('maidens sung' / 'Saxon tongue'), but then capping this effect by rhyming English and

Irish in conditions of enmity: 'Saxon foe' / '*craoibhin cno*'. The poignancy of the poem resides in its speaker's attempt to remember the Irish-language, which 'didst charm my ruptured ear', while still forced to make his complaint in the English language that had caused its rupture.

Thomas Davis and Young Ireland

Samuel Ferguson's 'Lament for Thomas Davis' was published anonymously in 1847. It was a belated *DUM* tribute to the then two-years-dead intellectual leader of the writers grouped round the *Nation* newspaper who were known as 'Young Ireland'. The elegy moves between personal grief and the necessary register for the commemoration of a public figure, mourning one future lost for Ireland through the death of a leader and thinker of integrity and promise. Ferguson had been ill at the time of Davis's death, and the poem's allusion to this fact contributes to its personal sense of events moving beyond the liberal virtues it celebrates. The ambition of Ferguson's 'Lament' was for a major mode, the pastoral elegy, and the assumption was that Davis was of sufficient stature to carry it. Written as the Great Famine began, and published as it reached its peak, the poem's commemorative urge is tempered not just by personal sorrow, but by the sense of foreboding of a poem which fears the fratricidal violence of civil war. Traversing the seasons before it confronts Davis's death, it is full of metaphors of interrupted fecundity and growth: the soul of Davis is addressed as 'Young Husbandman of Erin's fruitful seed-time, / In the fresh track of danger's plough!' Consolation lies in the renewed confidence borne out by the new synthetic form itself: according to Ferguson in the accompanying article, the poem is written in 'the peculiar Irish taste in his composition, which it was poor Davis's delight to inculcate'. Its generic distinctiveness is national: although it 'may seem rugged to English eyes, [it] possesses a regular melody for Irish ears, and we believe, comes home to the Irish heart'.[36]

The appearance of such a piece in the Tory *DUM* bears testimony to the great influence of Thomas Osborne Davis (1814–45) across all of mid-century Irish culture and politics. Davis's death was just one of the many catastrophes that were to befall the cultural nationalist project in the late 1840s, but his influence was not confined to his own time. In 1914, introducing selections from his writings, Arthur Griffith could contrast him with the 'gigantic figure' of O'Connell, 'who inspired no generation but his own. The spirit of Davis has raised in every generation since his death resistance to national subjection and effort for national liberty.'[37] Davis's fellow editor and publisher of the *Nation*, the critic and politician Charles Gavan Duffy (1816–1903), was from 1843 to publish the immensely successful *Spirit of the Nation* series, newly written patriotic poems to ballad measures or in simple public registers. These were sold in cheap sixpenny editions to all who could read, and came with suggested melodies to be sung to those who could not. The melodies were to be those of 'a proud and fierce character', as distinct from an Irish music which 'too much loves to weep'.[38] The tunes were also aimed at the bands and choral singing of the temperance movement, a cause the *Nation* supported with great zeal. Consequently, the spirit of Davis was to be matched by the marching music and slogans of Irish nationalism: the title of a typical poem by John O'Hagan (1822–90), 'Ourselves Alone', could be translated back into Irish to provide the name of the political party that Griffith would lead, Sinn Féin.

Davis's own 'A Nation Once Again' and 'The West's Asleep' are typical of the songs printed in the *Nation* and collected in *The Spirit of the Nation*, looking forward to a new epoch or commemorative of great events in the past. In Davis's hands these might be as likely to be defeats as victories ('Lament for the Death of Eoghan Ruadh O'Neill', 'The Sack of Baltimore'), but there was ambivalence in other versions of history. Duffy's ballad 'The Muster of the North' replays the notorious massacre of Protestants in Ulster in 1641 from the point of view of the insurgents; 'The Croppy Boy' by William McBurney and 'The Memory of the Dead' by John Kells Ingram (1823–1907) were both answers to the famous and not-so-rhetorical question in the first line of Ingram's ballad 'Who fears to speak of '98?' The first printed appearance of the popular ballad 'The Shan Van Vocht' was in the *Nation* in 1842.[39]

In one respect, the poets of the *Nation* were, as Griffith was later to say, writers of 'poems, vibrant with manliness and passion . . . written deliberately to re-awaken and strengthen the national spirit and inform the national mind'. Davis's nationalism was an inclusive one, not just that of 'ourselves alone'. For all that the *Nation* invoked an imagery of blood and race, Davis for one knew that such exclusivity would impoverish the emerging nation. His poem 'Celts and Saxons' finds legitimate nationhood simply in the fact of being born in Ireland, and claims to rise above the factions of Irish society, of ethnicity, sect or class: 'We heed not blood, nor creed, nor clan.' The poem's sense of utopian possibility envisages a future of tolerant hybridity:

> And oh! It were a gallant deed
>   To show before mankind,
> How every race and every creed
>   Might be by love combined –

> Might be combined, yet not forget
>   The fountains whence they rose,
> And, filled by many a rivulet,
>   The stately Shannon flows.[40]

That final image of rivulets flowing into one river performs two functions, allowing differing cultural or sectarian identities while actively promoting their mixing. 'Love' in this stanza is, on the one hand, the Christian gospel which all sects in Ireland shared, and on the other, a principle of the intermarriage which will bring about the hybrid future of the modern nation.

Davis was Protestant, half-Welsh, half-Irish (thus signing himself 'The Celt') and Trinity-educated. To his own model mixed background might be added the European source of his ideas. The influence of the nationalism of Johann Gottfried von Herder, Augustin Thierry or Guiseppe Mazzini was heard in the *Nation* along with specifically Irish complaints. The nickname for the writers gathered round Davis, 'Young Ireland', was coined as an English joke, contrasting their liberalism with Young England, the conservative grouping in the Tory party gathered round Benjamin Disraeli. But European nationalist movements of the 1830s, like Young Germany or Young Italy, were certainly in mind. Davis's thinking was placed squarely in the contexts of a western liberal tradition of nationality founded in Romantic subjectivism, recreating in the public sphere an emphasis on individual qualities of spirit, will and emotion. Only liberty could allow the growth of both individual and nation, and Davis constructs an Irish version of Victorian notions of the compulsion to duty and heroism. He could write in the *Nation* in 1843:

> To speak, look and do what your own soul from its depths orders you, are credentials of greatness which all men understand and acknowledge . . . Why should not nations be judged thus? Is not a full indulgence of its natural tendencies essential to a *people's* greatness?[41]

In style and substance, this is Carlylean hero-worship transformed into the spirit of the nation, a sounding of a *zeitgeist* heard across post-Napoleonic Europe, where nationalism is a vital principle of the will both of self and of history. In the words of O'Hagan's refrain, 'To do at once what is to do, / And trust OURSELVES ALONE'.

Both music and poetry come to play the vital role in this emergence of the nation: while the poems and songs in *The Spirit of the Nation* were envisaged as expressive of spirit, it might be more likely that they were that spirit itself. Davis, after all, held that 'National poetry is the very flowering of the soul.'[42] Duffy's publishing projects thus gained a near-mystical imperative. In 1845 he published his immensely popular *Ballad Poetry of Ireland*, which by its thirty-ninth edition in 1866, had sold 76,000 copies.[43] Both in its preface and selection, this anthology contributes much to the increasingly nationalist version of the arguments put forward by Samuel Ferguson a decade earlier. Davis wrote passionately on the need to revive the Irish-language: 'A nation without a language of its own is only half a nation.'[44] But both Duffy and fellow Young Ireland poet and anthologist Denis Florence MacCarthy (1817–82), editor of the 1846 *Book of Irish Ballads*, published only English-language poems through Duffy's press.

For Duffy and MacCarthy (and Davis reviewing Duffy in the *Nation*[45]) the resultant literature is called 'Anglo-Irish' and it is written in the 'Anglo-Irish' language. According to Duffy, 'There is an Anglo-Irish-language as easily discriminated from London English as the dialect of Saxon spoken in the Lowlands of Scotland . . . It is a dialect fired with the restless imagination, and coloured with the strong passions of our nation.'[46] This new use of the term 'Anglo-Irish' speaks from the pragmatic side of the *Nation* writers, a typical Davis-like accommodation, describing the distinctively Celtic features (imagination, passion) of a poetry which nevertheless must pay due respect to the English language which was, in MacCarthy's terms, 'the nursing mother of our minds'. English had its uses, none less than the fact that it bore the advantages of being 'widely-diffused' as well as 'genius-consecrated'. To its gathering international dominance might be added the Irish mode. MacCarthy speaks of this in terms reminiscent of Ferguson's strictures on translation, or Walsh's macaronic practice: 'An Irish word or an Irish phrase, even appositely introduced, will not be sufficient; it must pervade the entire poem, and must be seen and felt in the construction, the sentiment and the expression.' Invoking a cliché of authenticity and rooted, organic form, MacCarthy says that Irish writers must 'endeavour to be racy of their native soil'.[47]

For a brief period this criticism indeed fertilised a large amount of original ballad poetry written by Irish men and women: Stopford Brooke and T. W. Rolleston's classic 1900 anthology *A Treasury of Irish Poetry* includes nineteen *Nation* poets, while still giving the most famous, James Clarence Mangan, a section to himself. In addition to the more revolutionary tone of O'Hagan, McBurney and Ingram, the religious topics broached by John Keegan (1809–49) and the historical subjects dramatised in ballad by Thomas D'Arcy McGee (1825–68) or Richard D'Alton Williams (1822–62) show the focus of these writers on a self-improving and educational mission which was essentially bourgeois in class and ethics. Women poets, too, initially wrote within this focused range of subject matter, on polemical, historical or devotional matters, following the *Nation's* middle-class curriculum: receiving the first unsightly and ill-punctuated manuscripts from the seventeen-year-old Ellen Mary Patrick Downing (1828–69), Duffy sent her Davis's *Essays* and his own *Ballad Poetry*, along with Percy's *Reliques* and Lamb's *Tales from Shakespeare*.[48] Following conventional practice, Downing published pseudonymously, as 'Mary of the Nation', and was joined by other young women, Mary Kelly (*c*.1825–1910), also known as 'Eva', Olivia Knight (later Hope Connolly, *c*.1830–1909), known as 'Thomasine', and, after 1850, Elizabeth Willoughby Treacy (later Varian, *c*.1830–96), whose pen-name was 'Finola'. The most famous of these was Jane Elgee (*c*.1821–96), later Lady Wilde, mother of Oscar, who wrote as 'Speranza'.

The subject matter for all of these poets was to be transformed by one historical event which brought a remarkable period of cultural and intellectual growth to an end. This was the failure of the potato crop in 1845 and the succeeding years, and the subsequent years of famine. After the deaths of Davis and O'Connell, an increasingly militant faction followed John Mitchel (1815–75), powerful polemicist and founder of the *United Irishman* paper. Of the early writing of the youthful Downing and Kelly in the *Nation*, Kelly's 'Tipperary' is a typical poem in praise of home and place which gives way only intermittently to nationalist anger in a Catholic idiom: 'Our land it is theirs by plunder, but, by Brigid, ourselves are free.'[49] Kelly's own growing politicisation, however, where she was to play the steadfast Sarah Curran to her exiled fiancée O'Doherty's Emmet, can be seen in her famine poetry. 'A Scene for Ireland' pictures a starving family evicted from a burnt-out home with the note of sarcasm reserved for the rich lady landowner:

> For all the grace of silks and lace
> > Some wretches naked shiver;
> For every smile upon her face
> > Some death-blue lips will quiver!
>
> There's not a scene of lordly pride
> > (Did heaven's good light illumine)
> But we should know had, far and wide,
> > Its meed of victims human.[50]

As social and economic conditions slid towards catastrophe, so the level of rhetorical indignation increased in Young Ireland poetry. For some literary historians the cultural consequences of famine were an accentuation of the gaps and discontinuities of Victorian Irish writing, where famine writing is marked by a sense of the inadequacy of representation before the enormity of the subject.[51] However, as Chris Morash's 1989 anthology *The Hungry Voice* shows, famine poetry practically amounts to a sub-genre of Irish poetry. The approach varied, from the barely controlled ironies of a poet like Kelly to the more oblique treatments of Mangan. Perhaps the most direct responses were written by Elgee, who was later allied with the more revolutionary elements of Young Ireland which followed the death of Davis. She became politicised only after witnessing Davis's funeral, but by 1848 she was serving as editor of the *Nation*, writing revolutionary leader articles and printing 'Jacta Alea Est' (The Die is Cast) which was to cause the paper's brief suppression. Certainly this Anglo-Irish Protestant in her mid-twenties struck an impressive figure as a type of the new nationalist woman. As Duffy remembered her, she was 'a tall girl . . . whose stately carriage and figure, flashing brown eyes, and features cast in an heroic mould, seemed fit for the genius of poetry, or the spirit of revolution'.[52]

Elgee's best-known poem on the subject, 'The Famine Year', is a dialogue poem, in which the victims reproach the questioning first speaker of the poem, thus moving between the silence of the observer and the anger of the suffering. The speaker is revealed as dumbly English at the end, since the poem is left with the dead bearing witness for themselves in eternity:

> We are wretches, famished, scorned, human tools to build your pride,
> But God will yet take vengeance for the souls for whom Christ died.
> Now is your hour of pleasure, bask ye in the world's caress;
> But our whitening bones against ye will arise as witnesses,
> From the cabins and the ditches, in their charred, uncoffined masses,
> For the ANGEL OF THE TRUMPET will know them as he passes.
> A ghastly, spectral army before great God we'll stand
> And arraign ye as our murderers, O spoilers of our land![53]

The power of this writing lies in the sonic string of near, slightly out-of-control sibilant rhymes, 'caress / witnesses / masses / passes', which lend semantic force to the speech of those about to die and go to heaven. 'Caress / witnesses' reinforces the discomfort and guilt of the better-off, who themselves must bear witness as soon as they become readers of this poem.

A collected *Poems by Speranza* was published in 1864, and the volume opens with a dedication to her sons, Willie and Oscar Wilde, offering them up for sacrifice to the nation: 'I made them indeed, / Speak plain the word COUNTRY. I taught them, no doubt, / That a Country's a thing men should die for at need!' The opening poem, 'The Brothers', then presents a bloodthirsty tale of 1798, which ends with the severed heads of both brothers preserved in adjoining coffins, talking to each other still. Elgee's poetry is perhaps too attracted to this macabre note, but it was symptomatic of the later move of Young Ireland away from peaceful political means through the horrors of famine. William Smith O'Brien's failed uprising at Ballingarry, Ireland's one ignominious contribution to 1848, a year of revolutions in Europe, saw the effective ending of Young Ireland as a political force and a combination of deportations and escape depleted the leadership. They were matched by the thousands fleeing starvation, and the massive emigration throughout the rest of the century which, with the million deaths at home, was practically to halve the population of Ireland. Ellen Downing's sentimental classic of 1849, 'The Old Chapel at Lismore',[54] written before she herself became a nun, is in a way prophetic of the return of popular Irish nationalism to a Catholic faith and fatherland, while also effectively giving up on the imaginative experiments and utopian thinking of the 1840s.

James Clarence Mangan

The year 1849 was also the date of the death of the most famous poet associated with Young Ireland and the period of famine, James Clarence Mangan (1803–49). For someone like John Mitchel, who was to edit an American edition of Mangan in 1859, he was to become the type of the unfulfilled and abject Irish artist, whose short life and strange career would serve as representative of the failures of Irish culture in times of degradation and insurrection.[55] Mitchel's portrait was to carry on down through to the end of the century and the beginning of the next. Ten years after Yeats expressed his desire to be counted one with Davis, Mangan and Ferguson, in 1902 the twenty-year-old James Joyce read a paper on Mangan to the Royal University's Literary and Historical Society.

Joyce associated himself with the Mitchel version of a poet who alternated between tragedy and bathos. For Charles Gavan Duffy, among others, Mangan's poetry was held up as the significant literary achievement of Young Ireland ballad poetry, and he makes extraordinary claims for its prosodic successes: 'he has not, and perhaps never had, any rival in mastery of the metrical and rhythmical resources of the English tongue'.[56] The young Joyce brought this appreciation of Mangan together with the mystical side of the spirit of the *Nation*, seeing that stylistic mastery alternated with a corresponding self-abnegation before historical circumstance and Romantic poetics: 'Mangan is the type of his race. History encloses him so straitly that even his fiery moments do not set him free from it.'[57]

Mangan spent all of his life in Dublin, working variously as a scrivener and a librarian, but mainly as contributor to the periodical press. Until late in his life he was to publish almost exclusively in magazines and newspapers, and the majority of his writing is hackwork, written to finance the eccentric, unhealthy and alcoholic existence which was to lead to his death from cholera at the end of the famine. His prose works are in the main pastiche, veering between Gothic and a humour that was highly dependent on wordplay and frequent lapses into riddle, verse or translation. He wrote his own autobiography twice in the last months of his life. One version, a sort of confession for his friend Fr C. P. Meehan, was written between the staves of a music score. It typically vacillates between tales of a squalid childhood, his brilliance at school and the drudgery of his work as a scrivener. It is structured in brief chapters headed by epigraphs from Massinger, the New Testament and *Othello* ('Farewell the tranquil mind! Farewell content!'), as if to hold together a life written through Renaissance tragedy, German Romanticism and Irish Catholic mysticism.[58] A sketch of Mangan's character appeared in the *Irishman* newspaper after his death in 1850, but it was a piece of journalism written by Mangan himself, his so-called 'impersonal autobiography'. By way of contrast with the more elevated tone and the self-pity of the longer 'Autobiography', it is full of macabre jokes about the impending death of its subject.

In its way, the impersonal autobiography refutes the value which Joyce and Mitchel placed on Mangan, bound to what Joyce called a 'narrow and hysterical nationality',[59] compelled to write out of the national sadness. Mangan's poetry was founded in the translations, from Persian and German as much as Irish, that he provided for periodicals, and he frequently invented poems and poets when pecuniary circumstances demanded. In forgery, translation and original poems, Mangan's habit of pseudonymous publication results, though, in what he calls 'the antithesis of plagiarism', which comes from one who says he '*must* write in a variety of styles' (Mangan's emphasis). In an Irish version of a mid-Victorian conception of the 'sympathy' of the Romantic artist, the poet becomes the medium through which the 'original' is transmitted. Asking himself, as it were, the question "'And do you really sympathise with your subject?"' he answers:

> 'Yes, always, always . . . When I write as a Persian, I feel as a Persian, and am transported back to the days of Diemsheed and the Genii; when I write as a Spaniard, I forget, for the moment, everything but the Cid, the Moors, and the Alhambra; for when I translate from the Irish, my heart has no pulses except for the wrongs and sorrows of my own stricken land.'[60]

This list of clichés doesn't neglect a common Irish one, reading like a sarcastic version of Romantic negative capability. Rewriting his Mangan address in 1907, Joyce directly suggested a Keatsian poet whose desire for anonymity is balanced only by his anger: 'He is a Romantic, a would-be herald, a prototype for a would-be nation; but for all that, one who expressed the sacred indignation of his soul in a dignified form cannot have written his name in water.'[61] In Joyce's rhyming, punning prose, only 'sacred indignation' achieves 'dignified form'. Compulsive punning runs also throughout everything Mangan does, however, and he was not above turning the Keats epitaph into a joke. In a piece published in the *Irishman* in July 1849, a month after his death, Mangan's sketch of William Maginn imagines his subject's imminent obscurity and the reasons for his failure in terms which are prescient of his own loss of identity through journalism, illness and drink: 'His name, like Keats, has been "written in water"; or, more properly speaking, in gin-and-water. By the cognomen, in fact, of Maginn-and-water he *was* familiarly known among his literary associates and boon companions in later years.'[62]

Such a turn to the dismissive joke, of a tonal whimsy which pushes bad taste towards bad faith, is typical of all of Mangan's writing, a writing not just in a variety of styles but also of genres and modes, frequently within the same text. Much of the poetry seems deliberately spoiled by a maddening compulsion to remind us of its linguistic artifice, through the jokes, the puns and the outrageous rhymes pushed towards outright doggerel. The effect is paradoxical, of a bogus authenticity, an incessant inventiveness which suggests complete stylistic originality for each poem, yet is usually written as translation through the texts of others. Even stunning original poems written in a time of famine, like 'A Vision of Connaught in the Thirteenth Century', or 'Siberia', dislocate their nightmare allegories into other times, other places, other styles. Yet neither could be mistaken for the work of any poet other than Mangan.

Speaking of the extraordinary mixture of classical allusion and local political events in the celebrated street ballads of Mangan's Dublin neighbour Zozimus (Michael Moran, 1795–1846), David Lloyd points out that 'Tonal instability . . . is common, as is a similarly vertiginous mixture of realism and burlesque, "high language" and slang.'[63] For Lloyd, such instabilities are evidence of an anxiety about the inauthenticity of the Young Ireland ballads, their nationalist fear of adulteration and, paradoxically, their bourgeois desire to invent an Anglo-Irish ballad canon which might avoid the literary and social embarrassments of the street ballad tradition. For Mangan, however, who '*must* write in a variety of styles', this is hardly an issue. It is hard to feel securely 'at home' in a Mangan poem, and he produces poetry as strange and original as anything produced in English in the nineteenth century. Joyce suggests a musical inventiveness to match that of Poe, and Mangan's contemporary Duffy had heard a combination of German ballad metres, oriental verse forms, and the metres both of Gaelic poetry, learnt from the imitations of Callanan, Ferguson and Walsh, and the street ballads of the poet's Dublin. Add in the fact of regular anonymous publication, the striving through translation for identification of the poet with a speaker from widely differing poetic and linguistic cultures, and we also have the cultivation of the deliberate impersonality of prosopopoeia, or the dramatic monologue, which by mid-century was becoming the dominant post-Romantic mode of British and American verse.

One celebrated poem of Mangan demonstrates the use he made of Irish-language texts, nationalist song and the highly inventive translating practice through which translation appears as dramatic monologue. Thomas Furlong's version of the lyric of the song 'Róisín Dubh' had appeared in Hardiman's *Irish Minstrelsy* in 1831. Hardiman glossed the song as an eighteenth-century Jacobite allegory of Irish history, in which the Ulster chieftain Red Hugh O'Donnell addresses the Ireland from which he was forced into exile after the Battle of Kinsale of a century before, in 1602. The reading attracted the ire of Samuel Ferguson in his *DUM* reviews, even if he couldn't resist telling O'Donnell's story at some length as a Waverley-style romance for his *DUM* readers. For Ferguson, Furlong's translation and Hardiman's reading of it removed the erotic charge of the poem. Indeed he read it as a love poem of transgressive desire between the speaker, an exiled priest, and his lover, figured as a little black rose. Closely following the Irish, Ferguson translated the speaker as saying that he would read the gospel in mass for her, take her 'youth' and 'make delights behind the fort'. Blasphemy shades into illicit desire, while pandering to one sectarian prejudice of Ferguson's Protestant *DUM* readers, of the shortcomings of Roman Catholicism's celibate priesthood. Furlong's coy version had written the desire of the song's celebrated final verse with misty mountains and 'the crimson hue' of 'the wild waves of old ocean'.[64] Merely through literal translation, Ferguson's speaker renders the sexual excitement of the geography of the entire country in an extraordinary surfeit of pathetic fallacy:

> The Erne shall be in its strong flood – the hills shall be uptorn;
> And the sea shall have its waves red, and blood shall be spilled;
> Every mountain-valley, and every moor throughout Ireland shall be on high,
> Some day before (you) shall perish, my Roiseen Dubh.[65]

Mangan ran together these conflicting readings of the Irish song in three versions, and the best-known, 'Dark Rosaleen', appeared in the *Nation* in May 1846. He had contributed his translations in annotated series in the *Anthologia Germanica* and *Literae Orientales* to the *DUM* from 1835, and his *Anthologia Hibernica* was also to appear there from 1847. But like others in the time of the famine, he was to follow John Mitchel to the *United Irishman* and his one book-length collection, *The Poets and Poetry of Munster*, was developed for the interest of Young Ireland in the Jacobite dissent of the previous century. Mangan's version of 'Róisín Dubh' thus lends the note of indignation that Joyce had seen in his poetry to its new contexts, where the Hardiman/Furlong Jacobite version of the poem in turn becomes a Young Ireland allegory. The eroticised politics of the *aisling* tradition, of the bereft girl pining for her exiled Stuart prince, emerge in the new conditions of Irish nationalism, which, given Young Ireland's rehabilitation of the United Irishmen, was now republican and militant.

Mangan is quite happy to follow Furlong, and keep the girl and her lover at a platonic distance in 'Dark Rosaleen'. The mounting sexual excitement, however, is kept as an index of feeling for the resurgence which would transform the speaker of the poem's complaint of abject 'pain and woe'. The speaker sees that a smile would give him 'A second life, a soul anew', and the poem then appears to shed both allegory and fidelity to the 'original' in its final stanza as it contemplates an insurgent national desire. 'Dark Rosaleen' ends with a contemporary, mid-1840s speaker, where the sexual excitement of Ferguson's lines has been transferred on to the nation-as-woman trope, now contemplating a violent apocalypse:

> O! the Erne shall run red
>   With redundance of blood,
> The earth shall rock beneath our tread,
>   And flames wrap hill and wood,
> And gun-peal, and slogan cry,
>   Wake many a glen serene,
> Ere you shall fade, ere you shall die,
>   My Dark Rosaleen!
>   My own Rosaleen!
> The judgement hour must first be nigh,
> Ere you can fade, ere you can die,
>   My Dark Rosaleen![66]

Neither 'gun-peal, and slogan cry' nor 'judgement hour' appears in any previous versions, but they are adaptations for new contexts: the *Nation* newspaper, the growing crisis of famine, the falling apart of nationalist consensus after the death of Davis.

Mangan does more than just update the text, however. Like his great version of 'O'Hussey's Ode to the Maguire', the poem is ostensibly a translation, but it reads more like an impersonation or a dramatic monologue. He weaves together loose, Gaelic-approximated sound patterns along with the transforming powers of metaphor implicit in subversive uses of the Jacobite tradition. A modulated assonance sounds quietly within the indignation, as Joyce might put it, of the envisaged apocalypse: 'blood', for instance, takes only half-rhymes, with 'tread' and 'wood'. There is a delicate string of related sounds suggested from the anglicised name of the river Éirne onwards: the sounds in 'Erne', 'run', and 'red' are reordered in their very excess, 'redundance', and the sounds are accented on through the stanza, in 'gun', 'slogan', 'glen' and 'serene'. The latter modulation gains full rhyming association with the poem's title, the anglicised name 'Rosaleen', thus linking back with the English rhymes Rosaleen had taken throughout all seven stanzas of the poem. These patterns, not out of place in a sound poem, serve then to echo the transformations that have been worked in the metaphor through the possible two hundred and fifty years of the poem's textual history, from the defeat and exile of the Gaelic aristocracy after Kinsale, the underground allegories of the *aisling* tradition, and on through the coy bourgeois sexuality that had provoked the contempt of Ferguson. Yet throughout, the text also questions the powers of certain types of figuration in the national tradition, as it plays with the dangerous content of those figures. While not exactly writing agit-prop, the speaker of 'Dark Rosaleen' certainly gets agitated, all in the insecure, inauthentic surrounds of what is now a synthetic English poem.

Narrative and epic: the Fenians, De Vere, Allingham

After quoting Mangan's supposed Turkish 'translation', the wonderful *tour de force* 'The Karamanian Exile' ('I see thee ever in my dreams, / Karaman! / Thy hundred hills, thy thousand streams, / Karaman! O Karaman!'), Frank O'Connor felt that the effect was laughable. But he does point to its 'extraordinary rhythmical freedom', while only slightly misrepresenting the political point of such innovation: 'it is not English poetry'.[67] The best of Mangan's poems sound mannered to the ear because they are so original. Yet while the sources, actual or spoof, may be from other languages, the final results are a deliberate synthesis of a number of competing cultural influences which produced an ultimately creative form born out of the chafing irritation at its enclosure within English. Nevertheless, rather like Scots poetry after the sim- ilarly short career of Robert Burns, Mangan's example was so strong, and in his case, his contribution so idiosyncratic, that the quality of the short-lived alliance of English-language poetry with the nationalist tradition through the 1830s and 1840s did not last after his death in 1849. Despite the amount of writing it provoked, the famine had much to do with this, and a combination of the horror with which liberal unionist opinion viewed British mismanage- ment of the situation and the dispersal of the Young Ireland intellectuals after 1848, led to the political and cultural vacuum in which there was little poetry of distinction composed within Ireland for the next thirty or so years.

Denis Florence MacCarthy continued to write and publish for the *Nation* and other journals, continuing the publication for Irish audiences of Irish and European texts in English versions. His versions of the dramas of Calderon, for instance, attempt to replicate in English the unusual rhyming of the originals, in ways which the example of Mangan had suggested to the Irish translator.[68] But his versions of Irish myth and legend are conventional if competent. A typical example is his verse translation of the Latin Irish *immram*, the *Navigatio Sancti Brendani*, which ends up in a 'Hy Brasil' which sounds suspiciously like the New York which was then receiving thousands of Irish emigrants after the famine: '"But in the end upon that land shall fall / A bitter scourge, a lasting flood of tears,"' he has St Brendan say of Ireland; so, '"Then shall this land prove thy poor country's friend, / And shine a second Eden in the west."'[69] Timothy Daniel Sullivan (1827–1914) also showed that this medieval Catholic material had an audience in Ireland: his verse translation of the *immram* 'The Voyage of the O'Corras' posits only sacramental absolution for sins of violence and seemingly unquenchable revenge.[70]

The increasingly violent events of the Fenians of the 1860s and then the Land League in the 1880s were echoed in an Irish national poetry influenced alike by a quiescent Catholic hierarchy and a leadership which tempted insurrection when it wasn't in exile. The poetry of John Francis O'Donnell (1837–74) was composed for the various periodicals for which he had worked from the age of fourteen, a life of hackwork which was to lead to an early death at thirty-seven. While the verse has a mid-Victorian competence, quite unlike the textures of Mangan, and was published in English as well as Irish journals, O'Donnell's national poems, like 'In the Night-Time', 'In Exile', 'The Question', or his best-known poem 'A Spinning Song', echo the tone of Young Ireland indignation. Again rather like Mangan, O'Donnell's poetry came to be associated with a political movement of which he was not entirely a member, in his case the Fenians. Thematically incoherent while stylistically conventional, the poetry shows the pressures of producing large amounts of occasional verse: introducing a selection of poems after O'Donnell's death, the novelist and poet Richard Dowling (1846–98) speaks of the possible three volumes of uncollected poems scattered across periodicals in Ireland, Britain and the USA.[71]

Even in exile, however, the careers of the Young Irelanders were not always those of the irreconcilable Mitchel, who continued to write powerful autobiographical polemic from the United States, or the other great oratorical figure of Young Ireland, Thomas Francis Meagher (1823–67), who ended up leading the Irish Brigade in the American Civil War. Perhaps more typical were Duffy, who became prime minister of Victoria in Australia and accepted a knighthood in 1873, John O'Hagan who followed his fellow Ulster Catholic, patron and Gladstone's Lord Chancellor, Thomas O'Hagan, to the judiciary, or Thomas D'Arcy McGee, who was to become a minister in the Canadian government and was assassinated after denouncing the Fenians. The movement of Irish poetry, like that of the Irish population, became centrifugal, a great diasporic scattering of energies from their Irish centre. In 1887, the Irish-American publisher and poet Daniel Connolly published his vast anthology, the *Household Library of Ireland's Poets with Full and Choice Selections from the Irish-American Poets*. By then, he could claim Irishness of birth or descent for some fifty-nine American poets.

Even an eccentric figure like Thomas Caulfield Irwin (1823–92), who published his often whimsical poetry (or *Versicles* as his first volume of 1856 was called) in both the *DUM* and the *Nation*, turned briefly to the new phenomenon of global Irishness in his *Irish Poems and Legends* of 1869. This was dedicated to his 'Countrymen, Native & Emigrant' and reserved one stanza of 'The Potato Digger's Song' ('The blessed fruit / That grows at the root / Is the real gold / of Ireland') for the Australian Irish. He goes on to envisage the humour of a British empire which is also an Irish one, in his characteristically odd lineation:

> As the great Sun sets in glory furled,
>   Faith, it's great to think as I watch his face –
> If he never sets on the English World,
>   He never, lad, sets on the Irish Race,
>   In the West, in the South, New Ireland's still
>   Growing up in his light; – come, work with a will.[72]

Even in a 'New Ireland', no matter how it is still 'Growing up', the potato must still be dug.

However, the best poetry of the period following the famine was written by two Irish poets with unionist sympathies who published for British as well as

Irish audiences. Aubrey de Vere (1814–1902) and William Allingham (1824–89) spent much of their literary lives in British intellectual circles, working with British publishers yet writing on Irish subjects. De Vere's long life saw friendships with two poets laureate, Wordsworth and Tennyson, but most significant was his friendship with John Henry Newman. Cardinal Manning received him into the Catholic church in 1851. While not an unusual move for an English Tory, de Vere's was a rare Irish conversion, brought up as he was in the much more entrenched sectarian atmosphere of the nineteenth-century Anglo-Irish landed class. This unusual social and cultural position makes it difficult to accommodate de Vere's poetry within either English or Irish literary histories, most of it written as long poems on religious or classical as well as Irish subjects. Active in famine relief, de Vere produced a polemic on the subject, the title of which betrays some of the ambivalence of his position: *English Misrule and Irish Misdeeds* (1848). He also wrote one of the most powerful famine poems, 'The Year of Sorrow: 1849', the four parts of which follow the seasons which brought the failure of the potato crop for a fifth successive year.

De Vere also appropriated the figural practice of the Irish Catholic tradition, and in particular the black rose trope of Furlong and Mangan. Thomas Davis had hoped that in the place of a modern epic, Irish poets might write a 'Ballad History of Ireland'. De Vere was an unlikely candidate for such a task, but his *Inisfail: A Lyrical Chronicle of Ireland* (1861) was a 180-page sequence of lyrics and ballads which told the history of Ireland from the Norman invasion to the end of the eighteenth century. *Inisfail* has its *longeurs*, but its most effective passages are those which suit its author's Tory temperament, in the Romance elements of heroic events, or of lament for religious persecution and the Penal Laws. 'A Ballad of Sarsfield', for instance, imagines 'The Bursting of the Guns' in 1690 in the near-doggerel rhymes of the street ballad. It follows 'Archbishop Plunkett', written in the same metre, but mixing elegy with anger over Oliver Plunkett's betrayal and execution by the English monarch: 'His Faith King Charles partakes – and hides!' *Inisfail* returns throughout to the black rose motif and two of its lyrics are called 'Roisin Dubh'. Its best-known lyric, called simply 'Song', is another treatment of the theme, and is reserved for the poem's ending at the late-eighteenth century:

Song

The Little Black Rose shall be red at last!
    What made it black but the East wind dry
And the tear of the widow that fell on it fast?
    It shall redden the hills when June is nigh!

The Silk of the Kine shall rest at last!
      What drave her forth but the dragon-fly?
In the golden vale she shall feed full fast
      With her mild gold horn, and her slow dark eye.

The wounded wood-dove lies dead at last:
      The pine long-bleeding, it shall not die!
– This song is secret. Mine ear it pass'd
      In a wind o'er the stone-plain of Athenry.[73]

The delicately inventive use of the repetition of rhyme scheme and rhyme words here sounds a precariously rare note of hope in the Irish poetry of the period, looking back to the deliverance of the Catholics through the gradual repeal of the Penal Laws in the eighteenth century just as it hopes for the deliverance of a blighted Ireland in the nineteenth.

The very isolation of de Vere's position in both British and Irish society belies his short-lived hope for peace and prosperity. The rise of political violence in the years immediately following the publication of *Inisfail* seemed to forestall the solution promoted by his other long poem of 1861, *The Sisters*, of a Catholic unionist quietism fostering peace through an acceptance of the cultural union with a Great Britain now tolerant of Ireland's Catholicism. In 1858, a combination of the remnants of the Young Irelanders, nationalist journalists and small-scale Catholic landowners had formed the Irish Republican Brotherhood, or IRB. Loosely allied with the agrarian secret societies, the Ribbonmen, which had persisted throughout the nineteenth century, this popular movement had a broader social and geographical base than Young Ireland. Known commonly as Fenians, its members were based not only in Ireland, but in Britain and America. Small-scale insurrections in Munster and Dublin in 1867 were matched by atrocities linked to Fenianism in Manchester and London and no fewer than two invasions of Canada in 1866 and 1870. The best-known Fenian poem was another invocation of 1798 for a new nationalist movement, 'The Rising of the Moon' by John Keegan Casey (1846–70). Casey's imprisonment in 1867 and early death also provided a poet-martyr for his generation.

The Fenian journal, *The Irish People*, was edited by John O'Leary (1830–1907), who, like Davis and Duffy before him, was a vigorous promoter of Irish verse. Along with O'Donnell, its best-known writers were Charles Joseph Kickham (1828–82) and Fanny Parnell (1848–82). The mode of Kickham's verse is closer to that of earlier poet-novelists Banim and Griffin, drawn to the narrative ballad just as he was drawn to a life of political activism. With understated acuity, his political gratitude struggling slightly with his literary generosity, O'Leary said that Kickham was 'a patriot first and a poet after . . . He found other and what he deemed more pressing work to do for Ireland: and it is certainly not for me to quarrel with his choice.'[74] Parnell was the *Irish People*'s own teenage poet, but left for Paris and then America. There she became, according to Daniel Connolly, 'the "Speranza" of the new Ireland in America'.[75] It was in the 1880s, the decade of her brother Charles Stewart Parnell's pre-eminence, that her *Land League Songs* gained their full propagandist audience. The imprisonment or political exile of the Fenian leaders after 1867 meant that literary Fenianism was not to achieve its very real literary influence until the return of O'Leary from exile in 1885, when he was to serve as a formative influence on the young William Butler Yeats.

In the midst of this renewed political activity, William Allingham's *Lawrence Bloomfield in Ireland: A Modern Poem* appeared serially in London, in *Fraser's Magazine* from 1862 to 1863. It was revised, republished and slightly retitled in one volume as *Laurence Bloomfield in Ireland* in 1864. It is the most important long Irish poem of the 1860s, if not in the Victorian period before Yeats, raising matters of land, proprietorship, political violence and social inequality. The condition-of-Ireland poem challenged a number of Victorian Irish poets, particularly those of an imperialist persuasion, drawn to Victorian versions of epic. De Vere's *The Sisters* mixes blank verse dialogue with narrative and Samuel Ferguson's long poems based in Irish mythical material, *Congal* (1872) or *Conary* (1880), lend themselves to Victorian allegorical interpretations, mixing Irish epic and imperialism.[76] Neither poet fully solves the formal problem of the long poem, and Allingham's contribution – as one enthusiastic reader, George Eliot, pointed out – was to revive the manner of the English poetry of the provincial, presenting an Irish version of George Crabbe's *The Village*. Thus his poem mixes the social critique both of repressive landlordism and of agrarian secret societies in a mode of poetic realism which has little precedent in Victorian Irish poetry. It suggested an eclogic solution, of the perfect landlord reconciled in mild feudal relation with a well-managed tenantry, and as with the similarly peaceful suggestion made by de Vere in *The Sisters*, it did not win many adherents in a time of increasingly violent political divisions. O'Leary, however, recognised the power of its diagnosis of social ills and reprinted large sections in *The Irish People*. Not only does *Laurence Bloomfield* picture Ireland between the famine and the rise of Parnell in frequently harrowing detail, it also suggests an Irish verse form open to the varying currents of Victorian poetry and culture, pre-Raphaelite and realist as much as Celtic: its subtitle is *A Modern Poem*.

Laurence Bloomfield is the one successful formal break from the lyrics which dominate the Irish mode. When Yeats approached Allingham's wife, Helen, the English painter, for permission to publish *Sixteen Poems* of Allingham, he called him 'my own master in Irish verse'.[77] His choice, though, was exclusively lyric. Allingham himself, though, never settled on one style. This is not quite the restless, mannerist impersonation of Mangan, rather a poet working for an English market in which he half-occupied an establishment role and half-presented a lack of a perceptible identity. He was later to edit *Fraser's Magazine*, and his *Diary* mixes a delightful memoir of his early life in Donegal with lengthy transcripts of conversations with his English friends, practically every writer of substance in Victorian literary society. These conversations present a series of vivid pictures of Victorian literary opinion, mediated through Allingham's modest persona, of the culturally removed, questioningly respectful or politely amused provincial. According to Geoffrey Taylor, Allingham was 'that rare thing, an Irish liberal',[78] and the *Diary* only infrequently lapses into impatient soliloquy.

Like Ferguson, Allingham was also a linguist and collector of Irish music and ballad, producing *The Ballad Book* (1864) for the English market. This differs from similar anthologies by Duffy and MacCarthy in that it includes many Scottish and English as well as Irish ballads, seeking the common British ground across this shared genre that might be expected from someone of Allingham's liberal unionist persuasion. His 1860 anthology of British verse, *Nightingale Valley*, was an inspiration for Francis Turner Palgrave's (and Alfred Tennyson's) *Golden Treasury*, that index of Victorian lyrical taste, full as it is of Scottish, English and Irish ballad poetry. Allingham's youthful experiences at fairs in Ireland, listening to ballads and picking up tunes, greatly influenced his own writing. One of his best-known lyrics, 'Lovely Mary Donnelly', was originally printed by Allingham himself and distributed on ballad sheets, so that it could be granted authentic performance: 'Songs for a people must find their natural element beside the cottage hearth.'[79]

In *Laurence Bloomfield*, he was no less aware than Davis of the power of the popular song tradition and its responsibilities for heightened political feeling. The impressionable peasant hero, Neal Doran, is drawn to Ribbon politics through story and song:

> With this, Old Ireland's glories, and her wrongs,
> Her famous dead, her landscapes, and her songs,
> Were fever'd fancy's beverage, – things well known
> Mingled with names and dreams confus'dly shown.

Poetic visions hover'd; every page
For Erin's glory, every fireside sage
Whose *shanahus* a brooding audience drew,
Were pleasant to his soul, and gospel-true.[80]

The couplet form, which has deterred readers from the poem, is here perfectly adapted as an ironic narrative device which can carry the subversive melody of which it warns, where legend, 'Old Ireland's glories and her wrongs', becomes 'gospel-true'.

The spectre of a coming modernity lies behind much of the poem and many of its pragmatic, attentive portrayals of social fact and the dangers of political fantasy. Neal Doran is attracted to a violence which might appear to be delusory, prompted by an ideology in which 'Poetic visions hover'd'. It results in a Ribbon assassination later in the poem, an act from which Neal recoils to become the ideal tenant. Allingham also provided his British readers with a scathing account of the oppressive social conditions in which the peasant class lived, forgotten by the British government, and in the arbitrary grip of a system of landownership which was compounded in equal parts by the irresponsibility of absentee landlords and the remorselessness of local land agents. In a long poem filled with a number of virtuoso set-pieces, the eviction scene in the seventh chapter is a piece of writing made all the more penetrating by its controlled and precise narration. It is a mark of the modernity of the poem that Allingham allows another, symbolist, mode to mix with its realist narrative drive. The narration pauses at the moment of the leaving of the home:

The strong stand ready; now appear the rest,
Girl, matron, grandsire, baby on the breast,
And Rosy's thin face on a pallet borne;
A motley concourse, feeble and forlorn.
One old man, tears upon his wrinkled cheek,
Stands trembling on a threshold, tries to speak,
But, in defect for any word for this,
Mutely upon the doorpost prints a kiss,
Then passes out for ever.[81]

Jane Elgee had granted her famine victims indignation and eloquence in the face of their suffering. In a moment more representative of the speechless suffering of modernity – the emigrant, the refugee, the holocaust victim – Allingham simply shows his peasants silent, the narration flat: 'in defect of any word for this'. The mute kissing of the doorpost is certainly Victorian, but it is followed by the last domestic act of the old man who 'passes out for ever', an outcast crossing the threshold. For the poet Paul Muldoon, 'This image of a critically positioned figure, a figure who is neither here nor there, may be traced back . . . to some deep-rooted sense of liminality that was, and is, central to the Irish psyche.'[82]

The 1880s: crossing the threshold

The framing in the doorway is in its way representative both of Allingham's own relation to Irish culture and of a society poised with trepidation before the next stage of its history. The occupation of such liminal spaces was one of the ways in which Revival Irish poetry was to invigorate itself by embracing its own marginality. Allingham's best-known poem, 'The Fairies', was immensely successful in England as well as Ireland, lending a Celtic note to a Victorian culture drawn to the picturesque and the Otherworldly. From mid-century, it echoed his friend Samuel Ferguson's 'The Fairy Thorn', but it also predated another treatment of the same theme, 'The Stolen Child', first published in 1886 and written by William Butler Yeats (1865–1939). Allingham's fairies had lived between land and water, 'along the rocky shore' or 'in the reeds / Of the black mountain lake'. Allingham's poem is far less doom-laden than Ferguson's twilit treatment, celebrating the mischievous 'Wee folk, good folk, / Trooping all together'. The metre is nursery rhyme, and the subject matter is childlike, and Allingham moves between natural and supernatural worlds, drawn to the escapism of the material. Yeats's early poetry was to occupy just such half-lit, half-natural, half-supernatural worlds, seeming actively to desire an escape through the liminal to alternative worlds.

Writing in 1889 about Yeats's first full volume, *The Wanderings of Oisin*, the Irish novelist and poet Rosa Mulholland (1841–1921) stated that, 'Ireland is in need of a great poet; surely he is already on the wing towards us.' Her hope was tempered by the experience of the previous century: 'We cannot deny that, up to the present, our poets have been only the fragments and beginnings of poets, each after each a promise and a disappointment.'[83] Even for those who did show promise, the Ireland of the 1880s appeared to be a place in which a literary career could only result in disappointment. Educated in Oxford, and consciously losing his accent, the major Irish-born writer of the last decades of the nineteenth century, Speranza's son Oscar Wilde (1854–1900), published first as a poet in London in 1881, and chose to continue his subsequent career as playwright, novelist, and reviewer outside of Ireland. Apart from the quality of the young Yeats's work, therefore, there was no reason in the 1880s to think that this moment might not be another period of promise which ended in disappointment: the febrile political atmosphere of the failed 1886 Home Rule Bill, in which an Irish issue brought down a British government, was followed swiftly by the seeming ending of political hopes with the fall of Parnell in 1889. No matter that Mulholland's hope for change was based in one precocious talent, there was cause for optimism, and the 1890s, of course, were to bring something more than fragments and beginnings. Two important editorial figures laid the groundwork for poetic revival in the 1870s and 1880s. The first was Jesuit priest and sometime-poet Fr Matthew Russell (1834–1912), who in 1873 began to edit the *Irish Monthly*. The second was the Fenian John O'Leary, who in 1885 returned from France twenty years after he had been exiled from Ireland.

A glimpse at the *Irish Monthly* around the time of the Home Rule crisis might not at first provide evidence of radical literary change. Beside translations of Shakespeare's songs into Latin by the little known 'GH' (Gerard Manley Hopkins, Jesuit colleague of Russell), the reader might find serialised publications of Mulholland's novels and stories and appreciative reviews of the Catholic poetry that she and Russell wrote. Russell's editorial policy was fairly plural, though, a fact underlined by the breadth of theme, nationalist as well as Catholic, that the concentration of women's writing brought to the journal. The young poets Katharine Tynan (1861–1931) and Rose Kavanagh (1859–91) joined Ellen O'Leary (1831–89) who had come from Tipperary to live with her brother John on his return to Dublin. The careers of O'Leary and Kavanagh seemed to fulfil the template of the short career of the Irish poet, as they died within two years of each other at the turn of the decade, but Tynan was to play a crucial part in the Revival, as poet and editor right up to the early years of the Irish Free State. The pluralism can also be seen in Russell's obituary for Samuel Ferguson, who had died in 1886. On the one hand he praises Ferguson's 'The Widow's Cloak', an Irish mode poem dedicated to Queen Victoria, and on the other hand quotes letters from Ferguson bemoaning a lifetime's loyalism unrewarded by recognition in England. The preceding poem in that issue was Yeats's 'Meditation of the Old Fisherman', seeming vindication of the elderly Ferguson's desire as expressed to Russell, 'regardless of such discouragements, to do what I can for the formation of a characteristic school of letters for my own country'.[84] 'The Stolen Child' appeared at the end of the year in the December issue.

Within two years, the poems by Tynan, Kavanagh, O'Leary, Yeats and others were to move out of the pages of the *Irish Monthly* and into a new publication. This was the seminal *Poems and Ballads of Young Ireland*, quite deliberately evoking the 1840s and dedicated to John O'Leary. It was filled with a new style of poetry for a new cultural nationalism. This extended to the Gaelic Athletic Association (GAA) as shown by the inclusion of 'Marching Song of the Gaelic Athletes' by Douglas Hyde (1860–1949), later first president of both the Gaelic League, from 1893, and Ireland from 1938. Since 1887, O'Leary had been editor of *The Gael*, newspaper of the GAA, but this didn't stop him publishing poems in it. His public life since his return was dedicated to an updating of a Davisite educational mission, as the titles of his lectures show: 'How Irishmen Should Feel', or 'What Irishmen Should Know'. The younger poets in the *Poems and Ballads*, such as Yeats, Kavanagh and Tynan, were also joined by more established writers such as Ellen O'Leary, John Todhunter (1839–1916) and T. W. Rolleston (1857–1920), all of whom were to play a part in this transitional moment.

The forms and subject matter of the volume were within now-accepted synthetic English-language Irish styles and subjects, either the recreation of historical events or the rewriting of Gaelic poetry. This can be seen in Kavanagh's elegiac 'St Michan's Churchyard', its subject matter raised only obliquely for those who knew the significance of the location, the graveyard in which Robert Emmet is reputed to be buried; or Hyde's English version of the Gaelic *óglachas* form as Fenian elegy, in the 'Death Lament for John O'Mahony'. Tynan's 'Shameen Dhu' was more familiar ballad monologue, spiced with the synthetic Hiberno-English dialect. It is Yeats's contributions, though, which are the most impressive, borrowing from these Gaelic or folksong examples and writing them through the oblique allegories of a nationalist literary tradition that he was all too keen to appropriate. 'The Stolen Child', in particular, points to the consolidation of Victorian verse forms and the new confidence which O'Leary's influence was to instil in this younger generation of writers.

> We foot it all the night,
> Weaving olden dances,
> Mingling hands, and mingling glances,
> Till the moon has taken flight;
> To and fro we leap,
> And chase the frothy bubbles
> While the world is full of troubles
> And is anxious in its sleep.
> Come away O human child!
> To the waters and the wild
> With a faery hand in hand,
> For the world's more full of weeping than you can understand.[85]

From Ferguson or Allingham, Yeats borrows locations which cross over between possible worlds, folk or fairy, modern or antique, finding in the mingling of identities a cultural form which pleads to be released from modernity just as it acknowledges its determination by it.

The world is still a place of sorrow and Yeats knew that the Irish poet could not remain away with the fairies. The interest of European Romanticism in things Celtic from Goethe through Ernest Renan to Matthew Arnold might be traced to the eighteenth century, and James Macpherson's forged presentation of Irish epic material as the poems of the imagined poet Ossian, mourning the passing of an epic time. Irish antiquarians throughout the nineteenth century reclaimed this material, and versions by Ferguson or Hyde, and translations by Standish Hayes O'Grady (1832–1915) were keen to restore some authenticity to them. In 1889, Yeats presented his version of the story as the title poem of *The Wanderings of Oisin and Other Poems*. The publication of the poem was coincident with the fall of Parnell, and the passing away of heroes from the earth is a constant theme of Irish poetry. In its Ossianic subject matter, though, it is more directly associated with the Fenians, for whom, of course, Ossian was said to mourn.

Yeats's rewriting of literary Celticism was to conceive of a poetry no longer attuned merely to loss, but to look forward to a new epic in the liberated future of national revival. *The Wanderings of Oisin* is a poem of doors, of thresholds, which for all that it does escape to a utopian place, the Tír na nÓg to which Niamh tempts the hero, it then strives to return to the world. On return, Oisin faces the passing of his own heroic epoch and vents his rage against a pallid Christianity, represented by the St Patrick who has been prompting him for his story throughout the poem's mixture of dialogue and epic. The poem's allegory can be vague, but one paradox of its poet's emerging symbolic technique is that Oisin seeks a return to a poetry freed from elegy, defeat and allegorical obscurity. In the first part of the poem, Niamh's people ask the warrior-poet to play a human song on a harp, and Oisin tells St Patrick what happened:

> And when I sang of human joy
> They hushed them every man and maid.
> Oh, Patrick, by thy beard, they wept,
> And one came close, a tearful boy.
> 'A sadder creature never stept
> Than this strange bard,' he cried, and caught
> The harp away. A dolorous pool
> Lay 'neath us; of its hollow cool

No creature had familiar thought
Save deer towards noon that water sought.
Therein the silver harp he hurled,
And each one said, with a long, long sigh,
'The saddest harp in all the world!'[86]

This is the 1889 version, and the resting place of the harp was later revised to 'a leaf-hid, hollow place / That kept dim waters from the sky', the place of obscurity and the secrecy of symbol. The sorrow imparted by the inherent pathos of Irish national music – whatever its ostensible subject – is a recurrent theme throughout eighteenth- and nineteenth-century Irish cultural criticism. The hurling away of the national instrument after the performance of the sorrowful song of human joy is in one sense the recognition of defeat at the heart of this culture. Another sense, of course, given Yeats's Fenian sympathies throughout the 1880s, is that in order to think about the future of the nation, its 'coming times', there must be a repudiation of a national culture constructed around a history which tells only of colonisation, repression and defeat. That culture cannot shake off its dominant elegiac mode, its perpetual commemorations of defeat in the past.

Yeats has one particular achievement in that culture in mind, that of Thomas Moore. Moore's harp cannot but be sorrowful; as he says in his 1815 farewell to music, 'Dear Harp of My Country! In darkness I found thee.' Its first stanza had ended with sorrow inevitably sounded from the strings of the national instrument and the melodies of the national music: 'But, so oft hast thou echo'd the deep sigh of sadness, / That ev'n in thy mirth it will steal from thee still.' Moore's surreptitious stealing of sadness from the instrument is like the movement of symbolism itself, secreting sadness in joy. Niamh's people see straight through this, as it were, and banish it to the 'leaf-hid hollow place', which is the fitting end for all such wanton obscurity. Moore's harp, which still sounds in its memory the echoes of its previous songs, carries about it too much defeat for the young Yeats, no matter how he too is attracted to the obscurity of a symbolist poetic. For the wind passing over the strings of the human instrument, the harp, he will substitute the wind passing over reeds, where the symbolic significance carries the supernatural import of epochal change.

Notes

1. Thomas Kinsella, 'The Irish Writer', in W. B. Yeats and Thomas Kinsella, *Davis, Mangan, Ferguson: Tradition and the Irish Writer* (Dublin: Dolmen, 1970), pp. 58, 66.

2. Thomas Davis, 'A Nation Once Again', *The Spirit of the Nation*, new edn. (Dublin: Duffy, 1845, reprinted Poole: Woodstock, 1998), p. 274.

3. Seamus Deane, *Strange Country: Modernity and Nationhood in Irish Writing since 1790* (Oxford: Clarendon Press, 1997), p. 127.

4. Thomas Davis, 'Ballad Poetry of Ireland', in *Literary and Historical Essays of Thomas Davis* (Dublin: Duffy, 1846), pp. 222–3.

5. Geoffrey Schirmer, *Out of What Began: A History of Irish Poetry in English* (Ithaca: Cornell University Press, 1998), pp. 69–70.

6. *Collected Poems of W. B. Yeats* (London: Macmillan, 1958), p. 57.

7. Seamus Deane, ed., 'Poetry and Song, 1800–1890', Deane, general ed. *Field Day Anthology of Irish Literature*, 3 vols. (Field Day: Derry, 1991), II, p. 2.

8. Thomas MacDonagh, *Literature in Ireland*, ed. Gerald Dawe (Nenagh: Relay, 1996), pp. 56, 40–1.

9. George Darley, *Complete Poetical Works*, ed. Ramsey Colles (London: Routledge, 1908). See 'Introduction', pp. ix–xxxvii.

10. Robert Welch, *A History of Verse Translation from the Irish, 1789–1897* (Gerrards Cross: Colin Smythe, 1988), p. 7.

11. Jeremiah Joseph Callanan, *The Recluse of Inchidony and Other Poems* (London: Hurst, Chance, 1829), p. 128.

12. W. B. Yeats, 'Modern Irish Poetry' (1894), in *Prefaces and Introductions*, ed. William H. O'Donnell (London: Macmillan, 1988), p. 103.

13. The translation is Robert Welch's, *History of Verse Translation*, p. 67.

14. *Dublin University Magazine (DUM)* 3 (March 1834), pp. 331–2.

15. Samuel Ferguson, 'Dialogue between the Heart and Head of an Irish Protestant', *DUM* 2 (November 1833), p. 591.

16. George Denis Zimmermann, *Songs of Irish Rebellion*, 2nd edn. (Dublin: Four Courts Press, 2002).

17. Frontispiece to *The Reliques of Fr Prout* (London: Bell and Daldy, 1866).

18. William Maginn, *Miscellanies*, ed. R. W. Montague, 2 vols. (London: Sampson Low, 1885), I, pp. 260–74; II, pp. 373–84.

19. 'The Watergrasshill Carousal', *Reliques of Fr Prout*, p. 66.

20. This is the title in the *Reliques*, p. 159, although it is frequently known as 'The Bells of Shandon' after its refrain.

21. MacDonagh, *Literature in Ireland*, p. 173.

22. Samuel Lover, *Songs and Ballads*, 4th edn (London: David Bryce, 1858), pp. 3–4.

23. Charles Gavan Duffy, *Young Ireland: A Fragment of Irish History, 1840–1850*, 2nd edn. (London; Cassell, 1880), p. 169.

24. Samuel Lover, *Legends and Stories of Ireland* (1831, 1834) (London: Bohn, n.d.), p. 248.

25. Ibid., pp. 251–2.

26. Peter Denman, *Samuel Ferguson, the Literary Achievement* (Gerrards Cross: Colin Smythe, 1990), p. 18.

27. Deane, *Strange Country*, p. 109.

28. Samuel Ferguson, 'Hardiman's Irish Minstrelsy, III', *DUM* 4 (October 1834), p. 455.

29. James Hardiman, ed. *Irish Minstrelsy, or Bardic Remains of Ireland; with English Poetical Translations*, 2 vols. (London: Robins, 1831), I, p. lxxxvii.

30. Ferguson, 'Hardiman, II', *DUM* 4 (August 1834), pp. 154, 162.

31. Ferguson, 'Hardiman, III', p. 453.

32. Ferguson, 'Hardiman, II', p. 154; 'Hardiman, III', p. 467.

33. Hardiman, *Irish Minstrelsy*, I, p. 239. On p. 238, the title of the poem is given as 'Caisiol Mumhan'.

34. Edward Walsh, *Irish Popular Songs* (Dublin: J. McGlashan, 1847), p. 32.

35. Gerald Griffin, *The Poetical and Dramatic Works of Gerald Griffin* (Duffy: Dublin, 1895).

36. Printed with Anon. [Ferguson], 'Portrait Gallery, XLII – Thomas Davis', *DUM* 29 (February 1847), p. 198.

37. Arthur Griffith, ed. *Thomas Davis: The Thinker and Teacher: The Essence of his Writings in Prose and Poetry* (Dublin: Gill, 1914), p. xii.

38. 'Preface' to *The Spirit of the Nation*, pp. v–vi.

39. See Zimmermann, *Songs of Irish Rebellion*, pp. 228–9, 226–7, 133–7.

40. *The Spirit of the Nation*, p. 191.

41. Thomas Davis in the *Nation*, 1 April 1843, quoted in T. W. Moody, *Thomas Davis: A Centenary Address* (Dublin: Hodges Figgis, 1945), p. 46.

42. Davis, *Literary and Historical Essays*, p. 223.

43. Charles Gavan Duffy, 'Preface to the 39th Edn', in Duffy, *The Ballad Poetry of Ireland* (Dublin: Duffy, 1866), p. 11.

44. Davis, *Literary and Historical Essays*, p. 174.

45. Davis, 'Ballad Poetry of Ireland', in Davis, *Literary and Historical Essays*, pp. 220–40.

46. Duffy, *Ballad Poetry*, p. 24.

47. Denis Florence MacCarthy, introduction to *The Book of Irish Ballads* (Dublin: Duffy, 1846), p. 23.

48. Charles Gavan Duffy, *Four Years of Irish History, 1845–1849* (London: Cassell, 1883), p. 89.

49. Stopford A. Brooke and T. W. Rolleston, *A Treasury of Irish Poetry in the English Tongue* (London: Macmillan, 1900), p. 154.

50. Christopher Morash, ed. *The Hungry Voice: The Poetry of the Irish Famine* (Dublin: Irish Academic Press, 1989), p. 61.

51. See Christopher Morash, *Writing the Irish Famine* (Oxford: Oxford University Press, 1995); Terry Eagleton, *Heathcliff and the Great Hunger* (London: Verso, 1995); Margaret Kelleher, *The Feminization of Famine* (Cork: Cork University Press, 1997); Melissa Fegan, *Literature and the Irish Famine, 1845–1919* (Oxford: Oxford University Press, 2002).

52. Duffy, *Four Years*, p. 95.

53. Lady Wilde (Jane Elgee), *Poems by Speranza* (Dublin: Duffy, 1864).

54. Brooke and Rolleston, *Treasury*, p. 150.

55. John Mitchel, introduction to James Clarence Mangan, *Poems* (New York: Haverty, 1859).

56. Duffy, *Ballad Poetry*, p. 29.

57. James Joyce, 'James Clarence Mangan' (1902), in Joyce, *Occasional, Critical and Political Writing*, ed. Kevin Barry (Oxford: Oxford University Press, 2000), p. 59.

58. Morgan, *The Collected Works of James Clarence Mangan*, ed. Jacques Chuto, Peter van de Kamp, Augustine Martin and Ellen Shannon-Mangan, 7 vols. (Dublin: Irish Academic Press, 1997–2002), *Prose 1840–1882*, pp. 226–39.

59. Joyce, 'Mangan', p. 60.

60. Mangan, *Prose 1840–1882*, p. 224.

61. Joyce, 'Mangan', p. 136.

62. Mangan, *Prose 1840–1882*, p. 221.

63. David Lloyd, *Anomalous States: Irish Writing and the Post-Colonial Moment* (Dublin: Lilliput Press, 1993), p. 95.

64. Hardiman, *Irish Minstrelsy*, I, p. 257.

65. Ferguson, 'Hardiman, II', pp. 157–8.

66. Mangan, *Collected Works, Poems*, III, pp. 167–70.

67. Frank O'Connor, *The Backward Look: A Survey of Irish Literature* (London: Macmillan, 1967), p. 152.

68. *Dramas of Calderon*, trans. Denis Florence MacCarthy, 2 vols. (London: Dolman, 1853).

69. Denis Florence MacCarthy, 'The Voyage of St. Brendan', ll. 721–8, in *Ballads, Poems and Lyrics, Original and Translated* (Dublin: McGlashan, 1850).

70. Timothy Daniel Sullivan, *Poems* (Dublin: Sullivan, 1888).

71. John Francis O'Donnell, *Poems* (London: Ward and Downey, 1891).

72. Thomas Caulfield Irwin, *Irish Poems and Legends; Historical and Traditionary* (Glasgow: Cameron and Ferguson, 1869), pp. 96–8.

73. Aubrey de Vere, *Inisfail*, new edn (London: Macmillan, 1897), pp. 1–183.

74. John O'Leary, 'Charles J. Kickham', in Brooke and Rolleston, eds. *Treasury*, pp. 199–200.

75. Daniel Connolly, 'Irish American Poets', *Irish Monthly* 14 (1886), p. 200.

76. See Colin Graham, *Ideologies of Epic: Nation, Empire and Victorian Epic Poetry* (Manchester: Manchester University Press, 1998), pp. 72–123.

77. *The Collected Letters of W. B. Yeats, vol. III*, eds. John Kelly and Ronald Schuchard (Oxford: Clarendon, 1994), pp. 68–73.

78. Geoffrey Taylor, ed. *Irish Poets of the Nineteenth Century* (London: Routledge and Kegan Paul, 1951), p. 4.

79. See Hugh Shiels, 'William Allingham and Folk Song', *Hermathena* 117 (1974), pp. 26, 30.

80. William Allingham, *Laurence Bloomfield in Ireland: A Modern Poem* (London: Macmillan, 1864), ch. VI, ll. 21–8.

81. Allingham, *Laurence Bloomfield*, ch. VII, ll. 83–91.

82. Paul Muldoon, *To Ireland, I* (Oxford: Clarendon Press, 2000), pp. 8–9.

83. Rosa Mulholland, 'William Butler Yeats', *Irish Monthly* 17 (1889), pp. 365–71.

84. Matthew Russell, 'Sir Samuel Ferguson. In Memoriam', *Irish Monthly* 14 (1886), p. 534.

85. *Poems and Ballads of Young Ireland*, ed. John O'Leary and others (Dublin: Gill, 1888), pp. 12–13.

86. *The Variorum Edition of the Poems of W. B. Yeats*, eds. Peter Allt and Russell K. Alspach (New York: Macmillan, 1957), p. 17.

Select bibliography

Brooke, Stopford A. and T. W. Rolleston, *A Treasury of Irish Poetry in the English Tongue*, London: Macmillan, 1900.

Brown, Malcolm, *The Politics of Irish Literature: From Thomas Davis to W. B. Yeats*, London: Allen and Unwin, 1972.

Colman, Anne Ulry, *A Dictionary of Nineteenth-Century Irish Women Poets*, Galway: Kenny's, 1996.

Davis, Thomas, *Literary and Historical Essays of Thomas Davis*, Dublin: Duffy, 1846.

Deane, Seamus, ed. 'Poetry and Song 1800–1890', in Seamus Deane, general ed., *The Field Day Anthology of Irish Writing*, 3 vols. (Derry: Field Day, 1991), II, pp. 1–114.

  Strange Country: Modernity and Nationhood in Irish Writing since 1790, Oxford: Clarendon Press, 1997.

Denman, Peter, *Samuel Ferguson, the Literary Achievement*, Gerrards Cross: Colin Smythe 1990.

Duffy, Charles Gavan, *The Ballad Poetry of Ireland*, 39th edn. Dublin: Duffy, 1866.

  Four Years of Irish History, 1845–1849, Cassell: London, 1883.

  Young Ireland: A Fragment of Irish History, 1840–1850, 2nd edn. London: Cassell, 1880.

Eagleton, Terry, *Heathcliff and the Great Hunger*, London: Verso, 1995.

Fegan, Melissa, *Literature and the Irish Famine, 1845–1919*, Oxford: Oxford University Press, 2002.

Ferguson, Samuel, 'Hardiman's Irish Minstrelsy', *Dublin University Magazine*, 3–4 (1834).

Graham, Colin, *Ideologies of Epic: Nation, Empire and Victorian Epic Poetry*, Manchester: Manchester University Press, 1998.

Griffith, Arthur, ed. *Thomas Davis: The Thinker and Teacher: The Essence of his Writings in Prose and Poetry*, Dublin: Gill, 1914.

Hardiman, James, ed. *Irish Minstrelsy, or Bardic Remains of Ireland; with English Poetical Translations*, 2 vols. London: Robins, 1831.

Kelleher, Margaret, *The Feminization of Famine*, Cork: Cork University Press, 1997.

Kinsella, Thomas, 'The Irish Writer', in W. B. Yeats and Thomas Kinsella, *Davis, Mangan, Ferguson: Tradition and the Irish Writer*, Dublin: Dolmen, 1970.

Kinsella, Thomas and Seán Ó Tuama, eds. & trans. *An Duanaire 1600–1900: Poems of the Dispossessed*, Portlaoise: Dolmen, 1981.

Leerssen, Joep, *Remembrance and Imagination: Patterns in the Historical and Literary Representation of Ireland in the Nineteenth Century*, Cork: Cork University Press, 1997.

Lloyd, David, *Anomalous States: Irish Writing and the Post-Colonial Moment*, Dublin: Lilliput Press, 1993.

  Nationalism and Minor Literature: James Clarence Mangan and the Emergence of Irish Cultural Nationalism, Berkeley: University of California Press, 1987.

MacCarthy, Denis Florence, *The Book of Irish Ballads*, Dublin: Duffy, 1846.

MacDonagh, Thomas, *Literature in Ireland*, ed. Gerald Dawe, Nenagh: Relay, 1996.

Morash, Christopher, ed. *The Hungry Voice: The Poetry of the Irish Famine*, Dublin: Irish Academic Press, 1989.

  Writing the Irish Famine, Oxford: Oxford University Press, 1995.

Muldoon, Paul, *To Ireland, I*, Oxford: Clarendon Press, 2000.

Murphy, James H., *Ireland: A Social, Cultural and Literary History, 1791–1891*, Dublin: Four Courts Press, 2003.

O'Connor, Frank, *The Backward Look: A Survey of Irish Literature*, London: Macmillan, 1967.

Poems and Ballads of Young Ireland, ed. John O'Leary and others, Dublin: Gill, 1888.

Regan, Stephen, ed. *Irish Writing: An Anthology of Irish Literature in English, 1789–1939*, Oxford: Oxford University Press, 2004.

Schirmer, Geoffrey, *Out of What Began: A History of Irish Poetry in English*, Ithaca: Cornell University Press, 1998.

The Spirit of the Nation, new edn. Dublin: Duffy, 1845; reprinted Poole: Woodstock, 1998.

Taylor, Geoffrey, ed. *Irish Poets of the Nineteenth Century*, London: Routledge and Kegan Paul, 1951.

Welch, Robert, *A History of Verse Translation from the Irish, 1789–1897*, Gerrards Cross: Colin Smythe, 1988.

Irish Poetry from Moore to Yeats, Gerrards Cross: Colin Smythe, 1980.

Zimmermann, George Denis, *Songs of Irish Rebellion*, 2nd edn. (Dublin: Four Courts Press, 2002).

13

Literature in Irish, 1800–1890: from the Act of Union to the Gaelic League

GEARÓID DENVIR

Remarking on his own sense of discontinuity and uprootedness as a writer of English, resulting from what he calls the great linguistic rift of the shift from Irish to English, Thomas Kinsella refers to 'the silence of the nineteenth century'.[1] Joep Leerssen, in his widely acclaimed Field Day monograph *Remembrance and Imagination*, asserts from the outset that 'the native tradition in the nineteenth century is almost silent, having been pauperised into virtual illiteracy'.[2] While the use of words like 'almost' and 'virtual' can be said to leave an ideological escape clause, Seamus Deane leaves his readers in no doubt when he definitively states in his *Short History of Irish Literature* that Irish 'was well and truly dead by the end of the eighteenth century'.[3] The direct result of such a claim is of course that, as literature in Irish no longer exists, it is intellectually acceptable to redefine the very notion and nature of 'Irish literature'. Thus, in his study of 'Irish National Character 1790–1900', Deane draws solely on literature in English and claims that 'the idea of an Irish national character took shape in response to the earlier and aggressive English (or British) definition'.[4] Irish literature of the period as a result becomes a progression from Edmund Burke through the first Celtic Revival and the antiquarian movement, followed by the novels of Maria Edgeworth, the stories of William Carleton, the writings of Samuel Ferguson and Standish O'Grady, and finishes up with W. B. Yeats. In the same vein, Norman Vance, in the introductory chapter of his *Irish Literature since 1800*, gives a mere eleven lines to the nineteenth century in a twelve-page background section on 'The Irish Language Tradition' and refers only to the 'rescue activity' of scholars and translators.[5]

Even linguistically well-informed scholars like Leerssen continue to read nineteenth-century Ireland in anglocentric terms. In his recent pamphlet *Hidden Ireland, Public Sphere*, he argues that 'a massive cultural transfer took place in Ireland between the Gaelic tradition and the urban, English-speaking, educated classes . . . a complete Gaelic re-orientation of Ireland's public space and public sphere',[6] and that:

The period 1760–1845 witnesses a crucial transformation in Irish culture in that the native Gaelic tradition, with its pre-modern attitudes, with its historical vision leading back to Ireland's primal Milesian settlement, with its catastrophic interpretation of history and its Messianic hopes for a deliverance from English rule, is interiorized by a modernizing, urban-centred, English-speaking and essentially Victorian Ireland.[7]

This simplistic binary opposition between a 'pauperized and seditious, largely Gaelic-speaking peasantry' and an 'English-speaking urban middle class'[8] can also be found in the work of scholars of Irish itself, who, like R. A. Breatnach, see even eighteenth-century literature in Irish as 'the end of a tradition'.[9] This conceptual framework has more to do with the politics and ideology which justify a colonial (or indeed colonised) 'Irish' identity for the middle-class, urbanised, English-speaking intelligentsia, both Catholic and Protestant, which came to prominence during the nineteenth century in Ireland, and whose present-day successors hold sway in contemporary cultural and literary discourse, than with a proper analysis of the 'Hidden Ireland' of the period.

The above-mentioned silence about the nineteenth century extends far beyond the time-frame of the century itself, and the period has been largely neglected by scholars of the Irish tradition. Despite the recent imaginative and scholarly work of Ó Buachalla,[10] Leerssen[11] and Mac Craith[12] on the seventeenth and eighteenth centuries, and of Hutchinson[13] and O'Leary[14] on the Irish Revival of the late nineteenth to early twentieth century, and despite the historical, literary, cultural and linguistic work mentioned in Ó Ciosáin's research review of the nineteenth century,[15] the period remains under-researched. One of the principal difficulties is the lack of primary written sources from the inside (although a considerable number, mostly untapped, do exist, as we shall see). Written accounts of the period in English are quite common, mostly from travellers, proselytisers, state officials and other non-Irish speakers, and most describe in detail the poverty and constant begging, bad housing, ragged clothing and general ill health of the 'natives'. The problem with sources such as these, apart from their impressionistic nature, is that the world of the native is mediated through the mindset of outsiders who neither speak the language nor understand the culture of the people they describe. In a sense, of course, the same can be said for present-day scholars of the period who neglect sources in Irish.

Another fundamental problem in the area is the definition of what constitutes discourse in Irish tradition, and the difficulties associated with over-simplified, falsely based or anachronistic categorisation of so-called literary genres. Modern literary discourse in general defines creative literary works as 'novels', 'plays', 'poetry', 'short stories' and various related sub-categories, and can thus fail to admit to the canon works which do not fit this conceptual framework. This is why, for example, the section entitled 'Poetry 1800–1890' in *The Field Day Anthology of Irish Writing* is dominated by the history and assumptions of the established canon of 'Anglo-Irish Literature', whereas literature in Irish is represented solely by a handful of 'Popular Songs', and not a single *file* deserves a mention in a section devoted to the poetry of the period.[16] The modes of discourse in Irish-language literature in the nineteenth century (and before) emanate from a different conceptual framework and from a different world-view to modern concepts of the function and aims of the literary act. In 'reading' this literature, therefore, one must read from within and not impose literary concepts and methodologies extraneous to the Gaelic tradition.

Simplistic polarities or dichotomies, such as the binary opposition of 'traditional' to 'modern', 'oral' to 'print', 'rural' to 'urban', 'illiterate peasant' to 'middle-class educated', 'Irish' to 'English' (which is often portrayed as the essential cultural change, or the process of modernisation in Ireland of the nineteenth century), fail to take account of the cultural complexity and intellectual and aesthetic sophistication of the native or Irish-speaking Irish population of the period. As Máirtín Ó Cadhain, in a famous lecture to the Folklore Society of Ireland, An Cumann le Béaloideas Éireann, in 1950, stated with no little ire, it was not peasants who preserved the oral literature. Studiously avoiding the pejorative terms 'folk literature' or 'folklore', he reminds us of the fact that the *file* and *seanchaí* were heirs to a conscious literary and intellectual tradition very different from the English tradition, but not inferior because of that fact.[17] The *seanchaí*, for example, was the repository of a particular society's knowledge of itself over a wide range of the human condition as lived over generations by that community. Subject to critical analysis and appreciation by his peers, he was entitled to give voice to that knowledge in his stories, riddles, proverbs, sayings, songs, etc. The *file*, or poet, was heir to the same tradition and also gave voice, though in a more creative, innovative and challenging way than the *seanchaí*, to his own vision of his world through his poems and songs. Thus, despite the general acceptance in much contemporary thought of the concept of 'imagined community', which is, in essence, the claim that identity formation is a process which is brought about from without rather than from within – one defines oneself supposedly in opposition to another rather than in conscious knowledge of one's own essential self – this chapter will argue that Irish-language literary activity in the nineteenth century constitutes, in the first place, a conscious, intellectual, ideological space for 'us' in the universe as a first principle, while also, although by secondary rather than by primary function, in many ways also distinguishing 'us' from 'them'.[18] This space is where the internal cultural logic of Irish-speaking Ireland of the period is to be found, and moreover, as language as a repository of cultural meaning is vital to both society and to the individuals and groups that constitute that society, the only means of 'reading' or understanding that society in its own terms from within is through its language.

Such a reading will give due credence to the complex and rich range of cultural practices in Ireland at the time. It will also acknowledge that the native population was in many ways both a society on the margins and, at the same time, in rapid transition – in language, popular culture, religion, education, administration, politics and economics – and that many seemingly contradictory practices and beliefs existed side by side. Belief in magic and ritual and in the existence of fairies and other supernatural beings, while beginning to erode, existed, for example, side by side with dogmatic Christian belief regulated by ever-centralising churches, and a gradually modernising, urbanising society was still 'regulated by seasonal and calendar rituals; its cosmology was deeply local and supernatural, emphasising the powers inherent in places, objects and people'.[19] Such apparent contradictions are not, however, mutually exclusive but rather give an indication of the complex cultural mosaic that is Irish-speaking Ireland in the nineteenth century.

Learning in the Gaelic understanding of that word was a textual activity, and therefore most of the material in manuscripts tends to be copies of canonical works from within the tradition, and not new literary creations in their own right. This is particularly true of nineteenth-century manuscripts, although of course, much new material is also contained in the manuscripts of this period. The material copied reveals the world-view and attitude to what constitutes learning, or valid literary activity, within the Gaelic world of the Irish scribes at the time, over a range of matters that were of fundamental importance. It is also evident in the manuscripts that the scribes were very possessive of their manuscript collections and immensely proud of this inherited tradition.

Language shift

One of the major cultural changes of the nineteenth century in Ireland was unquestionably the language shift from Irish to English which was by any standards swift and dramatic. In the period from 1800 to 1891, a mere three generations, the number of Irish speakers declined from some three million or more, the great majority of whom would have almost certainly been monoglot, to the 38,121 monoglot speakers recorded in the census of 1891. Strangely enough in a country often consumed by the past, there is no definitive work on this most important event in Irish history, although, as Niall Ó Ciosáin has shown, some significant research has been published, particularly in recent years.[20] Despite the fact that the actual number of Irish speakers increased in the first half of the century, and that possibly the greatest absolute number of speakers ever existed on the eve of the Great Famine (1845–7), the percentage of the population speaking Irish began to decrease well before 1800 and this decline gathered pace as the century progressed. This shift was most noticeable among the Catholic middle and upper classes and educated social elites, and was more gradual among the less privileged masses, particularly in the western half of the country. This can be seen, for example, in the fact that many of Daniel O'Connell's supporters in the Catholic Association, young, mainly middle-class Catholic radicals, had little or no knowledge of Irish nor any inclination to learn the language.

It must be pointed out, however, that the Irish and English languages were not completely cut off from one another in private or in public discourse throughout the period, and that both languages are central to an understanding of the cultural, political and social life of the period. As Ó Ciosáin has pointed out for the period 1750–1850, 'Ireland was at all points . . . an intensely bilingual and diglossic society',[21] and this observation is also true for the rest of the period under discussion here, as will be obvious from even a short account of the literary and language-related activity recounted below. The intermingling of the two languages as a means of everyday communication can be seen in the person of Daniel O'Connell, who, on the one hand, proclaimed himself a utilitarian who dismissed without a sigh the gradual disuse of Irish, but who, on the other hand, interacted like many of his class with his own tenants through Irish in the manner of an Irish chieftain. In addition, it is obvious that bilingualism was common even among the uneducated classes, as can be seen from the number of macaronic songs from the period.[22] This diglossia extended also to the literary and cultural world where most of the scribes and scholars and many of the poets were equally at home in both languages. Moreover, the language shift was not uniform, and it is a great exaggeration to state with absolute certainty that the language survived only in the more remote regions. Apart from the fact that circles of scholars were active in cities like Dublin, Cork, Belfast and Limerick, Irish continued to be spoken in many areas where it is often presumed that the language was extinct. The census of 1851, for example, shows that Irish was still spoken commonly even in the north-eastern counties, with 1,153 native speakers recorded for County Down, and Dr William Neilson, who was appointed as a Presbyterian minister in Dundalk in 1795 as 'it was considered essential that the minister of this congregation should be able to speak Irish', tells of delivering sermons in Irish throughout Ulster in the early part of the nineteenth century.[23] In the south-east, Irish is reported spoken in business transactions in Kilkenny City in 1822, with some strong farmers unable to speak any English.[24] It is also worth noting in this context of societal bilingualism that Irish was not solely confined to the Catholic population and that many Protestants either spoke Irish from birth or learned the language for various reasons, mostly cultural or religious.

The famine had a huge impact on the fate of the Irish language, with the decimation through death or emigration of the poorer, rural classes, particularly in the stronger Irish-speaking regions of the west, and such a traumatic event must have had major psychological and psycho-cultural repercussions. The national school system, founded in 1831, and the consequent growth of literacy in English, was without doubt another important cause of language shift, and as Patrick Keenan, chief inspector for National Education, noted in his annual report to the Commissioners for 1855, 'We are quietly but certainly destroying the national legend, the national music and the national language of the country.'[25] It must also be stated, however, that while the national schools neither taught Irish nor gave instruction through Irish, the same held true generally for the earlier hedge schools, many of whose teachers would not only have known Irish but were in many cases scholars of the language, and for the various Catholic schools which were founded in the early part of the century before the foundation of the national school system. Moreover, as Ó Ciosáin has shown, by 'the late eighteenth century . . . the Catholic church in most places was functioning primarily in English'.[26] The Catholic clergy were highly influential in the spread of English and of literacy in that language, despite the fact that many individual priests and a few bishops were either patrons to scribes or poets, or indeed scribes and poets in their own right. Tomás Ó Fiaich has referred to the anglicising influence of the 'Maynooth dandies' of the nineteenth century, despite the fact that Irish was the home language of many of the student priests and also supposedly a part of their priestly training.[27] John O'Donovan, writing in 1834 while working on the Ordnance Survey of Ireland, tells of Maynooth-educated priests in County Down being able to speak Irish, but who thought it more fashionable to conceal that fact. Other factors in the language shift were the growing urbanisation, commercialisation and consumerism of the country, the great improvement in communications through the developing infrastructure of roads and railways, the unprecedented increase in literacy in English allied to the growth of the newspaper and publishing industries, and the almost totally dominant role of English in the public domain – political, legal and administrative.

Thus, as the nineteenth century progressed, Irish became the language of the outsider, the marginalised, the dispossessed, the rural backward poor, and English during this same period became the language of political and cultural hegemony, spoken by the insider, the privileged, the ruler and the urban middle and upper classes. As the scribe, scholar and poet Dáibhí de Barra put it succinctly in a letter to the Waterford language activist and publisher Phillip Barron: 'in my part of the country (and I suppose it is so in other parts) any man who can afford meat to his dinner and deem himself an Esq., thinks it degrading to utter one syllable of such a despicable language, but they effect to understand it not'.[28] Native speakers of Irish no longer perceived themselves as being at the centre should they adhere to the native language, and therefore focused on another linguistic reality. I have argued elsewhere that this process of language shift is a classic postcolonial endgame, and that the nineteenth century saw the cultural and linguistic assimilation of much of the native population into a provincial or Victorian version of the culture of the coloniser.[29]

Scholarly societies

It is one of the ironies of the history of the nineteenth century in Ireland that the language shift and the process of cultural assimilation took place at the same time as the development of Irish political and cultural nationalism and also during a period which saw a remarkable growth in Irish scholarship. The late eighteenth and all of the nineteenth century saw a major flourishing in the field of Irish learning, both among scholars trained in the native tradition and among English-speaking intellectuals and scholars of a philanthropical bent, and also among others whose aim was the creation of a distinctive Anglo-Irish identity through the production of a literature in English based on the older Gaelic tradition.

The various scholarly societies which were established throughout the century must be seen in the context of the contemporary intellectual climate in Europe where the 'exaltation of elements relating to nationalism – local custom and landscape, folk traditions, episodes from national history, the high passion for patriotism'[30] associated with Romanticism inspired scholars and others to engage with the ancient traditions – literary, linguistic, visual – of their own countries. Other reasons for the increase in interest in the Irish language at the turn of the century were the growing output of published

Irish literature in the post-Macpherson era; the growing importance of the new science of linguistics which attracted many scholars to Irish as a vernacular with a long-established written tradition; and the religious movement in Ireland at the time which led to the production of much printed material, mainly religious but with some secular texts, and to the employment of many Irish scholars as teachers of Irish in various religious societies. Much of the intellectual and scholarly debate of the early period of the century crystallised in the later development of cultural nationalism and linguistic revivalism in the latter part of the century. Most of the people active in the learned societies were 'gentlemen' – Protestant aristocrats or members of the Protestant upper middle class – or educated Catholics who were becoming prominent with the rise of the Catholic middle class, and there is no doubt that their activities had much to do with the politics of identity formation in a changing society. It must be stressed, also, that these societies were concerned solely with 'the bardic remains' of Ireland, that their agenda was purely scholarly and cultural with almost no hint of the revivalism that was to emerge towards the end of the century. As Máirín Nic Eoin has noted, the period 'marked a shift from the status of Irish as a living language among the general population to that of a symbolic code to be collected, studied, and treated as a subject of antiquarian interest by a growing body of well-to-do scholars'.[31]

As Ó Ciosáin has remarked of the nineteenth century, 'literate culture was widespread, and more manuscripts were produced than in any other century',[32] and there was also a marked increase in the number of books published in Irish. The material produced, both in manuscript and in print, much of which was probably a question of 'collectors working before nightfall',[33] shows a world in transition and gives an interesting perspective on Ireland at the time not found in official documents. The most publicly visible, and also the most commented upon aspect of this movement among scholars of literature and history, is without doubt the establishment of scholarly societies throughout the period. Following on what Hutchinson[34] calls the first wave of cultural nationalism in the eighteenth century, which saw the establishment of the Royal Irish Academy in 1785 and the holding of the Belfast Harp Festival in 1792, allied to the publication of translations from Irish literature such as Joseph Cooper Walker's *Historical Memoirs of the Irish Bards* (1786) and Charlotte Brooke's *Reliques of Irish Poetry* (1789), not to mention Edward Bunting's *General Collection of the Ancient Irish Music* (1796), a series of antiquarian and scholarly societies was established throughout the nineteenth century.

The Gaelic Society of Dublin, founded in 1807, was the earliest of the learned societies in our period and was founded with the aim of promoting knowledge of the ancient traditions of Ireland through the study and publication of material from manuscripts. This interaction between the older, individual-oriented world of scribal activity and the modern, collectivised world of print culture can be seen as a paradigm for much Irish-language activity in the nineteenth century, and illustrates the fact that the separation between the two cultures was not as great as is sometimes presumed and that there was 'a complementary relationship between the written and the printed media'.[35] The first secretary of the society was Theophilus O'Flanagan (*c.*1760–1814), a native speaker from County Clare, educated in the manuscript tradition by his father, Mathúin, by Seán Ó Nuanáin, reputedly the best teacher in Munster at the time, and by Peadar Ó Conaill (1755–1826), whose life's work was the compilation of a dictionary, and whose kinsman Daniel O'Connell famously refused a grant to aid its publication, claiming 'that his uncle was an old fool to have spent so much of his life on so useless a work'.[36] The Gaelic Society published only one volume, *The Transactions of the Gaelic Society* (1808), but many of those involved in the activities of the society were prominent in later antiquarian activities: Fr Pól Ó Briain (*c.*1763–1820, a grand-nephew of Turlough O'Carolan), poet, first professor of Irish at St Patrick's College, Maynooth and author of *A Practical Grammar of the Irish Language* (1809); Revd William Neilson (1774–1821), Presbyterian minister, professor of the classical, Hebrew and Irish languages at the Royal Belfast Academical Institution, and author of *Introduction to the Irish Language* (1808); William Haliday (1788–1812), a Dublin solicitor who began learning Irish aged seventeen without his family's knowledge, and later published *Uraicecht na Gaedhilge: A Grammar of the Gaelic Language* (1808) and a volume from Keating's *Foras Feasa ar Éirinn* (1811), both under pseudonyms; and Edward O'Reilly (1765–1830), treasurer of the society, scribe and author of the Irish/English dictionary, *Sanas Gaoidhilge/Sags-Bhéarla* (1817).

The Iberno-Celtic society was founded in Dublin in 1818 with the same general aims as the Gaelic Society, the preservation and publication of ancient Irish literature, and, as was common among such societies, stated from the outset that no religious or political debates whatsoever would be tolerated in the activities of the society, a difficult aspiration in a country sharply divided on religious and political lines at the time. Despite the patronage and support of such aristocratic figures as the duke of Leinster, the earl of Talbot, the marquis of Sligo and others, the society published only one volume, Edward O'Reilly's well-known *Chronological Account of Nearly Four Hundred Irish Writers with a Descriptive Catalogue of their Works* (1820). Other similar societies were established regularly in Dublin and other places until the mid-century: a branch of the Gaelic Society in Cork (1818), The Society for the Revival of Ancient

Irish Literature (Limerick, *c.*1820), The Irish Archaeological Society (1840), The Celtic Society (1845), the Kilkenny Archaeological Society (1849), and the Ossianic Society (1853).

Of particular interest, especially in the context of later historical developments, are the various scholarly societies and other cultural activities in Belfast and Ulster generally, especially during the first half of the nineteenth century. Following on the work of the Belfast Harp Festival and the musical publications of Edward Bunting towards the end of the eighteenth century, Irish-language activity gathered pace in the region over the following fifty years. Belfast City saw a flowering of literary, historical, philosophical and musical societies, some more lasting than others, founded and funded in the main by a group of well-educated, wealthy, middle-class Protestants, which indicates that Irish was an integral part of the life of the city at the time. Some of this group were convinced unionists, others less so, and still others were sympathetic to the United Irishmen. Certain among them would have had a native or near-native knowledge of Irish, while others were avid learners of the language, and much of their scholarly work was underpinned by scholars educated in the native tradition.

Chief among the patrons and activists in these learned societies was Dr James Mac Donnell (1763–1845), probably the most influential member of the Irish cultural movement in Ulster in his time. Born to a Catholic father and a Protestant mother in the Glens of Antrim, he was raised a Protestant and educated in the first instance at home, where he was taught music by the famous Art Ó Néill, one of the most important participants in the Belfast Harp Festival, and later in Belfast. Mac Donnell qualified as a medical doctor but his heart lay in the cultural and scholarly movements of the time. A generous patron of scribes and scholars, he was one of the founders of the Linenhall Library in 1788 and was the main force behind the Belfast Harp Festival in 1792. In 1808 he co-founded the Irish Harp Society with Edward Bunting and others and he paid a stipend to Art Ó Néill in the last few years of his life. He was also involved in many charitable and cultural organisations, including the Royal Belfast Academical Institution in 1810, in which Irish was taught by William Neilson (from 1818 to 1821) and Tomás Ó Fiannachta (from 1833 to 1849) and which later became the Queen's College.

Robert Shipboy Mac Adam (1808–95), described by Ó Buachalla as 'the first Gaelic Leaguer', and by the poet and scribe Peadar Ó Gealacáin as 'Cosantóir na Sean-Ghaeilge'[37] (The Protector of Old Irish), was, along with Mac Donnell, one of the most important patrons of scholars and scholarly societies in nineteenth-century Belfast. He was educated at the Royal Belfast Academical

Institution, where he was probably taught Irish by William Neilson. He was co-owner, along with his brother James, of the Soho Foundry in Belfast which, at its height, employed over 250 people, and he travelled much of the country in connection with his business. He was totally apolitical and he saw as his life's work 'the resuscitation of our long lost national literature'.[38] Mac Adam could read, write and speak Irish very well and was sufficiently proficient in interpreting and translating a seventeenth-century text for it to be called 'tolerably correct' by none other than John O'Donovan. He wrote *An Introduction to the Irish Language* for use in his old school in 1835 and was editor of the *Ulster Journal of Archaeology* (1853–62) where he published some material of his own, including a collection of 600 proverbs collected during his travels in the North. He also put together an English–Irish dictionary of 1,388 pages, still unpublished, a project he took upon himself, as he says in the introduction, on account of 'méad mo ghean ar mo thír dhúchais . . . agus teasghrádh don teangaidh' (my deep attachment to my native land and my warm love for the language). Mac Adam was known throughout Ulster, and indeed further afield, as a generous patron and gave both scribal patronage and employment to many Irish scholars, including Aodh Mac Domhnaill, Nioclás Ó Cearnaigh, Art Mac Bionaid and Peadar Ó Gealacáin. He also put together a large collection of manuscripts, many of which are still in the Belfast Central Library. Other notable members of this Northern Irish coterie of influential scholars and intellectuals were the above-mentioned Revd William Neilson, Dr Samuel Bryson (1776–1853), medical doctor and apothecary, scribe, scholar and copyist and collector of manuscripts, who knew Irish from a very young age in his native County Down, and Edward A. Maginiss (1821–77), a wealthy Catholic merchant with a bakery in Newry, County Down, for whom Art Mac Bionaid wrote ten manuscripts, including his history of Ireland.

The first of the learned societies in our period in the North was the Belfast Literary Society, founded in 1801 by James Mac Donnell and others of the intellectual middle class of the city. The society, though without a specific headquarters, survived for many years and hosted an immense range of lectures from the many scholars who lived in or frequented the city. The Irish Harp Society followed in 1808 and taught both harp and Irish lessons. They established a school with the piper and scribe Séamus Mac Óda as teacher from 1809 until 1813 when the school closed as a result of financial problems. The society itself lasted until 1831 (with a short break, 1813–19) and is credited as being an important link in ensuring the continuation of the harping tradition. Without any doubt, the most important of the scholarly societies in Belfast in the first half of the nineteenth century was the Cuideacht Gaedhilge Uladh, or the Ulster Gaelic Society, founded in 1830 with the third marquis of Downshire (who in all probability knew Irish) as president, James Mac Donnell as chairman, and as co-secretaries Robert Mac Adam and Dr Rueben Bryce, professor of classical languages at the Belfast Academy and a significant educational thinker of the period. The aims of the society were quite radical for the time: the establishment of schools through the medium of Irish, the publication of books in Irish, the collection of books and manuscripts in Irish, and the maintenance of a teacher of Irish in Belfast. The first publication to appear was Tomás Ó Fiannachta's translation of Maria Edgeworth's *Forgive and Forget* (*Maith agus Dearmad*) and *Rosanna* in one volume in 1833. This was followed by, among others, Mac Adam's *Introduction to the Irish Language* in 1835 (as an aid to teaching the Irish classes), and in 1841 by *Casán na Gaedhilge: An Introduction to the Irish Language*, 'for the use of the Native Irish, and for those who wish to acquire a knowledge of our sweet and venerable mother-tongue'.[39] Ó Buachalla has shown that in all likelihood the many anthologies of translations from Irish poetry, which appeared after this time, from the likes of Samuel Ferguson, Thomas O'Hagan, George Fox and others, were inspired by the work of the Cuideacht. It should also be noted that Belfast served as a centre of learning for the whole north-east region, and that Irish scholarship was being pursued in many outlying towns in the region such as Newry, Dundalk and Drogheda, as can be seen, for example in the activities of the Drogheda Gaelic Society (1843), a short-lived offshoot of the Ulster Gaelic Society whose stated aim was to publish the bardic remains of Ireland, together with grammar and religious books in Irish.

The activities of the learned societies were not confined to the urban centres of Dublin and Belfast alone. The work of modern scholars such as Breandán Ó Conchúir,[40] Meidhbhín Ní Úrdail,[41] Breandán Ó Madagáin,[42] Cornelius Buttimer[43] and others has shown that there was intense scribal activity in other urban centres of intellectual activity throughout the country, particularly in Cork, Kilkenny and Limerick – although Galway, the county with the greatest number of Irish speakers at the time, and which had a rich literary tradition in the seventeenth century, saw little scholarly activity in the period, apart from the significant work of James Hardiman and some other minor scribal activity. Moreover, these centres did not operate in isolation, and even a short perusal of either nineteenth-century manuscripts themselves or the copious correspondence between patrons and scholars indicates an intricate and wide-ranging network of committed people with a common literary, aesthetic and cultural agenda. A notable example of this scholarly brotherhood can be seen in the correspondence of John Windele (1801–65), the Cork-born scholar, antiquarian and collector of manuscripts whose voluminous correspondence with other scholars throughout the country survives in the Royal Irish Academy. This activity indicates that, despite the fact that the language was rapidly losing speakers, Irish was still a significant element in public and intellectual discourse during the nineteenth century throughout the whole island of Ireland and across the political and religious divides of the time.

The work of the societies modernised Irish scholarship through the introduction of print-based, scientific methodologies, as well as conserving a vast amount of the manuscript tradition. The societies also introduced Gaelic Ireland to English-speaking intellectuals and artists, many of whom were from the Protestant middle class, and created the ideological and intellectual climate which led to the emergence of a new sense of cultural, and eventually, political awareness as the century progressed. Thus, the nationalistic poetry in English, described in chapter 12 of this history, the national iconography found in much of the visual art of the period, and the political ideology of movements such as the Young Ireland of Thomas Davis, whose aim was 'a moral regeneration of Irish life by its return to its traditional language, literature, music and arts',[44] are all ideologically underpinned and, as it were, validated by the research of the scholars.

Native scholars

Gaelic learning in the nineteenth century was not, however, confined to the somewhat rarefied atmosphere of these urban-based learned societies. A fundamental aspect of the scholarly movement of the period was the intimate and island-wide interaction between the above-mentioned educated, middle-class antiquarians, mostly, though not all, from an English-speaking background, and scholars educated in the native literary tradition whose knowledge of the manuscripts underpinned the publications of the scholarly societies. Indeed, the activities of these societies would not have been possible without the active participation of scholars trained in the native tradition. Thus, we have already seen the scholar Theophilus O'Flanagan as the mainstay of the Gaelic Society of Dublin in the early part of the century, a role performed by the likes of the scholar, publisher and antiquarian bookseller John O'Daly, whose shop at Angelsea Street was a meeting place for 'Irishians', and scholars such as Eugene O'Curry, John O'Donovan and James Hardiman, for the Irish Archaeological Society, The Celtic Society, the Ossianic Society and others in the mid-century.

This process is particularly evident in the participation of native scholars such as Art Mac Bionaid (1793–1879), Peadar Ó Gealacáin (1792–1860) and

Aodh Mac Domhnaill (1802–67), in the work of the learned societies in Belfast, discussed above. These scholars, and many others, were from the Oirialla district of south-east Ulster, north Meath and Louth, which was an extremely literate part of Gaelic Ireland from the late seventeenth to the late nineteenth century. Art Mac Bionaid, the last of the poets of Oirialla, was descended from scholars and born into a literate household in Forkhill, south Armagh. A stonemason by trade, and extremely cantankerous by nature, his real life's work was the preservation of the Ulster poetry of the preceding century, poetry in which he took a fierce pride – the work of Séamus Dall Mac Cuarta, Cathal Buí Mac Giolla Ghunna, Peadar Ó Doirnín, Pádraig Mac Giolla Fhiondain and Art Mac Cumhaigh. He began to write at the age of twenty and made a copy in 1819 of Seathrún Céitinn's canonical version of nativist Irish history, *Foras Feasa ar Éirinn*, which still survives in the National Library in Dublin (Ms. G536). Over the following forty years he copied many manuscripts, mainly for three patrons, Robert Mac Adam, Edward Augustus Maginnis and the scribe, collector, poet and Catholic priest An tAthair Pádraig Ó Luain. He copied mainly Ulster texts and his *oeuvre* contains stories and poems, folklore, place lore or *dinnseanchas*, religious material, grammar treatises and lexicographical matter. His *magnum opus* is without doubt his history of Ireland from the Vikings to the Treaty of Limerick, *Comhrac na nGael agus na nGall le Chéile*, which will be discussed later. While fiery in temperament and prone to argumentation, as seen in his falling-out with his fellow poet Aodh Mac Domhnaill, and in his often revealing correspondence with Robert Mac Adam and John O'Daly, he was held in high regard for his knowledge and learning by fellow scribes, poets and patrons.

The aforementioned Aodh Mac Domhnaill, poet, scribe, teacher and philosopher from County Meath, though a Catholic, taught for many years for the Irish Society and other Bible societies, thus, like a significant number of his fellow scholars, earning the odium of many of his co-religionists. He was an adviser to George Field, who published *Casán na Gaedhilge: An Introduction to the Irish Language* in 1841, and by 1842 was engaged by Robert Mac Adam to teach Irish, and to collect and transcribe manuscripts, for which purpose he travelled throughout Ireland. He also composed poetry, much of it on topical events, and his *Fealsúnacht*, or philosophical treatise, will be discussed later.

Peadar Ó Gealacáin was one of the most important and prolific scribes of the nineteenth century. Twenty-five of his manuscripts are extant, although it is known that he wrote many more, and his life and times give a deep insight into the native learning of the period. He was born in north County Meath, which was on the fringe of the Oirialla district, still strongly Irish-speaking at the time, and he was educated in a hedge school where he learned English, Latin, mathematics, astrology and music. His father's home was frequented by local poets, and Peadar became acquainted from a young age with the native tradition. Like many scribes of his time, he made a precarious living as a teacher, moving from place to place, between the years 1814 and 1826, and despite being a devoted Catholic, he also spent some time as a teacher for the Irish Society. His friend Aodh Mac Domhnaill recommended him as a scribe and scholar to Robert Mac Adam in 1844 and for the following ten years he copied manuscripts for Mac Adam, and for Bernard Tumelty and J. T. Rowland of the Drogheda Gaelic Society. The range of Ó Gealacáin's work is illustrative of the native learning of his time. His scribal career extended from *c.*1822 until his death in 1860 and his work covers poetry and prose, religious material (saints' Lives and prayers – as well, interestingly, as charms), history and legend, heroic and tragic stories, Fenian lays, and other miscellaneous material such as riddles, cures for people and animals, lists of goods and prices, and mathematical problems. Most of his work is copied but he also includes his own poetic compositions, and many scholars have commented on his beautiful penmanship.

Another fundamental element in the mosaic that is Irish scholarship and literary discourse in the nineteenth century was the Ordnance Survey, established in Ireland in 1824 in order to establish the acreage and boundaries of every townland in Ireland for taxation purposes, and which incidentally provides the cultural and linguistic background to Brian Friel's wonderful, though historically dubious, play about human language and communication, *Translations*. Under the direction of Thomas Larcom (1801–79) the survey was extended to include historical and other details, and George Petrie (1789–1866) was engaged to oversee the topographical section. Petrie in turn oversaw two of the giants of Irish scholarship in the nineteenth century, John O'Donovan (1806–61) and Eugene O'Curry (1794–1862). Born in Kilkenny, O'Donovan was educated in a local hedge-school, became a teacher himself and moved to Dublin, where he worked as a scribe for James Hardiman. Thomas Larcom appointed him, in succession to Edward O'Reilly, to the topographical section of the Ordnance Survey and he travelled the country between 1834 and 1842, sending back detailed accounts of the history, lore, language and literary tradition of the twenty-nine counties he visited. He also collected manuscripts, and in the early 1840s he edited texts for the Irish Archaeological Society, including *The Banquet of Dun na nGedh* (1842) on which Ferguson based his long narrative poem *Congal* in 1872. In 1847 he published *Leabhar na gCeart or The Book of Rights*, followed by the seven volumes of the *Annals of the Kingdom of Ireland*,

1848–51, and in 1852 he edited and translated for John O'Daly the satire composed by Aonghus Rua Ó Dálaigh under the title *The Tribes of Ireland*, with a poetical translation by James Clarence Mangan. He also began work around this time, with O'Curry, on ancient Irish law texts, although neither lived to see them published by Robert Atkinson as *Ancient Laws of Ireland* (1865–1901). Interestingly enough in the all-Ireland context of the network of scholars, O'Donovan was appointed professor of Irish in Queen's College, Belfast, in 1849, and although he never lived there, nor had any students, he did deliver regular lectures, some of which were published by Mac Adam in the *Ulster Journal of Archaeology*.

Eugene O'Curry, brother-in-law and colleague of O'Donovan, was born and educated in County Clare, and after a short spell in Limerick City, moved to Dublin in the early 1830s where he quickly made the acquaintance of many of the prominent people in Gaelic and literary circles such as Samuel Ferguson and J. H. Todd, for whom he catalogued the manuscripts in the Royal Irish Academy. Like O'Donovan, he also acted as an editorial advisor to the Irish Archaeological Society and to the Celtic Society. He worked with O'Donovan in the topographical section of the Ordnance Survey and on the *Annals of the Four Masters*. In 1854 he was appointed professor of Irish history and archaeology at the newly founded Catholic University where he delivered in 1855–6 a famous series of lectures, later published as *Lectures on the Manuscript Materials of Ancient Irish History*, which strongly influenced Matthew Arnold's equally famous *On the Study of Celtic Literature* (1866). A further series of lectures was published posthumously as *On the Manners and Customs of the Ancient Irish* (3 vols., 1873), and both series 'amount to an authoritative interpretation of Gaelic society and culture based on a comprehensive survey of all the sources available in his day'.[45] O'Curry and O'Donovan established the basis for much of modern Irish-language scholarship, although it should be noted that both their interests were basically antiquarian, focused on the older historical tradition, rather than on the later language and tradition. Moreover, although both were native speakers of Irish, and obviously emotionally and ideologically attached to the language as a scholarly discourse, neither O'Donovan nor O'Curry felt any attachment to the language as a medium of day-to-day communication. They always spoke English to one another and none of their children was able to speak Irish. O'Donovan expressed the belief in 1851 that Irish 'will become obsolete in about fifty years'[46] and that 'it is no longer necessary to the exigencies of modern society, with which the Irish race must either amalgamate or perish ... in ... the progress of our ancestors from rude primeval simplicity to true civilization and positive science'.[47] As already noted, this would have been a common attitude among members of the urban-based learned societies throughout the country, with little or no language revival ideology evident until the founding of The Society for the Preservation of the Irish Language in 1876 and other later societies.

The nineteenth century was a period of intense scribal activity in Irish. Much of this activity was a result of the influence of the learned societies and was, undoubtedly, an act of retrieval of a culture and tradition believed to be on the verge of extinction. However, this explanation alone does not account for the fact that so many manuscripts continued to be written, particularly in the early and mid-century. Without doubt much of the work of the scribes and native scholars of the period had a more positive *causa scribendi*. Their activity was a continuation of a cultural, literary, aesthetic and ideological tradition, to which they were heirs, in a communal, familial and personal sense, and the practice and continuation of their hereditary craft was part of their very *raison d'être*. While accepting that many manuscripts of this late period were but loose collections of leaves, and that as the nineteenth century progressed so too did the amount of English material in the manuscripts, not to mention the instances of phonetic script based on English spelling (particularly in the west, where one finds, for example, the poetry of Raiftearaí and the Ó Callanáin brothers, Marcus and Patsaí), at the same time, there is unquestionably a vitality and a contemporary world-view in the scribal activity of the period that has not yet been sufficiently recognised or commented upon. Moreover, not all the material copied at the time was from older manuscripts and much new material relating to the 'hidden Ireland' of the day is to be found in these manuscripts, a significant number of which await the perusal of modern scholars.

Most of the scribes, scholars and poets of the period earned their main income as poorly paid farm labourers and teachers – and it is not without historical irony that many Catholic scribes and poets taught Irish in Protestant Bible schools throughout the country, often ignoring grave warnings and threats of excommunication from their priests. One also encounters more comfortable men among the scribes, priests and farmers in the main, especially in the 'fat lands' of Munster. Ó Conchúir notes many priests among Cork scribes,[48] Ó hÓgáin does likewise for Kilkenny,[49] and Ó Néill has described the life and work of the Kilkenny farmer, miller, music collector and scribe Pádraig Ó Néill (1765–1832), who published *Bláithfhleasg na Milseán* (1816), which contains two long poems in Irish. He also composed a series of poems in praise of the ancestors of one Sheffield Grace, claiming that they were originally composed in the seventeenth century (a fraud not exposed until 1940), and Ó hOgáin lists eight manuscripts in his hand that are still extant. In further illustration of the network of scholarship and native learning at the time, Ó Néill was married to the sister of his fellow farmer and scribe Séamas Ó Scoireadh (?–1828), according to John O'Donovan 'a respectable farmer, and a man of so vigorous a mind that he acquired an extensive knowledge of philology and general literature',[50] and both men had regular contact with the members of the Iberno-Celtic Society in Dublin and other scholars. Eoghan Ó Néill argues that the case of Pádraig Ó Néill represents 'a small self-contained world . . . a *mikrocosmos* of Irish Ireland, a hidden Ireland of the time', and claims that many other such regions existed in nineteenth-century Ireland.[51]

Another interesting example of this type of scholarly network, involving both native and 'gentlemen' scholars, can be seen in the circle around the wealthy Cork scribe and patron Donnchadh Ó Floinn (1760–1830), whose copious correspondence with a multitude of scholars still survives. The scholars include Mícheál Óg Ó Longáin, Peadar Ó Conaill, Fr Pól Ó Briain, James Hardiman, Edward O'Reilly, the lexicographer who was treasurer of the Irish Society, and Patrick Lynch (1754–1818), author of *The Pentaglot Perceptor* (1810), *The Life of Saint Patrick* (1810) and other works, and secretary of the Gaelic Society. As Ó Conchúir[52] has shown, he knew most of the poets and scribes of Cork during his time, collected many manuscripts, of which twenty are still extant, and established a small printing press in his own home, as Hardiman stated, 'for the patriotic purpose of multiplying copies of some favourite Irish poems as a means of their preservation'.[53]

The Ó Longáin family of scribes from Carraig na bhFear in County Cork, who span the late eighteenth and nineteenth century, are representative of their time and craft, particularly in the Munster region. Mícheál Óg Ó Longáin (1766–1837) was one of the most important scholars, scribes and poets of the early nineteenth century, and the family tradition was carried on by his twin sons, Peadar (1801–c.1861) and Pól (1801–66) and their younger brother, Seosamh (1816–80). Son of the scribe and scholar Mícheál Mac Pheadair, who died when his son was four years old, Mícheál Óg was the local secretary of the United Irishmen and a committed activist for the movement, as seen in many of his poems and other writings. He was highly politically aware, had a particular aversion to the Act of Union and hoped for help from Republican France for his political views to be implemented. A strong pride in his Irishness, allied to a strong wish for freedom from England, permeates his work:

Go bhfeiceam Éire saor gan daoirse
'S a bratuinn uaithne i n-uachtar scaoilte
Gach tíoránach claoincheárdach coimhtheach
I n-ainm an diabhail 's gan Dia dá gcuimhdheacht.

(May we see Ireland free from bondage
And her green flag raised and flaunting;
Every evil-doing foreign tyrant
Gone to the devil and may God not protect them.)[54]

Mícheál Óg was often in difficult personal circumstances and to supplement his meagre income worked as a labourer, teacher and translator, mostly in his native Cork. Bishop John Murphy of Cork employed him as a scribe from 1817 to 1820, work in which he was assisted by his sons Peadar and Pól. Mícheál Óg was a most productive scribe, writing some 150 manuscripts. He also composed over 350 poems, most of which remain unpublished, and therefore not easily accessible to scholars for critical commentary. It is fair to say, however, that Daniel Corkey fails to do him justice in his study *The Hidden Ireland*. Like his father, Peadar, about whom relatively little is known, he commenced his scribal career at the tender age of fifteen, and worked as a teacher and farm labourer to supplement his income. He copied manuscripts regularly throughout his life for many different patrons, mainly in the Cork area, and spent most of his life in the native Ó Longáin district of Carraig na bhFear. Like his twin, Pól started writing at an early age and also worked as a teacher, but unlike Peadar, he travelled to Dublin – where it is said that he taught Irish to Thomas Davis – and was appointed official scribe to the Royal Irish Academy in the post-famine period, during what Ní Úrdail refers to as a 'Golden Age' of manuscript transcription in the capital.[55] Seosamh, often referred to as the last of the professional Irish scribes, was also a teacher (in the national school system) and lived, like his father and brothers, in a constant state of penury, particularly in his earlier years. He was appointed as a scribe in the Royal Irish Academy in 1865 on the death of Eugene O'Curry, a position he held until his death. During this time he produced copies of some of the most ancient manuscripts, some of which were published in print form by the Academy – *Leabhar na hUidhre* (1870), *Leabhar Breac* (1872–6), *Leabhar Laighneach* (1880) – thus illustrating what Ní Úrdail calls 'the changing times' in the nineteenth century during which 'a script-oriented rural context in Carraig na bhFear came to be replaced by its print-oriented counterpart in the city of Dublin where the last Ó Longáin plied his pen'.[56]

The Ó Longáin family also illustrate another notable feature of the manuscript culture of the nineteenth century, which was the mobility of the schoolmasters and scribes who moved around the country as employment became available, whether it be teaching, labouring or transcribing for patrons, and this mobility facilitated the circulation and transmission of learning. As to the material to be found in the manuscripts, religious texts such as Lives of saints, prayer books, biblical stories, sermons and other catechetical material, most of them translations from other languages, are the largest single category,[57] the majority of which is overwhelmingly Catholic, although some Protestant material does also exist. Much of this material is in English-based phonetic spelling and was written by priests who could speak Irish but who were unlettered in that language – examples from throughout the country are still to be found in the library at St Patrick's College, Maynooth.[58] The manuscripts also contain the normal range of traditional material: genealogical material, historical material, word lists (proverbs, sayings and even some dictionaries) and other grammatical and linguistic material, charms, incantations and other 'folk' material popularly believed to be beneficial to people.

One particularly interesting, and also largely unstudied, body of work is *Materia Medica*, including 'folk medicine', and information on medicinal plants and herbs, conditions and diseases, which in the case of Mícheál Ó Longáin reflects the growing interest in science (and in botany, medicine and agriculture in particular) of the period.[59] This material is but another example of the interplay of the written and the oral, of print and manuscript culture, and warns yet again against a simplistic distinction between the traditional and the modern in Irish-speaking Ireland at the time.

Fiannaíocht literature is the most popular native literary genre in evidence in the manuscripts which contain Fenian lays and stories from the prose cycle (*Tóraíocht Dhiarmada agus Ghráinne, Cath Fionntrá, Bruidhean Chaorthainn, Eachtra an Ghiolla Dheacair, Eachtra Lomnochtáin* being to the fore), some stories from the Ulster Cycle, and romantic prose tales (*Cath Chluana Tairbh, Deargruathar Chonaill Chearnaigh, Oidheadh Chonnlaoich*). The manuscripts also contain some tales not known from earlier sources and, thus, most likely emanating from the oral tradition. There is also a large body of poems, songs and stand-alone stanzas (*burdúin*) – some newly composed, others copied – together with warrant poems and some historical poems, and also copious verse correspondence between poets. The newly created material in the manuscripts is mostly poetry, although some prose texts do exist as well. Céitinn's *Foras Feasa ar Éirinn* is the main text copied, and its influence is all-pervasive in the poetry of the period.

Some scribes, such as Amhlaoibh Ó Súilleabháin, Pádraig Ó Néill and others, wrote their own material, although most wrote for patrons. Many prepared material which they hoped to see in print (either traditional texts or compositions or books of their own), Mac Bionaid's History of Ireland and Peadar Ó Conaill's Dictionary being two representative examples. Most of this work never saw the printer's press, however, and certainly not in the lifetime of the scribe or composer. Moreover, despite the language decline of the period, and despite the growing amount of English in the manuscripts over the century, most of the material is in Irish, although increasingly as the century progressed, commentary and other notations on the margins of the texts are in English.

The main interest and focus of most of the nineteenth-century language activity in Irish was without question scholarly and antiquarian, even among scholars immersed in the tradition. Most had a sentimental and cultural adherence to the language which they wished to preserve through their scholarship as a cultural memory for future generations. The language attitude of scribes and scholars can be seen in colophon notes to their manuscripts and in the introductions to their various publications, most of which are written solely in English. They invariably show a romantic, backward-looking attachment to the language and regret dolefully what they see as its swiftly approaching demise. There is also a strong emphasis on the beauty of the language itself and on its effectiveness as a literary medium through the ages, allied to a sense of the importance of learning for tribal memory.

Nioclás Ó Cearnaigh, a native speaker and also a poet, wrote the explanatory notes in his manuscripts almost exclusively in English. Although his introduction to *The Bardic Remains of Louth* (with Matthew Graham) in the 1830s shows a proto-revivalist attitude which predates Thomas Davis – he suggests the teaching of Irish in the schools and the use of Irish by politicians, lawyers, farmers, landlords, church leaders and clergy, and also claims that the eradication of Irish was a deliberate policy of the English government[60] – his main interest in the language was without any doubt scholarly. Similarly, Amhlaoibh Ó Súilleabháin also complains about the loss of the language: 'Ta an Bearla Sasanach ag breith barr gach la air ár tteangan dilis bunudhasach fein' (English is overcoming our own dear native language every day)[61] – but his own agenda was also primarily scholarly. Ní Úrdail notes that there is a preoccupation with the Irish language as a cultural-political cause in the Ó Longáin manuscripts and that Mícheál Óg saw his role as that of retriever of sources from the Gaelic world from the darkness of the past 'ar mhaithe leis an nGaoidheilg 7 d'fhonn coghnamh fuasgalta do thabhairt uirthi ón ndorchadas ndearmadach ndanardha ionna bhfuil le cian d'aimsir' (for the good of the Irish language in order to help revive it from the foreign darkness of oblivion in which it has been for a long time).[62]

By contrast, the language attitude apparent in the poetry, with its more radical world-view and tendency towards millennial sentiments, is more akin to the revivalist attitude of the later part of the century and, perhaps, illustrates the fact that the private and intimate life, the life of the 'hidden Ireland of the time', is to be found mainly in the poetry. The poets are very conscious of the fact that Irish is the medium of their poetic discourse and the language itself is a fundamental part of the sense of self, both personal and communal, that permeates all of the poetry.

The influence of print culture on Irish began on a small scale in the seventeenth century, continued to grow in the eighteenth century, and became more pronounced with the massive growth of literacy and print culture among all classes in the nineteenth century. As Ní Úrdail has noted, while scribes were still commissioned to transcribe manuscripts during the nineteenth century, the influence of print culture was widespread, with form, style and lay-out of manuscripts imitating print through, for example, the use of indices, translations, annotations in English and other editorial techniques associated with print media. Despite the fact that there was no development of strong popular literacy in Irish in the nineteenth century, as happened in Wales, two kinds of literacy in Irish existed at this time, particularly in the earlier period: manuscript literacy and print literacy.[63] In addition to the flourishing of manuscript production, there was also a small but significant increase in the number of books printed in Irish during the period. At the same time, literacy in Irish was often viewed with suspicion by Catholics, and in particular by the clergy, because of its association with the proselytism of the Bible societies. However, the popularity of texts such as Tadhg Gaelach Ó Súilleabháin's *The Pious Miscellany* shows that print literacy and orthodox Catholicism existed side by side in the early nineteenth century. Moreover, it should also be remembered that the Bible societies were an important source of patronage for impoverished scribes at the time and as such helped keep the native tradition of learning alive.

The most common printed material in Irish was scriptures in Irish (mostly the product of the Bible societies) and other religious material, in the main prayer books and catechisms (both original and translations from other languages). There were also some sermons for the use of priests – suggesting a certain amount of priestly literacy in Irish. Although Whitley Stokes estimated that some 20,000 people could read Irish in 1806 from 1.5 million Irish-speaking households,[64] and despite the fact that this material was undoubtedly used for personal devotion, there is no doubt that most of the Irish-speaking population would have come into contact with such works by listening to them being read out, or in the case of devotional verse, being recited from memory.

Printed material of a secular nature is represented mostly by the scholarly publications, already mentioned, of the various learned societies and their members throughout the century. Very few of these books would have received any mass circulation outside the rarified middle- and upper-class world of these same societies. They include prose texts, poetry (mostly with facing translations into English), primers and grammars intended as teaching aids,[65] and also various broadsheets, mostly of poetry, many of which were written in a phonetic script. In the mid-century the Ossianic Society published some Fenian poetry and prose tales – *Cath Gabhra* (1853), *Feis Tighe Chonáin* (1855), *Tóruigheacht Dhiarmuda agus Ghráinne* (1857) – which were more accessible to readers not versed in the literary tradition. This development in turn prepared the way for the introduction of mainline print culture into Irish with the founding of the journals *An Gaodhal* (The Gael) in the USA in 1881 and *Irisleabhar na Gaedhilge* (The Gaelic Journal) in 1882 in Dublin. Nevertheless, the gradual decline of Irish as a spoken language during the century led inevitably to a decline in literacy in the language, a change exacerbated by increased literacy levels in English. This indeed was one of the fundamental issues addressed by the language revival societies of the final quarter of the century, beginning with the Society for the Preservation of the Irish Language (1876) and culminating in Conradh na Gaeilge/Gaelic League (1893), whose main strategies were the introduction of Irish as a subject at all levels of the education system and the establishment of a dedicated Publications Committee in 1900.

Prose literature in Irish

One of the main characteristics of nineteenth-century literature in Irish is the lack of what might be called newly created prose. While there is a large amount of prose material in the manuscripts, very little is new. Cathal Ó Háinle, in an article entitled 'The Novel Frustrated',[66] analyses the romantic prose tales of the seventeenth and eighteenth centuries, and the few surviving texts from the nineteenth century, and laments the fact that such stories did not develop into a prose genre that could, in the fullness of time, have become the modern genre of the novel. Indeed, as will be seen in volume II, this lack of a continuous prose tradition proved to be a fundamental problem for the writers of the Revival generation in their efforts to establish modern prose genres in the new writing in Irish of the time. Most of the prose written in the nineteenth century is a continuation of the scribal activity of copying earlier texts.

There are, however, some notable exceptions to this general pattern. Cornelis Buttimer has shown that the manuscript tradition in Cork between 1700 and 1840 dealt with important matters of the day – city affairs, the politics of the day (he cites electioneering in Cork City as an example), economics, morality and religion. He also demonstrates that the scribes and scholars had a keen awareness of the greater world outside Ireland and that they commented upon the international affairs of the time, including the Seven Years War, the life and times of Napoleon and other matters.[67] He argues convincingly that these manuscript materials amount to the native world-view of the time through the linguistic lens of Irish in an urban context, thus showing that the vibrant manuscript culture was highly politically aware and in no way insular.

The literary output of Dáibhí de Barra (1757 / 8–1851), the Cork poet, scribe and scholar, is illustrative both of the scope of native learning in the nineteenth century and also of the present state of the study of the literature of the period. He is best known to us as a scribe and writer of prose, and thirteen manuscripts from his hand survive, mostly from the period 1821–35. *Parlaimint na bhFíodóirí* (published in 1902) is a rollicking satire on Cork weavers, much in the tradition of the earlier *Pairlement Chloinne Tomáis*, and *Cath na nDeachún ar Thráigh Rosa Móire* (published in 1960) is an account of a tithe affray in Cork in 1833, written in the style of the aforementioned romantic tales with verse interspersed through the text in the traditional manner, and illustrates the resistance of Catholic Irish-speaking Ireland to the tithe system. One of his best-known works is *Corraghliocas na mBan Léirmhínithe*, a translation of Edward Ward's *Female Policy Detected, or the Arts of a Designing Woman Laid Open* (1695), not published, however, until 1991. Despite his large output of prose, de Barra's contemporaries would have regarded him as 'file agus fear léinn' (a poet and man of learning) and over a hundred of his poems, mostly unpublished, are extant and unstudied in manuscript form, including devotional verse, occasional poems and *barántais* (warrant poems).

Another interesting prose text is Art Mac Bionaid's history of Ireland, *Comhrac na nGael agus na nGall le chéile*, written in 1857–8. The text, to quote Mac Bionaid from his introduction to 'Triamhain na hÉirinne', an *aisling* poem of his, outlines 'the savage atrocities, the shocking barbarities, the lawless oppression . . . exercised over the Irish Catholics from the Danish invasion to the desertion of the Irish nobility after the capitulation of Limerick, partly by foreigners and partly by natives who denied the religion of their forefathers'.[68] Mac Bionaid was no historian, even in the Gaelic understanding of the word.

His text is but a litany of the supposed woes inflicted on the poor misfortu-nate Gael over the century, and it is full of factual errors. He makes no secret of his ideological stance and perhaps the only relief is provided by the liter-ary style, which also draws on the romantic tales, and by his obvious love of country and of the Gaelic literary tradition. Another text from the same region and timeframe also worth mentioning is Aodh Mac Domhnaill's trea-tise on natural philosophy, *Fealsúnacht Aoidh Mhic Dhomhnaill*, described by Aodán Mac Póilín as 'one of the last original prose texts in Irish to come out of the native tradition, and probably the most important of the nineteenth century'.[69]

Without any doubt the most intriguing, and indeed the most 'modern' prose text of the nineteenth century is *Cín Lae Amhlaoibh Uí Shúilleabháin*, a personal diary for the years 1827–34 by Amhlaoibh Ó Súilleabháin (1780–1837), written during a period of rapid change in Ireland. Ó Súilleabháin was the son of a schoolmaster and scholar and was himself trained in the native learning. Born in Kerry, he spent most of his adult life as a shopkeeper in Callan, County Kilkenny, where he pursued his scholarly interests in some comfort. He copied and collected manuscripts and was particularly interested in the poetry of Munster in the seventeenth and eighteenth century. He also copied devotional material and composed some original poems of his own. He read widely in Irish and in English, but, despite his emotional and intellectual attachment to the Irish language, he was a pragmatist who accepted the growing domination of English in the public sphere, particularly in education and business. He was strongly influenced by the contemporary European intellectual climate of the Enlightenment, Romanticism and the general antiquarian movement, and many critics have alluded to the influence of Gilbert White's *The Natural History of Selbourne* on the discussion of nature in his *Cín Lae*. His work offers a rare insight into the intellectual and social history of the period through the eyes of a scholar trained in the native tradition who was also open to contemporary European thought. Ó Súilleabháin follows the systematic, schematic thought processes of the 'scientific' age of reason, common in European thought at the time, and he is extremely disparaging of the pre-modern non-systematic thought of the Gaelic tradition. At the same time, however, Ó Súilleabháin remains embedded in the Gaelic world, as seen for example in his frequent sectarian outbursts against the English and the Protestant faith. Thus his work provides an interesting insight into the question of Irish identity at a critical moment in Irish cultural and political history.

A likeable personality shines through the *Cín Lae* as Ó Súilleabháin records details concerning everyday matters and occurrences – the weather, games, information on local people and events, local customs and practices. He also casts an eye on local, national and even international politics, often recounting happenings on mainland Europe – the wars in Turkey and Greece (1828) and the insurrections in Belgium and Poland (1830–1), for example. Also evident is his interest in improving means of farming, thus demonstrating the mindset of the Catholic, Gaelic middle class with a modernising agenda. In this regard, although steeped in the Gaelic tradition, he was against wake amusements and the passive, fatalistic attitude to God's will as the dominant force in human affairs common among the Catholic underclass, an attitude he perceived as counter-productive. Written in an easy, readable style, unlike the verbose romantic tales he composed, the *Cín Lae* can be placed in the common diary genre in contemporary English and European writing. Although a one-off in literary terms within the Irish tradition, it can also be seen as the precursor of the emergence of the centrality of the individual in literature in Irish, but as it remained in manuscript form until its publication in 1936, its influence could not be exerted in that direction in the nineteenth century. The same holds true for the other prose texts mentioned above, all of which were first published in scholarly editions in the twentieth century. The only other original prose text which might be considered in the context of the evolution of modern literature in Irish in a print culture during this period is the biography of John Mac Hale, the first of its kind in Irish, published by his nephew and protegé, Uileag de Búrca, in *Irisleabhar na Gaedhilge* (1882–6). Interestingly, de Búrca also published a biography in book form in English, *The Life and Times of the Most Rev. John Mac Hale*, in 1882.

Poetry in Irish

Poetry in Irish was the public voice of Gaelic Ireland during the nineteenth century, although even scholars well versed in the Gaelic tradition are wont to peasantise both the poetry itself and the community that produced it. They regard it as 'the end of a tradition', instead of accepting it as the contemporary response to the situation in which those still within the Gaelic tradition found themselves. Many dismiss it as a mere literary survival from greater, loftier times, the last miserable hurrah of a once great tradition. Piaras Béaslaí, in his *Éigse Nua-Ghaedhilge*, dismisses it as 'minor verse',[70] and Máirín Ní Mhuiríosa and Caerwyn Williams in *Traidisiún Liteartha na nGael* claim that it is 'gan doimhneacht smaointe ná snas liteartha' (without depth of thought or literary polish).[71] More recently, Art Hughes dismisses poetry from the Oirialla district of Ulster in the period as 'the class of peasant poetry that was . . . practised in this area for well over two centuries',[72] and Ó Háinle states that verse 'continued to be produced, often by non-lettered poets; but most of it was doggerel about local events and concerns'.[73] Certainly, much of the poetry of the period was composed orally and, as it were, outside the direct influence of the old learned tradition, and much of this work has come down through oral transmission. However, as Niall Ó Ciosáin for the Irish tradition, and Ruth Finnegan[74] and others in discussing oral literature in general, have cogently argued, the so-called divide between 'oral' and 'literary' is not so great as is often claimed, and, despite the different scope of each, both use many of the same literary devices and techniques.

Filíocht in the Irish tradition, as distinct from what we understand today as poetry, particularly in a modern context, remains a cultural constant in the period from the seventeenth to the nineteenth century. It, rather than prose, is the principal medium for public discourse within the tradition and it carries the 'nativist world-view', the ideology of Irish-speaking Ireland at the time. This understanding of the cultural significance of *filíocht* emanates from the traditional function of the poet throughout the entirety of the Gaelic tradition, which was to give voice to the community, whose representative he was, in a manner that was culturally and aesthetically acceptable to that community. Thus, the Irish poetry of the nineteenth century can be read as Gaelic Ireland representing itself through the medium of the word in accordance with traditional modes, thereby simultaneously engaging with the past and the present. This continuing importance of *filíocht* within the Irish-speaking world of the nineteenth century can be seen in the number of poems composed and copied in the period (the vast majority of which are still only in manuscript form) and also in the significant number of poems and songs that continued to be transmitted in the oral tradition, many of which were collected in the early part of the twentieth century by the Irish Folklore Commission. It must be emphasised again that this cultural activity continued during a time of great poverty and hardship in rural Gaelic Ireland, and that many Irish-speaking emigrants brought manuscripts of Irish poetry and other material (some in phonetic English-based scripts) with them to the new world, thus indicating their continuing importance as significant cultural objects. The native belief in the inherent superiority of poetry over prose can be seen in our period in the attitude of Nioclás Ó Cearnaigh, who refers in a letter to his fellow scholar and poet John O'Daly to Archbishop John Mac Hale's translation into Irish of Moore's *Melodies* as 'mere prose', while at the same time suggesting that it would be more praiseworthy to study the older poets in order 'to learn their sweet secret'.[75]

The greatest corpus of poetry in the nineteenth century comes from Munster, where the native tradition of scholarship and learning survived the longest, and where most of the copying of manuscripts occurred during the period. It is also worth noting that part of the prominence of Munster poetry comes, no doubt, from the publication of such canonical works as John O'Daly's *The Poets and Poetry of Munster* in 1849, from the various translations of Irish poetry into English during the century, and also from the work of scholars from the early part of the twentieth century who edited and published much Munster poetry under the auspices of the Gaelic League.

Mícheál Óg Ó Longáin, as already noted, is the poet/scribe *par excellence* of this period. Over 350 of his poetic compositions survive, most still in manuscript form. Much of this material is in fact correspondence in verse concerning scribal material and scholarship, as was normal in eighteenth and nineteenth-century literary circles. His work contains *aisling* poems, devotional verse, and elegies on the deaths of friends and fellow scholars, but he is best known for his political poetry, which shows a strong republican ideology.[76]

The Waterford poet Pádraig Denn (1756–1828) is best known for his religious poetry with a strong emphasis on sin, human frailty and the wrath of God. A schoolteacher, sacristan and instructor in catechetics to young people in the parish of Cappoquin, he published an edition of Tadhg Gaelach Ó Súilleabháin's *Pious Miscellany* (first published in 1805) in 1819, adding some of his own poems. He was one of the first Irish-language poets to see his own compositions in print, as *Aighneas an Pheacaig leis an mBás* (1814), some of which survived in oral tradition until the early twentieth century in Waterford, and *Stiúrthóir an Pheacaig* (1824). Séamus Mac Cruitín (1815–70) from County Clare referred to himself in 1860 as 'The last of the hereditary Bards of Thomand'. He claimed kinship with the poet Aindrias Mac Cruitín (his great-grand-uncle) and with the well-known eighteenth-century poet Aodh Buí Mac Cruitín. He composed what could be called 'official poetry' in the main, *caointe* or lament poems, praise poems, love songs and humorous songs. He also composed some poems and songs in English, reflecting the linguistic reality of his time, and like many of the poets he was in despair as to the future of the language.

Pádraig Phiarais Cúndún (1777–1856) is a most interesting poet. Born in County Cork, he was a comfortable farmer, even employing two workers, but was seemingly more interested in learning than in farming, and his business failed. He was literate in Irish and taught for a period, but he was forced by financial circumstances to emigrate to the United States with his wife and family in 1826. He settled in Utica, New York, and his many letters home give a unique insight into the mind of an Irish-speaking emigrant coping with the new world – one such letter containing 278 lines in verse in praise of the American way of life. Unlike many of his fellow poets and scholars, he was more interested in contemporary poetry than in the earlier tradition, and his own well-known and much-anthologised poem 'Tórramh an Bharraille' is a song of praise to his home place of Baile Mhic Óda where in typical emigrant fashion he wished to die and be buried.

No account of the Munster poetry of the period would be complete without a mention of Máire Bhuí Ní Laoghaire (c.1774–c.1849), one of the few female poets from whom a significant body of poetry survives and who was also well thought of in the tradition. She is most famous for her poem 'Cath Chéim an Fhia', a lively if somewhat exaggerated account of a bloody encounter between local Whiteboys and the yeomanry on 11 January 1822, a song sung to this day in the same Gaeltacht region, and a defining poem in her life and her poetic work. She was born at Túirín na nÉan, Béal Átha an Ghaorthaidh, in west Cork, and showed her independent mind when she eloped with and married Séamus de Búrca. They were quite wealthy by the early 1820s, farming some 150 acres at Céim an Fhia and employing servant labour. After the aforementioned battle of Céim an Fhia, her sons were forced to go on the run, their rent was increased and they were eventually evicted in 1847. Unlike most of the Munster poets, Máire Bhuí was unable to read or write. Nevertheless, the narrative modes and techniques, and the literary style of her poetry are completely in keeping with the poetry of her time and place. She composed *aisling* poems in accordance with the Munster tradition, *caointe*, lullabies, love songs, humorous songs and religious songs. Her strong personality and forthright views emerge clearly throughout the poetry, and this is seen most clearly in the political message of strong support for Catholic emancipation and repeal infused, as was the norm for the poetic tradition, with a clear millenarian message.

Other Munster poets worth mentioning in the period are the Kerry poet Diarmaid na Bolgaighe Ó Séaghdha (c.1755–1846), author of many religious poems, who though literate did not write down his own poetry, who received patronage from a local chieftain, Sylvester Ó Súilleabháin (the last Mac Fínín Duibh), in the early part of his career, and who died almost destitute during the famine; and Tomás Rua Ó Súilleabháin (1785–1848), the Kerry schoolteacher, poet and friend of Daniel O'Connell, whose career he records in the traditional, often belligerent, manner of the official Gaelic poet. Ó Súilleabháin's poem 'Amhrán na Leabhar' (The Song of the Books), which laments the loss of all his books during a sea crossing, gives an insight into the literary leanings and learning of the Irish poet and scholar of his time, listing as it does an eclectic mix of printed and manuscript works, both secular and religious.

The poetic tradition in the nineteenth century also survived in the Oirialla district where we have already noted the flourishing of manuscript copying and native learning during the period. As was the case in Munster, these scholars considered poetry as traditional learning and therefore they both copied older poetry and composed verse of their own within that same tradition. The period saw the production of much poetry, the organisation of some poetic festivals, and also a number of 'Iomarbhánna Filí', poetic contentions between the poets of Munster and their Ulster counterparts, and among local poets themselves. Much of this poetry is, however, pedantic, laboured and smacking of the contrived learning of poets for whom making poems was a pastime rather than an essential part of the life of the society of the time. It is certainly less immediate, less rooted in the community at large, and it did not receive wide circulation among the Irish-speaking population in general, unlike Connacht or Munster poetry of the period. Art Hughes calls this Oirialla poetry 'the swansong of the vibrant Gaelic tradition of the South Armagh hinterland at the end of the nineteenth century',[77] and there is no doubt that much of the poetic activity of the period declined with the language itself after the 1850s, despite the fact that some of the poets themselves lived on until the 1880s, the period which saw the beginnings of the Irish Revival movement.

Nioclás Ó Cearnaigh called himself 'The last of the Bards of Louth', and was, according to Tomás Ó Fiaich, 'the best northern poet writing in Irish in the nineteenth century'.[78] He composed many poems, including one over a hundred verses long on the Great Famine, and a hauntingly beautiful elegy on a murdered child, 'Cumha na máthara fán leanbh', arguably 'one of the finest poems, in Irish or English, written in this country in the nineteenth century'.[79] Although it is sometimes difficult to establish exactly what poems he composed, because of his propensity for ascribing his own compositions to earlier poets, a sufficient corpus of work exists to enable us to establish an overview of his work. As with many poets throughout the country, political comment permeates his poetry, and the underlying message is that of the cultural and political nationalism common in the English-language poetry of the time, from a strong Ulster perspective. He claims, for example, in one poem, 'Beidh Éire gan mhearbhall le feara Thír Eoghain'[80] (Ireland shall be won without doubt by the men of Tyrone). There are also strong sectarian overtones in the poetry, allied to themes such as emigration and the importance of retaining the Irish language as a marker of identity. While Ó Cearnaigh's poetry is immersed in the tradition, it also shows the influence in both form and content of nineteenth-century English Romantic poetry and, in particular, the rhetoric of the *Nation* poets. He was strongly influenced by Thomas Davis for whom he composed some poems in English, and some of Ó Cearnaigh's poems were published in the *Nation*. This active engagement with the ideas, form and public forum of such political poetry in English can be read as an answer to those who might have presumed that Irish poetry was to be written henceforth in English only after the fashion of the likes of Moore, Mangan and Ferguson.

Peadar Ó Gealacáin, poet and scribe, was described by a contemporary as 'a natural Irish bard, tho' a man of no great erudition'.[81] As Ó Fiaich has noted, his poetry contains less of the pseudo-learning and antiquarianism of Ó Cearnaigh[82] and is closer to the type of oral poetry composed by the later oral poets. Like that of his fellow poets, his work is also sectarian, with a traditional Catholic religiosity. His politics are strongly nationalistic, with a robust, oft-repeated hatred of the English (Clann Bhullaí, Clann Liútair, Clann Sheáin Bhuí, Gallbhodaigh an Bhéarla) and he could be extremely scathing, as witnessed in some personalised denunciations in the Irish tradition of *aoir* or satire. He also composed love songs in the traditional manner, and a winning sense of humour permeates much of his poetry, as seen for example in a humorous poem on the death of a cat, and its supposed deep effect on the community,[83] and also in the robust, Rabelaisian sense of sexuality portrayed in the following advice to young women:

> A chailíní na scéimhe, glacaigí mo scéal,
> Agus cumhdaigí féin bhur n-íochtar,
> Ná ligigí choíche Tadhg a sheilg fá bhur mbléin,
> Nó is doiligh daoibh an gadhar a mháistreacht.

(O beautiful girls, listen to what I say, and protect your lower region; don't let Tim go hunting in your groin, or you will find it hard to master the dog.)[84]

The poetry of Art Mac Bionaid is virulently anti-Protestant and sectarian and illustrates a strong sense of Ulster identity in both the geographical and cultural senses – a fact also true of most of the material he copied. Moreover, he particularly favoured the typical Ulster metre of *Trí Rainn is Amhrán*. Over half his poems are either on a religious theme or dedicated to a priest, and they are intensely serious with no sense of the mischief and humour found in the likes of Ó Gealacáin and others. His cantankerous nature and difficult personality made satire his natural mode of expression, and he satirises priests whom he disliked, the Bible societies which he particularly hated along with their teachers, and other Gaelic scholars with whom he disagreed, including his one-time friend and co-scholar, Aodh Mac Domhnaill, whom he satirised in a well-known poem, 'An tOllamh Úr – or reflections upon Hugh Mac Donnell's conduct for assuming the name of poet'.

Aodh Mac Domhnaill saw himself in his poetry as a spokesman for his community, the Gaeldom of Ulster. His compositions are conservative and learned, are heavily influenced by the Ulster poets of the preceding century, and are suffused with literary references to the older historical and literary tradition. Unlike Mac Bionaid and Ó Cearnaigh, they show no influence of English on language or prosody. The poems are very Ulster-centric, with a strong emphasis on the Irish language and culture. In politics Mac Domhnaill was a committed supporter of Daniel O'Connell, although unlike many of his fellow poets, he disapproved of violence. He composed praise poems and elegies in the traditional mode for various political figures. He laments Thomas Davis in the traditional heroic style, claiming "Sí Éire a chaill a céile fíor' (Ireland has lost her true spouse),[85] and a long elegy on O'Connell full of traditional clichés argues that he was 'An Guaire a d'fhuascail Éirinn' (The Guaire, *i.e.* the King of Connacht, who freed Ireland).[86] He notes in the same poem that it is the function of the poet to ensure the continuing fame of such heroes through the medium of poetry. Similarly, his religious poems are strongly Catholic and narrated in the traditional discourse, with an emphasis on piety and the need for repentance. The Catholic church is portrayed as the one true church, and thus the poems are invariably anti-Protestant and anti-English. The one note of relief in the poetry is the good humour of the local poems.

Many other poets were active at the time, and merit at least a mention in any survey of the Ulster poetry of the period: Séamas Mac Giolla Choille (*c.*1759–1828), apothecary and lover of learning and all things Gaelic, who organised poetic contentions in Dundalk in 1825 and 1826, but whose own verse leaves much to be desired; Art Mór Mac Murchaidh (?–1844), Murchadh na nDán, the poet and satirist who, despite living in straitened circumstances, called his humble abode 'Grottoplace Castle', where he taught, among others, Mac Giolla Choille, Ó Cearnaigh and Matthew Moore Graham, one of the founders of the Drogheda Gaelic Society; Fr Pádraig Ó Luain, poet, scholar and patron to Mac Bionaid; Fr Pól Ó Briain, the aforementioned professor of Irish at Maynooth, whose light-hearted early poems show a fondness for wine and female company but whose later poems are more stilted and archaic, rather like his grammar.

Although Connacht had the highest number of Irish speakers in the entire country, and despite the fact that the province also had a significant tradition of scholarly activity down to the seventeenth century, there was relatively little scholarly activity in the region in the nineteenth century. This is a result, in no small part, of the poverty of the region and the lack of a suitable infrastructure of patronage which was much more available to scholars in what Ó Buachalla has called the 'fat lands' of Munster. William Mahon has shown that only a mere thirty or so manuscripts survive from County Galway in our period, as against more than five hundred for the province of Munster, and most of these are from the east Galway plain. The manuscripts themselves are rather less learned than in Munster or Ulster, and many of them are from the oral tradition and written in a phonetic script based on English. One interesting scribe is Pádraig Mag Fhloinn (*fl.* 1828–35) who wrote down, from oral tradition, songs by Toirialach Ó Cearbhalláin and Antaine Raiftearaí, and copied *Doctor Kirwan's Irish Catechism* and *Iomarbháigh na bhFilí*. He also wrote an English–Irish dictionary of over 700 pages which contained 'upwards of 100,000 words which have never been published in any dictionary of our vernacular language'.[87]

The most important scholar associated with the region at this time is, without doubt, James Hardiman (1782–1855), librarian at the Queen's College, Galway, and author of *The History of the Town and County of Galway from the Earliest Period to the Present Time* (1820), and editor of Roderick O'Flaherty's *Chorographical Description of West or h-Iar-Connaught* (1846). His most important work is *Irish Minstrelsy or Bardic Remains of Ireland* (two volumes, 1831), which contains Irish poetry from the earliest time down to the oral poetry of the day, including the work of Connacht poets of the nineteenth century such as Raiftearaí (whom Hardiman knew well), Mícheál Mac Suibhne and Riocard Bairéad. Hardiman, himself a scholar of national standing and a founder member of the Irish Archaeological Society and the Celtic Society, was also an assiduous collector of manuscripts and a patron to some scribes whom he paid to copy manuscripts. A staunch Catholic and supporter of Catholic emancipation, and strongly nationalistic in outlook, he blamed British policy in Ireland for the destruction, as he saw it, of the ancient Irish civilisation, views which were famously criticised by the strongly unionist Samuel Ferguson in the *Dublin University Magazine* in 1834.

The dearth of formal scholarship in the west of Ireland in general in the nineteenth century does not indicate that there was any shortage of poetic activity or that there was no reception for poetry and other native literary forms among the mostly monoglot Irish-speaking population who were in the main illiterate in their own language. As a result, the poetry of this period and place tends to be rather less pedantic and precious – and certainly less formally learned – than that of both Munster and Ulster. It is also much lighter in tone, and more grounded in local communities, with a strong emphasis on local events and characters. It is also worth noting that many songs of Raiftearaí and Bairéad and their like can still be heard in Gaeltacht areas, having come down through oral tradition.

The poetry of Antaine Raiftearaí (1779–1835) speaks from and for the Gaelic world of his time, a period when the Catholic Irish-speaking masses were becoming more politicised than in previous generations. Firmly rooted in his own place, the region, as he says himself, between the Shannon and the sea, the consciousness of his work is an introduction to the native *Weltanschauung* not visible in state papers and visitors' accounts – sources invariably either blind or hostile to that world. He constantly addresses his listeners in the authoritative voice of the traditional poet, insisting that it is his function to interpret the world for them, which he does in no uncertain terms:

> Fear gan radharc gan léann a mhíníos daoibh an scéal,
> Raiftearaí a d'éist ler dúradh
> a deir go flaitheas Dé nach rachaidh neach go héag
> a bhéas ag plé le leabhra Liútair.

(A man without sight or learning explains the matter for you, Raiftearaí who listened to what was said; who says that those who have anything to do with the books of Luther will never go to heaven.)[88]

Raiftearaí believed, like the poets of the seventeenth and eighteenth century, that Ireland was lost through 'clisiam Gall', the trickery of the Gall, and he gives in poem after poem the 'nationalist' or 'nativist' version of history following Seathrún Céitinn, one of his oft-mentioned heroes, and others of that same tradition. His poetry is, therefore, often venomously sectarian and this fact caused problems for his first editor, the son of a Church of Ireland minister, none other than Douglas Hyde, founder of the Gaelic League.

Raiftearaí apart, the best-known Connacht poet of this era is the north Mayo schoolmaster and sheebeen owner Riocard Bairéad (1740–1819), who according to tradition fits the image of the poet as rake. His poetry has a strong sense of *joie de vivre*, and he is best remembered for his rollicking drinking song 'Preab san Ól', still sung to this day, and for his ironic praise poem, in reality a satire, 'Eoghan Cóir', a merciless putdown of a pitiless, tyrannical land agent. Mícheál Mac Suibhne (*c.*1760–1820) is the best known of a group of poets in the mountainous area of north Galway / south Mayo. His songs and poems are full of good humour and wit, and he is remembered mostly for love songs, in particular 'Bainis Pheigí Ní Eaghra', a lighthearted wish list of all the luxurious items he would require if he were to marry Peggy, including the best of fine clothing, twenty-four musicians, good strong drink and tobacco, and the nobility of the countryside to be present!

The brothers Marcus (*c.*1789–*c.*1846) and Patsaí (*c.*1791–1865) Ó Callanáin, from Craughwell, County Galway, are best remembered for their poetic contention with Raiftearaí. Marcas composed a biting satire on Raiftearaí and his wife, Siobhán, 'Scioladh Mharcais Uí Challanáin',[89] Raiftearaí answered in kind, and the contention continued. According to tradition, this was no formal poetic duel of words, and there was a real enmity between the parties. Lady Gregory recounts in *Poets and Dreamers* overhearing two old ladies in the poorhouse in Gort, County Galway, arguing the poetic merits of both parties. Apart from the contention with Raiftearaí, the brothers' poetry was mostly localised, concerned with the small events of everyday life. Marcas's best-known poem is a witty dialogue between the poet and his spade, while Patsaí composed a poem on the failure of the potato crop in 1846 in which he refers to the common belief at the time, often expressed in the poetry, that the famine was a visitation of the wrath of God on a sinful people:

> Is iad ár bpeacaí a tharraing gach sciúirse orainn,
> Agus d'fhág faoi chluain sin ag an Áibhirseoir,
> Is iad ár bpeacaí a dhíbríonns uainne,
> Na grástaí a fuair muid ón Slánaitheoir.

(Our sins brought every scourge upon us, and left us deceived by the Devil, it is our sins that banish from us, the grace we received from the Saviour.)[90]

One of the fundamental, underlying tenets of Irish poetry of the nineteenth century, and indeed of the poetry of the previous two centuries, is the oft-repeated statement that the native Irish had been wrongfully dispossessed of their land and heritage by an outside interloper. As Tom Dunne has argued, this poetry contains 'a significant corpus of political songs and poems in Irish [which] illustrates the continuing strength of the seventeenth-century anti-colonial tradition, but also how it was adapted to meet the profound cultural and social changes of this period'.[91] As with the poets of the preceding centuries, the nineteenth-century poets claim that Ireland's present state is entirely a result of the sins of its people. The basic message of the poetry is, however, that the native Irish, the rightful heirs to the country, will defeat the interloper and, moreover, exact revenge in no uncertain terms for all the wrongs inflicted, and that Ireland will eventually be restored to its rightful, ancestral owners. The poetry of this period is thus the public voice of the dispossessed, a discourse of rights and revolt from below, continuing from the preceding centuries, and narrated in the traditional manner and mode. It is also the complete and public rejection of the prevailing status quo and is simultaneously forward- and backward-looking in that it justifies the rights of the historical entity which is Gaeldom while also anticipating the day when the Gael will reign supreme once more and achieve his vengeance.

Raiftearaí, for example, draws upon the historical authority of the Psalter of Cashel and Seathrún Céitinn at the outset of his poem of more than four hundred lines, 'Seanchas na Sceiche', which recounts the history of Ireland from the Flood down to the era of Patrick Sarsfield. He declares that his account is totally true, and finishes with his usual authoritative poetical assertion, 'Sin mar chuir Raiftearaí síos ar Éirinn' (That is how Raiftearaí described the case of Ireland).[92] This sense of the poetic authority and of the truth of poetic declarations is a constant in the poetry not just of the nineteenth century, but throughout the tradition. Traditionally the *file*, as possessor of *imbas forasnai*, (the wisdom that illuminates), drew upon the ancestral power of the poetic vocation in his poetry and he was never loath to remind his listeners of this fact. Thus, in a similar vein to Raiftearaí, Peadar Ó Gealacáin claims that his poetic vocation is to explain the truth through the medium of his poetry, 'Ag míniú na fírinne, síos insa dán seo',[93] and Tomás Rua Ó Súilleabháin declares:

> Mar is duine beag mór mé, is ba dhual dom bheith faobhrach
> Is do roinn Dia liom bua thar an slua bhí ar an aonach.

(For I am a little big man, and I was wont to be sharp, and God gave me a greater gift than the crowd at the fair.)[94]

The political objective of the poets is seldom left in any doubt – 'réabadh Danar as Clár Luirc' (the rending of the English from Ireland)[95] as Pádraig Phiarais Cúndún succinctly expressed it. In this same context, Raiftearaí refers to himself frequently as the spokesperson for his people, whom he identifies as the Irish-speaking Catholic population of the whole island, the descendants of Clanna Mhíle and the rightful inheritors of the whole island by dint of their lineage, a fundamental, even defining element in Irish poetry from the seventeenth to the nineteenth century. In this role as spokesperson and prophet he forecasts the fall of the English:

> Raiftearaí a mhínigh agus a chuir síos an bealach seo
> is a deir go mbeidh Galla le fána.

(Raiftearaí explained and put it down in this way, and says that the English shall be tumbled.)[96]

Moreover, his message is crystal clear as to the means of achieving this end. 'Lasfaidh Éire le faobhar lann' (Ireland will flare up with sharpened blades) and the Gael will have 'pléisiúr ar *Orangemen*' (the pleasure of revenge on the Orangemen). There is also a triumphalist note to the poetry. It is not sufficient that the Gael succeed; the English must also be seen to fall:

> . . . beidh Galla suaite sínte gan duine lena gcaoineadh,
> ach tinte cnámh thíos againn ag lasadh suas go hard.

(. . . the English shall be agitated and flattened, without anyone to keen them, but we shall have bonfires flaming up high.)[97]

This note of strong certitude of a future redemption to be achieved when the rightful rulers take over in Ireland is, as Ó Buachalla has noted, the fundamental message of Irish Jacobite poetry from the eighteenth century down to poetic declarations concerning Daniel O'Connell, the greatest political leader of nationalist Catholic Ireland, in the nineteenth century. O'Connell is represented in the work of many poets throughout the country as the great Irish hero. Hundreds of songs (and, indeed, many tales) were composed about him, a body of poems which, as Dunne has pointed out, 'constitutes crucial evidence of the enduring power of the Gaelic political and literary traditions'.[98] He is praised in the traditional manner of Irish chieftains in the earlier bardic poetry. He is portrayed as the great leader who will lead the Irish out of bondage, just as Moses led his own people to the promised land:

> Ó Conaill ina lár is Ó Briain ar a láimh,
> Mar Mhaoise ag sárú Éigipt,
> Nó Iósua bhí láidir ag leagan na bpálás
> Le stoirm is toirneach na n-adharca.

(O'Connell at the centre and O'Brien at his side, as Moses defeating Egypt, or strong Joshua destroying the palaces with the storm and thunder of the trumpets.)[99]

The language and sentiments are prophetic throughout and frequently draw on the earlier *aisling* poetry, even in Ulster where the Jacobite *aisling* poetry was almost unknown in the previous century. Thus, Tomás Rua Ó Súilleabháin, a friend and neighbour of O'Connell in Derrynane, County Kerry, and almost an official poet to the Liberator, draws on many of the themes in Irish poetry over the previous two centuries in what is, perhaps, the best-known of the O'Connellite poems. The key note is Gaelic and Catholic triumphalism, and freedom will be achieved by the sword for those of Irish blood – sentiments which would no doubt have discomfited O'Connell greatly:

> Sé Dónall binn Ó Conaill caoin
> An planda fíor den Ghaelfhuil,
> Gur le feabhas a phinn is meabhair a chinn
> Do scól sé síos an craos-shliocht;
> Go bhfuil sé scríofa i bPastorini
> Go maithfear cíos do Ghaelaibh
> Is go mbeidh farraigí breac le flít ag teacht
> Isteach thar Pointe Chléire.

(Sweet, gentle Daniel O'Connell is the prince of Gaelic blood, who by the excellence of his pen and his intelligence has destroyed the avaricious foreigners; it is written in Pastorini that the Irish will not have to pay rent, and the sea will be awash with a fleet of ships coming around the headland of Cape Clear.)[100]

Another interesting and fairly representative song from County Clare, where O'Connell was elected to parliament, also draws on the idea of violent revolt with help from abroad (another traditional political concept in the poetry and mentioned by many poets). It also refers to the installation of O'Connell as high king of Ireland, comparing him at the same time to Napoleon, another well-regarded political leader among nineteenth-century Irish poets:

> Agus dá dtagadh suathadh beart ins an tír seo agus go bhfilleadh an flít isteach,
> Agus go gcruinneoidís inár dtimpeall mar dhíon don bhfathach inár measc;
> Go dtroidfimis go dílis iad ar chlaidheamh nó ar phúdar ceart,
> Is go ndéanfaimis Ardrí de ins an tír seo mar *Bhónaparte*.

(And if matters became agitated in this country and if the fleet were to arrive, and if they were to assemble around us as a roof over the giant in our midst; we would fight them loyally with sword or proper powder, and we would make him High King of the country like Bonaparte.)[101]

The political world-view of this poetry is not 'republican' in the accepted sense of nineteenth-century political discourse, but rather royalist in the sense of rule by chieftain in the traditional Gaelic mode – a further indication of the continuance of what Ó Buachalla calls the Jacobite mentality in Irish literary and political discourse.[102] There is also in this political poetry a strong Messianic attitude, an absolute belief in the truth of the prophecy that the Catholic Church, and thus the Irish, will eventually win the day. In this regard, the poets frequently refer to the prophecies of Pastorini, which were widely circulated in pamphlet and broadsheet form in the early nineteenth century in Ireland.

These prophecies were based on the writings of the English Benedictine bishop Charles Walmesley whose *General History of the Christian Church* (1771) forecast the destruction of Protestant churches in 1825.

Another fundamental aspect of the political poetry of the period is its sectarian nature, particularly in poems where history, politics and religion interface. Most of the poetry is staunchly pro-Catholic and virulently anti-Protestant, as for example in this verse from a warrant poem ('barántas') by Dáibhí de Barra to Tomás Ó Murchú na nAmhrán:

> Buail siar chum Bandan, is ann tá an gasra
> Is measa sa dúiche de chomplacht *Orangemen*,
> Paca gan riail, chuir an diabhal chun mearathaill,
> Do ghoidfeadh an iall, an scian 's a' meanaithe.

(Go back to Bandon, it is there you will find the worst band of Orangemen in the area, a pack without order who drove the Devil demented, who would rob the strap, the knife and the awl.)[103]

Raiftearaí composed a series of poems on politico-religious themes where he leaves his listeners in no doubt as to his beliefs. Protestants are damned to hellfire for eternity as their religion is based completely on falsehood, he claims. They read a false Bible, do not fast on Fridays and even eat meat on Good Friday. Moreover, they do not render obedience to the Blessed Virgin, nor to the true church of Rome. Raiftearaí constantly takes an almost malicious pleasure in asserting that the days of Protestant supremacy are numbered in Ireland, as Pastorini prophesied, and that the day is about to dawn on which the Orangemen will be defeated. It must be remembered, in the context of such blatant sectarianism, that the nineteenth century in Ireland, and indeed throughout Europe, was a period of rampant sectarianism. This period in Ireland saw a movement of intense religious proselytisation which in turn led to much sectarian strife throughout the country. Between 1806 and 1820, for example, when Raiftearaí was in his prime, seven Bible societies were founded in Ireland with the sole aim of showing the native Irish-speaking population the errors of Catholicism and releasing them from what their founders believed to be the bondage of Rome.

Despite this all-pervasive presence of religion in everyday life, and apart from the aforementioned elements of millenarianism and prophecy (a fundamental part of much religiosity of the time across the sectarian divide), it is most remarkable that there is very little of the 'popular religion' of the time as described by Connolly[104] in the poetry of Raiftearaí or his fellow poets. In fact, their poetry is firmly in the mainstream of the orthodox Catholicism of the time, reflecting the influence of the Tridentine Reform which began in Ireland in the late eighteenth century and continued through into the nineteenth. The poets probably either read or heard read many of the various standardising Irish-language Catholic texts readily available at the time. Chief among them was *The Pious Miscellany*, well known throughout Munster and in other places, including Galway, which 'embodied and partially created a regional religious culture, a type of reformed Catholicism in the Irish language'.[105] Bishop Gallagher's sermons were also in widespread use, as were the various catechisms commonly available at the time: *Doctor Kirwan's Irish Catechism*, published in 1830, but in manuscript before that and frequently read aloud, even before 1800; Andrew Dunlevy's *Teagusg Críostuidhe*, first published in 1742, but still in common use in the following century; and later John Mac Hale's catechism *An Teagasg Criosdaighe* (1839), which replaced Dunlevy in common use.

As a result, much of the devotional and religious poetry is didactic in nature. There is a strong emphasis on the sinful nature of man, who is depraved by nature, and thus in dire need of reform and repentance (the *aithrí* or repentance poem being de rigueur for any poet worth his poetic salt!) in order to achieve ultimate redemption. Lists of sins in the poems illustrate the moral failings of the Irish, and therefore devotional poetry is at one with the above-mentioned poetry of a political and historical nature. The poetry of Raiftearaí is typical of the native Irish Catholic religiosity of his time. As with his political poetry, where he draws on the authority of past historians and authors, his religious poetry, like that of his fellow poets, refers constantly to the authority of the traditional Catholic world-view, as witnessed in sacred scripture and tradition. Thus, he constantly underpins his own authoritative statements concerning religious matters with justifications such as 'Thug na húdair naofa cuntas dúinn sa scéal seo' (The sacred authors gave an account of this matter), or 'Gurb é a dúirt an t-údar naofa Naomh Seán sa *Revelation*' (As the holy author St John said in the Revelation).[106] He portrays man as unfree, sinful and in need of the grace of God to achieve redemption. There is an almost Jansenistic attitude of fatalism in the poems which regularly implore God or Jesus Christ through the intercession of Mary, the Blessed Virgin, to save humankind, to grant grace to a people who seem to have a mere passive role in the process. The transience of life is frequently alluded to and the poems often describe the final days, 'na críocha déanacha', indicating a religion focused on death and on the next world rather than on the present world of humankind. Heaven is seen as the reward for a life well lived, and as with the ultimate redemption of the Gael which is prophesied in the political realm, the good Catholic shall enter into the kingdom.

All, however, is not gloom, doom and other weighty matters of life and death in the poetry. Despite the emphasis on politics and religion, there is also a range of other matters addressed. The poems often express a strong sense of *joie de vivre*, particularly in the many humorous poems and also in much of the love poetry, which is frequently a joyous celebration of sexuality, as seen, for example, in a poem like Raiftearaí's well-known 'Máire Ní Eidhin'.[107] Indeed, this type of poem exists comfortably side by side with the many poems extolling the virtues of sanctity and purity. In the same way, one finds many drinking songs and poems featuring the traditional image of the poet as rake – Riocard Bairéad's 'Preab san Ól' being a particularly apt example – while other compositions echo the official anti-drink church views of the time during the halcyon days of Fr Theobald Mathew's temperance movement. Interestingly, this sophisticated 'read' on issues fundamental to everyday life as lived in the flesh is far more liberal and relaxed in many ways than the attitude of most of the so-called modernisers of the later Revival movement, whose attitude to these matters was generally far more puritanical, even positively Victorian.

Much of this poetry is also local, with a strong celebration of the sense of place, a fundamental element in Irish literature throughout the tradition. Thus, Máire Bhuí Ní Laoghaire is very much of west Cork, Raiftearaí of the area west of the Shannon, and the northern poets all show an unflinching Ulster-centric attitude throughout their work. The following verse by Tomás Rua Ó Súilleabháin, although from a religious song, is representative of the attitude to place:

> Céad moladh le hÍosa, le Muire is le Bríde
> Go bhfeicfeadsa arís mo ghaolta,
> Tá go fairsing sa líon ón gCathair go Snaidhm,
> Is i nDoir' Fhionáin aoibhinn aerach,
> Cois Beannach an naoimh bhí i ngradam ag Críost,
> I Sceilg Mhichíl ghil naofa,
> Mar a bhfaighinnse mé shíneadh, mo chur is mo chaoineadh
> I measc gasra dem mhuintir féinig.

(All praise to Jesus, Mary and Bridget, until I see again my relations, who are plentiful in the area between Caher and Sneem, and in beautiful airy Derrynane, beside Banna of the saint well regarded by Christ, in bright and holy Skellig Michael, where I would be buried and keened among my own people.)[108]

In addition, the poetry also describes many other elements of the life of Irish-speaking society of the time – praise poems to local heroes, accounts of local and personal events and happenings (often reflecting events on the national stage), *caointe*, and poems that illustrate the ordinary life of the time, to name but a few – and thus allows access to the public and indeed private space that was Gaelic Ireland, or indeed Ireland from below in the nineteenth century.

Post-famine writing

After the Great Famine, as the language declined, scholarly activity, and indeed literary poetry, diminished rapidly. Belfast, where the learned societies had flourished, for example, saw many changes at this time – the rapid growth of the city as a result of a large influx of poor Catholics and the consequent significant increase in sectarian tensions – which led indirectly to the gradual fading away of the scholarly societies as scholars and their patrons passed away. Irish was now commonly equated with Catholicism in the North, and as early as the 1840s the Ulster Gaelic Society ceased activities, the Academical Institution ceased teaching Irish, and, even though John O'Donovan was appointed to the chair of Irish at the Queen's College in 1849 and gave some public lectures, he had no students. Ó Buachalla has estimated that the last Irish was written in Belfast in 1854.[109] While some scholarly activity did continue throughout the country, and even in America, it was concentrated mainly on Dublin where the scholarly societies and the Royal Irish Academy continued their work. It was in the capital that the later societies, the Society for the Preservation of the Irish Language (1876), the first society which sought to 'preserve' the language as a vernacular, and the Gaelic Union (1880), were founded. In so far as they encouraged Irish speakers to retain their language and others to learn it, these societies were the ideological precursors of Conradh na Gaeilge, the Gaelic League, which was to become the most important of the societies in the language and literary revival of the turn of the century.

John Mac Hale (1791–1881), a native speaker of Irish, Catholic archbishop of Tuam (1834–81), and a staunch supporter of both O'Connellite politics and the Irish language, was one of the few significant figures in language activities outside Dublin in the mid-century. He published his pastoral letters in Irish, insisted that religious ceremonies take place in Irish in his diocese, and part of his resistance to the national school system was owing to language considerations. His catechism, which An tAthair Peadar Ó Laoghaire, one of the giants of the Revival movement and author of the first novel published in Irish, *Séadna*, claims inspired him to write in Irish,[110] was the most popular catechism of its time and was still used in places in Connacht until the 1950s. Among his other translations into Irish were *The Iliad* (eight volumes, 1844–71), the *Pentateuch* (1861) and a selection of Moore's *Melodies* (1871). Although Mac Hale was no Irish scholar – indeed some of his translations, and particularly his renderings of Moore's *Melodies*, are most infelicitous – he is rightly seen as a bridge between the earlier patrons (both priests and bishops) from before the famine and the generation of language activists and scholars that was to emerge in the Revival era from the late 1870s onwards.

Similarly, most of the poets referred to thus far flourished in the first half of the nineteenth century, and indeed many of them were coming to their maturity as the century dawned. In the mid-century, the personal, cultural, social and political trauma of the Great Famine saw a great acceleration in the process of language decay, with its associated cultural loss. Nonetheless, the famine was commented upon countrywide both by scribes and scholars in the manuscripts and by the poets in poem and song, and there is both a national and a local dimension to the discourse. Most of the songs and poems show a fierce anger and an almost apocalyptic despair while at the same time accepting that it is God's will that the potato failed and that the people were dying as a result. There is also a strong sense of outrage at the civil authorities, and at the English government in particular, that allowed such a disaster to happen. Nioclás Ó Cearnaigh, for example, sees himself – in a long poem on the famine – as the spokesperson for his downtrodden community, and reacts in the traditional literary mode of the *file* by making his public statement through the medium of verse. He blames the English government for the situation in no uncertain terms:

> Seán beag Ruiséal pocán gan éifeacht
> Bhí an tan ina cheannfort ós na réigiúin;
> Fear ionaid an Rí i nÁth Cliath níorbh fhearr é
> Clarendon ciapach, cíorloch, scléipeach.

> (Little John Russell, a bloated, ineffectual fellow
> Was at that time commander of the regions;
> The King's deputy in Dublin was no better,
> The tormenting, upsetting braggart, Clarendon.)[111]

Patsaí Ó Callanáin in his poem 'Na Fataí Bána' denigrates the upper classes who continued to live well during the famine, in utter contrast to the lot of the poor starving masses:

Tá daoine uaisle i mbuaic an tsaoil seo,
Tá puins is fíon acu dá n-ól ar chlár,
Tá feoil dá halpadh acu go méirleach craosach,
Gan trua ná daonnacht do fhear an chaill.

(There are nobility at the top of this life, they are drinking punch and wine at table, they are greedily devouring meat like thieves, without pity or humanity for those who have lost everything.)[112]

The debilitating impact of the famine on personal relationships and on the human spirit is evident in many songs, and in particular in the following interesting verse from the song 'Amhrán an Ghorta' collected in west Kerry, and mentioned by Ó Gráda in his study of famine memory in Irish folklore:

Tá scamall éigin os cionn na hÉireann
Nár fhan dúil i gcéilíocht ag fear ná ag mnaoi;
Ní aithníonn éinne des na daoine a chéile,
Is tá an suan céanna ar gach uile ní.
Ní miste spéirbhean bheith amuigh go déanach,
Níor fhan aon tréine ins na fir a bhí,
Níl ceol in aon áit ná suim ina dhéanamh,
Is ní aithním glao cheart ag bean chun bídh.

(There is a cloud of some sort over Ireland, neither man nor woman has any desire for companionship, none of the people recognise one another, and the same slumber is upon all things. No matter if a beautiful woman is out late, there is no virility left in the men as once there was, there is no music anywhere nor interest in making it, and I do not hear the proper call to table from a woman.)[113]

It is evident, therefore, that the poetic voice, although under severe pressure, was not silenced during the famine, and much research remains to be done in this area. Most of the poetry of this period can be classified as oral poetry, *filíocht bhéil*, which continued to be composed in the Irish-speaking areas – an art form, it is worth noting, that still survives to this day in the Gaeltacht. Seosamh Mac Grianna has called the Ulster poets of this period 'Filí gan Iomrá' (poets of little renown). Their poems speak in the main of local rather than national happenings and Tomás Ó Fiaich has called them 'songs of the open air, of the countryside and especially of the sea, without the smell of the scholar's midnight oil'.[114]

The same can be said for the poetry of the Connemara poet Colm de Bhailís, born in 1796, who died at the great age of 109 years and 10 months in the poorhouse at Oughterard, County Galway. De Bhailís, who once saw

Raiftearaí on a street in Galway City, and thought him rough and uncouth, was himself no doubt to the outsider an unlettered, bedraggled peasant, who could not sign his own son's death certificate on the latter's death of consumption at the age of twenty years in 1877, and therefore had to merely make his mark on the document. As heir to Raiftearaí and the other poets before him, de Bhailís speaks with the authority of the traditional Gaelic poet in his songs and constantly reminds his listeners that his voice must be listened to when he talks of matters that merit a poem. He recounts in his songs the everyday happenings of the local community and interprets that life through the critical eye of the hereditary poet. He praises or chastises the people of the area as appropriate, reminds them of their social, cultural and religious duties, and entertains them in some amusing songs, all recounted in the well-wrought verses that his community had a right to expect from him. De Bhailís's poetry lacks the national consciousness, and indeed the technical and linguistic verve, of Raiftearaí, but at the same time the best of his songs, like 'Amhrán an Tae' and 'Cúirt an tSrutháin Bhuí', are worthwhile artistic statements which articulate the inner world, the perceived reality of his community to such an extent that, as with some of the songs of Raiftearaí, they are still sung in the Connemara Gaeltacht today.[115]

Seán Ó Duinnshléibhe (1812–89), the Blasket poet mentioned by Tomás Ó Criomhthain in his groundbreaking Gaeltacht autobiography *An tOileánach*, is another example of the Gaeltacht poet who fulfilled the traditional function as spokesman to and for his own community. His song 'Beauty Deas an Oileáin', concerning a *naomhóg* or rowing boat from the island that won a famous race in nearby Ventry sometime during the 1880s, is still sung in the Kerry Gaeltacht. Like many of his peers, he lived a very precarious existence and his poems tell of the everyday life of the island with great good humour. He also reflects the prevailing political ideology of his community in a manner reminiscent of the earlier poets of the nineteenth century. In a poem about a cow stolen from the local police, whom he calls 'Orangemen from the end of Ireland', he opens with a strong statement on the politics of the day, drawing on many of the literary devices and traditional messages already seen in the earlier poetry:

> Is fada fé scamall dúinn ceangailte síos,
> Fé mar bhí Maois age Phaoró,
> Is gan againn dá lorg ach toradh na dlí,
> A bhí scríbhte i leabhar an tSáirséalaigh;
> Tá súil ag Mac Muire 'gainn go dtiocfaidh sé i gcrích,

Landlordí s'lacha bheith ag imeacht gan chíos,
O'Brien is é i dteideal ag riarú na dlí,
Is beidh Parnell mar rí 'gainn in Éirinn.

(We are a long time in bondage under a cloud, as was Moses under Pharaoh,
and all we have as a result is the fruit of the law, which was written in Sarsfield's
book; we hope to God that the day will come, when the dirty landlords will
go without rent, O'Brien will be in charge and will regulate the law, and we
will have Parnell as king of Ireland.)[116]

Bob Weldon (1835–1914) from Waterford is another Gaeltacht poet from
the late nineteenth century who lived to see his poetry, like that of de Bhailís
and Ó Duinnshléibhe, appreciated and, moreover, published by the Revival
generation. Most of Weldon's surviving poems were composed in his later
years under the influence of Gaelic Leaguers. His oldest surviving poem is,
however, from 1856, a time when he says himself that he 'composed poems as
a pastime for the local people, as enjoyable incidents happened . . . keeping
the language alive among the people'.[117] His poems are, nonetheless, fairly
typical of the oral poetry of his day – praise poems, love poems, elegies and
other occasional poetry, with a strong local dimension and a winning sense of
humour. Another interesting poet from the same region as Weldon is Pádraig
Ó Miléadha (1877–1947), most of whose work, although written and published
in the twentieth century, was imbedded firmly in form and content in the
earlier period. Ó Miléadha, a native speaker of Irish and literate in English
from his national school education, learned to read and write Irish by reading
John O'Daly's The Poets and Poetry of Munster, which contains many poems Ó
Miléadha would have known from the oral tradition. His collection of poems
and songs, Duanta Aneas (1934), is very reminiscent in tone, outlook and indeed
revivalist attitude to the type of poems composed by Weldon, and includes
some songs still sung in the region and known nationally, for example 'Sliabh
Geal gCua na Féile' and 'Na Tincéirí'. His long poem Trí Glúine Gaedheal is
a nativist version of nineteenth-century history in well-wrought verse which
has its roots in the long narrative political poems in Irish from the seventeenth
century down to Raiftearaí's 'Seanchas na Sceiche'.

Poets such as de Bhailís, Ó Duinnshléibhe, Weldon, Ó Miléadha and the
many other oral poets who continued with the native craft, an cheird dúchais,
in the latter part of the nineteenth century are part of the unbroken tradition
of filíocht which continues in the Gaeltacht to this day, and they were also
the inspiration for the first generation of poets in the Revival period who

introduced the notion of modern poetry, *nuafhilíocht*, to the Irish literary tradition. The fact that the poetic tradition continued in the Gaeltacht through the late nineteenth century, even if radically altered in comparison with the learned poetry of previous generations, means that the poetic chain was never quite broken, and this sense of literary and historical continuity was to be a fundamental aspect of the literary output of the revivalist generation of writers in Irish. For, as Ó Fiaich has noted, in the year that Art Mac Bionaid died, Patrick Pearse was born.

Leerssen argues throughout *Hidden Ireland, Public Sphere* that 'historical memory' is contained in (printed) books and that the 'information or literary art' of the manuscripts was 'practically cut off from the public sphere' in nineteenth-century Ireland. Noting the growth of the practice of anthologising Irish literature into English, the rise of the 'national tale', the popularity of Moore's *Melodies*, and the collecting and editing of manuscripts as a 'retrieval of the Gaelic past', he also argues that nineteenth-century literary activity in Irish was 'translated (that is to say re-contextualized) . . . from its original, now dwindling frame of reference' into a wider currency, that of print culture in English, which he calls a 'public sphere'.[118] He also points out the lack of public markers of nationalist 'lieux de mémoire' within the native tradition, and claims that by this time '*native Ireland had no public space*'.[119] There is no question but that the architecture of identity referred to by Leerssen within the Irish tradition is primarily textual or verbal. Thus the *filíocht* and other literary activity in Irish during the nineteenth century, when viewed from within the tradition and in its own terms, is far more than the 'inchoate, informal and diffuse lore' or the mere 'oral channels of ballad and *seanchas*' referred to by Leerssen.[120] It is the public voice of the historical memory, be that oral or written, even in a manuscript tradition, that was listened to in the Irish-speaking community. Thus a poet like Raiftearaí could commence a lament such as 'Eanach Dhúin' by stating:

> Má fhaighimse sláinte beidh caint is tráchtadh
> ar an méid a báthadh as Eanach Dhúin.

(If I remain healthy the community will continue to speak, of those drowned at Annaghdown.)[121]

Raiftearaí remained healthy, composed the poem, and the poetic boast rang true. The tragic drowning in the river Corrib on 4 September 1828 happened in a remote area to an insignificant group of Irish speakers bound for the fair in Galway City. Many greater tragedies occurred in the intervening period and were forgotten with the passage of time. The drowning at Eanach Dhúin, however, lives on in the memory because a blind, old, unlettered poet composed a poem which, by being aesthetically pleasing according to the literary conventions of the inherited tradition, entered into the canon of that tradition.

Raiftearaí and his fellow poets, and the scribes and scholars who continued the native tradition of learning in the nineteenth century, were men of their time, who engaged with the world around them according to the exigencies and understandings of their native craft and in the manner expected of them by the community to whom and for whom they spoke. They lived in a rapidly changing society, and were often at pains to understand some of the changes that were taking place, but nonetheless their work is an expression from within their own world of the *mentalité* of the Irish-speaking Ireland of their day. The corpus of their work is Gaelic Ireland verbally representing itself in accordance with tradition and thus engaging with the present, the past and indeed the future in a discourse which can be traced back directly to the seventeenth century and beyond. It is not so much the search for an identity as the reiteration of an already existing sense of identity, in both a cultural and a political sense, the nation, or as Hobsbawn might express it, the 'proto-nation' in the period before the growth of nationalism, continuing to write rather than writing back. The Gaelic poets proclaimed through their art a message of hope and redemption for the underclass, the downtrodden, the 'little people' of Ireland, and they promised heaven on earth to those who listened. And it should be noted that their people did listen. Without any doubt, more people in nineteenth-century Ireland listened to Raiftearaí and the poets, and recited their poems from memory, than read the novels of Maria Edgeworth or the politico-philosophical treatises of Edmund Burke. Thus the native learning, and in particular the poetry, is the native 'public space' and 'tribal memory' in nineteenth-century Ireland, which the poets found, as Raiftearaí puts it, 'scríofa i leabhar na daonnachta' (written in the book of humanity).[122]

Notes

1. Thomas Kinsella, *The Irish Writer* (New York: PMLA, 1966), pp. 58–9.
2. Joep Leerssen, *Remembrance and Imagination: Patterns in the Historical and Literary Representation of Ireland in the Nineteenth Century* (Cork: Cork University Press, 1996), p. 1.
3. Seamus Deane, *A Short History of Irish Literature* (London: Hutchinson, 1986), p. 28.
4. Seamus Deane, 'Irish National Character 1790–1900', in Tom Dunne, ed. *The Writer as Witness*, Historical Studies XVI (Cork: Cork University Press, 1987), p. 91.
5. Norman Vance, *Irish Literature since 1800* (London: Longman, 2002), p. 19.
6. Joep Leerssen, *Hidden Ireland, Public Sphere*, Research Papers in Irish Studies (Galway: Arlen House, 2002), p. 13.

7. Ibid., p. 34.

8. Ibid., p. 16.

9. R. A. Breatnach, 'The End of a Tradition: A Survey of Eighteenth-Century Irish Literature', *Studia Hibernica* 1 (1961), pp. 128–50.

10. Breandán Ó Buachalla, *Aisling Ghéar: Na Stíobhartaigh agus an tAos Léinn* (Dublin: An Clóchomhar, 1984); 'Annála Ríoghachta Éireann is Foras Feasa ar Éirinn: An Comhthéacs Comhaimseartha', *Studia Hibernica* 22/23 (1985), pp. 59–105; 'Na Stíobhartaigh agus an tAos Léinn: Cing Séamus', *Proceedings of the Royal Irish Academy*, 83, c (1983), pp. 81–134; 'Cúlra is Tábhacht an Dáin *A leabhráin ainmnighthear d'Aodh*', *Celtica* 21 (1990), pp. 402–16; 'Poetry and Politics in Early Modern Ireland', *Eighteenth Century Ireland* 7 (1992), pp. 149–75; 'James Our True King: The Ideology of Irish Royalism in the Seventeenth Century', in D. G. Boyce, ed. *Political Thought in Ireland since the Seventeenth Century* (London: Routledge, 1993), pp. 1–30.

11. Joep Leerssen, *Mere Irish and Fíor-Ghael: Studies in the Idea of Irish Nationality, its Development and Literary Expression prior to the Nineteenth Century* (1986; Cork: Cork University Press, 1996).

12. Mícheál Mac Craith, *Lorg na hIasachta ar na Dánta Grádha* (Dublin: An Clóchomhar, 1989); 'Gaelic Ireland and the Renaissance', in G. Williams and R. O. Jones, eds., *The Celts and the Renaissance: Tradition and Innovation* (Cardiff: University of Wales Press, 1990), pp. 57–89; 'The Gaelic Reaction to the Reformation', in S. G. Ellis and S. Barber, eds. *Conquest and Union: Fashioning a British State, 1485–1725* (London: Longman, 1995), pp. 139–61; 'Litríocht an 17ú haois: Tonnbhriseadh an tSeanghnáthaimh nó Tonnchruthú an Nuaghnáthaimh?', *Léachtaí Cholm Cille* XXVI (Maynooth: An Sagart, 1996), pp. 50–82.

13. John Hutchinson, *The Dynamics of Cultural Nationalism: The Gaelic Revival and the Creation of the Irish Nation-State* (London: Allen and Unwin, 1987).

14. Philip O'Leary, *The Prose Literature of the Gaelic Revival 1881–1921: Ideology and Innovation* (University Park: Pennsylvania State University Press, 1994).

15. Niall Ó Ciosáin, 'Gaelic Culture and Language Shift', in L. Geary and M. Kelleher, eds. *Nineteenth-Century Ireland: A Guide to Recent Research* (Dublin: University College Dublin Press, 2005), pp. 136–52.

16. Seamus Deane, general ed. *The Field Day Anthology of Irish Writing*, 3 vols. (Derry: Field Day Publications, 1991), II, pp. 1–97.

17. Máirtín Ó Cadhain, 'Béaloideas', *Feasta* (March 1950), pp. 9–12, 19–25.

18. See Benedict Anderson, *Imagined Communities: Reflections on the Origins and Spread of Nationalism* (London: Verso, 1983). Lillis Ó Laoire discusses this idea of self-definition from within Tory Island in his *Ar Chreag i Lár na Farraige* (Inverin: Cló Iar-Chonnachta, 2002), p. 189.

19. Niall Ó Ciosáin, *Print and Popular Culture in Ireland, 1750–1850* (London: Macmillan, 1997), p. 7.

20. Ó Ciosáin, 'Gaelic Culture and Language Shift'.

21. Ó Ciosáin, *Print and Popular Culture*, p. 6.

22. See Diarmaid Ó Muirithe, *An tAmhrán Macarónach* (Dublin: An Clóchomhar, 1980).

23. Breandán Ó Buachalla, *I mBéal Feirste Cois Cuain* (Dublin: An Clóchomhar, 1968), p. 61.

24. Máirín Nic Eoin, 'Irish Language and Literature in County Kilkenny in the Nineteenth Century', in William Nolan and Kevin Whelan, eds. *Kilkenny, History and Society: Interdisciplinary Essays on the History of an Irish County* (Dublin: Geography Publications, 1990), pp. 465–79, p. 467.

25. *Report of the Commissioners for National Education* (1855), p. 75.

26. Ó Ciosáin, *Print and Popular Culture*, p. 167.

27. Tomás Ó Fiaich, 'The Ulster Poetic Tradition in the Nineteenth Century', *Léachtaí Cholm Cille III* (Maynooth: An Sagart, 1972), p. 30.

28. Breandán Ó Conchúir, *Scríobhaithe Chorcaí 1700–1850* (Dublin: An Clóchomhar, 1982), p. 12.

29. See Gearóid Denvir, 'Decolonising the Mind: Language and Literature in Ireland', *New Hibernia Review*, I, I (1997), pp. 44–68.

30. S. Kirkpatrick, 'Spanish Romanticism', in Roy Porter and Mikulas Teich, eds. *Romanticism in National Context* (Cambridge: Cambridge University Press, 1988), p. 269.

31. Nic Eoin, 'Irish Language and Literature', p. 465.

32. Ó Ciosáin, 'Gaelic Culture and Language Shift', p. 136.

33. Gearóid Ó Tuathaigh, 'An Chléir Chaitliceach, an Léann Dúchais agus an Cultúr in Éirinn, *c.*1750–*c.*1850', *Léachtaí Cholm Cille XVI* (Maynooth: An Sagart, 1986), pp. 110–39, p. 110.

34. Hutchinson, *The Dynamics of Cultural Nationalism*.

35. Meidhbhín Ní Úrdail, *The Scribe in Eighteenth- and Nineteenth-century Ireland* (Münster: Nodus, 2000), p. 203.

36. Eugene O'Curry, *Catalogue of Irish Manuscripts of the Royal Irish Academy*, Part 10 (1843), p. 42.

37. Ó Buachalla, *I mBéal Feirste*, p. 267.

38. Roger Blaney, *Presbyterians and the Irish Language* (Belfast: Ulster Historical Foundation, 1996), p. 127.

39. Ó Buachalla, *I mBéal Feirste*, p. 103.

40. Ó Conchúir, *Scríobhaithe Chorcaí*.

41. Ní Úrdail, *The Scribe in Ireland*.

42. Breandán Ó Madagáin, *An Ghaeilge i Luimneach 1700–1900* (Dublin: An Clóchomhar, 1974); *Teagasc ar an Sean-Tiomna* (Dublin: An Clóchomhar, 1974).

43. Cornelius Buttimer, 'Gaelic Literature and Contemporary Life in Cork, 1700–1840', in Patrick O'Flanagan, Cornelius Buttimer and Gerald O'Brien, eds. *Cork, History and Society: Interdisciplinary Essays on the History of an Irish County* (Dublin: Geography Publications, 1993), pp. 585–653. See also Sean Beecher, *An Ghaeilge in Cork City: An Historical Perspective to 1894* (Cork: Angel Press, 1993).

44. Hutchinson, *The Dynamics of Cultural Nationalism*, p. 96.

45. Robert Welch, ed. *The Oxford Companion to Irish Literature* (Oxford: Clarendon Press, 1996), p. 417.

46. Ó Buachalla, *I mBéal Feirste*, p. 239

47. John O'Donovan, 'On the Traditions of the County of Kilkenny', *Journal of the Royal Society of Antiquarians in Ireland* I (1949–51), p. 369.

48. Ó Conchúir, *Scríobhaithe Chorcaí*, p. 225.

49. Éamonn Ó hÓgáin, 'Scríobhaithe Lámhscríbhinní Gaeilge i gCill Chainnigh 1700–1870', in Nolan and Whelan, eds. *Kilkenny: History and Society*, pp. 405–36.

50. Ibid., 424.

51. Eoghan Ó Néill, *Gleann an Óir: Ar Thóir na Staire agus na Litríochta in Oirthear Mumhan agus i nDeisceart Laighean* (Dublin: An Clóchomhar, 1988), p. 9.

52. Ó Conchúir, *Scríobhaithe Chorcaí*, p. 69–77.

53. Máire Ní Mhurchú and Diarmuid Breathnach, eds. *1782–1881 Beathaisnéis* (Dublin: An Clóchomhar, 1999), p. 105.

54. Ní Úrdail, *The Scribe in Ireland*, p. 49.

55. Ibid., p. 118.

56. Ibid., p. 209.

57. Buttimer, 'Gaelic Literature', p. 628.

58. Pádraig Ó Fiannachta, 'Litríocht an Lae 1800–1850', in *Léachtaí Cholm Chille III* (Maynooth: An Sagart, 1972), pp. 5–8.

59. Ní Úrdail, *The Scribe in Ireland*, p. 180.

60. Seán Ó Dufaigh and Diarmaid Ó Doibhlin, eds. *Nioclás Ó Cearnaigh: Beatha agus Saothar* (Dublin: An Clóchomhar, 1989), pp. 21–3, 30–3.

61. Michael McGrath, ed. *Cinnlae Amhlaoibh Uí Shúileabháin*, 4 vols. Irish Texts Society, XXX–XXXIII (London: Irish Texts Society, 1936–7), I, p. 198.

62. Ní Úrdail, *The Scribe in Ireland*, p. 98.

63. Ó Ciosáin, *Print and Popular Culture*, pp. 157, 168–9.

64. Brian Ó Cuív, 'Irish Language and Literature 1691–1845', in W. E. Vaughan, ed. *A New History of Ireland vol. V: Ireland Under the Union*, I (Oxford: Clarendon Press, 1989), pp. 374–473, p. 381.

65. For example, Paul O'Brien, *A Practical Grammar of the Irish Language* (Dublin, 1809), Owen Connellan, *A Dissertation on Irish Grammar* (Dublin, 1834), and John O'Donovan, *Grammar of the Irish Language* (Dublin, 1845).

66. Cathal Ó Háinle, 'The Novel Frustrated', in Cathal Ó Háinle and Donald E. Meek, eds. *Unity in Diversity: Studies in Irish and Scottish Gaelic Language, Literature and History* (Dublin: School of Irish, Trinity College, 2004), pp. 125–51.

67. Buttimer, 'Gaelic Literature'.

68. Réamonn Ó Muirí, *Lámhscríbhinn Stairiúil an Bhionadaigh* (Monaghan: Éigse Oirialla, 1994), p. 83.

69. Aodán Mac Póilín, 'The Irish Language in Belfast until 1900', in Nicholas Allen and Aaron Kelly, eds. *The Cities of Belfast* (Dublin: Four Courts Press, 2003), p. 56.

70. Piaras Béaslaí, *Éigse Nua-Ghaedhilge*, 2 vols. (Dublin: Oifig an tSoláthair, 1934), p. 225.

71. Máirín Ní Mhuiríosa and Caerwyn Williams, *Traidisiún Liteartha na nGael* (Dublin: An Clóchomhar, 1979), p. 305.

72. A. J. Hughes, 'Gaelic Poets and Scribes of the South Armagh Hinterland in the Eighteenth and Nineteenth Centuries', in A. J. Hughes and William Nolan, eds. *Armagh, History and Society: Interdisciplinary Essays on the History of an Irish County* (Dublin: Geography Publications, 2001), pp. 509–56, p. 509.

73. Ó Háinle, 'The Novel Frustrated', p. 127.

74. Ruth Finnegan, *Literacy and Orality: Studies in the Technology of Communication* (Oxford: Basil Blackwell, 1988).

75. Ó Dufaigh and Ó Doibhlin, *Nioclás Ó Cearnaigh*, pp. 41–2.

76. Ní Úrdail, *The Scribe in Ireland*, p. 94–5. Ní Úrdail claims that this emphasis on the political nature of the work comes from the ideological agenda of early twentieth-century editors who sympathised with Ó Longáin's catholicity, his republicanism and his 'revivalist' language attitude.

77. Hughes, 'Gaelic Poets and Scribes', p. 547.

78. Ó Fiaich 'The Ulster Poetic Tradition', p. 31.

79. Ibid., p. 29.

80. 'Ógfhir Thír Eoghain', in Ó Dufaigh and Ó Doibhlin, *Nioclás Ó Cearnaigh*, p. 99.

81. Ciarán Dawson, *Peadar Ó Gealacáin, Scríobhaí* (Dublin: An Clóchomhar, 1992), p. 12.

82. Ó Fiaich 'The Ulster Poetic Tradition', p. 32.

83. 'Cat Phara Héat' (Para Héat's Cat), in Dawson, *Peadar Ó Gealacáin*, pp. 33–5.

84. 'Eachtra Philib Uí Shiridean' (The Adventure of Philip Sheridan), ibid., p. 38.

85. Colm Beckett, *Aodh Mac Domhnaill: Dánta* (Dublin: An Clóchomhar, 1987), p. 44.

86. Ibid, p. 151.

87. William Mahon, 'Scríobhaithe Lámhscríbhinní Gaeilge i nGaillimh 1700–1900', in Gerard Moran and Raymond Gillespie, eds. *Galway, History and Society: Interdisciplinary Essays on the History of an Irish County* (Dublin: Geography Publications, 1996), pp. 623–50, p. 630.

88. Ciarán Ó Coigligh, ed. *Raiftearaí: Amhráin agus Dánta* (Dublin: An Clóchomhar, 1967), p. 108.

89. Seán Ó Ceallaigh, *Filíocht na gCallanán* (Dublin: An Clóchomhar, 1967), pp. 77–84.

90. Ibid., p. 70.

91. Tom Dunne, '"Tá Gaedhil bhocht cráidhte": Memory, Tradition and the Politics of the Poor in Gaelic Poetry and Song', in Laurence M. Geary, ed. *Rebellion and Remembrance in Modern Ireland* (Dublin: Four Courts Press, 2001), pp. 93–111, 94.

92. Ó Coigligh, *Raiftearaí*, p. 148.

93. Dawson, *Peadar Ó Gealacáin*, p. 110.

94. Máire Ní Shúilleabháin, ed. *Amhráin Thomáis Rua Uí Shúilleabháin* (Maynooth: An Sagart, 1985), p. 36.

95. Risteard Ó Foghludha, ed. *Pádraig Phiarais Cúndún* (Dublin: Oifig Díolta Foillseacháin Rialtais, 1932), p. 106.

96. Ó Coigligh, *Raiftearaí*, p. 99.

97. Ibid., p. 104.

98. Dunne, '"Tá Gaedhil bhocht cráidhte"', p. 104.

99. Beckett, *Aodh Mac Domhnaill*, p. 32.

100. Ní Shúilleabháin, *Amhráin Thomáis Rua*, p. 57.

101. Marion Gunn, *A Chomharsain Éistigí* (Dublin: An Clóchomhar, 1984), p. 91.

102. Ó Buachalla, *Aisling Ghéar*. Mícheál Óg Ó Longáin, a United Irishman activist, is an interesting exception to this.

103. Pádraig Ó Fiannachta, *An Barántas* (Maynooth: An Sagart, 1978), p. 142.

104. S. J. Connolly, *Priests and People in Pre-Famine Ireland* (Dublin: Four Courts Press, 1982, 2001).

105. Ó Ciosáin, *Print and Popular Culture*, p. 131.

106. Ó Coigligh, *Raiftearaí*, p. 104.

107. Ibid., pp. 84–5.
108. Ní Shúilleabháin, *Amhráin Thomáis Rua*, p. 13.
109. Ó Buachalla, *I mBéal Feirste*, p. 272.
110. Peadar Ua Laoghaire, *Mo Sgéal Féin* (Dublin: Brún agus Ó Nualláin, 1915), pp. 104–5.
111. Cornelius Buttimer, 'A Stone on the Cairn: The Great Famine in Later Gaelic Manuscripts', in Chris Morash and Richard Hayes, eds. *New Perspectives on the Famine* (Dublin: Irish Academic Press, 1996), pp. 93–109, pp. 106–7.
112. Ó Ceallaigh, *Filíocht na gCallanán*, p. 68.
113. Cormac Ó Gráda, *An Drochshaol: Béaloideas agus Amhráin* (Dublin: Coiscéim, 1994), p. 73.
114. Ó Fiaich, 'The Ulster Poetic Tradition', p. 35.
115. See Gearóid Denvir, ed. *Amhráin Choilm de Bhailís* (Inverin: Cló Iar-Chonnachta, 1996).
116. Seán Ó Dubhda, ed. *Duanaire Duibhneach* (Dublin: Oifig Díolta Foillseacháin Rialtais, 1933), p. 62.
117. Pádraig Ó Macháin, ed. *Riobard Bheldon: Amhráin agus Dánta* (Dublin, The Poddle Press, 1995), p. 95.
118. Leerssen, *Hidden Ireland, Public Sphere*, p. 25, 27.
119. Ibid., p. 28–31, italics in original.
120. Ibid., p. 29–30.
121. Ó Coigligh, *Raiftearaí*, p. 134.
122. Ibid., p. 84.

Select bibliography

Beckett, Colm, *Aodh Mac Domhnaill: Dánta*, Dublin: An Clóchomhar, 1987.

Blaney, Roger, *Presbyterians and the Irish Language*, Belfast: Ulster Historical Foundation, 1996.

Buttimer, Cornelius, 'Gaelic Literature and Contemporary Life in Cork, 1700–1840', in Patrick O'Flanagan, Cornelius Buttimer and Gerald O'Brien, eds. *Cork, History and Society: Interdisciplinary Essays on the History of an Irish County*, Dublin: Geography Publications, 1993, pp. 585–653.

'A Stone on the Cairn: The Great Famine in Later Gaelic Manuscripts', in Chris Morash and Richard Hayes, eds. *New Perspectives on the Famine*, Dublin: Irish Academic Press, 1996, pp. 93–109.

Dawson, Ciarán, *Peadar Ó Gealacáin, Scríobhaí*, Dublin: An Clóchomhar, 1992.

Denvir, Gearóid, ed. *Amhráin Choilm de Bhailís*, Inverin: Cló Iar-Chonnachta, 1996.

'Decolonising the Mind: Language and Literature in Ireland', *New Hibernia Review*, I, I (1997), pp. 44–68.

Doherty, Gillian M., *The Irish Ordnance Survey: History, Culture and Memory*, Dublin: Four Courts Press, 2004.

Dunne, Tom, '"Tá Gaedhil bhocht cráidhte"': Memory, Tradition and the Politics of the Poor in Gaelic Poetry and Song', in Laurence M. Geary, ed. *Rebellion and Remembrance in Modern Ireland*, Dublin: Four Courts Press, 2001, pp. 93–111.

Hughes, A. J., 'Gaelic Poets and Scribes of the South Armagh Hinterland in the Eighteenth and Nineteenth Century', in A. J. Hughes and William Nolan, eds. *Armagh, History* and Society: Interdisciplinary Essays on the History of an Irish County, Dublin: Geography Publications, 2001, pp. 505–56.

Hutchinson, John, The Dynamics of Cultural Nationalism: The Gaelic Revival and the Creation of the Irish Nation-State, London: Allen and Unwin, 1987.

Leerssen, Joep, Hidden Ireland, Public Sphere, Galway: Arlen House, 2002.

Remembrance and Imagination: Patterns in the Historical and Literary Representation of Ireland in the Nineteenth Century, Cork: Cork University Press, 1996.

Mac Lochlainn, Antain, 'The Famine in Gaelic Tradition', Irish Review 17/18 (1995), pp. 90–108.

Mac Póilín, Aodán, 'The Irish Language in Belfast until 1900', in Nicholas Allen and Aaron Kelly, eds. The Cities of Belfast, Dublin: Four Courts Press, 2003, pp. 41–61.

Mahon, William, 'Scríobhaithe Lámhscríbhinní Gaeilge i nGaillimh 1700–1900', in Gerard Moran and Raymond Gillespie, eds. Galway, History and Society: Interdisciplinary Essays on the History of an Irish County, Dublin: Geography Publications, 1996, pp. 623–50.

Nic Eoin, Máirín, 'Irish Language and Literature in County Kilkenny in the Nineteenth Century', in William Nolan and Kevin Whelan, eds. Kilkenny: History and Society: Interdisciplinary Essays on the History of an Irish County, Dublin: Geography Publications, 1990, pp. 465–79.

Ní Mhurchú, Máire and Diarmuid Breathnach, eds. 1782–1881 Beathaisnéis, Dublin: An Clóchomhar, 1999.

Ní Úrdail, Meidhbhín, The Scribe in Eighteenth- and Nineteenth-Century Ireland, Münster: Nodus, 2000.

Ó Buachalla, Breandán, I mBéal Feirste Cois Cuain, Dublin: An Clóchomhar, 1968.

Ó Ciosáin, Niall, 'Gaelic Culture and Language Shift', in L. Geary and M. Kelleher, eds. Nineteenth-Century Ireland: A Guide to Recent Research, Dublin: UCD Press, 2005, pp. 136–52.

Print and Popular Culture in Ireland, 1750–1850, London: Macmillan Press, 1997.

Ó Conchúir, Breandán, Scríobhaithe Chorcaí 1700–1850, Dublin: An Clóchomhar, 1982.

Ó Cuív, Brian, 'Irish Language and Literature 1691–1845', in W. E. Vaughan, ed. A New History of Ireland, vol. V: Ireland under the Union, I, Oxford, Oxford University Press, 1989, pp. 374–473.

'Irish Language and Literature 1845–1921', in W. E. Vaughan, ed., A New History of Ireland, vol. VI: Ireland under the Union, II, 1870–1921, ed. Oxford, Oxford University Press, 1986, pp. 385–435.

Ó Drisceoil, Proinsias, Ar Scaradh Gabhail: An Fhéiniúlacht in 'Cín Lae Amhlaoibh Uí Shúilleabháin', Dublin: An Clóchomhar, 2000.

Ó Dufaigh, Seán and Diarmaid Ó Doibhlin, eds. Nioclás Ó Cearnaigh: Beatha agus Saothar, Dublin: An Clóchomhar, 1989.

Ó Fiaich Tomás, 'The Ulster Poetic Tradition in the Nineteenth Century', in Léachtaí Cholm Cille III, Maynooth: An Sagart, 1972, pp. 20–37.

Ó Fiannachta, Pádraig, ed. Léachtaí Cholm Cille III: Litríocht an 19ú hAois Maynooth: An Sagart, 1972.

Ó Gráda, Cormac, An Drochshaol: Béaloideas agus Amhráin, Dublin: Coiscéim, 1994.

Ó Háinle, Cathal, 'The Novel Frustrated', in Cathal Ó Háinle and Donald E. Meek, eds. Unity in Diversity: Studies in Irish and Scottish Gaelic Language, Literature and History, Dublin: School of Irish, Trinity College, 2004, pp. 125–51.

Ó hÓgáin, Éamonn, 'Scríobhaithe Láimhscríbhinní Gaeilge i gCill Chainnigh 1700–1870', in William Nolan and Kevin Whelan, eds. *Kilkenny, History and Society: Interdisciplinary Essays on the History of an Irish County*, Dublin: Geography Publications, 1990, pp. 405–36.

Ó Muirí, Réamonn, *Láimhscríbhinn Stairiúil an Bhionadaigh*, Monaghan: Éigse Oirialla, 1994.

Ó Néill, Eoghan, *Gleann an Óir: Ar Thóir na Staire agus na Litríochta in Oirthear Mumhan agus i nDeisceart Laighean*, Dublin: An Clóchomhar, 1988.

Ó Snodaigh, Pádraig, *The Hidden Ulster: Protestants and the Irish Language*, Belfast: Lagan Press, 1995.

Ó Tuathaigh, Gearóid, 'An Chléir Chaitliceach, an Léann Dúchais agus an Cultúr in Éirinn, c.1750–c.1850', in *Léachtaí Cholm Cille XVI*, Maynooth: An Sagart, 1986, pp. 110–39.

14

Historical writings, 1690–1890

CLARE O'HALLORAN

There is general agreement among historians that 1690 marked a watershed in Irish history in general, but no such decisive break can be seen in historical writing. Many of the same themes and debates continued, notably over the nature of pre-colonial Gaelic society.[1] These were sharpened by the incorporation of the wars and rebellions of the late sixteenth and seventeenth centuries into the available narrative, as evidence in support of the English colonial diagnosis of Edmund Spenser and Sir John Davies that the conquest had been imperfectly carried out and that consequently the native Irish remained fundamentally untouched by the civilising process.[2] Oliver MacDonagh's argument that early nineteenth-century historical writing lacked a 'developmental or sequential view of past events', and thus treated the past ahistorically as 'an arsenal of weapons' with which to fight contemporary political battles, can equally be applied to previous centuries. This also produced a habit of interpreting historical events and actions as if they were contemporary: 'In such a view, no statute of limitations softens the judgement to be made upon past events, however distant [and] no prescriptive rights can be established by the passage of time, however lengthy.'[3] This concept of history as, in some ways, contemporaneous is to be found in almost all the texts discussed below.

Seventeenth-century legacies

The most prominent histories published in the immediate aftermath of the Williamite success came from the victors' camp. They were characterised by a noticeable sense of history as an unfinished, still-unfolding process which incorporated the present in all its uncertainties. The pattern was established, when the outcome of the Williamite wars was still unclear, in *Hibernia Anglicana* (1689–90) by Richard Cox (1650–1733). A judge and landowner in Cork, Cox had left Ireland following the accession of James II because, it was said, of anti-Catholic statements made by him while presiding at the quarter sessions.[4]

Subtitled 'the History of Ireland from the Conquest thereof by the English to the present time', the book was written in the full knowledge that the conquest might well be undone before its publication, unless urgent action was taken by the Williamite forces. He dedicated the work to William and Mary, reminding them that the loss of Ireland would be 'incompatible with your Glory' and urging an intensive 're-conquering' of Ireland for strategic reasons.[5] In the second part, published in 1690, he again addressed William and looked forward to 'a happy Restitution of your poor Protestant Subjects of *Ireland* to their Native Homes'.[6] In the 'Address to the Reader', he made plain his awareness of the contingent nature of the project he had embarked on: 'Where the Windings and Revolutions will end, God Almighty only knows.' While he ended with the hope that in the future he might be able to give 'a *joyful Account* of *all* these *Things*', there is a clear sense that news of a final Jacobite victory would have required a radical reshaping of his narrative.[7]

The fragmentary and fluid nature of this work was characteristic of much Irish historical writing in the following two hundred years. While historians in less troubled times lacked this acute sense of the uncertainty of the end point of their histories, they nonetheless still wrote in the fear, or expectation, of fundamental change to the Williamite political settlement. In the eighteenth century, for example, Catholics and Protestants represented the past, both modern and pre-colonial, in ways which were shaped by the Williamite victory and the subsequent penal legislation against Catholics and Dissenters put in place to ensure an enduring Protestant ascendancy. All felt the need to comment, even indirectly, on contemporary political realities and perspectives. While historical writing did undergo change in this period, notably as a result of the development from the 1820s of more scientific approaches to documentary and material evidence, many of the preoccupations of historians and antiquaries continued to be determined or framed by the turbulent events of the late sixteenth and seventeenth centuries, and by the hostile colonial commentaries by Spenser and Davies on the nature of Gaelic society.

Cox's *Hibernia Anglicana* provides a useful summary of established Protestant thinking, and therefore became emblematic for Catholic writers of the interpretations which they sought to overturn. According to Cox, the native Irish were distinguished by their 'Rudeness, Ignorance and Barbarity', as evidenced in Gaelic custom and law, and had remained in that state until 'the English Conquest', which ushered in a great 'Improvement' to their 'Manners and Conditions', since which time they had lived 'far happier than ever they did under the Tyranny of their own Lords'. While he conceded that scholarship had flourished in the Middle Ages, this was because of the 'many Learned Men fleeing persecution who flocked to Ireland'. When they left, 'Ireland soon returned to its former Ignorance', so that long before the English conquest 'there were hardly any Footsteps of Learning left in that Kingdom'. Thus, the concession of a golden age of 'saints and scholars' was made compatible with his thesis of the indispensable civilising influence of the English. However, these English colonists were themselves soon to 'degenerate', by adopting Gaelic customs, habits and names and intermarrying with the natives, to the extent that the Irish were now 'a mixt people', there being 'hardly a Gentleman among them, but has English Blood in his Veins'. This assertion was further supported by Cox's contention that in remote times 'the World was inhabited by degrees, and from the adjacent Countries', and hence that England, or more widely Britain, had always functioned as the *origines gentium* for Ireland. While other northern peoples, 'Danes, Norwegians, Oastmen', might have settled in small numbers, ''tis certain, that most of the Original Inhabitants of Ireland came out of Britain'. This was reflected in their language, which 'is the most compound Language in the World, (the English only excepted)'. History, seen as a set of recurrent patterns or cycles, therefore ordained the Williamite reconquest of Ireland, for the Irish 'are but the same People our Ancestors have so often triumphed over'. This claim of a long-rooted Irish past for the English in Ireland was buttressed by the argument that the reformed religion of the new settlers remained true to the tenets and practices of the early Irish church. In Cox's *Hibernia Anglicana* this took the form of a chapter-by-chapter summary of Archbishop James Ussher's *Discourse of the Religion anciently professed by the Irish and British* (1622), the first authoritative demonstration of this thesis.[8]

Cox's attempts to root the recent settlers as securely as possible in an Irish past were taken up in the following decade by William Molyneux (1656–98) in his *Case of Ireland being Bound by Acts of Parliament in England, Stated* (1698), which used historical and juridical arguments in support of the legislative independence of the Irish parliament. Amongst these was Molyneux's contention that 'the great Body of the present People of *Ireland*, are the Progeny of the *English* and *Britains*, that from time to time have come over into this Kingdom; and there remains but a meer handful of the Antient *Irish* at this day'.[9] On this basis he claimed for the new settlers the rights to parliamentary sovereignty allegedly granted to the Anglo-Normans by Henry II. The drive to give themselves a rooted and continuous Irish past was, thus, a reflection of unabated Protestant anxiety to secure their position of political dominance. It is, therefore, appropriate that Cox's characterisation of the Irish pre-colonial past as a catalogue of 'the most Unnatural, Bloody, Everlasting, Destructive Fewds [*sic*]'[10] seems little different from the 'innumerable Fewds, Wars and

Rebellions' that make up most of his narrative of the colonial period.[11] This covers the first half of the seventeenth century in some detail, but focuses in particular on the rebellion of 1641 and on the allegations of Catholic atrocities, which had long been a source of contention between Protestant and Catholic writers. Significantly, Cox prefaced the narrative with a long essay 'touching the controverted points in this history', which was both a rebuttal of a number of 'popish' authors' interpretations of the causes and events of the 1641 rebellion, and an exhortation to government to ensure that the rebels, who had 'less cause to rebel in 1641, than at any time before', must 'never be able to Rebel any more'.[12] In Cox's formulation, which mixed past, present and possible future Irish insurgents without conscious distinction, can be seen the successful government strategy of keeping the memory of the 1641 rebellion alive, through annual commemoration on 23 October, the day it broke out.[13] One important lesson of the past for Irish Protestants was eternal vigilance in the face of the Catholic threat.

As an exile, Cox could not report directly on the Protestant experience of the period of Jacobite control in Ireland, following the accession of James II. An eye-witness account by William King (1650–1729), *The State of the Protestants of Ireland under the late King James' Government* (1691), lent support to the thesis of the unchanged nature of Irish Catholic perfidy, by cataloguing numerous incidents of unlawful and threatening behaviour (often described as 'barbarous') by Catholics towards Protestants during the previous four years.[14] Yet King's work had other and more pressing concerns than the illustration of Protestant suffering and Catholic misdeeds, for which it later became known. He also wrote in self-defence against the Tory charge that the removal of James II as monarch was an unlawful usurpation. The king's removal was essential, he alleged, because of his waging a 'War for the advancement of Popery', which, if allowed to succeed, would have left Irish Protestants 'in the Condition of the Vilest of Slaves'.[15] He also defended those Protestants, like himself, who had remained peaceably in Ireland, rather than fleeing when James II landed, against the Whig charge of suspect loyalty to William and the Protestant monarchy. They had done so out of a sense of public service, and he cited as evidence of this the preservation of state records, including 'the very Outlawryes of the Rebels and Murtherers [*sic*] in 1641', in spite of Jacobite orders for their destruction.[16] Thus, the safeguarding of the state records of 1641 functioned as a touchstone of Protestant loyalty, further underlining the centrality of the rebellion for that community's identity. The classic Protestant account of 1641 was Sir John Temple's *Irish Rebellion* (1646), which represented it as an attempt to restore Catholicism, and, using the sworn statements of survivors, catalogued in gory detail the alleged premeditated massacre of 300,000 Protestants.[17] It was reissued regularly over the next 130 years, often at times of Jacobite unrest, and with subtle modifications of sub-title or frontispiece to emphasise its continuing significance.[18]

The Catholic response to such charges was muted for many decades, but in 1746 John Curry (d.1780), a physician in Dublin, published anonymously *A Brief Account from the most authentic Protestant Writers of the Causes, Motives and Mischiefs of the Irish Rebellion*. Using a tactic much favoured by later apologists, Curry eschewed Catholic testimony and used mainly Protestant accounts of 1641 where they either showed Catholic actions in a favourable light, or revealed contradictions and inconsistencies in the accepted Protestant record. He also included a list of massacres 'committed on the Irish', as further evidence of the inaccuracy of traditional accounts. Having procured a London publisher for the book, Curry was intent on appealing to English opinion, over the heads of Irish Protestants, for a fresh approach to the Catholic question based on rational principles rather than age-old prejudices. The book provoked a rejoinder from the Protestant antiquary and historian Walter Harris (1686–1761), who, in *Fiction Unmasked* (1752), accused 'the Popish physician' of virulently defaming 'the Protestant Religion and English interest of this kingdom' and of inciting the Irish to rebellion. Harris claimed he was only drawn into the controversy when he met 'many real and well disposed Protestants' who said that Curry's work had impressed them.[19] Perhaps emboldened by this, Curry's *Historical Memoirs of the Irish Rebellion in the year 1641* (1758) adopted a more forthright approach, defending both the rebels and their leaders by reference to the prior iniquitous conduct of government ministers.[20] Similarly, in his later work, *A Historical and Critical Review of the Civil Wars in Ireland from the Reign of Queen Elizabeth to the Settlement under King William* (1775), he argued that the ill-treatment of settlers in Ulster had been sparked off by atrocities carried out by Scottish troops on the Catholics of Islandmagee in County Antrim.[21] He also tried to discredit the depositions – sworn statements taken from Protestants shortly after the rebellion – upon which the case for Catholic atrocities rested. In the following century the depositions were to become the subject of sharp controversy among historians.

Protestants and the Gaelic past

Explorations of the recent past remained contentious, and, in the eighteenth century at least, even dangerous for the few Catholics brave enough to meddle in it. In these circumstances the remote past seemed a safer location for scholarly research. This is one explanation for the flowering of interest in the pre-colonial period, which was led, in the main, by Irish Protestant writers. It was also part of the pattern identified earlier, of Protestant efforts to create a usable Irish history for themselves. The best example of this is the English translation of Geoffrey Keating's *Foras Feasa ar Éirinn*, which appeared in 1723 as *The General History of Ireland*. Written in the 1630s by a Catholic Counter Reformation priest of Old English (or Anglo-Norman) descent, this narrative history, which ended with the coming of the Anglo-Normans in the twelfth century, had circulated in manuscript for almost one hundred years. The translator, Dermod O'Connor, a controversial and somewhat disreputable figure, put together an expensive folio volume, handsomely bound and containing the pedigrees of the Gaelic noble families, most of whom were subscribers.[22] The conversion to Protestantism of many of these was reflected in the translation, which replaced the original term 'Catholic' with 'Christian' or omitted it altogether.[23] Other changes stemmed partly from the fact that by the 1720s the Old English had long ceased to be a separate and recognisable group in Ireland, so that 'old English nobility' was changed to 'Irish nobility' throughout. While religion was still the bedrock of identity, there was a move to make birth in Ireland a transcending basis for a shared patriotism. Thus, the translator claimed, for those of Irish descent, this work would 'support the Honour of their Ancestors' and for more recent arrivals, it would 'give the World a just Idea of the Dignity of the Country where they were born'.[24] In its first appearance in print, Keating's *Foras Feasa* was reconfigured, not only to make the Gaelic world more accessible for Protestants, but also to legitimate its incorporation into their own heritage.

The process by which Irish Protestants harnessed the past to their project of forging a stable and prosperous society in eighteenth-century Ireland can be seen in the publications of the Physico-Historical Society. Established in 1744 to survey Ireland's 'antient and present state', it complemented the Dublin Society, founded ten years earlier, which followed a classic Enlightenment programme for the improvement of the Irish economy. A number of studies published under the auspices of the Physico-Historical Society focused on the topography, antiquities, natural history and economy of particular counties.[25] The aim was not only to demonstrate economic potential, but also to highlight the progress that had already been made since the troubled times of the previous century. This reflected growing Protestant concerns that the emphasis on Irish backwardness cast a shadow on all those living in Ireland, regardless of ancestry, and was off-putting to prospective Protestant settlers.[26] As part of this strategy, Irish antiquities were lavishly described as proof of a rich and interesting history, symbolised by the many monuments scattered throughout the countryside. The possession of such an ancient heritage, carefully repackaged, was in itself synonymous with civility.

While the need to remove the association of Irishness with a state of barbarism was crucial to Protestant engagement with the pre-colonial Irish past and the Gaelic world from the 1730s, some Protestant historical works were written to address more universal concerns. On the basis of its title, Francis Hutchinson's *Defence of the Antient Historians, with a particular application of it to the History of Ireland and Great Britain, and other Northern Nations* (1734) appears to be a justification of the accuracy of Gaelic traditional accounts of the history of Ireland. One might expect it to follow the argument of Hugh MacCurtin's *A Brief Discourse in Vindication of the Antiquity of Ireland* (1717), which was a defence of the version of Irish history to be found in the medieval manuscript tradition. In fact, Hutchinson's focus was directed towards a wider European debate on the authority of scripture as an authentic account of the beginnings of the world.[27] Hutchinson (1660–1739), who was bishop of Down and Connor, deplored the tendency of 'Moderns' to dismiss both the question of the origins of a people, and the 'antient historians' who wrote about it, as unworthy of scholarly attention. Doubts cast on such writings were of use to free thinkers who would 'banter us out of the Belief in the Creation'.[28] Thus, for Hutchinson, the Gaelic tradition, which conformed to Mosaic orthodoxy on the creation, was a powerful weapon in a larger struggle against heterodoxy and atheism, and it was for that reason he defended it against the overly severe censures of 'Modern Criticks'.[29]

While not stated explicitly, a similar outlook lay behind James Parsons's *Remains of Japhet* (1767). Although English-born, Parsons (1705–70) was educated in Ireland, trained as a physician and later became foreign secretary of the Royal Society.[30] *Remains of Japhet* was an investigation into the origins of European languages, which claimed that the Irish and Welsh, as descendants of Noah's third son, Japhet, were the 'original nations' of Europe and that their languages were dialects of 'Japhetan', which, together with Hebrew, was the tongue spoken before Babel.[31] As the 'only unmixed remains of the children of Japhet, upon the globe', he argued, they deserved 'more liberal treatment' by English writers.[32]

This claim that the Gaelic tradition of the peopling of Ireland from the east deserved greater respect because of its conformity to biblical history was to animate the most important of these Protestant writers, Charles Vallancey (1721–1812). Like Hutchinson and Parsons, Vallancey was an outsider, born in Flanders to French Huguenot parents who moved to England when he was a child. He first came to Ireland in 1750 as an officer in the Royal Engineers, and remained there for the rest of his long life, attaining the rank of general, and combining his military work of fortification design and cartography with antiquarian pursuits.[33] An interest in Gaelic place-names, sparked off by the military surveying he carried out, developed into an obsession with Irish antiquities and particularly with the Irish language, in which he claimed great expertise. In his first and most influential work, *An Essay on the Antiquity of the Irish Language* (1772), Vallancey announced his discovery of close links between Gaelic and the almost lost Phoenician (or Punic) language, and through the latter he tied Gaelic into a line of descent from Hebrew, making it an older tongue than Latin or any of the languages generally associated with civilisation. It was thus 'the most copious Language extant' and 'most desirable to be acquired by all Antiquarians and Etymologists'.[34]

Although the general thrust of Vallancey's thesis lent support to the traditional account of the eastern origins of the original inhabitants of the island and to the claim of an early high civilisation, this was in many ways incidental to his project as it developed. As the 1770s progressed, Vallancey pushed Irish origins further eastwards, on the basis of increasingly dubious etymologies, so that by 1786 he could claim that manuscript histories recorded the epic journey of the Irish from Asia to the outer reaches of western Europe. The failure to recognise that they contained the key to all the great civilisations of the world had been a result of the errors of scribes and translators who had misunderstood the term 'Eirin', taking it to mean Ireland, when it really referred to Iran or Persia.[35] By this sleight of hand, Vallancey wholly orientalised his project and at the same time actively identified himself with Sir William Jones and other scholars of the East India Company who were engaged in a major project of recovering and translating early Indian and Persian history and literature. However, they too were motivated by religious zeal and aimed at no less than reconciling the history of Asia with that put forward in the Bible.[36] The serious purpose behind Vallancey's imperial project has been obscured by his increasingly ludicrous claims and publications. It is only recently that his position as military strategist in Ireland and links with the East India Company have been emphasised as a means of contextualising his obsessions and bringing out their colonialist nature.[37]

Golden ages

For Catholic antiquaries, any interest shown by Protestant writers in the Gaelic past and language was to be welcomed enthusiastically, even if, as with Vallancey, it went far beyond Catholic concerns. It was interpreted as a softening in attitude from the harsh and dismissive views of Cox and others who had branded pre-colonial Irish society as barbaric and in need of English reform. Most Catholic antiquaries wrote primarily to counteract such perspectives, and this pattern of native Irish or Catholic reaction to first English and then Irish Protestant negative representations of Gaelic society and its past was dominant in the eighteenth century as it had been in the seventeenth.[38] The most influential Catholic antiquary of the period was Charles O'Conor (1710–91), who also collaborated with John Curry in a series of pamphlets opposing the Penal Laws. O'Conor was a descendant of the last nominal high king of Ireland, Ruaidhrí Ó Conchobhair (Rory O'Conor), who was defeated by the Anglo-Normans. Although much of the family's land in County Roscommon was confiscated because of their Jacobite loyalty, Charles's father had managed to consolidate their remaining small estate, a task which his son continued in his role as gentleman farmer. O'Conor received a training in classical Irish, at a time when such a bardic education was dying out. He remained deeply conscious all his life of the need to preserve medieval Gaelic manuscripts, which he collected and which, as time went on, he alone seemed to have the tools to decipher, and even then only imperfectly. He was increasingly asked by non-Gaelic-speaking historians to make extracts and translations of them. In this sense, he was an important link in a tradition of scribal activity stretching back to the Middle Ages.

O'Conor's historical publications were few but influential. His *Dissertations on the Antient History of Ireland* (1753) was published anonymously, in keeping with the prevalent Catholic strategy in the mid-century of keeping a low public profile. By the early 1760s, however, his reputation as an expert on early Ireland had grown, and he had become a friend of George Faulkner, the veteran Dublin publisher of Jonathan Swift, joining his circle whenever he could visit Dublin.[39] At Faulkner's instigation, O'Conor put together a second edition of the *Dissertations* (1766), but reworked the original text to remove any material which might appear controversial to liberal Protestant eyes. The theme of both editions of the *Dissertations* was the existence of a sophisticated and literate civilisation in pre-Christian Ireland. Working from the manuscript tradition, but also borrowing from Keating's *Foras Feasa* (although he affected to despise it) and Roderic O'Flaherty's *Ogygia* (1685), O'Conor argued that the art of writing had arrived in Ireland with their founding ancestors, the sons of Míl, who had learned it in the east, among the Phoenicians and Egyptians from whom they were descended. The arrival of these adventurers in 1013 BC had ushered in the Milesian civilisation which subsequently embraced

Christianity with enthusiasm, survived the depredations of the Vikings, but was fatally weakened by the Anglo-Normans. Thus, O'Conor posited a continuous golden age which reached back from the Christian era into the mists of prehistory and which was ruptured by the greed and venality of Henry II's barons, and then systematically destroyed by successive English governments in Ireland. Far from being the barbarians represented in Giraldus Cambrensis (?1146–?1220) and later writers, the Milesian Irish of O'Conor's account were cultured, and their indigenous society, for the most part, a model of order. This was in contrast to the Teutonic tribes who were in possession of much of the rest of northern Europe at this time, and who were the real barbarians.[40]

In this way, O'Conor turned the charge of barbarism against the ancestors of those who made it, although by implication only, as his aim was to enlist, rather than alienate, liberal English and Irish Protestant support. Mindful of the allegation that Catholics gave their first loyalty to Rome rather than to the Hanoverians, which was used to justify the Penal Laws, O'Conor stressed the independence of the early Irish church from Rome, much as Keating had done previously. However, by contrast, O'Conor wrote of the period of 'saints and scholars' in a deliberately secular way, downplaying miraculous elements which Protestants associated with a degenerate Catholicism. In his account, St Patrick was 'a *Statesman*, as well as *Apostle*', who resembled a progressive eighteenth-century Whig politician, and whose rational religion was eminently suitable to the maintenance of liberty and of social order; in other words, the antithesis of popery.[41] O'Conor's sensitivity on these issues was characteristic of Catholic historians living and writing in Ireland, who were directly concerned with the pragmatic politics of surviving, and repealing, the Penal Laws. This was in contrast to the French-based Jacobite priest, Abbé James MacGeoghegan (1702–63), whose three-volume *Histoire de l'Irlande* was published in Paris between 1758 and 1762. MacGeoghegan was attached to the Irish College in Paris and for a time was chaplain to the Irish Brigade in France, to whom the *Histoire* was dedicated.[42] He espoused a forthright Catholic position in his work, which had as its principal theme the heroism and devoutness of Irish Catholicism throughout history, and was an undisguised attack on the Penal Laws. His assertion that close links had existed between Ireland and Rome throughout almost the entire early Middle Ages laid Catholics in Ireland open to the charge of age-old popery and buttressed Protestant arguments against any relaxation of the Penal Laws.[43] But for MacGeoghegan the Jacobite defeat was not yet part of the past. Thus, for example, the final sentence of the work was couched in the present tense, and complained that the Irish, having exerted themselves in favour of 'their lawful prince', were now 'forced to submit to a hateful yoke', and had lost 'their estates and properties'.[44] This ominous ending, with its reference to the most recent land settlement and implied hope of its reversal, was unthinkable in the work of an Irish-based Catholic historian of the same period.

By contrast, O'Conor's instinctive caution was reflected in the measured prose style of the second edition of the *Dissertations*, which also attempted to emulate the best Enlightenment historians, by interrogating received ideas about the past and discarding what seemed fanciful. This was at odds with his need to prove the historicity of the controversial pre-Christian golden age, but it shaped the way he presented his argument, so that on the surface, at least, it conformed to the kind of sceptical approach then in vogue. Other Catholics were not so constrained, notably Sylvester O'Halloran (1728–1807), who wrote several historical works in the 1770s and 1780s. O'Conor was unenthusiastic about them, but he was not to know that, in their romanticism, they constituted a major shift in the way that Catholics would write about their past, which would continue in the following century. O'Halloran represented a break with tradition in other ways too. As an eye surgeon in Limerick who had received his training in London and Paris, he was a member of the new middle class which dominated Catholic politics from the late eighteenth century. He also had a very different background in Gaelic culture, having been taught some Irish language and history by his family connection, the Gaelic poet Seán Clárach Mac Domhnaill, one of the eighteenth-century writers who developed new popular forms of Gaelic poetry in place of the aristocratic bardic tradition with which O'Conor identified.[45]

This may explain O'Halloran's enthusiasm for the poems of Ossian, which the Scot James Macpherson had published in the early 1760s and presented as translations of epic poems by a Highland bard of the third century. Macpherson's highly refined and sentimentalised versions of the *Fiannaíocht* poetry of Scotland were calculated to appeal to eighteenth-century sensibilities, which valued the ancient over the modern, and the primitive over the sophisticated. The histories of the pre-colonial period which O'Halloran went on to produce were influenced by Macpherson's vision of a noble warrior society with its own strict codes of honour. He set out to prove that the most distinctive and civilised of the military customs of medieval Europe, including chivalry and knighthood, had originated among the Irish Celts.[46] O'Halloran's histories were unscholarly but entertaining, and they enjoyed a renewed success in the nineteenth century, when colourful popular narratives of Irish history became more acceptable.

Ossianic influences

By highlighting a rich and all-but-vanished literary tradition, Macpherson's Ossian poems were also crucial in the development of Irish Protestant romanticism about the Gaelic world and its past. While Catholic writers tended to have ambivalent feelings about the poems, in that they believed that Macpherson was claiming for Scotland what rightfully belonged to their cultural tradition, Protestants had less strong feelings of territoriality.[47] The poems, therefore, became an impetus for a group of liberal Protestant writers to appropriate the Gaelic past (now seen primarily in terms of its music and poetry) for their own heritage. Among the most prominent was Joseph Cooper Walker (1761–1810), whose *Historical Memoirs of the Irish Bards* (1786) was an elegy to a literature that had disappeared as a result of the English conquest, written in the form of an imaginative recreation of the training of the bards in the distant past, and a disquisition on their music. This claimed that the melancholic tone associated with Irish song was reflective of the 'sword of oppression' wielded by successive English governments.[48] Walker's many hostile references to English rule were in line with 'patriot' feeling in Ireland in the 1780s. They are also a measure of the extent to which Irish Protestant identification with Gaelic culture in the late eighteenth century seemed to be attached to that political stance.[49]

This same process of identification can be seen in the work of Charlotte Brooke (?1740–93). As its name suggests, her *Reliques of Irish Poetry* (1789), a collection of translations from the Gaelic, was modelled on Thomas Percy's *Reliques of English Poetry* (1765), as well as on Macpherson's Ossian poems. In her detailed footnotes, Brooke harnessed the poetry as a means of discrediting the imputation of barbarism to the Irish. She argued vehemently against the 'anti-Hibernian' critics who represented 'our early ancestors' as 'Barbarians, descended from barbarians, and ever continuing the same'. The use of the first person plural by Protestants when referring to the early Irish past was another measure of their efforts to root themselves more securely in it. Brooke's aim in translating the poetry was to vindicate the claim to an ancient and glorious history renowned for its 'scientific and military' achievements. Thus, the 'productions of Irish Bards' could help to restore the reputation of Ireland, because they exhibited 'a glow of cultivated genius [and] manners of a degree of refinement, totally astonishing, at a period when the rest of Europe was nearly sunk into barbarism'.[50]

'Enlightened' histories

The early phase of Romanticism had, therefore, a considerable influence on historical writing in Ireland. Charles O'Conor, however, was less enthusiastic than most, although he helped both Walker and Brooke with their projects and welcomed the favourable attention that they brought to Gaelic literature. His preference was for a work on the modern period which would counter the historically based arguments of conservative Protestants in favour of the retention of the Penal Laws. When his plans to write such a book himself came to naught, he decided that a modern history from the pen of a liberal Protestant would be more successful in promoting a favourable view of recent Catholic actions. Thomas Leland (1722–85), a fellow of Trinity College, Dublin, was chosen and courted, not only by O'Conor, but also by Edmund Burke and by the liberal Protestant circle around George Faulkner, to do for Ireland what the great Scottish historians David Hume and John Robertson had done for England and Scotland respectively, that is to write a 'philosophic' modern history, giving an ostensibly objective, or non-party, narrative of the colonial period.

Leland's three-volume *History of Ireland from the Invasion of Henry II* (1773) was addressed to an English audience and aimed to trace 'the progress of English power in Ireland' from Henry II to William III. He strove for an appropriate balance in his method, which was to pay careful attention to evidence, use his 'private judgement' and avoid 'controversial discussion'. In this enlightened age, he claimed (with a mistaken optimism), the 'passions and prejudice', which had hitherto made it impossible to write a narrative of the modern period, had faded; time and 'an increasing liberality of sentiment' had rendered the public 'indifferent' to previously contentious issues.[51] The most significant of these was the 1641 rebellion, on which his supporters were expecting him to adopt an unbiased approach. On Catholic conduct in 1641 he was more moderate than previous commentators such as Temple and Cox. He argued that while the rebels' conduct had indeed been barbarous, they had been provoked by a government policy of 'injustice and oppression' which was in itself 'a barbarous iniquity'. However, he did highlight Catholic atrocities, using vivid language to capture the horror involved.[52] Worse still, Leland demolished the case Curry had made for the early occurrence of the Islandmagee massacre by Protestant forces, assigning it instead to January 1642, and he compounded the injury by having recourse to the depositions in order to do so.[53] Mainly because of this attempted evenhandedness, which also induced a certain leadenness into the narrative style, Leland's *History* pleased neither Protestants nor Catholics.[54] Enlightenment 'philosophic' history was no match for the prejudices and passions which the seventeenth century could still arouse.

Two further Protestant writers also claimed to be following an Enlightenment approach in their campaign against what they saw as the pernicious and overwhelming acceptance of a Milesian golden age that was destroyed by English intervention. Thomas Campbell (1733–95) and Edward Ledwich (1738–1823) were clergymen, who, in the late 1770s, were prepared to go along with the dominant consensus. However, they came to regret this, and the extreme scepticism which they afterwards espoused was a means of distancing themselves from positions which had come to embarrass them. Thus, while in 1777 Campbell was prepared to allow that civilisation had made 'a considerable progress' before the arrival of the Anglo-Normans, in 1789 he wrote that such a claim was itself an indicator of the continuing failure of the civilising process in Ireland.[55] In 1781 Ledwich had claimed that recently discovered *brehon* law manuscripts freed 'us from the charge of barbarism'.[56] By the time he came to write *Antiquities of Ireland* (1790), he had repudiated such views, and dropping the first person plural (signalling the end of his identification with the Gaelic past), he dismissed them as a 'wretched code of laws' which gave 'a picture of rude life [of] a barbarous people'.[57] Ledwich modelled his position on the enlightened scepticism of Pierre Bayle and Jean de Launoy, to the extent of following the latter in doubting the existence of St Patrick, whose life story he brushed aside as 'a fiction invented long after the time in which he is supposed to live'.[58] Yet the scepticism of Campbell and Ledwich appears as little short of posturing, in the light of their enthusiastic adoption of the myth of the *Christian* golden age of 'saints and scholars'.[59] As clergymen of the established church they felt a strong sense of ownership of Ireland's early Christian heritage, and were advancing James Ussher's project of forging an origin legend for the Church of Ireland.[60]

Impact of the 1798 rebellion

Ledwich maintained that the promotion of a Milesian golden age destroyed by colonisation was incompatible with loyalism.[61] In the turbulent 1790s this became clear to one of its foremost Protestant supporters, Joseph Cooper Walker, who abandoned Irish topics and retired into the calmer waters of Italian literature. In 1795 he proffered and then withdrew support for the subscription appeal of the Revd Charles O'Conor (1764–1828) for a memoir of his grandfather (who had died in 1791), because the grandson planned to highlight O'Conor's propaganda against the Penal Laws, rather than his historical scholarship, and also to call for the vote for Catholics.[62] Walker's comment on the published *Memoirs*, that 'it breathes the spirit of bigotry, broaches dangerous doctrines, and reflects with acrimony on the English settlers, and the Irish parliament', is an indication of how far he had moved from his earlier 'patriot' position.[63] The newly established Royal Irish Academy (1785), which promoted antiquities as one of its three specialities, was similarly buffeted by the political crises of the decade. The Antiquities Committee of the Academy was riven by political differences, as well as by antagonism between Ledwich and Vallancey, which often resulted in poor attendances and little business being carried out.[64] When the rebellion of 1798 happened, those Protestant historians who, unlike Walker, had not renounced their controversial views, were tainted by association. The most prominent of these was Vallancey, even though by this stage his orientalist writings bore no relation to the traditional account of a Milesian golden age. In a letter to a correspondent, Walker mused that Vallancey must have been 'hurt at the conduct of those whose champion he has been', and used the term 'Milesian' to refer to the rebels.[65]

The 1798 rebellion made it impossible for the Royal Irish Academy to continue to sponsor antiquarian research, and, after being moribund for over a decade, the Antiquities Committee was disbanded in 1810.[66] The rebellion also ushered in a more overtly partisan scholarship, in which Ledwich took a leading role, bringing out a second and expanded edition of his *Antiquities of Ireland* in 1804. But by far the most important publication of the immediate post-rebellion period was the monumental history of 1798, *Memoirs of the Different Rebellions in Ireland from the Arrival of the English* (1801) by Richard Musgrave (c.1757–1818), magistrate and Orangeman. As its title made clear, this sought to connect 1641, 1688–91 and 1798, and was closely modelled on Temple's *Irish Rebellion* (1646), being based on a large number of sworn affidavits, many of these collected by Musgrave himself from Protestant eye-witnesses and victims, who gave testimony of the 'dreadful barbarities' perpetrated by the rebels.[67] Musgrave's basic thesis was identical to Temple's: the rebellion was an attempt by Catholics to achieve 'the extirpation or expulsion of the Protestants [and] the exclusive occupation of the island for themselves'. Musgrave also provided damning evidence of Presbyterian participation in the rebellion in Ulster, thus underlining the position of the established church as the lone upholder of loyalty to king and constitution.[68] The lessons to be drawn were clear: constant vigilance against a resurgent Irish barbarism, no further repeal of the Penal Laws, and the eradication of Catholicism from Ireland.

Musgrave's *Memoirs* had a considerable impact on conservative opinion in Ireland and Britain.[69] However, he was not allowed to hold the field alone; a Catholic counter-narrative of the rebellion appeared almost immediately. This was in contrast to the seventeenth century, when Catholic repudiations of Temple did not appear until the 1670s.[70] The rise of middle-class Catholic self-confidence, evident long before the rebellion and only partially checked by it, can be seen in Edward Hay's *History of the Insurrection of the County of Wexford* (1803). Hay (*c*.1761–1826) was a member of a wealthy Catholic family, who had been active in radical politics in Wexford throughout the 1790s and played a shadowy role in the rebellion, for which he was imprisoned.[71] His *History* purported to be a 'fair and impartial account' which was designed to overthrow the 'hateful misrepresentations' of loyalist narratives.[72] More a vindication of his own conduct, it nevertheless subverted the view of the rebellion as a Catholic conspiracy by representing it as the outcome of the brutal conduct of magistrates, yeomanry and militia, which had driven the peasantry to insurrection.[73] Hay sent five hundred copies to London so that the king and members of parliament could read his counter-narrative,[74] a clear recognition of the importance of influencing metropolitan elite opinion, which had also preoccupied John Curry and Charles O'Conor in their attempts to gain public acceptance for their version of 1641.

Post-Union Catholic histories

Hay's public self-vindication so soon after the rebellion was unusual; most of those implicated laid low for many years and the few who wrote their memoirs did so decades later. Indeed, Hay was accused by Musgrave of having published his *History* in order to prepare the ground for the Emmet rebellion which broke out three months later.[75] However, the fraught political climate after the Union did not, in general, deter Catholic historians. Histories produced in the first three decades of the nineteenth century reflect the growing sense of grievance among Catholics at the failure to grant emancipation. In this highly charged and sectarian atmosphere, it became almost obligatory for the most partisan works to claim a strict attitude of scholarly impartiality. Thus, Denis Taaffe (*c*.1743–1813) identified his *Impartial History of Ireland* (1809–11) with the Renaissance historiographical tradition of 'philosophy teaching by example', but also allied himself with 'the liberal spirit of our Irish annalists' who, he claimed, always wrote of 'the English and their Irish colonists' with great detachment. This was in contrast to Musgrave, always and understandably the chief target of Catholic ire, whom he put in a line of 'English libeller[s]' from the time of Giraldus Cambrensis, on whom it was necessary to practise a kind of forensic exposure of 'the false evidence of lying history'.[76]

Edward Ledwich was also attacked, notably as the purveyor of 'palpably malevolent falsehoods' by John Lanigan (1758–1828) in his *Ecclesiastical History of Ireland* (1822). While Lanigan's claim to have divested himself of 'all national or religious prejudices' before embarking on this project is not sustained, he at least had embraced critical methods of research (learned during his time at the university of Pavia[77]) and consulted documents widely from what he termed 'foreign and domestic sources'. He was equally prepared to criticise the inaccuracies of Catholic as well as Protestant historians, but reserved his heaviest guns for Ledwich as one of the main 'slanderers of the Irish character, and vilifiers of the ancient religion of the *Island of Saints*'.[78] While Lanigan wished to restore the religious golden age to adherents of Catholicism, many of the Catholic works written during this time showed little interest in 'golden age' history. For example, John Lawless (1773–1837), despite entitling his book *A Compendium of the History of Ireland from the earliest period to the reign of George I* (1814), announced that he would pass rapidly over the earliest ages as being 'more interesting to the curious antiquarian than to the practical politician'. 'Those days of greatness' would not provide the kind of 'useful information' to be found in 'our modern history', which consisted of 'the recorded sufferings of Ireland'.[79] Similarly, while Matthew O'Conor (1773–1844), in his *History of Irish Catholics* (1813), began with a 'View of the State of Ireland from the Invasion of Henry II', his main focus was on the period since 1691, recounting a story of 'incomparable misery', in which the many violations of the Treaty of Limerick were listed in detail. A grandson of Charles O'Conor, Matthew nevertheless identified more with John Curry's historical work on 1641 and saw himself as carrying that torch, but without the constraints of the previous century, when 'it was perilous to speak against existing tyranny'.[80] In contrast to his eighteenth-century forebears, this O'Conor displayed little of their customary deference. The dedication to George, prince of Wales, demanded that he finish the work begun by his father in dismantling the Penal Laws, in the name of 'Justice that avenges the deeds and misdeeds of nations'.[81] Protestations of Irish Catholic loyalty and gratitude to George III mitigated, but did not negate, this accompanying threat of revenge if the demand was not met.

In 1810 Curry's late work, *Historical and Critical Review of the Civil Wars in Ireland*, was published in a 'new and improved' third edition with a long dedication to 'the Committee of Catholics of Ireland'. This recommended Curry as 'your first *Vindicator*' and the book as 'your code, your political bible, your magazine of arguments, your repository of facts'.[82] The increased prominence accorded to Curry's work can be seen in Taaffe, Lawless, O'Conor and virtually all other Catholic historical writers in this period. Taaffe quoted long extracts and went to great lengths to assert the accuracy of Curry's contention that the Islandmagee massacre of Catholics had happened towards the beginning of the rebellion.[83] In spite of Leland's dismissal of it, Islandmagee became an icon of Catholic martyrdom and a touchstone, first of emancipationist, and then of Catholic nationalist, politics.

The new antiquarianism

The increasingly sectarian politics of the first two decades of the nineteenth century had revealed obvious fault-lines in the joint antiquarian Milesian 'golden age' enterprise of the 1770s and 1780s, and temporarily halted the Royal Irish Academy's sponsorship of research. In its place emerged an exclusively Catholic and middle-class enterprise, the Gaelic Society, which, although of brief duration, was ambitious in its plans for the publication of translations of Gaelic manuscripts with the originals.[84] Its successor, founded in 1820, the equally short-lived Iberno-Celtic Society, also produced just one volume of transactions, but had the patronage of the duke of Leinster as president, along with a number of peers and two Catholic bishops.[85] Clearly, as the 1798 rebellion receded into the past, Ascendancy involvement in antiquarianism became once again permissible, which was also signalled by the resumption of antiquarian activities by the Royal Irish Academy from the mid-1820s. The equally respectable Irish Archaeological Society, founded in 1840, whose membership overlapped with that of the Academy, oversaw the production of an important series of editions of Gaelic texts with translations. This merged with the Celtic Society (founded in 1845) in 1854, in the aftermath of the famine, when money for such scholarly ventures was in short supply. Finally in 1853 the Ossianic Society was established to provide popular editions and translations of many of the *Fiannaíocht* and other tales made fashionable by Macpherson's Ossian.[86]

This new spirit of inquiry was reinforced by the election to Academy membership of George Petrie (1789–1866), a landscape artist with a special interest in ecclesiastical architecture. Petrie transformed Irish antiquarianism by adopting a scientific method based on detailed observation of monuments in their topographical context, combined with evidence taken from manuscripts. In 1832, using this approach, he won the Academy essay competition on the subject of the origin and uses of the round towers. The essay was eventually published in a much expanded form in his *Ecclesiastical Architecture of Ireland, anterior to the Anglo-Norman Invasion* (1845). He concluded that the towers were of Christian origin, built as belfries and refuges from 'sudden predatory attack', but recognised that Vallancey's Phoenicianist theory – that they were built in pagan times for the performance of oriental forms of fire worship – would retain the status of holy writ among some sections of the public. While this proved correct, Petrie's exposition of what he termed 'the science . . . of architectural antiquities' gradually became the dominant model of historical research.[87]

Petrie's methods had been honed at the Ordnance Survey of Ireland, where, from 1835 to 1846, he was superintendent of the Topographical Section, which was charged with research into topography, place-names and antiquities, to be incorporated into historical memoirs to accompany each of the six-inch county maps.[88] Petrie drew on the expertise of a number of Gaelic scholars, notably John O'Donovan (1806–61) and Eugene O'Curry (1794–1862), who were employed as researchers in the Survey, and also edited and translated manuscripts for other bodies, such as the Irish Archaeological Society. O'Donovan's major achievement was a six-volume edition and translation of the seventeenth-century *Annals of the Four Masters* (1848–51), hitherto partially available in print only in the Revd Charles O'Conor's defective Latin edition.[89] O'Curry was appointed professor of Irish history and archaeology at the newly established Catholic University in 1854, and O'Donovan to a chair at Queen's College, Belfast, testament to the growing acceptance of Gaelic scholarship as essential to the two emerging disciplines of history and archaeology in place of the earlier amateur antiquarianism.

O'Curry's *Lectures on the Manuscript Materials of Ancient Irish History* (1861) aimed to present a comprehensive account of the 'records and remains' of the Gaelic manuscript tradition, to show that they were indispensable for 'the accurate study of the History of the country'.[90] A further lecture series, *On the Manners and Customs of the Ancient Irish* (1873), published posthumously, was more traditional in its approach, and hardly disturbed the framework of 'golden age' history laid down in previous centuries. Thus, he used the widespread acceptance of a Christian 'island of saints and scholars' as an argument 'beyond any reasonable doubt' for the Milesian establishment of a social, political and legal system from 'a very remote period', which lasted, in spite of vicissitudes, down to the end of the sixteenth century.[91] This seems to bear out Petrie's resigned acknowledgement in the preface to his *Ecclesiastical Architecture of Ireland* that his less colourful version of the remote past would not prove attractive to a significant portion of his intended audience. He expected 'the great majority of the middle classes of the Irish people' to be unreceptive to his 'dry facts [which] have too little poetry in them to reach the judgment through the medium of the imagination'.[92]

Popular histories

The unenthusiastic reception of Petrie's findings can clearly be seen in *An Illustrated History of Ireland* (1868) by Mary Francis Cusack (1832–99), which adhered to the Phoenicianist theory on round towers. An extremely popular work (with copious illustrations of Irish antiquities from the collections of the Royal Irish Academy), it went into a second edition within a year. Among the corrections made was the inclusion of an admission that scholars 'are all but unanimous in ascribing a Christian origin to these remarkable buildings'. She did this with obvious reluctance at the prompting of Petrie's friend Lord Dunraven.[93] Elsewhere she noted Petrie's opinions only to cast doubt on them.[94] She was a champion of O'Curry's expertise, on the basis that he was more likely to use his learning in support of 'the popular account' of a high literary culture in Milesian Ireland.[95] Thus, while Cusack had imbibed, and benefited from, the new scholarship – she quoted at length from O'Donovan's translation of the *Annals of the Four Masters* and included facsimile samples from manuscripts in the Royal Irish Academy collection – it featured mainly as an overlay on a traditionalist interpretation of both ancient and modern history that was largely derived from eighteenth-century templates.

Other writers also remoulded the new scholarship to create a highly coloured and romantic past. The most interesting of these was Standish James O'Grady (1846–1928), whose *History of Ireland* (1878–80) influenced the circle around Yeats in the following decades. The sub-titles of its two volumes, 'Cuculain and his Contemporaries' and 'The Heroic Period', epitomised his interests. He complained that Irish archaeology, which he defined as the 'accumulation of names, dates, events' and the 'testing of statements and traditions', had 'swallowed up the domain of pure history', thus leaving the field open to 'novelists and romancers' to revivify the past. These latter were ignorant of the new scholarship and had no interest in truth or accuracy. O'Grady, by contrast, had absorbed the translations of bardic poetry and tales published by the scholarly societies, and claimed to be using 'sympathy, imagination [and] creation' to form 'a more or less faithful and vivid picture' of the pre-Christian past in Ireland as a 'heroic age' filled 'with great heroic personages of a dignity and power more than human'. He argued that the 'heroic history' to be found in the manuscript tradition was true, because 'the uncivilised mind', which had produced it, was incapable of invention.[96] This recalls the primitivist arguments used to support the authenticity of the Ossian poems, and underlines the continuing influence of James Macpherson.

The numerous reprints of eighteenth-century works by O'Halloran and others kept classic 'golden age' history to the forefront.[97] After 1850 there was also a growing market for new popular histories which reworked that traditional narrative by soldering it onto the kind of embittered accounts of the seventeenth and eighteenth centuries first produced in the post-Union and pre-emancipation period. John Mitchel (1815–75), radical former Young Irelander, described his *History of Ireland from the Treaty of Limerick to the Present Time* (1868) as a continuation of the Abbé MacGeoghegan's Jacobite *Histoire de l'Irlande* (1758–62). MacGeoghegan, Mitchel claimed, would have desired 'the dark record of English atrocity in Ireland, which he left unfinished, to be daily brought down through all its subsequent scenes of horror and slaughter, which have been still more terrible after his day than they were before'. Mitchel's account of the 'naked truth concerning English domination since the Treaty of Limerick' climaxed with the recent famine, seen as the *ne plus ultra* of English policy towards Ireland.[98]

The only significant study of the famine in this period was Canon John O'Rourke's *The Great Irish Famine* (1874), which focused on the operation of relief schemes as well as on the political and policy dimensions of the crisis. The famine otherwise functioned either as a metaphor of English government neglect or malevolence, or, in the case of Emily Lawless (1845–1913), for example, as a trauma which had resulted in the obliteration of the past: 'Whole phases of life, whole types of character, whole modes of existence and ways of thought passed away then and have never been renewed.'[99] It was hard to accommodate the famine within a framework that stressed the glories and continuities of Irish history. Thus, for A. M. Sullivan (1830–84), a moderate nationalist who, like John Mitchel, had edited the *Nation* newspaper, the famine was never more than a tragic but brief stopping point in his narratives of stirring battles and brave Irish deeds. Significantly, Sullivan incorporated Sylvester O'Halloran's heroic *General History of Ireland* (1778) into his own *Pictorial History of Ireland, from the Landing of the Milesians to the Present Time* (1884). Although Sullivan mined the same seam as Standish James O'Grady, the latter's aesthetic sense and unionist politics ensured that they produced very different kinds of works.

Sullivan's best-known, and best-selling, historical work, *The Story of Ireland* (1869), was explicit in presenting the Irish past as a popular and uplifting story designed for 'our young people', to convince them that Irish history, far from being a 'wild, dreary, and uninviting monotony of internecine slaughter', was 'an entertaining and instructive narrative of stirring events, abounding with episodes thrilling, glorious, and beautiful'.[100] It was dedicated to 'My young fellow-countrymen, at home and in exile', a recognition of the growing importance of the emigrant Irish in America, both politically and as a market for populist works of Irish history. Significantly, Sullivan made the Irish military in exile a theme of the book, calling the early Irish missionaries on the continent 'the missionary saint-army of Ireland', forerunners of the Flight of the Earls in 1607 and the departure of the Irish Jacobites in 1691 for 'the battle fields of Europe'.[101] The Irish Brigade of the French *Ancien Régime* army exerted a potent hold on the nationalist imagination. It featured in the poetry of Thomas Davis, for example, and Mitchel had chosen to continue MacGeoghegan's history, owing to his role as chaplain to that 'renowned corps of exiles, whose dearest wish and prayer was always to encounter and overthrow the British power upon any field'.[102] For Sullivan, the support given to the Fenians by the Irish in America was emblematic of the continuation of that tradition of resistance-in-exile, 'For England had filled the western continent with an Irish population burning for vengeance upon the power that had hunted them from their own land'.[103]

Sullivan's historical tour began with the arrival of the Milesians, continued through the '"Golden age" of pre-Christian Erin', followed by the only bloodless Christian conversion in Europe, and the defeat of the Danes by Brian Boru. It reserved for the Anglo-Norman colonisation the status of a transcendent event of 'ulterior and enduring consequences'.[104] Three-quarters of the book dealt with the colonial period, cast as a continuous and gallant struggle by Irish princes against English domination, in which 'Milesian Ireland' only 'disappeared from history' with the Flight of the Earls.[105] Unlike most eighteenth-century histories by Catholics, nineteenth-century works included an element of contemporaneity, and thus Sullivan closed his narrative with the Fenian rising of 1867, which he imbued with the same characteristics of heroism and humanity as previous rebellions, emphasising the purity and virtue of the 'Men of '67', and claiming that their 'insane and hopeless enterprise' had made Irish nationality 'a more visible and potential reality than it had been for centuries'. Like Sir Richard Cox's open-ended account written in the midst of the Williamite military campaign, Sullivan refused to conclude his Milesians-to-Fenians narrative; the story of Ireland could only be paused, 'not ended, because *"Ireland is not dead yet"*'.[106] Sullivan's *Story of Ireland* is only one of a large number of popular histories which appeared in the second half of the nineteenth century. These included Thomas D'Arcy McGee's *Popular History of Ireland* (1862), Justin McCarthy's *History of Our Own Times* (1879), and

Charles Gavan Duffy's *Young Ireland* (1880) and *Bird's Eye View* (1882). All shared that same sense of the past as ever-present, its intransigent problems only to be resolved by the future-to-come, which was a characteristic of almost all history writing in this two-hundred-year period.

Archive-based histories

A lack of firm boundaries between past, present and future can also be seen in the more scholarly works of Irish historians who were part of the growing international trend towards writing archive-based histories. Research carried out in state papers became a growing desideratum from the 1820s, although many works in that and succeeding decades continued in the old ways, notably Tom Moore's four-volume *History of Ireland* (1835–46), a rather turgid recycling of Keating et al., which lacks the verve of his mock history and political satire on English and Ascendancy misgovernment, *Memoirs of Captain Rock* (1824). The concept of historical research in state records came relatively late to Ireland. In Britain, an Act passed in 1838 established a central Public Records Office; its Irish equivalent was not enacted until 1867. This was in part owing to reluctance in Dublin Castle to undertake any centralising of record-keeping which would involve the undermining of vested interests among the several branches of the existing state archives. However, it was also a symptom of a wider refusal in the first half of the nineteenth century to countenance the opening of politically sensitive state papers to public scrutiny. This applied not only to relatively recent events, such as the 1798 rebellion, but even to records concerning landownership in the seventeenth century, to which researchers of good standing were regularly refused access.[107]

The result was that the first histories to use state records in a methodical way were produced by those who had privileged access by virtue of their employment as record-keepers. James Hardiman (1782–1855), who was also a noted translator of Gaelic manuscripts, worked in the State Paper Office when he produced his *History of the Town and County of Galway* (1820). This allowed him access to town charters and other documents which he supplemented by material from repositories in England. While Hardiman was consciously producing a new kind of historical writing, he was nevertheless as present-minded as any of the more historiographically limited writers such as Lawless and Matthew O'Conor, in that he envisaged the book as making a contribution to the emancipation campaign, by proving Irish Catholics' 'most unalterable attachment to the Protestant monarchs of Great Britain'.[108] Hardiman's work was the beginning of a growing fashion for county histories based on official sources. John D'Alton (1792–1867), stalwart of the Royal Irish Academy and proponent of Phoenicianist theories (in his *Essay on the History, Religion, Learning, Arts, and Government of Ireland* (1830)), had ambitious plans for a series of such county histories financed by local subscription. Although 'the apathy of the gentry' forced him to scale down the undertaking, in 1844 Drogheda Corporation made him a grant of two hundred guineas to write a history of the town. He also received funding from the directors of the newly established Dublin and Drogheda Railway Company, making this the first known example in Ireland of commercial sponsorship of history writing. For that reason he prefaced the work with a long and convoluted peroration on the history of transport in Ireland from pre-Christian times, claiming, with obvious wonder and excitement, that the power of steam had 'within a very few years, annihilated all previous calculations of time and space'.[109] As if to prove this, D'Alton also included a lengthy illustrated itinerary of the railway line, describing the antiquarian and historical associations of the landscape through which it travelled.[110]

Hardiman and D'Alton were to the forefront of the two main historiographical developments of the nineteenth century – the use of official sources, on the one hand, and of the newly emerging Gaelic annals in translation, on the other – in the production of more scholarly works. Significantly, in the early part of the century this was not incompatible with fully subscribing to the 'golden age' version of the early Irish past. From the mid-nineteenth century, however, growing professionalisation and the emphasis on records and evidence led to a split between the producers of popular histories and those who accepted the need for archival research and standards of accuracy. This was aided by the opening of the Public Records Office in Dublin in 1869, and by the steady publication of calendars of Irish state papers held in Dublin and elsewhere.[111] The towering figure here was John Gilbert (1829–98), who, in his multiple roles in the Public Record Office, the Historic Manuscripts Commission and Dublin Corporation, was responsible for calendaring and publishing a wealth of valuable historical documentation. Best remembered for his still essential *History of the City of Dublin* (1861), Gilbert maintained that the best way to ensure the fading away of 'those romances styled "Irish histories"' was to publish 'the facts, still slumbering in . . . obscure record repositories'.[112] This he mainly did, not through narrative histories, but by editing previously unknown texts for other scholars to incorporate into their accounts.

Gilbert was preoccupied with the seventeenth century and especially with the still controversial events of 1641–2. As a Catholic and nationalist, he was determined to put into print documents which would provide a corrective to the received Protestant version of the period.[113] This new phase of the controversy was sharpened by contemporary political developments, notably the focus on the land question and possible British Liberal responses to it. John P. Prendergast (1808–93), barrister and one of the new generation of historians, who was acutely conscious of the parallels between past and present, began his *Cromwellian Settlement of Ireland* (1865) by acknowledging the continuing centrality of land as the wellspring of political power in Ireland. The Cromwellian period, with its large-scale confiscations, was still relevant because it was the 'foundation of the present settlement of Ireland'. Land (and greed for land) motivated all parties in the 1640s. Thus, the rebels wished 'to recover their ancient lands', not to kill Protestant settlers, while reports of Catholic atrocities were invented by the English, who 'hungered after Irish estates'.[114] The fact that Prendergast, a Protestant, denied the massacre claims might suggest that attempted historical impartiality and archival research were related developments. However, he replaced the usual sectarian bias by an unusual ethnic loyalty to his ancestors, the Old English, who took the Confederate side in the 1640s.

Prendergast aimed, in part, to elucidate the tragedy of this group and thus highlighted the story of a settler family who had held land in Tipperary 'from the days of King John'. Having, like all the 'ancient English of Ireland', been forced by 'long-continued injuries and insults . . . into the same ranks with the Irish in defence of the King's cause in 1641', they lost their estate to a Cromwellian adventurer.[115] The Restoration settlement (the subject of his second book) did not restore such people to their estates, and thus confirmed the Cromwellian 'social revolution' by destroying the Catholic landed class. Prendergast made no attempt to hide the contemporary political message of this work: Gladstonian land reform threatened the current landowners, including Catholics who, 'through thrift', had managed to build up estates again. This would usher in another social revolution which would drive out 'the only class accustomed to government' and ensure the impoverishment of the country.[116]

Although Prendergast intended his works to impart political lessons for his own time, his denial of the 1641 massacres helped to reanimate the old dispute. The flames were fanned by the English historian James Anthony Froude (1818–94), in his three-volume *The English in Ireland in the Eighteenth Century* (1872–4), another present-minded work that warned, in the context of a growing English debate about the Irish question, of the dangers of granting self-government to Ireland, using the example of the descent into the chaos of the 1790s which followed the granting of legislative independence in 1782. Froude's controversial

first and second chapters had made the 1641 massacres central to his characterisation of the Irish as irredeemably barbarous and prone to violence unless
treated with consistent discipline and force, which, he maintained, had only
happened under Cromwellian rule.[117] His lurid account of the 1641 massacres
was straight out of Temple and other seventeenth-century works, but overall
the book was based on a considerable amount of research in the Irish Public
Record Office. The result was a revival of the bitter controversy, but on new
terms, in which research methods and evidence played a greater part than
before.[118]

While Froude had not himself consulted the depositions taken from witnesses in 1641, he encouraged an Irish Protestant historian (and only the fourth
female writer to feature in this survey), Mary Hickson, to edit a selection of
them, providing a characteristically trenchant foreword which diagnosed the
denial of the massacres as part of the grievance mentality of 'the Irish race'.[119]
The title of Hickson's book, *Ireland in the Seventeenth Century, or, the Irish Massacres of 1641–1642, their Causes and Results* (1884), underlines the way in which
the events of 1641 were made to define the entire century. Indeed her ambitious
aim was not only to reinstate the depositions as the authoritative source for
the massacres, but to establish them as the key to the history of Ireland and
of Anglo-Irish relations since 1600.[120] Hickson represented this as an act of
historical justice, following two hundred years of Catholic denunciations of
the depositions as unreliable.[121]

It fell to W. E. H. Lecky (1838–1903) to inject a note of scholarly detachment
into what was fast becoming a rerun of earlier acerbic Protestant–Catholic
exchanges. In a major review of Froude's *English in Ireland* published in 1873–4
Lecky had systematically challenged Froude's findings as partisan and his use
of evidence as slipshod.[122] When Lecky came to write the Irish chapters for
his *History of England in the Eighteenth Century* (1878–90), which were later
published in five volumes as *A History of Ireland in the Eighteenth Century* (1892),
he responded to Froude by providing a more measured account of the 1641
rebellion, in which he greatly reduced the estimates of Protestant deaths and
stressed the cruelties of both rebel and government sides.[123] It is fitting to end
this survey of two hundred years of history writing with Lecky's *History of
Ireland*, since it marks a real departure from the avowedly partisan approaches
that had dominated, as well as the establishment of archival research as essential
to the discipline. In addition, Lecky adopted a broad intellectual framework
(developed in his earlier writings on the history of rationalism and of European
morals), which, while focused largely on the politics of the period, uncovered
the economic and social factors underlying political developments. The result is

a work which is still used by historians more than a century after its publication. However, Lecky's *History of Ireland* is very much a work of its time. Written during the upheavals of Parnellite politics and the land war, it is as present-minded in its preoccupations as any other work of the period.

As a young man Lecky had nationalist sympathies and, under the influence of the *Risorgimento*, wrote a study of the growth of 'nationality' in Ireland, focusing on the contributions of Jonathan Swift, Henry Flood, Henry Grattan and Daniel O'Connell. His *Leaders of Public Opinion in Ireland* (1861) was belatedly taken up by nationalists in the 1870s and 1880s in support of their campaign for self-government. However, Fenianism and the land war had caused Lecky to repudiate his early views and work, and to become an opponent of Home Rule and of radical land reform.[124] In his *History of Ireland* Lecky concentrated mainly on the second half of the eighteenth century and represented the Protestant political elite, and in particular Henry Grattan (who was his hero and role model), as the guardians of political progress and civility. It was Lecky who was most responsible for the myth of 'Grattan's parliament' as a lost golden age. But, aware that some supporters of home rule were promoting their project as the rebirth of Grattan's parliament, Lecky sought to destroy the attempted parallel. Grattan, he emphasised, had believed it essential that political power should remain 'in the hands of Irish property and Irish intelligence'. While he had supported the inclusion of the leading members of the 'Catholic gentry' in the Irish House of Commons, he had feared that 'the ignorant and excitable Catholic population might be one day detached from the influence of property and respectability, and might become a prey to designing agitators and demagogues'. In 1798, this fear became reality. For Lecky the extension of the franchise to Catholics in 1793 had also laid the foundation for the 'political anarchy' of his own day.[125] Democracy involved the collapse of society; that was the message relayed by Irish history.

Thus, the Renaissance belief that political lessons might be learned from history became, in Irish historical writing, a fear that the past, in its manifestations of war and bloodshed, would endlessly repeat itself. That sense of apocalypse was never far from the works under discussion here. As Seamus Deane has argued, the fragmented nature of Irish history, as well as the series of political, social and economic crises that were ongoing through the nineteenth century, meant that there was never 'a climactic moment' from which a 'Whig interpretation' of the Irish past could be derived.[126] As long as the central question of who on the island should hold political and economic power remained to be answered, Irish history could never be safely contained within the covers of a book.

Notes

1. For the purpose of analysing the texts under discussion here, I use the term 'pre-colonial' to denote the period prior to the Anglo-Norman conquest of the twelfth century, 'colonial' for the period from 1169 to the end of the sixteenth century, and 'modern' for times closer to when these writers lived.
2. Joep Leerssen, *Mere Irish and Fíor-Ghael: Studies in the Idea of Irish Nationality, its Development and Literary Expression prior to the Nineteenth Century* (first published 1986; Cork: Cork University Press, 1996), pp. 32–76, 254–93.
3. Oliver MacDonagh, *States of Mind* (London: George Allen and Unwin, 1983), pp. 6–7.
4. *Dictionary of National Biography*, XII, p. 414.
5. Richard Cox, *Hibernia Anglicana* (London: Joseph Watts, 1689–90), part I, Epistle Dedicatory, n.p.
6. Ibid., part II, Dedication, n.p.
7. Ibid., part II, 'Address to the Reader', n.p.
8. Ibid., part I, 'Apparatus: or Introductory Discourse to the History of Ireland, concerning the State of that Kingdom before the Conquest thereof by the English', n.p.
9. William Molyneux, *The Case of Ireland being Bound by Acts of Parliament in England, Stated* (1698; Dublin: Cadenus Press, 1977), pp. 34–5.
10. Cox, *Hibernia Anglicana*, part I, 'Apparatus: or Introductory Discourse to the History of Ireland', n.p.
11. Ibid., part II, 'Address to the Reader', n.p.
12. Ibid., part II, 'Apparatus, or Introductory Discourse; touching the Controverted Points in this History', n.p.
13. T. C. Barnard, 'The Uses of 23 October 1641 and Irish Protestant Celebrations', *English Historical Review* 106 (1991), pp. 889–920.
14. William King, *The State of the Protestants of Ireland under the late King James' Government* (London: Robert Clavell, 1691), pp. 88–96.
15. Ibid., p. 117.
16. Ibid., pp. 233, 234, 238, 236.
17. Sir John Temple, *The Irish Rebellion: or, an History of the Beginnings and first Progresse of the General Rebellion raised within the Kingdom of Ireland, upon the three and twentieth day of October, in the year, 1641. Together with the Barbarous Cruelties and Bloody Massacres which ensued thereupon* (London: Samuel Gillibrand, 1646).
18. Reissues or new editions appeared in 1679, 1713, 1724, 1746, 1766 and 1812.
19. Walter Harris, *Fiction Unmasked* (Dublin: E. Bate, 1752), pp. vii–viii.
20. John Curry, *Historical Memoirs of the Irish Rebellion in the Year 1641* (London: n.p., 1758), pp. 63–71.
21. John Curry, *An Historical and Critical Review of the Civil Wars in Ireland from the Reign of Queen Elizabeth to the Settlement under King William*, 2 vols. (1775; 2nd edn, Dublin: Luke White, 1786), I, pp. 195–205.
22. Diarmaid Ó Catháin, 'Dermot O'Connor, Translator of Keating', *Eighteenth-Century Ireland* 2 (1987), pp. 67–88.
23. J. R. Hill, 'Popery and Protestantism, Civil and Religious Liberty: The Disputed Lessons of Irish History 1690–1812', *Past & Present* 118 (1988), pp. 102–3.

24. Dermod O'Connor, translator's preface, in Geoffrey Keating, *A General History of Ireland* (London: B. Creake, 1723), p. ii.

25. Eoin Magennis, '"A Land of Milk and Honey": The Physico-Historical Society, Improvement and the Surveys of Mid-Eighteenth Century Ireland', *Proceedings of the Royal Irish Academy*, 102C, 6 (2002), pp. 199–200.

26. Charles Smith, *The Antient and Present State of the County and City of Waterford* (Dublin: A. Reilly, 1746), p. ix; Smith, *The Antient and Present State of the County of Kerry* (Dublin: n.p., 1756), pp. ix–x.

27. See Colin Kidd, *British Identities before Nationalism: Ethnicity and Nationhood in the Atlantic World, 1600–1800* (Cambridge: Cambridge University Press, 1999), pp. 9–33.

28. Francis Hutchinson, *A Defence of the Antient Historians, with a particular application of it to the History of Ireland and Great Britain, and other Northern Nations* (Dublin: John Smith and William Bruce, 1734), pp. viii, x.

29. Ibid., pp. vi–vii, x, v.

30. *Dictionary of National Biography*, xv, pp. 403–4.

31. James Parsons, *Remains of Japhet* (London: n.p., 1767), pp. viii, x, xix–xx.

32. Ibid., p. x.

33. J. H. Andrews, 'Charles Vallancey and the Map of Ireland', *Geographical Journal* 132 (1966), pp. 48–61; Monica Nevin, 'The Defence of the Southern Part of Ireland by General Vallancey, Chief Engineer', *Journal of the Royal Society of Antiquaries of Ireland* 125 (1995), pp. 5–9.

34. Charles Vallancey, *An Essay on the Antiquity of the Irish Language. Being a Collation of Irish with the Punic Language* (Dublin: S. Powell, 1772), pp. 1–2.

35. Charles Vallancey, *A Vindication of the Ancient History of Ireland* (Dublin: Luke White, 1786), reprinted in Vallancey, ed. *Collectanea de Rebus Hibernicis* IV (Dublin: Luke White, 1786), no. xiv, pp. xlvi, 50.

36. Thomas Trautmann, *Aryans and British India* (Berkeley, Los Angeles and London: University of California Press, 1997), p. 42.

37. Clare O'Halloran, *Golden Ages and Barbarous Ages: Antiquarian Debate and Cultural Politics in Ireland c.1750–1800* (Cork: Cork University Press, 2004), chapter 2.

38. Leerssen, *Mere Irish*, pp. 255–93.

39. The correspondence of O'Conor and Faulkner can be read in two modern editions: *Prince of Dublin Printers: The Letters of George Faulkner*, ed. R. E. Ward (Lexington: University of Kentucky Press, 1972) and *The Letters of Charles O'Conor of Belanagare*, ed. C. C. Ward and R. E. Ward, 2 vols. (Ann Arbor, MI: Irish American Cultural Institute/University Microfilms, 1980).

40. Charles O'Conor, *Dissertations on the History of Ireland* (Dublin: G. Faulkner, 1766), pp. 24–5, 96–108, 238–9, 231.

41. Charles O'Conor, *Dissertations on the Antient History of Ireland* (Dublin: James Hoey, 1753), p. xxiv.

42. Vincent Geoghegan, 'A Jacobite History: The Abbé MacGeoghegan's *History of Ireland*', *Eighteenth-Century Ireland* 6 (1991), pp. 37–9.

43. Abbé [James] MacGeoghegan, *The History of Ireland, Ancient and Modern*, trans. Patrick O'Kelly (Dublin: J. Duffy, 1849), pp. 147, 155, 181–2, 235, 243–7. See also Clare O'Halloran, '"The Island of Saints and Scholars": Views of the Early Church and

Sectarian Politics in Late-Eighteenth Century Ireland', *Eighteenth-Century Ireland* 5 (1990), p. 10.

44. MacGeoghegan, *History of Ireland*, p. 616.

45. J. B. Lyons, 'Sylvester O'Halloran, 1728–1807', *Eighteenth-Century Ireland* 4 (1989), pp. 65–6.

46. Sylvester O'Halloran, *An Introduction to the Study of the History and Antiquities of Ireland* (London: J. Murray, 1772), pp. 5–6, 40, 124–5.

47. See Clare O'Halloran, 'Irish Re-creations of the Gaelic Past: The Challenge of Macpherson's Ossian', *Past & Present* 124 (1989), pp. 69–95.

48. Joseph Cooper Walker, *Historical Memoirs of the Irish Bards*, 2 vols. (1786; 2nd edn, Dublin: J. Christie, 1818), I, pp. 147, 181, 185.

49. Joep Leerssen, 'Antiquarian Research: Patriotism to Nationalism', in Cyril Byrne and Margaret Harry, eds. *Talamh an Éisc: Canadian and Irish Essays* (Halifax, Nova Scotia: Nimbus, 1986), pp. 80–1.

50. Charlotte Brooke, *Reliques of Irish Poetry* (Dublin: George Bonham, 1789), pp. 27, iv–v, vii–viii.

51. Thomas Leland, *The History of Ireland from the Invasion of Henry II with a Preliminary Discourse on the Antient State of that Kingdom*, 3 vols. (1773; Dublin: Brett Smith, 1814), I, pp. ii–iii.

52. Ibid., III, pp. 88, 127.

53. Ibid., pp. 128–9.

54. Joseph Liechty, 'Testing the Depth of Catholic/Protestant Conflict: The Case of Thomas Leland's *History of Ireland*, 1773', *Archivium Hibernicum* 42 (1987), pp. 20–1.

55. Thomas Campbell, *A Philosophical Survey of the South of Ireland* (London: W. Strahan & D. Cadell, 1777), pp. 67–8; Campbell, *Strictures on the Ecclesiastical and Literary History of Ireland* (Dublin: Luke White, 1789), p. 227.

56. Edward Ledwich, 'An Essay on the Study of Irish Antiquities', in Vallancey, *Collectanea de Rebus Hibernicis*, II (Dublin: Luke White, 1781), no. vi, pp. 88–9.

57. Edward Ledwich, *Antiquities of Ireland* (Dublin: Arthur Grueber, 1790), pp. 118, 270.

58. Ibid., pp. 160–1.

59. O'Halloran, '"The Island of Saints and Scholars"', pp. 14–15.

60. On Ussher, see Alan Ford, 'James Ussher and the Creation of an Irish Protestant Identity', in Brendan Bradshaw and Peter Roberts, eds. *British Consciousness and Identity: The Making of Britain, 1533–1707* (Cambridge: Cambridge University Press, 1998), pp. 200–2.

61. Ledwich to Joseph Cooper Walker, 17 April 1787, Ms. 1461(2), f. 225, Trinity College, Dublin.

62. Revd Charles O'Conor, *Advertisement* (1795), bound with a copy of *Memoirs of the Life and Work of Charles O'Conor of Belanagare* (Dublin: J. Mehain, 1796) in National Library of Ireland, Dublin, catalogue no. J92 0; Walker to Revd Charles O'Conor, 24 August 1795, Ms. OCD 8.4.HL.146, Clonalis House, County Roscommon.

63. Walker to Pinkerton, 25 March 1800, in *The Literary Correspondence of John Pinkerton*, 2 vols. (London: H. Colburn, 1830), II, pp. 137–8.

64. Minutes of the Antiquities Committee, *passim*, Royal Irish Academy, Dublin; Charles Vallancey to J. C. Walker, 10 January 1798, Ms. 1461(4), f. 74, Trinity College, Dublin.

65. Walker to Pinkerton, 31 October 1798, in *Literary Correspondence of John Pinkerton*, II, p. 37.

66. O'Halloran, *Golden Ages*, chapter 7.
67. David Dickson, 'Foreword' in Richard Musgrave, *Memoirs of the different Rebellions in Ireland, from the Arrival of the English: also a particular detail of that which broke out the 23rd of May, 1798; with a History of the Conspiracy which preceded it* (1801; 4th edn, Fort Wayne, IN: Round Tower Books, 1995), pp. vi–vii; Musgrave, *Memoirs of the different Rebellions*, p. 881, note.
68. Ibid., pp. 851, 161–89, 513–25, 621.
69. See James J. Sack, *From Jacobite to Conservative: Reaction and Orthodoxy in Britain, c.1760–1832* (Cambridge: Cambridge University Press, 1993), pp. 96–8, 240–2.
70. Toby Barnard, '1641: A Bibliographical Essay', in Brian Mac Cuarta, ed. *Ulster 1641: Aspects of the Rising* (Belfast: Institute of Irish Studies, 1993), p. 175.
71. Margaret Ó hÓgartaigh, 'Edward Hay: Historian of 1798', *Eighteenth-Century Ireland* 13 (1998), pp. 121–6.
72. Edward Hay, *History of the Insurrection of the County of Wexford* (Dublin: n.p., 1803), p. 1. Hay also wrote a pamphlet attacking Musgrave (*Authentic Detail of the Extravagant and Inconsistent Conduct of Sir Richard Musgrave* (?Dublin: n.p., ?1803)).
73. Hay, *History*, pp. 61–4.
74. Ó hÓgartaigh, 'Edward Hay', p. 127.
75. Kevin Whelan, *The Tree of Liberty* (Cork: Cork University Press, 1996), p. 160.
76. Denis Taaffe, *An Impartial History of Ireland, from the period of the English Invasion to the year 1810*, 4 vols. (Dublin: J. Christie, 1809–11), I, pp. iv–vi.
77. Donal McCartney, 'The Writing of History in Ireland, 1800–30', *Irish Historical Studies* 10 (1957), pp. 347–62, p. 350.
78. John Lanigan, *An Ecclesiastical History of Ireland*, 4 vols. (Dublin: D. Graisberry, 1822), I, pp. vii, title page, ix–x.
79. John Lawless, *A Compendium of the History of Ireland from the earliest period to the reign of George I*, 2 vols. (1813; Edinburgh: Michael Anderson, 1823), I, p. viii.
80. Matthew O'Conor, *The History of the Irish Catholics from the Settlement in 1691* (Dublin: J. Stockdale, 1813), advertisement.
81. Ibid., pp. vii–viii.
82. John Curry, *An Historical and Critical Review of the Civil Wars in Ireland* (1775; Dublin: R. Connolly, 1810), dedication.
83. Taaffe, *Impartial History*, II, pp. 556–64.
84. Leerssen, *Mere Irish*, p. 366.
85. Joep Leerssen, *Remembrance and Imagination: Patterns in the Historical and Literary Representation of Ireland in the Nineteenth Century* (Cork: Cork University Press, 1996), p. 76.
86. Damian Murray, *Romanticism, Nationalism and Irish Antiquarian Societies, 1840–80* (Maynooth: National University of Ireland, Maynooth, 2000).
87. George Petrie, *The Ecclesiastical Architecture of Ireland, anterior to the Anglo-Norman Invasion; comprising an Essay on the Origin and Uses of the Round Towers of Ireland, which obtained the gold medal and prize of the Royal Irish Academy* (2nd edn 1845; reprinted Shannon: Irish University Press, 1970), pp. 2–3, 13, viii, 24–5.
88. J. H. Andrews, *A Paper Landscape: The Ordnance Survey in Nineteenth-Century Ireland* (1975; Dublin: Four Courts Press, 2002), pp. 144–79.

89. Revd Charles O'Conor, *Rerum Hibernicarum Scriptores Veteres*, 4 vols. (Buckingham: J. Seeley and T. Payne, 1814–26), III; *Annála Ríoghachta Éireann: Annals of the Kingdom of Ireland by the Four Masters from the earliest period to 1616*, ed. and trans. John O'Donovan, 7 vols. (1848–51; reprinted Dublin: De Burca, 1990).

90. Eugene O'Curry, *Lectures on the Manuscript Materials of Ancient Irish History* (Dublin: J. Duffy, 1861), pp. viii–ix.

91. Eugene O'Curry, *On the Manners and Customs of the Ancient Irish*, 3 vols. (1873; facsimile edn, Dublin: Edmund Burke, 1996), II, pp. 2–3, 3–33.

92. Petrie, *Ecclesiastical Architecture of Ireland*, p. ix.

93. Mary Francis Cusack, *An Illustrated History of Ireland* (2nd edn, 1868; reprinted London: Bracken Books, 1995), pp. 152–3.

94. Ibid., pp. 144–5.

95. Ibid., pp. 38–9, 144–5.

96. Standish [James] O'Grady, *History of Ireland*, 2 vols. (London: Sampson Low, Searle, Marston and Rivington, 1878–80), I, pp. iii, iv, vi, xvii.

97. Editions of O'Halloran's *History of Ireland* appeared in 1803, 1819 and 1820; a second edition of Walker's *Historical Memoirs of the Irish Bards* in 1818, and of Charlotte Brooke's *Reliques of Irish Poetry* in 1816. The nationalist publisher James Duffy brought out a new edition of Dermod O'Connor's translation of Keating's *Foras Feasa* under the title *The General History of Ireland* in 1841, and the first English translation of James MacGeoghegan's *Histoire de l'Irlande* in 1849.

98. John Mitchel, *The History of Ireland from the Treaty of Limerick to the Present Time* (Glasgow: Cameron, Ferguson, 1868), Introduction, n.p.

99. Emily Lawless, *Ireland* (1885; London: T. Fisher Unwin; New York: G. P. Puttnam's Sons, 1888), pp. 401–2.

100. A. M. Sullivan, *The Story of Ireland* (Dublin: A. M. Sullivan, n.d. [1867]), p. 7.

101. Ibid., pp. 343, 75, 342, 471.

102. Mitchel, *History of Ireland*, Introduction, n.p.

103. Sullivan, *Story of Ireland*, pp. 570–1.

104. Ibid., p. 137.

105. Ibid., p. 342.

106. Ibid., pp. 580–1.

107. Gréagóir Ó Dúill, 'Gilbert and the Public Record Office of Ireland', in Mary Clarke, Yvonne Desmond and Nodlaig P. Hardiman, eds. *Sir John T. Gilbert, 1829–98: Historian, Archivist and Librarian* (Dublin: Four Courts Press, 1999), pp. 25–7.

108. James Hardiman, *The History of the City and County of Galway* (1820; reprinted Galway: Connacht Tribune, 1985), pp. vii–viii.

109. John D'Alton, *The History of Drogheda*, 2 vols. (Dublin: n.p., 1844), I, p. xvii.

110. Ibid., pp. l–cxxxiv.

111. Ó Dúill, 'Gilbert and the Public Record Office', pp. 30–3.

112. Quoted in Toby Barnard, 'Sir John Gilbert and Irish Historiography', in Clarke et al., *Sir John T. Gilbert*, p. 92.

113. Ibid., pp. 100–1. Gilbert's two main publications in this area were *A Contemporary History of Affairs in Ireland from 1641 to 1652*, 3 vols. (Dublin: Irish Archaeological and Celtic Society, 1879–80), and *History of the Irish Confederation and the War in Ireland, 1641–43*, 7 vols. (Dublin: n.p., 1882–91).

114. John P. Prendergast, *The Cromwellian Settlement of Ireland* (London: Longman, Green, Longman, Roberts & Green, 1865), pp. iii, v–vi, 4, 7.

115. Ibid., pp. ix–x, xiii–xvi.

116. John P. Prendergast, *Ireland from the Restoration to the Revolution, 1660–1690* (London: Longmans, Green, 1887), pp. vi–ix.

117. James Anthony Froude, *The English in Ireland in the Eighteenth Century*, 3 vols. (London: Longmans, Green, 1872–4), I, pp. 66–140.

118. Donal McCartney, 'James Anthony Froude and Ireland: A Historiographical Controversy of the Nineteenth Century', in T. D. Williams, ed. *Historical Studies VIII* (Dublin: Gill and Macmillan, 1971), pp. 171–90. See also Ciaran Brady, 'James Anthony Froude (1818–1894), Moral Obligation, and the Uses of Irish History', in Vincent P. Carey and Ute Lotz-Heumann, eds. *Taking Sides? Colonial and Confessional Mentalités in Early Modern Ireland* (Dublin: Four Courts Press, 2003), pp. 266–90.

119. J. A. Froude, 'Preface' to Mary Hickson, *Ireland in the Seventeenth Century, or, the Irish Massacres of 1641–2, their Causes and Results*, 2 vols. (London: Longmans, Green, 1884), I, pp. v–vi.

120. Hickson, *Ireland in the Seventeenth Century*, I, p. 164.

121. Ibid., p. 121.

122. Donal McCartney, *W. E. H. Lecky: Historian and Politician, 1838–1903* (Dublin: Lilliput Press, 1994), pp. 67–8, 71–4.

123. W. E. H. Lecky, *A History of Ireland in the Eighteenth Century*, 5 vols. (London: Longmans, Green, 1892), I, pp. 46–89.

124. Donal McCartney, 'Lecky's *Leaders of Public Opinion in Ireland*', *Irish Historical Studies* 14 (1964), pp. 119–41.

125. Lecky, *History of Ireland*, III, pp. 18, 254–5.

126. Seamus Deane, *Strange Country: Modernity and Nationhood in Irish Writing since 1790* (Oxford: Clarendon Press, 1997), p. 146.

Select bibliography

Barnard, T. C., 'The Uses of 23 October 1641 and Irish Protestant Celebrations', *English Historical Review* 106 (1991), pp. 889–920.

Deane, Seamus, *Strange Country: Modernity and Nationhood in Irish Writing since 1790*, Oxford: Clarendon Press, 1997.

Foster, R. F., *The Irish Story: Telling Tales and Making It Up in Ireland*, London: Allen Lane, The Penguin Press, 2001.

Hill, J. R., 'Popery and Protestantism, Civil and Religious Liberty: The Disputed Lessons of Irish History 1690–1812', *Past & Present* 118 (1988), pp. 96–129.

Hutchinson, John, *The Dynamics of Cultural Nationalism: The Gaelic Revival and the Creation of the Irish Nation State*, London: Allen & Unwin, 1987.

Kidd, Colin, *British Identities before Nationalism: Ethnicity and Nationhood in the Atlantic World, 1600–1800*, Cambridge: Cambridge University Press, 1999.

Leerssen, Joep, *Mere Irish and Fíor-Ghael: Studies in the Idea of Irish Nationality, its Development and Literary Expression prior to the Nineteenth Century*, first published 1986; Cork: Cork University Press, 1996.

Remembrance and Imagination: Patterns in the Historical and Literary Representation of Ireland in the Nineteenth Century, Cork: Cork University Press, 1996.

McCartney, Donal, *W. E. H. Lecky: Historian and Politician, 1838–1903*, Dublin: Lilliput Press, 1994.

'The Writing of History in Ireland, 1800–30', *Irish Historical Studies* 10 (1957), pp. 347–62.

Mac Cuarta, Brian, ed. *Ulster 1641: Aspects of the Rising*, Belfast: Institute of Irish Studies, 1993.

MacDonagh, Oliver, *States of Mind*, London: George Allen and Unwin, 1983.

Murray, Damian, *Romanticism, Nationalism and Irish Antiquarian Societies, 1840–80* (Maynooth: National University of Ireland, 2000).

O'Halloran, Clare, *Golden Ages and Barbarous Nations: Antiquarian Debate and Cultural Politics in Ireland, c.1750–1800*, Cork: Cork University Press, 2004.

Sheehy, Jeanne, *The Rediscovery of Ireland's Past: The Celtic Revival, 1830–1930*, London: Thames and Hudson, 1980.

15

Literature and the oral tradition

DONNA WONG

Introduction

The title of this chapter recognises that the Irish literary tradition encompasses both 'literature', which a modern audience generally thinks of as prose or poetry that is attributable, datable, written and fixed in one authoritative form, and 'oral tradition', which a modern audience rarely thinks of at all, but which encompasses prose, poetry, sayings, superstitions and many other genres of folklore, whose composers may or may not be known, whose date of creation may or may not be estimated, and which circulates in multiple versions through the interaction of performer and listener. Such distinctions between them – and there are many more[1] – imply that literature and oral tradition exist discretely, neither one affecting nor being affected by the other. But what one person writes may be read aloud and heard by others, just as what one person speaks may be written and read silently by others. Even a quick survey of the Irish literary tradition confirms that such interaction has occurred for centuries.

The concept of literature described above is peculiar to members of a highly literate society, in which the majority are taught to read, write and rely on print to guarantee the accuracy, longevity and availability of information.[2] Literature in oral form, however, is familiar to populations in virtually all places and times. In pre-Christian Ireland, literature and all other knowledge worth retaining may well have been memorised by professional scholars. Evidence from the Christian period shows that jurists, historians, physicians and poets secured their data 'in repetitions and mnemonics, in alliterations, rhymes, and formulaic closures'[3] to ease its passage and ensure its fidelity from one generation to the next. Verse was used to document everything from business contracts to victories in battle. Metrical and prose *dindshenchas*, stories that explain the origins of place-names, provided a narrative map that evoked and was evoked by features of the landscape. Similar items were grouped into a triad, under the heading of a shared trait that made it as easy to list three things as one. These well-crafted words were memorable and say-able and still endure in folk-tales and proverbs.

Scholars who had relied on oral tradition for centuries did not abandon it because they suddenly awoke to the merits of literacy. That they could write but had limited use for letters is attested by the abundance of fourth-century inscriptions in *ogam*, a writing system based on the Latin alphabet. What caused them to take up reading and writing in a serious way was their discovery in the fifth century that these skills were prerequisites for the adoption of Christianity: 'Christianity, which is a "religion of the book", simply cannot survive without a literate class, even if the mass of the faithful are illiterate.'[4]

Christianity's apparatus of books, however, did not instantly undermine oral tradition. Because of the scarcity of manuscripts and reading ability, it was usual for one person to read aloud to a group, so that until at least the twelfth century texts were more commonly heard than read.[5] Nor did the skills of reading and writing cause a *fer léginn* (literally 'man of reading', a scholar of Christian texts) to devalue oral tradition. A vellum trail of obituaries, eulogies and stories in which poets and saints show mutual respect demonstrates that colleagues who entered the church still esteemed the learning of those who did not.[6] At first transcription may have been a mark of status, a declaration that native tradition was as worthy as the new religion of the effort and resources that book production required. But as centuries passed, and scholars died of plague or violence, the survivors set out to create a written back-up for human memory. Probably their best-known failsafe is *Acallam na Senórach* (The Colloquy of the Ancients), an enormous collection of stories about Fionn mac Cumaill and the fíana, related by the very last of the fíana to a very interested St Patrick.

Inevitably the concentration of learning in Irish monasteries blurred the boundaries between oral and written, Irish and Latin, secular and religious knowledge, to such an extent that the feasibility of drawing such distinctions has incited a furious contention among Celtic scholars of the modern period. The late James Carney wrote of 'nativists' and 'anti-nativists' in 1955, but these terms were largely ignored until Kim McCone published The Anti-Nativist Manifesto, a.k.a. *Pagan Past and Christian Present in Early Irish Literature*, in 1991. In a bombshell, McCone divides scholars of early and medieval Irish texts into two categories: nativists, who focus on insular Irish tradition, conservative oral transmission, pre-Christian and Indo-European survivals, versus anti-nativists, who focus on contemporary continental trends, creative written transmission, biblical and local influences. He denigrates scholars such as

D. A. Binchy, Gerard Murphy and Proinsias Mac Cana for unquestioningly and untenably perpetuating nativist misconceptions, while praising scholars such as Donnchadh Ó Corráin, Liam Breatnach and Proinsias Mac Cana (not a typo; Mac Cana is alternately given horns and a halo) for insightfully and plausibly advancing anti-nativist analyses.[7] The strengths and weaknesses of McCone's argument are summarised in a review by Patrick Sims-Williams. While acknowledging some brilliant insights, he states': 'I am not convinced... that it is helpful to lump these very diverse scholars together as a "nativist school" and as opponents of James Carney', since all critics follow theoretical trends, develop different perspectives, and advance interpretations that may need to be modified in light of later developments.[8] McCone's wake-up-or-be-damned call would have been more effective had not the acidity of his prose impeded the absorption of his ideas, and to this day 'nativist' remains the 'N-word' of Celtic studies.

Although the controversy engulfed medieval Irish texts, the contrasts it posited, e.g. secular/religious, oral/written, and Irish/European – debatable even in the earlier period – could hardly be maintained in Ireland after 1200. By then, religious reformers had arrived from the continent, 'audited' the monasteries and put an end to much of the in-house work on Irish litera-ture. Henceforth aspects of the native manuscript tradition were entrusted to the same secular learned families who preserved oral tradition. Scholarly professions being hereditary, generations of poets drew on both streams of literature, displaying their command of the material in bardic poetry, the elite literary genre that claimed centre stage in the thirteenth century and relin-quished it during the seventeenth. A bardic poem is a first-person address by a professional poet to an aristocratic patron, and it may discuss any topic from political advice to personal apology, although more praise poems have survived than any other type. Notwithstanding the fact that it was sometimes written down, bardic poetry was oral from its conception to its presentation. Descriptions of the proper practices dating from the end of the bardic period stipulate composing in a dark room, ruling out the possibility of written drafts, and the patterns of assonance, alliteration, rhyme and metre are arranged for the ear, not the eye. A finished poem was always performed before the patron and his guests, by a professional reciter accompanied on the harp. The event was never merely entertainment. On the contrary, the most respected bards were confidential advisers to the heads of noble families, and encoded in their verse were military recommendations, intelligence reports and messages from potential allies. Ultimately their influence over Irish and Old English aristocrats impelled the New English to destroy them, and their strength was critically diminished once their last powerful patrons went into exile in 1607.

Although 'folk tradition' was as distinctively Irish as bardic poetry and far more pervasive, it flourished among commoners rather than nobles, and the New English did not feel threatened by a population lacking political or military clout. In any case the methods that had dismantled the institution of bardic poetry could not have succeeded against folk tradition, which was sustained by very different means. Bardic poetry, while oral in composition, was the product of a highly visible group of scholars who could read and write Irish and English,[9] whereas folk tradition was common property, its performers indistinguishable from their audience, with all participants relying on spoken Irish. The last formally educated bards complain of a turncoat aristocracy and a vulgar middle class whom ambition persuaded to speak English. But the lower class was consistently Irish-speaking right up until the 1840s famine, and the devastation of this population was a blow from which the language has never recovered.

Movements to promote Modern Irish and Irish tradition began in the late nineteenth century, with mixed success. Amateur antiquarians and professional folklorists have collected a great deal of oral tradition, in Irish and in English, their efforts co-ordinated in 1935 by the Irish Folklore Commission, and lodged since 1971 in the renowned Folklore Archives in University College Dublin. The Gaelic League (*Conradh na Gaeilge*), founded in 1893, awakened national interest in the language and made classes widely available. The Irish Literary Revival, spanning approximately 1890 to 1922, brought international attention to the literature. In the past few decades, periodicals, newspapers, radio and television programmes in Irish have made it possible to practise spoken and written Irish far outside the *Gaeltacht* areas (officially recognised Irish-speaking communities). There have also been some truly spectacular backfires. For generations, Modern Irish bore the stigma of a compulsory subject, and the school edition of *Peig* was the most hated book in Ireland. Often those appointed to teach Irish knew nothing about teaching a language, resulting in such dreary, unforgiving instruction that students developed a life-long resistance to the subject. During the twentieth century, the most insidious disaster was the left-handed iconisation of the native Irish speaker as a simple-minded peasant, giving rise to the absurd misconception that embracing Modern Irish means renouncing prosperity, modernity and globalism.

The turbulent history of the language has unavoidably complicated the writing of literature in Irish. In the years around 1900, the success of organisations such as the Gaelic League created a demand for reading material in contemporary Modern Irish. Concerned primarily with instruction, early authors wrote stories crammed with examples of grammar, vocabulary and idiom, or transcribed orally composed folk-tales to illustrate dialect. Predictably, this approach produced texts, not art. Authors such as Patrick Pearse and Pádraic Ó Conaire soon realised that abandoning the folk-tale's oral style and rural concerns was a prerequisite to composing a modern literature. Choosing the international over the insular, they looked to Russia, France and Norway for models of polished written narratives.[10] This new style of story-telling showed them how to write about urban life, personal conflicts, early and medieval legends, refuting the charge that Modern Irish was an outmoded and inadequate language. The composition of world-class literature in Modern Irish has proved it a viable creative medium, as versatile in print as it is in speech, and it is gratifying that since the founding of the Gaelic League, action and purpose have exchanged roles: learners used to read the literature in order to practise the language, and now people learn the language in order to read the literature.

The fine print

Texts that illustrate the relationship between literature and oral tradition are as numerous as periwinkles on the beach, but the authors discussed below meet very specific criteria. All of them had sufficient proficiency in Irish at the time of writing to consult original sources, whether manuscript, audiotape or human. When they made creative or editorial decisions, it was with full awareness of the options available to them. Most of them use oral tradition in a variety of ways, and the ones that are rare or subtle are the ones that will be pointed out. In addition, to avoid unnecessary shedding of ink, this study limits remarks about authors and works that are already awash in critical attention.

Táin Bó Cúailnge (The Cattle Raid of Cooley)

Three-quarters of the way through the oldest surviving version of Táin Bó Cúailnge (TBC), Súaltaim, a father of the Ulster champion Cú Chulainn, bounds into the presence of Conchobar, king of Ulster, and summarises the events of the preceding 3,400 lines: 'Fir gontair, mná brattar, baí agthar!' (Men are slain, women carried off, cattle driven away!).[11] Arrested by this oral headline, Conchobar and company ask to hear all about it. As they discuss how to respond to the attack, Súaltaim becomes fatally fidgety, leaps up and is decapitated on the edge of his shield, in a unique instance of the bearer of bad news being held blameless by listeners only accidentally to kill himself. The grotesque humour of this scene is extended by the narrator's comment, 'Dob*eir* i nEmain aitherroch a chend forsin scíath isa teach 7 asbeir an cend an focol cétna. – Cia asberat alaili is inna c[h]otlud ro boí-som forsind liaic, 7 is de dorochair fora scíath oc diuchtrad' (The horse brought his head on the shield back into Emain, and the head uttered the same words. – Though others say that he had been asleep on the stone and on waking had fallen from it on to his shield).[12]

Featuring tale-bearing, cattle-rustling, foe-slaying, head-chopping and alternate versions, this passage is a microcosm of the whole. *TBC*, the longest more-or-less-continuous Irish narrative from this period, relates the exploits of Cú Chulainn, a savage noble who singlehandedly fends off an invading army until his mysteriously stricken comrades can come to his aid. The portrayal of Cú Chulainn as his people's saviour, the glorification of single combat, and the cast of thousands suggest an Irish *Aeneid*, with the same patina of venerability and finesse. A shadow had hung over the authenticity of Celtic literature since James Macpherson's 'translations' of ancient Scottish epic were exposed as his own inventions (1760).[13] A romantic mist had clung to the character of Celtic peoples since Matthew Arnold's unforgivably unforgettable typing of 'The Celt' as passionate, poetic and doomed to subservience by his own sensitivity (1867).[14] A bona fide Irish epic of classical grandeur would have refuted scepticism and stereotype, and a definitive edition of it would have deified scholars who had been editing and translating Old and Middle Irish texts since the end of the eighteenth century. Even partial translations had inspired writers such as James Stephens, who very freely retells *TBC* in *In the Land of Youth*, while Cú Chulainn's significance for Patrick Pearse and W. B. Yeats has been so often written about that nothing more will be written about it here. Moreover, *TBC* interested European academics as well as the Irish public. In the nineteenth century, linguists had identified Celtic as a very old branch of the Indo-European language tree, and comparativists were eager to autopsy early Irish texts for Indo-European archaisms. *TBC* should have been a goldmine for nationalist propaganda, international scholarship and at least one major press.

Yet contrary to every rule of marketing, no full-length edition or English translation of *TBC* was published until 1976. In her account of *TBC*'s drunken wandering towards unexpurgated, bilingual existence in print, Maria Tymoczko argues that the delay was a result of uneasiness about the story's contents and narrative style.[15] Regarding its subject matter, it will suffice to note that a grandfather named Iliach goes naked into battle with his genitals sagging through the bottom of his chariot, Cú Chulainn forces a charioteer to walk back to camp carrying his master's severed head, and Freud would have a field day with the theft by Ailill, king of Connacht, of the sword of Fergus mac Róich, an expatriate Ulsterman who has become very friendly with the thighs of Medb, queen of Connacht. In sum, those who were able to read *TBC* were reluctant to place it before the public because its primitiveness was too primitive, its violence was too violent, and its sex was too sexy.

'Able to read *TBC*' refers to more than the difficulty of Old and Middle Irish. For just as the Súaltaim episode typifies the themes and structure of *TBC*, *TBC* exemplifies the best, the worst and the most trying features of early medieval Irish literature. While the main events of the tale are believed to have coalesced by the eighth century, the oldest manuscript copy was compiled in the late eleventh century.[16] Four hundred years of contemplation and revision might seem sufficient to perfect even a doctoral dissertation; nevertheless, it is as plain as a pillar-stone that there was no definitive *TBC* by the time the first, second or third recension was written. Judging from the tellings that have survived, *TBC* existed in numerous variants, oral and written, which continually interacted and generated new ones. Since there was no consensus on *TBC*, every version had an equal claim to authority. A narrator was free to combine and modify all the material at his disposal as long as he preserved the main elements of the story, e.g. Cú Chulainn's combats can differ in order and detail, provided he wins them. With so many variables to consider, the effort that storytellers put into recreating *TBC* is matched by the effort that scholars put into deciphering it.

Firstly, modern scholars face a dilemma that is the exact opposite of James Macpherson's, an excess rather than an absence of originals. *TBC* has come down to us in multiple manuscripts, which among them offer three distinct recensions of the tale. To complicate matters, Recension 1, the oldest, had to be reconstructed from a portion in the eleventh-century *Lebor na hUidre* that happens to overlap the portion in the fourteenth-century Yellow Book of Lecan. It is this version that Cecile O'Rahilly tackled first, that Thomas Kinsella later renovated, and that is the focus of discussion below.[17]

Secondly, *TBC* is prosimetric, alternating prose and verse. While the bulk of the story is third-person narrative prose, at key points *TBC* leaps into first-person dramatic verse that is always spoken aloud by a character. Prose describes action, sets out events in order and moves the plot along, whereas poetry expresses emotion, reveals intimate thoughts, and pauses to explore the moment fully. The prose gives context to the poetry, the poetry gives voice to sentiments missing from the prose, and both components are interwoven in all three recensions, confirming that this is the intended written form.

Thirdly, far from being a seamlessly woven narrative, *TBC* is a crazy quilt of episodes worthy of the title '32 Short Stories about Cú Chulainn'. Events are related in a sequence that is bewildering to a modern reader, the narrator even acknowledging that others might tell them in a different order. For example, having stated that the invaders felled trees in Slechta to make way for their chariots, he offers an earlier incident as an equally acceptable explanation: 'Mad iar n-arailib immorro dorala and so imacallaim eter Medb 7 Fedelm banfháith, amal ro innisimar remoind, 7 dano is iarsind frecra do rat-si for Medb ro slechtad in fid' (According to others, however, it was here that the dialogue between Medb and Feidelm Banfháith as we have related above took place, and it was after the answer Feidelm made to Medb that the wood was cut down).[18] That *TBC*'s episodes are self-contained rather than interconnected is emphasised by their titles, e.g. 'The Harrying of Cooley', 'The Death of Nechta Scéne's Three Sons', 'The Fight of Fer Diad and Cú Chulainn', some of which are listed elsewhere as the titles of short stories.[19]

Fourthly, *TBC* is full of features characteristic of oral storytelling. There is repetition of memorable words and phrases, e.g. the one-line announcement made by Súaltaim is also made by Cú Chulainn,[20] quite possibly because the declaration is plausible and dramatic whether it is delivered by the anxious father or the impatient son. Descriptions are recycled rather than personalised, e.g. Cú Chulainn's punk hairstyle in battle mirrors that of Fer Cailliu, a character in 'The Destruction of Da Derga's Hostel',[21] for spiky-haired Irishmen are always supernatural and dangerous. Some events happen repeatedly, e.g. the rivers Cronn, Colptha and Glais Gatlaig rise in turn to halt the invaders.[22] Likewise, the same narrative function is over-fulfilled by more than one episode, as three of Cú Chulainn's combats are meant to be climactic.[23] Whereas his other opponents are dead men walking, Fer Báeth, Lóch Mac Mo Femis and Fer Diad are described as capable of killing him, and each of them has a personal stake in the match: Fer Báeth and Fer Diad are Cú Chulainn's fosterbrothers, while Lóch seeks to avenge the death of a bloodbrother who fought Cú Chulainn in his stead.

This is not to say that Recension 1 is an oral rather than a written composition. Rather, it appears to be a snapshot of *TBC* at a point in its manuscript history when the conventions of oral storytelling were still visible. Some idea of how profound was the adjustment from what was heard to what was seen may be gleaned from Patrick Ford's suggestion that episodes of *TBC* had no fixed order until they were written down.[24] In oral tradition, tales about the same cast of characters can be told singly or severally, on one or multiple occasions, or as part of a group of stories linked only by a theme, such as birth or death. Turning this material into text required the imposition of sequence upon it because written narrative requires a progression from beginning to end. The need to order free-range stories doubtless underlies the references to other versions and authorities (written or oral), implicit admissions that *TBC* had no history in a final form. Certainly this inference is supported by the roles of speaking and writing within the narrative itself: agreements are oral, orders are spoken, messengers tell their errands, and crucial speech is uttered in first-person verse. In contrast, nothing is written other than brief inscriptions on gravestones and withes, which must be deciphered by the few nobles who are able to read. If Recension 1 is emerging from oral tradition, it is no more than halfway into written tradition.

This is what Thomas Kinsella set out to make palatable to a modern audience, by attempting a compromise between the two customary types of translation: popular, which, being aimed at a general audience, tends to be 'eminently readable, constituting stylistic achievements in English, but departing radically from the textual material, formal properties, and linguistic structures of the Irish sources', versus scholarly, which, being aimed at the academic community, often results in 'nearly unreadable gloss translations, utterly lacking in literary interest or merit'.[25] The 'versus' is deliberate, for these categories imply a separation of artistry and accuracy, necessitating a choice between a large, varied readership and a small, specialised one. Kinsella's introduction to *The Táin* delineates an approach that unites both sets of opposites. Foremost he sets out 'to give a living and readable version of the story',[26] and this means abandoning literal translation: 'sentence structure and tense, for example, have been changed without hesitation; elements are occasionally shifted from one sentence to another; proper names have been substituted for pronouns, and vice versa; a different range of verbs has been used; and so on'.[27] On the other hand, wanting 'to give an idea of the simple force of the story at its best',[28] he opted to translate Recension 1, the earliest and starkest version. Rather than clear away its clutter of duplication, digression and commentary, he 'tries not to deviate significantly at any point from the original' and emphasises that 'nothing has been added in the translation beyond a very occasional word or phrase designed to keep the narrative clear'.[29] He has also preserved *TBC*'s prosimetric form, with the qualification that 'greater freedom has been taken with the verse than with the prose, though the sense and structural effects are followed with reasonable faithfulness'.[30]

Yet Kinsella makes sweeping editorial changes whenever fidelity to the original would imperil artistry. His statement that 'As far as possible the story has been freed of inconsistencies and repetitions. Obscurities have been cleared up and missing parts supplied from other sources, generally the Book of Leinster text'[31] is deceptively frank, for he at once confesses and downplays his narrative tidying of 'the original disarray'.[32] When he sets episodes in order, individually and as part of a sequence, he is not restoring coherence but creating it. Additionally, since he presents *The Tain* as a translation of Recension 1, he undermines his own claims by 'correcting' it with readings from Recension 2 (the version that runneth over in the Book of Leinster). In truth he has constructed his translation much as a medieval redactor must have constructed a version in Irish, surveying all available material, favouring one telling, consulting others when in doubt, then cutting, pasting and patching to produce a new *TBC* that is as inclusive and coherent to his contemporaries as he can make it. Like the monks who wrote glosses in the margins – glosses incorporated into the text by later monks – Kinsella anticipates audience questions in endnotes and in a preface of eight independent tales, drawn from various manuscripts and neatened in various ways, that give the background of major characters and events. These tales are not part of *TBC* proper and it is very unlikely that they would have been told in a group to their original audience. Ultimately *The Tain* is as much Recension K(insella) as Recension 1.

In his introduction to the book, Kinsella details the narrative habits of medieval redactors and how they affected his own decisions. Yet he merely lists the authors and titles of previous translations, remarking that he chose Recension 1 partly because Joseph Dunn, Lady Gregory and others had chosen Recension 2. From this it appears that their sole influence on Kinsella was to incite him to do what they had not. But there is translation tradition as well as oral tradition and manuscript tradition, and all three reveal borrowing, divergence and amendment. Joep Leerssen points out that 'between the Gaelic Táin and Kinsella lie the filters of Lady Gregory and of the many authors inspired by her. These earlier Anglo-Irish renderings of the Táin in turn become parameters in a tradition which partly defines Kinsella's own position vis-à-vis his source text.'[33] Every new translation of *TBC* reacts to its predecessors and aims to achieve something they did not. Kinsella wanted to improve on Winifred Faraday's translation of Recension 1, and advances in scholarship enabled him to resolve many of the uncertainties Faraday herself bemoaned. For example, in Faraday's time, the location of episodes and the progress of the invaders could not be traced, 'a careful working-out of the topography of the *Táin* being much needed, many names being still unidentified'.[34] Kinsella had the opportunity to consult experts who correlated *TBC* place-names with geographical locations, finally mapping 'The Route of the Tain'.

Other improvements reflect Kinsella's talent as a poet. Faraday omits the *roscada*, a type of cryptic, alliterative verse, on the grounds that it consists of 'usually meaningless strings of words, with occasional intelligible phrases. In all probability the passages aimed at sound, with only a general suggestion of the drift.'[35] Her argument that it would be pointless to translate poetry that is incoherent in Irish ignores the fact that *TBC* is prosimetric, so omitting verse of any kind damages the narrative. Kinsella reproduced the effect and the enigma of *roscada* by creating equivalents in English, 'passages of verse which more or less match the original for length, ambiguity and obscurity, and which carry the phrases and motifs and occasional short runs that are decipherable in the Irish'.[36] Thus Faraday's footnote 'Here follows about two columns of rhetoric [= *roscada*], consisting of a taunting dialogue between Ailill, Fergus and Medb'[37] is replaced in Kinsella's version by six pages of tense, insinuating verse, Ailill declaring 'not even if you win / can you take my place',[38] Fergus replying with strained dignity 'A pity friend / we hack each other / with sharp words'.[39] When the poetry is included, the characters' accusations incandesce the strong personal conflicts beneath their nominal alliance.

A third influence on translation is what society allows. As mentioned above, all translators try to avoid upsetting their audience: Lady Gregory keeps mum on Cú Chulainn's bizarre distortion in battle, Cecile O'Rahilly balks at translating *macraille* (testicles), and Faraday's euphemisms for sex are gentle enough to pass Disney censors. Since their editions, standards of decency have relaxed, tolerance of graphic violence has increased, and Indo-European comparativists have reclassified as honourably primitive what was once denounced as unprintably disgusting. Today frank text banishes coy ellipses, to the extent that

> what obviously fascinates Kinsella most are the differences between the modern European ethos and the barbarism and heroism of the Táin . . . with its grotesque descriptions of battle frenzy, its cold, matter-of-fact brutality, its enigmatic feats of prowess, its casual, off-hand honesty in matters of sex and excretion. Here as in the nomenclature, Kinsella attempts to show how deeply different ancient Celtic culture was from our own christian/humanist tradition.[40]

Translators once sought to diminish the distance between the 'us' of the audience and the 'them' of *TBC* by rewriting the characters and their actions to meet our approval. Kinsella emphasises the unfamiliarity of *TBC* to evoke our wonder at a world that, like Louis le Brocquy's inkblot illustrations, will never be fully coherent to us. Consider how differently we react to Medb when, as she seduces Fer Diad into fighting Cú Chulainn, she ends her list of promised rewards with Faraday's discreet 'you shall get my love if you need it over and above',[41] versus Kinsella's uninhibited 'and my own friendly thighs on top of that if needs be'[42] – double entendre apt, if accidental.

Bardic poetry and Aogán Ó Rathaille

Far more people are acquainted with *TBC* than with bardic poetry, although their histories suggest that the opposite should be true. Cecile O'Rahilly's full-length edition and English translation of *TBC*, Recension 1 was published in 1976. Decades earlier, the Irish Texts Society had produced multi-volume editions of bardic poetry in the original Irish with accompanying English translations. Among its offerings were the collected verse of Dáibhí Ó Bruadair (three volumes in 1910, 1913 and 1917), Tadhg Dall Ó hUiginn (two volumes in 1922 and 1926), and a bardic miscellany (two volumes in 1939 and 1940). The intricacy of the verse is such that it tends to be translated with obsessive accuracy, if only to prove that the translator has a grip on the syntax. Nevertheless, the language of this poetry – Early Modern Irish – is more accessible to readers with a knowledge of Modern Irish than is the language of *TBC*. Additionally, whereas almost nothing is known of *TBC*'s creation or transmission, the text of a bardic poem is often accompanied by the name of the poet, the name of the patron and the year in which it was composed, while the verses themselves refer to contemporary events. The nearly 2,000 surviving bardic poems offer a panoramic view of the last formal institution of native poetry and occupy a pivotal place in the Irish literary tradition.

Unfortunately, the reasons why bardic poetry should be widely read are also the reasons why it is not. The features that its intended audience found exquisite and engaging are unavailable or incomprehensible to twenty-first-century readers. A bardic poem printed on a page lacks the dimensions of a performance before a patron and his guests, a skilful recitation adorned with music, well-timed pauses, and nuances of tone and gesture that reveal the intentions behind words. Such an experience is incommunicable by text, which tends to accent inherent difficulties and create new ones. The most immediate problem is orthography. Bardic poems were transcribed centuries before the invention of the simplified spelling system (1947), and since there is no dictionary of Early Modern Irish, words may be unrecognisable until they are pronounced aloud. This kind of confusion is trebled by the bards' use of many more forms of words than the current official standard contains. Bards consistently composed in a literary dialect of Irish, which they themselves had designed. To maximise their metrical options, and to ensure that their work would be understood throughout the island, they adopted numerous regional variants that have since fallen out of use. Likewise, the kind of verse they favoured has since fallen out of taste. Bards composing for aristocratic patrons shared the aesthetic of English Enlightenment poets: the ideal is to express the party line cleverly and memorably. To a bard, the style mattered more than the substance. For in the absence of newspapers, radio and television, nobles who craved fame paid high prices for poems that celebrated their attributes, accomplishments and ancestry. The worst eulogies are an avalanche of adjectives, grandiose titles and fawning explanations; the best are the verbal equivalent of eloquent and creditable applause.

Bardic poetry cannot be appreciated without a certain amount of effort by the modern reader, and even in its own time, only a sophisticated, savvy listener would have been attuned to the layers of sound and meaning. One scholar has assured readers that 'after the first fifty or a hundred poems, a fascination, an addiction even, develops',[43] conceding that addiction rather than withdrawal can be agonisingly slow. Since a bardic poem may consist of more than a hundred four-line stanzas, if a newcomer must wade through 'fifty or a hundred' such poems before s/he is hooked, then bardic poetry is a vice that is far easier to decline than to develop. Only a fraction of the existing material has been edited and translated, and the difficulty of approaching this genre has been compounded by a shortage of rhetorical analysis. Whereas the bards' world-view, political awareness and factual reliability have been examined in detail, there have been few attempts to explain how their poems function. How is a matter broached and an argument built up, from the opening to the final stanza? How are titles constructed and placed to prick a patron's conscience or chip away his resistance? How does the recital of a mythological story, an ancestor's fate or the history of a place-name create the impression of a destiny that it would be disastrous to refuse? In the absence of arguments to the contrary, descriptions of bardic poetry as monotonous, unimaginative and insincere have prevailed. Yet bards produced the humorous and lively *Iomarbhágh na bhFileadh* (The Contention of the Bards), an island-wide debate about everything from propriety in poetry to the place of the New English in Irish society; and the last formally trained poets, educated for a trade that had nearly vanished, parodied the English legal warrant in the *barántas*, authorising lethal redress for the theft of cheese, dungheaps and old hats. Contrary to stereotype, those who had been schooled in the tradition of bardic poetry did not produce an undifferentiated mass of verse. The quality and content of each poem depend on the composer's skill.

For instance, Giolla Brighde Mac Con Midhe (d.1272) could make a marvel of a praise poem. One of his finest was addressed to Aodh mac Feidhlimidh Ó Conchobhair, a patron who resided at Cruachain. Beginning 'Dearmad do fhágbhas ag Aodh; / triallam dá fhios don athtaom' (I left behind with Aodh something I forgot; let us go to visit him again),[44] the poet appears to be casually recalling an instance of carelessness and taking practical steps to correct it. Once he has done so, however, he confides 'Mar bheirim uidhe ar m'aghaidh / 's mo chúl ris Ó gConchobhair, / bídh mo rún ag triall óm thoigh / siar ar mo chúl go Cruachoin' (As I make my way forward with my back to Ó Conchobhair, my heart is ever journeying from my house back behind me to Cruachain).[45] The image of the poet heading home while longing to backtrack hints that his memory is not as faulty as he claims. When in succeeding stanzas he confesses to leaving behind a needle, a brooch and a glove, each oversight justifying another visit to Ó Conchobhair, suspicion gels into certainty: Mac Con Midhe has been inventing excuses to return to Cruachain because Ó Conchobhair is such a delightful host. This sly, amusing prologue leads gracefully into praise of Ó Conchobhair, with whom Mac Con Midhe has the ideal poet–patron relationship. The poet's art and the patron's worthiness are mutually sustaining, for whenever the poet calls on his patron with a praise poem, he is so lavishly rewarded that he is inspired to compose another. Reminded of Aodh's feasting hall – note that his memory is as accurate now as it was unreliable before – Mac Con Midhe takes the opportunity to describe the famous artefacts upon its walls, a horn, gold cups, a standard, each a testament to the owner's glory. Burnishing them with his refrain 'mór an dearmad nár dhéachsam' (great my omission not to have seen it), 'mo dhearmad gan a ndéachsoin' (my omission it was not have seen), 'Do budh mór an dearmad damh / gan . . . d'fhéachadh' (It was a great oversight on my part not to see),[46] the poet neatly sets up a second series of pretexts. Having neglected these wonders, he must plan future visits in order to examine them. Beginning and ending with the same ploy is the thematic equivalent of *dúnadh* (closure), a device in which the first and last word/s of a poem are exactly the same. This is a conventional praise poem, but its wit, charm and personality make it a pleasure to read. It must have brought down the house when it was vocally unfolded, line by line, before Ó Conchobhair and his guests. One can easily imagine the host casting amused glances around the feasting hall and returning the smiles of his visitors, who would have recognised in the poem the comical reflection of their own desire to remain.

At the opposite end of the emotional spectrum is Tadhg Óg Ó hUiginn's (d.1448) elegy for Tadhg Mac Cathail. As Ó Conchobhair was to Mac Con Midhe, Mac Cathail was a beloved patron to Ó hUiginn, and Mac Con Midhe's delight in Ó Conchobhair's company is matched by Ó hUiginn's desolation at Mac Cathail's death. Unprepared for the unthinkable, Ó hUiginn initially believed that the messenger was mistaken: 'Truagh mar thargamar a ceilt / oighidh laoich Locha Deirgdeirc; / nochar léigheas a lomadh / an céidfhios do-chualomar' (I tried to discredit the death of the hero of Deirgdeirc; I would not listen to the telling of that first account of it)[47] until proof made denial impossible. Aware that cynics may dismiss his sorrow as lip-service, the poet declares 'Is cian ó chumhaidh fhallsa / an toirse a-tá ormsa; / gan éanduine gum fheitheamh / ar ndéaraine dáilfithear' (No feigned grief mine, my tears will flow while no one sees me).[48] It is his duty publicly to mourn a patron, but he has practical and emotional reasons for sadness. The deceased was a devoted patron who treated Ó hUiginn as 'ollamh 's a fhear cumuinn' (his chief poet and friend).[49] So close was their relationship that others were jealous, and without Mac Cathail's protection, his favourite is as miserable as he once was merry, exclaiming 'Tugais doimheanma 'n-a díol / mo mhoirn ó mhac an airdríogh' (A sorrow, O prince, hast thou inflicted on me equal to all the joy I ever got from thee).[50] He is anguished too on behalf of his patron, who 'Do-ghéabhadh inmhe a athar . . . gan chumhgachadh' (would have got his father's place without trouble)[51] had not death overtaken him as it did Cormac Connloingeas, a legendary doomed prince. Cormac, son of the Ulster king Conchobhar mac Nessa, had gone into exile in Connacht. When Conchobhar died, Cormac accepted the Ulstermen's invitation to return and rule them. But his reverse-defection angered Medb, the Connacht ruler who had granted him refuge, and she had him killed on his way home to take the kingship. From Ó hUiginn's perspective, his patron's death is a duplicate tragedy of wasted promise. He bolsters the comparison with a recital of Mac Cathail's victories that renews his fame and hints at his capacity for still greater achievements. Ó hUiginn's lament exposes layer upon layer of loss, of a friend, of a patron, of thwarted potential, of the glorious era that Mac Cathail's rule would have been. By voicing every consequence of his death, the poet speaks for all who mourn Mac Cathail and creates a verbal monument to his memory. In print it is as striking and affecting as it must have been in performance that he refers to Mac Cathail in the third person for fifty of the fifty-one stanzas, the one exception being a reproach that the poet would never have needed to utter were his patron alive.

The work of Dáibhí Ó Bruadair (d.1698) is marked by the fact that poetry ceased to be a viable profession during his lifetime. Since there was no demand for poems on the standard topics, he composed verse on whatever preoccupied him. Likewise, instead of having them performed for patrons in feasting halls, he recited them to fellow poets at meetings they held in friendly houses and taverns. Only colleagues could have appreciated Ó Bruadair's artistry and

concerns, and understood his inner turbulence in 'Is mairg nár chrean' (Woe
Unto Him who Hath Failed), as he remembers the wealth and popularity of
his youth: 'An tamall im ghlaic do mhair an ghléphinginn / ba geanamhail
gart dar leat mo thréighthesí' (As long as a coin of bright silver remained in
this hand of mine / Attractive and witty, thou well mayst surmise, were my
qualities).[52] With a mixture of pride and regret he recalls a welcome in every
house, an admiring audience, and lavish spending as befits a noble – until a
downturn in his fortunes painfully altered his faith in prosperity and in friends:
'D'athruigh 'na ndearcaibh dath mo néimhe anois / ar aiste nach aithnid ceart
im chéimeannaibh' (Immediately changed in their eyes was the hue of my
character, / No longer do they recognise in my muse's steps excellence).[53]
Bewildered that 'an bleachtas bréige' (fallacious success)[54] could wreak such
havoc in his life, he strives to comprehend what has happened by distilling and
ordering his thoughts in verse. Sustained by the structure of the poem, which
proves that he is truly an artist, he admits to the humiliation of digging ditches
to earn a living: 'le harm nár chleachtas feacht ba mhéithe mé, / d'atadar
m'ailt ó rath na crélainne / is do mharbh a feac ar fad mo mhéireanna' (With
an implement ne'er by me wielded in days of prosperity, / From guiding the
run of the clay-blade my knuckles all swollen are / And the spade-shaft hath
deadened my fingers),[55] the same fingers with which 'do tharrainginn dais
ba cleas ar chléireachaibh' (I used to draw dashes which wholly outwitted
the other clerks).[56] That he is earnestly trying to discern the path that led to
his downfall is clear from his willingness to accept blame as well as to assign
it. His friends deserted him, but he squandered money that he should have
saved for an uncertain future. Now he can only pray that resignation to his
fate in this life will win him mercy in the next: 'ós éigion dúinn iomchar na
daoirse atá / réidh a rúin m'ionntrust i dtír na ngrás' (Since I must endure
the present pitiless captivity, / Prepare my interest, O Darling, for me in the
land of grace).[57] It is startling to imagine this honest, elegant poem forming
in the mind of a labourer shovelling mud, a contrast mirrored by the glory
of Heaven being requested by a bard sunk to the bottom of society. Realists
like Ó Bruadair did not expect a divine reprieve, and he acknowledges that
even if God esteems bards as men do not, He will not reward them until their
harsh lives are over. The real hope in Ó Bruadair's work is its sheer existence:
by continuing to compose as expertly as if he were in a patron's employ, he
reaffirms the value of his art and guards its place in Irish culture.

Michael Hartnett had considered the Irish language 'merely another school
subject, not a key to another culture' until a friend quoted, then translated
some of Dáibhí Ó Bruadair's poetry.[58] That recital impressed upon Hartnett

the historical and literary reality of poetry in Irish, with Ó Bruadair its foremost representative. Consequently he was more than a little disconcerted by the text of Ó Bruadair's poems: 'When I read him . . . I was shocked. I could not understand his verse! It seemed a gnarled, concertina'd kind of Gaelic written for a distant and savage people.'[59] *Seeing* bardic poetry undid the enchantment of *hearing* it; Hartnett's perception of the balance of sense and sound was blocked by the syntactic jungle made visible in print. Years later, determined 'to unravel his language'[60] once and for all, Hartnett began with what originally attracted him: 'I did to his poems what should be done to all poems: I read them aloud – and slowly began to understand them.'[61] Listening led to insight into the poetry and the poet, whose snobbery was another challenge: 'this aristocratic *hauteur* was something I disliked . . . but I was making the mistake of judging him by mid-twentieth-century liberal standards – I had to reconsider his real position within his *own* society'.[62] Hartnett realised that Ó Bruadair's arrogance was integrity according to a tradition in which 'the Holy Trinity was not so much Father, Son and Holy Ghost as Prince, Prelate and Poet'.[63] Moreover, since Ó Bruadair's personality infused his poetry, smoothing over his abrasive traits would render any translation of his work bland and false. In order to translate the verse, Hartnett would have to translate the man who spoke through it: 'I want to find a way to make his poetry acceptable to our taste, and to employ as much of his technique as I can master, [and] I also want to find a "voice" for him; and this task is most important of all.'[64]

The translations in Hartnett's *O Bruadair* do convey a sense of the poet as well as the poetry, of an individual concentrating his experiences and emotions into lines strong enough to contain them. This impression that composing was an instinctive reaction is enhanced by the varied and vivid selections from Ó Bruadair's work. Along with mournful elegies, shrewd observations and philosophical musings are deeply serrated satires. 'Seirbhíseach seirgthe' (A shrivelled-up skivvy),[65] aimed at a serving-girl who refused Ó Bruadair beer on credit, is a burr in verse that demonstrates why a poet's curse was as feared as his praise was desired. His descriptions of her plummet from bad to horrendous, 'Seirbhíseach seirgthe íogair srónach seasc' (A shrivelled-up skivvy, snappy, nosy, dry),[66] 'an deilbhín gan deirglí' (wizened old midget),[67] 'Meirgíneach bheirbhthe í gan ceol na cab' (over-done slut with no note in her throat),[68] and finally 'Reilgín an eilitín nach d'ord na mban / is seisce gnaoi dá bhfeiceamaoid i ród re maith / a beith na daoi ós deimhin dí go deo na dtreabh' (no woman at all, that club-footed bitch, / with the driest old face you could meet on a trip / she talks apishly now and she always will).[69] These caricatures are accented by the percussive repetition of consonants and vowels, e.g. 'seirgthe' (shrivelled) and 'seirbhíseach' (skivvy), 'gan deirglí' (wizened), and 'deilbhín' (midget). Similarly, generosity being the mark of nobility, he believes her stinginess bespeaks bloodlines so base that her lovers or offspring would have to be subhuman: 'ba bheag an díth dá mbeireadh sí do ghósta cat' (small harm if she pupped a cat to a ghost).[70] The physicality of Ó Bruadair's imagery avenges her rough treatment of him, and however long her outrage rankled, his reprisal has lasted far longer. No paper that bears this satire is truly acid-free. But when this short, packed and very pointed satire was hurled aloud, in tones as cutting as its insults and as vehement as its curses, it must have struck the skivvy like a flight of arrows. Moreover, these verses would have lodged in the memories of witnesses, whose every retelling would have helped immortalise her in ridicule.

Hartnett has also translated poetry by Aogán Ó Rathaille. Born forty-five years after Ó Bruadair, Ó Rathaille experienced many of the same hardships, foremost a shortage of patronage, and responded to adversity with powerful and often experimental verse. Instead of composing in *dán díreach*, the traditional bardic metres, Ó Rathaille preferred *amhrán*, newer metres that the bards had considered unsuitable for formal poetry. Owing to Frank O'Connor's much-anthologised 'Brightness of Brightness', 'A Sleepless Night' and 'Last Lines', Ó Rathaille is best known for his *aisling* (vision) poems and bitter complaints. But folk tradition remembers his keen sense of humour, which manifested in pranks and exuberantly funny poems. He was one of the first to take up the *barántas*, a Munster genre in which the poet assumes a sheriff's authority, uses English and Latin legalese, and issues formal complaints about a crime, in a manner that celebrates oral Irish poetry at the expense of written English law. No patron is praised more highly than the victim and his pilfered property, whose character, value and history are invested with every conceivable virtue. Conversely, the criminal is lynched by satire, adjudged physically and morally deficient, deformed and disgusting. Whatever transgression he has committed, a posse is ordered to bring him back, none too gently, for summary execution. Composing a *barántas* must have given a poet far greater satisfaction than he ever received from the real enforcers of English law, and such a poem would delight anyone who had been victimised by a criminal or an officer. The genre's wide appeal supports Pádraig Ó Fiannachta's theory that the *barántas* circulated mainly by word of mouth.

'On a Cock Stolen from a Good Priest' is Hartnett's version of Ó Rathaille's earliest *barántas*, inspired by a priest who bought a rooster at a fair, asked the sheriff's servant to deliver it to his home, and was confounded when it failed to appear. When Ó Rathaille heard of the incident, he must have been tickled by the irony that the presumed thief was an employee of the man responsible for apprehending him. The poet undertook the job for the sheriff by composing a *barántas*, whose very first stanza displays the characteristic mixture of authenticity and improvisation:

> whereas Aonghus, fáithchliste,
>   Sagart cráibhtheach, críostaightheach,
> Do theacht indiu im láithir-se,
>   le gearán cáis is fírinne

> (*Whereas* Aonghus, wise in prophecy,
>   a pious priest and Christian man;
> today into my presence came
>   complaining, stating truthfully)[71]

The official 'whereas', the complainant's name and the formal request for action are retained, but are accompanied by superfluous praise of the victim, who is accounted 'fáithchliste' (wise in prophecy) and 'cráibhtheach' (pious). This small step beyond the bounds of protocol is followed by a giant leap as the stolen bird is rapturously described as 'Ba bhreághta scread is bláthmhaise / Is baic le scáil gach líondatha' (of lovely crow, and beautiful / and his nape was gleaming, colour-full),[72] 'b'aoibhinn cúilbhrice' (speckle-backed delightfully),[73] and worth 'caogad mínscilling' (fifty shillings).[74] Glorifying the rooster turns its theft into the abduction of a prizewinner, and to drive home the gravity of the crime, Ó Rathaille reminds the audience that of all people a priest 'Ba ghábhadh dá shamhuil dáirithe / Coileach screaduighthe is dúistighthe / Do bheith dá fhaireadh ar shámhchodhladh / I n-am gach easpuirt úrnaighthe' (needs a crowing cock to wake him up, / to watch in case of dozing off / every time that Vespers call).[75] Aonghus may be unable to fulfil his religious duties for want of his alarm-cock, and it is imperative that the thief be punished appropriately. Ó Rathaille orders his bailiffs 'Tugaidh chugham-sa é ar ruainseachán, / Go gcrochadh é mar dhreoileacán' (bring him here in cords tied up / that I may hang him for the wretch he is)[76] – a harsh penalty for stealing, perhaps, but no harsher than the penalty meted out to bards in 1570 by John Perrot, the first president of Munster, for the crime of having no permanent employer. Note that there is no mention of an investigation or a trial; since officers of the law are never mistaken, a man's capture is sufficient proof of his guilt. To legitimise the procedure he has outlined, Ó Rathaille announces 'For your so doing, d'oibliogáid, / Ag so uaim díbh bhur n-ughdarás' (For your so doing as your duty 'tis / you now by me are authorised)[77] and this, along with his closing lines 'Mar scríobhas mo lámh le cleiteachán, / An lá so d'aois an Uachtaráin' (Written by my hand and quill / in this era of the President),[78] reminds his audience that the *barántas* is as valid and unbiased as the document on which it is modelled. Both the sheriff and the priest would have appreciated these playful verses, which by putting the theft in perspective might have made a real warrant unnecessary. Aonghus has lost a rooster, but not nearly as excellent a one as Ó Rathaille describes; Aonghus would like to see the thief punished, but not hanged; and Aonghus's hens will be lonely, but Aonghus is no more likely than usual to sleep through Vespers. The theft of the bird is an inconvenience, but the sequel to the crime is sheer delight.

It was noted earlier that medieval Irish scholars energetically debate whether Irish tales from the early medieval period were composed orally and then mechanically transcribed or were composed as they were written down. In the case of medieval Irish verse, there is less dispute that professional poets composed orally for an audience of listeners. To bards, poetry was always an architecture of sound, not to be read silently from the page but to be perceived in performance like music or drama. Trained poets did not record their own work in writing until they perceived that it would not be heard, memorised and recited by a continuous line of successors, such as had existed for centuries before. Modern readers must resist the assumption that this poetry was intended to be presented as text. The inevitable blank margins surrounding a printed poem are a healthy reminder that it has come down to us divested of its aural effects, formal setting, social and personal context. We are too far removed from its performance to fill in all the gaps, but we can at least bear in mind that there is many a slip between text and lip, and that what we see is not what the audience was intended to receive.

Folklore and the Irish language

The introduction to this chapter emphasised that the separation of 'literature' and 'oral tradition' requires a careful definition of terms, awareness of the preconceptions attached to them, and acceptance that this exercise is literally and figuratively 'academic', i.e. an aim of professional scholars and understood to be theoretical rather than practical. Similarly, this section subverts its title by warning that the separation of 'folklore' and 'Irish language' is at best conditional and at worst impossible. From the nineteenth century onward, these two were considered the most indigenous, ancient and authentic aspects of Irish culture and therefore the core of Irish identity. This perspective explains why 'the revival of the Irish language and the preservation of Irish folklore were parallel undertakings', the term and the concept evolving together:

> The word *béaloideas* has been established as the Irish for folklore probably from the early years of the Gaelic League (founded in 1893). The word has been used at least since the late 1620s, when Geoffrey Keating (Seathrún Céitinn) used it in his Irish history, *Forus Feasa ar Éirinn*. But the concept of folklore did not then exist . . . its rebirth with a contemporary meaning was typical of efforts to renew the Irish language.[79]

The Gaelic League was not alone in linking the language and the folklore ingrained in it. Gaeltacht teacher, writer and activist Máirtín Ó Cadhain declared in exasperation 'Ní hé tábhacht na Gaeltachta gur féidir Gaeilge a fhoghlaim inti. Ná gur féidir an Ghaeilge a scéitheadh amach aisti ar an gcuid eile den tír. Beag baol. Is inti a chleachtaítear na seannósanna. Is inti is mó atá béaloideas. Níl sa nGaeltacht ach brainse den bhéaloideas' (The importance of the Irish-speaking community isn't that Irish can be learned there. Nor that Irish can spread from there to the rest of the country. Fat chance. It's there that the old customs are practised. It's there that folklore is most plentiful. The Irish-speaking community is only a branch of folklore).[80] Such a claim may seem extravagant, but the fact remains that the majority of Irish folklore, like the majority of Irish literature, exists in the Irish language. Moreover, James Delargy – a founding member of the Folklore of Ireland Society (1927) and editor of its famed journal *Béaloideas* – held that knowledge of Modern Irish was scarcely separable from knowledge of Irish folklore, and together these were the wellspring of Irish literature: 'Dar linn-ne, pé leitríocht Ghaedhilge a sgríofar feasta i n-Éirinn muna mbeidh sí Gaedhealach agus muna mbeidh a préamhacha bunuithe, greamaithe i leitríocht agus i mbéaloideas na Gaedhilge, ní bheidh innti ach rud leamh-neamblasta gan áird' (It seems to us that whatever literature in Irish will be written in Ireland from now on will be dull, bland and insignificant unless it will be Irish and unless its roots are based and fixed in the literature and folklore of Irish).[81] Although modern authors rejected oral narrative style, the plots, characters and themes of folklore have been very successfully integrated into compositions by writers from W. B. Yeats and Flann O'Brien to Seamus Heaney and Vincent Woods.

In 1935, the groundbreaking rescue-work carried out in *Béaloideas* was aided and abetted by the Irish government. Its funding of the Irish Folklore Commission made possible the employment of full-time and part-time collectors, and the enlistment of primary school students and teachers in a survey carried out in 1937–8 that resulted in the 500,000-page 'Schools Collection'. During

the 1970s folklore departments were established in what are now University
College Dublin and University College Cork, the Dublin department being
the successor to the Irish Folklore Commission itself. Integration into the university system has greatly facilitated the study of folklore, providing skilled
instruction, access to collections and the opportunity to explore supplemen-
tary disciplines, such as history and art. Since then, there has been growing
recognition that 'literature has always been enriched by folklore, and the history of narratives passes from the oral to the literary and back again'.[82]

Yet if folklore has escaped obscurity, it has not escaped preconceptions
about oral tradition as 'implicitly or explicitly opposed to the world of reading
and writing', even though, as Diarmuid Ó Giolláin observes, 'the growing
proximity to each other of the "oral" and the "literary" is a feature of the
development of all modern societies'.[83] The first three volumes of *The Field
Day Anthology of Irish Writing* (1991) met with a notoriously critical reception
for their glaring and glared-at sins of omission, chief among them a lack of
works in Irish and works by women. Two additional volumes were compiled
to redress these problems, their title, *The Field Day Anthology of Irish Writing:
Irish Women's Writing and Traditions* (2002), emphasising that literature by Irish
women encompasses two languages and two media. Women's art in oral
composition, in Irish and in English, is asserted by the inclusion of spoken
or sung reminiscences, folk-tales, poems, songs and prayers. The pronounced
split between volumes one to three and volumes four to five of *The Field
Day Anthology* will convince many – especially those who have relied on the
reviews – that female composers, the Irish language and oral tradition stand
in opposition to male composers, the English language and written literature.
This view is a convenience of critics who ignore prominent exceptions such
as Gabriel Rosenstock, a man who writes poetry in Irish, and Mary Lavin, a
woman who wrote short stories in English. It is far easier to posit consistent
combinations of gender, language and medium in the Irish literary tradition
than to prove that they prevail.

Likewise, it should be understood that the scarcity of literature ascribed
to women during the medieval centuries reflects only what has survived in
writing; absence from manuscripts does not prove either a former dearth
or a former abundance. On the other hand, we do know enough about the
manuscript tradition to surmise what kinds of material were less likely to be
written down. Whether the recorders were monks, scribes or impoverished
bards, they transcribed an utterance because its contents were vitally important, its composition was exemplary, and/or it was at risk of being lost forever.
Pride in its value, then dread of its disappearance appears to have motivated

the writing of early Irish law, history and literature. During the period of bardic poetry, patrons had verse recorded for the purpose of documenting their family's fame. When patrons became scarce, professional poets who continued to compose, including Dáibhí Ó Bruadair and Aogán Ó Rathaille, wrote out their poems because there was no next generation to memorise and recite them.

Therefore the written tradition should be poor in material that recorders considered ordinary in content, poor in quality or assured of oral transmission. Undoubtedly a trivial or faulty composition would have been excluded from memory as naturally as from manuscript, unless it were retained for amusement or as a negative exemplar. But a great deal of information would have been commonly known without being inconsequential. If the formal tradition governed professions and institutions, codifying law, religious teachings and trade rules, folk tradition was the manual for everyday life, from the uses of seaweed to protection against supernatural dangers. These keys to health, safety and prosperity passed orally from generation to generation in the normal course of life, as children observed their elders, participated alongside them and eventually taught children of their own. Its sheer ordinariness would have disqualified folk tradition from being recorded by professional scholars, who prioritised the literature of their own elite institutions and rarely concerned themselves with compositions that were authored and orally circulated within the general population; the large-scale recording of narratives about the folk-hero Fionn mac Cumaill did not occur until its aristocratic rival, the Ulster Cycle, had fallen out of fashion. 'At any time in the history of Irish', comments Seán Ó Coileáin, 'we may suppose the existence of different levels of oral tradition, closely associated with their corresponding social classes, which would not have been regarded as fit material for inclusion in manuscript.'[84] Indeed, a strong oral existence might have kept a genre out of books altogether. Since folk tradition flourished in every community, there would have been a continual supply of new participants, and writing would have seemed an unnecessary precaution. In fact when the Gaelic League undertook to publish collections of folk-tales, the abundance of material soon flooded the market and may have whetted the public's taste for modern literature in Irish.

The earliest written mention of some oral genres indicates that they were already well developed and established. When subsequent records, however intermittent, give the same impression, it is small risk to reason that the genre has been practised and refined for many generations.[85] A prime example is the *caoineadh* or keen, a verse lament for the dead that was composed and performed in the presence of the assembled mourners. It consisted of testimony by those who knew the deceased intimately, e.g. as spouse, child or sibling, each participant contributing to a composite portrait of him. His closest female relatives, often assisted by noted experts in the art, sat around the body and sorted themselves into 'a soloist who established the rhythm and sang or chanted along, and two, four, or more other women who listened carefully and answered her in chorus'.[86] Note that 'solo' and 'chorus' were roles that any member of the group could assume; the same voice was not always dominant, nor the rest solely responsive. Much of the lament was composed extemporaneously as a performer took up the current theme, modified it or introduced a new one. Their collaboration produced what critic Angela Bourke has called 'a long, ragged rant, rhymed and rhythmic; interspersed with stylized sobs and wailings, chanted, sung or spoken'.[87] The inarticulate cries that punctuated the lament were part of the keening women's freedom to manifest all symptoms of distress, 'dealing with all the stages of what modern psychology recognizes as a process of grieving: denial, anger, bargaining, sadness and acceptance'.[88] There were also non-vocal dramatic gestures, such as rocking back and forth or tearing at one's own hair and clothing. This vicarious indulgence helped onlookers purge their grief and eased their adjustment to the new absence in their lives. Because many of the techniques used to effect this release cannot be written, 'perhaps the most important point to bear in mind is that what may appear to us as a text . . . is not a literary composition, nor merely an oral composition either, but part of a dramatic performance of which the verbal element is but one factor'.[89]

It may come as a surprise that the keen could be critical and humorous as well as affectionate and respectful. But a certain amount of irreverence must have been irresistible because the lament was made by the women who were most familiar with the personality, habits and opinions of the deceased. No one was better able to give due praise and blame, and keening a man gave them a unique opportunity to voice long-held and long-suppressed grievances. Directly addressing him in the keen gave them the satisfaction of the very last word. Their privileges on this occasion allowed them to speak ill of the dead, provided the ill was obliquely expressed. Because the language of keening was formulaic, even a subtle change to a stock phrase could transform its meaning so that 'the most devastating criticism could be made to seem quite innocuous by clever turns of the traditional formulas'.[90]

Rachel Bromwich warns that 'keens are to be sharply distinguished from the dignified and formal *Marbhnaí*, or elegies, which were the work of professional poets'[91] and so too Tomás Ó hAilín notes in his article about the keen 'níor thagair mé sa léacht seo don mharbhna, don chaoineadh liteartha (nó léannta), a cheapadh na filí ar dhaoine iomráiteacha' (I didn't refer in this study to the *marbhna*, the literary (or learned) keen, which the poets made about prominent people).[92] While the keen of folk tradition and the elegy of formal tradition were distinct genres and were performed in disparate social contexts, these two types of verse nevertheless share significant features. Both were composed by specialists who spoke in the first person, reviewed the life of the deceased, utilised stock epithets and sound effects, provided the official statement of grief, and left a lasting impression of grace or disgrace. In terms of public perception, the keen was as indispensable to the honour of the deceased as was bardic poetry to that of the patron. As Angela Bourke has pointed out, 'Women's lament poetry of the Irish tradition [was recognised] as belonging to the order of powerful utterance: praise and blame which must be carefully wrought because they are not simply ephemeral compositions of verbal art, but powerful instruments.'[93] In spite of its long history, however, the lament tradition was little studied outside the Gaeltacht until nineteenth-century folklorists made available *Caoineadh Airt Uí Laoghaire* (The Lament for Art O'Leary).

Of the several versions they recorded, the fullest was recited by a woman who was herself an expert keener, well able to appreciate and remember a superb piece of work. An Irish version edited by Seán Ó Tuama and translations by Frank O'Connor, Thomas Kinsella and Éilís Dillon have made the poem and its background familiar to most. As a nudge to memory: Art O'Leary, a 21-year-old officer in the Austrian army, returned to Ireland around 1767 and insisted on retaining both his sword and his prize horse. Having thus broken two of the infamous Penal Laws, he was pursued by Abraham Morris, high sheriff of Cork. He was still on the run in 1773 when he was informed on by a man named John Cooney and shot to death by a pursuing soldier. In all probability this event would have been remembered propagandistically as the killing of a handsome, defiant Irishman by an envious, ruthless Englishman, had not the words of Art's widow, Eibhlín Ní Chonaill, recast it as a personal tragedy. When she keens him, his violent end is not the focus but the lens that sharpens her memory and intensifies her passion.

Long before she alludes to his death, Eibhlín enables her audience to grasp the depth of her feelings for Art. She begins by relating their history in terms that are simultaneously realistic and idealistic: 'Thug mo shúil aire dhuit, / Thug mo chroí taitneamh duit, / D'ealaíos óm athair leat' (My eye observed you, / My heart approved you, / I fled from my father with you).[94] Love at first sight did not blind her to the sacrifice she would have to make: since her father disliked him, she had to decide which man had the greater claim on her affection. Aware that others might have decided differently, she declares 'Is domhsa nárbh aithreach' (I never repented it)[95] because her spouse's behaviour vindicated her attachment to him. With real pleasure she describes how well he provided for her, supplying specific, concrete details about the beauty of their house, the quality of the food, and the luxury of sleeping late, knowing that servants would perform the early morning tasks. Proud as she is of Art's virtues as a husband, she is even prouder of his virtues as a man, boasting: 'D'umhlaídís Sasanaigh / Síos go talamh duit' (The Saxons bowed to you),[96] fearing and hating him for being their superior. Interspersed with Eibhlín's expressions of tenderness, the Englishmen's 'aon-chorp eagla' (deadly fear)[97] and 'aon-chorp gráine' (deadly hatred)[98] are as jarring as wrong notes in a serenade, and the dissonance artfully reflects her state of mind. The polar reactions Art evokes collide on the day his mare returns home, bearing only a bloody saddle. Loving him and knowing that others loathe him, Eibhlín is filled with foreboding, and her one thought is to find him: 'Thugas léim go tairsigh, / An dara léim go geata, / An tríú léim ar mo chapall' (My first leap reached the threshold, / My second reached the gateway, / My third leap reached the saddle).[99] Heedless of her own safety, she rides to where his body lies. Her previous statements of affection decipher her claim 'Do chuid fola leat 'na sraithibh; / Is níor fhanas le hí ghlanadh / Ach í ól suas lem basaibh' (Your heart's blood was still flowing; / I did not stay to wipe it / But filled my hands and drank it)[100] as an act of devotion in which she embraces her last possible union with him. But these alarmed and alarming actions may owe more to keening conventions than to factual deeds. Since the greater the love, the greater the loss, it is usual for a keener to claim she was deranged by grief, and Eibhlín is still in the first stage of denial. Even with the corpse before her, she urges 'éirigh suas id sheasamh / Is tar liom féin abhaile' (Rise up from where you're lying / And we'll be going homewards).[101]

This desperate plea ends Eibhlín's first series of lines, and from here on others add to the keen, Art's father briefly, his sister extensively. There is unmistakable rivalry between the two women, for the sister immediately challenges the wife's portrayal of herself as a devoted widow. Prefacing injury with insult, the sister recalls that Art had his pick of pretty, wealthy women, any of whom would have been a credit to him as a wife. Then in a knife-twist as neat as the turn in a sonnet, she reveals in the last two lines that Eibhlín was not one of them. His death so little affected her that she slept while everyone else – including the sister, of course – was awake mourning him. Stung and perhaps caught off-guard, Eibhlín energetically refutes these charges, declaring that she went to bed to comfort the children. Her conduct was that of a good mother, not a derelict wife. Unconvinced, the sister continues to vie with her. When

Eibhlín avows she would have taken the bullet in his stead, the sister makes the same claim. Eibhlín praises him as a husband and a father, whereupon his sister idolises him as a son, a brother and a bachelor. Expertise and her status as widow give Eibhlín the edge to close the keen. Vowing revenge, cursing John Cooney and all who played a part in Art's death, she asserts that the end of her lament is not the end of her grief. This tragic loss has left her heart 'Dúnta suas go dlúth / Mar a bheadh glas a bheadh ar thrúnc / 'S go raghadh an eochair amú' (Closed up tight and firm / Like a trunk that is locked / And the key is mislaid).[102] Her heart is shut forever, as his coffin will be, and her sorrow is as lasting as his absence. Having finally accepted the fact of his death, Eibhlín stops addressing her remarks to him and invites the mourners to give him a final toast. They too must say goodbye because the man whom she incited – 'éirigh suas' (rise up) – is soon to be 'ag iompar cré agus cloch' (weighed down by earth and stones).[103]

The first performance of the Lament must have been riveting, with different voices rising and falling, the excitement of artistic improvisation, and the atmosphere charged with the tension between Art's wife and sister. On the page, their lines still resound with passion and pride, but in print the Lament is presented as a poem by Eileen O'Leary rather than as a traditional keen by Eibhlín Ní Chonaill *et alia*. Dealing first with the issue of single authorship, it has been shown that the stanzas by Art's sister are a crucial counterpoint to the stanzas by Eibhlín. The sister is a capable competitor because her skill in keening is supplemented by a knowledge of Art that his wife cannot match. In addition, habitually naming Eibhlín as the author of the keen gives her sole creative credit not only for the Lament for Art O'Leary, but for the lament tradition within which she composed it. Thus, 'The uniqueness of Eibhlín's composition has been stressed to such an extent that her participation in a communal women's performance tradition is almost forgotten.'[104] Focusing on her individual talent and ignoring her use of keening conventions implies that hers was a lone gifted voice crying in an inept wilderness. But since the Lament is part of a long tradition, its excellence derives from the excellence of every keen from which its composers learned their craft. In terms of quality, as poet Nuala Ní Dhomhnaill declares, 'Eibhlín Dubh's composition is not a fluke; it just happens to be one of the very few (almost) complete keens that is extant.'[105]

'(Almost) complete' is perniciously true of the Lament's published versions. To accommodate readers of written literature, editors chose one of the recorded oral versions to serve as the printed standard, fixing the order of the stanzas, the speakers of the stanzas, and the lines of which those stanzas consist.

Furthermore, they brought that single version into line with their ideal of the Lament by leaving out the unsatisfactory portions. How drastic these changes could be may be understood from a single instance. In what Seán Ó Tuama calls the 'B' version of the Lament, Eibhlín remembers that Art used to hit her with a stick, for spending too freely yet failing to keep the larder full.[106] Her protestations that she gave him cause to beat her and is neither complaining nor reproaching him for it hints that that is exactly what she is doing: in the doublespeak of keening language, she is announcing that she did not deserve to be struck and that he expected her to do too much with too small a housekeeping allowance. Criticism of this sort is entirely consonant with keening, which sets out to provide a full and true description of the deceased. But these lines are regularly omitted because Art would seem less sympathetic and Eibhlín less in love if she portrayed him as an abusive skinflint. Removing the Lament from its origin in the keening tradition has allowed it to be recast to such an extent that far more readers think of it as a written work in English than as an oral composition in Irish.

In 1998 Breandán Ó Buachalla put forth a third conception, namely, the Lament as a written composition in Irish. Tellingly, his book *An Caoine agus an Chaointeoireacht* (The Keen and the Practice of Keening) is the first volume in a series called *Lúb ar Phár*, a punning combination of two Irish phrases, *lúb ar lár* (literally 'a loop on the floor'), meaning 'an omission or mistake', and *ar phár* (literally 'on paper'), meaning 'written down'. Deducing from its components, a *lúb ar phár* should be a publication that aims to correct a scholarly oversight. This is an apt characterisation of *An Caoine*. Mirroring McCone's revisionist reading of medieval Irish literature, Ó Buachalla examines the history of the Lament, finds little or no foundation for views that have become standard, then proposes a radical new interpretation. To take just a few points, Ó Buachalla argues that, firstly, the Lament was composed by Eibhlín alone, secondly, the Lament was composed after Art was buried, thirdly, the Lament was a written composition, because, fourthly, written keens constituted an upper-class literary genre largely confined to eighteenth-century Munster and completely dissociated from the lower-class practice of keening.

Curiously, Ó Buachalla's vigorous critique of the scholarship exposes how easily the evidence cuts both ways. Often it does not sustain his arguments any better than it does the ones he wishes to refute. A typical instance is his exposure of the lack of consensus on how many verses of the Lament were composed by Art's sister: 'dhá véarsa a leag an Feiritéarach ar dheirfiúr Airt ina chéad leagan, ocht véarsa ina dhara leagan; cúig véarsa a leag Ó Cróinín ar dheirfiúr Airt, ocht véarsa a chum sí, dar le Ó Tuama' (Feiritéar attributes two stanzas to Art's sister in his first version (of the Lament), eight stanzas in his second version; Ó Cróinín attributes five stanzas to Art's sister, and she composed eight stanzas according to Ó Tuama).[107] To Ó Buachalla, disagreement about which stanzas should be ascribed to Art's sister makes it doubtful that she composed any of them, and uncertainty about her contribution to the Lament in turn weakens the case for multiple authorship. But it is common for editors to have different readings of a text, especially one that exists in several versions; and besides, as was noted of translations of *TBC* above, each new version of a text must diverge from its predecessors in order to justify its existence. Elsewhere, Ó Buachalla rightly points out 'tá coibhneas nó ceangal idir an seánra agus ócáid chinnte ach ní fhágann sin gur le linn na n-ócáidí sin a bhfuiltear ag cur síos orthu a cumadh aon dán acu' (there's a relationship or connection between the genre and a specific occasion but that doesn't mean any of the poems were composed during the occasions that they describe).[108] He is reminding readers that there is no law of literature requiring that a poem mourning a dead man be composed literally over his dead body. Conversely, of course, there is no law of literature that forbids it. At other times, Ó Buachalla's claims undermine themselves: 'ní mór . . . idirdhealú a dhéanamh idir an caoine agus an chaointeoireacht: seánra liteartha is ea an caoine, riotuál poiblí is ea – dob ea – an chaointeoireacht. Agus faoi mar a tharraing an barántas liteartha as béarlagair agus as gothaí na cúirte, tharraing an caoine as béarlagair agus as gothaí na caointeoireachta' (it's necessary to distinguish the keen from the practice of keening: the keen is a literary genre, the practice of keening is – was – a public ritual. And just as the literary *barántas* drew on the jargon and attitudes of the court, the keen drew on the jargon and attitudes of the practice of keening).[109] Relying on distinctions of social class to prove distinctions of literary genres, Ó Buachalla admits that highbrow written laments display traits of lowbrow oral lamenting, but denies that their resemblance is a result of the one being a record of the other. Instead, he contends that the written lament borrowed and refined the best features of oral lamenting. The underlying assumption is unfortunate and familiar: the Lament and its kindred are too eloquent to have been composed aloud and impromptu. Nor is his position strengthened by his strained comparison of the keen, a native Irish lament composed by the deceased's close female relatives, and the *barántas*, an Irish spoof of an English document composed by irreverent professional poets. While *An Caoine* demonstrates Ó Buachalla's grasp of Lament criticism, it inadvertently confirms that it is far easier to challenge opinions than it is to posit convincing alternatives.

How the Lament has fared illustrates the vulnerability of any oral work once it is locked in print, and the peril increases exponentially once it has been translated. Its original language anchors a composition in context with the history of its own words, from specialised terminology to local pronunciation, and the link between Modern Irish and oral tradition was further strengthened by practical need. 'Ba bheag ab fhiú an traidisiún foirmiúil léinn sa Ghaeilge, amach ó correisceacht thábhachtach thall is abhus, le céad éigin bliain roimh thús na hAthbheochana. Cha raibh de léann go forleathan i measc lucht na Gaeilge ach an léann béil amháin' (There was scarcely a formal tradition of learning in Irish, apart from the occasional important exception here and there, for a century before the start of the Revival. Among Irish speakers the only widespread education was oral).[110] Folklore preserved and transmitted vocabulary, grammar and traditional knowledge, merging fluency in the language with understanding of the culture.[111] Simply recognising the components of a place-name, for example, can transform an ordinary location into the site of wonders. 'Words and names in Irish [are] doorways into stories. Ardee in County Louth [is] *Áth Fhirdia*: the place where the hero Cú Chulainn killed his boyhood companion Ferdia in single combat at the ford. Kildare [is] *Cill Dara*, the oak church built by St Brigid in the sixth century.'[112]

Folklore and modern Irish literature

Happily, articles, books and dissertations analysing the use of Irish folklore in modern Irish literature make it unnecessary for the current writer singlehandedly to convince the current reader that Irish folklore is an integral component of twentieth-century Irish literature. Countless surveys of Irish literature give a nod to the subject, and scholars have commented on the use of folklore by authors such as Liam O'Flaherty and Máirtín Ó Cadhain. Therefore, all things being finite, the final portion of this study will highlight some of the innovative literary uses of two pervasive categories of oral tradition: folk-tales and proverbs.

As mentioned above, the first wave of Modern Irish writers turned instinctively to folk-tales, mindful that they held riches of imagination, diversity and expression. The problem was not their choice of material but their failure to realise how much of the magic of an oral performance is lost when its words alone are transcribed. Without the storyteller's gestures, facial expressions, changes of tone and volume, the corresponding shifts of humour, suspense and emphasis are largely undetectable. Likewise, some of the devices that are charming to hear – long, alliterative strings of adjectives, stock descriptions, repetitive dialogue – are monotonous when read laboriously instead of being heard fleetingly. Perceiving these obstacles, the second wave of Modern Irish writers turned away from folk-tales in search of a style suitable for written composition. The third wave has reaped double dividends by incorporating elements of folk-tales into original written narratives. Interest in folk-tales for the purposes of modern writing has coincided with a growing understanding of the ways in which seemingly simple oral tales explore complicated issues. Folklorists, psychologists and literary scholars are recognising that the folk-tale, like the keen, provides an acceptable disguise for the discussion of awkward or forbidden subjects. In *Strange Terrain: The Fairy World in Newfoundland*, Barbara Rieti presents case studies in which the ostensible shifting of agency to fairies allows the storyteller and the audience to contemplate disturbing events such as vandalism, abduction, physical and mental injury. An excellent companion to Rieti's book is *The Good People: New Fairylore Essays*, edited by Peter Narváez. This collection of studies covers the interpretations as well as the functions of fairy legend, including attempts to link changelings to infant medical conditions, the co-existence of fairy belief alongside the 'official religion' of Christianity, and the messages of modern spin-offs such as the Tooth Fairy. What the current trend of folklore scholarship is revealing has been summarised by Bo Almqvist: 'folk legends rather than expressing a single attitude to a particular problem, due to the flexibility and variation which is their very essence, often serve as vehicles for discussion of different solutions to questions of vital interest to tellers and audience'.[113] In oral tradition, multiple versions of a story exist because multiple resolutions of a problem are possible. This same trait of adaptability has enabled thousands of folk-tales to remain current and spread by changing their details to fit different times, locations and cultures.

There has always been a ready market for translations and retellings of folk-tales, for children, for adults and for that entirely separate audience, tourists, whose effect on literary development will make a tenure-winning book for some eccentric academic. But growing appreciation of the sophistication of folk-tales has inspired some authors to create remarkable narrative hybrids in which the oral traditional version of a story, minimally altered for readability, is interleaved with a thoroughly modern retelling of it. When it is well done, this combination of contrast (e.g. oral/written, long ago/today, rural/urban) and convergence (e.g. same personalities, same dilemma, same morals) shows what miraculous offspring can result from the marriage of unlikely partners.

Probably the best-known success is Benedict Kiely's *Cards of the Gambler*, based on the folk-tale about a card-player who meets God and Death, then makes a deal that allows him to prosper on earth but seriously complicates his afterlife. Instalments of this alternate with the same story digitally remastered in a modern urban setting, with Modernist psychological depth. The gambler is a dissolute doctor, God is a priest, and Death is a 'contact man' who knows all the right and all the wrong people to grant a request. Souls are judged at the gate of an airport, by security guards who determine whether or not a person qualifies for ascent to Heaven. The book is worth reading for its originality alone. But with the two tellings side by side, what seems fanciful and remote in the folk-tale becomes disturbingly imminent, while the familiarity of the modern setting melts into surreality; anything is possible if a man can look through the doorway of a pub and recognise Death waiting for him outside. Far from seeming quaint, the folk-tale has the compelling force of a premonition, allowing readers to (fore)see the gambler's fate and offering successively assurances of humour, suspense, and the unexpected possibility of breaking even.

An ingenious variation on this technique is *The Inland Ice and Other Stories*, in which Éilís Ní Dhuibhne interleaves fourteen segments of a folk-tale and thirteen short stories. The folk-tale describes a nameless heroine's pursuit of her enchanted lover. As she endures hardship after hardship, her counterparts in the short stories – a cross-section of modern women – confront their own obstacles in the forms of neglect, depression and dependence on uncertain relationships. It is no surprise that the folk-tale and the book end with the heroine finally trumping the spell-casting witch. But having done so, she finds herself even more disenchanted than the man whom she has freed. Literally on the brink of a fairy-tale ending, she sees her past mistakes, realises where true happiness lies, and refuses to be trapped by traditional expectations. She matures far more than do any of the 'real' women in the short stories, exemplifying the wisdom folk-tales still have to offer. It is the paradox of a traditional heroine setting a radical new example that amplifies Ní Dhuibhne's wake-up call: women are responsible for their own happiness and must learn to take control of their lives.

As in the case of folk-tales, proverbs have become increasingly conspicuous thanks to collections. The assortments include An Seabhac's *Seanfhocail na Muimhneach* (Munster Proverbs), which is entirely in Modern Irish; *Ireland of the Proverb*, text by Liam Mac Con Iomaire, delightful photographs by Bill Doyle, which gives proverbs in Irish with translations and commentary in English; and *The Wasp in the Mug: Unforgettable Irish Proverbs*, a facing-page bilingual book with whimsical footnotes by Gabriel Rosenstock and whimsical drawings by Pieter Sluis. That the proverb is less generally recognised than the folk-tale is a result of its greater resistance to translation: few who do not know Modern Irish realise the extent to which the proverbs permeate the Irish literary tradition. Although proverbs in different languages can have the same meaning – e.g. *níl aon tinteán mar do thinteán féin* (there's no hearth like your own hearth) = 'there's no place like home', *céard a dhéanfadh mac an chait ach luch a mharú?* (what would the cat's son do but kill a mouse?) = 'the apple doesn't fall far from the tree' – the actual wording of a proverb is highly inflexible and specific to its native culture. Whereas the story of a folk-tale can survive drastic changes of discourse,[114] the proverb is so concise that it tolerates very few substitutions. 'He who is not strong must be clever' is rendered as both *an té nach bhfuil láidir, <u>caithfidh sé</u> bheith glic* and *an té nach bhfuil láidir, <u>ní foláir dó</u> bheith glic*, but the only variation is of equivalent regional idioms – *caithfidh sé* and *ní foláir dó* are two ways of indicating necessity or obligation, here translated 'must'. Likewise, *mada rua* might be substituted for *sionnach* in a proverb such as *dá fhad a ritheann an sionnach/mada rua, beirtear air sa deireadh* (however long the fox may run, he's caught in the end), but these are interchangeable names for the same animal, and the choice does not affect the structure of the proverb. Identification of a proverb requires recognition of synonyms, knowledge of its basic meaning and a grasp of the kind of situation in which it would be quoted, ironically or not. When it is cited appropriately in a text, it has the combined force of a history of validity, applicability to the current situation and the perfect fit of recognition by the audience. Duelling proverbs have decided many an argument, and in a creative work it can provide a punchline, a judgement or a skylight into the speaker's state of mind.

Máirtín Ó Cadhain's mastery of Modern Irish led to a natural and liberal sprinkling of Irish proverbs throughout his writing. But they are not merely the narrator's commentary, nor a means of pedantically summarising the moral of a story. Rather, they occur where they would occur normally in speech, defining both the speaker and the situation at hand. Some of his most memorable characters are noted for their ability to distil an opinion or a problem into the shot-glass of a proverb. At other times, the casual surfacing of a proverb in reflection or conversation causes the absurdity, gravity or inevitability of the matter in question to leap out as suddenly as a Jack-in-the-box. Like the final pun of a Myles na gCopaleen 'Keats and Chapman' anecdote, the proverb brings clarity and order where previously there was confusion. While Ó Cadhain had the greatest scope for speech in *Cré na Cille* (1949), proverbs are deployed with exquisite timing in some of his short stories, and often in the most unexpected circumstances. A personal favourite occurs near the end of 'An Eochair' (The Key) in his collection *An tSraith ar Lár*.[115] By this point in this tale, the breaking of a key in the lock has left 'J.', a junior file clerk in the Civil Service, trapped in a windowless room full of old files. For days he has been stuck there without food, water or a washroom, initially because his superior 'S.' is on vacation, next because of a government holiday, and finally because Civil Service authorities are more concerned about following proper procedure than about saving his life. As J. waits for Godot, a parade of officials stops outside the jammed door to explain why he cannot be let out: memos must be sent, official permission must be given to call a locksmith, and every alternative must be explored before the door can be broken down, because the door is the valuable property of the Civil Service. When J. is so weak that he can only slump against the door, he hears the Undersecretary on the other side cheerfully remind him 'Ba ghaire cabhair Dé ná an doras' (God's help would be nearer than the door).[116] Given J.'s predicament, the irony of this proverb is outrageous. As he slowly dies on the other side of an actual locked door, tormented by the voices of ineffectual, indifferent officials babbling about protocol and precedent, the nearest thing to him is obstruction, not rescue. This proverb is meant to hearten those in despair, assuring them that a benevolent higher authority is always close at hand. But the God of the Civil Service is Old Testament rather than New, demanding such rigid adherence to the rules that J. for 'Junior' begins to seem like J. for 'Job'; a message of hope becomes a counsel of despair when uttered by one of the very superiors who is ensuring that J.'s imprisonment will end in death rather than deliverance. Although the proverb is given no emphasis in the Undersecretary's chatter, it throws the whole tragicomical history of J.'s career in the Civil Service into bas-relief, as his delusional dread of turning into a file is fulfilled by his entombment in the paper catacombs.

Like Ó Cadhain, Nuala Ní Dhomhnaill tends to understate the role of proverbs because she expects them to be recognised and understood. In many of her poems they arch out of the lines like dolphins, slightly altered to follow the course of her thoughts, so that meaning materialises along with the original wording. 'Dán do Mhelissa' (Poem for Melissa) concludes with 'seasfainn le mo chorp idir dhá bhró an mhuilinn / i muilte Dé chun nach meilfí tú mín mín' (I would stand with my body between the mill's two grindstones / in the mills of God to save you from being ground too finely),[117] expressing her desire to protect her daughter against the merciless fate alluded to in the proverb *meileann muilte Dé go mall ach meileann siad go mín* (God's mills grind slowly but finely), i.e. no one can avoid what is in store for her/him, whether it be vindication, ill luck or poetic justice. In 'Sionnach' (Fox), Ní Dhomhnaill speaks directly to the subject of the proverb *dá fhad a ritheann an sionnach, beirtear air sa deireadh* (no matter how long the fox runs, he is caught in the end), telling him:

nach breá nach bhfuil fhios agat,
dá mhéid a ritheann leat,
sa deireadh
gurb é siopa an fhionnadóra
a bheidh mar chríoch ort.

(isn't it a good thing you don't know,
however long you run,
in the end
the furrier's shop
will be your last stop.)[118]

In the second and third stanzas, she takes an exit off the highway of the proverb's message that justice will always, if eventually, overtake the wicked. Already it is clear that her sympathies lie with the fox – she is glad he does not know the 'sod of his death' (the exact spot where he is fated to die) – but her reflection that people are as prone to preen themselves by quoting poems as they are by wearing fur coats establishes a link between the outlaw of the woods and the outlaw of the intellect.[119] Making common cause with the fox, she issues a joint warning to hunters: 'Bainim snap / as láimh mo chothaithe' (I bite / the hand that feeds me).[120] Neither foxes nor poets will tamely submit to exploitation, and the controversy that surrounds translation of Modern Irish works gives teeth to her translation into Irish of a widely known English expression for treachery, 'to bite the hand that feeds you'. In 'Sionnach' it is better to be a traitor, as it is better to be a fugitive, because the provider has his own reasons for feeding the fox, just as politicians and others have their own motives for endorsing poems. The hand that rocks the cradle deserves no gratitude when at any moment it may tip out the occupant.

Biddy Jenkinson's *An Grá Riabhach* includes the hilarious short story 'Lúidín an Phíobaire' (The Piper's Little Finger), titled after and plot-driven by the saying *chomh díomhaoin le lúidín an phíobaire* (as idle as a piper's little finger), an expression for laziness or uselessness based on the pinky's limited role in traditional piping. Protagonist and narrator Flora McCrimmon, an extremely liberated female piper, falls in love with an extremely conservative male piper after trading tunes with him in a pub. Eager to follow their hot session of music with an equally hot session of sex, she peppers their conversation with a series of invitations that would be transparent to a younger man. Her question 'An fíor go mbíonn lúidín an phíobaire díomhaoin?' (Is it true that the piper's little finger is idle?) evokes a disappointingly matter-of-fact reply in the affirmative.[121] Determinedly, she becomes his piping pupil in order to continue her campaign of musical seduction. Both of them make such progress that by the end, when she seizes his hand to make him feel her *imoibriú* – the position of a piper's lips for blowing – her challenge 'Samhlaigh é sin anois ar an mbéalóg!' (Now imagine that on the mouthpiece!) causes him to clear his throat, unable to think of a bland response.[122] In their final exchange, Flora's reminder 'Níor thaispeáin tú go fóill dom cén nóta a sheinntear le lúidín an phíobaire' (You still haven't shown me what note is played with the piper's little finger) causes him to shoot back 'Taispeánfad lá éigin, ambaist!' (I'll show you some day, I swear!) – a welcome indication that he will yet show her his virtuosity with an instrument other than the pipes.[123]

As brief as a proverb can be, it is not the smallest unit of the Irish language that can focus a surrounding composition. Angela Bourke's 'Le Soleil et le Vent' is the story of how a widow, Rosemary, comes to terms with two tragedies, the recent death of her husband Dónall and the subsequent discovery that he and a lover had had a child. Since Rosemary had been unable to conceive, she is devastated by guilt and envy as well as by grief and anger. Overwhelmed by the ruin of her past, she takes refuge with friends on the coast of Brittany, where certain families carry on the tradition of harvesting salt from the sea. She learns that women were entitled to sell the *fleur de sel* – the finest salt skimmed from the *oeillets* (little eyes), the clay basins that hold seawater for evaporation – and the knowledge brings an unexpected benefit. Thinking about the sea and the profit women derived from its drying, burning residue of salt causes Rosemary to consider her tears from a completely different perspective:

> I thought of the Irish words for tide, spring tide, sea-water: *taoille, rabharta, sáile* . . . 'Goirt,' my mind said silently, the Irish world for salty. 'Is goirt iad na deora a shiltear,' they say, 'ach is goirte na deora nach siltear.' The tears that are shed are salty, but unshed tears are even saltier. Of course *goirt* means everything from salt to bitter.[124]

Because the semantic range of *goirt* matches her mixed emotions, the word itself is a significant release, enabling her finally to articulate what she is feeling. She takes a second step towards recovery when *goirt* brings to mind a proverb, a reminder that peace comes to the person who cries to purge consuming anguish. Previously her tears have been a confirmation of enduring pain. Now they are a release, and letting go of the past frees her to imagine a future that may take her 'where [she] had never been, but maybe [she] could go now'.[125] She vows to close this episode in her life with a gesture reminiscent of communion: 'I would open the blue ribbon on the white cotton bag of *fleur de sel*, moisten my finger and dip it in. I wanted to taste one perfect salt crystal on my tongue',[126] an act that will combine language, experience and emotion. Her new awareness merges with that of the audience, for whom *goirt* resonates throughout the book: its title *By Salt Water* refers to 'not only the sea, but also tears, sweat, and the amniotic fluid where we first swim'.[127] Although all the stories in this collection are in English, they are united by an Irish word encrusted with folklore, and there could be no more compelling demonstration of the ongoing synergy of literature and oral tradition.

Notes

1. The standard introduction to composition in oral tradition is Albert Lord's *The Singer of Tales* (1960; New York: Atheneum, 1983).
2. For an overview of how the functions of oral tradition have been transferred to print technologies see Walter Ong, *Orality and Literacy: The Technologizing of the Word* (New York: Methuen, 1982).
3. Angela Bourke, 'Introduction', in A. Bourke, S. Kilfeather, M. Luddy, M. Mac Curtain, G. Meaney, M. Ní Dhonnchadha, M. O'Dowd and C. Wills, eds. *The Field Day Anthology of Irish Writing, vols. IV and V: Irish Women's Writing and Traditions* (Cork: Cork University Press in association with Field Day, 2002), IV, p. 1195.
4. Jane Stevenson, 'The Beginnings of Literacy in Ireland', *Proceedings of the Royal Irish Academy* 89C (1989), pp. 127–65, p. 134.
5. See M. B. Parkes, 'The Literacy of the Laity', in David Daiches and Anthony Thorlby, eds. *Literature and Western Civilization, vol. II: The Medieval World* (London: Aldus Books, 1973), pp. 555–77; Raymond Gillespie, 'The Circulation of Print in Seventeenth-Century Ireland', *Studia Hibernica* 29 (1995–7), pp. 31–58.
6. A well-known example is the *Amra Choluimb Chille*, a eulogy of St Columba composed by Dallán Forgaill, a professional poet, which monks not only recorded but glossed to the point of obfuscation. The verse and its retinue of comments were bravely edited by Whitley Stokes in 'The Bodleian Amra Choluimb Chille', *Revue celtique* 20 (1899), pp. 30–55, 133–83, 248–87.
7. See Kim McCone, *Pagan Past and Christian Present in Early Irish Literature*, Maynooth Monographs III (Maynooth: An Sagart, 1991). The first three chapters present his views of broad categories, e.g. scholarship, history and narrative, while the remaining seven chapters apply them to more specific topics, e.g. laws, kingship, politics.
8. See Patrick Sims-Williams, 'Léirmheas [Review]: *Pagan Past and Christian Present in Early Irish Literature*, Kim McCone', *Éigse* 29 (1996), pp. 179–96, p. 180.
9. See Nicholas Canny, 'The Formation of the Irish Mind: Religion, Politics and Gaelic Irish Literature 1580–1750', *Past & Present* 95 (1982), p. 91–116, p. 105.
10. Their campaign was vigorously opposed on linguistic as well as literary grounds. For the full cast and libretto of this long-running feud see Philip O'Leary, *The Prose Literature of the Gaelic Revival, 1881–1921: Ideology and Innovation* (University Park, PA: Pennsylvania State University Press, 1994), pp. 19–162.
11. Cecile O'Rahilly, ed. and trans. *Táin Bó Cúailnge: Recension 1* (Dublin: Dublin Institute for Advanced Studies, 1976), l. 3425, p. 104 (translation p. 217).
12. Ibid., ll. 3443–7, p. 104 (translation p. 217).

13. For an examination of what Macpherson published, claimed and appears to have actually used see Derick S. Thomson, *The Gaelic Sources of Macpherson's 'Ossian'*, Aberdeen University Studies XXX (Edinburgh: University Press, 1951).

14. Matthew Arnold, *The Study of Celtic Literature* (1905; London: Kennikat Press, 1970). Find its cure in John Kelleher, 'Matthew Arnold and the Celtic Revival', in Harry Levin, ed. *Perspectives of Criticism* (Cambridge, MA: Harvard University Press, 1950), pp. 197–221.

15. Maria Tymoczko, *Translation in a Postcolonial Context* (Manchester: St Jerome Publishing, 1999), pp. 62–89.

16. A principal scribe of *Lebor na hUidre*, the manuscript containing the earliest version of *TBC*, died in 1106; it is not known to what extent the writing of this particular tale hastened his demise or the demise of the later scribe who altered the text. For the details see O'Rahilly, *Táin Bó Cúailnge*, pp. vii–xviii.

17. O'Rahilly also edited and translated the other two recensions in 1978 and 1984, thereby fulfilling the three-miracle requirement for canonisation.

18. O'Rahilly, *Táin Bó Cúailnge*, ll. 303–5, p. 10 (translation p. 133).

19. Ibid., pp. 154, 142, 195. For the tale-lists, see Proinsias Mac Cana, *The Learned Tales of Medieval Ireland* (Dublin: Dublin Institute for Advanced Studies, 1980), esp. pp. 41–65.

20. O'Rahilly, *Táin Bó Cúailnge*, l. 1214, p. 38 (translation p. 158).

21. Compare O'Rahilly, *Táin Bó Cúailnge*, ll. 2268–72, p. 69 (translation p. 187) to Jeffrey Gantz, trans. *Early Irish Myths and Sagas* (New York: Penguin, 1981), p. 71.

22. O'Rahilly, *Táin Bó Cúailnge*, ll. 1000–1, p. 31 (translation p. 153), l. 1164, p. 36 (translation p. 157) and ll. 1017–24 (translation p. 154).

23. Ibid., ll. 1737–806 (translation pp. 173–5), ll. 1874–2037 (translation pp. 177–81) and ll. 2567–3153 (translation pp. 195–208). For a fuller comparison of these combats see Donna Wong, 'Combat between Fosterbrothers in *Táin Bó Cúailnge*', *Proceedings of the Harvard Celtic Colloquium* 13 (1995), pp. 119–44.

24. Patrick Ford, 'Oral to Literary: The Route of the Táin', unpublished paper presented at a meeting of the Celtic Studies Association of North America at the University of Washington, April 1993. Reduplicated thanks to Dr Ford for making the text of this talk available to me.

25. Tymoczko, *Translation*, p. 122.

26. Thomas Kinsella, trans. *The Tain* (1969; Oxford: Oxford University Press, 1970), p. xi. Kinsella's translation will be referred to subsequently as *The Tain*, as distinct from the Irish-language *Táin* or *TBC*.

27. Ibid., p. xi.

28. Ibid.

29. Ibid.

30. Ibid., pp. xi–xii.

31. Ibid., p. xi.

32. Ibid.

33. Joep Leerssen, 'Táin after Táin: The Mythical Past and the Anglo Irish', in Joris Duytschaever and Geert Lernout, eds. *History and Violence in Anglo-Irish Literature* (Amsterdam: Rodori, 1983), pp. 29–46.

34. L. Winifred Faraday, trans. *The Cattle-Raid of Cúalnge* (Táin Bó Cúailnge): *An Old Irish Prose-Epic* (London: David Nutt, 1904), p. xviii.

35. Ibid., p. xx.
36. Kinsella, *The Tain*, p. xii.
37. Faraday, *The Cattle-Raid*, p. 4, note 1.
38. Kinsella, *The Tain*, p. 105.
39. Ibid., p. 107.
40. Leerssen, 'Táin after Táin', p. 40.
41. Faraday, *The Cattle-Raid*, p. 101.
42. Kinsella, *The Tain*, p. 169.
43. Katharine Simms, 'Bardic Poetry as a Historical Source', in T. Dunne, ed. *The Writer as Witness: Literature as Historical Evidence* (Cork: Cork University Press, 1987), pp. 58–75, p. 71.
44. N. J. A. Williams, ed. and trans. *The Poems of Giolla Brighde Mac Con Midhe*, Irish Texts Society LI (Dublin: Irish Texts Society, 1980), ll. 1–2, p. 162 (translation p. 163).
45. Ibid., ll. 5–8, p. 162 (translation p. 163).
46. Ibid., ll. 74, 78, p. 166 (translation p. 167) and ll. 97–8, p. 168 (translation p. 169).
47. Lambert McKenna, ed. and trans. *Aithdioghluim Dána, Parts 1 and 2*, Irish Texts Society XXXVII and XL (London: Irish Texts Society, 1939 and 1940), Part 1, ll. 9–12, p. 17 (translation Part 2, p. 10).
48. Ibid., Part 1, ll. 33–6, p. 17 (translation Part 2, p. 10).
49. Ibid., Part 1, l. 58, p. 18 (translation Part 2, p. 11).
50. Ibid., Part 1, ll. 93–4, p. 19 (translation Part 2, p. 11).
51. Ibid., Part 1, ll. 109–10, p. 19 (translation Part 2, p. 12).
52. John Mac Erlean, ed. and trans. *Duanaire Dháibhidh Uí Bhruadair: The Poems of David Ó Bruadair, Part 2*, Irish Texts Society XIII (London: Irish Texts Society, 1913), ll. 9–10, p. 26 (translation p. 27). Mac Erlean's torturous translations have been retained for comparison with Michael Hartnett's, to follow.
53. Ibid., ll. 33–4, p. 28 (translation p. 29).
54. Ibid., l. 31, p. 26 (translation p. 27).
55. Ibid., ll. 50–2, p. 28 (translation p. 29).
56. Ibid., l. 12, p. 26 (translation p. 27).
57. Ibid., ll. 83–4, p. 32 (translation p. 33).
58. Michael Hartnett, 'Wrestling with Ó Bruadair', in Seán Mac Réamoinn, ed. *The Pleasures of Gaelic Poetry* (London: Allen Lane, 1982), pp. 65–78, p. 65.
59. Ibid., p. 65.
60. Ibid.
61. Ibid., p. 72.
62. Ibid., p. 70.
63. Ibid., pp. 70–1.
64. Ibid., p. 73.
65. Mac Erlean, *Ó Bruadair, Part 2*, l. 1, p. 220 and translation from Michael Hartnett, *O Bruadair* (Dublin: Gallery Books, 1985), p. 21. Hartnett follows the scholarly practice of using the first line of a bardic poem as its makeshift title, since bards did not give titles to their compositions.
66. Mac Erlean, *Ó Bruadair, Part 2*, l. 1, p. 220 (translation Hartnett, *O Bruadair*, p. 21).
67. Mac Erlean, *Ó Bruadair, Part 2*, l. 4, p. 220 (translation Hartnett, *O Bruadair*, p. 21).

68. Mac Erlean, *Ó Bruadair, Part 2*, l. 19, p. 220 (translation Hartnett, *O Bruadair*, p. 21).

69. Mac Erlean, *Ó Bruadair, Part 2*, ll. 13–15, p. 220 (translation Hartnett, *O Bruadair*, p. 21).

70. Mac Erlean, *Ó Bruadair, Part 2*, l. 12, p. 220 (translation Hartnett, *O Bruadair*, p. 21).

71. Revd Patrick Dinneen and Tadhg O'Donoghue, eds. and trans. *The Poems of Egan O'Rahilly*, Irish Texts Society III (London: Irish Texts Society, 1911), ll. 1–4, p. 258 and translation from Michael Hartnett, *O Rathaille* (Loughcrew, County Meath: Gallery Books, 1998), p. 36.

72. Dinneen and O'Donoghue, *O'Rahilly*, l. 7, p. 258 (translation Hartnett, *O Rathaille*, p. 36).

73. Dinneen and O'Donoghue, *O'Rahilly*, l. 10, p. 258 (translation Hartnett, *O Rathaille*, p. 36).

74. Dinneen and O'Donoghue, *O'Rahilly*, l. 9, p. 258 (translation Hartnett, *O Rathaille*, p. 36).

75. Dinneen and O'Donoghue, *O'Rahilly*, ll. 13–16, p. 258 (translation Hartnett, *O Rathaille*, p. 36).

76. Dinneen and O'Donoghue, *O'Rahilly*, ll. 23–4, p. 260 (translation Hartnett, *O Rathaille*, p. 36).

77. Dinneen and O'Donoghue, *O'Rahilly*, l. 30, p. 260 (translation Hartnett, *O Rathaille*, p. 37).

78. Dinneen and O'Donoghue, *O'Rahilly*, ll. 31–2, p. 260 (translation Hartnett, *O Rathaille*, p. 37).

79. Diarmuid Ó Giolláin, *Locating Irish Folklore: Tradition, Modernity, Identity* (Cork: Cork University Press, 2000), p. 48.

80. Máirtín Ó Cadhain, 'An Chré', in Seán Ó Laighin, ed. *Ó Cadhain i bhFeasta* (Dublin: Clódhanna Teoranta, 1990), pp. 129–40, p. 139. My translation.

81. James Delargy/Séamus Ó Duilearga, 'Ó'n bhFear Eagair [Editorial]', *Béaloideas* 1–2 (1927–30), pp. 3–6, p. 3. My translation.

82. Ó Giolláin, *Locating*, p. 34.

83. Ibid., p. 165.

84. Seán Ó Coileáin, 'The Irish Lament: An Oral Genre', *Studia Hibernica* 24 (1984–8), pp. 97–117, p. 114.

85. See Rachel Bromwich, 'The Keen for Art O'Leary, its Background and its Place in the Tradition of Gaelic Keening', *Éigse* 5, 4 (1947), pp. 236–52.

86. Angela Bourke, 'More in Anger than in Sorrow: Irish Women's Lament Poetry', in Joan Newlon Radner, ed. *Feminist Messages: Coding in Women's Folk Culture* (Urbana and Chicago: University of Illinois Press, 1993), pp. 160–82, p. 162.

87. Angela Bourke, 'Performing, Not Writing: The Reception of an Irish Woman's Lament', in Yopie Prins and Maeera Shreiber, eds. *Dwelling in Possibility: Women Poets and Critics on Poetry* (Ithaca and London: Cornell University Press, 1997), pp. 132–46, p. 135.

88. Angela Bourke, 'Lamenting the Dead', in Bourke et al., *The Field Day Anthology*, IV, pp. 1365–6, p. 1366.

89. Ó Coileáin, 'The Irish Lament', p. 103.

90. Bourke, 'More in Anger', p. 161.

91. Bromwich, 'The Keen for Art O'Leary', p. 241.

92. Tomás Ó hAilín, 'Caointe agus Caointeoirí', *Feasta* 23, 10 (1971), pp. 7–11, p. 9. My translation.

93. Angela Bourke, 'The Irish Traditional Lament and the Grieving Process', *Women's Studies International Forum* 11, 4 (1988), pp. 287–91, p. 290.

94. Seán Ó Tuama, ed. *Caoineadh Airt Uí Laoghaire* (1961; Dublin: An Clóchomhar, 1979), ll. 4–6, p. 33 and note 6, p. 55, and translation from Eilís Dillon, trans. 'The Lament for Arthur O'Leary', in Peter Levi, *The Lamentation of the Dead*, Poetica XIX (London: Anvil Press Poetry, 1984), pp. 23–35, p. 23.

95. Ó Tuama, *Caoineadh*, l. 8, p. 33 (translation Dillon, 'The Lament', p. 23).

96. Ó Tuama, *Caoineadh*, l. 30, p. 34 (translation Dillon, 'The Lament', p. 24).

97. Ó Tuama, *Caoineadh*, l. 33, p. 34 (translation Dillon, 'The Lament', p. 24).

98. Ó Tuama, *Caoineadh*, l. 43, p. 34 and note 43, p. 56 (translation Dillon, 'The Lament', p. 24).

99. Ó Tuama, *Caoineadh*, ll. 69–71, p. 35 and notes 69–71, p. 57 (translation Dillon, 'The Lament', p. 25).

100. Ó Tuama, *Caoineadh*, ll. 82–4, p. 35 (translation Dillon, 'The Lament', p. 25).

101. Ó Tuama, *Caoineadh*, ll. 86–7, p. 36 (translation Dillon, 'The Lament', p. 25).

102. Ó Tuama, *Caoineadh*, ll. 381–3, p. 45 (translation Dillon, 'The Lament', p. 35).

103. Ó Tuama, *Caoineadh*, l. 390, p. 45 (translation Dillon, 'The Lament', p. 35).

104. Bourke, 'Performing, Not Writing', p. 140.

105. Nuala Ní Dhomhnaill, 'What Foremothers?', in Theresa O'Connor, ed. *The Comic Tradition in Irish Women Writers* (Gainesville, FL: University Press of Florida, 1996), pp. 8–20, p. 12.

106. 'Cé nárbh é do leathadh ort / Ach go dtugthá an maide dhom, / Ach ba mise fá ndeara san / Mar do bhíos ró-rabairneach / 'S an stór ró-ghearra agam, / Agus nílimse dá chasadh leat' from Ó Tuama, *Caoineadh*, p. 78.

107. Breandán Ó Buachalla, *An Caoine agus an Chaointeoireacht*, Lúb ar Phár I (Dublin: Cois Life Teoranta, 1998), p. 13. Translations from this work are my own.

108. Ibid., p. 51.

109. Ibid., p. 49.

110. Nollaig Mac Congáil, 'Finscéalta faoin Osnádúr i Nualitríocht na Gaeilge', *Béaloideas* 60 (1992–3), pp. 1–17, p. 1. My translation.

111. Modern Irish dictionaries often quote proverbs, and as Tomás Ó Cathasaigh has observed, Father Dinneen's *Foclóir Gaedhilge agus Béarla* (1927; 2nd edn Dublin: Irish Texts Society, 1934) 'is the only dictionary in the world with a folktale in it'. I hand him laurels for referring me to Dinneen's marvellous entry for *riabhach*, which concludes '*laetheanta na riaibhche*, the days of the brindled cow, .i. March; the legend is that the brindled cow complained at the dawn of April of the harshness of March, whereupon March borrowed a few days from April and these were so wet and stormy that the *bó riabhach* was drowned, hence March has a day more than April, and the borrowed days are called *laetheanta na riaibhche*', p. 893.

112. Angela Bourke, 'Language, Stories, Healing', in Anthony Bradley and Maryann Gialanella Valiulis, eds. *Gender and Sexuality in Modern Ireland* (Amherst, MA: University of Massachusetts Press, 1997), pp. 299–314, p. 301.

113. Bo Almqvist, 'Of Mermaids and Marriages', *Béaloideas* 58 (1990), pp. 1–74, p. 39. My translation.

114. These terms are as used in Seymour Chatman, *Story and Discourse: Narrative Structure in Fiction and Film* (Ithaca and London: Cornell University Press, 1978). Briefly, 'story'

is the fixed aspect, whereas 'discourse' is the changeable way in which the story is told.

115. Máirtín Ó Cadhain, *An tSraith ar Lár* (1967; Dublin: Sáirséal-Ó Marcaigh, 1986), pp. 203–60.

116. Ibid., p. 246.

117. Nuala Ní Dhomhnaill, *Féar Suaithinseach* (Maynooth: An Sagart, 1988), p. 104. Translations from this work are my own.

118. Nuala Ní Dhomhnaill, *An Dealg Droighin* (Dublin and Cork: Cló Mercier, 1981), p. 86. Translations from this work are my own.

119. For a view of the uneatable turning the tables on the unspeakable, see Linda L. Revie, 'The Little Red Fox, Emblem of the Irish Peasant in Poems by Yeats, Tynan and Ní Dhomhnaill', in Deborah Fleming, ed. *Learning the Trade: Essays on W. B. Yeats and Contemporary Poetry* (West Cornwall, CT: Locust Hill Press, 1993), pp. 133–4, specifically pp. 126–8.

120. Ní Dhomhnaill, *An Dealg*, p. 86

121. Biddy Jenkinson, *An Grá Riabhach* (Dublin: Coiscéim, 2000), pp. 82–8, p. 86. Translations from this work are my own.

122. Ibid., p. 88.

123. Ibid., p. 88.

124. Angela Bourke, *By Salt Water* (Dublin: New Island Books, 1996), pp. 90–8, p. 97.

125. Ibid., p. 97.

126. Ibid., p. 98.

127. This quotation is from the back cover of *By Salt Water. Goirt* is a personal favourite of mine because I first heard it from Séamas Ó Cualáin, an unforgettable teacher and native speaker from Baile Mór an Spidéil, County Galway, who defined it as *blas na farraige* (the taste of the sea). For this reason, it also became for me *blas na Gaeilge* in its literal sense, 'the taste of the Irish language'.

Select bibliography

Almqvist, Bo, 'Of Mermaids and Marriages', *Béaloideas* 58 (1990), pp. 1–74.

Arnold, Matthew, *The Study of Celtic Literature*, 1866; London: Kennikat Press, 1970.

Bromwich, Rachel, 'The Keen for Art O'Leary, its Background and its Place in the Tradition of Gaelic Keening', *Éigse* 5, 4 (1947), pp. 236–52.

Bourke, Angela, 'The Irish Traditional Lament and the Grieving Process', *Women's Studies International Forum* 11, 4 (1988), pp. 287–91.

'Language, Stories, Healing', in Anthony Bradley and Maryann Gialanella Valiulis, eds. *Gender and Sexuality in Modern Ireland*, Amherst, MA: University of Massachusetts Press, 1997, pp. 299–314.

'More in Anger than in Sorrow: Irish Women's Lament Poetry', in Joan Newlon Radner, ed. *Feminist Messages: Coding in Women's Folk Culture*, Urbana and Chicago: University of Illinois Press, 1993, pp. 160–82.

'Performing, Not Writing: The Reception of an Irish Woman's Lament', in Yopie Prins and Maeera Shreiber, eds. *Dwelling in Possibility: Women Poets and Critics on Poetry*, Ithaca and London: Cornell University Press, 1997, pp. 132–46.

Breatnach, Pádraig, 'The Chief's Poet', *Proceedings of the Royal Irish Academy* 83c (1983), pp. 37–79.

Canny, Nicholas, 'The Formation of the Irish Mind: Religion, Politics and Gaelic Irish Literature 1580–1750', *Past & Present* 95 (1982), pp. 91–116.

Dunne, T. J., 'The Gaelic Response to Conquest and Colonisation: The Evidence of the Poetry', *Studia Hibernica* 20 (1980), pp. 7–30.

Hartnett, Michael, 'Wrestling with Ó Bruadair', in Seán Mac Réamoinn, ed. *The Pleasures of Gaelic Poetry*, London: Allen Lane, 1982, pp. 65–78.

Kelleher, John, 'Matthew Arnold and the Celtic Revival', in Harry Levin, ed. *Perspectives of Criticism*, Cambridge, MA: Harvard University Press, 1950, pp. 197–221.

Leerssen, Joep, 'Táin after Táin: The Mythical Past and the Anglo Irish', in Joris Duytschaever and Geert Lernout, eds. *History and Violence in Anglo-Irish Literature*, Amsterdam: Rodori, 1983, pp. 29–46.

Lord, Albert, *The Singer of Tales*, 1960; New York: Atheneum, 1983.

Mac Congáil, Nollaig, 'Finscéalta faoin Osnádúr i Nualitríocht na Gaeilge', *Béaloideas* 60–1 (1992–3), pp. 1–17.

Mac Eoin, Gearóid, 'Poet and Prince in Medieval Ireland', in Evelyn Mullally and John Thompson, eds. *The Court and Cultural Diversity: Selected Papers from the Eighth Triennial Congress of the International Courtly Literature Society*, Cambridge: D. S. Brewer, 1997, pp. 3–16.

McWilliams, Jim, 'Nuala Ní Dhomhnaill's Poems: An Appreciation', in Alexander G. Gonzalez, ed. *Contemporary Irish Women Poets: Some Male Perspectives*, Contributions in Women's Studies CLXXIV, Westport, CT: Greenwood Press, 1999, pp. 135–41.

Narváez, Peter, ed. *The Good People: New Fairylore Essays*, 1991; Lexington: University Press of Kentucky, 1997.

Ní Dhomhnaill, Nuala, 'What Foremothers?', in Theresa O'Connor, ed. *The Comic Tradition in Irish Women Writers*, Gainesville, FL: University Press of Florida, 1996, pp. 8–20.

  'Why I Choose to Write in Irish, the Corpse That Sits Up and Talks Back', in Susan Shaw Sailer, ed. *Representing Ireland: Gender, Class, Nationality*, Gainesville, FL: University Press of Florida, 1997, pp. 45–56.

  'Ó Liombó go dtí Sráid Grafton: Comhrá le Nuala Ní Dhomhnaill', *Innti* 12 (1989), pp. 39–54.

O'Connor, Laura, ed. 'Medbh McGuckian and Nuala Ní Dhomhnaill: *Comhrá*, with a Foreword and Afterword by Laura O'Connor', *The Southern Review* 31, 3 (1995), pp. 581–614.

Ó Fiannachta, Pádraig, *An Barántas, I*, Maynooth: An Sagart, 1978.

  'The Poetic Warrant', *Studia Celtica Japonica* 4 (1991), pp. 1–14.

O'Leary, Philip, *The Prose Literature of the Gaelic Revival, 1881–1921: Ideology and Innovation*, University Park, PA: Pennsylvania State University Press, 1994.

Ong, Walter, *Orality and Literacy: The Technologizing of the Word*, New York: Methuen, 1982.

Parkes, M. B., 'The Literacy of the Laity', in David Daiches and Anthony Thorlby, eds. *Literature and Western Civilization, Vol II: The Medieval World*, London: Aldus Books, 1973, pp. 555–77.

Rieti, Barbara, *Strange Terrain: The Fairy World in Newfoundland*, St John's, Newfoundland: Institute of Social and Economic Research, 1991.

Simms, Katharine, 'Bardic Poetry as a Historical Source', in T. Dunne, ed. *The Writer as Witness: Literature as Historical Evidence*, Cork: Cork University Press, 1987, pp. 58–75.

Stevenson, Jane, 'The Beginnings of Literacy in Ireland', *Proceedings of the Royal Irish Academy* 89C (1989), pp. 127–65.

Thomson, Derick S., *The Gaelic Sources of Macpherson's 'Ossian'*, Aberdeen University Studies CXXX, Edinburgh: University Press, 1951.

Tymoczko, Maria, *Translation in a Postcolonial Context*, Manchester: St Jerome Publishing, 1999.

Guide to major subject areas

Index

Authorship, where known, has been identified in the index below. In many cases in Irish literature, particularly in the earlier periods, authorship was anonymous. Untitled poems are indicated by the poem's first line (in italics).